Marketing text in the world?

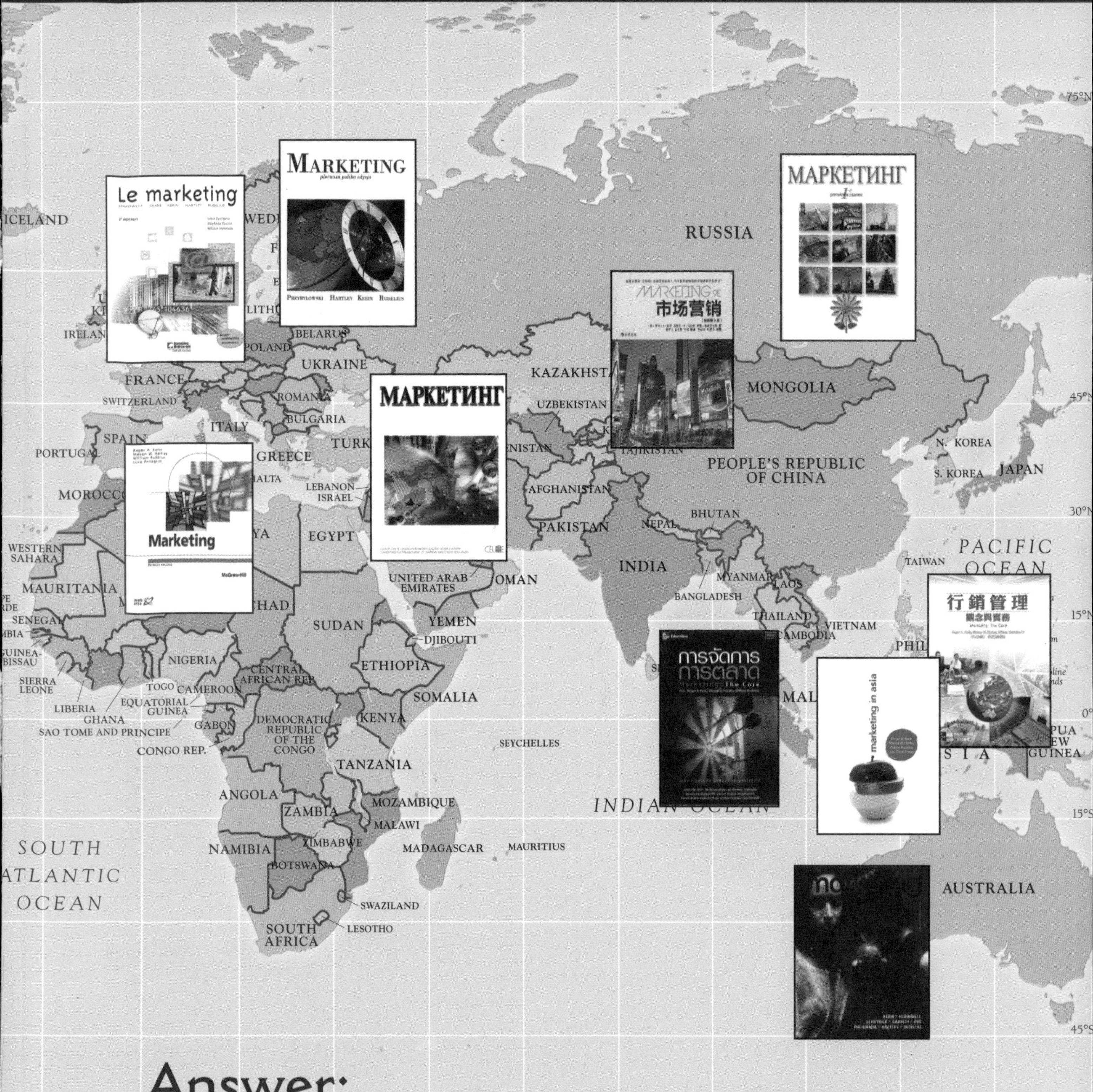

Answer:
Experience. Leadership. Innovation.

MARKETING

12/e

Roger A. Kerin
Southern Methodist University

Steven W. Hartley
University of Denver

William Rudelius
University of Minnesota

MARKETING, TWELFTH EDITION

Published by McGraw-Hill Education, 2 Penn Plaza, New York, NY 10121.

This book is printed on acid-free paper.

1 2 3 4 5 6 7 8 9 0 DOW/DOW 1 0 9 8 7 6 5 4

ISBN 978-0-07-786103-2
MHID 0-07-786103-5

Senior Vice President, Products & Markets: *Kurt L. Strand*
Vice President, Content Production & Technology Services: *Kimberly Meriwether David*
Managing Director: *Paul Ducham*
Executive Brand Manager: *Sankha Basu*
Executive Director of Development: *Ann Torbert*
Development Editor: *Sean M. Pankuch*
Development Editor: *Gina Huck Siegert*
Marketing Manager: *Donielle Xu*
Director, Content Production: *Terri Schiesl*
Content Project Manager: *Christine A. Vaughan*
Senior Buyer: *Carol A. Bielski*
Design: *Matthew Baldwin*
Cover Image: © *Getty Images/Mike Theiss*
Content Licensing Specialist: *Joanne Mennemeier*
Typeface: *10.5/12 Times Roman*
Compositor: *Aptara®, Inc.*
Printer: *R. R. Donnelley*

All credits appearing on page or at the end of the book are considered to be an extension of the copyright page.

Library of Congress Cataloging-in-Publication Data

Kerin, Roger A.
Marketing/Roger A. Kerin, Southern Methodist University, Steven W. Hartley, University of Denver, William Rudelius, University of Minnesota.—Twelfth edition.
pages cm
Includes index.
ISBN-13: 978-0-07-786103-2 (alk. paper)
ISBN-10: 0-07-786103-5 (alk. paper)
1. Marketing. I. Hartley, Steven William. II. Rudelius, William. III. Title.
HF5415.M29474 2015
658.8—dc23

2013039848

A MESSAGE FROM THE AUTHORS

Welcome to the next step in your journey to learn about the exciting world of marketing! You could not have chosen a more dynamic time to become involved in the discipline. Changes in consumers' values, efforts at an economic recovery, new technologies related to social media and data analytics, global competition, and increasing regulation related to privacy and e-commerce are all contributing to a marketing environment that changes every day. In addition, the relationships between capitalism and democracy and other market and governance perspectives are evolving rapidly. We are thrilled to provide a textbook that helps you navigate the challenges of studying marketing during the next several months, and possibly your entire career!

Our efforts to provide you with exceptional learning resources have focused on three important elements of the text and its supplements: Engagement, Leadership, and Innovation. We believe that each of these elements is essential to students and instructors and can contribute to the development of marketing expertise while facilitating the integration of the many complexities of marketing.

Engagement. Our experiences with thousands of students, managers, and instructors have given us many insights into important aspects of education in colleges and universities around the globe. For example, active, high-involvement, real-life, and current materials are essential to effective teaching and learning. In addition, we believe that higher education must embrace a new "age of engagement" in which interactions hold your attention and integrate all elements of study. Our text and supplements encourage interaction between students and four learning partners—the instructor, other students, businesses, and the publisher. In-class activities, an interactive web page and blog, "building-your-marketing-plan" guides, and an online learning center are just a few examples of our efforts to encourage engagement in the learning process.

Leadership. Through 12 U.S. editions and 18 international editions in 10 languages, we have been committed to taking a leadership role in the development and presentation of new ideas, principles, theories, and practices in marketing. We are at the forefront of coverage of ethics, social responsibility, technology, social media, marketing dashboards and metrics, and new research in the marketing discipline. Perspectives from an extraordinary variety of companies, industries, trading blocs, and countries are integrated in our package to create learning resources that help students become leaders in marketing.

Innovation. We have been diligent in our efforts to use innovation in our text and its supplements to serve the many learning styles of today's students. For example, we have included QR (quick response) codes in the margins of each chapter to allow easy access to online materials; we added new videos about Chobani Greek Yogurt, X-1 audio equipment, Secret Deodorant, the LA Galaxy soccer club, Carmex lip balm, and StuffDOT social loyalty service, and made them available through streaming links; and we increased the visual impact of text, PowerPoint, and testing materials to facilitate visual learning styles.

We believe these and many other aspects of *Marketing* and its supplements create a unique learning package, and we are very excited to have this opportunity to share our interests, insights, and experiences with you. We hope you enjoy your marketing studies. Welcome to the 12th edition of *Marketing*!

Roger A. Kerin
Steven W. Hartley
William Rudelius

PREFACE

Marketing utilizes a unique, innovative, and effective pedagogical approach developed by the authors through the integration of their combined classroom, college, and university experiences. The elements of this approach have been the foundation for each edition of *Marketing* and serve as the core of the text and its supplements as they evolve and adapt to changes in student learning styles, the growth of the marketing discipline, and the development of new instructional technologies. The distinctive features of the approach are illustrated below:

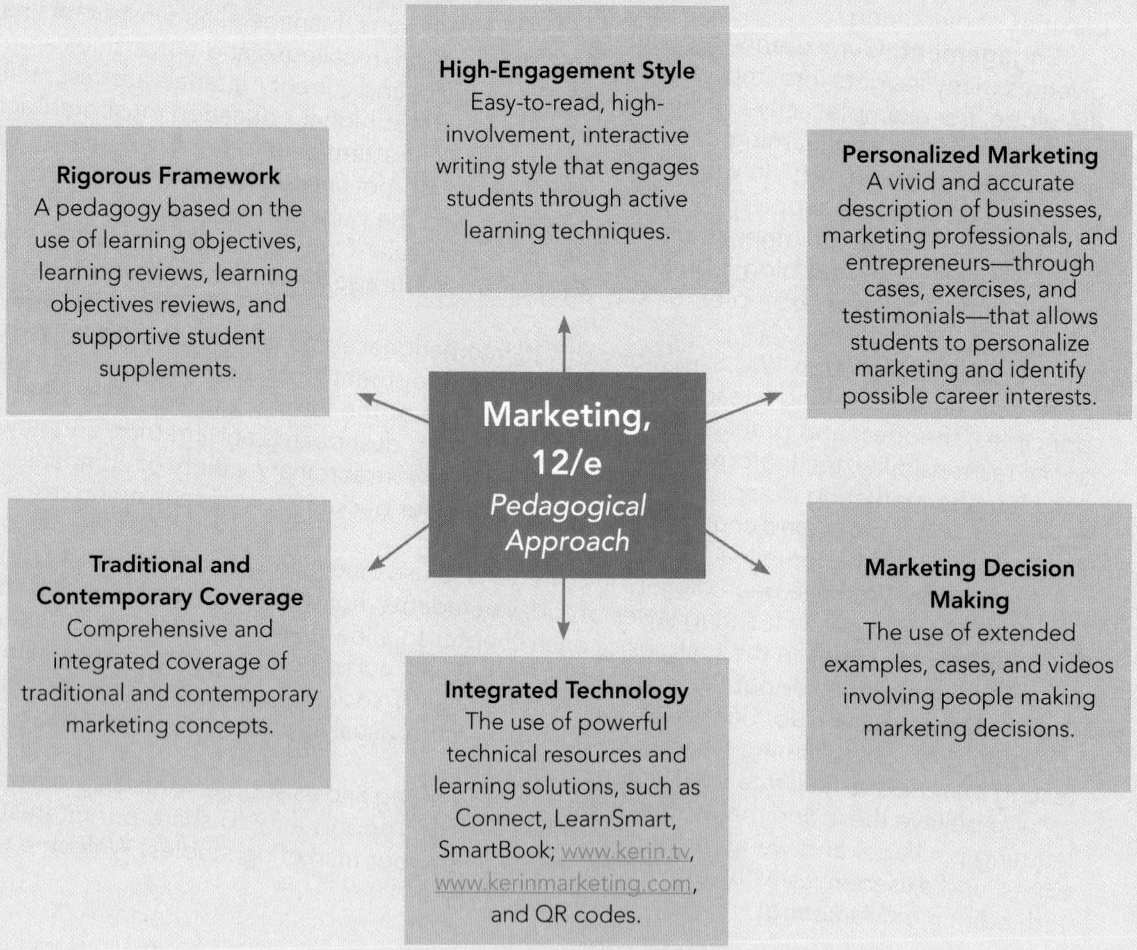

Marketing, 12/e
Pedagogical Approach

High-Engagement Style
Easy-to-read, high-involvement, interactive writing style that engages students through active learning techniques.

Personalized Marketing
A vivid and accurate description of businesses, marketing professionals, and entrepreneurs—through cases, exercises, and testimonials—that allows students to personalize marketing and identify possible career interests.

Marketing Decision Making
The use of extended examples, cases, and videos involving people making marketing decisions.

Integrated Technology
The use of powerful technical resources and learning solutions, such as Connect, LearnSmart, SmartBook; www.kerin.tv, www.kerinmarketing.com, and QR codes.

Traditional and Contemporary Coverage
Comprehensive and integrated coverage of traditional and contemporary marketing concepts.

Rigorous Framework
A pedagogy based on the use of learning objectives, learning reviews, learning objectives reviews, and supportive student supplements.

The goal of the 12th edition of *Marketing* is to create an exceptional experience for today's students and instructors of marketing. The development of *Marketing* was based on a rigorous process of assessment, and the outcome of the process is a text and package of learning tools that are based on *engagement, leadership*, and *innovation* in marketing education.

ENGAGEMENT

The members of this author team have benefited from extraordinary experiences as instructors, researchers, and consultants, as well as the feedback of users of previous editions of *Marketing*—now more than one million students! The authors believe that success in marketing education in the future will require the highest levels of engagement. They ensure engagement by facilitating interaction between students and four learning partners—the instructor, other students, businesses, and the publisher. Some examples of high-engagement elements of *Marketing* include:

ICA 1-1: IN-CLASS ACTIVITY

Designing a Candy Bar

Learning Objectives. To have students work in teams to (1) define a target market for a candy bar and (2) develop a simple marketing program for it.

Nature of the Activity. To engage students actively in a realistic marketing task in their first class meeting and have them share their ideas with classmates.

In-Class Activities. These activities are designed to engage students in discussions with the instructor and among themselves. They involve surveys, online resources, out-of-class assignments, and personal observations. Each activity illustrates a concept from the textbook and can be done individually or as a team. Examples include: Designing a Candy Bar, Marketing Yourself, Pepsi vs. Coke Taste Test, and What Makes a Memorable TV Commercial?

Interactive Web Page and Blog (www.kerinmarketing.com). Students can access recent articles about marketing and post comments for other students. The site also provides access to the videos and a *Marketing* Twitter feed!

BUILDING YOUR MARKETING PLAN

If your instructor assigns a marketing plan for your class, don't make a face and complain about the work—for two special reasons. First, you will get insights into trying to actually "do marketing" that often go beyond what you can get by simply reading the textbook. Second, thousands of graduating students every year get their first job by showing prospective employers a "portfolio" of samples of their written work from college—often a marketing plan if they have one. This can work for you.

This "Building Your Marketing Plan" section at the end of each chapter suggests ways to improve and focus your marketing plan. You will use the sample marketing plan in Appendix A (following Chapter 2) as a guide, and this section after each chapter will help you apply those Appendix A ideas to your own marketing plan.

The first step in writing a good marketing plan is to have a business or product that enthuses you and for which you can get detailed information, so you can avoid

Building Your Marketing Plan. The Building Your Marketing Plan guides at the end of each chapter are based on the format of the Marketing Plan presented in Appendix A. On the basis of self-study or as part of a course assignment, students can use the activities to organize interactions with businesses to build a marketing plan. Students and employers often suggest that a well-written plan in a student's portfolio is an asset in today's competitive job market.

Online Learning Center (www.kerin.tv). The Online Learning Center provides a connection between students and the text publisher, McGraw-Hill Education. The Learning Center provides Marketing Dashboard practice activities, QR code links, video case transcripts, links to stream the video cases, and PowerPoint presentations and quizzes for each chapter. The center also offers "Help" and "Feedback" functions.

LEADERSHIP

The popularity of *Marketing* in the United States and around the globe is the result, in part, of the leadership role of the authors in developing and presenting new marketing content and pedagogies. For example, *Marketing* was the first text to integrate ethics, technology, and interactive marketing. It was also the first text to develop custom-made videos to help illustrate marketing principles and practices and bring them to life for students as they read the text. The authors have also been leaders in developing new learning tools such as a three-step learning process that includes learning objectives, learning reviews, and learning objectives reviews; and new testing materials that are based on Bloom's learning taxonomy and include questions with figures and images from the text. Other elements that show how *Marketing* is a leader in the discipline include:

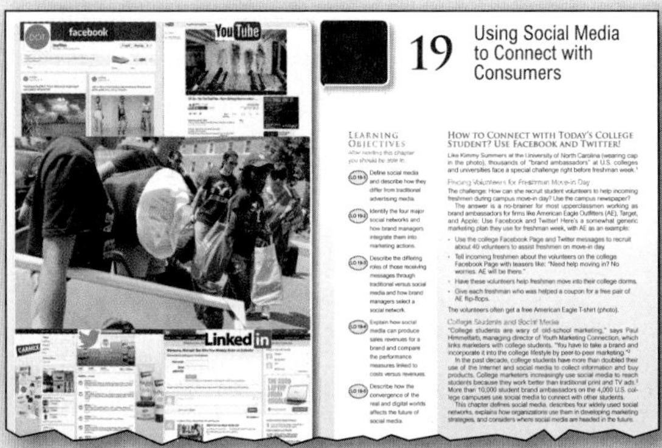

Chapter 19: Using Social Media to Connect with Consumers. *Marketing* features a dedicated chapter for social media marketing. This new environment is rapidly changing and constantly growing. The authors cover the building blocks of social media marketing and provide thorough, relevant content and examples. The authors discuss major social media platforms like Twitter, Facebook, LinkedIn, and YouTube. They explain how managers and companies can use those outlets for marketing purposes. Also discussed in Chapter 19 are methods of measuring a company's success with social media marketing. This chapter is one of many ways *Marketing* is on the cutting edge of the field.

Marketing Dashboards and Marketing Metrics. The *Using Marketing Dashboards* feature in the text delivers two of the newest elements of the business and marketing environment today—performance metrics and dashboards to visualize them. Some of the metrics included in the text are: Category Development Index (CDI), Brand Development Index (BDI), Load Factor (a capacity management metric), Price Premium, Sales per Square Foot, Same-Store Sales Growth, Promotion-to-Sales Ratio, and Cost per Thousand (CPM) impressions. The Dashboard feature is designed to allow readers to learn, practice, and apply the concepts.

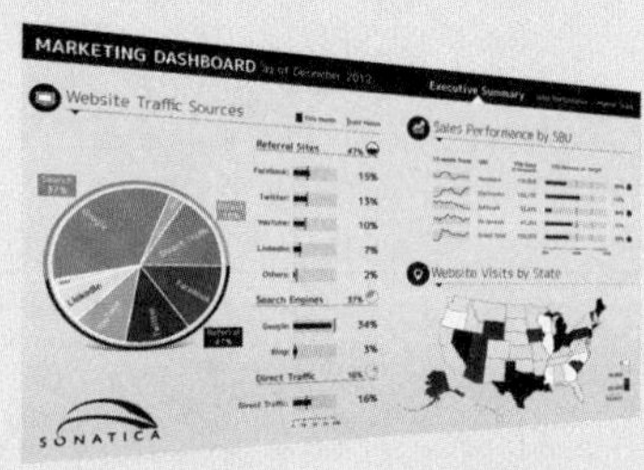

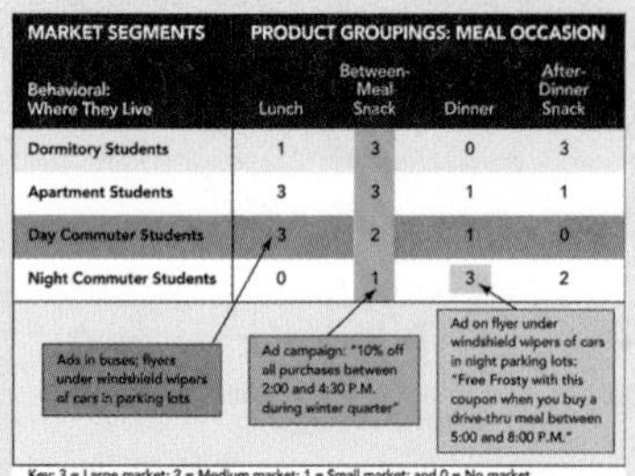

MARKET SEGMENTS	PRODUCT GROUPINGS: MEAL OCCASION			
Behavioral: Where They Live	Lunch	Between-Meal Snack	Dinner	After-Dinner Snack
Dormitory Students	1	3	0	3
Apartment Students	3	3	1	1
Day Commuter Students	3	2	1	0
Night Commuter Students	0	1	3	2

Ads in buses; flyers under windshield wipers of cars in parking lots

Ad campaign: "10% off all purchases between 2:00 and 4:30 P.M. during winter quarter"

Ad on flyer under windshield wipers of cars in night parking lots: "Free Frosty with this coupon when you buy a drive-thru meal between 5:00 and 8:00 P.M."

Key: 3 = Large market; 2 = Medium market; 1 = Small market; and 0 = No market

Color-Coded Graphs and Tables. The use of color in the graphs and tables enhances their readability and adds a visual level of learning to the textbook for readers. In addition, these color highlights increase student comprehension by linking the text discussion to colored elements in the graphs and tables.

New Video Cases. Each chapter ends with a case that is supported by a video to illustrate the issues in the chapter. New cases such as Chobani Greek Yogurt, X-1 Audio, Secret Deodorant, LA Galaxy, Carmex lip balm, and StuffDOT, and recent cases such as IBM, Groupon, Trek Bicycles, Google, and Mountain Dew provide current and relevant examples that are familiar to students.

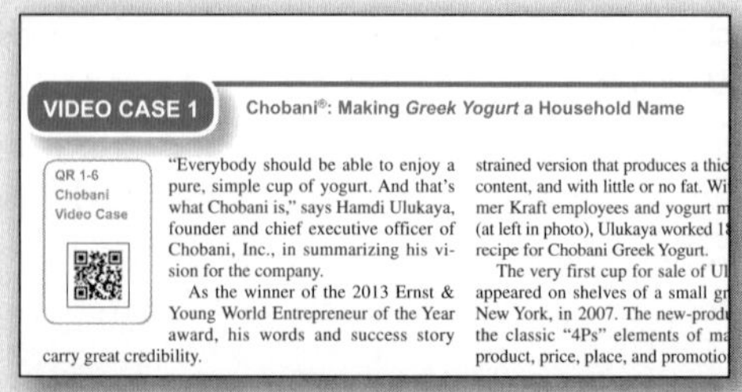

VIDEO CASE 1 Chobani®: Making *Greek Yogurt* a Household Name

QR 1-6 Chobani Video Case

"Everybody should be able to enjoy a pure, simple cup of yogurt. And that's what Chobani is," says Hamdi Ulukaya, founder and chief executive officer of Chobani, Inc., in summarizing his vision for the company.

As the winner of the 2013 Ernst & Young World Entrepreneur of the Year award, his words and success story carry great credibility.

strained version that produces a thic content, and with little or no fat. Wi mer Kraft employees and yogurt m (at left in photo), Ulukaya worked 1 recipe for Chobani Greek Yogurt.

The very first cup for sale of Ul appeared on shelves of a small gr New York, in 2007. The new-prod the classic "4Ps" elements of ma product, price, place, and promotio

INNOVATION

In today's fast-paced and demanding educational environment, innovation is essential to effective learning. To maintain *Marketing*'s leadership position in the marketplace, the author team consistently creates innovative pedagogical tools that match contemporary students' learning styles and interests. The authors keep their fingers on the pulse of technology to bring real innovation to their text and package. Innovations such as QR codes, a Twitter feed, hyperlinked PowerPoint slides, and an online blog augment the McGraw-Hill Education online innovations such as Connect, LearnSmart, and SmartBook.

QR Codes. You can see QR codes in magazine ads; on television programming; as part of catalogs, in-store displays, and product packaging; and throughout *Marketing,* 12/e! These codes bring the text to life with ads and videos about products and companies that are discussed in the text. These videos also keep the text even more current. While each code in the text has a caption (as shown to the right), the links are updated to reflect new campaigns and market changes. In addition, the QR codes provide links to stream the video cases at the end of each chapter. You can use your smartphone to download any QR code reader to use the QR codes found throughout the book. If you don't have access to a smartphone, go to www.kerin.tv to find the links through your computer.

QR 1-2
Terrafugia
Transition
Video

Twitter Feed and Online Blog. Visit www.kerinmarketing.com to participate in *Marketing*'s online blog discussion and to see Twitter feed updates. You can also subscribe to the Twitter feed to receive the Marketing Question of the Day and respond with the #QotD hashtag.

Connect, LearnSmart, and SmartBook Integration. These McGraw-Hill Education products provide a comprehensive package of online resources to enable students to learn faster, study more efficiently, and increase knowledge retention. The products represent the gold standard in online, interactive, and adaptive learning tools and have received accolades from industry experts for their Library and Study Center elements, filtering and reporting functions, and immediate student feedback capabilities. In addition, the authors have developed book-specific interactive assignments, including (a) auto-graded applications based on the marketing plan exercises, and (b) activities based on the Marketing Dashboards and marketing metrics presented in the text.

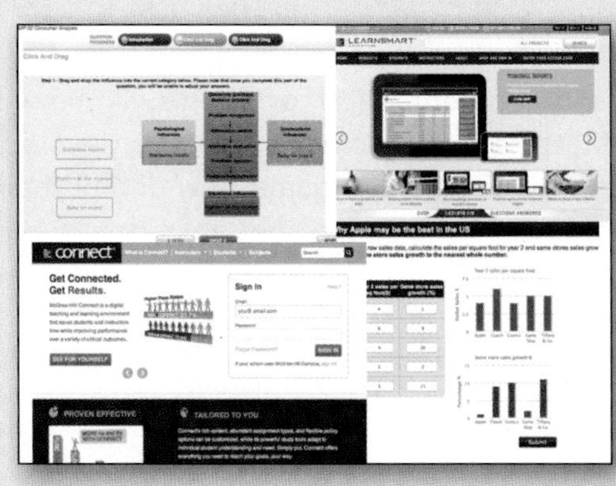

CHAPTER 2: MASTER TEST BANK

DEVELOPING SUCCESSFUL ORGANIZATIONAL AND MARKETING STRATEGIES

Test Item Table by Learning Objective and Bloom's Level of Learning

Learning Objective (LO)	Bloom's Level of Learning (LL)		
	Level 1 Knowledge (Knows Basic Terms & Facts)	Level 2 Comprehension (Understands Concepts & Principles)	Level 3 Application (Applies Principles)
LO 1-1 Describe two kinds of organizations and the three levels of strategy in them. (pp. 22-24)	9, 10, 11, 12, 13, 14, 15, 16, 17, 18, 19, 20, 24, 25, 28, 29, 30, 32, 33, 41, 42, 49, 50, 51, 52, 54, 55, 59, 62, 63, 354	21, 22, 26, 27, 31, 34, 35, 36, 37, 38, 39, 40, 43, 44, 45, 47, 48, 53, 56, 57, 60, 61, 64 **358, 359, 361**	23, 46, 58, 65, 66 **360**

NOTE: **Bold** numbers indicate short essay questions. Underlined numbers indicate visually enhanced questions.

Innovative Test Bank. Containing almost 7,000 multiple-choice and essay questions, the *Marketing,* 12/e Test Bank reflects more than two decades of innovations. The Test Bank includes two Test Item Tables for each chapter that organize all the chapter's test items by Bloom's three levels of learning against both (1) the main sections in the chapter, and (2) the chapter's learning objectives. In addition, a number of "visual test questions" for each chapter reward students who have spent the effort to understand key graphs, tables, and images in the chapter.

New and Revised Content

Chapter 1: New Chapter Opening Example and New Case on Chobani Greek Yogurt. Chapter 1 begins by describing Chobani's development of its Greek Yogurt as a new food category and its use of word-of-mouth advertising, sponsorship of the Olympics, and Facebook as marketing activities to help it grow to a brand with more than $1 billion in sales. New examples from Domino's, Target, and US Bank have been added, and the discussion of the customer relationship era has been expanded. The chapter ends with a new case and supporting video about Chobani.

Chapter 2: New Coverage of B-Corp Certification and Business Definition, and New Application of BCG Model to Apple Products. The Chapter 2 opening example now includes discussion of Ben & Jerry's "B-Corp" certification, which reflects its efforts to solve social and environmental problems. A new Marketing Matters box discusses how the developers of the Angry Birds video game now define their business. The chapter also includes an in-depth application of the Boston Consulting Group's business portfolio analysis model to selected Apple products (including the iPod, iMac, iPhone, and iPad) and a planning gap analysis for Apple's goals and results.

Chapter 3: Update of Environmental Scan for Facebook and Discussion of New Trends in Marketing. Facebook's management mantra, "Move fast and break things," is discussed in the context of a rapidly changing marketing environment. In addition, discussion of new trends such as consumers constantly switching media, robots becoming viable technologies, and peer-to-peer websites generating growth in microbusinesses has been added. Coverage of changes in the regulatory environment, such as proposed legislation related to the labeling of genetically modified food, has also been included.

Chapter 4: New Discussion of Anheuser-Busch's Practices Related to Ethics and Social Responsibility. Chapter 4 now includes a discussion of the Anheuser-Busch "Our World: Our Responsibility" campaign designed to help Anheuser-Busch become the "Best Beer Company in a Better World." Other new examples include green marketing and cause marketing activities by Levi Strauss and Procter & Gamble.

Chapter 5: Update of Evaluative Criteria Example and Addition of Brand Community Discussion. The discussion of alternative evaluation and evaluative criteria has been updated with recent smartphone ratings and Apple iPhone-versus-Motorola Dröid comparisons. In addition, the Reference Group Influence section now includes a new discussion of associative, aspiration, and dissociative groups and the definition and description of a brand community.

Chapter 6: Updated Coverage of Buyer–Seller Relationships and Supply Partnerships. An updated discussion describes the supply partnership between Harley-Davidson and Milsco Manufacturing, a company that has designed and manufactured Harley-Davidson motorcycle seats for 80 years. The chapter also includes new examples related to Siemens, AT&T, IBM, and Macy's.

Chapter 7: New Material on Dell's Retail Stores in India and China's Growth in World Trade. The chapter-opening example has been updated to describe Dell's retail growth strategy in India, which includes shop-in-a-shop stores and Dell-exclusive stores. In addition, the discussion on world trade flows describes how China will become the country with the largest amount of world trade by 2015.

Chapter 8: Updated Test Screening Examples, New In-Depth Example Using LEGO, and New Coverage of the Impact of Social Media and the Use of Cross Tabulations. The discussion of movie studios using marketing research is updated with movies such as *The Hobbit*, *The Surrogate*, and *The Hunger Games* sequels (*Catching Fire* and *Mockingjay*). The discussions related to Step 1 and Step 2 of the Marketing Research Approach are completely updated with LEGO's research as an example. In addition, the discussion of the use of social media in marketing research has been expanded to include Frito-Lay's use of Facebook as a substitute for focus groups. Finally, an extensive discussion of the use of cross tabulations has been added.

Chapter 9: Updated Zappos, Wendy's, and Apple Examples. The chapter-opening example has been updated to reflect Zappos's expansion to products other than shoes. In addition, the Wendy's example now includes discussion of Wendy's new upscale menu, and the Apple examples include updated discussions of the Apple product-market grid.

Chapter 10: Expanded Discussions of Disruptive Innovation, Idea Generation, Crowdfunding, and Development; a New Marketing Matters Box; and New X-1 Audio Video Case. Chapter 10 has added new examples of disruptive innovation, a discussion about using internal training to generate new-product ideas, a description of crowdsourcing sites where inventors can obtain early-stage funding, and a detailed discussion of Google's driverless car in the development stage of the new-product process. A new Marketing Matters box describes the source of the idea for Netflix and how its business model keeps changing. A new case, X-1 Audio, gives a detailed description of the development of new waterproof audio equipment for athletes of any kind!

Chapter 11: Updated Examples, New Counterfeit Product and Brand Name Discussions, and New Secret Deodorant Video. Chapter 11 includes new examples about General Motors, Microsoft, LEGO, Unilever, Android, Caress, ConAgra Foods, and Pepsi-Cola. In addition, an expanded discussion describes the most counterfeited branded products and adds to the list of criteria to use when selecting a good brand name. The chapter ends with a new video case about Secret deodorant.

Chapter 12: New Chapter-Opening Example about the Sharing Economy, Updated Concepts, and New LA Galaxy Video Case. The "sharing economy" being pioneered by service companies such as Airbnb, Sidecar, Parking Panda, DogVacay, SnapGoods, and TaskRabbit is introduced and discussed in the chapter-opening example. New concepts such as co-creation of services, innovation of core and supplementary services, and service blueprints are now included in Chapter 12. The chapter ends with a new video case that describes the sports marketing activities of the LA Galaxy soccer team.

Chapters 13 and 14: New Marketing Matters Boxes, Updated Discussions of Price Elasticity, Break-Even Analysis, and Dynamic Pricing, and New Video Case on Carmex lip balm. A new Marketing Matters box describing the Dollar Shave Club illustrates how price transparency has led to new online businesses that use price and convenience to attract customers. Another new Marketing Matters box explains how some retailers are using price-match guarantees to stop "showrooming"—the practice of shopping in a store and then buying online. New and expanded discussions include the factors that determine price elasticity, a "color-coded" explanation of break-even analysis and a break-even chart, and updated use of dynamic pricing and fixed-pricing terminology. A new case discusses pricing practices for Carmex lip balm.

Chapter 15. Updated Examples and Advertisements. The chapter-opening example has been updated to reflect that Callaway Golf's online store is now one of the largest Internet retailers, with $30 million in annual sales. New examples and ads include IBM, Eddie Bauer, Jiffy Lube, and PetSmart.

Chapter 16. New Chapter-Opening Example, Updated Material on Green Retailing, and Expanded Marketing inSite Box on Showrooming and Flash Sales. Google Glass(es) and its potential impact on retailing are now the topic of the chapter-opening example. The discussion of green retailing now includes the *Newsweek* ranking of retailers with the best green practices, and the Marketing inSite box describes "showrooming" and watching for "flash" sales as new forms of shopping.

Chapter 17: New Chapter-Opening Example, Updated Coverage of Mobile Marketing, and Updated Discussion of Privacy Issues in Marketing. Taco Bell's integrated marketing campaign is discussed in the chapter-opening example. In addition, an updated discussion of the use of mobile marketing to reach today's college students is part of the Marketing Matters box, and expanded coverage of do-not-call, do-not-mail, and do-not-track legislation is provided.

Chapter 18: New Coverage of Online Television, New Advertising Campaigns, and New Discussion of Advertising Agency of the Year. Chapter 18 begins with a discussion of the dramatic changes in television, a medium that is now available through broadcast, cable, satellite, and the Internet. New examples of advertising include campaigns from Dasani, Fidelity, Coca-Cola, Samsung, GoDaddy, K-Swiss, and Hilton. In addition, the chapter includes a new discussion of *Advertising Age*'s Agency of the Year—72andSunny.

Chapter 19: New Material on Facebook, Twitter, LinkedIn, YouTube, and Other Social Media, and New StuffDOT Video Case. This chapter, new in the last edition, is completely updated to reflect the incredible impact of social media on marketing. New examples include Facebook Home, YouTube channels, near field communications, and many others. The chapter ends with a new StuffDOT video case.

Chapter 20: Update about the Sales Organization at GE Healthcare and New Discussion on Genetic Predisposition to Create Value. The chapter-opening example has been updated to describe the success of sales professional Lindsey Smith at General Electric's Healthcare division. In addition, the chapter now includes new material about genetic markers that may indicate a salesperson's predisposition or willingness to interact with customers and learn about their problems in order to meet their needs.

Chapter 21: Updated Examples, Data, and Information about Interactive Marketing. The chapter-opening example is updated to describe the interactive marketing process at custom bike builder, Seven Cycles. In addition, new data on the number of online shoppers and the level of online retail sales emphasize the growth and importance of interactive marketing. New data regarding what online consumers buy indicate that just five product categories account for two-thirds of all online sales.

Chapter 22: New Coverage of Disruptive Innovations, New Learning Objectives, and New Marketing Matters Box on Implementation. New material and a Marketing Matters box provide coverage of disruptive innovations, which create new markets by displacing low-end products. New and updated material address two new learning objectives—"Use a time-based agenda and action item lists to conduct a meeting," and "Describe an organization's marketing department and the role of a product manager." A new Marketing Matters box describes how successful implementation requires that managers reward success rather than punish failure.

ENGAGING FEATURES

Chapter-opening vignettes introduce students to chapter concepts by using an exciting company as an example. Students are immediately engaged while learning about real-world companies.

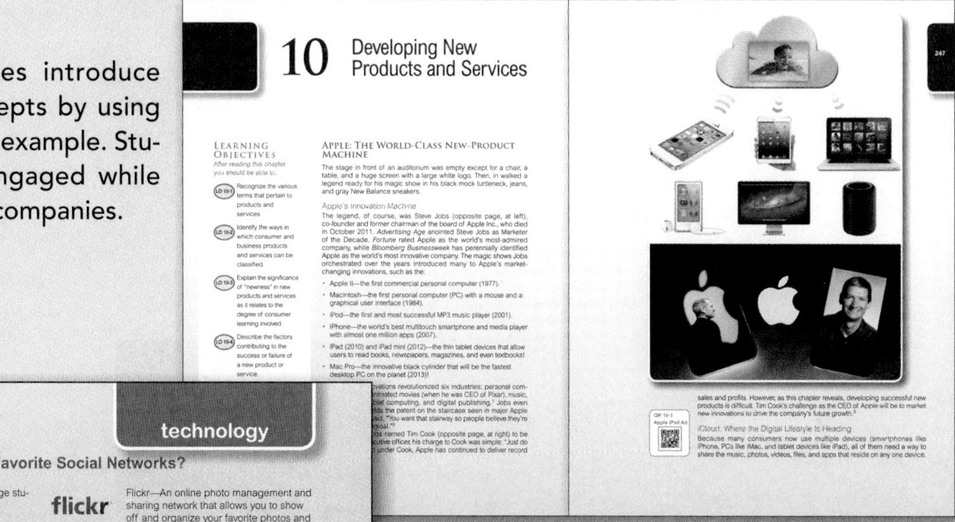

10 Developing New Products and Services

LEARNING OBJECTIVES
After reading this chapter you should be able to:

LO 10-1 Recognize the various terms that pertain to products and services.
LO 10-2 Identify the ways in which consumer and business products and services can be classified.
LO 10-3 Explain the significance of "newness" in new products and services as it relates to the degree of consumer learning involved.
LO 10-4 Describe the factors contributing to the success or failure of a new product or service.

APPLE: THE WORLD-CLASS NEW-PRODUCT MACHINE

The stage in front of an auditorium was empty except for a chair, a table, and a huge screen with a large white logo. Then, in walked a legend ready for his magic show in his black mock turtleneck, jeans, and gray New Balance sneakers.

Apple's Innovation Machine

The legend, of course, was Steve Jobs (opposite page, at left), co-founder and former chairman of the board of Apple Inc., who died in October 2011. *Advertising Age* anointed Steve Jobs as Marketer of the Decade. *Fortune* rated Apple as the world's most-admired company, while *Bloomberg Businessweek* has perennially identified Apple as the world's most innovative company. The magic shows Jobs orchestrated over the years introduced many to Apple's market-changing innovations, such as the:

- Apple II—the first commercial personal computer (1977).
- Macintosh—the first personal computer (PC) with a mouse and a graphical user interface (1984).
- iPod—the first and most successful MP3 music player (2001).
- iPhone—the world's best multitouch smartphone and media player with almost one million apps (2007).
- iPad (2010) and iPad mini (2012)—the thin tablet devices that allow users to read books, newspapers, magazines, and even textbooks!
- Mac Pro—the innovative black cylinder that will be the fastest desktop PC on the planet (2013)!

247

Marketing Matters

technology

What Are Some of Your Other Favorite Social Networks?

Other social networks that are popular among college students with diverse interests include the following:

Vimeo—A community of creative people who are passionate about sharing the videos they make.

Google+—A social-sharing network from Google that allows you to organize friends in "circles" for easy sharing, host "hangouts," and more.

Foursquare—A location-based mobile platform that helps you explore cities through "check-ins" and rewards.

StumbleUpon—A discovery engine for finding and sharing the best content on the Web.

Flickr—An online photo management and sharing network that allows you to show off and organize your favorite photos and videos.

Pinterest—A content sharing network where members "pin" images, videos, and more to "boards" they create, which are categorized into different themes.

Tumblr—A feature-rich, micro-blogging platform that allows users to share text, photos, music, links, videos, and more.

Instagram—A fast and fun way to share photos; users simply snap a photo, choose a specialized filter to alter the look and feel of the image, and share the image with family and friends.

Marketing Matters boxes highlight real-world examples of customer value creation and delivery, entrepreneurship, and technology that give students further insight into the practical world of marketing.

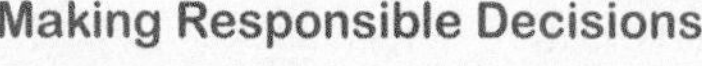

Making Responsible Decisions

sustainability

Millennials Are Going to Change the World—through Environmental Sustainability!

Millennials are determined to make a difference in the world and, by doing so, make the world a better place. They are idealistic and eager to get started, particularly when it comes to environmental sustainability, which millennials believe is part of what it means to be socially responsible. The group includes students in college and graduate school and many early career employees. In different ways each group is making its voice heard.

There are approximately 17 million undergraduate millennials who expect sustainable campus communities that include LEED (Leadership in Energy and Environmental Design)-certified housing, campus transit systems, and recycling programs. They view themselves as part of the "ecoRenaissance" movement. Graduate students are looking for programs with sustainability electives, case studies, and potential for involvement with organizations such as Net Impact (www.netimpact.org), as social responsibility officer, environmental consultant, and sustainability database specialist at companies that are eco-conscious and advocate good citizenship.

Sara Hochman is a typical example. She was interested in environmental issues in college, and her first job was as an environmental consultant. To make a bigger impact on her clients, she decided she needed to "beef up" her business skills, so she enrolled in graduate school at the University of Chicago where she could take an elective on renewable energy and join the Energy Club. Similarly, a recent college graduate joined the Peace Corps because, she said, "I want to be part of something bigger than just me-me-me."

Have you made similar choices or decisions based on your interest and concern about sustainability? What will the world look like after the millennials have made their changes? It is difficult to predict.

71

CHAPTER 3 Scanning the Marketing Environment

Making Responsible Decisions boxes focus on social responsibility, sustainability, and ethics. These boxes provide exciting, current examples of how companies approach these subjects in their marketing strategy.

Marketing inSite

Identifying Your VALS Profile: What Motivates You?

The VALS™ system run by Strategic Business Insights has identified eight unique consumer segments based on a person's primary motivation and resources. The text provides a brief description of each segment.

Do you wish to know your VALS profile? If you do, respond to the questions on the

VALS survey at www.strategicbusinessinsights.com. Simply click "VALS." Next, click the "Take the VALS Survey" link. In addition to obtaining your profile in real time, you can examine the characteristics of your own and other profiles in greater detail.

Marketing inSite exercises are integrated in the text and ask students to go online and think critically about a specific company's use of the Internet, helping students apply knowledge of key chapter concepts, terms, and topics, as well as evaluate the success or failure of the company's efforts.

BUILDING YOUR MARKETING PLAN

To develop the promotion strategy for your marketing plan, follow the steps suggested in the planning phase of the promotion decision process described in Figure 17–6.

1 You should (*a*) identify the target audience, (*b*) specify the promotion objectives, (*c*) set the promotion budget, (*d*) select the right promotion tools, (*e*) design the promotion, and (*f*) schedule the promotion.

2 Also specify the pretesting and posttesting procedures needed in the implementation and evaluation phases.

3 Finally, describe how each of your promotion tools is integrated to provide a consistent message.

Building Your Marketing Plan is an end-of-chapter feature that requires students to go through the practical application of creating their own marketing plan.

INSTRUCTOR RESOURCES

Marketing, 12/e *Instructor Resources*

Instructor's Manual
The IM includes lecture notes, video case teaching notes, Appendix D case teaching notes, and In-Class Activities.

Video Cases
A unique series of 22 marketing video cases includes new videos featuring Chobani, X-1 Audio, Secret, LA Galaxy, Carmex, and StuffDOT.

Appendix D Cases
www.12e.kerin.tv/AppD
Alternate cases for each chapter for instructors who elect to assign additional cases.

Test Bank
We offer almost 7,000 test questions categorized by topic learning objectives, and level of learning.

Blog
www.kerinmarketing.com
A blog written specifically for use in the classroom! Throughout each term we post new examples of marketing campaigns, along with a classroom discussion and participation guide.

Connect, LearnSmart, and SmartBook
The unique content platform delivering powerful technical resources and adaptive learning solutions.

Online Learning Center
www.kerin.tv
Online access to all course materials.

In-Class Activities
Chapter-specific in-class activities for today's students who learn from active, participative experiences.

PowerPoint Slides
Media-enhanced and hyperlinked slides enable engaging and interesting classroom discussions.

Practice Marketing (Simulation)
Practice Marketing is a 3D, online, multiplayer game that enables students to gain practical experiences in an interactive environment.

The *Marketing 12/e Course Planning Roadmap* is designed to help you select elements from the textbook and supplements to plan and deliver a course tailored to your students' needs. The Roadmap is available for download at www.12e.kerin.tv/roadmap.

Course Planning Checklist

Chapters (CH)	Video Cases (VC)	Using Marketing Dashboards (UMD)	Quick Response Codes (QR)	In-Class Activities (ICA)
CH 1: Creating Customer Relationships and Value through Marketing	☐ VC 1: Chobani®: Making *Greek Yogurt* a Household Name		☐ QR 1-1: Chobani Ad ☐ QR 1-2: Terrafugia Transition Video ☐ QR 1-3: Pepsi Next Ad ☐ QR 1-4: 3M Flag Highlighters Ad ☐ QR 1-5: Hermitage Tour Video ☐ QR-1-6: Chobani Video Case	☐ ICA 1-1: Designing a Candy Bar ☐ ICA 1-2: What Makes a Better Mousetrap?
CH 2: Developing Successful Organizational and Marketing Strategies	☐ VC 2: IBM: Using Strategy to Build a "Smarter Planet"	☐ UMD 2: How Well is Ben & Jerry's Doing?: Dollar Sales and Dollar Market Share	☐ QR 2-1: Cree LED Bulb Ad ☐ QR 2-2: Medtronic Video ☐ QR 2-3: Angry Birds Video ☐ QR 2-4: B&J's Bonnaroo Buzz Ad ☐ QR 2-5: IBM Video Case	☐ ICA 2-1: Calculating a "Fog Index" for Your Own Writing ☐ ICA 2-2: Marketing Yourself

Connect

Connect is an all-digital teaching and learning environment designed from the ground up to work with the way instructors and students think, teach, and learn. As a digital teaching, assignment, and assessment platform, Connect strengthens the link among faculty, students, and coursework, helping everyone accomplish more in less time.

LearnSmart

The smartest way to get from B to A

LearnSmart is the most widely used and intelligent adaptive learning resource. It is proven to strengthen memory recall, improve course retention, and boost grades by distinguishing between what students know and what they don't know, and honing in on the concepts that they are most likely to forget. LearnSmart continuously adapts to each student's needs by building an individual learning path. As a result, students study smarter and retain more knowledge.

SmartBook

A revolution in learning

Fueled by LearnSmart, SmartBook is the first and only adaptive reading experience available today. SmartBook personalizes content for each student in a continuously adapting reading experience. Reading is no longer a passive and linear experience, but an engaging and dynamic one where students are more likely to master and retain important concepts, coming to class better prepared.

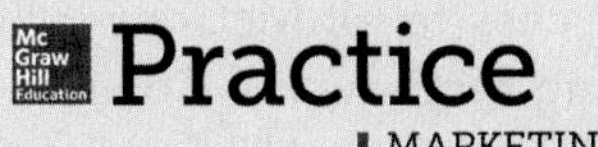

Practice Marketing

McGraw-Hill's Practice Marketing is a 3D, online, multiplayer game that enables students to gain practical experience by applying the skills they learn in a highly interactive and engaging environment. Using the knowledge built on their course, students become the marketing manager for a company entering the backpack market. By making decisions and seeing the results, players get feedback on their actions and learn by doing. Practice Marketing is the first in this series of new digital products from McGraw-Hill. Contact your local rep for more details.

Create

Instructors can now tailor their teaching resources to match the way they teach! With McGraw-Hill Create, www.mcgrawhillcreate.com, instructors can easily rearrange chapters, combine material from other content sources, and quickly upload and integrate their own content-like course syllabi or teaching notes. Find the right content in Create by searching through thousands of leading McGraw-Hill textbooks. Arrange the material to fit your teaching style. Order a Create book and receive a complimentary print review copy in 3–5 business days or a complimentary electronic review copy (echo) via e-mail within one hour. Go to www.mcgrawhillcreate.com today and register.

Tegrity Campus

Tegrity makes class time available 24/7 by automatically capturing every lecture in a searchable format for students to review when they study and complete assignments. With a simple one-click start-and-stop process, you capture all computer screens and corresponding audio. Students can replay any part of any class with easy-to-use browser-based viewing on a PC or Mac. Educators know that the more students can see, hear, and experience class resources, the better they learn. In fact, studies prove it. With patented Tegrity "search anything" technology, students instantly recall key class moments for replay online or on iPods and mobile devices. Instructors can help turn all their students' study time into learning moments immediately supported by their lecture. To learn more about Tegrity, watch a two-minute Flash demo at http://tegritycampus.mhhe.com.

Blackboard® Partnership

McGraw-Hill Education and Blackboard have teamed up to simplify your life. Now you and your students can access Connect and Create right from within your Blackboard course—all with one single sign-on. The grade books are seamless, so when a student completes an integrated Connect assignment, the grade for that assignment automatically (and instantly) feeds your Blackboard grade center. Learn more at www.domorenow.com.

McGraw-Hill Campus™

McGraw-Hill Campus is a new one-stop teaching and learning experience available to users of any learning management system. This institutional service allows faculty and students to enjoy single sign-on (SSO) access to all McGraw-Hill Higher Education materials, including the award-winning McGraw-Hill Connect platform, from directly within the institution's website. With McGraw-Hill Campus, faculty receive instant access to teaching materials (e.g., ebooks, test banks, PowerPoint slides, animations, learning objects, etc.), allowing them to browse, search, and use any instructor ancillary content in our vast library at no additional cost to instructor or students. In addition, students enjoy SSO access to a variety of free content (e.g., quizzes, flash cards, narrated presentations, etc.) and subscription-based products (e.g., McGraw-Hill Connect). With McGraw-Hill Campus enabled, faculty and students will never need to create another account to access McGraw-Hill products and services. Learn more at www.mhcampus.com.

Assurance of Learning Ready

Many educational institutions today focus on the notion of *assurance of learning,* an important element of some accreditation standards. *Marketing* is designed specifically to support instructors' assurance of learning initiatives with a simple yet powerful solution. Each test bank question for *Marketing* maps to a specific chapter learning objective listed in the text. Instructors can use our test bank software, EZ Test and EZ Test Online, to easily query for learning objectives that directly relate to the learning outcomes for their course. Instructors can then use the reporting features of EZ Test to aggregate student results in similar fashion, making the collection and presentation of assurance of learning data simple and easy.

AACSB Tagging

McGraw-Hill Education is a proud corporate member of AACSB International. Understanding the importance and value of AACSB accreditation, *Marketing*'s Test Bank recognizes the curricula guidelines detailed in the AACSB standards for business accreditation by connecting selected questions in the text and the test bank to six of the general knowledge and skill guidelines in the AACSB standards. The statements contained in *Marketing* are provided only as a guide for the users of this textbook. The AACSB leaves content coverage and assessment within the purview of individual schools, the mission of the school, and the faculty. While the *Marketing* teaching package makes no claim of any specific AACSB qualification or evaluation, we have within *Marketing* labeled selected questions according to the six general knowledge and skills areas.

McGraw-Hill Customer Experience Group Contact Information

At McGraw-Hill, we understand that getting the most from new technology can be challenging. That's why our services don't stop after you purchase our products. You can e-mail our Product Specialists 24 hours a day to get product training online. Or you can search our knowledge bank of Frequently Asked Questions on our support website. For Customer Support, call **800-331-5094**, e-mail **mhsupport@mcgraw-hill.com**, or visit www.mhhe.com/support. One of our Technical Support Analysts will be able to assist you in a timely fashion.

Acknowledgments

To ensure continuous improvement of our textbook and supplements we have utilized an extensive review and development process for each of our past editions. Building on that history, the *Marketing*, 12th edition development process included several phases of evaluation and a variety of stakeholder audiences (e.g., students, instructors, etc.).

Reviewers who were vital in the changes that were made to the twelfth edition and its supplements include:

Dr. Priscilla G. Aaltonen
Hampton University

Aysen Bakir
Illinois State University

Cathleen H. Behan
Northern Virginia Community College

Patricia Bernson
County College of Morris

Charles Bodkin
UNC Charlotte

Nancy Boykin
Colorado State University

Barry Bunn
Valencia College

Michael Callow
Morgan State University

Rae Caloura
Johnson & Wales University

Catherine Campbell
University of Maryland-University College

Lindell Phillip Chew
University of Missouri-St. Louis

Frank A. Chiaverini
County College of Morris

Diana Joy Colarusso
Daytona State College

Francisco Coronel
Hampton University

Jane Cromartie
University of New Orleans

Andrew Dartt
Texas Tech University

Tom Deckelman
Owens Community College

Mary Beth DeConinck
Western Carolina University

Timothy Donahue
Chadron State College

Beibei Dong
Lehigh University

Sundaram Dorai
Northeastern Illinois University

Katalin Eibel-Spanyi
Eastern Connecticut State University

Ronald A. Feinberg
Suffolk Community College

Jeff Finley
California State University-Fresno

Kasia Firlej
Purdue University-Calumet

John Fitzpatrick
Northwestern Michigan College

Eugene Flynn
Harper Community College

William Foxx
Troy University Montgomery

Amy Frank
Wingate University

Anthony R. Fruzzetti
Johnson & Wales University

Joe M. Garza
University of Texas-Pan American

John Gaskins
Longwood University

Annette George
Morgan State University

Richard Hargrove
High Point University

Yi He
California State University-East Bay

Steve Hertzenberg
James Madison University

Donald Hoffer
Miami University

Cathleen Hohner
College of DuPage

Pamela Hulen
Johnson County Community College

Jianfeng Jiang
Northeastern Illinois University

Vahwere Kavota
Hampton University

Walter Kendall
Tarleton State University

Sylvia Keyes
Bridgewater State University

John C. Keyt
Gardner-Webb University

Imran Khan
University of South Alabama

Greg Kitzmiller
Indiana University

Anthony Koh
University of Toledo

Helen Koons
Miami University-Ohio

Linda N. LaMarca
Tarleton State University

Sue Lewis
Tarleton State University

Guy Lochiatto
MassBay Community College

Jun Ma
Indiana University-Purdue University Fort Wayne

Ahmed Maamoun
University of Minnesota-Duluth

Cesar Maloles
California State University-East Bay

Raymond Marzilli
Johnson & Wales University

Sanal Mazvancheryl
American University

Diane T. McCrohan
Johnson & Wales University

Sue McGorry
DeSales University

Mary Ann McGrath
Loyola University-Chicago

Terrance Kevin McNamara
Suffolk County Community College

Sanjay S. Mehta
Sam Houston State University

Juan (Gloria) Meng
Minnesota State University-Mankato

Kathy Meyer
Dallas Baptist University

Victoria Miller
Morgan State University

Robert Morris
Florida State College at Jacksonville

Carol M. Motley
University of Alabama at Birmingham
Jean Murray
Bryant University
Keith B. Murray
Bryant University
Elaine Notarantonio
Bryant University
Joanne Orabone
Community College of Rhode Island
Nikolai Ostapenko
University of the District of Columbia
Richard D. Parker
High Point University
Jerry Peerbolte
University of Arkansas-Fort Smith
Deepa Pillai
Northeastern Illinois University
Michael Pontikos
Youngstown State University
Milton Pressley
University of New Orleans
Bruce Ramsey
Franklin University
Maria Randazzo-Nardin
State University of New York-Farmingdale College
Clay Rasmussen
Texas A&M University System-Tarleton State University

Chris Ratcliffe
Bryant University
Deana Ray
Forsyth Technical Community College
Kristen Regine
Johnson & Wales University
Ruth Rosales
Miami University
Abhik Roy
Quinnipiac University
Kumar Sarangee
Santa Clara University
Mary Schramm
Quinnipiac University
Sandipan Sen
Southeast Missouri State University
Kunal Sethi
University of Minnesota-Duluth
Abhay Shah
Colorado State University-Pueblo
Ravi Shanmugam
Santa Clara University
Lisa Siegal
Texas A&M University-San Antonio
Sally Sledge
Norfolk State University
James Garry Smith
Tarleton State University
Kimberly Smith
County College of Morris

Julie Sneath
University of South Alabama
Janice Taylor
Miami University
Mary Tripp
Wisconsin Indianhead Technical College
Lisa Troy
Texas A&M University
Ann Veeck
Western Michigan University
Jeffrey W. von Freymann
Wingate University
Judy Wagner
East Carolina University
Erin Wilkinson
Johnson & Wales University
Jacqueline Williams
North Carolina A&T State University
Tina L. Williams
East Carolina University
Van Wood
Virginia Commonwealth University
Jefrey R. Woodall
York College of Pennsylvania
George Young
Liberty University
Shabnam Zanjani
Northeastern Illinois University
Srdan Zdravkovic
Bryant University

The preceding section demonstrates the amount of feedback and developmental input that went into this project, and we are deeply grateful to the numerous people who have shared their ideas with us. Reviewing a book or supplement takes an incredible amount of energy and attention. We are glad so many of our colleagues took the time to do it. Their comments have inspired us to do our best.

Reviewers who contributed to the first 11 editions of this book include:

Nadia J. Abgrab
Kerri Acheson
Wendy Achey
Roy Adler
Christie Amato
Linda Anglin
Chris Anicich
Ismet Anitsal
Godwin Ariguzo
William D. Ash
Corinne Asher
Gerard Athaide
Tim Aurand
Andy Aylesworth
Patricia Baconride
Siva Balasubramanian
A. Diane Barlar
James H. Barnes
Suman Basuroy
Connie Bateman
Leta Beard
Karen Becker-Olsen
Frederick J. Beier
Thom J. Belich
Joseph Belonax
John Benavidez
Ellen Benowitz
Karen Berger
Thomas M. Bertsch
Parimal Bhagat
Carol Bienstock
Abhi Biswas
Kevin W. Bittle
Christopher Blocker
Jeff Blodgett
Nancy Bloom
Charles Bodkin
Larry Borgen
Koren Borges
Nancy Boykin
John Brandon
Thomas Brashear
Martin Bressler
Glen Brodowsky
Bruce Brown
William Brown
William G. Browne
Judy Bulin
David J. Burns
Alan Bush
Stephen Calcich
William J. Carner
Gary Carson
Larry Carter
Tom Castle
Gerald O. Cavallo

Carmina Cavazos
Erin Cavusgil
S. Tamer Cavusgil
Kirti Celly
Bruce Chadbourne
S. Choi Chan
Donald Chang
Sang Choe
Kay Chomic
Janet Ciccarelli
Melissa Clark
Reid Claxton
Debbie Coleman
Mark Collins
Howard Combs
Clare Comm
Clark Compton
Mary Conran
Cristanna Cook
Sherry Cook
John Coppett
John Cox
Scott Cragin
Ken Crocker
Joe Cronin
James Cross
Lowell E. Crow
Brent Cunningham
John H. Cunningham
Bill Curtis
Bob Dahlstrom
Dan Darrow
Neel Das
Mayukh Dass
Hugh Daubek
Martin Decatur
Francis DeFea
Joseph Defilippe
Beth Deinert
Linda M. Delene
Tino DeMarco
Frances Depaul
Jobie Devinney-Walsh
Irene Dickey
Paul Dion
William B. Dodds
James H. Donnelly
Casey Donoho
Ron Dougherty
Diane Dowdell
Paul Dowling
Michael Drafke
Lawrence Duke
Bob Dwyer
Laura Dwyer
Rita Dynan
Eddie V. Easley
Eric Ecklund
Alexander Edsel
Roger W. Egerton
Kellie Emrich
Steven Engel
David Erickson
Barbara Evans
Ken Fairweather
Larry Feick
Lori Feldman
Kevin Feldt
John Finlayson
Karen Flaherty
Theresa Flaherty
Elizabeth R. Flynn
Charles Ford
Renee Foster
Michael Fowler
Judy Foxman
Tracy Fulce
Donald Fuller
Bashar Gammoh
Stan Garfunkel
Stephen Garrott
James Gaubert
Glen Gelderloos
David Gerth
James Ginther
Susan Godar
Dan Goebel
Marc Goldberg
Leslie A. Goldgehn
Larry Goldstein
Kenneth Goodenday
Karen Gore
Darrell Goudge
James Gould
Kimberly Grantham
Nancy Grassilli
Stacia Gray
Barnett Greenberg
James L. Grimm
Pamela Grimm
Pola B. Gupta
Mike Hagan
Richard Hansen
Donald V. Harper
Dotty Harpool
Lynn Harris
Robert C. Harris
Ernan Haruvy
Santhi Harvey
Ron Hasty
Julie Haworth
Bryan Hayes
James A. Henley, Jr.
Ken Herbst
Jonathan Hibbard
Richard M. Hill
Nathan Himelstein
Adrienne Hinds
Donald Hoffer
Al Holden
Fred Honerkamp
Kristine Hovsepian
Jarrett Hudnal
Fred Hurvitz
Mike Hyman
Rajesh Iyer
Donald R. Jackson
Paul Jackson
Kenneth Jameson
David Jamison
Deb Jansky
Keith Jones
Cydney Johnson
James C. Johnson
Wesley Johnston
Robert Jones
Mary Joyce
Jacqueline Karen
Janice Karlen
Sudhir Karunakaran
Rajiv Kashyap
Herbert Katzenstein
Philip Kearney
George Kelley
Katie Kemp
Ram Kesaran
Joe Kim
Brian Kinard
Martyn Kingston
Roy Klages
Chiranjeev Kohli
Christopher Kondo
Douglas Kornemann
Kathleen Krentler
Terry Kroeten
David Kuhlmeier
Anand Kumar
Nanda Kumar
Michelle Kunz
Ann Kuzma
John Kuzma
Priscilla LaBarbera
Duncan G. LaBay
Christine Lai
Jay Lambe
Tim Landry
Jane Lang
Irene Lange
Richard Lapidus
Donald Larson
Ron Larson
Ed Laube
J. Ford Laumer
Debra Laverie
Marilyn Lavin
Gary Law
Robert Lawson
Wilton Lelund
Karen LeMasters
Cecil Leonard
Richard C. Leventhal
Cindy Leverenz
Leonard Lindenmuth
Ann Little
Eldon L. Little
Jason Little
Yunchuan Liu
James Lollar
Paul Londrigan
Lynn Loudenback
Ann Lucht
Harold Lucius
Mike Luckett
Robert Luke
Michael R. Luthy
Richard J. Lutz
Jun Ma
Marton L. Macchiete
Rhonda Mack
Patricia Manninen
James Marco
Kenneth Maricle
Larry Marks
Tom Marshall
Elena Martinez
Carolyn Massiah
Tamara Masters
Charla Mathwick

Michael Mayo
James McAlexander
Peter J. McClure
Maria McConnell
Phyllis McGinnis
Jim McHugh
Jane McKay-Nesbitt
Gary F. McKinnon
Roger McIntyre
Ed McLaughlin
Jo Ann McManamy
Kristy McManus
Bob McMillen
Samuel E. McNeely
Lee Meadow
Havva Jale Meric
James Meszaros
Matt Meuter
Fekri Meziou
George Miaoulis
Soon Hong Min
Ronald Michaels
Jennie Mitchell
Herbert A. Miller
Stephen W. Miller
Theodore Mitchell
William G. Mitchell
Steven Moff
Kim Montney
Rex Moody
Melissa Moore
Linda Morable
Fred Morgan
Farrokh Moshiri
Gordon Mosley
William Motz
Donald F. Mulvihill
James Munch
James A. Muncy
Jeanne Munger
Linda Munilla
Bill Murphy
Brian Murray
Janet Murray
Keith Murray
Suzanne Murray
Paul Myer
Joseph Myslivec
Sunder Narayanan
Edwin Nelson
Jennifer Nelson
Bob Newberry
Eric Newman
Donald G. Norris
Carl Obermiller
Dave Olson
James Olver
Ben Oumlil
Notis Pagiavlas
Allan Palmer
Yue Pan
Anil Pandya
Dennis Pappas
June E. Parr
Philip Parron
Vladimir Pashkevich
Thomas Passero
David Terry Paul
Richard Penn
John Penrose
William Pertula
Michael Peters
Bill Peterson
Susan Peterson
Renee Pfeifer-Luckett
Chuck Pickett
William S. Piper
Stephen Pirog
Gary Poorman
Vonda Powell
Carmen Powers
Susie Pryor
Joe Puzi
Abe Qastin
Edna Ragins
Priyali Rajagopal
Daniel Rajaratnam
James P. Rakowski
Rosemary Ramsey
Kristen Regine
Timothy Reisenwitz
Alicia Revely
Barbara Ribbens
Cathie Rich-Duval
Kim Richmond
Joe Ricks
Heikki Rinne
Bruce Robertson
Sandra Robertson
Linda Rochford
William Rodgers
Jean Romeo
Teri Root
Dennis Rosen
Tom Rossi
Vicki Rostedt
Heidi Rottier
Larry Rottmeyer
Robert W. Ruekert
Maria Sanella
Eberhard Scheuling
Charles Schewe
Kathryn Schifferle
Starr F. Schlobohm
Roberta Schultz
Lisa M. Sciulli
Stan Scott
Kim Sebastiano
Harold S. Sekiguchi
Doris M. Shaw
Eric Shaw
Ken Shaw
Dan Sherrel
Philip Shum
Susan Sieloff
Lisa Simon
Bob E. Smiley
Allen Smith
David Smith
Kimberly D. Smith
Ruth Ann Smith
Sandra Smith
Norman Smothers
Gonca Soysal
James V. Spiers
Pat Spirou
Martin St. John
Craig Stacey
Miriam B. Stamps
Susan Stanix
Cheryl Stansfield
Angela Stanton
Joe Stasio
Tom Stevenson
John Striebich
Andrei Strijnev
Randy Stuart
Kathleen Stuenkel
Scott Swan
Rick Sweeney
Michael Swenson
Robert Swerdlow
Vincent P. Taiani
Clint Tankersley
Ruth Taylor
Steve Taylor
Andrew Thacker
Tom Thompson
Scott Thorne
Hsin-Min Tong
Dan Toy
Fred Trawick
Thomas L. Trittipo
Gary Tucker
Sue Umashankar
Bronis Verhage
Bronis J. Verhage
Ottilia Voegtli
Jeff von Freymann
Gerald Waddle
Randall E. Wade
Blaise Waguespack, Jr.
Harlan Wallingford
Mark Weber
Don Weinrauch
Robert S. Welsh
Ron Weston
Michelle Wetherbee
Sheila Wexler
Max White
James Wilkins
Erin Wilkinson
Janice Williams
Joan Williams
Kaylene Williams
Kathleen Williamson
Robert Williams
Jerry W. Wilson
Joseph Wisenblit
Robert Witherspoon
Van R. Wood
Wendy Wood
Kim Wong
Lauren Wright
Lan Wu
William R. Wynd
Poh-Lin Yeoh
Mark Young
Sandra Young
Gail M. Zank
James Zemanek
Christopher Ziemnowicz
Lisa Zingaro
Leon Zurawicki

Thanks are due to many people, including students, instructors, university staff, librarians and researchers, business periodical authors and editors, company representatives, and marketing professionals of every kind. Their assistance has been essential in our efforts to continue to provide the most comprehensive and up-to-date teaching and learning package available. We have been fortunate to have so many people be part of our team!

Our long-time collaborator, Michael Vessey, led our efforts on the Instructor's Manual, PowerPoint slides, In-Class Activities, and the Test Bank. In addition, he provided cases, research assistance, and many special images. Michael is an exceptional education and learning consultant who brings an extraordinary familiarity with marketing and contemporary pedagogies to our project.

Thanks are also due to many other colleagues who contributed to the text, cases, and supplements. They include: Richard Lutz of the University of Florida; Linda Rochford of the University of Minnesota-Duluth; Kevin Upton of the University of Minnesota-Twin Cities; Nancy Nentl of Metropolitan State University; David Brennan of the University of St. Thomas; Leslie Kendrik of Johns Hopkins University; Lau Geok Theng of the National University of Singapore; and Leigh McAlister of the University of Texas at Austin. Anders Sandholm and Kirk Huizenga provided assistance with the Test Bank. Rick Armstrong of Armstrong Photography, Dan Hundley and George Heck of Token Media, Nick Kaufman and Michelle Morgan of NKP Media, Bruce McLean of World Class Communication Technologies, Paul Fagan of Fagan Productions, Martin Walter of White Room Digital, Scott Bolin of Bolin Marketing, and Andrew Schones of Pure Imagination produced the videos.

Many businesspeople also provided substantial assistance by making available information that appears in the text, videos, and supplements—much of it for the first time in college materials. Thanks are due to Chris Klein, Jaime Cardenas, Casey Leppanen, Heather Peace, and Lori Nevares of LA Galaxy; Carl Thomas, Peter Dirksing, and Dana Swanson of X-1 Audio, Inc.; Ian Wolfman and Jana Boone of meplusyou; David Ford and Don Rylander of Ford Consulting Group; Mark Rehborg of Tony's Pizza; Vivian Callaway, Sandy Proctor, and Anna Stoesz of General Mills; David Windorski, Tom Barnidge, and Erica Schiebel of 3M; Nicholas Skally, Jeremy Stonier, and Joe Olivas of Prince Sports; David Montgomery, David Buck, and Bonnie Clark of the Philadelphis Phillies; Ian Wolfman of imc^2; Brian Niccol of Pizza Hut; Kim Nagele of JCPenney, Inc.; Charles Besio of the Sewell Automotive Group, Inc.; Lindsey Smith of GE Healthcare; Beverly Roberts of the U.S. Census Bureau; Carla Silveira of Ghirardelli Chocolate Company; Michael Kuhl of 3M Sports and Leisure; Kerry Barnett of Valassis Communications; Sheryl Adkins-Green of Mary Kay, Inc.; Mattison Crowe of Seven Cycles, Inc.; Alisa Allen, Kirk Hodgdon, Jeff Gerst, Holly Matson, Nick Naumann, and Dane Hartzell of Bolin Marketing; Jennifer Katz, Amanda Axvig and Brian Stucky of AOI Marketing; and Nelson Ng from Dundas Data Visualization, Inc.

Those who provided the resources for use in both the *Marketing:* 12th Edition textbook, Instructor's Manual, and/or PowerPoint presentations include: Kevin Upton of the University of Minnesota; Nancy Nentl of Metropolitan State University; David Windorski of 3M Company; Becky Bolin of Bolin Marketing; Todd Walker and Jean Golden of Million Dollar Idea; Karen Cohick of Susan G. Komen for the Cure; Liz Stewart of Ben & Jerry's; John Formella and Patricia Lipari of Kodak; Nelson Ng of Dundas Data Visualizations; Apple, Inc.; Erica Schiebel of 3M; Karen Cohick of Susan G. Komen for the Cure; Joe Diliberti of *Consumer Reports;* Patricia Breman of Strategic Business Insights (VALS); Brian Nielsen of the Nielsen Company; David Walonick of StatPac; Becky Labitzky and Kirsten Knutson of Bolin Marketing;Mark Rehborg of Schwan's Consumer Brands (Tony's Pizza); David Ford of Ford Consulting Group; Jennifer Olson of Experian Simmons; Kitty Munger and Mary Wykoff of Wendy's; Mark Heller of RetailSails; Nicky Hutcheon of ZenithOptimedia; Amy Thompson and Jennifer Allison of Dell, Inc.; Adriana Carlton of Walmart and Rick Hill of Bernstein-Rein Advertising (Walmart); Janine Bolin of Saks, Inc.; Dr. Yory Wurmser of the Direct Marketing Association; Elizabeth Clendenin of Unilever (Caress); Jennifer Katz, Kelsey Fisher, and Amanda Axvig of AOI Marketing (StuffDOT), and Eric Fleming of Segway.

We also want to thank the following people who generously provided assistance and digital images for use in our *Marketing: 12th* Edition In-Class Activities (ICAs) and associated PowerPoint presentations: Mitch Forster and Carla Silveira of Ghirardelli Chocolate Company; Karolyn Warfel and Betsy Boyer of Woodstream Corp. (Victor Pest); Leonard Fuld of Fuld & Co.; Maggie Jantzen of Starbucks Coffee Company; Barbara Jo Davis, formerly of Ken Davis Products; Dr. Aelred Kurtenbach, Nichole Bjerke, and LaVetta Foster of Daktronics; Jeff Gerst of Bolin Marketing (Carmex); Michelle Green and Victoria Glazier of the U.S. Census Bureau; Lisa Castaldo of Pepsi; Muffie Taggert of General Mills; David Windorski, Cathy Jeske, and Erica Schiebel of 3M (3M Post-it® Flag Highlighter); Robert M. McMath, formerly of NewProductWorks; Becky Hickel and Katherine Hamilton of Magnetic Poetry; Kerry Sell of GlaxoSmithKline (Breathe Right) and Nick Naumann of Bolin Marketing (Breathe Right); Greg Rodriguez; Jeremy Tucker, Julia Wells, and Lisa Cone of Frito-Lay (Doritos); Susan Carroll and Bob Robinson of Apple, Inc.; Willard Oberton of Fastenal Company; Dave Peterson of 3M New Ventures (Ultrathon); Scott Wosniak and Jennifer Arnold of Toro; Kim Eskro of Fallon Worldwide (Gold'n Plump); Robin Grayson of TBWA/Chiat/Day (Apple); Katie Kramer of Valassis Communications, Inc. (Nutella/Advil); Triestina Greco of Nutella/Ferrero; Tim Stauber of Wyeth Consumer Healthcare (Advil); Yvonne Pendleton and Lucille Storms of Mary Kay; Stephanie Bailey, Jasmine Stringer, and Garland Hill of General Mills; and Agustin Matos of Gordon Food Service for procuring several of the ISK items.

Staff support from the Southern Methodist University, the University of Denver, and the University of Minnesota was essential. We gratefully acknowledge the help of Wanda Hanson, Jeanne Milazzo, Gloria Valdez, and Jill Johnson for their many contributions.

Checking countless details related to layout, graphics, clear writing, and last-minute changes to ensure timely examples is essential for a sound and accurate textbook. This also involves coordinating activities of authors, designers, editors, compositors, and production specialists. Christine Vaughan, our Content Project Manager, of McGraw-Hill Education's production staff and editorial consultant, Gina Huck Siegert of Imaginative Solutions, Inc., provided the necessary oversight and hand-holding for us, while retaining a refreshing sense of humor, often under tight deadlines. Thank you again!

Finally, we acknowledge the professional efforts of the McGraw-Hill Education staff. Completion of our book and its many supplements required the attention and commitment of many editorial, production, marketing, and research personnel. Our Burr Ridge-based team included Paul Ducham, Sankha Basu, Sean Pankuch, Matt Baldwin, Carol Bielski, Joanne Mennemeier, Joyce Chappetto, Donielle Xu, and many others. In addition, we relied on Michael Hruby for constant attention regarding photo elements of the text. Handling the countless details of our text, supplement, and support technologies has become an incredibly complex challenge. We thank all these people for their efforts!

Roger A. Kerin
Steven W. Hartley
William Rudelius

BRIEF CONTENTS

DETAILED CONTENTS

Part 1 Initiating the Marketing Process

Facebook
students
million
active
users
site
service
networking
friends
Web
U.S.
college
billion
Zuckerberg
Mark
people

Part 2 Understanding Buyers and Markets

6 UNDERSTANDING ORGANIZATIONS AS CUSTOMERS 138

I CHOOSE TO
TAKE MY OWN PATH
I CHOOSE DELL
I CHOOSE TO
TAKE MY OWN PATH
I CHOOSE DELL

Part 3 Targeting Marketing Opportunities

Part 4 Satisfying Marketing Opportunities

11 MANAGING SUCCESSFUL PRODUCTS, SERVICES, AND BRANDS 270

INSIDE THIS WEEK: TECHNOLOGY QUARTERLY
The Economist
Hugo Chávez's rotten legacy
Is the stockmarket right?
Management tips for the Vatican
Getting Britain to grow
The comet that could hit Mars
The sharing economy
On the internet, everything is for hire

San Francisco Giants

VIZIO
COLLECTION

15 MANAGING MARKETING CHANNELS AND SUPPLY CHAINS 384

COOL RANCH
Doritos LOCOS TACOS
BIG BOX
COOL RANCH

facebook
YouTube
LinkedIn

20 PERSONAL SELLING AND SALES MANAGEMENT 530

Part 5 Managing the Marketing Process

Marketing

1 Creating Customer Relationships and Value through Marketing

LEARNING OBJECTIVES

After reading this chapter you should be able to:

- **LO 1-1** Define marketing and identify the diverse factors that influence marketing actions.
- **LO 1-2** Explain how marketing discovers and satisfies consumer needs.
- **LO 1-3** Distinguish between marketing mix factors and environmental forces.
- **LO 1-4** Explain how organizations build strong customer relationships and customer value through marketing.
- **LO 1-5** Describe how today's customer relationship era differs from prior eras.

LAUNCHING A *NEW* BILLION-DOLLAR FOOD CATEGORY—IN JUST SEVEN YEARS!

Thousands of newly launched consumer products quietly fail every year. How could an entirely new food category skyrocket to success? The answer: Look at Chobani® Greek Yogurt!

In 2005, Turkish immigrant Hamdi Ulukaya opened his mail in New Berlin, New York, and saw an ad that said, "Fully equipped yogurt factory for sale." He bought it, painted the walls, hired a yogurt master from Turkey, and turned his attention to the task of developing high-quality Greek yogurt. He named it Chobani, which means "shepherd" in Turkish.[1]

Developing Chobani's Unique Greek Yogurt

Hamdi Ulukaya is not fond of American-style yogurt. "It was full of sugar and preservatives, nothing like I had enjoyed growing up," he says. "In Turkey we eat strained yogurt, which is rich and creamy, at every meal." The straining process removes much of the liquid whey while leaving behind more protein than the unstrained American yogurts marketed by Yoplait and Dannon.

"I was very picky. It took us 18 months to get the recipe right. But in 2007, we had it. I knew I had only one shot, and it had to be perfect," says Ulukaya.[2]

Reaching Customers

From the very beginning, Ulukaya and team pushed for distribution in major grocery chains and in their main dairy cases, *not* confined to the specialty or health food sections of these chains or in smaller, niche stores. He was convinced that Americans would really like Greek yogurt if they tried it. Ulukaya's conviction paid off. By 2009, Chobani could be found in the main dairy cases of chains like Stop & Shop, BJ's, and Costco. And by 2013, Chobani Greek Yogurt was sold nationwide in the United States, the United Kingdom, and Australia.[3]

Chobani had little money for traditional advertising at the start, so it relied on positive word of mouth, with one happy customer telling another about this new Chobani Greek Yogurt. In 2010, Chobani's "CHOmobile" started to tour the country, handing out free samples

from the van at events to encourage consumers to try Chobani's Greek Yogurt for the first time. Perhaps the biggest breakthrough in gaining public awareness was its sponsorship of the 2012 and 2014 U.S. Olympic and Paralympic Teams. During the 2012 opening ceremonies, Chobani premiered its "Proudly with You" TV advertisement.

To access this QR code link, see the instructions in the Preface.

QR 1-1
Chobani Ad

Just over five years from launch, Chobani boasts nearly 800,000 Facebook fans. The company has created a YouTube channel that features "Just Add Good" recipes to show customers how to use its tasty products in meals and desserts. It also interacts with consumers through a half-dozen other social media sites such as Twitter and Instagram, acknowledging everyone who mentions the brand.[4]

Located in New York City, Chobani SoHo is the brand's first-of-its-kind retail concept, serving yogurt creations with innovative toppings.

Chobani Today

In 2010, Chobani introduced its Champions Greek Yogurt line of 3.5-ounce cups for kids as a good source of vitamin D and protein. To promote the Champions brand, in 2012 Chobani hired former two-time U.S. Olympian women's softball pitcher—and mother—Jennie Finch as spokesperson for the first television commercial for Champions. Also in 2012, Chobani opened Chobani SoHo in a New York City neighborhood, a unique retail store featuring a collection of yogurt creations with original Chobani toppings.[5]

For Chobani, 2013 was a banner year that included introducing several new product lines, which are described in the video case at the end of the chapter. Chobani also expanded its main product line by adding more flavors like coconut, banana, and key lime, which were suggested by customers.[6]

So how successful has Chobani been? In 2013, Chobani, with sales of over $1 billion annually, held 20 percent of the entire U.S. yogurt market. Greek yogurt accounted for about 36 percent of all yogurt sales in the United States, and Chobani garnered a huge 39 percent share of this segment—ahead of both Yoplait's Greek and Dannon's Oikos brands.[7]

Chobani, Marketing, and You

Will Hamdi Ulukaya and his Chobani Greek Yogurt continue this fantastic success—especially with the recent appearance of competing Greek yogurts from Yoplait, Dannon, and PepsiCo? For Ulukaya, one key factor will be how well Chobani understands and uses marketing—the subject of this book.

WHAT IS MARKETING?

The good news is that you are already a marketing expert! You perform many marketing activities and make marketing-related decisions every day. For example, would you sell more LG 55-inch 3D OLED HD Smart TVs at $9,999 or $999 each? You answered $999, right? So your experience in shopping gives you some expertise in marketing. As a consumer, you've been involved in thousands of marketing decisions, but mostly on the buying and not the selling side. But to test your expertise, answer the "marketing expert" questions posed in Figure 1–1. You'll find the answers within the next several pages.

Are you a marketing expert? If so, what would you pay for this cutting-edge TV?

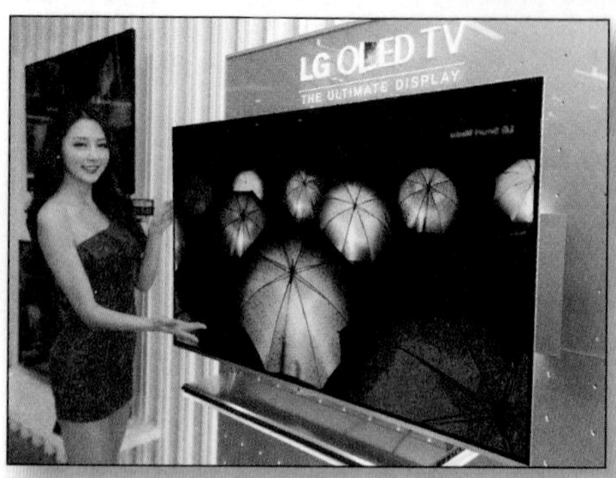

The bad news is that good marketing isn't always easy. That's why every year thousands of new products fail in the marketplace and then quietly slide into oblivion.

Marketing and Your Career

Marketing affects all individuals, all organizations, all industries, and all countries. This book seeks to teach you marketing concepts, often by having you actually "do marketing"—by putting you in the shoes of a marketing manager facing actual marketing decisions. The book also shows marketing's many applications and how it affects our lives. This knowledge should make you a

FIGURE 1–1
The see-if-you're-really-a-marketing-expert test.

Answer the questions below. The correct answers are given later in the chapter.

1. True or false. In 2014, you will be able to buy a flying car for about $279,000 that takes off or lands at most airports, has a safety parachute, drives on any roadway, gets 35 mpg, and can fill up at most gasoline stations.
2. True or false. The 60-year lifetime value of a loyal Kleenex customer is $994.
3. To be socially responsible, 3M puts what recycled material into its very successful Scotch-Brite® Never Rust™ soap pads? (*a*) aluminum cans, (*b*) steel-belted tires, (*c*) plastic bottles, (*d*) computer screens.

For time to think and write software code, the chief executive officer of the world's largest social media company sometimes hides out at a restaurant near his Silicon Valley headquarters.

better consumer and enable you to be a more informed citizen, and it may even help you in your career planning.

Perhaps your future will involve doing sales and marketing for a large organization. Working for a well-known company—Apple, Ford, Facebook, or General Mills—can be personally satisfying and financially rewarding, and you may gain special respect from your friends.

Small businesses also offer marketing careers. Small businesses are the source of the majority of new U.S. jobs. So you might become your own boss by being an entrepreneur and starting your own business.

In February 2004, a 19-year-old college sophomore from Harvard University started his own small web service business from his dorm room. He billed it as "an online directory that connects people through social networks at colleges." That student, of course, was Mark Zuckerberg.[8] The success of the Facebook launch defies comprehension. Zuckerberg's Thefacebook.com website signed up 900 Harvard students in the four days after it appeared in early 2004. By the second week, there were almost 5,000 members. Unlike Facebook, not every Internet start-up reaches over a billion users a few years after its launch. In fact, more than half of all new businesses fail within five years of their start-up.

Marketing: Delivering Benefits to the Organization, Its Stakeholders, and Society

LO 1-1 Define marketing and identify the diverse factors that influence marketing actions.

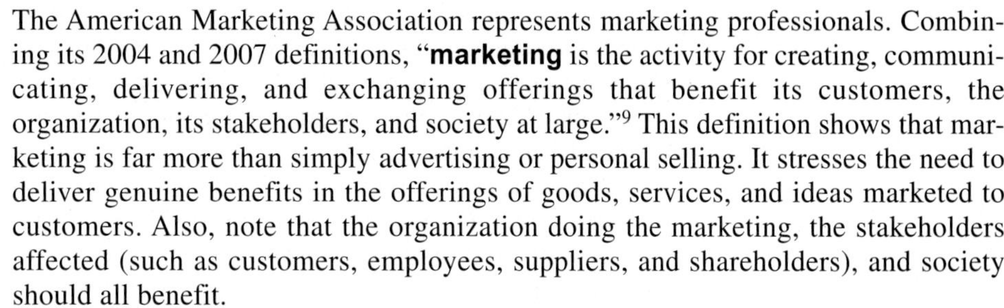

The American Marketing Association represents marketing professionals. Combining its 2004 and 2007 definitions, "**marketing** is the activity for creating, communicating, delivering, and exchanging offerings that benefit its customers, the organization, its stakeholders, and society at large."[9] This definition shows that marketing is far more than simply advertising or personal selling. It stresses the need to deliver genuine benefits in the offerings of goods, services, and ideas marketed to customers. Also, note that the organization doing the marketing, the stakeholders affected (such as customers, employees, suppliers, and shareholders), and society should all benefit.

To serve both buyers and sellers, marketing seeks (1) to discover the needs and wants of prospective customers and (2) to satisfy them. These prospective customers include both individuals, buying for themselves and their households, and organizations, buying for their own use (such as manufacturers) or for resale (such as wholesalers and retailers). The key to achieving these two objectives is the idea of **exchange**, which is the trade of things of value between a buyer and a seller so that each is better off after the trade.[10]

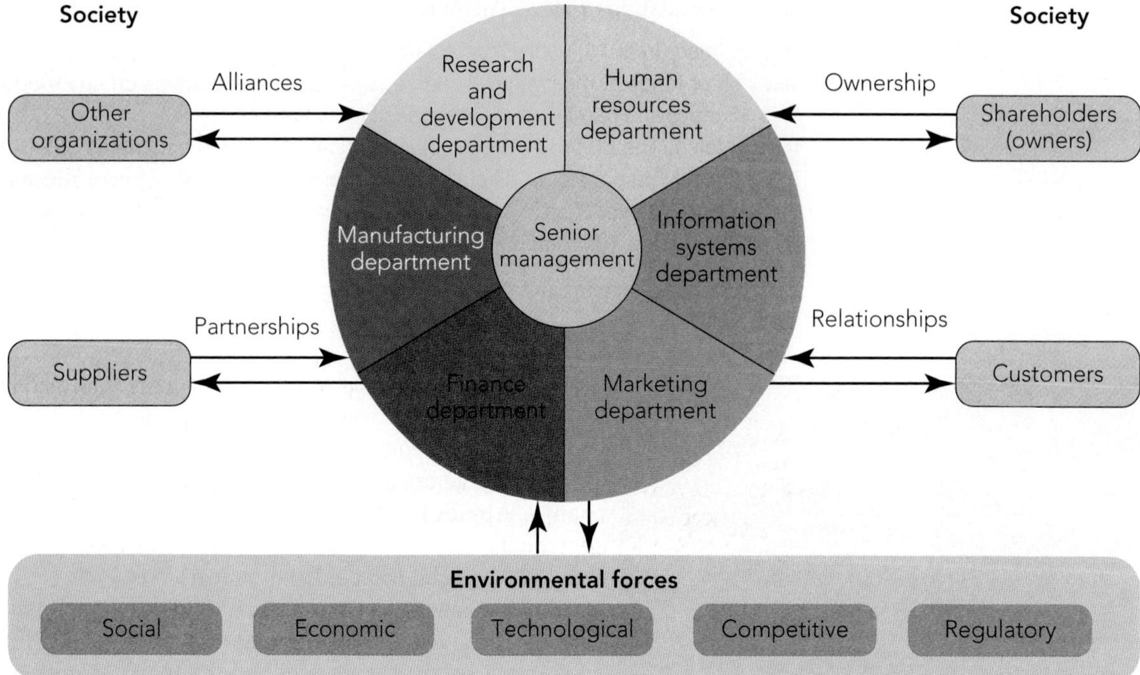

FIGURE 1–2
A marketing department relates to many people, organizations, and forces. Note that the marketing department both *shapes* and *is shaped by* its relationship with these internal and external groups.

The Diverse Elements Influencing Marketing Actions

Although an organization's marketing activity focuses on assessing and satisfying consumer needs, countless other people, groups, and forces interact to shape the nature of its actions (see Figure 1–2). Foremost is the organization itself, whose mission and objectives determine what business it is in and what goals it seeks. Within the organization, management is responsible for establishing these goals. The marketing department works closely with a network of other departments and employees to help provide the customer-satisfying products required for the organization to survive and prosper.

Figure 1–2 also shows the key people, groups, and forces outside the organization that influence its marketing activities. The marketing department is responsible for facilitating relationships, partnerships, and alliances with the organization's customers, its shareholders (or often representatives of nonprofit organizations), its suppliers, and other organizations. Environmental forces involving social, economic, technological, competitive, and regulatory considerations also shape an organization's marketing actions. Finally, an organization's marketing decisions are affected by and, in turn, often have an important impact on society as a whole.

The organization must strike a balance among the sometimes differing interests of these groups. For example, it is not possible to simultaneously provide the lowest-priced and highest-quality products to customers and pay the highest prices to suppliers, the highest wages to employees, and the maximum dividends to shareholders.

What Is Needed for Marketing to Occur

For marketing to occur, at least four factors are required: (1) two or more parties (individuals or organizations) with unsatisfied needs, (2) a desire and ability on their part to have their needs satisfied, (3) a way for the parties to communicate, and (4) something to exchange.

Two or More Parties with Unsatisfied Needs Suppose you've developed an unmet need—a desire for a late-night dinner after studying for an exam—but you don't yet know that Domino's Pizza has a location in your area. Also unknown to you is that Domino's recently introduced its tasty Handmade Pan Pizza, just waiting to be ordered, handmade, and delivered. This is an example of two parties with unmet needs: you, desiring a meal, and your local Domino's Pizza owner, needing someone to buy a Handmade Pan Pizza.

Desire and Ability to Satisfy These Needs Both you and the Domino's Pizza owner want to satisfy these unmet needs. Furthermore, you have the money to buy the Domino's Handmade Pan Pizza and the time to order it online or over the telephone. The Domino's owner has not only the desire to sell its Handmade Pan Pizza but also the ability to do so since the pizza is easily made and delivered to (or picked up by) you.

A Way for the Parties to Communicate The marketing transaction of purchasing a Domino's Handmade Pan Pizza will never occur unless you know the product exists and its location (street/web address and/or phone number). Similarly, the Domino's Pizza owner won't sell the Handmade Pan Pizza unless there's a market of potential buyers nearby. When you receive a coupon in the mail or drive by the Domino's store location, this communication barrier between you (the buyer) and the Domino's Pizza owner (the seller) is overcome.

Marketing doesn't happen in a vacuum. The text describes the four factors needed to buy a product like a Domino's Handmade Pan Pizza.

Something to Exchange Marketing occurs when the transaction takes place and both the buyer and seller exchange something of value. In this case, you exchange your money ($7.99) for the Domino's Handmade Pan Pizza. Both you and the Domino's Pizza owner have gained and also given up something, but you are both better off because each of you has satisfied the other's unmet needs. You have the opportunity to eat a Domino's Handmade Pan Pizza to satisfy your hunger, but you gave up some money to do so; the Domino's Pizza owner gave up the Handmade Pan Pizza but received money, which will help the owner remain in business. The ethical and legal foundations of this exchange process are central to marketing and are discussed in Chapter 4.

learning review

1-1. What is marketing?

1-2. Marketing focuses on ________ and ________ consumer needs.

1-3. What four factors are needed for marketing to occur?

HOW MARKETING DISCOVERS AND SATISFIES CONSUMER NEEDS

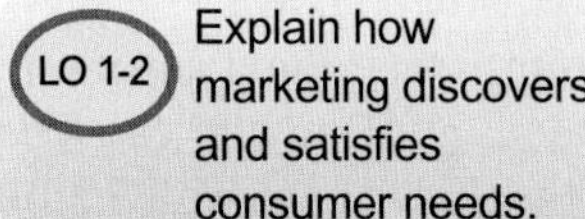

The importance of discovering and satisfying consumer needs in order to develop and offer successful products is so critical to understanding marketing that we look at each of these two steps in detail next. Let's start by asking you to analyze the three products below.

For these three products, identify (1) what benefits the product provides buyers and (2) what factors or "showstoppers" might doom the product in the marketplace. Answers are discussed in the text.

Vanilla-mint-flavored toothpaste in an aerosol container

A flying car—available in 2014

A mid-calorie diet cola

Discovering Consumer Needs

The first objective in marketing is discovering the needs of prospective customers. But these prospective customers may not always know or be able to describe what they need and want. When Apple built its first Apple II personal computer and started a new industry, consumers didn't really know what the benefits would be and had to be educated about how to use personal computers. In contrast, Bell, a U.S. bicycle helmet maker, listened to its customers, collected hundreds of their ideas, and put several into its new products.[11] This is where effective marketing research, the topic of Chapter 8, can help.

The Challenge: Meeting Consumer Needs with New Products

New-product experts generally estimate that up to 94 percent of the more than 40,000 new consumer products (food, beverage, health, beauty, and other household and pet products) introduced in the United States annually "don't succeed in the long run."[12] Robert M. McMath, who has studied more than 110,000 of these new-product launches, has two key suggestions: (1) focus on what the customer benefit is, and (2) learn from past mistakes.[13]

The solution to preventing product failures seems embarrassingly obvious. First, find out what consumers need and want. Second, produce what they need and want, and don't produce what they don't need and want. The three products shown above illustrate just how difficult it is to achieve new-product success, a topic covered in more detail in Chapter 10.

Without reading further, think about the potential benefits to customers and possible "showstoppers"—factors that might doom the product—for each of the three products pictured. Some of the products may come out of your past, and others may be on your horizon. Here's a quick analysis of the three products:

- *Dr. Care Toothpaste.* After extensive research, Dr. Care family toothpaste in its aerosol container was introduced more than two decades ago. The vanilla-mint-flavored product's benefits were advertised as being easy to use and sanitary. Pretend for a minute that you are five years old and left alone in the bathroom to brush your teeth using your Dr. Care toothpaste. Hmm! Apparently, surprised parents were not enthusiastic about the bathroom wall paintings sprayed by their future Rembrandts—a showstopper that doomed this creative product.[14]
- *Terrafugia Transition.* In 2014, Terrafugia plans to introduce the Transition® roadable aircraft, the world's first combination personal airplane and car. The Transition's flexibility allows it to land at most of the 5,200 general aviation airports in the United States. As a car, it can fold its wings, making it drivable on

QR 1-2
Terrafugia Transition Video

a roadway—from highways to residential streets! The Transition comes with a safety parachute and has a 23-gallon tank that can be filled at most gasoline stations. The proposed cost? About $279,000; you can reserve one for just a $10,000 deposit (see question 1, Figure 1–1). Potential showstoppers: The price and a potential buyer's concern that a vehicle bumped in a fender bender on a road might not be something to fly around in.[15]

QR 1-3
Pepsi Next Ad

- *Pepsi Next.* In early 2012, PepsiCo launched a new cola brand—Pepsi Next. It is "tastefully" sweetened with a combination of high fructose corn sugar and three artificial sweeteners, resulting in a soft drink that has 60 calories—60 percent less than regular Pepsi-Cola. Pepsi Next will battle for market share in the mid-calorie segment of soft drinkers who want both taste and low calories. A potential showstopper: In the past, mid-calorie soft drinks Pepsi XL (1995), Pepsi Edge (2004), and Coca-Cola C2 (2004) all failed as "transition" sodas from regular to diet. Will Pepsi Next be next? As always, you'll be the judge![16]

Firms spend billions of dollars annually on marketing and technical research that significantly reduces, but doesn't eliminate, new-product failure. So meeting the changing needs of consumers is a continuing challenge for firms around the world.

Consumer Needs and Consumer Wants Should marketing try to satisfy consumer needs or consumer wants? Marketing tries to do both. Heated debates rage over this question, fueled by the definitions of needs and wants and the amount of freedom given to prospective customers to make their own buying decisions.

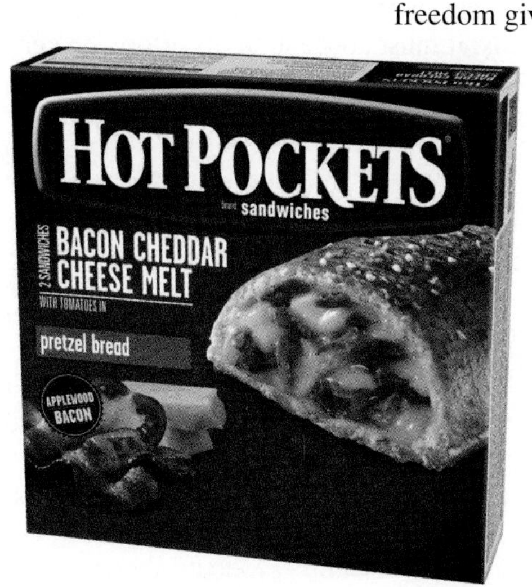

Studying late at night for an exam and being hungry, you decide to microwave a Hot Pockets Bacon Cheddar Cheese Melt sandwich. Is this a need or want? The text discusses the role of marketing in influencing decisions like this.

A *need* occurs when a person feels deprived of basic necessities such as food, clothing, and shelter. A *want* is a need that is shaped by a person's knowledge, culture, and personality. So if you feel hungry, you have developed a basic need and desire to eat something. Let's say you then want to eat an apple or a Hot Pockets Bacon Cheddar Cheese Melt microwave sandwich because, based on your past experience, you know these will satisfy your hunger need. Effective marketing, in the form of creating an awareness of good products at convenient locations, can clearly shape a person's wants.

Certainly, marketing tries to influence what we buy. A question then arises: At what point do we want government and society to step in to protect consumers? Most consumers would say they want government to protect us from harmful drugs and unsafe cars but not from candy bars and soft drinks. To protect college students, should government restrict their use of credit cards?[17] Such questions have no clear-cut answers, which is why legal and ethical issues are central to marketing. Because even psychologists and economists still debate the exact meanings of *need* and *want*, we shall use the terms interchangeably throughout the book.

As shown in the left side of Figure 1–3 on the next page, discovering needs involves looking carefully at prospective customers, whether they are children buying M&Ms candy, college students buying Chobani Greek Yogurt, or firms buying Xerox color copiers. A principal activity of a firm's marketing department is to scrutinize its consumers to understand what they need and want and the forces that shape those needs and wants.

What a Market Is Potential consumers make up a **market**, which is people with both the desire and the ability to buy a specific offering. All markets ultimately are people. Even when we say a firm bought a Xerox copier, we mean one or several people in the firm decided to buy it. People who are aware of their unmet needs may have the desire to buy the product, but that alone isn't sufficient. People must also have the ability to buy, such as the authority, time, and money. People may even "buy" an idea that results in an action, such as having their blood pressure checked annually or turning down their thermostat to save energy.

FIGURE 1–3 Marketing seeks first to discover consumer needs through extensive research. It then seeks to satisfy those needs by successfully implementing a marketing program possessing the right combination of the marketing mix—the four Ps.

Satisfying Consumer Needs

Marketing doesn't stop with the discovery of consumer needs. Because the organization obviously can't satisfy all consumer needs, it must concentrate its efforts on certain needs of a specific group of potential consumers. This is the **target market**—one or more specific groups of potential consumers toward which an organization directs its marketing program.

LO 1-3 Distinguish between marketing mix factors and environmental forces.

The Four Ps: Controllable Marketing Mix Factors Having selected its target market consumers, the firm must take steps to satisfy their needs, as shown in the right side of Figure 1–3. Someone in the organization's marketing department, often the marketing manager, must develop a complete marketing program to reach consumers by using a combination of four elements, often called "the four Ps"—a useful shorthand reference to them first published by Professor E. Jerome McCarthy:[18]

- *Product.* A good, service, or idea to satisfy the consumer's needs.
- *Price.* What is exchanged for the product.
- *Promotion.* A means of communication between the seller and buyer.
- *Place.* A means of getting the product to the consumer.

We'll define each of the four Ps more carefully later in the book, but for now it's important to remember that they are the elements of the **marketing mix**. These four elements are the controllable factors—product, price, promotion, and place—that can be used by the marketing manager to solve a marketing problem. For example, when a company puts a product on sale, it is changing one element of the marketing mix—namely, the price. The marketing mix elements are called *controllable factors* because they are under the control of the marketing department in an organization.

Designing an effective marketing mix also conveys to potential buyers a clear **customer value proposition**, which is a cluster of benefits that an organization promises customers to satisfy their needs. For example, Walmart's customer value proposition can be described as "everyday low prices for a broad range of products that are always in stock in convenient locations." Michelin's customer value proposition can be summed up as "providing safety-conscious parents greater security in tires at a premium price."[19]

The Uncontrollable, Environmental Forces While marketers can control their marketing mix factors, there are forces that are mostly beyond their control (see Figure 1–2). These are the **environmental forces** that affect a marketing decision, which consist of social, economic, technological, competitive, and regulatory forces. Examples are what consumers themselves want and need, changing technology, the state of the economy in terms of whether it is expanding or contracting, actions that competitors take, and government restrictions. Covered in detail in Chapter 3, these five forces may serve as accelerators or brakes on marketing, sometimes expanding an organization's marketing opportunities and at other times restricting them.

Traditionally, many marketing executives have treated these environmental forces as rigid, absolute constraints that are entirely outside their influence. However, recent studies and marketing successes have shown that a forward-looking, action-oriented firm can often affect some environmental forces by achieving technological or competitive breakthroughs, such as Apple's iPhone and iPad.

THE MARKETING PROGRAM: HOW CUSTOMER RELATIONSHIPS ARE BUILT

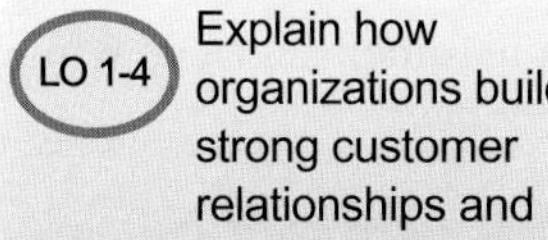

LO 1-4
Explain how organizations build strong customer relationships and customer value through marketing.

An organization's marketing program connects it with its customers. To clarify this link, we will first discuss the critically important concepts of customer value, customer relationships, and relationship marketing. Then we will illustrate these concepts using 3M's marketing program for its new Post-it® Flag Highlighter products.

Relationship Marketing: Easy to Understand, Hard to Do

Intense competition in today's fast-paced global markets has prompted many successful U.S. firms to focus on "customer value." Gaining loyal customers by providing unique value is the essence of successful marketing. What is new is a more careful attempt at understanding how a firm's customers perceive value and then actually creating and delivering that value to them.[20] **Customer value** is the unique combination of benefits received by targeted buyers that includes quality,

Target, Starbucks, and U.S. Bank provide customer value using three very different approaches. For their strategies, see the text.

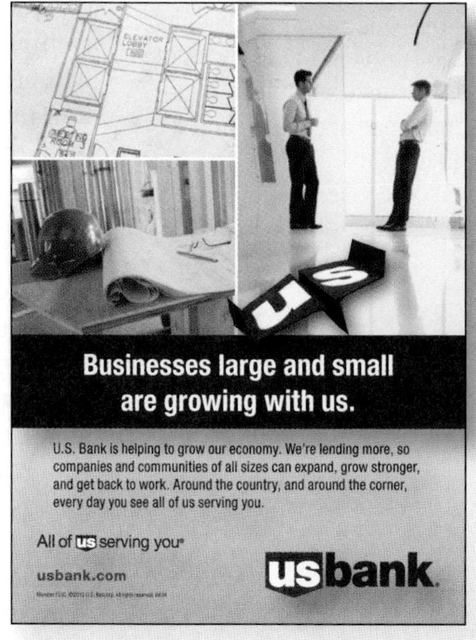

convenience, on-time delivery, and both before-sale and after-sale service at a specific price. Firms now actually try to place a dollar value on the purchases of loyal, satisfied customers during their lifetimes. For example, loyal Kleenex customers average 6.7 boxes a year, about $994 over 60 years in today's dollars (see question 2, Figure 1–1).[21]

Research suggests that firms cannot succeed by being all things to all people. Instead, firms seek to build long-term relationships with customers by providing unique value to them. Many successful firms deliver outstanding customer value with one of three value strategies: best price, best product, or best service.[22]

With the intense competition among U.S. businesses, being seen as "best" is admittedly difficult. Still, the three firms shown in the ads on the previous page have achieved great success as reflected in the mission, vision, and values statements they stress and live by:[23]

- Best price: Target. It uses the Target brand promise of "Expect More, Pay Less®" to "make Target the preferred shopping destination for our guests by delivering outstanding value."
- Best product: Starbucks. Starbucks seeks "to inspire and nurture the human spirit—one person, one cup and one neighborhood at a time," stressing quality coffee and ethics in the process.
- Best service: U.S. Bank. The brand-line in the U.S. Bank ad—"All of US serving you®"—reinforces its commitment to best-in-class customer service, while providing a complete array of financial products and services.

Remaining among the "best" is a continuing challenge for today's businesses.

A firm achieves meaningful customer relationships by creating connections with its customers through careful coordination of the product, its price, the way it's promoted, and how it's placed.

Apple uses relationship marketing concepts with its iMac—tailoring the product to the taste of an individual customer and delivering it quickly.

The hallmark of developing and maintaining effective customer relationships is today called **relationship marketing**, which links the organization to its individual customers, employees, suppliers, and other partners for their mutual long-term benefit. Relationship marketing involves a personal, ongoing relationship between the organization and its individual customers that begins before and continues after the sale.[24]

Huge manufacturers find this rigorous standard of relationship marketing difficult to achieve. Today's information technology, along with cutting-edge manufacturing and marketing processes, has led to tailoring products or services to the tastes of individual customers in high volumes at a relatively low cost. So you can place an Internet order for an Apple iMac and have it delivered in four or five days—in a configuration tailored to your unique wants. But with today's Internet purchases, you will probably have difficulty achieving the same personal, tender-loving-care connection that you once had with your neighborhood computer store, bookstore, or other local retailer.[25]

The Marketing Program and Market Segments

Effective relationship marketing strategies help marketing managers discover what prospective customers need and convert these ideas into marketable products (see Figure 1–3). These concepts must then be converted into a tangible **marketing program**—a plan that integrates the marketing mix to provide a good, service, or idea to prospective buyers. Ideally, they can be formed into **market segments**, which are relatively homogeneous groups of prospective buyers that (1) have common needs and (2) will respond similarly to a marketing action. This action might be a product feature, a promotion, or a price. As shown in Figure 1–3, in an effective organization this process is continuous: Consumer needs trigger product concepts that are translated into actual products that stimulate further discovery of consumer needs.

learning review

1-4. An organization can't satisfy the needs of all consumers, so it must focus on one or more subgroups, which are its _________.

1-5. What are the four marketing mix elements that make up the organization's marketing program?

1-6. What are environmental forces?

3M's Strategy and Marketing Program to Help Students Study

"How do college students *really* study?" asked David Windorski, a 3M inventor of Post-it® brand products, when thinking about adding a new item to the Post-it® line.[26]

To answer this question, Windorski worked with a team of four college students. Their task was to observe and question dozens of students about their study behavior, such as how they used their textbooks, took notes, wrote term papers, and reviewed for exams. Often, they watched students highlight a passage and then mark the page with a Post-it® Note or Post-it® Flag. Windorski realized he could pair an existing Post-it® product with a highlighter—merging the functions of two products into one to help students study!

Moving from Ideas to a Marketable Highlighter Product After working on 15 or 20 wood and clay models, Windorski concluded he had to build a highlighter product that would dispense Post-it® Flags because the Post-it® Notes were simply too large to put inside the barrel of a highlighter.

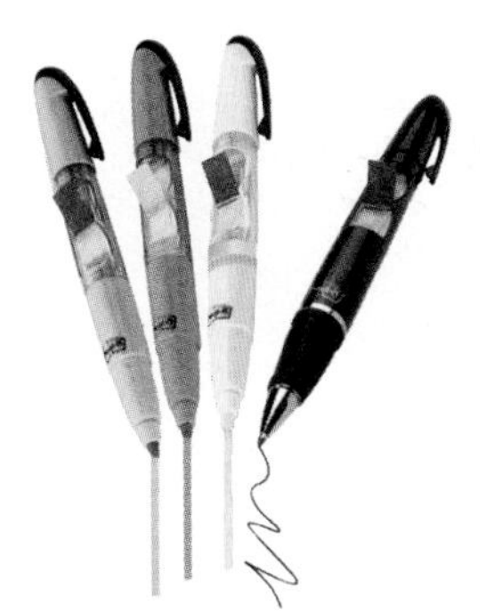

3M's initial product line of Post-it® Flag Highlighters and Post-it® Flag Pens includes variations in color and line widths.

Hundreds of the initial highlighter prototypes with Post-it® Flags inside were produced and given to students—and also office workers—to get their reactions. This research showed users wanted a convenient, reliable cover to protect the Post-it® Flags in the highlighter. So Windorski's rotating cover for the Post-it® Flag Highlighter was born.

Adding the Post-it® Flag Pen Most of David Windorski's initial design energies had gone into his Post-it® Flag Highlighter research and development. But Windorski also considered other related products. Many people in offices need immediate access to Post-it® Flags while writing with pens. Students are a potential market for this product, too, but probably a smaller market segment than office workers.

A Marketing Program for the Post-it® Flag Highlighter and Pen After several years of research, development, and production engineering, 3M introduced its new products. Figure 1–4 on the next page outlines the strategies for each of the four marketing mix elements in 3M's program to market its Post-it® Flag Highlighters and Post-it® Flag Pens. Although similar, we can compare the marketing program for each of the two products:

QR 1-4
3M Post-it® Flag Highlighters Ad

- *Post-it® Flag Highlighter.* The target market shown in the orange column in Figure 1–4 is mainly college students, so 3M's initial challenge was to build student awareness of a product that they didn't know existed. The company used a mix of print ads in college newspapers and a TV ad and then relied on word-of-mouth advertising—students telling their friends about how great the product is. Gaining distribution in college bookstores was also critical. Plus, 3M charged a price to distributors that it hoped would give a reasonable bookstore price to students and an acceptable profit to distributors and 3M.
- *Post-it® Flag Pen.* The primary target market shown in the green column in Figure 1–4 is people working in offices. The Post-it® Flag Pens are mainly business products—bought by the purchasing department in an organization and stocked as office supplies for employees to use. So the marketing program for Post-it® Flag Pens emphasizes gaining distribution in outlets used by an organization's purchasing department.

MARKETING MIX ELEMENT	MARKETING PROGRAM ACTION TO REACH: COLLEGE STUDENT MARKET SEGMENT	MARKETING PROGRAM ACTION TO REACH: OFFICE WORKER MARKET SEGMENT	RATIONALE FOR MARKETING PROGRAM ACTION
Product strategy	Offer Post-it® Flag Highlighter to help college students in their studying	Offer Post-it® Flag Pen to help office workers in their day-to-day work activities	Listen carefully to the needs and wants of potential customer segments to use 3M technology to introduce a useful, innovative product
Price strategy	Seek retail price of about $3.99 to $4.99 for a single Post-it® Flag Highlighter or $5.99 to $7.99 for a three-pack	Seek retail price of about $3.99 to $4.99 for a single Post-it® Flag Pen; wholesale prices are lower	Set prices that provide genuine value to the customer segment being targeted
Promotion strategy	Run limited promotion with a TV ad and some ads in college newspapers and then rely on student word-of-mouth messages	Run limited promotion among distributors to get them to stock the product	Increase awareness among potential users who have never heard of this new, innovative 3M product
Place strategy	Distribute Post-it® Flag Highlighters through college bookstores, office supply stores, and mass merchandisers	Distribute Post-it® Flag Pens through office wholesalers and retailers as well as mass merchandisers	Make it easy for prospective buyers to buy at convenient retail outlets (both products) or to get at work (Post-it® Flag Pens only)

FIGURE 1–4
Marketing programs for the launch of two Post-it® brand products targeted at two target market segments.

How well did these new 3M products do in the marketplace? They have done so well that 3M bestowed a prestigious award on David Windorski and his team. And in what must be considered any inventor's dream come true, Oprah Winfrey flew Windorski to Chicago to appear on her TV show and thank him in person. She told Windorski and her audience that the Post-it® Flag Highlighter is changing the way she does things at home and at work—especially in going through potential books she might recommend for her book club. "David, I know you never thought this would happen when you were in your 3M lab . . . but I want you to take a bow before America for the invention of this . . . (highlighter). It's the most incredible invention," she said.[27]

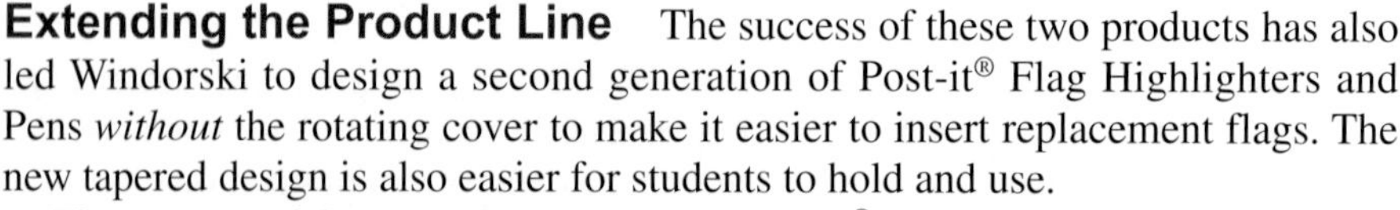

Extending the Product Line The success of these two products has also led Windorski to design a second generation of Post-it® Flag Highlighters and Pens *without* the rotating cover to make it easier to insert replacement flags. The new tapered design is also easier for students to hold and use.

The success of the second generation of Post-it® Flag Highlighters, in turn, has spawned a family of related products. One is a line of Post-it® Flag Pens with yellow, pink, or blue inks, available individually or in a three-pack.

Is it too much trouble when you're studying to grab for a 3M Post-it® Flag, then a highlighter, and then your pen? You're in luck! New to the family of 3M products is the latest generation of David Windorski's innovations: A 3-in-1 combination that has a highlighter on one end, a pen on the other, and 3M Post-it® Flags in the removable cap, as shown in the photo. In addition, 3M recently introduced two more products to its Post-it® Flag Highlighter line: a Post-it Flag + Gel Pen and a Post-it® Flag + Permanent Marker. Each includes a comfortable grip, up to four different colors, and 50 flags.

Welcome to the third generation of Post-it® Flag Highlighters: the 3-in-1 Post-it® Flag Pen and Highlighter. The cap contains the Post-it® flags.

HOW MARKETING BECAME SO IMPORTANT

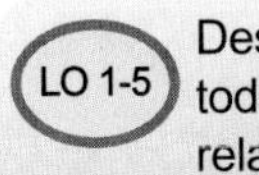

Describe how today's customer relationship era differs from prior eras.

To understand why marketing is a driving force in the modern global economy, let us look at (1) the evolution of the market orientation, (2) ethics and social responsibility in marketing, and (3) the breadth and depth of marketing activities.

Evolution of the Market Orientation

Many American manufacturers have experienced four distinct stages in the life of their firms.[28] The first stage, the *production era*, covers the early years of the United States up until the 1920s. Goods were scarce and buyers were willing to accept virtually any goods that were available and make do with them.[29] In the *sales era* from the 1920s to the 1960s, manufacturers found they could produce more goods than buyers could consume. Competition grew. Firms hired more salespeople to find new buyers. This sales era continued into the 1960s for many American firms.

Starting in the late 1950s, marketing became the motivating force among many American firms and the *marketing concept era* dawned. The **marketing concept** is the idea that an organization should (1) strive to satisfy the needs of consumers while also (2) trying to achieve the organization's goals. General Electric probably launched the marketing concept and its focus on consumers when its 1952 annual report stated: "The concept introduces . . . marketing . . . at the beginning rather than the end of the production cycle and integrates marketing into each phase of the business."[30]

Firms such as General Electric, Marriott, and Facebook have achieved great success by putting huge effort into implementing the marketing concept, giving their firms what has been called a *market orientation*. An organization that has a **market orientation** focuses its efforts on (1) continuously collecting information about customers' needs, (2) sharing this information across departments, and (3) using it to create customer value.[31] Today's *customer relationship era*, the brown bar in Figure 1–5, started in the 1980s and occurs as firms continuously seek to satisfy the high expectations of customers.

A recent focus in the customer relationship era has been the advent of social networking, in which organizations and their customers develop relationships through social media websites such as Facebook, Twitter, and YouTube, among others. This focus has allowed organizations to understand and market to current and prospective customers in ways that are still evolving, such as in using social media.

An important outgrowth of this focus on the customer is the recent attention placed on **customer relationship management (CRM)**, the process of identifying prospective buyers, understanding them intimately, and developing favorable long-term perceptions of the organization and its offerings so that buyers will choose them in the marketplace.[32] This process requires the involvement and commitment of managers and employees throughout the organization[33] and a growing application of information,

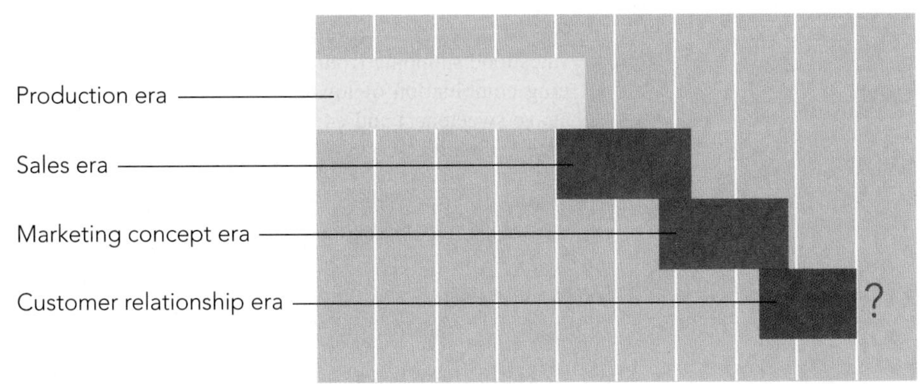

FIGURE 1–5
Four different orientations in the history of American business. Today's customer relationship era focuses on satisfying the high expectations of customers.

Fortune magazine recently named Trader Joe's its "hottest retailer." This reflects the company's focus on providing a great customer experience, as described in the text.

communication, and Internet technology, as will be described throughout this book. Unfortunately, many expensive CRM computer systems have not provided the expected benefits because they failed to identify exactly which customer segments the company wanted to reach.

The foundation of customer relationship management is really **customer experience**, which is the internal response that customers have to all aspects of an organization and its offering. This internal response includes both the direct and indirect contacts of the customer with the company. Direct contacts include the customer's contacts with the seller through buying, using, and obtaining service. Indirect contacts most often involve unplanned "touches" with the company through word-of-mouth comments from other customers, reviewers, and news reports.

In terms of outstanding customer experience, Trader Joe's is high on the list and was recently named "America's hottest retailer" by *Fortune* magazine:

> But Trader Joe's is no ordinary grocery chain. It's an offbeat, fun discovery zone that elevates food shopping from a chore to a cultural experience. It stocks its shelves with a winning combination of low-cost, yuppie-friendly staples (cage-free eggs and organic blue agave sweetener) and exotic, affordable luxuries—Belgian butter waffle cookies or Thai lime-and-chili cashews—that you simply can't find anyplace else.[34]

Trader Joe's has about 400 stores in over 30 states. It started in California and then expanded on the West Coast before jumping to the East Coast in 1996 and the Midwest in 2000.

What makes the customer experience and loyalty of shoppers at Trader Joe's unique? The reasons include:

- Setting low prices, made possible by offering its own brands rather than well-known national ones.

3M's Scotch-Brite® Never Rust™ soap pads—made from recycled plastic bottles—reflect the increasing concern among today's organizations for society's well-being.

- Offering unusual, affordable products not available from other retailers, like the Thai lime-and-chili cashews mentioned by *Fortune* magazine.
- Providing rare employee "engagement" to help customers, like actually walking them to where the roasted chestnuts are—rather than saying "aisle five."

This commitment to providing a *real* customer experience, rather than just paying lip service to it, is what gives Trader Joe's its *Fortune* rating.

The disconnect between what companies *think they are providing* versus what customers *say they are receiving* shows how important customer experience is. In a recent survey of 362 companies, only 8 percent of customers described the experience they received as being "superior," but 80 percent of the companies believed they were supplying a "superior" customer experience.[35]

Ethics and Social Responsibility in Marketing: Balancing the Interests of Different Groups

As organizations have changed their orientation, society's expectations of marketers have also changed. Today, the standards of marketing practice have shifted from an emphasis on producers' interests to consumers' interests. Guidelines for ethical and socially responsible behavior can help managers balance consumer, organizational, and societal interests.

Ethics Many marketing issues are not specifically addressed by existing laws and regulations. Should information about a firm's customers be sold to other organizations? Should advertising by professional service providers, such as accountants and attorneys, be restricted? Should consumers be on their own to assess the safety of a product? These questions raise difficult ethical issues. Many companies, industries, and professional associations have developed codes of ethics to assist managers.

Social Responsibility While many ethical issues involve only the buyer and seller, others involve society as a whole. For example, suppose you change the oil in your old Chevy yourself and dump the used oil in a corner of your backyard. Is this just a transaction between you and the oil manufacturer? Not quite! The used oil will contaminate the soil, so society will bear a portion of the cost of your behavior. This example illustrates the issue of *social responsibility*, the idea that organizations are accountable to a larger society.

The well-being of society at large should also be recognized in an organization's marketing decisions. In fact, some marketing experts stress the **societal marketing concept**, the view that organizations should satisfy the needs of consumers in a way that provides for society's well-being.[36] For example, Scotch-Brite® Never Rust™ soap pads from 3M—which are made from recycled plastic bottles—are more expensive than those offered by competitors (SOS and Brillo) but are superior because they don't rust or scratch (see question 3, Figure 1–1).

Strategies in marketing art museums include planning new "satellite" museums like this one for the Louvre in Abu Dhabi . . .

The Breadth and Depth of Marketing

Marketing today affects every person and organization. To understand this, let's analyze (1) who markets, (2) what is marketed, (3) who buys and uses what is marketed, (4) who benefits from these marketing activities, and (5) how consumers benefit.

Who Markets? Every organization markets. It's obvious that business firms involved in manufacturing (Heinz), retailing (Trader Joe's), and providing services

. . . or taking a "virtual tour" of Russia's State Hermitage Museum—courtesy of IBM.

(Marriott) market their offerings. And nonprofit organizations such as your local hospital or college, places (cities, states, countries), and even special causes (Race for the Cure) also engage in marketing. Finally, individuals such as political candidates often use marketing to gain voter attention and preference.

What Is Marketed? Goods, services, and ideas are marketed. *Goods* are physical objects, such as toothpaste, cameras, or computers, that satisfy consumer needs. *Services* are intangible items such as airline trips, financial advice, or art museums. *Ideas* are thoughts about concepts, actions, or causes.

In this book, goods, services, and ideas are all considered "products" that are marketed. So a **product** is a good, service, or idea consisting of a bundle of tangible and intangible attributes that satisfies consumers' needs and is received in exchange for money or something else of value.

Services like those offered by art museums, hospitals, and sports teams are relying more heavily on effective marketing. For example, financial pressures have caused art museums to innovate to market their unique services—the viewing of works of art by visitors—to increase revenues. This often involves levels of rare creativity unthinkable several decades ago.

This creativity ranges from establishing a global brand identity by launching overseas museums to offering sit-at-home video tours. France's Louvre, home to the *Mona Lisa* painting, is developing a new satellite museum in Abu Dhabi housed in an architecturally space-age building.[37] Russia's world-class 1,000-room State Hermitage Museum wanted to find a way to market itself to potential first-time visitors. So it partnered with IBM to let you take a "virtual tour" of its exhibits while watching on your iPad and relaxing.

QR 1-5
Hermitage
Tour Video

Ideas are most often marketed by nonprofit organizations or the government. So the Nature Conservancy markets the cause of protecting the environment. Charities market the idea that it's worthwhile for you to donate your time or money. The Peace Corps markets to recruit qualified volunteers. And state governments in Arizona and Florida market taking a warm, sunny winter vacation in their states.

Who Buys and Uses What Is Marketed? Both individuals and organizations buy and use products that are marketed. **Ultimate consumers** are the people—whether 80 years or eight months old—who use the products and services purchased for a household. In contrast, **organizational buyers** are those manufacturers, wholesalers, retailers, and government agencies that buy products and services for their own use or for resale. Although the terms *consumers, buyers,* and *customers* are sometimes used for both ultimate consumers and organizations, there is no consistency on this. In this book you will be able to tell from the example whether the buyers are ultimate consumers, organizations, or both.

Marketing the idea of volunteering for the Peace Corps can benefit society.

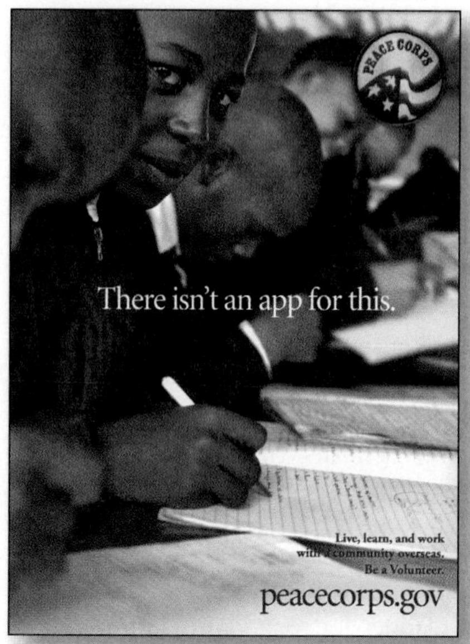

PEACE CORPS
There isn't an app for this.
Live, learn, and work
Be a Volunteer.
peacecorps.gov

Who Benefits? In our free-enterprise society, there are three specific groups that benefit from effective marketing: consumers who buy, organizations that sell, and society as a whole. True competition between products and services in the marketplace ensures that consumers can find value from the best products, the lowest prices, or exceptional service. Providing choices leads to the consumer satisfaction and quality of life that we expect from our economic system.

Organizations that provide need-satisfying products with effective marketing programs—for example, Target, IBM, and Avon—have blossomed. But competition creates problems for ineffective competitors, including the hundreds of dot-com businesses, such as Pets.com, that failed over a decade ago.

Finally, effective marketing benefits society.[38] It enhances competition, which both improves the quality of products and services and lowers their prices. This makes countries more competitive in world markets and provides jobs and a higher standard of living for their citizens.

How Do Consumers Benefit? Marketing creates **utility**, the benefits or customer value received by users of the product. This utility is the result of the marketing exchange process and the way society benefits from marketing. There are four different utilities: form, place, time, and possession. The production of the product or service constitutes *form utility. Place utility* means having the offering available where consumers need it, whereas *time utility* means having it available when needed. *Possession utility* is the value of making an item easy to purchase through the provision of credit cards or financial arrangements. Marketing creates its utilities by bridging space (place utility) and hours (time utility) to provide products (form utility) for consumers to own and use (possession utility).

learning review

1-7. What are the two key characteristics of the marketing concept?

1-8. What is the difference between ultimate consumers and organizational buyers?

LEARNING OBJECTIVES REVIEW

LO 1-1 *Define marketing and identify the diverse factors that influence marketing actions.*
Marketing is an organizational function and a set of processes for creating, communicating, and delivering value to customers and for managing customer relationships in ways that benefit the organization and its stakeholders. This definition relates to two primary goals of marketing: (*a*) discovering the needs of prospective customers and (*b*) satisfying them. Achieving these two goals also involves the four marketing mix factors largely controlled by the organization and the five environmental forces that are generally outside its control.

LO 1-2 *Explain how marketing discovers and satisfies consumer needs.*
The first objective in marketing is discovering the needs and wants of consumers who are prospective buyers and customers. This is not easy because consumers may not always know or be able to describe what they need and want. A need occurs when a person feels deprived of basic necessities such as food, clothing, and shelter. A want is a need that is shaped by a person's knowledge, culture, and personality. Effective marketing can clearly shape a person's wants and tries to influence what he or she buys. The second objective in marketing is satisfying the needs of targeted consumers. Because an organization obviously can't satisfy all consumer needs, it must concentrate its efforts on certain needs of a specific group of potential consumers or target market—one or more specific groups of potential consumers toward which an organization directs its marketing program. It then selects its target market segment(s), which are relatively homogeneous groups of prospective buyers that (1) have common needs and (2) will respond similarly to a marketing action. Finally, the organization develops a set of marketing actions in the form of a unique marketing program to reach them.

LO 1-3 *Distinguish between marketing mix factors and environmental forces.*
Four elements in a marketing program designed to satisfy customer needs are product, price, promotion, and place. These elements are called the marketing mix, the four Ps, or the marketer's controllable variables. The marketing mix also provides a clear customer value proposition—a cluster of benefits that an offering satisfies. Environmental forces, also called uncontrollable variables, are largely beyond the organization's control. These include social, economic, technological, competitive, and regulatory forces.

LO 1-4 *Explain how organizations build strong customer relationships and customer value through marketing.*
The essence of successful marketing is to provide sufficient value to gain loyal, long-term customers. Customer value is the unique combination of benefits received by targeted buyers that usually includes quality, price, convenience, on-time delivery, and both before-sale and after-sale service. Marketers do this by using one of three value strategies: best price, best product, or best service.

LO 1-5 *Describe how today's customer relationship era differs from prior eras.*
U.S. business history is divided into four overlapping periods: the production era, the sales era, the marketing concept era, and the current customer relationship era. The production era covers the period up until the 1920s, when buyers were willing to accept virtually any goods that were available. The central notion was that products would sell themselves. The sales era lasted from the

1920s to the 1960s. Manufacturers found they could produce more goods than buyers could consume, and competition grew, so the solution was to hire more salespeople to find new buyers. In the late 1950s, the marketing concept era dawned when organizations adopted a strong market orientation and integrated marketing into each phase of their business. In today's customer relationship era, organizations continuously seek to satisfy the high expectations of customers—an aggressive extension of the marketing concept era. This is increasingly done through social media.

FOCUSING ON KEY TERMS

customer experience p. 16
customer relationship management (CRM) p. 15
customer value p. 11
customer value proposition p. 10
environmental forces p. 11
exchange p. 5
market p. 9
market orientation p. 15
market segments p. 12
marketing p. 5
marketing concept p. 15
marketing mix p. 10
marketing program p. 12
organizational buyers p. 18
product p. 18
relationship marketing p. 12
societal marketing concept p. 17
target market p. 10
ultimate consumers p. 18
utility p. 19

APPLYING MARKETING KNOWLEDGE

1 What consumer wants (or benefits) are met by the following products or services? (*a*) 3M Post-it® Flag Highlighter, (*b*) Nike running shoes, (*c*) Hertz Rent-A-Car, and (*d*) television home shopping programs.

2 Each of the four products, services, or programs in question 1 has substitutes. Respective examples are (*a*) a Bic™ highlighter, (*b*) regular tennis shoes, (*c*) taking a bus, and (*d*) a department store. What consumer benefits might these substitutes have in each case that some consumers might value more highly than those mentioned in question 1?

3 What are the characteristics (e.g., age, income, education) of the target market customers for the following products or services? (*a*) *National Geographic* magazine, (*b*) Chobani Greek Yogurt, (*c*) New York Giants football team, and (*d*) Facebook.

4 A college in a metropolitan area wishes to increase its evening-school offerings of business-related courses such as marketing, accounting, finance, and management. Who are the target market customers (students) for these courses?

5 What actions involving the four marketing mix elements might be used to reach the target market in question 4?

6 What environmental forces (uncontrollable variables) must the college in question 4 consider in designing its marketing program?

7 Does a firm have the right to "create" wants and try to persuade consumers to buy goods and services they didn't know about earlier? What are examples of "good" and "bad" want creation? Who should decide what is good and what is bad?

BUILDING YOUR MARKETING PLAN

If your instructor assigns a marketing plan for your class, don't make a face and complain about the work—for two special reasons. First, you will get insights into trying to actually "do marketing" that often go beyond what you can get by simply reading the textbook. Second, thousands of graduating students every year get their first job by showing prospective employers a "portfolio" of samples of their written work from college—often a marketing plan if they have one. This can work for you.

This "Building Your Marketing Plan" section at the end of each chapter suggests ways to improve and focus your marketing plan. You will use the sample marketing plan in Appendix A (following Chapter 2) as a guide, and this section after each chapter will help you apply those Appendix A ideas to your own marketing plan.

The first step in writing a good marketing plan is to have a business or product that enthuses you and for which you can get detailed information, so you can avoid glittering generalities. We offer these additional bits of advice in selecting a topic:

- *Do* pick a topic that has personal interest for you—a family business; a business, product, or service you or a friend might want to launch; or a student organization that needs marketing help.
- *Do not* pick a topic that is so large it can't be covered adequately or so abstract it will lack specifics.

1 Now to get you started on your marketing plan, list four or five possible topics and compare these with the criteria your instructor suggests and those shown above. Think hard, because your decision will be with you all term and may influence the quality of the resulting marketing plan you show to a prospective employer.

2 When you have selected your marketing plan topic, whether the plan is for an actual business, a possible business, or a student organization, write the "company description" in your plan, as shown in Appendix A (following Chapter 2).

VIDEO CASE 1 Chobani®: Making *Greek Yogurt* a Household Name

QR 1-6
Chobani
Video Case

"Everybody should be able to enjoy a pure, simple cup of yogurt. And that's what Chobani is," says Hamdi Ulukaya, founder and chief executive officer of Chobani, Inc., in summarizing his vision for the company.

As the winner of the 2013 Ernst & Young World Entrepreneur of the Year award, his words and success story carry great credibility.

THE IDEA

Hamdi Ulukaya came to the United States in 1994 to learn English and study business. He started a feta cheese company, Euphrates, when his visiting father complained about the quality of American feta cheese. In 2005, Kraft Foods closed its New Berlin, New York, yogurt plant built in 1885. While tidying up his office, Ulukaya stumbled upon a postcard about the sale of the shuttered Kraft plant and threw it out. After sleeping on the decision, he fished it out of the wastebasket, visited the plant, and purchased it with the help of a United States Small Business Administration loan.

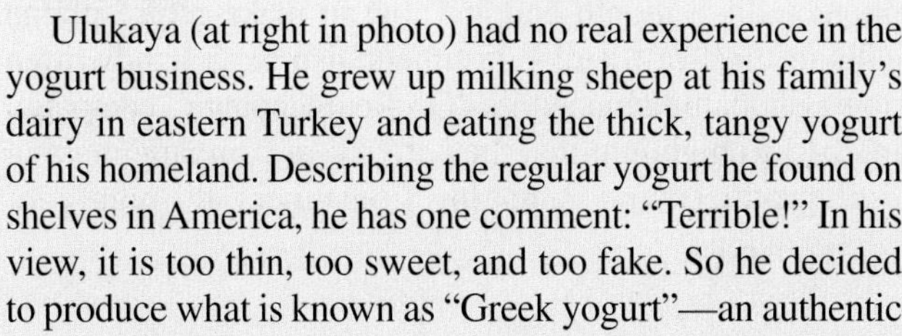

Ulukaya (at right in photo) had no real experience in the yogurt business. He grew up milking sheep at his family's dairy in eastern Turkey and eating the thick, tangy yogurt of his homeland. Describing the regular yogurt he found on shelves in America, he has one comment: "Terrible!" In his view, it is too thin, too sweet, and too fake. So he decided to produce what is known as "Greek yogurt"—an authentic strained version that produces a thick texture, high protein content, and with little or no fat. With the help of four former Kraft employees and yogurt master Mustafa Dogan, (at left in photo), Ulukaya worked 18 months to perfect the recipe for Chobani Greek Yogurt.

The very first cup for sale of Ulukaya's Greek yogurt appeared on shelves of a small grocer on Long Island, New York, in 2007. The new-product launch focused on the classic "4Ps" elements of marketing mix actions: product, price, place, and promotion.

PRODUCT STRATEGY

From the start Ulukaya's Greek yogurt carried the brand name "Chobani." There was no room for error, and the product strategy for the Chobani brand focused on the separate elements of (1) the product itself and (2) its packaging.

The Chobani product strategy stresses its authentic straining process that removes excess liquid whey. This results in a thicker, creamier yogurt that yields 13 to 18 grams of protein per single-serve cup, depending on the flavor. Chobani is free of ingredients like milk protein concentrate and animal-based thickeners, which some manufacturers add to make "Greek-style" yogurts.

Chobani uses three pounds of milk to make one pound of Chobani Greek Yogurt. Some other features that make Chobani Greek Yogurt *"nothing but good,"* to quote its tagline:

- Higher in protein than regular yogurt.
- Made with real fruit and only natural ingredients.
- Preservative-free.

- No artificial flavors or artificial sweeteners.
- Contains five live and active cultures, including three probiotics.

Then, and still today, Ulukaya obsesses about Chobani's packaging of the original cups. In 2007, Ulukaya concluded that *not any cup* would do. He insisted on a European-style cup with a circular opening *exactly* 95 millimeters across. This made for a shorter, wider cup that was more visible on retailer's shelves. Also, instead of painted-on labels, Ulukaya chose shrink-on plastic sleeves that adhere to the cup and offer eye-popping colors.

"With our packaging people would say, 'You're making it all look different and why are you doing that?' " says Kyle O'Brien, executive vice president of sales. "If people pay attention to our cups—bright colors and all—we know we have won them, because what's inside the cup is different from anything else on the shelf."

PRICE STRATEGY

To keep control of their product, Ulukaya and O'Brien approached retailers directly rather than going through distributors. Prices were set high enough to recover Chobani's costs and give reasonable margins to retailers but not so high that future rivals could undercut its price. Today, prices remain at about $1.29 for a single-serve cup.

PLACE STRATEGY

The decision of Ulukaya and O'Brien to get Chobani Greek Yogurt into the conventional yogurt aisle of traditional supermarkets—not on specialty shelves or in health food stores—proved to be sheer genius. Today Chobani sees its Greek Yogurt widely distributed in both conventional and mass supermarkets, club stores, and natural food stores. On the horizon: growing distribution in convenience and drug stores, as well as schools. Chobani is also focused on educating food service directors at schools across the United States about Greek yogurt's health benefits for schoolkids.

The Chobani growth staggers imagination. From the company's first order of 200 cases in 2007, its 2013 sales have grown to over 2 million cases per week. To increase capacity and bring new products to market faster, in 2012 Chobani opened a nearly one million square foot plant in Idaho. Built in just 326 days, it is the largest yogurt manufacturing facility in the world.

Along the way Chobani faced a strange glitch: Demand for Chobani's Greek yogurt far surpassed supply, leading to unhappy retailers with no Chobani cups to sell. Kyle O'Brien launched Operation Bear Hug. "Instead of hiding behind letters to retailers, we decided to get on a plane and to communicate with them within 24 hours about the problem and what we proposed to do about it," says O'Brien. "So we found it critical to be very transparent and open with our communication at times like that."

PROMOTION STRATEGY

In its early years Chobani had no money for traditional advertising, so it relied on word-of-mouth recommendation from enthusiastic customers. The brand harnessed consumer passion on social media channels early on and found that people loved the taste of Chobani once they tried it. So in 2010, Chobani kicked off its CHOmobile tour: a mobile vehicle sampling Chobani at events across the country, encouraging consumers to taste Greek yogurt for the first time. As Chobani grew, it began to launch new promotional activities tied to (1) traditional advertising, (2) social media, and (3) direct communication with customers.

In 2011, Chobani launched its first national advertising campaign, "Real Love Stories." The only problem: apparently it was *too* successful! The resulting additional consumer demand for Chobani Greek Yogurt exceeded its production capacity, leaving retailers unhappy because of complaining consumers. What did Chobani do then? It stopped the advertising campaign and sent in another Operation Bear Hug team to communicate with retailers. Since then it has run other successful national advertising campaigns, including sponsorship of the 2012 and 2014 U.S. Olympic Teams.

"Social media has been important to Chobani, which has embraced a high-touch model that emphasizes positive communication with its customers," says Sujean Lee, head of corporate affairs. Today, Chobani's Customer Loyalty Team receives about 7,000 inbound customer e-mails and phone calls a month and are able to make return phone calls to most of them. Consumers also get a handwritten note. Chobani launched its "Go Real Chobani" campaign in 2013 to highlight that they are a *real* company making *real* products and engaging consumers through *real* conversations.

Aside from Facebook (www.Facebook.com/Chobani), the company interacts with its consumers through Twitter, Pinterest, Instagram, Foursquare, and other social media platforms. Chobani Kitchen (www.chobanikitchen.com) is an online resource with recipes, videos, and tips on how to use its Greek yogurt in favorite recipes.

AGGRESSIVE INNOVATION AND POSITIVE SOCIAL CHANGE

Dannon, Yoplait, and PepsiCo were shocked by the success of Chobani Greek Yogurt. Each now offers its own competing Greek yogurt. With giant competitors like these, what can Chobani do? Chobani's focus: Innovate! And with creative, new Greek yogurt products!

"Today we offer our Chobani Greek Yogurt in single-serve and multi-serve sizes, while expanding our authentic strained Greek yogurt to new occasions and forms." says Joshua Dean, vice-president of brand advertising. Its recent new-product offerings include:

- Chobani Bite®—3.5-ounce 4-packs to reach the new "indulgent" segment of Chobani customers—those wanting a healthy afternoon or evening snack. Sample flavor: Raspberry with Dark Chocolate Chips.
- Chobani Champions® Tubes—made for kids, the 2.25-ounce tubes offer low-fat, blended Chobani flavors with fruit in grab-and-go packaging. Sample flavor: Jammin' Strawberry.
- Chobani Flip™ (photo above)—a 5.3-ounce, two-compartment package that lets consumers bend or "flip" mix-ins like granola or hazelnuts into the Chobani Greek Yogurt compartment. Sample flavor: Almond Coco Loco, a coconut low-fat yogurt paired with dark chocolate and sliced toasted almonds.

Chobani gives 10 percent of all profits to its Shepherd's Gift Foundation to support people and organizations working for positive, long-lasting change. The name comes from the "spirit of a shepherd," an expression in Turkey used to describe people who give without expecting anything in return. To date the foundation has supported over 50 projects—from local ones to international famine relief efforts.

WHERE TO NOW?

International operations and a unique test-market boutique in New York City give a peek at Chobani's future.

International markets provide a growth opportunity. Already sold internationally in Australia, Chobani opened its international headquarters office in 2013. Other countries have far greater annual per capita consumption than that for U.S. consumers. For example, some Europeans eat five or six times as much on average. So while entrenched competitors exist in many foreign countries, the markets are often huge, too.

How do you test ideas for new Greek yogurt flavors? In Chobani's case, it opened what it calls a "first-of-its-kind Mediterranean yogurt bar"—called Chobani SoHo—in a trendy New York City neighborhood. Here, customers can try new yogurt creations—from Strawberry + Granola to Toasted Coconut + Pineapple. The Chobani marketing team obtains consumer feedback at Chobani SoHo, leading to potential new flavors or products in the future.

Hmmm! Ready to schedule a visit to New York City and Chobani SoHo? And then sample a creation made with Pistachio + Chocolate (plain Chobani topped with pistachios, dark chocolate, honey, oranges, and fresh mint leaves), and perhaps influence what Chobani customers will be buying in the future?

Questions

1. From the information about Chobani in the case and at the start of the chapter, (*a*) whom did Hamdi Ulukaya identify as the target for his first cups of Greek yogurt and (*b*) what was his initial "4Ps" marketing strategy?

2. (*a*) What marketing actions would you expect the companies selling Yoplait, Dannon, and PepsiCo yogurts to take in response to Chobani's appearance and (*b*) how might Chobani respond?

3. What are (*a*) the advantages and (*b*) the disadvantages of Chobani's Customer Loyalty Team that handles communication with customers—from phone calls and e-mails to Facebook and Twitter messages?

4. As Chobani seeks to build its brand, it opened a unique retail store in New York City: Chobani SoHo. Why did Chobani do this?

5. (*a*) What criteria might Chobani use when it seeks markets in new countries and (*b*) what three or four countries meet these criteria?

2 Developing Successful Organizational and Marketing Strategies

LEARNING OBJECTIVES

After reading this chapter you should be able to:

LO 2-1 Describe three kinds of organizations and the three levels of strategy in them.

LO 2-2 Describe core values, mission, organizational culture, business, and goals.

LO 2-3 Explain why managers use marketing dashboards and marketing metrics.

LO 2-4 Discuss how an organization assesses where it is now and where it seeks to be.

LO 2-5 Explain the three steps of the planning phase of the strategic marketing process.

LO 2-6 Describe the four components of the implementation phase of the strategic marketing process.

LO 2-7 Discuss how managers identify and act on deviations from plans.

STARTING A BUSINESS BY GETTING AN "A" IN AN ICE CREAM-MAKING COURSE!

Ben & Jerry's started in 1978 when longtime friends Ben Cohen and Jerry Greenfield headed north to Vermont to start an ice cream parlor business in a renovated gas station. Buoyed with enthusiasm, $12,000 in borrowed and saved money, and ideas from a $5 Penn State correspondence course in ice cream making, Ben and Jerry were off and scooping. Their first flavor? Vanilla—because it's a universal best seller.[1]

The two founding entrepreneurs of Ben & Jerry's have successfully implemented some highly creative organizational and marketing strategies over the years. These include:

- *Caring Dairy.* Their milk and cream are bought from a cooperative that guarantees its supplies are bovine growth hormone free.
- *PartnerShops.* Their "social entrepreneurship" PartnerShop programs enable community-based nonprofit organizations to own and operate Scoop Shops that help employ at-risk youth and young adults to better their lives.
- *Fair Trade.* Their belief that "people should get their fair share of the pie" has led them to practice Fair Trade-certified sourcing of key ingredients—cocoa, coffee, and vanilla—for their deliciously unique flavors like Chocolate Therapy. These items are purchased from producers in developing countries who practice sustainable farming techniques.
- *B-Corp Certified.* Their social mission has earned them "B-Corp" certification. This is a designation from B-Lab, a nonprofit organization whose purpose is to "use the power of business to solve social and environmental problems" in order to positively impact the community and environment within which the organization operates.[2]

As you can see, Ben & Jerry's Homemade Holdings, Inc., links its three-part mission statement to social causes designed to improve humanity by offering consumers delicious products with creatively funky names.

Today, Ben & Jerry's is owned by Unilever, which is the market leader in the global ice cream industry—one that is expected to reach $68 billion by 2015.[3] While customers love Ben & Jerry's rich premium ice cream, many buy its products to support its social mission. As a

Ben & Jerry's Mission

Ben & Jerry's is founded on & dedicated to a sustainable corporate concept of linked prosperity. Our mission consists of 3 interrelated parts:

SOCIAL *mission*

To operate the Company in a way that actively recognizes the central role that business plays in society by initiating innovative ways to improve the quality of life locally, nationally and internationally.

PRODUCT *mission*

To make, distribute and sell the finest quality all natural ice cream and euphoric concoctions with a continued commitment to incorporating wholesome, natural ingredients and promoting business practices that respect the Earth and the Environment.

ECONOMIC *mission*

To operate the Company on a sustainable financial basis of profitable growth, increasing value for our stakeholders and expanding opportunities for development and career growth for our employees.

Underlying the Mission is the determination to seek new & creative ways of addressing all 3 parts, while holding a deep respect for individuals inside & outside the company, & for the communities of which they are a part.

testament to its success, Ben & Jerry's has over 7 million fans on Facebook—the most of any premium ice cream marketer!

Chapter 2 describes how organizations set goals to provide an overall direction to their organizational and marketing strategies. The marketing department of an organization converts these strategies into plans that must be implemented and then evaluated so deviations can be exploited or corrected based on the marketing environment.

TODAY'S ORGANIZATIONS

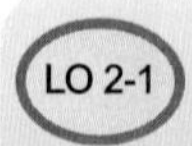

LO 2-1 Describe three kinds of organizations and the three levels of strategy in them.

In studying today's visionary organizations, it is important to recognize (1) the kinds of organizations that exist, (2) what strategy is, and (3) how this strategy relates to the three levels of structure found in many large organizations.

Kinds of Organizations

An *organization* is a legal entity that consists of people who share a common mission. This motivates them to develop *offerings* (goods, services, or ideas) that create value for both the organization and its customers by satisfying their needs and wants.[4] Today's organizations are of three types: (1) for-profit organizations, (2) nonprofit organizations, and (3) government agencies.

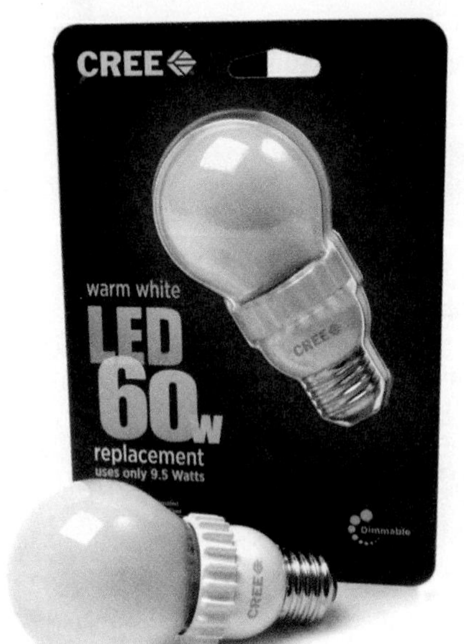

Cree is an example of a for-profit organization. Its Cree LED light bulb, launched in 2013, replaces the traditional incandescent bulb. The Cree LED 60w bulb is 84 percent more energy efficient, lasts for 25,000 hours, and initially sold for about $12.

A *for-profit organization,* often called a *business firm,* is a privately owned organization such as Target, Nike, or Cree that serves its customers to earn a profit so that it can survive. **Profit** is the money left after a for-profit organization subtracts its total expenses from its total revenues and is the reward for the risk it undertakes in marketing its offerings.

In contrast, a *nonprofit organization* is a nongovernmental organization that serves its customers but does not have profit as an organizational goal. Instead, its goals may be operational efficiency or client satisfaction. Regardless, it also must receive sufficient funds above its expenses to continue operations. Social entrepreneurs like Teach For America and SightLife, described in the Making Responsible Decisions box, seek to solve the practical needs of society and are usually structured as nonprofit organizations.[5] For simplicity in the rest of the book, the terms *firm, company*, and *organization* are used interchangeably to cover both for-profit and nonprofit organizations.

Lastly, a *government agency* is a federal, state, county, or city unit that provides a specific service to its constituents. For example, the Census Bureau, a unit of the U.S. Department of Commerce, is a federal government agency that provides population and economic data.

Organizations that develop similar offerings create an *industry*, such as the computer industry or the automobile industry.[6] As a result, organizations make strategic decisions that reflect the dynamics of the industry to create a compelling and sustainable advantage for their offerings relative to those of competitors to achieve a superior level of performance.[7] Much of an organization's marketing strategy is having a clear understanding of the industry within which it competes.

What Is Strategy?

QR 2-1 Cree LED Bulb Ad

An organization has limited human, financial, technological, and other resources available to produce and market its offerings—it can't be all things to all people! Every organization must develop strategies to help focus and direct its efforts to accomplish its goals. However, the definition of strategy has been the subject of debate among management and marketing theorists. For our purpose, **strategy** is an organization's long-term course of action designed to deliver a unique customer experience while achieving its goals.[8] All organizations set a strategic direction. And marketing helps to both set this direction and move the organization there.

The Structure of Today's Organizations

Large organizations are extremely complex. They usually consist of three organizational levels whose strategies are linked to marketing, as shown in Figure 2–1.

social responsibility

Making Responsible Decisions

Using Social Entrepreneurship to Help People

What do Teach For America and SightLife have in common?

The answer: They are "social entrepreneurs" that are actively practicing—you guessed it!—social entrepreneurship. In a nutshell, social entrepreneurship applies innovative approaches to organize, create, and manage a venture to solve the practical needs of society. These usually are nonprofit organizations and focus on issues facing people who lack the financial or political means to solve their own problems. Let's look at the two social entrepreneurs mentioned above, models of creative nonprofit organizations.

TEACHFORAMERICA

Launched by college senior Wendy Kopp, Teach For America is the national corps of outstanding recent college graduates who commit to teach for two years in urban and rural public schools and become lifelong leaders in expanding educational opportunity. In 2013, more than 10,000 corps members taught 750,000 students, while nearly 28,000 Teach For America alumni continue working from inside and outside the field of education for the fundamental changes necessary to ensure educational excellence and equity.

The mission of SightLife is incredibly clear and specific: "To end cornea blindness." Cornea blindness, affecting 10 million people globally, can be cured by transplanting a donated, healthy cornea to replace a diseased one. Seattle-based SightLife finds cornea donors and prepares the tissues for surgery. SightLife works with eye surgeons and health organizations in about 30 countries. In 2012, SightLife provided almost 14,000 corneas for transplant—improving the lives of their recipients.

Corporate Level The *corporate level* is where top management directs overall strategy for the entire organization. "Top management" usually means the board of directors and senior management officers with a variety of skills and experiences that are invaluable in establishing the organization's overall strategy.

The president or chief executive officer (CEO) is the highest ranking officer in the organization and is usually a member of its board of directors. This person must possess leadership skills ranging from overseeing the organization's daily operations to spearheading strategy planning efforts that may determine its very survival.

FIGURE 2–1
The board of directors oversees the three levels of strategy in organizations: corporate, strategic business unit, and functional.

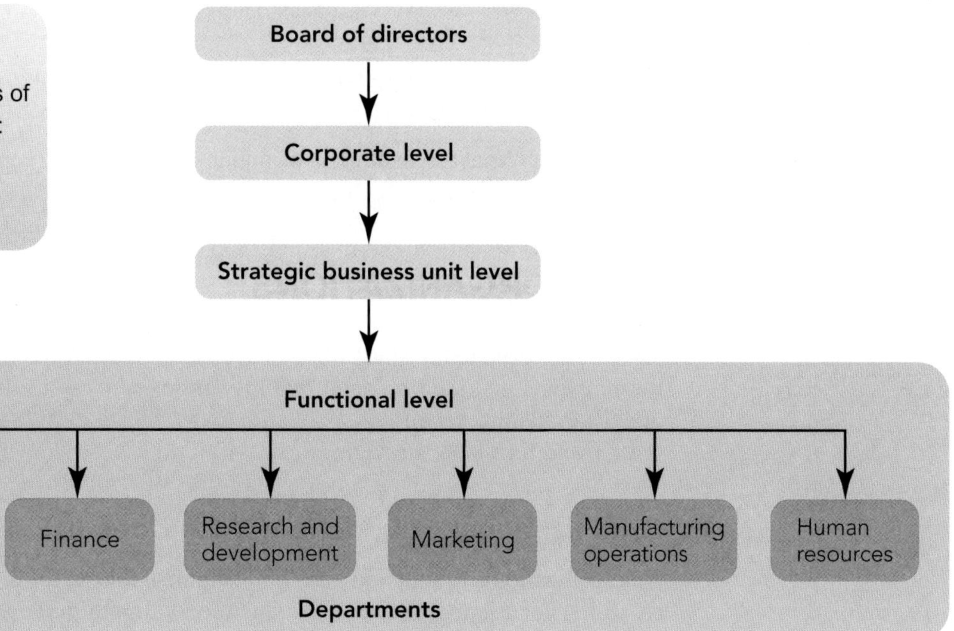

Prada manages a portfolio or group of businesses—including perfume, leather goods, and luggage—each of which may be viewed as a strategic business unit (SBU).

In recent years, many large firms have changed the title of the head of marketing from vice president of marketing to chief marketing officer (CMO). These CMOs have an increasingly important role in top management because of their ability to think strategically. Most bring multi-industry backgrounds, cross-functional management expertise, analytical skills, and intuitive marketing insights to their job. These CMOs are increasingly called upon to be their organizations' "visionaries for the future" by staying in touch with consumers' needs and wants.[9]

Strategic Business Unit Level Some multimarket, multiproduct firms, such as Prada and Johnson & Johnson, manage a portfolio or group of businesses. Each group is a *strategic business unit (SBU)*, which is a subsidiary, division, or unit of an organization that markets a set of related offerings to a clearly defined target market. At the *strategic business unit level*, managers set a more specific strategic direction for their businesses to exploit value-creating opportunities. For less complex firms with a single business focus, such as Ben & Jerry's, the corporate and business unit levels may merge.

Functional Level Each strategic business unit has a *functional level*, where groups of specialists actually create value for the organization. The term *department* generally refers to these specialized functions such as marketing and finance (see Figure 2–1). At the functional level, the organization's strategic direction becomes its most specific and focused. Just as there is a hierarchy of levels within an organization, there is a hierarchy of strategic directions set by managers at each level.

A key role of the marketing department is to look outward by listening to customers, developing offerings, implementing marketing program actions, and then evaluating whether those actions are achieving the organization's goals. When developing marketing programs for new or improved offerings, an organization's senior management may form *cross-functional teams*. These consist of a small number of people from different departments who are mutually accountable to accomplish a task or a common set of performance goals. Sometimes these teams will have representatives from outside the organization, such as suppliers or customers, to assist them.

learning review

2-1. What is the difference between a for-profit and a nonprofit organization?

2-2. What are examples of a functional level in an organization?

STRATEGY IN VISIONARY ORGANIZATIONS

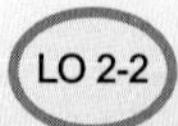
LO 2-2 Describe core values, mission, organizational culture, business, and goals.

To be successful, today's organizations must be forward-looking. They must anticipate future events and then respond quickly and effectively to those events. A visionary organization must specify its foundation (why does it exist?), set a direction (what will it do?), and formulate strategies (how will it do it?), as shown in Figure 2–2.[10]

Organizational Foundation: Why Does It Exist?

An organization's foundation is its philosophical reason for being—why it exists. Successful visionary organizations use this foundation to guide and inspire their employees through three elements: core values, mission, and organizational culture.

Organizational foundation (why)		Organizational direction (what)		Organizational strategies (how)

• Core values
• Mission (vision)
• Organizational culture
	+	• Business
		• Goals (objectives)
		  ○ Long-term
		  ○ Short-term
			=	• By level
				  ○ Corporate
				  ○ SBU
				  ○ Functional
				• By product
				  ○ Good
				  ○ Service
				  ○ Idea

FIGURE 2–2
Today's visionary organizations use key elements to (1) establish a foundation and (2) set a direction using (3) strategies that enable them to develop and market their products successfully.

Core Values An organization's **core values** are the fundamental, passionate, and enduring principles that guide its conduct over time.[11] A firm's founders or senior management develop these core values, which are consistent with their essential beliefs and character.[12] They capture the firm's heart and soul and serve to inspire and motivate its *stakeholders*—employees, shareholders, board of directors, suppliers, distributors, creditors, unions, government, local communities, and customers. Core values also are timeless and guide the organization's conduct. To be effective, an organization's core values must be communicated to and supported by its top management and employees; if not, they are just hollow words.[13]

Mission By understanding its core values, an organization can take steps to define its **mission**, a statement of the organization's function in society that often identifies its customers, markets, products, and technologies. Often used interchangeably with *vision*, a *mission statement* should be clear, concise, meaningful, inspirational, and long-term.[14]

QR 2-2
Medtronic
Video

Medtronic is a world leader in producing heart pacemakers and other electrical stimulation devices to treat diabetes, Parkinson's disease, and chronic back pain.[15] Medtronic almost died in infancy when it was trying to raise start-up capital. A world-renowned consulting company surveyed doctors and "concluded there was no foreseeable market for pacemakers."[16] Earl Bakken, its founder, wrote this mission statement for Medtronic when it was launched a half century ago (and which today remains virtually unchanged):

> To contribute to human welfare by application of biomedical engineering in the research, design, manufacture, and sale of instruments or appliances that alleviate pain, restore health, and extend life.

Similar inspiration and focus appear in the mission statements of other for-profit organizations, as well as nonprofit organizations and government agencies:

- Southwest Airlines: "To be dedicated to the highest quality of Customer Service delivered with a sense of warmth, friendliness, individual pride, and Company Spirit."
- American Red Cross: "To prevent and alleviate human suffering in the face of emergencies by mobilizing the power of volunteers and the generosity of donors."[17]

At Medtronic, senior executives give each new employee worldwide this medallion. On the front is a rising figure along with a motto that reads, "Medtronic: Alleviating Pain—Restoring Health—Extending life." On the back is Medtronic's abridged mission statement. What does this medallion signify to employees? For insights, see the text.

Each statement exhibits the qualities of a good mission: a clear, challenging, and compelling picture of an envisioned future.[18]

Recently, many organizations have added a social element to their mission statements to reflect an ideal that is morally right and worthwhile. This is what Ben & Jerry's social mission statement shows in the chapter opener. Stakeholders, particularly customers, employees, and now society, are asking organizations to be exceptional citizens by providing long-term value while solving society's problems.

In the first half of the 20th century, what "business" did railroad executives believe they were in? The text reveals their disastrous error.

Organizational Culture An organization must connect with all of its stakeholders. Thus, an important corporate-level marketing function is communicating its core values and mission to them. Medtronic presents every new employee with a medallion depicting a "rising figure" on one side and the company's mission statement on the other. And each December, several patients describe to a large employee holiday celebration how Medtronic devices have changed their lives.[19] These activities send clear messages to employees and other stakeholders about Medtronic's **organizational culture**—the set of values, ideas, attitudes, and norms of behavior that is learned and shared among the members of an organization.

Organizational Direction: What Will It Do?

As shown in Figure 2–2, the organization's foundation enables it to set a direction in terms of (1) the "business" it is in and (2) its specific goals.

Business A **business** describes the clear, broad, underlying industry or market sector of an organization's offering. To help define its business, an organization looks at the set of organizations that sell similar offerings—those that are in direct competition with each other—such as "the ice cream business." The organization can then begin to answer the questions, "What do we do?" or "What business are we in?"

Professor Theodore Levitt saw that 20th century American railroads defined their business too narrowly, proclaiming, "We are in the railroad business!" This myopic focus caused them to lose sight of who their customers were and what they needed. So railroads failed to develop strategies to compete with airlines, barges, pipelines, and trucks. As a result, many railroads merged or went bankrupt. Railroads should have realized they were in "the transportation business."[20]

With today's increased global competition, many organizations are rethinking their *business model*, the strategies an organization develops to provide value to the customers it serves. Technological innovation is often the trigger for this business model change. American newspapers are looking for a new business model as former subscribers now get their news online.[21] Bookstore retailer Barnes & Noble, too, is rethinking its *business model* as e-book readers like Amazon's Kindle and Apple's iPad have gained widespread popularity.[22]

Why is Rovio altering its business model by developing an Angry Birds Land amusement park in Finland? See the text and the Marketing Matters box for the answer.

The Marketing Matters box describes how Rovio Entertainment Ltd., the Finnish developer of the Angry Birds video games, has defined the business it is in. Taking a lesson from Theodore Levitt, Rovio sees itself as being an "entertainment company," *not* a "gaming company." Time will tell whether the Angry Birds brand and image that works so well with its video games will carry over to amusement parks, clothing, toys, soda, candy, and movies![23]

Marketing Matters

entrepreneurship

Angry Birds: Discovering Its "Business" and . . . Business Model!

By 2008, three Finnish 20-somethings had developed 50 video games for Rovio Entertainment Ltd. without much success. Then in 2009, along came their Angry Birds video game, which skyrocketed to success. Rovio wondered how to build on that very success.

What Business Are We In?

Looking for growth opportunities, one clear strategy was to launch spin-offs of the original Angry Birds video game. In April 2012, Rovio introduced Angry Birds Space, which set a record by becoming the first app to hit 50 million downloads in only 35 days. By then, across all platforms, Angry Birds could boast of over 700 million downloads.

If you are traveling in Finland, you can expect to see at least one of more than 30 Angry Birds amusement parks. These came about through Rovio partnering with a Finnish playground equipment maker, putting Rovio clearly outside the video game business. "We stopped looking at ourselves as a gaming company a long time ago," says Peter Vesterbacka, Rovio's chief marketing officer. "We are an entertainment company."

Dreaming Big: Angry Birds—the Movie?

So what's next? Some of the companies that Rovio has partnered with so far include a Swedish clothing manufacturer, an American toy maker (Hasbro), and a Finnish beverage company. By 2013, the round birds with big eyebrows and orange beaks were showing up on T-shirts, soda cans, flip flops, toys, hoodies, and candy—not only in Finland but around the world. On the horizon for a 2016 summer release is an Angry Birds movie. The Angry Birds animated film will be targeted at kids, while also hoping to entertain their parents.

Will this entertainment business model succeed? The answer depends on whether the powerful Angry Birds brand and image can cross diverse product categories without offending existing customers.

QR 2-3
Angry Birds
Video

Goals **Goals** or **objectives** (terms used interchangeably in this book) are statements of an accomplishment of a task to be achieved, often by a specific time. Goals convert an organization's mission and business into long- and short-term performance targets. Business firms can pursue several different types of goals:

- *Profit.* Most firms seek to maximize profits—to get as high a financial return on their investments (ROI) as possible.
- *Sales* (dollars or units). If profits are acceptable, a firm may elect to maintain or increase its sales even though profits may not be maximized.
- *Market share.* **Market share** is the ratio of sales revenue of the firm to the total sales revenue of all firms in the industry, including the firm itself.
- *Quality.* A firm may offer the highest quality, as Medtronic does with its implantable medical devices.
- *Customer satisfaction.* Customers are the reason the organization exists, so their perceptions and actions are of vital importance. Satisfaction can be measured with surveys or by the number of customer complaints.
- *Employee welfare.* A firm may recognize the critical importance of its employees by stating its goal of providing them with good employment opportunities and working conditions.
- *Social responsibility.* Firms may seek to balance the conflicting goals of stakeholders to promote their overall welfare, even at the expense of profits.

Nonprofit organizations (such as museums and hospitals) also have goals, such as to serve consumers as efficiently as possible. Similarly, government agencies set goals that seek to serve the public good.

Rovio, the maker of Angry Birds, is altering its "business model," which requires entirely new organizational strategies.

Organizational Strategies: How Will It Do It?

As shown in Figure 2–2, the organizational foundation sets the "why" of organizations and the organizational direction sets the "what." To convert these into actual results, the organizational strategies are concerned with the "how." These organizational strategies vary in at least two ways, depending on (1) a strategy's level in the organization and (2) the offerings an organization provides to its customers.

Variation by Level Moving down the levels in an organization involves creating increasingly specific, detailed strategies and plans. So, at the corporate level, top managers may struggle with writing a meaningful mission statement; while at the functional level, the issue is who makes tomorrow's sales call.

Variation by Product Organizational strategies also vary by the organization's products. The strategy will be far different when marketing a very tangible physical good (a Medtronic heart pacemaker), a service (a Southwest Airlines flight), or an idea (a donation to the American Red Cross). This is Rovio's challenge as it tries to extend its new business model of becoming an "entertainment company" to encompass stuffed toys, amusement parks, and movies.

Most organizations develop a marketing plan as a part of their strategic marketing planning efforts. A **marketing plan** is a road map for the marketing actions of an organization for a specified future time period, such as one year or five years. The planning phase of the strategic marketing process (discussed later) usually results in a marketing plan that directs the marketing actions of an organization. Appendix A at the end of this chapter provides guidelines for writing a marketing plan.

learning review

2-3. What is the meaning of an organization's mission?

2-4. What is the difference between an organization's business and its goals?

Tracking Strategic Performance with Marketing Dashboards

LO 2-3 Explain why managers use marketing dashboards and marketing metrics.

Although marketing managers can set strategic directions for their organizations, how do they know if they are making progress in getting there? One answer is to measure performance by using marketing dashboards.

Car Dashboards and Marketing Dashboards A **marketing dashboard** is the visual computer display of the essential information related to achieving a marketing objective.[24] Often, active hyperlinks provide further detail. An example is when a chief marketing officer (CMO) wants to see daily what the effect of a new TV advertising campaign is on a product's sales.[25]

The idea of a marketing dashboard really comes from the display of information found on a car's dashboard. On a car's dashboard, we glance at the fuel gauge and take action when our gas is getting low. With a marketing dashboard, a marketing manager glances at a graph or table and makes a decision whether to take action or to analyze the problem further.[26]

Dashboards, Metrics, and Plans The marketing dashboard of Sonatica, a hypothetical hardware and software firm, appears in Figure 2–3. It shows graphic displays of key performance indicators linked to its product lines.[27] Each display in a marketing dashboard shows a **marketing metric**, which is a measure of the quantitative

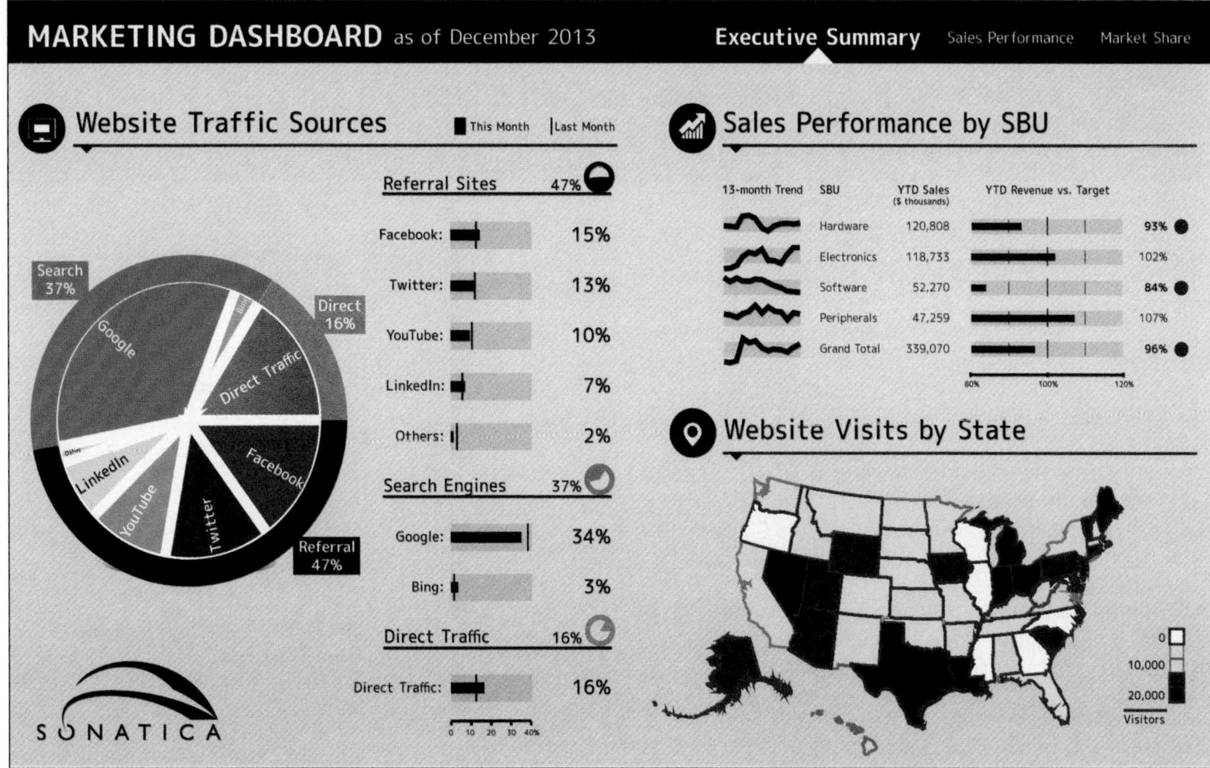

Source: Dundas Data Visualization, Inc.

FIGURE 2–3
An effective marketing dashboard, like this one from Sonatica, a hypothetical hardware and software firm, helps managers assess a business situation at a glance.

value or trend of a marketing action or result.[28] Choosing which marketing metrics to display is critical for a busy manager, who can be overwhelmed with irrelevant data.[29]

Today's marketers use *data visualization,* which presents information about an organization's marketing metrics graphically so marketers can quickly (1) spot deviations from plans during the evaluation phase and (2) take corrective actions.[30] This book uses data visualization in many figures to highlight in color key points described in the text. The Sonatica marketing dashboard in Figure 2–3 uses data visualization tools like a pie chart, a line or bar chart, and a map to show how parts of its business are performing as of December 2013:

- *Website Traffic Sources.* The color-coded perimeter of the pie chart shows the three main sources of website traffic (referral sites at 47 percent, search engines at 37 percent, and direct traffic at 16 percent). These three colors link to those of the circles in the column of website traffic sources. Of the 47 percent of traffic coming from referral sites, the horizontal *bullet graphs* to the right show that Sonatica's Facebook visits comprise 15 percent of total website traffic, up from a month ago (as shown by the vertical line).
- *Sales Performance by SBU.* The *spark lines* (the wavy lines in the far left column) show the 13-month trends of Sonatica's strategic business units (SBUs). For example, the trends in electronics and peripherals are generally up, causing their sales to exceed their YTD (year to date) targets. Conversely, both software and hardware sales failed to meet YTD targets, a problem quickly noted by a marketing manager seeing the red "warning" circles in their rows at the far right. This suggests that immediate corrective actions are needed for the software and hardware SBUs.
- *Website Visits by State.* The U.S. map shows that the darker the state, the greater the number of website visits for the current month. For example, Texas has close to 20,000 visits per month, while Illinois has none.

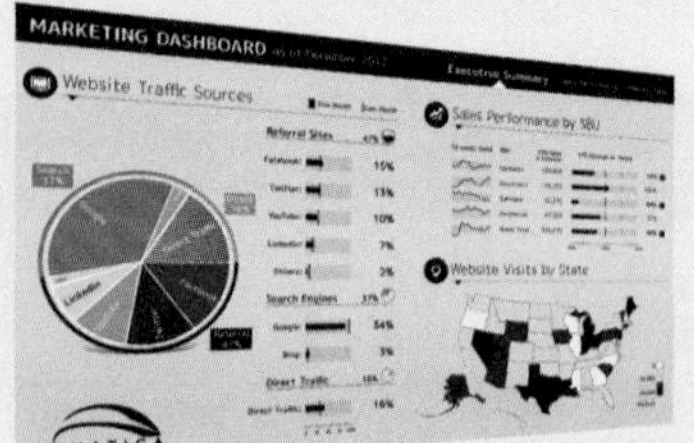

Using Marketing Dashboards

How Well Is Ben & Jerry's Doing?

As the marketing manager for Ben & Jerry's, you need to assess how it is doing within the United States in the super-premium ice cream market in which it competes. For this, you choose two marketing metrics: dollar sales and dollar market share.

Your Challenge Scanner data from checkout counters in supermarkets and other retailers show the total industry sales of super-premium ice cream were $1.25 billion in 2013. Internal company data show you that Ben & Jerry's sold 50 million units at an average price of $5.00 per unit in 2013. A "unit" in super-premium ice cream is one pint.

Your Findings Dollar sales and dollar market share can be calculated for 2013 using simple formulas and displayed on the Ben & Jerry's marketing dashboard as follows:

$$\begin{aligned}\text{Dollar sales(\$)} &= \text{Average price} \times \text{Quantity sold}\\ &= \$5.00 \times 50 \text{ million units}\\ &= \$250 \text{ million}\end{aligned}$$

$$\begin{aligned}\text{Dollar market share(\%)} &= \frac{\text{Ben \& Jerry's sales (\$)}}{\text{Total industry sales (\$)}}\\ &= \frac{\$250 \text{ million}}{\$1.25 \text{ billion}}\\ &= 0.20 \text{ or } 20\%\end{aligned}$$

Your dashboard displays show that from 2012 to 2013 dollar sales increased from $240 million to $250 million and that dollar market share grew from 18.4 to 20.0 percent.

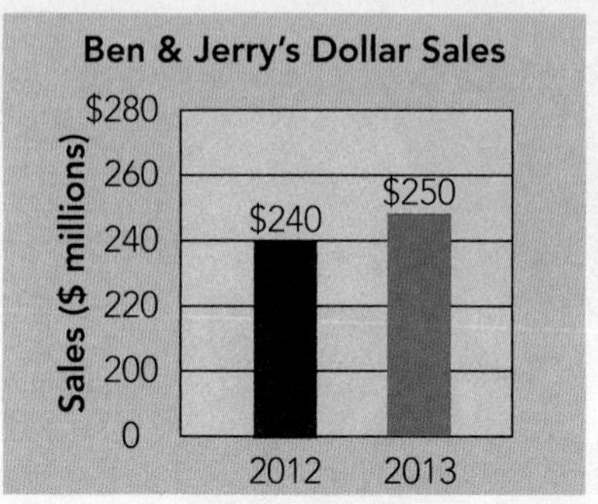

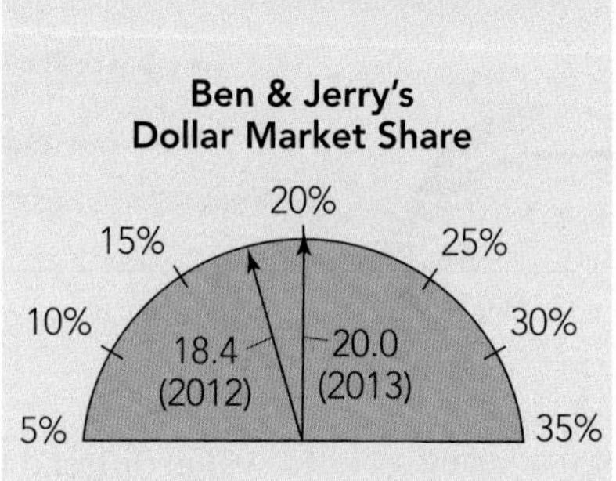

Your Action The results need to be compared with the goals established for these metrics. In addition, they should be compared with previous years' results to see if the trends are increasing, flat, or decreasing. This will lead to marketing actions.

The Ben & Jerry's dashboard in the Using Marketing Dashboards box shows how the two widely used marketing metrics of dollar sales and dollar market share can help the company assess its growth performance from 2012 to 2013. The Using Marketing Dashboard boxes in later chapters highlight other key marketing metrics and how they can lead to marketing actions.

SETTING STRATEGIC DIRECTIONS

Discuss how an organization assesses where it is now and where it seeks to be.

To set a strategic direction, an organization needs to answer two difficult questions: (1) Where are we now? and (2) Where do we want to go?

A Look Around: Where Are We Now?

Asking an organization where it is at the present time involves identifying its competencies, customers, and competitors.

Lands' End's unconditional guarantee for its products highlights its focus on customers.

Competencies Senior managers must ask the question: What do we do best? The answer involves an assessment of the organization's core *competencies*, which are its special capabilities—the skills, technologies, and resources—that distinguish it from other organizations and provide customer value. Exploiting these competencies can lead to success.[31]

Medtronic's competencies include world-class technology, training, and service that respond to life-threatening medical needs. *Bloomberg Businessweek* magazine has called Medtronic "the standard setter for quality."[32] Competencies should be distinctive enough to provide a *competitive advantage*, a unique strength relative to competitors that provides superior returns, often based on quality, time, cost, or innovation.[33]

Customers Ben & Jerry's customers are ice cream and frozen yogurt eaters who have different preferences (form, flavor, health, and convenience). Medtronic's pacemaker customers include cardiologists and heart surgeons who serve patients that need this type of device. Lands' End communicates a remarkable commitment to its customers and its product quality with these unconditional words:

Guaranteed. Period.®

The Lands' End website points out that this guarantee has always been an unconditional one. It reads: "If you're not satisfied with any item, simply return it to us at any time for an exchange or refund of its purchase price." But to get the message across more clearly to its customers, it created the two-word guarantee. The point is that Lands' End's strategy must provide genuine value to customers to ensure that they have a satisfying experience.[34]

Competitors In today's global marketplace, the distinctions among competitors are increasingly blurred. Lands' End started as a catalog retailer. But today, Lands' End competes with not only other clothing catalog retailers but also traditional department stores, mass merchandisers, and specialty shops. Even well-known clothing brands such as Liz Claiborne now have their own chain stores. Although only some of the clothing in any of these stores directly competes with Lands' End offerings, all of these retailers have websites to sell their offerings over the Internet. This means there's a lot of competition out there.

Growth Strategies: Where Do We Want to Go?

Knowing where the organization is at the present time enables managers to set a direction for the firm and allocate resources to move in that direction. Two techniques to aid managers with these decisions are (1) business portfolio analysis and (2) diversification analysis.

Business Portfolio Analysis Successful organizations have a portfolio or range of offerings (products and services) that possess different growth rates and market shares within the industry in which they operate. The Boston Consulting Group (BCG), an internationally known management consulting firm, has developed **business portfolio analysis**. It is a technique that managers use to quantify performance measures and growth targets to analyze their firms' strategic business units (SBUs) as though they were a collection of separate investments.[35] The purpose of this tool is to determine which SBU or offering generates cash and which one requires cash to fund the organization's growth opportunities.

Marketing Matters

technology

Filling the Shoes of Apple CEO Tim Cook: Where Will Apple's Projected Future Growth for Its Major SBUs Come From?

Every CEO of a for-profit organization faces one problem in common: trying to find ways to increase future sales and profits to keep it growing!

Put yourself in Tim Cook's shoes. One of his jobs is to search for new growth opportunities. Using your knowledge about Apple products, do a quick analysis of its four SBUs shown below to determine where Apple should allocate its time and resources. Rate these growth opportunities from highest to lowest in terms of percentage growth in unit sales from 2013 to 2016:

We'll walk you through possible answers. You then can evaluate your performance over the next two pages and decide whether you're really ready for Mr. Cook's job!

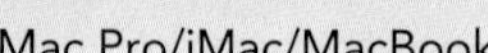
Mac Pro/iMac/MacBook

iPod

iPhone

iPad/iPad mini

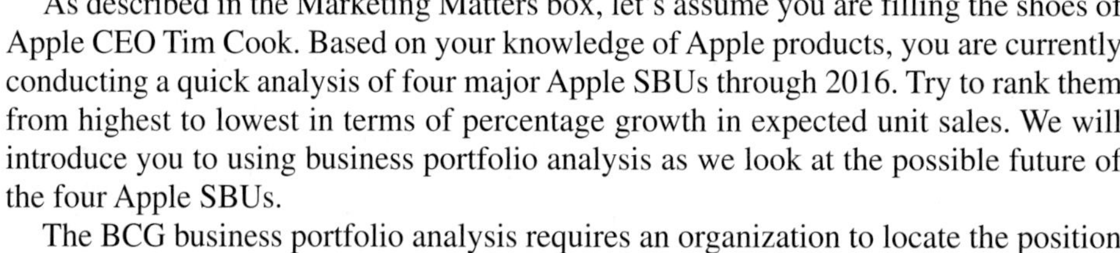

As described in the Marketing Matters box, let's assume you are filling the shoes of Apple CEO Tim Cook. Based on your knowledge of Apple products, you are currently conducting a quick analysis of four major Apple SBUs through 2016. Try to rank them from highest to lowest in terms of percentage growth in expected unit sales. We will introduce you to using business portfolio analysis as we look at the possible future of the four Apple SBUs.

What can Apple expect in future growth of sales revenues from its Mac Pro/iMac/MacBook products...

The BCG business portfolio analysis requires an organization to locate the position of each of its SBUs on a growth-share matrix (see Figure 2–4). The vertical axis is the *market growth rate*, which is the annual rate of growth of the SBU's industry. The horizontal axis is the *relative market share*, defined as the sales of the SBU divided by the sales of the largest firm in the industry. A relative market share of 10× (at the left end of the scale) means that the SBU has 10 times the share of its largest competitor, whereas a share of 0.1× (at the right end of the scale) means it has only 10 percent of the share of its largest competitor.

The BCG has given specific names and descriptions to the four resulting quadrants in its growth-share matrix based on the amount of cash they generate for or require from the organization:

- *Cash cows* are SBUs that generate large amounts of cash, far more than they can use. They have dominant shares of slow-growth markets and provide cash to cover the organization's overhead and to invest in other SBUs.
- *Stars* are SBUs with a high share of high-growth markets that may need extra cash to finance their own rapid future growth. When their growth slows, they are likely to become cash cows.
- *Question marks* are SBUs with a low share of high-growth markets. They require large injections of cash just to maintain their market share, much less increase it. The name implies management's dilemma for these SBUs: choosing the right ones to invest in and phasing out the rest.
- *Dogs* are SBUs with low shares of slow-growth markets. Although they may generate enough cash to sustain themselves, they may not become real winners

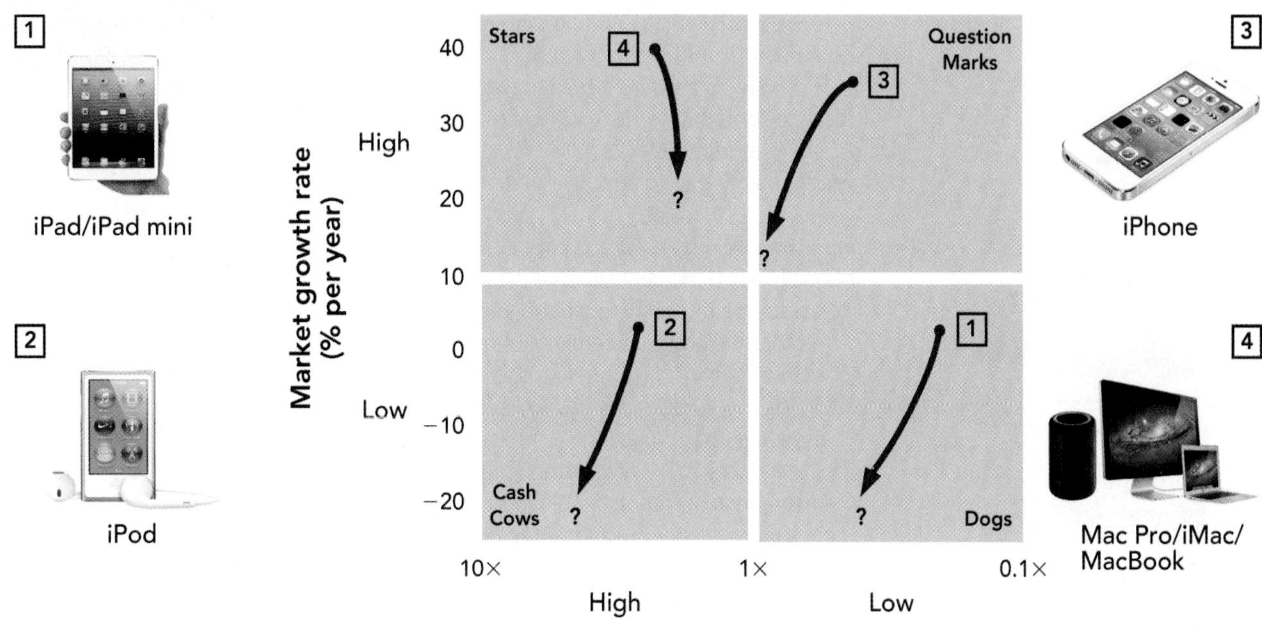

FIGURE 2–4 Boston Consulting Group (BCG) business portfolio analysis for four of Apple's consumer-related SBUs. Starting in 2013, the lines show where the sales revenues for each SBU are projected to be by 2016.

for the organization. Dropping SBUs that are dogs may be required if they consume more cash than they generate, except when relationships with other SBUs, competitive considerations, or potential strategic alliances exist.[36]

An organization's SBUs often start as question marks and go counterclockwise around Figure 2–4 to become stars, then cash cows, and finally dogs. Because an organization has limited influence on the market growth rate, its main objective is to try to change its relative dollar or unit market share. To do this, management decides what strategic role each SBU should have in the future and either injects cash into or removes cash from it.

According to Interbrand, a leading brand management consulting firm, Apple has been consistently cited as one of the top global brands over the past decade in its annual Best Global Brands survey. What has made Apple so iconic is not only its revolutionary products but also its commitment to infusing the "human touch" with its technology such that its customers connect with the brand on both a cognitive *and* an emotional level. The late Steve Jobs was instrumental in creating Apple's organizational culture and core values that will continue to guide its future.[37]

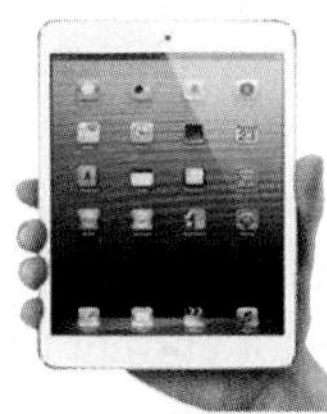

... or its iPad/iPad mini tablet devices?

Using the BCG business portfolio analysis framework, Figure 2–4 shows that the Apple picture might look this way from 2013 to 2016 for its four strategic business units:[38]

1. *Mac Pro/iMac/MacBook* (desktop and laptop personal computers or PCs). By mid-2013, Apple offered three lines of desktops (Mac Pro, iMac, and Mac mini) and two lines of laptops (MacBook Pro and MacBook Air). Global PC unit sales have declined during the past few years due to the growth of tablet devices. However, Apple's Macs have bucked this trend, increasing its global unit market share from 10 to 12 percent. By 2016, global PC unit sales are expected to fall dramatically due to the explosion in tablet device sales. As a result, Apple's Mac PC SBU appears to be a *dog* (low market share in a low-growth market).[39]
2. *iPod* (MP3 music players). Apple entered the MP3 player market with its iPod device in 2001. Today, Apple sells four iPod product lines (classic, nano, shuffle, and touch). As of mid-2013, Apple had a 70 percent share of this market! However, global MP3 music player unit sales are falling and are expected to decline

further by 2016. Why? Smartphones will continue to replace MP3 devices, and the launch of additional wearable digital watches may impact sales. For Apple, its iPod SBU is a *cash cow* (high market share in a low-growth market) and is likely to remain one for the near future.[40]

3. *iPhone* (smartphones). Apple launched its revolutionary iPhone in 2007, the first smartphone that used a multi-touch user interface. iPhone unit sales skyrocketed but have since leveled off. By 2017, the smartphone market is expected to grow at a compound annual rate of 13 percent due to dropping average smartphone prices. Apple's iPhone had a 15 percent share of the global smartphone market in mid-2013—second to Samsung, whose share was 41 percent. Apple's iPhone is on the *question mark-star* borderline and may remain so for the next few years unless or until it introduces new, compelling models such as the rumored iPhone 5S and iPhone 6.[41]
4. *iPad/iPad mini* (tablet devices). In 2010, Steve Jobs once again revolutionized an industry when he launched the iPad. Unit sales reached an astonishing 40 percent market share by mid-2013—leading both Samsung's Galaxy (18 percent) and Amazon's Kindle (4 percent). Global tablet unit sales are expected to more than double by 2016 as consumers switch from desktop and laptop PCs to tablet devices, with Apple still the market share leader. As these products mature, Apple's iPad/iPad mini SBU may move from a *star* toward a *cash cow* as its growth begins to subside after 2016.[42]

How can Ben & Jerry's develop new products and social responsibility programs that contribute to its mission? The text describes how the strategic marketing process and its SWOT analysis can help.

So, how did you—as Tim Cook—rank the growth opportunity for each of Apple's four SBUs for the future? In terms of priority, perhaps Apple will "milk" the cash generated from the Mac Pro/iMac/MacBook PC SBU [1] and iPod MP3 player SBU [2] to fund the investments needed to exploit the growth opportunities projected for the iPhone smartphone SBU [3] and the iPad/iPad mini tablet devices SBU [4]. Is Apple concerned? With its history of pulling exotic new-product "rabbits out of its hat," let's wait and see!

The primary strength of business portfolio analysis lies in forcing a firm to place each of its SBUs in the growth-share matrix, which in turn suggests which SBUs will be cash producers and cash users in the future. Weaknesses of this analysis arise from the difficulty in (1) getting the needed information and (2) incorporating competitive data into business portfolio analysis.[43]

QR 2-4
B&J's Bonnaroo Buzz Ad

Diversification Analysis **Diversification analysis** is a technique that helps a firm search for growth opportunities from among current and new markets as well as current and new products.[44] For any market, there is both a current product (what the firm now sells) and a new product (what the firm might sell in the future). And for any product there is both a current market (the firm's existing customers) and a new market (the firm's potential customers). As Ben & Jerry's seeks to increase sales revenues, it considers all four market-product strategies shown in Figure 2–5:

- *Market penetration* is a marketing strategy to increase sales of current products in current markets, such as selling more Ben & Jerry's Bonnaroo Buzz Fair

FIGURE 2–5 Four market-product strategies: alternative ways to expand sales revenues for Ben & Jerry's using diversification analysis.

MARKETS	PRODUCTS: Current	PRODUCTS: New
Current	**Market penetration** Selling more Ben & Jerry's super-premium ice cream to Americans	**Product development** Selling a new product such as children's clothing under the Ben & Jerry's brand to Americans
New	**Market development** Selling Ben & Jerry's super-premium ice cream to Brazilians for the first time	**Diversification** Selling a new product such as children's clothing under the Ben & Jerry's brand to Brazilians for the first time

Trade–sourced ice cream to U.S. consumers. There is no change in either the basic product line or the markets served. Increased sales are generated by selling either more ice cream (through better promotion or distribution) *or* the same amount of ice cream at a higher price to its current customers.

- *Market development* is a marketing strategy to sell current products to new markets. For Ben & Jerry's, Brazil is an attractive new market. There is good news and bad news for this strategy: As household incomes of Brazilians increase, consumers can buy more ice cream; however, the Ben & Jerry's brand may be unknown to Brazilian consumers.
- *Product development* is a marketing strategy of selling new products to current markets. Ben & Jerry's could leverage its brand by selling children's clothing in the United States. This strategy is risky because Americans may not see the company's expertise in ice cream as extending to children's clothing.
- *Diversification* is a marketing strategy of developing new products and selling them in new markets. This is a potentially high-risk strategy for Ben & Jerry's if it decides to try to sell Ben & Jerry's branded clothing in Brazil. Why? Because the firm has neither previous production nor marketing experience from which to draw in marketing clothing to Brazilian consumers.

learning review

2-5. What is the difference between a marketing dashboard and a marketing metric?

2-6. What is business portfolio analysis?

2-7. Explain the four market-product strategies in diversification analysis.

THE STRATEGIC MARKETING PROCESS

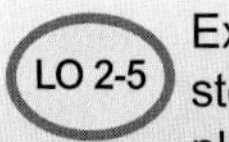

Explain the three steps of the planning phase of the strategic marketing process.

After an organization assesses where it is and where it wants to go, other questions emerge, such as:

1. How do we allocate our resources to get where we want to go?
2. How do we convert our plans into actions?
3. How do our results compare with our plans, and do deviations require new plans?

To answer these questions, an organization uses the **strategic marketing process**, whereby an organization allocates its marketing mix resources to reach its target markets. This process is divided into three phases: planning, implementation, and evaluation, as shown in Figure 2–6 on the next page.

The Planning Phase of the Strategic Marketing Process

Figure 2–6 shows the three steps in the planning phase of the strategic marketing process: (1) situation (SWOT) analysis, (2) market-product focus and goal setting, and (3) the marketing program.

Step 1: Situation (SWOT) Analysis The essence of **situation analysis** is taking stock of where the firm or product has been recently, where it is now, and where it is headed in terms of the organization's marketing plans and the external forces and trends affecting it. An effective summary of a situation analysis is a **SWOT analysis**, an acronym describing an organization's appraisal of its internal **S**trengths and **W**eaknesses and its external **O**pportunities and **T**hreats.

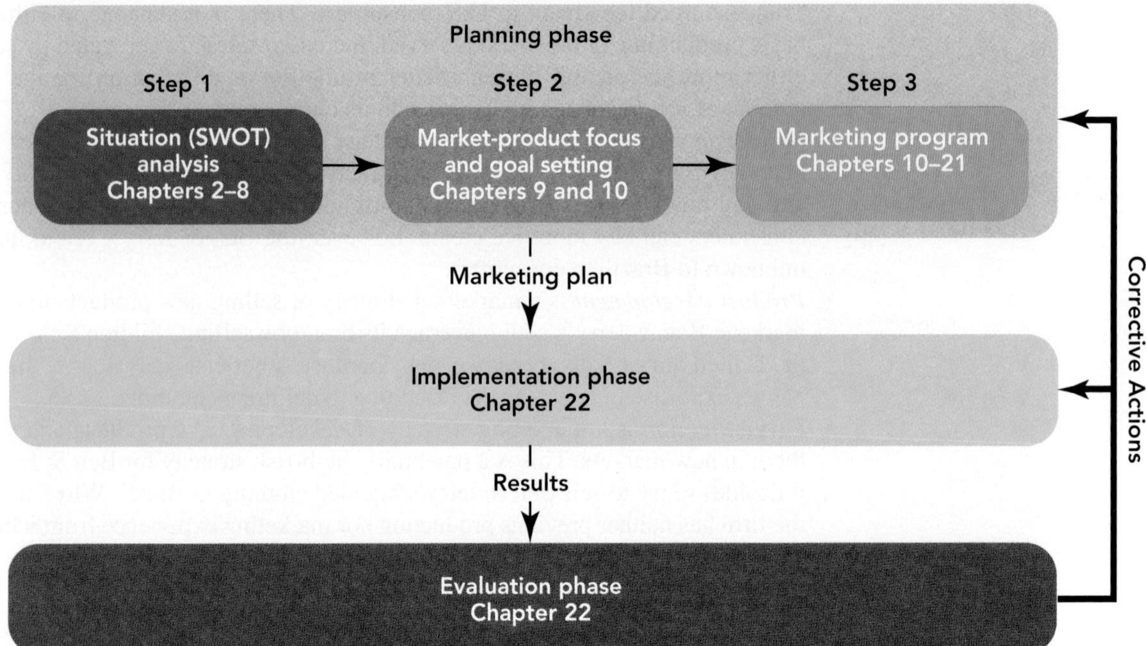

FIGURE 2–6
The strategic marketing process has three vital phases: planning, implementation, and evaluation. The figure also indicates the chapters in which these phases are discussed in the text.

The SWOT analysis is based on an exhaustive study of four areas that form the foundation upon which the firm builds its marketing program:

- Identify trends in the organization's industry.
- Analyze the organization's competitors.
- Assess the organization itself.
- Research the organization's present and prospective customers.

Assume you are responsible for doing the SWOT analysis for Ben & Jerry's shown in Figure 2–7. Note that the SWOT table has four cells formed by the combination of internal versus external factors (the rows) and favorable versus unfavorable factors (the columns) that identify Ben & Jerry's strengths, weaknesses, opportunities, and threats.

The task is to translate the results of the SWOT analysis into specific marketing actions that will help the firm grow. The ultimate goal is to identify the *critical* strategy-related factors that impact the firm and then build on vital strengths, correct glaring weaknesses, exploit significant opportunities, and avoid disaster-laden threats.

The Ben & Jerry's SWOT analysis in Figure 2–7 can be the basis for these kinds of specific marketing actions. An action in each of the four cells might be:

- *Build on a strength.* Find specific efficiencies in distribution with parent-company Unilever's existing ice cream brands.
- *Correct a weakness.* Recruit experienced managers from other consumer product firms to help stimulate growth.
- *Exploit an opportunity.* Develop new product lines of low-fat, low-carb frozen Greek-style yogurt flavors to respond to changes in consumer tastes.
- *Avoid a disaster-laden threat.* Focus on less risky international markets, such as Brazil and Argentina.

Step 2: Market-Product Focus and Goal Setting Determining which products will be directed toward which customers (step 2 of the planning phase in Figure 2–6) is essential for developing an effective marketing program (step 3). This decision is often based on **market segmentation**, which involves aggregating

FIGURE 2–7
Ben & Jerry's: A SWOT analysis to keep it growing. The picture painted in this SWOT analysis is the basis for management actions.

LOCATION OF FACTOR	TYPE OF FACTOR	
	Favorable	Unfavorable
Internal	**Strengths** • Prestigious, well-known brand name among U.S. consumers • Complements Unilever's other ice cream brands • Recognized for its social mission, values, and actions	**Weaknesses** • B&J's social responsibility actions could reduce focus • Experienced managers needed to help growth • Modest sales growth and profits in recent years
External	**Opportunities** • Growing demand for quality ice cream in overseas markets • Increasing U.S. demand for Greek-style yogurt • Many U.S. firms successfully use product and brand extensions	**Threats** • B&J customers read nutritional labels and are concerned with sugary and fatty desserts • Competes with General Mills and Nestlé brands • Increasing competition in international markets

prospective buyers into groups, or segments, that (1) have common needs and (2) will respond similarly to a marketing action. This enables an organization to focus specific marketing programs on its target market segments.

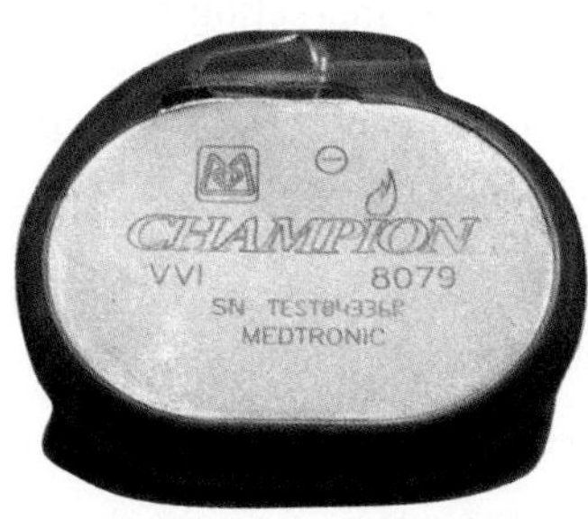

The Champion: Medtronic's high-quality, long-life, low-cost heart pacemaker for Asian market segments.

In the case of Medtronic, executives researched a potential new market in Asia by talking extensively with doctors in India and China. Medtronic discovered that these doctors wanted an affordable pacemaker that was reliable and easy to implant. So Medtronic developed and marketed a new product, the Champion heart pacemaker, directed at satisfying their needs.

Goal setting involves specifying measurable marketing objectives to be achieved. For example, the goal may be to introduce Medtronic's Champion pacemaker in emerging markets, starting in Asia. Let's examine Medtronic's five-year plan to reach the "affordable and reliable" pacemaker segment that results in its marketing program:[45]

- *Set marketing and product goals.* Chances of new-product success are increased by specifying both market and product goals. Based on their market research, Medtronic executives set the following goal: Market the Chinese-produced Champion pacemaker to Asian markets within three years.
- *Select target markets.* The Champion pacemaker will be targeted at cardiologists and heart surgery clinics in India, China, and other Asian countries.
- *Find points of difference.* **Points of difference** are those characteristics of a product that make it superior to competitive substitutes. Just as a competitive advantage is a unique strength of an entire organization compared to its competitors, points of difference are unique characteristics of one of its products that make it superior to competitive products it faces in the marketplace. For the Champion pacemaker, the key points of difference are its high quality, long life, reliability, ease of use, and low cost.
- *Position the product.* The pacemaker will be "positioned" in cardiologists' and patients' minds as a medical device that is high quality and reliable with a long, nine-year life. The name Champion was selected after testing acceptable names among doctors in India, China, Pakistan, Singapore, and Malaysia.

So step 2 in the planning phase of the strategic marketing process—deciding which products will be directed toward which customers—is the foundation for step 3, developing the marketing program.

FIGURE 2–8
The four Ps elements of the marketing mix must be blended to produce a cohesive marketing program.

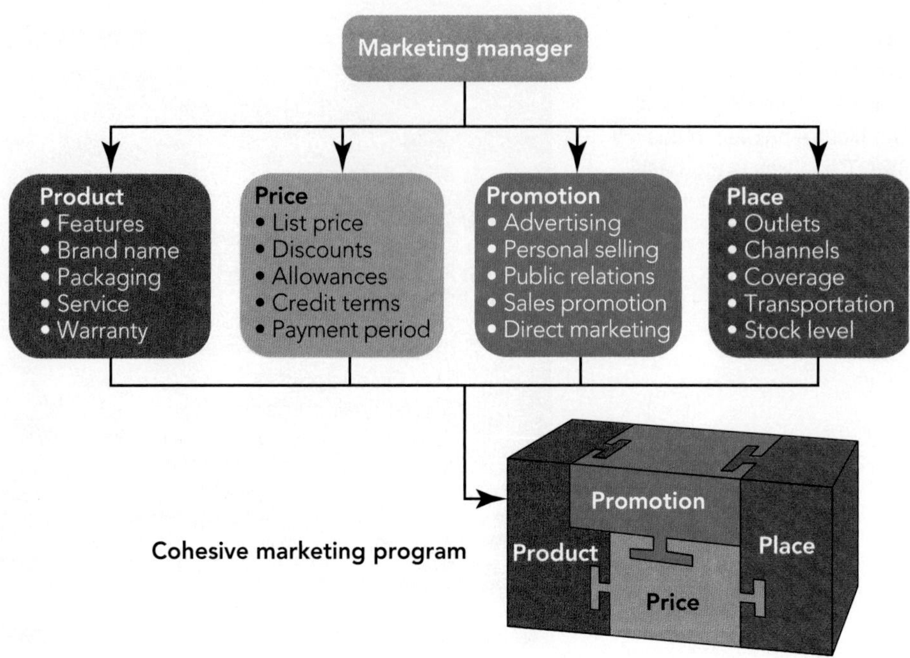

Step 3: Marketing Program Activities in step 2 tell the marketing manager which customers to target and which customer needs the firm's product offerings can satisfy—the *who* and *what* aspects of the strategic marketing process. The *how* aspect—step 3 in the planning phase—involves developing the program's marketing mix (the four Ps) and its budget. Figure 2–8 shows that each marketing mix element is combined to provide a cohesive marketing program. The five-year marketing plan for Medtronic's Champion pacemaker includes these marketing mix actions:

- *Product strategy.* Offer a Champion brand heart pacemaker with only those features needed by Asian patients.
- *Price strategy.* Manufacture the Champion to control costs so that it can be priced below $1,000 (in U.S. dollars)—an affordable price for Asian markets.
- *Promotion strategy.* Introduce the Champion at medical conventions across Asia to demonstrate its many beneficial features.
- *Place (distribution) strategy.* Search out, utilize, and train reputable medical device distributors across Asia to call on cardiologists and medical clinics.

Putting this marketing program into effect requires that the firm commit time and money to it in the form of a sales forecast (see Chapter 8) and budget that must be approved by top management.

learning review

2-8. What are the three steps of the planning phase of the strategic marketing process?

2-9. What are points of difference and why are they important?

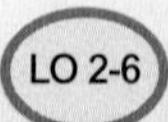
LO 2-6 Describe the four components of the implementation phase of the strategic marketing process.

The Implementation Phase of the Strategic Marketing Process

As shown in Figure 2–6, the result of the hours spent in the planning phase of the strategic marketing process is the firm's marketing plan. Implementation, the second phase of the strategic marketing process, involves carrying out the marketing plan that emerges from the planning phase. If the firm cannot execute the marketing plan—in the implementation phase—the planning phase wasted time and resources.

There are four components of the implementation phase: (1) obtaining resources, (2) designing the marketing organization, (3) defining precise tasks, responsibilities, and deadlines, and (4) actually executing the marketing program designed in the planning phase.

Obtaining Resources A key task in the implementation phase of the strategic marketing process is finding adequate human and financial resources to execute the marketing program successfully. Small business owners often obtain funds from savings, family, friends, and bank loans. Marketing managers in existing organizations obtain these resources by getting top management to divert profits from BCG stars or cash cows.

Designing the Marketing Organization A marketing program needs a marketing organization to implement it. Figure 2–9 shows the organization chart of a typical manufacturing firm, giving some details of the marketing department's structure. Four managers of marketing activities are shown to report to the vice president of marketing or CMO. Several regional sales managers and an international sales manager may report to the manager of sales. The product or brand managers and their subordinates help plan, implement, and evaluate the marketing plans for their offerings. However, the entire marketing organization is responsible for converting these marketing plans into realistic marketing actions.[46]

Defining Precise Tasks, Responsibilities, and Deadlines Successful implementation requires that team members know the tasks for which they are responsible and the deadlines for completing them. To implement the thousands of tasks on a new aircraft design, Lockheed Martin typically holds weekly program meetings. The outcome of each of these meetings is an *action item list*, an aid to implementing a marketing plan consisting of four columns: (1) the task, (2) the person responsible for completing that task, (3) the date to finish the task, and (4) what is to be delivered. Within hours of completing a program meeting, the action item list is circulated to those attending. This then serves as the starting agenda for the next meeting. Meeting minutes are viewed as secondary and backward-looking. Action item lists are forward-looking, clarify the targets, and put strong pressure on people to achieve their designated tasks by the deadline.

FIGURE 2–9
Organization of a typical manufacturing firm, showing a breakdown of the marketing department.

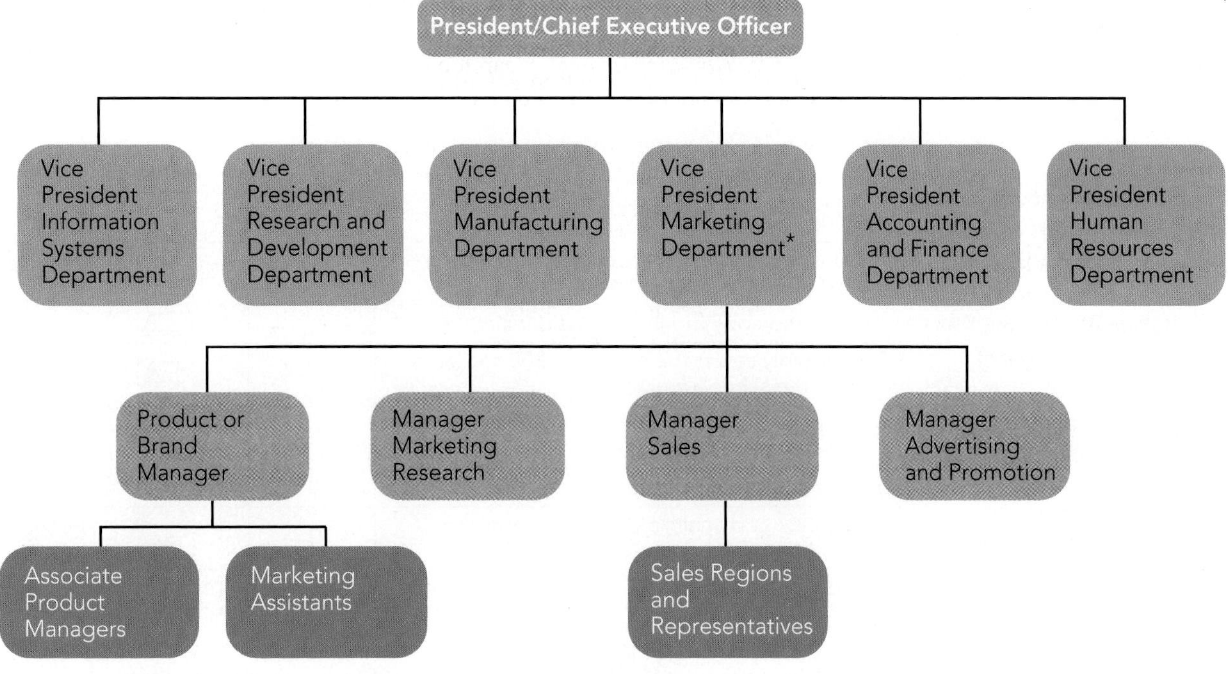

Suppose, for example, that you and two friends undertake a term project on the problem, "How can the college increase attendance at its performing arts concerts?" The instructor says the term project must involve a mail survey of a sample of students, and the written report with the survey results must be submitted by the end of the 11-week quarter. To begin, you identify all the project tasks and then estimate the time required to complete each one. To complete it in 11 weeks, your team must plan which activities can be done concurrently (at the same time) to save time.

Scheduling activities can be done efficiently with a *Gantt chart*, which is a graph of a program schedule. Figure 2–10 shows a Gantt chart—invented by Henry L. Gantt—used to schedule the class project, demonstrating how the concurrent work on several tasks enables the students to finish the project on time. Software programs such as Microsoft Project simplify the task of developing a program schedule or Gantt chart.

The key to all scheduling techniques is to distinguish tasks that *must* be done sequentially from those that *can* be done concurrently. For example, Tasks 1 and 2 that are shaded yellow in Figure 2–10 *must* be done sequentially. This is because in order to type and copy the final questionnaire before mailing (Task 2), the student *must* have a final draft of the questionnaire (Task 1). In contrast, Tasks 6 and 7 that are shaded blue *can* be done concurrently. So writing the final report (Task 7) *can* be started before tabulating the questions (Task 6) is completed. This overlap speeds up project completion.

Executing the Marketing Program Marketing plans are meaningless without effective execution of those plans. This requires attention to detail for both marketing strategies and marketing tactics. A **marketing strategy** is the means by which a marketing goal is to be achieved, usually characterized by a specified target market and a marketing program to reach it. The term implies both the end sought (target market) and the means or actions to achieve it (marketing program).

To implement a marketing program successfully, hundreds of detailed decisions are often required to develop the actions that comprise a marketing program for an offering. These actions, called **marketing tactics**, are detailed day-to-day operational marketing actions for each element of the marketing mix that contribute to the overall success of marketing strategies. Writing ads and setting prices for new product lines are examples of marketing tactics.

LO 2-7 Discuss how managers identify and act on deviations from plans.

The Evaluation Phase of the Strategic Marketing Process

The evaluation phase of the strategic marketing process seeks to keep the marketing program moving in the direction set for it (see Figure 2–6). Accomplishing this

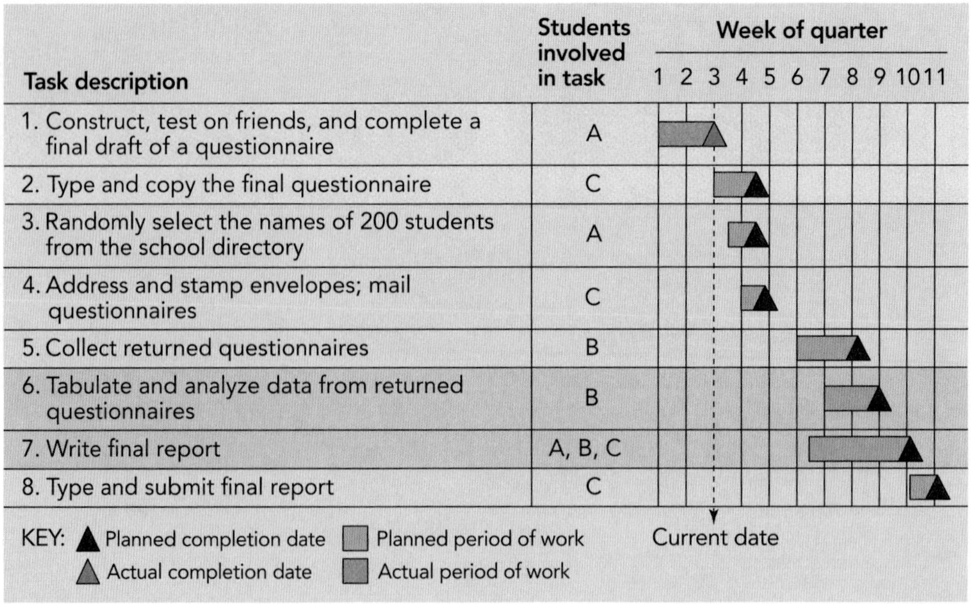

FIGURE 2–10
This Gantt chart shows how three students (A, B, and C) can schedule tasks to complete a term project on time. Software programs, such as Microsoft Project, simplify the task of developing a program schedule or Gantt chart.

Task description	Students involved in task	Week of quarter: 1 2 3 4 5 6 7 8 9 10 11
1. Construct, test on friends, and complete a final draft of a questionnaire	A	
2. Type and copy the final questionnaire	C	
3. Randomly select the names of 200 students from the school directory	A	
4. Address and stamp envelopes; mail questionnaires	C	
5. Collect returned questionnaires	B	
6. Tabulate and analyze data from returned questionnaires	B	
7. Write final report	A, B, C	
8. Type and submit final report	C	

Current date

KEY: Planned completion date; Planned period of work; Actual completion date; Actual period of work requires the marketing manager to (1) compare the results of the marketing program with the goals in the written plans to identify deviations and (2) act on these deviations—exploiting positive deviations and correcting negative ones.

Comparing Results with Plans to Identify Deviations At the end of its fiscal year, which is September 30, Apple begins the evaluation phase of its strategic marketing process. Suppose you are on an Apple task force in late 2005 that is responsible for making plans through 2012. You observe that extending the 2000–2005 trend of Apple's recent sales revenues (line AB in Figure 2–11) to 2012 along line BC shows an annual growth in sales revenue unacceptable to Apple's management.

Looking at potential new products in the Apple pipeline, your task force set an aggressive annual sales growth target of 25 percent per year—the line BD in Figure 2–11. This would give sales revenues of $34 billion in 2009 and $66 billion in 2012.

This reveals a gray wedge-shaped gap DBC in the figure. Planners call this the *planning gap*, the difference between the projection of the path to reach a new sales revenue goal (line BD) and the projection of the path of a plan already in place (line BC). The ultimate purpose of the firm's marketing program is to "fill in" this planning gap—in the case of your Apple task force, to move its future sales revenue line from the slow-growth line BC up to the more challenging target of line BD.

This is the essence of evaluation: comparing actual results with goals set. To reach aggressive growth targets in sales revenues, firms like Apple must continuously look for a new BCG SBU or product *cash cow* or *star*.

Acting on Deviations When evaluation shows that actual performance differs from expectations, managers need to take immediate marketing actions—exploiting positive deviations and correcting negative ones. Comparing the explosion in Apple's actual sales revenues from 2006 to 2012 (line BE in Figure 2–11) to its target sales revenues (line BD) shows Apple's rare, world-class ability to both generate and anticipate

FIGURE 2–11
The evaluation phase of the strategic marketing process requires that the organization compare actual results with goals to identify and act on deviations to fill in its "planning gap." The text describes how Apple is working to fill in its planning gap.

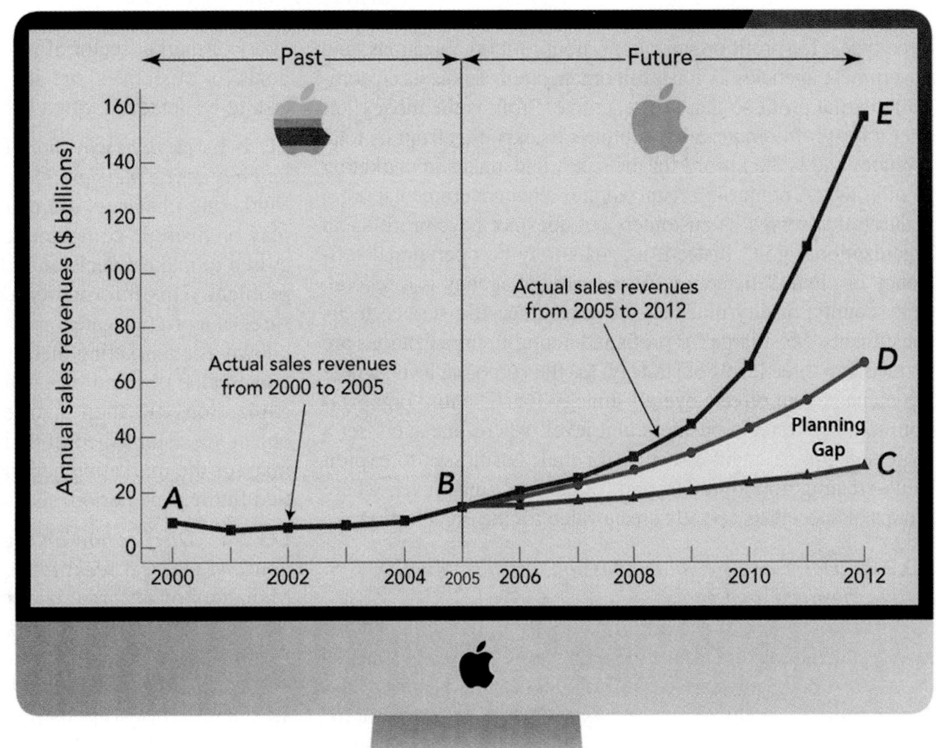

consumer demand and commercialize new technologies for its revolutionary offerings. Let's consider some of its marketing actions:

- *Exploiting a positive deviation.* Favorable customer reactions to Apple's iPhone (2007) and its iPad (2010) enable it to sell the products globally and to introduce improved versions and models, such as the iPad mini (2012).
- *Correcting a negative deviation.* As Apple's desktop PCs became dated, it moved aggressively to replace them with new iMacs (2012) and Mac Pro (2013). Also, Apple refreshed its MacBook Air and MacBook Pro lines of laptops (2013). Moreover, Apple introduced an iPhone mini in 2013 to spur sales in China, a huge market for smartphones.

As we saw earlier in the BCG business portfolio analysis of the four Apple product lines, the firm has several *stars* and *cash cows* to fill in its planning gap. We shall explore Apple's market-product strategies in more detail later in Chapters 9 and 10.

learning review

2-10. What is the implementation phase of the strategic marketing process?

2-11. How do the goals set for a marketing program in the planning phase relate to the evaluation phase of the strategic marketing process?

LEARNING OBJECTIVES REVIEW

LO 2-1 *Describe three kinds of organizations and the three levels of strategy in them.*
An organization is a legal entity that consists of people who share a common mission. It develops offerings (goods, services, or ideas) that create value for both the organization and its customers by satisfying their needs and wants. Today's organizations are of three types: for-profit organizations, nonprofit organizations, and government agencies. A for-profit organization serves its customers to earn a profit so that it can survive. Profit is the money left after a for-profit organization subtracts its expenses from its total revenues and is the reward for the risk it undertakes in marketing its offerings. A nonprofit organization is a nongovernmental organization that serves its customers but does not have profit as an organizational goal. Instead, its goals may be operational efficiency or client satisfaction. A government agency is a federal, state, county, or city unit that provides a specific service to its constituents. Most large for-profit and nonprofit organizations are divided into three levels of strategy: (*a*) the corporate level, where top management directs overall strategy for the entire organization; (*b*) the strategic business unit level, where managers set a more specific strategic direction for their businesses to exploit value-creating opportunities; and (*c*) the functional level, where groups of specialists actually create value for the organization.

LO 2-2 *Describe core values, mission, organizational culture, business, and goals.*
Organizations exist to accomplish something for someone. To give organizations direction and focus, they continuously assess their core values, mission, organizational culture, business, and goals. Today's organizations specify their foundation, set a direction, and formulate strategies—the "why," "what," and "how" factors, respectively. Core values are the organization's fundamental, passionate, and enduring principles that guide its conduct over time. The organization's mission is a statement of its function in society, often identifying its customers, markets, products, and technologies. Organizational culture is a set of values, ideas, attitudes, and norms of behavior that is learned and shared among the members of an organization. To answer the question, "What business are we in?" an organization defines its "business"—the clear, broad, underlying industry category or market sector of its offering. Finally, the organization's goals (or objectives) are statements of an accomplishment of a task to be achieved, often by a specific time.

LO 2-3 *Explain why managers use marketing dashboards and marketing metrics.*
Marketing managers use marketing dashboards to visually display on a single computer screen the essential information required to make a decision to take an action or further analyze a problem. This information consists of key performance measures of a product category, such as sales or market share, and is known as a marketing metric, which is a measure of the quantitative value or trend of a marketing activity or result. Most organizations tie their marketing metrics to the quantitative objectives established in their marketing plan, which is a road map for the marketing activities of an organization for a specified future time period, such as one year or five years.

LO 2-4 *Discuss how an organization assesses where it is now and where it seeks to be.*
Managers of an organization ask two key questions to set a strategic direction. The first question, "Where are we now?" requires an organization to (*a*) reevaluate its competencies to ensure that its special capabilities still provide a competitive advantage; (*b*) assess its present and prospective customers to ensure they have a satisfying customer experience—the central goal of marketing today; and (*c*) analyze its current and potential competitors from a global perspective to determine whether it needs to redefine its business.

The second question, "Where do we want to go?," requires an organization to set a specific direction and allocate resources to move it in that direction. Business portfolio and diversification analyses help an organization do this. Managers use business portfolio analysis to assess the organization's strategic business units (SBUs), product lines, or individual products as though they were a collection of separate investments (*cash cows*, *stars*, *question marks*, and *dogs*) to determine the amount of cash each should receive. Diversification analysis is a tool that helps managers use one or a combination of four strategies to increase revenues: market penetration (selling more of an existing product to existing markets); market development (selling an existing product to new markets); product development (selling a new product to existing markets); and diversification (selling new products to new markets).

LO 2-5 *Explain the three steps of the planning phase of the strategic marketing process.*
An organization uses the strategic marketing process to allocate its marketing mix resources to reach its target markets. This process is divided into three phases: planning, implementation, and evaluation. The planning phase consists of (*a*) a situation (SWOT) analysis, which involves taking stock of where the firm or product has been recently, where it is now, and where it is headed and focuses on the organization's internal factors (strengths and weaknesses) and the external forces and trends affecting it (opportunities and threats); (*b*) a market-product focus through market segmentation (grouping buyers into segments with common needs and similar responses to marketing programs) and goal setting, which in part requires creating points of difference (those characteristics of a product that make it superior to competitive substitutes); and (*c*) a marketing program that specifies the budget and actions (marketing strategies and tactics) for each marketing mix element.

LO 2-6 *Describe the four components of the implementation phase of the strategic marketing process.*
The implementation phase of the strategic marketing process carries out the marketing plan that emerges from the planning phase. It has four key components: (*a*) obtaining resources; (*b*) designing the marketing organization to perform product management, marketing research, sales, and advertising and promotion activities; (*c*) developing schedules to identify the tasks that need to be done, the time that is allocated to each one, the people responsible for each task, and the deadlines for each task—often with an action item list and Gantt chart; and (*d*) executing the marketing strategies, which are the means by which marketing goals are to be achieved, and their associated marketing tactics, which are the detailed day-to-day marketing actions for each element of the marketing mix that contribute to the overall success of a firm's marketing strategies. These are the marketing program actions a firm takes to achieve the goals set forth in its marketing plan.

LO 2-7 *Discuss how managers identify and act on deviations from plans.*
The evaluation phase of the strategic marketing process seeks to keep the marketing program moving in the direction that was established in the marketing plan. This requires the marketing manager to compare the results from the marketing program with the marketing plan's goals to (*a*) identify deviations or "planning gaps" and (*b*) take corrective actions to exploit positive deviations or correct negative ones.

FOCUSING ON KEY TERMS

APPLYING MARKETING KNOWLEDGE

1 *(a)* Using Medtronic as an example, explain how a mission statement gives it a strategic direction. *(b)* Create a mission statement for your own career.

2 What competencies best describe (*a*) your college or university and (*b*) your favorite restaurant?

3 Compare the advantages and disadvantages of Ben & Jerry's attempting to expand sales revenues by using (*a*) a product development strategy or (*b*) a market development strategy.

4 Select one strength, one weakness, one opportunity, and one threat from the Ben & Jerry's SWOT analysis shown in Figure 2–7. Suggest an action that a B&J marketing manager might take to address each factor.

5 What is the main result of each of the three phases of the strategic marketing process? (*a*) planning, (*b*) implementation, and (*c*) evaluation.

6 Parts of Tasks 5 and 6 in Figure 2–10 are done both concurrently and sequentially. (*a*) How can this be? (*b*) How does it help the students meet the term paper deadline? (*c*) What is the main advantage of scheduling tasks concurrently rather than sequentially?

7 The goal-setting step in the planning phase of the strategic marketing process sets quantified objectives for use in the evaluation phase. What does a manager do if measured results fail to meet objectives? Exceed objectives?

BUILDING YOUR MARKETING PLAN

1 Read Appendix A, "Building an Effective Marketing Plan." Then write a 600-word executive summary for the Paradise Kitchens marketing plan using the numbered headings shown in the plan. When you have completed the draft of your own marketing plan, write a 600-word executive summary to go in the front of your own marketing plan.

2 Using Chapter 2 and Appendix A as guides, focus your marketing plan by (*a*) writing your mission statement in 25 words or less, (*b*) listing three nonfinancial goals and three financial goals, (*c*) writing your competitive advantage in 35 words or less, and (*d*) creating a SWOT analysis table.

3 Draw a simple organization chart for your organization.

VIDEO CASE 2 IBM: Using Strategy to Build a "Smarter Planet"

QR 2-5
IBM Video Case

"'Smarter Planet' is not an advertising campaign, it's not even a marketing campaign, it is a business strategy," explains Ann Rubin, vice president of advertising at IBM.

The "Smarter Planet" strategy is based on the idea that the next major revolution in the global marketplace will be the instrumentation and integration of the world's processes and infrastructures, generating unprecedented amounts of data. The data captured and analyzed in industries such as banking, energy, health care, and retailing will allow IBM to help businesses be more efficient, productive, and responsive.

THE COMPANY

Founded in 1911, IBM has a history of innovation and focus on customers. The blue covers on its computers, blue letters in the IBM logo, and dark blue suits worn by IBM salespeople led to the now popular company nickname, "Big Blue." Today, it has over 430,000 employees in more than 170 countries. *Forbes* magazine ranks IBM as the fourth most valuable brand in the world. The company is a leading developer of new business technologies, receiving more than 5,000 patents each year. Some of its well-known inventions include the automated teller machine (ATM), the hard disk drive, the magnetic stripe card, relational databases, and the Universal Product Code (UPC). In addition, IBM recently gained attention for its artificial intelligence program called Watson, which challenged two *Jeopardy!* game show champions and won! According to Virginia Rometty, the current CEO of IBM, "IBM is an innovation company."

VALUES, MISSION, AND STRATEGY

Recently, IBM initiated a project to facilitate online discussions of key business issues among 50,000 employees to identify common themes and perspectives. According to Sam Palmisano, former CEO of IBM, "We needed to affirm IBM's reason for being, what sets the company apart, and what should drive our actions as individual IBMers." The results were three underlying values of IBM's business practices: (1) dedication to every client's success, (2) innovation that matters—for our company and for the world, and (3) trust and personal responsibility in all relationships. These values now come to life at IBM in its "policies, procedures, and daily operations," explains Palmisano.

IBM's core values also help to define its mission, or its general function in society. In clear, concise, inspirational language, IBM's mission statement is:

- At IBM, we strive to lead in the invention, development and manufacture of the industry's most advanced information technologies, including computer systems, software, storage systems, and microelectronics.
- We translate these advanced technologies into value for our customers through our professional solutions, services, and consulting businesses worldwide.

The mission, and the values it represents, helps define the organizational culture at IBM. Executives, managers, and all employees create the culture through the strategies they select and the detailed plans for accomplishing them.

IBM's strategies are based on its assessment of fundamental changes in the business environment. First, IBM sees global changes such as fewer trade barriers, the growth of developing economies, and increasing access to the World Wide Web. These changes necessitate a new type of corporation that IBM calls the "globally integrated enterprise." Second, IBM foresees a new model of computing that includes computational capability in phones, cameras, cars, and other appliances and allows economic, social, and physical systems to be connected. This connectivity creates a "smarter planet." Finally, IBM predicts a growing demand for custom-made technological solutions that help organizations measure and achieve specific outcomes.

As a result, IBM began to shift from commodity-based businesses such as PCs and hard disk drives, to "customizable" businesses such as software and services. The change in IBM was so substantial that it has described its plan in a document called the *2015 Road Map*. The Map describes four strategic opportunities: (1) growth markets such as China, India, Brazil, and Africa, (2) business analytics and optimization, (3) cloud and smarter computing, and (4) the connected, "smarter" planet. These opportunities suggest a strategy that delivers value through business and IT innovation to selected industries with an integrated enterprise. The overarching strategy that highlights IBM's capabilities is called "Building a Smarter Planet."

BUILDING A SMARTER PLANET

The Smarter Planet initiative is designed for clients who value IBM's industry and process expertise, systems integration capability, and research capacity. A smarter planet, while global by definition, happens on the industry level. It is driven by forward-thinking organizations that share a common outlook: They see change as an opportunity, and they act on possibilities, not just react to problems.

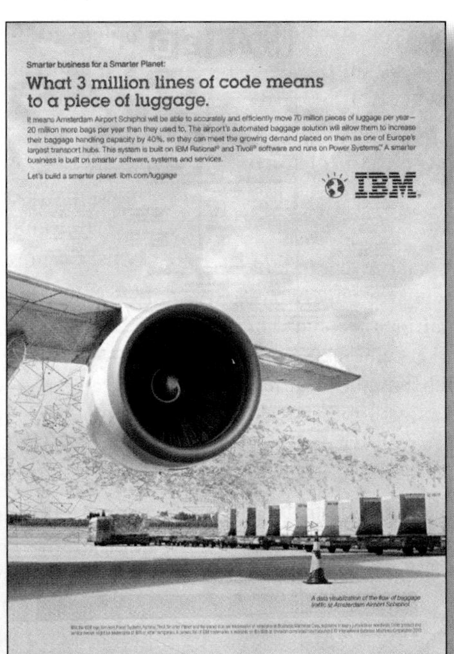

John Kennedy, vice president of marketing, explains, "'A Smarter Planet' actually surfaced from observing what was happening in our clients. They were looking to take the vast amount of data that was being generated inside their companies and looking to better understand it." To IBM "smart" solutions have three characteristics. They are instrumented, they are intelligent, and they are interconnected. Millions of digital devices, now connected through the Internet, produce data that can be turned into knowledge through advanced computational power. IBM believes that this knowledge can help reduce costs, cut waste, improve efficiency, and increase productivity for companies, industries, and cities.

Since introducing the Smarter Planet strategy, IBM has collaborated with more than 600 organizations around the globe. The success of the strategy is evident in the broad range of industries where "smart" solutions are being implemented. They include banking; communications; electronics, automotive and aerospace; energy and utilities; government; health care; insurance; oil and gas; retailing; and transportation. Each industry has reported a variety of applications.

In a study of 439 cities, for example, smart solutions such as ramp metering, signal coordination, and accident management reduced travel delays by more than 700,000 annually, saving each city $15 million. A study by the U.S. Department of Energy found that consumers with smart electric meters cut their power usage and saved 10 percent on their power bills. Retailers who implemented smart systems to analyze buying behavior, merchandise assortment, and demand were able to cut supply chain costs by 30 percent, reduce inventory levels by 25 percent, and increase sales by 10 percent.

THE BUILDING A SMARTER PLANET MARKETING PLAN

Marketing and communications professionals at IBM have developed the marketing plan for IBM's "Smarter Planet" strategy. The general goal is to describe the company's view of the next era of information technology and its impact on business and society. The execution of the plan includes messaging from IBM leaders, an advertising campaign, an Internet presence, and public relations communications. In addition, IBM measures and tracks the performance of the marketing activities.

The importance of the Smarter Planet strategy was first communicated through a message from the top. Palmisano prepared a "Letter from the Chairman" for the annual report. His message was a powerful statement. Smarter Planet, according to Palmisano, "is not a metaphor. It describes the infusion of intelligence into the way the world actually works."

IBM also used a print and television advertising campaign to add detail to the general message. The ads focused on the ability to improve the world now, with IBM's help. "I think what's different about Smarter Planet," says Ann Rubin, "is that it was not inward facing, it was looking out at what the world needed. We felt like we could go out there and influence the world for the better."

IBM recently celebrated its 100th anniversary! Its record of success is testimony to the resilience of a business model that encourages long-term strategies that can say "Welcome to a Smarter Planet."

Questions

1 What is IBM's "Smarter Planet" business strategy? How does this strategy relate to IBM's mission and values?

2 Conduct a SWOT analysis for IBM's Smarter Planet initiative. What are the relevant trends to consider for the next three to five years?

3 How can IBM communicate its strategy to companies, cities, and governments?

4 What are the benefits of the Smarter Planet initiative to (*a*) society and (*b*) IBM?

5 How should IBM measure the results of the Smarter Planet strategy?

APPENDIX A

BUILDING AN EFFECTIVE MARKETING PLAN

"New ideas are a dime a dozen," observes Arthur R. Kydd, "and so are new products and new technologies." Kydd should know. As chief executive officer of St. Croix Venture Partners, he and his firm have provided the seed money and venture capital to launch more than 60 start-up firms in the last 30 years. Today, those firms have more than 5,000 employees. Kydd explains:

> I get 200 to 300 marketing and business plans a year to look at, and St. Croix provides start-up financing for only two or three. What sets a potentially successful idea, product, or technology apart from all the rest is markets and marketing. If you have a real product with a distinctive point of difference that satisfies the needs of customers, you may have a winner. And you get a real feel for this in a well-written marketing or business plan.[1]

This appendix (1) describes what marketing and business plans are, including the purposes and guidelines in writing effective plans, and (2) provides a sample marketing plan.

MARKETING PLANS AND BUSINESS PLANS

After explaining the meanings, purposes, and audiences of marketing plans and business plans, this section describes some writing guidelines for them and what external funders often look for in successful plans.

Meanings, Purposes, and Audiences

A *marketing plan* is a road map for the marketing actions of an organization for a specified future time period, such as one year or five years.[2] No single "generic" marketing plan applies to all organizations and all situations. Rather, the specific format for a marketing plan for an organization depends on the following:

- *The target audience and purpose*. Elements included in a particular marketing plan depend heavily on (1) who the audience is and (2) what its purpose is. A marketing plan for an internal audience seeks to point the direction for future marketing activities and is sent to all individuals in the organization who must implement the plan or who will be affected by it. If the plan is directed to an external audience, such as friends, banks, venture capitalists, crowdfunding sources like Kickstarter, or other potential investors for the purpose of raising capital, it has the additional function of being an important sales document. In this case, it contains elements such as the strategic plan/focus, organization, structure, and biographies of key personnel that would rarely appear in an internal marketing plan. Also, the financial information is far more detailed when the plan is used to raise outside capital. The elements of a marketing plan for each of these two audiences are compared in Figure A–1.
- *The kind and complexity of the organization*. A small neighborhood restaurant has a somewhat different marketing plan than Medtronic, which serves international markets. The restaurant's plan would be relatively simple and directed at serving customers in a local market. In Medtronic's case, because there is a hierarchy of marketing plans, various levels of detail would be used—such as the entire organization, the strategic business unit, or the product/product line.
- *The industry*. Both the restaurant serving a local market and Medtronic, selling heart pacemakers globally, analyze competition. However, their geographic scopes are far different, as are the complexities of their offerings and, hence, the time periods likely to be covered by their plans. A one-year marketing plan may be adequate for the restaurant, but Medtronic may need a five-year planning horizon because product development cycles for complex, new medical devices may be three or four years.

In contrast to a marketing plan, a **business plan** is a road map for the entire organization for a specified future period of time, such as one year or five years.[3] A key difference between a marketing plan and a business plan is that the business plan contains details on the research and development (R&D)/operations/manufacturing activities of the organization. Even for a manufacturing business, the marketing plan is probably 60 or 70 percent of the entire business plan. For firms like a small restaurant or an auto repair shop, their marketing and

Element of the plan	Marketing plan		Business plan	
	For internal audience (to direct the firm)	For external audience (to raise capital)	For internal audience (to direct the firm)	For external audience (to raise capital)
1. Executive summary	✓	✓	✓	✓
2. Description of company		✓		✓
3. Strategic plan/focus		✓		✓
4. Situation analysis	✓	✓	✓	✓
5. Market-product focus	✓	✓	✓	✓
6. Marketing program strategy and tactics	✓	✓	✓	✓
7. R&D and operations program			✓	✓
8. Financial projections	✓	✓	✓	✓
9. Organization structure		✓		✓
10. Implementation plan	✓	✓	✓	✓
11. Evaluation	✓		✓	
Appendix A: Biographies of key personnel		✓		✓
Appendix B, etc.: Details on other topics	✓	✓	✓	✓

FIGURE A–1
Elements in typical marketing and business plans targeted at different audiences.

business plans are virtually identical. The elements of a business plan typically targeted at internal and external audiences appear in the two right-hand columns in Figure A–1.

The Most-Asked Questions by Outside Audiences

Lenders and prospective investors reading a business or marketing plan that is used to seek new capital are probably the toughest audiences to satisfy. Their most-asked questions include the following:

1. Is the business or marketing idea valid?
2. Is there something unique or distinctive about the product or service that separates it from substitutes and competitors?
3. Is there a clear market for the product or service?
4. Are the financial projections realistic and healthy?
5. Are the key management and technical personnel capable, and do they have a track record in the industry within which they must compete?
6. Does the plan clearly describe how those providing capital will get their money back and make a profit?

Rhonda Abrams, author of *The Successful Business Plan,* observes, "Although you may spend five months preparing your plan, the cold, hard fact is that an investor or lender can dismiss it in less than five minutes. If you don't make a positive impression in those critical first five minutes, your plan will be rejected."[4] While her comments apply to plans seeking to raise capital, the first five questions listed above apply equally well to plans prepared for internal audiences.

Writing and Style Suggestions

There are no magic one-size-fits-all guidelines for writing successful marketing and business plans. Still, the following writing and style guidelines generally apply:[5]

- Use a direct, professional writing style. Use appropriate business terms without jargon. Present and future tenses with active voice ("I will write an effective marketing plan") are generally better than past tense and passive voice ("An effective marketing plan was written by me").
- Be positive and specific to convey potential success. At the same time, avoid superlatives ("terrific," "wonderful"). Specifics are better than glittering generalities.

- Use numbers for impact, justifying projections with reasonable quantitative assumptions, where possible.
- Use bullet points for succinctness and emphasis. As with the list you are reading, bullets enable key points to be highlighted effectively.
- Use A-level (the first level) and B-level (the second level) headings under the numbered section headings to help readers make easy transitions from one topic to another. This also forces the writer to organize the plan more carefully. Use these headings liberally, inserting at least one every 200 to 300 words.
- Use visuals where appropriate. Photos, illustrations, graphs, and charts enable massive amounts of information to be presented succinctly.
- Shoot for a plan 15 to 35 pages in length, not including financial projections and appendices. An uncomplicated small business may require only 15 pages, while a high-technology start-up may require more than 35 pages.
- Use care in layout, design, and presentation. Laser printers give a more professional look than ink-jet printers do. Use 11- or 12-point type (you are now reading 10.5-point type) in the text. Use a serif type (with "feet," like that you are reading now) in the text because it is easier to read, and sans serif (without "feet") in graphs and charts like Figure A–1. A bound report with a nice cover and a clear title page adds professionalism.

These guidelines are used, where possible, in the sample marketing plan that follows.

SAMPLE FIVE-YEAR MARKETING PLAN FOR PARADISE KITCHENS, INC.

To help interpret the marketing plan for Paradise Kitchens, Inc., that follows, we will describe the company and suggest some guidelines for interpreting the plan.[6]

Background on Paradise Kitchens, Inc.

With a degree in chemical engineering, Randall F. Peters spent 15 years working for General Foods and Pillsbury with a number of diverse responsibilities: plant operations, R&D, restaurant operations, and new business development. His wife, Leah, with degrees in both molecular cellular biology and food science, held various Pillsbury executive positions in new category development, packaged goods, and restaurant R&D. In the company's start-up years, Paradise Kitchens survived on the savings of Randy and Leah, the co-founders. Based on their backgrounds, they decided Randy should serve as president and CEO of Paradise Kitchens and Leah should focus on R&D and corporate strategy.

Interpreting the Marketing Plan

The marketing plan on the next pages, based on an actual Paradise Kitchens plan, is directed at an external audience (see Figure A–1). To protect proprietary information about the company, some details and dates have been altered, but the basic logic of the plan has been kept.

Notes in the margins next to the Paradise Kitchens plan fall into two categories:

1. *Substantive notes* are in blue boxes. These notes elaborate on the significance of an element in the marketing plan and are keyed to chapter references in this textbook.
2. *Writing style, format, and layout notes* are in red boxes and explain the editorial or visual rationale for the element.

A word of encouragement: Writing an effective marketing plan is hard but also challenging and satisfying work. Dozens of the authors' students have used effective marketing plans they wrote for class in their interviewing portfolio to show prospective employers what they could do and to help them get their first job.

Color-Coding Legend

Blue boxes explain significance of marketing plan elements.

Red boxes give writing style, format, and layout guidelines.

The Table of Contents provides quick access to the topics in the plan, usually organized by section and subsection headings.

Seen by many experts as the single most important element in the plan, the two-page Executive Summary "sells" the plan to readers through its clarity and brevity. For space reasons, it is not shown here, but the Building Your Marketing Plan exercise at the end of Chapter 2 asks the reader to write an Executive Summary for this plan.

The Company Description highlights the recent history and recent successes of the organization.

The Strategic Focus and Plan sets the strategic direction for the entire organization, a direction with which proposed actions of the marketing plan must be consistent. This section is not included in all marketing plans. See Chapter 2.

The qualitative Mission statement focuses the activities of Paradise Kitchens for the stakeholder groups to be served. See Chapter 2.

FIVE-YEAR MARKETING PLAN
Paradise Kitchens,® Inc.

Table of Contents

2. Company Description

Paradise Kitchens,® Inc., was started by co-founders Randall F. Peters and Leah E. Peters to develop and market Howlin' Coyote® Chili, a unique line of single serve and microwavable Southwestern/Mexican style frozen chili products. The Howlin' Coyote line of chili was first introduced into the Minneapolis–St. Paul market and expanded to Denver two years later and Phoenix two years after that.

To the Company's knowledge, Howlin' Coyote is the only premium-quality, authentic Southwestern/Mexican style, frozen chili sold in U.S. grocery stores. Its high quality has gained fast, widespread acceptance in its targeted markets. In fact, same-store sales doubled in the last year for which data are available. The Company believes the Howlin' Coyote brand can be extended to other categories of Southwestern/Mexican food products, such as tacos, enchiladas, and burritos.

Paradise Kitchens believes its high-quality, high-price strategy has proven successful. This marketing plan outlines how the Company will extend its geographic coverage from 3 markets to 20 markets by the year 2016.

3. Strategic Focus and Plan

This section covers three aspects of corporate strategy that influence the marketing plan: (1) the mission, (2) goals, and (3) core competency/sustainable competitive advantage of Paradise Kitchens.

Mission

The mission of Paradise Kitchens is to market lines of high-quality Southwestern/Mexican food products at premium prices that satisfy consumers in this fast-growing food segment while providing challenging career opportunities for employees and above-average returns to stockholders.

The Goals section sets both the nonfinancial and financial targets—where possible in quantitative terms—against which the company's performance will be measured. See Chapter 2.

Lists use parallel construction to improve readability—in this case a series of infinitives starting with "To . . ."

Goals

For the coming five years Paradise Kitchens seeks to achieve the following goals:

- Nonfinancial goals
  1. To retain its present image as the highest-quality line of Southwestern/Mexican products in the food categories in which it competes.
  2. To enter 17 new metropolitan markets.
  3. To achieve national distribution in two convenience store or supermarket chains by 2014 and five by 2015.
  4. To add a new product line every third year.
  5. To be among the top five chili lines—regardless of packaging (frozen or canned)—in one-third of the metro markets in which it competes by 2015 and two-thirds by 2017.
- Financial goals
  1. To obtain a real (inflation-adjusted) growth in earnings per share of 8 percent per year over time.
  2. To obtain a return on equity of at least 20 percent.
  3. To have a public stock offering by the year 2015.

Photos or sample ads can illustrate key points effectively, even if they are not in color as they appear here.

A brief caption on photos and sample ads ties them to the text and highlights their reason for being included.

Core Competency and Sustainable Competitive Advantage

In terms of core competency, Paradise Kitchens seeks to achieve a unique ability to (1) provide distinctive, high-quality chilies and related products using Southwestern/Mexican recipes that appeal to and excite contemporary tastes for these products and (2) deliver these products to the customer's table using effective manufacturing and distribution systems that maintain the Company's quality standards.

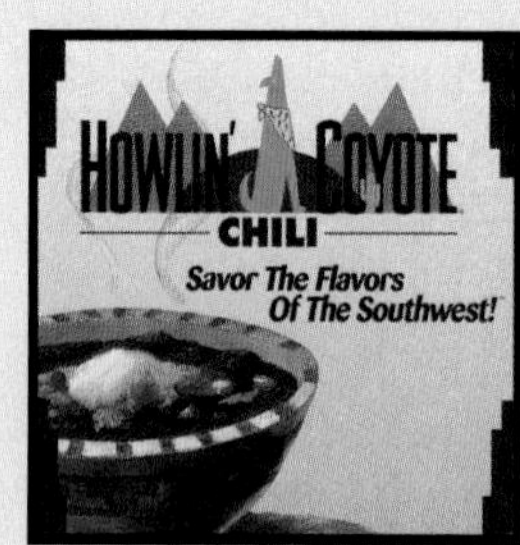

To help achieve national distribution through chains, Paradise Kitchens introduced this point-of-purchase ad that adheres statically to the glass door of the freezer case.

To translate these core competencies into a sustainable competitive advantage, the Company will work closely with key suppliers and distributors to build the relationships and alliances necessary to satisfy the high taste standards of our customers.

To improve readability, each numbered section usually starts on a new page. (This is not done in this plan to save space.)

The Situation Analysis is a snapshot to answer the question, "Where are we now?" See Chapter 2.

The SWOT analysis identifies strengths, weaknesses, opportunities, and threats to provide a solid foundation, which is the springboard to identify subsequent actions in the marketing plan. See Chapter 2.

Each long table, graph, or photo is given a figure number and title. It then appears as soon as possible after the first reference in the text, accommodating necessary page breaks. This avoids breaking long tables like this one in the middle. Short tables or graphs are often inserted in the text without figure numbers because they don't cause serious problems with page breaks.

Effective tables seek to summarize a large amount of information in a short amount of space.

4. Situation Analysis

This situation analysis starts with a snapshot of the current environment in which Paradise Kitchens finds itself by providing a brief SWOT (strengths, weaknesses, opportunities, threats) analysis. After this overview, the analysis probes ever-finer levels of detail: industry, competitors, company, and consumers.

SWOT Analysis

Figure 1 shows the internal and external factors affecting the market opportunities for Paradise Kitchens. Stated briefly, this SWOT analysis highlights the great strides taken by the company since its products first appeared on grocers' shelves.

Figure 1. SWOT Analysis for Paradise Kitchens

Internal Factors	Strengths	Weaknesses
Management	Experienced and entrepreneurial management and board	Small size can restrict options
Offerings	Unique, high-quality, high-price products	Many lower-quality, lower-price competitors
Marketing	Distribution in three markets with excellent consumer acceptance	No national awareness or distribution; restricted shelf space in the freezer section
Personnel	Good workforce, though small; little turnover	Big gap if key employee leaves
Finance	Excellent growth in sales revenues	Limited resources may restrict growth opportunities when compared to giant competitors
Manufacturing	Sole supplier ensures high quality	Lack economies of scale of huge competitors
R&D	Continuing efforts to ensure quality in delivered products	Lack of canning and microwavable food processing expertise
External Factors	**Opportunities**	**Threats**
Consumer/Social	Upscale market, likely to be stable; Southwestern/Mexican food category is fast-growing segment due to growth in Hispanic American population and desire for spicier foods	Premium price may limit access to mass markets; consumers value a strong brand name
Competitive	Distinctive name and packaging in its markets	Not patentable; competitors can attempt to duplicate product; others better able to pay slotting fees
Technological	Technical breakthroughs enable smaller food producers to achieve many economies available to large competitors	Competitors have gained economies in canning and microwavable food processing
Economic	Consumer income is high; convenience important to U.S. households	More households "eating out," and bringing prepared take-out into home
Legal/Regulatory	High U.S. Food & Drug Administration standards eliminate fly-by-night competitors	Mergers among large competitors being approved by government

The text discussion of Figure 1 (the SWOT Analysis table) elaborates on its more important elements. This "walks" the reader through the information from the vantage point of the plan's writer.

The Industry Analysis section provides the backdrop for the subsequent, more detailed analysis of competition, the company, and the company's customers. Without an in-depth understanding of the industry, the remaining analysis may be misdirected. See Chapter 2.

Sales of Mexican entrees are significant and provide a variety of future opportunities for Paradise Kitchens.

Even though relatively brief, this in-depth treatment of sales of Mexican foods in the U.S. demonstrates to the plan's readers the company's understanding of the industry within which it competes.

The Competitor Analysis section demonstrates that the company has a realistic understanding of its major chili competitors and their marketing strategies. Again, a realistic assessment gives confidence that subsequent marketing actions in the plan rest on a solid foundation. See Chapters 2, 3, 8, and 9.

In the Company's favor internally are its strengths: an experienced management team and board of directors, excellent acceptance of its product line in the three metropolitan markets within which it competes, and a strong manufacturing and distribution system to serve these limited markets. Favorable external factors (opportunities) include the increasing appeal of Southwestern/Mexican foods, the strength of the upscale market for the Company's products, and food-processing technological breakthroughs that make it easier for smaller food producers to compete.

Among unfavorable factors, the main weakness is the limited size of Paradise Kitchens relative to its competitors in terms of the depth of the management team, the available financial resources, and the national awareness and distribution of product lines. Threats include the danger that the Company's premium prices may limit access to mass markets and competition from the "eating-out" and "take-out" markets.

Industry Analysis: Trends in Frozen and Mexican Foods

Frozen Foods. According to *Grocery Headquarters*, consumers are flocking to the frozen food section of grocery retailers. The reasons: hectic lifestyles demanding increased convenience and an abundance of new, tastier, and nutritious products.[7] By 2007, the latest year for which data are available, total sales of frozen food in supermarkets, drugstores, and mass merchandisers, such as Target and Costco (excluding Walmart), reached $29 billion. Prepared frozen meals, which are defined as meals or entrees that are frozen and require minimal preparation, accounted for $8.1 billion, or 26 percent of the total frozen food market.

Sales of Mexican entrees totaled $506 million in 2007.[8] Heavy consumers of frozen meals, those who eat five or more meals every two weeks, tend to be kids, teens, and adults 35–44 years old.[9]

Mexican Foods. Currently, Mexican foods such as burritos, enchiladas, and tacos are used in two-thirds of American households. These trends reflect a generally more favorable attitude on the part of all Americans toward spicy foods that include red chili peppers. The growing Hispanic population in the United States, over 50 million and almost $1.2 trillion in purchasing power in 2012, partly explains the increasing demand for Mexican food. This Hispanic purchasing power is projected to be over $1.7 trillion in 2017.[10]

Competitor Analysis: The Chili Market

The chili market represents over $500 million in annual sales. On average, consumers buy five to six servings annually, according to the NPD Group. The products fall primarily into two groups: canned chili (75 percent of sales) and dry chili (25 percent of sales).

This page uses a "block" style and does *not* indent each paragraph, although an extra space separates each paragraph. Compare this page with page 56, which has indented paragraphs. Most readers find that indented paragraphs in marketing plans and long reports are easier to follow.

Bluntly put, the major disadvantage of the segment's dominant product, canned chili, is that it does not taste very good. A taste test described in an issue of *Consumer Reports* magazine ranked 26 canned chili products "poor" to "fair" in overall sensory quality. The study concluded, "Chili doesn't have to be hot to be good. But really good chili, hot or mild, doesn't come out of a can."

The Company Analysis provides details of the company's strengths and marketing strategies that will enable it to achieve the mission and goals identified earlier. See Chapters 2 and 8.

Company Analysis

The husband-and-wife team that co-founded Paradise Kitchens, Inc., has 44 years of experience between them in the food-processing business. Both have played key roles in the management of the Pillsbury Company. They are being advised by a highly seasoned group of business professionals, who have extensive understanding of the requirements for new-product development.

The Company now uses a single outside producer with which it works closely to maintain the consistently high quality required in its products. The greater volume has increased production efficiencies, resulting in a steady decrease in the cost of goods sold.

The "A heading" for this section ("4. Situation Analysis," which appears on p. 55) identifies the major section of the plan. The "B heading" of Customer Analysis has a more dominant typeface and position than the lower-level "C heading" of Customer Characteristics. These headings introduce the reader to the sequence and level of topics covered within each major "A level" section. The organization of this textbook uses this kind of structure and headings.

Customer Analysis

In terms of customer analysis, this section describes (1) the characteristics of customers expected to buy Howlin' Coyote products and (2) health and nutrition concerns of Americans today.

Satisfying customers and providing genuine value to them is why organizations exist in a market economy. This section addresses the questions "Who are the customers for Paradise Kitchens's products?" See Chapters 5, 6, 7, 8, and 9.

Customer Characteristics. Demographically, chili products in general are purchased by consumers representing a broad range of socioeconomic backgrounds. Howlin' Coyote chili is purchased chiefly by consumers who have achieved higher levels of education and whose income is $50,000 and higher. These consumers represent 50 percent of canned and dry mix chili users.

The household buying Howlin' Coyote has one to three people in it. Among married couples, Howlin' Coyote is predominantly bought by households in which both spouses work. While women are a majority of the buyers, single men represent a significant segment.

The five Howlin' Coyote entrees offer a quick, tasty meal with high-quality ingredients.

Because the chili offers a quick way to make a tasty meal, the product's biggest users tend to be those most pressed for time. Howlin' Coyote's premium pricing also means that its purchasers are skewed toward the higher end of the income range. Buyers range in age from 25 to 54 years old and often live in the western United States where spicy foods are more readily eaten.

This section demonstrates the company's insights into a major trend that has a potentially large impact.

Health and Nutrition Concerns. Coverage of food issues in the U.S. media is often erratic and occasionally alarmist. Because Americans are concerned about their diets, studies from organizations of widely varying credibility frequently receive significant attention from the major news organizations. For instance, a study of fat levels of movie popcorn was reported in all the major media. Similarly, studies on the healthfulness of Mexican food have received prominent play in print and broadcast reports. The high caloric levels of much Mexican and Southwestern-style food have been widely reported and often exaggerated. Some Mexican frozen-food competitors, such as Don Miguel, Mission Foods, Ruiz Foods, and José Olé, plan to offer or have recently offered more "carb-friendly" and "fat-friendly" products in response to this concern.

Howlin' Coyote is already lower in calories, fat, and sodium than its competitors, and those qualities are not currently being stressed in its promotions. Instead, in the space and time available for promotions, Howlin' Coyote's taste, convenience, and flexibility are stressed.

The size of headings should give a professional look to the report and not overwhelm the reader. These two headings are too large.

5. Market-Product Focus

This section describes the five-year marketing and product objectives for Paradise Kitchens and the target markets, points of difference, and positioning of its lines of Howlin' Coyote chilies.

Marketing and Product Objectives

As noted in Chapters 2, 9, and 10, the chances of success for a new product significantly increase if objectives are set for the product itself and if target market segments are identified for it. Diversification analysis, discussed in Chapter 2, helps identify the market segments to target. This section makes these explicit for Paradise Kitchens. The objectives also serve as the planned targets against which marketing activities are measured in program implementation and evaluation.

Howlin' Coyote's marketing intent is to take full advantage of its brand potential while building a base from which other revenue sources can be mined—both in and out of the retail grocery business. These are detailed in four areas below:

- *Current markets.* Current markets will be grown by expanding brand and flavor distribution at the retail level. In addition, same-store sales will be grown by increasing consumer awareness and repeat purchases, thereby leading to the more efficient broker/warehouse distribution channel.
- *New markets.* By the end of Year 5, the chili, salsa, burrito, and enchilada business will be expanded to a total of 20 metropolitan areas, which represent 53 percent of the 38 major U.S. metropolitan markets. This will represent 70 percent of U.S. food store sales.
- *Food service.* Food service sales will include chili products and smothering sauces. Sales are expected to reach $693,000 by the end of Year 3 and $1.5 million by the end of Year 5.
- *New products.* Howlin' Coyote's brand presence will be expanded at the retail

A heading should be spaced closer to the text that follows (and that it describes) than the preceding section to avoid confusion for the reader. This rule is not followed for the Target Markets heading, which now unfortunately appears to "float" between the preceding and following paragraphs.

This section identifies the specific niches or target markets toward which the company's products are directed. When appropriate and when space permits, this section often includes a market-product grid. See Chapter 9.

An organization cannot grow by offering only "me-too products." The greatest single factor in a new product's failure is the lack of significant "points of difference" that set it apart from competitors' substitutes. This section makes these points of difference explicit. See Chapter 10.

A positioning strategy helps communicate the unique points of difference of a company's products to prospective customers in a simple, clear way. This section describes this positioning. See Chapters 8 and 9.

level through the addition of new products in the frozen-foods section. This will be accomplished through new-product concept screening in Year 1 to identify new potential products. These products will be brought to market in Years 2 and 3.

Target Markets

The primary target market for Howlin' Coyote products is households with one to three people, where often both adults work, and with individual income typically above $50,000 per year. These households contain more experienced, adventurous consumers of Southwestern/Mexican food and want premium quality products.

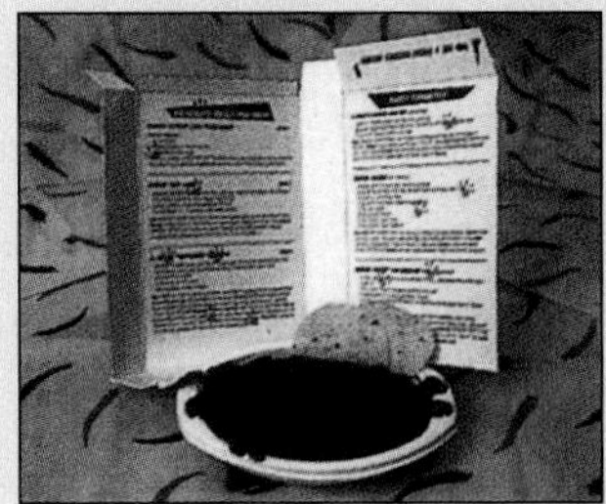

To help buyers see the many different uses for Howlin' Coyote chili, recipes are even printed on the *inside* of the packages.

Points of Difference

The "points of difference"—characteristics that make Howlin' Coyote chilies unique relative to competitors—fall into three important areas:

- *Unique taste and convenience.* No known competitor offers a high-quality, "authentic" frozen chili in a range of flavors. And no existing chili has the same combination of quick preparation and home-style taste that Howlin' Coyote does.
- *Taste trends.* The American palate is increasingly intrigued by hot spices. In response to this trend, Howlin' Coyote brands offer more "kick" than most other prepared chilies.
- *Premium packaging.* Howlin' Coyote's packaging graphics convey the unique, high-quality product contained inside and the product's nontraditional positioning.

Positioning

In the past, chili products have been either convenient or tasty, but not both. Howlin' Coyote pairs these two desirable characteristics to obtain a positioning in consumers' minds as very high-quality "authentic Southwestern/Mexican tasting" chilies that can be prepared easily and quickly.

Everything that has gone before in the marketing plan sets the stage for the marketing mix actions—the four Ps—covered in the marketing program. See Chapters 10 through 21.

This section describes in detail three key elements of the company's product strategy: the product line, its quality and how this is achieved, and its "cutting edge" packaging. See Chapters 10 and 11.

This Price Strategy section makes the company's price point very clear, along with its price position relative to potential substitutes. When appropriate and when space permits, this section might contain a break-even analysis. See Chapters 13 and 14.

This "introductory overview" sentence tells the reader the topics covered in the section—in this case in-store demonstrations, recipes, and cents-off coupons. While this sentence may be omitted in short memos or plans, it helps readers see where the text is leading. These sentences are used throughout this plan. This textbook also generally uses these introductory overview sentences to aid your comprehension.

6. Marketing Program

The four marketing mix elements of the Howlin' Coyote chili marketing program are detailed below. Note that "chile" is the vegetable and "chili" is the dish.

Product Strategy

After first summarizing the product line, the approach to product quality and packaging is covered.

Product Line. Howlin' Coyote chili, retailing for $3.99 for an 11-ounce serving, is available in five flavors: Green Chile Chili, Red Chile Chili, Beef and Black Bean Chili, Chicken Chunk Chili, and Mean Bean Chili.

Unique Product Quality. The flavoring systems of the Howlin' Coyote chilies are proprietary. The products' tastiness is due to extra care lavished upon the ingredients during production. The ingredients used are of unusually high quality. Meats are low-fat cuts and are fresh, not frozen, to preserve cell structure and moistness. Chilies are fire-roasted for fresher taste. Tomatoes and vegetables are of select quality. No preservatives or artificial flavors are used.

Packaging. Reflecting the "cutting edge" marketing strategy of its producers, Howlin' Coyote bucks conventional wisdom in its packaging. It specifically avoids placing predictable photographs of the product on its containers. Instead, Howlin' Coyote's package shows a Southwestern motif that communicates the product's out-of-the-ordinary positioning.

The Southwestern motif makes Howlin' Coyote's packages stand out in a supermarket's freezer case.

Price Strategy

At $3.99 for an 11-ounce package, Howlin' Coyote chili is priced comparably to the other frozen offerings but higher than the canned and dried chili varieties. However, the significant taste advantages it has over canned chilies and the convenience advantages over dried chilies justify this pricing strategy.

Promotion Strategy

Key promotion programs feature in-store demonstrations, recipes, and cents-off coupons.

Elements of the Promotion Strategy are highlighted in terms of the three key promotional activities the company is emphasizing: in-store demonstrations, recipes, and cents-off coupons. For space reasons, the company's online strategies are not shown in the plan. See Chapters 17, 18, and 19.

Another bulleted list adds many details for the reader, including methods of gaining customer awareness, trial, and repeat purchases as Howlin' Coyote enters new metropolitan areas.

The Place Strategy is described here in terms of both (1) the present method and (2) the new one to be used when the increased sales volume makes it feasible. See Chapters 15 and 16.

All the marketing mix decisions covered in the just-described marketing program have both revenue and expense effects. These are summarized in this section of the marketing plan.

Note that this section contains no introductory overview sentence. While the sentence is not essential, many readers prefer to see it to avoid the abrupt start with Past Sales Revenues.

In-Store Demonstrations. In-store demonstrations enable consumers to try Howlin' Coyote products and discover their unique qualities. Demos will be conducted regularly in all markets to increase awareness and trial purchases.

Recipes. Because the products' flexibility of use is a key selling point, recipes are offered to consumers to stimulate use. The recipes are given at all in-store demonstrations, on the back of packages, through a mail-in recipe book offer, and in coupons sent by direct-mail or freestanding inserts.

Cents-Off Coupons. To generate trial and repeat purchase of Howlin' Coyote products, coupons are distributed in four ways:

- *In Sunday newspaper inserts*. These inserts are widely read and help generate awareness.
- *In-pack coupons*. Each box of Howlin' Coyote chili will contain coupons for $1 off two more packages of the chili. These coupons will be included for the first three months the product is shipped to a new market. Doing so encourages repeat purchases by new users.
- *Direct-mail chili coupons*. Those households that fit the Howlin' Coyote demographics described previously will be mailed coupons.
- *In-store demonstrations*. Coupons will be passed out at in-store demonstrations to give an additional incentive to purchase.

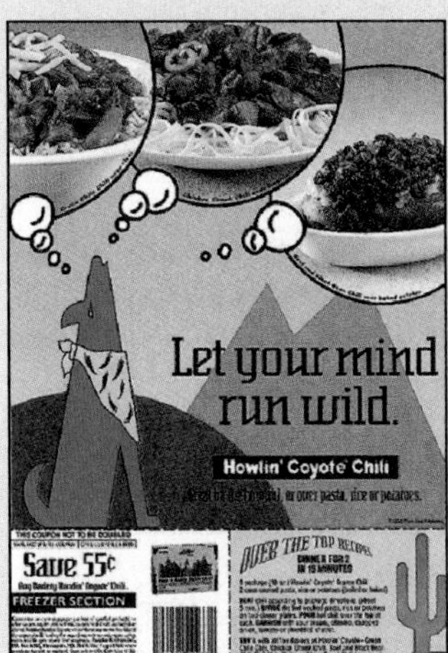

Sunday newspaper inserts encourage consumer trial and provide recipes to show how Howlin' Coyote chili can be used in summer meals.

Place (Distribution) Strategy

Howlin' Coyote is distributed in its present markets through a food distributor. The distributor buys the product, warehouses it, and then resells and delivers it to grocery retailers on a store-by-store basis. As sales grow, we will shift to a more efficient system using a broker who sells the products to retail chains and grocery wholesalers.

7. Financial Data and Projections

Past Sales Revenues

Historically, Howlin' Coyote has had a steady increase in sales revenues since its introduction in 2005. In 2009, sales jumped spectacularly, due largely to new

The graph shows more clearly the dramatic growth of sales revenue than data in a table would do.

The Five-Year Projections section starts with the judgment forecast of cases sold and the resulting net sales. Gross profit and then operating profit—critical for the company's survival—are projected. An actual plan often contains many pages of computer-generated spreadsheet projections, usually shown in an appendix to the plan.

Because this table is very short, it is woven into the text, rather than given a figure number and a title.

Because the plan proposes to enter 17 new metropolitan markets in the coming five years (for a total of 20), it is not possible to simply extrapolate the trend in Figure 2. Instead, management's judgment must be used. Methods of making sales forecasts—including the "lost horse" technique used here—are discussed in Chapter 8.

The Organization of Paradise Kitchens appears here. It reflects the bare-bones organizational structure of successful small businesses. Often a more elaborate marketing plan will show the new positions expected to be added as the firm grows.

promotion strategies. Sales have continued to rise, but at a less dramatic rate. Sales revenues appear in Figure 2.

Figure 2. Sales Revenues for Paradise Kitchens, Inc.

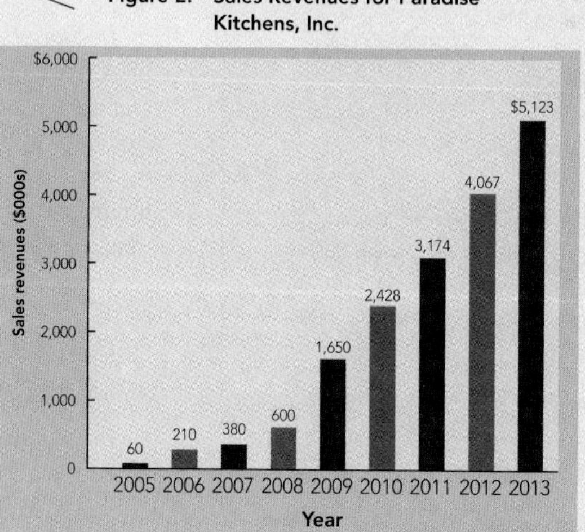

Five-Year Projections

Five-year financial projections for Paradise Kitchens appear below. These projections reflect the continuing growth in the number of cases sold (with eight packages of Howlin' Coyote chili per case).

		Projections (000s)				
Financial Element	Actual 2013	Year 1 2014	Year 2 2015	Year 3 2016	Year 4 2017	Year 5 2018
Cases sold (000s)	353	684	889	1,249	1,499	1,799
Net sales ($000s)	$5,123	$9,913	$12,884	$18,111	$21,733	$26,080
Gross profit ($000s)	$2,545	$4,820	$6,527	$8,831	$10,597	$12,717
Operating profit ($000s)	$339	$985	$2,906	$2,805	$3,366	$4,039

8. Organization

Paradise Kitchens's present organization appears in Figure 3. It shows the four people reporting to the President. Below this level are both the full-time and part-time employees of the Company.

Figure 3. The Paradise Kitchens Organization

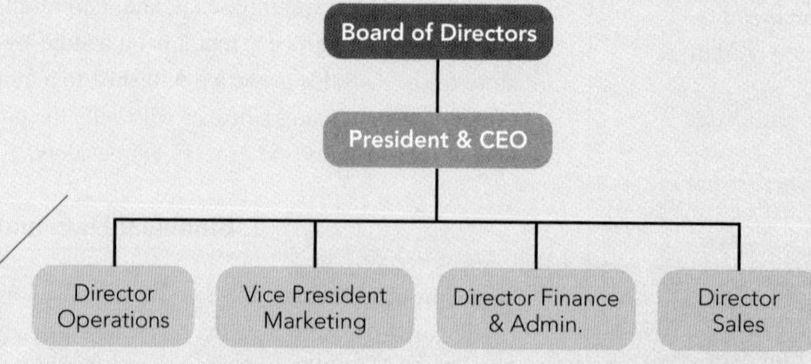

The Implementation Plan shows how the company will turn its plan into results. Charts are often used to set deadlines and assign responsibilities for the many tactical marketing decisions needed to enter a new market.

The essence of Evaluation is comparing actual sales with the targeted values set in the plan and taking appropriate actions. Note that the section briefly describes a contingency plan for alternative actions, depending on how successful the entry into a new market turns out to be.

Various appendices may appear at the end of the plan, depending on the plan's purpose and audience. For example, résumés of key personnel or detailed financial spreadsheets often appear in appendices. For space reasons these are not shown here.

At present, Paradise Kitchens operates with full-time employees in only essential positions. It now augments its full-time staff with key advisors, consultants, and subcontractors. As the firm grows, people with special expertise will be added to the staff.

9. Implementation Plan

Introducing Howlin' Coyote chilies to 17 new metropolitan markets is a complex task and requires that creative promotional activities gain consumer awareness and initial trial. Counting the three existing metropolitan markets in which Paradise Kitchens competes, by 2018 it will be in 20 metropolitan markets or 53 percent of the top 38 U.S. metropolitan markets. The anticipated rollout schedule to enter these metropolitan markets appears in Figure 4.

Figure 4. Rollout Schedule to Enter New U.S. Markets

Year	New Markets Added Each Year	Cumulative Markets	Cumulative Percentage of 38 Major U.S. Markets
Today (2013)	2	5	16
Year 1 (2014)	3	8	21
Year 2 (2015)	4	12	29
Year 3 (2016)	2	14	37
Year 4 (2017)	3	17	45
Year 5 (2018)	3	20	53

The diverse regional tastes in chili will be monitored carefully to assess whether minor modifications may be required in the chili recipes. As the rollout to new metropolitan areas continues, Paradise Kitchens will assess manufacturing and distribution trade-offs. This is important in determining whether to start new production with selected high-quality regional contract packers.

10. Evaluation

Monthly sales targets in cases have been set for Howlin' Coyote chili for each metropolitan area. Actual case sales will be compared with these targets and tactical marketing programs modified to reflect the unique sets of factors in each metropolitan area.

Appendix A. Biographical Sketches of Key Personnel

Appendix B. Detailed Financial Projections

3 Scanning the Marketing Environment

Learning Objectives

After reading this chapter you should be able to:

LO 3-1 Explain how environmental scanning provides information about social, economic, technological, competitive, and regulatory forces.

LO 3-2 Describe how social forces such as demographics and culture can have an impact on marketing strategy.

LO 3-3 Discuss how economic forces such as macroeconomic conditions and consumer income affect marketing.

LO 3-4 Describe how technological changes can affect marketing.

LO 3-5 Discuss the forms of competition that exist in a market and the key components of competition.

LO 3-6 Explain the major legislation that ensures competition and regulates the elements of the marketing mix.

How Do You Attract 1 Billion Customers? Move Fast and Break Things!

In just nine years since he started Facebook from his Harvard dorm room, Mark Zuckerberg has one-seventh of the world's population as customers.

How did Facebook grow so quickly? Zuckerberg's management mantra "move fast and break things" was perfectly matched with a rapidly changing marketing environment! Let's take a look at how environmental forces influenced Facebook and where Facebook is headed in the future.

Facebook and the Influence of Environmental Forces

There are many forces that influenced Facebook:

- *Social forces* changed as almost every aspect of our society moved toward transparency. People wanted tools for obtaining information, offering opinions, and interacting with friends, and they began sharing more and more information about themselves.
- *Economic forces* also influenced the demand for Facebook as the cost of wireless connectivity, Internet service, and smartphones rapidly declined and made social networking affordable for consumers around the world.
- *Technological advances* in data storage, server speed, and software integration made Facebook fast and convenient. Its mega-data centers in Oregon, North Carolina, and Sweden offered increasingly efficient energy and heat management.
- *Competitive forces* by companies such as MySpace encouraged rapid expansion. Today, Google and Facebook are becoming fierce competitors for the role of society's depository of information.
- *Legal and regulatory forces* also influenced the development of Facebook. The company obtained rights to the name, developed privacy guidelines, and adapted to many Securities and Exchange Commission regulations when it became a publicly traded company.

Zuckerberg's rapid response to changes in the environment and his willingness to "break" old things by trying new things resulted in a unique social network that quickly connected the world.

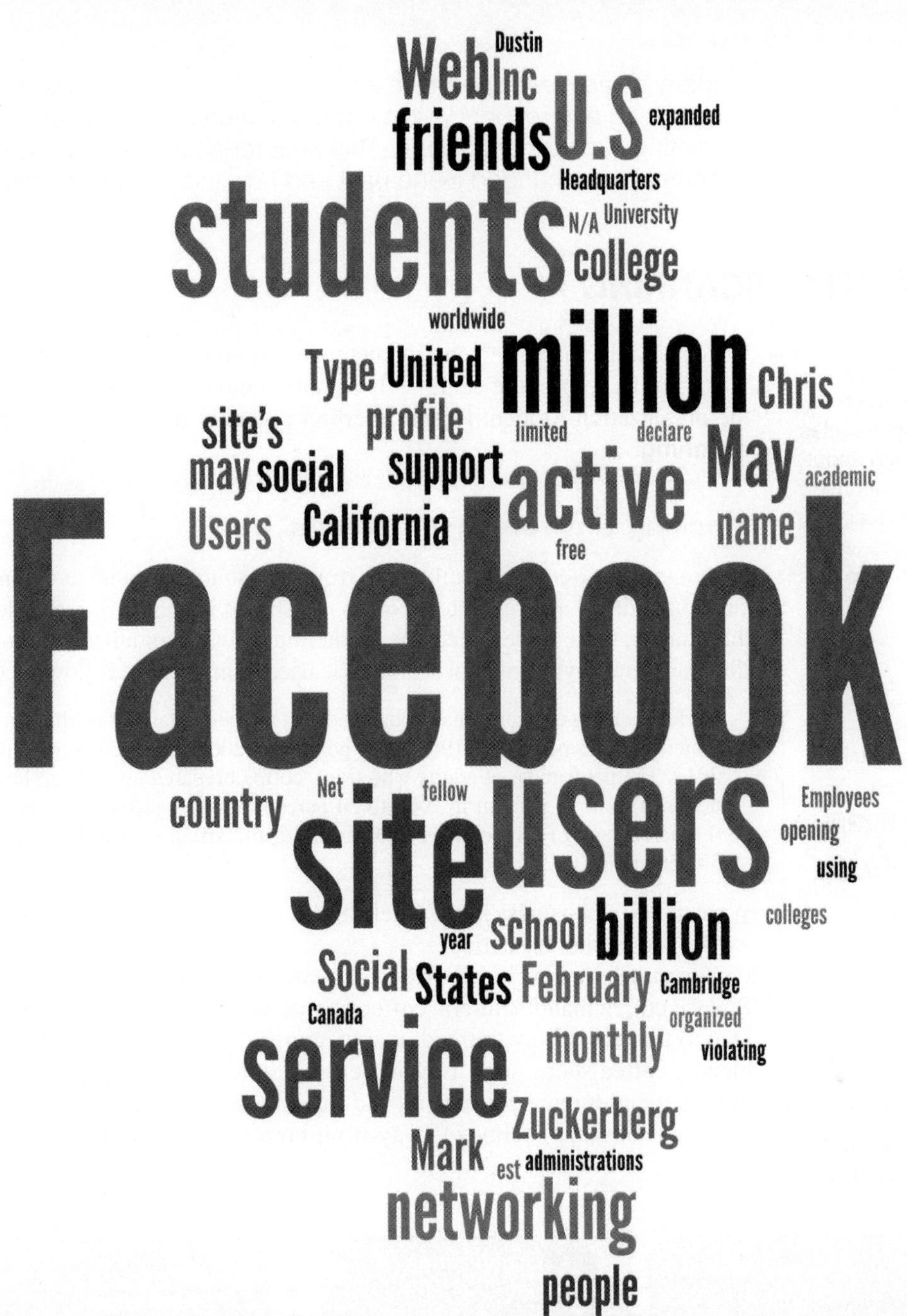

Facebook in the Future

Facebook is likely to respond to many changes in the future also. Mike Vernal, a Facebook engineer, explains that "We are trying to map out the graph of everything in the world and how it relates to each other." As people post more information about themselves, for example, Facebook will become more predictive about individual preferences and facilitate interactions with people who have similar interests. The future Facebook is also likely to include expansion into all international markets, including China, where it is currently banned, and other countries where Internet service is just becoming available. Finally, Facebook will become increasingly mobile as smartphones grow in popularity.[1] Chapter 19 provides additional discussion on social networks and social media.

Many businesses operate in environments where important forces change. Anticipating and responding to changes often means the difference between marketing success and failure. This chapter describes how the marketing environment has changed in the past and how it is likely to change in the future.

ENVIRONMENTAL SCANNING

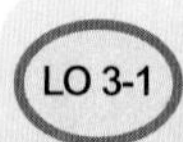

Explain how environmental scanning provides information about social, economic, technological, competitive, and regulatory forces.

Changes in the marketing environment are a source of opportunities and threats to be managed. The process of continually acquiring information on events occurring outside the organization to identify and interpret potential trends is called **environmental scanning**.

Tracking Environmental Trends

Environmental trends typically arise from five sources: social, economic, technological, competitive, and regulatory forces. As shown in Figure 3–1 and described later in this chapter, these forces affect the marketing activities of a firm in numerous ways. To illustrate how environmental scanning is used, consider the following trends:[2]

QR 3-1
Starbucks
Video

> Coffee industry marketers have observed that the percentage of adults who drink coffee declined from 75 percent in 1962 to 49 percent in 2004, and then increased to 64 percent in 2012. The percentage of adults who drink coffee prepared away from home, however, has declined from 31 percent in 2008 to 24 percent today. Age-specific analysis indicates that the percentage of 18- to 24-year-olds that drink coffee rose from 16 percent in 2003 to 50 percent in 2012.

What types of businesses are likely to be influenced by these trends? What future would you predict for coffee?

You may have concluded that these changes in coffee consumption are likely to influence coffee manufacturers, coffee shops, and supermarkets. If so, you are correct. Due to the recent growth trend, manufacturers are offering new flavors and seasonal blends, coffee shops such as Starbucks are automating to prepare drinks faster and make purchases more convenient, and supermarkets are adding boutiques and gourmet brands. The recent decline in away-from-home consumption has also led to changes.

FIGURE 3–1
Environmental forces affect the organization, as well as its suppliers and customers.

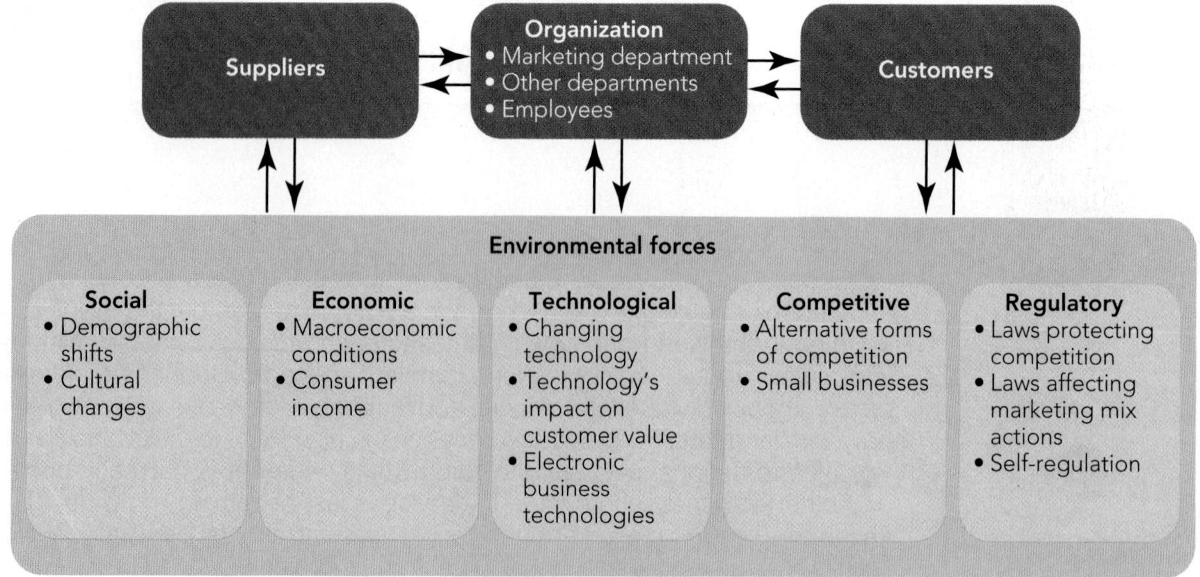

McDonald's, for example, has recently started selling bags of ground coffee in some of its stores. Predicting the future requires assumptions about the number of years the trends will continue and their rate of increase or decline. Do you believe the recent growth in coffee consumption by the 18- to 24-year-old age group will continue?

Environmental scanning also involves explaining trends. Why did coffee consumption decline for many years and then increase again recently? One explanation for the decline is that consumers switched from coffee to other beverages such as tea, soft drinks, juices, and bottled water. The increase may be the result of new coffee products distributed in coffee shops, supermarkets, and vending machines. The recent decline in away-from-home consumption may be the result of economic forces that cause consumers to reduce discretionary expenditures and also the growing use of single-cup brewing formats at home. Identifying and interpreting trends, such as the changes in coffee consumption, and developing explanations (such as those offered in this paragraph) are essential to successful environmental scanning.[3]

An Environmental Scan of Today's Marketplace

What other trends might affect marketing in the future? A firm conducting an environmental scan of the marketplace might uncover key trends such as those listed in Figure 3–2 for each of the five environmental forces.[4] Although the list of trends in Figure 3–2 is far from complete, it reveals the breadth of an environmental scan—from the way consumers are changing how they use media, to the increasing impact of new technologies such as robots, to the growth of online privacy advocacy and regulation. These trends affect consumers and the organizations that serve them. Trends such as these are described in the following discussion of the five environmental forces.

FIGURE 3–2
An environmental scan of today's marketplace shows the many important trends that influence marketing.

ENVIRONMENTAL FORCE	TREND IDENTIFIED BY AN ENVIRONMENTAL SCAN
Social	• Consumers are increasingly switching media (up to 27 times per hour) as they search for short, engaging messages. • High unemployment and reduced income are increasing demand at discount retailers for lower-cost and smaller-sized products. • Crowdfunding, online concept testing, and preordering are becoming important ways for consumers to participate in brand and product development.
Economic	• During the recession, the consumer savings rate rose to 8.3%; the rate has since declined to 3.7%, indicating more spending. • The clean energy sector of the global economy is growing as countries begin to meet their Kyoto Protocol commitments. • The United States, Japan, China, and EU countries will increase investments in sustainable living infrastructure.
Technological	• Robots are becoming viable technologies for housework, surgery, and many forms of labor. • 3D printing and on-demand capabilities are creating a resurgence in domestic manufacturing. • There is a growing availability of new smartphone tools such as mobile advertising, mobile barcode scanning, and mobile payment apps.
Competitive	• Customer-generated content (feedback, reviews, etc.) is growing as a competitive advantage. • Microbusiness impact will increase through peer-to-peer websites. • Partnerships, collaboration, and co-creation of value are becoming important dimensions of competition.
Regulatory	• Online privacy protection advocacy and regulation is increasing. • There is increasing regulatory guidance regarding green and environmental marketing claims. • Health care, gun-control, and marijuana regulation debates are receiving more attention.

SOCIAL FORCES

Describe how social forces such as demographics and culture can have an impact on marketing strategy.

The **social forces** of the environment include the demographic characteristics of the population and its culture. Changes in these forces can have a dramatic impact on marketing strategy.

Demographics

Describing a population according to selected characteristics such as age, gender, ethnicity, income, and occupation is referred to as **demographics**. Several organizations such as the Population Reference Bureau and the United Nations monitor the world population profile, while many other organizations such as the U.S. Census Bureau provide information about the American population.

The World Population at a Glance The most recent estimates indicate there are 7.1 billion people in the world today, and the population is likely to grow to 9.6 billion by 2050. While this growth has led to the term *population explosion*, the increases have not occurred worldwide; they are primarily in the developing countries of Africa, Asia, and Latin America. In fact, India is predicted to have the world's largest population in 2050 with 1.69 billion people, and China will be a close second with 1.31 billion people. World population projections show that the proportion of the world's population in more developed countries such as the United States, Japan, Australia, and those in Europe is declining.[5]

What are the implications of the shifting age structure of the world population?

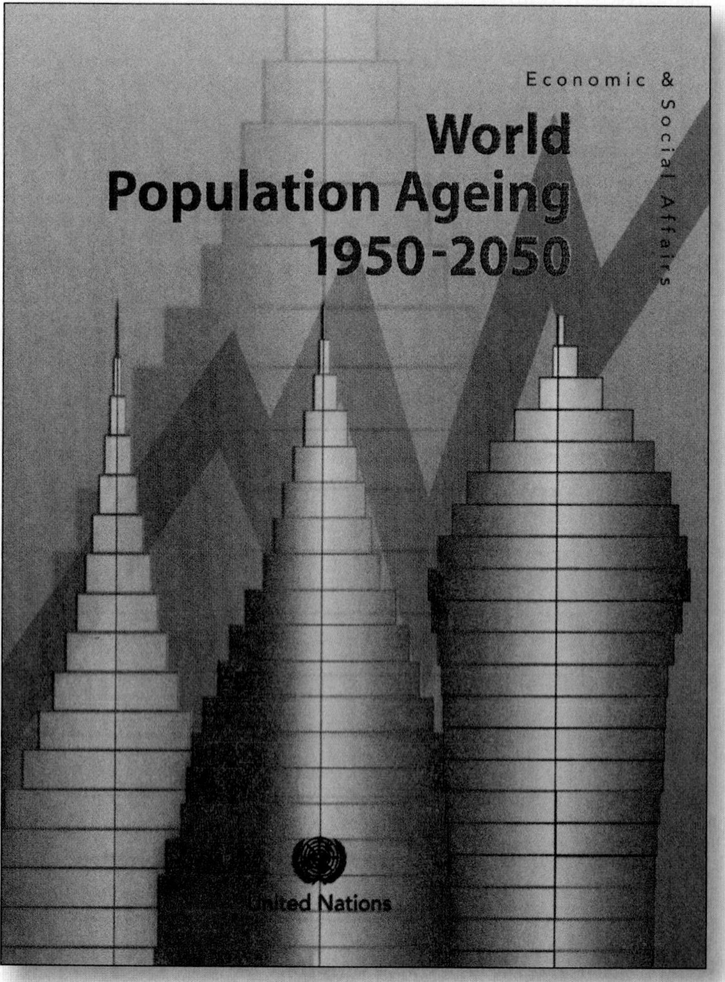

Economic & Social Affairs
World Population Ageing 1950-2050
United Nations

Another important global trend is the shifting age structure of the world population. Worldwide, the number of people 60 years and older is expected to more than triple in the coming decades and reach 2 billion by 2050. Again, the magnitude of this trend varies by region, and developed countries such as the United States are expected to face the highest growth rates of the elderly age group. Global income levels and living standards have also been increasing, although the averages across countries are very different. Per capita income, for example, ranges from \$88,890 in Norway, to \$45,560 in Canada, to \$370 in Ethiopia.

For marketers, global trends such as these have many implications. Obviously, the relative size of countries such as India and China will mean they represent huge markets for many product categories. Elderly populations in developed countries are likely to save less and begin spending their funds on health care, travel, and other retirement-related products and services. Economic progress in developing countries will lead to growth in entrepreneurship, new markets for infrastructure related to manufacturing, communication, and distribution, and the growth of exports.[6]

The U.S. Population Studies of the demographic characteristics of the U.S. population suggest several important trends. Generally, the population is becoming larger, older, and more diverse. The U.S. Census Bureau estimates that the current population of the United States is 316 million people. If current trends in life expectancy, birthrates, and immigration continue, by 2030 the U.S. population will exceed 358 million people. This growth suggests that niche markets based on age, life stage, family structure, geographic location, and ethnicity will become increasingly important.

The global trend toward an older population is particularly true in the United States. Today, there are more than 41 million people age 65 and older. By 2030, this age group will include more than 72 million people or 20 percent of the population. You may have noticed companies trying to attract older consumers by making typefaces larger, lowering store shelves, and avoiding colors that are difficult to read (yellow and blue). Finally, the term *minority* as it is currently used is likely to become obsolete as the size of most ethnic groups will double during the next two decades.[7]

Generational Cohorts A major reason for the graying of America is that the 76 million **baby boomers**—the generation of children born between 1946 and 1964—are growing older. Baby boomers are retiring at a rate of 10,000 every 24 hours, and they will all be 65 or older by 2030. Their participation in the workforce has made them the wealthiest generation in U.S. history, accounting for an estimated 50 percent of all consumer spending.

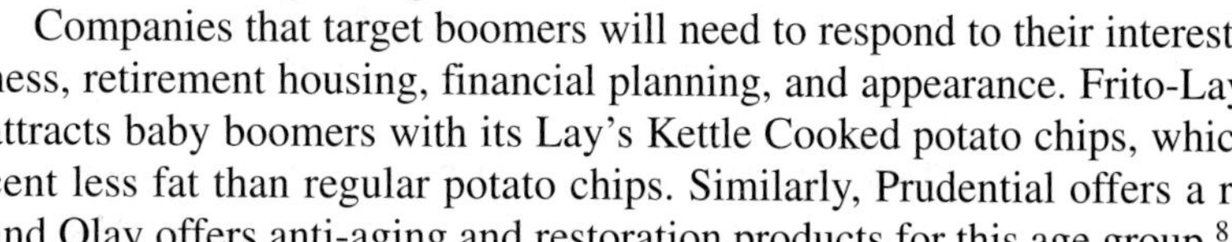

Companies that target boomers will need to respond to their interests in health, fitness, retirement housing, financial planning, and appearance. Frito-Lay, for example, attracts baby boomers with its Lay's Kettle Cooked potato chips, which have 40 percent less fat than regular potato chips. Similarly, Prudential offers a retirement plan and Olay offers anti-aging and restoration products for this age group.[8]

The baby boom cohort is followed by **Generation X**, which includes the 50 million people born between 1965 and 1976. This period is also known as the *baby bust*, because during this time the number of children born each year was declining. This is a generation of consumers who are self-reliant, supportive of racial and ethnic diversity, and better educated than any previous generation. They are not prone to extravagance and are likely to pursue lifestyles that are a blend of caution, pragmatism, and traditionalism.

In terms of net worth, Generation X is the first generation to have less than the previous generation. As baby boomers move toward retirement, however, Generation X is becoming a dominant force in many markets. Generation X, for example, spends more

Which generational cohorts are these three advertisers trying to reach?

on food, housing, apparel, and entertainment than other generations. In addition, this generation is on the Internet more than any other generation and also leads in terms of online spending. Surveys of Generation X consumers indicate they want online customer support; websites that are comprehensive, professional, and interactive; and advertising that is authentic, family-oriented, and unique. Generation X is also replacing baby boomers as the largest segment of business travelers. In response, American Airlines is offering travelers in-flight Wi-Fi, entertainment on demand, and personal powerports.[9]

The generational cohort labeled **Generation Y** includes the 72 million Americans born between 1977 and 1994. This was a period of increasing births, which resulted from baby boomers having children, and it is often referred to as the *echo-boom* or *baby boomlet.* Generation Y exerts influence on music, sports, computers, video games, and all forms of communication and networking. Generation Y members are interested in distinctive, memorable, and personal experiences and are very adept at managing their lives to create a work–life balance. They are strong-willed, passionate about the environment, and optimistic. This is also a group that is attracted to purposeful work where they have control. The Making Responsible Decisions box describes how millennials' interest in sustainability is influencing colleges, graduate schools, and employers. The term *millennials* is used, with inconsistent definitions, to refer to younger members of Generation Y and sometimes to Americans born since 1994.[10]

Because the members of each generation are distinctive in their attitudes and consumer behavior, marketers have been studying the many groups or cohorts that make up the marketplace and have developed *generational marketing* programs for them.

The American Household As the population age profile has changed, so has the structure of the American household. In 1960, 75 percent of all households consisted of married couples. Today, that type of household is just 48 percent of the population. Only 20 percent of households are married couples with children, and only 10 percent are households with working fathers and stay-at-home moms. Some of the fastest-growing types of households are those with an adult child who has moved back home with his or her parents and those with unmarried partners. These two categories included 5.5 million individuals and 7.7 million couples, respectively.

Analysis by the U.S. Bureau of the Census indicates that young people are postponing marriage and parenthood and that the increase in households with unmarried partners reflects that "pooling resources by moving in together may be one method of coping with extended unemployment." Businesses are adjusting to the changes because they have implications for purchases related to weddings, homes, baby and child products, and many other industries.[11]

Hallmark

The increase in cohabitation (households with unmarried partners) may be one reason the national divorce rate has declined during recent years. Even so, the likelihood that a couple will divorce exceeds 40 percent, and divorce among baby boomers—what is being called *gray divorce*—appears to be increasing. The majority of divorced people eventually remarry, which has created the **blended family**, one formed by merging two previously separated units into a single household. Today, one of every three Americans is a stepparent, stepchild, stepsibling, or some other member of a blended family. Hallmark Cards, Inc., now has specially designed cards and sentiments for blended families.[12]

Population Shifts A major regional shift in the U.S. population toward Southern and Western states is under way. The most recent Census Bureau estimates indicate that the populations of Texas, Utah, North Dakota, and Colorado grew at the fastest rates, while the populations of Rhode Island and Michigan declined in size. Nearly a century ago each of the top 10 most populous cities in the United States was within 500 miles of the Canadian border. Today, 7 of the top 10 are in states that border Mexico. Last year, Texas gained more people than any other state—its population increased by more than 400,000![13]

Populations are also shifting within states. In the early 1900s, the population shifted from rural areas to cities. From the 1930s through the 2000s, the population shifted sustainability

Making Responsible Decisions

Millennials Are Going to Change the World—through Environmental Sustainability!

Millennials are determined to make a difference in the world and, by doing so, make the world a better place. They are idealistic and eager to get started, particularly when it comes to environmental sustainability, which millennials believe is part of what it means to be socially responsible. The group includes students in college and graduate school and many early career employees. In different ways each group is making its voice heard.

There are approximately 17 million undergraduate millennials who expect sustainable campus communities that include LEED (Leadership in Energy and Environmental Design)-certified housing, campus transit systems, and recycling programs. They view themselves as part of the "ecoRenaissance" movement. Graduate students are looking for programs with sustainability electives, case studies, and potential for involvement with organizations such as Net Impact (www.netimpact.org), a nonprofit for students who want to "use business to improve the world." Early career employees want "green" jobs such as social responsibility officer, environmental consultant, and sustainability database specialist at companies that are eco-conscious and advocate good citizenship.

Sara Hochman is a typical example. She was interested in environmental issues in college, and her first job was as an environmental consultant. To make a bigger impact on her clients, she decided she needed to "beef up" her business skills, so she enrolled in graduate school at the University of Chicago where she could take an elective on renewable energy and join the Energy Club. Similarly, a recent college graduate joined the Peace Corps because, she said, "I want to be part of something bigger than just me-me-me."

Have you made similar choices or decisions based on your interest and concern about sustainability? What will the world look like after the millennials have made their changes? It is difficult to predict. As experts Peter Leyden and Ruy Teixeira advise, however, we should, "Hang on for the ride!"

---

from cities to suburbs and then from suburbs to more remote suburbs called *exurbs*. The recent recession, however, has made it difficult for families to move, causing a reverse in the trend and revived growth in urban areas. Today, 30 percent of all Americans live in central cities, 50 percent live in suburbs, and 20 percent live in rural locations.[14]

To assist marketers in gathering data on the population, the Census Bureau has developed a classification system to describe the varying locations of the population. The system consists of two types of *statistical areas*:

- A *metropolitan statistical area* has at least one urbanized area of 50,000 or more people and adjacent territory that has a high degree of social and economic integration.
- A *micropolitan statistical area* has at least one urban cluster of at least 10,000 but less than 50,000 people and adjacent territory that has a high degree of social and economic integration.

If a metropolitan statistical area contains a population of 2.5 million or more, it may be subdivided into smaller areas called *metropolitan divisions*. In addition, adjacent metropolitan statistical areas and micropolitan statistical areas may be grouped into *combined statistical areas*.[15]

There are currently 388 metropolitan statistical areas, which include 85 percent of the population, and 541 micropolitan statistical areas, which include 9 percent of the population.

Racial and Ethnic Diversity A notable trend is the changing racial and ethnic composition of the U.S. population. Approximately one in three U.S. residents belongs to the following racial or ethnic groups: African American, Native American or Alaska Native, Asian American, or Native Hawaiian or Pacific Islander. Diversity is further evident in the variety of peoples that make up these groups. For example, Asians consist of Asian Indians, Chinese, Filipinos, Japanese, Koreans, and Vietnamese.

The 2010 Census allowed respondents to choose more than one of the five race options, and more than 5 million people reported more than one race. Hispanics, who may be from any race, currently make up 16 percent of the U.S. population and are represented by Mexicans, Puerto Ricans, Cubans, and others of Central and South American ancestry. While the United States is becoming more diverse, Figure 3–3 suggests that the minority racial and ethnic groups tend to be concentrated in geographic regions.[16]

The racial and ethnic composition of the United States is expected to change even more in the future. By 2030, the Hispanic population will grow from 51 million to more than 78 million, or 22 percent of the population. The number of Asians in the United States will almost double to 23 million, or 6 percent of the population, and the African American population will be approximately 49 million, or 14 percent of the population. The multiracial category currently makes up 1.7 percent of the population and is expected to grow to 3.6 percent. Overall, the trends in the composition of the population suggest that the U.S. market will no longer be dominated by one group and that non-Hispanic Caucasians will be a declining majority over the next 15 years.

While the growing size of these groups has been identified through new Census data, their economic impact on the marketplace is also very noticeable. By 2015, Hispanics, African Americans, and Asian Americans will spend $1.3 trillion, $1.1 trillion, and $880 billion each year, respectively. To adapt to this new marketplace, many companies are developing **multicultural marketing** programs, which are combinations of the marketing mix that reflect the unique attitudes, ancestry, communication preferences, and lifestyles of different races. Because businesses must now market their products to a consumer base with many racial and ethnic identities, in-depth marketing research that allows an accurate understanding of each culture is essential.[17]

Additional analysis of population demographic data, such as the information shown in Figure 3–3, suggests that racial and ethnic groups tend to be concentrated in geographic regions. This information allows companies to combine their multicultural marketing efforts with regional marketing activities. Consider, for example, that 48 percent of Asian Americans live in Los Angeles, New York City, and San Francisco and that two-thirds of Hispanics live in Florida, Texas, and California. *Advertising*

FIGURE 3–3
Racial and ethnic groups (excluding Caucasians) are concentrated in geographic regions of the United States.

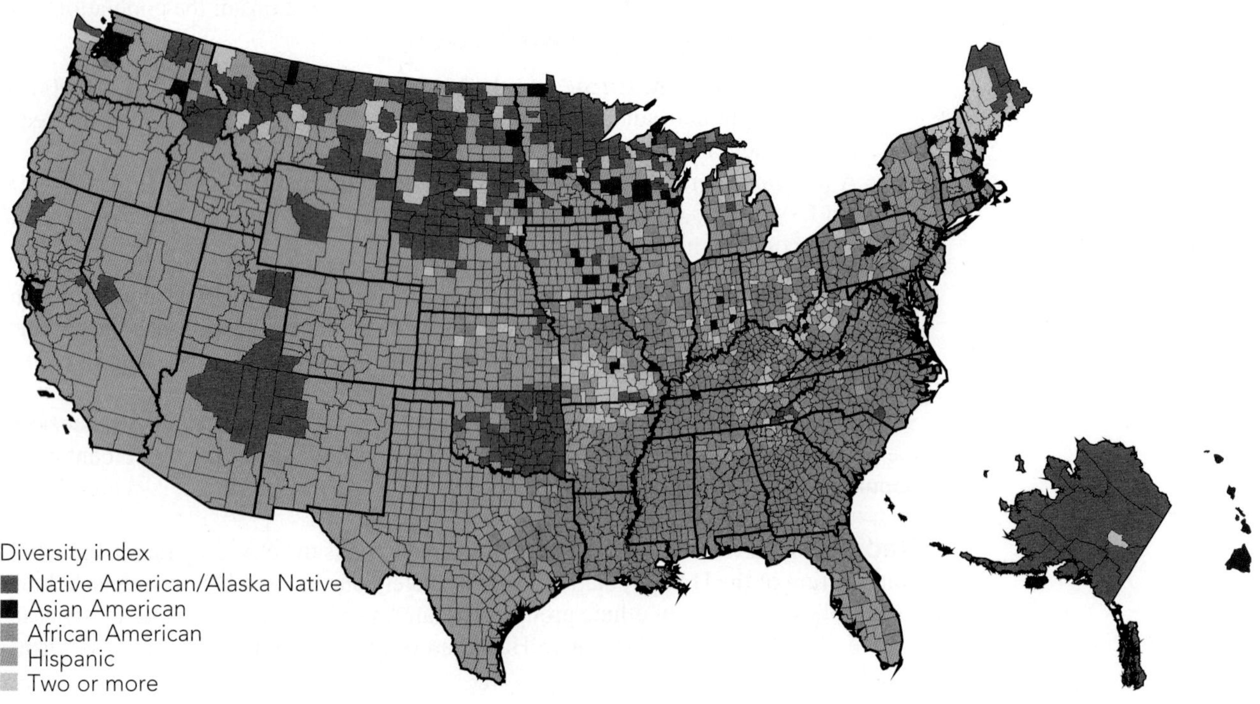

Chevrolet combines ethnic and regional marketing by using Spanish-language promotions like this one in some states.

QR 3-2 Chevrolet Video

Age's Multicultural Agency of the Year, LatinWorks, describes itself as "passionate about helping brands navigate today's cultural landscape." The agency uses its expertise to create Hispanic campaigns for Anheuser-Busch, Domino's Pizza, Chevrolet, Heinz, Lowe's, Target, and many others. For example, LatinWorks created a series of ads for Chevrolet, such as the ad for the Chevy Cruze Eco shown above.

Similarly, companies such as General Mills, Sears, and TAG Heuer are using mobile marketing to reach geographic concentrations of ethnic groups on their mobile phones. Some companies, however, are encouraging their agencies to develop the "total market," with messages that appeal to the general market and multicultural markets as well. Walmart, for example, ran its "Every Cart Tells a Story" campaign with only small differences between the English and Spanish versions.[18]

Culture

A second social force, **culture**, incorporates the set of values, ideas, and attitudes that are learned and shared among the members of a group. Because many of the elements of culture influence consumer buying patterns, monitoring national and global cultural trends is important for marketing. Cross-cultural analysis needed for global marketing is discussed in Chapter 7.

The Changing Attitudes and Roles of Men and Women One of the most notable cultural changes in the United States in the past 30 years has been in the attitudes and roles of men and women in the marketplace. Some experts predict that as this trend continues, the buying patterns of men and women will eventually be very similar.

Your mothers and grandmothers probably remember advertising targeted at them that focused on the characteristics of household products—like laundry detergent that got clothes "whiter than white." In the 1970s and 1980s, ads began to create a bridge between genders with messages such as Secret's "strong enough for a man, but made for a woman." In the 1990s, marketing to women focused on their challenge of balancing family and career interests. Since then, women and men have encouraged the slow movement toward equality in the marketplace. As a result, today's Generation Y represents the first generation of women

Diesel is making changes to appeal to women as well as men.

who have no collective memory of the dramatic changes we have undergone. As one expert explains, "Feminism today is like fluoride; we scarcely notice that we have it."

Several factors have contributed to the shift in attitudes. First, many young women had career mothers who provided a reference point for lifestyle choices. Second, increased participation in organized sports eliminated one of the most visible inequalities in opportunities for women. And finally, the Internet has provided exposure to the marketplace through a mechanism that makes gender, race, and ethnicity invisible. Recent surveys, however, suggest that many of the 35 million Generation Y women believe that there is still a need for equal opportunities and treatment in the workplace and in politics.[19]

Many companies that had a consumer base that was primarily women or primarily men in the past are preparing for growth from the other gender. Grocery stores, car dealers, investment services, video game developers, and many others hope to appeal to both groups in the future. UGG boots, for example, built a strong reputation among women with its distinctive boot and is now trying to attract men with new products, advertising, and endorsements from football star Tom Brady. Similarly, LEGO, which had been selling almost exclusively to boys, recently introduced its "Friends" line for girls.

QR 3-3
Diesel Video

Some industries are trying to avoid creating separate products for men and women. Professional sports leagues are targeting women, and spas are targeting men. Dolce & Gabbana recently introduced its Anthology fragrance line, for men and women. In general, the trend is toward fewer gender distinctions, particularly in marketing directed at young consumers. For example, Diesel's "Be Stupid" advertising campaign typically depicts men and women in partnership roles rather than portraying either one in a dominant or subordinate role.[20]

Changing Values Culture also includes values that may differ over time and between countries. During the 1970s, a list of values in the United States included achievement, work, efficiency, and material comfort. Today, commonly held values include personal control, continuous change, equality, individualism, self-help, competition, future orientation, and action. These values are useful in understanding most current behaviors of U.S. consumers, particularly when they are compared to values in other countries. Contrasting values outside the United States, for example, include belief in fate, the importance of tradition, the importance of rank and status, a focus on group welfare, and acceptance of birthright.

An increasingly important value for consumers in the United States and around the globe is sustainability and preserving the environment. Concern for the environment is one reason consumers are buying hybrid gas-electric automobiles, such as the Toyota Prius, the Chevy Volt, and the Ford C-MAX. Companies are also changing their business practices to respond to trends in consumer values. Coca-Cola has been working on alleviating global water scarcity, Facebook has committed to reducing the carbon footprint of its data centers by 25 percent by 2015, and Wal-Mart Stores, Inc., has set ambitious goals to cut energy use by buying more local products, reducing packaging, and switching to renewable power. Recent research also indicates that consumers are committed to brands with a strong link to social action. For example, Brita's "Filter For Good" campaign asks consumers to take a pledge to reduce their plastic bottle waste.[21]

A change in consumption orientation is also apparent. In the past, consumers often used debt to make many of their purchases. High unemployment, lower real estate prices, and tax increases, however, have changed their perspective. Today, U.S. consumers have become cautious buyers. **Value consciousness**—or the concern for obtaining the best quality, features, and performance of a product or service for a given price—is driving consumption behavior for many products at all price levels. For example, the recent recession led consumers to cut back on brand-name products such as toothpaste, shampoo, and toilet paper so that they could still afford discretionary products such as high-definition televisions and smartphones. Likewise, the recent recession and slow economic recovery prompted consumers to reduce the distances they would drive to shop.

Innovative marketers have responded to this new value-conscious orientation in numerous ways. Dollar General, for example, opened new stores in convenient locations and installed taller shelves so that it could build up its stock of name-brand food, health, and beauty products. The store quickly saw sales increase by 6 percent. Similarly, Walmart and other retailers began providing special deals to customers who shop for bargains online.[22]

learning review

3-1. Describe three generational cohorts.

3-2. Why are many companies developing multicultural marketing programs?

3-3. How are important values such as sustainability reflected in the marketplace today?

ECONOMIC FORCES

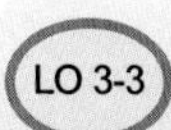

Discuss how economic forces such as macroeconomic conditions and consumer income affect marketing.

The second component of the environmental scan, the **economy**, pertains to the income, expenditures, and resources that affect the cost of running a business and household. We'll consider two aspects of these economic forces: a macroeconomic view of the marketplace and a microeconomic perspective of consumer income.

Macroeconomic Conditions

Of particular concern at the macroeconomic level is the performance of the economy based on indicators such as GDP (gross domestic product), unemployment, and price changes (inflation or deflation). In an inflationary economy, the cost to produce and buy products and services escalates as prices increase. From a marketing standpoint, if prices rise faster than consumer incomes, the number of items consumers can buy decreases. This relationship is evident in the cost of a college education. The College Board reports that since 2000 college tuition and fees have increased 146 percent (from \$3,508 to \$8,655) while family incomes have increased less than 19 percent. The share of family income required to pay for tuition at public four-year colleges has risen from 8 percent in 2000 to 17 percent today.[23]

Periods of declining economic activity are referred to as recessions. During recessions, businesses decrease production, unemployment rises, and many consumers have less money to spend. The U.S. economy experienced recessions from 1973–75, 1981–82, 1990–91, and in 2001. Most recently, a recessionary period began in 2007 and ended in 2009, becoming the longest in recent history.[24]

Consumer expectations about the economy are an important element of environmental scanning. Consumer spending, which accounts for two-thirds of U.S. economic activity, is affected by expectations of the future. The two most popular surveys of consumer expectations are the Consumer Confidence Index, conducted by a nonprofit business

FIGURE 3–4
The Index of Consumer Sentiment (ICS) is closely related to economic conditions.

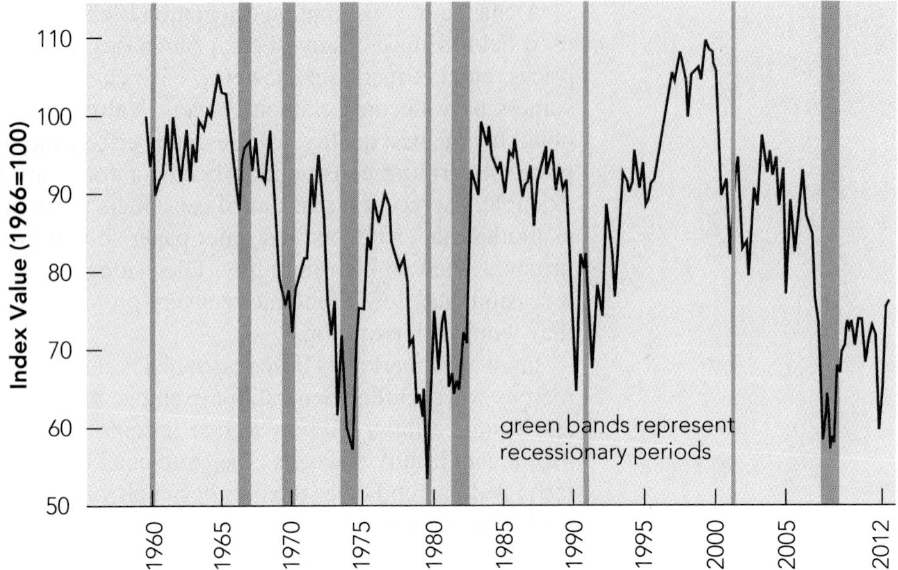

research organization called the Conference Board, and the Index of Consumer Sentiment, conducted by the Survey Research Center at the University of Michigan. The surveys track the responses of consumers to specific questions about their expectations, and the results are reported once each month. For example, the Index of Consumer Sentiment asks, "Looking ahead, do you think that a year from now you will be better off financially, worse off, or just about the same as now?" The answers to the questions are used to construct an index. The higher the index, the more favorable are consumer expectations. Figure 3–4 shows the fluctuation in the Index of Consumer Sentiment and its close relationship to economic conditions (green areas represent recessionary periods). The consumer expectations surveys are closely monitored by many companies, particularly manufacturers and retailers of cars, furniture, and major appliances.[25]

Consumer Income

The microeconomic trends in terms of consumer income are also important issues for marketers. Having a product that meets the needs of consumers may be of little value if they are unable to purchase it. A consumer's ability to buy is related to income, which consists of gross, disposable, and discretionary components.

Gross Income The total amount of money made in one year by a person, household, or family unit is referred to as **gross income** (or "money income" at the Census Bureau). While the typical U.S. household earned only about $8,700 of income in 1970, it earned about $50,054 in 2011. When gross income is adjusted for inflation, however, income of that typical U.S. household was relatively stable. In fact, inflation-adjusted income has only varied between $45,146 and $54,489 since 1970. Approximately 54 percent of U.S. households have an annual income between $25,000 and $99,999.[26] Are you from a typical household? Read the Marketing inSite box to learn how you can determine the median household income in your hometown.

Disposable Income The second income component, **disposable income**, is the money a consumer has left after paying taxes to use for necessities such as food, housing, clothing, and transportation. Thus, if taxes rise or fall faster than income, consumers are likely to have more or less disposable income. Similarly, dramatic changes in the prices of products can require spending adjustments. In recent years, for example, as the price of gasoline increased, consumers found themselves adjusting their spending in other categories. In addition, the decline in home prices has had a

Marketing inSite

American FactFinder: Your Source for Economic Information

Marketers collect and use environmental information to better understand consumers. One way to begin an environmental scan is to compare economic and demographic data about a particular segment of the population to what is "typical" or "average" for the entire population. Do you think your hometown is typical? To find out, visit the American FactFinder at http://factfinder2.census.gov and use the "Community Facts" tool to obtain information about your hometown. Just type in the zip code of your hometown and FactFinder will give you population size, median age, and median income information from the U.S. Census. You can also click on links listed under *American Community Survey* for more detailed information. Use the tool to look up information about your state or the United States to make comparisons.

psychological impact on consumers, who tend to spend more when they feel their net worth is rising and postpone purchases when it declines. During a recessionary period, spending, debt, and use of credit all decline. The recent downturn has led many consumers to switch from premium brands to lower-priced brands.[27]

Discretionary Income The third component of income is **discretionary income**, the money that remains after paying for taxes and necessities. Discretionary income is used for luxury items such as a Cunard cruise. An obvious problem in defining discretionary versus disposable income is determining what is a luxury and what is a necessity.

The Department of Labor monitors consumer expenditures through its annual Consumer Expenditure Survey. In 2011, consumers spent about 13 percent of their income on food, 34 percent on housing, and 4 percent on clothes. While an additional 24 percent is often spent on transportation and health care, the remainder is generally viewed as discretionary. The percentage of income spent on food and housing typically declines as income increases, which can provide an increase in discretionary income. Discretionary expenditures also can be increased by reducing savings.

QUEEN MARY 2
THE GRANDEST OCEAN LINER AT SEA

As consumers' discretionary income increases, so does the opportunity to indulge in the luxurious leisure travel marketed by Cunard.

Cunard Cruise Line
www.cunard.com

The Bureau of Labor Statistics observed that during the 1990s and early 2000s the savings rate declined to zero. That trend was reversed in 2008 when the government issued stimulus checks designed to improve the economy and, instead of spending the money, consumers saved it. Recent data on consumer expenditures indicate that the savings rate is now approximately 3.7 percent.[28]

TECHNOLOGICAL FORCES

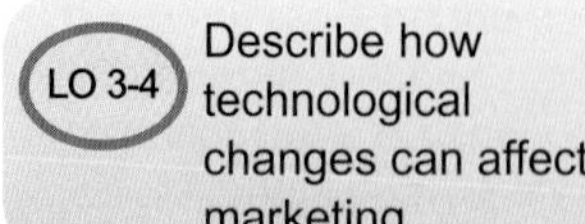

Describe how technological changes can affect marketing.

Our society is in a period of dramatic technological change. **Technology**, the third environmental force in Figure 3–2, refers to inventions or innovations from applied science or engineering research. Each new wave of technological innovation can replace existing products and companies. Do you recognize the items pictured below and what they may replace?

Technology of Tomorrow

Technological change is the result of research, so it is difficult to predict. Some of the most dramatic technological changes occurring now, however, include the following:

- Connectivity will grow to include all customers, machines, vehicles, appliances, and mobile devices to create the "Internet of Things."
- Computers will develop all five senses to create intelligent data collection and personalized predictive capabilities.
- Green technologies such as smart grid electricity services, online energy management, and consumer-generated energy (e.g., home wind turbines) will gain widespread acceptance among American consumers.
- 3D technologies will move from movie theaters and televisions to many new and useful applications.

Some of these trends in technology are already being realized in today's marketplace. Vail Ski Resort, for example, uses sensors in ski passes to track skiers and to monitor how many vertical feet they cover in a day. The phone app MindMeld uses speech recognition to listen to your phone calls and pull up search data related to your conversations. Bloomingdale's is trying virtual dressing rooms that use 3D technology to allow shoppers to try different clothes, colors, and accessories. Other technologies such

Technological change leads to new products. What products might be replaced by these innovations?

as Skype's television cameras, Chevy's electric cars, and Nike's biometric wristbands are likely to replace or become substitutes for existing products and services such as telephones, gasoline-powered vehicles, and traditional medical equipment.[29]

Technology's Impact on Customer Value

Advances in technology have important effects on marketing. First, the cost of technology is plummeting, causing the customer value assessment of technology-based products to focus on other dimensions such as quality, service, and relationships. *PC Magazine* (www.pcmag.com) publishes an article titled, "The Best Free Software," each year to tell readers about companies that give their software away, with the expectation that advertising or upgrade purchases will generate revenue. A similar approach is used by many U.S. mobile phone vendors, who charge little for the telephone if the purchase leads to a long-term telephone service contract.[30]

Technology also provides value through the development of new products. More than 3,000 companies recently unveiled 20,000 new products at the Consumer Electronics Show held in Las Vegas. New products included Samsung's phones with a flexible screen, transparent 3D televisions by Hisense, and driverless vehicle technologies from Audi and Lexus. *Better Homes and Gardens* magazine announced 63 best new product award winners in four categories: beauty, food and beverage, health and personal care, and household. Some of the winners included Taste Nirvana's coconut water, the Nestlé Crunch Girl Scout Thin Mint candy bar, and Tide's single-dose laundry detergent pods. Other new products likely to be available soon include injectable health monitors that will send glucose, oxygen, and other clinical information to a wristwatch-like monitor and robots that use artificial intelligence to master specific tasks.[31]

Technology can also change existing products and the ways they are produced. Many companies are using technological developments to recycle products through the manufacturing cycle several times. The National Association for PET Container Resources, for example, estimates that 29 percent of all plastic bottles are now recycled, usually to make polyester fibers that are spun into everything from sweaters to upholstery. Tomra Systems has installed more than 67,000 reverse vending machines in North America, Europe, Japan, South America, and the Middle East, facilitating the collection of more than 30 billion cans and bottles annually. In California, there are more than 450 rePLANET recycling centers where consumers can bring back their empty beverage containers and redeem them for the deposit paid when the products were

Tomra and rePLANET offer recycling through its kiosks and centers.

purchased. Another approach is *precycling*, or efforts by manufacturers and consumers to avoid creating waste. For manufacturers, this includes decreasing the amount of packaging they use; and for consumers, it means buying products that last longer, avoiding products with excess packaging, and reusing as much as possible. According to marketing expert Melissa Lavigne, "It's about being conscious about products you buy in the first place. That's the idea behind precycling."[32]

Electronic Business Technologies

The transformative power of technology may be best illustrated by the rapid growth of the **marketspace**, an information- and communication-based electronic exchange environment mostly occupied by sophisticated computer and telecommunication technologies and digitized offerings. Any activity that uses some form of electronic communication in the inventory, exchange, advertisement, distribution, and payment of products and services is often called **electronic commerce**. Network technologies are now used for everything from filing expense reports, to monitoring daily sales, to sharing information with employees, to communicating instantly with suppliers.

Many companies have adapted Internet-based technology internally to support their electronic business strategies. An *intranet*, for example, is an Internet-based network used within the boundaries of an organization. It is a private network that may or may not be connected to the public Internet. *Extranets*, which use Internet-based technologies, permit communication between a company and its suppliers, distributors, and other partners (such as advertising agencies).

COMPETITIVE FORCES

The fourth component of the environmental scan, **competition**, refers to the alternative firms that could provide a product to satisfy a specific market's needs. There are various forms of competition, and each company must consider its present and potential competitors in designing its marketing strategy.

Alternative Forms of Competition

LO 3-5 Discuss the forms of competition that exist in a market and the key components of competition.

Four basic forms of competition form a continuum from pure competition to monopolistic competition to oligopoly to pure monopoly. Chapter 13 contains further discussions on pricing practices under these four forms of competition.

At one end of the continuum is *pure competition*, in which there are many sellers and they each have a similar product. Companies that deal in commodities common to agribusiness (for example, wheat, rice, and grain) often are in a pure competition position in which distribution (in the sense of shipping products) is important but other elements of marketing have little impact.

In the second point on the continuum, *monopolistic competition*, many sellers compete with substitutable products within a price range. For example, if the price of coffee rises too much, consumers may switch to tea. Coupons or sales are frequently used marketing tactics.

Oligopoly, a common industry structure, occurs when a few companies control the majority of industry sales. The wireless telephone industry, for example, is dominated by four carriers that serve more than 90 percent of the U.S. market. Verizon, AT&T, Sprint, and T-Mobile have 117, 107, 55, and 34 million subscribers, respectively. Similarly, the entertainment industry in the United States is dominated by Viacom, Disney, and Time Warner, and the major firms in the U.S. defense contractor industry are Boeing, Northrop Grumman, and Lockheed Martin. Critics of oligopolies suggest that because there are few sellers, price competition among firms is not desirable because it leads to reduced profits for all producers.[33]

The final point on the continuum, *pure monopoly*, occurs when only one firm sells the product. Monopolies are common for producers of products and services considered essential to a community: water, electricity, and cable service. Typically, marketing plays a small role in a monopolistic setting because it is regulated by the state or federal government. Government control usually seeks to ensure price protection for the buyer, although deregulation in recent years has encouraged price competition in the electricity market. Concern that Microsoft's 86 percent share of the PC operating system market was a monopoly that limited consumer access to competitors' Internet browsers led to lawsuits and consent decrees from the U.S. Justice Department and investigations and fines from the European Union. A recent Federal Trade Commission investigation of Google found that although the company's market share of the online search market exceeds 70 percent, it had not harmed competition in the marketplace. An investigation by the European Union, however, is still in progress.[34]

Components of Competition

In developing a marketing program, companies must consider the factors that drive competition: entry, the bargaining power of buyers and suppliers, existing rivalries, and substitution possibilities.[35] Scanning the environment requires a look at all of them. These factors relate to a firm's marketing mix decisions and may be used to create a barrier to entry, increase brand awareness, or intensify a fight for market share.

Entry In considering the competition, a firm must assess the likelihood of new entrants. Additional producers increase industry capacity and tend to lower prices. A company scanning its environment must consider the possible **barriers to entry** for other firms, which are business practices or conditions that make it difficult for new firms to enter the market. Barriers to entry can be in the form of capital requirements, advertising expenditures, product identity, distribution access, or the cost to customers of switching suppliers. The higher the expense of the barrier, the more likely it will deter new entrants. For example, Western Union and MoneyGram dominate the $529 billion money transfer market because of their huge distribution networks of branch offices and global pickup locations. Potential competitors find it difficult to enter the market because lack of distribution limits consumer access.[36]

Power of Buyers and Suppliers A competitive analysis must consider the power of buyers and suppliers. Powerful buyers exist when they are few in number, there are low switching costs, or the product represents a significant share of the buyer's total costs. This last factor leads the buyer to exert significant pressure for price competition. A supplier gains power when the product is critical to the buyer and when it has built up the switching costs.

Existing Competitors and Substitutes Competitive pressures among existing firms depend on the rate of industry growth. In slow-growth settings, competition is more heated for any possible gains in market share. High fixed costs also create competitive pressures for firms to fill production capacity. For example, airlines offer discounts for making early reservations and charge penalties for changes or cancellations in an effort to fill seats, which represent a high fixed cost.

Small Businesses as Competitors

While large companies provide familiar examples of the forms and components of competition, small businesses make up the majority of the competitive landscape for most businesses. Consider that there are approximately 28 million small businesses in the United States, which employ half of all private sector employees. In addition, small businesses generate 64 percent of all new jobs and 44 percent of the gross domestic product (GDP). Research has shown a strong correlation between national economic growth and the level of new small business activity in previous years.[37]

learning review

3-4. What is the difference between a consumer's disposable and discretionary income?

3-5. How does technology impact customer value?

3-6. In pure competition there are a ____________ number of sellers.

REGULATORY FORCES

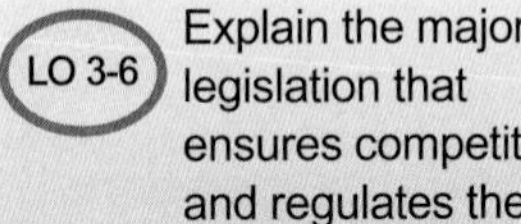

LO 3-6 Explain the major legislation that ensures competition and regulates the elements of the marketing mix.

For any organization, the marketing and broader business decisions are constrained, directed, and influenced by regulatory forces. **Regulation** consists of restrictions state and federal laws place on business with regard to the conduct of its activities. Regulation exists to protect companies as well as consumers. Much of the regulation from the federal and state levels is the result of an active political process and has been passed to ensure competition and fair business practices. For consumers, the focus of legislation is to protect them from unfair trade practices and ensure their safety.

Protecting Competition

Major federal legislation has been passed to encourage competition, which is deemed desirable because it permits the consumer to determine which competitor will succeed and which will fail. The first such law was the *Sherman Antitrust Act* (1890). Lobbying by farmers in the Midwest against fixed railroad shipping prices led to the passage of this act, which forbids (1) contracts, combinations, or conspiracies in restraint of trade and (2) actual monopolies or attempts to monopolize any part of trade or commerce. Because of vague wording and government inactivity, however, there was only one successful case against a company in the nine years after the act became law, and the Sherman Act was supplemented with the *Clayton Act* (1914). This act forbids certain actions that are likely to lessen competition, although no actual harm has yet occurred.

In the 1930s, the federal government had to act again to ensure fair competition. During that time, large chain stores appeared, such as the Great Atlantic & Pacific Tea Company (A&P). Small businesses were threatened, and they lobbied for the *Robinson-Patman Act* (1936). This act makes it unlawful to discriminate in prices charged to different purchasers of the same product, where the effect may substantially lessen competition or help to create a monopoly.

Product-Related Legislation

Various federal laws in existence specifically address the product component of the marketing mix. Some are aimed at protecting the company, some at protecting the consumer, and at least one at protecting both.

A company can protect its competitive position in new and novel products under the patent law, which gives inventors the right to exclude others from making, using, or selling products that infringe the patented invention. The federal copyright law is another way for a company to protect its competitive position in a product. The copyright law gives the author of a literary, dramatic, musical, or artistic work the exclusive right to print, perform, or otherwise copy that work. Copyright is secured automatically when the work is created. However, the published work should bear an appropriate copyright notice, including the copyright symbol, the first year of publication, and the name of the copyright owner, and it must be registered under the federal copyright law.

Digital technology has necessitated additional copyright legislation, called the *Digital Millennium Copyright Act* (1998), to improve protection of copyrighted digital products. In

These products are identified by protected trademarks. Are any of these trademarks in danger of becoming generic?

addition, producers of DVD movies, music recordings, and software want protection from websites and devices designed to circumvent antipiracy elements of their products.[38]

There are many consumer-oriented federal laws regarding products. The various laws include more than 30 amendments and separate laws relating to food, drugs, and cosmetics, such as the *Infant Formula Act* (1980), the *Nutritional Labeling and Education Act* (1990), and new labeling requirements for dietary supplements (1997) and trans fats (2006). Recently, several states have proposed new legislation that would require the labeling of genetically modified food.[39] Various other consumer protection laws have a broader scope, such as the *Fair Packaging and Labeling Act* (1966), the *Child Protection Act* (1966), and the *Consumer Product Safety Act* (1972), which established the Consumer Product Safety Commission to monitor product safety and establish uniform product safety standards. Many of these laws came about because of **consumerism**, a grassroots movement started in the 1960s to increase the influence, power, and rights of consumers in dealing with institutions. This movement continues and is reflected in the growing consumer demand for ecologically safe products and ethical and socially responsible business practices. One hotly debated issue concerns liability for environmental abuse.

Trademarks are intended to protect both the firm selling a trademarked product and the consumer buying it. A Senate report states:

> The purposes underlying any trademark statute [are] twofold. One is to protect the public so that it may be confident that, in purchasing a product bearing a particular trademark which it favorably knows, it will get the product which it asks for and wants to get. Secondly, where the owner of a trademark has spent energy, time, and money in presenting to the public the product, he is protected in this investment from misappropriation in pirates and cheats.

This statement was made in connection with another product-related law, the *Lanham Act* (1946), which provides for registration of a company's trademarks. Historically, the first user of a trademark in commerce had the exclusive right to use that particular word, name, or symbol in its business. Registration under the Lanham Act provides important advantages to a trademark owner that has used the trademark in interstate or foreign commerce, but it does not confer ownership. A company can lose its trademark if it becomes *generic*, which means that it has primarily come to be merely a common descriptive word for the product. Coca-Cola, Whopper, and Xerox are registered trademarks, and competitors cannot use these names. Aspirin and escalator are former trademarks that are now generic terms in the United States and can be used by anyone.

In 1988, the *Trademark Law Revision Act* resulted in a major change to the Lanham Act, allowing a company to secure rights to a name before actual use by declaring an intent to use the name.[40] In 2003, the United States agreed to participate in the *Madrid Protocol*, which is a treaty that facilitates the protection of U.S. trademark rights throughout the world. Currently, more than 91 nations are members of the Madrid Protocol, including the United States, Australia, China, the European Union, France, Germany, Japan, and the United Kingdom.[41]

One of the most recent changes in trademark law is the U.S. Supreme Court's ruling that companies may obtain trademarks for colors associated with their products. Over time, consumers may begin to associate a particular color with a specific brand. Examples of products that may benefit from the new law include NutraSweet's sugar substitute in pastel blue packages and Owens-Corning Fiberglas Corporation's pink insulation.[42] Another recent addition to trademark law is the *Federal Trademark Dilution Act* (1995, 2006), which is used to prevent someone from using a trademark on a noncompeting product (e.g., "Cadillac" brushes).[43]

Pricing-Related Legislation

The pricing component of the marketing mix is the focus of regulation from two perspectives: price fixing and price discounting. Although the Sherman Act did not outlaw price fixing, the courts view this behavior as *per se illegal* (*per se* means "through or of itself"), which means the courts see price fixing itself as illegal.

Certain forms of price discounting are allowed. Quantity discounts are acceptable; that is, buyers can be charged different prices for a product provided there are differences in manufacturing or delivery costs. Promotional allowances or services may be given to buyers on an equal basis proportionate to volume purchased. Also, a firm can meet a competitor's price "in good faith." Legal and regulatory aspects of pricing are covered in more detail in Chapter 14.

Distribution-Related Legislation

The government has four concerns with regard to distribution—earlier referred to as "place" actions in the marketing mix—and the maintenance of competition. The first, *exclusive dealing*, is an arrangement a manufacturer makes with a reseller to handle only its products and not those of competitors. This practice is illegal under the Clayton Act only when it substantially lessens competition.

Requirement contracts require a buyer to purchase all or part of its needs for a product from one seller for a time period. These contracts are not always illegal but depend on the court's interpretation of their impact on distribution.

Exclusive territorial distributorships are a third distribution issue often under regulatory scrutiny. In this situation, a manufacturer grants a distributor the sole rights to sell a product in a specific geographical area. The courts have found few violations with these arrangements.

QR 3-4
FTC Video

The fourth distribution strategy is a *tying arrangement*, whereby a seller requires the purchaser of one product to also buy another item in the line. These contracts may be illegal when the seller has such economic power in the tying product that the seller can restrain trade in the tied product. Legal aspects of distribution are reviewed in greater detail in Chapter 15.

Advertising- and Promotion-Related Legislation

Promotion and advertising are aspects of marketing closely monitored by the Federal Trade Commission (FTC), which was established by the *FTC Act of 1914*. The FTC is concerned with deceptive or misleading advertising and unfair business practices and has the power to (1) issue cease and desist orders and (2) order corrective advertising. In issuing a *cease and desist order*, the FTC orders a company to stop practices the commission considers unfair. With *corrective advertising*, the FTC can require a company to spend money on advertising to correct previous misleading ads. The enforcement powers of the FTC are so significant that often just an indication of concern from the commission can cause companies to revise their promotion.

Marketing Matters

technology

Online Tracking: Is Big Brother Watching?

Have you ever wondered how your web browser determines which advertisements appear on your screen? The answer is that your actions are "tracked" to create a profile of your interests. Each of the major browser makers—Microsoft, Google, Mozilla, and Apple—can keep a record of the web pages you visit or the topics you discuss in your e-mail. The information allows advertisers to match their advertising specifically to you. So, ideally, you only see advertising that offers products or services of interest to you. You see dog food ads if you are a dog owner and cat food ads if you are a cat owner, for example.

The collection of this information, however, has also raised the issue of privacy. Privacy advocates suggest that many consumers do not realize that the information is being collected and used without their consent. They also argue that in extreme situations the information could lead to unintended outcomes for the consumers—being turned down for a mortgage or a health insurance policy because of online book or food purchases, for example.

To facilitate the debate, the Federal Trade Commission (FTC) recently released a report calling for better self-regulation of online information collection. In its report, the FTC suggests that each browser should offer users a "Do Not Track" option to signal a computer user's desire not to be tracked. Advertisers would be asked to comply with the request. This opt-out system would be very similar to the current "Do Not Call" system. In Europe, the guidelines are more restrictive, requiring consumers to explicitly "opt-in."

The questions related to this issue are not simple. Consumers will need to decide if giving up some privacy by sharing data is a reasonable trade-off for targeted advertising, customized news sites, and online social networks. Organizations in the $24 billion advertising industry will need to evaluate their ability to self-regulate, and the FTC eventually will need to decide whether legislation is needed. The situation is likely to become even more complicated in the near future as consumers, and especially children, increase their use of smartphone mobile apps that generate tracking data. How do you think the debate will be resolved?

A landmark legal battle regarding deceptive advertising involved the Federal Trade Commission and Campbell Soup Co. It had been Campbell's practice to insert clear glass marbles into the bottom of soup containers used in print advertisements to bring the soup ingredients (e.g., noodles or chicken) to the surface. The FTC ruled that the advertising was deceptive because it misrepresented the amount of solid ingredients in the soup, and it issued a cease and desist order. Campbell and its advertising agency agreed to discontinue the practice. Future ads used a ladle to show the ingredients.[44]

Other laws have been introduced to regulate promotion practices. The *Deceptive Mail Prevention and Enforcement Act* (1999), for example, provides specifications for direct-mail sweepstakes, such as the requirement that the statement "No purchase is necessary to enter" be displayed in the mailing, in the rules, and on the entry form. Similarly, the *Telephone Consumer Protection Act* (1991) provides requirements for telemarketing promotions, including fax promotions. Telemarketing is also subject to a law that created the *National Do Not Call Registry*, which is a list of consumer phone numbers of people who do not want to receive unsolicited telemarketing calls.

Finally, new laws such as the *Children's Online Privacy Protection Act* (1998), the *European Union Data Protection Act* (1998), and the *Controlling the Assault of Non-Solicited Pornography and Marketing (CAN-SPAM) Act* (2004) are designed to restrict information collection and unsolicited e-mail promotions and specify simple opt-out procedures on the Internet. See the Marketing Matters box to learn about the Federal Trade Commission's effort to create a "Do Not Track" system to ensure online privacy.[45] A related Internet issue, taxation, has generated an ongoing debate and temporary laws such as the *Internet Tax Freedom Act* (2007).[46]

Control through Self-Regulation

The government has provided much legislation to create a competitive business climate and protect the consumer. An alternative to government control is **self-regulation**,

Companies must meet certain requirements before they can display this logo on their websites.

Better Business Bureau
www.bbbonline.com

where an industry attempts to police itself. The major television networks, for example, have used self-regulation to set their own guidelines for TV ads for children's toys. These guidelines have generally worked well. There are two problems with self-regulation, however: noncompliance by members and enforcement. In addition, if attempts at self-regulation are too strong, they may violate the Robinson-Patman Act.

The best-known self-regulatory group is the Better Business Bureau (BBB). This agency is a voluntary alliance of companies whose goal is to help maintain fair practices. Although the BBB has no legal power, it does try to use "moral suasion" to get members to comply with its standards. The BBB recently developed a reliability assurance program, called BBB Online, to provide objective consumer protection for Internet shoppers. Before they display the BBB Accredited Business logo on their website, participating companies must be members of their local Better Business Bureau, have been in business for at least one year, agree to participate in BBB's advertising self-regulation program, abide by the BBB Code of Business Practices, respect the privacy and e-mail preferences of their visitors, and work with the BBB to resolve consumer disputes that arise over products or services promoted or advertised on their site.[47]

learning review

3-7. The __________ Act was punitive toward monopolies, whereas the __________ Act was preventive.

3-8. Describe some of the recent changes in trademark law.

3-9. How does the Better Business Bureau encourage companies to follow its standards for commerce?

LEARNING OBJECTIVES REVIEW

LO 3-1 *Explain how environmental scanning provides information about social, economic, technological, competitive, and regulatory forces.*
Many businesses operate in environments where important forces change. Environmental scanning is the process of acquiring information about these changes to allow marketers to identify and interpret trends. There are five environmental forces businesses must monitor: social, economic, technological, competitive, and regulatory. By identifying trends related to each of these forces, businesses can develop and maintain successful marketing programs. Several trends that most businesses are monitoring include the way consumers are changing how they use media, the increasing impact of new technologies such as robots, and the growth of online privacy advocacy and regulation.

LO 3-2 *Describe how social forces such as demographics and culture can have an impact on marketing strategy.*
Demographic information describes the world population; the U.S. population; the generational cohorts such as baby boomers, Generation X, and Generation Y; the structure of the American household; the geographic shifts of the population; and the racial and ethnic diversity of the population, which has led to multicultural marketing programs. Cultural factors include the trend toward fewer differences in male and female consumer behavior and the impact of values such as sustainability on consumer preferences.

LO 3-3 *Discuss how economic forces such as macroeconomic conditions and consumer income affect marketing.*
Economic forces include the strong relationship between consumers' expectations about the economy and their spending. Gross income has remained stable for more than 40 years although the rate of saving has fluctuated, declining to zero before rising to 3.7 percent recently.

LO 3-4 *Describe how technological changes can affect marketing.*
Technological innovations can replace existing products and services. Changes in technology can also have an impact on customer value by reducing the cost of products, improving the quality of products, and providing new products that were not previously feasible. Electronic commerce is transforming how companies do business.

LO 3-5 *Discuss the forms of competition that exist in a market and the key components of competition.*
There are four forms of competition: pure competition, monopolistic competition, oligopoly, and monopoly. The key components of competition include the likelihood of new competitors, the power of buyers and suppliers, and the presence of competitors and possible substitutes. While large companies are often used as examples of marketplace competitors, there are 28 million small businesses in the United States, which have a significant impact on the economy.

LO 3-6 *Explain the major legislation that ensures competition and regulates the elements of the marketing mix.*
Regulation exists to protect companies and consumers. Legislation that ensures a competitive marketplace includes the Sherman Antitrust Act. Product-related legislation includes copyright and trademark laws that protect companies and packaging and labeling laws that protect consumers. Pricing- and distribution-related laws are designed to create a competitive marketplace with fair prices and availability. Regulation related to promotion and advertising reduces deceptive practices and provides enforcement through the Federal Trade Commission. Self-regulation through organizations such as the Better Business Bureau provides an alternative to federal and state regulation.

FOCUSING ON KEY TERMS

baby boomers p. 69
barriers to entry p. 81
blended family p. 70
competition p. 80
consumerism p. 83
culture p. 73
demographics p. 68
discretionary income p. 77
disposable income p. 76
economy p. 75
electronic commerce p. 80
environmental scanning p. 66
Generation X p. 69
Generation Y p. 70
gross income p. 76
marketspace p. 80
multicultural marketing p. 72
regulation p. 82
self-regulation p. 85
social forces p. 68
technology p. 78
value consciousness p. 75

APPLYING MARKETING KNOWLEDGE

1 For many years Gerber has manufactured baby food in small, single-sized containers. In conducting an environmental scan, (*a*) identify three trends or factors that might significantly affect this company's future business, and (*b*) propose how Gerber might respond to these changes.

2 Describe the new features you would add to an automobile designed for consumers in the 55+ age group. In what magazines would you advertise to appeal to this target market?

3 The population shift from suburbs to exurbs and small towns was discussed in this chapter. What businesses and industries are likely to benefit from this trend? How will retailers need to change to accommodate these consumers?

4 New technologies are continuously improving and replacing existing products. Although technological change is often difficult to predict, suggest how the following companies and products might be affected by the Internet and digital technologies: (*a*) Kodak cameras and film, (*b*) American Airlines, and (*c*) the Metropolitan Museum of Art.

5 In recent years in the brewing industry, a couple of large firms that have historically had most of the beer sales (Anheuser-Busch and Miller) have faced competition from many small "micro" brands. In terms of the continuum of competition, how would you explain this change?

6 The Johnson Company manufactures buttons and pins with slogans and designs. These pins are inexpensive to produce and are sold in retail outlets such as discount stores, hobby shops, and bookstores. Little equipment is needed for a new competitor to enter the market. What strategies should Johnson consider to create effective barriers to entry?

7 Why would Xerox be concerned about its name becoming generic?

8 Develop a "Code of Business Practices" for a new online vitamin store. Does your code address advertising? Privacy? Use by children? Why is self-regulation important?

BUILDING YOUR MARKETING PLAN

Your marketing plan will include a situation analysis based on internal and external factors that are likely to affect your marketing program.

1 To summarize information about external factors, create a table similar to Figure 3–2 and identify three trends related to each of the five forces (social, economic, technological, competitive, and regulatory) that relate to your product or service.

2 When your table is completed, describe how each of the trends represents an opportunity or a threat for your business.

VIDEO CASE 3 Geek Squad: A New Business for a New Environment

QR 3-5
Geek Squad
Video Case

"As long as there's innovation there is going to be new kinds of chaos," explains Robert Stephens, founder of the technology support company Geek Squad. The chaos Stephens is referring to is the difficulty we have all experienced trying to keep up with the many changes in our environment, particularly those related to computers, technology, software, communication, and entertainment. Generally, consumers have found it difficult to install, operate, and use many of the electronic products available today. "It takes time to read the manuals," Stephens says. "I'm going to save you that time because I stay home on Saturday nights and read them for you!"

THE COMPANY

The Geek Squad story begins when Stephens, a native of Chicago, passed up an Art Institute scholarship to pursue a degree in computer science. While Stephens was a computer science student he took a job fixing computers for a research laboratory, and he also started consulting. He could repair televisions, computers, and a variety of other items, although he decided to focus on computers. His experiences as a consultant led him to realize that most people needed help with technology and that they saw value in a service whose employees would show up at a specified time, be friendly, use understandable language, and solve the problem. So, with just $200, Stephens formed Geek Squad in 1994.

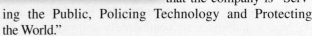

Geek Squad set out to provide timely and effective help with all computing needs regardless of the make, model, or place of purchase. Geek Squad employees were called "agents" and wore uniforms consisting of black pants or skirts, black shoes, white shirts, black clip-on ties, a badge, and a black jacket with a Geek Squad logo to create a "humble" attitude that was not threatening to customers. Agents drove black-and-white Volkswagen Beetles, or Geekmobiles, with a logo on the door, and charged fixed prices for services, regardless of how much time was required to provide the service. The "house call" services ranged from installing networks, to debugging a computer, to setting up an entertainment system, and cost from $100 to $300. "We're like 'Dragnet'; we show up at people's homes and help," Stephens says. "We're also like *Ghostbusters* and there's a pseudogovernment feel to it like *Men in Black*."

In 2002, Geek Squad was purchased by leading consumer electronics retailer Best Buy for about $3 million. Best Buy had observed very high return rates for most of its complex products. Shoppers would be excited about new products, purchase them and take them home, get frustrated trying to make them actually work, and then return them to the store demanding a refund. In fact, Best Buy research revealed that consumers were beginning to see service as a critical element of the purchase. The partnership was an excellent match. Best Buy consumers welcomed the help. Stephens became Geek Squad's chief inspector and a Best Buy vice president and began putting a Geek Squad "precinct" in every Best Buy store, creating some stand-alone Geek Squad Stores, and providing 24-hour telephone support. There are now more than 20,000 agents in the United States, Canada, the United Kingdom, and China, and return rates have declined by 25 to 35 percent. Geek Squad service plans are also being sold on eBay and in some Target stores. The Geek Squad website proclaims that the company is "Serving the Public, Policing Technology and Protecting the World."

THE CHANGING ENVIRONMENT

Many changes in the environment occurred to create the need for Geek Squad's services. Future changes are also likely to change the way Geek Squad operates. An environmental scan helps illustrate the changes.

The most obvious changes may be related to technology. Wireless broadband technology, high-definition televisions, products with Internet interfaces, and a general trend toward computers, smartphones, entertainment systems, and even appliances being interconnected are just a few examples of new products and applications for consumers to learn about. There are also technology-related problems such as viruses, spyware, lost data, and "crashed" or inoperable computers. New technologies have also created a demand for new types of maintenance such as password management, operating system updates, disk cleanup, and "defragging."

Another environmental change that contributes to the popularity of Geek Squad is the change in social factors such as demographics and culture. In the past many electronics manufacturers and retailers focused primarily on men. Women, however, are becoming increasingly interested in personal computing and home entertainment and, according to the Consumer Electronics Association, are likely to outspend men in the near future. Best Buy's consumer research indicates that women expect personal service during the purchase as well as during the installation after the purchase—exactly the service Geek Squad is designed to provide. Our culture is also embracing the Geek Squad concept. For example, in the recently discontinued television series *Chuck* (2007–2012), one of the characters worked for the "Nerd Herd" at "Buy More" and drove a car like a Geekmobile on service calls!

Competition, economics, and the regulatory environment have also had a big influence on Geek Squad. As discount stores such as Walmart and PC makers such as Dell began to compete with Best Buy, new services such as in-home installation were needed to create value for customers. Now, just as change in competition created an opportunity for Geek Squad, it is also leading to another level of competition as Staples has introduced EasyTech services and Office Depot has introduced Tech Depot services. The economic situation for electronics continues to improve as prices decline and demand increases. Consumers purchased 2 million 3D TVs in 2010, and sales of all consumer electronics exceeded $180 billion. Finally, the regulatory environment continues to change with respect to the electronic transfer of copyrighted materials such as music and movies and software. Geek Squad must monitor the changes to ensure that its services comply with relevant laws.

THE FUTURE FOR GEEK SQUAD

The combination of many positive environmental factors helps explain the extraordinary success of Geek Squad. Today, it repairs more than 3,000 PCs a day and generates more than $2 billion in revenue. Because Geek Squad services have a high profit margin they contribute to the overall performance of Best Buy, and they help generate traffic in the store and create store loyalty. To continue to grow, however, Geek Squad will need to continue to scan the environment and try new approaches to creating customer value.

One possible new approach is to create new partnerships. Geek Squad and Ford, for example, have developed a partnership to help consumers install in-car communication systems. In the future, Best Buy will offer 240-volt home charging stations for Ford's electric vehicle, the Focus. Geek Squad will offer electrical audits and residential installations for the car owners. Geek Squad is also using new technology to improve. Agents now use a smartphone to access updated schedules, log in their hours, and run diagnostics tests on clients' equipment. Best Buy is also testing a "Solutions Central" desk, similar to the Genius Bar concept in Apple stores, and staffing it with Geek Squad agents. Finally, to attract the best possible employees, Geek Squad and Best Buy are trying a "results-only work environment" that has no fixed schedules and no mandatory meetings. By encouraging employees to make their own work–life decisions, the Geek Squad hopes to keep morale and productivity high.

Other changes and opportunities are certain to appear soon. However, despite the success of the Geek Squad and the potential for additional growth, Robert Stephens is modest and claims, "Geeks may inherit the Earth, but they have no desire to rule it!"

Questions

1 What are the key environmental forces that created an opportunity for Robert Stephens to start the Geek Squad?
2 What changes in the purchasing patterns of (*a*) all consumers and (*b*) women made the acquisition of Geek Squad particularly important for Best Buy?
3 Based on the case information and what you know about consumer electronics, conduct an environmental scan for Geek Squad to identify key trends. For each of the five environmental forces (social, economic, technological, competitive, and regulatory), identify trends likely to influence Geek Squad in the near future.
4 What promotional activities would you recommend to encourage consumers who currently use independent installers to switch to Geek Squad?

4 Ethical and Social Responsibility in Marketing

Learning Objectives

After reading this chapter you should be able to:

LO 4-1 Explain the differences between legal and ethical behavior in marketing.

LO 4-2 Identify factors that influence ethical and unethical marketing decisions.

LO 4-3 Describe the different concepts of social responsibility.

LO 4-4 Recognize unethical and socially irresponsible consumer behavior.

Anheuser-Busch: Becoming the Best Beer Company in a Better World

Why would a company spend more than $980 million since 1982 trying to persuade people to use its products responsibly and tens of millions of dollars more to protect and preserve the environment? Ask Anheuser-Busch, the leading American brewer.

Alcohol Responsibility

Anheuser-Busch has been an advocate for responsible drinking for more than three decades. The company began an aggressive campaign to fight alcohol misuse and underage drinking with its landmark "Know When to Say When" campaign in 1982. In 1989, a Consumer Awareness and Education department was established within the company. This department, now called Corporate Social Responsibility (CSR), is charged with developing and implementing programs, advertising, and partnerships that promote responsible drinking; helping prevent drunk driving; and helping curb underage drinking before it starts. For example, millions of copies of the company's *Family Talk About Drinking* guidebook have been distributed free to parents and educators. The *Family Talk About Drinking* program helps parents and other adults talk with children about underage drinking; in 2011, it was extended to social media to include a dedicated Facebook Page (see www.facebook.com/ABFamilyTalk).

In 2004, the brewer began a new chapter in its awareness and education efforts with the launch of its "Responsibility Matters" campaign. This effort emphasized and implemented effective education and awareness programs that promoted responsibility and responsible behaviors. Anheuser-Busch believes these efforts have helped contribute—at least in part—to declines in drunk-driving fatalities, underage drinking, and other forms of alcohol misuse since 1982.

In 2012, Anheuser-Busch launched NationofResponsibleDrinkers.com, an online responsible drinking campaign with social media components to engage adult drinkers and raise awareness. The website asks adults to pledge their commitment to drink responsibly and then share it through Facebook to encourage friends to do the same. The pledge is threefold:

- Respect the legal drinking age.
- Enjoy responsibly and know when to say when.
- Be or use a designated driver.

Each pledge is then populated on an interactive map, showing those who have taken the pledge in their communities.

In 2013, Budweiser launched its first-ever responsible drinking blimp. The airship, which carried the "Designate a Driver" message, embarked on a 17-week tour across much of the country. The blimp's flight plan coincided with major festivals, outdoor celebrations, and sporting events in tour cities.

QR 4-1
Responsibility Matters Ad

Consumers 21 and older could follow the Budweiser Designate a Driver blimp on Twitter with @budblimp throughout the tour and tweet photos of the vessel in their city using hashtags. Adults could also log on to www.budblimp.com to pledge to drink responsibly and always designate a driver and then share their pledge through Facebook to encourage friends to do the same.

Anheuser-Busch also implements programs to help prevent underage drinking by providing retailers with tools to properly check IDs and help prevent sales to minors. The company also helps parents start and continue conversations about alcohol with their children; supports law enforcement in upholding the law; and, through a variety of community speakers, assists schools in building self-esteem among teens.

Community Support

Charitable outreach is at the core of Anheuser-Busch's business philosophy, and employees are an integral part of the corporate responsibility mission. Actively involving its employees in such initiatives increases public awareness, engages employees, and provides a direct contribution to the community. For example, Anheuser-Busch employees volunteer with national charitable organizations, such as Habitat for Humanity and River Network. In 2012, Anheuser-Busch employees and their families volunteered nearly 120,000 hours in support of a variety of community organizations.

Also in 2012, Anheuser-Busch donated more than 1.4 million cans of emergency drinking water in 27 communities in 11 U.S. states to support disaster relief related to tornadoes, storms, wildfires, and floods affecting 48 communities. Between 1988 and 2012, Anheuser-Busch packaged and donated more than 72 million cans of emergency drinking water to communities and relief organizations in response to natural disasters.

Environmental Preservation

Anheuser-Busch is committed to brewing the highest quality beers, improving its environmental performance, and making a positive impact in communities across the country. The company focuses environmental efforts both inside and outside its breweries on the key issues of water, energy, and recycling.

Water is a key ingredient in beer, and Anheuser-Busch strives to protect this natural resource. In 2013, the company reported that its breweries had reduced water use by 40 percent over the prior five years and had a 99.6 percent recycling rate. In fact, 130 of its operations worldwide are zero-waste. Anheuser-Busch has been a leading recycler of aluminum cans for more than 30 years, recycling nearly 15 billion cans annually. Other items, such as grain, beechwood chips, plastic, cardboard, glass, and metals also are being reduced, reused, and recycled by the company. In fact, from 2009 to 2012, Anheuser-Busch reduced its packaging materials by nearly 73,000 tons.

Nearly one out of every six beers made by Anheuser-Busch is brewed with renewable fuels, including biogas and landfill gas. The company is one of the world's largest operators of the Bio-Energy Recovery System (BERS), a method of turning the nutrients in wastewater from the brewing process into renewable biogas.

In 2011, the Fairfield, California, brewery added a wind turbine, which can provide up to 20 percent of the necessary electricity for brewery operations. The addition of the turbine represents the third source of renewable energy for the Fairfield facility, which also utilizes BERS and solar panels. When combined with the solar array at its Newark, New Jersey, brewery, this makes Anheuser-Busch one of the largest users of solar power in the U.S. brewing industry.

Anheuser-Busch clearly acts on what it views as an ethical obligation to its customers and the general public with its alcohol awareness and education programs and community support. At the same time, the company's efforts to protect the natural environment and improve societal well-being reflect its broader social responsibility.[1]

NATURE AND SIGNIFICANCE OF MARKETING ETHICS

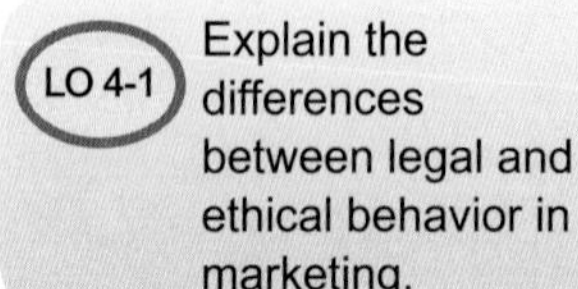

LO 4-1
Explain the differences between legal and ethical behavior in marketing.

Ethics are the moral principles and values that govern the actions and decisions of an individual or group.[2] They serve as guidelines on how to act rightly and justly when faced with moral dilemmas.

An Ethical/Legal Framework for Marketing

A good starting point for understanding the nature and significance of ethics is the distinction between the legality and the ethicality of marketing decisions. Figure 4–1 helps visualize the relationship between laws and ethics.[3] Whereas ethics deal with personal moral principles and values, **laws** are society's values and standards that are

FIGURE 4–1
Four ways to classify marketing decisions according to ethical and legal relationships.

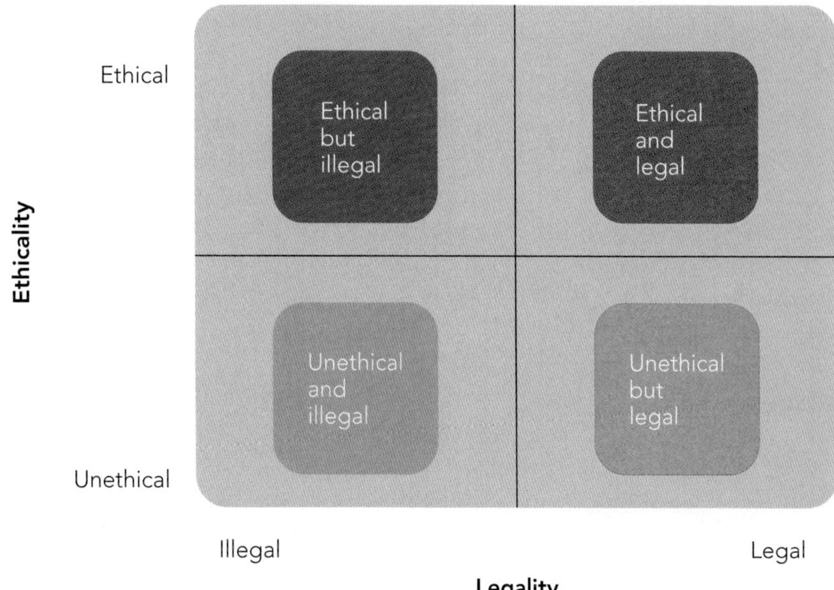

enforceable in the courts. This distinction can sometimes lead to the rationalization that if a behavior is within reasonable ethical and legal limits, then it is not really illegal or unethical. When a recent survey asked the question, "Is it OK to get around the law if you don't actually break it?" about 61 percent of businesspeople who took part responded "yes."[4] How would you answer this question?

Judgment plays a large role in numerous situations in defining ethical and legal boundaries. Consider the following situations. After reading each, assign it to the cell in Figure 4–1 that you think best fits the situation along the ethical–legal continuum.[5]

1. More than 70 percent of the physicians in the Maricopa County (Arizona) Medical Society agreed to establish a maximum fee schedule for health services to curb rising medical costs. All physicians were required to adhere to this schedule as a condition for membership in the society. The U.S. Supreme Court ruled that this agreement to set prices violated the Sherman Act and represented price fixing, which is illegal. Was the society's action ethical?
2. A company in California sells a computer program to auto dealers showing that car buyers should finance their purchase rather than pay cash. The program omits the effect of income taxes and misstates the interest earned on savings over the loan period. The finance option always provides a net benefit over the cash option. Company employees agree that the program does mislead buyers, but they say the company will "provide what [car dealers] want as long as it is not against the law." Is this practice ethical?
3. China is the world's largest tobacco-producing country and has 300 million smokers. Approximately 700,000 Chinese die annually from smoking-related illnesses. This figure is expected to rise to more than 2 million by 2025. China legally restricts tobacco imports. U.S. trade negotiators advocate free trade, thus allowing U.S. tobacco companies to market their products in China. Is the Chinese trade position ethical?
4. A group of college students recorded movies at a local theater and then uploaded the movies to the Internet. Federal statutes state that the unauthorized reproduction, distribution, or exhibition of copyrighted motion pictures is illegal. The students then directed friends and family to a peer-to-peer Internet network that allowed them to download the movies for free, which they did. Is the students' behavior ethical? Is the behavior of their friends and family ethical?

Did these situations fit neatly into Figure 4–1 as clearly ethical and legal or unethical and illegal? Probably not. As you read further in this chapter, you will be asked to consider other ethical dilemmas.

Critical Perceptions of Ethical Behavior

There has been a public outcry about the ethical practices of businesspeople.[6] Public opinion surveys show that 58 percent of U.S. adults rate the ethical standards of business executives as only "fair" or "poor"; 76 percent say the lack of ethics in businesspeople contributes to tumbling societal moral standards; and advertising practitioners and car salespeople are thought to be among the least ethical occupations. Surveys of corporate employees generally confirm this public perception. When asked if they are aware of ethical misconduct in their companies, 45 percent say "yes."

There are at least four possible reasons the state of perceived ethical business conduct is at its present level. First, there is increased pressure on businesspeople to make decisions in a society characterized by diverse value systems. Second, there is a growing tendency for business decisions to be judged publicly by groups with different values and interests. Third, the public's expectations of ethical business behavior have increased. Finally, and most disturbing, ethical business conduct may have declined.

learning review

4-1. What are ethics?

4-2. What are four possible reasons for the present state of ethical conduct in the United States?

FACTORS THAT AFFECT ETHICAL MARKETING BEHAVIOR

LO 4-2 Identify factors that influence ethical and unethical marketing decisions.

Researchers have identified numerous factors that influence ethical marketing behavior.[7] Figure 4–2 presents a framework that shows these factors and their relationships.

Societal Culture and Norms

As described in Chapter 3, *culture* refers to the set of values, ideas, and attitudes that are learned and shared among the members of a group. Culture also serves as a socializing force that dictates what is morally right and just. This means that moral standards are relative to particular societies.[8] These standards often reflect the laws and regulations that affect social and economic behavior, which can create ethical dilemmas. Companies that compete in the global marketplace recognize this fact. Consider UPS, the world's largest package delivery company operating in more than 200 countries and territories worldwide.[9] According to the company's global compliance and ethics coordinator, "Although languages and cultures around the world may be different, we do not change

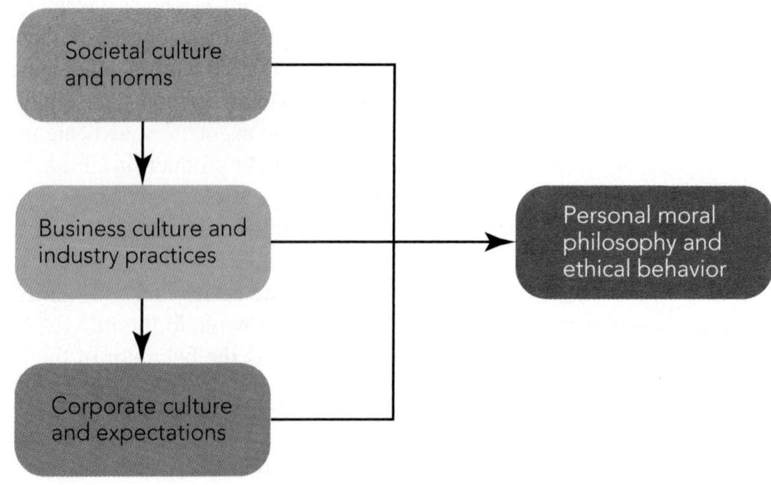

FIGURE 4–2 A framework for understanding ethical behavior. Each of these influences has an effect on ethical marketing behavior, as described in the text.

our ethical standards at UPS. Our ethics program is global in nature." Not surprisingly, UPS is consistently ranked among the world's most ethical companies.

Societal values and attitudes also affect ethical and legal relationships among individuals, groups, and business institutions and organizations. Consider the copying of another's copyright, trademark, or patent. These are viewed as intellectual property. Unauthorized use, reproduction, or distribution of intellectual property is illegal in the United States and most countries and can result in fines and prison terms for perpetrators. The owners of intellectual property also lose. For example, annual worldwide lost sales from the theft of intellectual property amount to $12.5 billion in the music industry, $20.5 billion in the movie industry, and $63 billion in the software industry.[10] Lost sales, in turn, result in lost jobs, royalties, wages, and tax revenue.

But what about downloading copyrighted music, movies, and software over the Internet or from peer-to-peer file-sharing programs without paying the owner of this property? Is this an ethical or unethical act? It depends on who you ask. Surveys of the U.S. public indicate that the majority consider these acts unethical. However, only a third of U.S. college students say these acts are unethical.[11]

Business Culture and Industry Practices

Societal culture provides a foundation for understanding moral behavior in business activities. *Business cultures* "comprise the effective rules of the game, the boundaries between competitive and unethical behavior, [and] the codes of conduct in business dealings."[12] Consumers have witnessed instances where business cultures in the financial (insider trading), insurance (deceptive sales practices), and defense (bribery) industries went awry. Business culture affects ethical conduct both in the exchange relationship between sellers and buyers and in the competitive behavior among sellers.

Ethics of Exchange The exchange process is central to the marketing concept. Ethical exchanges between sellers and buyers should result in both parties being better off after a transaction.

Before the 1960s, the legal concept of **caveat emptor**—let the buyer beware—was pervasive in the American business culture. In 1962, President John F. Kennedy outlined a **Consumer Bill of Rights** that codified the ethics of exchange between buyers and sellers. These were the right (1) to safety, (2) to be informed, (3) to choose, and (4) to be heard. Consumers expect and often demand that these rights be protected, as have American businesses.

The *right to safety* manifests itself in industry and federal safety standards for most products sold in the United States. In fact, the U.S. Consumer Product Safety Commission routinely monitors the safety of 15,000 consumer products. However, even the most vigilant efforts to ensure safe products cannot foresee every possibility. Personal claims and property damage from consumer product safety incidents cost companies more than $700 billion annually. Consider the case of batteries used in laptop and notebook computers. Dell Inc. learned that the lithium-ion batteries in its notebook computers, made by Sony Energy Devices Corporation of Japan, posed a fire hazard to consumers. The company recalled 2.7 million batteries and gave consumers a replacement before any personal injuries resulted.[13]

The Federal Trade Commission plays an active role in educating consumers and businesses about the importance of personal information privacy on the Internet. FTC initiatives, including recent proposals concerning children's online privacy, are detailed on its website.

Federal Trade Commission
www.ftc.gov

The *right to be informed* means that marketers have an obligation to give consumers complete and accurate information about products and services. This right also applies to the solicitation of personal information over the Internet and its subsequent use by marketers.[14] An FTC survey of websites indicated that 92 percent collect personal information such as consumer e-mail addresses, telephone numbers, shopping habits, and financial data.

Making Responsible Decisions

ethics

Corporate Conscience in the Cola War

Suppose you are a senior executive at Pepsi-Cola and a Coca-Cola employee offers to sell you the marketing plan and sample for a new Coke product at a modest price. Would you buy it knowing Pepsi-Cola could gain a significant competitive edge in the cola war?

When this question was posed in an online survey of marketing and advertising executives, 67 percent said they would buy the plan and product sample if there were no repercussions. What did Pepsi-Cola do when this offer actually occurred? The company immediately contacted Coca-Cola, which contacted the FBI. An undercover FBI agent paid the employee $30,000 in cash stuffed in a Girl Scout cookie box as a down payment and later arrested the employee and accomplices. When asked about the incident, a Pepsi-Cola spokesperson said: "We only did what any responsible company would do. Competition must be tough, but must always be fair and legal."

Why did the 33 percent of respondents in the online survey say they would decline the offer? Most said they would prefer competing ethically so they could sleep at night. According to a senior advertising agency executive who would decline the offer: "Repercussions go beyond potential espionage charges. As long as we have a conscience, there are repercussions."

So what happened to the Coca-Cola employee and her accomplices? She was sentenced to eight years in prison and ordered to pay $40,000 in restitution. Her accomplices were each sentenced to five years in prison.

Yet, only two-thirds of websites inform consumers of what is done with this information once obtained. The FTC wants more than posted privacy notices that merely inform consumers of a company's data-use policy, which critics say are often vague, confusing, or too legalistic to be understood. This view is shared by two-thirds of consumers who worry about protecting their personal information online. The consumer right to be informed has spawned much federal legislation, such as the *Children's Online Privacy Protection Act* (1998) and self-regulation initiatives restricting disclosure of personal information.

Relating to the *right to choose*, today many supermarket chains demand "slotting allowances" from manufacturers, in the form of cash or free goods, to stock new products.[15] This practice could limit the number of new products available to consumers and interfere with their right to choose. One critic of this practice remarked, "If we had had slotting allowances a few years ago, we might not have had granola, herbal tea, or yogurt."

Finally, the *right to be heard* means that consumers should have access to public-policy makers regarding complaints about products and services. This right is illustrated in limitations put on telemarketing practices. The FTC established the Do Not Call Registry in 2003 for consumers who do not want to receive unsolicited telemarketing calls. Today, over 218 million U.S. telephone numbers are listed in the registry, which is managed by the FTC. A telemarketer can be fined up to $16,000 for each call made to a telephone number posted on the registry.

Ethics of Competition Business culture also affects ethical behavior in competition. Two kinds of unethical behavior are most common: (1) economic espionage and (2) bribery.

Economic espionage is the clandestine collection of trade secrets or proprietary information about a company's competitors. This practice is illegal and unethical and carries serious criminal penalties for the offending individual or business. Espionage

Marketing inSite

The Bribe Payers Index

Bribery as a means to win and retain business varies widely by country. Transparency International periodically polls employees of multinational firms and institutions and political analysts and ranks countries on the basis of their perceived level of bribery to win or retain business. To obtain the most recent ranking, visit the Transparency International website at www.transparency.org and click Bribe Payers Index.

Scroll the Bribe Payers Index to see where the United States stands in the worldwide rankings. How does the United States compare in relation to its neighbors, Canada and Mexico? Any surprises? Which country listed in the index has the highest ranking and which has the lowest ranking?

activities include illegal trespassing, theft, fraud, misrepresentation, wiretapping, the search of a competitor's trash, and violations of written and implicit employment agreements with noncompete clauses. More than half of the largest firms in the United States have uncovered espionage in some form, costing them $300 billion annually in lost sales.[16]

Economic espionage is most prevalent in high-technology industries, such as electronics, specialty chemicals, industrial equipment, aerospace, and pharmaceuticals, where technical know-how and trade secrets separate industry leaders from followers. But espionage can occur anywhere—even in the soft drink industry! Read the Making Responsible Decisions box to learn how Pepsi-Cola responded to an offer to obtain confidential information about its archrival's marketing plans.[17]

The second form of unethical competitive behavior is giving and receiving bribes and kickbacks. Bribes and kickbacks are often disguised as gifts, consultant fees, and favors. This practice is more common in business-to-business and government marketing than in consumer marketing.

In general, bribery is most evident in industries experiencing intense competition and in countries in the earlier stages of economic development. According to a United Nations study, 15 percent of all companies in industrialized countries have to pay bribes to win or retain business. In Asia, this figure is 40 percent. In Eastern Europe, 60 percent of all companies must pay bribes to do business. A recent poll of senior executives engaged in global marketing revealed that Russia was the most likely country to engage in bribery to win or retain business. The Netherlands, Switzerland, and Belgium were the least likely.[18] Bribery on a worldwide scale is monitored by Transparency International. Visit its website described in the Marketing inSite box to view the most recent country rankings on its Bribe Payers Index.

The prevalence of economic espionage and bribery in international marketing has prompted laws to curb these practices. Two significant laws, the *Economic Espionage Act* (1996) and the *Foreign Corrupt Practices Act* (1977), address these practices in the United States. Both are detailed in Chapter 7.

Corporate Culture and Expectations

A third influence on ethical practices is corporate culture. *Corporate culture* is the set of values, ideas, and attitudes that is learned and shared among the members of an organization. The culture of a company demonstrates itself in the dress ("We don't wear ties"), sayings ("The IBM Way"), and manner of work (team efforts) of employees. Culture is also apparent in the expectations for ethical behavior present in formal codes of ethics and the ethical actions of top management and co-workers.

AMERICAN MARKETING ASSOCIATION STATEMENT OF ETHICS

Preamble

The American Marketing Association commits itself to promoting the highest standard of professional ethical norms and values for its members. Norms are established standards of conduct that are expected and maintained by society and/or professional organizations. Values represent the collective conception of what people find desirable, important, and morally proper. Values serve as the criteria for evaluating the actions of others. Marketing practitioners must recognize that they not only serve their enterprises but also act as stewards of society in creating, facilitating, and executing the efficient and effective transactions that are part of the greater economy. In this role, marketers should embrace the highest ethical *norms* of practicing professionals and the ethical *values* implied by their responsibility toward stakeholders (e.g., customers, employees, investors, channel members, regulators, and the host community).

General Norms

1. Marketers must do no harm. This means doing work for which they are appropriately trained or experienced so that they can actively add value to their organizations and customers. It also means adhering to all applicable laws and regulations and embodying high ethical standards in the choices they make.
2. Marketers must foster trust in the marketing system. This means that products are appropriate for their intended and promoted uses. It requires that marketing communications about goods and services are not intentionally deceptive or misleading. It suggests building relationships that provide for the equitable adjustment and/or redress of customer grievances. It implies striving for good faith and fair dealing so as to contribute toward the efficacy of the exchange process.
3. Marketers must embrace, communicate, and practice the fundamental ethical values that will improve consumer confidence in the integrity of the marketing exchange system. These basic *values* are intentionally aspirational and include honesty, responsibility, fairness, respect, openness, and citizenship.

Ethical Values

Honesty—to be truthful and forthright in our dealings with customers and stakeholders.

- We will tell the truth in all situations and at all times.
- We will offer products of value that do what we claim in our communications.
- We will stand behind our products if they fail to deliver their claimed benefits.
- We will honor our explicit and implicit commitments and promises.

Responsibility—to accept the consequences of our marketing decisions and strategies.

- We will make strenuous efforts to serve the needs of our customers.
- We will avoid using coercion with all stakeholders.
- We will acknowledge the social obligations to stakeholders that come with increased marketing and economic power.

FIGURE 4–3
American Marketing Association Statement of Ethics.

American Marketing Association
www.marketingpower.com

Codes of Ethics A **code of ethics** is a formal statement of ethical principles and rules of conduct. It is estimated that 86 percent of U.S. companies have some sort of ethics code and one of every four large companies has corporate ethics officers. Ethics codes typically address contributions to government officials and political parties, customer and supplier relations, conflicts of interest, and accurate recordkeeping.

At United Technologies, for example, 400 business practices officers distribute the company's ethics code, translated into 24 languages, to about 200,000 employees who work for this defense and engineering giant in some 180 countries. In 2010, United Technologies dismissed 330 employees for violations related to its code of ethics.[19]

However, an ethics code is rarely enough to ensure ethical behavior. Coca-Cola has an ethics code and emphasizes that its employees be ethical in their behavior. But that did not stop some Coca-Cola employees from rigging the results of a test market for a frozen soft drink to win Burger King's business. Coca-Cola subsequently agreed to pay Burger King and its operators more than $20 million to settle the matter.[20]

Lack of specificity is a major reason for the violation of ethics codes. Employees must often judge whether a specific behavior is unethical. The American Marketing Association has addressed this issue by providing a detailed statement of ethics, which all members agree to follow. This statement is shown in Figure 4–3.

FIGURE 4–3
(Continued)

- We will recognize our special commitments to economically vulnerable segments of the market such as children, the elderly, and others who may be substantially disadvantaged.

Fairness—to try to balance justly the needs of the buyer with the interests of the seller.

- We will represent our products in a clear way in selling, advertising, and other forms of communication; this includes the avoidance of false, misleading, and deceptive promotion.
- We will reject manipulations and sales tactics that harm customer trust.
- We will not engage in price fixing, predatory pricing, price gouging, or "bait-and-switch" tactics.
- We will not knowingly participate in material conflicts of interest.

Respect—to acknowledge the basic human dignity of all stakeholders.

- We will value individual differences even as we avoid stereotyping customers or depicting demographic groups (e.g., gender, race, sexual orientation) in a negative or dehumanizing way in our promotions.
- We will listen to the needs of our customers and make all reasonable efforts to monitor and improve their satisfaction on an ongoing basis.
- We will make a special effort to understand suppliers, intermediaries, and distributors from other cultures.
- We will appropriately acknowledge the contributions of others, such as consultants, employees, and co-workers, to our marketing endeavors.

Openness—to create transparency in our marketing operations.

- We will strive to communicate clearly with all our constituencies.
- We will accept constructive criticism from our customers and other stakeholders.
- We will explain significant product or service risks, component substitutions, or other foreseeable eventualities that could affect customers or their perception of the purchase decision.
- We will fully disclose list prices and terms of financing as well as available price deals and adjustments.

Citizenship—to fulfill the economic, legal, philanthropic and societal responsibilities that serve stakeholders in a strategic manner.

- We will strive to protect the natural environment in the execution of marketing campaigns.
- We will give back to the community through volunteerism and charitable donations.
- We will work to contribute to the overall betterment of marketing and its reputation.
- We will encourage supply chain members to ensure that trade is fair for all participants, including producers in developing countries.

Implementation

Finally, we recognize that every industry sector and marketing subdiscipline (e.g., marketing research, e-commerce, direct selling, direct marketing, advertising) has its own specific ethical issues that require policies and commentary. An array of such codes can be accessed through links on the AMA website. We encourage all such groups to develop and/or refine their industry and discipline-specific codes of ethics to supplement these general norms and values.

Ethical Behavior of Top Management and Co-Workers A second reason for violating ethics codes rests in the perceived behavior of top management and co-workers.[21] Observing peers and top management and gauging responses to unethical behavior play an important role in individual actions. A study of business executives reported that 45 percent had witnessed ethically troubling behavior. About 22 percent of those who reported unethical behavior were penalized, through either outright punishment or a diminished status in the company.[22] Clearly, ethical dilemmas can bring personal and professional conflict. For this reason, states have enacted laws designed to protect **whistle-blowers**, employees who report unethical or illegal actions of their employers.

Your Personal Moral Philosophy and Ethical Behavior

Ultimately, ethical choices are based on the personal moral philosophy of the decision maker. Moral philosophy is learned through the process of socialization with friends and family and by formal education. It is also influenced by the societal, business, and corporate culture in which a person finds him- or herself. Two prominent personal moral philosophies have direct bearing on marketing practice: (1) moral idealism and (2) utilitarianism.

What does 3M's Scotchgard have to do with ethics, social responsibility, and a $200 million loss in annual sales? Read the text to find out.

Moral Idealism **Moral idealism** is a personal moral philosophy that considers certain individual rights or duties as universal, regardless of the outcome. This philosophy exists in the Consumer Bill of Rights and is favored by moral philosophers and consumer interest groups. For example, the right to know applies to probable defects in an automobile that relate to safety.

This philosophy also applies to ethical duties. A fundamental ethical duty is to do no harm. Adherence to this duty prompted the recent decision by 3M executives to phase out production of a chemical 3M had manufactured for nearly 40 years. The substance, used in far-ranging products from pet food bags, candy wrappers, carpeting, and 3M's popular Scotchgard fabric protector, had no known harmful health or environmental effect. However, the company discovered that the chemical appeared in minuscule amounts in humans and animals around the world and accumulated in tissue. Believing that the substance could be possibly harmful in large doses, 3M voluntarily stopped its production, resulting in a $200 million loss in annual sales.[23]

Utilitarianism An alternative perspective on moral philosophy is **utilitarianism**, which is a personal moral philosophy that focuses on "the greatest good for the greatest number" by assessing the costs and benefits of the consequences of ethical behavior. If the benefits exceed the costs, then the behavior is ethical. If not, then the behavior is unethical. This philosophy underlies the economic tenets of capitalism and, not surprisingly, is embraced by many business executives and students.[24]

Utilitarian reasoning was apparent in Nestlé Food Corporation's marketing of Good Start infant formula, sold by Nestlé's Carnation Company. The formula, promoted as hypoallergenic, was designed to prevent or reduce colic caused by an infant's allergic reaction to cow's milk, a condition suffered by 2 percent of babies. However, some severely milk-allergic infants experienced serious side effects after using Good Start, including convulsive vomiting. Physicians and parents charged that the hypoallergenic claim was misleading, and the Food and Drug Administration investigated the matter.

A Nestlé vice president defended the claim and product, saying, "I don't understand why our product should work in 100 percent of cases. If we wanted to say it was foolproof, we would have called it allergy-free. We call it hypo-, or less, allergenic."[25] Nestlé officials seemingly believed that most allergic infants would benefit from Good Start—"the greatest good for the greatest number." But, other views prevailed. The claim was dropped from the product label.

An appreciation for the nature of ethics, coupled with a basic understanding of why unethical behavior arises, alerts a person to when and how ethical issues arise in marketing decisions. Ultimately, ethical behavior rests with the individual, but the consequences affect many.

learning review

4-3. What rights are included in the Consumer Bill of Rights?

4-4. Economic espionage includes what kinds of activities?

4-5. What is meant by moral idealism?

UNDERSTANDING SOCIAL RESPONSIBILITY IN MARKETING

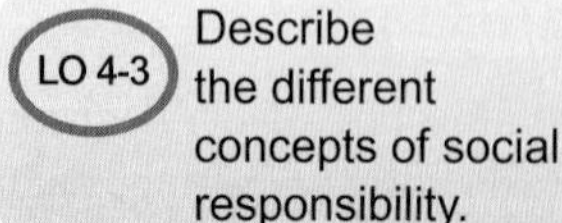
LO 4-3 Describe the different concepts of social responsibility.

As we saw in Chapter 1, the societal marketing concept stresses marketing's social responsibility by not only satisfying the needs of consumers but also providing for society's welfare. **Social responsibility** means that organizations are part of a larger society and are accountable to that society for their actions. Like ethics, agreement on the nature and scope of social responsibility is often difficult to come by, given the diversity of values present in different societal, business, and corporate cultures.

Three Concepts of Social Responsibility

Figure 4–4 shows three concepts of social responsibility: (1) profit responsibility, (2) stakeholder responsibility, and (3) societal responsibility.

Profit Responsibility *Profit responsibility* holds that companies have a simple duty: to maximize profits for their owners or stockholders. This view is expressed by Nobel Laureate Milton Friedman, who said, "There is one and only one social responsibility of business—to use its resources and engage in activities designed to increase its profits so long as it stays within the rules of the game, which is to say, engages in open and free competition without deception or fraud."[26]

Genzyme, the maker of Cerezyme, a drug that treats a genetic illness called Gaucher's disease that affects 10,000 people worldwide, has been criticized for apparently adopting this view in its pricing practices. Genzyme charges up to $200,000 for a year's worth of Cerezyme. A Genzyme spokesperson responded saying the company spends about $150 million annually to manufacture Cerezyme and freely gives the drug to patients without insurance. Also, the company invested considerable dollars in research over several years to develop Cerezyme, and the drug's profits are reinvested in ongoing R&D programs.[27]

Stakeholder Responsibility Criticism of the profit view has led to a broader concept of social responsibility. *Stakeholder responsibility* focuses on the obligations an organization has to those who can affect achievement of its objectives. These constituencies include consumers, employees, suppliers, and distributors. Source Perrier S.A., the supplier of Perrier bottled water, exercised this responsibility when it recalled 160 million bottles of water in 120 countries after traces of a toxic chemical were found in 13 bottles. The recall cost the company $35 million, as well as the profit from $40 million in lost sales. Even though the chemical level was not harmful to humans, Source Perrier's president believed he acted in the best interests of the firm's consumers, distributors, and employees by removing "the least doubt, as minimal as it might be, to weigh on the image of the quality and purity of our product"—which it did.[28]

FIGURE 4–4
Three concepts of social responsibility. Each concept of social responsibility relates to particular constituencies. There is often conflict in satisfying all three constituencies at the same time.

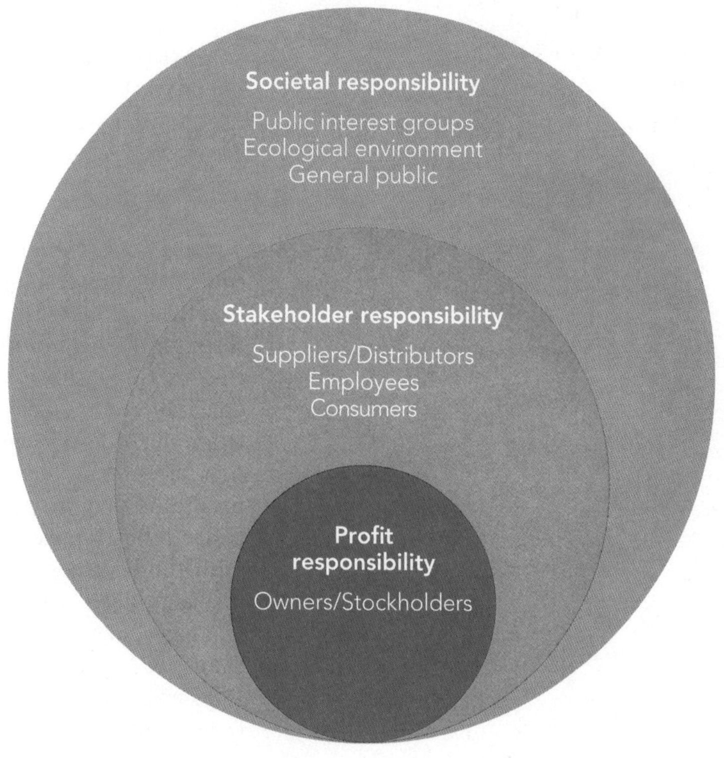

Failure to consider a company's broader constituencies can have negative consequences. For example, Toyota Motor Corporation executives were widely criticized for how they responded to complaints about the safety of selected Toyota brands. These cars had been linked to sticky gas pedals, which can lead to sudden acceleration problems. The company recalled over 9 million cars worldwide under pressure from the National Highway Traffic Safety Administration. After the recall, Toyota sales fell, which affected Toyota employees, suppliers, shareholders, and distributors.[29]

Societal Responsibility An even broader concept of social responsibility has emerged in recent years. *Societal responsibility* refers to obligations that organizations have (1) to the preservation of the ecological environment and (2) to the general public. Today, emphasis is placed on the **triple-bottom line**—recognition of the need for organizations to improve the state of people, the planet, and profit simultaneously if they are to achieve sustainable, long-term growth.[30] Growing interest in green marketing, cause marketing, social audits, and sustainable development reflects this recognition.

Green marketing—marketing efforts to produce, promote, and reclaim environmentally sensitive products—takes many forms.[31] At 3M, product development opportunities emanate both from consumer research and its "Pollution Prevention Pays" (3P) program. This program solicits employee suggestions on how to reduce pollution and recycle materials. Since 1975, this program has generated over 9,000 3P projects that have eliminated more than 3.5 billion pounds of air, water, and solid-waste pollutants from the environment. Levi Strauss & Co. uses 8 recycled plastic bottles in each pair of Waste<Less jeans, which are composed of at least 20 percent recycled plastic. This practice has eliminated millions of discarded plastic bottles from landfills and reduced the water consumed in the manufacturing process.

Walmart has instituted buying practices that encourage its suppliers to use containers and packaging made from corn, not oil-based, resins. The company expects this initiative will save 800,000 barrels of oil annually. These voluntary responses to environmental issues have been implemented with little or no additional cost to consumers and have resulted in cost savings to companies.

A cause marketing pioneer for more than three decades, Procter & Gamble focuses on supporting disadvantaged youth and disaster relief. A successful brand campaign includes the Pampers 1 Pack = 1 Vaccine initiative, protecting 100 million women and their babies against maternal and neonatal tetanus since 2006.

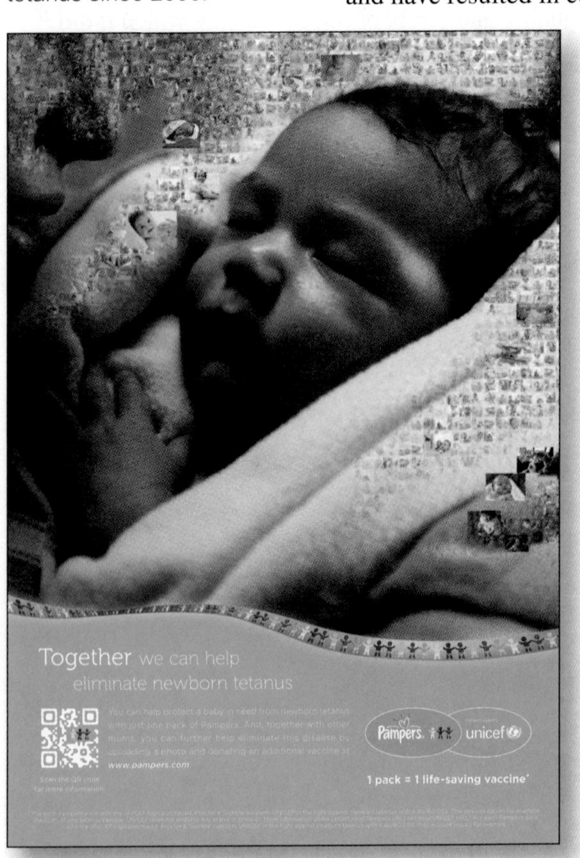

A global undertaking to further green marketing efforts is the *ISO 14000* initiative developed by the International Standards Organization (ISO) in Geneva, Switzerland. *ISO 14000* consists of worldwide standards for environmental quality and green marketing practices. These standards are embraced by 158 countries, including the United States. More than 260,000 companies have met *ISO 14000* standards for environmental quality and green marketing.[32]

Socially responsible efforts on behalf of the general public are becoming more common. A formal practice is **cause marketing**, which occurs when the charitable contributions of a firm are tied directly to the customer revenues produced through the promotion of one of its products.[33] This definition distinguishes cause marketing from a firm's standard charitable contributions, which are outright donations. For example, when consumers purchase selected company products, Procter & Gamble directs part of that revenue toward programs that support disadvantaged youth and provide disaster relief. MasterCard International links usage of its card with fund-raising for institutions that combat cancer, heart disease, child abuse, drug abuse, and muscular dystrophy. Häagen-Dazs supports the "help the honey bees" campaign, Barnes & Noble promotes literacy, and Coca-Cola sponsors local Boys and Girls Clubs. Avon Products, Inc., focuses on different issues in different countries, including breast cancer, domestic violence, and disaster relief, among many others.

Marketing Matters

customer value

Will Consumers Switch Brands for a Cause? Yes, If . . .

American Express Company pioneered cause marketing when it sponsored the renovation of the Statue of Liberty. This effort raised $1.7 million for the renovation, increased card usage among cardholders, and attracted new cardholders. In 2001, U.S. companies raised more than $5 billion for causes they champion. It is estimated that cause marketing raised over $10 billion in 2012.

Cause marketing benefits companies as well as causes. Research indicates that 85 percent of U.S. consumers say they have a more favorable opinion of companies that support causes they care about. Also, 80 percent of consumers say they will switch to a brand or retailer that supports a good cause if the price and quality of brands or retailers are equal. In short, cause marketing may be a valued point of difference for brands and companies, all other things being equal.

For more information, including news, links, and case studies, visit the Cause Marketing Forum website at www.causemarketingforum.com.

QR 4-2
Häagen-Dazs
Video

Cause marketing programs incorporate all three concepts of social responsibility by addressing public concerns and satisfying customer needs. They can also enhance corporate sales and profits as described in the Marketing Matters box.[34]

The Social Audit and Sustainable Development: Doing Well by Doing Good

Converting socially responsible ideas into actions involves careful planning and monitoring of programs. Many companies develop, implement, and evaluate their social responsibility efforts by means of a **social audit**, which is a systematic assessment of a firm's objectives, strategies, and performance in terms of social responsibility. Frequently, marketing and social responsibility programs are integrated. Consider McDonald's. The company's concern for the needs of families with children who are chronically or terminally ill was converted into some 350 Ronald McDonald Houses around the world. These facilities, located near treatment centers, enable families to stay together during the child's care. In this case, McDonald's is contributing to the welfare of a portion of its target market.

A social audit consists of five steps:[35]

1. Recognition of a firm's social expectations and the rationale for engaging in social responsibility endeavors.
2. Identification of social responsibility causes or programs consistent with the company's mission.
3. Determination of organizational objectives and priorities for programs and activities it will undertake.
4. Specification of the type and amount of resources necessary to achieve social responsibility objectives.
5. Evaluation of social responsibility programs and activities undertaken and assessment of future involvement.

Corporate attention to social audits will increase as companies seek to achieve sustainable development and improve the quality of life in a global economy. **Sustainable development** involves conducting business in a way that protects the natural environment while making economic progress.

Marketing and social responsibility programs are often integrated, as is the case with McDonald's. Its concern for children worldwide is apparent at the Ronald McDonald House in Baltimore, Maryland. This facility has housed over 30,000 families since 1982. Each night, 36 families call the facility home.

McDonald's
www.mcdonalds.com

Ecologically responsible initiatives such as green marketing represent one such initiative. Recent initiatives related to working conditions at offshore manufacturing sites that produce goods for U.S. companies focus on quality-of-life issues. Public opinion surveys show that 90 percent of U.S. citizens are concerned about working conditions under which products are made in Asia and Latin America. Companies such as Reebok, Nike, Liz Claiborne, Levi Strauss, and Mattel have responded by imposing codes of conduct to reduce unsafe, harsh, or abusive working conditions at offshore manufacturing facilities.[36] Still, poor working conditions exist. For example, over 1,000 garment workers in Bangladesh died when their factory collapsed in 2013.

Companies that evidence societal responsibility have been rewarded for their efforts. Research has shown that these companies (1) benefit from favorable word of mouth among consumers and (2) typically outperform less responsible companies in terms of financial performance.[37]

Turning the Table: Consumer Ethics and Social Responsibility

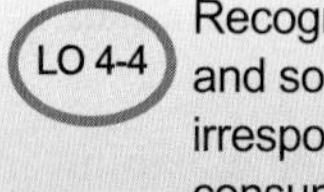

LO 4-4 Recognize unethical and socially irresponsible consumer behavior.

Consumers also have an obligation to act ethically and responsibly in the exchange process and in the use and disposition of products. Unfortunately, consumer behavior is spotty on both counts.

Unethical practices of consumers are a serious concern to marketers.[38] These practices include filing warranty claims after the claim period; misredeeming coupons; making fraudulent returns of merchandise; providing inaccurate information on credit applications; tampering with utility meters; tapping cable TV lines; pirating music, movies, and software from the Internet; and submitting phony insurance claims.

The cost to marketers of such behavior in lost sales and prevention expenses is huge. For example, consumers who redeem coupons for unpurchased products or use coupons for other products cost manufacturers $1 billion each year. Fraudulent automobile insurance claims cost insurance companies more than $10 billion annually. In addition, retailers lose about $13 billion yearly from shoplifting and $9.6 billion annually from fraudulent returns of merchandise. Consumers also act unethically toward each other. According to the FBI, consumer complaints about online auction fraud, in which consumers misrepresent their goods to others, outnumber all other reports of online crime.

Nike has been a leader in improving workplace conditions in Asian factories that produce its sporting apparel and equipment.

Nike
www.nike.com

Research on unethical consumer behavior indicates that these acts are rarely motivated by economic need. This behavior appears to be influenced by (1) a belief that a consumer can get away with the act and it is worth doing and (2) the rationalization that the act is justified or driven by forces outside the individual—"everybody does it." These reasons were vividly expressed by a 24-year-old who pirated a movie and was sentenced to six months of house arrest, three years of probation, and a $7,000 fine. He said, "I didn't like paying for movies," and added, "so many people do it, you never think you're going to get caught."[39]

Consumer purchase, use, and disposition of environmentally sensitive products relate to consumer social responsibility. Research indicates that consumers are sensitive to ecological issues.[40] For example, a recent survey of U.S. consumers indicated that 50 percent were personally willing to change their lifestyle to improve the environment. However, only 28 percent could identify personal changes in their own shopping or living habits over the past five years to illustrate their supposed commitment. Related research shows that consumers (1) may be unwilling to sacrifice convenience and pay higher prices to protect the environment and (2) lack the knowledge to make informed decisions dealing with the purchase, use, and disposition of products.

Consumer confusion over which products are environmentally safe is also apparent, given marketers' rush to offer "green products." For example, few consumers realize that nonaerosol "pump" hair sprays are the second-largest cause of air pollution, after drying paint. In California alone, 27 tons of noxious hair spray fumes are expelled every day. And some environmentally safe claims made by marketers have been labeled *greenwashing*—the practice of making an unsubstantiated or misleading claim about the environmental benefits of a product, service, technology, or company practice.[41]

QR 4-3
Corporate Greenwashing Video

To address such claims, the FTC has drafted guidelines that describe the circumstances under which environmental claims can be made without constituting misleading information in regard to recyclable, biodegradable, and sustainable products and processes.[42] For example, an advertisement or product label touting a package as "50 percent more recycled content than before" could be misleading if the recycled content has increased from 2 percent to 3 percent.

Ultimately, marketers and consumers are accountable for ethical and socially responsible behavior. The 21st century will prove to be a testing period for both.

learning review

4-6. What is meant by social responsibility?

4-7. Marketing efforts to produce, promote, and reclaim environmentally sensitive products are called ______________.

4-8. What is a social audit?

LEARNING OBJECTIVES REVIEW

LO 4-1 *Explain the differences between legal and ethical behavior in marketing.*
A good starting point for understanding the nature and significance of ethics is the distinction between the legality and the ethicality of marketing decisions. Whereas ethics deal with personal moral principles and values, laws are society's values and standards that are enforceable in the courts. This distinction can lead to the rationalization that if a behavior is within reasonable ethical and legal limits, then it is not really illegal or unethical. Judgment plays a large role in defining ethical and legal boundaries in marketing. Ethical dilemmas arise when acts or situations are not clearly ethical and legal or unethical and illegal.

LO 4-2 *Identify factors that influence ethical and unethical marketing decisions.*
Four factors influence ethical marketing behavior. First, societal culture and norms serve as socializing forces that dictate what is morally right and just. Second, business culture and industry practices affect ethical conduct in both the exchange relationships between buyers and sellers and the competitive behavior among sellers. Third, corporate culture and expectations are often defined by corporate ethics codes and the ethical behavior of top management and co-workers. Finally, an individual's personal moral philosophy, such as moral idealism or utilitarianism, will dictate ethical choices. Ultimately, ethical behavior rests with the individual, but the consequences affect many.

LO 4-3 *Describe the different concepts of social responsibility.*
Social responsibility means that organizations are part of a larger society and are accountable to that society for their actions. There are three concepts of social responsibility. First, profit responsibility holds that companies have a simple duty: to maximize profits for their owners or stockholders. Second, stakeholder responsibility focuses on the obligations an organization has to those who can affect achievement of its objectives. Those constituencies include consumers, employees, suppliers, and distributors. Finally, societal responsibility focuses on obligations that organizations have to the preservation of the ecological environment and the general public. Companies are placing greater emphasis on societal responsibility today and are reaping the rewards of positive word of mouth from their consumers and favorable financial performance.

LO 4-4 *Recognize unethical and socially irresponsible consumer behavior.*
Consumers, like marketers, have an obligation to act ethically and responsibly in the exchange process and in the use and disposition of products. Unfortunately, consumer behavior is spotty on both counts. Unethical consumer behavior includes filing warranty claims after the claim period; misredeeming coupons; pirating music, movies, and software from the Internet; and submitting phony insurance claims, among other behaviors. Unethical behavior is rarely motivated by economic need. Rather, research indicates that this behavior is influenced by (*a*) a belief that a consumer can get away with the act and it is worth doing and (*b*) the rationalization that such acts are justified or driven by forces outside the individual—"everybody does it." Consumer purchase, use, and disposition of environmentally sensitive products relate to consumer social responsibility. Even though consumers are sensitive to ecological issues they (*a*) may be unwilling to sacrifice convenience and pay potentially higher prices to protect the environment and (*b*) lack the knowledge to make informed decisions dealing with the purchase, use, and disposition of products.

FOCUSING ON KEY TERMS

cause marketing p. 102
caveat emptor p. 95
code of ethics p. 98
Consumer Bill of Rights p. 95
economic espionage p. 96
ethics p. 92
green marketing p. 102
laws p. 92
moral idealism p. 100
social audit p. 103
social responsibility p. 100
sustainable development p. 103
triple-bottom line p. 102
utilitarianism p. 100
whistle-blowers p. 99

APPLYING MARKETING KNOWLEDGE

1 What concepts of moral philosophy and social responsibility are applicable to the practices of Anheuser-Busch described in the introduction to this chapter? Why?

2 Five ethical situations were presented in this chapter: (*a*) a medical society's decision to set fee schedules, (*b*) the use of a computer program by auto dealers to arrange financing, (*c*) smoking in China, (*d*) downloading movies, and (*e*) the pricing of Cerezyme for the treatment of a rare genetic illness. Where would each of these situations fit in Figure 4–1?

3 The American Marketing Association Statement of Ethics shown in Figure 4–3 details the rights and duties of parties in the marketing exchange process. How do these rights and duties compare with the Consumer Bill of Rights?

4 Compare and contrast moral idealism and utilitarianism as alternative personal moral philosophies.

5 How would you evaluate Milton Friedman's view of the social responsibility of a firm?

6 The text lists several unethical practices of consumers. Can you name others? Why do you think consumers engage in unethical conduct?

7 Cause marketing programs have become popular. Describe two such programs with which you are familiar.

BUILDING YOUR MARKETING PLAN

Consider these potential stakeholders that may be affected in some way by the marketing plan on which you are working: shareholders (if any), suppliers, employees, customers, and society in general. For each group of stakeholders:

1 Identify what, if any, ethical and social responsibility issues might arise.

2 Describe, in one or two sentences, how your marketing plan addresses each potential issue.

VIDEO CASE 4 Toyota: Building Cleaner, Greener Cars

QR 4-4
Toyota Video Case

"Toyota's mission is to become the most respected and admired car company in America," explains Jana Hartline, manager of environmental communications at Toyota. To accomplish this, Jana and her colleagues at Toyota are working toward a future where a wide range of innovative vehicles, fuel technologies, and partnerships converge to create an economically vibrant, mobile society in harmony with the environment. It's a challenge Jana finds exciting and the result is cleaner, greener cars!

THE COMPANY

Kiichiro Toyoda began research on gasoline-powered engines in 1930. By 1935 he had developed passenger car prototypes, and in 1957 he introduced the "Toyopet" in the United States. The Toyopet was not successful and was discontinued. In 1965, however, the Corona was introduced, and it was followed by the Corolla in 1968. The Corolla went on to become the best-selling passenger car in the world, with 27 million purchased in more than 140 countries!

The popularity of Toyota's automobiles continued to grow in the United States and in 1975 it surpassed Volkswagen to become the number one import brand. In 1998 Toyota launched its first full-sized pickup, the Toyota Tundra. Toyota also expanded its product line by adding the Lexus brand, which became known for its exceptional quality and customer service. By 2000, Lexus was one of the best-selling luxury brands in the United States, competing with both Mercedes-Benz and BMW. Toyota also introduced the Scion brand of moderately priced vehicles for the youth market.

The company opened a national sales headquarters in Torrance, California, and also opened manufacturing facilities so it could produce cars in the United States. By 2012 Toyota had the capacity to build 2.2 million cars and trucks and 1.45 million engines in 15 plants across North America. Toyota's sales and distribution organization includes 1,500 Toyota, Lexus, and Scion dealers. Toyota's marketing organization has led to many memorable marketing campaigns. Some of its early taglines included "You Asked For It, You Got It!" and "Oh What a Feeling!" which included the "Toyota Jump." The Lexus tagline, "The Relentless Pursuit of Perfection," is still in use today, while Toyota's ads now exclaim, "Let's Go Places."

Today, Toyota is the world's largest automobile manufacturer. The company is ranked the tenth largest corporation by *Fortune* magazine. The company's core principle is "to contribute to society and the economy by producing high-quality products and services." Its success is often attributed to a business philosophy referred to as "The Toyota Way."

THE TOYOTA WAY

The Toyota Way is a business philosophy used to (1) improve processes and products, (2) build trust, and (3) empower individuals and teams. There are two values that act as pillars of The Toyota Way. They are continuous improvement and respect for people. These values are evident in five business practices:

- *Challenge*: To build a long-term vision and meet challenges with courage and creativity.
- *Kaizen*: To continuously improve business operations, always striving for innovation and evolution.
- *Genchi Genbutsu*: To always go to the source to find the facts and make correct decisions; to build consensus and expeditiously achieve goals.
- *Respect*: To respect others and the environment, to build trust and to take responsibility.
- *Teamwork*: To stimulate personal and professional growth, maximize individual and team performance.

In fact, according to Jana Hartline, the two values are "integrated into everything that we do on a daily basis," creating "a unique corporate environment."

As the company has grown it has also sought a larger role in society. For example, Toyota created the Toyota USA Foundation with a $10 million endowment and a mission to make Toyota a leading corporate citizen. The foundation supports programs focused on the environment, education, and safety that help strengthen communities. Since 1991 Toyota has contributed over $500 million to philanthropic programs in the United States. Combining The Toyota Way with its corporate philanthropy has been very successful. Toyota believes that the foundation of its success involves a constant spirit of challenge and enthusiasm for new ideas. For example, Toyota's environmental vision includes the concept of sustainable mobility.

ENVIRONMENTAL VISION AND THE PRIUS

To make its environmental vision actionable, Toyota developed a five-year Environmental Action Plan. The plan is structured around five key areas:

- Energy and Climate Change
- Recycling and Resource Management
- Air Quality
- Environmental Management
- Cooperation with Society

For each area Toyota creates goals and measurable targets based on a life-cycle view of vehicles: from design, to manufacturing, to sales and distribution, to use, and finally to how the vehicle is recycled at end-of-life. One of its top

goals has been to develop advanced vehicle technologies to complement traditional automobile technologies. Ed LaRocque, national manager of vehicle marketing, describes how Toyota started one of these initiatives:

> *In the early 90s Toyota developed what we called the G21 vision. The goal of the G21 plan was to bring a vehicle to market that represented a great value, and had great environmental benefits, not just in Japan but globally.*

The concept was eventually introduced as the Prius, a hybrid vehicle with a gasoline engine and an electric motor combination called the Hybrid Synergy Drive. The car received an EPA-estimated mileage rating of 50 mpg. Initially the Prius was attractive to very eco-conscious consumers but met with some resistance from the press and the general population. The cars were fuel efficient, but they were not attractive. Since the first introduction, Toyota has made changes and introduced two new generations of the Prius to help it become the world's most-popular hybrid, selling more than three million of the vehicles.

Toyota's development of new technologies such as the Hybrid Synergy Drive helped it recognize the implications for the entire mobility system. A strategy for sustainable mobility affects not only new technologies and vehicles, but also new energy sources, new transportation systems, and the many partnerships of involved stakeholders. Advertising for the Prius emphasizes this point, claiming the car provides "Harmony between man, nature, and machine." In the long-term, however, this strategy will not be successful if consumers are not aware of or knowledgeable about advanced technologies. To increase awareness and knowledge Toyota specified the development of partnerships as a goal.

STRATEGIC PARTNERSHIPS

Toyota believes that partnerships with relevant organizations help increase awareness of its technologies and products. These programs are designed to educate people so they can reduce their environmental footprint. One of these programs, for example, is *Together Green*—a

$20 million, five-year alliance with Audubon to fund projects, train leaders, and offer volunteer opportunities. Similarly, Toyota has partnered with the World Wildlife Fund to establish hybrid energy systems, oil recycling programs, and renewable energy outreach campaigns. The exposure from these programs is often much more effective than other communication options. Mary Nickerson, National Manager of Advanced Technology, explains: "we [have] used partnerships with the American Lung Association, with the Electric Drive Transportation Association, Environmental Media Association, and the national parks to help touch many more millions of people than we ever could have done with a traditional advertising campaign."

Toyota recently announced a grant of $5 million and 25 Toyota vehicles in support of U.S. National Parks. Parks included in this grant and other Toyota partnerships are Yellowstone National Park, Great Smoky Mountains National Park, Everglades National Park, Yosemite National Park, the Grand Canyon, the Santa Monica National Recreation Area, and the Golden Gate Bridge Foundation. The national parks partnership offers an opportunity to enhance the experiences of visitors through education and hybrid vehicle use (park employees use the donated Toyota vehicles to reduce noise and emissions in the parks).

Generally, the goal of the national parks partnership program is to make a personal connection with park visitors about Toyota's hybrid vehicles when they are in a natural setting in which they are receptive to receiving a message about sustainable mobility. The message implies important links:

"Green" Vehicles > Cleaner Air > Preservation of Parks

In addition, Toyota believes that the programs have other benefits, including:

- Strengthening Toyota's image as an environmental leader among automakers.
- Communicating a message of environmental stewardship.
- Building awareness of the Prius and other Toyota hybrids.
- Educating park visitors on the benefits of advanced vehicle technology.

Research by Toyota indicates that the program is working. A recent corporate image study indicated that among four leading automakers (Toyota, Honda, Ford, and GM), Toyota was rated highest on dimensions such as "Leader in High MPG," "Leader in Technology Development," "Environmentally Friendly Vehicles," and "Wins Environmental Awards."

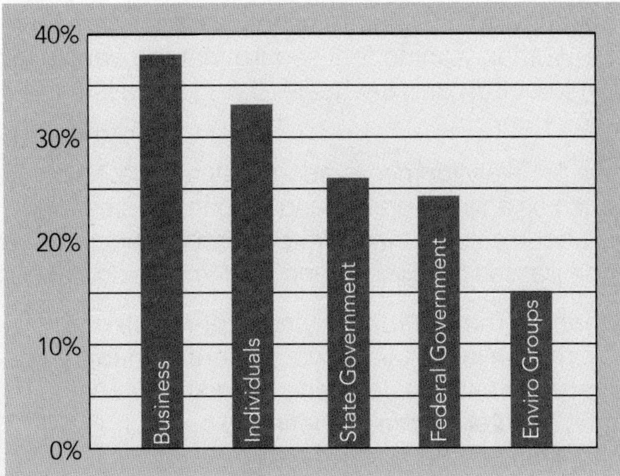

FIGURE 1
Who should take the lead in addressing environmental issues?

THE FUTURE

Figure 1 shows the results of a survey of consumer interests and their response to the question, "Who should take the lead in addressing environmental issues?" The results suggest that in the future consumers will expect businesses to be proactive about the environment and sustainability.

For Toyota, a focus on sustainability will mean considering the environmental, social, and economic consequences of the auto business and continuously working to reduce the negative and increase the positive impacts of its activities and decisions. The increasing importance of sustainability will challenge Toyota to look at these impacts from all stages of the vehicle life cycle. It will also encourage Toyota's managers to consider the opinions of many stakeholders such as consumers, regulators, local communities, and nongovernmental organizations.

The recent concerns about Toyota vehicle product quality, which led to the recall of 16 million vehicles, have hurt Toyota's reputation. In the future, all activities, including the partnership strategy and the national parks program, will determine if Toyota can become "the most respected car company in the world."

Questions

1 How does Toyota's approach to social responsibility relate to the three concepts of social responsibility described in the text (profit responsibility, stakeholder responsibility, and societal responsibility)?

2 How does Toyota's view of sustainable mobility contribute to the company's overall mission?

3 Has Toyota's National Parks project been a success? What indicators suggest that the project has had an impact?

4 What future activities would you suggest for Toyota as it strives to improve its reputation?

5 Understanding Consumer Behavior

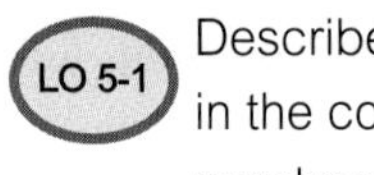

Learning Objectives

After reading this chapter you should be able to:

LO 5-1 Describe the stages in the consumer purchase decision process.

LO 5-2 Distinguish among three variations of the consumer purchase decision process: routine, limited, and extended problem solving.

LO 5-3 Identify the major psychological influences on consumer behavior.

LO 5-4 Identify the major sociocultural influences on consumer behavior.

Enlightened Carmakers Know What Custom(h)ers Value

Who makes 60 percent of new-car buying decisions? Who influences 80 percent of new-car buying decisions? Women. Yes, women.

Women are a driving force in the U.S. automobile industry. Enlightened carmakers have hired women designers, engineers, and marketing executives to better understand and satisfy this valuable car buyer and influencer. What have they learned? While car price and quality are important, women and men think and feel differently about car features and key elements of the new-car buying decision process and experience.

- *The sense of styling.* Women and men care about styling. For men, styling is more about a car's exterior lines and accents or "curb appeal." Women are more interested in interior design and finishes. Designs that fit their proportions, provide good visibility, offer ample storage space, and make for effortless parking are particularly important.
- *The need for speed.* Both sexes want speed, but for different reasons. Men think about how many seconds it takes to get from zero to 60 miles per hour. Women want to feel secure that the car has enough acceleration to outrun an 18-wheeler trying to pass them on a freeway entrance ramp.
- *The substance of safety.* Safety for men is about features that help avoid an accident, such as antilock brakes and responsive steering. For women, safety is about features that help to survive an accident. These features include passenger airbags and reinforced side panels.
- *The shopping experience.* The new-car-buying experience differs between men and women in important ways. Generally, men decide up front what car they want and set out alone to find it. By contrast, women approach it as an intelligence-gathering expedition. Referred to as *CROPing*, women shoppers look for *CR*edible *OP*inions. They actively seek information and postpone a purchase decision until all options have been evaluated. Women, more frequently than men, visit auto-buying websites, read car-comparison articles, and scan car advertisements. Still, recommendations of friends and relatives matter most to women. Women typically shop three dealerships before making a purchase decision—one more than men.

Carmakers have learned that women, more than men, dislike the car-buying experience—specifically, the experience of dealing with car salespeople. In contrast to many male car buyers, women do not typically revel in the gamesmanship of car buying. "Men get all excited about going out to buy a car and talk about how they're going to one-up the salesman and get a great deal," said Anne Fleming, president of www.women-drivers.com, a consumer ratings site. "I've never heard or seen any comments from women like that." In particular, women dread the price negotiations that are often involved in buying a new car. Not surprisingly, about half of women car buyers take a man with them to finalize the terms of sale.[1]

This chapter examines **consumer behavior**, the actions a person takes in purchasing and using products and services, including the mental and social processes that come before and after these actions. This chapter shows how the behavioral sciences help answer questions such as why people choose one product or brand over another, how they make these choices, and how companies use this knowledge to provide value to consumers.

CONSUMER PURCHASE DECISION PROCESS AND EXPERIENCE

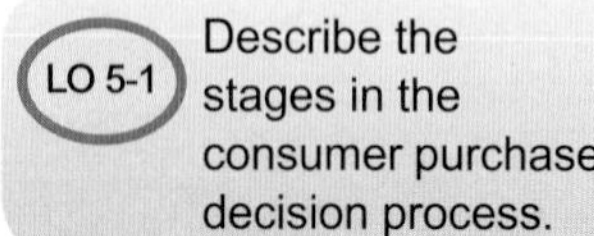

LO 5-1
Describe the stages in the consumer purchase decision process.

Behind the visible act of making a purchase lies an important decision process and consumer experience that must be investigated. The stages a buyer passes through in making choices about which products and services to buy is the **purchase decision process**. This process has the five stages shown in Figure 5–1: (1) problem recognition, (2) information search, (3) alternative evaluation, (4) purchase decision, and (5) postpurchase behavior.

Problem Recognition: Perceiving a Need

Problem recognition, the initial step in the purchase decision, is perceiving a difference between a person's ideal and actual situations big enough to trigger a decision.[2] This can be as simple as finding an empty milk carton in the refrigerator; noting, as a first-year college student, that your high school clothes are not in the style that other students are wearing; or realizing that your notebook computer may not be working properly.

In marketing, advertisements or salespeople can activate a consumer's decision process by showing the shortcomings of competing (or currently owned) products. For instance, an advertisement for a new generation smartphone could stimulate problem recognition because it emphasizes "maximum use from one device."

Information Search: Seeking Value

After recognizing a problem, a consumer begins to search for information, the next stage in the purchase decision process. First, you may scan your memory for previous experiences with products or brands.[3] This action is called *internal search*. For frequently purchased products such as shampoo and conditioner, this may be enough.

In other cases, a consumer may undertake an *external search* for information.[4] This is needed when past experience or knowledge is insufficient, the risk of making a wrong purchase decision is high, and the cost of gathering information is low. The primary sources of external information are (1) *personal sources*, such as relatives and friends whom the consumer trusts; (2) *public sources*, including various product-rating organizations such as *Consumer Reports*, government agencies, and TV "consumer programs"; and (3) *marketer-dominated sources*, such as information from sellers including advertising, company websites, salespeople, and point-of-purchase displays in stores.

Suppose you are considering buying a new smartphone. You will probably tap several of these information sources: friends and relatives, advertisements, brand and company websites, and stores carrying these phones (for demonstrations). You also

FIGURE 5–1
The purchase decision process consists of five stages.

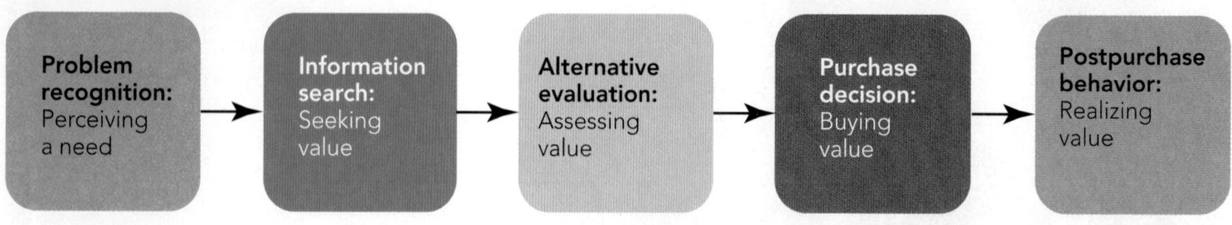

BRAND	MODEL	PRICE	DISPLAY QUALITY	VOICE QUALITY	MESS-AGING	WEB BROWSING	CAMERA IMAGE QUALITY	BATTERY LIFE
Apple	iPhone 5	$300	Excellent	Good	Very Good	Excellent	Excellent	Good
Apple	iPhone 4S	100	Excellent	Good	Very Good	Good	Very Good	Good
BlackBerry	Q 10	200	Excellent	Fair	Very Good	Very Good	Very Good	Very Good
LG	Intuition	50	Excellent	Good	Excellent	Excellent	Good	Good
Motorola	Dröid Razr Maxx HD	200	Excellent	Good	Excellent	Excellent	Very Good	Excellent
Motorola	Dröid 4	100	Very Good	Good	Excellent	Excellent	Very Good	Good
Samsung	Galaxy S 4	200	Excellent	Good	Excellent	Excellent	Excellent	Very Good
Samsung	Stratosphere II	50	Very Good	Fair	Excellent	Excellent	Good	Good

Rating: Excellent · Very Good · Good · Fair · Poor

Source: "Ratings: Smart Phones," *Consumer Reports* (August 2013), p. 39. This excerpted list of smartphones is *only* for Verizon customers. These smartphones are listed alphabetically and not in the order of their ratings.

FIGURE 5–2
Consumer Reports provides an evaluation of smartphones for consumers.

might study the comparative evaluation of selected smartphones appearing in *Consumer Reports*, a portion of which appears in Figure 5–2.[5]

Alternative Evaluation: Assessing Value

Consumer Reports
www.consumerreports.org

The alternative evaluation stage clarifies the problem for the consumer by (1) suggesting criteria to use for the purchase, (2) yielding brand names that might meet the criteria, and (3) developing consumer value perceptions. Given only the information shown in Figure 5–2, which selection criteria would you use in buying a smartphone? Would you use price, display quality, voice quality, messaging, web browsing, camera image quality, battery life, or some other combination of these or other criteria?

For some of you, the information provided may be inadequate because it does not contain all the factors you might consider when evaluating smartphones. These factors are a consumer's **evaluative criteria**, which represent both the objective attributes of a brand (such as display) and the subjective ones (such as prestige) you use to compare different products and brands.[6] Firms try to identify and capitalize on both types of criteria to create the best value for the money paid by you and other consumers. These criteria are often displayed in advertisements.

Consumers often have several criteria for evaluating brands. Knowing this, companies seek to identify the most important evaluative criteria that consumers use when comparing brands. For example, among the seven criteria shown in Figure 5–2, suppose you use four in considering smartphones: (1) a retail price of $200 or less, (2) excellent messaging capability, (3) good voice quality, and (4) very good to excellent camera image quality. These criteria establish the brands in your **consideration set**—the group of brands a consumer would consider acceptable from among all the brands in the product class of which he or she is aware.[7]

This advertisement for the Dröid Razr Maxx HD by Motorola focuses on the brand's extended battery life, which limits the need for frequent charging, often at awkward times and places.

Your evaluative criteria result in two brands, Samsung and Motorola, and their respective models (the Samsung Galaxy S4 and the Motorola Dröid Razr Maxx HD and Dröid 4) in your consideration set. If the brand alternatives are equally attractive based on your original criteria, you might expand your list of desirable features. For example, you might decide that battery life is also important and compare the alternatives based on that criterion as well.

Purchase Decision: Buying Value

Having examined the alternatives in the consideration set, you are almost ready to make a purchase decision. Two choices remain: (1) from whom to buy and (2) when to buy. For a product like a smartphone, the information search process probably involved visiting retail stores, seeing different brands advertised on television and newspapers, and viewing a smartphone on a seller's website. The choice of which seller to buy from will depend on such considerations as the terms of sale, your past experience buying from the seller, and the return policy. Often a purchase decision involves a simultaneous evaluation of both product attributes and seller characteristics. For example, you might choose the second-most preferred smartphone brand at a store or website with a liberal refund and return policy versus the most preferred brand from a seller with more conservative policies.

Deciding when to buy is determined by a number of factors. For instance, you might buy sooner if one of your preferred brands is on sale or its manufacturer offers a rebate. Other factors such as the store atmosphere, pleasantness or ease of the shopping experience, salesperson assistance, time pressure, and financial circumstances could also affect whether a purchase decision is made now or postponed.[8]

Use of the Internet to gather information, evaluate alternatives, and make buying decisions adds a technological dimension to the consumer purchase decision process and buying experience. For example, 45 percent of consumers with price comparison smartphone apps routinely compare prices for identical products across different sellers at the point of purchase prior to making a purchase decision.[9]

Postpurchase Behavior: Realizing Value

After buying a product, the consumer compares it with his or her expectations and is either satisfied or dissatisfied. If the consumer is dissatisfied, marketers must determine whether the product was deficient or consumer expectations were too high. Product deficiency may require a design change. If expectations are too high, a company's advertising or the salesperson may have oversold the product's features and benefits.

Sensitivity to a customer's consumption or use experience is extremely important in a consumer's value perception. For example, research on telephone services provided by Sprint and AT&T indicates that satisfaction or dissatisfaction affects consumer value perceptions.[10] Studies show that satisfaction or dissatisfaction affects consumer communications and repeat-purchase behavior. Satisfied buyers tell three other people about their experience. In contrast, about 90 percent of dissatisfied buyers will not buy a product again and will complain to nine people.[11] Satisfied buyers also tend to buy from the same seller each time a purchase occasion arises. The financial impact of repeat-purchase behavior is significant, as described in the Marketing Matters box.[12]

Firms such as General Electric (GE), Johnson & Johnson, Coca-Cola, and British Airways focus attention on postpurchase behavior to maximize customer satisfaction and retention. These firms, among many others, now provide toll-free telephone numbers, offer liberalized return and refund policies, and engage in extensive staff training to handle complaints, answer questions, record suggestions, and solve consumer problems. For example, GE has a database that stores 750,000 answers regarding about 8,500 of its models in 120 product lines to handle 3 million calls annually. Such efforts produce positive postpurchase communications among consumers and foster relationship building between sellers and buyers.

Marketing Matters

How Much Is a Satisfied Customer Worth?

Customer satisfaction and experience underlie the marketing concept. But how much is a satisfied customer worth?

This question has prompted firms to calculate the financial value of a satisfied customer over time. Frito-Lay, for example, estimates that the average loyal consumer in the Southwestern United States eats 21 pounds of snack chips a year. At a price of $2.50 a pound, this customer spends $52.50 annually on the company's snacks such as Lay's and Ruffles potato chips, Doritos and Tostitos tortilla chips, and Fritos corn chips. Exxon estimates that a loyal customer will spend $500 annually for its branded gasoline, not including candy, snacks, oil, or repair services purchased at its gasoline stations. Kimberly-Clark reports that a loyal customer will buy 6.7 boxes of its Kleenex tissues each year and will spend $994 on facial tissues over 60 years, in today's dollars.

These calculations have focused marketer attention on the buying experience, customer satisfaction, and retention. Ford Motor Company set a target of increasing customer retention—the percentage of Ford owners whose next car is also a Ford—from 60 percent to 80 percent. Why? Ford executives say that each additional percentage point is worth a staggering $100 million in profits.

This calculation is not unique to Ford. Research shows that a 5 percent improvement in customer retention can increase a company's profits by 70 to 80 percent.

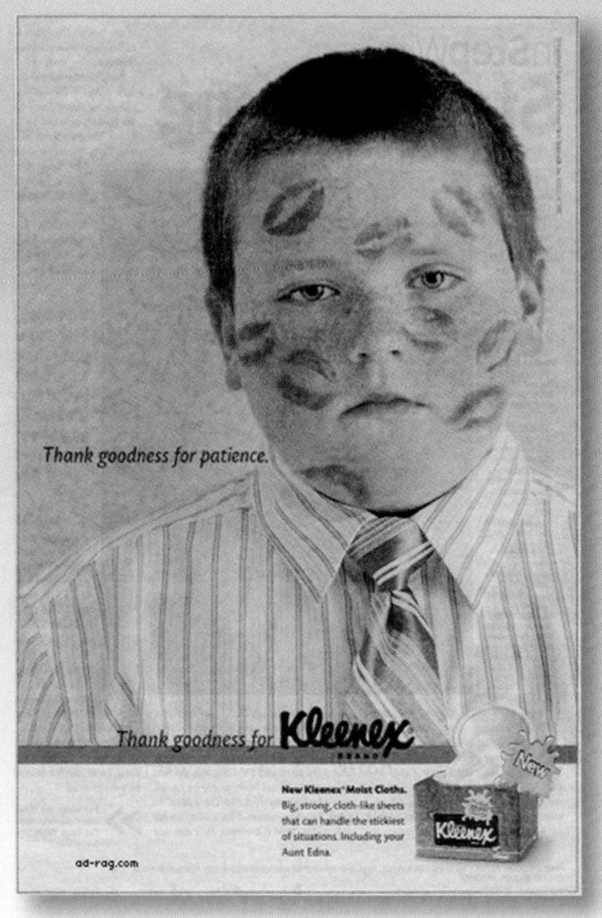

Thank goodness for patience.
Thank goodness for Kleenex
New
New Kleenex Moist Cloths.
Big, strong, cloth-like sheets that can handle the stickiest of situations. Including your Aunt Edna.
ad-rag.com

Often a consumer is faced with two or more highly attractive alternatives, such as an Samsung Galaxy S4 or Motorola Dröid Razr Maxx HD. If you choose the Galaxy S4, you might think, "Should I have purchased the Dröid Razr Maxx HD?" This feeling of postpurchase psychological tension or anxiety is called **cognitive dissonance**. To alleviate it, consumers often attempt to applaud themselves for making the right choice. So after your purchase, you may seek information to confirm your choice by asking friends questions like, "Don't you like my new phone?" or by reading ads of the brand you chose. You might even look for negative features about the brands you didn't buy and decide that the Dröid Razr Maxx HD smartphone did not feel right. Firms often use ads or follow-up calls from salespeople in this postpurchase behavior stage to comfort buyers that they made the right decision. For many years, Buick ran an advertising campaign with the message, "Aren't you really glad you bought a Buick?"

LO 5-2 Distinguish among three variations of the consumer purchase decision process: routine, limited, and extended problem solving.

Consumer Involvement Affects Problem Solving

Sometimes consumers don't engage in the five-stage purchase decision process. Instead, they skip or minimize one or more stages depending on the level of **involvement**, the personal, social, and economic significance of the purchase to the consumer.[13] High-involvement purchase occasions typically have at least one of three characteristics: The item to be purchased (1) is expensive, (2) can have serious personal

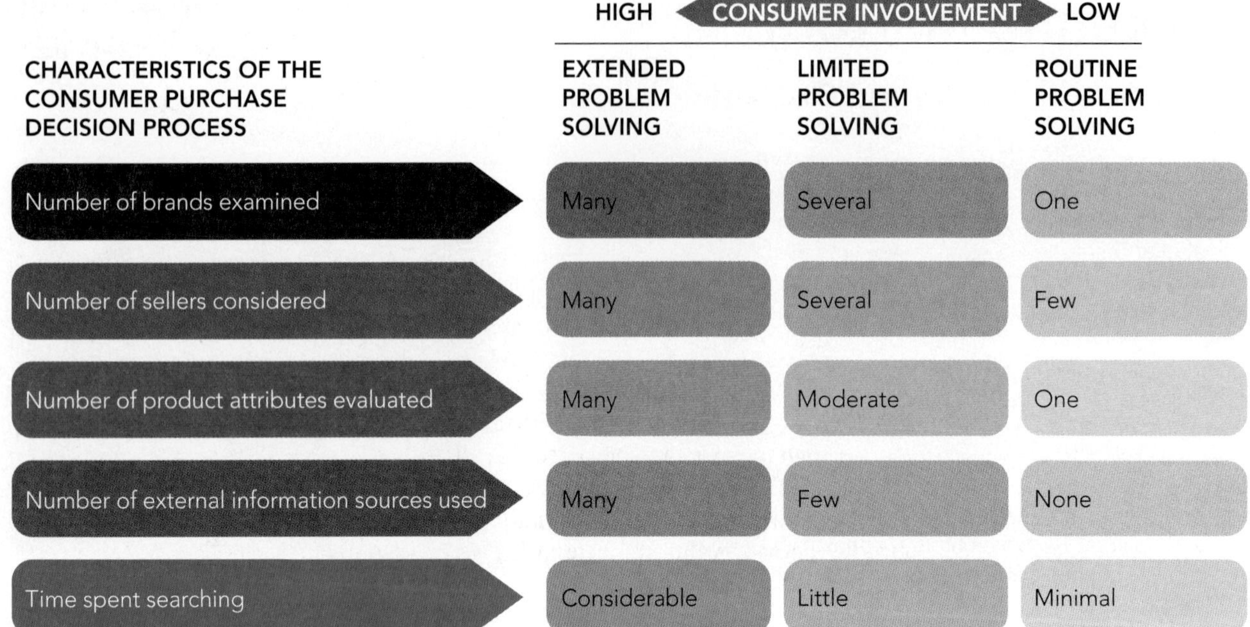

HIGH
CONSUMER INVOLVEMENT
LOW
CHARACTERISTICS OF THE CONSUMER PURCHASE DECISION PROCESS
EXTENDED PROBLEM SOLVING
LIMITED PROBLEM SOLVING
ROUTINE PROBLEM SOLVING
Number of brands examined
Many
Several
One
Number of sellers considered
Many
Several
Few
Number of product attributes evaluated
Many
Moderate
One
Number of external information sources used
Many
Few
None
Time spent searching
Considerable
Little
Minimal

FIGURE 5–3
Comparison of problem-solving variations: extended problem solving, limited problem solving, and routine problem solving.

consequences, or (3) could reflect on one's social image. For these occasions, consumers engage in extensive information searches, consider many product attributes and brands, form attitudes, and participate in word-of-mouth communication. Low-involvement purchases, such as toothpaste and soap, barely involve most of us, but audio and video systems and automobiles are very involving.

There are three general variations in the consumer purchase decision process based on consumer involvement and product knowledge. Figure 5–3 shows some of the important differences between the three problem-solving variations.

Extended Problem Solving In extended problem solving, each of the five stages of the consumer purchase decision process is used and considerable time and effort are devoted to the search for external information and the identification and evaluation of alternatives. Several brands are in the consideration set, and these are evaluated on many attributes. Extended problem solving exists in high-involvement purchase situations for items such as automobiles and audio systems.

Limited Problem Solving In limited problem solving, consumers typically seek some information or rely on a friend to help them evaluate alternatives. Several brands might be evaluated using a moderate number of attributes. Limited problem solving is appropriate for purchase situations that do not merit a great deal of time or effort, such as choosing a toaster or a restaurant for lunch.

Routine Problem Solving For products such as table salt and milk, consumers recognize a problem, make a decision, and spend little effort seeking external information and evaluating alternatives. The purchase process for such items is virtually a habit and typifies low-involvement decision making. Routine problem solving is typically the case for low-priced, frequently purchased products.

Consumer Involvement and Marketing Strategy Low and high consumer involvement have important implications for marketing strategy. If a company markets a low-involvement product and its brand is a market leader, attention is placed on (1) maintaining product quality, (2) avoiding stockout situations so that buyers don't substitute a competing brand, and (3) repetitive advertising messages that reinforce

DELICIOUS DRINK WITH GREAT BODY.
(YOURS)
70 calories
0g fat
3g dietary fiber
Could've had a V8.

What does this ad for V8 vegetable juice and its slogan, "Could've Had a V8," have to do with getting the brand into a consumer's consideration set? Read the text to find out.

a consumer's knowledge or assure buyers they made the right choice. Market challengers have a different task. They must break buying habits by using free samples, coupons, and rebates to encourage trial of their brand. Advertising messages will focus on getting their brand into a consumer's consideration set. For example, Campbell's V8 vegetable juice advertising message—"Could've Had a V8"—is targeted at consumers who routinely consider only fruit juices and soft drinks for purchase. Marketers can also link their brand attributes with high-involvement issues. Post Cereals does this by linking consumption of its whole grain cereals with improved heart health and protection against major diseases.

Marketers of high-involvement products know that their consumers constantly seek and process information about objective and subjective brand attributes, form evaluative criteria, rate product attributes in various brands, and combine these ratings for an overall brand evaluation—like that described in the smartphone purchase decision. Market leaders ply consumers with product information through advertising and personal selling and use social media to create online experiences for their company or brand. Market challengers capitalize on this behavior through comparative advertising that focuses on existing product attributes and often introduce novel evaluative criteria for judging competing brands. Challengers also benefit from Internet search engines such as Microsoft Bing and Google that assist buyers of high-involvement products.

Situational Influences That Affect Purchase Decisions

Often the purchase situation will affect the purchase decision process. Five **situational influences** have an impact on the purchase decision process: (1) the purchase task, (2) social surroundings, (3) physical surroundings, (4) temporal effects, and (5) antecedent states.[14]

The purchase task is the reason for engaging in the decision. The search for information and the evaluation of alternatives may differ depending on whether the purchase is a gift, which often involves social visibility, or for the buyer's own use. Social surroundings, including the other people present when a purchase decision is made, may also affect what is purchased. Consumers accompanied by children buy about 40 percent more items than consumers shopping by themselves. Physical surroundings such as decor, music, and crowding in retail stores may alter how purchase decisions are made. Temporal effects such as time of day or the amount of time available will influence where consumers have breakfast and lunch and what is ordered. Finally, antecedent states, which include the consumer's mood or the amount of cash on hand, can influence purchase behavior and choice. For example, consumers with credit cards purchase more than those with cash or debit cards.

Figure 5–4 on the next page shows the many influences that affect the consumer purchase decision process. In addition to situational influences, the decision to buy a product also involves and is affected by important psychological and sociocultural influences. These two influences are covered in the remainder of this chapter. Marketing mix influences are described in Chapters 10 through 20. Chapter 21 elaborates on consumer behavior in the context of online information search and buying.

learning review

5-1. What is the first stage in the consumer purchase decision process?

5-2. The brands a consumer considers buying out of the set of brands in a product class of which the consumer is aware are collectively called the ______________.

5-3. What is the term for postpurchase anxiety?

FIGURE 5–4
Influences on the consumer purchase decision process come from both internal and external sources.

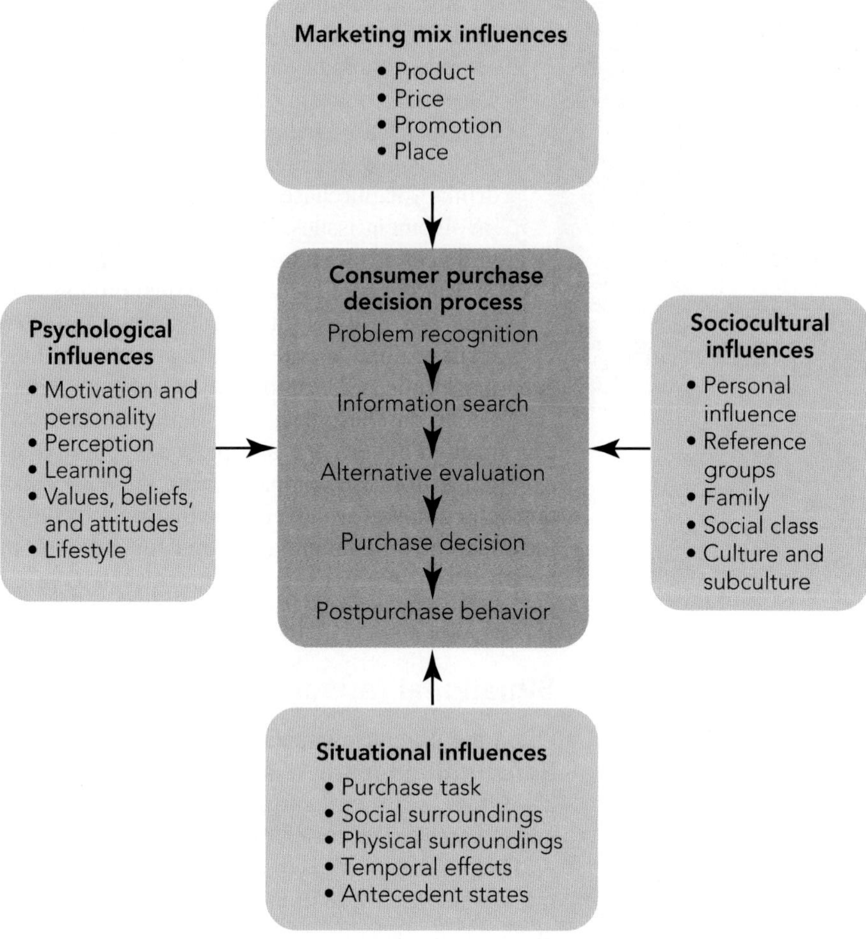

PSYCHOLOGICAL INFLUENCES ON CONSUMER BEHAVIOR

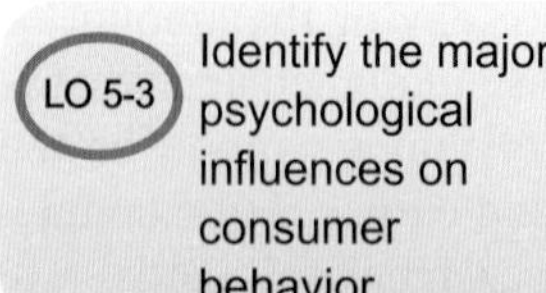

Identify the major psychological influences on consumer behavior.

Psychology helps marketers understand why and how consumers behave as they do. In particular, psychological concepts such as motivation and personality; perception; learning; values, beliefs, and attitudes; and lifestyle are useful for interpreting buying processes and directing marketing efforts.

Consumer Motivation and Personality

Motivation and personality are two familiar psychological concepts that have specific meanings and marketing implications. These concepts are closely related and are used to explain why people do some things and not others.

Motivation **Motivation** is the energizing force that stimulates behavior to satisfy a need. Because consumer needs are the focus of the marketing concept, marketers try to arouse these needs.

An individual's needs are boundless. People possess physiological needs for basics such as water, shelter, and food. They also have learned needs, including self-esteem, achievement, and affection. Psychologists point out that these needs may be hierarchical; that is, once physiological needs are met, people seek to satisfy their learned needs.

FIGURE 5–5
The Maslow hierarchy of needs is based on the idea that motivation comes from a need. If a need is met, it's no longer a motivator, so a higher-level need becomes the motivator. Higher-level needs demand support of lower-level needs.

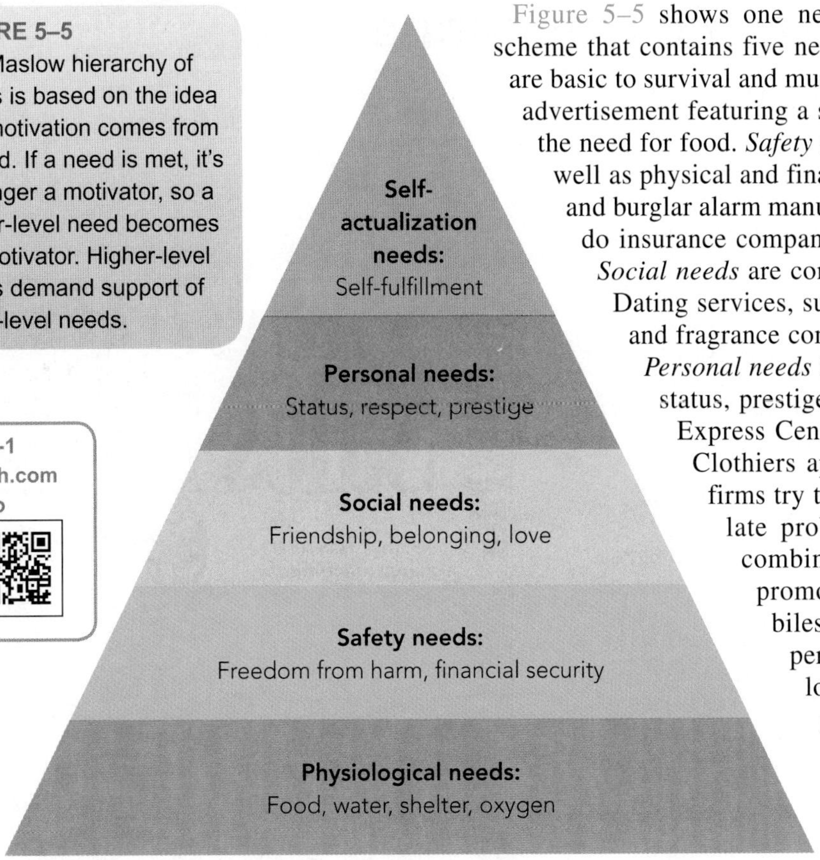

QR 5-1
Match.com
Video

Figure 5–5 shows one need hierarchy and classification scheme that contains five need classes.[15] *Physiological needs* are basic to survival and must be satisfied first. A Red Lobster advertisement featuring a seafood salad attempts to activate the need for food. *Safety needs* involve self-preservation as well as physical and financial well-being. Smoke detector and burglar alarm manufacturers focus on these needs, as do insurance companies and retirement plan advisors. *Social needs* are concerned with love and friendship. Dating services, such as Match.com and eHarmony, and fragrance companies try to arouse these needs. *Personal needs* include the need for achievement, status, prestige, and self-respect. The American Express Centurian Card and Brooks Brothers Clothiers appeal to these needs. Sometimes firms try to arouse multiple needs to stimulate problem recognition. Michelin has combined safety with parental love to promote tire replacement for automobiles. *Self-actualization needs* involve personal fulfillment. For example, a long-running U.S. Army recruiting program invited enlistees to "Be all you can be."

Personality While motivation is the energizing force that makes consumer behavior purposeful, a consumer's personality guides and directs behavior. **Personality** refers to a person's consistent behaviors or responses to recurring situations.

Although many personality theories exist, most identify *key traits*—enduring characteristics within a person or in his or her relationships with others. Such traits include assertiveness, extroversion, compliance, dominance, and aggression, among others. These traits are inherited or formed at an early age and change little over the years. Research suggests that compliant people prefer known brand names and use more mouthwash and toilet soaps. Aggressive types use razors, not electric shavers, apply more cologne and aftershave lotions, and purchase signature goods such as Gucci and Yves St. Laurent as an indicator of status.[16]

These personality characteristics are often revealed in a person's **self-concept**, which is the way people see themselves and the way they believe others see them. Marketers recognize that people have an actual self-concept and an ideal self-concept. The actual self refers to how people actually see themselves. The ideal self describes how people would like to see themselves.

These two self-images—actual and ideal—are reflected in the products and brands a person buys, including automobiles, home appliances and furnishings, magazines, consumer electronics, clothing, grooming and leisure products, and frequently, the stores in which a person shops. The importance of self-concept is summed up by a senior marketing executive at Lenovo, a global supplier of notebook computers: "The notebook market is getting more like cars. The car you drive reflects you, and notebooks are becoming a form of self-expression as well."[17]

Making Responsible Decisions

ethics

The Ethics of Subliminal Messages

For over 50 years, the topic of subliminal perception and the presence of subliminal messages and images embedded in commercial communications have sparked heated debate.

The Federal Communications Commission has denounced subliminal messages as deceptive. Still, consumers spend $50 million a year for subliminal messages designed to help them raise their self-esteem, stop compulsive buying, quit smoking, or lose weight. Almost two-thirds of U.S. consumers think subliminal messages are present in commercial communications; about half are firmly convinced that this practice can cause them to buy things they don't want.

Subliminal messages are not illegal in the United States, however, and marketers are often criticized for pursuing opportunities to create these messages in both electronic and print media. A book by August Bullock, *The Secret Sales Pitch,* is devoted to this topic. Bullock identifies images and advertisements that he claims contain subliminal messages and describes techniques that can be used for conveying these messages. Do you "see" the subliminal message that is embedded in the book's cover?

Do you believe that a marketer's attempts to implant subliminal messages in electronic and print media are a deceptive practice and unethical, regardless of their intent?

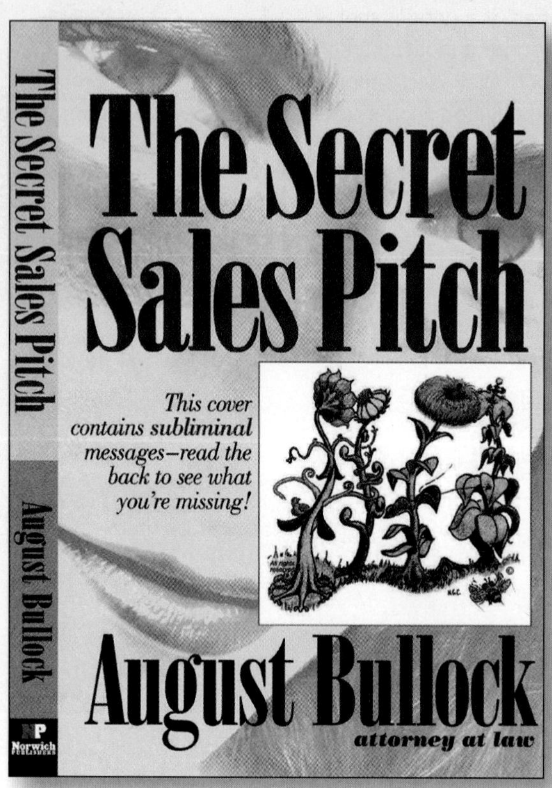

Consumer Perception

One person sees a Cadillac as a mark of achievement; another sees it as ostentatious. This is the result of **perception**—the process by which an individual selects, organizes, and interprets information to create a meaningful picture of the world.

Selective Perception Because the average consumer operates in a complex environment, the human brain attempts to organize and interpret information with a process called *selective perception,* a filtering of exposure, comprehension, and retention. *Selective exposure* occurs when people pay attention to messages that are consistent with their attitudes and beliefs and ignore messages that are inconsistent with them. Selective exposure often occurs in the postpurchase stage of the consumer decision process, when consumers read advertisements for the brand they just bought. It also occurs when a need exists—you are more likely to "see" a McDonald's advertisement when you are hungry rather than after you have eaten a pizza.

Selective comprehension involves interpreting information so that it is consistent with your attitudes and beliefs. A marketer's failure to understand this can have disastrous results. For example, Toro introduced a small, lightweight snowblower called the Snow Pup. Even though the product worked, sales failed to meet expectations. Why? Toro later found out that consumers perceived the name to mean that Snow Pup was a toy or too light to do any serious snow removal. When the product was renamed Snow Master, sales increased sharply.[18]

Selective retention means that consumers do not remember all the information they see, read, or hear, even minutes after exposure to it. This affects the internal and external information search stage of the purchase decision process. This is why furniture and automobile retailers often give consumers product brochures to take home with them when they leave the showroom.

Because perception plays an important role in consumer behavior, it is not surprising that the topic of subliminal perception is a popular item for discussion. **Subliminal perception** means that you see or hear messages without being aware of them. The presence and effect of subliminal perception on behavior is a hotly debated issue, with more popular appeal than scientific support. Indeed, evidence suggests that such messages have limited effects on behavior.[19] If these messages did influence behavior, would their use be an ethical practice? (See the Making Responsible Decisions box.)[20]

Why does Clorox tout the Good Housekeeping Seal for its Fresh Step cat litter? Why does Mary Kay, Inc., offer a free sample of its Velocity brand fragrance through its website? The answers appear in the text on the next page.

The Clorox Company
www.freshstep.com

Mary Kay, Inc.
www.marykay.com

Perceived Risk Perception plays a major role in the perceived risk in purchasing a product or service. **Perceived risk** represents the anxiety felt because the consumer cannot anticipate the outcomes of a purchase but believes there may be negative consequences. Examples of possible negative consequences are the size of the financial outlay required to buy the product (can I afford $500 for those skis?), the risk of physical harm (is bungee jumping safe?), and the performance of the product (will the whitening toothpaste work?). A more abstract form is psychosocial (what will my friends say about my tattoo?). Perceived risk affects a consumer's information search. The greater the perceived risk, the more extensive the external search stage is likely to be.

Fresh Step
Cats everywhere are having a hard time smelling their litter boxes.
freshstep.com

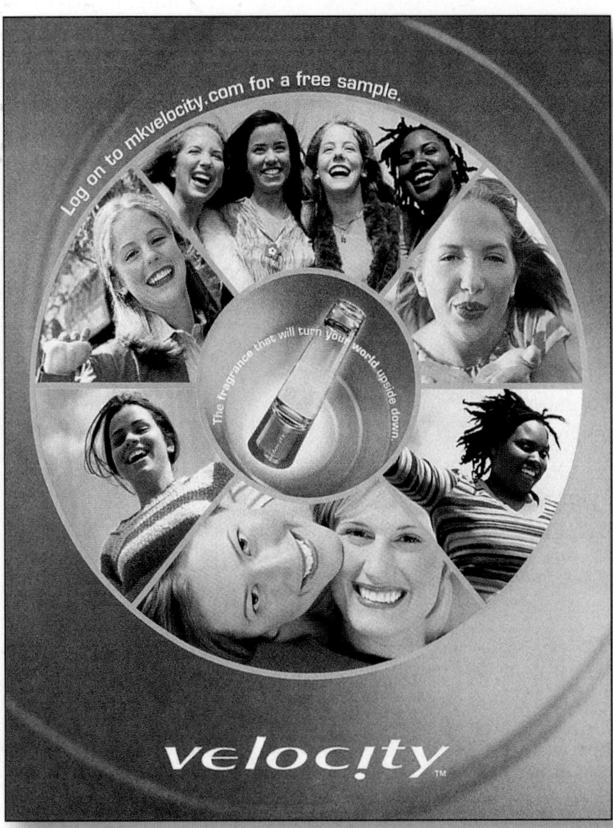

Log on to mkvelocity.com for a free sample.
The fragrance that will turn your world upside down.
velocity

Recognizing the importance of perceived risk, companies develop strategies to reduce the consumer's perceived risk and encourage purchases. These strategies and examples of firms using them include the following:

- *Obtaining seals of approval:* The Good Housekeeping Seal for Fresh Step cat litter.
- *Securing endorsements from influential people:* Endorsements for Promise soft spread from 9 out of 10 cardiologists.
- *Providing free trials of the product:* Samples of Mary Kay's Velocity fragrance.
- *Giving extensive usage instructions:* Clairol hair coloring.
- *Providing warranties and guarantees:* Kia Motors's 10-year, 100,000-mile warranty.

Consumer Learning

Much consumer behavior is learned. Consumers learn which information sources to consult for information about products and services, which evaluative criteria to use when assessing alternatives, and, more generally, how to make purchase decisions. **Learning** refers to those behaviors that result from (1) repeated experience and (2) reasoning.

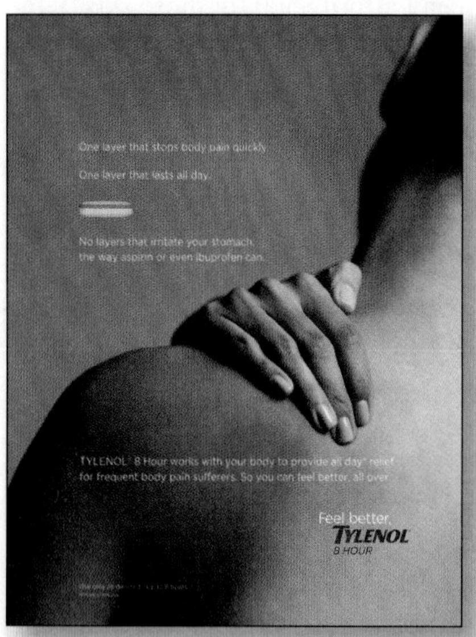

How does this advertisement for Tylenol 8-Hour apply to cognitive learning? Read the text to find out.

Tylenol
www.tylenol.com

Behavioral Learning *Behavioral learning* is the process of developing automatic responses to a situation built up through repeated exposure to it. Four variables are central to how consumers learn from repeated experience: drive, cue, response, and reinforcement. A *drive* is a need that moves an individual to action. Drives, such as hunger, might be represented by motives. A *cue* is a stimulus or symbol perceived by consumers. A *response* is the action taken by a consumer to satisfy the drive. *Reinforcement* is the reward. Being hungry (drive), a consumer sees a cue (a billboard), takes action (buys a sandwich), and receives a reward (it tastes great!).

Marketers use two concepts from behavioral learning theory. *Stimulus generalization* occurs when a response elicited by one stimulus (cue) is generalized to another stimulus. Using the same brand name for different products is an application of this concept, such as Tylenol Cold & Flu and Tylenol P.M. *Stimulus discrimination* refers to a person's ability to perceive differences in stimuli. Consumers' tendency to perceive all light beers as being alike led to Budweiser Light commercials that distinguished between many types of "light beers" and Bud Light.

Cognitive Learning Consumers also learn through thinking, reasoning, and mental problem solving without direct experience. This type of learning, called *cognitive learning*, involves making connections between two or more ideas or simply observing the outcomes of others' behaviors and adjusting your own accordingly. Firms also influence this type of learning. Through repetition in advertising, messages such as "Feel Better, Tylenol 8-Hour" link a brand (Tylenol 8-Hour) and an idea (pain reliever) by showing someone using the brand and finding relief.

Brand Loyalty Learning is also important to marketers because it relates to habit formation—the basis of routine problem solving. Furthermore, there is a close link between habits and **brand loyalty**, which is a favorable attitude toward and consistent purchase of a single brand over time. Brand loyalty results from the positive reinforcement of previous actions. A consumer reduces risk and saves time by consistently purchasing the same brand of shampoo and has favorable results—healthy, shining hair. There is evidence of brand loyalty in many commonly

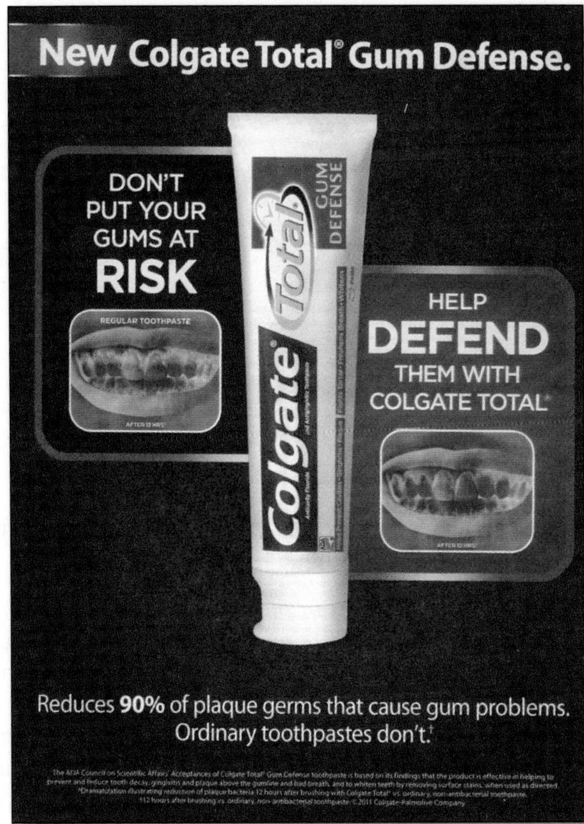

Attitudes toward Colgate Total toothpaste and Hellmann's Real Mayonnaise were successfully changed by these ads. How? Read the text on the next page to find out how marketers can change consumer attitudes toward products and brands.

Colgate-Palmolive
www.colgate.com

Hellmann's
www.hellmanns.com

purchased products in the United States and the global marketplace. However, the incidence of brand loyalty appears to be declining in North America, Western Europe, and Japan.[21]

Consumer Values, Beliefs, and Attitudes

Values, beliefs, and attitudes play a central role in consumer decision making and related marketing actions.

Attitude Formation An **attitude** is a "learned predisposition to respond to an object or class of objects in a consistently favorable or unfavorable way."[22] Attitudes are shaped by our values and beliefs, which are learned. Values vary by level of specificity. We speak of American core values, including material well-being and humanitarianism. We also have personal values, such as thriftiness and ambition. Marketers are concerned with both but focus mostly on personal values. Personal values affect attitudes by influencing the importance assigned to specific product attributes. Suppose thriftiness is one of your personal values. When you evaluate cars, fuel economy (a product attribute) becomes important. If you believe a specific car brand has this attribute, you are likely to have a favorable attitude toward it.

Beliefs also play a part in attitude formation. **Beliefs** are a consumer's subjective perception of how a product or brand performs on different attributes. Beliefs are based on personal experience, advertising, and discussions with other people. Beliefs about product attributes are important because, along with personal values, they create the favorable or unfavorable attitude the consumer has toward certain products, services, and brands.

Marketing inSite

Identifying Your VALS Profile: What Motivates You?

The VALS™ system run by Strategic Business Insights has identified eight unique consumer segments based on a person's primary motivation and resources. The text provides a brief description of each segment.

Do you wish to know your VALS profile? If you do, respond to the questions on the VALS survey at www.strategicbusinessinsights.com. Simply click "VALS." Next, click the "Take the VALS Survey" link. In addition to obtaining your profile in real time, you can examine the characteristics of your own and other profiles in greater detail.

Attitude Change Marketers use three approaches to try to change consumer attitudes toward products and brands, as illustrated in the following examples.[23]

1. *Changing beliefs about the extent to which a brand has certain attributes.* To allay mothers' concerns about ingredients in its mayonnaise, Hellmann's successfully communicated the product's high Omega 3 content, which is essential to human health.
2. *Changing the perceived importance of attributes.* Pepsi-Cola made freshness an important product attribute when it stamped freshness dates on its cans. Before doing so, few consumers considered cola freshness an issue. After Pepsi spent about $25 million on advertising and promotion, a consumer survey found that 61 percent of cola drinkers believed freshness dating was an important attribute.
3. *Adding new attributes to the product.* Colgate-Palmolive included a new antibacterial ingredient, triclosan, in its Colgate Total toothpaste and spent $100 million marketing the brand. The result? Colgate Total toothpaste is now a billion-dollar-plus global brand.

Consumer Lifestyle

Lifestyle is a mode of living that is identified by how people spend their time and resources, what they consider important in their environment, and what they think of themselves and the world around them. The analysis of consumer lifestyles, called *psychographics*, provides insights into consumer needs and wants. Lifestyle analysis has proven useful in segmenting and targeting consumers for new and existing products and services (see Chapter 9).

Psychographics, the practice of combining psychology, lifestyle, and demographics, is often used to uncover consumer motivations for buying and using products and services. A prominent psychographic system is VALS from Strategic Business Insights (SBI).[24] The VALS system identifies eight consumer segments based on (1) their primary motivation for buying and having certain products and services and (2) their resources.

According to SBI researchers, consumers are motivated to buy products and services and seek experiences that give shape, substance, and satisfaction to their lives. But not all consumers are alike. Consumers are inspired by one of three primary motivations—ideals, achievement, and self-expression—that give meaning to their self or the world and govern their activities. The different levels of resources enhance or constrain a person's expression of his or her primary motivation.

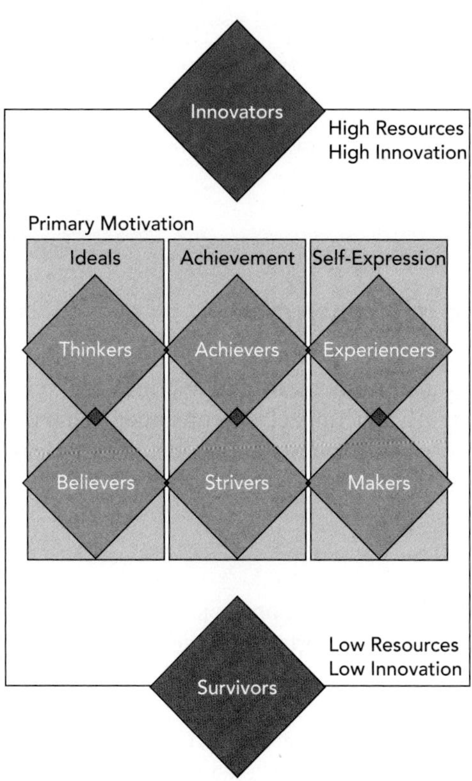

The VALS classification system places consumers with abundant resources—psychological, physical, and material means and capacities—near the top of the chart and those with minimal resources near the bottom. The chart segments consumers by their basis for decision making: ideals, achievement, or self-expression. The boxes intersect to indicate that some categories may be considered together. For instance, a marketer may categorize Thinkers and Believers together.

A person's resources include psychological, physical, demographic, and material capacities such as income, self-confidence, and risk-taking. Before reading further, visit the VALS website discussed in the Marketing inSite box. Complete the short survey to learn which segment best describes you.

The VALS system seeks to explain why and how consumers make purchase decisions.

- *Ideals-motivated groups.* Consumers motivated by ideals are guided by knowledge and principles. *Thinkers* are mature, reflective, and well-educated people who value order, knowledge, and responsibility. They are practical consumers and deliberate information-seekers who value durability and functionality in products over styling and newness. *Believers*, with fewer resources, are conservative, conventional people with concrete beliefs based on traditional, established codes: family, religion, community, and the nation. They choose familiar products and brands, favor American-made products, and are generally brand loyal.
- *Achievement-motivated groups.* Consumers motivated by achievement look for products and services that demonstrate success to their peers or to a peer group they aspire to. *Achievers* have a busy, goal-directed lifestyle and a deep commitment to career and family. Image is important to them. They favor established, prestige products and services and are interested in time-saving devices given their hectic schedules. *Strivers* are trendy, fun-loving, and less self-confident than Achievers. They also have lower levels of education and household income. Money defines success for them. They favor stylish products and are as impulsive as their financial circumstances permit.
- *Self-expression-motivated groups.* Consumers motivated by self-expression desire social or physical activity, variety, and risk. *Experiencers* are young, enthusiastic, and impulsive consumers who become excited about new possibilities but are equally quick to cool. They savor the new, the offbeat, and the risky. Their energy finds an outlet in exercise, sports, outdoor recreation, and social activities. Much of their income is spent on fashion items, entertainment, and socializing and particularly on looking good and having the latest things. *Makers*, with fewer resources, express themselves and experience the world by working on it—raising children or fixing a car. They are practical people who have constructive skills, value self-sufficiency, and are unimpressed by material possessions except those with a practical or functional purpose.
- *High- and low-resource groups.* Two segments stand apart. *Innovators* are successful, sophisticated, take-charge people with high self-esteem and abundant resources of all kinds. Image is important to them, not as evidence of power or status, but as an expression of cultivated tastes, independence, and character. They are receptive to new ideas and technologies. Their lives are characterized by variety. *Survivors*, with the least resources of any segment, focus on meeting basic needs (safety and security) rather than fulfilling desires. They represent a modest market for most products and services and are loyal to favorite brands, especially if they can be purchased at a discount.

Each of these segments exhibits unique media preferences. Experiencers and Strivers are the most likely to visit Internet chat rooms. Innovators, Thinkers, and Achievers tend to read business and news magazines such as *Fortune* and *Time*. Makers read automotive magazines. Believers are the heaviest readers of *Reader's Digest*. GeoVALS™ estimates the percentage of each VALS group by zip code.

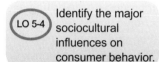

learning review

5-4. The problem with the Toro Snow Pup was an example of selective ______________.

5-5. What three attitude-change approaches are most common?

5-6. What does *lifestyle* mean?

SOCIOCULTURAL INFLUENCES ON CONSUMER BEHAVIOR

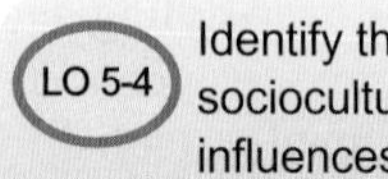

LO 5-4 Identify the major sociocultural influences on consumer behavior.

Sociocultural influences, which evolve from a consumer's formal and informal relationships with other people, also exert a significant impact on consumer behavior. These involve personal influence, reference groups, family influence, social class, culture, and subculture.

Personal Influence

A consumer's purchases are often influenced by the views, opinions, or behaviors of others. Two aspects of personal influence are very important to marketing: opinion leadership and word-of-mouth activity.

Opinion Leadership Individuals who exert direct or indirect social influence over others are called **opinion leaders**. Opinion leaders are considered to be knowledgeable about or users of particular products and services, so their opinions influence others' choices.[25] Opinion leadership is widespread in the purchase of cars and trucks, entertainment, clothing and accessories, club membership, consumer electronics, vacation destinations, food, and financial investments. A study by *Popular Mechanics* magazine identified 18 million opinion leaders who influence the purchases of some 85 million consumers for do-it-yourself products.

About 10 percent of U.S. adults are opinion leaders. Identifying, reaching, and influencing opinion leaders is a major challenge for companies. Some firms use actors or sports figures as spokespersons to represent their products. Others promote

Firms use world-class athletes as spokespersons to represent their products, such as football player Eli Manning and tennis player Victoria Azarenka for Citizen watches.

Citizen Watch Company
www.citizenwatch.com

Marketing Matters

customer value

BzzAgent—The Buzz Experience

Have you recently heard about a new product, movie, website, book, or restaurant from someone you know . . . or a complete stranger? If so, you may have had a word-of-mouth experience.

Marketers recognize the power of word of mouth. The challenge has been to harness that power. BzzAgent Inc. does just that. Its worldwide volunteer army of one million natural-born talkers channel their chatter toward products and services they deem authentically worth talking about, either online or in person. "Our goal is to capture honest word of mouth," says David Balter, BzzAgent's founder, "and to build a network that turns passionate customers into brand evangelists."

BzzAgent's method is simple. Once a client signs on with BzzAgent, the company searches its "agent" database for those who match the demographic and psychographic profile of the target market for a client's offering. Agents then can sign up for a buzz campaign and receive a sample product and a training manual for buzz-creating strategies. Each time an agent completes an activity, he or she is expected to file an online report describing the nature of the buzz and its effectiveness. BzzAgent coaches respond with encouragement and feedback on additional techniques.

Agents keep the products they promote. They also earn points redeemable for books, CDs, and other items by filing detailed reports. Who are the agents? About 65 percent are older than 25 and 70 percent are women. All are gregarious and genuinely like the product or service, otherwise they wouldn't participate in the buzz campaign.

Estée Lauder, Monster.com, Anheuser-Busch, Penguin Books, Lee, Michelin, Wrigley, Arby's, Nestlé, Hershey Foods, Procter & Gamble, Danone, and Volkswagen have used BzzAgent. But BzzAgent's buzz isn't cheap, and not everything is buzz worthy. Deploying 1,000 agents on a 12-week campaign can cost a company $95,000, exclusive of product samples. BzzAgent researches a product or service before committing to a campaign and rejects about 80 percent of the companies that seek its service. It also refuses campaigns for politicians, religious groups, and certain products, such as firearms. Interested in BzzAgent? Visit its website at www.bzzagent.com or www.facebook.com/bzzagent.

their products in media believed to reach opinion leaders. Still others use more direct approaches. For example, a carmaker recently invited influential community leaders and business executives to test-drive its new models. Some 6,000 accepted the offer, and 98 percent said they would recommend their tested car. The company estimated that the number of favorable recommendations totaled 32,000.

Word of Mouth The influencing of people during conversations is called **word of mouth**. Word of mouth is the most powerful and authentic information source for consumers because it typically involves friends viewed as trustworthy. About 75 percent of all consumer conversations about brands happen face-to-face, 15 percent happen over the phone, and 10 percent happen online.[26] According to a recent study, 67 percent of U.S. consumer product sales are directly based on word-of-mouth activity among friends, family, and colleagues.[27]

QR 5-2
Dove Video

The power of personal influence has prompted firms to promote positive and retard negative word of mouth. For instance, "teaser" advertising campaigns are run in advance of new-product introductions to stimulate conversations. Other techniques such as advertising slogans, music, and humor also heighten positive word of mouth. Many commercials shown during the Super Bowl are created expressly to initiate conversations about the advertisements and featured product or service the next day. Increasingly, companies recruit and deploy people to produce *buzz*—popularity created by consumer word of mouth. Read the Marketing Matters box to learn how this is done by BzzAgent.[28] Then scan the quick response code in the margin to see a video of BzzAgent's campaign for Dove hair care products.

Unfortunately, word of mouth can also be a source of negative information. For example, consider the damaging (and untrue) rumors that have plagued Kmart (snake eggs in clothing), Taco Bell (beef content in taco meat filling), Corona Extra beer (contamination), and Snickers candy bars in Russia (a cause of diabetes). Overcoming or neutralizing negative word of mouth is difficult and costly. However, supplying factual information, providing toll-free numbers for consumers to call the company, and giving appropriate product demonstrations have proven helpful.

The power of word of mouth is magnified by the Internet through online forums, blogs, social media, and websites. In fact, companies use special software to monitor online messages and find out what consumers are saying about their products, services, and brands. They have found that 30 percent of people spreading negative information have never owned or used the product, service, or brand![29]

Reference Group Influence

Reference groups are people to whom an individual looks as a basis for self-appraisal or as a source of personal standards. Reference groups affect consumer purchases because they influence the information, attitudes, and aspiration levels that help set a consumer's standards. For example, one of the first questions one asks others when planning to attend a social occasion is, "What are you going to wear?" Reference groups influence the purchase of luxury products rather than necessities—particularly when the use or consumption of a chosen brand will be highly visible to others.

The Harley Owners Group (HOG) has over 1 million members and is a prototypical brand community. Read the text to learn about the characteristics of a brand community.

Consumers have many reference groups, but three groups have clear marketing implications.[30] An *associative group* is one to which a person actually belongs, including fraternities and sororities and alumni associations. Such groups are easily identifiable and are targeted by firms selling insurance, insignia products, and charter vacations.

Associative reference groups can also form around a brand, as is the case with clubs like the HOG (Harley Owners Group), which is made up of Harley-Davidson fans. A **brand community** is a specialized group of consumers with a structured set of relationships involving a particular brand, fellow customers of that brand, and the product in use. A consumer who is a member of a brand community thinks about brand names (e.g., Harley-Davidson), the product category (e.g., motorcycles), other customers who use the brand (e.g., HOG members), and the marketer that makes and promotes the brand.

An *aspiration group* is one that a person wishes to be a member of or wishes to be identified with, such as a professional society or sports team. Firms frequently rely on spokespeople or settings associated with their target market's aspiration group in their advertising.

A *dissociative group* is one that a person wishes to maintain a distance from because of differences in values or behaviors. Firms often avoid dissociative reference groups in their marketing. For example, retailer Abercrombie & Fitch offered to pay cast members of the controversial TV reality show *Jersey Shore* to *not* wear its clothing. "We understand that the show is for entertainment purposes, but believe this association is contrary to the aspirational nature of our brand, and may be distressing to many of our fans," the retailer stated.[31]

Family Influence

Family influences on consumer behavior result from three sources: consumer socialization, passage through the family life cycle, and decision making within the family or household.

Consumer Socialization The process by which people acquire the skills, knowledge, and attitudes necessary to function as consumers is called **consumer**

socialization.[32] Children learn how to purchase (1) by interacting with adults in purchase situations and (2) through their own purchasing and product usage experiences. Research shows that children evidence brand preferences at age two, and these preferences often last a lifetime. This knowledge prompted the licensing of the well-known Craftsman brand name to MGA Entertainment for its children's line of My First Craftsman toys and power tools and Time Inc.'s *Sports Illustrated Kids.*

Family Life Cycle Consumers act and purchase differently as they go through life. The **family life cycle** concept describes the distinct phases that a family progresses through from formation to retirement, each phase bringing with it identifiable purchasing behaviors.[33] Figure 5–6 illustrates the traditional progression as well as contemporary variations of the family life cycle. Today, the *traditional family*—married couple with children younger than 18 years—constitutes just 21 percent of all U.S. households. The remaining 78 percent of U.S. households include single parents; unmarried couples; divorced, never-married, or widowed individuals; and older married couples whose children no longer live at home.

Young singles' buying preferences are for nondurable items, including prepared foods, clothing, personal care products, and entertainment. They represent a target market for recreational travel, automobile, and consumer electronics firms. Young married couples without children are typically more affluent than young singles because usually both spouses are employed. These couples exhibit preferences for furniture, housewares, and gift items for each other. Young marrieds with children are driven by the needs of their children. They make up a sizable market for life insurance, various children's products, and home furnishings. Single parents with children are the least financially secure of households with children. Their buying preferences are often affected by a limited economic status and tend toward convenience foods, child care services, and personal care items.

Middle-aged married couples with children are typically better off financially than their younger counterparts. They are a significant market for leisure products and home improvement items. Middle-aged couples without children typically have a large

FIGURE 5–6
Modern family life cycle stages and flows. Can you identify people you know in different stages? Do they follow the purchase patterns described in the text?

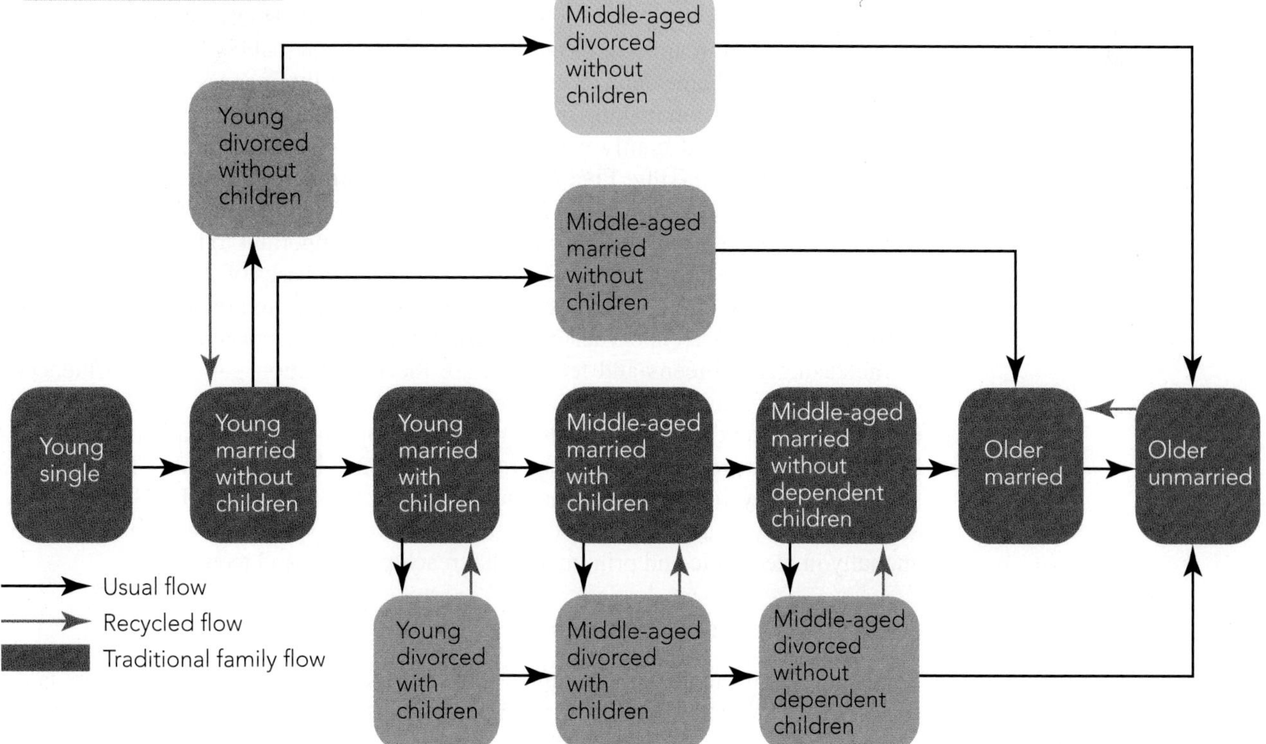

Today, 31 percent of men are the primary grocery shoppers in their households. Marketers that supply the $560 billion retail food industries are now adjusting store layouts and shelf placements to cater to men.

amount of discretionary income. These couples buy better home furnishings, status automobiles, and financial services. Persons in the last two phases—older married and older unmarried—make up a sizable market for prescription drugs, medical services, vacation trips, and gifts for younger relatives.

Family Decision Making A third source of family influence on consumer behavior involves the decision-making process that occurs within the family.[34] Two decision-making styles exist: spouse-dominant and joint decision making. With a joint decision-making style, most decisions are made by both husband and wife. Spouse-dominant decisions are those for which either the husband or the wife is mostly responsible. Research indicates that wives tend to have more say when purchasing groceries, children's toys, clothing, and medicines. Husbands tend to be more influential in home and car maintenance purchases. Joint decision making is common for cars, vacations, houses, home appliances and electronics, family finances, and medical care. As a rule, joint decision making increases with the education of the spouses.

Roles of individual family members in the purchase process are another element of family decision making. Five roles exist: (1) information gatherer, (2) influencer, (3) decision maker, (4) purchaser, and (5) user. Family members assume different roles for different products and services. This knowledge is important to firms. For example, 89 percent of wives either influence or make outright purchases of men's clothing. Even though women are often the grocery decision makers, they are not necessarily the purchasers. Today, 31 percent of men are the primary grocery shoppers in their households.

Increasingly, preteens and teenagers are the information gatherers, influencers, decision makers, and purchasers of products and services for the family, given the prevalence of working parents and single-parent households. The market for products bought by or for preteens and teenagers surpasses $208 billion annually. These figures help explain why, for example, Johnson & Johnson, Apple, Kellogg, P&G, Nike, Sony, and Oscar Mayer, among countless other companies, spend more than $70 billion annually in electronic and print media that reach preteens and teens.

Social Class Influence

A more subtle influence on consumer behavior than direct contact with others is the social class to which people belong. **Social class** may be defined as the relatively permanent, homogeneous divisions in a society into which people sharing similar values, interests, and behavior can be grouped. A person's occupation, source of income (not level of income), and education determine his or her social class. Generally speaking, three major social class categories exist—upper, middle, and lower—with subcategories within each. This structure has been observed in the United States, Great Britain, Western Europe, and Latin America.[35]

To some degree, persons within social classes exhibit common values, attitudes, beliefs, lifestyles, and buying behaviors. Compared with the middle classes, people in the lower classes have a more short-term time orientation, think in concrete rather than abstract terms, and see fewer personal opportunities. Members of the upper classes focus on achievements and the future and think in abstract or symbolic terms.

Companies use social class as a basis for identifying and reaching particularly good prospects for their products and services. For instance, JCPenney has historically appealed to the middle classes. *New Yorker* magazine reaches the upper classes. In general, people in the upper classes are targeted by companies for items such as financial investments, expensive cars, and formal evening wear. The middle classes represent a target market for home improvement centers, automobile parts stores, and personal hygiene products. Firms also recognize differences in media preferences among classes: lower and working classes prefer tabloid magazines; middle classes read fashion, romance, and celebrity (*People*) magazines; and upper classes tend to subscribe to literary, travel, and news magazines.

QR 5-3
Nissan Ad

Culture and Subculture Influences

As described in Chapter 3, *culture* refers to the set of values, ideas, and attitudes that are learned and shared among the members of a group. Thus, we often refer to the American culture, the Latin American culture, or the Japanese culture. Cultural underpinnings of American buying patterns were described in Chapter 3; Chapter 7 will explore the role of culture in global marketing.

Subgroups within the larger, or national, culture with unique values, ideas, and attitudes are referred to as **subcultures**. Various subcultures exist within the American culture. The three largest racial/ethnic subcultures in the United States are Hispanics, African Americans, and Asian Americans. Collectively, they are expected to account for one in four U.S. consumers and to spend about $2.5 trillion for goods and services in 2017, which will represent 16.4 percent of the United States' total buying power.[36] Each group exhibits sophisticated social and cultural behaviors that affect buying patterns, which provides the basis for multicultural marketing programs described in Chapter 3.

Why does Best Foods advertise its Mazola Corn Oil in Spanish? Read the text for the answer.

Mazola Corn Oil
www.mazola.com

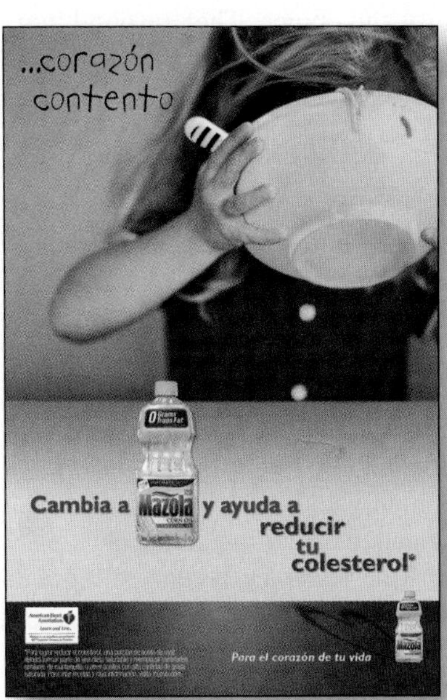

Hispanic Buying Patterns Hispanics represent the largest racial/ethnic subculture in the United States in terms of population and spending power. About 50 percent of Hispanics in the United States are immigrants, and the majority are under the age of 29. One-third of Hispanics are younger than 18.

Research on Hispanic buying practices has uncovered several consistent patterns:[37]

1. Hispanics are quality and brand conscious. They are willing to pay a premium price for premium quality and are often brand loyal.
2. Hispanics prefer buying American-made products, especially those offered by firms that cater to Hispanic needs.
3. Hispanic buying preferences are strongly influenced by family and peers.
4. Hispanics consider advertising a credible product information source, and U.S. firms spend about $8 billion annually on advertising to Hispanics.
5. Convenience is not an important product attribute to Hispanic homemakers with respect to food preparation or consumption, nor is low caffeine in coffee and soft drinks, low fat in dairy products, or low cholesterol in packaged foods.

Despite some consistent buying patterns, marketing to Hispanics has proven to be a challenge for two reasons. First, the Hispanic subculture is diverse and composed of Mexicans, Puerto Ricans, Cubans, and others of Central and South American ancestry. Cultural differences among these nationalities often affect product preferences. For example, Campbell Soup Company sells its Casera line of soups, beans, and sauces using different recipes to appeal to Puerto Ricans on the East Coast and Mexicans in the Southwest. Second, a language barrier exists, and commercial messages are frequently misinterpreted when translated into Spanish. Volkswagen learned this lesson when the Spanish translation of its "Drivers Wanted" slogan suggested "chauffeurs wanted." The Spanish slogan was changed to "*Agarra Calle*," a slang expression that can be loosely translated as "let's hit the road."

Sensitivity to the unique needs of Hispanics by firms has paid huge dividends. For example, Metropolitan Life Insurance is the largest insurer of Hispanics. Goya Foods dominates the market for ethnic food products sold to Hispanics. Best Foods's Mazola Corn Oil captures two-thirds of the Hispanic market for this product category. Time, Inc., has more than 750,000 subscribers to its *People en Español*.

African American Buying Patterns African Americans have the second-largest spending power of the three racial/ethnic subcultures in the United States. Consumer research on African American buying patterns has focused on similarities and differences with Caucasians. When socioeconomic status differences between African Americans and Caucasians are removed, there are more similarities than points of difference. Differences in buying patterns are greater within the African American subculture, due to levels of socioeconomic status, than between African Americans and Caucasians of similar status.

Even though similarities outweigh differences, there are consumption patterns that do differ between African Americans and Caucasians.[38] For example, African Americans spend far more than Caucasians on boys' clothing, rental goods, and audio equipment. African American women spend three times more on health and beauty products than Caucasian women. Furthermore, the typical African American family is five years younger than the typical Caucasian family. This factor alone accounts for some of the observed differences in preferences for clothing, music, shelter, cars, and many other products, services, and activities. Finally, it must be emphasized that, historically, African Americans have been deprived of employment and educational opportunities in the United States. Both factors have resulted in income disparities between African Americans and Caucasians, which influence purchase behavior.

African American women represent a large market for health and beauty products. Cosmetics companies such as Maybelline actively seek to serve this market.

Maybelline
www.maybelline.com

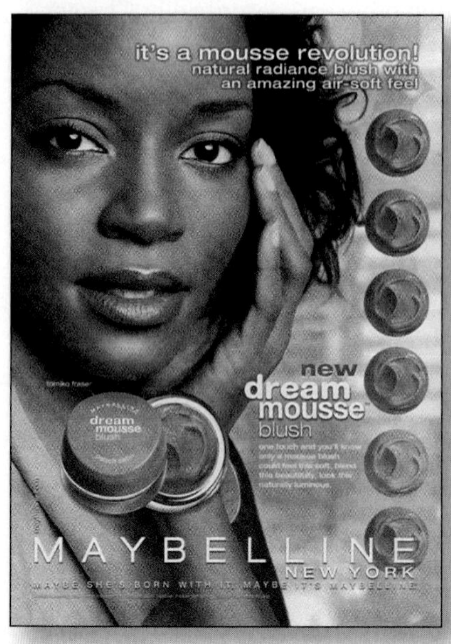

Recent research indicates that while African Americans are price conscious, they are strongly motivated by quality and choice. They respond more to products and advertising that appeal to their African American pride and heritage as well as address their ethnic features and needs regardless of socioeconomic status.

Asian American Buying Patterns Asian Americans are the fastest growing racial/ethnic subculture in the United States. About 70 percent of Asian Americans are immigrants. Most are under the age of 30.

The Asian subculture is composed of Chinese, Japanese, Filipinos, Koreans, Asian Indians, people from Southeast Asia, and Pacific Islanders. The diversity of the Asian subculture is so great that generalizations about buying patterns of this group are difficult to make.[39] Consumer research on Asian Americans suggests that individuals and families can be divided into two groups. *Assimilated* Asian Americans are conversant in English, highly educated, hold professional and managerial positions, and exhibit buying patterns very much like the typical American consumer. *Nonassimilated* Asian Americans are recent immigrants who still cling to their native languages and customs.

The diversity of Asian Americans evident in language, customs, and tastes requires marketers to be sensitive to different Asian nationalities. For example,

Anheuser-Busch's agricultural products division sells eight varieties of California-grown rice, each with a different Asian label to cover a range of nationalities and tastes. The company's advertising also addresses the preferences of Chinese, Japanese, and Koreans for different kinds of rice bowls. McDonald's actively markets to Asian Americans. According to a company executive, "We recognize diversity in this market. We try to make our messages in the language they prefer to see them."

Studies show that the Asian American subculture as a whole is characterized by hard work, strong family ties, appreciation for education, and median family incomes exceeding those of any other ethnic group. This subculture is also the most entrepreneurial in the United States, as evidenced by the number of Asian-owned businesses. These qualities led Metropolitan Life Insurance to identify Asian Americans as a target for insurance following the company's success in marketing to Hispanics.

learning review

5-7. What are the two primary forms of personal influence?

5-8. Marketers are concerned with which types of reference groups?

5-9. What two challenges must marketers overcome when marketing to Hispanic consumers?

LEARNING OBJECTIVES REVIEW

LO 5-1 *Describe the stages in the consumer purchase decision process.*
The consumer purchase decision process consists of five stages. They are problem recognition, information search, alternative evaluation, purchase decision, and postpurchase behavior. Problem recognition is perceiving a difference between a person's ideal and actual situation big enough to trigger a decision. Information search involves remembering previous purchase experiences (internal search) and external search behavior such as seeking information from other sources. Alternative evaluation clarifies the problem for the consumer by (*a*) suggesting the evaluative criteria to use for the purchase, (*b*) yielding brand names that might meet the criteria, and (*c*) developing consumer value perceptions. The purchase decision involves the choice of an alternative, including from whom to buy and when to buy. Postpurchase behavior involves the comparison of the chosen alternative with a consumer's expectations, which leads to satisfaction or dissatisfaction and subsequent purchase behavior.

LO 5-2 *Distinguish among three variations of the consumer purchase decision process: routine, limited, and extended problem solving.*
Consumers don't always engage in the five-stage purchase decision process. Instead, they skip or minimize one or more stages depending on the level of involvement—the personal, social, and economic significance of the purchase. For low-involvement purchase occasions, consumers engage in routine problem solving. They recognize a problem, make a decision, and spend little effort seeking external information and evaluating alternatives. For high-involvement purchase occasions, each of the five stages of the consumer purchase decision process is used and considerable time and effort are devoted to the search for external information and the identification and evaluation of alternatives. With limited problem solving, consumers typically seek some information or rely on a friend to help them evaluate alternatives.

LO 5-3 *Identify the major psychological influences on consumer behavior.*
Psychology helps marketers understand why and how consumers behave as they do. In particular, psychological concepts such as motivation and personality, perception, learning, values, beliefs and attitudes, and lifestyle are useful for interpreting buying processes. Motivation is the energizing force that stimulates behavior to satisfy a need. Personality refers to a person's consistent behaviors or responses to recurring situations. Perception is the process by which an individual selects, organizes, and interprets information to create a meaningful picture of the world. Consumers filter information through selective exposure, comprehension, and retention.

Much consumer behavior is learned. Learning refers to those behaviors that result from (*a*) repeated experience and (*b*) reasoning. Brand loyalty results from learning. Values, beliefs, and attitudes are also learned and influence how consumers evaluate products, services, and brands. A more general concept is lifestyle. Lifestyle, also called psychographics, combines psychology and demographics and focuses on how people spend their time and resources, what they consider important in their environment, and what they think of themselves and the world around them.

LO 5-4 *Identify the major sociocultural influences on consumer behavior.*
Sociocultural influences, which evolve from a consumer's formal and informal relationships with other people, also affect

consumer behavior. These involve personal influence, reference groups, the family, social class, culture, and subculture. Opinion leadership and word-of-mouth behavior are two major sources of personal influence on consumer behavior. Reference groups are people to whom an individual looks as a basis for self-approval or as a source of personal standards. Family influences on consumer behavior result from three sources: consumer socialization, passage through the family life cycle, and decision making within the family or household. A more subtle influence on consumer behavior than direct contact with others is the social class to which people belong. Persons within social classes tend to exhibit common values, attitudes, beliefs, lifestyles, and buying behaviors. Finally, a person's culture and subculture have been shown to influence product preferences and buying patterns.

FOCUSING ON KEY TERMS

attitude p. 123
beliefs p. 123
brand community p. 128
brand loyalty p. 122
cognitive dissonance p. 115
consideration set p. 113
consumer behavior p. 112
consumer socialization p. 128
evaluative criteria p. 113
family life cycle p. 129
involvement p. 115
learning p. 122
lifestyle p. 124
motivation p. 118
opinion leaders p. 126
perceived risk p. 121
perception p. 120
personality p. 119
purchase decision process p. 112
reference groups p. 128
self-concept p. 119
situational influences p. 117
social class p. 130
subcultures p. 131
subliminal perception p. 121
word of mouth p. 127

APPLYING MARKETING KNOWLEDGE

1 Review Figure 5–2, which shows the smartphone attributes identified by *Consumer Reports*. Which attributes are important to you? What other attributes might you consider? Which brand would you prefer?

2 Suppose research at Panasonic reveals that prospective buyers are anxious about buying high-definition television sets. What strategies might you recommend to the company to reduce consumer anxiety?

3 A Porsche salesperson was taking orders on new cars because he was unable to satisfy the demand with the limited number of cars in the showroom and lot. Several persons had backed out of the contract within two weeks of signing the order. What explanation can you give for this behavior, and what remedies would you recommend?

4 Which social class would you associate with each of the following items or actions? (*a*) tennis club membership, (*b*) an arrangement of plastic flowers in the kitchen, (*c*) *True Romance* magazine, (*d*) *Smithsonian* magazine, (*e*) formally dressing for dinner on a routine basis, and (*f*) being a member of a bowling team.

5 Assign one or more levels of the Maslow hierarchy of needs described in Figure 5–5 to the following products: (*a*) life insurance, (*b*) cosmetics, (*c*) *The Wall Street Journal*, and (*d*) hamburgers.

6 With which stage in the family life cycle would the purchase of the following products and services be most closely identified? (*a*) bedroom furniture, (*b*) life insurance, (*c*) a Caribbean cruise, (*d*) a house mortgage, and (*e*) children's toys.

7 "The greater the perceived risk in a purchase situation, the more likely that cognitive dissonance will result." Does this statement have any basis given the discussion in the text? Why?

BUILDING YOUR MARKETING PLAN

To conduct a consumer analysis for the product—the good, service, or idea—in your marketing plan:

1 Identify the consumers who are most likely to buy your product—the primary target market—in terms of (*a*) their demographic characteristics and (*b*) any other kind of characteristics you believe are important.

2 Describe (*a*) the main points of difference of your product for this group and (*b*) what problem they help solve for the consumer in terms of the first stage in the consumer purchase decision process in Figure 5–1.

3 For each of the four outside boxes in Figure 5–4 (marketing mix, psychological, sociocultural, and situational influences), identify the one or two key influences with respect to your product.

This consumer analysis will provide the foundation for the marketing mix actions you develop later in your plan.

VIDEO CASE 5 Groupon: Helping Consumers with Purchase Decisions

QR 5-4
Groupon
Video Case

University of Chicago graduate student Andrew Mason was in a rut. "There's so much to do in Chicago," he explains, "but I found myself going to the same movie theaters and restaurants."

To help people like him try new places, Mason started a website that offered coupons to large groups. He reasoned that people would try something new if the price was low enough, and that businesses would offer low prices if they knew they could sell a large quantity. The result was Groupon, a company that offers "group coupons" in deal-of-the-day offerings for local or national businesses. Consumers love the concept, buying everything from restaurant certificates, to yoga lessons, to tickets to a museum exhibit. "We think the Internet has the potential to change the way people discover and buy from local businesses," says Mason.

THE COMPANY AND GROUPON CONCEPT

Mason started with a website called ThePoint.org, which was designed to organize campaigns, protests, boycotts, and fund-raising drives for important social issues. ThePoint was not successful but it provided the concept of making offers that are only carried out if enough people commit to participate in them. With that idea Mason launched Groupon in October 2008 with a two-pizzas-for-the-price-of-one offer at the Motel Bar, located in the same building where ThePoint rented space. The concept quickly grew in Chicago and Groupon expanded into other U.S. cities and then into other countries. Today Groupon is available in 375 American cities and 48 countries, and its subscriber base has grown from 400 in 2008 to 200 million today. In its fourth full year of operation, Groupon generated $5.4 billion in gross billings.

Part of Groupon's success is the simplicity of its business model—offer subscribers at least one deal in their city each day. The unique aspect of the concept is that a certain number of people need to buy into the offer before the coupon discount is valid. Approximately 95 percent of Groupon offers "tip," or reach the number of buyers required by the merchant. Once the minimum number is met, Groupon and the merchant split the revenue. For example, a yoga studio might offer a $100 membership for $50 if 200 people participate in the offer. Once 200 consumers have indicated interest, the deal "tips" and Groupon and the yoga studio each receive 50 percent of the revenue. Everyone wins. Consumers receive an exceptional value, the merchant obtains new customers without any advertising cost, and Groupon generates revenue for creating value in the marketplace.

Many of the deals have generated extraordinary demand. The Joffrey Ballet, for example, sold 2,338 season subscriptions, doubling its subscriber base in one day! Similarly, consumers purchased 445,000 Groupons offering $50 worth of merchandise for $25 at the Gap and 6,561 tickets to a King Tut exhibit in New York's Times Square for half price at $18 apiece. The most popular

offering so far was a $25 ticket for an architectural boat tour in Chicago for $12. Groupon sold 19,822 tickets in eight hours! The company's attention to customer satisfaction ensures success stories like these. "We have a policy called 'The Groupon Promise' that any customer can return a Groupon, no questions asked—even if they used it—if they feel like Groupon has let them down," explains Mason. Groupon's success has attracted many more merchants than it can accommodate. In fact, only about 12 percent of all merchants that contact Groupon are selected to offer a deal.

In addition to the deal-of-the-day offerings, Groupon has several other services. GrouponLive offers deals to obtain tickets to sporting events, concerts, theatrical performances, and other forms of live entertainment. Groupon Getaways offers travel experiences in two forms—as a specific booking or as a voucher where consumers make a separate reservation. Groupon Goods features deals on new and innovative products. Finally, Groupon is testing a concept it calls "Pull," which enables customers to search among thousands of deals that they can buy and use instantly. To use the service, consumers log on to the Groupon Mobile app on their smartphone and select "Nearby." The app then determines the location of the consumer and displays a map of nearby deals. More than 40 million people have downloaded the Groupon Mobile app, and approximately 45 percent of Groupon's transactions in the United States are completed from a mobile device.

Groupon's growth is evident in some amazing numbers. The company has offered more than 400 million deals, with over 500,000 merchant partners, and employs 11,000 people around the globe. In addition, Groupon has created a market of consumer deal hunters that includes its 41.7 million active customers, and an industry of approximately 500 competitive deal services. The competitors include LivingSocial, Amazon Local, Google Offers, Plum District, Tippr, Bloomspot, Scoutmob, and many others. While the industry is large and growing, the competition has been intense, leading Facebook, Yahoo!, and others to test social-buying deal services but discontinue the offerings.

USING COUPONS TO INFLUENCE CONSUMERS' BUYING BEHAVIOR

"Part of the reason that Groupon has grown as quickly as it has is because we really understand consumer behavior," explains Julie Mossler, public relations & consumer marketing manager at Groupon. Generally, Groupon consumers follow the same purchase decision process common to many consumer purchases. The first stage, problem recognition, may be triggered by an e-mail or an appointment to have lunch with friends. Groupon deal-of-the-day e-mail messages, for example, often present consumers with an opportunity to do something they wouldn't ordinarily do—take sky-diving lessons or subscribe to the ballet. Groupon Nearby presents real-time offers on smartphone apps in response to an immediate need in a specific location. While the two types of offers generate different types of purchases, they both begin the purchase process.

The second stage, information search, may simply be a review of previous experiences with the merchant making the offer, online comparisons with competitors, or discussions with friends on Facebook or Twitter. In fact, the collective buying aspect of Groupon encourages subscribers to share promotions with family and friends to increase the chances of reaching the required number of buyers.

In the alternative evaluation stage many Groupon customers focus on price as the most important evaluative criteria, although other aspects such as quantity or time restrictions may be considered. The Groupon Nearby offers, for example, may only be valid on specific days or during short windows of time. Piece Brewery & Pizzeria in Chicago, for example, used Groupon to sell a $30 coupon for $20 valid only during its slow periods—11 a.m. to 3 p.m. Tuesday through Thursday.

The fourth stage, the purchase decision, is made online and then confirmed when the deals tip. Bo Hurd, national sales manager at Groupon, believes that the purchase stage is unique for Groupon users. He explains, "the fact that [consumers] have put money on the line. . . is driving them from the online piece, to the computers. . . to do something, to try something." Finally, after the purchase consumers compare their experience with their expectations to determine if they are satisfied or dissatisfied.

Psychological, sociocultural, and situational factors also influence Groupon users' purchase behavior. The recession has increased the importance of personal values such as thriftiness, so deal-prone people who were attracted to websites such as Gilt in fashion and Woot in consumer electronics are also attracted to Groupon. The typical Groupon user is an 18- to 34-year old woman with an average income of about $70,000. This is significant because this group's affinity to social media enables the use of Groupon, which depends on e-mail and smartphone apps to reach its customers. Specific situations such as planning entertainment activities, finding a close restaurant for lunch, or buying a gift are also common to Groupon users. As Groupon has learned more about its subscribers, it has begun personalizing the deals they see. The company uses variables such as gender, location of residence or office, and buying history to match deals with the customers. This process provides offers that are more likely to be of interest to consumers and allows Groupon to serve more merchants.

GROUPON CHALLENGES

As popular as Groupon has become, it does face three challenges. The first challenge is related to the use of coupons. Some consumers buy the coupons but never use them, eventually leaving them dissatisfied and unlikely to use Groupon again. Some consumers use the coupons but do not become regular customers. Because of the deep discounts used to sell the Groupons, most of the deals are not profitable for the merchants, so they are dissatisfied if the Groupon users do not make repeat purchases. David Perlman, owner of the Essex restaurant in New York City, for example, offered deals on Groupon and Open Table, selling 1,500 and 1,000 coupons, respectively. Now he is comparing the diners each deal brought in to determine which group has generated more repeat customers. Some merchants are also concerned that frequent discounting could discourage customers from ever making purchases without a discount.

Another challenge facing Groupon is managing its growth. The company has expanded into Europe, Latin America, Asia, and Russia by acquiring local daily deal services. For example, in Europe it purchased CityDeal, in Russia it purchased Darberry, and in Japan it purchased Qpod. It also acquired sites with customer bases in Hong Kong, Singapore, Taiwan, and the Philippines. As a result, Groupon currently has more subscribers abroad than in the United States, although more deals are still sold in the United States. According to Groupon Co-CEO Eric Lefkofsky, "We're applying our North American playbook to our international business in order to standardize systems and processes." As Groupon continues to grow, it anticipates that it must also develop a comprehensive understanding of the differences in international buying behaviors.

Finally, Groupon faces an extraordinary level of competition. Part of the problem is that the daily deal technology is not very sophisticated and the model is easy to copy. Manufacturers, large retailers, and small businesses are all trying the concept. ConAgra has offered a group coupon deal for its Healthy Choice brand through a Facebook app, Walmart launched its own deal-of-the-day coupon service, and some businesses use recently developed plug-and-play software that helps build deals into their websites. Mason hopes that Groupon Nearby is one answer to this challenge because it is much more difficult to replicate. "We have always been thinking about how to solve these fundamental problems of our model. We have known since very early on that some form of real-time deal optimization is where this had to go," he explains.

Groupon's success is the result of a simple and effective business model and an insightful understanding of consumer behavior. In the future Groupon's strategies will require continued attention to understanding consumers around the globe. Mossler explains: "Groupon has been heralded as the fastest growing company of all time, and the reason for that is because we have solved this unsolvable problem, which is how do you engage with local customers. The model really works anywhere as long as you adapt for local communities."

Questions

1 How has an understanding of consumer behavior helped Groupon grow from 400 subscribers in Chicago in 2008 to 200 million subscribers in 48 countries today?

2 What is the Groupon Promise? How does the Groupon Promise affect a consumer's perceived risk and cognitive dissonance?

3 Describe the five-stage purchase decision process for a typical Groupon user.

4 What are possible psychological and sociological influences on the Groupon consumer purchase decision process?

5 What challenges does Groupon face in the future? What actions would you recommend related to each challenge?

6 Understanding Organizations as Customers

LEARNING OBJECTIVES

After reading this chapter you should be able to:

LO 6-1 Distinguish among industrial, reseller, and government organizational markets.

LO 6-2 Describe the key characteristics of organizational buying that make it different from consumer buying.

LO 6-3 Explain how buying centers and buying situations influence organizational purchasing.

LO 6-4 Recognize the importance and nature of online buying in industrial, reseller, and government organizational markets.

BUYING IS MARKETING TOO! PURCHASING PUBLICATION PAPER FOR JCPENNEY

Kim Nagele views paper differently than most people do. As the senior purchasing manager at JCPMedia, Inc., he and a team of purchasing professionals bought more than 150,000 tons of publication paper in 2012.

JCPMedia, Inc., is responsible for print and paper purchasing at jcpenney, one of the largest department store retailers in the United States. Paper purchasing is a serious marketing responsibility for JCPMedia, Inc., which buys publication paper for jcpenney newspaper inserts and direct-mail pieces. Some 10 companies from around the world—including Verso Paper in the United States, Catalyst Paper, Inc., in Canada, Norske Skog in Norway, and UPM-Kymmene, Inc., in Finland—supply paper to jcpenney.

"The choice of paper and suppliers is also a significant marketing decision given the sizable revenue and expense consequences," notes Tom Cassidy, Vice President-Marketing Production at JCPMedia, Inc. JCPMedia, Inc., paper buyers work closely with senior jcpenney marketing executives and within budget constraints to assure that the right appearance, quality, and quantity of publication paper is purchased at the right price point for merchandise featured in the millions of jcpenney newspaper inserts and direct-mail pieces distributed every year in the United States.

JCPMedia, Inc., paper buyers themselves are thoroughly trained in many facets of purchasing. For example, Kim Nagele is a Certified Professional in Supply Management (CPSM). The CPSM designation is awarded to those individuals who have demonstrated competence in such areas as contracting and negotiation, cost management, forecasting, and materials and inventory management through a rigorous examination process.

In addition to paper appearance, quality, quantity, and price, JCPMedia paper buyers formally evaluate paper supplier capabilities, often by extended visits to supplier facilities in the United States, Canada, and Europe. Supplier capabilities include the capacity to deliver on-time selected grades of paper from specialty items to magazine papers, the availability of specific types of paper to meet printing deadlines, and formal programs focused on the life cycle of paper products. For example, a supplier's forestry management and sustainability practices are considered in the paper buying process. In fact, paper

bought by JCPMedia, Inc., is certified through the Sustainable Forestry Initiative, Forest Stewardship Council, or the Programme for the Endorsement of Forest Certification—three prominent certification programs for forest management.[1]

The next time you thumb through a jcpenney newspaper insert or direct-mail piece, take a moment to notice the paper. Considerable effort and attention was given to its selection and purchase decision by Tom Cassidy, Kim Nagele, and JCPMedia, Inc., paper buyers.

Purchasing paper for JCPMedia is one example of organizational buying. This chapter examines the different types of organizational buyers; key characteristics of organizational buying, including online buying; buying situations; unique aspects of the organizational buying process compared with the consumer purchase process; and some typical buying procedures and decisions in today's organizational markets.

THE NATURE AND SIZE OF ORGANIZATIONAL MARKETS

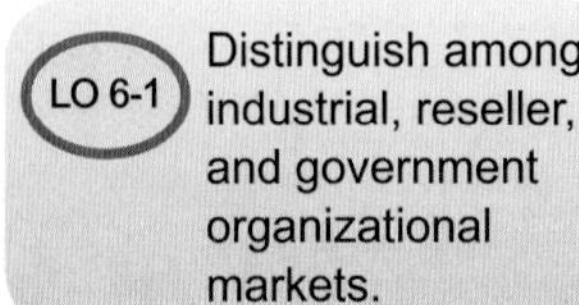

LO 6-1
Distinguish among industrial, reseller, and government organizational markets.

Understanding organizational markets and buying behavior is a necessary prerequisite for effective business marketing. **Business marketing** is the marketing of goods and services to companies, governments, or not-for-profit organizations for use in the creation of goods and services that they can produce and market to others. Because over half of all U.S. business school graduates take jobs in firms that engage in business marketing, it is important to understand the characteristics of organizational buyers and their buying behavior.

Organizational buyers are those manufacturers, wholesalers, retailers, and government agencies that buy goods and services for their own use or for resale. For example, these organizations buy computers and telephone services for their own use. However, manufacturers buy raw materials and parts that they reprocess into the finished goods they sell. Wholesalers and retailers resell the goods they buy without reprocessing them.

Organizational buyers include all buyers in a nation except ultimate consumers. These organizational buyers purchase and lease large volumes of capital equipment, raw materials, manufactured parts, supplies, and business services. In fact, because they often buy raw materials and parts, process them, and sell the upgraded product several times before it is purchased by the final organizational buyer or ultimate consumer, the total annual purchases of organizational buyers are far greater than those of ultimate consumers. IBM alone buys nearly $35 billion in goods and services each year for its own use or resale.[2]

Organizational buyers are divided into three markets: (1) industrial, (2) reseller, and (3) government.[3] Each market is described next.

Industrial Markets

There are about 7.5 million firms in the industrial, or business, market. These *industrial firms* in some way reprocess a product or service they buy before selling it again to the next buyer. This is certainly true of Corning, Inc., which transforms an exotic blend of materials to create optical fiber capable of carrying much of the telephone traffic in the United States on a single strand. It is also true (if you stretch your imagination) of a firm selling services, such as a bank that takes money from its depositors, reprocesses it, and "sells" it as loans to borrowers.

The importance of services in the United States today is emphasized by the composition of industrial markets. Companies that primarily sell physical goods (manufacturers; mining; construction; and farms, timber, and fisheries) represent 25 percent of all the industrial firms. The services market sells diverse services such as legal advice, auto repair, and dry cleaning. Service companies—finance, insurance, and real estate businesses; transportation, communication, and public utility firms; and not-for-profit organizations—represent 75 percent of all industrial firms. Because of the size and importance of service companies and not-for-profit organizations (such as the American Red Cross), services marketing is discussed in detail in Chapter 12.

Reseller Markets

Wholesalers and retailers that buy physical products and resell them again without any reprocessing are *resellers*. In the United States there are about 1.1 million retailers and 435,000 wholesalers. In Chapters 15 and 16 you will see how manufacturers use wholesalers and retailers in their distribution ("place") strategies as channels through which their products reach ultimate consumers. In this chapter, we look at these resellers mainly as organizational buyers in terms of (1) how they make their own buying decisions and (2) which products they choose to carry.

The Orion lunar spacecraft to be designed, developed, tested, and evaluated by Lockheed Martin Corp. is an example of a purchase by a government unit, namely the National Aeronautics and Space Administration (NASA). Read the text to find out how much NASA will pay for the Orion lunar spacecraft prior to its launch in 2017.

Lockheed Martin Corporation
www.lockheedmartin.com

QR 6-1
NASA Video

Government Markets

Government units are the federal, state, and local agencies that buy goods and services for the constituents they serve. There are about 89,500 of these government units in the United States. These purchases include the $10.5 billion the National Aeronautics and Space Administration (NASA) intends to pay Lockheed Martin to develop and produce the Orion lunar spacecraft scheduled for launch in 2017 as well as lesser amounts spent by local school and sanitation districts.[4]

Global Organizational Markets

Industrial, reseller, and government markets also exist on a global scale. International trade statistics indicate that the largest exporting industries in the United States focus on organizational buyers, not ultimate consumers. Capital equipment (such as construction equipment, computers, and telecommunications) and industrial supplies (such as machine parts) account for about one-half of all U.S. product exports.

The majority of world trade involves exchange relationships that span the globe. Consider the ingredients found in Kellogg's popular Nutri-Grain cereal bar. Kellogg buyers purchase ingredients from farmers, food processors, and wholesalers in eight countries on three continents.[5] Additional examples of business marketing in the global arena appear in Chapter 7.

MEASURING DOMESTIC AND GLOBAL INDUSTRIAL, RESELLER, AND GOVERNMENT MARKETS

The measurement of industrial, reseller, and government markets is an important first step for a firm interested in gauging the size of one, two, or all three of these markets in the United States and around the world. This task has been made easier with the **North American Industry Classification System (NAICS)**.[6] The NAICS provides common industry definitions for Canada, Mexico, and the United States, which makes it easier to measure economic activity in the three member

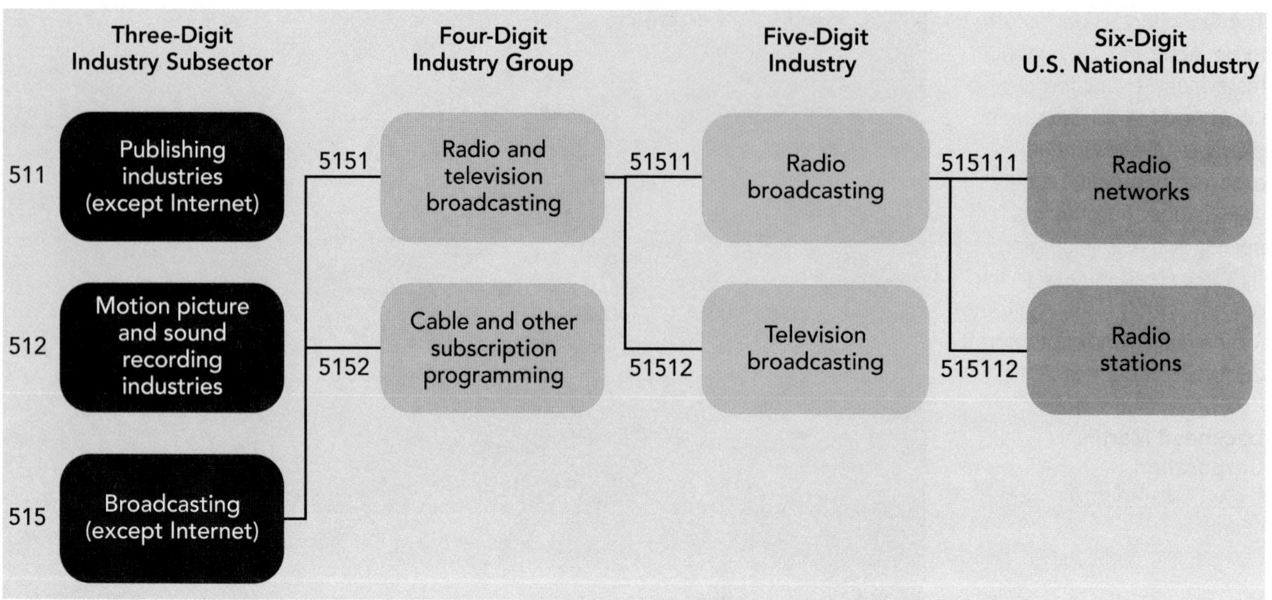

FIGURE 6–1
NAICS breakdown for the information industries sector: NAICS code 51 (abbreviated).

countries of the North American Free Trade Agreement (NAFTA). The NAICS replaced the Standard Industrial Classification (SIC) system, a version of which has been in place for more than 50 years in the three NAFTA member countries. The SIC neither permitted comparability across countries nor accurately measured new or emerging industries. Furthermore, the NAICS is consistent with the International Standard Industrial Classification of All Economic Activities, which is published by the United Nations and designed to facilitate the measurement of global economic activity.

The NAICS groups economic activity to permit studies of market share, demand for goods and services, import competition in domestic markets, and similar studies. It designates industries with a numerical code in a defined structure. A six-digit coding system is used. The first two digits designate a sector of the economy, the third digit designates a subsector, and the fourth digit represents an industry group. The fifth digit designates a specific industry and is the most detailed level at which comparable data are available for Canada, Mexico, and the United States. The sixth digit designates individual country-level national industries. Figure 6–1 shows the breakdown within the information industries sector (code 51) to illustrate the NAICS classification scheme.

The NAICS permits a firm to find the NAICS codes of its present customers and then obtain NAICS-coded lists for similar firms. Also, it is possible to monitor NAICS categories to determine the growth in various sectors and industries to identify promising marketing opportunities. However, the NAICS has an important limitation. Five-digit national industry codes are not available for all three countries because the respective governments will not reveal data when too few organizations exist in a category.

learning review

6-1. What are the three main types of organizational buyers?

6-2. What is the North American Industry Classification System (NAICS)?

CHARACTERISTICS OF ORGANIZATIONAL BUYING

LO 6-2 Describe the key characteristics of organizational buying that make it different from consumer buying.

Organizations are different from individuals, so buying for an organization is different from buying for yourself or your family. In both cases the objective in making the purchase is to solve the buyer's problem—to satisfy a need or want. However, the unique objectives and policies of an organization put special constraints on how it makes buying decisions. Understanding the characteristics of organizational buying is essential in designing effective marketing programs to reach these buyers. Key characteristics of organizational buying are listed in Figure 6–2 and discussed next.[7]

Demand Characteristics

Consumer demand for products and services is affected by their price and availability and by consumers' personal tastes and discretionary income. By comparison, industrial demand is derived. **Derived demand** means that the demand for industrial products and services is driven by, or derived from, demand for consumer products and services. For example, the demand for Weyerhaeuser's pulp and paper products is based on consumer demand for newspapers, FedEx packages, and disposable diapers. Derived demand is based on expectations of future consumer demand. For instance, Whirlpool buys parts for its washers and dryers in anticipation of consumer demand, which is affected by the replacement cycle for these products and by consumer income.

FIGURE 6–2
Key characteristics and dimensions of organizational buying behavior.

CHARACTERISTICS	DIMENSIONS
Market characteristics	• Demand for industrial products and services is derived. • Few customers typically exist, and their purchase orders are large.
Product or service characteristics	• Products or services are technical in nature and purchased on the basis of specifications. • Many of the goods purchased are raw and semifinished. • Heavy emphasis is placed on delivery time, technical assistance, and postsale service.
Buying process characteristics	• Technically qualified and professional buyers follow established purchasing policies and procedures. • Buying objectives and criteria are typically spelled out, as are procedures for evaluating sellers and their products or services. • There are multiple buying influences, and multiple parties participate in purchase decisions. • There are reciprocal arrangements, and negotiation between buyers and sellers is commonplace. • Online buying over the Internet is widespread.
Marketing mix characteristics	• Direct selling to organizational buyers is the rule, and distribution is very important. • Advertising and other forms of promotion are technical in nature. • Price is often negotiated, evaluated as part of broader seller and product/service qualities, and frequently affected by quantity discounts.

Size of the Order or Purchase

The size of the purchase involved in organizational buying is typically much larger than that in consumer buying. The dollar value of a single purchase made by an organization often runs into thousands or millions of dollars. For example, Siemens was recently awarded a $300 million contract to build a natural-gas-fired power plant in Texas.[8]

With so much money at stake, most organizations place constraints on their buyers in the form of purchasing policies or procedures. Buyers must often get competitive bids from at least three prospective suppliers when the order is above a specific amount, such as $5,000. When the order is above an even higher amount, such as $50,000, it may require the review and approval of a vice president or even the president of the company. Knowing how order size affects buying practices is important in determining who will participate in the purchase decision, who will make the final decision, and the length of time that will be required to arrive at a purchase agreement.

Number of Potential Buyers

Firms selling consumer products or services often try to reach thousands or millions of individuals or households. For example, your local supermarket or bank probably serves thousands of people. Kellogg tries to reach 80 million North American households with its breakfast cereals and probably succeeds in selling to a third or half of these in any given year. Firms selling to organizations are often restricted to far fewer buyers. Gulfstream Aerospace Corporation can sell its business jets to a few thousand organizations throughout the world, and Goodyear sells its original equipment tires to fewer than 10 car manufacturers.

Organizational Buying Objectives

Organizations buy products and services for one main reason: to help them achieve their objectives. For business firms, the buying objective is usually to increase profits through reducing costs or increasing revenues. For example, 7-Eleven buys automated inventory systems to increase the number of products that can be sold through its convenience stores and to keep them fresh. Nissan Motor Company switched its advertising agency because it expects the new agency to devise a more effective ad campaign to help it sell more cars and increase revenues. To improve executive decision making, many firms buy advanced computer systems to process data. The objectives of nonprofit firms and government agencies are usually to meet the needs of the groups they serve.

Many companies today have broadened their buying objectives to include an emphasis on buying from minority- and women-owned suppliers and vendors. Companies such as Pitney Bowes, PepsiCo, Coors, and jcpenney report that sales, profits, and customer satisfaction have increased because of their minority- and women-owned supplier and vendor initiatives. Learn about AT&T's commitment to and the success of its supplier diversity efforts in the Marketing inSite box.[9]

Pitney Bowes is a leader in supplier diversity. The company has over 800 diverse suppliers that account for $63 million in annual purchases.

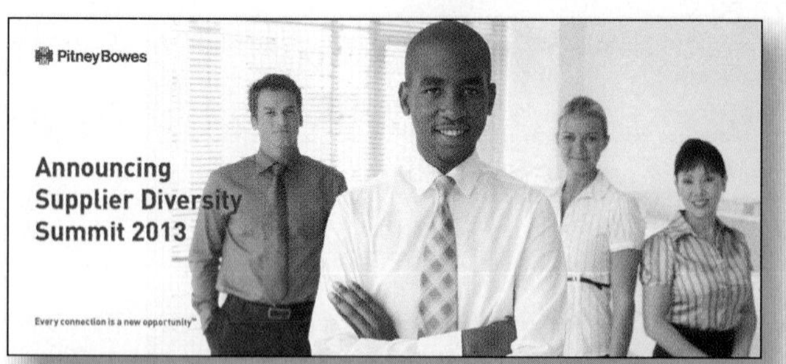

Other companies include environmental sustainability initiatives. For example, Lowe's and Home Depot no longer purchase lumber from companies that harvest timber from the world's endangered forests. Successful business marketers recognize that understanding a company's buying objectives is a necessary first step in marketing to organizations.

Organizational Buying Criteria

In making a purchase, the buying organization must weigh key buying criteria that apply to the potential supplier and what it wants to sell. **Organizational buying criteria**

Marketing inSite

Supplier Diversity Is a Strategic Initiative at AT&T

AT&T is a pioneer and national leader in developing and implementing supplier diversity best practices. The company's Minority Business Enterprise (MBE) Program was formed in 1968. In 1980, AT&T's Women Business Enterprise (WBE) Program was started, followed by the Disabled Veteran Business Enterprise (DVBE) Program in 1993.

AT&T has spent over $50 billion with businesses through its supplier diversity initiatives since 1968, and for good reason. Supplier diversity is a critical initiative in AT&T's business strategy and a key component of the company's plan to deliver the best products and services to its customers. Today, AT&T purchases about 23 percent of products and services from diversity-owned enterprises.

at&t

To learn more about AT&T's supplier diversity initiatives and its goals, visit www.attsuppliers.com and scroll down to Supplier Diversity Programs.

are the objective attributes of the supplier's products and services and the capabilities of the supplier itself. These criteria serve the same purpose as the evaluative criteria used by consumers and described in Chapter 5. The most commonly used criteria are (1) price, (2) ability to meet the quality specifications required for the item, (3) ability to meet required delivery schedules, (4) technical capability, (5) warranties and claim policies in the event of poor performance, (6) past performance on previous contracts, and (7) production facilities and capacity.[10] Suppliers that meet or exceed these criteria create customer value.

Organizational buyers who purchase products and services in the global marketplace often supplement their buying criteria with supplier ISO 9000 standards certification. **ISO 9000** standards, developed by the International Standards Organization (ISO) in Geneva, Switzerland, refer to standards for registration and certification of a manufacturer's quality management and assurance system based on an on-site audit of practices and procedures. The 3M Co., which buys and markets its products globally, has over 80 percent of its manufacturing and service facilities ISO 9000 certified. This certification gives 3M confidence in the consistent quality of its suppliers' manufacturing systems and products.[11]

Many organizational buyers today are transforming their buying criteria into specific requirements that are communicated to prospective suppliers. This practice, called **supplier development**, involves the deliberate effort by organizational buyers to build relationships that shape suppliers' products, services, and capabilities to fit a buyer's needs and those of its customers. Consider Deere & Company, the maker of John Deere farm, construction, and lawn-care equipment. Deere employs supplier-development engineers who work full-time with the company's suppliers to improve their efficiency and quality and reduce their costs. According to a Deere senior executive, "Their quality, delivery, and costs are, after all, our quality, delivery, and costs."[12]

Buyer–Seller Relationships and Supply Partnerships

Another distinction between organizational and consumer buying behavior lies in the nature of the relationship between organizational buyers and suppliers. Specifically, organizational buying is more likely to involve complex negotiations concerning delivery schedules, price, technical specifications, warranties, and claim policies. These negotiations also can last for an extended period. This was the case when the Lawrence Livermore National Laboratory acquired an IBM Sequoia supercomputer at a cost of about $250 million. In terms of processing speed, the amount of data that the Sequoia can process in one hour is equivalent to what 6.7 billion people would be able to calculate (using calculators)—if they had 320 years to do their work![13]

Marketing Matters

customer value

At Milsco Manufacturing, "Our Marketing Philosophy Is Designed to Develop Partnerships" and Deliver a Great Ride for Customers' Seats

Form, fit, and functionality are the hallmarks of a proper seating solution. Just ask the executives and engineers at Milsco Manufacturing.

Whether you are cruising the wide open spaces on your Harley-Davidson motorcycle or mowing your backyard on a John Deere lawn tractor, you're getting a comfortable ride thanks to a company you may have never heard of. Milsco is a Wisconsin-based designer and producer of seating solutions. Its customers include Harley-Davidson, John Deere, Yamaha, Caterpillar, Arctic Cat, Kubata, Toro, and Toyota, as well as numerous other well-known and respected household names in the motorcycle, power sports, agricultural, construction, marine recreation, turf care, industrial lift, golf cart, and mobility markets.

Milsco's marketing philosophy is designed to develop partnerships with its customers. The 80-year partnership between Harley-Davidson and Milsco is a case in point. Since 1934, Milsco has been the sole source of original equipment motorcycle seats and a major supplier of after-market parts and accessories, such as saddlebags, for Harley-Davidson. Milsco engineers and designers work closely with their Harley counterparts in the design of each year's new products.

In fact, Milsco partners with each of its customers to design and manufacture the most effective and functional seating solution. Every year, the company launches over 100 new products, many of which are crafted by hand, in response to new and changing customer requirements.

The next time you sit down on a Harley or a John Deere lawn tractor (or any other product involving a partnership with Milsco Manufacturing), notice the seat and remember that it was designed and manufactured for your form, fit, and functionality—and, of course, comfort.

Reciprocal arrangements also exist in organizational buying. **Reciprocity** is an industrial buying practice in which two organizations agree to purchase each other's products and services. The U.S. Justice Department disapproves of reciprocal buying because it restricts the normal operation of the free market. However, the practice exists and can limit the flexibility of organizational buyers in choosing alternative suppliers.

Long-term contracts are also prevalent. Hewlett-Packard has a 10-year, $3 billion contract to manage Procter & Gamble's information technology in 160 countries.[14]

QR 6-2
Starbucks Sustainability Video

In some cases, buyer–seller relationships evolve into supply partnerships. A **supply partnership** exists when a buyer and its supplier adopt mutually beneficial objectives, policies, and procedures for the purpose of lowering the cost or increasing the value of products and services delivered to the ultimate consumer. A classic example of a supply partnership is the one between Harley-Davidson and Milsco Manufacturing. Milsco has designed and manufactured Harley-Davidson motorcycle seats for 80 years. The importance of supply partnerships for Milsco is described in the Marketing Matters box.[15]

Retailers, too, have forged partnerships with their suppliers. Walmart has such a relationship with Procter & Gamble for ordering and replenishing P&G's products in its stores. By using computerized cash register scanning equipment and direct

Making Responsible Decisions

sustainability

Sustainable Procurement for Sustainable Growth

Manufacturers, retailers, wholesalers, and governmental agencies are increasingly sensitive to how their buying decisions affect the environment. Concerns about the depletion of natural resources; air, water, and soil pollution; and the social consequences of economic activity have given rise to the concept of sustainable procurement. Sustainable procurement aims to integrate environmental considerations into all stages of an organization's buying process with the goal of reducing the negative impact on human health and the physical environment.

Starbucks is a pioneer and worldwide leader in sustainable procurement. The company's attention to quality coffee extends to its coffee growers located in more than 20 countries. This means that Starbucks pays coffee farmers a fair price for the beans; that the coffee is grown in an ecologically sound manner; and that Starbucks invests in the farming communities where its coffees are produced. In this way, Starbucks focuses on the sustainable growth of its suppliers.

electronic linkages to P&G, Walmart can tell P&G what merchandise is needed, along with how much, when, and to which store to deliver it on a daily basis.

Supply partnerships often include provisions for what is called *sustainable procurement*. This buying practice is described in the Making Responsible Decisions box.[16] Because supply partnerships also involve the physical distribution of goods, they are again discussed in Chapter 15 in the context of supply chain management.

The Buying Center: A Cross-Functional Group

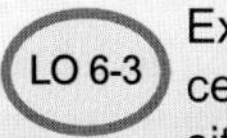

Explain how buying centers and buying situations influence organizational purchasing.

For routine purchases with a small dollar value, a single buyer or purchasing manager often makes the purchase decision alone. In many instances, however, several people in the organization participate in the buying process. The individuals in this group, called a **buying center**, share common goals, risks, and knowledge important to a purchase decision. For most large multistore chain resellers, such as Macy's, 7-Eleven, Target, or Safeway, the buying center is highly formalized and is called a *buying committee*. However, most industrial firms or government units use informal groups of people or call meetings to arrive at buying decisions.

A firm marketing to many industrial firms and government units needs to recognize the importance of buying centers and understand the structure, the technical and business functions represented, and the behavior of these groups.[17] Four questions provide guidance in understanding the buying center in these organizations: (1) Which individuals are in the buying center for the product or service? (2) What is the relative influence of each member of the group? (3) What are the buying criteria of each member? and (4) How does each member of the group perceive our company, our products and services, and our salespeople?

People in the Buying Center The composition of the buying center in a given organization depends on the specific item being bought. Although a buyer or purchasing manager is almost always a member of the buying center, individuals from other functional areas are also included, depending on what is to be purchased. In buying a million-dollar machine tool, the president (because of the size of the purchase) and the manufacturing vice president would probably be members of the buying center. For key components to be included in a final manufactured product, a cross-functional group of

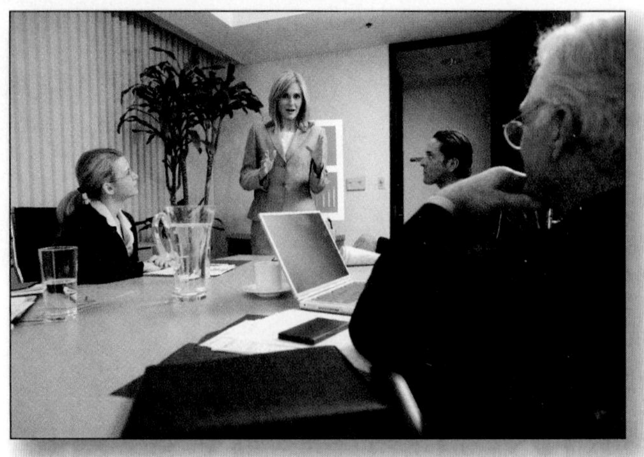

Effective marketing to organizations requires an understanding of buying centers and their role in purchase decisions.

individuals from research and development (R&D), engineering, and quality control are likely to be added. For new word-processing equipment, experienced secretaries who will use the equipment would be included as members. Still, a major question in penetrating the buying center is finding and reaching the people who will initiate, influence, and actually make the buying decision.

Roles in the Buying Center Individuals in a buying center play five specific roles. In some purchases, the same person may perform two or more of these roles.

- *Users* are the people in the organization who actually use the product or service, such as a secretary who will use a new word processor.
- *Influencers* affect the buying decision, usually by helping define the specifications for what is bought. The information systems manager would be a key influencer in the purchase of a new mainframe computer.
- *Buyers* have formal authority and responsibility to select the supplier and negotiate the terms of the contract. Kim Nagele performs this role as senior sourcing manager at JCP Media, as described in the chapter opening example.
- *Deciders* have the formal or informal power to select or approve the supplier that receives the contract. In routine orders the decider is usually the buyer or purchasing manager; in important technical purchases it is more likely to be someone from R&D, engineering, or quality control. The decider for a key component being incorporated in a final manufactured product might be any of these three people.
- *Gatekeepers* control the flow of information in the buying center. Purchasing personnel, technical experts, and secretaries can all keep salespeople or information from reaching people performing the other four roles.

Buying Situations and the Buying Center The number of people in the buying center largely depends on the specific buying situation. Researchers who have studied organizational buying identify three types of buying situations, called **buy classes**. These buy classes vary from the routine reorder, or *straight rebuy*, to the completely new purchase, termed *new buy*. In between these extremes is the *modified rebuy*. Some examples will clarify the differences.[18]

- *New buy*. Here the organization is a first-time buyer of the product or service. This involves greater potential risks in the purchase, so the buying center is enlarged to include all those who have a stake in the new buy. Procter & Gamble's purchase of a multimillion-dollar fiber-optic network from Corning, Inc., for its corporate offices in Cincinnati, represented a new buy.[19]
- *Straight rebuy*. Here the buyer or purchasing manager reorders an existing product or service from the list of acceptable suppliers, probably without even checking with users or influencers from the engineering, production, or quality control departments. Office supplies and maintenance services are usually obtained as straight rebuys.
- *Modified rebuy*. In this buying situation the users, influencers, or deciders in the buying center want to change the product specifications, price, delivery schedule, or supplier. Although the item purchased is largely the same as with the straight rebuy, the changes usually necessitate enlarging the buying center to include people outside the purchasing department.

Figure 6–3 summarizes how buy classes affect buying center tendencies.[20]

BUYING CENTER DIMENSION	BUY-CLASS SITUATION: NEW BUY	STRAIGHT REBUY	MODIFIED REBUY
People involved	Many	One	Two to three
Decision time	Long	Short	Moderate
Problem definition	Uncertain	Well-defined	Minor modifications
Buying objective	Good solution	Low-priced supplier	Low-priced supplier
Suppliers considered	New/present	Present	Present
Buying influence	Technical/operating personnel	Purchasing agent	Purchasing agent and others

FIGURE 6–3
The buying situation affects buying center behavior in different ways. Understanding these differences can pay huge dividends for companies that market to organizations.

The marketing and sales strategies of the sellers facing each of these three buying situations can vary greatly because the importance of personnel from functional areas such as purchasing, engineering, production, and R&D often varies with (1) the type of buying situation and (2) the stage of the purchasing process. If it is a new buy for the manufacturer, you should be prepared to act as a consultant to the buyer, work with technical personnel, and expect a long time for a buying decision to be reached. However, if the manufacturer has bought the item from you before (a straight or modified rebuy), you might emphasize a competitive price and a reliable supply in meetings with the purchasing agent.

learning review

6-3. What one department is almost always represented by a person in the buying center?

6-4. What are the three types of buying situations or buy classes?

CHARTING THE ORGANIZATIONAL BUYING PROCESS

Organizational buyers, like consumers, engage in a decision process when selecting products and services. **Organizational buying behavior** is the decision-making process that organizations use to establish the need for products and services and identify, evaluate, and choose among alternative brands and suppliers. There are important similarities and differences between the two decision-making processes. To better understand the nature of organizational buying behavior, we first compare it with consumer buying behavior and then detail an actual organizational purchase.

Stages in the Organizational Buying Process

As shown in Figure 6–4 (and covered in Chapter 5), the five stages a student might use in buying a smartphone also apply to organizational purchases. However, comparing the two right-hand columns in Figure 6–4 reveals key differences. For example, when a smartphone manufacturer buys earbud headsets for its units from a supplier, more individuals are involved, supplier capability becomes more important, and the postpurchase evaluation behavior is more formalized.

The headset-buying decision process is typical of the steps made by organizational buyers. Let's now examine in detail the decision-making process for a more complex product—machine vision systems.

Buying a Machine Vision System

Machine vision is widely regarded as one of the keys to the 21st century factory. The chief elements of a machine vision system are its optics, light source, camera, video processor, and computer software. Vision systems are mainly used for product inspection. They are also becoming important as one of the chief elements in the information feedback loop of systems that control manufacturing processes. Vision systems, selling for $5,000 to $20,000, are mostly sold to original equipment manufacturers

FIGURE 6–4
Comparing the stages in a consumer and organizational purchase decision process.

STAGE IN THE BUYING DECISION PROCESS	CONSUMER PURCHASE: SMARTPHONE FOR A STUDENT	ORGANIZATIONAL PURCHASE: EARBUD HEADSET FOR A SMARTPHONE
Problem recognition	Student doesn't like the features of the smartphone now owned and desires a new one.	Marketing research and sales departments observe that competitors are improving the earbud headsets for their smartphones. The firm decides to improve the earbud headsets on its own new models, which will be purchased from an outside supplier.
Information search	Student uses personal past experience and that of friends, ads, the Internet, and *Consumer Reports* to collect information and uncover alternatives.	Design and production engineers draft specifications for earbud headsets. The purchasing department identifies suppliers of earbud headsets.
Alternative evaluation	Alternative smartphones are evaluated on the basis of important attributes desired in a phone, and several stores are visited.	Purchasing and engineering personnel visit with suppliers and assess (1) facilities, (2) capacity, (3) quality control, and (4) financial status. They drop any suppliers not satisfactory on these attributes.
Purchase decision	A specific brand of smartphone is selected, the price is paid, and the student leaves the store.	They use (1) quality, (2) price, (3) delivery, and (4) technical capability as key buying criteria to select a supplier. Then they negotiate terms and award a contract.
Postpurchase behavior	Student reevaluates the purchase decision and may return the phone to the store if it is unsatisfactory.	They evaluate suppliers using a formal vendor rating system and notify a supplier if the earbud headsets do not meet their quality standard. If the problem is not corrected, they drop the firm as a future supplier.

(OEMs) who incorporate them in still larger industrial automation systems, which sell for millions of dollars. Companies worldwide are expected to spend nearly $5 billion for machine vision components in 2015.[21]

Finding productive applications for machine vision involves the constant search for technology and designs that satisfy user needs. The buying process for machine vision components and assemblies is frequently a new buy because many machine vision systems contain elements that require some custom design. Let's track five purchasing stages that a company such as the Industrial Automation Division of Maschine GmbH, a large German industrial firm, would follow when purchasing components and assemblies for the machine vision systems it produces and installs.

Problem Recognition Sales engineers constantly canvass industrial automation equipment users for leads on upcoming industrial automation projects. They also keep these users current on technology, products, and services provided by Maschine. When a firm needing a machine vision capability identifies a project that would benefit from Maschine's expertise, company engineers typically work with the firm to determine the kind of system required to meet the customer's need.

After a contract is won, project personnel must often make a **make-buy decision**—an evaluation of whether components and assemblies will be purchased from outside suppliers or built by the company itself. (Maschine GmbH produces many components and assemblies.) When these items are to be purchased from outside suppliers, the company engages in a thorough supplier search and evaluation process.

Information Search Companies such as Maschine GmbH employ a sophisticated process for identifying outside suppliers of components and assemblies. For standard items such as connectors, printed circuit boards, and components such as resistors and capacitors, the purchasing agent consults the company's purchasing databank, which contains information on hundreds of suppliers and thousands of products. All products in the databank have been prenegotiated as to price, quality, and delivery time, and many have been assessed using **value analysis**—a systematic appraisal of the design, quality, and performance of a product to reduce purchasing costs.

For one-of-a-kind components or assemblies such as new optics, cameras, and light sources, the company relies on its engineers to keep current on new developments in product technology. This information is often found in technical journals and industry magazines or at international trade shows where suppliers display their most recent innovations. In some instances, supplier representatives might be asked to make presentations to the buying center at Maschine GmbH. Such a group often consists of a project engineer; several design, system, and manufacturing engineers; and a purchasing agent.

Alternative Evaluation The main buying criteria used to select machine vision suppliers and products are displayed in Figure 6–5 on the next page.[22] Product performance, a supplier's technical support, and ease of use are the three most frequently mentioned important buying criteria for machine vision suppliers and products. Interestingly, price is among the least frequently mentioned. Typically, two or three suppliers for each standard component and assembly are identified from a **bidder's list**—a list of firms believed to be qualified to supply a given item. This list is generated from the company's purchasing databank as well as from engineering inputs. Specific items that are unique may be obtained from a single supplier after careful evaluation by the buying center.

Firms selected from the bidder's list are sent a quotation request from the purchasing agent, describing the desired quantity, delivery date(s), and specifications of the components or assemblies. Suppliers are expected to respond within 30 days.

FIGURE 6–5
Product and supplier selection criteria for buying machine vision equipment emphasize factors other than price.

A machine vision inspection camera is used in the automotive industry to perform a gear inspection. In this case, to check if the notches are correctly angled and sized.

Percentage of machine vision buyers citing individual selection criteria as most important when making a product or supplier decision.

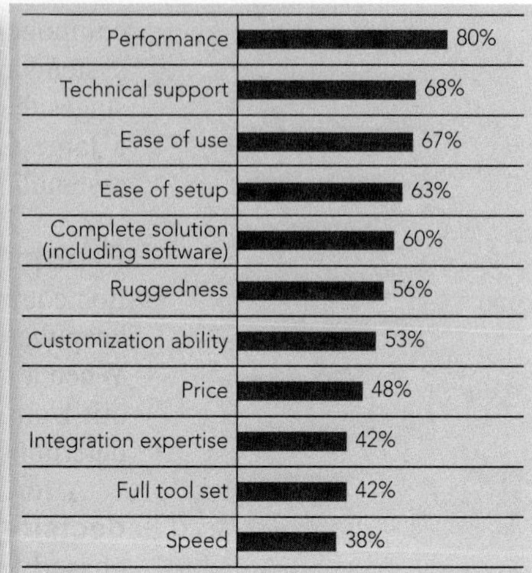

Purchase Decision Unlike the short purchase stage in a consumer purchase, the period from supplier selection to order placement to product delivery can take several weeks or even months. Even after bids for components and assemblies are submitted, further negotiation concerning price, performance, and delivery terms is likely. Sometimes conditions related to warranties, indemnities, and payment schedules have to be agreed on. The purchase decision is further complicated by the fact that two or more suppliers of the same item might be awarded contracts. This practice can occur when large orders are requested. Suppliers who are not chosen are informed why their bids were not selected.

Postpurchase Behavior As in the consumer purchase decision process, postpurchase evaluation occurs in the industrial purchase decision process, but it is formalized and often more sophisticated. All items purchased are examined in a formal product acceptance process. The performance of the supplier is also monitored and recorded. Performance on past contracts determines a supplier's chances of being asked to bid on future purchases, and poor performance may result in a supplier's name being dropped from the bidder's list.

This example of an organizational purchase suggests four lessons for marketers who want to increase their chances of selling products and services to organizations. Firms selling to organizations must (1) understand the organization's needs, (2) get on the right bidder's list, (3) find the right people in the buying center, and (4) provide value to organizational buyers.

learning review

6-5. What is a make-buy decision?

6-6. What is a bidder's list?

ONLINE BUYING IN ORGANIZATIONAL MARKETS

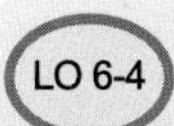

Recognize the importance and nature of online buying in industrial, reseller, and government organizational markets.

Organizational buying behavior and business marketing continues to evolve with the application of Internet technology. Organizations dwarf consumers in terms of online transactions made, average transaction size, and overall purchase volume. In fact, organizational buyers account for about 80 percent of the global dollar value of all online transactions.

Prominence of Online Buying in Organizational Markets

Online buying in organizational markets is prominent for three major reasons.[23] First, organizational buyers depend heavily on timely supplier information that describes product availability, technical specifications, application uses, price, and delivery schedules. This information can be conveyed quickly via Internet technology. Second, this technology has been shown to substantially reduce buyer order processing costs. At General Electric, online buying has cut the cost of a transaction from $50 to $100 per purchase to about $5. Third, business marketers have found that Internet technology can reduce marketing costs, particularly sales and advertising expense, and broaden their potential customer base for many types of products and services.

For these reasons, online buying is popular in all three kinds of organizational markets. For example, airlines electronically order over $400 million in spare parts from the Boeing Company each year. Customers of W. W. Grainger, a large U.S. wholesaler of maintenance, repair, and operating supplies, buy more than $2 billion worth of these products annually online. Supply and service purchases totaling $650 million each year are made online by the Los Angeles County government.

Online buying can assume many forms. Organizational buyers can purchase directly from suppliers. For instance, a buyer might acquire a dozen desktop photocopiers from Xerox at www.xerox.com. This same buyer might purchase office furniture and supplies through a reseller such as Office Depot at www.officedepot.com. Increasingly, organizational buyers and business marketers are using e-marketplaces and online auctions to purchase and sell products and services.

E-Marketplaces: Virtual Organizational Markets

A significant development in organizational buying has been the creation of online trading communities, called **e-marketplaces**, that bring together buyers and supplier organizations. These online communities go by a variety of names, including *B2B exchanges* and *e-hubs*, and make possible the real-time exchange of information, money, products, and services.

E-marketplaces can be independent trading communities or private exchanges. Independent e-marketplaces act as a neutral third party and provide an Internet technology trading platform and a centralized market that enable exchanges between buyers and sellers. They charge a fee for their service and exist in settings that have one or more of the following features: (1) thousands of geographically dispersed buyers and sellers, (2) volatile prices caused by demand and supply fluctuations, (3) time sensitivity due to perishable offerings and changing technologies, and (4) easily comparable offerings between a variety of sellers.

Examples of independent e-marketplaces include PlasticsNet (plastics), Hospital Network.com (health care supplies and equipment), and TextileWeb (garment and apparel products). Small business buyers and sellers, in particular, benefit from independent e-marketplaces. These e-marketplaces offer them an economical way to expand their customer base and reduce the cost of products and services. For example,

Marketing Matters

entrepreneurship

eBay Means Business for Entrepreneurs

San Jose, California–based eBay Inc. is a true Internet phenomenon. By any measure, it is the predominant person-to-person trading community in the world. But there is more.

eBay offers a trading platform for millions of small businesses in the United States and even greater numbers around the world.

The eBay trading platform has proven to be a boon for small businesses. According to an eBay-commissioned survey conducted by ACNielsen, 82 percent of small businesses using eBay report that it has helped their business grow and expand, 78 percent say it has helped to reduce their costs, and 79 percent say it has helped their business become more profitable.

In addition, eBay promotes entrepreneurship. According to a spokesperson from the American Enterprise Institute for Public Policy Research, "The potential for entrepreneurs to realize success through eBay is significant."

eBay provides an electronic platform for entrepreneurs and the small business market in the United States and other countries. Read the Marketing Matters box to learn more about how eBay promotes entrepreneurship.[24]

Large companies tend to favor private exchanges that link them with their network of qualified suppliers and customers. Private exchanges focus on streamlining a company's purchase transactions with its suppliers and customers. Like independent e-marketplaces, they provide a technology trading platform and central market for buyer–seller interactions. They are not a neutral third party, however, but represent the interests of their owners. For example, NeoGrid is an international business-to-business private exchange. It connects more than 250 retail customers with 80,000 suppliers. Its members include Best Buy, Campbell Soup, Costco, RadioShack, Safeway, Target, Tesco, and Walgreens. The Global Healthcare Exchange engages in the buying and selling of health care products for over 4,000 hospitals and more than 400 health care suppliers, such as Abbott Laboratories, GE Medical Systems, Johnson & Johnson, Medtronic USA, and McKesson Corporation in North America.

Online Auctions in Organizational Markets

Online auctions have grown in popularity among organizational buyers and business marketers. Many e-marketplaces offer this service. Two general types of auctions are common: (1) a traditional auction and (2) a reverse auction.[25] Figure 6–6 shows how buyer and seller participants and price behavior differ by type of auction. Let's look at each auction type more closely to understand the implications of each for buyers and sellers.

In a **traditional auction** a seller puts an item up for sale and would-be buyers are invited to bid in competition with each other. As more would-be buyers become involved, there is an upward pressure on bid prices. Why? Bidding is sequential. Prospective buyers observe the bids of others and decide whether or not to increase the bid price. The auction ends when a single bidder remains and "wins" the item with its highest price. Traditional auctions are often used to dispose of excess merchandise. For example, Dell Inc. sells surplus, refurbished, or closeout computer merchandise at its www.dellauction.com website.

A reverse auction works in the opposite direction from a traditional auction. In a **reverse auction**, a buyer communicates a need for a product or service and would-be suppliers are invited to bid in competition with each other. As more would-be suppliers

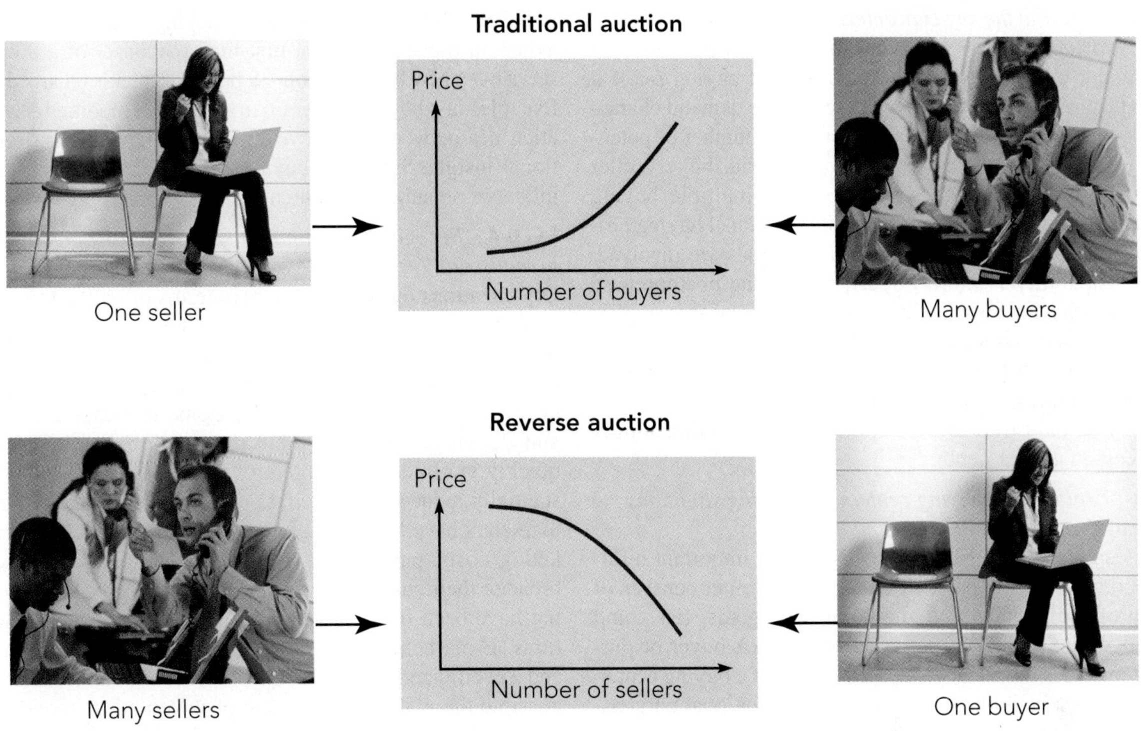

Traditional auction

One seller → Price / Number of buyers ← Many buyers

Reverse auction

Many sellers → Price / Number of sellers ← One buyer

FIGURE 6–6
Buyer and seller participants and price behavior differ by type of online auction. As an organizational buyer, would you prefer to participate in a traditional auction or a reverse auction?

become involved, there is a downward pressure on bid prices for the buyer's business. Why? Like traditional auctions, bidding is sequential and prospective suppliers observe the bids of others and decide whether or not to decrease the bid price. The auction ends when a single bidder remains and "wins" the business with its lowest price. Reverse auctions benefit organizational buyers by reducing the cost of their purchases. As an example, United Technologies Corp. estimates that it has saved $600 million on the purchase of $6 billion in supplies using online reverse auctions.[26]

Clearly, buyers welcome the lower prices generated by reverse auctions. Suppliers often favor reverse auctions because they give them a chance to capture business that they might not have otherwise had, perhaps because of a long-standing purchase relationship between the buyer and another supplier. On the other hand, suppliers say reverse auctions put too much emphasis on prices, discourage consideration of other important buying criteria, and may threaten supply partnership opportunities.[27]

learning review

6-7. What are e-marketplaces?

6-8. In general, which type of online auction creates upward pressure on bid prices and which type creates downward pressure on bid prices?

LEARNING OBJECTIVES REVIEW

LO 6-1 *Distinguish among industrial, reseller, and government organizational markets.*

There are three different organizational markets: industrial, reseller, and government. Industrial firms in some way reprocess a product or service they buy before selling it to the next buyer. Resellers—wholesalers and retailers—buy physical products and resell them again without any reprocessing. Government agencies, at the federal, state, and local levels, buy goods and services for the constituents they serve. The North American Industry Classification System (NAICS) provides common industry definitions for Canada, Mexico, and the United States, which facilitates the measurement of economic activity for these three organizational markets.

LO 6-2 *Describe the key characteristics of organizational buying that make it different from consumer buying.*
Seven major characteristics of organizational buying make it different from consumer buying. These include demand characteristics, the size of the order or purchase, the number of potential buyers, buying objectives, buying criteria, buyer–seller relationships and supply partnerships, and multiple buying influences within organizations. The organizational buying process itself is more formalized, more individuals are involved, supplier capability is more important, and the postpurchase evaluation behavior often includes performance of the supplier and the item purchased. Figure 6–4 details how the purchase decision process differs between a consumer and an organization. The example describing the purchase of a machine vision system by an industrial firm illustrates the organizational buying process in greater depth.

LO 6-3 *Explain how buying centers and buying situations influence organizational purchasing.*
Buying centers and buying situations have an important influence on organizational purchasing. A buying center consists of a group of individuals who share common goals, risks, and knowledge important to a purchase decision. A buyer or purchasing manager is almost always a member of a buying center. However, other individuals may affect organizational purchasing due to their unique roles in a purchase decision. Five specific roles that a person may play in a buying center include users, influencers, buyers, deciders, and gatekeepers. The specific buying situation will influence the number of people and the different roles played in a buying center. For a routine reorder of an item—a straight rebuy situation—a purchasing manager or buyer will typically act alone in making a purchasing decision. When an organization is a first-time purchaser of a product or service—a new buy situation—a buying center is enlarged and all five roles in a buying center often emerge. A modified rebuy situation lies between these two extremes. Figure 6–3 offers additional insights into how buying centers and buying situations influence organizational purchasing.

LO 6-4 *Recognize the importance and nature of online buying in industrial, reseller, and government organizational markets.*
Organizations dwarf consumers in terms of online transactions made and purchase volume. Online buying in organizational markets is popular for three reasons. First, organizational buyers depend on timely supplier information that describes product availability, technical specifications, application uses, price, and delivery schedules. This information can be conveyed quickly via Internet technology. Second, this technology substantially reduces buyer order processing costs. Third, business marketers have found that Internet technology can reduce marketing costs, particularly sales and advertising expense, and broaden their customer base. Two developments in online buying have been the creation of e-marketplaces and online auctions. E-marketplaces provide a technology trading platform and a centralized market for buyer–seller transactions and make possible the real-time exchange of information, money, products, and services. These e-marketplaces can be independent trading communities, such as PlasticsNet, or private exchanges, such as the Global Healthcare Exchange. Online traditional and reverse auctions represent a second major development. With traditional auctions, the highest-priced bidder "wins." Conversely, the lowest-priced bidder "wins" with reverse auctions.

FOCUSING ON KEY TERMS

bidder's list p. 151
business marketing p. 140
buy classes p. 148
buying center p. 147
derived demand p. 143
e-marketplaces p. 153
ISO 9000 p. 145
make-buy decision p. 151
North American Industry Classification System (NAICS) p. 141
organizational buyers p. 140
organizational buying behavior p. 149
organizational buying criteria p. 144
reciprocity p. 146
reverse auction p. 154
supplier development p. 145
supply partnership p. 146
traditional auction p. 154
value analysis p. 151

APPLYING MARKETING KNOWLEDGE

1 Describe the major differences among industrial firms, resellers, and government units in the United States.

2 Explain how the North American Industry Classification System (NAICS) might be helpful in understanding industrial, reseller, and government markets, and discuss the limitations inherent in this system.

3 List and discuss the key characteristics of organizational buying that make it different from consumer buying.

4 What is a buying center? Describe the roles assumed by people in a buying center and what useful questions should be raised to guide any analysis of the structure and behavior of a buying center.

5 Effective marketing is of increasing importance in today's competitive environment. How can firms more effectively market to organizations?

6 A firm that is marketing multimillion-dollar wastewater treatment systems to cities has been unable to sell a

new type of system. This setback has occurred even though the firm's systems are cheaper than competitive systems and meet U.S. Environmental Protection Agency (EPA) specifications. To date, the firm's marketing efforts have been directed to city purchasing departments and the various state EPAs to get on approved bidder's lists. Talks with city-employed personnel have indicated that the new system is very different from current systems and therefore city sanitary and sewer department engineers, directors of these two departments, and city council members are unfamiliar with the workings of the system. Consulting engineers, hired by cities to work on the engineering and design features of these systems and paid on a percentage of system cost, are also reluctant to favor the new system. (*a*) What roles do the various individuals play in the purchase process for a wastewater treatment system? (*b*) How could the firm improve the marketing effort behind its new system?

BUILDING YOUR MARKETING PLAN

Your marketing plan may need an estimate of the size of the market potential or industry potential (see Chapter 8) for a particular product market in which you compete. Use these steps:

1 Define the product market precisely, such as ice cream.
2 Visit the NAICS website at www.census.gov.
3 Click "NAICS" and enter a keyword that describes your product market (e.g., ice cream).
4 Follow the instructions to find the specific NAICS code for your product market and the economic census data that detail the dollar sales and provide the estimate of market or industry potential.

VIDEO CASE 6 Trek: Building Better Bikes through Organizational Buying

QR 6-3
Trek Video Case

"Let me tell you a little bit about the history of Trek," says Mark Joslyn, vice president of human resources at Trek Bicycle Corporation. "It's a fantastic story," he continues proudly, "It's a story about a business that started in response to a market opportunity." That opportunity was to build bicycles with the highest-quality frames. In fact, Trek's mission was simple: "Build the best bikes in the world." To do this Trek needed to find the best raw materials from the best vendors. Michael Leighton, a Trek product manager, explains, "Our relationship with our vendors is incredibly important, and one of our recipes for success!"

THE COMPANY

Trek Bicycle was founded in 1976 by Richard Burke and Bevill Hogg. With just five employees they began manufacturing bicycles in a Wisconsin barn. From the beginning they targeted the high-quality, prestige segment of the bicycle market, using only the best materials and components for their bicycles. The first year they manufactured 900 custom-made bicycles which sold quickly. Soon, Trek exceeded its manufacturing capacity. It built a new 26,000-square-foot factory and corporate headquarters to help meet growing demand.

Trek's focus on quality meant that it was very sensitive to the materials used to manufacture the bicycles. The first models, for example, used hand-brazed steel for the frames. Then, borrowing ideas from the aerospace industry, Trek soon began making frames out of bonded aluminum. Following on the success of its aluminum bicycles, Trek began manufacturing bicycles out of carbon fiber. The idea was to be "at the front of technology," explains Joslyn.

The company also expanded its product line. Its first bikes were designed to compete directly with Japanese and Italian bicycles and included road racing models. In 1983 Trek manufactured its first mountain bike. In 1990 Trek developed a new category of bicycle—called a multitrack—that combined the speed of road bikes with the ruggedness of mountain bikes. The company also began manufacturing children's bikes, tandem bikes, BMX bikes, and models used by police departments and the U.S. Secret Service. In addition, it added a line of cycling apparel called Trek Wear and cycling accessories such as helmets. Recently, Trek also undertook an Eco Design initiative to build bicycles and parts that are "green" in terms of the environmental impact of manufacturing them, how long they last, and how they can be recycled. To accommodate these production demands, Trek expanded its facilities two more times.

As Trek's popularity increased, it began to expand outside of the United States. For example, the company

acquired a Swiss bicycle company called Villiger and the oldest bicycle company in Germany, Diamant. It also expanded into China, opening two stores and signing deals with 20 Chinese distributors.

Today, Trek is one of the leading manufacturers of bicycles and cycling products, with more than $800 million in sales and 2,000 employees. Trek's products, are now marketed through 1,700 dealers in North America and wholly owned subsidiaries in seven countries, and through distributors in 90 other countries. Its brands include Trek, Gary Fisher, and Bontrager. As a global company, Trek's mission has evolved also, and today the mission is to "help the world use the bicycle as a simple solution to complex problems." Trek employees believe that the bicycle is the most efficient form of human transportation and that it can combat climate change, ease urban congestion, and build human fitness. Their motto: "We believe in bikes." Mark Joslyn explains:

> In the world today we are faced with a number of challenges. We are faced with congestion, issues with mobility, issues with the environment, and quite frankly, issues with health. We believe that the bicycle is a simple solution to all of those things. We are clearly an alternative to other forms of transportation and that's evident in the way that people are embracing cycling not just for recreation but also for transportation. And more and more, particularly in the United States, we are seeing people move to the bike as a way to get around and get to the places they need to ultimately get their life done.

ORGANIZATIONAL BUYING AT TREK

Trek's success at accomplishing its mission is the result of many important business practices, including its organizational buying process. The process begins when managers specify types of materials such as carbon fiber, component parts such as wheels and shifters, and finishing materials such as paint and decals needed to produce a Trek product. In addition, they specify quality requirements, sizing standards, and likely delivery schedules. According to Leighton, once the requirements are known, the next step is to "go to our buying center and say 'can you help us find this piece?'"

The buying center is the group of individuals who are responsible for finding the best suppliers and vendors for the organization's purchases. At Trek the buying center consists of a purchasing manager, buyers who identify domestic and international sources of materials and components, and representatives from research and development, production, and quality control. The communication between the product managers and the buying center is important. "I work very closely with our buying centers to ensure that we're partnering with vendors who can supply reliable quality, and they are actually the ones who, with our quality control team, go in and say 'yes this vendor is building product to the quality that meets Trek's standards,' and they also negotiate the pricing. Our buying center domestically is a relatively small team of people and they are focused on specific components."

When potential suppliers are identified, they are evaluated on four criteria—quality, delivery capabilities, price, and environmental impact of their production process. This allows Trek to compare alternative suppliers and to select the best match for Trek and its customers. Once a business is selected as a Trek supplier, it is continuously evaluated on elements of the four criteria. For example, current suppliers might receive scores on the number of defects in a large quantity of supplies, whether just-in-time orders made their deadlines, if target prices were maintained, and if recycled packaging was used. At Trek the tool that is used to record information about potential and existing suppliers is called a "white paper." Michael Leighton describes how they work: "Our buying center is tasked with developing what we call white papers. It's a sheet that managers can look at that shows issues and benefits related to working with these people." Every effort is made to develop long-term relationships with suppliers so that they become partners with Trek. These partnerships mean that Trek's success also contributes to the partner's success.

Trek's product managers and the buying center are involved in three types of organizational purchases. First, new buys are purchases that are made for the first time. Second, modified rebuys involve changing some aspect of a previously ordered product. Finally, straight rebuys are reorders of existing products from the list of acceptable suppliers. Leighton offers examples of each type of purchase at Trek:

> So, [for] a new buy, we work with our buying centers to find new products, something we've never done before whether it's a new saddle with a new material or a new technology that goes into the frame that damps vibration or gives a better ride. Another case might be electric bikes—maybe we are putting a motor in a bike, that's a new thing, so our buying center will help us go find those vendors. A modified rebuy is basically a saddle with a little bit different material but we are sharing some components of it, so the existing components of the saddle [are the same] but the cover is new, so it's a little bit different, but it's just the evolution of the product. A straight rebuy is looking at our strategic vision for the component further on down the line where we are just buying the same component and the volume goes up. We look at how can we make this a better business; can we save some money or can we make it more worth our while to keep buying the same product rather than buying something new.

While each of the types of purchases may occur frequently at Trek, the criteria that are used to select or evaluate a vendor may vary by the type of purchase and the type of product, making the buying process a dynamic challenge for managers.

ECO BUYING AND THE FUTURE AT TREK

One of Trek's criteria for evaluating existing and potential vendors is their environmental impact. Joslyn says it well: "We evaluate our vendors on many criteria including, increasingly, the elements that we would consider to be the 'green' part" of their offering. For example, Trek recently selected a supplier that (1) owned a quarry for extracting material, (2) used its own manufacturing facilities, and (3) used natural gas instead of coal in its production process. This was appealing to Trek because it suggested that the supplier had a "thorough understanding" of the impact of the product on the environment from start to finish.

Trek's organizational buying reflects the growing importance of its "Eco" perspective. Its bikes are becoming "smarter" as it adds electric-assist components to help them become a practical transportation alternative. Its bikes are also becoming "greener" as more low-impact materials and components are used and as packaging size and weight are reduced. Trek is also addressing the issue of recycling by building the bikes to last longer, using its dealers to help recycle tires and tubes, and funding a nonprofit organization called Dream Bikes to teach youth to fix and repair donated bikes.

In addition to changing bikes and the way it makes them, Trek faces several other challenges as it strives to improve its organizational buying process. For example, the growing number of suppliers and vendors necessitates constant, coordinated, and real-time communication to ensure that all components are available when they are needed. In addition, changes in consumer interests and economic conditions mean that Trek must anticipate fluctuations in demand and make appropriate changes in order sizes and delivery dates. As Mark Joslyn explains, "Everything we do all the time can and should be improved. So the search for ideas inside of our business and outside of our business, always looking for ways that we can improve and bring new technology and new solutions to the marketplace, is just a core of who we are."

Questions

1 What is the role of the buying center at Trek? Who is likely to comprise the buying center in the decision to select a new supplier at Trek?

2 What selection criteria does Trek utilize when it selects a new supplier or evaluates an existing supplier?

3 How has Trek's interest in the environmental impact of its business influenced its organizational buying process?

4 Provide an example of each of the three buying situations—straight rebuy, modified rebuy, and new buy—at Trek.

7 Understanding and Reaching Global Consumers and Markets

LEARNING OBJECTIVES

After reading this chapter you should be able to:

LO 7-1 Describe the nature and scope of world trade from a global perspective and identify the major trends that have influenced world trade and global marketing.

LO 7-2 Identify the environmental forces that shape global marketing efforts.

LO 7-3 Name and describe the alternative approaches companies use to enter global markets.

LO 7-4 Explain the distinction between standardization and customization when companies craft worldwide marketing programs.

BUILDING A BILLION DOLLAR BUSINESS IN INDIA THE DELL INC. WAY

Why did Dell Inc. embark on a bold global growth initiative in 2007? In the words of Steve Felice, former president of Dell Asia-Pacific and Japan, "Our success was going to be largely dependent on our ability to expand globally."

Dell's global initiative focused on emerging economies in Asia, Africa, and Latin America. Compared with mature economies in North America and Western Europe, emerging economies offered significant growth potential, according to Michael Dell, Dell's founder and chief executive officer. And Dell's global strategy has proven successful. India is a major growth market for Dell Inc. and posts annual sales over $1.5 billion. In 2013, Dell employed some 25,000 people in India, which represented about one-fourth of its global workforce.

Dell's global initiative was bold in its departure from prior product development practices. Prior to its global initiative, Dell designed products for global requirements and distributed the same product globally. The company now routinely designs low-cost notebook, laptop, and desktop personal computers for customers in China, India, and other emerging economies.

Dell's global initiative also required many changes in its signature direct sales, service, and distribution strategy. The company built its U.S. business with telephone- and Internet-based sales—without retailers. However, in emerging economies and India, customers prefer to see, touch, and use a personal computer before they buy. In response, Dell uses individual sales affiliates who reach out to customers in person and give them a firsthand product experience at their doorstep.

At the same time, Dell has joined hands with Indian chain retailers such as Croma and eZone for a shop-in-a-shop counter for its products. Dell backs this hybrid retail model by offering extended onsite service (technicians who visit individuals' homes) in over 650 cities to both retail and small business customers.

Dell also opened Dell exclusive stores in 2008. According to a company spokesperson, "The exclusive Dell store is a step towards enhancing the overall purchase experience for consumers in India. We have rapidly increased our presence in the consumer market here with new products and by expanding our reach. With the launch of Dell exclusive stores, we offer our customers the touch and feel for Dell branded products within a unique shopping experience."

Each Dell exclusive store offers the advantages of Dell's direct purchasing model with the additional benefit of retail availability—allowing

customers to browse, touch, and feel the product. Dell's approach makes it possible for customers to see the products on the retail shelves and then place an order for the preferred model with the choice to customize the looks and configuration of the unit. By early 2013, Dell had 60 exclusive stores in India.

Dell's global initiative also involved a new advertising campaign, with Dell opting for real-life successful entrepreneurs in India to endorse its products. The "Take Your Own Path" advertising campaign has proven to be highly effective. Dell's success in India illustrates the importance of understanding global customers and reaching them by adapting to their specific needs and preferences.[1]

This chapter describes today's complex and dynamic global marketing environment. It begins with an overview of world trade and the emergence of a borderless economic world. Attention is then focused on prominent cultural, economic, and political-regulatory factors that present both an opportunity and a challenge for global marketers. Four major global market entry strategies are then detailed, including the advantages and disadvantages of each. Finally, the task of designing, implementing, and evaluating worldwide marketing programs for companies such as Dell Inc. is described.

DYNAMICS OF WORLD TRADE

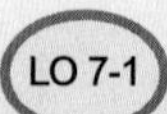

LO 7-1 Describe the nature and scope of world trade from a global perspective and identify the major trends that have influenced world trade and global marketing.

The dollar value of world trade has more than doubled in the past decade. Manufactured products and commodities account for 75 percent of world trade. Service industries, including telecommunications, transportation, insurance, education, banking, and tourism, represent the other 25 percent.

World Trade Flows

All nations and regions of the world do not participate equally in world trade. World trade flows reflect interdependencies among industries, countries, and regions. These flows manifest themselves in country, company, industry, and regional exports and imports. The dynamics of world trade are evolving. China will replace the United States as the biggest country measured by trade in 2015. Asia will overtake Western Europe as the largest region measured by trade in 2015.

Global Perspective on World Trade The United States, China, Japan, Western Europe, and Canada together account for more than two-thirds of world trade in manufactured products and commodities.[2] China is the world's leading exporter, followed by the United States and Germany. The United States is the world's leading importer, followed by China and Germany. China, Germany, and the United States remain well ahead of other countries in terms of imports and exports, as shown in Figure 7–1.

A global perspective on world trade views exports and imports as complementary economic flows: A country's imports affect its exports and exports affect its imports. Every nation's imports arise from the exports of other nations. As the exports of one country increase, its national output and income rise, which in turn leads to an increase in the demand for imports. This nation's greater demand for imports stimulates the exports of other countries. Increased demand for exports of other nations energizes their economic activity, resulting in higher national income, which stimulates their demand for imports. In short, imports affect exports and vice versa. This phenomenon is called the *trade feedback effect* and is one argument for free trade among nations.

Not all trade involves the exchange of money for products or services. In a world where 70 percent of all countries do not have convertible currencies or where government-owned enterprises lack sufficient cash or credit for imports, other means of payment are used. An estimated 10 to 15 percent of world trade involves **countertrade**, the practice of using barter rather than money for making global sales.[3]

Countertrade is popular with many Eastern European nations, Russia, and Asian countries. For example, Daimler AG agreed to sell 30 trucks to Romania in exchange for 150 Romanian-made jeeps. Daimler then sold the jeeps in Ecuador in exchange for bananas, which it brought back to Germany and sold to a German supermarket chain in exchange for cash. Volvo of North America delivered automobiles to the Siberian police force when Siberia had no cash to pay for them. It accepted payment in oil, which it then sold for cash to pay for media advertising in the United States.

United States Perspective on World Trade The United States has been the world's perennial leader in terms of **gross domestic product (GDP)**, which is the monetary value of all products and services produced in a country during one year. The United States is also among the world's leaders in exports due in large part to its global prominence in the aerospace, chemical, office equipment, information technology, pharmaceutical, telecommunications, and professional service industries.

FIGURE 7–1
The United States, China, and Germany are the leaders in global merchandise trade by a wide margin. China exports more manufactured products and commodities than it imports. The United States imports more manufactured products and commodities than it exports. Read the text to learn about trends in U.S. exports and imports and the competitive advantage of nations.

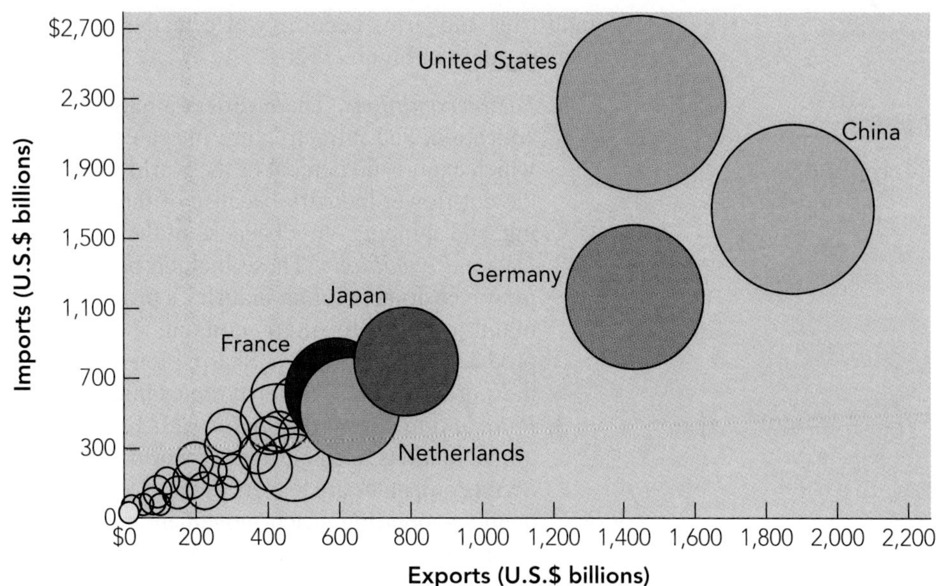

However, the U.S. percentage share of world exports has shifted downward over the past 30 years, whereas its percentage share of world imports has increased. Therefore, the relative position of the United States as a supplier to the world has diminished despite an absolute growth in exports. At the same time, its relative role as a marketplace for the world has increased, particularly for automobile, oil, textile, apparel, and consumer electronics products.

The difference between the monetary value of a nation's exports and imports is called the **balance of trade**. When a country's exports exceed its imports, it incurs a surplus in its balance of trade. When imports exceed exports, a deficit results. World trade trends in U.S. exports and imports are reflected in the U.S. balance of trade.

Two important things have happened in U.S. exports and imports over the past 30 years. First, imports have exceeded exports each year, indicating that the United States has a continuing balance of trade deficit. Second, the volume of both exports and imports has increased dramatically, showing why almost every American is significantly affected. The effect varies from the products they buy (Samsung DVD players from South Korea, Waterford crystal from Ireland, Louis Vuitton luggage from France) to those they sell (Cisco Systems's Internet technology to Europe, DuPont's chemicals to the Far East, Merck pharmaceuticals to Africa) and the jobs and improved standard of living that result.

World trade flows to and from the United States reflect demand and supply interdependencies for goods and services among nations and industries.[4] The four largest importers of U.S. products and services are, in order: Canada, Mexico, China, and Japan. These countries purchase approximately 67 percent of U.S. exports. The four largest exporters to the United States are, in order: China, Canada, Mexico, and Japan.

Competitive Advantage of Nations

As companies in many industries find themselves competing against foreign competitors at home and abroad, government policymakers around the world are increasingly asking why some companies and industries in a country succeed globally while others lose ground or fail. Harvard Business School professor Michael Porter suggests a "diamond" to explain a nation's competitive advantage and why some industries and firms become world leaders.[5] He has identified four key elements, which appear in Figure 7–2:

1. *Factor conditions.* These reflect a nation's ability to turn its natural resources, education, and infrastructure into a competitive advantage. Consider Holland, which exports 60 percent of the world's cut flowers. The Dutch lead the world in the cut-flower industry because of their research in flower cultivation, packaging, and shipping—not because of their weather.
2. *Demand conditions.* These include both the number and sophistication of domestic customers for an industry's product. Japan's sophisticated consumers demand quality in their consumer electronics, thereby making Japan's producers—Sony, Sanyo, Sharp, Pioneer, JVC, Matsushita, and Hitachi—among the world leaders in the electronics industry.
3. *Related and supporting industries.* Firms and industries seeking leadership in global markets need clusters of world-class suppliers that accelerate innovation. Swiss companies are leaders in the global watch market, in part, because of high-quality supporting watch-movement makers.
4. *Company strategy, structure, and rivalry.* These factors include the conditions governing the way a nation's businesses are organized and managed, along with the intensity of domestic competition. The Italian shoe industry has become a world leader because of intense domestic competition among firms such as MAB, Bruno Magli, and Rossimoda, which has made shoes for Christian Dior and Anne Klein Couture.

Case histories of firms in more than 100 industries were analyzed in Porter's study. While the strategies used by successful global competitors differed in many respects, a

FIGURE 7–2
Porter's diamond of national competitive advantage contains four key elements that explain why some industries and firms in different countries become world leaders.

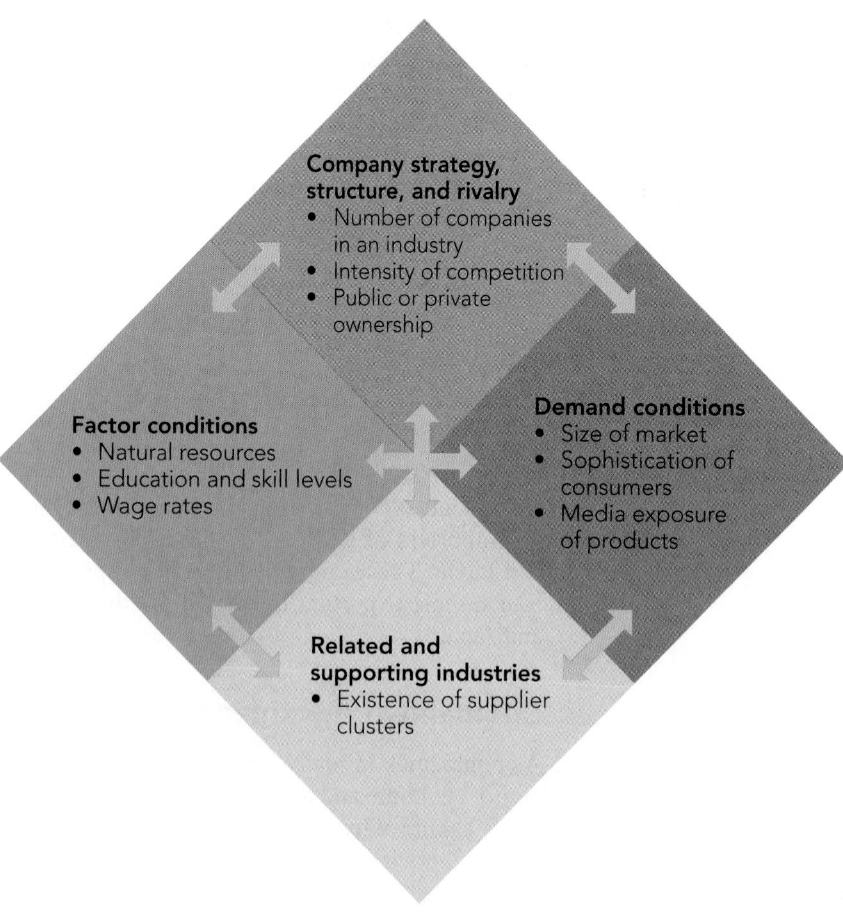

Sony and Bruno Magli have succeeded in the global marketplace as well as in their domestic markets.

Sony Corporation
www.sony.com

Bruno Magli
www.brunomagli.it

common theme emerged: A firm that succeeds in global markets has first succeeded in intense domestic competition. Hence, competitive advantage for global firms grows out of continuous improvement, innovation, and change.

The Dark Side of Global Competitive Advantage

Pursuit of a country's competitive advantage in global markets also has a dark side—economic espionage.[6] *Economic espionage* is the clandestine collection of trade secrets or proprietary information about competitors. This practice is common in high-technology industries such as electronics, specialty chemicals, industrial equipment, aerospace, and pharmaceuticals, where technical know-how and trade secrets separate global industry leaders from followers.

It is estimated that economic espionage costs U.S. firms upwards of $250 billion a year in lost sales. The intelligence services of some 23 nations routinely target U.S. firms for information about research and development efforts, manufacturing and marketing plans, and customer lists. To counteract this threat, the **Economic Espionage Act (1996)** makes the theft of trade secrets by foreign entities a federal crime in the United States. This act prescribes prison sentences of up to 15 years and fines up to $500,000 for individuals. Agents of foreign governments found guilty of economic espionage face a 25-year prison sentence and a $10 million fine.

learning review

7-1. What is the trade feedback effect?

7-2. What variables influence why some companies and industries in a country succeed globally while others lose ground or fail?

MARKETING IN A BORDERLESS ECONOMIC WORLD

Global marketing has been and continues to be affected by a growing borderless economic world. Four trends in the past decade have significantly influenced the landscape of global marketing:

Trend 1: Gradual decline of economic protectionism by individual countries.

Trend 2: Formal economic integration and free trade among nations.

Trend 3: Global competition among global companies for global customers.

Trend 4: Emergence of a networked global marketspace.

Decline of Economic Protectionism

Protectionism is the practice of shielding one or more industries within a country's economy from foreign competition through the use of tariffs or quotas. The argument for protectionism is that it limits the outsourcing of jobs, protects a nation's political security, discourages economic dependency on other countries, and promotes development of domestic industries. Read the Making Responsible Decisions box and decide for yourself if protectionism has an ethical dimension.[7]

Tariffs and quotas discourage world trade as depicted in Figure 7–3. **Tariffs**, which are a government tax on products or services entering a country, primarily serve to raise prices on imports. The average tariff on manufactured products in industrialized countries is 4 percent. However, wide differences exist across nations. For example, European Union countries have a 10 percent tariff on cars imported from Japan, which is about four times higher than the tariff imposed by the United States on Japanese cars.

The effect of tariffs on consumer prices is substantial. Consider U.S. rice exports to Japan. The U.S. Rice Millers' Association claims that if the Japanese rice market were opened to imports by lowering tariffs, lower prices would save Japanese consumers $6 billion annually, and the United States would gain a large share of the Japanese rice market. Tariffs imposed on bananas by European Union countries cost consumers $2 billion a year. U.S. consumers pay $5 billion annually for tariffs on

FIGURE 7–3
How does protectionism affect world trade? Protectionism hinders world trade through tariff and quota policies of individual countries. Tariffs increase prices and quotas limit supply.

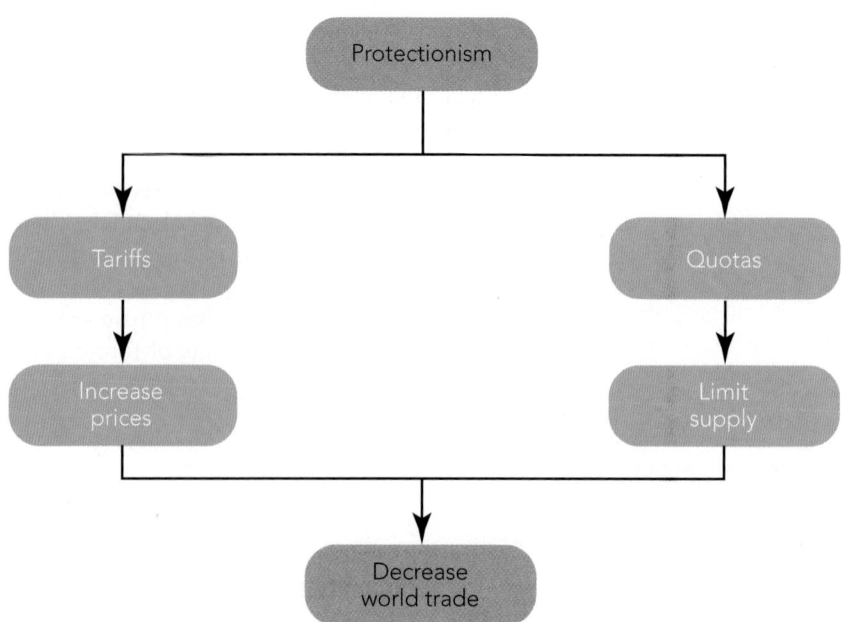

Making Responsible Decisions

ethics

Global Ethics and Global Economics—The Case of Protectionism

World trade benefits from free and fair trade among nations. Nevertheless, governments of many countries continue to use tariffs and quotas to protect their various domestic industries. Why? Protectionism earns profits for domestic producers and tariff revenue for the government. There is a cost, however. Protectionist policies cost Japanese consumers between $75 billion and $110 billion annually. U.S. consumers pay about $70 billion each year in higher prices because of tariffs and other protective restrictions.

Sugar and textile import quotas in the United States, automobile and banana import tariffs in European countries, shoe and automobile tire import tariffs in the United States, beer import tariffs in Canada, and rice import tariffs in Japan protect domestic industries but also interfere with world trade for these products. Regional trade agreements, such as those found in the provisions of the European Union and the North American Free Trade Agreement, may also pose a situation whereby member nations can obtain preferential treatment in quotas and tariffs but nonmember nations cannot.

Protectionism, in its many forms, raises an interesting global ethical question. Is protectionism, no matter how applied, an ethical practice?

imported shoes. Incidentally, 99 percent of shoes worn in the United States are imported.

A **quota** is a restriction placed on the amount of a product allowed to enter or leave a country. Quotas can be mandated or voluntary and may be legislated or negotiated by governments. Import quotas seek to guarantee domestic industries access to a certain percentage of their domestic market. For example, there is a limit on Chinese dairy products sold in India, and in Italy there is a quota on Japanese motorcycles. China has import quotas on corn, cotton, rice, and wheat.

The United States also imposes quotas. For instance, U.S. sugar import quotas have existed for more than 70 years and preserve about half of the U.S. sugar market for domestic producers. American consumers pay $3 billion annually in extra food costs because of this quota. U.S. quotas on textiles are estimated to add 50 percent to the wholesale price of clothing for American consumers—which, in turn, raises retail prices.

The major industrialized nations of the world formed the **World Trade Organization (WTO)** in 1995 to address an array of world trade issues.[8] There are 159 WTO member countries, including the United States, which account for more than 90 percent of world trade. The WTO is a permanent institution that sets rules governing trade between its members through panels of trade experts who decide on trade disputes between members and issue binding decisions. The WTO reviews more than 200 trade disputes annually.

Rise of Economic Integration

A number of countries with similar economic goals have formed transnational trade groups or signed trade agreements for the purpose of promoting free trade among member nations and enhancing their individual economies. Three of the best-known examples are the European Union (or simply EU), the North American Free Trade Agreement (NAFTA), and the Asian Free Trade Areas.

European Union The European Union consists of 28 member countries that have eliminated most barriers to the free flow of products, services, capital, and labor across their borders (see Figure 7–4).[9] This single market houses more than 500 million consumers with a combined gross domestic product larger than that of the United States. In addition, 16 countries have adopted a common currency called the *euro*. Adoption of the euro has been a boon to electronic commerce in the EU by eliminating the need to continually monitor currency exchange rates.

The EU creates abundant marketing opportunities because firms do not need to market their products and services on a nation-by-nation basis. Rather, pan-European marketing strategies are possible due to greater uniformity in product and packaging standards; fewer regulatory restrictions on transportation, advertising, and promotion imposed by countries; and the removal of most tariffs that affect pricing practices. For example, Colgate-Palmolive Company now markets its Colgate toothpaste with one formula and package across EU countries at one price. Black & Decker—the maker of electrical hand tools, appliances, and other consumer products—now produces 8, not 20, motor sizes for the European market, resulting in production and marketing cost savings. These practices were previously impossible because of

FIGURE 7–4
The European Union in early 2014 consists of 28 countries with more than 500 million consumers.

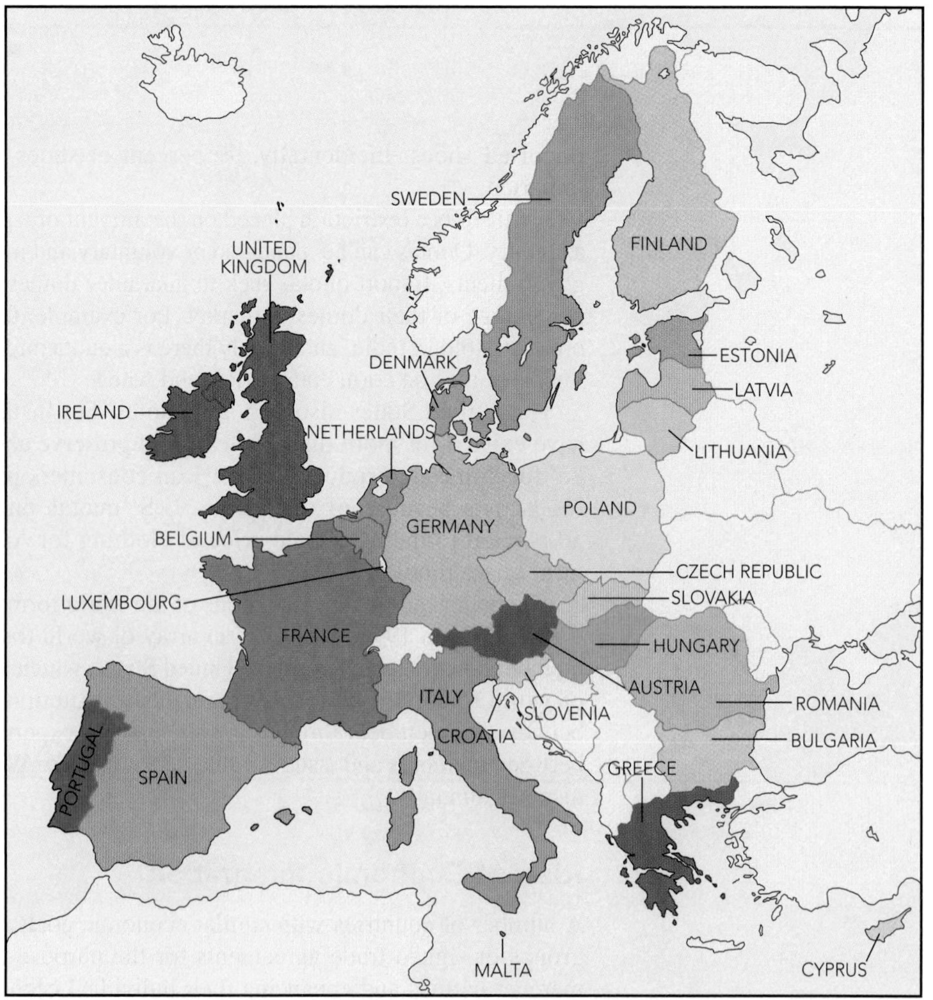

European Union
www.europa.eu.int

different government and trade regulations. Europeanwide distribution from fewer locations is also feasible given open borders. French tire maker Michelin closed 180 of its European distribution centers and now uses just 20 to serve all EU countries.

North American Free Trade Agreement The North American Free Trade Agreement (NAFTA) lifted many trade barriers between Canada, Mexico, and the United States and created a marketplace with more than 450 million consumers. NAFTA has stimulated trade flows among member nations as well as cross-border retailing, manufacturing, and investment.[10] For example, NAFTA paved the way for Walmart to move to Mexico, Target to enter Canada, and Mexican supermarket giant Gigante to move into the United States. Whirlpool Corporation's Canadian subsidiary stopped making washing machines in Canada and moved that operation to Ohio. Whirlpool then shifted the production of kitchen ranges and compact dryers to Canada. Ford invested $60 million in its Mexico City manufacturing plant to produce smaller cars and light trucks for global sales.

In 2006, a comprehensive free trade agreement among Costa Rica, the Dominican Republic, El Salvador, Guatemala, Honduras, Nicaragua, and the United States extended many NAFTA benefits to Central American countries and the Dominican Republic. Called CAFTA-DR, this agreement is viewed as a step toward a 34-country Free Trade Area of the Americas for the Western Hemisphere.

Asian Free Trade Agreements Efforts to liberalize trade in East Asia—from Japan and the four "Little Dragons" (Hong Kong, Singapore, South Korea, and Taiwan) through Thailand, Vietnam, Malaysia, and Indonesia—are also growing. Although the trade agreements are less formal than those underlying the EU and NAFTA, they have reduced tariffs among countries and promoted trade.

A New Reality: Global Competition among Global Companies for Global Consumers

The emergence of a largely borderless economic world has created a new reality for marketers of all shapes and sizes. Today, world trade is driven by global competition among global companies for global consumers.

Global Competition **Global competition** exists when firms originate, produce, and market their products and services worldwide. The automobile, pharmaceutical, apparel, electronics, aerospace, and telecommunication fields represent well-known industries with sellers and buyers on every continent. Other industries that are increasingly global in scope include soft drinks, cosmetics, ready-to-eat cereals, snack chips, and retailing.

Global competition broadens the competitive landscape for marketers. The familiar "cola war" waged by Pepsi-Cola and Coca-Cola in the United States has been repeated around the world, including in India, China, and Argentina. Procter & Gamble's Pampers and Kimberly-Clark's Huggies have taken their disposable diaper rivalry from the United States to Western Europe. Boeing and Europe's Airbus vie for lucrative commercial aircraft contracts on virtually every continent.

Collaborative relationships also are a common way to meet the demands of global competition. Global **strategic alliances** are agreements among two or more independent firms to cooperate for the purpose of achieving common goals such as a competitive advantage or customer value creation. For example, General Mills and Nestlé of Switzerland created Cereal Partners Worldwide to fine-tune Nestlé's European cereal marketing and distribute General Mills cereals worldwide. Today this global alliance produces almost $3 billion in annual sales in more than 140 countries.

Pepsi-Cola, now available in about 160 countries and territories, accounts for a quarter of all soft drinks sold internationally. This Brazilian ad—"How to make jeans last 10 years"—features the popular Diet Pepsi brand targeted at weight-conscious consumers.

PepsiCo, Inc.
www.pepsico.com

Global Companies Three types of companies populate and compete in the global marketplace: (1) international firms, (2) multinational firms, and (3) transnational firms.[11] All three employ people in different countries, and many have administrative, marketing, and manufacturing operations (often called *divisions* or *subsidiaries*) around the world. However, a firm's orientation toward and strategy for global markets and marketing defines the type of company it is or attempts to be.

An *international firm* engages in trade and marketing in different countries as an extension of the marketing strategy in its home country. Generally, these firms market their existing products and services in other countries the same way they do in their home country. Avon, for example, successfully distributes its product line through direct selling in Asia, Europe, and South America, employing virtually the same marketing strategy used in the United States.

A *multinational firm* views the world as consisting of unique parts and markets to each part differently. Multinationals use a **multidomestic marketing strategy**, which means that they have as many different product variations, brand names, and advertising programs as countries in which they do business. For example, Lever Europe, a division of Unilever, markets its fabric softener known as Snuggle in the United States in 10 European countries under seven brand names, including Kuschelweich in Germany, Coccolino in Italy, and Mimosin in France. These products have different packages, different advertising programs, and occasionally different formulas. Procter & Gamble markets Mr. Clean, its popular multipurpose cleaner, in North America and Asia. But you won't necessarily find the Mr. Clean brand in other parts of the world. In many Latin American countries, Mr. Clean is Maestro Limpio. Mr. Clean is Mr. Proper in most parts of Europe, Africa, and the Middle East.

A *transnational firm* views the world as one market and emphasizes cultural similarities across countries or universal consumer needs and wants rather than differences. Transnational marketers employ a **global marketing strategy**—the practice of standardizing marketing activities when there are cultural similarities and adapting them when cultures differ. This approach benefits marketers by allowing them to realize economies of scale from their production and marketing activities.

Global marketing strategies are popular among many business-to-business marketers such as Caterpillar and Komatsu (heavy construction equipment) and Texas Instruments,

Intel, and Hitachi (semiconductors). Consumer product marketers such as Timex, Seiko, and Swatch (watches), Coca-Cola and Pepsi-Cola (cola soft drinks), Mattel and LEGO (children's toys), Nike and Adidas (athletic shoes), Gillette (personal care products), L'Oréal and Shiseido (cosmetics), and McDonald's (quick-service restaurants) successfully execute this strategy.

Each of these companies markets a **global brand**—a brand marketed under the same name in multiple countries with similar and centrally coordinated marketing programs.[12] Global brands have the same product formulation or service concept, deliver the same benefits to consumers, and use consistent advertising across multiple countries and cultures. This isn't to say that global brands are not sometimes tailored to specific cultures or countries. However, adaptation is used only when necessary to better connect the brand to consumers in different markets.

Consider McDonald's.[13] This global marketer has adapted its proven formula of "food, fun, and families" across 123 countries on six continents. Although the Golden Arches and Ronald McDonald appear worldwide, McDonald's tailors other aspects of its marketing program. It serves beer in Germany, wine in France, and coconut, mango, and tropical mint shakes in Hong Kong. Hamburgers are made with different meat and spices in Japan, Thailand, India, and the Philippines. But McDonald's world-famous french fry is standardized. Its french fry in Beijing, China, tastes like the one in Paris, France, which tastes like the one in your hometown.

Global Consumers Global competition among global companies often focuses on the identification and pursuit of global consumers, as described in the Marketing Matters box on the next page.[14] **Global consumers** consist of consumer groups living in many countries or regions of the world who have similar needs or seek similar features and benefits from products or services. Evidence suggests the presence of a global middle-income class, a youth market, and an elite segment, each consuming or using a common assortment of products and services, regardless of geographic location.

A variety of companies have capitalized on the global consumer. Whirlpool, Sony, and IKEA have benefited from the growing global middle-income class desire for kitchen appliances, consumer electronics, and home furnishings, respectively. Levi Strauss, Nike, Adidas, Coca-Cola, and Apple have tapped the global youth market. DeBeers, Chanel, Gucci, Rolls-Royce, and Sotheby's and Christie's, the world's largest fine art and antique auction houses, cater to the elite segment for luxury products worldwide.

Sweden's IKEA is capitalizing on the home-improvement trend sweeping through China. The home-furnishings retailer is courting young Chinese consumers who are eagerly updating their housing with modern, colorful but inexpensive furniture. IKEA entered China in 1998. The company expects to have at least 18 stores open in China by 2015.

IKEA
www.ikea.com

Marketing Matters

customer value

The Global Teenager—A Market of 2 Billion Voracious Consumers

The "global teenager" market consists of 2 billion 13- to 19-year-olds in Europe, North and South America, and industrialized nations of Asia and the Pacific Rim who have experienced intense exposure to television (MTV broadcasts in 169 countries in 28 languages), movies, travel, social media, and global advertising by companies such as Apple, Sony, Nike, and Coca-Cola. The similarities among teens across these countries are greater than their differences. For example, a global study of middle-class teenagers' rooms in 25 industrialized countries indicated it was difficult, if not impossible, to tell whether the rooms were in Los Angeles, Mexico City, Tokyo, Rio de Janeiro, Sydney, or Paris. Why? Teens spend $250 billion annually for a common gallery of products: Nintendo video games, Tommy Hilfiger apparel, Levi's blue jeans, Nike and Adidas athletic shoes, Swatch watches, Apple iPhones (shown in the photo), Benetton apparel, and Cover Girl cosmetics.

Teenagers around the world appreciate fashion and music, and they desire novelty and trendier designs and images. They also acknowledge an Americanization of fashion and culture based on another study of 6,500 teens in 26 countries. When asked what country had the most influence on their attitudes and purchase behavior, 54 percent of teens from the United States, 87 percent of those from Latin America, 80 percent of the Europeans, and 80 percent of those from Asia named the United States. This phenomenon has not gone unnoticed by parents. As one parent in India said, "Now the youngsters dress, talk, and eat like Americans."

Emergence of a Networked Global Marketspace

The use of Internet technology as a tool for exchanging products, services, and information on a global scale is the fourth trend affecting world trade. Almost 3 billion businesses, educational institutions, government agencies, and households worldwide are expected to have Internet access by 2015. The broad reach of this technology attests to its potential for promoting world trade.

A networked global marketspace enables the exchange of products, services, and information from sellers *anywhere* to buyers *anywhere* at *any time* and at a lower cost. In particular, companies engaged in business-to-business marketing have spurred the growth of global electronic commerce.[15] Ninety percent of

Nestlé is an innovator in customizing website content and communicating with consumers in their native languages. Read the text to learn how many country websites Nestlé operates. The website shown here is for Hungary.

Nestlé Company
www.nestle.com

global electronic commerce revenue arises from business-to-business transactions among a dozen countries in North America, Western Europe, and the Asia/Pacific Rim region.

Industries that have benefited from Internet technology include industrial chemicals and controls; maintenance, repair, and operating supplies; computer and electronic equipment and components; aerospace parts; and agricultural and energy products. The United States, China, Canada, the United Kingdom, Germany, Sweden, Japan, India, and Taiwan are among the most active participants in worldwide business-to-business electronic commerce.

QR 7-1
Nestlé
Hungary Ad

Marketers recognize that the networked global marketspace offers unprecedented access to prospective buyers on every continent. Companies that have successfully capitalized on this access manage multiple country and language websites that customize content and communicate with consumers in their native tongue. Nestlé, the world's largest packaged food manufacturer, coffee roaster, and chocolate maker, is a case in point. The company operates 65 individual country websites in more than 20 languages that span five continents.

learning review

7-3. What is protectionism?

7-4. The North American Free Trade Agreement was designed to promote free trade among which countries?

7-5. What is the difference between a multidomestic marketing strategy and a global marketing strategy?

A GLOBAL ENVIRONMENTAL SCAN

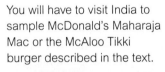

Identify the environmental forces that shape global marketing efforts.

Global companies conduct continuing environmental scans of the five sets of environmental factors described earlier in Figure 3–1 (social, economic, technological, competitive, and regulatory forces). This section focuses on three kinds of uncontrollable environmental variables—cultural, economic, and political-regulatory—that affect global marketing practices in strikingly different ways than those in domestic markets.

Cultural Diversity

Marketers must be sensitive to the cultural underpinnings of different societies if they are to initiate and consummate mutually beneficial exchange relationships with global consumers. A necessary step in this process is **cross-cultural analysis**, which involves the study of similarities and differences among consumers in two or more nations or societies.[16] A thorough cross-cultural analysis involves an understanding of and an appreciation for the values, customs, symbols, and language of other societies.

You will have to visit India to sample McDonald's Maharaja Mac or the McAloo Tikki burger described in the text.

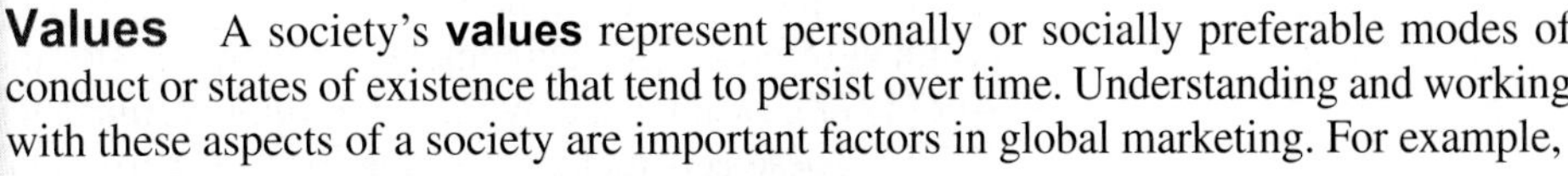

Values A society's **values** represent personally or socially preferable modes of conduct or states of existence that tend to persist over time. Understanding and working with these aspects of a society are important factors in global marketing. For example,

- McDonald's does not sell beef hamburgers in its restaurants in India because the cow is considered sacred by almost 85 percent of the population. Instead, McDonald's sells the Maharaja Mac: two all-chicken patties, special sauce, lettuce, cheese, pickles, onions on a sesame-seed bun. For the 40 percent of Indian consumers who eat no meat of any kind, McDonald's offers the McAloo Tikki burger, which features a spicy breaded potato patty, and the McPuff, a vegetable and cheese pastry.

Cultural symbols evoke deep feelings. What cultural lesson did Coca-Cola executives learn when they used the Eiffel Tower and the Parthenon in a global advertising campaign? Read the text to find the answer.

- Germans have not been overly receptive to the use of credit cards such as Visa or MasterCard and installment debt to purchase products and services. Indeed, the German word for debt, *Schuld*, is the same as the German word for guilt.

These examples illustrate how cultural values can influence behavior in different societies. Cultural values become apparent in the personal values of individuals that affect their attitudes and beliefs and the importance assigned to specific behaviors and attributes of products and services. These personal values affect consumption-specific values, such as the use of installment debt by Germans, and product-specific values, such as the importance assigned to credit card interest rates.

Customs **Customs** are what is considered normal and expected about the way people do things in a specific country. Clearly customs can vary significantly from country to country. For example, 3M Company executives were perplexed when the company's Scotch-Brite floor-cleaning product initially produced lukewarm sales in the Philippines. When a Filipino employee explained that consumers there customarily clean floors by pushing coconut shells around with their feet, 3M changed the shape of the pad to a foot and sales soared. Some other customs may seem unusual to Americans. Consider, for example, that in France, men wear more than twice the number of cosmetics than women do and that Japanese women give Japanese men chocolates on Valentine's Day.

The custom of giving token business gifts is popular in many countries where they are expected and accepted. However, bribes, kickbacks, and payoffs offered to entice someone to commit an illegal or improper act on behalf of the giver for economic gain is considered corrupt in any culture.

The prevalence of bribery in global marketing has led to an agreement among the world's major exporting nations to make bribery of foreign government officials a criminal offense. This agreement is patterned after the **Foreign Corrupt Practices Act (1977)**, as amended by the *International Anti-Dumping and Fair Competition Act* (1998). These acts make it a crime for U.S. corporations to bribe an official of a foreign government or political party to obtain or retain business in a foreign country. For example, the German engineering company Siemens AG paid an $800 million fine for $1 billion in alleged bribes of government officials around the globe.[17]

Cultural Symbols **Cultural symbols** are things that represent ideas and concepts. Symbols and symbolism play an important role in cross-cultural analysis because different cultures attach different meanings to things. So important is the role of symbols that a field of study, called **semiotics**, has emerged that examines the correspondence between symbols and their role in the assignment of meaning for people. By adroitly using cultural symbols, global marketers can tie positive symbolism to their products, services, and brands to enhance their attractiveness to consumers. However, improper use of symbols can spell disaster. A culturally sensitive global marketer will know that:[18]

- North Americans are superstitious about the number 13, and Japanese feel the same way about the number 4. *Shi*, the Japanese word for four, is also the word for death. Knowing this, Tiffany & Company sells its fine glassware and china in sets of five, not four, in Japan.
- "Thumbs-up" is a positive sign in the United States. However, in Russia and Poland, this gesture has an offensive meaning when the palm of the hand is shown, as AT&T learned. The company reversed the gesture depicted in ads, showing the back of the hand, not the palm.

Cultural symbols evoke deep feelings. Consider how executives at Coca-Cola Company's Italian office learned this lesson. In a series of advertisements directed at Italian vacationers, the Eiffel Tower, the Empire State Building, and the Tower of Pisa were turned into the familiar Coca-Cola bottle. However, when the white marble columns in the Parthenon that crowns the Acropolis in Athens were turned into Coca-Cola bottles, the Greeks were outraged. Greeks refer to the Acropolis as the "holy rock," and a government official said the Parthenon is an "international symbol of excellence" and that "whoever insults the Parthenon insults international culture." Coca-Cola apologized for the ad.[19]

Global marketers are also sensitive to the fact that the country of origin or manufacture of products and services can symbolize superior or poor quality in some countries. For example, Russian consumers believe products made in Japan and Germany are superior in quality to products from the United States and the United Kingdom. Japanese consumers believe Japanese products are superior to those made in Europe and the United States. About a third of Americans say the quality of products from other countries is not as good as products made in the United States.[20]

What does the Nestlé Kit Kat bar have to do with academic achievement in Japan? Read the text on the next page to find out.

Nestlé Company
www.nestle.com

QR 7-2
Nestlé
Japan Ad

Language Global marketers should know not only the native tongues of countries in which they market their products and services but also the nuances and idioms of a language. Even though about 100 official languages exist in the world, anthropologists estimate that at least 3,000 different languages are spoken. There are 23 official languages spoken in the European Union, and Canada has two official languages (English and French). Seventeen major languages are spoken in India alone.

English, French, and Spanish are the principal languages used in global diplomacy and commerce. However, the best language to use to communicate with consumers is their own, as any seasoned global marketer will attest to. Unintended meanings of brand names and messages have ranged from the absurd to the obscene:

- When the advertising agency responsible for launching Procter & Gamble's successful Pert shampoo in Canada realized that the name means "lost" in French, it substituted the brand name Pret, which means "ready."
- In Italy, Cadbury Schweppes, the world's third-largest soft-drink manufacturer, realized that its Schweppes Tonic Water brand had to be renamed Schweppes Tonica because "il water" turned out to be the idiom for a bathroom.
- The Vicks brand name common in the United States is German slang for sexual intimacy; therefore, Vicks is called Wicks in Germany.

Experienced global marketers use **back translation**, where a translated word or phrase is retranslated into the original language by a different interpreter to catch

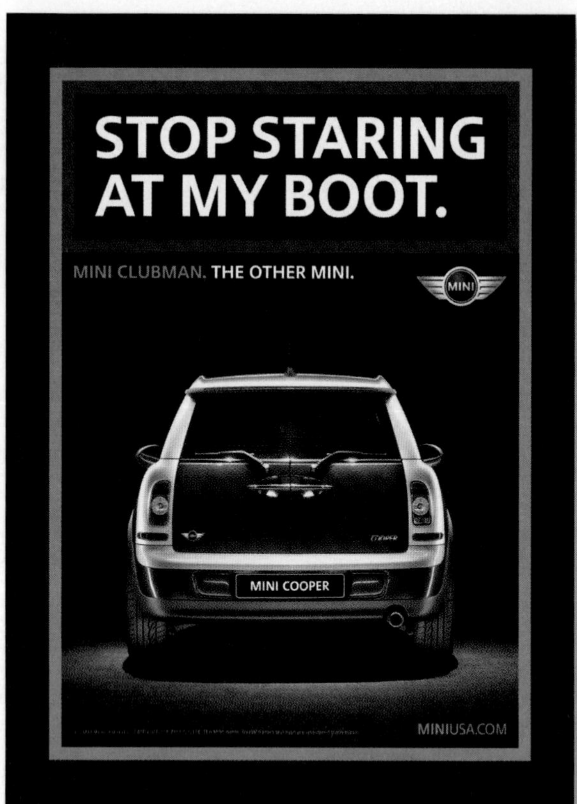

The Mini is marketed in many countries using many languages, such as English and Italian. The Italian translation is "Stop Looking at My Rear."

errors. For example, IBM's first Japanese translation of its "Solution for a small planet" advertising message yielded "Answers that make people smaller." The error was corrected. Nevertheless, unintended translations can produce favorable results. Consider Kit Kat bars marketed by Nestlé worldwide. Kit Kat is pronounced "kitto katsu" in Japanese, which roughly translates to "Surely win." Japanese teens eat Kit Kat bars for good luck, particularly when taking crucial school exams.[21]

Cultural Ethnocentricity The tendency for people to view their own values, customs, symbols, and language favorably is well known. However, the belief that aspects of one's culture are superior to another's is called *cultural ethnocentricity* and is a sure impediment to successful global marketing.

An outgrowth of cultural ethnocentricity exists in the purchase and use of products and services produced outside of a country. Global marketers are acutely aware that certain groups within countries disfavor imported products, not on the basis of price, features, or performance, but purely because of their foreign origin.

Consumer ethnocentrism is the tendency to believe that it is inappropriate, indeed immoral, to purchase foreign-made products.[22] Ethnocentric consumers believe that buying imported products is wrong because such purchases are unpatriotic, harm domestic industries, and cause domestic unemployment. Consumer ethnocentrism has been observed among a segment of the population in the United States, France, Japan, Korea, and Germany as well as other parts of Europe and Asia. Consumer ethnocentrism makes the job of global marketers more difficult.[23]

Consumer ethnocentrism is common in many countries. This bumper sticker is just one illustration of how ethnocentric consumers express themselves in the United States.

Economic Considerations

Global marketing is also affected by economic considerations. Therefore, a scan of the global marketplace should include (1) a comparative analysis of the economic development in different countries, (2) an assessment of the economic infrastructure in these countries, (3) measurement of consumer income in different countries, and (4) recognition of a country's currency exchange rates.

Stage of Economic Development There are 195 independent countries in the world today, each of which is at a slightly different point in terms of its stage of economic development. However, they can be classified into two major groupings that will help the global marketer better understand their needs:

- *Developed* countries have somewhat mixed economies. Private enterprise dominates, although they have substantial public sectors as well. The United States, Canada, Japan, and most of Western Europe can be considered developed.
- *Developing* countries are in the process of moving from an agricultural to an industrial economy. There are two subgroups within the developing category: (1) those that have already made the move and (2) those that remain locked in a preindustrial economy. Countries such as Brazil, Poland, Hungary, India, China, Slovenia, Australia, Israel, Venezuela, and South Africa fall into the first group. In the second group are Afghanistan, Sri Lanka, Ethiopia, Tanzania, and Chad, where living standards are low and improvement will be slow.

About 86 percent of the world's population of roughly 7.1 billion people reside in developing countries and live on one-fifth of total world income. Four billion of these people live on less than $2 per day.[24] In global marketing terms, they are viewed as being at the **bottom of the pyramid**, which is the largest, but poorest, socioeconomic group of people in the world.[25]

Today, global companies are choosing to serve people at the bottom of the pyramid by being responsive to their conditions and needs. Motorola is an example. The company developed a low-cost cell phone with battery life as long as 500 hours for rural villagers without regular electricity and an extra-loud volume for use in noisy markets. Motorola's cell phone, a no-frills design priced at $40, has a standby time of two weeks and conforms to local languages and customs. Motorola has been successful selling this cell phone design in rural areas across China, India, and Turkey. Still, the task facing global marketers is not easy. A country's stage of economic development affects and is affected by other economic factors, as described next.

Economic Infrastructure The *economic infrastructure*—a country's communications, transportation, financial, and distribution systems—is a critical consideration in determining whether to try to market to a country's consumers and organizations. Parts of the infrastructure that North Americans or Western Europeans take for granted can be huge problems elsewhere—not only in developing nations but even in Eastern Europe, the Indian subcontinent, and China, where such an infrastructure is assumed to be in place. Two-lane roads outside major urban centers that limit average speeds to 35 to 40 miles per hour are common and a nightmare for firms requiring prompt truck delivery in these countries. In China, the bicycle is the preferred mode of transportation. This is understandable because China has few navigable roads outside its major cities—where 80 percent of the population lives. In India, Coca-Cola uses large tricycles to distribute cases of Coke along narrow streets in many cities. Wholesale and retail institutions tend to be small. In many of these countries, the majority are operated by new owner–managers, who are still learning the ways of a free market system.

The communication infrastructures in these countries also differ. This infrastructure includes telecommunication systems and networks in use, such as telephones, cable television, broadcast radio and television, computer, satellite, and wireless telephone.

The Coca-Cola Company has made a huge financial investment in bottling and distribution facilities in Russia.

The Coca-Cola Company
www.thecoca-colacompany.com

In general, the communication infrastructure in many developing countries is limited or antiquated compared with that of developed countries.

Even the financial and legal system can cause problems. Formal operating procedures among financial institutions and the notion of private property are still limited. As a consequence, it is estimated that two-thirds of the commercial transactions in Russia involve nonmonetary forms of payment. The legal red tape involved in obtaining titles to buildings and land for manufacturing, wholesaling, and retailing operations also has been a huge problem. Still, the Coca-Cola Company plans to invest $1 billion by 2015 for bottling facilities in Russia, and Frito-Lay spent $60 million to build a plant outside Moscow to make Lay's potato chips.

Consumer Income and Purchasing Power A global marketer selling consumer products must also consider what the average per capita or household income is among a country's consumers and how the income is distributed to determine a nation's purchasing power. Per capita income varies greatly between nations. Average yearly per capita income in EU countries is about $33,000 and is less than $500 in some developing countries such as Liberia. A country's income distribution is important because it gives a more reliable picture of a country's purchasing power. Generally, as the proportion of middle-income households in a country increases, the greater that nation's purchasing capability tends to be.

In established market economies such as those in North America and Western Europe, 65 percent of households have an annual purchasing capability of $20,000 or more. In comparison, 75 percent of households in the developing countries of Sub-Saharan Africa have an annual purchasing power of less than $5,000.[26]

Seasoned global marketers recognize that people in developing countries often have government subsidies for food, housing, and health care that supplement their income. So people with seemingly low incomes are actually promising customers for a variety of products. For instance, a consumer in South Asia earning the equivalent of $250 per year can afford Gillette razors. When that consumer's income rises to $1,000, a Sony television becomes affordable, and a new Volkswagen or Nissan automobile can be bought with an annual income of $10,000. In developing countries of Eastern Europe, a $1,000 annual income makes a refrigerator affordable, and $2,000 brings an automatic washer within reach—good news for Whirlpool, the world's leading manufacturer and marketer of major home appliances.

Levi Strauss & Co. launched its Denizen brand jeans in China in late 2010. Created for teens and young adults in emerging markets who cannot afford Levi-branded jeans, Denizen is now sold in the United States.

Levi Strauss & Co.
www.levistrauss.com

QR 7-3
Denizen
Video

Efforts to raise household incomes in developing countries is evident in the popularity of microfinance. **Microfinance** is the practice of offering small, collateral-free loans to individuals who otherwise would not have access to the capital necessary to begin small businesses or other income-generating activities. An example of microfinance is found in Hindustan Lever's Project Shakti initiative in India. The company realized it could not sell to the rural poor in India unless it found ways to distribute its products such as soap, shampoos, and laundry detergents. Lever provided start-up loans to women to buy stocks of products to sell to local villagers. Today, over 45,000 women entrepreneurs sell Lever products to 600,000 Indian consumers in 135,000 villages in India. Equally important, these women now have a source of income, whereas before they had nothing.[27]

Hindustan Lever's Project Shakti initiative in India has resulted in over 45,000 women entrepreneurs selling Lever products in 135,000 villages—with more to come.

Unilever
www.unilever.com

Income growth in developing countries of Asia, Latin America, and Eastern Europe is expected to stimulate world trade. The number of consumers in these countries earning the equivalent of $10,000 per year is expected to surpass the number of consumers in the United States, Japan, and Western Europe combined by 2015. By one estimate, half of the world's population has now achieved "middle-class" status.[28] For this reason, developing countries represent a prominent marketing opportunity for global companies.

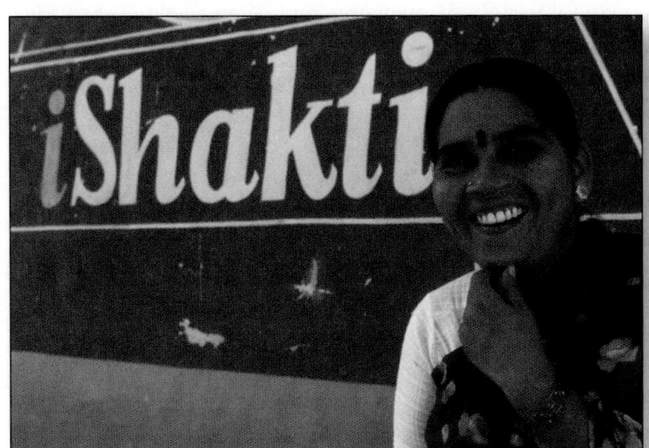

Currency Exchange Rates Fluctuations in exchange rates among the world's currencies are of critical importance in global marketing. Such fluctuations affect everyone, from international tourists to global companies.

A **currency exchange rate** is the price of one country's currency expressed in terms of another country's currency, such as the U.S. dollar expressed in Japanese yen, euros, or Swiss francs. Failure to consider exchange rates when pricing products for global markets can have dire consequences. Mattel learned this lesson the hard way. The company was recently unable to sell its popular Holiday Barbie doll and accessories in some international markets because they were too expensive. Why? Barbie prices, expressed in U.S. dollars, were set without regard for how they would convert into foreign currencies and were too high for many buyers.[29]

Marketing inSite

Checking a Country's Political Risk Rating

The political climate in every country is regularly changing. Governments can make new laws or enforce existing policies differently. Numerous consulting firms prepare political risk analyses that incorporate a variety of variables such as the risk of internal turmoil, external conflict, government restrictions on company operations, and tariff and nontariff trade barriers.

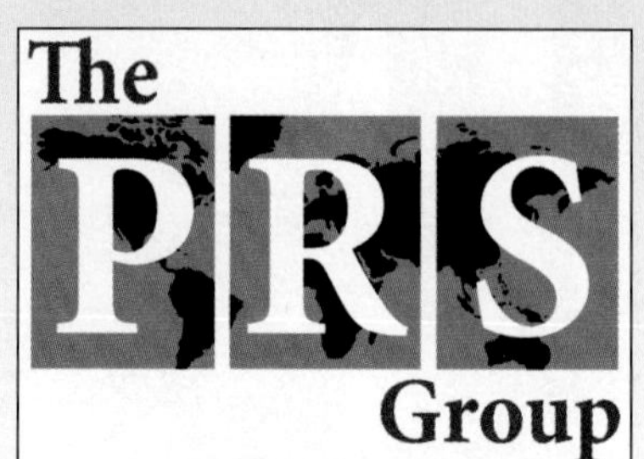

The PRS Group, Inc., maintains multiple databases of country-specific information and projections, including country political risk ratings for 140 countries. These ratings can be accessed at www.prsgroup.com. Click "Intl. Country Risk Guide" followed by "Free Samples and Downloads." Then click "Table 1: Country Risk, Ranked by Composite Rating" (you will need to give your name and e-mail address to obtain the table).

Which three countries have the highest rating (lowest risk), and which three have the lowest rating (highest risk)? Which countries have risk ratings closest to the United States?

Exchange rate fluctuations affect the sales and profits made by global companies. When foreign currencies can buy more U.S. dollars, for example, U.S. products are less expensive for the foreign customer. Short-term fluctuations, however, can have a significant effect on the profits of global companies.[30] Hewlett-Packard recently gained nearly a half million dollars of additional profit through exchange rate fluctuation in one year. On the other hand, Honda lost $408 million on its European operations alone in one year because of currency swings in the Japanese yen compared with the euro and British pound.

Political-Regulatory Climate

Assessing the political and regulatory climate for marketing in a country or region of the world involves not only identifying the current climate but also determining how long a favorable or unfavorable climate will last. An assessment of a country or regional political-regulatory climate includes an analysis of its political stability and trade regulations.

Political Stability Trade among nations or regions depends on political stability. Billions of dollars in trade have been lost in the Middle East and Africa as a result of internal political strife, terrorism, and war. Losses such as these encourage careful selection of politically stable countries and regions of the world for trade.

Political stability in a country is affected by numerous factors, including a government's orientation toward foreign companies and trade with other countries. These factors combine to create a political climate that is favorable or unfavorable for marketing and financial investment in a country or region of the world. Marketing managers monitor political stability using a variety of measures and often track country risk ratings supplied by agencies such as the PRS Group, Inc. Visit the PRS Group, Inc., website shown in the Marketing inSite box to see political risk ratings for 140 countries. Expect to be surprised by the ranking of countries, including the United States.

Trade Regulations Countries have a variety of rules that govern business practices within their borders. These rules often serve as trade barriers.[31] For example, Japan has some 11,000 trade regulations. Japanese car safety rules effectively require all automobile replacement parts to be Japanese and not American or European; public health rules make it illegal to sell aspirin or cold medicine without a pharmacist present. The Malaysian government has advertising regulations stating that "advertisements must not project or promote an excessively aspirational lifestyle," Sweden outlaws all advertisements to children, and Saudi Arabia bans Mattel's Barbie dolls because they are a symbol of Western decadence.

Trade regulations also appear in free trade agreements among countries. EU nations abide by some 10,000 rules that specify how products are to be made and marketed. For instance, the rules for a washing machine's electrical system are detailed on more than 100 typed pages. Regulations related to contacting consumers via telephone, fax, and e-mail without their prior consent also exist.

The European Union's ISO 9000 quality standards, though not a trade regulation, have the same effect on business practice. These standards, described in Chapter 6, involve registration and certification of a manufacturer's quality management and quality assurance system. Many European companies require suppliers to be ISO 9000 certified as a condition of doing business with them.

learning review

7-6. Semiotics involves the study of ________.

7-7. When foreign currencies can buy more U.S. dollars, are U.S. products more or less expensive for a foreign consumer?

COMPARING GLOBAL MARKET-ENTRY STRATEGIES

Name and describe the alternative approaches companies use to enter global markets.

Once a company has decided to enter the global marketplace, it must select a means of market entry. Four general options exist: (1) exporting, (2) licensing, (3) joint venture, and (4) direct investment.[32] As Figure 7–5 demonstrates, the amount of financial commitment, risk, marketing control, and profit potential increases as the firm moves from exporting to direct investment.

Exporting

Exporting is producing products in one country and selling them in another country. This entry option allows a company to make the least number of changes in terms of its product, its organization, and even its corporate goals. Host countries usually do not like this practice because it provides less local employment than under alternative means of entry.

Indirect exporting is when a firm sells its domestically produced products in a foreign country through an intermediary. It has the least amount of commitment and risk but will

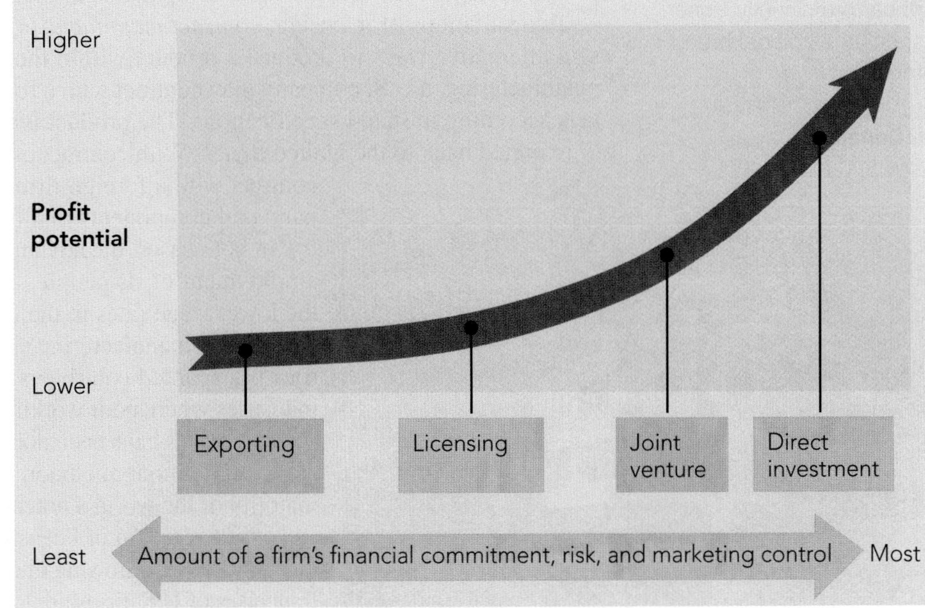

FIGURE 7–5
A firm's profit potential and control over marketing activities increase as it moves from exporting to direct investment as a global market-entry strategy. But so does a firm's financial commitment and risk. Firms often engage in exporting, licensing, and joint ventures before pursuing a direct investment strategy.

probably return the least profit. Indirect exporting is ideal for a company that has no overseas contacts but wants to market abroad. The intermediary is often a distributer that has the marketing know-how and resources necessary for the effort to succeed. Fran Wilson Creative Cosmetics uses an indirect exporting approach to sell its products in Japan. Read the Marketing Matters box to find out how this innovative marketer and its Japanese distributors sell 20 percent of the lipsticks exported to Japan by U.S. cosmetics companies.[33]

Direct exporting is when a firm sells its domestically produced products in a foreign country without intermediaries. Companies become involved in direct exporting when they believe their volume of sales will be sufficiently large and easy to obtain that they do not require intermediaries. For example, the exporter may be approached by foreign buyers that are willing to contract for a large volume of purchases. Direct exporting involves more risk than indirect exporting for the company but also opens the door to increased profits. The Boeing Company applies a direct exporting approach. Boeing is the world's largest aerospace company and the largest U.S. exporter.

Even though exporting is commonly employed by large firms, it is the prominent global market-entry strategy among small- and medium-sized companies. For example, 60 percent of U.S. firms exporting products have fewer than 500 employees. These firms account for about 34 percent of total U.S. merchandise exports.[34]

Licensing

Under licensing, a company offers the right to a trademark, patent, trade secret, or other similarly valued item of intellectual property in return for a royalty or a fee. The advantages to the company granting the license are low risk and a capital-free entry into a foreign country. The licensee gains information that allows it to start with a competitive advantage, and the foreign country gains employment by having the product manufactured locally. For instance, Yoplait yogurt is licensed from Sodima, a French cooperative, by General Mills for sales in the United States.

There are some serious drawbacks to this mode of entry, however. The licensor forgoes control of its product and reduces the potential profits gained from it. In addition, while the relationship lasts, the licensor may be creating its own competition. Some licensees are able to modify the product somehow and enter the market with product and marketing knowledge gained at the expense of the company that got them started. To offset this disadvantage, many companies strive to stay innovative so that the licensee remains dependent on them for improvements and successful operation. Finally, should the licensee prove to be a poor choice, the name or reputation of the company may be harmed.

Two variations of licensing, *contract manufacturing* and *contract assembly*, represent alternative ways to produce a product within the foreign country. With contract manufacturing, a U.S. company may contract with a foreign firm to manufacture products according to stated specifications. The product is then sold in the foreign country or exported back to the United States. With contract assembly, the U.S. company may contract with a foreign firm to assemble (not manufacture) parts and components that have been shipped to that country. In both cases, the advantage to the foreign country is the employment of its people, and the U.S. firm benefits from the lower wage rates in the foreign country.

Contract manufacturing and assembly in developing countries has sparked controversy in the toy, textile, and apparel industries where poor working conditions, low pay, and child labor practices have been documented. However, this practice has been an economic boon to Taiwan and China, where the majority of the world's notebook computers are made.[35]

A third variation of licensing is *franchising*. Franchising is one of the fastest-growing market-entry strategies. Over 75,000 franchises of U.S. firms are located in countries throughout the world. Franchises include soft-drink, motel, retailing, fast-food,

McDonald's uses franchising as a market-entry strategy, and about two-thirds of the company's sales come from non–U.S. operations. Note that the golden arches appear prominently—one aspect of its global brand promise.

McDonald's
www.mcdonalds.com

Marketing Matters

entrepreneurship

Creative Cosmetics and Creative Export Marketing in Japan

How does a medium-sized U.S. cosmetics firm sell 1.5 million tubes of lipstick in Japan annually? Fran Wilson Creative Cosmetics can attribute its success to a top-quality product, effective advertising, and a novel export marketing program. The firm's Moodmatcher lip coloring comes in green, orange, silver, black, and six other hues that change to a shade of pink, coral, or red, depending on a woman's chemistry when it's applied.

The company does not sell to department stores. According to a company spokesperson, "Shiseido and Kanebo (two large Japanese cosmetics firms) keep all the other Japanese or import brands out of the major department stores." Rather, the company sells its Moodmatcher lipstick through a network of Japanese distributors that reach Japan's 40,000 beauty salons.

The result? The company, with its savvy Japanese distributors, accounted for 20 percent of the lipsticks exported annually to Japan by U.S. cosmetics companies.

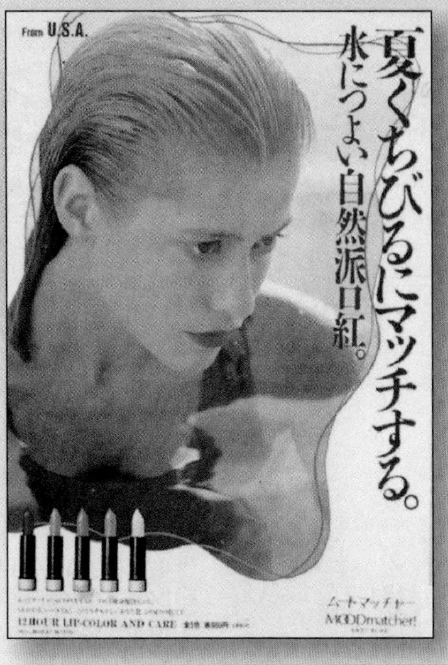

Strauss Group's joint venture with PepsiCo markets Frito-Lay's Cheetos, Ruffles, Doritos, and other snacks in Israel.

Strauss Group
www.strauss-group.com

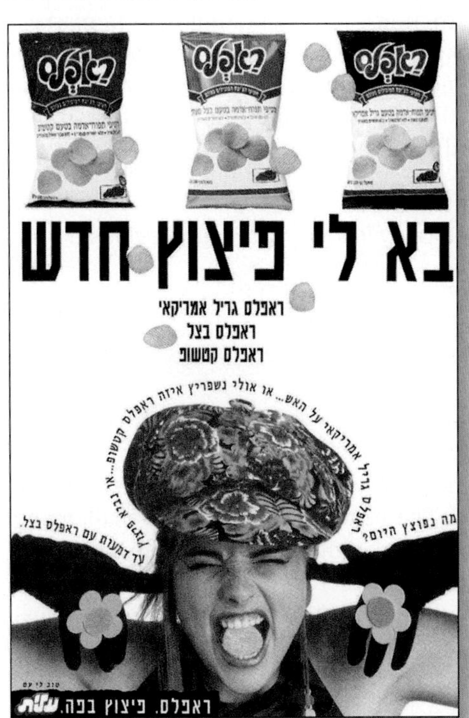

and car rental operations and a variety of business services. McDonald's is a premier global franchiser, with some 14,000 franchised units outside the United States.

Joint Venture

When a foreign company and a local firm invest together to create a local business, it is called a **joint venture**. These two companies share the ownership, control, and profits of the new company. For example, the Strauss Group has a joint venture with PepsiCo to market Frito-Lay's Cheetos, Ruffles, Doritos, and other snacks in Israel.[36]

The advantages of this option are twofold. First, one company may not have the necessary financial, physical, or managerial resources to enter a foreign market alone. The joint venture between Ericsson, a Swedish telecommunications firm, and CGCT, a French switch maker, enabled them together to beat out AT&T for a $100 million French contract. Ericsson's money and technology combined with CGCT's knowledge of the French market helped them to win the contract. Second, a government may require or strongly encourage a joint venture before it allows a foreign company to enter its market. For example, in China, international giants such as Procter & Gamble, Starbucks, and General Motors operate wholly or in part through joint ventures.

The disadvantages arise when the two companies disagree about policies or courses of action for their joint venture or when governmental bureaucracy bogs down the effort. For example, U.S. firms often prefer to reinvest earnings gained, whereas some foreign companies may want to spend those earnings. Or a U.S. firm may want to return profits earned to the United States, while the local firm or its government may oppose this—a problem faced by many potential joint ventures. The collapse of the joint venture between France's Group Danone and a local company in China is a case in point. The joint venture partners could not agree on the distribution of profits.[37]

Nestlé has made a sizable direct investment in ice cream manufacturing in China to produce its global brands such as Drumstick. Nestlé operates 31 factories in China.

Nestlé Company
www.nestle.com

Direct Investment

The biggest commitment a company can make when entering the global market is **direct investment**, which entails a domestic firm actually investing in and owning a foreign subsidiary or division. Examples of direct investment are Nissan's Smyrna, Tennessee, plant that produces pickup trucks and the Mercedes-Benz factory in Vance, Alabama, that makes the M-class sports utility vehicle. Many U.S.–based global companies also use this mode of entry. Reebok entered Russia by creating a subsidiary known as Reebok Russia.

For many companies, direct investment often follows one of the other three market-entry strategies.[38] For example, both FedEx and UPS entered China through joint ventures with Chinese companies. Each subsequently purchased the interests of its partner and converted the Chinese operations into a division. Following on the success of its European and Asian exporting strategy, Harley-Davidson now operates wholly owned marketing and sales subsidiaries in Germany, Italy, the United Kingdom, and Japan, among other countries.

The advantages to direct investment include cost savings, a better understanding of local market conditions, and fewer local restrictions. Firms entering foreign markets using direct investment believe that these advantages outweigh the financial commitments and risks involved. However, sometimes they don't. Tesco, the British supermarket giant, entered the United States in 2007 only to withdraw in 2012 after sizable operating losses and an investment of $1.6 billion.[39]

learning review

7-8. What mode of entry could a company follow if it has no previous experience in global marketing?

7-9. How does licensing differ from a joint venture?

CRAFTING A WORLDWIDE MARKETING PROGRAM

LO 7-4 Explain the distinction between standardization and customization when companies craft worldwide marketing programs.

The choice of a market-entry strategy is a necessary first step for a marketer when joining the community of global companies. The next step involves the challenging task of planning, implementing, and evaluating marketing programs worldwide.

Successful global marketers standardize global marketing programs whenever possible and customize them wherever necessary. The extent of standardization and customization is often rooted in a careful global environment scan supplemented with judgment based on experience and marketing research.

FIGURE 7–6
Five product and promotion strategies for global marketing exist based on whether a company extends or adapts its product and promotion message for consumers in different countries and cultures. Read the text to learn how different companies employ these strategies.

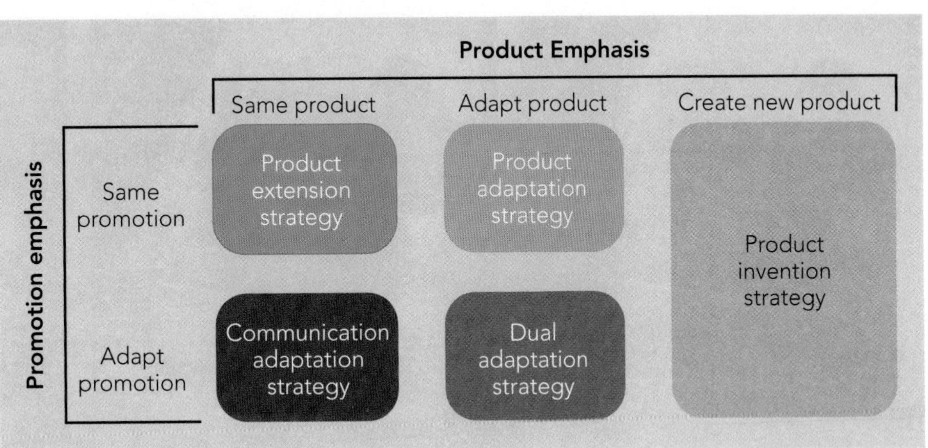

Product and Promotion Strategies

Global companies have five strategies for matching products and their promotion efforts to global markets. As Figure 7–6 shows, the strategies focus on whether a company extends or adapts its product and promotion message for consumers in different countries and cultures.

A product may be sold globally in one of three ways: (1) in the same form as in its home market, (2) with some adaptations, or (3) as a totally new product:[40]

1. *Product extension.* Selling virtually the same product in other countries is a product extension strategy. It works well for products such as Coca-Cola, Gillette razors, Wrigley's gum, Sony consumer electronics, Harley-Davidson motorcycles, Nike apparel and shoes, and Nokia cell phones. As a general rule, product extension seems to work best when the consumer market target for the product is alike across countries and cultures—that is, consumers share the same desires, needs, and uses for the product.
2. *Product adaptation.* Changing a product in some way to make it more appropriate for a country's climate or consumer preferences is a product adaptation strategy. Exxon sells different gasoline blends based on each country's climate. Frito-Lay produces and markets its potato chips in Russia, but don't expect them to taste like the chips eaten in North America. Russians prefer dairy, meat, and seafood-flavored potato chips. Gerber baby food comes in different varieties in different countries. Popular Gerber varieties outside the United States include vegetables and rabbit meat in Poland and freeze-dried sardines and rice in Japan. Maybelline's makeup is adapted to local skin types and weather across the globe, including an Asia-specific mascara that doesn't run during the rainy season.
3. *Product invention.* Alternatively, companies can invent totally new products designed to satisfy common needs across countries. Black & Decker did this with its Snake Light flexible flashlight. Created to address a global need for portable lighting, the product became a best seller in North America, Europe, Latin America, and Australia and is the most successful new product developed by Black & Decker. Similarly, Whirlpool developed a compact, automatic clothes washer specifically for households in developing countries with annual household incomes of $2,000. Called Ideale, the washer features bright colors because washers are often placed in home living areas, not hidden in laundry rooms (which don't exist in many homes in developing countries).

An identical promotion message is used for the product extension and product adaptation strategies around the world. Gillette uses the same global message for its men's toiletries: "Gillette, the Best a Man Can Get." Even though Exxon adapts its gasoline blends for different countries based on climate, the promotion message is unchanged: "Put a Tiger in Your Tank."

Gillette delivers the same global message whenever possible as shown in the Gillette for Women Venus ads from the United States, Mexico, and France.

The Gillette Company
www.gillette.com

QR 7-4
Nescafé
China Video

Global companies may also adapt their promotion message. For instance, the same product may be sold in many countries but advertised differently. As an example, L'Oréal, a French health and beauty products marketer, introduced its Golden Beauty brand of sun care products through its Helena Rubenstein subsidiary in Western Europe with a *communication adaptation strategy*. Recognizing that cultural and buying motive differences related to skin care and tanning exist, Golden Beauty advertising features dark tanning for northern Europeans, skin protection to avoid wrinkles among Latin Europeans, and beautiful skin for Europeans living along the Mediterranean Sea, even though the products are the same.

Other companies use a *dual adaptation strategy* by modifying both their products and promotion messages. Nestlé does this with Nescafé coffee. Nescafé is marketed using different coffee blends and promotional campaigns to match consumer preferences in different countries. For example, Nescafé, the world's largest brand of coffee, generally emphasizes the taste, aroma, and warmth of shared moments in its advertising around the world. However, Nescafé is advertised in Thailand as a way to relax from the pressures of daily life.

These examples illustrate the simple rule applied by global companies: Standardize product and promotion strategies whenever possible and customize them wherever necessary. This is the art of global marketing.[41]

Distribution Strategy

Distribution is of critical importance in global marketing. The availability and quality of retailers and wholesalers as well as transportation, communication, and warehousing facilities are often determined by a country's stage of economic development. Figure 7–7 outlines the channel through which a product manufactured in one country must travel to reach its destination in another country. The first step involves the seller; its headquarters is the starting point and is responsible for the successful distribution to the ultimate consumer.

The next step is the channel between two nations, moving the product from one country to another. Intermediaries that can handle this responsibility include resident buyers in a foreign country, independent merchant wholesalers who buy and sell the product, or agents who bring buyers and sellers together.

Once the product is in the foreign nation, that country's distribution channels take over. These channels can be very long or surprisingly short, depending on the product line. In Japan, fresh fish go through three intermediaries before getting to a retail outlet. Conversely, shoes only go through one intermediary. In other cases, the channel does not even involve the host country. Procter & Gamble sells its soap door-to-door in the Philippines because there are no other alternatives in many parts of that country.

FIGURE 7–7
Channels of distribution in global marketing are often long and complex.

Dell has had to revise its direct-marketing channel that originally featured online and phone buying in India, as described in the chapter-opening example.

Pricing Strategy

Global companies also face many challenges in determining a pricing strategy as part of their worldwide marketing effort. Individual countries, even those with free trade agreements, may impose considerable competitive, political, and legal constraints on the pricing latitude of global companies. For example, antitrust authorities in Germany limited Walmart from selling some items below cost to lure shoppers. Without this advantage, Walmart was unable to compete against German discount stores. This, and other factors, led Walmart to leave Germany following eight years without a profit.[42] Of course, economic factors such as the costs of production, selling, and tariffs, plus transportation and storage costs, also affect global pricing decisions.

Pricing too low or too high can have dire consequences. When prices appear too low in one country, companies can be charged with dumping, a practice subject to severe penalties and fines. **Dumping** is when a firm sells a product in a foreign country below its domestic price or below its actual cost. This is often done to build a company's share of the market by pricing at a competitive level. Another reason is that the products being sold may be surplus or cannot be sold domestically and, therefore, are already a burden to the company. The firm may be glad to sell them at almost any price.

A recent trade dispute involving U.S. apple growers and Mexico is a case in point. Mexican trade officials claimed that U.S. growers were selling their red and golden delicious apples in Mexico below the actual cost of production. They imposed a 101 percent tariff on U.S. apples, and a severe drop in U.S. apple exports to Mexico resulted. Subsequent negotiations set a floor on the price of U.S. apples sold to Mexico.[43]

When companies price their products very high in some countries but competitively in others, they face a gray market problem. A **gray market**, also called *parallel importing*, is a situation where products are sold through unauthorized channels of distribution. A gray market comes about when individuals buy products in a lower-priced country from a manufacturer's authorized retailer, ship them to higher-priced countries, and then sell them below the manufacturer's suggested retail price through unauthorized retailers. Many well-known products have been sold through gray markets, including Seiko watches, Chanel perfume, and Mercedes-Benz cars. Parallel importing is legal in the United States. It is illegal in the European Union.

learning review

7-10. Products may be sold globally in three ways. What are they?

7-11. What is dumping?

LEARNING OBJECTIVES REVIEW

LO 7-1 *Describe the nature and scope of world trade from a global perspective and identify the major trends that have influenced world trade and global marketing.*
A global perspective on world trade views exports and imports as complementary economic flows: A country's imports affect its exports and exports affect its imports. World trade flows to and from the United States reflect demand and supply interdependencies for products among nations and industries. The four largest importers of U.S. products and services are Canada, Mexico, China, and Japan. The four largest exporters to the

United States are China, Canada, Mexico, and Japan. The United States imports more products than it exports.

Four major trends have influenced the landscape of global marketing in the past decade. First, there has been a gradual decline of economic protectionism by individual countries, leading to a reduction in tariffs and quotas. Second, there is growing economic integration and free trade among nations, reflected in the creation of the European Union and the North American Free Trade Agreement. Third, there exists global competition among global companies for global consumers, resulting in firms adopting global marketing strategies and promoting global brands. And finally, a networked global marketspace has emerged using Internet technology as a tool for exchanging products, services, and information on a global scale.

LO 7-2 *Identify the environmental forces that shape global marketing efforts.*

Three major environmental forces shape global marketing efforts. First, there are cultural forces, including values, customs, cultural symbols, and language. Economic forces also shape global marketing efforts. These include a country's stage of economic development and economic infrastructure, consumer income and purchasing power, and currency exchange rates. Finally, political-regulatory forces in a country or region of the world create a favorable or unfavorable climate for global marketing efforts.

LO 7-3 *Name and describe the alternative approaches companies use to enter global markets.*

Companies have four alternative approaches for entering global markets. These are exporting, licensing, joint venture, and direct investment. Exporting involves producing products in one country and selling them in another country. Under licensing, a company offers the right to a trademark, patent, trade secret, or similarly valued item of intellectual property in return for a royalty or fee. In a joint venture, a foreign company and a local firm invest together to create a local business. Direct investment entails a domestic firm actually investing in and owning a foreign subsidiary or division.

LO 7-4 *Explain the distinction between standardization and customization when companies craft worldwide marketing programs.*

Companies distinguish between standardization and customization when crafting worldwide marketing programs. Standardization means that all elements of the marketing program are the same across countries and cultures. Customization means that one or more elements of the marketing program are adapted to meet the needs or preferences of consumers in a particular country or culture. Global marketers apply a simple rule when crafting worldwide marketing programs: Standardize marketing programs whenever possible and customize them wherever necessary.

FOCUSING ON KEY TERMS

back translation p. 175
balance of trade p. 163
bottom of the pyramid p. 177
consumer ethnocentrism p. 176
countertrade p. 162
cross-cultural analysis p. 173
cultural symbols p. 174
currency exchange rate p. 179
customs p. 174
direct investment p. 184
dumping p. 187
Economic Espionage Act (1996) p. 165
exporting p. 181
Foreign Corrupt Practices Act (1977) p. 174
global brand p. 171
global competition p. 169
global consumers p. 171
global marketing strategy p. 170
gray market p. 187
gross domestic product (GDP) p. 162
joint venture p. 183
microfinance p. 179
multidomestic marketing strategy p. 170
protectionism p. 166
quota p. 167
semiotics p. 175
strategic alliances p. 169
tariffs p. 166
values p. 173
World Trade Organization (WTO) p. 167

APPLYING MARKETING KNOWLEDGE

1 Consider the following statement: "Quotas are a hidden tax on consumers, whereas tariffs are a more obvious one." What does this mean?

2 Is the trade feedback effect described in the text a long-run or short-run view on world trade flows? Explain your answer.

3 The United States is considered to be a global leader in the development and marketing of pharmaceutical products, and Merck & Co. of New Jersey is a world leader in prescription drug sales. What explanation can you give for this situation based on the text discussion concerning the competitive advantage of nations?

4 How successful would a television commercial in Japan be if it featured a husband surprising his wife in her dressing area on Valentine's Day with a small box of chocolates containing four candies? Explain.

5 As a novice in global marketing, which global market-entry strategy would you be likely to start with? Why? What other alternatives do you have for a global market entry?

6 Coca-Cola is sold worldwide. In some countries, Coca-Cola owns the bottling facilities; in others, it has signed contracts with licensees or relies on joint ventures. When selecting a licensee in each country, what factors should Coca-Cola consider?

BUILDING YOUR MARKETING PLAN

Does your marketing plan involve reaching global customers outside the United States? If the answer is no, read no further and do not include a global element in your plan. If the answer is yes, try to identify the following:

1 What features of your product are especially important to potential customers?

2 In which countries do these potential customers live?

3 What special marketing issues are involved in trying to reach them?

Answers to these questions will help in developing more detailed marketing mix strategies described in later chapters.

VIDEO CASE 7 Mary Kay, Inc.: Building a Brand in India

QR 7-5
Mary Kay
Video Case

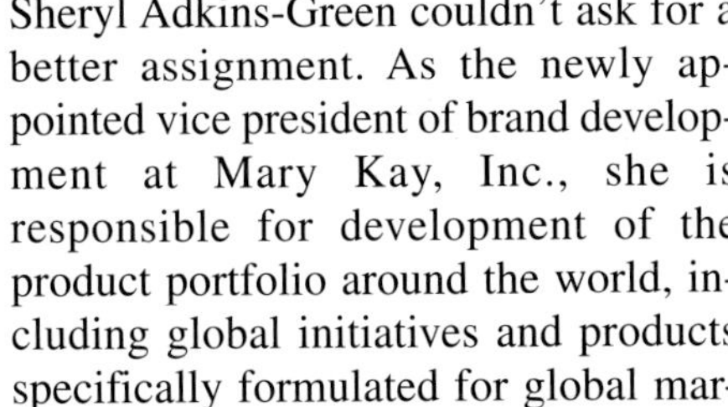

Sheryl Adkins-Green couldn't ask for a better assignment. As the newly appointed vice president of brand development at Mary Kay, Inc., she is responsible for development of the product portfolio around the world, including global initiatives and products specifically formulated for global markets. She is enthusiastic about her position, noting that, "There is tremendous opportunity for growth. Even in these economic times, women still want to pamper themselves, and to look good is to feel good."

Getting up to speed on her new company and her new position topped her short-term agenda. She was specifically interested in the company's efforts to date to build the Mary Kay brand in India.

THE MARY KAY WAY

Mary Kay Ash founded Mary Kay Cosmetics in 1963 with her life savings of $5,000 and the support of her 20-year-old son, Richard Rogers, who currently serves as executive chairman of Mary Kay, Inc. Mary Kay, Inc., is one of the largest direct sellers of skin care and color cosmetics in the world with more than $2.5 billion in annual sales. Mary Kay brand products are sold in more than 35 markets on five continents. The United States, China, Russia, and Mexico are the top four markets served by the company. The company's global independent sales force exceeds 2 million. About 65 percent of the company's independent sales representatives reside outside the United States.

Mary Kay Ash's founding principles were simple, time-tested, and remain a fundamental company business philosophy. She adopted the Golden Rule as her guiding principle, determining the best course of action in virtually any situation could be easily discerned by "doing unto others as you would have them do unto you." She also steadfastly believed that life's priorities should be kept in their proper order, which to her meant "God first, family second, and career third." Her work ethic, approach to business, and success have resulted in numerous awards and recognitions including, but not limited to, the Horatio Alger American Citizen Award, recognition as one of "America's 25 Most Influential Women," and induction into the National Business Hall of Fame.

Mary Kay, Inc., engages in the development, manufacture, and packaging of skin care, makeup, spa and body, and fragrance products for men and women. It offers anti-aging, cleanser, moisturizer, lip and eye care, body care, and sun care products. Overall, the company produces more than 200 premium products in its state-of-the-art manufacturing facilities in Dallas, Texas, and Hangzhou, China. The company's approach to direct selling employs the "party plan," whereby independent sales representatives host parties to demonstrate or sell products to consumers.

GROWTH OPPORTUNITIES IN ASIA-PACIFIC MARKETS

Asia-Pacific markets represent major growth opportunities for Mary Kay, Inc. These markets for Mary Kay, Inc., include Australia, China, Hong Kong, India, Korea, Malaysia, New Zealand, the Philippines, Singapore, and Taiwan.

China accounts for the largest sales revenue outside the United States, representing about 25 percent of annual Mary Kay, Inc., worldwide sales. The company entered China in 1995 and currently has some 200,000 independent sales representatives or "beauty consultants" in that country.

Part of Mary Kay's success in China has been attributed to the company's message of female empowerment and femininity, which has resonated in China, a country where young women have few opportunities to start their own businesses. Speaking about the corporate philosophy at Mary Kay, Inc., KK Chua, President, Asia-Pacific, said, "Mary Kay's corporate objective is not only to create a market, selling skin care and cosmetics; it's all about enriching women's lives by helping women reach their full potential, find their inner beauty and discover how truly great they are." This view is echoed by Sheryl Adkins-Green, who notes that the Mary Kay brand has

FIGURE 1
Social and economic statistics for India in 2007 and China in 1995.

	India 2007	China 1995
Population (million)	1,136	1,198
Population age distribution (0–24; 25–49; 50+)	52%, 33%, 15%	43%, 39%, 18%
Urban population	29.2%	29.0%
Population/square mile	990	332
Gross domestic product (U.S.$ billion)	3,113	728
Per capita income (U.S.$)	$950	$399
Direct selling sales percent of total cosmetics/skin care sales	3.3%	3.0%

"transformational and aspirational" associations for users and beauty consultants alike.

Mary Kay, Inc., learned that adjustments to its product line and message for women were necessary in some Asia-Pacific markets. In China, for example, the order of life's priorities—"God first, family second, and career third"—has been modified to "Faith first, family second, and career third." Also, Chinese women aren't heavy users of makeup. Therefore, the featured products include skin cream, anti-aging cream, and whitening creams. As a generalization, whitening products are popular among women in China, India, Korea, and the Philippines, where lighter skin is associated with beauty, class, and privilege.

MARY KAY, INDIA

Mary Kay, Inc., senior management believed that India represented a growth opportunity for three reasons. First, the Indian upper and consuming classes were growing and were expected to total over 500 million individuals. Second, the population was overwhelmingly young and optimistic. This youthful population continues to push consumerism as the line between luxury and basic items continues to blur. Third, a growing number of working women have given a boost to sales of cosmetics, skin care, and fragrances in India's urban areas, where 70 percent of the country's middle-class women reside.

Senior management also believed that India's socioeconomic characteristics in 2007 were similar in many ways to China's in 1995, when the company entered that market (see Figure 1). The Mary Kay culture was viewed as a good fit with the Indian culture, which would benefit the company's venture into this market. For example, industry research has shown that continuing modernization of the country has led to changing aspirations. As a result, the need to be good looking, well-groomed, and stylish has taken on a newfound importance.

Mary Kay initiated operations in India in September 2007 with a full marketing launch in early 2008. The initial launch was in Delhi, the nation's capital and the second most populated metropolis in India, and Mumbai, the nation's most heavily populated metropolis. Delhi, with per capita income of U.S. $1,420, and Mumbai, with per capita income of $2,850, were among the wealthiest metropolitan areas in India.

According to Rhonda Shasteen, chief marketing officer at Mary Kay, Inc., "For Mary Kay to be successful in India, the company had to build a brand, build a sales force, and build an effective supply chain to service the sales force."

Building a Brand

Mary Kay, Inc., executives believed that brand building in India needed to involve media advertising; literature describing the Mary Kay culture, the Mary Kay story, and the company's image; and educational material for Mary Kay independent sales representatives. In addition, Mary Kay, Inc., became the cosmetics partner of the Miss India Worldwide Pageant 2008. At this event, Mary Kay Miss Beautiful Skin 2008 was crowned.

Brand building in India also involved product mix and pricing. Four guidelines were followed:

1. Keep the offering simple and skin care focused for the new Indian sales force and for a new operation.
2. Open with accessibly priced basic skin care products in relation to the competition in order to establish Mary Kay product quality and value.
3. Avoid opening with products that would phase out shortly after launch.
4. Address the key product categories of Skin Care, Body Care, and Color based on current market information.

Brand pricing focused on offering accessibly priced basic skin care to the average middle-class Indian consumer between the ages of 25 and 54. This strategy, called "mass-tige pricing," resulted in product price points that were above mass but below prestige competitive product prices. Following an initial emphasis on offering high-quality, high-value products, Mary Kay introduced more technologically advanced products that commanded higher price points. For example, the company introduced the Mary Kay MelaCEP Whitening System, consisting of seven products, which was specifically formulated for Asian skin in March 2009. This system was ". . . priced on the lower price end of the prestige category with a great value for money equation," said Hina Nagarajan, country manager for Mary Kay India.

Building a Sales Force

According to Adkins-Green, "Mary Kay's most powerful marketing vehicle is the direct selling organization," which is a key component of the brand's marketing strategy. Mary Kay relied on its Global Leadership Development Program directors and National Sales directors and the Mary Kay Sales Education staff from the United States and Canada for the initial recruitment and training of independent sales representatives in India. New independent sales representatives received 2 to 3 days of intensive training and a starter kit that included not only products, but also information pertaining to product demonstrations, sales presentations, professional demeanor, the company's history and culture, and team building.

"Culture training is very important to Mary Kay (independent sales representatives) because they are going to be the messengers of Mary Kay," said Hina Nagarajan. "As a direct-selling company that offers products sold person-to-person, we recognize that there's a personal relationship between consultant and client with every sale," added Rhonda Shasteen. By late 2009, there were some 4,000 independent sales representatives in India present in some 200 cities mostly in the northern, western, and northeastern regions of the country.

Creating a Supply Chain

Mary Kay, India, imported products into India from China, Korea, and the United States. Products were shipped to regional distribution centers in Delhi and Mumbai, India, where Mary Kay Beauty Centers were located. Beauty Centers served as order pickup points for the independent sales representatives. Mary Kay beauty consultants purchased products from the company and, in turn, sold them to consumers.

LOOKING AHEAD

Mary Kay, Inc., plans to invest around $20 million in the next five years on product development, company infrastructure, and building its brand in India. "There is a tremendous opportunity for growth," says Sheryl Adkins-Green. India represents a particularly attractive opportunity. Developing the brand and brand portfolio and specifically formulating products for Indian consumers will require her attention to brand positioning and brand equity.

Questions

1 Is Mary Kay an international firm, a multinational firm, or a transnational firm based on its marketing strategy? Why?

2 What global market-entry strategy did Mary Kay use when it entered India?

3 Is Mary Kay a global brand? Why or why not?

8 Marketing Research: From Customer Insights to Actions

Learning Objectives

After reading this chapter you should be able to:

LO 8-1 Identify the reason for conducting marketing research.

LO 8-2 Describe the five-step marketing research approach that leads to marketing actions.

LO 8-3 Explain how marketing uses secondary and primary data.

LO 8-4 Discuss the uses of observations, questionnaires, panels, experiments, and newer data collection methods.

LO 8-5 Explain how information technology and data mining lead to marketing actions.

LO 8-6 Describe three approaches to developing a company's sales forecast.

Reducing the Risk of a Movie's Failure with Test Screenings and Tracking Studies

The Hunger Games, *Star Trek*, and *The Hobbit* are movies that rewarded their studios with huge profits.[1] Unfortunately, not every movie has such favorable results. So what can these studios do to try to reduce the costly risk that a movie will be a box-office flop?

What's in a Movie Name?

Fixing bad names for movies—like *The Surrogate*, *Rope Burns*, and *Shoeless Joe*—can turn potential disasters into hugely successful blockbusters. Don't remember seeing these movies? Well, test screenings—a form of marketing research—found that moviegoers like you had problems with these original titles. Here's what happened:

- The 2012 movie *The Surrogate*, which garnered Helen Hunt an Academy Award nomination, became *The Sessions* because a rival studio controlled the rights to the name *The Surrogate*.
- *Rope Burns* became *Million Dollar Baby* because audiences didn't like the original name. The movie won the 2005 Academy Award for Best Picture and starred Hilary Swank as a woman boxer and Clint Eastwood as her trainer.
- Shown frequently on television now, *Shoeless Joe* became the baseball classic *Field of Dreams* because audiences thought Kevin Costner was playing a homeless person.

To reduce risks to the studio, filmmakers want movie titles that are concise, grab attention, capture the essence of the film, and have no legal restrictions—the same factors that make a good brand name.[2]

QR 8-1
***The Hunger Games* Movie Trailer**

The Risks of Today's (and Tomorrow's) Blockbuster Movies

Bad titles, poor scripts, temperamental stars, costly special effects, and several blockbuster movies released at the same time are just a few of the nightmares studio executives face. They try to reduce their risks by developing appealing sequels, like *Iron Man 3*, *Transformers 4*, and *Despicable Me 2*. And,

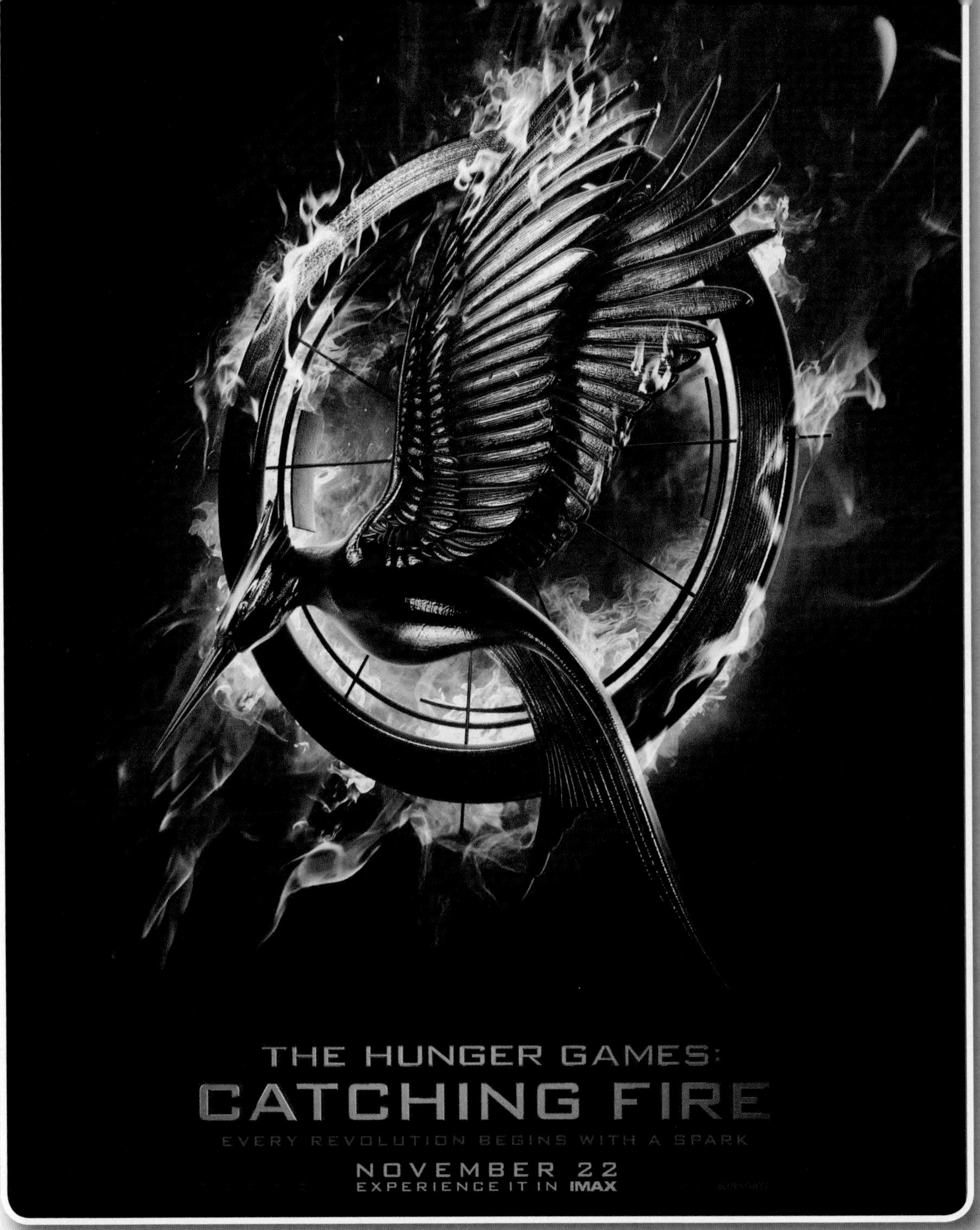

you guessed it: *The Hunger Games* will have sequels in 2013 (*Catching Fire*), 2014 (*Mockingjay*, *Part 1*), and 2015 (*Mockingjay*, *Part 2*).

With a typical film costing over $100 million to produce and market,[3] studios also try to reduce their risks by:

- *Conducting test screenings*. In test screenings, 300 to 400 prospective moviegoers are recruited to attend a "sneak preview" of a film before its release.[4] After viewing the movie, the audience fills out an exhaustive survey to critique its title, plot, characters, music, and ending to identify improvements to make in the final edit.[5]

The text describes how its "mini" test screening brought *Avatar* to life.

- *Using tracking studies*. Immediately before an upcoming film's release, studios will ask prospective moviegoers in the target audience three key questions: (1) Are you aware of the film? (2) Are you interested in seeing the film? and (3) Will you see the film this weekend?[6] Studios use these data to forecast the movie's opening weekend box-office sales and, if necessary, run last-minute ads to promote the film.

Converting Marketing Research Results into Actions

Sometimes marketing research can mean the difference between having a blockbuster hit and having no movie at all. Consider the fact that director James Cameron had to produce a short "mini" test screening of a 3D segment of *Avatar* to convince four Twentieth Century Fox executives to fund his movie. The studio made the right choice; *Avatar* became #1 in all-time worldwide gross ticket sales.[7]

Test screenings resulted in the now-classic *Fatal Attraction* movie having one of the most successful "ending switches" of all time. In these sneak previews, audiences liked everything but the ending, which had Alex (Glenn Close) committing suicide and framing Dan (Michael Douglas) as her murderer. The studio shot $1.3 million of scenes for a new ending, which led to *Fatal Attraction*'s box-office success.

These examples show how marketing research leads to decisive marketing actions, the main topic of this chapter. Also, marketing research is often used to help a firm develop its sales forecasts, the final topic of this chapter.

THE ROLE OF MARKETING RESEARCH

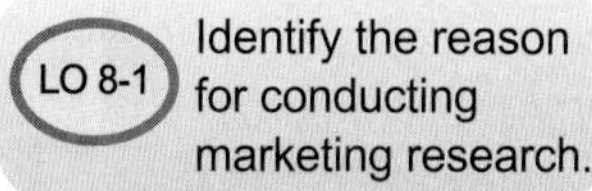
LO 8-1 Identify the reason for conducting marketing research.

Let's (1) look at what marketing research is, (2) identify some difficulties with it, and (3) describe the five steps marketers use to conduct it.

What Is Marketing Research?

Marketing research is the process of defining a marketing problem and opportunity, systematically collecting and analyzing information, and recommending actions.[8] Although imperfect, marketers conduct marketing research to reduce the risk of and thereby improve marketing decisions.

The Challenges in Doing Good Marketing Research

Whatever the marketing issue involved—whether discovering consumer tastes or setting the right price—good marketing research is challenging. For example:

- Suppose your firm is developing a new product never before seen by consumers. Will consumers really know whether they are likely to buy a product that they have never thought about before?
- Imagine if you, as a consumer, were asked about your personal hygiene habits. Even though you know the answers, will you reveal them? When personal or status questions are involved, will people give honest answers?
- Will consumers' actual purchase behaviors match their stated interests or intentions? Will they buy the same brand they say they will?

Marketing research must overcome these difficulties and obtain the information needed so that marketers can assess what consumers want and will buy.

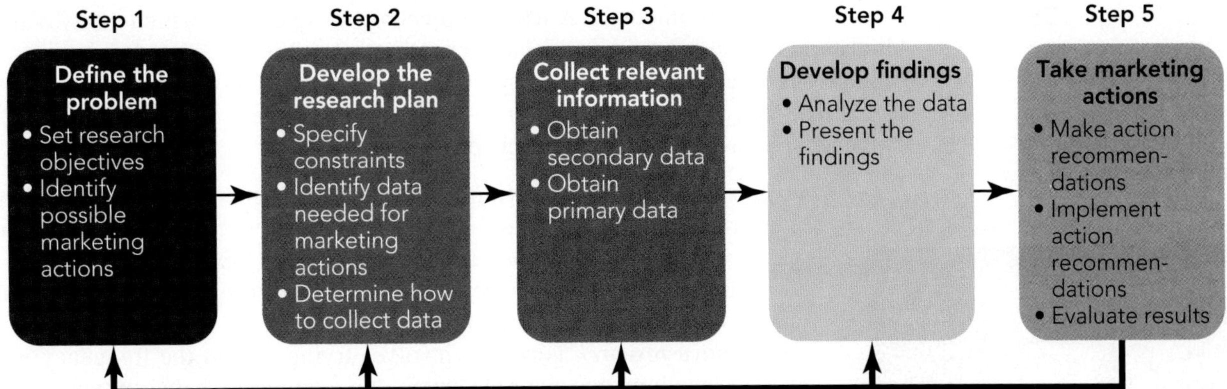

FIGURE 8–1
Five-step marketing research approach leading to marketing actions. Lessons learned from past research mistakes are fed back to improve each of the steps.

Describe the five-step marketing research approach that leads to marketing actions.

Five-Step Marketing Research Approach

A *decision* is a conscious choice from among two or more alternatives. All of us make many such decisions daily. At work we choose from alternative ways to accomplish an assigned task. At college we choose from alternative courses. As consumers we choose from alternative brands. No magic formula guarantees correct decisions.

Managers and researchers have tried to improve the outcomes of decisions by using more formal, structured approaches to *decision making*, the act of consciously choosing from among alternatives. The systematic marketing research approach used to collect information to improve marketing decisions and actions described in this chapter uses five steps and is shown in Figure 8–1. Although the five-step approach described here focuses on marketing decisions, it provides a systematic checklist for making both business and personal decisions.

STEP 1: DEFINE THE PROBLEM

Every marketing problem faces its own research challenges. For example, the marketing strategy used by LEGO's toy researchers and designers in Denmark illustrates the wide variations possible in collecting marketing research data to build better toys.

LEGO Mindstorms EV3: From TRACK3R, whose interchangeable bazooka and hammer can operate after only 20 minutes of assembly . . .

LEGO's definition of "toy" has changed dramatically in the last half century—far beyond the 40 billion LEGO bricks sitting in rooms around the world today. In 1998, LEGO introduced the Mindstorms kit, a "toy" that integrates electronics, computers, and robots with LEGO bricks. Developed with the help of the Media Lab at the Massachusetts Institute of Technology, the Mindstorms kit appeals to a diverse market—from elementary school kids to world-class robotics experts. The kits can be found in homes, schools, universities, and industrial laboratories.[9]

A simplified look at the marketing research for the LEGO Mindstorms EV3—introduced in late 2013 at a price of $350—shows the two key elements in defining a problem: setting the research objectives and identifying possible marketing actions.

Set the Research Objectives

Research objectives are specific, measurable goals the decision maker, in this case a LEGO manager, seeks to achieve in conducting the marketing research. For LEGO, let's assume the immediate research objective is to decide which of two new Mindstorms designs should be selected for marketing.

In setting research objectives, marketers have to be clear on the purpose of the research that leads to marketing actions. The three main types of marketing research, explained in more detail later in the chapter, are as follows:

. . . to EV3RSTORM, whose infrared sensors let it walk or skate.

1. *Exploratory research* provides ideas about a vague problem. LEGO was concerned that middle school kids would be overwhelmed by the 500-plus pieces in Mindstorms kits and quickly lose interest. LEGO's brainstorming—an example of exploratory research—revealed kids need to have a basic device up, running, and doing tricks in 20 minutes.
2. *Descriptive research* generally involves trying to find the frequency with which something occurs or the extent of a relationship between two factors. So if LEGO wants to know which of the two Mindstorms kits is of greatest interest to middle school versus high school students, it might ask them. LEGO can then assess the relationship by doing a cross tabulation (discussed later in the chapter) of school level versus kit preference.
3. *Causal research* tries to determine the extent to which the change in one factor changes another one. Changing key pieces in a Mindstorms kit affects how quickly the newly built device can do tricks—affecting acceptance by kit users. Test markets, discussed later, use causal research.

Identify Possible Marketing Actions

Effective decision makers develop specific **measures of success**, which are criteria or standards used in evaluating proposed solutions to the problem. Different research outcomes, based on the measure of success, lead to different marketing actions. For LEGO, assume the measure of success is the total time middle schoolers spend playing with each of the two Mindstorms kits until they produce a device that can do simple tricks. This measure of success leads to a clear-cut marketing action: Market the design that produces an acceptable device in the least amount of playing time.

Marketing researchers know that defining a problem is an incredibly difficult task. If the objectives are too broad, the problem may not be researchable. If they are too narrow, the value of the research results may be seriously lessened. This is why marketing researchers spend so much time defining a marketing problem precisely and writing a formal proposal that describes the research to be done.[10]

STEP 2: DEVELOP THE RESEARCH PLAN

The second step in the marketing research process requires that the researcher (1) specify the constraints on the marketing research activity, (2) identify the data needed for marketing actions, and (3) determine how to collect the data.

Specify Constraints

The **constraints** in a decision are the restrictions placed on potential solutions to a problem. Examples include the limitations on the time and money available to solve the problem.

What constraints might LEGO set in mid-2012 in developing the LEGO Mindstorms EV3, whose market launch is scheduled for late 2013? LEGO might establish the following constraints on its decision to select one of the two improved designs: The decision (1) must be made in five weeks (2) using 10 teams of middle schoolers playing with the two improved Mindstorms kits.

Identify Data Needed for Marketing Actions

Effective marketing research studies focus on collecting data that will lead to effective marketing actions. In the Mindstorms case, LEGO's marketers might want to know students' math skills, time spent playing video games, and so on. But that information, while nice to know, is largely irrelevant because the study should focus on collecting only those data that will help them make a clear choice between the two Mindstorms designs.

Determine How to Collect Data

Determining how to collect useful marketing research data is often as important as actually collecting the data—Step 3 in the process, which is discussed later. Two key elements in deciding how to collect the data are (1) concepts and (2) methods.

Concepts In the world of marketing, *concepts* are ideas about products or services. To find out about consumer reactions to a potential new product, marketing researchers frequently develop a *new-product concept*, which is a picture or verbal description of a product or service the firm might offer for sale. For example, the LEGO designers might develop a new-product concept for an innovative Mindstorms EV3 robot, like that shown, capable of walking or skating, perhaps by adding an infrared sensor.

Methods *Methods* are the approaches that can be used to collect data to solve all or part of a problem. To collect data, the LEGO designers might use a combination of (1) observing the behavior of Mindstorms users and (2) asking them questions to meet its "20-minute" measure of success for young users. Observing people and asking them questions—the two main data collection methods—are discussed in the section that follows.

How successful is LEGO's marketing research and design strategy for its Mindstorms robots? Among younger users alone, in 2012 more than 20,000 elementary and middle school teams faced off in competitions around the world.

How can you find and use the methods that other marketing researchers have found successful? Information on useful methods is available in tradebooks, textbooks, and handbooks that relate to marketing and marketing research. Some periodicals and technical journals, such as the *Journal of Marketing* and the *Journal of Marketing Research*, both published by the American Marketing Association, summarize methods and techniques valuable in addressing marketing problems.

Special methods vital to marketing are (1) sampling and (2) statistical inference. For example, marketing researchers often use *sampling* by selecting a group of distributors, customers, or prospects, asking them questions, and treating their answers as typical of all those in whom they are interested. They may then use *statistical inference* to generalize the results from the sample to much larger groups of distributors, customers, or prospects to help decide on marketing actions.

learning review

8-1. What is marketing research?

8-2. What is the five-step marketing research approach?

8-3. What are constraints, as they apply to developing a research plan?

STEP 3: COLLECT RELEVANT INFORMATION

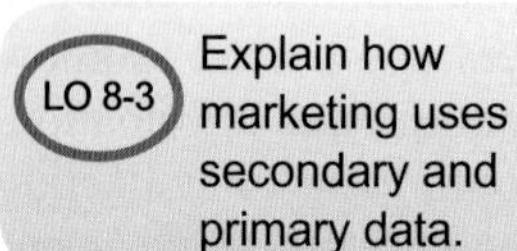

Explain how marketing uses secondary and primary data.

Collecting enough relevant information to make a rational, informed marketing decision sometimes simply means using your knowledge to decide immediately. At other times it entails collecting an enormous amount of information at great expense.

Figure 8–2 shows how the different kinds of marketing information fit together. **Data**, the facts and figures related to the project, are divided into two main parts: secondary data and primary data. **Secondary data** are facts and figures that have already been recorded prior to the project at hand. As shown in Figure 8–2, secondary data are divided into two parts—internal and external secondary data—depending on whether the data come from inside or outside the organization needing the research. **Primary data** are facts and figures that are newly collected for the project. Figure 8–2 shows that primary data can be divided into observational data, questionnaire data, and other sources of data.

Secondary Data: Internal

The internal records of a company generally offer the most easily accessible marketing information. These internal sources of secondary data may be divided into two related parts: (1) marketing inputs and (2) marketing outcomes.

Marketing input data relate to the effort expended to make sales. These range from sales and advertising budgets and expenditures to salespeople's call reports, which describe the number of sales calls per day, who was visited, and what was discussed.

Marketing outcome data relate to the results of the marketing efforts. These involve accounting records on shipments and include sales and repeat sales, often broken down by sales representative, industry, and geographic region. In addition, e-mails, phone calls, and letters from customers can reveal both complaints and what is working well.[11]

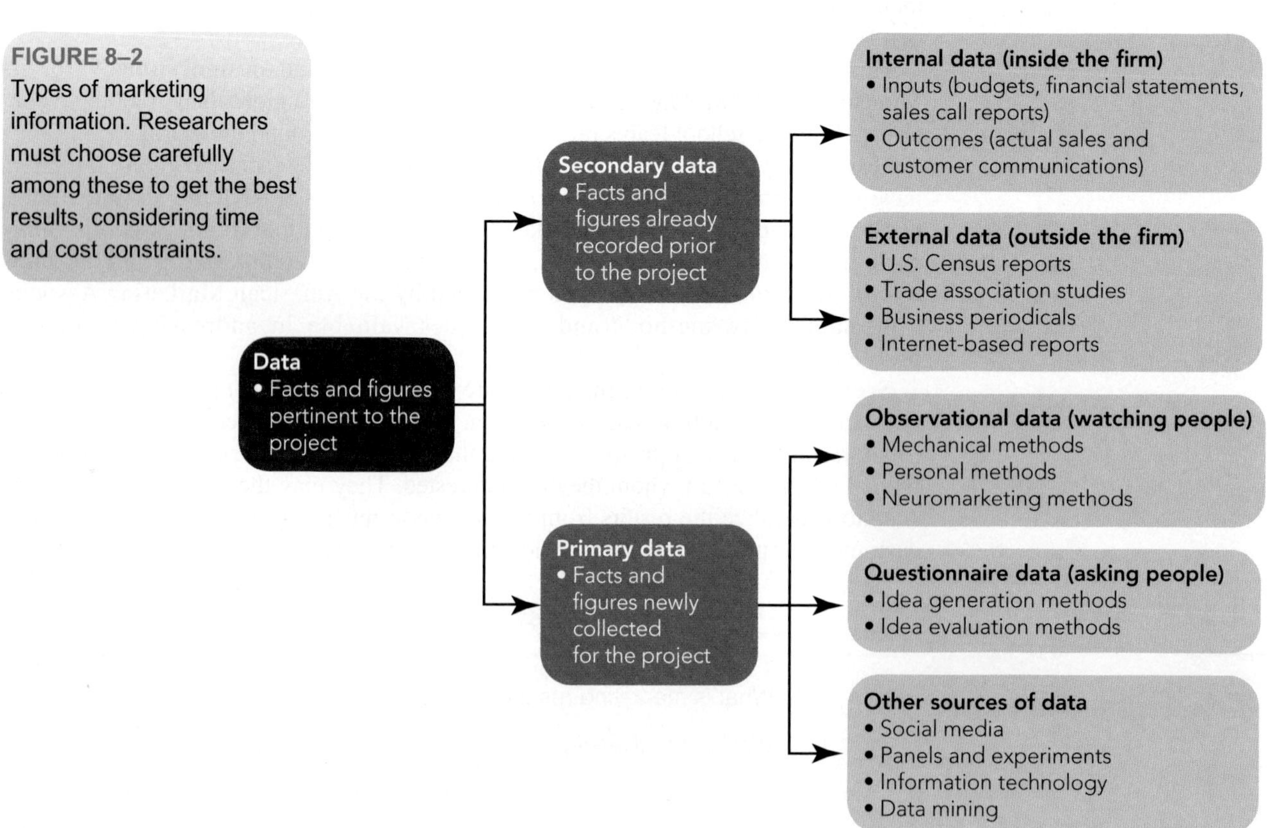

FIGURE 8–2
Types of marketing information. Researchers must choose carefully among these to get the best results, considering time and cost constraints.

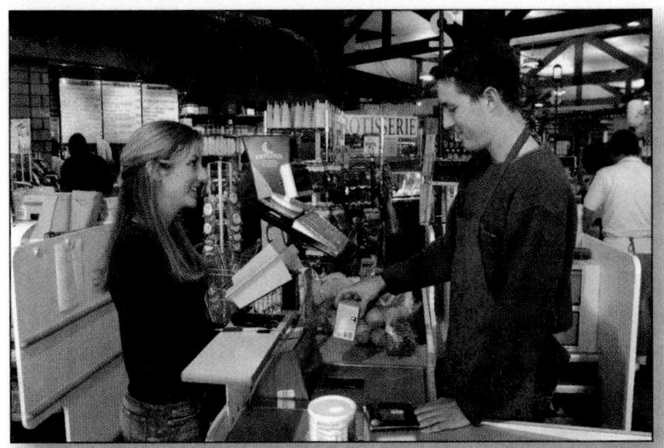

Scanner data at supermarket checkout counters provide valuable information for marketing decisions.

QR 8-2
Census 2010
Video

Secondary Data: External

Published data from outside the organization are external secondary data. The U.S. Census Bureau publishes a variety of useful reports. Best known is the Census 2010, which is the most recent count of the U.S. population that occurs every 10 years. Recently, the Census Bureau began collecting data annually from a smaller number of people through the American Community Survey. Both surveys contain detailed information on American households, such as the number of people per household and the age, sex, race/ethnic background, income, occupation, and education of individuals within the household. Marketers use these data to identify characteristics and trends of ultimate consumers.

The Census Bureau also publishes the Economic Census, which is conducted every five years. These reports are vital to business firms selling products and services to organizations. The 2012 Economic Census contains data on the number and sales of establishments in the United States that produce a product or service based on each firm's geography (state, county, zip code, etc.), industry sector (manufacturing, retail trade, etc.), and North American Industry Classification System (NAICS) code. Data for the 2012 Economic Census will be released beginning in 2014.

Several market research companies pay households and businesses to record all their purchases using a paper or electronic diary. Such *syndicated panel* data economically answer questions that require consistent data collection over time, such as, "How many times did our customers buy our products this year compared to last year?" Examples of syndicated panels that provide a standard set of data on a regular basis are the Nielsen TV ratings and J.D. Power's automotive quality and customer satisfaction surveys.

Some data services provide comprehensive information on household demographics and lifestyle, product purchases, TV viewing behavior, and responses to coupon and free-sample promotions. Their advantage is that a single firm can collect, analyze, interrelate, and present all this information. For consumer product firms such as Procter & Gamble, sales data from various channels are critical to allocate scarce marketing resources. As a result, they use tracking services such as IRI's InfoScan to collect product sales and coupon/free-sample redemptions that have been scanned at the checkout counters of supermarket, drug, convenience, and mass merchandise retailers.

Finally, trade associations, universities, and business periodicals provide detailed data of value to market researchers and planners. These data are now available online via the Internet and can be identified and located using a search engine such as Google or Bing. The Marketing inSite box on the next page provides examples.

Advantages and Disadvantages of Secondary Data

A general rule among marketing people is to obtain secondary data first and then collect primary data. Two important advantages of secondary data are (1) the tremendous time savings because the data have already been collected and published or exist internally and (2) the low cost, such as free or inexpensive Census reports. Furthermore, a greater level of detail is often available through secondary data, especially U.S. Census Bureau data.

However, these advantages must be weighed against some significant disadvantages. First, the secondary data may be out of date, especially if they are U.S. Census data collected only every 5 or 10 years. Second, the definitions or categories might not be quite right for a researcher's project. For example, the age groupings or product categories might be wrong for the project. Also, because the data have been collected for another purpose, they may not be specific enough for the project. In such cases, it may be necessary to collect primary data.

Marketing inSite

Online Databases and Internet Resources Useful to Marketers

Marketers today in search of secondary data can consult online databases available via the Internet. Indexes to articles in periodicals and statistical or financial data on markets, products, and organizations can be accessed either directly or via Internet search engines or portals through keyword searches.

Statistical and financial data on markets, products, and organizations include:

- *The Wall Street Journal* (www.wsj.com), CNBC (www.cnbc.com), and *Fox Business* (www.foxbusiness.com), which provide up-to-the-minute business news and video clips about companies, industries, and trends that affect the marketing environment.
- STAT-USA (www.stat-usa.gov) and the Census Bureau (www.census.gov) of the U.S. Department of Commerce, which provide information on U.S. business, economic, and trade activity collected by the federal government.

Portals and search engines include:

- USA.gov (www.usa.gov), the portal to all U.S. government websites. Users can click on links to browse by topic or enter keywords for specific searches.
- Google (www.google.com), the most popular portal to the entire Internet. Users enter keywords for specific searches and then click on results of interest.

Some of these websites are accessible only if you or your educational institution have paid a subscription fee. Check with your institution's website.

learning review

8-4. What is the difference between secondary and primary data?

8-5. What are some advantages and disadvantages of secondary data?

Discuss the uses of observations, questionnaires, panels, experiments, and newer data collection methods.

Primary Data: Watching People

Observing people and asking them questions are the two principal ways to collect new or primary data for a marketing study. Facts and figures obtained by watching, either mechanically or in person, how people actually behave is the way marketing researchers collect **observational data**. Observational data can be collected by mechanical (including electronic), personal, or neuromarketing methods.

Mechanical Methods National TV ratings, such as those of Nielsen shown in Figure 8–3, are an example of mechanical observational data collected by a "people meter." The device measures what channel and program is tuned in and who is watching. The people meter (1) is a box that is attached to TV sets, VCRs, DVRs (digital video recorders), cable boxes, and satellite dishes in about 20,000 households across the country;[12] (2) has a remote that operates the meter when a viewer begins and finishes watching a TV program; and (3) stores and then transmits the viewing information each night to Nielsen. Data are also collected on TV viewing using less sophisticated meters or TV diaries (a paper-pencil measurement system).

In early 2012, Nielsen introduced "cross-platform television ratings," which combine Nielsen's existing TV ratings with its new online ratings. These ratings include consumer viewing of TV programs seen not only on regular TV but also streamed online or wirelessly on PCs, smartphones, tablet devices, and video game consoles.[13]

On the basis of all these observational data, Nielsen then calculates the rating and share of each TV program.

What determines if *American Idol* stays on the air? For the importance of the TV "ratings game," see the text.

FIGURE 8–3
Nielsen Television Index Ranking Report for network TV prime-time households for the week ending May 19, 2013. The difference of a few share points in Nielsen TV ratings affects the cost of a TV ad on a show and even whether the show remains on the air.

Rank	Program	Network	No. of Viewers (millions)	Rating	Share
1	*NCIS*	CBS	13.5	11.8	20
2	*The Big Bang Theory*	CBS	11.0	9.6	17
3	*Dancing with the Stars*	ABC	10.1	8.8	14
4	*American Idol*—Thursday	FOX	9.9	8.7	14
5	*NCIS: Los Angeles*	CBS	9.7	8.5	13
6	*Dancing with the Stars*—Results	ABC	8.9	7.8	12
7	*American Idol*—Wednesday	FOX	8.6	7.5	13
8	*The Big Bang Theory*—Special	CBS	8.4	7.4	12
9	*Castle*	ABC	8.4	7.4	12
10	*Voice*	NBC	7.9	6.9	11

Source: Nielsen © 2013. The Nielsen Company Broadcast Ranking Report for the week ending May 19, 2013. Viewing estimates include live viewing and DVR playback on the same day, defined as 3 A.M. to 3 A.M. Rank is based on the number of U.S. viewers (in millions) from Nielsen's National People Meter Sample.

With 115.6 million TV households in the United States, a single rating point equals 1 percent, or 1,156,000 TV households.[14] For TV viewing, a share point is the percentage of TV sets in use tuned to a particular program. Because TV and cable networks sell over $64 billion annually in advertising and set advertising rates to advertisers on the basis of those data, precision in the Nielsen data is critical.[15]

A change of 1 percentage point in a rating can mean gaining or losing millions of dollars in advertising revenues because advertisers pay rates on the basis of the size of the audience for a TV program. So as shown by the green rows in Figure 8–3, we might expect to pay more for a 30-second TV ad on *NCIS* than one on *Castle*. Broadcast and cable networks may change the time slot or even cancel a TV program if its ratings are consistently poor and advertisers are unwilling to pay a rate based on a higher guaranteed rating.

But TV advertisers today have a special problem: With about three out of four TV viewers skipping ads with TiVo and DVRs, or channel surfing during commercials, how many people are actually seeing their TV ads? Now services such as Nielsen offer advertisers minute-by-minute measurement of how many viewers stay tuned during commercials. Recently, TiVo also expanded its service to allow TV advertisers to see how many and what kind of users are watching their commercials.[16] The viewership data in Figure 8–3 include not only live TV but also programs recorded on DVRs. With these more precise measures of who is likely to see a TV ad, buying TV ads is becoming more scientific.[17]

Is this *really* marketing research? A mystery shopper at work.

Personal Methods Observational data can take some strange twists. Jennifer Voitle, a laid-off investment bank employee with four advanced degrees, responded to an Internet ad and found a new career: *mystery shopper*. Companies pay mystery shoppers to check on the quality and pricing of their products and the integrity of and customer service provided by their employees. Jennifer gets paid to travel to exotic hotels, eat at restaurants, play golf, test-drive new cars, shop for clothes, and play arcade games. But her role posing as a customer gives her client unique marketing research information that can be obtained in no other way. Says Jennifer, "Can you believe they call this work?"[18]

Watching consumers in person or recording them are two other observational approaches. For example, Procter & Gamble watches women do their laundry, clean the floor, put on makeup, and so on because they comprise 80 percent of its customers! And Gillette records consumers brushing their teeth in their own bathrooms to see how they really brush—not just how they say they brush. The new-product result: Gillette's Oral-B CrossAction toothbrush.[19]

Ethnographic research is a specialized observational approach in which trained observers seek to discover subtle behavioral and emotional reactions as consumers encounter products in their "natural use environment," such as in their home or car.[20] Recently, Kraft launched Deli Creations, which are sandwiches made with its Oscar Mayer meats, Kraft cheeses, and Grey Poupon mustard, after spending several months with consumers in their kitchens. Kraft discovered that consumers wanted complete, ready-to-serve meals that are easy to prepare—and it had the products to create them.[21]

Personal observation is both useful and flexible, but it can be costly and unreliable when different observers report different conclusions when watching the same event. And while observation can reveal *what* people do, it cannot easily determine *why* they do it. This is the principal reason for using neuromarketing and questionnaires, our next topics.

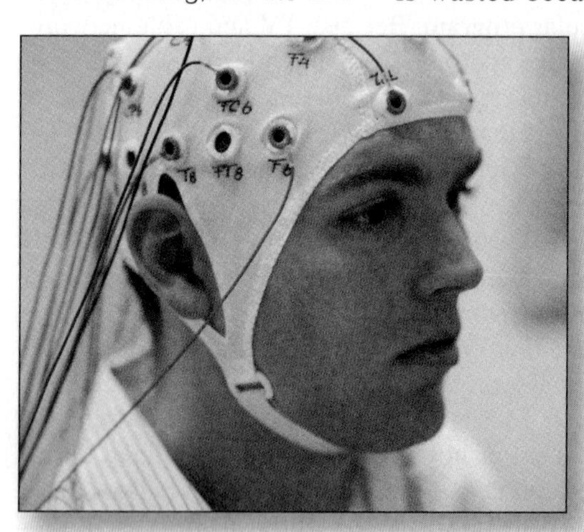

"Neuromarketing" often uses a cap with dozens of sensors to measure brain waves to try to understand consumers better. For some changes made by Campbell Soup Company based on neuromarketing, see the text.

Neuromarketing Methods Global brand expert Martin Lindstrom believes that most traditional marketing research—like focus groups and surveys—is wasted because consumers' feelings toward products and brands reside deep within the subconscious part of their brains. Lindstrom used brain scanning to analyze the buying processes of more than 2,000 participants. Lindstrom merged neuroscience—the study of the brain—with marketing! His controversial findings using "neuromarketing" are summarized in his breakthrough book *Buyology*.[22]

Based on the results of neuromarketing studies, Campbell Soup Company recently changed the labels of most of its soup cans. Some of the changes: Steam now rises from more vibrant images of soup; the "unemotional spoons" have disappeared; and the script logo is smaller and has been moved to the bottom of the can.[23]

Primary Data: Asking People

How many dozens of times have you filled out some kind of a questionnaire? Maybe a short survey at school or a telephone or e-mail survey to see if you are pleased with the service you received. Asking consumers questions and recording their answers is the second principal way of gathering information.

We can divide this primary data collection task into (1) idea generation methods and (2) idea evaluation methods, although they sometimes overlap and each has a number of special techniques.[24] Each survey method results in valuable **questionnaire data**, which are facts and figures obtained by asking people about their attitudes, awareness, intentions, and behaviors.

Idea Generation Methods—Coming Up with Ideas In the past, the most common way of collecting questionnaire data to generate ideas was through an *individual interview*, which involves a single researcher asking questions of one respondent. This approach has many advantages, such as being able to probe for additional ideas using follow-up questions to a respondent's initial answers. However, this method is very expensive. Later in the chapter we'll discuss some alternatives.

Focus groups of students and instructors were used in developing this textbook. To see the specific suggestion that may help you study, read the text.

QR 8-3 Trend Hunter Video

Wendy's spent over two years remaking its 42-year-old burger. The result: Dave's Hot 'N Juicy, named after Wendy's founder, Dave Thomas. See Figure 8–4 for some questions that Wendy's asked consumers in a survey to discover their fast-food preferences, behaviors, and demographics.

General Mills sought ideas about why Hamburger Helper didn't fare well when it was introduced. Initial instructions called for cooking a half-pound of hamburger separately from the noodles or potatoes, which were later mixed with the hamburger. So General Mills researchers used a special kind of individual interview, called a *depth interview*, in which researchers ask lengthy, free-flowing kinds of questions to probe for underlying ideas and feelings. These depth interviews showed consumers (1) didn't think it contained enough meat and (2) didn't want the hassle of cooking in two different pots. The Hamburger Helper product manager changed the recipe to call for a full pound of meat and to allow users to prepare it in one dish, leading to product success.

Focus groups are informal sessions of 6 to 10 past, present, or prospective customers in which a discussion leader, or moderator, asks for opinions about the firm's products and those of its competitors, including how they use these products and special needs they have that these products don't address. Often recorded and conducted in special interviewing rooms with a one-way mirror, these groups enable marketing researchers and managers to hear and watch consumer reactions.

The informality and peer support in an effective focus group help uncover ideas that are often difficult to obtain with individual interviews. For example, to improve understanding and learning by students using this textbook, focus groups were conducted among both marketing instructors and students. Both groups recommended providing answers to each chapter's set of Learning Review questions. This suggestion was followed, so you can see the answers by turning to a section at the back of the textbook or by tapping your finger on the question in the textbook's iPad version.

Finding "the next big thing" for consumers has caused marketing researchers to turn to some less traditional techniques. For example, "fuzzy front end" methods attempt early identification of elusive consumer tastes or trends. Trend Hunter is a firm that seeks to anticipate and track "the evolution of cool." Trend hunting (or watching) is the practice of identifying "emerging shifts in social behavior," which are driven by changes in pop culture that can lead to new products. Trend Hunter has identified about 200,000 "micro-trends" through its global network of 118,000 members and features several of these trends on its daily Trend Hunter TV broadcast via its YouTube channel (trendhuntertv).[25]

Idea Evaluation Methods—Testing an Idea In idea evaluation, the marketing researcher tries to test ideas discovered earlier to help the marketing manager recommend marketing actions. Idea evaluation methods often involve conventional questionnaires using personal, mail, telephone, fax, and online (e-mail or Internet) surveys of a large sample of past, present, or prospective consumers. In choosing among them, the marketing researcher balances the cost of the particular method against the expected quality of the information and the speed with which it can be obtained.

Personal interview surveys enable the interviewer to be flexible in asking probing questions or getting reactions to visual materials but are very costly. *Mail surveys* are usually biased because those most likely to respond have had especially positive or negative experiences with the product or brand. While *telephone interviews* allow flexibility, unhappy respondents may hang up on the interviewer, even with the efficiency of computer-assisted telephone interviewing (CATI).

Increasingly, marketing researchers have begun to use *online surveys* (e-mail and Internet) to collect primary data. The reason: Most consumers have an Internet connection and an e-mail account. Marketers can embed a survey in an e-mail sent to targeted respondents. When they open the e-mail, consumers can either see the survey or click on a link to access it from a website. Marketers can also ask consumers to complete a "pop up" survey in a separate browser window when they access an organization's

1. What things are most important to you when you decide to eat out and go to a fast-food restaurant?

____

____

____

2. Have you eaten at a fast-food restaurant in the past month?

☐ Yes ☐ No

3. If you answered yes to question 2, how often do you eat at a fast-food restaurant?

☐ Once a week or more ☐ 2 to 3 times a month ☐ Once a month or less

4. How important is it to you that a fast-food restaurant satisfies you on the following characteristics? [Check the box that describes your feelings for each item listed.]

CHARACTERISTIC	VERY IMPORTANT	SOMEWHAT IMPORTANT	IMPORTANT	UNIMPORTANT	SOMEWHAT UNIMPORTANT	VERY UNIMPORTANT
• Taste of food	☐	☐	☐	☐	☐	☐
• Cleanliness	☐	☐	☐	☐	☐	☐
• Price	☐	☐	☐	☐	☐	☐
• Variety of menu	☐	☐	☐	☐	☐	☐

5. For each of the characteristics listed below, check the space on the scale that describes how you feel about Wendy's. Mark an X on only **one** of the five spaces for each item listed.

CHARACTERISTIC	CHECK THE SPACE THAT DESCRIBES THE DEGREE TO WHICH WENDY'S IS . . .						
• Taste of food	Tasty	____	____	____	____	____	Not tasty
• Cleanliness	Clean	____	____	____	____	____	Dirty
• Price	Inexpensive	____	____	____	____	____	Expensive
• Variety of menu	Broad	____	____	____	____	____	Narrow

FIGURE 8–4
To obtain the most valuable information from consumers, this Wendy's survey utilizes four different kinds of questions discussed in the text *(continued on the next page).*

website. Many organizations use this method to have consumers assess their products and services or evaluate the design and usability of their websites.

The advantages of online surveys are that the cost is relatively minimal and the turnaround time from data collection to report presentation is much quicker than the traditional methods discussed earlier. However, online surveys have serious drawbacks: Some consumers may view e-mail surveys as "junk" or "spam" and may either choose to not receive them (if they have a "spam blocker") or purposely or inadvertently delete them, unopened. For Internet surveys, some consumers have a "pop-up blocker" that prohibits a browser from opening a separate window that contains the survey; thus, they may not be able to participate in the research. For both e-mail and Internet surveys, consumers can complete the survey multiple times, creating a significant bias in the results. This is especially true for online panels. In response, research firms such as SurveyMonkey have developed sampling technology to prohibit this practice.[26]

The foundation of all research using questionnaires is developing precise questions that get clear, unambiguous answers from respondents.[27] Figure 8–4 shows a number

6. Check one box that describes your agreement or disagreement with each statement listed below:

STATEMENT	STRONGLY AGREE	AGREE	DON'T KNOW	DISAGREE	STRONGLY DISAGREE
• Adults like to take their families to fast-food restaurants	☐	☐	☐	☐	☐
• Our children have a say in where the family chooses to eat	☐	☐	☐	☐	☐

7. How important are each of the following sources of information to you when selecting a fast-food restaurant at which to eat? [Check one box for each source listed.]

SOURCE OF INFORMATION	VERY IMPORTANT	SOMEWHAT IMPORTANT	NOT AT ALL IMPORTANT
• Television	☐	☐	☐
• Newspapers	☐	☐	☐
• Radio	☐	☐	☐
• Billboards	☐	☐	☐
• Internet	☐	☐	☐
• Social networks	☐	☐	☐

8. How often do you eat out at each of the following fast-food restaurants? [Check one box for each source listed.]

RESTAURANT	ONCE A WEEK OR MORE	2 TO 3 TIMES A MONTH	ONCE A MONTH OR LESS
• Burger King	☐	☐	☐
• McDonald's	☐	☐	☐
• Wendy's	☐	☐	☐

9. As head of the household, please answer the following questions about you and your household. [Check only one for each item.]
   a. What is your gender? ☐ Male ☐ Female
   b. What is your marital status? ☐ Single ☐ Married ☐ Other (widowed, divorced, etc.)
   c. How many children under age 18 live in your home? ☐ 0 ☐ 1 ☐ 2 ☐ 3 or more
   d. What is your age? ☐ Under 25 ☐ 25–44 ☐ 45 or older
   e. What is your total annual individual or household income?
   ☐ Less than $15,000 ☐ $15,000–49,000 ☐ Over $49,000

FIGURE 8–4 *(continued)*

of formats for questions taken from a Wendy's survey that assessed fast-food restaurant preferences among present and prospective consumers.

Question 1 is an example of an *open-ended question*, which allows respondents to express opinions, ideas, or behaviors in their own words without being forced to choose among alternatives that have been predetermined by a marketing researcher. This information is invaluable to marketers because it captures the "voice" of respondents, which is useful in understanding consumer behavior, identifying product benefits, or developing advertising messages.

In contrast, *closed-end* or *fixed alternative questions* require respondents to select one or more response options from a set of predetermined choices. Question 2 is an example of a *dichotomous question*, the simplest form of a fixed alternative question that allows only a "yes" or "no" response.

A fixed alternative question with three or more choices uses a *scale.* Question 5 is an example of a question that uses a *semantic differential scale*, a five-point scale in which the opposite ends have one- or two-word adjectives that have opposite

Visitors to Frito-Lay's Facebook Page voted on new potato chip flavors by clicking on "I'd Eat That" to show their preferences.

meanings. For example, depending on the respondent's opinion regarding the cleanliness of Wendy's restaurants, he or she would check the left-hand space on the scale, the right-hand space, or one of the three other intervening points. Question 6 uses a *Likert scale*, in which the respondent indicates the extent to which he or she agrees or disagrees with a statement.

The questionnaire in Figure 8–4 provides valuable information to the marketing researcher at Wendy's. Questions 1 to 8 inform him or her about the respondent's likes and dislikes in eating out, frequency of eating out at fast-food restaurants generally and at Wendy's specifically, and sources of information used in making decisions about fast-food restaurants. Question 9 gives details about the respondent's personal or household characteristics, which can be used in trying to segment the fast-food market, a topic discussed in Chapter 9.

Marketing research questions must be worded precisely so that all respondents interpret the same question similarly. For example, in a question asking whether you eat at fast-food restaurants regularly, the word *regularly* is ambiguous. Two people might answer "yes" to the question, but one might mean "once a day" while the other means "once or twice a month." However, each of these interpretations suggests that dramatically different marketing actions be directed to these two prospective consumers.

The high cost of using personal interviews in homes has increased the use of *mall intercept interviews*, which are personal interviews of consumers visiting shopping centers. These face-to-face interviews reduce the cost of personal visits to consumers in their homes while providing the flexibility to show respondents visual cues such as ads or actual product samples. A disadvantage of mall intercept interviews is that thc people interviewed may not be representative of the consumers targeted, giving a biased result.

Electronic technology has revolutionized traditional concepts of interviews or surveys. Today, respondents can walk up to a kiosk in a shopping center, read questions off a screen, and key their answers into a computer on a touch screen. Fully automated telephone interviews exist in which respondents key their replies on a touch-tone telephone.

Primary Data: Other Sources

Four other methods of collecting primary data exist that overlap somewhat with the methods just discussed. These involve using (1) social media, (2) panels and experiments, (3) information technology, and (4) data mining.

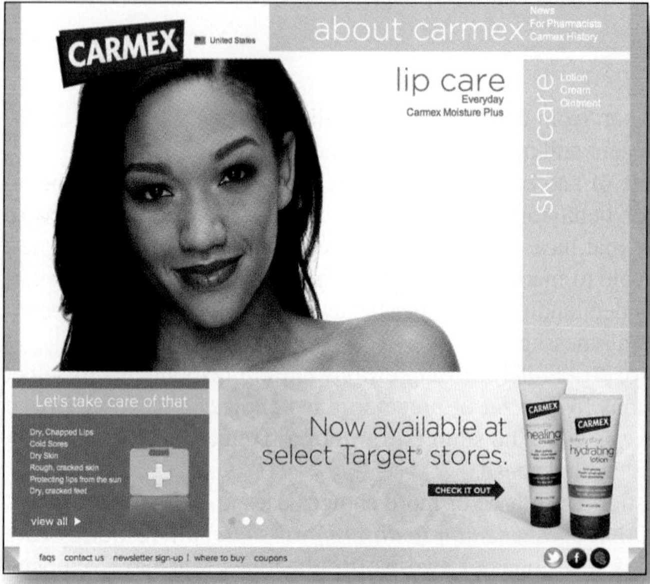

Carmex's home page topics range from its Twitter Giveaways to win Carmex products to its family history. For how it uses social media marketing research, see the Using Marketing Dashboards box.

Social Media Facebook, Twitter, and other social media are revolutionizing the way today's marketing research is done. In developing a new potato chip flavor, Frito-Lay substituted Facebook research for its usual focus groups. Visitors to its Facebook Page were polled, allowing them to suggest new flavors, three of which appeared in 2013. All they had to do was click an "I'd Eat That" button to show their preferences. And Estée Lauder asked social media users to vote on which discontinued shades to bring back.[28]

Carma Laboratories, Inc., the maker of Carmex lip balm, is a third generation, family-owned business with a history of accessibility to customers. In fact, founder Alfred Woelbing personally responded to every letter he received from customers. Today, Carma Labs relies on social media programs to help promote its products.[29]

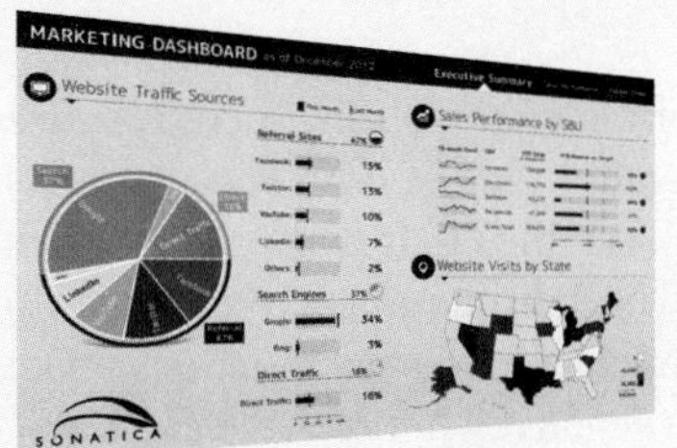

Using Marketing Dashboards

Are the Carmex Social Media Programs Working Well?

As a marketing consultant to Carmex, you've just been asked to assess its social media activities for its lip balm product line.

Carmex has recently launched new social media programs and promotions to tell U.S. consumers more about its line of lip balm products. These include Facebook and Twitter contests that allow Carmex fans and followers to win free samples by connecting with Carmex. A creative "Carmex Kiss" widget allows users to upload their photo and to send an animated kiss to a friend.

Your Challenge To assess how the Carmex social media programs are doing, you choose these five metrics: (1) Carmex conversation velocity—total Carmex mentions on the Internet; (2) Facebook fans—the number of Facebook users in a time period who have liked Carmex's Facebook brand page; (3) Twitter followers—the number of Twitter users in a time period who follow Carmex's Twitter feed; (4) Carmex share of voice—Carmex mentions on the Internet as a percentage of mentions of all major lip balm brands; and (5) Carmex sentiment—the percentage of Internet Carmex share-of-voice mentions that are (*a*) positive, (*b*) neutral, or (*c*) negative.

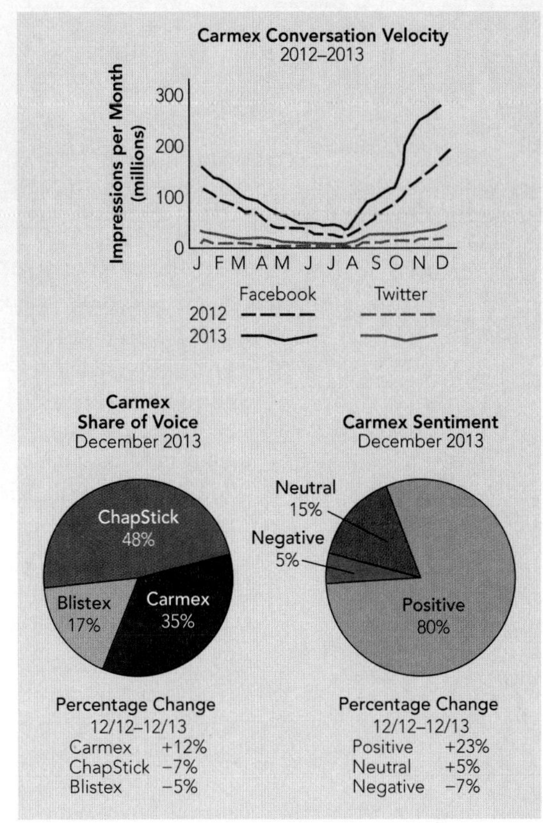

Your Findings Analyzing the marketing dashboard here, you reach these conclusions. First, the number of both Facebook fans and Twitter followers for Carmex is up significantly for 2013 compared to 2012, which is good news. Second, the Carmex share of voice of 35 percent is good, certainly relative to the 48 percent for the #1 brand ChapStick. But especially favorable is Carmex's 12 percent increase in share of voice compared to a year ago. Third, the Carmex sentiment dashboard shows 80 percent of the mentions are positive, and only 5 percent are negative. Even more significant is that positive mentions are up 23 percent over last year.

Your Actions You conclude that Carmex's social media initiatives are doing well. Your next step is to probe deeper into the data to see which ones—such as free samples or the Carmex Kiss—have been especially effective in triggering the positive results and build on these successes in the future.

Carmex lip balm is meant to reduce cold sore symptoms and soothe dry and chapped lips. It is packaged in jars, sticks, and squeezable tubes. The U.S. Carmex product line includes original, strawberry, lime twist, vanilla, pomegranate, and cherry flavors. Although Carmex lip balm sales trend behind ChapStick and Blistex, Carmex consumers tend to be loyalists—true zealots.

One opportunity for Carmex (www.mycarmex.com) is to conduct marketing research using social media listening tools to understand the nature of online lip balm conversations. Lip balm is a seasonal product, with both sales and online activity peaking during the cough–cold season of November through March.

The Using Marketing Dashboards box shows how Carmex uses marketing metrics to assess its social media programs for its line of products. Data have been modified to protect proprietary information.

To discover how Walmart used test markets to help develop its internationally successful supercenters, such as this one in China, see the text.

Carmex uses several social media metrics, such as *conversation velocity*, *share of voice*, and *sentiment*.[30] These metrics are tracked by electronic search engines that comb the Internet for consumers' behaviors and "brand mentions" to calculate share of voice and determine whether these brand mentions appear to be "positive," "neutral," or "negative" in order to calculate "sentiment." A widely used Facebook metric measures the number of *likes*, which refers to the number of Facebook users opting in to a brand's messages and liking the brand.

Marketing researchers increasingly want to glean information from sites to "mine" their raw consumer-generated content in real time. However, when relying on this consumer-generated content, the sample of individuals from whom this content is gleaned may not be statistically representative of the marketplace.[31]

Panels and Experiments Two special ways that observations and questionnaires are sometimes used are panels and experiments.

Marketing researchers often want to know if consumers change their behavior over time, so they take successive measurements of the same people. A *panel* is a sample of consumers or stores from which researchers take a series of measurements. For example, the NPD Group collects data about consumer purchases such as apparel, food, and electronics from its Online Panel, which consists of nearly 2 million individuals worldwide. So a firm like General Mills can count the frequency of consumer purchases to measure switching behavior from one brand of its breakfast cereal (Wheaties) to another (Cheerios) or to a competitor's brand (Kellogg's Special K). A disadvantage of panels is that the marketing research firm needs to recruit new members continually to replace those who drop out. These new recruits must match the characteristics of those they replace to keep the panel representative of the marketplace.

An *experiment* involves obtaining data by manipulating factors under tightly controlled conditions to test cause and effect. The interest is in whether changing one of the independent variables (a cause) will change the behavior of the dependent variable that is studied (the result). In marketing experiments, the independent variables of interest—sometimes called the marketing *drivers*—are often one or more of the marketing mix elements, such as a product's features, price, or promotion (like advertising messages or coupons). The ideal dependent variable usually is a change in the purchases (incremental unit or dollar sales) of individuals, households, or organizations. For example, food companies often use *test markets*, which offer a product for sale in a small geographic area to help evaluate potential marketing actions. In 1988, Walmart opened three experimental stand-alone supercenters to gauge consumer acceptance before deciding to open others. Today, Walmart operates over 4,000 supercenters around the world.

A potential difficulty with experiments is that outside factors (such as actions of competitors) can distort the results of an experiment and affect the dependent variable (such as sales). A researcher's task is to identify the effect of the marketing variable of interest on the dependent variable when the effects of outside factors in an experiment might hide it.

Information Technology **Information technology** involves operating computer networks that can store and process data. Today, information technology can extract hidden information from large databases, such as those containing retail sales collected through barcode scanners at checkout counters and households' product purchases and TV viewing behavior.

Figure 8–5 shows how marketers use information technology, data, models, and queries to obtain results that lead to marketing actions. Today's marketing managers can be drowned in an ocean of data; they need to adopt strategies for dealing with complex, changing views of the competition, the market, and the consumer.

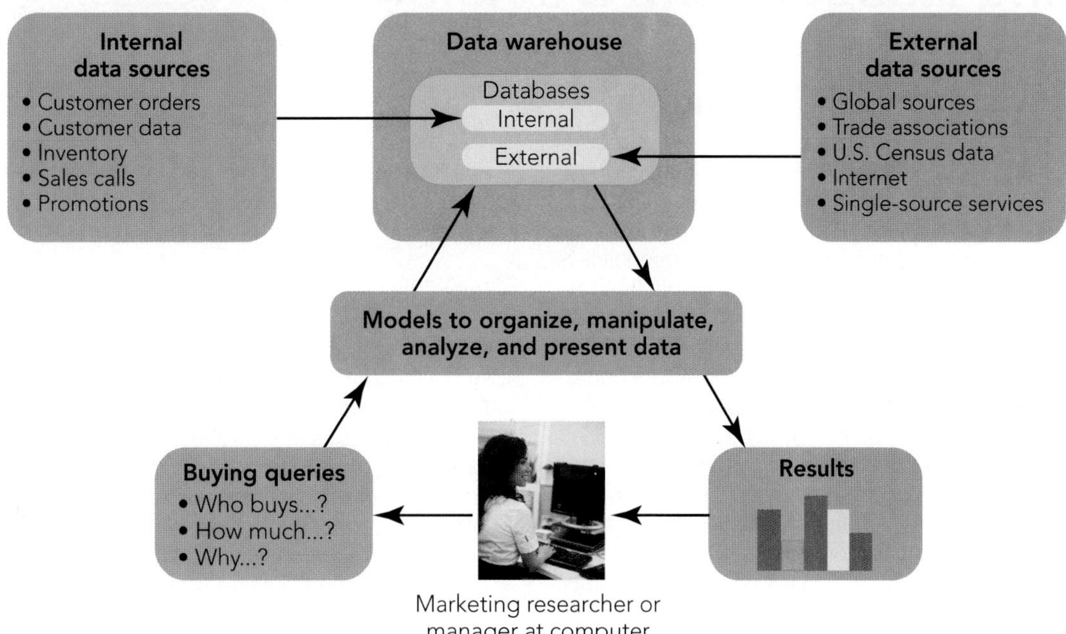

FIGURE 8–5
How marketing researchers and managers use information technology to turn information into action.

The Internet and PC help make sense out of this vast amount of information. The marketer's task is to convert it into useful information that will lead to marketing actions.[32]

As shown at the top of Figure 8–5, marketers use information technology that consists of computers linked together through sophisticated communication networks to access and retrieve data from internal and external sources. These data sources are stored, organized, and managed in databases. Collectively, these databases form a *data warehouse*.

As shown at the bottom of Figure 8–5, marketers use computers to query the databases in the data warehouse with marketing queries or questions. These questions go through statistical models that organize and manipulate the data to analyze and identify the relationships that exist. The results are then presented using tables and graphics for easier interpretation. When querying a database, marketers can use *sensitivity analysis* to ask "what if" questions to determine how hypothetical changes in *product* or *brand drivers*—the factors that influence the buying decisions of a household or organization—can affect sales.

Traditional marketing research typically involves identifying possible drivers and then collecting data. For example, we might collect data to test the hypothesis that increasing couponing (the driver) during spring will increase trials by first-time buyers (the result).

At 10 P.M., what is this man likely to buy besides these diapers? For the curious answer that data mining gives, see the text.

Data Mining In contrast, *data mining* is the extraction of hidden predictive information from large databases to find statistical links between consumer purchasing patterns and marketing actions. Some of these are common sense: Since many consumers buy peanut butter and grape jelly together, why not run a joint promotion between Skippy peanut butter and Welch's grape jelly? But would you have expected that men buying diapers in the evening sometimes buy a six-pack of beer as well? Supermarkets discovered

Making Responsible Decisions

ethics

No More Personal Secrets: The Downside of Data Mining

eXelate, Intellidyn, Rapleaf, Google Ad Preferences, Yahoo!, BlueKai, Alliance Data, reputation.com . . . yes . . . and Facebook and Twitter, too!

The common denominator for all these is their sophisticated data mining of the Internet and social media that reveals an incredible amount of personal information about any American. *Time* journalist Joel Stein, using both online and offline sources, discovered how easily outsiders could find his social security number and then found a number of other things about himself—some correct, some not.

For example, he likes hockey, rap, rock, parenting, recipes, clothes and beauty products, and movies. He makes most of his purchases online, averaging only $25 per purchase. He uses Facebook, Friendster, LinkedIn, MySpace, Pandora, and StumbleUpon. He bought his house in November, which is when his home insurance is up for renewal. His dad's wife has a traffic ticket.

And he uses an Apple iMac and is an 18- to 19-year-old woman???!!!

OK, OK, sometimes data mining errors occur!

These data are collected many ways from the Internet—from tracking devices (like cookies, discussed in Chapter 21) on websites to apps downloaded on a cellphone, PC, or tablet device that reveal a user's contact list and location.

These personal details have huge benefits for marketers. Data mining enables one-to-one personalization and now enables advertisers to target individual consumers. This involves using not only demographics such as age and sex but also "likes," past buying habits, social media used, brands bought, TV programs watched, and so on.

Want to do some sleuthing yourself? Download Ghostery at www.ghostery.com. It tells you all the companies grabbing your data when you visit a website.

this when they mined checkout data from scanners. So they placed diapers and beer near each other, then placed potato chips between them—and increased sales on all three items! On the near horizon is RFID (radio frequency identification) technology using "smart tags" on the diapers and beer to tell whether they wind up in the same shopping bag.

Data mining related to the Internet and social media is exploding. In 2012, companies were expected to spend $840 million for online data, double the 2009 amount. This increased investment in data mining also includes a greater focus on the more than $2 billion spent annually on social media advertising. And the cost to an advertiser for that one bit of special information about you? Two-fifths of a cent.[33] For how much online data mining can reveal about you personally and the ethical issues involved, see the Making Responsible Decisions box.

Advantages and Disadvantages of Primary Data

Compared with secondary data, primary data have the advantages of being more flexible and more specific to the problem being studied. The main disadvantages are that primary data are usually far more costly and time-consuming to collect than secondary data.

Wendy's Customer Satisfaction Survey allows customers to provide feedback on their meal experience. To take the survey, go to www.talktowendys.com. You'll need a receipt from a recent visit, which has an 8-digit code to start the survey. Your reward? A printable coupon that can be used on your next visit!

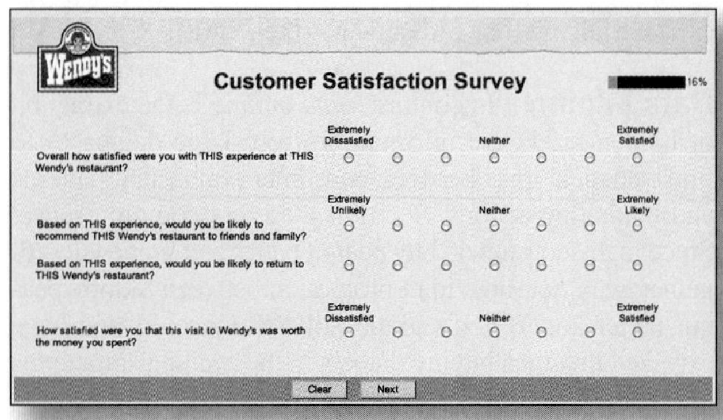

Analyzing Primary Data Using Cross Tabulations

Suppose top management at Wendy's wants to use the questionnaire in Figure 8–4 to survey a sample of U.S. households to assess how often customers of different ages eat at fast-food restaurants. Management suspects that as the age of the head of the household increases, visits to fast-food restaurants decline. The data provided by the questionnaire confirm this, but the information is not in a format that suggests ideas for viable marketing actions. Using cross tabulations will provide answers leading to actions.

A. ABSOLUTE FREQUENCIES

Age of Head of Household (Years)	Frequency of Visiting Fast-Food Restaurants			
	Once a Week or More	2 to 3 Times a Month	Once a Month or Less	Total
Under 25	144	52	19	215
25 to 44	46	58	29	133
45 or Older	82	69	87	238
Total	272	179	135	586

B. ROW PERCENTAGES: RUN HORIZONTALLY

Age of Head of Household (Years)	Frequency of Visiting Fast-Food Restaurants			
	Once a Week or More	2 to 3 Times a Month	Once a Month or Less	Total
Under 25	67.0%	24.2%	8.8%	100.0%
25 to 44	34.6%	43.6%	21.8%	100.0%
45 or Older	34.5%	29.0%	36.5%	100.0%
Total	46.5%	30.5%	23.0%	100.0%

FIGURE 8–6
Two forms of a cross tabulation relating age of head of household to frequency of fast-food restaurant patronage.

Developing Cross Tabulations A **cross tabulation**, or *cross tab*, is a method of presenting and analyzing data involving two or more variables to discover relationships in the data.

The Wendy's questionnaire in Figure 8–4 includes many questions that might be paired to understand the fast-food business better. For example, to try to answer the question in which Wendy's top management is interested, we can pair the question regarding the age of the head of the household in Figure 8–4 (question 9d) with the question that asks how often the respondent eats at a fast-food restaurant (question 3).

Using the answers to question 3 as the column headings and the answers to question 9d as the row headings gives the cross tabulation shown in Figure 8–6, based on answers from 586 respondents. The figure shows two forms of cross tabulations:

- The raw data or answers to the specific questions are shown in Figure 8–6A. For example, this cross tab shows that 144 households in the sample whose head was under 25 (shaded red) ate at fast-food restaurants once a week or more. It also shows the loyalty of many customers of fast-food restaurants; the number of customers who visit them once a week or more is more than double the number who visit them once a month or less, as indicated by the totals shaded brown in Figure 8–6A.
- Answers on a percentage basis, with the percentages running horizontally, are shown in Figure 8–6B. Of the 215 households headed by someone under 25, 67.0 percent ate at a fast-food restaurant at least once a week and only 8.8 percent ate there once a month or less. Also, across all age groups, 46.4 percent—almost half—ate in a fast-food restaurant once a week or more.

Two other forms of cross tabulation using the raw data shown in Figure 8–6A are described in problem 7 in Applying Marketing Knowledge at the end of the chapter.

Interpreting Cross Tabulations A careful analysis of Figures 8–6A and 8–6B shows that patronage of fast-food restaurants is related to the age of the head of the household. The percentages on the diagonal (in orange) in Figure 8–6B reveal that younger households are far more likely than older households to visit fast-food restaurants once a week or more.

So if we want to reach frequent users of fast-food restaurants, we should target those whose head of household is under 25 years of age and who tend to visit these restaurants once a week or more, as shown in Figure 8-6B. Marketers often use special efforts to reach these loyal, frequent users. So Wendy's might advertise to the segment of households headed by a man or woman under 25 years old. But Figures 8–6A and 8–6B *do not* tell us what media to use to reach them—such as by television ads or social networks. For those answers, we need to relate the age of the head of household again to the answers given to question 7 in Figure 8–4—the source of information that households use.

Probably the most widely used technique for organizing and presenting marketing data, cross tabulations have some important advantages. The simple format permits direct interpretation and an easy means of communicating data to management. Cross tabs offer great flexibility and can be used to summarize questionnaire, observational, and experimental data.

Cross tabulations also have some disadvantages. For example, they can be misleading if the percentages are based on too few observations. Also, cross tabulations can hide some relationships because each cross tab typically shows only two or three variables. Balancing both advantages and disadvantages, more marketing decisions are probably made using cross tabulations than any other method of analyzing data.

learning review

8-6. What is the difference between observational and questionnaire data?

8-7. Which type of survey provides the greatest flexibility for asking probing questions: mail, telephone, or personal interview?

8-8. What is cross tabulation?

STEP 4: DEVELOP FINDINGS

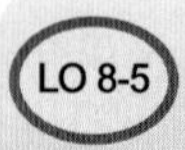

Explain how information technology and data mining lead to marketing actions.

Mark Twain once observed, "Collecting data is like collecting garbage. You've got to know what you're going to do with the stuff before you collect it." So, marketing data and information have little more value than garbage unless they are analyzed carefully and translated into findings, Step 4 in the marketing research approach.[34]

Analyze the Data

Schwan Food Company produces 3 million frozen pizzas a day under brand names that include Tony's and Red Baron. Let's see how Teré Carral, the marketing manager for the Tony's brand, might address a market segment question in early 2013. We will use hypothetical data to protect Tony's proprietary information.

How are sales doing? To see how marketers at Tony's Pizza assessed this question and the results, read the text.

Teré is concerned about the limited growth in the Tony's brand over the past four years. She hires a consultant to collect and analyze data to explain what's going on with her brand and to recommend ways to improve its growth. Teré asks the consultant to put together a proposal that includes the answers to two key questions:

1. How are Tony's sales doing on a household basis? For example, are fewer households buying Tony's pizzas, or is each household buying fewer Tony's pizzas? Or both?
2. What factors might be contributing to Tony's very flat sales over the past four years?

Facts uncovered by the consultant are vital. For example, is the average household consuming more or less Tony's pizza than in previous years? Is Tony's flat sales performance related to a specific factor? With answers to these questions Teré can take actions to address the issues in the coming year.

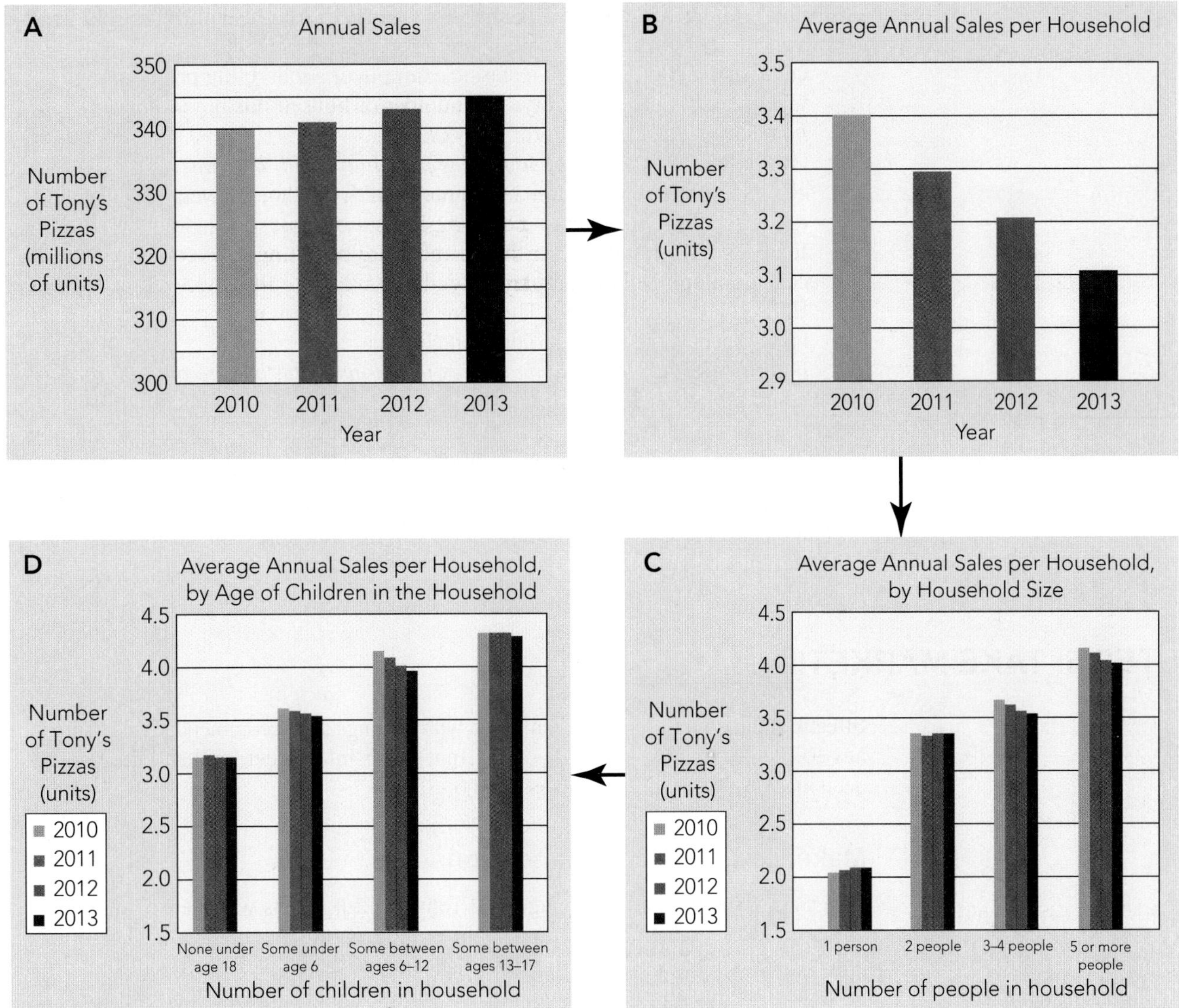

FIGURE 8–7
These marketing dashboards present findings to Tony's marketing manager that will lead to recommendations and actions.
Source: Teré Carral, Tony's Pizza.

Present the Findings

Findings should be clear and understandable from the way the data are presented. Managers are responsible for *actions*. Often it means delivering the results in clear pictures and, if possible, in a single page.

The consultant gives Teré the answers to her questions using the marketing dashboards in Figure 8–7, a creative way to present findings graphically. Let's look over Teré's shoulder as she interprets these findings:

- Figure 8–7A, *Annual Sales*—This shows the annual growth of Tony's Pizza is stable but virtually flat from 2010 through 2013.
- Figure 8–7B, *Average Annual Sales per Household*—Look closely at this graph. At first glance, it seems like sales in 2013 are *half* what they were in 2010, right? But be careful to read the numbers on the vertical axis. They show that household purchases of Tony's pizzas have been steadily declining over the past four years, from an average of 3.4 pizzas per household in 2010 to 3.1 pizzas per household in 2013. (Significant, but hardly a 50 percent drop.) Now the question is, if Tony's annual sales are stable, yet the average individual household is buying fewer Tony's pizzas, what's going on? The answer is, more

households are buying pizzas—it's just that each household is buying fewer Tony's pizzas. That households aren't choosing Tony's is a genuine source of concern. But again, here's a classic example of a marketing problem representing a marketing opportunity. The number of households buying pizza is *growing*, and that's good news for Tony's.

- Figure 8–7C, *Average Annual Sales per Household, by Household Size*—This chart starts to show a source of the problem: Even though average sales of pizza to households with only one or two people are stable, households with three or four people and those with five or more are declining in average annual pizza consumption. Which households tend to have more than two people? Answer: Households *with children*. Therefore, we should look more closely at the pizza-buying behavior of households with children.
- Figure 8–7D, *Average Annual Sales per Household, by Age of Children in the Household*—The real problem that emerges is the serious decline in average consumption in the households with younger children, especially in households with children in the 6-to-12-year-old age group.

Identifying a sales problem in households with children 6 to 12 years old is an important discovery, as Tony's sales are declining in a market segment that is known to be one of the heaviest in buying pizzas.

STEP 5: TAKE MARKETING ACTIONS

Effective marketing research doesn't stop with findings and recommendations—someone has to identify the marketing actions, put them into effect, and monitor how the decisions turn out, which is the essence of Step 5.

Make Action Recommendations

Teré Carral, the marketing manager for Tony's Pizza, meets with her team to convert the market research findings into specific marketing recommendations with a clear objective: Target households with children ages 6 to 12 to reverse the trend among this segment and gain strength in one of the most important segments in the frozen pizza category. Her recommendation is to develop:

- An advertising campaign that will target children 6 to 12 years old.
- A monthly promotion calendar with this age group target in mind.
- A special event program reaching children 6 to 12 years old.

Marketing research at Tony's Pizza helped develop this colorful, friendly ad targeted at families with children in the 6-to-12-year-old age group.

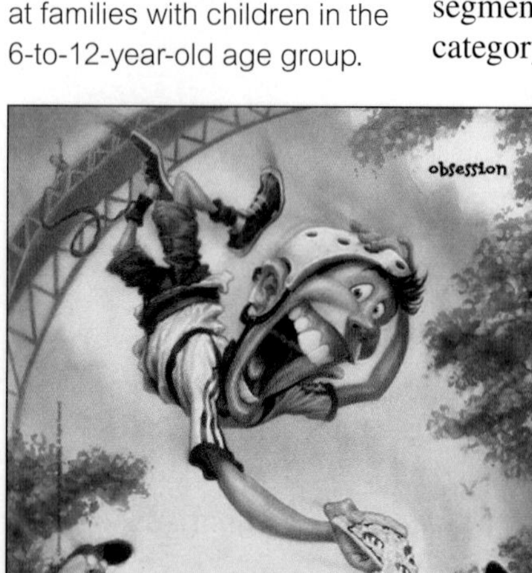

Implement the Action Recommendations

As her first marketing action, Teré undertakes advertising research to develop ads that appeal to children in the 6-to-12-year-old age group and their families. The research shows that children like colorful ads with funny, friendly characters. She gives these research results to her advertising agency, which develops several sample ads for her review. Teré selects three that are tested on children to identify the most appealing one, which is then used in her next advertising campaign for Tony's Pizza. This is the ad shown to the left.

Evaluate the Results

Evaluating results is a continuing way of life for effective marketing managers. There are really two aspects of this evaluation process:

- *Evaluating the decision itself.* This involves monitoring the marketplace to determine if action is necessary in the future. For Teré, is her new ad successful in appealing to 6-to-12-year-old children and their families? Are sales increasing to this target segment? The success of this strategy suggests Teré should add more follow-up ads with colorful, funny, friendly characters.
- *Evaluating the decision process used.* Was the marketing research and analysis used to develop the recommendations effective? Was it flawed? Could it be improved for similar situations in the future? Teré and her marketing team must be vigilant in looking for ways to improve the analysis and results—to learn lessons that might apply to future marketing research efforts at Tony's.

Again, systematic analysis does not guarantee success. But, as in the case of Tony's Pizza, it can improve a firm's success rate for its marketing decisions.

learning review

8-9. In the marketing research for Tony's Pizza, what is an example of (*a*) a finding and (*b*) a marketing action?

8-10. In evaluating marketing actions, what are the two dimensions on which they should be evaluated?

SALES FORECASTING TECHNIQUES

LO 8-6 Describe three approaches to developing a company's sales forecast.

Forecasting or estimating potential sales is often a key goal in a marketing research study. Good sales forecasts are important for a firm as it schedules production. The term **sales forecast** refers to the total sales of a product that a firm expects to sell during a specified time period under specified environmental conditions and its own marketing efforts. For example, Betty Crocker might develop a sales forecast of 4 million cases of cake mix for U.S. consumers in 2014, assuming consumers' dessert preferences remain constant and competitors don't change prices.

Three main sales forecasting techniques are often used: (1) judgments of the decision maker, (2) surveys of knowledgeable groups, and (3) statistical methods.

Judgments of the Decision Maker

Probably 99 percent of all sales forecasts are simply the judgment of the person who must act on the results of the forecast—the individual decision maker. *A direct forecast* involves estimating the value to be forecast without any intervening steps. Examples appear daily: How many quarts of milk should I buy? How much money should I withdraw at the ATM?

How might a marketing manager for the New Balance Minimus running shoe create a sales forecast through 2016? Read the text to find out.

A *lost-horse forecast* involves starting with the last known value of the item being forecast, listing the factors that could affect the forecast, assessing whether they have a positive or negative impact, and making the final forecast. The technique gets its name from how you'd find a lost horse: go to where it was last seen, put yourself in its shoes, consider those factors that could affect where you might go (to the pond if you're thirsty, the hayfield if you're hungry, and so on), and go there.

For example, New Balance recently introduced its Minimus, a shoe that is 50 percent lighter than other lightweight shoes. Its unique features are designed to make running easier and limit foot injuries. Suppose a New Balance marketing manager in early 2014 needs to make a sales forecast through 2016. She would take the known value of 2013 sales and list positive factors (good acceptance of its high-tech designs, great publicity) and the negative factors (the economic recession, competition from established name brands) to arrive at the final series of sales forecasts.[35]

Surveys of Knowledgeable Groups

If you wonder what your firm's sales will be next year, ask people who are likely to know something about future sales. Two common groups that are surveyed to develop sales forecasts are prospective buyers and the firm's salesforce.

A *survey of buyers' intentions forecast* involves asking prospective customers if they are likely to buy the product during some future time period. For industrial products with few prospective buyers, this can be effective. There are only a few hundred customers in the entire world for Boeing's large airplanes, so Boeing surveys them to develop its sales forecasts and production schedules.

A *salesforce survey forecast* involves asking the firm's salespeople to estimate sales during a forthcoming period. Because these people are in contact with customers and are likely to know what customers like and dislike, there is logic to this approach. However, salespeople can be unreliable forecasters—painting too rosy a picture if they are enthusiastic about a new product or too grim a forecast if their sales quota and future compensation are based on it.

Statistical Methods

The best-known statistical method of forecasting is *trend extrapolation*, which involves extending a pattern observed in past data into the future. When the pattern is described with a straight line, it is *linear trend extrapolation*. Suppose that in early 2000 you were a sales forecaster for the Xerox Corporation and had actual sales data running from 1988 to 1999 (see Figure 8–8). Using linear trend extrapolation, you draw a line to fit the past sales data and project it into the future to give the forecast values shown for 2000 through 2012.

If in 2013 you want to compare your forecasts with actual results, you are in for a surprise—illustrating the strength and weakness of trend extrapolation. Trend extrapolation assumes that the underlying relationships in the past will continue into the future, which is the basis of the method's key strength: simplicity. If this assumption proves correct, you have an accurate forecast. However, if this proves wrong, the forecast is likely to be wrong. In this case, your forecasts from 2000 through 2012 were too high, as shown in Figure 8–8, largely because of fierce competition in the photocopying industry. The spike in 2010 sales revenues is mainly due to new acquisitions.

FIGURE 8–8
Linear trend extrapolation of sales revenues at Xerox, made at the start of 2000.

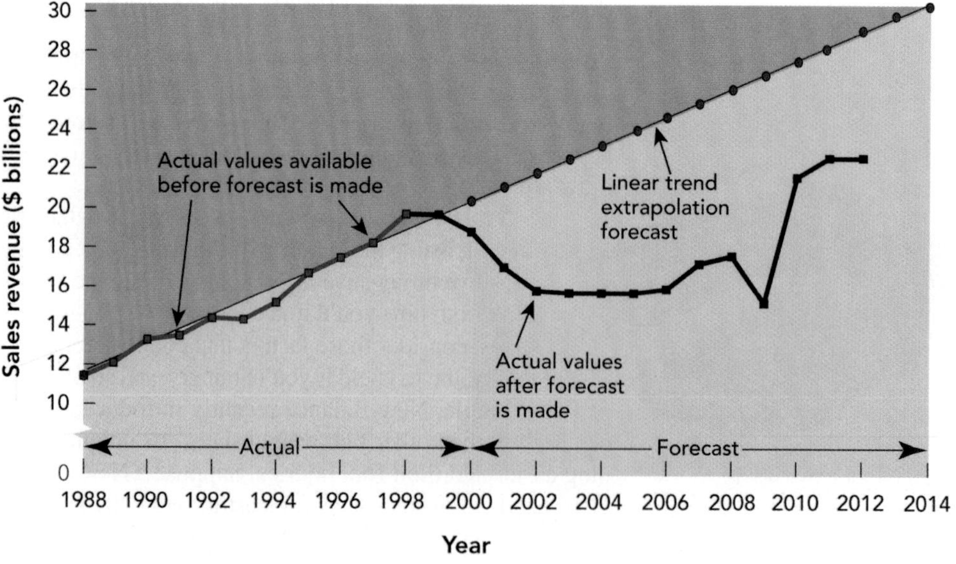

learning review

8-11. What are the three kinds of sales forecasting techniques?

8-12. How do you make a lost-horse forecast?

LEARNING OBJECTIVES REVIEW

LO 8-1 *Identify the reason for conducting marketing research.*

To be successful, products must meet the wants and needs of potential customers. So marketing research reduces risk by providing the vital information to help marketing managers understand those wants and needs and translate them into marketing actions.

LO 8-2 *Describe the five-step marketing research approach that leads to marketing actions.*

Marketing researchers engage in a five-step decision-making process to collect information that will improve marketing decisions. The first step is to define the problem, which requires setting the research objectives and identifying possible marketing actions. The second step is to develop the research plan, which involves specifying the constraints, identifying data needed for marketing decisions, and determining how to collect the data. The third step is to collect the relevant information, which includes considering pertinent secondary data (both internal and external) and primary data (by observing and questioning consumers) as well as using information technology and data mining to trigger marketing actions. The fourth step is to develop findings from the marketing research data collected. This involves analyzing the data and presenting the findings of the research. The fifth and last step is to take marketing actions, which involves making and implementing the action recommendations and then evaluating the results.

LO 8-3 *Explain how marketing uses secondary and primary data.*

Secondary data have already been recorded prior to the start of the project and consist of two parts: (*a*) internal secondary data, which originate from within the organization, such as sales reports and customer comments, and (*b*) external secondary data, which are created by other organizations, such as the U.S. Census Bureau (which provides data on the country's population, manufacturers, retailers, and so on) or business and trade publications (which provide data on industry trends, market size, etc.). Primary data are collected specifically for the project and are obtained by either observing or questioning people.

LO 8-4 *Discuss the uses of observations, questionnaires, panels, experiments, and newer data collection methods.*

Marketing researchers observe people in various ways, such as electronically using Nielsen people meters to measure TV viewing behavior or personally using mystery shoppers or ethnographic techniques. A recent electronic innovation is neuromarketing—using high-tech brain scanning to record the responses of a consumer's brain to marketing stimuli like packages or TV ads. Questionnaires involve asking people questions (*a*) in person using interviews or focus groups or (*b*) via a questionnaire using a telephone, fax, print, e-mail, Internet, or social media survey. A cross tabulation is often used with questionnaire data to analyze the relationships among two or more variables to lead to marketing actions. Panels involve a sample of consumers or stores that are repeatedly measured through time to see if their behaviors change. Experiments, such as test markets, involve measuring the effect of marketing variables such as price or advertising on sales. Collecting data from social networks like Facebook or Twitter is increasingly important because users can share their opinions about products and services with countless "friends" around the globe.

LO 8-5 *Explain how information technology and data mining lead to marketing actions.*

Today's marketing managers are often overloaded with data—from internal sales and customer data to external data on TV viewing habits or grocery purchases from the scanner data at checkout counters. Information technology enables this massive amount of marketing data to be stored, accessed, and processed. The resulting databases can be queried using data mining to find statistical relationships useful for marketing decisions and actions.

LO 8-6 *Describe three approaches to developing a company's sales forecast.*

One approach uses the subjective judgments of the decision maker, such as direct or lost-horse forecasts. A direct forecast involves estimating the value to be forecast without any intervening steps. A lost-horse forecast starts with the last known value of the item being forecast and then lists the factors that could affect the forecast, assesses whether they have a positive or negative impact, and makes the final forecast. Surveys of knowledgeable groups, a second method, involve obtaining information such as the intentions of potential buyers or estimates provided by the salesforce. Statistical methods involving extending a pattern observed in past data into the future are a third approach. The best-known statistical method is linear trend extrapolation.

FOCUSING ON KEY TERMS

constraints p. 196
cross tabulation p. 211
data p. 198
information technology p. 208
marketing research p. 194
measures of success p. 196
observational data p. 200
primary data p. 198
questionnaire data p. 202
sales forecast p. 215
secondary data p. 198

APPLYING MARKETING KNOWLEDGE

1 Suppose your dean of admissions is considering surveying high school seniors about their perceptions of your school to design better informational brochures for them. What are the advantages and disadvantages of doing (*a*) telephone interviews and (*b*) an Internet survey of seniors requesting information about the school?

2 Wisk detergent decides to run a test market to see the effect of coupons and in-store advertising on sales. The index of sales is as follows:

Element in Test Market	Weeks before Coupon	Week of Coupon	Week after Coupon
Without in-store ads	100	144	108
With in-store ads	100	268	203

What are your conclusions and recommendations?

3 Nielsen obtains ratings of local TV stations in small markets by having households fill out diary questionnaires. These give information on (*a*) who is watching TV and (*b*) the program being watched. What are the limitations of this questionnaire method?

4 The format in which information is presented is often vital. (*a*) If you were a harried marketing manager and queried your information system, would you rather see the results in tables or charts and graphs? (*b*) What are one or two strengths and weaknesses of each format?

5 (*a*) Why might a marketing researcher prefer to use secondary data rather than primary data in a study? (*b*) Why might the reverse be true?

6 Look back at Figure 8–4. Which questions would you pair to form a cross tabulation to uncover the following relationships? (*a*) Frequency of fast-food restaurant patronage and restaurant characteristics important to the customer, (*b*) Age of the head of household and source of information used about fast-food restaurants, (*c*) Frequency of patronage of Wendy's and source of information used about fast-food restaurants, and (*d*) How much children have to say about where the family eats and number of children in the household.

7 Look back at Figure 8–6A. (*a*) Run the percentages vertically and explain what they mean. (*b*) Express all numbers in the table as a percentage of the total number of people sampled (586) and explain what the percentages mean.

8 Which of the following variables would linear trend extrapolation be more accurate for? (*a*) Annual population of the United States or (*b*) annual sales of cars produced in the United States by Ford. Why?

BUILDING YOUR MARKETING PLAN

To help you collect the most useful data for your marketing plan, develop a three-column table:

1 In column 1, list the information you would ideally like to have to fill holes in your marketing plan.

2 In column 2, identify the source for each bit of information in column 1, such as an Internet search, talking to prospective customers, looking at internal data, and so forth.

3 In column 3, set a priority on information you will have time to spend collecting by ranking each item: 1 = most important; 2 = next most important, and so forth.

VIDEO CASE 8 Carmex® (A): Leveraging Facebook for Marketing Research

QR 8-4
Carmex (A)
Video Case

"What makes social media 'social' is its give and take," says Jeff Gerst of Bolin Marketing, who manages the Carmex® social media properties. By "give" Gerst is referring to the feedback consumers send on social media; "take" is what they receive—such as news and coupons. "For Carmex, Facebook isn't just a way to share coupons or the latest product news, but it is also a marketing research resource. We have instantaneous access to the opinions of our consumers."

"While some people think of social media as 'free,' that is not true. However, almost everything in social media can be faster and cheaper than in the offline world," adds Dane Hartzell, general manager of Bolin Digital. "Many platforms have been prebuilt and we marketers only need to modify them slightly."

CARMEX AND ITS PRODUCT LINE

Although Carmex has been making lip balm since 1937, only in the last five years has it made serious efforts to stress growth and become more competitive. For example, Carmex has:

- Extended its lip balm products into new flavors and varieties.
- Expanded into nearly 30 international markets.
- Developed the Carmex Moisture Plus line of premium lip balms for women.
- Launched a line of skin care products, its first venture outside of lip care.

Carmex has used social media tools in developing all of these initiatives, but the focus of this case is how Carmex might use Facebook marketing research to grow its lip balm varieties in the United States.

FACEBOOK MARKETING RESEARCH: TREND SPOTTING

Brands can leverage Facebook and all social media platforms to test what topics and themes its audience engages with the most as well as validate concepts and ideas. In 2012 Carmex identified the growing trend of consumers seeking product customization. Carmex combined research with Facebook engagement data, which helped to validate consumer interest and led it to develop two new lines of limited-edition lip balm products that launched in 2013.

The first line was a set of three different Carmex "City Sticks" featuring New York, Chicago, and Las Vegas versions of the Carmex lip balm stick with recognizable

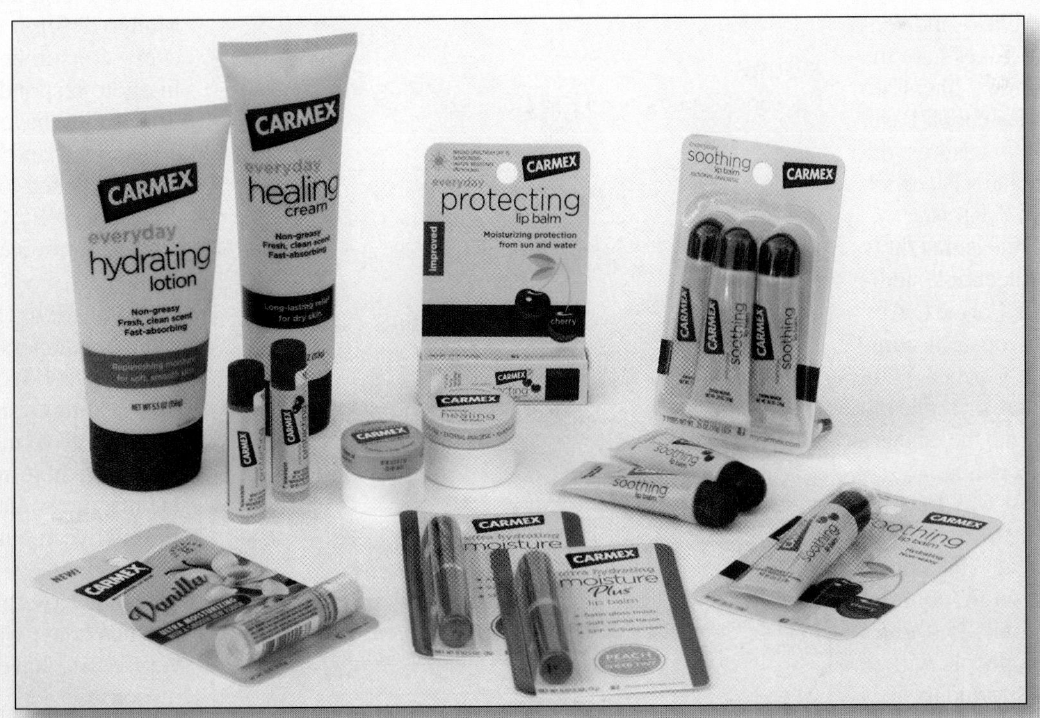

landmarks from each city on them. The brand partnered with Walgreens to exclusively sell the "City Sticks" in each of the three cities. During this time Carmex leveraged its social media channels on Facebook and Instagram to solicit photos of fans holding up their favorite style of Carmex in front of a landmark in their own city. Carmex then used these photos to help it decide on new locations for future limited-edition "City Sticks."

Carmex's second line of new products was four fashion-forward "glamorous" designs of Carmex Moisture Plus. Carmex researched current design trends in the women's fashion industry to come up with the four different styles, and it had seen good engagement from its Facebook community on "fashion themed" posts, which helped validate the concept. The four styles were: "Chic," a black and white houndstooth; "Fab," with bright purple circles; "Adventurous," a leopard print; and "Whimsical," with blue, orange, green, and pink intertwined ribbons. Carmex first announced the line to its Facebook fans to generate interest and they were brought to market in the summer of 2013.

FACEBOOK MARKETING RESEARCH: TWO KEY METRICS

"We have three potential new flavors and we can only put two into quantitative testing," explains Jeff Gerst to his team. "So we have two goals in doing marketing research on this. One is to use Facebook to help us determine which two flavors we should move forward with. The second goal is to drive our Facebook metrics."

The two key Facebook metrics the Carmex marketing team has chosen to help narrow the flavor choices from three to two are "likes" and "engagement." "Likes" are the number of new "likers" to the brand's Facebook Page. This metric measures the size of the brand's Facebook audience. In contrast, "engagement" measures how active its Facebook audience is with Carmex. Any time a liker posts a comment on the Carmex Wall, likes its status, or replies to one of its posts, the engagement level increases.

The easiest way for Carmex to grow the number of "likes" on its Facebook Page is through contests and promotions. If it gives away prizes, people will be drawn to its site and its likes will increase. However, these people may not actually be fans of the Carmex product so at the end of the promotion, they may "unlike" Carmex or they may remain fans but not engage with the Carmex Page at all.

"One of the biggest challenges facing Facebook Community Managers for brands is how to grow your likes without hurting the level of engagement," says Holly Matson, director of experience planning at Bolin Marketing.

"Depending on how we go about conducting the research," Gerst adds, "we can drive engagement with our existing Facebook community, we can use this as an opportunity to grow our Facebook community or, potentially, we could do both." The benefits of this Carmex Facebook strategy are twofold: (1) narrowing the number of flavors to be researched from three to two and (2) enhancing the connections with the Carmex Facebook community.

HOW THE METRICS MIGHT BE USED

Carmex's Facebook activity can benefit (1) by using a poll to increase engagement, (2) by launching a contest to increase the number of likers, and (3) by trying to increase both engagement and likers through combining a poll with a contest.

The "Engagement" Strategy: Use a Poll

Let's look at two ways to use the engagement strategy showing actual Facebook screens. First, Carmex can post a somewhat open-ended question on its Facebook Wall, such as, "Which Carmex lip balm flavor would you most like to see next: Watermelon, Green Apple, or Peach Mango?" (Figure 1). However, consumers are less likely to respond to a question if they have to type in a response and have their name attached to it.

Alternatively, Carmex can post the same question on its Wall as a fixed-alternative poll question (Figure 2). Then consumers need only click on a flavor to vote; this is quick, anonymous, and will drive more people to vote, where more votes means more engagement. Within five minutes Carmex will have several dozen votes and, by the end of a business day, Carmex can very easily have over 500 responses.

FIGURE 1
Facebook Open-Ended Poll Question

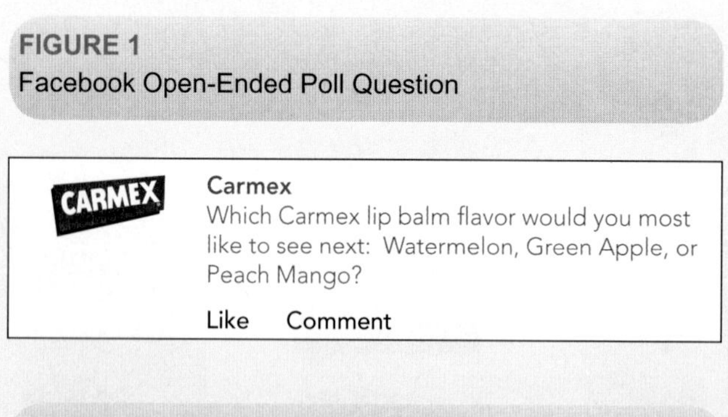
CARMEX
Carmex
Which Carmex lip balm flavor would you most like to see next: Watermelon, Green Apple, or Peach Mango?
Like Comment

FIGURE 2
Facebook Fixed-Alternative Poll Question

CARMEX
Carmex
Which Carmex lip balm flavor would you most like to see next?
Watermelon
Green Apple
Peach Mango

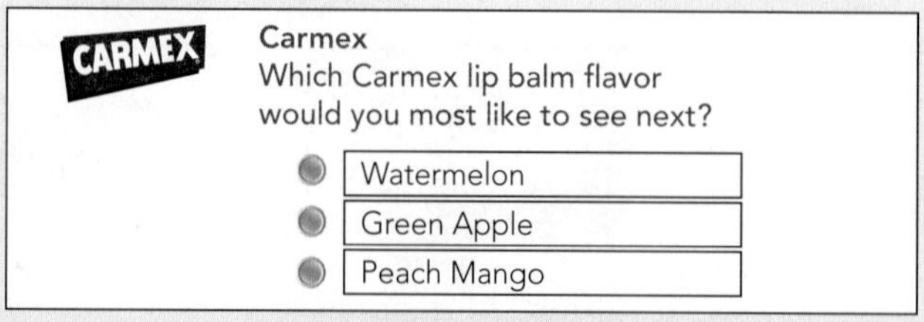

In this scenario, the consumers are content because they are able to engage with a brand they like and have their opinions heard. Carmex is content because it has engaged hundreds of its fans on its Facebook Page, and it gains results that are very helpful in deciding which flavors to put into testing. This scenario gets an answer quickly and drives fan engagement with existing fans but does not drive new likers to the Carmex Facebook Page.

FIGURE 3
Potential Results from Three Possible Facebook Strategies

FACEBOOK STRATEGY	POTENTIAL IMPACT ON...		
	Increased "Engagement"	Increased "Likes"	Cost
Poll Only	High	Low	Low
Contest Only	Low	High	Moderate
Poll + Contest	High	High	Moderate to High

Favorable Neutral Unfavorable

The "Likes" Strategy: Use a Contest

If Carmex wants to grow the size of its Facebook community, which means the number of its brand page "likes," it can adopt a different strategy. Carmex can announce a contest where, if consumers "like" Carmex on Facebook and share a comment, they will be entered to win three limited-edition flavors. The chance to win limited-edition flavors is exciting to Carmex enthusiasts, and a contest like this will draw new consumers to the page. Carmex can ask the winners to review the limited-edition flavors and see if there is a consensus on which flavors should move on to quantitative testing. Setting up a contest, developing official rules, promoting the contest through Facebook ads, and fulfilling a contest can be costly and time-consuming.

The Combined Strategy: Use Poll and Contest

Carmex can also choose to layer these two strategies into a combined strategy where it runs the limited-edition flavor contest to promote new likes and meanwhile posts the poll question on its Facebook Wall to drive engagement.

REACHING A DECISION

Figure 3 shows the potential results from the three Facebook strategies being considered—the poll only, the contest only, or both strategies together. Assume the Carmex marketing team has sought your help in selecting a strategy and needs your answers to the questions below.

Questions

1 What are the advantages and disadvantages for the Carmex marketing team in collecting data to narrow the flavor choices from three to two using (*a*) an online survey of a cross-section of Internet households or (*b*) an online survey of Carmex Facebook likers?

2 (*a*) On a Facebook brand page, what are "engagement" and "likes" really measuring? (*b*) For Carmex, which is more important and why?

3 (*a*) What evokes consumers' "engagement" on a brand page on Facebook? (*b*) What attracts consumers to "like" a brand page on Facebook?

4 (*a*) What are the advantages of using a fixed-alternative poll question on Facebook? (*b*) When do you think it would be better to use an open-ended question?

5 (*a*) If you had a limited budget and two weeks to decide which two flavors to put into quantitative testing, would you choose a "poll only" or a "contest only" strategy? Why? (*b*) If you had a sizable budget and two months to make the same decision, which scenario would you choose? Why?

9 Market Segmentation, Targeting, and Positioning

Learning Objectives

After reading this chapter you should be able to:

LO 9-1 Explain what market segmentation is and when to use it.

LO 9-2 Identify the five steps involved in segmenting and targeting markets.

LO 9-3 Recognize the bases used to segment consumer and organizational (business) markets.

LO 9-4 Develop a market-product grid to identify a target market and recommend resulting marketing actions.

LO 9-5 Explain how marketing managers position products in the marketplace.

Zappos.com's Strategy: Segments + Service = "Wow"

Tony Hsieh (opposite page) showed signs of being an entrepreneur early in life. Today, he's chief executive officer (CEO) of online retailer Zappos.com, now owned by Amazon.com. The company name is derived from the Spanish word *zapatos*, which means shoes.

In college, Hsieh sold pizzas out of his dorm room. Alfred Lin bought pizzas from Hsieh and then sold them by the slice to other students. Lin is now Hsieh's chief financial officer.[1]

A Clear Market Segmentation Strategy

Nick Swinmurn founded the online shoe store when he couldn't find a pair of Airwalk desert boots at a local mall. Hsieh, Lin, and Swinmurn have given Zappos.com a clear, specific market segmentation strategy: Offer a huge selection of shoes to people who will buy them online. Recently Zappos.com has added lines of clothes, accessories, beauty aids, and housewares. This focus on the segment of online buyers generates over $1 billion in sales annually.[2]

Pamela Leo, a New Jersey customer, says, "With Zappos I can try the shoes in the comfort of my own home. . . . It's fabulous."[3] Zappos .com also provides free shipping both ways and offers more than 1,000 brands to customers.

Delivering WOW Customer Service

Asked about Zappos.com, Hsieh says, "We try to spend most of our time on stuff that will improve customer-service levels."[4] This customer-service obsession for its market segment of online customers means that all new Zappos.com employees—whether the chief financial officer or the children's footwear buyer—go through four weeks of customer-loyalty training. Hsieh offers $2,000 to anyone completing the training who wants to leave Zappos.com. The theory: If you take the money and run, you're not right for Zappos.com. Few take the money!

Ten "core values" are the foundation for the Zappos.com culture, brand, and business strategies. Some examples:[5]

#1. Deliver WOW through service. This focus on exemplary customer service encompasses all 10 core values.

#3. Create fun and a little weirdness. In a Zappos.com day, cowbells ring, parades appear, and modified-blaster gunfights arise.

#6. Build open and honest relationships with communication. Employees are told to say what they think.

The other Zappos.com core values appear on its website: www.zappos.com. Tony Hsieh's strategy on core values and customer service appears on Twitter, where he has more than 2.6 million followers.[6]

The Zappos.com strategy illustrates successful market segmentation and targeting, the first topics in Chapter 9. The chapter ends with the topic of positioning the organization, product, or brand.

WHY SEGMENT MARKETS?

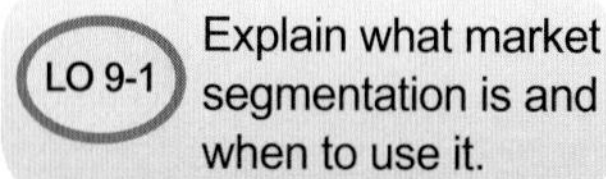
LO 9-1 Explain what market segmentation is and when to use it.

A business firm segments its markets so it can respond more effectively to the wants of groups of potential buyers and thus increase its sales and profits. Not-for-profit organizations also segment the clients they serve to satisfy client needs more effectively while achieving the organization's goals. Let's describe (1) what market segmentation is and (2) when to segment markets, sometimes using the Zappos.com segmentation strategy as an example.

What Market Segmentation Means

People have different needs and wants, even though it would be easier for marketers if they didn't. **Market segmentation** involves aggregating prospective buyers into groups that (1) have common needs and (2) will respond similarly to a marketing action. As defined in Chapter 1, *market segments* are the relatively homogeneous groups of prospective buyers that result from the market segmentation process. Each market segment consists of people who are relatively similar to each other in terms of their consumption behavior.

The existence of different market segments has caused firms to use a marketing strategy of **product differentiation**. This strategy involves a firm using different marketing mix actions, such as product features and advertising, to help consumers perceive the product as being different and better than competing products. The perceived differences may involve physical features, such as size or color, or nonphysical ones, such as image or price.

Segmentation: Linking Needs to Actions The process of segmenting a market and selecting specific segments as targets is the link between the various buyers' needs and the organization's marketing program, as shown in Figure 9–1. Market segmentation is only a means to an end: It leads to tangible marketing actions that can increase sales and profitability.

Market segmentation first stresses the importance of grouping people or organizations in a market according to the similarity of their needs and the benefits they are looking for in making a purchase. Second, such needs and benefits must be related to specific marketing actions that the organization can take, such as a new product or special promotion.

QR 9-1 Zappos Lady Gaga Video

The Zappos.com Segmentation Strategy The Zappos.com target customer segment originally consisted of people who wanted to (1) have a wide selection of shoes, (2) shop online in the convenience of their own homes, and (3) receive quick delivery and free returns. Zappos's actions include offering a huge inventory of shoes using an online selling strategy and providing overnight delivery. These actions have enabled Zappos.com to create a positive customer experience and generate repeat purchases. Zappos's success in selling footwear has enabled it to add lines of clothing, handbags, accessories (such as sunglasses), and housewares to reach new segments of buyers.

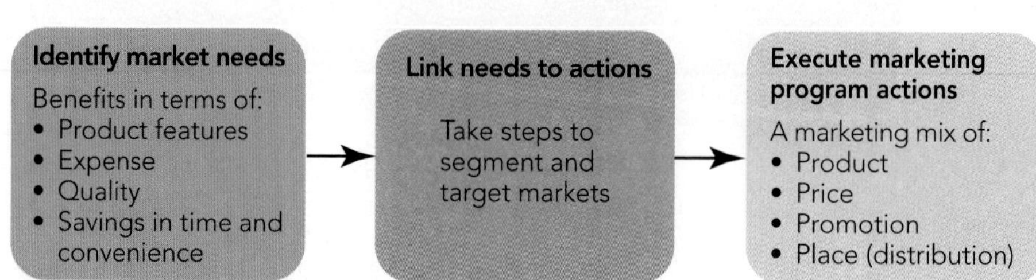

FIGURE 9–1 Market segmentation links market needs to an organization's marketing program—its specific marketing mix actions designed to satisfy those needs.

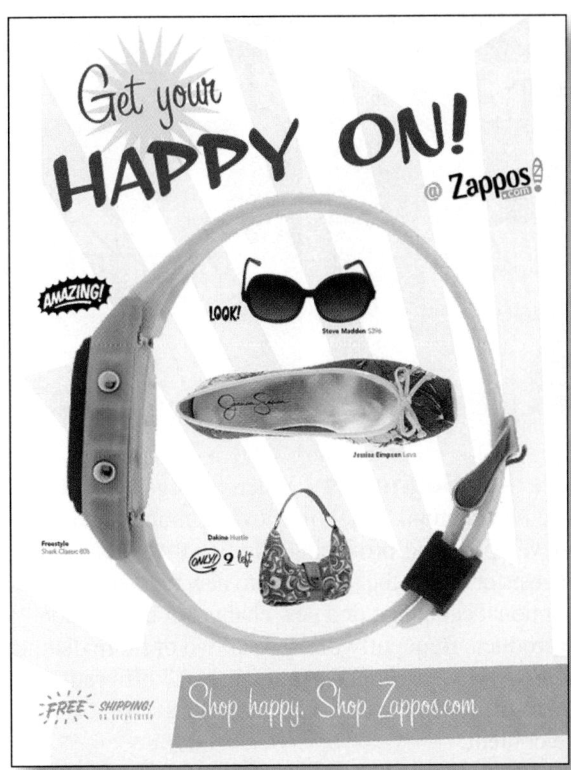

Zappos.com is reaching market segments beyond shoes with its edgy, attention-getting ads and WOW service.

With over 8 million customers and 5,000 calls daily to Zappos's service center, its executives believe the speed with which a customer receives an online purchase plays a big role in gaining repeat customers.[7] The company continues to stress this point of difference of providing the absolute best service among online sellers.

Using Market Product Grids How do you sleep—on your side, your back, or your stomach? These are really the key market segments of sleepers. Sleep researchers have discovered that you'll probably get a better night's sleep if you have the right firmness of pillow under your head. So we can develop the market-product grid shown in Figure 9–2.[8]

A **market-product grid** is a framework to relate the market segments of potential buyers to products offered or potential marketing actions. The market-product grid in Figure 9–2 shows the different market segments for bed pillows—the side, back, and stomach sleepers—in the horizontal rows. The product offerings—the pillows—appear in the vertical columns and are based on three different pillow firmnesses—firm, medium, and soft.

Market research reveals the size of each sleeper segment, as shown by both the percentages and circles in Figure 9–2. This tells pillow manufacturers the relative importance of each of the three market segments, which is critical information when scheduling production. It also emphasizes the importance of firm pillows, a product targeted at the side sleeper market segment. As Figure 9–2 shows, this segment is almost three times the size of the other two combined. Therefore, meeting the needs of this market segment with the right firmness of pillow is especially important.

When and How to Segment Markets

One-size-fits-all mass markets—like that for Tide laundry detergent 40 years ago—no longer exist. The marketing officer at Procter & Gamble, which markets Tide, says, "Every one of our brands is targeted." Due to the recent recession, the size of the middle-income market is shrinking. In response, P&G has begun implementing a new segmentation strategy: Offer different products to reach (1) high-income and (2) low-income families.[9]

A business goes to the trouble and expense of segmenting its markets when it expects that this extra effort will increase its sales, profit, and return on investment. When expenses are greater than the potentially increased sales from segmentation, a firm should not attempt to segment its market. Three specific segmentation strategies that illustrate this point are (1) one product and multiple market segments, (2) multiple products and multiple market segments, and (3) segments of one, or mass customization.

FIGURE 9–2
This market-product grid shows the kind of sleeper that is targeted for each of the bed pillow products. The percentages and sizes of the circles show that side sleepers are the dominant market segment and that they prefer firm pillows.

MARKET SEGMENTS	BED PILLOW PRODUCTS		
	Firm Pillows	Medium Pillows	Soft Pillows
Side sleepers	=73%		
Back sleepers		=22%	
Stomach sleepers			=5%

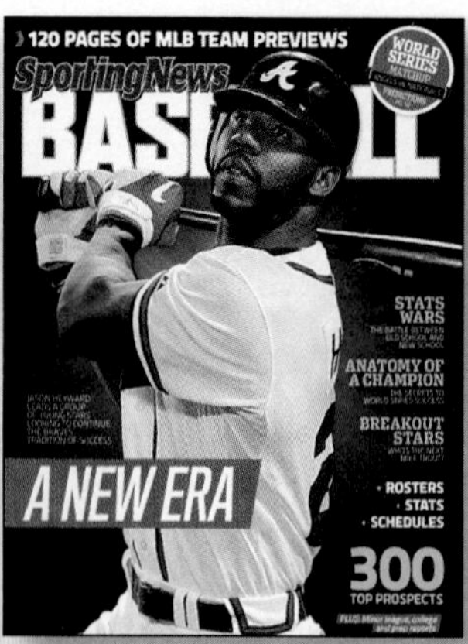

These *different* covers for the *same* magazine issue show a very effective market segmentation strategy. For which strategy it is and why it works, see the text.

One Product and Multiple Market Segments When an organization produces only a single product or service and attempts to sell it to two or more market segments, it avoids the extra costs of developing and producing additional versions of the product. In this case, the incremental costs of taking the product into new market segments are typically those of a separate promotional campaign or a new channel of distribution.

Magazines and books are single products frequently directed at two or more distinct market segments. The annual *Sporting News Baseball Yearbook* uses 17 different covers featuring a baseball star from each of its regions in the United States. Yet each regional issue has the same magazine content.

Harry Potter's phenomenal seven-book success is based on both author J. K. Rowling's fiction-writing wizardry and her publisher's creativity in marketing to preteen, teen, and adult segments of readers around the world. More than 450 million Harry Potter books, audio books, and e-books have been sold in 67 languages.[10] In the United States, the books were often at the top of *The New York Times* fiction best-seller list—for adults. Although separate covers for magazines or separate advertisements for books are expensive, these expenses are minor compared with the costs of producing multiple versions of magazines or books for several different market segments.

Multiple Products and Multiple Market Segments Ford's different lines of cars, SUVs, and pickup trucks are each targeted at a different type of customer—examples of multiple products aimed at multiple market segments. Producing these different vehicles is clearly more expensive than producing only a single vehicle. But this strategy is very effective *if* it meets customers' needs better, doesn't reduce quality or increase price, and adds to Ford's sales revenues and profits.

Unfortunately, this product differentiation strategy in the auto industry has a huge potential downside: The proliferation of different models and options can reduce quality and raise prices—especially in relation to foreign imports. Perhaps the extreme was in 1982, when the Ford Thunderbird had exactly 69,120 options compared with 32 (including colors) on the 1982 Honda Accord.[11]

Three decades later Ford is relearning its models and options lessons. Its current successful turnaround is partly related to a reduction in the number of frames, engines, and brands offered. As a result, Ford has reduced its number of models from 97 to 36 and sold off the Jaguar, Land Rover, and Volvo brands. Although there are fewer choices, Ford's simplified product line provides two benefits to consumers: (1) lower prices through producing a higher volume of fewer models and (2) higher quality because of the ability to debug fewer basic designs.[12]

Segments of One: Mass Customization American marketers are rediscovering today what their ancestors running the corner general store knew a century ago: Each customer has unique needs and wants and desires special tender loving care. Economies of scale in manufacturing and marketing during the past

ANN INC.'s LOFT chain tries to reach younger and value-conscious women with a casual lifestyle, while its Ann Taylor chain targets more sophisticated and relatively affluent women. For the potential dangers of this two-segment strategy, see the text.

century made mass-produced products so affordable that most customers were willing to compromise their individual tastes and settle for standardized products. Today's Internet ordering and flexible manufacturing and marketing processes have made *mass customization* possible, which means tailoring products or services to the tastes of individual customers on a high-volume scale.

Mass customization is the next step beyond *build-to-order* (BTO), manufacturing a product only when there is an order from a customer. Apple uses BTO systems that trim work-in-progress inventories and shorten delivery times to customers. To do this, Apple restricts its computer manufacturing line to only a few basic models that can be assembled in four minutes. This gives customers a good choice with quick delivery. But even this system falls a bit short of total mass customization because customers do not have an unlimited number of features from which to choose.

The Segmentation Trade-Off: Synergies versus Cannibalization

The key to successful product differentiation and market segmentation strategies is finding the ideal balance between satisfying a customer's individual wants and achieving *organizational synergy*, the increased customer value achieved through performing organizational functions such as marketing or manufacturing more efficiently. The "increased customer value" can take many forms: more products, improved quality of existing products, lower prices, easier access to products through improved distribution, and so on. So the ultimate criterion for an organization's marketing success is that customers should be better off as a result of the increased synergies.

The organization should also achieve increased revenues and profits from the product differentiation and market segmentation strategies it uses. When the increased customer value involves adding new products or a new chain of stores, the product differentiation–market segmentation trade-off raises a critical issue: Are the new products or new chain simply stealing customers and sales from the older, existing ones? This is known as *cannibalization*.

Marketers increasingly emphasize a two-tier, "Tiffany/Walmart" strategy. Many firms now offer different variations of the same basic offering to high-end and low-end segments. Gap's Banana Republic chain sells blue jeans for $58, whereas Old Navy stores sell a slightly different version for $22.

Unfortunately, the lines between customer segments can often blur and lead to problems. For example, consider the competition within the ANN INC. organization between stores in its two chains—Ann Taylor and LOFT. The Ann Taylor chain targets "successful, relatively affluent, fashion-conscious women," while its sister Ann Taylor LOFT chain targets "value-conscious women who want a casual lifestyle at work and home." The LOFT stores wound up stealing sales from the Ann Taylor chain. The result: More than 100 stores from both chains were recently closed.[13] Both chains are now aggressively targeting their customers by stressing online sales and opening new factory outlet stores.

The smaller Walmart Express format makes it easier for customers to take advantage of "everyday low prices."

Walmart is now operating 12 stores to test the concept of "Walmart Express," stores that are one-tenth the size of its supercenters and sell groceries. These smaller stores are intended to compete with the dollar chains and bare-bones outlets (like Germany's Aldi supermarket chain), which are stealing U.S. Walmart customers and causing lagging sales. Will its own Tiffany/Walmart strategy—or perhaps "Walmart/Aldi strategy"—prove successful or simply be another case of cannibalization?[14] Time will tell.

learning review

9-1. Market segmentation involves aggregating prospective buyers into groups that have two key characteristics. What are they?

9-2. In terms of market segments and products, what are the three market segmentation strategies?

STEPS IN SEGMENTING AND TARGETING MARKETS

LO 9-2 Identify the five steps involved in segmenting and targeting markets.

Figure 9–3 identifies the five-step process used to segment a market and select the target segments on which an organization wants to focus. Segmenting a market requires both detailed analysis and large doses of common sense and managerial judgment. So market segmentation is both science and art!

For the purposes of our discussion, assume that you have just purchased a Wendy's restaurant. Your Wendy's is located next to a large urban university, one that offers both day and evening classes. Your restaurant offers the basic Wendy's fare: hamburgers, chicken and deli sandwiches, salads, french fries, and Frosty desserts. Even though you are part of a chain that has some restrictions on menu and decor, you are free to set your hours of business and to develop local advertising. How can market segmentation help? In the sections that follow, you will apply the five-step process for segmenting and targeting markets to arrive at marketing actions for your Wendy's restaurant.

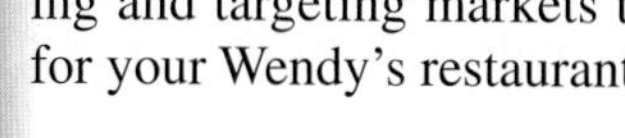

A local Wendy's restaurant near a large urban university campus—like yours!

Step 1: Group Potential Buyers into Segments

It's not always a good idea to segment a market. Grouping potential buyers into meaningful segments involves meeting some specific criteria that answer the questions, "Would segmentation be worth doing?" and "Is it possible?" If so, a marketer must find specific variables that can be used to create these various segments.

Criteria to Use in Forming the Segments A marketing manager should develop market segments that meet five essential criteria:[15]

- *Simplicity and cost-effectiveness of assigning potential buyers to segments.* A marketing manager must be able to put a market segmentation plan into effect. This means identifying the characteristics of potential buyers in a market and then cost-effectively assigning them to a segment.
- *Potential for increased profit.* The best segmentation approach is the one that maximizes the opportunity for future profit and return on investment (ROI). If this potential is maximized without segmentation, don't segment. For nonprofit organizations, the criterion is the potential for serving clients more effectively.
- *Similarity of needs of potential buyers within a segment.* Potential buyers within a segment should be similar in terms of common needs that, in turn, lead to common marketing actions, such as product features sought or advertising media used.
- *Difference of needs of buyers among segments.* If the needs of the various segments aren't very different, combine them into fewer segments. A different segment usually requires a different marketing action that, in turn, means greater

FIGURE 9–3
The five key steps in segmenting and targeting markets link the market needs of customers to the organization's marketing program.

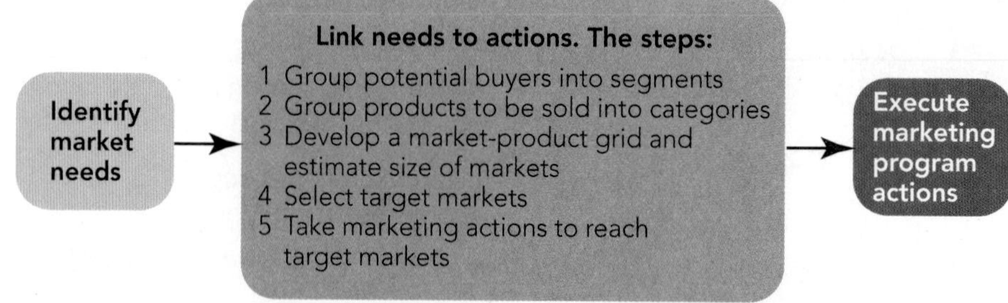

costs. If increased sales don't offset extra costs, combine segments and reduce the number of marketing actions.

- *Potential of a marketing action to reach a segment.* Reaching a segment requires a simple but effective marketing action. If no such action exists, don't segment.

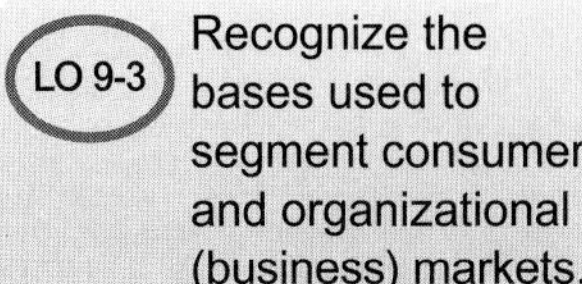

Recognize the bases used to segment consumer and organizational (business) markets.

Ways to Segment Consumer Markets Figure 9–4 shows four general bases of segmentation and the typical variables that can be used to segment U.S. consumer markets. These four segmentation bases are (1) *geographic segmentation*, which is based on where prospective customers live or work (region, city size); (2) *demographic segmentation*, which is based on some *objective* physical (gender, race), measurable (age, income), or other classification attribute (birth era, occupation) of prospective customers; (3) *psychographic segmentation*, which is based on some *subjective* mental or emotional attributes (personality), aspirations (lifestyle), or needs of prospective customers; and (4) *behavioral segmentation*, which is based on some observable actions or attitudes by prospective customers—such as where they buy, what benefits they seek, how frequently they buy, and why they buy. Some examples are:

- *Geographic segmentation: Region.* Campbell Soup Company found that its canned nacho cheese sauce, which could be heated and poured directly onto nacho chips, was too spicy for Americans in the East and not spicy enough for those in the West and Southwest. The result: Campbell's plants in Texas and California now produce a hotter nacho cheese sauce to serve their regions better.
- *Demographic segmentation: Household size.* More than half of all U.S. households are made up of only one or two persons, so Campbell packages meals with only one or two servings for this market segment.

FIGURE 9–4
Segmentation bases, variables, and breakdowns for U.S. consumer markets. Marketing managers should select segmentation variables that lead to marketing actions.

Basis of Segmentation	Segmentation Variables	Typical Breakdowns
Geographic	Region	Northeast; Midwest; South; West; etc.
	City size	Under 10,000; 10,000–24,999; 25,000–49,999; 50,000–99,999; etc.
	Statistical area	Metropolitan and micropolitan statistical areas; Census tract; etc.
	Media-television	210 designated market areas (DMA) in the U.S. (Nielsen)
	Density	Urban; suburban; small town; rural
Demographic	Gender	Male; female
	Age	Under 6 yrs; 6–11 yrs; 12–17 yrs; 18–24 yrs; 25–34 yrs; etc.
	Race/ethnicity	African American; Asian; Hispanic; White/Caucasian; etc.
	Life stage	Infant; preschool; child; youth; collegiate; adult; senior
	Birth era	Baby boomer (1946–1964); Generation X (1965–1976); etc.
	Household size	1; 2; 3–4; 5 or more
	Marital status	Never married; married; separated; divorced; widowed; domestic partner
	Income	Under \$15,000; \$15,000–\$24,999; \$25,000–\$34,999; etc.
	Education	Some high school or less; high school graduate (or GED); etc.
	Occupation	Managerial & professional; technical, sales; farming; etc.
Psychographic	Personality	Gregarious; compulsive; extroverted; aggressive; ambitious; etc.
	Values (VALS2)	Innovators; Thinkers; Achievers; Experiencers; Believers; Strivers; etc.
	Lifestyle (Nielsen PRIZM)	Blue Blood Estates; Single City Blues; etc. (66 total neighborhood clusters)
	Needs	Quality; service; price/value; health; convenience; etc.
Behavioral	Retail store type	Department; specialty; outlet; convenience; mass merchandiser; etc.
	Direct marketing	Mail order/catalog; door-to-door; direct response; Internet
	Product features	Situation-specific; general
	Usage rate	Light user; medium user; heavy user
	User status	Nonuser; ex-user; prospect; first-time user; regular user
	Awareness/intentions	Unaware; aware; interested; intending to buy; purchaser; rejection

Marketing Matters

technology

To Which "Flock" Do You Belong?

There is an old saying that "birds of a feather flock together." This also applies to the formation of market segments and gives rise to the following questions marketers must ask and answer: Who are your target customers? What are they like? Where do they live? How can you reach them?

These questions are answered in part by Nielsen, whose PRIZM® consumer segmentation system classifies every household into one of 66 demographically and behaviorally distinct neighborhood segments to identify lifestyles and purchase behavior within a defined geographic market area, such as zip code. Many organizations today use these neighborhood segments, especially with social media.

Want to know what your neighborhood is like? Go to www.claritas.com/MyBestSegments/Default.jsp and click the "ZIP Code Look-up" link or "Enter ZIP Code" button on the MyBestSegments home page. Then, type in your 5-digit zip code and security code. Last, click the "Submit" button to find out what the most common segments are in your neighborhood.

For a description of these segments, click the "Segment Explorer" tab. Is this your "flock"? What specific product or service organizations might be interested in targeting these segments?

- *Psychographic segmentation: Lifestyle.* Nielsen's lifestyle segmentation is based on the belief that "birds of a feather flock together." Thus, people of similar lifestyles tend to live near one another, have similar interests, and buy similar offerings. This is of great value to marketers. Nielsen PRIZM® classifies every household in the United States into one of 66 unique market segments. See the Marketing Matters box for a profile of where you live.
- *Behavioral segmentation: Product features.* Understanding what features are important to different customers is a useful way to segment markets because it can lead directly to specific marketing actions, such as a new product, an ad campaign, or a distribution channel. For example, college dorm residents frequently want to keep and prepare their own food to save money or have a late-night snack. However, their dorm rooms are often woefully short of space. MicroFridge understands this and markets a combination microwave, refrigerator, freezer, and charging station appliance targeted to these students.
- *Behavioral segmentation: Usage rate.* **Usage rate** is the quantity consumed or patronage—store visits—during a specific period. It varies significantly among different customer groups. Airlines have developed frequent-flier programs to encourage passengers to use the same airline repeatedly to create loyal customers. This technique, sometimes called *frequency marketing*, focuses on usage rate. One key conclusion emerges about usage: In market segmentation studies, some measurement of usage by, or sales obtained from, various segments is central to the analysis.

This appliance includes everything from a small refrigerator, freezer, and microwave oven to a charging station for laptops and mobile phones. To which market segment might this appeal? The answer appears in the text.

The Aberdeen Group recently analyzed which segmentation bases were used by the 20 percent most profitable organizations of the 220 surveyed. From highest to lowest, these were the segmentation bases they used:

- Geographic bases—88 percent.
- Behavioral bases—65 percent.
- Demographic bases—53 percent.
- Psychographic bases—43 percent.

The top 20 percent often use more than one of these bases in their market segmentation studies, plus measures such as purchase histories and usage rates of customers.[16]

Experian Simmons continuously surveys over 25,000 adults each year to obtain quarterly, projectable usage rate data from the U.S. national population for more than 500 consumer product categories and 8,000-plus brands. Its purpose is to discover how the products and services they buy and the media they use relate to their behavioral, psychographic, and demographic characteristics.

Patronage of Fast-Food Restaurants Figure 9–5 shows the results of a question Experian Simmons asked about adult respondents' frequency of use (or patronage) of fast-food restaurants.[17] As shown by the arrow in the far right column of Figure 9–5, the importance of the segment increases as we move up the table. Among nonusers of these restaurants, prospects (who might become users) are more important than nonprospects (who are never likely to become users). Moving up the rows to users, it seems logical that light users of these restaurants (0 to 5 times per month) are important but less so than medium users (6 to 13 times per month), who, in turn, are a less important segment than the critical group: heavy users (14 or more times per month). The Actual Consumption column in Figure 9–5 shows how much of the total monthly usage of these restaurants is accounted for by heavy, medium, and light users.

Usage rate is sometimes referred to in terms of the **80/20 rule**, a concept that suggests 80 percent of a firm's sales are obtained from 20 percent of its customers. The percentages in the 80/20 rule are not really fixed at exactly 80 percent and 20 percent, but they suggest that a small fraction of customers provides most of a firm's sales. For example, the orange shading in Figure 9–5 shows that the 36.1 percent of the U.S. population who are heavy users of fast-food restaurants provide 63.6 percent of the actual consumption volume. These high percentages are most likely due to the recession that began in 2007 as consumers increasingly patronized fast-food restaurants due to their inexpensive "value meal" offerings.

The Usage Index per Person column in Figure 9–5 emphasizes the importance of the heavy-user segment even more. Giving the light users (0 to 5 restaurant visits per month) an index of 100, the heavy users have an index of 640. In other words, for every $1.00 spent by a light user in one of these restaurants in a month, each heavy user spends $6.40. This is the reason that as a Wendy's restaurant owner, you want to focus most of your marketing efforts on reaching the highly attractive heavy-user market segment.

As part of its survey, Experian Simmons asked adults which fast-food restaurant(s) was (1) the sole or only restaurant, (2) the primary one, or (3) one of several secondary ones they patronized. As a Wendy's restaurant owner, the information depicted in Figure 9–6 on the next page should give you some ideas in developing a marketing program for your local market. For example, the Wendy's bar graph in Figure 9–6 shows that your sole (0.6 percent) and primary (12.5 percent) user segments are somewhat behind Burger King and far behind McDonald's. Thus, your challenge is to look at these two competitors and devise a marketing program to win customers from them.

FIGURE 9–5
Patronage of fast-food restaurants by adults 18 years and older. The table shows the critical importance of attracting heavy users and medium users to a fast-food restaurant.

User or Nonuser	Specific Segment	Number (1,000s)	Percent	Actual Consumption Percent	Usage Index per Person	Importance of Segment
Users	Heavy users (14 + per month)	82,502	36.1%	63.6%	640	High
	Medium users (6–13 per month)	68,634	30.0%	31.4%	380	↑
	Light users (0–5 per month)	41,264	18.1%	5.0%	100	
Total Users		**192,400**	**84.2%**	**100.0%**	—	
Nonusers	Prospects	2,708	1.2%	—	—	
	Nonprospects	33,459	14.6%	—	—	
Total Nonusers		**36,167**	**15.8%**	—	—	Low
Total	Users + Nonusers	**228,567**	**100.0%**	—	—	

Source: Experian Marketing Services Simmons Winter 2013 NHCS Full-Year Adult Survey 12-Month OneView[SM] Crosstabulation Report, Experian Marketing Services, 2013. See http://www.experian.com/marketing-services/consumer-insights.html.

FIGURE 9–6
Comparison of various kinds of users and nonusers for Wendy's, Burger King, and McDonald's fast-food restaurants. This table gives Wendy's restaurants a snapshot of its customers compared to those of its major competitors.

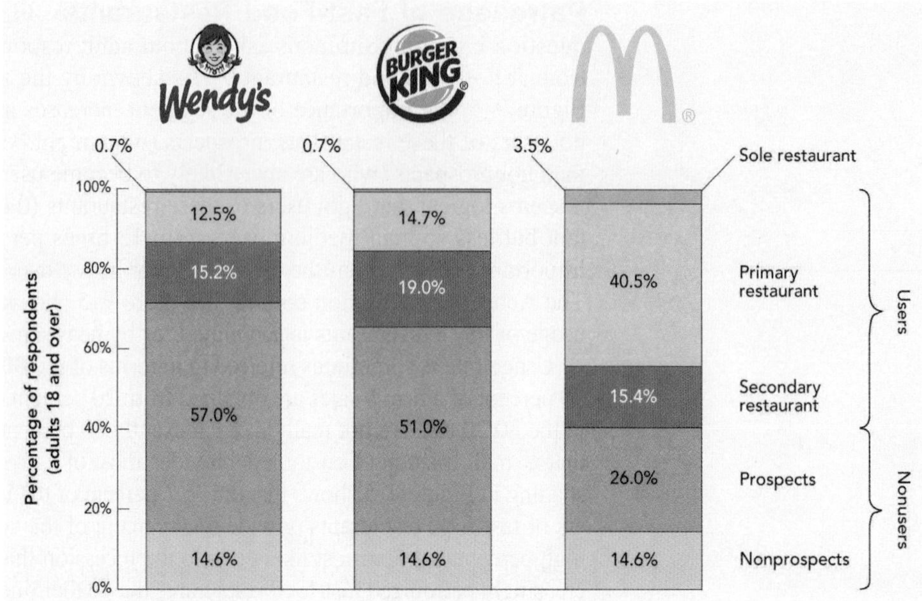

Source: Experian Marketing Services Simmons Winter 2013 NHCS Full-Year Adult Survey 12-Month OneView[SM] Crosstabulation Report, Experian Marketing Services, 2013. See http://www.experian.com/marketing-services/consumer-insights.html.

The nonusers part of the Wendy's bar graph in Figure 9–6 shows that 14.6 percent of adult Americans don't go to fast-food restaurants in a typical month and are really nonprospects—unlikely to ever patronize any fast-food restaurant. However, 57.1 percent of nonusers are prospects who may be worth a targeted marketing program. These adults use the product category (fast food) but do not yet patronize Wendy's. New menu items or promotional strategies may succeed in converting these prospects into users that patronize Wendy's.

What variables might Xerox use to segment organizational markets to respond to a firm's color copying problems? For the possible answer and related marketing actions, see the text.

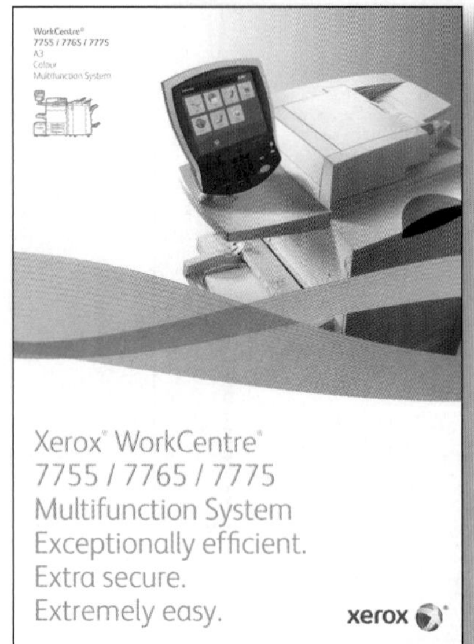

Xerox WorkCentre
7755 / 7765 / 7775
Multifunction System
Exceptionally efficient.
Extra secure.
Extremely easy.
xerox

Variables to Use in Forming Segments for Wendy's To analyze your Wendy's customers, you need to identify which variables to use to segment them. Because the restaurant is located near a large urban university, the most logical starting point for segmentation is really behavioral: Are the prospective customers students or nonstudents?

To segment the students, you could try a variety of (1) geographic variables, such as city or zip code; (2) demographic variables, such as gender, age, year in school, or college major; or (3) psychographic variables, such as personality or needs. But none of these variables really meets the five criteria listed previously—particularly, the fifth criterion about leading to a doable marketing action to reach the various segments. The behavioral basis of segmentation for the "students" segment really combines two variables: (1) where students live and (2) when they are on campus. This results in four "student" segments:

- Students living in dormitories (residence halls, sororities, fraternities).
- Students living near the university in apartments.
- Day commuter students living outside the area.
- Night commuter students living outside the area.

The three main segments of "nonstudents" include:

- Faculty and staff members who work at the university.
- People who live in the area but aren't connected with the university.
- People who work in the area but aren't connected with the university.

People in each of these nonstudent segments aren't quite as similar as those in the student segments, which makes them harder to reach with a marketing program or action. Think about (1) whether the needs of all these segments are different and (2) how various advertising media can be used to reach these groups effectively.

Ways to Segment Organizational (Business) Markets A number of variables can be used to segment organizational (business) markets (see Figure 9–7). For example, a product manager at Xerox responsible for its new line of multifunction color printers (MFPs) might use these segmentation bases and corresponding variables:

- *Geographic segmentation: Statistical area.* Firms located in a metropolitan statistical area might receive a personal sales call, whereas those in a micropolitan statistical area might be contacted by telephone.
- *Demographic segmentation: NAICS code.* Firms categorized by the North American Industry Classification System code as manufacturers that deal with customers throughout the world might have different document printing needs than retailers or lawyers serving local customers.
- *Demographic segmentation: Number of employees.* The size of the firm is related to the volume of digital documents produced, so firms with varying numbers of employees might be specific target markets for different Xerox MFPs.
- *Behavioral segmentation: Usage rate.* Similar to this segmentation variable for consumer markets, features are often of major importance in organizational markets. So Xerox can target organizations needing fast printing, copying, faxing, and scanning in color—the benefits and features emphasized in the ad for its Xerox Color WorkCentre 7775/7765/7775 Multifunction System.

FIGURE 9–7
Segmentation bases, variables, and breakdowns for U.S. organizational markets. These variables are used in business-to-business marketing.

Basis of Segmentation	Segmentation Variables	Typical Breakdowns
Geographic	Global region or country	European Union, South America, etc.; U.S., Japan, India, etc.
	Statistical area	Metropolitan and micropolitan statistical areas; Census tract; etc.
	Density	Urban; suburban; small town; rural
Demographic	NAICS code	2 digit: sector; 3 digit: subsector; 4 digit: industry group; etc.
	NAICS sector	Agriculture, forestry (11); mining (21); utilities (22); etc.
	Number of employees	1–99; 100–499; 500–999; 1,000–4,999; 5,000+
	Annual sales	Under $1 million; $1 million–$9.9 million; $10 million–$49.9 million; etc.
Behavioral	Number of locations	1–9; 10–49; 50–99; 100–499; 500–999; 1,000+
	Kind	Product; service
	Where used	Installation; component; supplies; etc.
	Application	Office; production; etc.
	Purchase location	Centralized; decentralized
	Who buys	Individual buyer; industrial buying group
	Type of buy	New buy; modified rebuy; straight rebuy

learning review

9-3. The process of segmenting and targeting markets is a bridge between which two marketing activities?

9-4. What is the difference between the demographic and behavioral bases of market segmentation?

QR 9-2
Dave's Hot 'n Juicy Ad

Step 2: Group Products to Be Sold into Categories

What does your Wendy's restaurant sell? Of course you are selling individual products such as Frostys, hamburgers, and fries. But for marketing purposes you're really selling combinations of individual products that become a "meal." This distinction is critical, so let's discuss both (1) individual Wendy's products and (2) groupings of Wendy's products.

Individual Wendy's Products When Dave Thomas founded Wendy's in 1969, he offered only four basic items: "Hot 'N Juicy" hamburgers, Frosty Dairy Desserts (Frostys), french fries, and soft drinks. Since then, Wendy's has introduced many new products and innovations to compete for customers' fast-food dollars. Some of these are shown in Figure 9–8. New products include salads, low trans fat chicken sandwiches, natural-cut fries with sea salt, and the "Dave's Hot 'N Juicy" hamburger. But there are also nonproduct innovations to increase consumer convenience like drive-thru services and E-Pay to enable credit card purchases.

Figure 9–8 also shows that each product or innovation is not targeted equally to all market segments based on gender, needs, or university affiliation. The cells in Figure 9–8 labeled "P" represent Wendy's primary target market segments when it introduced each product or innovation. The boxes labeled "S" represent the secondary target market segments that also bought these products or used these innovations. In some cases, Wendy's discovered that large numbers of people in a segment not originally targeted for a particular product or innovation bought or used it anyway.

Groupings of Wendy's Products: Meals Finding a means of grouping the products a firm sells into meaningful categories is as important as grouping customers into segments. If the firm has only one product or service, this isn't a problem. But when it has many, these must be grouped in some way so buyers can relate to them. This is why department stores and supermarkets are organized into product groups, with the departments or aisles containing related merchandise. Likewise, manufacturers organize products into groupings in the catalogs they send to customers.

FIGURE 9–8
Wendy's new products and other innovations target specific market segments based on a customer's gender, needs, or university affiliation.

MARKET SEGMENT		PRODUCT OR INNOVATION								
GENERAL	GROUP WITH NEED	HOT 'N JUICY HAMBURGER (1969)	DRIVE-THRU (1970)	99¢ SUPER VALUE MEALS (1989)	SALAD SENSATIONS (2002)	E-PAY (2003)	LOW TRANS FAT CHICKEN SANDWICHES (2006)	BREAKFAST SANDWICHES (2007)	NATURAL-CUT FRIES WITH SEA SALT (2010)	DAVE'S HOT 'N JUICY HAMBURGERS (2011)
GENDER	Male	P	P	P	S	P	S	P	P	P
	Female				P	P	P			
NEEDS	Price/Value			P	S					
	Health-Conscious				P		P			
	Convenience	S	P		S	P		P		S
	Meat Lovers	P		S			S	S	S	P
UNIVERSITY AFFILIATION	Affiliated (students, faculty, staff)	P	S	P	P	P	P	S		P
	Nonaffiliated (residents, workers)	S	P	S	S	S	S	P		S

Key: P = Primary market S = Secondary market

What are the product groupings for your Wendy's restaurant? It could be the item purchased, such as hamburgers, salads, Frostys, and french fries. This is where judgment—the qualitative aspect of marketing—comes in. Customers really buy an eating experience—a meal occasion that satisfies a need at a particular time of day. So the product groupings that make the most marketing sense are the five "meals" based on the time of day consumers buy them: breakfast, lunch, between-meal snack, dinner, and after-dinner snack. These groupings are more closely related to the way purchases are actually made and permit you to market the entire meal, not just your individual items such as french fries or hamburgers.

Step 3: Develop a Market-Product Grid and Estimate the Size of Markets

LO 9-4 Develop a market-product grid to identify a target market and recommend resulting marketing actions.

As noted earlier in the chapter, a market-product grid is a framework to relate the market segments of potential buyers to products offered or potential marketing actions by an organization. In a complete market-product grid analysis, each cell in the grid can show the estimated market size of a given product sold to a specific market segment. Let's first look at forming a market-product grid for your Wendy's restaurant and then estimate market sizes.

Forming a Market-Product Grid for Wendy's Developing a market-product grid means identifying and labeling the markets (or horizontal rows) and product groupings (or vertical columns), as shown in Figure 9–9. From our earlier discussion, we've chosen to divide the market segments into students versus nonstudents, with subdivisions of each. The columns—or "products"—are really the meals (or eating occasions) customers enjoy at the restaurant.

Estimating Market Sizes for Wendy's Now the size of the market in each cell (the unique market-product combination) of the market-product grid must be estimated. For your Wendy's restaurant, this involves estimating the sales of each kind of meal expected to be sold to each student and nonstudent market segment.

The market size estimates in Figure 9–9 vary from a large market ("3") to no market at all ("0") for each cell in the market-product grid. These may be simple guesstimates if you don't have the time or money to conduct formal marketing research (as discussed in Chapter 8). But even such crude estimates of the size of specific markets using a market-product grid are helpful in determining which target market segments to select and which product groupings to offer.

FIGURE 9–9
A market-product grid for your Wendy's fast-food restaurant next to an urban university. The numbers in the grid show the estimated size of the market in each cell, which leads to selecting the shaded target market.

MARKET SEGMENTS		PRODUCT OR INNOVATION				
General	Where They Live	Breakfast	Lunch	Between-Meal Snack	Dinner	After-Dinner Snack
Student	Dormitory	0	1	3	0	3
	Apartment	1	3	3	1	1
	Day Commuter	0	3	2	1	0
	Night Commuter	0	0	1	3	2
Nonstudent	Faculty or Staff	0	3	1	1	0
	Live in Area	0	1	2	2	1
	Work in Area	1	3	0	1	0

Key: 3 = Large market; 2 = Medium market; 1 = Small market; and 0 = No market

Wendy's has been aggressive in introducing new menu items to appeal to customers—such as making its classic cheeseburger thicker and offering new premium toppings.

Step 4: Select Target Markets

A firm must take care to choose its target market segments carefully. If it picks too narrow a set of segments, it may fail to reach the volume of sales and profits it needs. If it selects too broad a set of segments, it may spread its marketing efforts so thin that the extra expense exceeds the increased sales and profits.

Criteria to Use in Selecting the Target Segments Two kinds of criteria in the market segmentation process are those used to (1) divide the market into segments (discussed earlier) and (2) actually pick the target segments. Even experienced marketing executives often confuse them. Five criteria can be used to select the target segments for your Wendy's restaurant:

- *Market size.* The estimated size of the market in the segment is an important factor in deciding whether it's worth going after. There is really no market for breakfasts among dormitory students with meal plans, so you should not devote any marketing effort toward reaching this tiny segment. In your market-product grid (Figure 9–9), this market segment is given a "0" to indicate there is no market.
- *Expected growth.* Although the size of the market in the segment may be small now, perhaps it is growing significantly or is expected to grow in the future. Sales of fast-food meals eaten outside the restaurants are projected to exceed those eaten inside. And Wendy's has been shown to be the fast-food leader in average time to serve a drive-thru order—faster than McDonald's. This speed and convenience is potentially very important to night commuters in adult education programs.
- *Competitive position.* Is there a lot of competition in the segment now or is there likely to be in the future? The less the competition, the more attractive the segment is. For example, if the college dormitories announce a new policy of "no meals on weekends," this segment is suddenly more promising for your restaurant. Wendy's recently introduced the E-Pay pay-by-credit-card service at its restaurants to keep up with a similar service at McDonald's.
- *Cost of reaching the segment.* A segment that is inaccessible to a firm's marketing actions should not be pursued. For example, the few nonstudents who live in the area may not be reachable with ads in newspapers or other media. As a result, you should not waste money trying to advertise to them.
- *Compatibility with the organization's objectives and resources.* If your Wendy's restaurant doesn't yet have the cooking equipment to make breakfasts and has a policy against spending more money on restaurant equipment, then don't try to reach the breakfast segment. As is often the case in marketing decisions, a particular segment may appear attractive according to some criteria and very unattractive according to others.

Choose the Wendy's Segments Ultimately, a marketing executive has to use these criteria to choose the segments for special marketing efforts. As shown in Figure 9–9, let's assume you've written off the breakfast product grouping for two reasons: It's too small a market and it's incompatible with your objectives and resources. In terms of competitive position and cost of reaching the segment, you focus on the four student segments and *not* the three nonstudent segments (although you're certainly not going to turn their business away!). This combination of market-product segments—your target market—is shaded in Figure 9–9.

Step 5: Take Marketing Actions to Reach Target Markets

The purpose of developing a market-product grid is to trigger marketing actions to increase sales and profits. This means that someone must develop and execute an action plan in the form of a marketing program.

Your Immediate Wendy's Segmentation Strategy With your Wendy's restaurant you've already reached one significant decision: There is a limited market for breakfast, so you won't open for business until 10:30 A.M. In fact, Wendy's first attempt at a breakfast menu was a disaster and was discontinued in 1986. However, that strategy has changed yet again, with its new "fresh made breakfast" menu now being offered in most locations.

Another essential decision is where and what meals to advertise to reach specific market segments. An ad in the student newspaper could reach all the student segments, but it might be too expensive. If you choose three segments for special attention (Figure 9–10), advertising actions to reach them might include:

- *Day commuters* (an entire market segment). Run ads inside commuter buses and put flyers under the windshield wipers of cars in parking lots used by day commuters. These ads and flyers promote all the meals at your restaurant to the day commuter segment of students, a horizontal orange row through the product groupings or "meals" in your market-product grid.
- *Between-meal snacks* (directed to all four student market segments). To promote eating during this downtime for your restaurant, offer "Ten percent off all purchases between 2:00 and 4:30 P.M. during winter quarter." This ad promotes a single meal to all four student segments, a vertical blue column through the market-product grid.
- *Dinners to night commuters* (selecting a unique market-product combination). The most focused of all three campaigns, this strategy promotes a single meal to the single segment of night commuter students shaded green. The campaign uses flyers placed under the windshield wipers of cars in parking lots. To encourage eating dinner at Wendy's, offer a free Frosty with the coupon when the person buys a meal between 5 and 8 P.M. using the drive-thru window.

Depending on how your advertising actions work, you can repeat, modify, or drop them and design new campaigns for other segments you deem are worth the effort. This advertising example is just a small piece of a complete marketing program for your Wendy's restaurant.

FIGURE 9–10 Advertising actions to market various meals to a range of possible market segments of students.

MARKET SEGMENTS	PRODUCT GROUPINGS: MEAL OCCASION			
Behavioral: Where They Live	Lunch	Between-Meal Snack	Dinner	After-Dinner Snack
Dormitory Students	1	3	0	3
Apartment Students	3	3	1	1
Day Commuter Students	3	2	1	0
Night Commuter Students	0	1	3	2

Ads in buses; flyers under windshield wipers of cars in parking lots

Ad campaign: "10% off all purchases between 2:00 and 4:30 P.M. during winter quarter"

Ad on flyer under windshield wipers of cars in night parking lots: "Free Frosty with this coupon when you buy a drive-thru meal between 5:00 and 8:00 P.M."

Key: 3 = Large market; 2 = Medium market; 1 = Small market; and 0 = No market

There's always plenty of competition in the hamburger business. Five Guys Burgers and Fries has grown to more than 1,000 outlets in the past decade.

Keeping an Eye on Competition Other competitors are not sitting still, so in running your Wendy's you must be aware of their strategies as well. In 2012, McDonald's started posting the calories of its menu items.[18] In addition to offering free Wi-Fi in many of its locations, McDonald's is also aggressively marketing its "garden" snack wraps, McCafé coffee beverages, oatmeal, and high-margin fruit smoothies. And in 2013, it introduced its Egg White Delight McMuffin.[19] Meanwhile, Burger King has won awards for its "Subservient Chicken" and "Whopper Sacrifice" social media campaigns and is upgrading its outlets and broadening its Limited-Time-Only menus.[20]

Even new hamburger chains are popping up. In 1986, a Virginia husband-and-wife team started the Five Guys Burgers and Fries hamburger restaurant and 15 years later had only five restaurants in the Washington, D.C., area. But from 2003 to 2012, Five Guys exploded, with more than 1,000 locations nationwide and 1,500 new restaurants planned. Some of its points of difference: simple menu and decor, modest prices, only fresh ground beef (none frozen), and a trans-fat-free menu (cooking with peanut oil). But who's keeping track? The Big Three of McDonald's, Burger King, and Wendy's certainly are.

In addition to competition from traditional hamburger chains like Five Guys, all three are responding aggressively to reach the new "fast-casual" market segment. These customers want healthier food and lower prices in sit-down restaurants—a market segment being successfully targeted by fast-casual restaurants like Chipotle Mexican Grill and Panera Bread.[21]

Finally, a new source of competition is emerging from a variety of chains that aren't necessarily classified as restaurants at all. These include convenience store chains like 7-Eleven, coffee shops like Starbucks, smoothie outlets like Jamba Juice, and gas stations with prepared and reheatable packaged food.[22] Many of these outlets are now selling food items and trying to gain market share from the Big Three.

Future Strategies for Your Wendy's Restaurant Changing customer tastes and competition mean you must alter your strategies when necessary. This involves looking at (1) what Wendy's headquarters is doing, (2) what competitors are doing, and (3) what might be changing in the area served by your restaurant.

Wendy's recently introduced aggressive new marketing programs that include:[23]

- Refurbishing many of its restaurants and introducing new upscale menu items like its Bacon Portabella Melt sandwich.
- Offering coupons on higher-priced menu items to attract higher-income customers.
- Targeting 25- to 49-year-old customers, not just 18- to 24-year-old ones.
- Offering improved menu items like natural-cut fries with sea salt in 2010, the Dave's Hot 'N Juicy hamburger in 2011, and the Berry Almond Chicken Salad and Frosty Waffle Cone in 2013.

The Wendy's strategy has been remarkably successful, replacing Burger King as the #2 burger chain in terms of sales behind McDonald's. And Zagat's Fast-Food Survey recently rated Wendy's #1 on a number of key criteria among "mega" fast-food chains, including the Top Overall Chain for 2012.[24]

With these corporate Wendy's plans and new actions from competitors, maybe you'd better rethink your market segmentation decisions on hours of operation. Also, if new businesses have moved into your area, what about a new strategy to reach people that work in the area? Or you might consider a new promotion for the night owls and early birds—the 12 A.M. to 5 A.M. customers.

Marketing Matters

technology

Apple's Segmentation Strategy—Camp Runamok No Longer

Camp Runamok was the nickname given to Apple in the early 1980s because the innovative company had no coherent series of product lines directed at identifiable market segments. Today, Apple has targeted its various lines of Macintosh computers at specific market segments, as shown in the accompanying market-product grid.

Because the market-product grid shifts as a firm's strategy changes, the one here is based on Apple's product lines in mid-2013. The grid suggests the market segmentation strategy Apple is using to compete in the digital age.

MARKETS		COMPUTER PRODUCTS				
SECTOR	SEGMENT	Mac Pro	MacBook Pro	iMac	MacBook Air	Mac Mini
CONSUMER	Individuals			✓	✓	✓
	Small/ home office		✓	✓	✓	
	Students			✓	✓	✓
	Teachers		✓	✓		
PROFESSIONAL	Medium/ large business	✓	✓	✓	✓	✓
	Creative	✓	✓	✓		
	College faculty		✓	✓	✓	
	College staff			✓	✓	

How has Apple moved from its 1977 Apple II to today's iMac? The Marketing Matters box provides insights.

Apple's Ever-Changing Segmentation Strategy Steve Jobs and Steve Wozniak didn't realize they were developing today's multibillion-dollar PC industry when they invented the Apple I in a garage on April Fool's Day in 1976. However, when the Apple II was displayed at a computer trade show in 1977, consumers loved it and Apple Computer was born. Typical of young companies, Apple focused on its products and had little concern for its markets. Its creative, young engineers were often likened to "Boy Scouts without adult supervision."[25] Yet in 1984 the new Apple Macintosh revolutionized computers, and its 1984 Super Bowl TV ad is generally recognized as the best TV ad in history.

In 1997, Steve Jobs detailed his vision for a reincarnated Apple by describing a new market segmentation strategy that he called the "Apple Product Matrix." This strategy consisted of developing two general types of computer products (desktops and laptops) targeted at two market segments—the consumer and professional sectors.

In most segmentation situations, a single product does not fit into an exclusive market niche. Rather, product lines and market segments overlap. So Apple's market segmentation strategy enables it to offer different products to meet the needs of different market segments, as shown in the Marketing Matters box.

QR 9-3
Apple's 1984
Super Bowl Ad

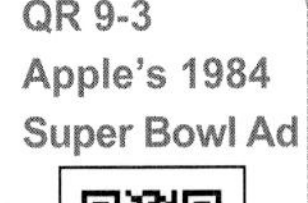

Market-Product Synergies: A Balancing Act

Recognizing opportunities for key synergies—that is, efficiencies—is vital to success in selecting target market segments and making marketing decisions. Market-product grids illustrate where such synergies can be found. How? Let's consider Apple's

What market-product synergies does Apple's iMac satisfy? Read the text to find out.

market-product grid in the Marketing Matters box on the previous page and examine the difference between marketing synergies and product synergies shown there.

- *Marketing synergies.* Running horizontally across the grid, each row represents an opportunity for efficiency in terms of a market segment. Were Apple to focus on just one group of consumers, such as the medium/large business segment, its marketing efforts could be streamlined. Apple would not have to spend time learning about the buying habits of students or college faculty. So it could probably create a single ad to reach the medium/large business target segment (the yellow row), highlighting the only products it would need to worry about developing: the Mac Pro, the MacBook Pro, the iMac, the MacBook Air, and the Mac mini. Although clearly not Apple's strategy today, new firms often focus only on a single customer segment.
- *Product synergies.* Running vertically down the market-product grid, each column represents an opportunity for efficiency in research and development (R&D) and production. If Apple wanted to simplify its product line, reduce R&D and production expenses, and manufacture only one computer, which might it choose? Based on the market-product grid, Apple might do well to focus on the iMac (the orange column), because every segment purchases it.

Marketing synergies often come at the expense of product synergies because a single customer segment will likely require a variety of products, each of which will have to be designed and manufactured. The company saves money on marketing but spends more on production. Conversely, if product synergies are emphasized, marketing will have to address the concerns of a wide variety of consumers, which costs more time and money. Marketing managers responsible for developing a company's product line must balance both product and marketing synergies as they try to increase the company's profits.

learning review

9-5. What factor is estimated or measured for each of the cells in a market-product grid?

9-6. What are some criteria used to decide which segments to choose for targets?

9-7. How are marketing and product synergies different in a market-product grid?

POSITIONING THE PRODUCT

LO 9-5 Explain how marketing managers position products in the marketplace.

When a company introduces a new product, a decision critical to its long-term success is how prospective buyers view it in relation to those products offered by its competitors. **Product positioning** refers to the place a product occupies in consumers' minds based on important attributes relative to competitive products. By understanding where consumers see a company's product or brand today, a marketing manager can seek to change its future position in their minds. This requires **product repositioning**, or *changing* the place a product occupies in a consumer's mind relative to competitive products.

Two Approaches to Product Positioning

Marketers follow two main approaches to positioning a new product in the market. *Head-to-head positioning* involves competing directly with competitors on similar product attributes in the same target market. Using this strategy, Dollar Rent A Car competes directly with Avis and Hertz.

More "zip" for chocolate milk? The text and Figure 9–11 describe how American dairies have successfully repositioned chocolate milk to appeal to adults.

Differentiation positioning involves seeking a less-competitive, smaller market niche in which to locate a brand. McDonald's tried to appeal to the health-conscious segment with its low-fat McLean Deluxe hamburger to avoid competing directly with Wendy's and Burger King. But this item was eventually dropped from the menu.

Writing a Positioning Statement

Marketing managers often convert their positioning ideas for the offering into a succinct written positioning statement. The positioning statement is used not only internally within the marketing department, but also for others outside it, such as research and development engineers or advertising agencies.[26] Here is the Volvo positioning statement for the North American market:

> For upscale American families who desire a carefree driving experience, Volvo is a premium-priced automobile that offers the utmost in safety and dependability.

This focuses Volvo's North American marketing strategy, so Volvo advertising almost always mentions safety and dependability.

Product Positioning Using Perceptual Maps

A key to positioning a product or brand effectively is discovering the perceptions in the minds of potential customers by taking four steps:

1. Identify the important attributes for a product or brand class.
2. Discover how target customers rate competing products or brands with respect to these attributes.
3. Discover where the company's product or brand is on these attributes in the minds of potential customers.
4. Reposition the company's product or brand in the minds of potential customers.

As shown in Figure 9–11, from these data it is possible to develop a **perceptual map**, a means of displaying in two dimensions the location of products or brands in the minds of consumers. This enables a manager to see how consumers perceive competing products or brands, as well as the firm's own product or brand.

FIGURE 9–11
The strategy American dairies are using to reposition chocolate milk to reach adults: Have adults view chocolate milk as both more nutritional and more "adult."

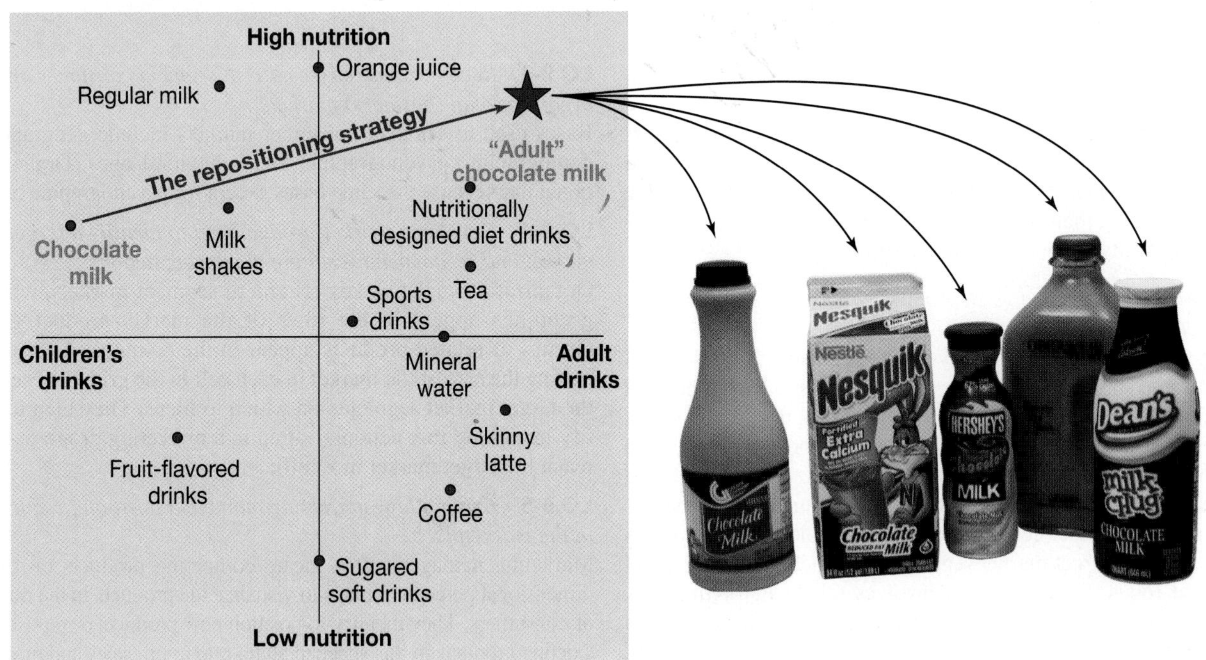

A Perceptual Map to Reposition Chocolate Milk for Adults

Recently, U.S. dairies decided to reposition chocolate milk in the minds of American adults to increase its sales. This is how dairies repositioned chocolate milk for American adults using the four steps listed on the previous page:

1. *Identify the important attributes (or scales) for adult drinks.* Research reveals the key attributes adults use to judge various drinks are (*a*) low versus high nutrition and (*b*) children's drinks versus adult drinks, as shown by the two axes in Figure 9–11.
2. *Discover how adults see various competing drinks.* Locate various adult drinks on these axes, as shown in Figure 9–11.
3. *Discover how adults see chocolate milk.* Figure 9–11 shows adults see chocolate milk as moderately nutritious (on the vertical axis) but as mainly a child's drink (on the horizontal axis).
4. *Reposition chocolate milk to make it more appealing to adults.* What actions did U.S. dairies take to increase sales? They repositioned chocolate milk to the location of the red star shown in the perceptual map in Figure 9–11.

The dairies' arguments are nutritionally powerful. For women, chocolate milk provides calcium, critically important in female diets. And dieters get a more filling, nutritious beverage than with a soft drink for about the same calories. The result: Chocolate milk sales increased dramatically, much of it because of adult consumption.[27] Part of this is due to giving chocolate milk "nutritional respectability" for adults, but another part is due to the innovative packaging that enables many new chocolate milk containers to fit in a car's cup holders.

learning review

9-8. What is the difference between product positioning and product repositioning?

9-9. Why do marketers use perceptual maps in product positioning decisions?

LEARNING OBJECTIVES REVIEW

LO 9-1 *Explain what market segmentation is and when to use it.*
Market segmentation involves aggregating prospective buyers into groups that (*a*) have common needs and (*b*) will respond similarly to a marketing action. Organizations go to the expense of segmenting their markets when it increases their sales, profits, and ability to serve customers better.

LO 9-2 *Identify the five steps involved in segmenting and targeting markets.*
Step 1 is to group potential buyers into segments. Buyers within a segment should have similar characteristics to each other and respond similarly to marketing actions like a new product or a lower price. Step 2 involves putting related products to be sold into meaningful groups. In step 3, organizations develop a market-product grid with estimated sizes of markets in each of the market-product cells of the resulting table. Step 4 involves selecting the target market segments on which the organization should focus. Finally, step 5 involves taking marketing mix actions—often in the form of a marketing program—to reach the target market segments.

LO 9-3 *Recognize the bases used to segment consumer and organizational (business) markets.*
Bases used to segment consumer markets include geographic, demographic, psychographic, and behavioral ones. Organizational markets use the same bases except for psychographic ones.

LO 9-4 *Develop a market-product grid to identify a target market and recommend resulting marketing actions.*
Organizations use five key criteria to segment markets, whose groupings appear in the rows of the market-product grid. Groups of related products appear in the columns. After estimating the size of the market in each cell in the grid, they select the target market segments on which to focus. They then identify marketing mix actions—often in a marketing program—to reach the target market most efficiently.

LO 9-5 *Explain how marketing managers position products in the marketplace.*
Marketing managers often locate competing products on two-dimensional perceptual maps to visualize the products in the minds of consumers. They then try to position new products or reposition existing products in this space to attain maximum sales and profits.

FOCUSING ON KEY TERMS

80/20 rule p. 231
market segmentation p. 224
market-product grid p. 225
perceptual map p. 241
product differentiation p. 224
product positioning p. 240
product repositioning p. 240
usage rate p. 230

APPLYING MARKETING KNOWLEDGE

1 What variables might be used to segment these consumer markets? (*a*) lawn mowers, (*b*) frozen dinners, (*c*) dry breakfast cereals, and (*d*) soft drinks.

2 What variables might be used to segment these industrial markets? (*a*) industrial sweepers, (*b*) photocopiers, (*c*) computerized production control systems, and (*d*) car rental agencies.

3 In Figure 9–9, the dormitory market segment includes students living in college-owned residence halls, sororities, and fraternities. What market needs are common to these students that justify combining them into a single segment in studying the market for your Wendy's restaurant?

4 You may disagree with the estimates of market size given for the rows in the market-product grid in Figure 9–9. Estimate the market size, and give a brief justification for these market segments: (*a*) dormitory students, (*b*) day commuters, and (*c*) people who work in the area.

5 Suppose you want to increase revenues for your fast-food restaurant even further. Referring to Figure 9–10, what advertising actions might you take to increase revenues from (*a*) dormitory students, (*b*) dinners, and (*c*) after-dinner snacks consumed by night commuter students?

6 Locate these drinks on the perceptual map in Figure 9–11: (*a*) cappuccino, (*b*) beer, and (*c*) soy milk.

BUILDING YOUR MARKETING PLAN

Your marketing plan needs a market-product grid to (*a*) focus your marketing efforts and (*b*) help you create a forecast of sales for the company. Use these steps:

1 Define the market segments (the rows in your grid) using the bases of segmentation used to segment consumer and organizational markets.

2 Define the groupings of related products (the columns in your grid).

3 Form your grid and estimate the size of the market in each market-product cell.

4 Select the target market segments on which to focus your efforts with your marketing program.

5 Use the information and the lost-horse forecasting technique (discussed in Chapter 8) to make a sales forecast (company forecast).

6 Draft your positioning statement.

VIDEO CASE 9 Prince Sports, Inc.: Tennis Racquets for Every Segment

QR 9-4
Prince Sports
Video Case

"Over the last decade we've seen a dramatic change in the media to reach consumers," says Linda Glassel, vice president of sports marketing and brand image of Prince Sports, Inc.

PRINCE SPORTS IN TODAY'S CHANGING WORLD

"Today—particularly in reaching younger consumers—we're now focusing so much more on social marketing and social networks, be it Facebook, Twitter, or internationally with Hi5, Bebo, and Orkut," she adds.

Linda Glassel's comments are a snapshot look at what Prince Sports faces in the changing world of tennis in the 21st century.

Prince Sports is a racquet sports company whose portfolio of brands includes Prince (tennis, squash, and badminton), Ektelon (racquetball), and Viking (platform/paddle tennis). Its complete line of tennis products alone is astounding: more than 150 racquet models; more than 50 tennis strings; over 50 footwear models; and countless types of bags, apparel, and other accessories.

Prince prides itself on its history of innovation in tennis—including inventing the first "oversize" and "longbody" racquets, the first "synthetic gut" tennis string, and the first "Natural Foot Shape" tennis shoe. Its challenge today is to continue to innovate to meet the needs of all levels of tennis players.

"One favorable thing for Prince these days is the dramatic growth in tennis participation—higher than it's been in many years," says Nick Skally (center in the photo below), senior marketing manager. A recent study by the Sporting Goods Manufacturers Association confirms this point: Tennis participation in the United States was up 43 percent—the fastest-growing traditional individual sport in the country.

TAMING TECHNOLOGY TO MEET PLAYERS' NEEDS

Every tennis player wants the same thing: to play better. But they don't all have the same skills, or the same ability to swing a racquet fast. So adult tennis players fall very broadly into three groups, each with special needs:

- *Those with shorter, slower strokes.* They want maximum power in a lightweight frame.
- *Those with moderate to full strokes.* They want the perfect blend of power and control.
- *Those with longer, faster strokes.* They want greater control with less power.

To satisfy all these needs in one racquet is a big order.

"When we design tennis racquets, it involves an extensive amount of market research on players at all levels," explains Tyler Herring, global business director for performance tennis racquets. Prince's research led it to introduce its breakthrough O^3 technology. "Our O^3 technology solved an inherent contradiction between racquet speed and sweet spot," he says. Never before had a racquet been designed that simultaneously delivers faster racquet speed with a dramatically increased "sweet spot." The "sweet spot" in a racquet is the middle of the frame that gives the most power and consistency when hitting. Recently, Prince introduced its latest evolution of the O^3 platform called EXO^3. Its newly patented design suspends the string bed from the racquet frame—thereby increasing the sweet spot by up to 83 percent while reducing frame vibration up to 50 percent.

SEGMENTING THE TENNIS MARKET

"The three primary market segments for our tennis racquets are our performance line, our recreational line, and our junior line," says Herring. He explains that within each of these segments Prince makes difficult design trade-offs to balance (1) the price a player is willing to pay, (2) what playing features (speed versus spin, sweet spot versus control, and so on) they want, and (3) what technology can be built into the racquet for the price point.

Within each of these three primary market segments, there are at least two subsegments—sometimes overlapping! Figure 1 gives an overview of Prince's market segmentation strategy and identifies sample racquet models. The three right-hand columns show the design variations of length, unstrung weight, and head size. The table shows the complexities Prince faces in converting its technology into a racquet with physical features that satisfy players' needs.

DISTRIBUTION AND PROMOTION STRATEGIES

"Prince has a number of different distribution channels—from mass merchants like Walmart and Target, to sporting goods chains, to smaller specialty tennis shops," says Nick Skally. For the large chains, Prince contributes co-op advertising for its in-store circulars, point-of-purchase displays, in-store signage, consumer brochures, and even "space planograms" to help the retailer plan the layout of Prince products in its tennis area. Prince aids for small tennis specialty shops include a supply of demo racquets, detailed catalogs, posters, racquet and string guides, merchandising fixtures, and hardware, such as racquet hooks and footwear shelves, in addition to other items. Prince also provides these shops with "player standees," which are corregated life-size cutouts of professional tennis players.

Prince reaches tennis players directly through its website (www.princetennis.com), which gives product information, tennis tips, and the latest tennis news. Besides using social networks like Facebook and Twitter, Prince runs ads in regional and national tennis publications and develops advertising campaigns for online sites and broadcast outlets.

In addition to its in-store activities, advertising, and online marketing, Prince invests heavily in its Teaching Pro program. These sponsored teaching pros receive all the latest product information, demo racquets, and equipment from Prince, so they can truly be Prince ambassadors in their community. Aside from their regular lessons, instructors and teaching professionals hold local "Prince Demo events" around the country to give potential customers a hands-on opportunity to see and try various Prince racquets, strings, and grips.

MARKET SEGMENTS				PRODUCT FEATURES IN RACQUET		
Main Segments	Subsegments	Segment Characteristics (Skill level, age)	Brand Name	Length (Inches)	Unstrung Weight (Ounces)	Head Size (Sq. in.)
Performance	Precision	For touring professional players wanting great feel, control, and spin	EXO³ Ignite 95	27.0	11.8	95
	Thunder	For competitive players wanting a bigger sweet spot and added power	EXO³ Red 95	27.25	9.9	105
Recreational	Small head size	For players looking for a forgiving racquet with added control	AirO Lightning MP	27.0	9.9	100
	Larger head size	For players looking for a larger sweet spot and added power	AirO Maria Lite OS	27.0	9.7	110
Junior	More experienced young players	For ages 8 to 15; somewhat shorter and lighter racquets than high school or adult players	AirO Team Maria 23	23.0	8.1	100
	Beginner	For ages 5 to 11; much shorter and lighter racquets; tennis balls with 50% to 75% less speed for young beginners	Air Team Maria 19	19.0	7.1	82

FIGURE 1
Prince targets racquets at specific market segments.

Prince also sponsors over 100 professional tennis players who appear in marquee events such as the four Grand Slam tournaments (Wimbledon and the Australian, French, and U.S. Opens). TV viewers can watch Russia's Maria Sharapova walk onto a tennis court carrying a Prince racquet bag or France's Gael Monfils hit a service ace using his Prince racquet.

Where is Prince headed in the 21st century? "As a marketer, one of the biggest challenges is staying ahead of the curve," says Glassel. And she stresses, "It's learning, it's studying, it's talking to people who understand where the market is going."

Questions

1 In the 21st century what trends in the environmental forces (social, economic, technological, competitive, and regulatory) (*a*) work for and (*b*) work against success for Prince Sports in the tennis industry?

2 Because sales of Prince Sports in tennis-related products depends heavily on growth of the tennis industry, what marketing activities might it use in the United States to promote tennis playing?

3 What promotional activities might Prince use to reach (*a*) recreational players and (*b*) junior players?

4 What might Prince do to gain distribution and sales in (*a*) mass merchandisers like Target and Walmart and (*b*) specialty tennis shops?

5 In reaching global markets outside the United States (*a*) what are some criteria that Prince should use to select countries in which to market aggressively, (*b*) what three or four countries meet these criteria best, and (*c*) what are some marketing actions Prince might use to reach these markets?

10 Developing New Products and Services

LEARNING OBJECTIVES

After reading this chapter you should be able to:

LO 10-1 Recognize the various terms that pertain to products and services.

LO 10-2 Identify the ways in which consumer and business products and services can be classified.

LO 10-3 Explain the significance of "newness" in new products and services as it relates to the degree of consumer learning involved.

LO 10-4 Describe the factors contributing to the success or failure of a new product or service.

LO 10-5 Explain the purposes of each step of the new-product process.

APPLE: THE WORLD-CLASS NEW-PRODUCT MACHINE

The stage in front of an auditorium was empty except for a chair, a table, and a huge screen with a large white logo. Then, in walked a legend ready for his magic show in his black mock turtleneck, jeans, and gray New Balance sneakers.

Apple's Innovation Machine

The legend, of course, was Steve Jobs (opposite page, at left), co-founder and former chairman of the board of Apple Inc., who died in October 2011. *Advertising Age* anointed Steve Jobs as Marketer of the Decade. *Fortune* rated Apple as the world's most-admired company, while *Bloomberg Businessweek* has perennially identified Apple as the world's most innovative company. The magic shows Jobs orchestrated over the years introduced many to Apple's market-changing innovations, such as the:

- Apple II—the first commercial personal computer (1977).
- Macintosh—the first personal computer (PC) with a mouse and a graphical user interface (1984).
- iPod—the first and most successful MP3 music player (2001).
- iPhone—the world's best multitouch smartphone and media player with almost one million apps (2007).
- iPad (2010) and iPad mini (2012)—the thin tablet devices that allow users to read books, newspapers, magazines, and even textbooks!
- Mac Pro—the innovative black cylinder that will be the fastest desktop PC on the planet (2013)!

Steve Jobs's innovations revolutionized six industries: personal computing, digitally animated movies (when he was CEO of Pixar), music, smartphones, tablet computing, and digital publishing.[1] Jobs even designed and holds the patent on the staircase seen in major Apple retail stores. He said, "You want that stairway so people believe they're in someplace magical."[2]

When Steve Jobs named Tim Cook (opposite page, at right) to be Apple's chief executive officer, his charge to Cook was simple: "Just do what's right." And under Cook, Apple has continued to deliver record

sales and profits. However, as this chapter reveals, developing successful new products is difficult. Tim Cook's challenge as the CEO of Apple will be to market new innovations to drive the company's future growth.[3]

QR 10-1
Apple iPad Ad

iCloud: Where the Digital Lifestyle Is Heading

Because many consumers now use multiple devices (smartphones like iPhone, PCs like iMac, and tablet devices like iPad), all of them need a way to share the music, photos, videos, files, and apps that reside on any one device.

Enter iCloud (opposite page), "which will now be the center of your digital life," as Steve Jobs explained in mid-2011. "iCloud stores all your content and wirelessly pushes any changes or purchases from one device automatically [up to the 'cloud' and then] down to all your other devices. Consumers won't have to worry about syncing their devices any longer to transfer their data. With iCloud, it will just work!"[4] Welcome to *cloud computing*, which involves moving the data and processing tasks normally hosted on your own device onto a remote data center server accessible via the Internet or Wi-Fi.[5]

The life of an organization depends on how it conceives, produces, and markets *new* products (goods, services, and ideas), the topic of this chapter. Many examples involve small businesses facing the difficult task of launching a successful start-up. Chapter 11 discusses the process of managing *existing* products, services, and brands.

WHAT ARE PRODUCTS AND SERVICES?

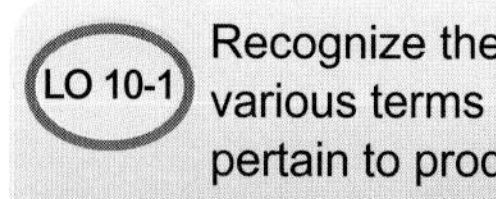

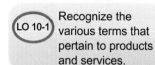

LO 10-1 Recognize the various terms that pertain to products and services.

The essence of marketing is in developing products and services to meet buyer needs. A **product** is a good, service, or idea consisting of a bundle of tangible and intangible attributes that satisfies consumers' needs and is received in exchange for money or something else of value. Let's clarify the meanings of goods, services, and ideas.

A Look at Goods, Services, and Ideas

Nondurable goods like chewing gum are easily consumed and rely on consumer advertising.

A *good* has tangible attributes that a consumer's five senses can perceive. For example, Apple's iPad can be touched and its features can be seen and heard. A good also may have intangible attributes consisting of its delivery or warranties and embody more abstract concepts, such as becoming healthier or wealthier. Goods also can be divided into nondurable goods and durable goods. A *nondurable* good is an item consumed in one or a few uses, such as food products and fuel. A *durable* good is one that usually lasts over many uses, such as appliances, cars, and smartphones. This classification method also provides direction for marketing actions. For example, nondurable goods, such as Wrigley's gum, rely heavily on consumer advertising. In contrast, costly durable goods, such as cars, generally emphasize personal selling.

Services are intangible activities or benefits that an organization provides to satisfy consumers' needs in exchange for money or something else of value. Services have become a significant part of the U.S. economy, reaching almost 50 percent of its gross domestic product.[6] Hence, a product may be the breakfast cereal you eat, whereas a service may be a tax return an accountant fills out for you.

Finally, in marketing, an *idea* is a thought that leads to a product or action, such as a concept for a new invention or getting people out to vote.

Throughout this book, *product* generally includes not only physical goods but services and ideas as well. When *product* is used in its narrower meaning of "goods," it should be clear from the example or sentence.

Classifying Products

LO 10-2 Identify the ways in which consumer and business products and services can be classified.

Two broad categories of products widely used in marketing relate to the type of user. **Consumer products** are products purchased by the ultimate consumer, whereas **business products** (also called *B2B products* or *industrial products*) are products organizations buy that assist in providing other products for resale. Some products can be considered both consumer and business items. For example, an Apple iMac computer can be sold to consumers for personal use or to business firms for office use. Each classification results in different marketing actions. Viewed as a consumer product, the iMac would be sold through Apple's retail stores or directly from its

BASIS OF COMPARISON	TYPE OF CONSUMER PRODUCT			
	CONVENIENCE PRODUCT	SHOPPING PRODUCT	SPECIALTY PRODUCT	UNSOUGHT PRODUCT
Product	Toothpaste, cake mix, hand soap, ATM cash withdrawal	Cameras, TVs, briefcases, airline tickets	Rolls-Royce cars, Rolex watches, heart surgery	Burial insurance, thesaurus
Price	Relatively inexpensive	Fairly expensive	Usually very expensive	Varies
Place (distribution)	Widespread; many outlets	Large number of selective outlets	Very limited	Often limited
Promotion	Price, availability, and awareness stressed	Differentiation from competitors stressed	Uniqueness of brand and status stressed	Awareness is essential
Brand loyalty of consumers	Aware of brand but will accept substitutes	Prefer specific brands but will accept substitutes	Very brand loyal; will not accept substitutes	Will accept substitutes
Purchase behavior of consumers	Frequent purchases; little time and effort spent shopping	Infrequent purchases; needs much comparison shopping time	Infrequent purchases; needs extensive search and decision time	Very infrequent purchases; some comparison shopping

FIGURE 10–1
How a consumer product is classified significantly affects which products consumers buy and the marketing strategies used.

online store. As a business product, an Apple salesperson might contact a firm's purchasing department directly and offer discounts for large volume purchases.

Consumer Products The four types of consumer products shown in Figure 10–1 differ in terms of (1) the effort the consumer spends on the decision, (2) the attributes used in making the purchase decision, and (3) the frequency of purchase. **Convenience products** are items that the consumer purchases frequently, conveniently, and with a minimum of shopping effort. **Shopping products** are items for which the consumer compares several alternatives on criteria such as price, quality, or style. **Specialty products** are items that the consumer makes a special effort to search out and buy. **Unsought products** are items that the consumer does not know about or knows about but does not initially want.

Figure 10–1 shows how each type of consumer product stresses different marketing mix actions, degrees of brand loyalty, and shopping effort. But how a consumer product is classified depends on the individual. One woman may view a camera as a shopping product and visit several stores before deciding on a brand, whereas her friend may view a camera as a specialty product and make a special effort to buy only a Nikon.

Business Products A major characteristic of business products is that their sales are often the result of *derived demand*; that is, sales of business products frequently result (or are derived) from the sale of consumer products. For example, as consumer demand for Ford cars (a consumer product) increases, the company may increase its demand for paint spraying equipment (a business product).

Business products may be classified as components or support products. *Components* are items that become part of the final product. These include raw materials such as lumber, as well as assemblies such as a Ford car engine. *Support products* are items used to assist in producing other products and services. These include:

- *Installations*, such as buildings and fixed equipment.
- *Accessory equipment*, such as tools and office equipment.
- *Supplies*, such as stationery, paper clips, and brooms.
- *Industrial services*, such as maintenance, repair, and legal services.

Strategies to market business products reflect both the complexities of the product involved (paper clips versus private jets) and the buy-class situations discussed in Chapter 6.

Classifying Services

Services can be classified according to whether they are delivered by (1) people or equipment, (2) business firms or nonprofit organizations, or (3) government agencies. These classifications are more thoroughly discussed in Chapter 12.

Product Classes, Forms, Items, Lines, and Mixes

QR 10-2
Crapola Video

Most organizations offer a range of products and services to consumers. Each set of offerings can be categorized according to the *product class* or industry to which they belong, like the iPad, which is classified as a tablet device. Products can exist in various *product forms* within a product class (see Chapters 2 and 11). A **product item** is a specific product that has a unique brand, size, or price. For example, Ultra Downy softener for clothes comes in different forms (liquid for the washer and sheets for the dryer) and load sizes (40, 60, etc.). Each of the different product items represents a separate *stock keeping unit* (SKU), which is a unique identification number that defines an item for ordering or inventory purposes.

A **product line** is a group of product or service items that are closely related because they satisfy a class of needs, are used together, are sold to the same customer group, are distributed through the same outlets, or fall within a given price range. Nike's product lines include shoes and clothing, whereas the Mayo Clinic's service lines consist of inpatient hospital care and outpatient physician services. Each product line has its own marketing strategy.

What company cheerfully tells its customers to "Have a crappy day"? Read the text to find out about this "tasty" offering!

Cranberry Apple Granola
"MAKES EVEN WEIRD PEOPLE REGULAR"
Crapola!
Net Wt 12 oz. (340 g)
MADE IN ELY MINNESOTA

The "Crapola Granola" product line started as an edgy party joke from Brian and Andrea Strom, owners of tiny Brainstorm Bakery. The dried **CR**anberries and **AP**ples gran**OLA**—hence the "Crapola" name—also contains nuts and five organic grains sweetened with maple syrup and honey. Its package promises that Crapola "Makes Even Weird People Regular."

Mentioned on TV by Jay Leno, Crapola is sold in retail outlets in the Midwest, California, and Oregon as well as online at www.crapola.us. The Stroms have a strategy of developing Crapola into a broader product line. Currently, they offer two other recipes: "Number Two" and "Red, White, and Blueberry." These product line extensions enable both consumers and retailers to simplify their buying decisions. So if a family has a good experience with Crapola, it might buy another product in the line. With a more extensive product line, the Stroms may manage to obtain distribution and shelf space in supermarket chains, which strive to increase efficiencies by dealing with fewer suppliers.[7]

Many firms offer a **product mix**, which consists of all of the product lines offered by an organization. For example, Cray Inc. has a small product mix of three product lines (supercomputers, storage systems, and a "data appliance") that are sold mostly to governments and large businesses. Procter & Gamble, however, has a large product mix that includes product lines such as beauty and grooming (Crest toothpaste and Gillette razors) and household care (Downy fabric softener, Tide detergent, and Pampers diapers).

learning review

10-1. What are the four main types of consumer products?

10-2. What is the difference between a product line and a product mix?

Marketing Matters

customer value

Feature Bloat: Geek Squad to the Rescue!

Adding more features to a product to satisfy more consumers seems like a no-brainer strategy for success. Right?

Feature Bloat

In fact, most marketing research with potential buyers of a product shows that while they *say* they want more features, in actuality they are overwhelmed with the mind-boggling complexity—or "feature bloat"—of some new products.

Computers pose a special problem for home users because there's no in-house technical assistance like that existing in large organizations. Ever call the manufacturer's toll-free "help" line? One survey showed that 29 percent of the callers swore at the customer service representative and 21 percent just screamed.

Geek Squad to the Rescue

Computer feature bloat has given rise to what TV's *60 Minutes* says is "the multibillion-dollar service industry populated by the very people who used to be shunned in the high school cafeteria: Geeks like Robert Stephens!"

More than a decade ago he turned his geekiness into the Geek Squad—a group of technically savvy people who can fix almost any computer problem.

"The biggest complaint about tech support people is rude, egotistical behavior," says Stephens. So he launched the Geek Squad to show some friendly humility by having team members work their wizardry while:

1. Showing genuine concern to customers.
2. Dressing in geeky white shirts, black clip-on ties, and white socks, a "uniform" borrowed from NASA engineers.
3. Driving to customer homes or offices in black-and-white VW "geekmobiles."

Do customers appreciate the 20,000-person Geek Squad, now owned by Best Buy? Robert Stephens answers by explaining, "People will say, 'They saved me . . . they saved my data.'" This includes countless college students working on their papers or theses with data lost somewhere in their computers—"data they promised themselves they'd back up next week."

See the video case that concludes Chapter 3 for more on the Geek Squad.

NEW PRODUCTS AND WHY THEY SUCCEED OR FAIL

LO 10-3 Explain the significance of "newness" in new products and services as it relates to the degree of consumer learning involved.

New products are the lifeblood of a company and keep it growing, but the financial risks can be large. Before discussing how new products reach the market, we'll begin by looking at *what* a new product is.

What Is a New Product?

The term *new* is difficult to define. Is Sony's PlayStation 4 *new* when there is already a PlayStation 3? Perhaps—because the PS4, Nintendo's Wii U, and Microsoft's new Xbox One will all position their consoles as entertainment "hubs" rather than just game consoles.[8] What does *new* mean for new-product marketing? Newness from several points of view are discussed next.

Newness Compared with Existing Products If a product is functionally different from existing products, it can be defined as new. Sometimes this newness is revolutionary and creates a whole new industry, as in the case of the Apple II computer. At other times more features are added to an existing product to try to appeal to more customers. And as HDTVs, smartphones, and tablet devices become more sophisticated, consumers' lives get far more complicated. This proliferation of extra features—sometimes called "feature bloat"—overwhelms many consumers. The Marketing Matters box describes how founder Robert Stephens launched his Geek Squad to address the rise of feature bloat.[9]

LOW — Degree of New Consumer Learning Needed — HIGH

BASIS OF COMPARISON	CONTINUOUS INNOVATION	DYNAMICALLY CONTINUOUS INNOVATION	DISCONTINUOUS INNOVATION
Definition	Requires no new learning by consumers	Disrupts consumer's normal routine but does not require totally new learning	Requires new learning and consumption patterns by consumers
Examples	New improved shaver, detergent, and toothpaste	Electric toothbrush, LED HDTVs, and smartphones	Wireless router, digital video recorder, and electric car
Marketing strategy	Gain consumer awareness and wide distribution	Advertise points of difference and benefits to consumers	Educate consumers through product trial and personal selling

FIGURE 10–2
The degree of "newness" in a new product affects the amount of learning effort consumers must exert to use the product and the resulting marketing strategy.

Newness from the Consumer's Perspective A second way to define new products is in terms of their effects on consumption. This approach classifies new products according to the degree of learning required by the consumer, as shown in Figure 10–2.

With a *continuous innovation*, consumers don't need to learn new behaviors. Toothpaste manufacturers can add new attributes or features like "whitens teeth" or "removes plaque" when they introduce a new or improved product, such as Colgate Total Advanced Gum Defense toothpaste. But the extra features in the new toothpaste do not require buyers to learn new tooth-brushing behaviors, so it is a continuous innovation. The benefit of this simple innovation is that effective marketing mainly depends on generating awareness, not re-educating customers.

With a *dynamically continuous innovation*, only minor changes in behavior are required. Heinz launched its EZ Squirt Ketchup in an array of unlikely hues—from green and orange to pink and teal—with kid-friendly squeeze bottles and nozzles.[10] Encouraging kids to write their names on hot dogs or draw dinosaurs on burgers as they use this new product requires only minor behavioral changes. So the marketing strategy here is to educate prospective buyers on the product's benefits, advantages, and proper use.

For how the kind of innovation present in this ketchup bottle affects its marketing strategy, see the text.

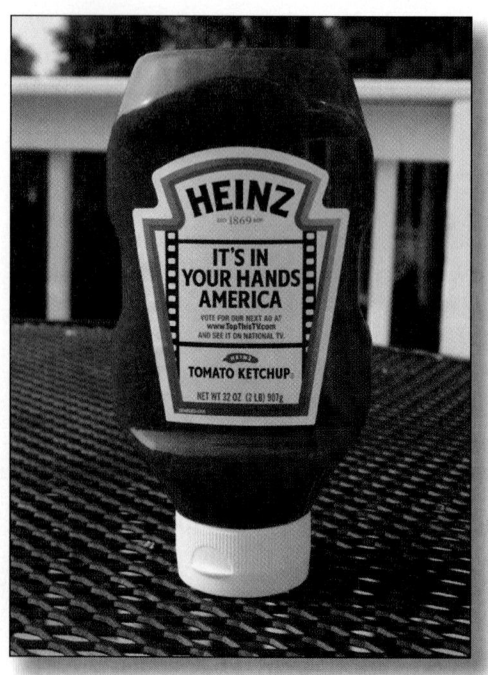

A *discontinuous innovation* involves making the consumer learn entirely new consumption patterns to use the product. Have you bought a wireless router for your computer? Congratulations if you installed it yourself! Recently, one-third of those bought at Best Buy were returned because they were too complicated to set up—the problem with a discontinuous innovation. So marketing efforts for discontinuous innovations usually involve not only gaining initial consumer awareness but also educating consumers on both the benefits and proper use of the innovative product, activities that can cost millions of dollars—and maybe require Geek Squad help.

Newness in Legal Terms The U.S. Federal Trade Commission (FTC) advises that the term *new* be limited to use with a product up to six months after it enters regular distribution. The difficulty with this suggestion is in the interpretation of the term *regular distribution.*

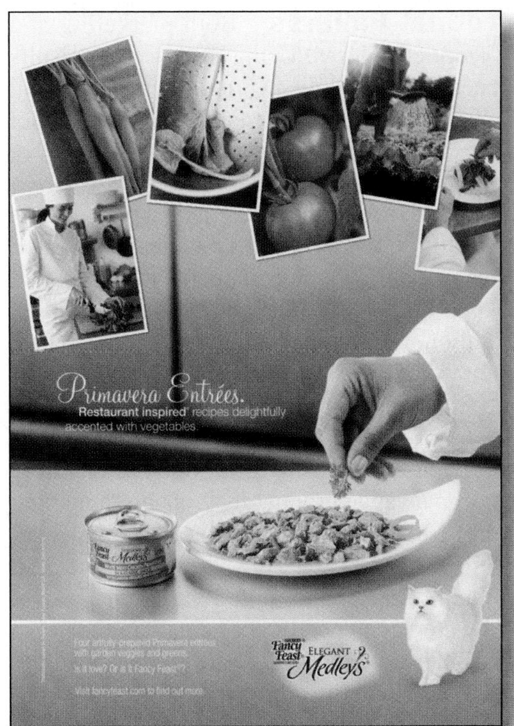

The text describes the potential benefits and dangers of an incremental innovation such as Purina's Elegant Medleys, its restaurant-inspired food for cats.

Newness from the Organization's Perspective Successful organizations view newness and innovation in their products at three levels. The lowest level, which usually involves the least risk, is a *product line extension*. This is an incremental improvement of an existing product line the company already sells. For example, Purina added its "new" line of Elegant Medleys, a "restaurant-inspired food for cats," to its existing line of 50 varieties of its Fancy Feast gourmet cat food. This has the potential benefit of adding new customers but the twin dangers of increasing expenses and cannibalizing products in its existing line.

At the next level is (1) a significant jump in innovation or technology or (2) a *brand extension* involving putting an established brand name on a new product in an unfamiliar market. In the first case, the significant jump in technology might be when a manufacturer offers new smartphones or digital cameras.

The second case—using an existing brand name to introduce a new product into an unfamiliar market—looks deceptively easy for companies with a powerful, national brand name. Colgate thought so. It puts its brand name on a line of frozen dinners called Colgate's Kitchen Entrees. The product line died quickly. A marketing expert calls this "one of the most bizarre brand extensions ever," observing that the Colgate brand name, which is strongly linked to toothpaste in people's minds, does not exactly get their "taste buds tingling." *Cosmopolitan's* yogurt had the same problem. The magazine, which has 58 international editions, is distributed in more than 100 countries. *Cosmopolitan* has the magazine business down pat. One thing *Cosmo* does not do best is brand and sell yogurt. Its *Cosmopolitan* Yogurt disappeared from retail shelves in 18 months.[11]

The third and highest level of innovation involves a radical invention, a truly revolutionary new product. Apple's Apple II, the first commercially successful "personal computer," and its iPad and iPod are examples of radical inventions. Effective new-product development in large firms exists at all three levels.

Why Products and Services Succeed or Fail

We all know the giant product and service successes—such as Apple's iPad, Google, and CNN. Yet the thousands of product failures every year that slide quietly into oblivion cost American businesses billions of dollars. Ideally, a new product or service needs a precise **protocol**, a statement that, before product development begins, identifies (1) a well-defined target market; (2) specific customers' needs, wants, and preferences; and (3) what the product will be and do to satisfy consumers.

A yogurt marketed by *Cosmopolitan* magazine? See the text for details.

Research reveals how difficult it is to produce a single commercially successful new product, especially among consumer packaged goods (CPG) that appear on supermarket shelves one month and are gone forever a few months later. Most American families buy the same 150 items over and over again—making it difficult to gain buyers for new products. So less than 3 percent of new consumer packaged goods exceed first-year sales of $50 million—the benchmark of a successful CPG launch.[12]

To learn marketing lessons and convert potential failures to successes, we can analyze why new products fail and then study several failures in detail. As we go through the new-product process later in the chapter, we can identify ways such failures might have been avoided—admitting that hindsight is clearer than foresight.

Describe the factors contributing to the success or failure of a new product or service.

Marketing Reasons for New-Product Failures Both marketing and nonmarketing factors contribute to new-product failures. Using the research results from several studies on new-product success and failure, we can identify critical marketing factors—which sometimes overlap—that often separate new-product winners and losers:[13]

1. *Insignificant point of difference.* Research shows that a distinctive point of difference is the single most important factor for a new product to defeat competing ones—having superior characteristics that deliver unique benefits to the user. In the mid-1990s, General Mills launched Fingos, a sweetened cereal flake about the size of a corn chip, with a $34 million promotional budget. Consumers were supposed to snack on them dry, but they didn't.[14] The point of difference was not important enough to get consumers to stop eating competing snacks such as popcorn and potato chips.
2. *Incomplete market and product protocol before product development starts.* Without this protocol, firms try to design a vague product for a phantom market. Developed by Kimberly-Clark, Avert Virucidal tissues contained vitamin C derivatives scientifically designed to kill cold and flu germs when users sneezed, coughed, or blew their noses into them. The product failed in test marketing. People didn't believe the claims and were frightened by the "cidal" in the brand name, which they connected to words like *suicidal*. A big part of Avert's failure was its lack of a product protocol that clearly defined how it would satisfy consumer wants and needs.[15]
3. *Not satisfying customer needs on critical factors.* Overlapping somewhat with point 1, this factor stresses that problems on one or two critical factors can kill the product, even though the general quality is high. For example, the Japanese, like the British, drive on the left side of the road. Until 1996, U.S. carmakers sent Japan few right-hand-drive cars—unlike German carmakers, which exported right-hand-drive models in several of their brands.
4. *Bad timing.* This results when a product is introduced too soon, too late, or when consumer tastes are shifting dramatically. Bad timing gives new-product managers nightmares. Microsoft, for example, introduced its Zune player a few years after Apple launched its iPod and other competitors offered their new MP3 players.
5. *No economical access to buyers.* Grocery products provide an example of this factor. Today's mega-supermarkets carry more than 30,000 different SKUs. With about 40,000 new consumer packaged goods (food, beverage, health and beauty aids, household, and pet items) introduced annually in the United States, the cost to gain access to retailer shelf space is huge. Because shelf space is judged in terms of sales per square foot, Thirsty Dog! (a zesty beef-flavored, vitamin-enriched, mineral-loaded, lightly carbonated bottled water for your dog) must displace an existing product on the supermarket shelves, a difficult task with the high sales-per-square-foot demands of these stores. Thirsty Dog! and its companion product Thirsty Cat! failed to generate enough sales to meet these requirements.
6. *Poor product quality.* This factor often results when a product is not thoroughly tested. The costs to an organization for poor quality can be staggering and include the labor, materials, and other expenses to fix the problem—not to mention the lost sales, profits, and market share that usually result. In early 2007, with a $500 million promotional budget, Microsoft launched its Windows Vista to replace its successful predecessor Windows XP. But the Vista software had so many quality problems with compatibility and performance, even Microsoft's most loyal users revolted. Today its problems would be highlighted even faster as Facebook and Twitter users post their complaints.[16]

New-product success or failure? Why might consumers choose *not* to buy sweetened corn flakes as a snack . . .

. . . or a vitamin-enriched carbonated bottled water for their dog or cat . . .

. . . or a spray to get rid of scary creatures from a child's bedroom? Answers appear in the text.

Introduce a Life Savers soda? The text asks if "groupthink" played a part in this new-product decision.

7. *Poor execution of the marketing mix: brand name, package, price, promotion, distribution.* Somewhere in the marketing mix there can be a showstopper that kills the product. Introduced by Gunderson & Rosario, Inc., Garlic Cake was supposed to be served as an hors d'oeuvre with sweet breads, spreads, and meats, but somehow the company forgot to tell this to potential consumers. Garlic Cake died because consumers were left to wonder just what a Garlic Cake is and when on earth a person would want to eat it.
8. *Too little market attractiveness.* The ideal is a large target market with high growth and real buyer need. But often the target market is too small or competitive to warrant the huge expenses necessary to reach it. OUT! International's Hey! There's A Monster In My Room spray was designed to rid scary creatures from a kid's bedroom and had a bubble-gum fragrance. While a creative and cute product, the brand name probably kept the kids awake at night more than their fear of the monsters because it implied the monster was still hiding in the bedroom. Also, was this a real market?

Simple marketing research should have revealed the problems in these new-product disasters. Developing successful new products may sometimes involve luck, but more often it involves having a product that really meets a need and has significant points of difference over competitive products.

Organizational Inertia in New-Product Failures Organizational problems and attitudes can also cause new-product disasters. Two key ones are:

- *Encountering "groupthink" in task force and committee meetings.* Someone in the new-product planning meeting knows or suspects the product concept is a dumb idea. But that person is afraid to speak up for fear of being cast as a "negative thinker," "not a team player," and then being ostracized from real participation in the group. Do you think someone on the Life Savers new-product team suspected a Life Savers soda wasn't a good idea but was afraid to speak up?[17] In the same way, a strong public commitment to a new product by its key advocate may make it difficult to kill the product even when new negative information comes to light.[18]
- *Avoiding the "NIH problem."* A great idea is a great idea, regardless of its source. Yet in the bureaucracy that can occur in large organizations, ideas from outside often get rejected simply because they come from outside—what has been termed the "not-invented-here (NIH) problem." NIH was never a problem for Steve Jobs. Part of his innovation genius was being open to ideas from everywhere. Jobs got the ideas for the mouse and the graphical user interface, which led to icons and pull-down menus for the Macintosh, from visits to the Xerox Corporation's Palo Alto Research Center, known as Xerox PARC.[19]

These organizational problems can contribute to the eight marketing reasons for new-product failures described above.

How Marketing Dashboards Can Improve New-Product Performance

The Using Marketing Dashboards box on the next page shows how marketers measure actual market performance versus the goals set in new-product planning. It shows that you have set a goal of 10 percent annual growth for the new snack you developed. You have chosen a marketing metric of "annual % sales change" to measure the annual growth rate from 2012 to 2013 for each of the 50 states.

Your special concerns in the marketing dashboard are the states shown in red, where sales have actually declined. As shown in the box, having identified the northeastern United States as a problem region, you can now conduct in-depth marketing research

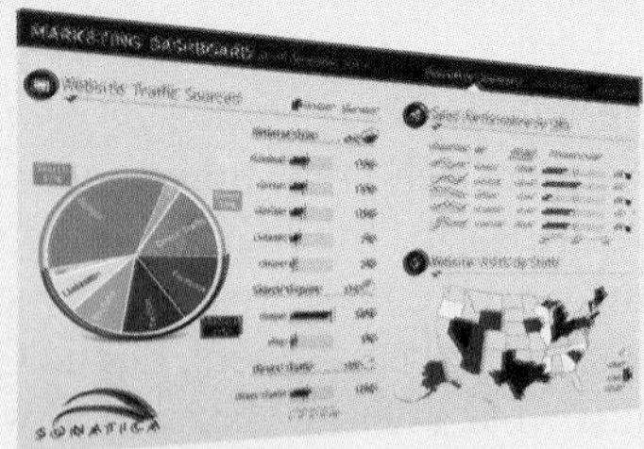

Using Marketing Dashboards

Which States Are Underperforming?

In 2010, you started your own company to sell a nutritious, high-energy snack you developed. It is now January 2014. As a marketer, you ask yourself, "How well is my business growing?"

Your Challenge The snack is sold in all 50 states. Your goal is 10 percent annual growth. To begin 2014, you want to quickly solve any sales problems that occurred during 2013. You know that states whose sales are stagnant or in decline are offset by those with greater than 10 percent growth.

Studying a table of the sales and percent change versus a year ago in each of the 50 states would work but be very time-consuming. A good graphic is better. You choose the following marketing metric, where "sales" are measured in units:

$$\text{Annual \% sales change} = \frac{(2013 \text{ Sales} - 2012 \text{ Sales}) \times 100}{2012 \text{ Sales}}$$

You want to act quickly to improve sales. In your map, growth that is greater than 10 percent is green, 0 to 10 percent growth is orange, and decline is red. Notice that you (1) picked a metric and (2) made your own rules that green is good, orange is bad, and red is very bad.

Your Findings You see that sales growth in the northeastern states is weaker than the 10 percent target, and sales are actually declining in many of the states.

Annual Percentage Change in Unit Volume, by State

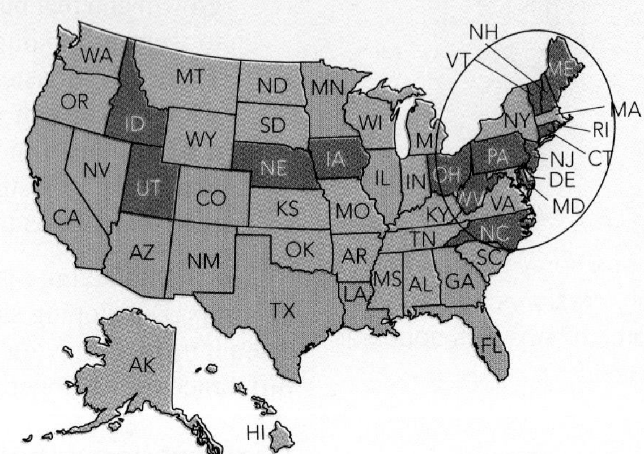

Your Action Marketing is often about grappling with sales shortfalls. You'll need to start by trying to identify and correct the problems in the largest volume states that are underperforming—in this case in the northeastern United States.

You'll want to do marketing research to see if the problem starts with (1) an external factor involving consumer tastes or (2) an internal factor such as a breakdown in your distribution system.

---

to lead to corrective actions. For example, is the decline in sales in this region due to an external factor, such as consumer preference? Perhaps consumers in the northeastern United States prefer more regional snack tastes or think your snack is too sweet. Or perhaps the problem is due to your own internal marketing strategy, such as poor distribution, prices that are too high, or ineffective advertising.

learning review

10-3. What kind of innovation would an improved electric toothbrush be?

10-4. Why can an "insignificant point of difference" lead to new-product failure?

10-5. What marketing metric might you use in a marketing dashboard to discover which states have weak sales?

THE NEW-PRODUCT PROCESS

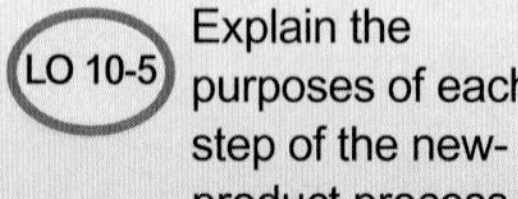

LO 10-5
Explain the purposes of each step of the new-product process.

To develop new products efficiently, companies such as General Electric and 3M use a specific sequence of steps to make their products ready for market. Figure 10–3 shows the **new-product process**, the seven stages an organization goes through to identify opportunities and convert them into salable products or services. Today many firms use a formal Stage-Gate® process to evaluate whether the results at each stage of the new-product

FIGURE 10–3
Carefully using the seven stages in the new-product process increases the chances of new-product success.

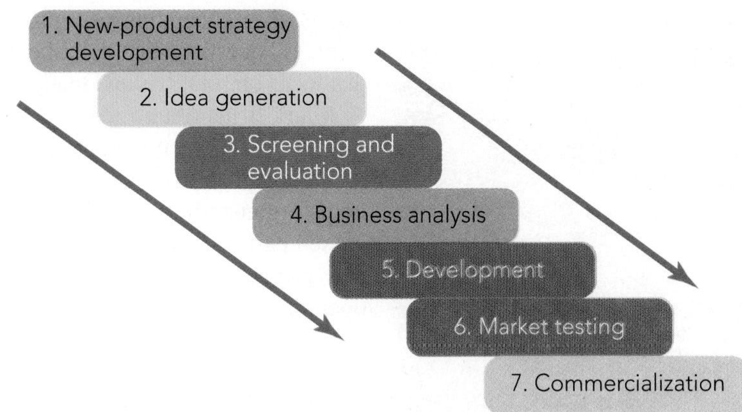

development process are successful enough to warrant proceeding to the next stage. If problems in a stage can't be corrected, the project doesn't proceed to the next stage and product development is killed.[20]

Stage 1: New-Product Strategy Development

For companies, **new-product strategy development** is the stage of the new-product process that defines the role for a new product in terms of the firm's overall objectives. During this stage, the firm uses both a SWOT analysis (Chapter 2) and environmental scanning (Chapter 3) to assess its strengths and weaknesses relative to the trends it identifies as opportunities or threats. The outcome not only defines the vital "protocol" for each new-product idea but also identifies the strategic role it might serve in the firm's business portfolio.

Occasionally a firm's Stage 1 activities can be blindsided by a revolutionary new product or technology that completely disrupts its business, sometimes called a "disruptive innovation." For example:

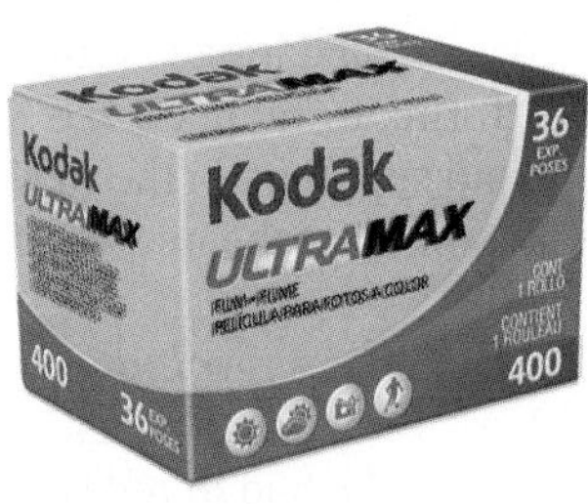

After inventing the digital camera in the mid-1970s, Kodak chose not to market it for fear of killing off its "cash cow" film business. Sadly, this led to a disastrous result, as the text describes.

- *Wikipedia.* This free and community-edited online encyclopedia caused Encyclopedia Britannica to cease print production after 244 years.
- *Digital photography.* Even though they were invented by Kodak, digital cameras made film and film cameras obsolete by the mid-2000s and drove Kodak into bankruptcy in 2012. Kodak did not actively market its digital cameras because it wanted to protect its film business, the firm's cash cow.
- *Personal computers.* Xerox's PARC never actively marketed personal computers (whose key components were actually invented at its Palo Alto Research Center) because top management didn't envision business opportunities beyond the photocopying business; this left the market open for Steve Jobs.[21]

Clearly, a firm's new-product strategy development must be on the lookout for innovative products or technology that might disrupt its plans.

New-product development for services, such as buying a stock or airline ticket or watching a National Football League game, is often difficult. Why? Because services are intangible and performance-oriented. Nevertheless, service innovations can have a huge impact on our lives. For example, the online brokerage firm E*TRADE has revolutionized the financial services industry through its online investment trading.

Stage 2: Idea Generation

Idea generation, the second stage of the new-product process, involves developing a pool of concepts to serve as candidates for new products, building upon the previous stage's results. Many forward-looking organizations have discovered that they are not generating enough useful new-product ideas. One internal approach for getting ideas within the firm is to train employees in the art and science of asking specific, probing questions.

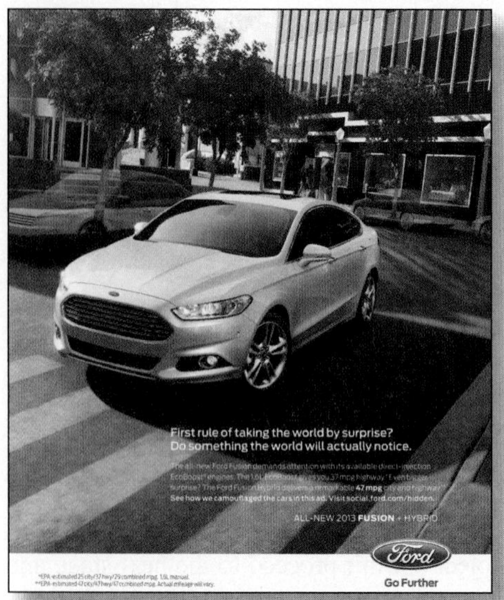

What method of idea generation did Ford use to create the new Ford Fusion? Read the text to find out.

The goal in generating new-product ideas and strategies is to move from "what is" questions that describe the present situation to "what if" questions that focus on solutions and marketing actions.[22]

Many firms obtain ideas externally using *open innovation*, in which they find and execute creative new-product ideas by developing strategic relationships with outside individuals and organizations. Open innovation helps organizations overcome the not-invented-here (NIH) barriers discussed earlier. The following discussion suggests methods of generating new-product ideas both internally and externally, the latter often using open innovation relationships.[23]

Employee and Co-Worker Suggestions Employees should be encouraged to suggest new-product ideas through suggestion boxes. The idea for Nature Valley granola bars from General Mills came when one of its marketing managers observed co-workers bringing granola to work in plastic bags.

An important part of Ford's current turnaround has been chief executive officer Alan Mulally's encouraging managers and employees to speak up and volunteer ideas to improve its technology and line of new cars—an openness lacking in U.S. auto companies in the past.[24] Further, Mulally has made clear that managers and employees in different departments aren't rivals. Instead of the not-invented-here (NIH) thinking of past years, Mulally has encouraged managers and employees to see themselves as part of the "One Ford" team and share information and help one another. This emphasis on improved employee communications has helped Ford launch new models, like its Fusion, add new technologies and redesign its supply chain.[25]

QR 10-3
P&G's Tide Pods Ad

Customer and Supplier Suggestions Firms ask their salespeople to talk to customers and ask their purchasing personnel to talk to suppliers to discover new-product ideas.[26] Whirlpool gets ideas from customers on ways to standardize components so that it can cut the number of different product platforms to reduce costs.[27] Business researchers tell firms to actively involve customers and suppliers in the new-product development process. This means the focus should be on what the new product will actually do for them rather than simply what they want.[28]

A. G. Lafley, CEO of Procter & Gamble (P&G), gave his executives a *revolutionary* thought: "Look outside the company for solutions to problems rather than insisting P&G knows best." When he ran P&G's laundry detergent business, he had to redesign the laundry boxes so they were easier to open. Why? While consumers *said* P&G's laundry boxes were "easy to open," cameras they agreed to have installed in their laundry rooms showed they opened the boxes with *screwdrivers*![29]

Procter & Gamble's new Tide Pods launch shows how it has improved both planning and implementation by involving consumers earlier in its innovation activities.

With a $150 million marketing budget, in 2012 P&G launched Tide Pods, a revolutionary three-chamber liquid dose that cleans, fights stains, and brightens. P&G describes Tide Pods as "its biggest laundry innovation in more than a quarter century." P&G says Tide Pods has produced the highest consumer-satisfaction scores the company has ever seen for a new laundry product. Following its successful new-product launch, however, P&G redesigned its packaging after discovering that some children thought the pods were candy and tried to eat them. How successful has Tide Pods been for P&G? After its first year, the product garnered a 73 percent share of the "unit dose" segment of the detergent market on estimated sales of $500 million—making it one of the most successful product launches of 2012![30]

"Crowdsourcing" is another creative idea-generation method if an R&D-marketing team wants ideas from 10,000 or 20,000 customers or suppliers. *Crowdsourcing* involves generating insights leading to actions based on ideas from massive numbers of people. It requires a precise question to focus the idea-generation process. Dell used crowdsourcing to develop an online site to generate 13,464 ideas for new products as well as website and marketing improvements, of which 402 were implemented.[31]

An IDEO innovation: A five-section, single-serve package for salads. Visit IDEO's website (www.ideo.com) to view its recent innovations.

Research and Development Laboratories Another source of new products is a firm's own research and development laboratories. Apple's sleek, cutting-edge designs for the iPad, iPhone, and iMac came out of its Apple Industrial Design Group, whose culture was established by the late Steve Jobs and is now guided by Senior Vice President of Design Jonathan Ive. What is the secret to Apple's world-class ability to convert vague concepts into tangible products? An action-item list from every meeting that focuses on *who* does *what* by *when*![32]

Professional R&D and innovation laboratories that are *outside* the walls of large corporations are also sources of open innovation and can provide new-product ideas.[33] IDEO is a world-class new-product development firm that uses "design thinking," which involves incorporating human behavior as well as building upon the ideas of others in the innovation-design process. As the most prolific and influential design firm in the world, IDEO has created thousands of new products for its clients. Brainstorming sessions conducted at IDEO can generate 100 new ideas in an hour!

IDEO designs include developing the standing Crest Neat Squeeze toothpaste dispenser and improving the original Apple mouse. Recently, Fresh Express asked IDEO to design an innovative single-serve package for salads. IDEO's solution: A five-section package—one large section for the salad greens and four smaller ones for proteins, dressings, and so on—with each section sealed in plastic (see the photo).[34]

Competitive Products Analyzing the competition can lead to new-product ideas. For six months, the Marriott Corporation sent a six-person intelligence team to travel and stay at economy hotels around the country. The team assessed the competition's strengths and weaknesses on everything from the soundproof qualities of the rooms to the softness of the towels. Marriott then budgeted $500 million for a new economy hotel chain—Fairfield Inns.

Smaller Firms, Universities, and Inventors Many firms look for outside visionaries that have inventions or innovative ideas that can become products. Some sources of this open innovation strategy include:

- *Smaller, nontraditional firms.* Small technology firms and even small, nontraditional firms in adjacent industries provide creative advances. General Mills partnered with Weight Watchers to develop Progresso Light soups, the first consumer packaged product in any grocery category to carry the Weight Watchers endorsement with a 0 points value per serving.[35]
- *Universities.* Many universities have technology transfer centers that often partner with business firms to commercialize faculty inventions. The first-of-its-kind carbonated yogurt Go-Gurt Fizzix was launched in late 2007 as a result of General Mills partnering with Brigham Young University to license the university's patent to put the "fizz" into the yogurt.[36]
- *Inventors.* Many lone inventors and entrepreneurs develop brilliant new-product ideas—like Gary Schwartzberg's tube-shaped bagel filled with cream cheese. A portable breakfast for the on-the-go person, the innovative bagel couldn't get widespread distribution. So Schwartzberg sold his idea to Kraft Foods, Inc., which now markets its Bagel-fuls filled with Kraft's best-selling Philadelphia cream cheese in supermarkets across the United States.[37]

Gary Schwartzberg partnered with Kraft Foods to get his cream cheese–filled bagels in stores across the United States.

Early-stage financing is almost always a problem for inventors and those starting a new business. *Crowdfunding* is a way to gather an online community of supporters to financially rally around a specific project that is unlikely to get resources from traditional sources such as banks or venture capital firms. For example, Kickstarter.com raised $1.2 million for start-up SmartThings to introduce a product that allows users to monitor their homes by remote control. But its biggest crowdfunding project

Crowdfunder Kickstarter.com enabled Pebble to market its customizable watch that runs a variety of apps.

was for the Pebble digital smartwatch with iPhone and Android smartphone integration: Almost 70,000 backers contributed over $10 million to develop this amazing product, which initially sold for $150! If *your* idea needs financing, here are five other crowdfunding sources and what they support:

- *Crowdrise.* Charitable causes.
- *Crowdtilt.* Anything.
- *Fundable.* Early-stage financing for start-up businesses.
- *Rally.* Nonprofits, artists, musicians, entrepreneurs.
- *GiveForward.* Medical causes.

If you want to donate to crowdfunding projects, that's fine, too: The average Kickstarter donor gives $25.[38]

Great ideas can come from almost anywhere—the challenge is recognizing and implementing them.

Stage 3: Screening and Evaluation

Screening and evaluation is the stage of the new-product process that internally and externally evaluates new-product ideas to eliminate those that warrant no further effort.

Internal Approach In this approach to screening and evaluation, a firm's employees evaluate the technical feasibility of a proposed new-product idea to determine whether it meets the objectives defined in the new-product strategy development stage. For example, 3M scientists develop many world-class innovations in the company's labs. A recent innovation was its microreplication technology—one that has 3,000 tiny gripping "fingers" per square inch. An internal assessment showed 3M that this technology could be used to improve the gripping of both batting and work gloves.

Organizations that develop service-dominated offerings need to ensure that employees have the commitment and skills to meet customer expectations and sustain customer loyalty—an important criterion in screening a new-service idea. This is the essence of **customer experience management (CEM)**, which is the process of managing the entire customer experience within the company. Marketers must consider employees' interactions with customers so that the new services are consistently delivered and experienced, clearly differentiated from other service offerings, and relevant and valuable to the target market.

External Approach Firms that take an external approach to screening and evaluation use *concept tests*, external evaluations with consumers that consist of preliminary testing of a new-product idea rather than an actual product. Generally, these tests are more useful with minor modifications of existing products than with new, innovative products with which consumers are not familiar.[39] Concept tests rely on written descriptions of the product but may be augmented with sketches, mockups, or promotional literature. Key questions for concept testing include: How does the customer perceive the product? Who would use it? and How would it be used?

learning review

10-6. What is the new-product strategy development stage in the new-product process?

10-7. What are the main sources of new-product ideas?

10-8. How do internal and external screening and evaluation approaches differ?

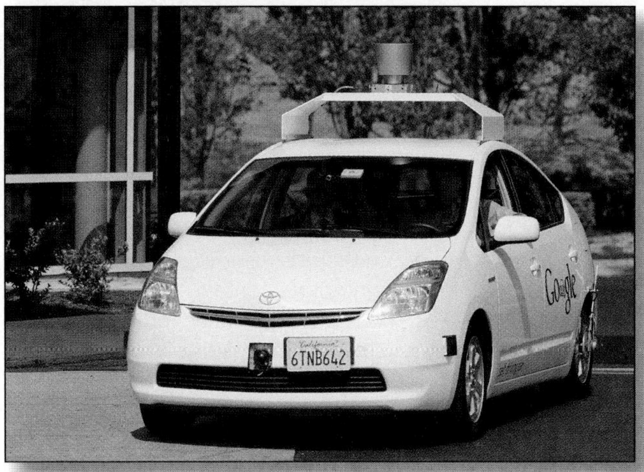

Is this what you'll be "driving" in 2020? Google's driverless cars have logged 300,000 miles without an accident!

QR 10-4
Google Car
Video

Stage 4: Business Analysis

Business analysis specifies the features of the product and the marketing strategy needed to bring it to market and make financial projections. This is the last checkpoint before significant resources are invested to create a *prototype*—a full-scale operating model of the product. The business analysis stage assesses the total "business fit" of the proposed new product with the company's mission and objectives—from whether the product can be economically developed and manufactured to the marketing strategy needed to have it succeed in the marketplace.

This process requires not only detailed financial projections but also assessments of the marketing and product synergies related to the company's existing operations. Will the new product require a lot of new machinery to produce it or can it be produced using the unused capacity of existing machines? Will the new product cannibalize sales of existing products or will it increase revenues by reaching new market segments? Can the new product be protected with a patent or copyright? Financial projections of expected profits require estimates of expected prices per unit and units sold, as well as detailed estimates of the costs of R&D, production, and marketing.

For services, business analysis involves using capacity management (discussed in Chapter 12) to find ways to match the availability of the service offering to when it is needed. For example, airlines and mobile phone service providers use *off-peak pricing* to charge different prices during different times of the day or during different days of the week to help match the supply and demand for their services.[40]

Stage 5: Development

Development is the stage of the new-product process that turns the idea on paper into a prototype. This results in a demonstrable, producible product that involves not only manufacturing the product efficiently but also performing laboratory and consumer tests to ensure the product meets the standards established for it in the protocol.

Google's driverless car is an extreme example of the complexity of the Stage 5 development process for a durable consumer good. The Google team consists of 15 engineers and has a fleet of 10 vehicles as the test models, among them the Toyota Prius and the Lexus RX 450h. In August 2012, the Google team announced its cars had completed over 300,000 miles of accident-free, "autonomous driving." These miles were "driven" by a driver with an unblemished driving record behind the wheel and a Google engineer in the passenger seat. A spinning, roof-mounted laser range finder and sophisticated software negotiated the steep hairpin turns in San Francisco and trips both across the Golden Gate Bridge and along the curvy Pacific Coast Highway.

Netflix is confronting changing markets, technologies, and competition. See the text and Marketing Matters box on the next page for a discussion of these changes at Netflix.

Where is Google's driverless car headed? Google has no plans to commercialize the vehicle itself but wants to market the technology to auto manufacturers. But it is clear Google will need to invest tens of millions of dollars into additional development and testing (see Stage 6 below) before anyone can buy a driverless car—typical of high-technology devices. Right now, only Nevada, California, and Florida have laws allowing driverless cars.

The good news for Google: safety. If its driverless car is perfected and allowed on U.S. highways, the 34,000 highway deaths and 240,000 hospitalizations caused by car accidents annually should fall.[41] This will surely be part of Google's marketing campaign!

Marketing Matters

technology

Netflix's Wild Roller-Coaster Ride

If in 1997, a customer had been charged a late fee of $40 for a VHS tape of *Apollo 13*, what might she or he have done? Maybe just grumble and pay it? Not Reed Hastings. Although he paid the $40 late fee, Hastings, unlike other disgruntled video store patrons, began "to investigate the idea of how to create a movie-rental business by mail."

Riding High

"Early on, the first concept we launched was rental by mail, but it wasn't subscription based so it worked more like Blockbuster," says Hastings, the founder and CEO of Netflix. It wasn't very popular. So in 1999, he relaunched his idea as a DVD-by-mail subscription service that delivered movies to customers for a fixed monthly fee. The business took off!

A Bump in the Road

But the Netflix business changed again in 2008 when advances in technology allowed subscribers to receive thousands of movies and TV shows "streamed" over the Internet via a television, set-top box, or video game console or wirelessly to a smartphone or tablet device.

This method caused a problem for Netflix because the firm is both a customer of and a competitor to broadcast and TV cable networks as well as movie studios—which can earn much more with their pay-per-view alternatives than with Netflix's streaming of its content. The result: higher licensing fees and reduced choices for Netflix, not to mention the copycat services from Apple (Apple TV/iTunes), Amazon (Instant Video), a new Verizon-Redbox venture, and others that add even more competition.

Where to Now? Up? Or Down?

As of mid-2013, Netflix's over 30 million U.S. subscribers love that they can view TV shows and movies for about $8 a month—far cheaper than pay-TV options. But to continue growing, Netflix believes that it must reinvent itself—again! Its solution? Offer original programming, starting with a political thriller called *House of Cards*—and deliver all 13 episodes at once rather than one per week. In 2013, this made-for-Netflix TV drama received nine Emmy nominations, the first time an online-only show has been in the running for TV's top award.

For services, improving the delivery of customer service is critical. This involves analyzing the entire sequence of steps or "service encounters" to improve the interactions between consumers and the service provider. High-contact services such as hotels, car rental agencies, and web providers use this approach to serve customers better.

The Marketing Matters box describes how Netflix founder and chief executive officer Reed Hastings got the idea for his start-up and how his business model has changed to reflect the way Internet breakthroughs are able to stream movies more conveniently to a consumer's TV set, game console, or iPad. Learning from its success with its *House of Cards* drama, Netflix signed an agreement in mid-2013 with DreamWorks Animation for over 300 hours of TV programming. But new competitors to Netflix are all around—including Amazon, a new Verizon-Redbox venture, and cable TV networks. What is Netflix's future? Stay tuned.[42]

Stage 6: Market Testing

Market testing is a stage of the new-product process that involves exposing actual products to prospective consumers under realistic purchase conditions to see if they will buy. If the budget permits, consumer packaged goods firms do this by *test marketing*, which involves offering a product for sale on a limited basis in a defined area for a specific time period. The three main kinds of test markets are (1) standard, (2) controlled, and (3) simulated.[43] Because standard test markets are so time-consuming and expensive and can alert competitors to a firm's plans, some firms skip test markets entirely or use controlled or simulated test markets.

Standard Test Markets In a *standard test market*, a company develops a product and then attempts to sell it through normal distribution channels in a number of test-market cities. Test-market cities must be demographically representative of markets targeted for the new product, have cable TV systems that can deliver different ads to different homes, and have retailers with checkout counter scanners to measure sales.

Consumer products, such as those from General Mills, often use controlled test markets to assess the likely success of new-product, promotional, or pricing strategies.

A distinguishing feature of a standard test market is that the producer sells the product to distributors, wholesalers, and retailers, just as it would do for other products.

Controlled Test Markets A *controlled test market* involves contracting the entire test program to an outside service. The service pays retailers for shelf space and can therefore guarantee a specified percentage of the test product's potential distribution volume. IRI is a leader in supplying controlled test markets to consumer packaged good firms like General Mills. Its BehaviorScan service uses five demographically representative cities to track sales made to a panel of households. In some cases the effectiveness of different TV commercials and other direct-to-consumer promotions can be measured.

Simulated Test Markets To save time and money, companies often turn to *simulated (or laboratory) test markets (STM)*, a technique that somewhat replicates a full-scale test market. STMs are often run in shopping malls, to find consumers who use the product class being tested. Next, qualified participants are shown the product or the product concept and are asked about usage, reasons for purchase, and important product attributes. They then see the company's and competitors' ads for the test product. Finally, participants are given money and allowed to choose between buying the firm's product or the products of competitors from a real or simulated store environment.

When Test Markets Don't Work Not all products can use test markets. Test marketing a service is very difficult because consumers can't see what they are buying. For example, how do you test market a new building for an art museum? Similarly, test markets for expensive consumer products, such as cars or costly industrial products such as jet engines, are impractical. For these products, reactions of potential buyers to mockups or one-of-a-kind prototypes are all that is feasible.

Stage 7: Commercialization

Finally, the product is brought to the point of **commercialization**—the stage of the new-product process that positions and launches a new product in full-scale production and sales. This is the most expensive stage for most new products. If competitors introduce a product that leapfrogs the firm's own new product or if cannibalization of its own existing products appears significant, the firm may halt the new-product launch. Companies can face disasters at the commercialization stage, regardless of whether they are selling business products or consumer products. Examples are Boeing's 787 Dreamliner and Burger King's french fries, which are discussed next.

Takeaway new-product lesson from the Boeing 787 Dreamliner: "Innovation . . . doesn't come easy." See the text for details.

The Boeing 787 Dreamliner Experience In 2004, Boeing announced the design for its Boeing 787 Dreamliner commercial airplane. Its technical advances would mean the plane would burn 20 percent less fuel and cost 30 percent less to maintain than present airliners. Boeing invested billions of dollars in the 787's development, and airlines had placed orders for almost 930 Dreamliners by mid-2013.

As the Dreamliner entered its commercialization stage, airlines around the world began taking deliveries. But with all the new technology in the Dreamliner, the new airplane was plagued by technical nightmares—even after extensive testing. Its wings, made with plastic-reinforced carbon fiber instead of aluminum, proved difficult to produce and attach to the fuselage. And with this new "high-tech skin," lightning doesn't dissipate like it did with the old aluminum skin. But an even more serious problem arose in early 2013: Lithium-ion batteries, which provide electrical power, caught fire on two Dreamliner aircraft, prompting regulators to ground all 50 Dreamliners in service around the world. Perhaps *The Wall Street Journal* gave the best new-product lesson from the Boeing 787 Dreamliner example: "Innovation—for all its value—doesn't come as easily as a catchphrase. It can get messy."[44]

To discover the downs and ups of commercializing a new product, see the text discussion of Burger King's 15-year search for a french fry recipe that can compete with McDonald's.

Burger King's French Fries: The Complexities of Commercialization Burger King's "improved french fries" are an example of what can go wrong with a consumer product at the commercialization stage. McDonald's french fries are the gold standard against which all other fries in the fast-food industry are measured. In 1997, Burger King decided to take on McDonald's fries and spent millions of R&D dollars developing a whey/starch-coated fry designed to retain heat longer and add crispiness. The launch, backed with a $70 million marketing campaign, turned into a disaster. The reason: Except under ideal conditions, the new fry proved too complicated to get right day after day in Burger King restaurants, and changes had to be made to get the "production" process correct to ensure consistent results.

Fast-forward to today. Over the past couple of years, Wendy's has introduced new fries in the fast-food war. Launched in late 2010, Wendy's Natural-Cut Fries with Sea Salt have become a huge hit.

Burger King, now the number three fast-food marketer after McDonalds and Wendy's, responded with its new thick-cut fries in late 2011. In development and testing for over two years, the new fries are "fluffier" on the inside for a more "potatoey" taste, have less sodium, and have a new "coating" on the outside. This was done to create a "crispy, golden-brown deliciousness" while retaining the heat longer—for at least 10 minutes because 75 percent of customers eat their fries "on the go" in their cars, offices, or homes.

A taste test conducted by an independent market research firm stated that the new Burger King fries were preferred over McDonald's fries by a 57 to 35 percent margin. Burger King also launched the largest TV advertising campaign in its history—featuring "spokespud" Mr. Potato Head—to promote the new fries.[45]

The Special Risks in Commercializing Grocery Products New grocery products pose special commercialization problems. Because shelf space is so limited, many supermarkets require a *slotting fee* for new products, a payment a manufacturer makes to place a new item on a retailer's shelf. This can run to several million dollars for a single product. But there's even another potential expense. If a new grocery product does not achieve a predetermined sales target, some retailers require a *failure fee*, a penalty payment a manufacturer makes to compensate a retailer for devoting valuable shelf space to a product that failed to sell.

These costly slotting fees and failure fees are further examples of why large grocery product manufacturers use regional rollouts. Companies selling consumer products using *regional rollouts* introduce a product sequentially into geographical areas of the United States to allow production levels and marketing activities to build up gradually, to minimize the risk of new-product failure. Grocery product manufacturers and telephone service providers use this strategy.

Speed as a Factor in New-Product Success Companies have discovered that speed or *time to market* (TtM) is often vital in introducing a new product. Recent studies have shown that high-tech products coming to market on time are far more profitable than those arriving late. So companies like Sony, BMW, 3M, and Hewlett-Packard often overlap the sequence of stages described in this chapter.

With this approach, termed *parallel development*, cross-functional team members who conduct the simultaneous development of both the product and the production process stay with the product from conception to production. This approach enabled Hewlett-Packard to reduce the development time for notebook computers from 12 to 7 months. In software development, *fast prototyping* uses a "do it, try it, fix it" approach—encouraging continuing improvement even after the initial design. To speed up time to market, many firms insulate their new-product teams from routine administrative tasks to keep them from bogging down in red tape.[46]

learning review

10-9. How does the development stage of the new-product process involve testing the product inside and outside the firm?

10-10. What is a test market?

10-11. What is the commercialization of a new product?

LEARNING OBJECTIVES REVIEW

LO 10-1 *Recognize the various terms that pertain to products and services.*

A product is a good, service, or idea consisting of a bundle of tangible and intangible attributes that satisfies consumers and is received in exchange for money or something else of value.

A good has tangible attributes that a consumer's five senses can perceive and intangible ones such as warranties; a laptop computer is an example. Goods also can be divided into nondurable goods, which are consumed in one or a few uses, and durable goods, which usually last over many uses.

Services are intangible activities or benefits that an organization provides to satisfy consumer needs in exchange for money or something else of value, such as an airline trip. An idea is a thought that leads to a product or action, such as eating healthier foods.

LO 10-2 *Identify the ways in which consumer and business products and services can be classified.*

By type of user, the major distinctions are consumer products, which are products purchased by the ultimate consumer, and business products, which are products that assist an organization in providing other products for resale.

Consumer products can be broken down based on the effort involved in the purchase decision process, marketing mix attributes used in the purchase, and the frequency of purchase: (*a*) convenience products are items that consumers purchase frequently and with a minimum of shopping effort; (*b*) shopping products are items for which consumers compare several alternatives on selected criteria; (*c*) specialty products are items that consumers make special efforts to seek out and buy; and (*d*) unsought products are items that consumers either do not know about or do not initially want.

Business products can be broken down into (*a*) components, which are items that become part of the final product, such as raw materials or parts, and (*b*) support products, which are items used to assist in producing other goods and services and include installations, accessory equipment, supplies, and industrial services.

Services can be classified in terms of whether they are delivered by (*a*) people or equipment, (*b*) business firms or nonprofit organizations, or (*c*) government agencies.

Firms can offer a range of products, which involve decisions regarding the product item, product line, and product mix.

LO 10-3 *Explain the significance of "newness" in new products and services as it relates to the degree of consumer learning involved.*

From the important perspective of the consumer, "newness" is often seen as the degree of learning that a consumer must engage in to use the product. With a continuous innovation, no new behaviors must be learned. With a dynamically continuous innovation, only minor behavioral changes are needed. With a discontinuous innovation, consumers must learn entirely new consumption patterns.

LO 10-4 *Describe the factors contributing to the success or failure of a new product or service.*

A new product or service often fails for these marketing reasons: (*a*) insignificant points of difference, (*b*) incomplete market and product protocol before product development starts, (*c*) a failure to satisfy customer needs on critical factors, (*d*) bad timing, (*e*) no economical access to buyers, (*f*) poor product quality, (*g*) poor execution of the marketing mix, and (*h*) too little market attractiveness.

LO 10-5 *Explain the purposes of each step of the new-product process.*

The new-product process consists of seven stages a firm uses to develop salable products or services: (1) *New-product strategy development* involves defining the role for the new product within the firm's overall objectives. (2) *Idea generation* involves developing a pool of concepts from consumers, employees, basic R&D, and competitors to serve as candidates for new products. (3) *Screening and evaluation* involves evaluating new-product ideas to eliminate those that are not feasible from a technical or consumer perspective. (4) *Business analysis* involves defining the features of the new product, developing the marketing strategy and marketing program to introduce it, and making a financial forecast. (5) *Development* involves not only producing a prototype product but also testing it in the lab and with consumers to see that it meets the standards set for it. (6) *Market testing* involves exposing actual products to prospective consumers under realistic purchasing conditions to see if they will buy the product. (7) *Commercialization* involves positioning and launching a product in full-scale production and sales with a specific marketing program.

FOCUSING ON KEY TERMS

business analysis p. 261
business products p. 248
commercialization p. 263
consumer products p. 248
convenience products p. 249
customer experience management (CEM) p. 260
development p. 261
idea generation p. 257
market testing p. 262
new-product process p. 256
new-product strategy development p. 257
product p. 248
product item p. 250
product line p. 250
product mix p. 250
protocol p. 253
screening and evaluation p. 260
services p. 248
shopping products p. 249
specialty products p. 249
unsought products p. 249

APPLYING MARKETING KNOWLEDGE

1 Products can be classified as either consumer or business products. How would you classify the following products? (*a*) Johnson's baby shampoo, (*b*) a Black & Decker two-speed drill, and (*c*) an arc welder.
2 Are Nature Valley granola bars and Eddie Bauer hiking boots convenience, shopping, specialty, or unsought products?
3 Based on your answer to question 2, how would the marketing actions differ for each product and the classification to which you assigned it?
4 In terms of the behavioral effect on consumers, how would a computer, such as an Apple iMac, be classified? In light of this classification, what actions would you suggest to the manufacturers of these products to increase their sales in the market?
5 What methods would you suggest to assess the potential commercial success for the following new products? (*a*) a new, improved ketchup; (*b*) a three-dimensional television system that took the company 10 years to develop; and (*c*) a new children's toy on which the company holds a patent.
6 Concept testing is an important step in the new-product process. Outline the concept tests for (*a*) an electrically powered car and (*b*) a new loan payment system for automobiles that is based on a variable interest rate. What are the differences in developing concept tests for products as opposed to services?

BUILDING YOUR MARKETING PLAN

In fine-tuning the product strategy for your marketing plan, do these two things:
1 Develop a simple three-column table in which (*a*) market segments of potential customers are in the first column and (*b*) the one or two key points of difference of the product to satisfy the segment's needs are in the second column.
2 In the third column of your table, write ideas for specific new products for your business in each of the rows in your table.

VIDEO CASE 10 X-1: Breaking the Barriers of Sound with New-Product Development

QR 10-5
X-1 Video
Case

X-1 started as a simple idea for a business school project and has quickly grown to become the foremost leader in waterproof, sweatproof, and weatherproof audio equipment for athletes. Many factors contribute to the success of X-1, "but new product development is the engine that drives it all," explains CEO Carl Thomas.

If you are a swimmer, runner, snowboarder, surfer, triathlete, climber, bicyclist, or any kind of sports enthusiast who enjoys music while you exercise, chances are you've seen X-1's products. The first product, a waterproof case for iPods, served as the starting point for a new-product development process that has added headphones, earbuds, cases, armbands, and accessories—an entire product line of audio solutions—to the company's offerings.

The commitment to new products has been so successful that the company now holds eight patents on its technology and was recognized by *Inc.* magazine as one of the top 500 fastest-growing companies in the United States. It is not surprising, then, to hear Thomas explain that marketing and new-product development "is a very key function for any company, but it's especially important for us."

THE COMPANY

X-1 has a fascinating history. Its founders were scuba divers who wanted to listen to music while they were diving, so they investigated how to use electronic devices and speakers underwater. The waterproof case they developed functioned to depths of 300 feet and led to a U.S. patent for a "waterproof enclosure for an audio device." At the same time, they were enrolled in a business school course that required the development of a business plan. They wrote the plan for their new technology, called their company Diver Entertainment, and began shipping products to other scuba divers.

It soon became obvious that the concept of waterproof audio equipment would appeal to many applications other than scuba diving. The company began developing waterproof headphones, changed its name to H2O Audio, and adopted the advertising tagline "Your Sport, Your Music." Swimmers, surfers, and triathletes were obvious potential customers, so Olympic swimmers Natalie Coughlin and Michael Phelps, professional surfer Laird Hamilton, and triathletes Greg and Laura Bennett were signed as official H2O Audio Ambassadors. The popularity of the brand grew rapidly as athletes in each of the sports learned about and tried the new products.

The success of H2O Audio products with aquatic athletes led the company to look for the next opportunity for growth. The obvious step was to expand to other sports and to attract athletes such as runners, kayakers, snowboarders, climbers, and weightlifters. In fact, H2O Audio soon came to realize that its market could be all athletes regardless of their sport.

The new strategy ran into an unexpected problem, however. While the H20 brand name was intuitive and descriptive and contributed to the initial success of the products, it also limited the perception of the products' uses to water sports. Applications to sports where the athletes were not actually underwater were not immediately obvious to retail store managers. Bicycle retailers and shoe stores, for example, would often decline to carry the products saying, "You're just a swim company," explains Thomas. As a result, H2O Audio undertook a six-month review of its brand.

The review process included interviews with athletes, retailers, manufacturers, and current customers. A branding agency was hired to help assess the information and to identify possible changes in the products and brand. It asked, "What characteristics are important to enable all athletes to train and perform at their peak with music?" The answer was to expand the original "waterproof" product concept to "waterproof, weatherproof, and sweatproof technology that is durable and comfortable."

According to Thomas, "We learned that every single one of the athletes out there needed the headphone to be not only durable and stable in whatever environment they were in, but they wanted it to be comfortable, they wanted it to fit, and they wanted it to not fall out." The process also identified a new brand name, X-1, which was inspired by the first aircraft to break the sound barrier—the Bell X-1. The new name led to a new advertising tag line—"Breaking the Barriers of Sound"—and immediately changed the perception of the products.

The X-1 product line was expanded to reflect the new, broader appeal to all athletes. The line included:

- *Momentum.* An in-ear ultralight headphone that is rinsable, weatherproof, and sweatproof.
- *Surge.* An in-ear headphone that is waterproof, weatherproof, and sweatproof and has bass amplified sound and sportwrap options.
- *Women's Momentum and Surge.* Headphones that are designed for petite ears.
- *Amphibx.* Armbands and cases that hold most audio devices including iPod Shuffle, iPod Touch, iPod Classic, and iPhone.
- *Interval.* A solution designed specifically for swimmers to attach to goggle straps.

All of the headphones are customizable with 3 to 5 different sizes of ear tips, and the cases all allow full function of touchscreens and buttons. The entire product line is the result of and reflects the importance of the product development process.

THE PRODUCT DEVELOPMENT PROCESS AT X-1

"Here at X-1, new-product development is essential. We are constantly monitoring and speaking with our retail buyers to make sure that we have the best product mix for the marketplace," explains Peter Dirksing, director of product development at X-1. Generally, the company follows a rigorous sequence of steps or stages.

X-1
POWERED BY H2O AUDIO
WATERPROOF
WEATHERPROOF
SWEATPROOF
SOUND.
12FT
WATERPROOF SWEATPROOF
SECURE FIT FOR ATHLETES
SEE THE PROOF
BREAKING THE BARRIERS OF SOUND AT X-1.COM

The first stage, new-product strategy development, reflects X-1's environmental scanning efforts. They observed that while the audio industry was mature, the advent of personal or mobile audio, created by products such as the Walkman, the Discman, the iPod, and now smartphones, represents an opportunity for new products.

The second stage is idea generation. X-1 uses many sources to help generate new ideas. Employees and coworkers, for example, can make suggestions at a "blue sky" meeting where, according to Dirksing, "No idea is a bad idea." The company also uses open innovation to generate new ideas by engaging retail buyers and soliciting ideas from a group of volunteer athletes called Team X-1.

The next stage, screening and evaluation, involves an evaluation of each idea to determine if it warrants further effort. X-1 assesses the feasibility of new technical requirements, synergy with existing technology, and the magnitude of resource requirements. All the factors "mix together to determine what is the greatest priority," explains Dirksing.

The fourth step, business analysis, involves creating a "business case" for the idea. The X-1 product development team works closely with sales and marketing to create a 12-month forecast that accounts for possible cannibalization of existing products and also estimates how long the product will be on the market before it reaches the break-even point.

In the development stage of the process, X-1 actually turns the idea into a prototype. The firm uses a 3D printer to check the aesthetics and the dimensions and to see how the product will actually fit on a person. Once the dimensions are determined, a functional prototype is needed. Dirksing explains, "After we've checked the outside dimensions on a 3D printed prototype, we'll actually send the final 3D drawings to a factory and get a functional prototype made."

The initial prototypes are used to conduct safety tests and the first functionality tests. "Part of my job is also making sure that the product functions as it's intended. So one of the really cool aspects of my job is that I'm taking prototypes out and hopping in the pool in the morning before work or getting in the water on my board and catching a wave or two before I get into the office just to make sure that these products we're developing are actually functioning in a real world environment," explains Dirksing.

Once production-quality prototypes are available, X-1 begins stage six, market testing. "We have a team of a few hundred amateur athletes that will get out and test the product and provide feedback," says Dirksing. X-1 also uses its website to connect with a cross-section of consumers and to get feedback as quickly as possible. Changes from this process lead to the final stage of the new-product development process, commercialization. X-1 develops a go-to-market plan, alerts the salesforce and retail buyers of the availability of new products, and begins production. Because X-1 is an international brand, this stage also includes developing the advertising and packaging for its customers in Europe, Asia, Australia, and around the world.

The new-product development process is an ongoing activity at X-1. At any given time the company may have 10 to 15 new-product ideas at various stages of the process. X-1's use of new technologies, such as 3D printers, as well as its fast-prototyping orientation has reduced product development time to about 12 months from start to commercialization. Once the new products are ready for consumers, the marketing department adds its expertise to ensure the success of the products.

MARKETING ADVANCED AUDIO SOLUTIONS

The marketing activities at X-1 are very comprehensive. "We do everything from print advertising, digital advertising, events, trade shows, social media, pretty much anything you can think of," says Dana Swanson, X-1 director of marketing. The many activities contribute to several different objectives, including changing the name of the company, rebranding the products, introducing new products, and communicating with different segments of consumers.

Changing the name from H2O Audio to X-1, for example, required marketing that helped get the product into people's hands so they could understand the value of the product. Swanson explains, "Something that is just going to splash our logo everywhere, like sponsoring a big race or an event, isn't as important to us as something like going to an event and having a booth where we can actually interact with people, talk about our product, and get our product into people's hands." This is also one of the reasons X-1 has product ambassadors. First, X-1 has contracts with selected professional and Olympic athletes who use X-1 products. Second, X-1 created a team of amateur athletes who receive product samples to use during amateur sporting events. In both cases, the ambassadors give X-1 products exposure to the marketplace and help demonstrate how they work.

X-1 also relies on social media, particularly to develop and introduce new products. "If it's out there, we've got a page, from Facebook to Twitter to Instagram," explains Swanson. "It's really all about just being where your people are and being there for them, interacting, talking, and answering questions," she goes on. Social media also allow X-1 to ask occasional questions about satisfaction with the products, color preferences, and even how the products are being used. Many of today's customers "love being involved," and their engagement is particularly helpful when X-1 introduces new products.

Communicating with different segments is also an important marketing objective. Currently, the three primary segments are:

- *Endurance Segment.* Includes athletes participating in all demanding athletic activities (e.g., marathons, triathalons, etc.) and training.
- *Outdoors Segment.* Includes all participants in activities that take place outside (e.g., hiking).
- *Club Segment.* Includes everyone who goes to a health club, fitness studio, or gymnasium.

One way X-1 ensures that it reaches these segments is through its sales channels. By offering its products through sporting goods stores (such as REI, Sports Chalet, and Eastern Mountain Sports), specialty retail stores, e-tailers (such as Amazon.com), and online through its own website, X-1 can reach the many potential consumers in each of the segments.

Public relations also helps provide a lot of exposure. X-1 is fortunate that it has many unique attributes such as reflective cables, customizable ear fit, ambient noise allowance, and special sizes for women to attract media interest. For example, *Fitness* magazine, *Women's Running* magazine, *MSN News, Fox News, The Wall Street Journal,* and *Travel Weekly* have all recently carried stories about X-1 products.

The combination of a great initial idea, a rigorous product development process, and excellent marketing actions all contribute to X-1's success. "I think X-1 products are successful because we actually are a solutions company," says Swanson, "We try to find a way that really works for athletes to bring their music with them while they're doing any activity."

Questions

1 What are the points of difference, or unique attributes, for X-1 products?

2 What are X-1's primary target markets?

3 Describe the new-product development process used at X-1. What are the similarities and differences to the process described in Figure 10–3?

4 Which of the eight reasons for new-product failure did X-1 avoid to ensure the success of X-1's products?

5 Identify one new-product idea you would suggest that X-1 evaluate.

11 Managing Successful Products, Services, and Brands

Learning Objectives

After reading this chapter you should be able to:

Explain the product life-cycle concept.

Identify ways that marketing executives manage a product's life cycle.

Recognize the importance of branding and alternative branding strategies.

Describe the role of packaging, labeling, and warranties in the marketing of a product.

Gatorade: Bringing Science to Sweat to Win from Within

Why is the thirst for Gatorade unquenchable? Look no further than constant product improvement and masterful brand development.

Like Kleenex in the tissue market, Jell-O among gelatin desserts, and Scotch for cellophane tape, Gatorade is synonymous with sports drinks. Concocted in 1965 at the University of Florida as a rehydration beverage for the school's football team, the drink was coined "Gatorade" by an opposing team's coach after watching his team lose to the Florida Gators in the Orange Bowl. The name stuck, and a new beverage product class was born. Stokely-Van Camp, Inc., bought the Gatorade formula in 1967 and commercialized the product.

Creating the Gatorade Brand

The Quaker Oats Company acquired Stokely-Van Camp in 1983 and quickly increased Gatorade sales through a variety of means. More flavors were added. Multiple package sizes were offered using different containers. Distribution expanded from convenience stores and supermarkets to mass merchandisers such as Walmart. Consistent advertising and promotion effectively conveyed the product's unique performance benefits and links to athletic competition. International opportunities were vigorously pursued.

Today, Gatorade is sold in more than 80 countries and is now a global brand. It is also the official sports drink of NASCAR, the National Football League, Major League Baseball, the National Basketball Association, the National Hockey League, Major League Soccer, and the Women's National Basketball Association.

Masterful brand management spurred Gatorade's success. Gatorade Frost was introduced in 1997 and aimed at expanding the brand's reach beyond organized sports to other usage occasions. Gatorade Fierce appeared in 1999. In the same year, Gatorade entered the bottled-water category with Propel Fitness Water, a lightly flavored water fortified with vitamins. The Gatorade Performance Series was introduced in 2001, featuring a Gatorade Energy Bar, Gatorade Energy Drink, and Gatorade Nutritional Shake.

Building the Gatorade Brand

Brand development accelerated after PepsiCo, Inc., purchased Quaker Oats and the Gatorade brand in 2001. Gatorade Xtremo, developed

I'VE BEEN YOUR BACKYARD GOALIE FOR 7 YEARS.
I'VE MADE THE SIDELINE MY SECOND HOME.
I'VE WINCED EVERY TIME YOU HEAD THE BALL.
I'VE WATCHED YOU LEARN FROM THE GAME.
I'LL DO WHATEVER IT TAKES TO HELP YOU
BECOME
UNLEASH POTENTIAL WITH CARBS TO REFUEL
AND ELECTROLYTES TO REHYDRATE, SO THEY
CAN GO LONGER. IT DOES WHAT WATER CAN'T.
G

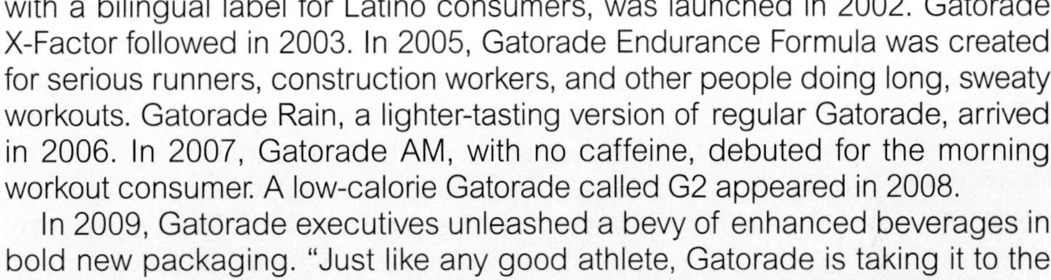

with a bilingual label for Latino consumers, was launched in 2002. Gatorade X-Factor followed in 2003. In 2005, Gatorade Endurance Formula was created for serious runners, construction workers, and other people doing long, sweaty workouts. Gatorade Rain, a lighter-tasting version of regular Gatorade, arrived in 2006. In 2007, Gatorade AM, with no caffeine, debuted for the morning workout consumer. A low-calorie Gatorade called G2 appeared in 2008.

In 2009, Gatorade executives unleashed a bevy of enhanced beverages in bold new packaging. "Just like any good athlete, Gatorade is taking it to the next level," said Gatorade's chief marketing officer. "Whether you're in it for the win, for the thrill or for better health, if your body is moving, Gatorade sees you as an athlete, and we're inviting you into the brand." According to a company announcement, "The new Gatorade attitude would be most visible through a total packaging redesign." For example, Gatorade Thirst Quencher now displays the letter G front and center along with the brand's iconic bolt. "For Gatorade, G represents the heart, hustle, and soul of athleticism and will become a badge of pride for anyone who sweats, no matter where they're active."

Gatorade's marketing performance is a direct result of continuous product improvement and masterful brand management as defined by the "Gatorade bath."

2
50
59

To differentiate the range of Gatorade offerings from the traditional Gatorade Thirst Quencher, newly enhanced beverages convey the attitude of a tough-love coach or personal trainer through in-your-face names on the label and nutrition benefits inside. For example, Gatorade Fierce is now Bring It and Gatorade X-Factor is now Be Tough. Continuing product development efforts guided the creation of the

G Series of products in 2010 and 2011 "that [go] beyond hydration to provide fuel, fluid, and nutrients before, during, and after the game." Gatorade Prime 01 was formulated to be consumed before a game. Gatorade Perform 02 was designed for consumption during a game. Gatorade Recover 03 was created for use after a game for rehydration and to promote muscle recovery. Starting in 2012, these products were supported with the "Win from Within" advertising campaign.[1]

QR 11-1
Gatorade Ad

The marketing of Gatorade illustrates continuous product development and masterful brand management in a dynamic marketplace. Not surprisingly, Gatorade remains a vibrant multibillion-dollar brand some 45 years after its creation. This chapter shows how the actions taken by Gatorade executives exemplify those made by successful marketers.

CHARTING THE PRODUCT LIFE CYCLE

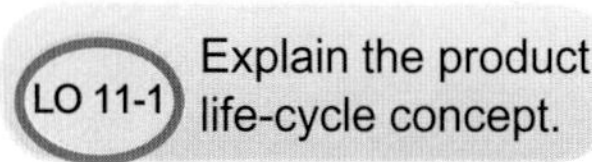

Products, like people, are viewed as having a life cycle. The concept of the **product life cycle** describes the stages a new product goes through in the marketplace: introduction, growth, maturity, and decline (Figure 11–1).[2] The two curves shown in this figure, total industry sales revenue and total industry profit, represent the sum of sales revenue and profit of all firms producing the product. The reasons for the changes in each curve and the marketing decisions involved are detailed next.

Introduction Stage

The introduction stage of the product life cycle occurs when a product is introduced to its intended target market. During this period, sales grow slowly, and profit is minimal. The lack of profit is often the result of large investment costs in product development, such as the millions of dollars spent by Gillette to develop the Gillette Fusion razor shaving system. The marketing objective for the company at this stage is to create consumer awareness and stimulate *trial*—the initial purchase of a product by a consumer.

The success of the Gillette Fusion shaving system can be understood using product life cycle concepts as discussed in the text.

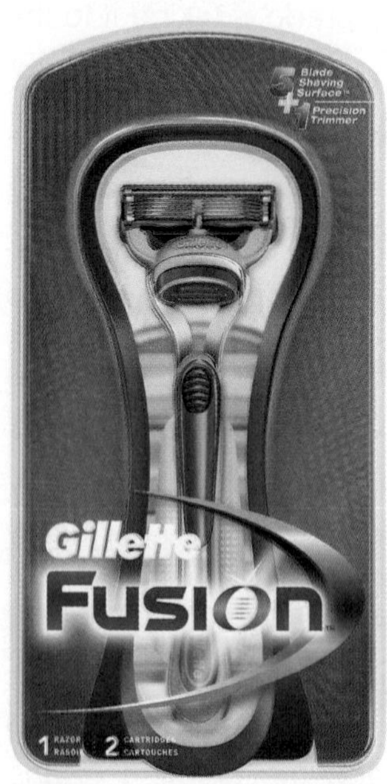

Companies often spend heavily on advertising and other promotion tools to build awareness and stimulate product trial among consumers in the introduction stage. For example, Gillette budgeted $200 million in advertising to introduce the Fusion shaving system to male shavers. The result? Over 60 percent of male shavers became aware of the new razor within six months and 26 percent tried the product.[3]

Advertising and promotion expenditures in the introduction stage are often made to stimulate *primary demand*, the desire for the product class rather than for a specific brand, since there are few competitors with the same product. As more competitors launch their own products and the product progresses along its life cycle, company attention is focused on creating *selective demand*, the preference for a specific brand.

Other marketing mix variables also are important at this stage. Gaining distribution can be a challenge because channel intermediaries may be hesitant to carry a new product. Also, a company often restricts the number of variations of the product to ensure control of product quality. As an example, the original Gatorade came in only one flavor—lemon-lime.

During introduction, pricing can be either high or low. A high initial price may be used as part of a *skimming* strategy to help the company recover the costs of development as well as capitalize on the price insensitivity of early buyers. A master of this strategy is 3M. According to a 3M manager, "We hit fast, price high, and get the heck out when the me-too products pour in."[4] High prices tend to attract competitors eager to enter the market because they see the opportunity for profit. To discourage competitive entry, a company can price low, referred to as *penetration pricing*. This pricing strategy helps build unit volume, but a company must closely monitor costs. These and other pricing techniques are covered in Chapter 14.

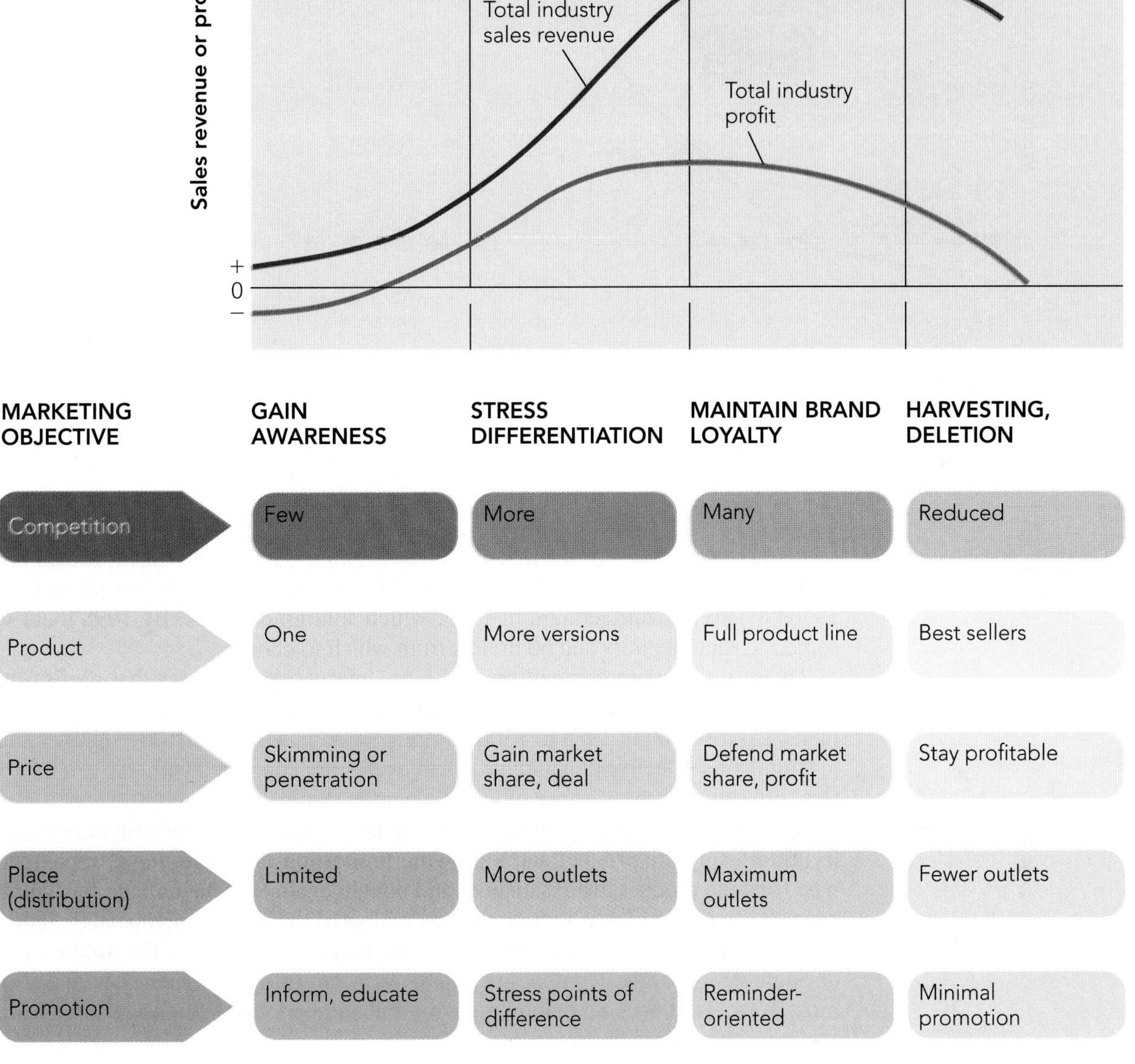

FIGURE 11–1
How stages of the product life cycle relate to a firm's marketing objectives and marketing mix actions.

Figure 11–2 on the next page charts the stand-alone fax machine product life cycle for business use in the United States from the early 1970s to 2014.[5] Sales grew slowly in the 1970s and early 1980s after Xerox pioneered the first portable fax machine. Fax machines were first sold direct to businesses by company salespeople and were premium priced. The average price for a fax machine in 1980 was a hefty $12,700, or almost $35,000 in today's dollars! Those fax machines were primitive by today's standards. They contained mechanical parts, not electronic circuitry, and offered few features seen in today's models.

Several product classes are in the introductory stage of the product life cycle today. These include smart TVs and all-electric-powered automobiles.

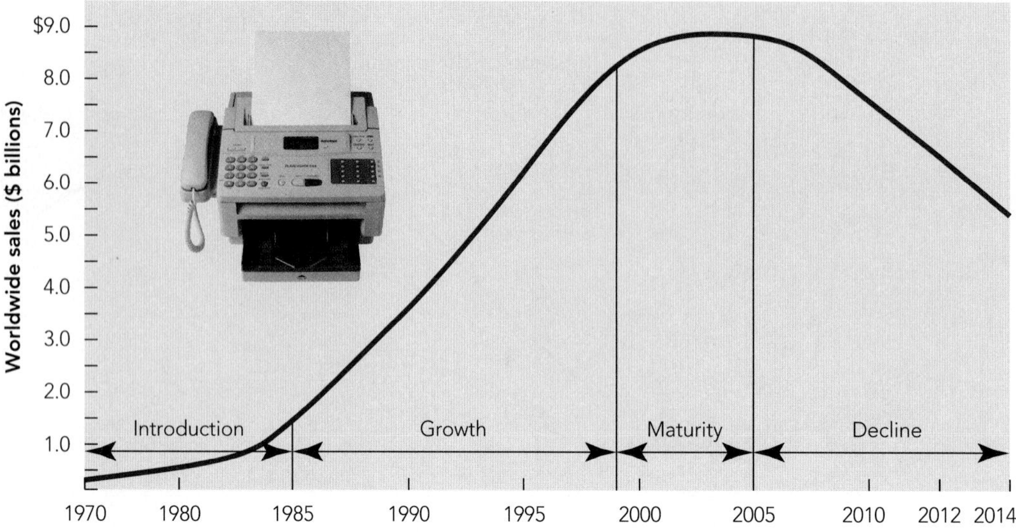

FIGURE 11–2
Product life cycle for the stand-alone fax machine for business use: 1970–2014. All four product life-cycle stages appear: introduction, growth, maturity, and decline.

Growth Stage

The growth stage of the product life cycle is characterized by rapid increases in sales. It is in this stage that competitors appear. For example, Figure 11–2 shows the dramatic increase in sales of fax machines from 1986 to 1998. The number of companies selling fax machines also increased, from one in the early 1970s to four in the late 1970s to seven manufacturers in 1983, which sold nine brands. By 1998 there were some 25 manufacturers and 60 brands from which to choose.

The result of more competitors and more aggressive pricing is that profit usually peaks during the growth stage. For instance, the average price for a fax machine plummeted from $3,300 in 1985 to $500 in 1995. At this stage, advertising shifts emphasis to stimulating selective demand; product benefits are compared with those of competitors' offerings for the purpose of gaining market share.

Product sales in the growth stage grow at an increasing rate because of new people trying or using the product and a growing proportion of *repeat purchasers*—people who tried the product, were satisfied, and bought again. For the Gillette Fusion razor, over 60 percent of men who tried the razor adopted the product permanently. For successful products, the ratio of repeat to trial purchases grows as the product moves through the life cycle. Durable fax machines meant that replacement purchases were rare. However, it became common for more than one machine to populate a business as the machine's use became more widespread.

Changes appear in the product in the growth stage. To help differentiate a company's brand from competitors, an improved version or new features are added to the original design, and product proliferation occurs. Changes in fax machines included (1) models with built-in telephones; (2) models that used plain, rather than thermal, paper for copies; and (3) models that integrated electronic mail.

In the growth stage, it is important to broaden distribution for the product. In the retail store, for example, this often means that competing companies fight for display and shelf space. Expanded distribution in the fax industry is an example. Early in the growth stage, just 11 percent of office machine dealers carried this equipment. By the mid-1990s, over 70 percent of these dealers sold fax equipment, and distribution was expanded to other stores selling electronic equipment, such as Best Buy and Office Depot.

Numerous product classes or industries are in the growth stage of the product life cycle today. Examples include smartphones, e-book readers, and other tablet devices such as the iPad.

Electric automobiles like the Chevrolet Spark made by General Motors are in the introductory stage of the product life cycle. By comparison, e-books such as Kindle offered by Amazon are in the growth stage of the product life cycle. Each product faces unique challenges based on its product life-cycle stage.

General Motors Company
www.gm.com

Amazon
www.amazon.com

Maturity Stage

The maturity stage is characterized by a slowing of total industry sales or product class revenue. Also, marginal competitors begin to leave the market. Most consumers who would buy the product are either repeat purchasers of the item or have tried and abandoned it. Sales increase at a decreasing rate in the maturity stage as fewer new buyers enter the market. Profit declines due to fierce price competition among many sellers, and the cost of gaining new buyers at this stage rises.

Marketing attention in the maturity stage is often directed toward holding market share through further product differentiation and finding new buyers. Fax machine manufacturers developed Internet-enabled multifunctional models with new features such as scanning, copying, and color reproduction. They also designed fax machines suitable for small and home businesses, which today represent a substantial portion of sales. Still, a major consideration in a company's strategy in this stage is to control overall marketing cost by improving promotional and distribution efficiency.

Fax machines entered the maturity stage in the late 1990s. At the time, about 90 percent of industry sales were captured by five producers (Hewlett-Packard, Brother, Sharp, Lexmark, and Samsung), reflecting the departure of marginal competitors. By 2004, 200 million stand-alone fax machines were installed throughout the world, sending more than 120 billion faxes annually.

Numerous product classes and industries are in the maturity stage of their product life cycle today. These include carbonated soft drinks and DVD players.

Decline Stage

The decline stage occurs when sales drop. Fax machines for business use moved to this stage in early 2005. By then, the average price for a fax machine had sunk below $100. Frequently, a product enters this stage not because of any wrong strategy on the part of companies, but because of environmental changes. For example, digital music players pushed compact discs into decline in the recorded music industry. Will Internet technology and e-mail make fax machines extinct any time soon? The Marketing Matters box on the next page offers one perspective on this question that may surprise you.[6]

Numerous product classes or industries are in the decline stage of their product life cycle. Two prominent examples include analog TVs and desktop personal computers.

Products in the decline stage tend to consume a disproportionate share of management and financial resources relative to their future worth. A company will follow one of two strategies to handle a declining product: deletion or harvesting.

Deletion Product *deletion*, or dropping the product from the company's product line, is the most drastic strategy. Because a residual core of consumers still consume or

Marketing Matters

customer value

Will E-mail Spell Extinction for Fax Machines?

Technological substitution that creates value for customers often causes the decline stage in the product life cycle. Will e-mail replace fax machines?

This question has been debated for years. Even though e-mail continues to grow with broadening Internet access, millions of fax machines are still sold each year. Industry analysts estimated that the number of e-mail mailboxes worldwide would be 3.3 billion in 2012 and will increase to 4.3 billion in 2016. However, the phenomenal popularity of e-mail has not brought fax machines to extinction. Why? The two technologies do not directly compete for the same messaging applications.

E-mail is used for text messages, and faxing is predominately used for communicating formatted documents by business users. Fax usage is expected to increase through 2014, even though unit sales of fax machines have declined on a worldwide basis. Internet technology and e-mail may eventually replace facsimile technology and paper and make fax machines extinct, but not in the immediate future.

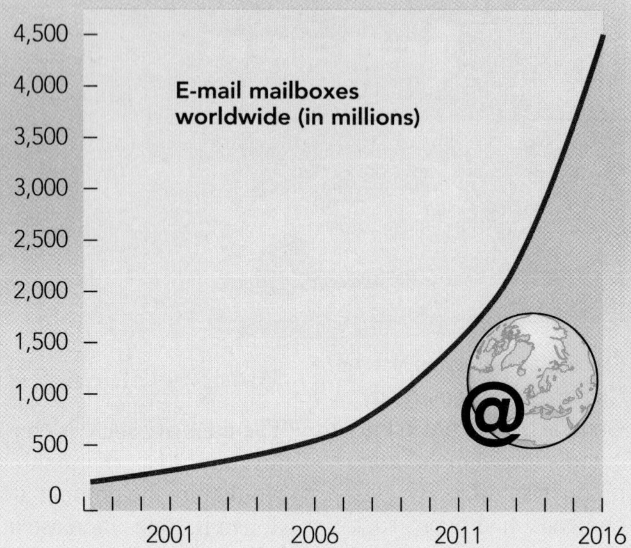

use a product even in the decline stage, product elimination decisions are not taken lightly. For example, Sanford Corporation continues to sell its Liquid Paper correction fluid for use with typewriters in the era of word-processing equipment.

Harvesting A second strategy, *harvesting*, is when a company retains the product but reduces marketing costs. The product continues to be offered, but salespeople do not allocate time in selling nor are advertising dollars spent. The purpose of harvesting is to maintain the ability to meet customer requests. Coca-Cola, for instance, still sells Tab, its first diet cola, to a small group of die-hard fans. According to Coke's CEO, "It shows you care. We want to make sure those who want Tab, get Tab."[7]

Four Aspects of the Product Life Cycle

Some important aspects of product life cycles are (1) their length, (2) the shape of their sales curves, (3) how they vary with different levels of products, and (4) the rate at which consumers adopt products.

Length of the Product Life Cycle There is no set time that it takes a product to move through its life cycle. As a rule, consumer products have shorter life cycles than business products. For example, many new consumer food products such as Frito-Lay's Baked Lay's potato chips move from the introduction stage to maturity in 18 months. The availability of mass communication vehicles informs consumers quickly and shortens life cycles. Also, technological change tends to shorten product life cycles as new-product innovation replaces existing products.

Shape of the Product Life Cycle The product life-cycle sales curve shown in Figure 11–1 is the *generalized life cycle*, but not all products have the same shape to their curve. In fact, there are several life-cycle curves, each type suggesting different marketing strategies. Figure 11–3 shows the shape of life-cycle sales curves for four different types of products: high-learning, low-learning, fashion, and fad products.

FIGURE 11–3
Alternative product life-cycle curves based on product types. Note the long introduction stage for a high-learning product compared with a low-learning product. Read the text for an explanation of the different product life-cycle curves.

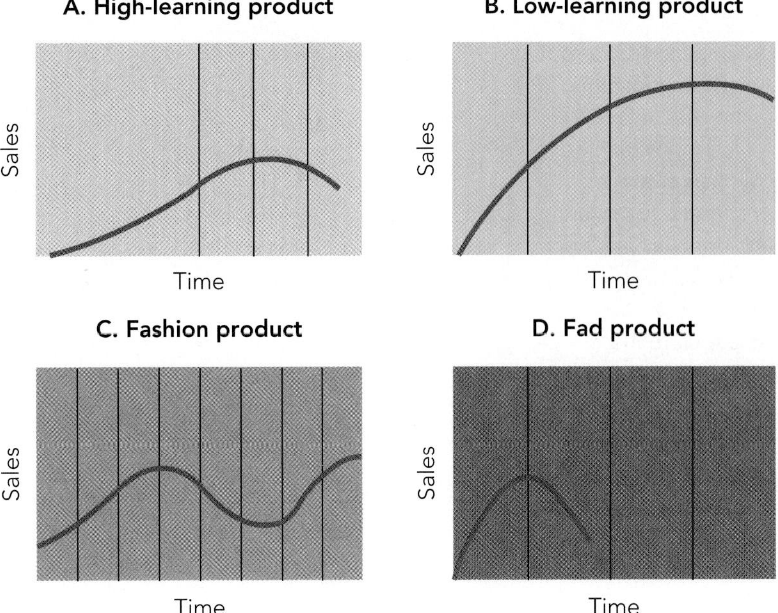

A *high-learning product* is one for which significant customer education is required and there is an extended introductory period (Figure 11–3A). It may surprise you, but personal computers had this life-cycle curve. Consumers in the 1980s had to learn the benefits of owning the product or be educated in a new way of performing familiar tasks. Convection ovens for home use required consumers to learn a new way of cooking and alter familiar recipes used with conventional ovens. As a result, these ovens spent years in the introductory period.

In contrast, sales for a *low-learning product* begin immediately because little learning is required by the consumer and the benefits of purchase are readily understood (Figure 11–3B). This product often can be easily imitated by competitors, so the marketing strategy is to broaden distribution quickly. In this way, as competitors rapidly enter, most retail outlets already have the innovator's product. It is also important to have the manufacturing capacity to meet demand. A successful low-learning product is Gillette's Fusion razor. This product achieved $1 billion in worldwide sales in less than three years.

A *fashion product* (Figure 11–3C) is a style of the times. Life cycles for fashion products frequently appear in women's and men's apparel. Fashion products are introduced, decline, and then seem to return. The length of the cycles may be months, years, or decades. Consider women's hosiery. Product sales have been declining for years. Women consider it more fashionable to not wear hosiery—bad news for Hanes brands, the leading marketer of women's sheer hosiery. According to an authority on fashion, "Companies might as well let the fashion cycle take its course and wait for the inevitable return of pantyhose."[8]

A *fad product* experiences rapid sales on introduction and then an equally rapid decline (Figure 11–3D). These products are typically novelties and have a short life cycle. They include car tattoos, sold in southern California and described as the first removable and reusable graphics for automobiles, and vinyl dresses and fleece bikinis made by a Minnesota clothing company.

The Product Level: Class and Form The product life cycle shown in Figure 11–1 is a total industry or generalized product class sales curve. Yet, in managing a product it is often important to distinguish among the multiple life cycles (class and form) that may exist.

FIGURE 11–4
Prerecorded music product life cycles by product form illustrate the effect of technological innovation on sales. Compact discs replaced cassette tapes, and digital music downloads will replace compact discs around 2015 if industry forecasts are correct. Do you even remember the cassette tape?

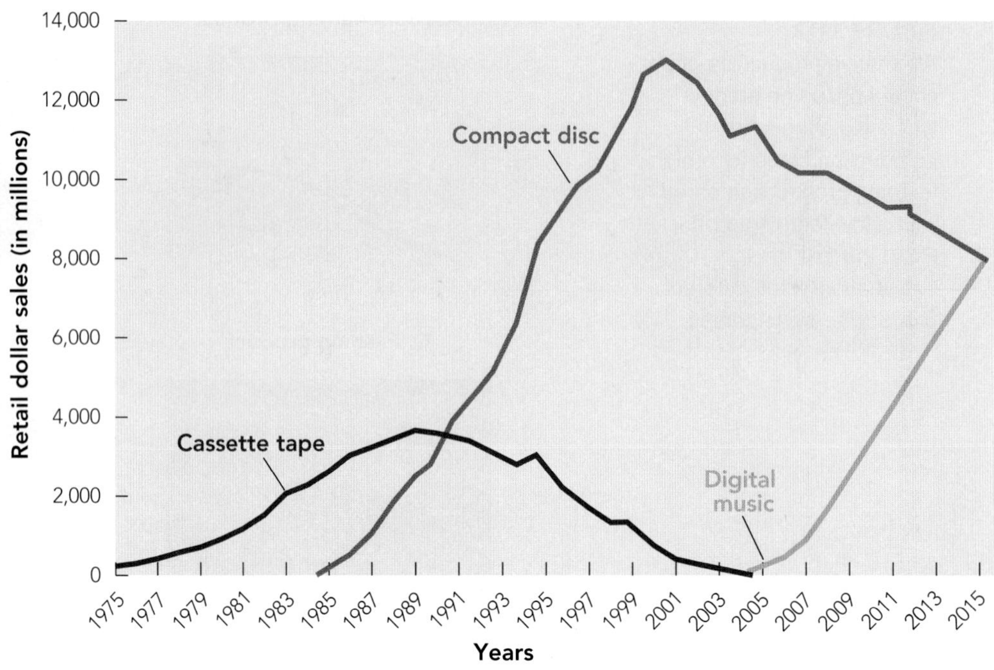

Product class refers to the entire product category or industry, such as prerecorded music. **Product form** pertains to variations within the product class. For prerecorded music, product form exists in the technology used to provide the music such as cassette tapes, compact discs, and digital music. Figure 11–4 shows the life cycles for these three product forms and the impact of technological innovation on sales.[9]

The Life Cycle and Consumers The life cycle of a product depends on sales to consumers. Not all consumers rush to buy a product in the introductory stage, and the shapes of the life-cycle curves indicate that most sales occur after the product has been on the market for some time. In essence, a product diffuses, or spreads, through the population, a concept called the *diffusion of innovation*.[10]

Some people are attracted to a product early. Others buy it only after they see their friends or opinion leaders with the item. Figure 11–5 shows the consumer population divided into five categories of product adopters based on when they adopt a new product. Brief profiles accompany each category. For any product to be successful, it must be purchased by innovators and early adopters. This is why manufacturers of new pharmaceuticals try to gain adoption by respected hospitals, clinics, and physicians. Once accepted by innovators and early adopters, successful new products move on to the early majority, late majority, and laggard categories.

Several factors affect whether a consumer will adopt a new product or not. Common reasons for resisting a product in the introduction stage are *usage barriers* (the product is not compatible with existing habits), *value barriers* (the product provides no incentive to change), *risk barriers* (physical, economic, or social), and *psychological barriers* (cultural differences or image).[11]

These factors help to explain the slow adoption of all-electric-powered automobiles in the United States. About one-third of one percent of cars sold in 2013 were all-electric-powered vehicles. Industry analysts cite the usage barrier for disappointing sales. They note that prospective buyers believe these cars are not compatible with existing driving habits. Analysts also mention a value barrier. Consumers have not recognized the superiority of all-electric cars over vehicles with internal combustion engines. Thirdly, a risk barrier exists in large measure to buyer uncertainty about the actual cost of all-electric-powered car ownership. According to one auto industry analyst, "The innovators and early adopters have purchased all-electric vehicles, but

FIGURE 11–5
Five categories and profiles of product adopters. For a product to be successful, it must be purchased by innovators and early adopters.

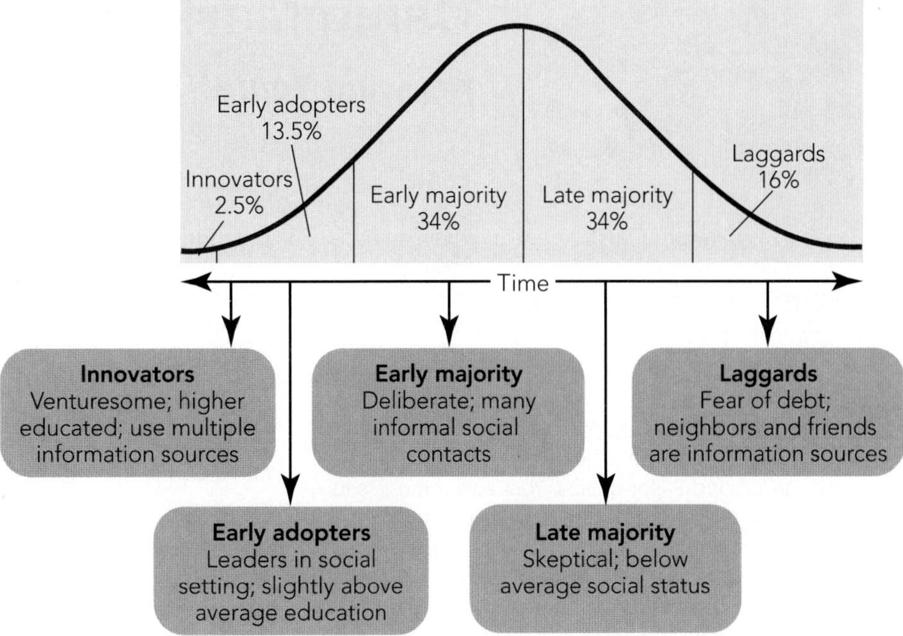

mainstream consumers have not followed." Not surprisingly, all-electric-powered automobiles remain in the introductory stage of the product life cycle.[12]

Companies attempt to overcome these barriers in numerous ways. For example, manufacturers of all-electric-powered automobiles provide low-cost leasing options to overcome usage, value, and risk barriers. Other companies provide warranties, money-back guarantees, extensive usage instructions, demonstrations, and free samples to stimulate initial trial of new products. For example, software developers offer demonstrations downloaded from the Internet. Cosmetics consumers can browse through the Cover Girl ColorMatch Custom Makeup Selector on its website to find out how certain makeup products will look. Free samples are one of the most popular means to gain consumer trial. In fact, 71 percent of consumers consider a sample to be the best way to evaluate a new product.[13]

learning review

11-1. Advertising plays a major role in the ______________ stage of the product life cycle, and ______________ plays a major role in maturity.

11-2. How do high-learning and low-learning products differ?

11-3. What are the five categories of product adopters in the diffusion of innovations?

MANAGING THE PRODUCT LIFE CYCLE

LO 11-2 Identify ways that marketing executives manage a product's life cycle.

An important task for a firm is to manage its products through the successive stages of their life cycles. This section describes the role of the product manager, who is usually responsible for this, and presents three ways to manage a product through its life cycle: modifying the product, modifying the market, and repositioning the product.

Role of a Product Manager

The product manager, sometimes called a *brand manager*, manages the marketing efforts for a close-knit family of products or brands. Introduced by Procter & Gamble in 1928, the product manager style of marketing organization is used by consumer

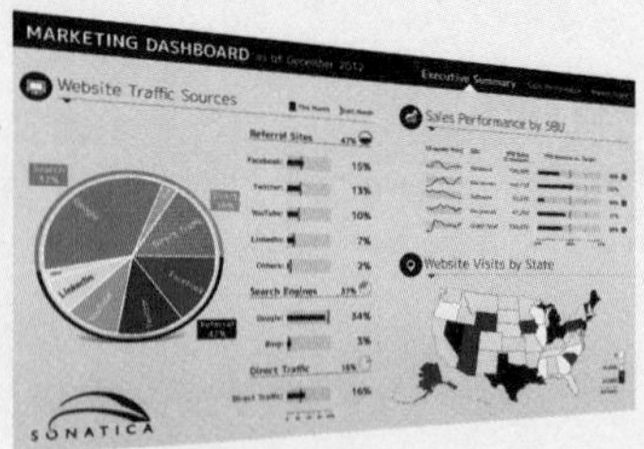

Using Marketing Dashboards

Knowing Your CDI and BDI

Where are sales for my product category and brand strongest and weakest? Data related to this question are displayed in a marketing dashboard using two indexes: (1) a category development index and (2) a brand development index.

Your Challenge You have joined the marketing team for Hawaiian Punch, the top fruit punch drink sold in the United States. The brand has been marketed to mothers with children under 13 years old. The majority of Hawaiian Punch sales are in gallon and 2-liter bottles. Your assignment is to examine the brand's performance and identify growth opportunities for the Hawaiian Punch brand among households that consume prepared fruit drinks (the product category).

Your marketing dashboard displays a category development index and a brand development index provided by a syndicated marketing research firm. Each index is based on the calculations below:

$$\text{Category Development Index (CDI)} = \frac{\text{Percent of a product category's total U.S. sales in a market segment}}{\text{Percent of the total U.S. population in a market segment}} \times 100$$

$$\text{Brand Development Index (BDI)} = \frac{\text{Percent of a brand's total U.S. sales in a market segment}}{\text{Percent of the total U.S. population in a market segment}} \times 100$$

A CDI over 100 indicates above-average product category purchases by a market segment. A number under 100 indicates below-average purchases. A BDI over 100 indicates a strong brand position in a segment; a number under 100 indicates a weak brand position.

You are interested in CDI and BDI displays for four household segments that consume prepared fruit drinks: (1) households without children; (2) households with children 6 years old or under; (3) households with children aged 7 to 12; and (4) households with children aged 13 to 18.

Your Findings The BDI and CDI metrics displayed below show that Hawaiian Punch is consumed by households with children, and particularly households with children under age 12. The Hawaiian Punch BDI is over 100 for both segments—not surprising since the brand is marketed to these segments. Households with children 13 to 18 years old evidence high fruit drink consumption with a CDI over 100. But Hawaiian Punch is relatively weak in this segment with a BDI under 100.

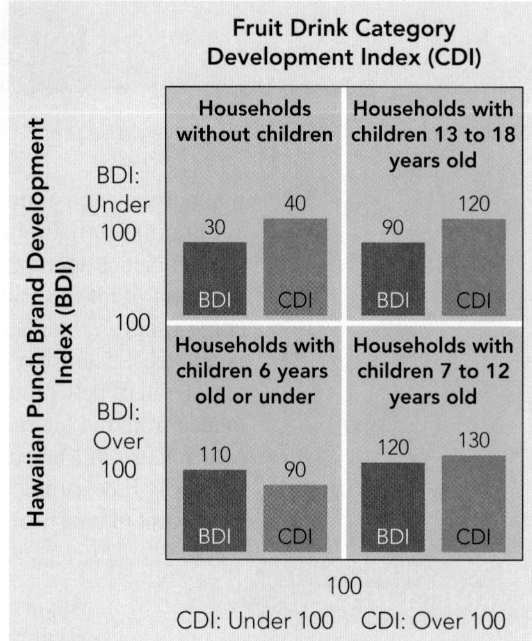

Your Action An opportunity for Hawaiian Punch exists among households with children 13 to 18 years old—teenagers. You might propose that Hawaiian Punch be repositioned for teens. In addition, you might recommend that Hawaiian Punch be packaged in single-serve cans or bottles to attract this segment, much like soft drinks. Teens might also be targeted for advertising and promotions.

goods firms, including General Mills and PepsiCo, and by industrial firms such as Intel and Hewlett-Packard.

All product managers are responsible for managing existing products through the stages of the life cycle. Some are also responsible for developing new products. Product managers' marketing responsibilities include developing and executing a marketing program for the product line described in an annual marketing plan and approving ad copy, media selection, and package design.

Product managers also engage in extensive data analysis related to their products and brands. Sales, market share, and profit trends are closely monitored. Managers often supplement these data with two measures: (1) a category development index

(CDI) and (2) a brand development index (BDI). These indexes help to identify strong and weak market segments (usually demographic or geographic segments) for specific consumer products and brands and provide direction for marketing efforts. The calculation, visual display, and interpretation of these two indexes for Hawaiian Punch are described in the Using Marketing Dashboards box on the facing page.

Harley-Davidson redesigned some of its motorcycle models to feature smaller hand grips, a lower seat, and an easier-to-pull clutch lever to create a more comfortable ride for women. According to Genevieve Schmitt, founding editor of WomenRidersNow.com, "They realize that women are an up-and-coming segment and that they need to accommodate them."

Harley-Davidson, Inc.
www.harley-davidson.com

Modifying the Product

Product modification involves altering one or more of a product's characteristics, such as its quality, performance, or appearance, to increase the product's value to customers and increase sales. Wrinkle-free and stain-resistant clothing made possible by nanotechnology revolutionized the men's and women's apparel business and stimulated industry sales of casual pants, shirts, and blouses. A common approach to product modification to increase a product's value to consumers is called *product bundling*—the sale of two or more separate products in one package. For example, Microsoft Office is sold as a bundle of computer software, including Word, Excel, and PowerPoint.

New features, packages, or scents can be used to change a product's characteristics and give the sense of a revised product. Procter & Gamble revamped Pantene shampoo and conditioner with a new vitamin formula and relaunched the brand with a multimillion-dollar advertising and promotion campaign. The result? Pantene, a brand first introduced in the 1940s, is now the top-selling shampoo and conditioner in the United States in an industry with more than 1,000 competitors.

Modifying the Market

With **market modification** strategies, a company tries to find new customers, increase a product's use among existing customers, or create new use situations.

Finding New Customers As part of its market modification strategy, LEGO is offering a new line of products to attract consumers outside of its traditional market. Known for its popular line of construction toys for young boys, LEGO has recently introduced a product line for young girls called LEGO Friends. Harley-Davidson has tailored a marketing program to encourage women to take up biking, thus doubling the number of potential customers for its motorcycles.

Increasing a Product's Use Promoting more frequent usage has been a strategy of Campbell Soup Company. Because soup consumption rises in the winter and declines during the summer, the company now advertises more heavily in warm months to encourage consumers to think of soup as more than a cold-weather food. Similarly, the Florida Orange Growers Association advocates drinking orange juice throughout the day rather than for breakfast only.

QR 11-2
Dockers Ad

Creating a New Use Situation Finding new uses for an existing product has been the strategy behind Dockers, the U.S. market leader in casual pants. Originally intended as a single pant for every situation, Dockers now promotes different looks for different usage situations: work, weekend, dress, and golf.[14]

Repositioning the Product

Often a company decides to reposition its product or product line in an attempt to bolster sales. *Product repositioning* changes the place a product occupies in a consumer's mind relative to competitive products. A firm can reposition a product by changing one or more of the four marketing mix elements. Four factors that trigger the need for a repositioning action are discussed next.

Reacting to a Competitor's Position One reason to reposition a product is because a competitor's entrenched position is adversely affecting sales and market share. New Balance, Inc., successfully repositioned its athletic shoes to focus on fit, durability, and comfort rather than competing head-on against Nike and Adidas on fashion and professional sports. The company offers an expansive range of shoes and networks with podiatrists, not sports celebrities.[15]

Reaching a New Market When Unilever introduced iced tea in Britain, sales were disappointing. British consumers viewed it as leftover hot tea, not suitable for drinking. The company made its tea carbonated and repositioned it as a cold soft drink to compete as a carbonated beverage and sales improved. Johnson & Johnson effectively repositioned its St. Joseph aspirin from a product for infants to an adult low-strength aspirin to reduce the risk of heart problems or strokes.[16]

Catching a Rising Trend Changing consumer trends can also lead to product repositioning. Growing consumer interest in foods that offer health and dietary benefits is an example. Many products have been repositioned to capitalize on this trend. Quaker Oats makes the FDA-approved claim that oatmeal, as part of a low-saturated-fat, low-cholesterol diet, may reduce the risk of heart disease. Calcium-enriched products, such as Kraft American cheese and Uncle Ben's Calcium Plus rice, emphasize healthy bone structure for children and adults. Weight-conscious consumers have embraced low-fat and low-calorie diets in growing numbers. Today, most food and beverage companies offer reduced-fat and low-calorie versions of their products.

Changing the Value Offered In repositioning a product, a company can decide to change the value it offers buyers and trade up or down. **Trading up** involves adding value to the product (or line) through additional features or higher-quality materials. Michelin, Bridgestone, and Goodyear have done this with a "run-flat" tire that can travel up to 50 miles at 55 miles per hour after suffering total air loss. Dog food manufacturers, such as Ralston Purina, also have traded up by offering super-premium foods based on "life-stage nutrition." Mass merchandisers, such as Target and Walmart, can trade up by adding a designer clothes section to their stores.

The Milk Processor Education Program (MilkPEP) promotes the replenishment and nutritional qualities of milk, in its advertising to capitalize on the growing consumer interest in foods that offer health and dietary benefits.

The Milk Processor Education Program
www.whymilk.com

Making Responsible Decisions

ethics

Consumer Economics of Downsizing—Get Less, Pay More

For more than 30 years, Starkist put 6.5 ounces of tuna into its regular-sized can. Today, Starkist puts 6.125 ounces of tuna into its can but charges the same price. Frito-Lay (Doritos and Lay's snack chips), PepsiCo (Tropicana orange juice), and Nestlé (Poland Spring and Calistoga bottled waters) have whittled away at package contents 5 to 10 percent while maintaining their products' package size, dimensions, and prices.

Procter & Gamble recently kept its retail price on its jumbo pack of Pampers and Luvs diapers, but reduced the number of diapers per pack from 140 to 132. Similarly, Unilever reduced the number of Popsicles in each package from 24 to 20 without changing the package price. Georgia-Pacific reduced the content of its Brawny paper towel six-roll pack by 20 percent without lowering the price.

Consumer advocates charge that downsizing the content of packages while maintaining prices is a subtle and unannounced way of taking advantage of consumer buying habits. They also say downsizing is a price increase in disguise and a deceptive, but legal, practice. Some manufacturers argue that this practice is a way of keeping prices from rising beyond psychological barriers for their products. Other manufacturers say prices are set by individual stores, not by them.

Is downsizing an unethical practice if manufacturers do not inform consumers that the package contents are less than they were previously?

Trading down involves reducing a product's number of features, quality, or price. For example, airlines have added more seats, thus reducing legroom, and limited meal service by only offering snacks on most domestic flights. Trading down also exists when companies engage in *downsizing*—reducing the package content without changing package size and maintaining or increasing the package price. Companies are criticized for this practice, as described in the Making Responsible Decisions box.[17]

learning review

11-4. How does a product manager help manage a product's life cycle?

11-5. What does "creating a new use situation" mean in managing a product's life cycle?

11-6. Explain the difference between trading up and trading down in product repositioning.

BRANDING AND BRAND MANAGEMENT

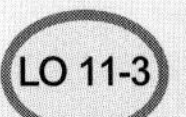
LO 11-3 Recognize the importance of branding and alternative branding strategies.

A basic decision in marketing products is **branding**, in which an organization uses a name, phrase, design, symbols, or combination of these to identify its products and distinguish them from those of competitors. A **brand name** is any word, device (design, sound, shape, or color), or combination of these used to distinguish a seller's products or services. Some brand names can be spoken, such as a Gatorade. Other brand names cannot be spoken, such as the white apple (the *logotype* or *logo*) that Apple puts on its machines and in its ads. A **trade name** is a commercial, legal

Can you describe brand personality traits for the successful Dr Pepper soft drink brand? Does the rock group KISS align with this brand personality? Read the text to learn what personality traits are often associated with the Dr Pepper brand.

Dr Pepper Snapple Group, Inc.
www.drpeppersnapplegroup.com

name under which a company does business. The Coca-Cola Company is the trade name of that firm.

A **trademark** identifies that a firm has legally registered its brand name or trade name so the firm has its exclusive use, thereby preventing others from using it. In the United States, trademarks are registered with the U.S. Patent and Trademark Office and protected under the *Lanham Act*. A well-known trademark can help a company advertise its offerings to customers and develop their brand loyalty.

Because a good trademark can help sell a product, *product counterfeiting*, which involves low-cost copies of popular brands not manufactured by the original producer, is a serious problem. Counterfeit products can steal sales from the original manufacturer or harm the company's reputation. U.S. companies lose about $250 billion each year to counterfeit products. The five most counterfeited branded products are, in order, handbags and wallets, watches and jewelry, clothing and accessories, consumer electronics, and shoes.[18] To counteract counterfeiting, the U.S. government passed the *Stop Counterfeiting in Manufactured Goods Act* (2006), which makes counterfeiters subject to 20-year prison sentences and $15 million in fines.

Consumers may benefit most from branding. Recognizing competing products by distinct trademarks allows them to be more efficient shoppers. Consumers can recognize and avoid products with which they are dissatisfied, while becoming loyal to other, more satisfying brands. As discussed in Chapter 5, brand loyalty often eases consumers' decision making by eliminating the need for an external search.

Brand Personality and Brand Equity

Product managers recognize that brands offer more than product identification and a means to distinguish their products from those of competitors.[19] Successful and established brands take on a **brand personality**, a set of human characteristics associated with a brand name. Research shows that consumers assign personality traits to products—traditional, romantic, rugged, sophisticated, rebellious—and choose brands that are consistent with their own or desired self-image. Marketers can and do imbue a brand with a personality through advertising that depicts a certain user or usage situation and conveys emotions or feelings to be associated with the brand. For example, personality traits linked with Coca-Cola are all-American and real; with Pepsi, young and exciting; and with Dr Pepper, nonconforming and unique. The traits often linked to Harley-Davidson are masculinity, defiance, and rugged individualism.

QR 11-3
Dr Pepper Ad

Brand name importance to a company has led to a concept called **brand equity**, the added value a brand name gives to a product beyond the functional benefits provided. This added value has two distinct advantages. First, brand equity provides a competitive advantage. The Sunkist brand implies quality fruit. The Disney name defines children's entertainment. A second advantage is that consumers are often willing to pay a higher price for a product with brand equity. Brand equity, in this instance, is represented by the premium a consumer will pay for one brand over another when the functional benefits provided are identical. Gillette razors and blades, Bose audio systems, Duracell batteries, and Louis Vuitton luggage all enjoy a price premium arising from brand equity.

Creating Brand Equity Brand equity doesn't just happen. It is carefully crafted and nurtured by marketing programs that forge strong, favorable, and unique customer associations and experiences with a brand. Brand equity resides in the minds of consumers and results from what they have learned, felt, seen, and heard about a brand over time. Marketers recognize that brand equity is not easily or quickly achieved. Rather, it arises from a sequential building process consisting of four steps (see Figure 11–6).[20]

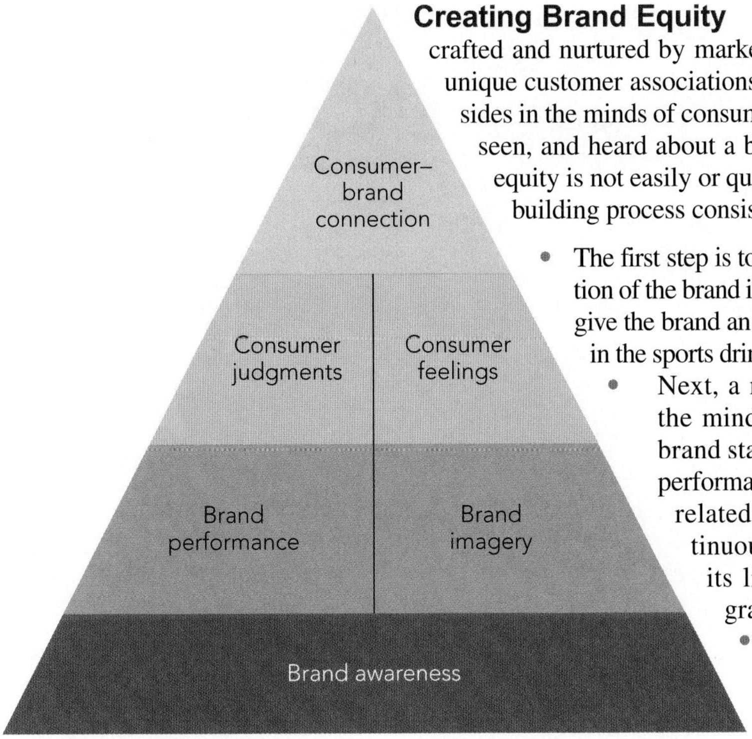

- The first step is to develop positive brand awareness and an association of the brand in consumers' minds with a product class or need to give the brand an identity. Gatorade and Kleenex have achieved this in the sports drink and facial tissue product classes, respectively.
- Next, a marketer must establish a brand's meaning in the minds of consumers. Meaning arises from what a brand stands for and has two dimensions—a functional, performance-related dimension and an abstract, imagery-related dimension. Nike has done this through continuous product development and improvement and its links to peak athletic performance in its integrated marketing communications program.
- The third step is to elicit the proper consumer responses to a brand's identity and meaning. Here attention is placed on how consumers think and feel about a brand. Thinking focuses on a brand's perceived quality, credibility, and superiority relative to other brands. Feeling relates to the consumer's emotional reaction to a brand. Michelin elicits both responses for its tires. Not only is Michelin thought of as a credible and superior-quality brand, but consumers also acknowledge a warm and secure feeling of safety, comfort, and self-assurance without worry or concern about the brand.
- The final, and most difficult, step is to create a consumer–brand connection evident in an intense, active loyalty relationship between consumers and the brand. A deep psychological bond characterizes a consumer–brand connection and the personal identification customers have with the brand. Brands that have achieved this status include Harley-Davidson, Apple, and eBay.

FIGURE 11–6
The customer-based brand equity pyramid shows the four-step building process that forges strong, favorable, and unique customer associations with a brand.

Valuing Brand Equity Brand equity also provides a financial advantage for the brand owner.[21] Successful, established brand names, such as Gillette, Nike, Gatorade, and Apple, have an economic value in the sense that they are intangible assets. The recognition that brands are assets is apparent in the decision to buy and sell brands. For example, Triarc Companies bought the Snapple brand from Quaker Oats for $300 million and sold it three years later to Cadbury Schweppes for $900 million. This example illustrates that brands, unlike physical assets that depreciate with time and use, can appreciate in value when effectively marketed. However, brands can lose value when they are not managed properly. Consider the purchase and sale of Lender's Bagels. Kellogg bought the brand for $466 million only to sell it to Aurora Foods for $275 million three years later following deteriorating sales and profits.

Financially lucrative brand licensing opportunities arise from brand equity.[22] **Brand licensing** is a contractual agreement whereby one company (licensor) allows its brand name(s) or trademark(s) to be used with products or services offered by another company (licensee) for a royalty or fee. For example, Playboy earns more than $62 million licensing its name and logo for merchandise. Disney makes billions of dollars each year licensing its characters for children's toys, apparel, and games. Licensing fees for Winnie the Pooh alone exceed $3 billion annually.

Successful brand licensing requires careful marketing analysis to ensure a proper fit between the licensor's brand and the licensee's products. World-renowned designer

Ralph Lauren has a long-term licensing agreement with Luxottica Group, S.p.A. of Milan for the design, production, and worldwide distribution of prescription frames and sunglasses under the Ralph Lauren brand. The agreement is an ideal fit for both companies. Ralph Lauren is a leader in the design, marketing, and distribution of premium lifestyle products. Luxottica is the global leader in the premium and luxury eyewear sector.

Luxottica Group, S.p.A.
www.luxottica.com

Ralph Lauren Corporation
www.ralphlauren.com

Ralph Lauren earns over $140 million each year by licensing his Ralph Lauren, Polo, and Chaps brands for dozens of products, including paint by Glidden, furniture by Henredon, footwear by Rockport, eyewear by Luxottica, and fragrances by L'Oreal.[23] Mistakes, such as Kleenex diapers, Bic perfume, and Domino's fruit-flavored bubble gum, are a few examples of poor matches and licensing failures.

Picking a Good Brand Name

We take brand names such as Red Bull, iPad, Android, and Axe for granted, but it is often a difficult and expensive process to pick a good name. Companies will spend between $25,000 and $100,000 to identify and test a new brand name. Six criteria are mentioned most often when selecting a good brand name.[24]

- *The name should suggest the product benefits.* For example, Accutron (watches), Easy Off (oven cleaner), Glass Plus (glass cleaner), Cling-Free (antistatic cloth for drying clothes), Chevrolet Spark (electric car), and Tidy Bowl (toilet bowl cleaner) all clearly describe the benefits of purchasing the product.
- *The name should be memorable, distinctive, and positive.* In the auto industry, when a competitor has a memorable name, others quickly imitate. When Ford named a car the Mustang, Pinto and Bronco soon followed. The Thunderbird name led to the Phoenix, Eagle, Sunbird, and Firebird from other car companies.
- *The name should fit the company or product image.* Sharp is a name that can apply to audio and video equipment. Bufferin, Excedrin, Anacin, and Nuprin are scientific-sounding names, good for analgesics. Eveready, Duracell, and DieHard suggest reliability and longevity—two qualities consumers want in a battery.
- *The name should have no legal or regulatory restrictions.* Legal restrictions produce trademark infringement suits, and regulatory restrictions arise through the improper use of words. For example, the U.S. Food and Drug Administration discourages the use of the word *heart* in food brand names. This restriction led to changing the name of Kellogg's Heartwise cereal to Fiberwise, and Clorox's Hidden Valley Ranch Take Heart Salad Dressing had to be modified to Hidden Valley Ranch Low-Fat Salad Dressing. Increasingly, brand names need a corresponding website address on the Internet. This further complicates name selection because about 250 million domain names are already registered globally.
- *The name should be simple* (such as Bold laundry detergent, Axe deodorant and body spray, and Bic pens) *and should be emotional* (such as Joy and Obsession perfumes and Caress soap, shower gel, and lotion).

Marketing inSite

So You Think You Have an Original Idea for a Brand or Trade Name? Better Check First!

More than a million brand names or trade names are registered with the U.S. Patent and Trademark Office. Thousands more are registered each year.

An important step in choosing a brand or trade name is to determine whether the name has been registered already. The U.S. Patent and Trademark Office (www.uspto.gov) offers a valuable service by allowing individuals and companies to quickly check to see if a name has been registered.

Do you have an idea for a brand or trade name for a new snack, software package, retail outlet, or service? Check to see if the name has been registered by clicking "Trademarks," then "Trademark Search." Enter your brand name to find out if someone has registered your chosen name(s). Or, for fun, put in your own last name to see if it has been trademarked!

- *The name should have favorable phonetic and semantic associations in other languages.* In the development of names for international use, having a nonmeaningful brand name has been considered a benefit. A name such as Exxon does not have any prior impressions or undesirable images among a diverse world population of different languages and cultures. The 7UP name is another matter. In Shanghai, China, the phrase means "death through drinking" in the local dialect. Sales have suffered as a result.

Do you have an idea for a brand name? If you do, check to see if the name (or your name) has been registered already with the U.S. Patent and Trademark Office by visiting its website. See the Marketing inSite box for details.

Branding Strategies

Companies can choose from among several different branding strategies, including multiproduct branding, multibranding, private branding, and mixed branding (see Figure 11–7).

FIGURE 11–7 Alternative branding strategies present both advantages and disadvantages to marketers. See the text for details.

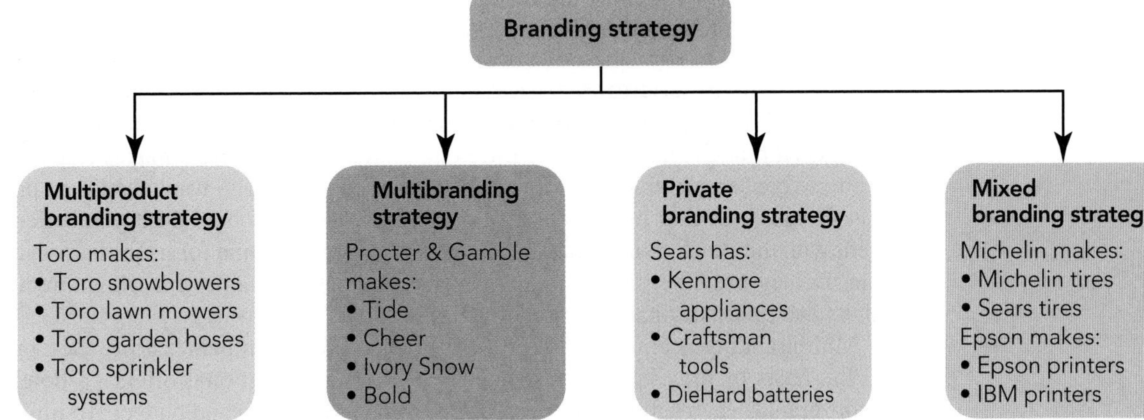

For how Kimberly-Clark has used a brand extension strategy to leverage its Huggies brand equity among mothers, see the text.

Kimberly-Clark Corporation
www.kimberly-clark.com

Multiproduct Branding Strategy With **multiproduct branding**, a company uses one name for all its products in a product class. This approach is sometimes called *family branding* or *corporate branding* when the company's trade name is used. For example, Microsoft, General Electric, Samsung, Gerber, and Sony engage in corporate branding—the company's trade name and brand name are identical. Church & Dwight uses the Arm & Hammer family brand name for all its products featuring baking soda as the primary ingredient.

There are several advantages to multiproduct branding. Capitalizing again on brand equity, consumers who have a good experience with the product will transfer this favorable attitude to other items in the product class with the same name. Therefore, this brand strategy makes possible *product line extensions*, the practice of using a current brand name to enter a new market segment in its product class.

Campbell Soup Company employs a multiproduct branding strategy with soup line extensions. It offers regular Campbell's soup, home-cooking style, and chunky varieties and more than 100 soup flavors. This strategy can result in lower advertising and promotion costs because the same name is used on all products, thus raising the level of brand awareness. A risk with line extension is that sales of an extension may come at the expense of other items in the company's product line. Line extensions work best when they provide incremental company revenue by taking sales away from competing brands or attracting new buyers.

Some multiproduct branding companies employ *subbranding*, which combines a corporate or family brand with a new brand, to distinguish a part of its product line from others. Gatorade successfully used subbranding with the introduction of Gatorade G2. Similarly, Porsche successfully markets its higher-end Porsche Carrera and its lower-end Porsche Boxster.

A strong brand equity also allows for *brand extension*: the practice of using a current brand name to enter a different product class. For instance, equity in the Huggies family brand name has allowed Kimberly-Clark to successfully extend its name to a full line of baby and toddler toiletries. This brand extension strategy generates $500 million in annual sales globally for the company. Honda's established name for motor vehicles has extended easily to snowblowers, lawn mowers, marine engines, and snowmobiles.

However, there is a risk with brand extensions. Too many uses for one brand name can dilute the meaning of a brand for consumers. Some marketing experts claim this has happened to the Arm & Hammer brand given its use for toothpaste, laundry detergent, gum, cat litter, air freshener, carpet deodorizer, and antiperspirant.[25]

A variation on brand extensions is the practice of *co-branding*: the pairing of two brand names of two manufacturers on a single product.[26] For example, Hershey Foods has teamed with General Mills to offer a co-branded breakfast cereal called Reese's Peanut Butter Puffs and with Nabisco to provide Chips Ahoy! cookies using Hershey's chocolate morsels. Co-branding benefits firms by allowing them to enter new product classes and capitalize on an already established brand name in that product class.

Multibranding Strategy Alternately, a company can engage in **multibranding**, which involves giving each product a distinct name. Multibranding is a useful strategy when each brand is intended for a different market segment. P&G makes Camay soap for those concerned with soft skin and Safeguard for those who want deodorant protection. Black & Decker markets its line of tools for the household do-it-yourselfer segment with the Black & Decker name but uses the DeWalt name for its professional tool line. Disney uses the Miramax and Touchstone Pictures names for films directed at adults and its Disney name for children's films.

Multibranding is applied in a variety of ways. Some companies array their brands on the basis of price-quality segments.[27] Marriott International offers 18 hotel and resort brands, each suited for a particular traveler experience and budget. To illustrate,

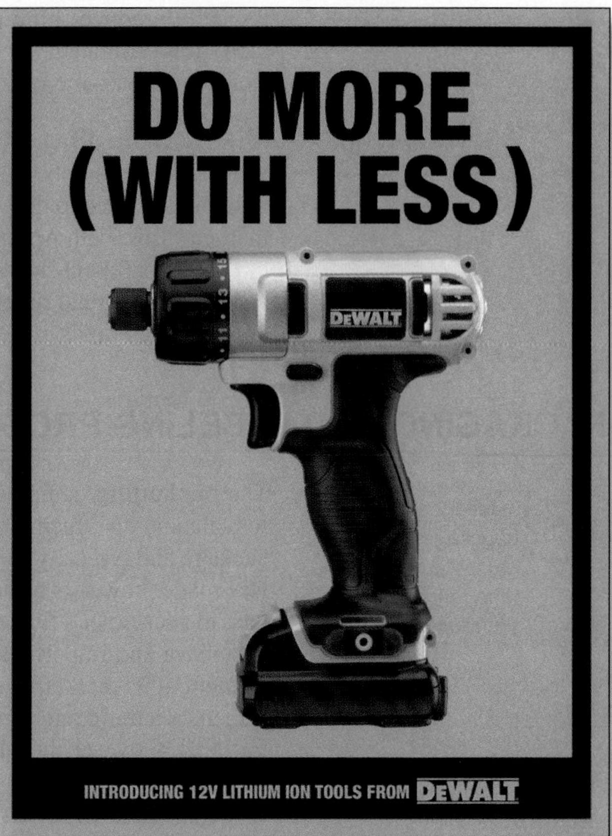

Black & Decker uses a multibranding strategy to reach different market segments. Black & Decker markets its tool line for the do-it-yourselfers with the Black & Decker name, but uses the DeWalt name for professionals.

Black & Decker
www.blackanddecker.com

Marriott EDITION hotels and Vacation Clubs offer luxury amenities at a premium price. Marriott and Renaissance hotels offer medium- to high-priced accommodations. Courtyard hotels and TownePlace Suites appeal to economy-minded travelers, whereas the Fairfield Inn is for those on a very low travel budget.

Other multibrand companies introduce new product brands as defensive moves to counteract competition. Called *fighting brands*, their chief purpose is to confront competitor brands.[28] For instance, Frito-Lay introduced Santitas brand tortilla chips to go head-to-head against regional tortilla chip brands that were biting into sales of its flagship Doritos and Tostitos brand tortilla chips. Ford launched its Fusion brand to halt the defection of Ford owners who were buying competitors' midsize cars. According to Ford's car group marketing manager, "Every year we're losing around 50,000 people from our products to competitors' midsize cars. We're losing Mustang, Focus, and Taurus owners. Fusion is our interceptor."[29]

Compared with the multiproduct strategy, advertising and promotion costs tend to be higher with multibranding. The company must generate awareness among consumers and retailers for each new brand name without the benefit of any previous impressions. The advantages of this strategy are that each brand is unique to each market segment and there is no risk that a product failure will affect other products in the line. Still, some large multibrand firms have found that the complexity and expense of implementing this strategy can outweigh the benefits. For example, Unilever recently pruned its brands from some 1,600 to 400 through product deletion and sales to other companies.[30]

Private Branding Strategy A company uses **private branding**, often called *private labeling* or *reseller branding*, when it manufactures products but sells them under the brand name of a wholesaler or retailer. Rayovac, Paragon Trade Brands, and ConAgra Foods are major suppliers of private-label alkaline batteries, diapers, and grocery products, respectively. RadioShack, Costco, Sears, Walmart, and Kroger are large retailers that have their own brand names. Private branding is popular because it typically produces high profits for manufacturers and resellers. Consumers also buy them. It is estimated that one of every five items purchased at U.S. supermarkets, drugstores, and mass merchandisers bears a private brand.[31]

Mixed Branding Strategy A fourth branding strategy is **mixed branding**, where a firm markets products under its own name(s) and that of a reseller because the segment attracted to the reseller is different from its own market. Beauty and fragrance marketer Elizabeth Arden is an example. The company sells its Elizabeth Arden brand through department stores, but its line of skin care products at Walmart is sold using the "skinsimple" brand name. Companies such as Del Monte, Whirlpool, and Dial produce private brands of pet foods, home appliances, and soap, respectively.

PACKAGING AND LABELING PRODUCTS

Describe the role of packaging, labeling, and warranties in the marketing of a product.

The **packaging** component of a product refers to any container in which it is offered for sale and on which label information is conveyed. A **label** is an integral part of the package and typically identifies the product or brand, who made it, where and when it was made, how it is to be used, and package contents and ingredients. To a great extent, the customer's first exposure to a product is the package and label, and both are an expensive and important part of marketing strategy. For Pez Candy, Inc., the central element of its marketing strategy is the character-head-on-a-stick plastic container that dispenses a miniature candy tablet. For more on how packaging creates customer value for Pez Candy, see the Marketing Matters box.[32]

Creating Customer Value and Competitive Advantage through Packaging and Labeling

Packaging and labeling cost U.S. companies about 15 cents of every dollar spent by consumers for products.[33] Despite their cost, packaging and labeling are essential because both provide important benefits for the manufacturer, retailer, and ultimate consumer. Packaging and labeling also can provide a competitive advantage.

Communication Benefits A major benefit of packaging is the label information it conveys to the consumer, such as directions on how, where, and when to use the product and the source and composition of the product, which is needed to satisfy legal requirements of product disclosure. For example, the labeling system for packaged and processed foods in the United States provides a uniform format for nutritional and dietary information. Many packaged foods contain informative recipes to promote usage of the product. Campbell Soup estimates that the green bean casserole recipe on its cream of mushroom soup can accounts for $20 million in soup sales each year![34] Other information consists of seals and symbols, either government-required or commercial seals of approval (such as the Good Housekeeping Seal).

For the functional benefits provided by Pringles' cylindrical packaging, see the text.

Functional Benefits Packaging often plays a functional role—providing storage, convenience, or protection or ensuring product quality. Stackable food containers are one example of how packaging can provide functional benefits. For example, beverage companies have developed lighter and easier ways to stack products on shelves and in refrigerators. Examples include Coca-Cola beverage packs designed to fit neatly onto refrigerator shelves and Ocean Spray Cranberries's rectangular juice bottles that allow 10 units per package versus 8 of its former round bottles.

The convenience dimension of packaging is increasingly important. Kraft Miracle Whip salad dressing, Heinz ketchup, and Skippy Squeez'It peanut butter are sold in squeeze bottles;

Marketing Matters

customer value

Creating Customer Value through Packaging—Pez Heads Dispense More Than Candy

Customer value can assume numerous forms. For Pez Candy, Inc. (www.pez.com), customer value manifests itself in some 450 Pez character candy dispensers. Each refillable dispenser ejects tasty candy tablets in a variety of flavors that delight preteens and teens alike in more than 60 countries.

Pez was formulated in 1927 by Austrian food mogul Edward Haas III and successfully sold in Europe as an adult breath mint. Pez, which comes from the German word for peppermint, *pfefferminz*, was originally packaged in a hygienic, headless plastic dispenser. Pez first appeared in the United States in 1953 with a headless dispenser, marketed to adults. After conducting extensive marketing research, Pez was repositioned with fruit flavors, repackaged with licensed character heads on top of the dispenser, and remarketed as a children's product in the mid-1950s. Since then, most top-level licensed characters and hundreds of other characters have become Pez heads. Consumers buy about 80 million Pez dispensers and 4.6 billion Pez tablets a year, and company sales growth exceeds that of the candy industry as a whole.

The unique Pez package dispenses a "use experience" for its customers beyond the candy itself, namely, fun. And fun translates into a 98 percent awareness level for Pez among teenagers and an 89 percent awareness level among mothers with children. Pez has not advertised its product for years. With that kind of awareness, who needs advertising?

microwave popcorn has been a major market success; and Chicken of the Sea tuna and Folgers coffee are packaged in single-serving portions. Nabisco offers portion-control package sizes for the convenience of weight-conscious consumers. It offers 100-calorie packs of Oreos, Cheese Nips, and other products in individual pouches.

Consumer protection is another important function of packaging, including the development of tamper-resistant containers. Today, companies commonly use safety seals or pop-tops that reveal previous opening. However, no package is truly tamper resistant. U.S. law now provides for maximum penalties of life imprisonment and $250,000 fines for package tampering. Consumer protection through labeling exists in "open dating," which states the expected shelf life of the product.

Functional features of packaging also can affect product quality. Pringles, with its cylindrical packaging, offers uniform chips, minimal breakage, and for some consumers, better value for the money than chips packaged in flex-bags.

Perceptual Benefits A third component of packaging and labeling is the perception created in the consumer's mind. Package and label shape, color, and graphics distinguish one brand from another, convey a brand's positioning, and build brand equity. According to the director of marketing for L'eggs hosiery, "Packaging is important to the positioning and equity of the L'eggs brand."[35] Why? Packaging and labeling have been shown to enhance brand recognition and facilitate the formation of strong, favorable, and unique brand associations.[36]

Successful marketers recognize that changes in packages and labels can update and uphold a brand's image in the customer's mind. Pepsi-Cola embarked on a packaging change to uphold its image among teens and young adults. Beginning in 2013, Pepsi-Cola introduced new package graphics that change every few weeks to reflect different themes, such as sports, music, fashion, and cars.[37]

Pepsi-Cola changes the graphics on its packages every few weeks to convey the brand's youthful positioning.

Because labels list a product's source, brands competing in the global marketplace can benefit from "country of origin or manufacture" perceptions as described in Chapter 7. Consumers tend to hold stereotypes about country-product pairings that they judge "best"—English tea, French perfume, Italian leather, and Japanese electronics—which can affect a brand's image. Increasingly, Chinese firms are adopting the English language and Roman letters for their brand labels sold in China. This is being done because of a common perception in many Asian countries that "things Western are good."[38]

Packaging and Labeling Challenges and Responses

Package and label designers face four challenges. They are (1) the continuing need to connect with customers; (2) environmental concerns; (3) health, safety, and security issues; and (4) cost reduction.

Connecting with Customers Packages and labels must be continually updated to connect with customers. The challenge lies in creating aesthetic and functional design features that attract customer attention and deliver customer value in their use. If done right, the rewards can be huge. For example, the marketing team responsible for Kleenex tissues converted its standard rectangular box into an oval shape with colorful seasonal graphics. Sales soared with this aesthetic change in packaging. After months of in-home research, Kraft product managers discovered that consumers often transferred Chips Ahoy! cookies to jars for easy access and to avoid staleness. The company solved both problems by creating a patented resealable opening on the top of the bag. The result? Sales of the new package doubled that of the old package with the addition of this functional feature.

Environmental Concerns Because of widespread global concern about the growth of solid waste and the shortage of viable landfill sites, the amount, composition, and disposal of packaging material continue to receive much attention. For example, PepsiCo, Coca-Cola, and Nestlé have decreased the amount of plastic in their beverage bottles to reduce solid waste.[39] Recycling packaging material is another major thrust. Procter & Gamble now uses recycled cardboard in over 70 percent of its paper packaging. Its Spic and Span liquid cleaner is packaged in 100 percent recycled material. Other firms, such as Walmart, are emphasizing the use of less packaging material. Since 2008, the company has been working with its 600,000 global suppliers to reduce overall packaging and shipping material by 5 percent by 2013.[40]

Health, Safety, and Security Issues A third challenge involves the growing health, safety, and security concerns of packaging materials. Today, most consumers believe companies should make sure products and their packages are safe and secure, regardless of the cost, and companies are responding in numerous ways. Most butane lighters sold today, like those made by Scripto, contain a child-resistant safety latch to prevent misuse and accidental fire. Childproof caps on pharmaceutical products and household cleaners and sealed lids on food packages are now common. New packaging technology and materials that extend a product's *shelf life* (the time a product can be stored) and prevent spoilage continue to be developed.

Cost Reduction About 80 percent of packaging material used in the world consists of paper, plastics, and glass. As the cost of these materials rises, companies are constantly challenged to find innovative ways to cut packaging costs while delivering value to their customers. As an example, Hewlett-Packard reduced the size and weight of its Photosmart product package and shipping container. Through design and material changes, packaging material costs fell by more than 50 percent. Shipping costs per unit dropped 41 percent.[41]

PRODUCT WARRANTY

A final component for product consideration is the **warranty**, which is a statement indicating the liability of the manufacturer for product deficiencies. There are various types of product warranties with different implications for manufacturers and customers.

Some companies, like Hyundai, offer *express warranties*, which are written statements of liabilities. In recent years, the FTC has required greater disclosure on express warranties to indicate whether the warranty is a limited-coverage or full-coverage alternative. A *limited-coverage warranty* specifically states the bounds of coverage and, more important, areas of noncoverage. A *full warranty* has no limits of noncoverage. The *Magnuson-Moss Warranty/FTC Improvement Act* (1975) regulates the content of consumer warranties and so has strengthened consumer rights with regard to warranties. Increasingly, manufacturers are being held to *implied warranties*, which assign responsibility for product deficiencies to the manufacturer. Studies show that the type of warranty can affect a consumer's product evaluation. Brands with limited warranties tend to receive less positive evaluations compared with full-warranty items.[42]

America's Best Warranty*

10-Year/100,000-Mile

Powertrain Limited Warranty

*Based on total package of warranty programs. See dealer for LIMITED WARRANTY details.

Hyundai has made a commitment to offer the best automobile warranty for buyers.

Hyundai Motor America
www.hyundaiusa.com

Warranties are also important in light of product liability claims. In the early part of the 20th century, the courts protected companies. The trend now is toward "strict liability" rulings, where a manufacturer is liable for any product defect, whether it followed reasonable research standards or not. This issue remains hotly contested between companies and consumer advocates.

Warranties represent much more than just protection from negative consequences for the buyer—they also offer a significant marketing advantage for the producer. Sears has built a strong reputation for its Craftsman tool line with a simple warranty: If you break a tool, it's replaced with no questions asked.

learning review

11-7. What are the six criteria mentioned most often when selecting a good brand name?

11-8. What are the three major benefits of packaging and labeling?

11-9. What is the difference between an express and an implied warranty?

LEARNING OBJECTIVES REVIEW

LO 11-1 *Explain the product life-cycle concept.*
The product life cycle describes the stages a new product goes through in the marketplace: introduction, growth, maturity, and decline. Product sales growth and profitability differ at each stage, and marketing managers have marketing objectives and marketing mix strategies unique to each stage based on consumer behavior and competitive factors. In the introductory stage, the need is to establish primary demand, whereas the growth stage requires selective demand strategies. In the maturity stage, the need is to maintain market share; the decline stage necessitates a deletion or harvesting strategy. Some important aspects of product life cycles are (*a*) their length, (*b*) the shape of the sales curve, (*c*) how they vary by product classes and forms, and (*d*) the rate at which consumers adopt products.

LO 11-2 *Identify ways that marketing executives manage a product's life cycle.*
Marketing executives can manage a product's life cycle three ways. First, they can modify the product itself by altering its characteristics, such as product quality, performance, or appearance. Second, they can modify the market by finding new customers for the product, increasing a product's use among existing customers, or creating new use situations for the product. Finally, they can reposition the product using any one or a combination of marketing mix elements. Four factors trigger a repositioning action. They include reacting to a competitor's position, reaching a new market, catching a rising trend, and changing the value offered to consumers.

LO 11-3 *Recognize the importance of branding and alternative branding strategies.*
A basic decision in marketing products is branding, in which an organization uses a name, phrase, design, symbols, or a combination of these to identify its products and distinguish them from those of its competitors. Product managers recognize that brands offer more than product identification and a means to distinguish their products from those of competitors. Successful and established brands take on a brand personality and acquire brand equity—the added value a given brand name gives to a product beyond the functional benefits provided—that is crafted and nurtured by marketing programs that forge strong, favorable, and unique consumer associations with a brand. A good brand name should suggest the product benefits, be memorable, fit the company or product image, be free of legal restrictions, be simple and emotional, and have favorable phonetic and semantic associations in other languages. Companies can and do employ several different branding strategies. With multiproduct branding, a company uses one name for all its products in a product class. A multibranding strategy involves giving each product a distinct name. A company uses private branding when it manufactures products but sells them under the brand name of a wholesaler or retailer. Finally, a company can employ mixed branding, where it markets products under its own name(s) and that of a reseller.

LO 11-4 *Describe the role of packaging, labeling, and warranties in the marketing of a product.*
Packaging, labeling, and warranties play numerous roles in the marketing of a product. The packaging component of a product refers to any container in which it is offered for sale and on which label information is conveyed. Manufacturers, retailers, and consumers acknowledge that packaging and labeling provide communication, functional, and perceptual benefits. Contemporary packaging and labeling challenges include (*a*) the continuing need to connect with customers, (*b*) environmental concerns, (*c*) health, safety, and security issues, and (*d*) cost reduction. Warranties indicate the liability of the manufacturer for product deficiencies and are an important element of product and brand management.

FOCUSING ON KEY TERMS

brand equity p. 284
brand licensing p. 285
brand name p. 283
brand personality p. 284
branding p. 283
label p. 290
market modification p. 281
mixed branding p. 290
multibranding p. 288
multiproduct branding p. 288
packaging p. 290
private branding p. 289
product class p. 278
product form p. 278
product life cycle p. 272
product modification p. 281
trade name p. 283
trademark p. 284
trading down p. 283
trading up p. 282
warranty p. 293

APPLYING MARKETING KNOWLEDGE

1 Listed here are three different products in various stages of the product life cycle. What marketing strategies would you suggest to these companies? (*a*) Canon digital cameras—growth stage, (*b*) Hewlett-Packard tablet computers—introductory stage, and (*c*) handheld manual can openers—decline stage.

2 It has often been suggested that products are intentionally made to break down or wear out. Is this strategy a planned product modification approach?

3 The product manager of GE is reviewing the penetration of trash compactors in American homes. After more than two decades in existence, this product is in relatively few homes. What problems can account for this poor acceptance? What is the shape of the trash compactor life cycle?

4 For years, Ferrari has been known as a manufacturer of expensive luxury automobiles. The company plans to attract the major segment of the car-buying market that purchases medium-priced automobiles. As Ferrari considers this trading-down strategy, what branding strategy would you recommend? What are the trade-offs to consider with your strategy?

5 The nature of product warranties has changed as the federal court system reassesses the meaning of warranties. How does the regulatory trend toward warranties affect product development?

BUILDING YOUR MARKETING PLAN

For the product offering in your marketing plan,

1 Identify (*a*) its stage in the product life cycle and (*b*) key marketing mix actions that might be appropriate, as shown in Figure 11–1.

2 Develop (*a*) branding and (*b*) packaging strategies, if appropriate for your offering.

VIDEO CASE 11 P&G's Secret Deodorant: Finding Inspiration in Perspiration

QR 11-4
Secret Video Case

How do you revitalize a 50-plus-year-old brand? By focusing the brand's marketing efforts on its core purpose—a purpose that is both benefit-driven and inspirational—and using that purpose to build essential one-to-one personal connections with consumers.

Procter & Gamble's (P&G's) Secret brand, launched in 1956, has dominated the women's antiperspirant deodorant category for many years. Secret maintains its leadership position as one of many products in what is typically considered a low-involvement product category. Underarm deodorant isn't traditionally the type of product consumers think about engaging with in an ongoing, meaningful way. However, Secret has demonstrated that delivering the product benefit is important to establish trust and build engagement. This type of engagement often results in amplifying the brand's marketing investment, or paid media. Since 2009, Secret's purpose has been at the center of its marketing efforts, resulting in tremendous growth and brand advocacy among consumers.

PRODUCT BACKGROUND

Secret was the first deodorant marketed exclusively to women. In the 1960s and 1970s, Secret's growth was supported by a recurring series of ads featuring a husband and wife dealing with issues of the day, such as having children and returning to work afterward. "It was all about empowering women to make the right choices for themselves and to embrace those choices fearlessly," according to Kevin Hochman, marketing director for skin and personal care at P&G North America at the time.

However, in 2004–2005, brand executives felt the theme was getting dated, so Secret backed off from that positioning. "We walked away," Hochman says. "We thought, women are empowered, and maybe this isn't so relevant. That was a mistake. Of course the idea was still relevant; we just hadn't modernized it in a contemporary way." Secret made a deliberate decision to go back to its roots.

THE ROAD TO PURPOSE

Secret started to experience slower growth in 2008 due to a down economy. The launch of a super-premium line of antiperspirant, Secret Clinical Strength, helped increase sales and market share, but competitors soon followed suit with similar products. Meanwhile, top P&G management began infusing the idea of purpose-driven marketing throughout the organization. The companywide vision focused on building brands through lifelong, one-to-one personal connections that ultimately build relationships and fulfill the company's purpose to "touch and improve more lives of more consumers more completely." With this in mind, Secret brand management realized it needed to get clear on defining who Secret was, why Secret existed, and what Secret's purpose was. The brand needed a reason for its consumers to care and wanted to give them a reason to share.

Through the leadership and efforts of its senior brand management and partner agencies, including MEplusYOU (formerly imc[2]), Leo Burnett Co., SMG, Marina Maher Communications, and consultancy group BrightHouse, the Secret brand team began to establish the brand's purpose and convey it across all marketing touch points in ways that resonated with target consumers' core values and beliefs. "It becomes about more than selling deodorant, or promoting functional benefits, and more about rallying around something higher-order," says Hochman.

The Secret team started by defining the brand's core beliefs: "We believe in the equality of the genders and that all people should be able to pursue their goals without fear. We believe that by acting courageously, supporting others, empathizing with their challenges and finding innovative solutions, we can help women be more fearless." Armed with Secret's core belief, the team developed a purpose statement that is grounded in the product benefit and allowed for fearlessness when you're not sweating: "Helping women of all ages to be more fearless."

"Just a few years ago, the majority of marketers' activities and expenditures occurred across unidirectional media channels that could only talk *at* consumers. This limited the role marketing could play in developing relationships between brands and people," says Ian Wolfman, principal and chief marketing officer of MEplusYOU. "Today, new media, in combination with mature media, allows marketers to play a more sophisticated role in facilitating deep, trusting relationships between brands and people as we simultaneously drive strong transactional activity. Brands like Secret realize that taking a stand on values it shares with consumers is the key to translating a brand's purpose into meaningful relationships and profit."

The brand carefully constructed an ecosystem of tactical marketing "ignitions." Each of these ignitions focused on sparking the interest of like-minded consumers and were designed to flex and surge with the needs of the brand. The brand's purpose served as the basis for each ignition in order to engage consumers across all channels (online and offline). With Facebook as the hub, Secret brand management used the Secret.com website, print advertising, public relations, creative and social media, and appropriate paid and organic search programs to complete each ignition.

DRIVING CONSUMER ENGAGEMENT AND SALES GROWTH THROUGH IGNITIONS

Secret brand management focused on activating brand purpose around the timeless idea of being more fearless and freshened it up with contemporary topics and pop culture. This effort included several ignitions. Two of these are Let Her Jump and Mean Stinks.

Let Her Jump

The first time Secret struck gold by focusing on purpose was through Let Her Jump, an effort to sanction women's ski jumping as an official Olympic sport. The Let Her Jump ignition was a companion piece to work P&G was already doing for the 2010 Winter Olympics in Vancouver.

Secret launched Let Her Jump with a small online media buy and a Facebook Page that included an inspirational video, petition, and Facebook Fan Page. The inspiring video encouraged viewers to visit LetHerJump.com (a custom fan page within Facebook), where they could lead the charge to get women's ski jumping included in the 2014 Winter Olympics. In 2011, the International Olympic Committee approved women's ski jumping for the 2014 Winter Games.

Let Her Jump was one of many elements that, in the spirit of a living brand purpose, helped fuel growth over the previous year. In addition to the video being viewed more than 700,000 times, 57 percent of visitors said this initiative improved brand perception, and Secret saw a double-digit purchase intent increase among women and teens. "This [ignition] was the first time we could pinpoint that activating against purpose generated a huge sales lift," Hochman said. "We saw the Clinical Sport [stock-keeping units] up 85 percent during the [2010] Olympics. We changed the world for the better. In a small way, yes, but a deodorant brand influencing pop culture is very exciting when you can then directly attribute it to business results." As an added bonus, the Let Her Jump program won the coveted Forrester Groundswell Award in 2010. The award recognizes excellence in achieving business and organizational goals with social technology applications and is awarded to some of the best social media programs in the world.

The success of Let Her Jump helped pave the way for investment in another ignition. After proving that purpose-driven work leads to profitable growth for the brand, the team was ready to tackle one of the biggest fears young girls face—bullying. While Let Her Jump was tied to a distinct event in time, the team was excited at the prospect of rallying behind something that could live on and continue to do good in the world.

Mean Stinks

The Secret brand waged a battle for niceness through its Mean Stinks program, the next and biggest step in Secret's fearless movement. Through media monitoring and social listening, the Secret team determined that bullying was a critical issue facing many teen girls—which led to the creation of the Mean Stinks ignition. Mean Stinks launched in early 2011 and focused on ending girl-to-girl meanness, encouraging girls to grow up to be fearless, while providing a safe hub for conversation and creating brand affinity for Secret among young women.

Through the Secret Mean Stinks movement, Secret brought a positive message to high school hallways, leading the charge to end the mean streak by showing teen girls that petty isn't pretty. Raising awareness of bullying is big, but "the need for education is tremendous—people aren't sure how to identify bullying, or what to do when it occurs," says Hochman. "And what's so compelling about the Mean Stinks program is how true it is to the brand's original essence."

The Secret team launched a Facebook media buy for Secret Mean Stinks to create awareness of the program, asking fans (primarily teen girls aged 13–24 and role models aged 25+) to share their stories. The Mean Stinks Facebook Wall was flooded with thousands of public apologies and heartfelt messages of empathy and encouragement. And as Secret continued to make a difference, women celebrities joined to take a stand, offering "nice advice" to girls through the Mean Stinks Facebook app and iAd.

In a single day, Secret gained over 200,000 Facebook fans—bringing its total number of fans to over a million, while its Mean Stinks Page gained over 20,000 new fans. Within the first two weeks, visitors accessed the Mean Stinks Facebook app more than 250,000 times and Secret became the second-fastest-growing Facebook Page globally for one week. This ignition also helped contribute to 10 percent overall sales growth for the entire fiscal year, 11.5 percent in the six-month period during which Mean Stinks was launched.

In the summer of 2011, Secret and Apple joined forces to create an iAd experience that tackled the issue for girls on the device that's most personal—their iPhone. The ignition received unusually high engagement levels and led to many "firsts" for Secret:

- First brand to create and share customized wallpapers via iPhone and iPod touch devices, which led to an "average time spent" rate that was 16 percent higher than average.
- First brand to use transition banners on the iAd Network, which resulted in exceeding benchmarks for banner "Tap through Rates" (50 percent higher than average for iAd).
- First brand to drive donations for a cause through the iAd, which resulted in donations to PACER's National Bullying Prevention Center.

In the first 10 days after launch, 23,000 consumers engaged with the Secret iAd, with more than eight page views per visit and an average of 80 seconds spent on the ad.

WHAT'S NEXT FOR SECRET

Secret executives saw success behind the purpose activation in the year after it was established, but they noticed it wasn't truly part of the brand's DNA or fully integrated into every marketing element. "[At first] we had a lot of grandiose ideas, but they were all added layers to our existing plan. Dollars were tight, and the purpose ideas started getting cut. Old Spice was ahead of us, and I wondered what they were doing differently," says Hochman. "By [working with our agency partners], we finally were able to ensure that [the ignitions] weren't just elements of our plans; they WERE our plan," Hochman says. "The way the Secret team operates now compared with four years ago—it's like day and night."

Hochman says the brand has more ideas that include educating, generating awareness, and empowering people to take meaningful action. Secret is recognized as being best in its class, something the brand is happy to tout. "But [success] isn't a Secret-only thing … it's a priority for all of our brands. And when people are living the brand, they're more excited to come to work. It's much more enabling and inspiring," Hochman says. And to continue in this success, Hochman suggests remembering that a brand's purpose is inextricably linked to the overall plan, it pervades everything about the business—including team culture—and it's in the company's roots.

Hochman also emphasizes the importance of transparency, something he believes Secret will continue to win out on in the future. "Today, information is free and plentiful. If there's a lack of sincerity, consumers know it," he says.

Questions

1 What is "purpose-driven marketing" from a product and brand management perspective at Procter & Gamble?

2 How does "purpose-driven" marketing for Secret deodorant relate to the hierarchy of needs concept detailed in Chapter 5?

3 What dimensions of the consumer-based brand equity pyramid have the Secret brand team focused on with its "Let Her Jump" and "Mean Stinks" ignitions?

12 Services Marketing

Learning Objectives

After reading this chapter you should be able to:

Describe four unique elements of services.

Recognize how services differ and how they can be classified.

Explain how consumers purchase and evaluate services.

Develop a customer contact audit to identify service advantages.

Explain the role of the seven Ps in the services marketing mix.

Discuss the important roles of internal marketing and customer experience management in service organizations.

New Services Can Help You Become Part of the Sharing Economy—and Maybe a Millionaire!

"We were just trying to solve our own problem," explains Brian Chesky, who started the first "sharing economy" business with co-founder Joe Gebbia in 2008.

Their problem was to make pocket cash as new residents in San Francisco. They didn't have anything except space in their apartment, so they created a website called Airbedandbreakfast.com to advertise floor space where people could temporarily sleep on air mattresses while attending a nearby conference. The idea was so successful they shortened the name to Airbnb.com and expanded the business to include many other kinds of spaces such as houses, villas, and even boats.

Initially, they focused on large events such as the Democratic and Republican national conventions where hotels were sold out. Airbnb offered to help visitors "Find a place to stay" by enabling them to rent from people who were willing to share their spaces. In exchange for providing the service, Airbnb charged the renter 3 percent and the traveler 6 to 12 percent. Demand for the service increased rapidly, and more than 141,000 people stayed at an Airbnb on New Year's Eve last year. Today, Airbnb has 300,000 listings available in 23,183 cities and 192 countries and books more than 10,000,000 guest nights each year. In addition, Chesky and Gebbia's shares of the company are valued at approximately $400 million each!

Airbnb was the genesis for what has come to be known as the sharing economy. It turns out that peer-to-peer sharing, or collaborative consumption, is a perfect match with the changes in consumer attitudes about ownership. Millennials typically don't buy newspapers, DVDs, or CDs; instead they find news on Facebook, stream movies from Hulu, and subscribe to music on Pandora. They are much more likely to borrow, rent, and share than previous generations of consumers.

As a result, many new services are being offered to accommodate these attitudes. Lyft and Sidecar now offer peer-to-peer ridesharing (similar to a taxi), while RelayRides and Getaround offer peer-to-peer car sharing (similar to a car rental). Parking Panda allows drivers to find homeowners who want to rent extra space in their driveway, and DogVacay helps pet owners find friendly places for canines to stay for a day. Rentoid, SnapGoods, and Liquid help people rent products, tools, and bicycles rather than purchase them. Similarly, TaskRabbit

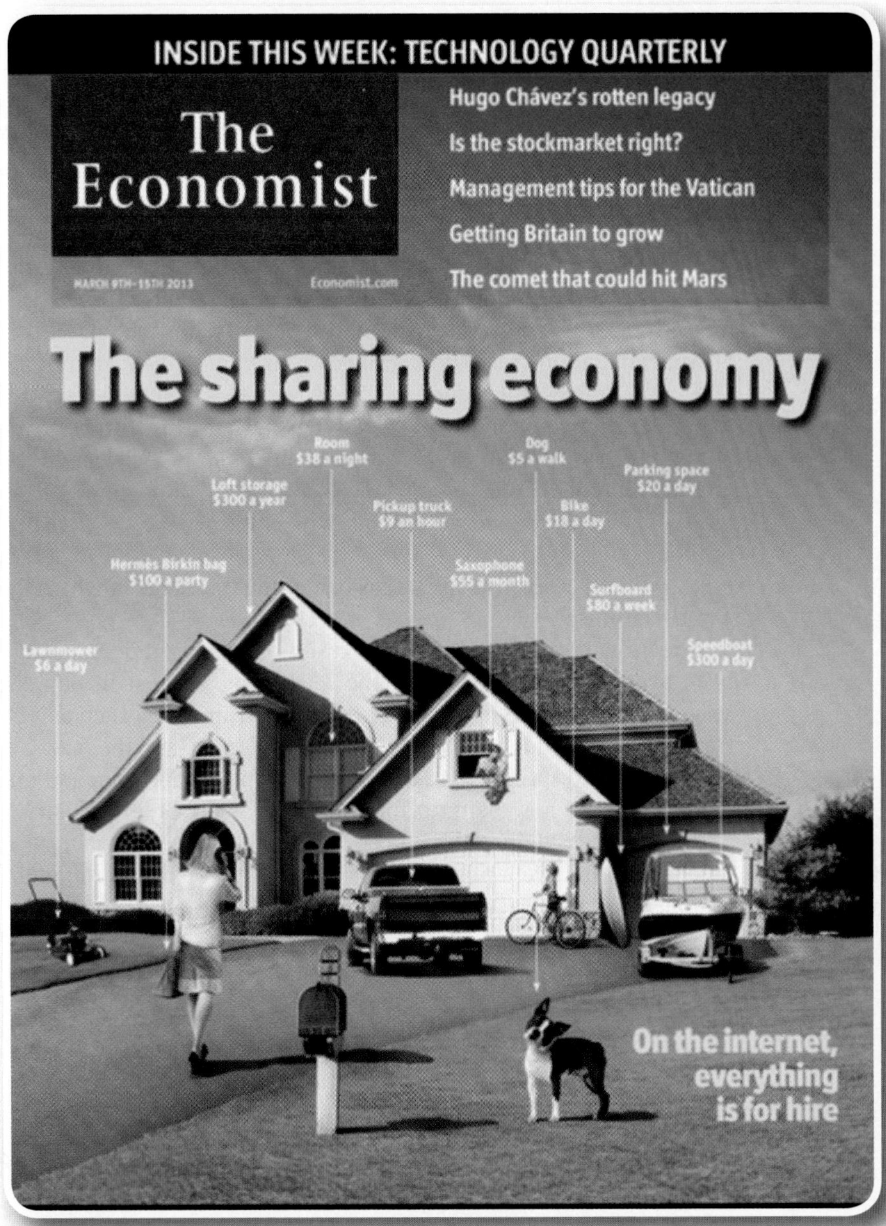

allows users to outsource small jobs and tasks to people in their neighborhood. There are even sharing sites that encourage free exchanges, such as couchsurfing.org, which is a network of volunteers who offer free hospitality, advice, and accommodation to international travelers.

Experts estimate that at least 100 new peer-to-peer sharing services are now in operation and that the revenue generated by the sharing economy exceeds $3.5 billion annually. Neil Turner, the founder and CEO of adverCar, a service that allows drivers to rent advertising space on their cars, suggests that "this is the way of the future." As we move from a perspective based on ownership to this new approach based on sharing and renting, traditional businesses will need to make changes. Avis Budget Group, for example, recently paid $500 million for Zipcar, while General Motors invested in Relay-Rides. Home Depot has introduced product rental in about half of its stores.[1]

QR 12-1
Airbnb Video

As these examples illustrate, services represent a dynamic and exciting component of our economy. In this chapter, we discuss how services differ from traditional products (goods), how service consumers make purchase decisions, and the ways in which the marketing mix is used for services.

THE UNIQUENESS OF SERVICES

Services are intangible activities or benefits (such as airline trips, financial advice, or automobile repair) that an organization provides to satisfy consumers' needs in exchange for money or something else of value.

Services today are a significant component of the global economy—and one of the most important components of the U.S. economy. The World Trade Organization estimates that, for all countries combined, exported merchandise and commercial services total \$14.8 trillion and \$3.7 trillion, respectively, despite one of the largest declines in 50 years due to the recession. As shown in Figure 12–1, more than 46 percent of the U.S. gross domestic product (GDP) now comes from services, exceeding goods and the three other components of GDP—business investment, government spending, and net exports (not shown in the figure). The value of services in the economy has increased more than 100 percent since 1990. Projections indicate that by 2020, goods-producing firms and service firms will employ 19.5 million people and over 130 million people, respectively. Services also represent a large export business—the \$647 billion of service exports in 2012 is one of the few areas in which the United States has a trade surplus.[2]

The growth of this sector is the result of increased demand for services that have been available in the past and the increasing interest in new services. Concierge services, for example, have long been popular in hotels such as The Breakers in Palm Beach, Florida, which has a staff of 11 concierges, and the Ritz-Carlton, which offers concierges who specialize in technology support, shopping, and medical issues. Similar services are now being offered outside of the hotel industry. For example, One Concierge offers individuals and corporations travel on private jets, yacht charters, gift purchasing, and event planning services in 115 countries around the globe. Concierge services are even available for daily lifestyle needs. Ace Concierge, for example, will

FIGURE 12–1
Services are now a larger part of the U.S. gross domestic product (GDP) than goods.

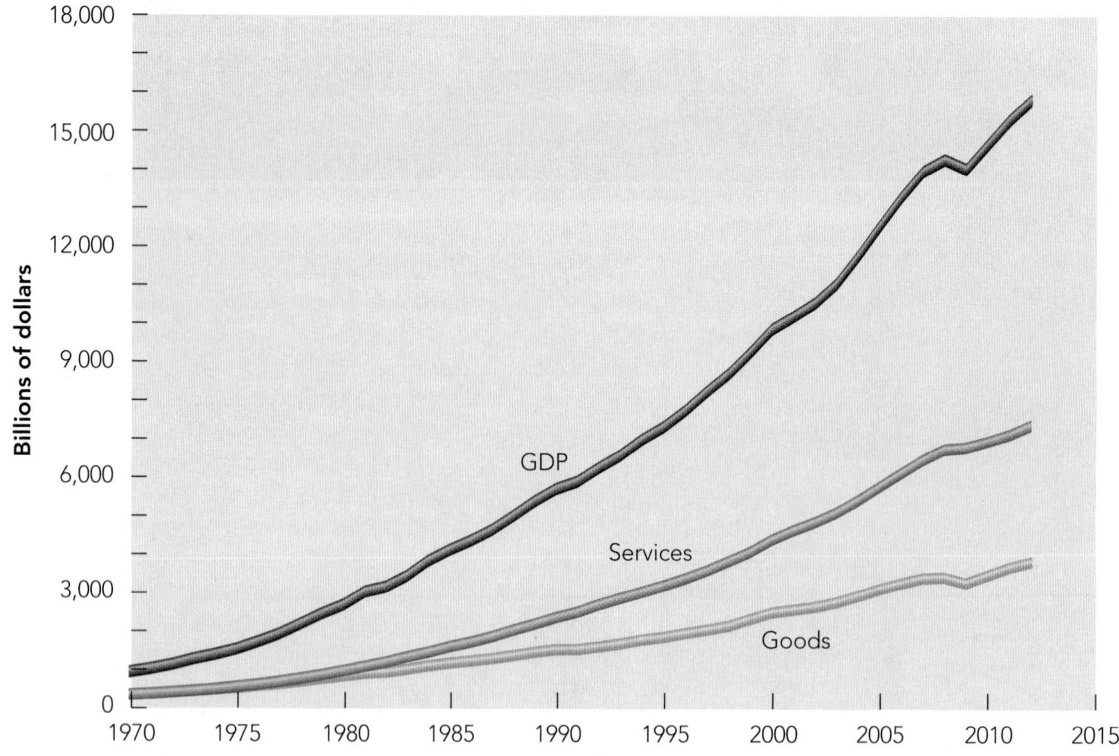

schedule car maintenance, pick up and deliver dry cleaning, walk your dog, or even shop for groceries! Other new services include: The Luggage Club, which offers door-to-door luggage delivery to and from 220 countries; Virgin Galactic, which offers private space travel; and Ubitus GameCloud, which recently launched its cloud-based gaming service to stream games to smartphones, tablets, and televisions. These firms and many others like them are providing the types of imaginative services that will play a role in our economy in the future.[3]

The Four I's of Services

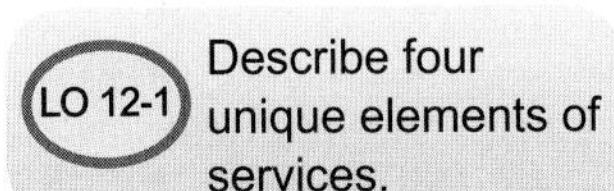

There are four unique elements to services—*intangibility, inconsistency, inseparability,* and *inventory*—referred to as the **four I's of services**.

Intangibility Services are intangible; that is, they can't be held, touched, or seen before the purchase decision. In contrast, before purchasing a traditional product, a consumer can touch a box of laundry detergent, kick the tire of an automobile, or sample a new breakfast cereal. Because services tend to be a performance rather than an object, they are much more difficult for consumers to evaluate. To help consumers assess and compare services, marketers try to make them tangible or show the benefits of using the service.

The American Airlines ad shows the airline's new seats and emphasizes their size and other tangible benefits. American Express also provides tangible benefits by allowing cardmembers to earn points for redemption of airline tickets, electronics, and gift cards through its Membership Rewards program.

Why do many services emphasize their tangible benefits? The answer appears in the text.

American Airlines
www.aa.com

American Express Co.
www.americanexpress.com

Inconsistency Developing, pricing, promoting, and delivering services is challenging because the quality of a service is often inconsistent. Because services depend on the people who provide them, their quality varies with each person's capabilities and day-to-day job performance. Inconsistency is much more of a problem in services than it is with tangible products. Tangible products can be good or bad in terms of quality, but with modern production lines the quality will at least be consistent. In contrast, the Philadelphia Phillies baseball team may have great hitting and pitching

and look like a pennant winner one day—and the next day they may lose by 10 runs. Or a soprano at New York's Metropolitan Opera may have a bad cold and give a less-than-perfect performance on the night that you attend. Whether the service involves tax assistance at H&R Block or guest relations at the Ritz-Carlton, organizations attempt to reduce inconsistency through standardization and training.[4]

Inseparability A third difference between services and products, and related to problems of consistency, is inseparability. In most cases, the consumer cannot (and does not) separate the deliverer of the service from the service itself. For example, Allstate's reminder that "You're in good hands" emphasizes the importance of its agents. Similarly, to receive an education, a person may attend a university. The quality of the education may be high, but if the student has difficulty interacting with instructors, finds counseling services poor, or does not receive adequate library or computer assistance, he or she may not be satisfied with the educational experience. Students' evaluations of their education will be influenced primarily by their perceptions of instructors, counselors, librarians, and other people at the university. This interaction between the service provider and the consumer means that they often *co-create* value together.[5]

The amount of interaction between the consumer and the service provider depends on the extent to which the consumer must be physically present to receive the service. Some services, such as haircuts, golf lessons, medical diagnoses, and food service, require the customer to participate in the delivery of the services. Other services, such as car repair, dry cleaning, and waste disposal, process tangible objects with less involvement from the customer. Finally, services such as banking, consulting, and insurance are often delivered electronically, requiring no face-to-face customer interaction. Even pharmacies may soon be automated for shoppers who are willing to submit to a fingerprint scan. While this approach can create value for consumers, a disadvantage of some *self-service technologies* such as ATMs, grocery store scanning stations, and self-service gas station pumps is that they are perceived as being less personal.[6]

Inventory Inventory of services is different from that of products. Inventory problems exist with products because many items are perishable and because there

People play an important role in the delivery of many services. Many services ads emphasize the personal element of the offering.

Merrill Lynch
www.wealthmanagement.ml.com

LOW COST — Cost of inventory — HIGH COST

Real estate agency / Hair salon | Insurance company | Dry cleaner | Auto repair center | Restaurant | Hotel | Amusement park | Airline / Hospital

FIGURE 12–2
Inventory carrying costs of services depend on the cost of employees and equipment.

are costs associated with handling inventory. With services, inventory carrying costs are more subjective and are related to **idle production capacity**, which is when the service provider is available but there is no demand for the service. The inventory cost of a service is the cost of paying the person used to provide the service along with any needed equipment. If a physician is paid to see patients but no one schedules an appointment, the fixed cost of the idle physician's salary is a high inventory carrying cost. In some service businesses, however, the provider of the service is on commission (a Merrill Lynch financial advisor) or is a part-time employee (a clerk at Macy's). In these businesses, inventory carrying costs can be significantly lower or nonexistent because the idle production capacity can be cut back by reducing hours or having no salary to pay because of the commission compensation system.

Figure 12–2 shows a scale of inventory carrying costs represented on the low end by real estate agencies and hair salons and on the high end by airlines and hospitals. The inventory carrying costs of airlines are high because of high-salaried pilots and very expensive equipment. In contrast, real estate agencies and hair salons have employees who work on commission and need little expensive equipment to conduct business. One reason service providers must maintain production capacity is because of the importance of time to today's customers.

The Service Continuum

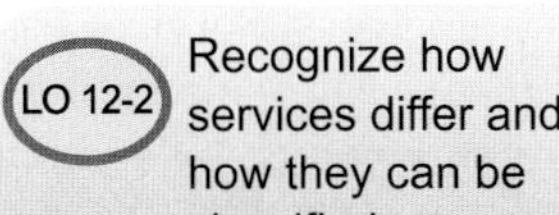

The four I's differentiate services from products in most cases, but many companies are not clearly service-based or product-based organizations. Is Hewlett-Packard a manufacturer or a service provider? Although Hewlett-Packard manufactures printers and other products, many of the company's employees work in its services division providing systems integration, networking, consulting, education, and product support.[7] What companies bring to the market ranges from the tangible to the intangible. This range of product-dominant to service-dominant offerings is referred to as the **service continuum** (see Figure 12–3 on the next page).

Teaching, nursing, and the theater are intangible, service-dominant activities, and intangibility, inconsistency, inseparability, and inventory are major concerns in their marketing. Salt, neckties, and dog food are tangible products, and the problems represented by the four I's are not relevant in their marketing. However, some businesses are a mix of intangible service and tangible product factors. A clothing tailor provides a service but also a product, the finished suit. How pleasant, courteous, and attentive the tailor is to the customer is an important component of the service, and how well the clothes fit is an important part of the product. As shown in Figure 12–3, a fast-food restaurant is about half tangible products (the food) and half intangible services (courtesy, cleanliness, speed, and convenience).

For many businesses today, it is useful to distinguish between their core offering—either a product or a service—and supplementary services. A core service offering such as a bank account, for example, also has supplementary services such as deposit

FIGURE 12–3
The service continuum shows how offerings can vary in their balance of products and services.

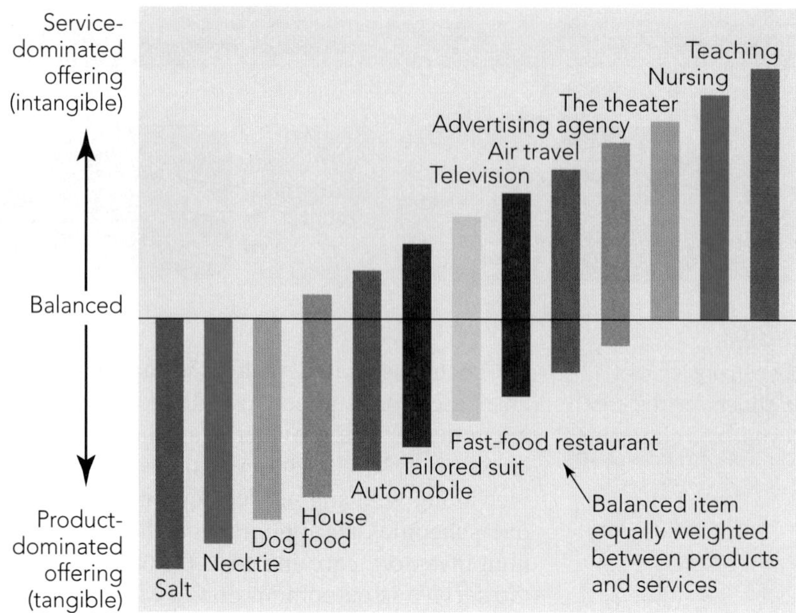

assistance, parking or drive-thru availability, ATMs, and monthly statements. Supplementary services often allow service providers to differentiate their offering from competitors, and they may add value for consumers. While there are many potential supplementary services, key categories of supplementary services include consultation, finance, shipping, installation, maintenance, and upgrades. Innovation in core services today often relies on the creative efforts of the organization. Understanding the impact of supplementary services, however, may be best accomplished through input from customers.[8]

Classifying Services

Throughout this book, marketing organizations, techniques, and concepts are classified to show the differences and similarities in an organized framework. Services can also be classified in several ways, according to whether (1) they are delivered by people or equipment, (2) they are for-profit or nonprofit, or (3) they are government sponsored.

Delivery by People or Equipment As seen in Figure 12–4, many companies offer services. Professional services include management consulting firms such as Booz Allen Hamilton or Accenture. Skilled labor is required by Sears in order to offer services such as appliance repair and by Sheraton in order to offer its catering service. Unskilled labor such as that used by Brink's store-security forces is also a service provided by people.

Equipment-based services do not have the marketing concerns of inconsistency because people are removed from the provision of the service. Electric utilities, for example, can provide service without frequent personal contact with customers. Motion picture theaters have projector operators that consumers never see. A growing number of customers use self-service technologies such as Home Depot's self checkout, Southwest Airlines's self check-in, and Schwab's online stock trading without interacting with any service employees.[9]

For-Profit or Nonprofit Organizations Many organizations involved in services also distinguish themselves by their tax status as for-profit or nonprofit organizations. In contrast to *for-profit organizations, nonprofit organizations'* excesses in

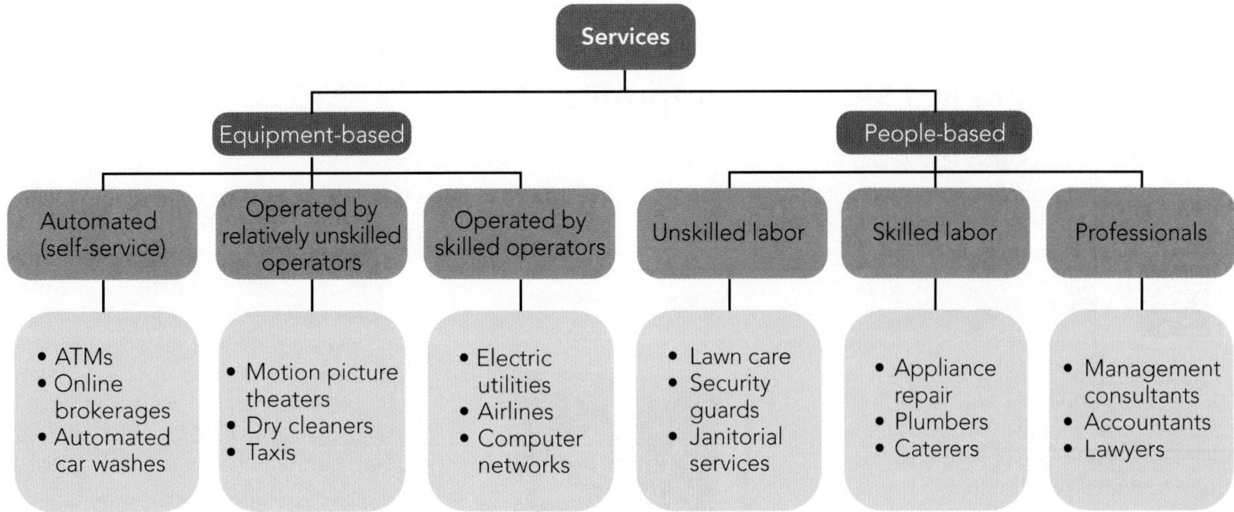

FIGURE 12–4
Services can be classified as equipment-based or people-based.

revenue over expenses are not taxed or distributed to shareholders. When excess revenue exists, the money goes back into the organization's treasury to allow continuation of the service. Based on the corporate structure of the nonprofit organization, it may pay tax on revenue-generating holdings not directly related to its core mission. Nonprofit organizations in the United States now have revenue of $1.77 trillion and account for 8 percent of all wages and salaries.[10]

United Way, Greenpeace, Outward Bound, The Salvation Army, and Girl Scouts are examples of nonprofit organizations. Historically, misconceptions have limited the use of marketing practices by such organizations.[11] In recent years, however, nonprofit organizations have turned to marketing to help achieve their goals. The American Red Cross is a good example. To increase blood donations and financial gifts, it hired creative agency BBDO to create its new Storytellers Campaign, which includes TV and print ads, direct marketing, public relations, and social media. In addition, to help its 700 field offices integrate their messages, the American Red Cross hired another agency to create a web portal called Brand Central, which offers

Nonprofit service organizations often advertise to help achieve their goals.

Outward Bound
www.outwardbound.org

Girl Scouts
www.girlscouts.org

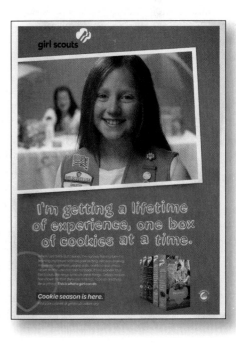

Marketing Matters

technology

Social Marketing Is a Must for Nonprofits

QR 12-2 American Red Cross Video

"Make It Social" is the mantra for many nonprofit organizations today. The recent recession has reduced charitable donations substantially, so many of the 1.5 million public charities, private foundations, universities, religious congregations, and other nonprofit organizations have turned to social marketing and social media to engage potential contributors.

The Susan G. Komen for the Cure organization has been one of the most successful in using new approaches. In addition to its familiar walks and races, the Komen Foundation uses Facebook, Twitter, YouTube, and Flickr to promote its cause and fund-raising activities. Its fragrance, Promise Me, for example, is promoted on its website and social media sites. It also allows mobile giving by texting the word KOMEN from a mobile phone. The success of the Komen organization's marketing actions has allowed it to raise more than $2 billion for breast cancer research and community outreach programs.

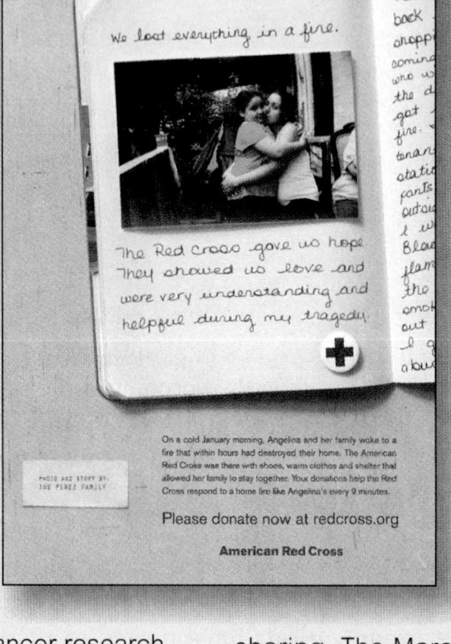

We lost everything in a fire.
The Red Cross gave us hope. They showed us love and were very understanding and helpful during my tragedy.
Please donate now at redcross.org
American Red Cross

The American Red Cross has also been quick to adopt social marketing tools. The organization recently opened a Social Media Digital Operations Center in Washington, D.C., to help it communicate with the general public, volunteers, and donors. In addition, the Red Cross has created tools such as the Hurricane app, which was downloaded by 235,000 people during Hurricane Sandy, and crowdfunding websites on IndieGoGo and Crowdrise, which raised millions in contributions for Sandy victims. Social media tools such as these are playing an increasingly important role in Red Cross operations as they become familiar to most people.

Nonprofit organizations should follow many of the same principles businesses use to engage people with social media. First, they should understand what motivates people to take up causes. One of the most important reasons is usually to feel like they are doing something, even if it is as simple as clicking the "like" button on Facebook. Second, nonprofit organizations need to be creative in their use of social media and incorporate digital photos, video, and gaming skills. As Jamie Henn, communications director for 350.org explains, "By using images and video we have been able to convey stories with emotional impact." The United Way, for example, partnered with CNN to deliver a live online panel discussion about its education goals. Finally, nonprofit campaigns should allow information sharing. The March of Dimes, for example, created on online forum where people can share stories, and it now has an average of 8,100 posts each month.

Social marketing campaigns and social media offer nonprofit organizations very effective tools for engaging their members, fans, friends, and the public. While the number of success stories is growing, it is important to remember to have a goal and measure progress toward that goal. Participation rates, donations, number of texts, posts on a blog, and other dimensions of effectiveness all contribute to the perception of the brand!

standardized templates for local communications materials. Other promotional activities include a campaign called Red Cross Racing, which is targeted at the 75 million NASCAR fans across the country, and the National Celebrity Cabinet, which currently includes Miley Cyrus, Pierce Brosnan, LL Cool J, Heidi Klum, Peyton Manning, and Patti LaBelle.

Other nonprofits have also been successful in using marketing to help achieve their goals. The American Marketing Association recently selected Anne Marie Dougherty as the recipient of the Nonprofit Marketer of the Year award for her extraordinary leadership of the Bob Woodruff Foundation, which has raised more than $10 million to support wounded veterans and their families.[12] See the Marketing Matters box to learn more about the social marketing activities of other nonprofit organizations, including Susan G. Komen for the Cure, the American Red Cross, and the March of Dimes.[13]

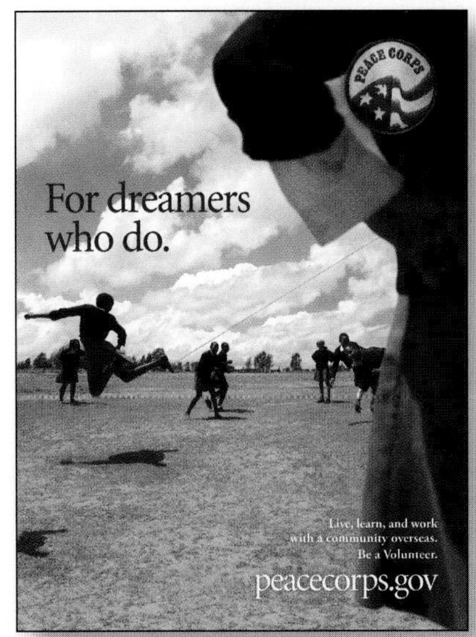
For dreamers
who do.
Live, learn, and work
with a community overseas.
Be a Volunteer.
peacecorps.gov

The Peace Corps has adopted many marketing activities.

Government Sponsored A third way to classify services is based on whether or not they are government sponsored. Although there is no direct ownership and they are nonprofit organizations, governments at the federal, state, and local levels provide a broad range of services. The United States Postal Service, for example, has adopted many marketing activities. First-class postage revenue has declined as postal service customers have increased their use of the Internet to send e-mail, pay bills, and file taxes. Rather than fight the trend, however, the U.S. Postal Service is embracing the Internet. Its website, www.usps.com, allows consumers to pay for postage, print shipping labels, and request a free package pickup. In addition, new post office boxes are being designed in sizes to better meet the needs of consumers who shop online, and greeting cards with a prepaid postage barcode are being offered through a partnership with Hallmark Cards. You may have noticed that many post offices are now also retail outlets that sell supplies, collector stamps, and even neckties. These marketing activities are designed to increase consumer use and to compete with UPS, FedEx, DHL, and foreign postal services for package delivery business. The U.S. Postal Service is also promoting online mailing list management and the use of direct mail.[14] The Peace Corps is another example of a government-sponsored service.

learning review

12-1. What are the four I's of services?

12-2. To eliminate service inconsistencies, companies rely on ______________ and ______________.

12-3. Would inventory carrying costs for an accounting firm with certified public accountants be (*a*) high, (*b*) low, or (*c*) nonexistent?

HOW CONSUMERS PURCHASE SERVICES

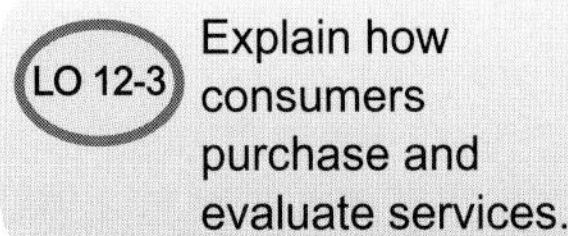
LO 12-3 Explain how consumers purchase and evaluate services.

Colleges, hospitals, hotels, and even charities are facing an increasingly competitive environment. Successful service organizations, like successful product-oriented firms, must (1) understand how the consumer makes a service purchase decision, (2) understand how the consumer evaluates quality, and (3) determine how to present a differential advantage relative to competing offerings.

The Purchase Process

Many aspects of services affect the consumer's evaluation of the purchase. Because services cannot be displayed, demonstrated, or illustrated, consumers cannot make a prepurchase evaluation of all the characteristics of services.[15] Similarly, because service providers may vary in their delivery of a service, an evaluation of a service may change with each purchase. Figure 12–5 on the next page portrays how different types of products and services are evaluated by consumers. Tangible products such as clothing, jewelry, and furniture have *search* properties, such as color, size, and style, which can be determined before purchase. Services such as restaurants and child care have *experience* properties, which can be discerned only after purchase or during consumption. Finally, services provided by specialized professionals such as medical diagnoses and legal services have *credence* properties, or characteristics that the consumer may find impossible to evaluate even after purchase and consumption.[16] To reduce the uncertainty created by these properties, service consumers turn to personal sources of information such as early adopters,

FIGURE 12–5
Consumers use search, experience, and credence properties to evaluate services.

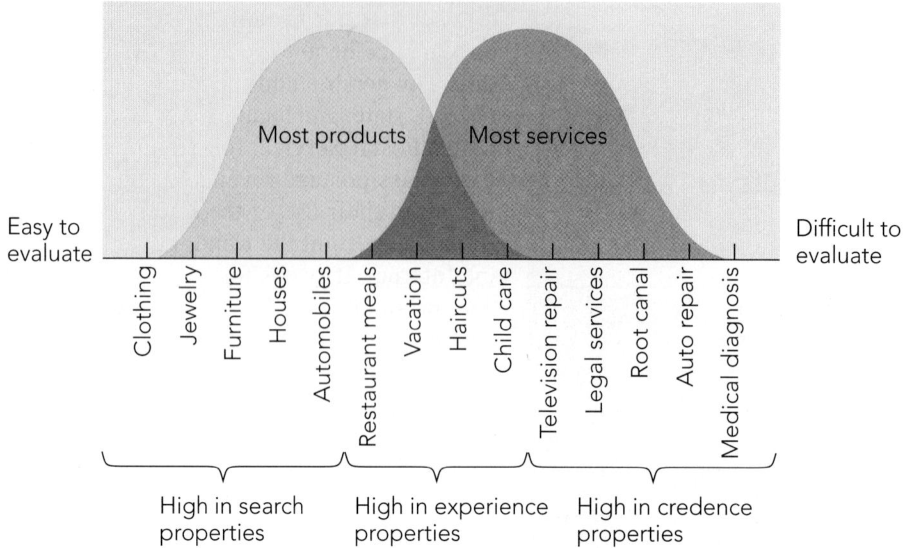

opinion leaders, and reference group members during the purchase decision process. Research indicates that consumers search for much more information when trying to evaluate services with credence properties.[17] In response to this need for more information, the Mayo Clinic uses an organized, explicit approach called "evidence management" to present customers with concrete and convincing evidence of its strengths.[18]

Assessing Service Quality

Once a consumer tries a service, how is it evaluated? Primarily, a consumer assesses service quality by comparing expectations about a service offering to his or her actual experience with the service.[19] Differences between the consumer's expectations and experience are identified through **gap analysis**. This type of analysis asks consumers to assess their expectations and experiences on dimensions of service quality such as those described in Figure 12–6.[20] Expectations are

FIGURE 12–6
There are five dimensions of service quality.

DIMENSION	DEFINITION	EXAMPLES OF QUESTIONS AIRLINE CUSTOMERS MIGHT ASK
Reliability	Ability to perform the promised service dependably and accurately	Is my flight on time?
Tangibility	Appearance of physical facilities, equipment, personnel, and communication materials	Are the gate, the plane, and the baggage area clean?
Responsiveness	Willingness to help customers and provide prompt service	Are the flight attendants willing to answer my questions?
Assurance	Knowledge and courtesy of employees and their ability to convey trust and confidence	Are the ticket counter attendants, flight attendants, and pilots knowledgeable about their jobs?
Empathy	Caring, individualized attention provided to customers	Do the employees determine if I have special seating, meal, baggage, transfer, or rebooking needs?

influenced by word-of-mouth communications, personal needs, past experiences, and promotional activities, while actual experiences are determined by the way an organization delivers its service.[21] The relative importance of the various dimensions of service quality varies by the type of service.[22] What if someone is dissatisfied and complains? Recent studies suggest that customers who experience a "service failure" will increase their satisfaction if the service provider makes a highly interactive service recovery effort, although they may not increase their intent to repurchase. In addition, service operators can increase customer satisfaction by explaining the cause of the service failure and letting customers choose between several recovery options.[23] See the Marketing inSite box on the next page for ideas about monitoring service failures.[24]

Customer Contact and Relationship Marketing

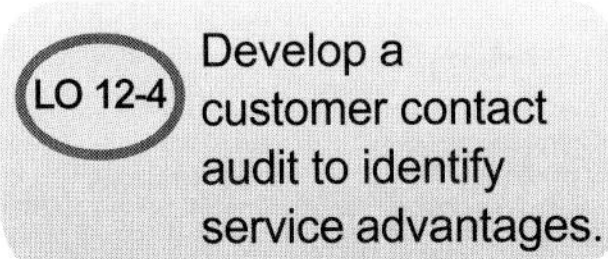

Develop a customer contact audit to identify service advantages.

Consumers judge services on the entire sequence of steps that make up the service process. To focus on these steps, or "service encounters," a firm can develop a **customer contact audit**—a flowchart of the points of interaction between consumer and service provider.[25] This is particularly important in high-contact services such as hotels, educational institutions, and automobile rental agencies. Figure 12–7 is a customer contact audit prepared for a car rental agency. The interactions identified in a customer contact audit often serve as the basis for developing relationships with customers. Recent research suggests that employees' competence and the authenticity and sincerity of their interactions affect the success of their customer relationships. Another version of a customer contact audit, called a *service blueprint*, includes all employee actions and acknowledges that services are designed to be "experiences."[26]

FIGURE 12–7
Customer contact audit for a car rental agency (green shaded boxes indicate customer activity).

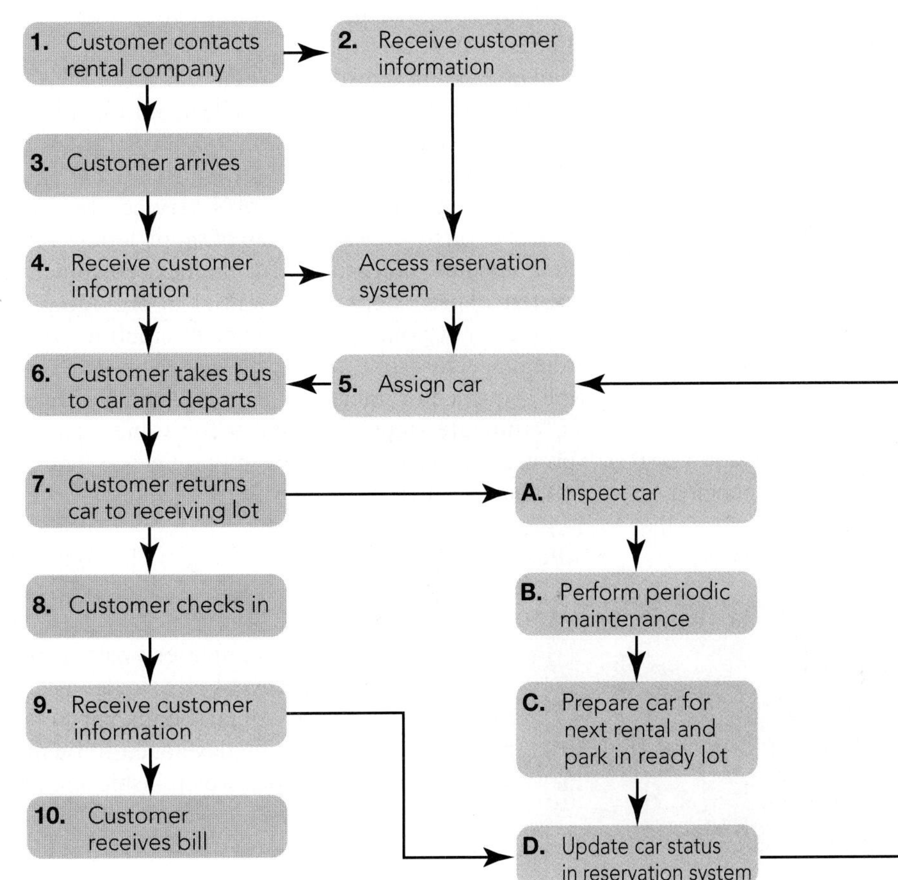

Hertz manages its customer contacts.

The Hertz Corporation
www.hertz.com

Marketing inSite

How Can You Learn about Service Failures? Media Monitoring!

Only 5 to 10 percent of dissatisfied customers choose to complain—the rest switch companies or make negative comments to other people. Increasingly, the forum for personal comments is on the many social media now available to consumers. Domino's Pizza, for example, discovered that consumers were publishing comments that its pizza was "like cardboard." Companies can search for comments using search engines such as www.blogsearch.google.com, and they can search for images on Google and videos on YouTube. Web services such as www.technorati.com and www.reputationdefender.com are available to monitor blogs, and media-monitoring firms will even watch for dissatisfied customers on Twitter.

Most public relations experts agree that it is best to respond to, rather than ignore, comments on the Internet. Regarding its product's comparison to cardboard, Domino's posted a response on YouTube, created a Twitter account, and then posted the real-time Twitter feed on a billboard in Times Square! To find out what consumers are saying about *your* favorite brands, try your own media search now.

A Customer's Car Rental Activities Let's look more closely at the customer contact audit illustrated in Figure 12–7. A customer decides to rent a car and (1) contacts the rental company. A customer service representative receives the information (2) and checks the availability of the car at the desired location. When the customer arrives at the rental site (3), the reservation system is again accessed, and the customer provides information regarding payment, address, and driver's license (4). A car is assigned to the customer (5), who proceeds by bus to the car pickup (6). On return to the rental location (7), the customer checks in (8), a customer service representative collects information on mileage, gas consumption, and damages (9), and a bill is printed (10).

Each of the steps numbered 1 to 10 is a customer contact point where the tangible aspects of the company's service are seen by the customer. Figure 12–7, however, also shows a series of steps lettered A to D that involve an inspection, maintenance, preparation for the next customer, and an update of the reservation system. These steps are essential in providing a clean, well-maintained car, but they are not points of customer interaction. To create a service advantage, a car rental agency—like any service company—must create a competitive advantage in the sequence of interactions with the customer. For example, Hertz has attempted to eliminate steps 4, 8, and 9 for some customers with its Gold Plus Rewards program. These customers simply pick up the car keys when they arrive and drop off the car when they return.

How many times will a Disney park visitor encounter a Disney employee? See the text for the answer.

Relationship Marketing The contact between a service provider and a customer represents a service encounter that is likely to influence the customer's assessment of the purchase. The number of encounters in a service experience may vary. Disney, for example, estimates that a park visitor will have 74 encounters with Disney employees in a single visit. These encounters represent opportunities to develop social bonds, or relationships, with customers. The relationship may also be developed through loyalty incentives such as airline frequent flyer programs. Relationship marketing provides several benefits for service customers, including the continuity of a single provider, customized service delivery, reduced stress due to a repetitive purchase process, and an absence of switching costs. Surveys of consumers have indicated that while customers of many services are interested in being "relationship customers," they require that the relationship be balanced in terms of loyalty, benefits, and respect for privacy,[27] and their expectations of the future benefits of the service influence the likelihood that they continue the relationship.[28] Understanding the service characteristics that lead to repeat purchases can help services managers allocate their resources to appropriate relationship marketing activities.[29]

learning review

12-4. What are the differences between search, experience, and credence properties?

12-5. Hertz created its differential advantage at the points of ________________ in its customer contact audit.

MANAGING THE MARKETING OF SERVICES

Explain the role of the seven Ps in the services marketing mix.

Just as the unique aspects of services necessitate changes in the consumer's purchase process, the marketing management process also requires special adaptation.[30] As we have seen in earlier chapters, the traditional marketing mix is composed of the four Ps: product, price, place, and promotion. Careful management of the four Ps is important when marketing services. However, the distinctive nature of services requires that other variables also be effectively managed by service marketers. The concept of an expanded marketing mix for services has been adopted by many service-marketing organizations. In addition to the four Ps, the services marketing mix includes people, the physical environment, and the process, or the **seven Ps of services marketing**.[31]

Logos and brand names help consumers identify services.

Product (Service)

The concepts of the product component of the marketing mix discussed in Chapters 10 and 11 apply equally well to Cheerios (a product) and American Express (a service). Managers of products and services must design the product concept with the features and benefits desired by customers. An important aspect of the product concept is branding. Because services are intangible, and more difficult to describe, the brand name or identifying logo of the service organization is particularly important when a consumer makes a purchase decision.[32] Therefore, service organizations, such as banks, hotels, rental car companies, and restaurants, rely on branding strategies to distinguish themselves in the minds of consumers. Strong brand names and symbols are important for service marketers, not only as a means of differentiation, but also to convey an image of quality. A service firm with a well-established brand reputation will also find it easier to introduce new services than firms without a brand reputation.[33]

Many services have undertaken creative branding activities. Hotels, for example, have begun to extend their branding efforts to consumers' homes through services such as *Hotels at Home*, an in-room catalog that offers Westin's "Heavenly Bed," Hilton's bathrobes, and even artwork from Sheraton hotel rooms for consumers to buy and use at home. Similarly, Fairmont Hotels has formed co-branding partnerships with Adidas, which provides athletic gear to loyalty program members, and BMW, which offers BMW Cruise Bikes for guest use.[34] Look at the logos on this page to determine how successful some companies have been in branding their service with a name and symbol.

Price influences perceptions of the quality of services.

Price

In service businesses, price is referred to in many ways. Hospitals refer to *charges*; consultants, lawyers, physicians, and accountants to *fees*; airlines to *fares*; hotels to *rates*; and colleges and universities to *tuition*. Because of the intangible nature of services, price is often perceived by consumers as a possible indicator of the quality of the service. Do you expect higher quality from an expensive restaurant? Would you wonder about the quality of a $100 surgery? In many cases, there may be few other available cues for the customer to judge, so price becomes very important as a quality indicator.[35]

Pricing of services goes beyond the traditional tasks of setting the selling price. When customers buy a service, they also consider nonmonetary costs, such as the mental and physical efforts required to consume the service. Service marketers must try to minimize the effort required to purchase and use the service. Pricing also plays a role in balancing consumer demand for services. Many service businesses use **off-peak pricing**, which consists of charging different prices during different times of the day or during different days of the week to reflect variations in demand for the service. Airlines, for example, offer discounts for weekend travel, while movie theaters offer matinee prices.

Place (Distribution)

Place, or distribution, is a major factor in developing a service marketing strategy because of the inseparability of services from the producer. Rarely are intermediaries involved in the distribution of a service; the distribution site and the service deliverer are the tangible components of the service. Until recently, customers generally had to go to the service provider's physical location to purchase the service. Increased competition, however, has forced many service firms to consider the value of convenient distribution and to find new ways of distributing services to customers. Hairstyling chains such as Cost Cutters Family Hair Salon, tax preparation offices such as H&R Block, and accounting firms such as Ernst & Young all use multiple locations for the distribution of services. Technology is also being used to deliver services beyond the provider's physical locations. In the banking industry, for example, customers of participating banks using the Cirrus system can access any one of 900,000 automatic teller machines in 93 countries. The availability of electronic distribution through the Internet also allows for global reach and coverage for a variety of services, including travel, education, entertainment, and insurance. With speed and convenience becoming increasingly important to customers when they select service providers, service firms can leverage the use of the Internet to deliver services on a 24/7 basis, in real time, on a global scale. This advantage varies by type of service, however: British grocery retailer Tesco has one million customers who shop online, while most health care services still rely on face-to-face interaction.[36]

Promotion

The value of promotion, especially advertising, for many services is to show consumers the benefits of purchasing the service. It is valuable to stress availability, location, consistent quality, and efficient, courteous service[37] and to provide a physical representation of the service or a service encounter.[38] The Accenture ad, for example, describes the benefits available to its customers—"High performance. Delivered."

Services use promotional programs to communicate benefits and provide a representation of the service encounter.

Accenture
www.accenture.com

Space Adventures
www.spaceadventures.com

QR 12-3
Space Adventures Video

The Space Adventures ad describes the benefit of its service as being "the world's first civilian explorer to circumnavigate the moon," and it provides a photo of the service encounter—a close-up view of the moon! In most cases, promotional concerns of services are similar to those of products.

Another form of promotion, *publicity*, has played a major role in the promotional strategy of many service organizations. Nonprofit organizations such as public schools, religious organizations, and hospitals, for example, often use publicity to disseminate their messages. For many of these organizations, the most common form of publicity is the *public service announcement* (PSA) because it is free.[39] As discussed later in Chapter 18, however, using PSAs as the foundation of a promotion program is unlikely to be effective because the timing and location of the PSA are under the control of the medium, not the organization.

Personal selling, sales promotion, and direct marketing also can play an important role in services marketing. Service firm representatives, such as hotel employees handling check-in services or waitstaff in restaurants, are often responsible for selling their services. Similarly, sales promotions such as coupons, free trials, and contests are often effective tools for service firms. Finally, direct marketing activities are often used to reach specific audiences with interest in specific types of services. Increasingly, service firms are adopting an integrated marketing communications approach (see Chapter 17), similar to the approach used by many consumer packaged goods firms, to ensure that the many forms of promotion are providing a consistent message and contributing to a common objective.

People

LO 12-6 Discuss the important roles of internal marketing and customer experience management in service organizations.

Many services depend on people for the creation and delivery of the customer service experience.[40] The nature of the interaction between employees and customers strongly influences the customer's perceptions of the service experience. Customers will often judge the quality of the service experience based on the performance of the people providing the service. This aspect of services marketing has led to a concept called internal marketing.[41]

Internal marketing is based on the notion that a service organization must focus on its employees, or internal market, before successful programs can be directed at customers.[42] Service firms need to ensure that employees have the attitude, skills, and commitment needed to meet customer expectations and to sustain customer loyalty. Employees with a commitment to mutually beneficial relationships with customers are most suitable for services today. This idea suggests that employee development through recruitment, training, communication, coaching, management, and leadership is critical to the success of service organizations.[43] Finally, many service organizations, such as educational institutions and athletic teams, must recognize that individual customer behavior may also influence the service outcome for other customers. These interactions suggest that the people element in services includes employees and all customers.

Once internal marketing programs have prepared employees for their interactions with customers, organizations can better manage the services they provide. **Customer experience management (CEM)**, introduced in Chapter 10, is the process of managing the entire customer experience with the company. CEM experts suggest that the process should be intentional and planned, consistent so that every experience is similar, differentiated from other service offerings, and relevant and valuable to the target market. Companies such as Disney, Southwest Airlines, the Ritz-Carlton, and Starbucks all manage the experience they offer customers. They integrate their activities to connect with customers at each contact point to move beyond customer relationships to customer loyalty.[44] For example, Zappos.com, the online retailer profiled in the opener to Chapter 9, requires that all employees complete a four-week customer loyalty training program to help deliver one of the company's core concepts—"Deliver WOW through Service."[45]

Physical Environment

The appearance of the environment in which the service is delivered and where the firm and customer interact can influence the customer's perception of the service. The physical evidence of the service includes all the tangibles surrounding the service: the buildings, landscaping, vehicles, furnishings, signage, brochures, and equipment. Service firms need to manage physical evidence carefully and systematically to convey the proper impression of the service to the customer. This is sometimes referred to as impression, or evidence, management.[46] For many services, the physical environment provides an opportunity for the firm to send consistent and strong messages about the nature of the service to be delivered.

Process

Process refers to the actual procedures, mechanisms, and flow of activities by which the service is created and delivered. The actual creation and delivery steps that the customer experiences provide customers with evidence on which to judge the service. These steps involve not only "what" gets created but also "how" it is created. The customer contact audit discussed earlier in the chapter is relevant to understanding the service process discussed here. The customer contact audit can serve as a basis for ensuring better service creation and delivery processes. Grease Monkey believes that it has the right process in the vehicle oil change and fluid exchange service business. Customers do not need appointments, stores are open six days per week, the service is completed in 15–20 minutes, and a waiting room allows customers to read or work while the service is being completed.

Most services have a limited capacity due to the inseparability of the service from the service provider and the perishable nature of the service. For example, to "buy" an appendectomy, a patient must be in the hospital at the same time as the surgeon and only one patient can be helped at that time. Similarly, no additional surgery can be

FIGURE 12–8
Different prices and packages help match hotel demand to capacity.

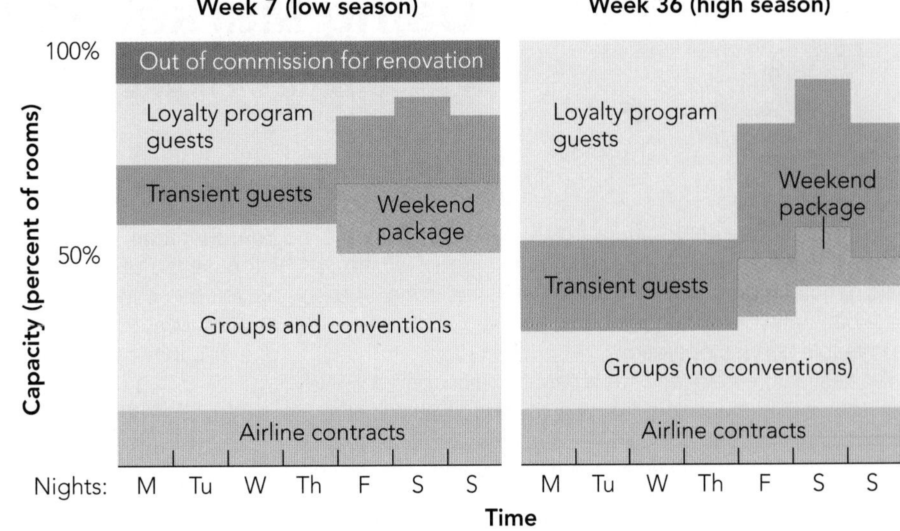

conducted tomorrow because of an unused operating room or an available surgeon today—the service capacity is lost if it is not used. So the service component of the marketing mix must be integrated with efforts to influence consumer demand.[47] This is referred to as **capacity management**.

Service organizations must manage the availability of the offering so that (1) demand matches capacity over the duration of the demand cycle (for example, one day, week, month, or year), and (2) the organization's assets are used in ways that will maximize the return on investment (ROI).[48] Figure 12–8 shows how a hotel tries to manage its capacity during the high and low seasons. Differing price structures are assigned to each segment of consumers to help moderate or adjust demand for the service. Airline contracts fill a fixed number of rooms throughout the year. In the low season, when more rooms are available, tour packages at appealing prices are used to attract groups or conventions, such as an offer for seven nights in Orlando at a reduced price. Weekend packages are also offered to vacationers. In the high-demand season, groups are less desirable because guests who will pay high prices travel to Florida on their own. The Using Marketing Dashboards box on the next page demonstrates how JetBlue Airways uses a capacity management measure called *load factor* to assess its profitability.

QR 12-4
Google TV
Video

SERVICES IN THE FUTURE

Google TV is one example of how services are changing. Read the text to learn more.

What can we expect from the services industry in the future? New and better services, of course, and an unprecedented variety of choices. Many of the changes will be the result of three factors: technological development, improved understanding of service delivery and consumption, and the social imperative for sustainability.

Technological advances are rapidly changing the services industry. The key elements of future services include mobility and personalization. AT&T, for example, recently introduced its mobile subscription service, Mobile TV, which allows consumers to view ESPN, Disney, Fox News, and other programs on their smartphones. Google TV has also introduced a new technology that uses sensors and voice recognition to determine who is viewing a program; based on this information, Google TV is able to customize the viewing experience.[49] Technology-mediated personalization can increase customers'

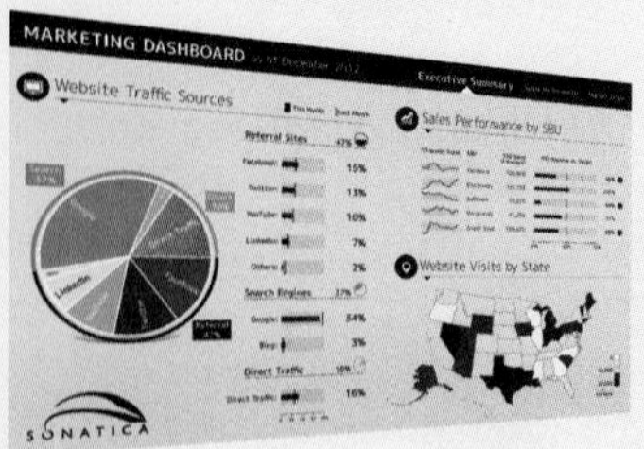

Using Marketing Dashboards

Are JetBlue's Flights Profitably Loaded?

Capacity management is critical in the marketing of many services. For example, having the right number of airline seats or hotel rooms available at the right time, price, and place can spell the difference between a profitable or unprofitable service operation.

Airlines feature *load factor* as a capacity management measure on their marketing dashboards, along with two other measures; namely, the *operating expense* per available seat flown one mile and the revenue generated by each seat flown one mile, called *yield*. Load factor is the percentage of available seats flown one mile occupied by a paying customer.

These three measures combine to show airline operating income or loss per available seat flown one mile:

Operating income (loss) per available seat flown one mile
= [Yield × Load factor] − Operating expense

Your Challenge As a marketing analyst for New York City–based JetBlue Airways, you have been asked to determine the operating income or loss per available seat flown one mile for the first six months of 2013. In addition, you have been asked to determine what load factor JetBlue must reach to break even assuming its current yield and operating expense will not change in the immediate future.

Your Findings JetBlue's yield, load factor, and operating expense marketing dashboard displays are shown below.

You can conclude from these measures that JetBlue Airways posted about a 0.21¢ loss per available seat flown one mile in the first six months of 2013:

Operating loss per available seat flown one mile
= [9.83¢ × 82.1%] − 8.28¢ = −.2096¢

Assuming JetBlue's yield and operating expenses will not change and using a little algebra, the airline's load factor will have to increase from 82.1 percent to 84.23 percent to break even:

Operating income (loss) per available seat flown one mile
= [9.83¢ × Load factor] − 8.28¢ = 0¢
Load factor = 84.23%

Your Action Assuming yield and operating expenses will not change, you should recommend that JetBlue consider revising its flight schedules to better accommodate traveler needs and advertise these changes. Consideration also might be given to how JetBlue utilizes its existing airplane fleet to serve its customers and produce a profit.

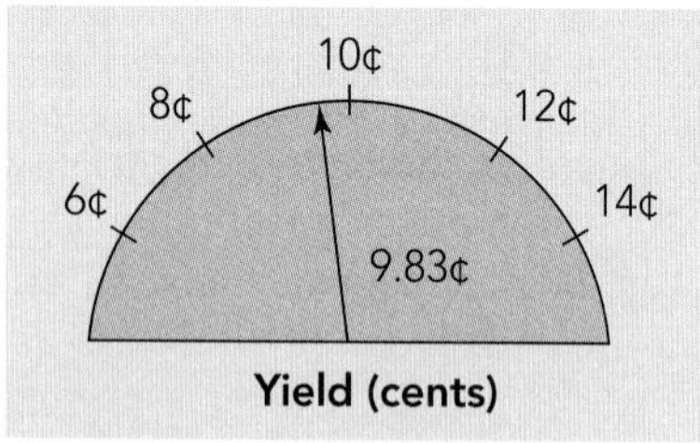

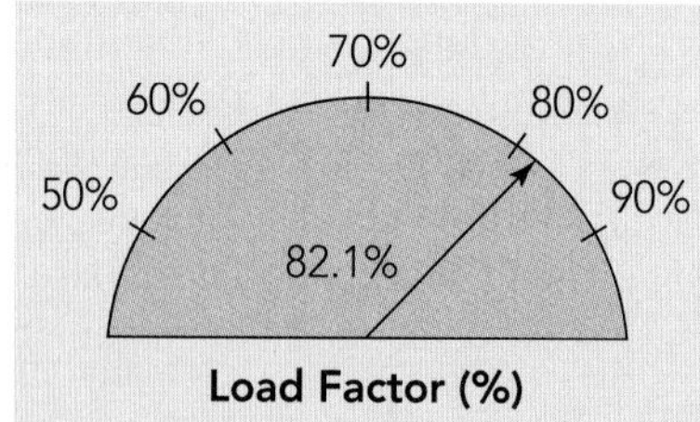

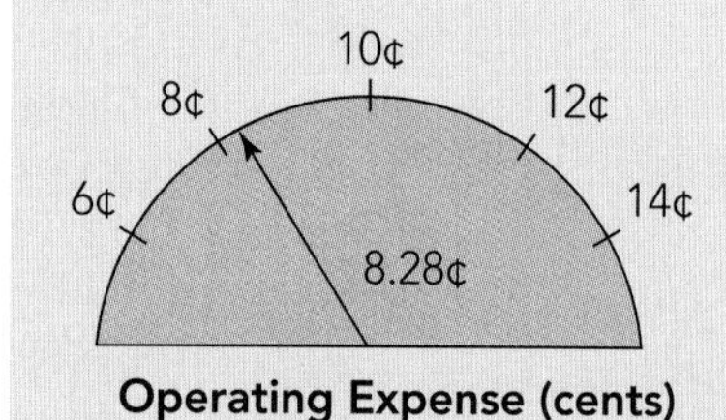

perceptions of value; however, excessive attempts at personalization can also trigger privacy concerns.[50]

New data and information about service consumers and providers is also leading to changes in service delivery and consumption. Physicians at the University of Virginia Health System discovered that cardiac patients learned more and reported 98 percent satisfaction when they shared a 90-minute appointment with other patients, rather than meeting the doctor in the traditional, shorter, one-on-one format. Other studies of services have discovered that in some businesses, such as retailing, restaurants, and repair and installation, customer satisfaction levels are inflated because employees often engage in "service sweethearting"—giving unauthorized free products or services to customers. Many of these businesses are now changing employee recruiting and training activities to limit this type of behavior. Both examples emphasize how understanding the details of service transactions will lead to new forms of service in the future.[51]

Finally, a growing interest in sustainability and "green" businesses is also changing the services industry. This trend began when consumers became aware of the environmental impact of many products such as automobiles, appliances, and cleaning solutions. Today, this trend has expanded to include consumers' assessment of services. Recent surveys indicate that green practices influence many consumer purchase decisions for services, including those provided by dry cleaners, contractors, and hotels. In response, many service providers are developing new approaches to their offerings. Hilton has set conservation goals to help its hotels achieve environmental management certification from the International Organization for Standardization (ISO). Similarly, the U.S. Postal Service has introduced sustainability initiatives to reduce energy, water, and petroleum use and to increase its recycling activities.[52] These and other approaches are likely to expand globally as services strive to create a competitive advantage.[53]

learning review

12-6. How does a movie theater use off-peak pricing?

12-7. Matching demand with capacity is the focus of ________________ management.

12-8. What factors will influence future changes in services?

LEARNING OBJECTIVES REVIEW

LO 12-1 *Describe four unique elements of services.*
The four unique elements of services—the four I's—are intangibility, inconsistency, inseparability, and inventory. Intangibility refers to the tendency of services to be a performance that cannot be held or touched, rather than an object. Inconsistency is a characteristic of services because they depend on people to deliver them, and people vary in their capabilities and in their day-to-day performance. Inseparability refers to the difficulty of separating the deliverer of the service (hair stylist) from the service itself (hair salon). Inventory refers to the need to have service production capability when there is service demand.

LO 12-2 *Recognize how services differ and how they can be classified.*
Services differ in terms of the balance of the part of the offering that is based on products and the part of the offering that is based on service. Services can be delivered by people or equipment, they can be provided by for-profit or nonprofit organizations, and they can be government sponsored.

LO 12-3 *Explain how consumers purchase and evaluate services.*
Because services are intangible, prepurchase evaluation is difficult for consumers. To choose a service, consumers use search, experience, and credence qualities to evaluate the product and service elements of an offering. Once a consumer tries a service, it is evaluated by comparing expectations with the actual experience on five dimensions of quality—reliability, tangibility, responsiveness, assurance, and empathy. Differences between expectations and experience are identified through gap analysis.

LO 12-4 *Develop a customer contact audit to identify service advantages.*
A customer contact audit is a flowchart of the points of interaction between a consumer and a service provider. The interactions identified in a customer contact audit often serve as the basis for developing relationships with customers.

LO 12-5 *Explain the role of the seven Ps in the services marketing mix.*
The services marketing mix includes seven Ps. An important aspect of the *product* element is branding—the use of a brand name or logo to help consumers identify a service. *Pricing* is reflected in charges, fees, fares, and rates and can be used to influence perceptions of the quality of a service and to balance demand for services. *Place* (or distribution) is used to provide access and convenience. *Promotional* tools such as advertising and publicity are a means of communicating the benefits of a service. *People* are responsible for the creation and delivery of the service. Internal marketing and customer experience management are concepts that result from a focus on people within the service organization and their interactions with customers. *Physical* environment refers to the appearance of the place where the services are delivered. *Process* refers to the actual procedures, mechanisms, and activities by which a service is created and delivered.

LO 12-6 *Discuss the important roles of internal marketing and customer experience management in service organizations.*

Because the employee plays a central role in creating the service experience and building and maintaining relationships with customers, services have adopted a concept called internal marketing. This concept suggests that services need to ensure that employees (the internal market) have the attitude, skills, and commitment needed to meet customer expectations. Customer experience management is the process of managing the entire customer experience with the company to ensure customer loyalty.

FOCUSING ON KEY TERMS

capacity management p. 315
customer contact audit p. 309
customer experience management (CEM) p. 314
four I's of services p. 301
gap analysis p. 308
idle production capacity p. 303
internal marketing p. 313
off-peak pricing p. 312
service continuum p. 303
services p. 300
seven Ps of services marketing p. 311

APPLYING MARKETING KNOWLEDGE

1 Explain how the four I's of services would apply to a Marriott Hotel.

2 Idle production capacity may be related to inventory or capacity management. How would the pricing component of the marketing mix reduce idle production capacity for (*a*) a car wash, (*b*) a stage theater group, and (*c*) a university?

3 Look back at the service continuum in Figure 12–3. Explain how the following points in the continuum differ in terms of consistency: (*a*) salt, (*b*) automobile, (*c*) advertising agency, and (*d*) teaching.

4 What are the search, experience, and credence properties of an airline for (*a*) the business traveler and (*b*) the pleasure traveler? What properties are most important to each group?

5 Outline the customer contact audit for the typical deposit you make at your neighborhood bank.

6 How does off-peak pricing influence demand for services?

7 Draw the channel of distribution for the following services: (*a*) a restaurant, (*b*) a hospital, and (*c*) a hotel.

8 The text suggests that internal marketing is necessary before a successful marketing program can be directed at consumers. Why is this particularly true for service organizations?

9 Outline the capacity management strategies that an airline must consider.

10 In recent years, many service businesses have begun to provide their employees with uniforms. Explain the rationale behind this strategy in terms of the concepts discussed in this chapter.

BUILDING YOUR MARKETING PLAN

In this section of your marketing plan you should distinguish between your core product—a good or a service—and supplementary services.

1 Develop an internal marketing program that will ensure that employees are prepared to deliver the core and supplementary services.

2 Using the flowchart in Figure 12–7 as a guide, create a customer contact audit to identify specific points of interaction with customers.

3 Describe marketing activities that will (*a*) address each of the four I's as they relate to your service and (*b*) encourage the development of relationships with your customers.

Add this section as an appendix to your marketing plan and use the results to develop your marketing mix strategy.

VIDEO CASE 12 LA Galaxy: Where Sports Marketing Is a Kick!

QR 12-5
LA Galaxy
Video Case

"We have a unique product for people," exclaims Chris Klein, president of the LA Galaxy soccer club. Soccer combines many elements of athleticism, teamwork, and competition to make it fast, exciting, engaging, fun, and increasingly popular. Klein goes on to explain, "This is a cool sport, and it's something that's growing." His enthusiasm is supported by a sophisticated strategy that Klein and his marketing team have designed to help people "experience the excitement" of their product!

THE LA GALAXY

The LA Galaxy is a professional soccer club competing in Major League Soccer (MLS). The club was one of ten charter clubs when the league began, and is now part of the league's Western Conference. "The LA Galaxy was founded in 1996," says Klein, and "through the course of the League's history, the Galaxy has been the most successful franchise in Major League Soccer." The team has been conference champions eight times, regular season champions four times, and the MLS championship winners four times.

The first Galaxy games were played at the Rose Bowl in Pasadena, California, until the team moved to its current location in the soccer-specific stadium StubHub Center in Carson, California. Players are primarily from the United States but also represent countries such as Brazil, Ireland, Italy, and Panama. "We have signed some of the biggest players, not only in our country, like Cobi Jones and Landon Donovan, but we've also signed some of the biggest players in the world," explains Klein. English soccer superstar David Beckham joined the LA Galaxy in 2007 and played through 2012, helping the team win two championships during that period.

Today, the LA Galaxy attracts an average of 23,000 fans to each of its games. While the hardcore fans tend to be 18- to 34-year-old men, the team also appeals to many other segments. For example, because soccer is the largest participant sport in the United States, many kids and youth soccer teams come to the games. In addition, many college students and families attend. According to Klein, it's a welcoming environment where "you can paint your face and yell" or you can bring your kids and just "have fun at the game." The team's mascot, Cozmo, is a frog-like extraterrestrial who entertains fans at the games and throughout Southern California.

MAJOR LEAGUE SOCCER

As part of its negotiation to hold the 1994 FIFA (Federation Internationale de Football Association) World Cup in the United States, the U.S. Soccer Federation promised to establish a professional soccer league. The result was Major League Soccer. Since its beginning with 10 teams in 1996, Major League Soccer has expanded to 19 teams, including 3 teams in Canada. Each team plays 34 games during the regular season from March to October, and the top 10 teams participate in the playoffs, which end with the MLS Cup in December.

Even though soccer is popular around the world, introducing professional soccer in the United States presented some difficulties. Klein describes the problem:

> Soccer is the biggest sport in the world, but here in the U.S. we have a lot of competition. Major League Soccer is the equivalent to Major League Baseball, the NFL, the NBA, and the NHL. These are established leagues and MLS is the fifth major sport. In 1996, we started thinking that we had to get every baseball fan, basketball fan, and football fan to enjoy our sport.

To attempt to attract fans from other sports, MLS experimented with changes to traditional soccer rules. For example, MLS added shootouts to resolve tie games, used a countdown (to zero) clock rather than a progressive clock, allowed extra substitutions, and even considered making the goals bigger to increase the scoring. Eventually, the league concluded that the changes had alienated some traditional soccer fans without attracting new fans from other sports, so it went back to the traditional rules for MLS games.

As the league shifted from an "attract all sports fans" philosophy to a focus on people with some existing interest in soccer, it made several other changes. First, it began moving MLS games from large, rented, football facilities to new, smaller, more intimate soccer-specific stadiums. In addition, the league made efforts to internationalize the teams by allowing up to eight players per team from outside of the United States. Finally, MLS encouraged all teams to create youth development programs to help find talented local players. To complement these efforts, each team manages its own marketing program.

THE LA GALAXY MARKETING PROGRAM

"The primary marketing objective for the Galaxy is ticket sales," says Casey Leppanen, senior director of marketing and broadcasting. "Our product is soccer," he goes on to explain, "but we are more than that. We are an experience." So, to sell single-game tickets and season tickets, the Galaxy developed a comprehensive marketing program. According to Leppanen, "Our marketing mix is pretty similar to any other sports team or company you're going to find." The key difference in marketing a sport, or any service, is that every game offers a different experience to fans. The players, the opponents, the weather, and the outcomes of the games change constantly.

How does the Galaxy sell a product that is constantly changing? The first step is to understand that different segments may attend a soccer game for different types of experiences. For example:

- *Supporter clubs.* Attend to watch the strategy of a game and see the Galaxy score.
- *Families.* Want to have fun, see the mascot, and get a souvenir.
- *Latino community.* Enjoy watching soccer and forming connections with players from Central and South America.
- *Trendsetting youth.* Attend to meet friends, enjoy an event, and see star players.
- *Groups* (teams, corporations, religious groups, etc.). Want an opportunity for networking and teambuilding.

The different interests combined with the changing "product" create a special marketing challenge.

The experience the Galaxy provides to fans is much more than watching a soccer game. It includes the quality of play, the individual members of the team, the merchandise, food, facilities, activities, and interactions with staff, other fans, and players. Some of the specific elements of the Galaxy game experience include:

- *Star players.* David Beckham, Cobi Jones, Landon Donovan, and Robbie Keane are all soccer stars that attract fans.
- *Team LA Store.* Offers LA Galaxy merchandise at StubHub Center and other locations.
- *Supporter clubs.* Three clubs—the Angel City Brigade, the Riot Squad, and the Galaxians—offer the opportunity to participate in an intense and festive fan experience, complete with songs and chants!
- *Promotional nights.* Special events include Family Nights, Bobblehead Nights, Jersey-Off-The-Back Auctions, and Student Nights.
- *"Name in Lights."* A donation gets your message on the home game scoreboard.
- *"Cozmo."* The team mascot who entertains all fans at every game.
- *StubHub Center.* The soccer-specific stadium offers a great atmosphere, amazing sight lines, event suites, terrace cabanas, restaurants, assigned seating, general admission seating, and an inclined lawn (also called the berm) for picnic-style seating.

Of course, there are many other elements that are all part of the experience the Galaxy marketing team manages and delivers at every game!

Next, the Galaxy must deliver relevant messages to each segment. Leppanen explains that the Galaxy "want to make sure that we're delivering an authentic message, but speak[ing] to them with what they want to be spoken about." One way they accomplish this is through direct marketing, which consists of email messages and direct-mail literature. These messages are complemented with traditional media advertising, outdoor advertising, and digital advertising. The traditional media include radio, TV,

and print. The outdoor advertising includes billboards and bus wraps. The digital platforms, which have a total of 1.3 million Galaxy fan users, include Facebook, Twitter, YouTube, Google+, Instagram, Pinterest, Flickr, and Foursquare. Digital is a very important part of the mix because "we can get really granular and sophisticated in who we're targeting and how we speak to them," explains Leppanen.

The Galaxy also use personal selling as part of their marketing program. A team of 25 people makes personal phone calls to help sell single-game tickets, family packs, group tickets, and season tickets. There are also two teams of brand ambassadors called the Star Squad and the Galaxy Street Team who are involved in about 500 events in the community each year. Lori Nevares, a marketing coordinator at Galaxy and former Street Team member, explains that "We got to go out and do all kinds of promotional events for different communities and see the fans and how much they were devoted to the Galaxy." A skills team called the Galaxy Futboleros provides high-energy performances throughout the community as well. Finally, Cozmo makes many appearances to deliver the Galaxy soccer message to current and potential fans.

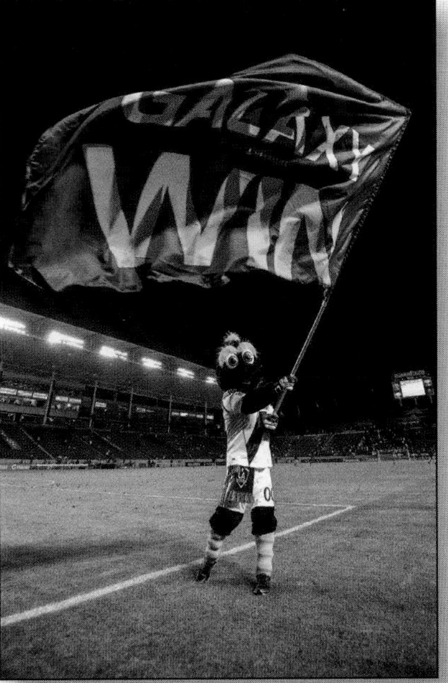

One of the final steps in the ticket sales process is setting the price. According to Heather Pease, director of ticketing, "Every year we conduct a very in-depth analysis of our ticket sales. We go seat-by-seat, row-by-row, and category-by-category to see how many people have purchased seats and at what price." The analysis also includes a comparison of ticket prices at other sports teams in the area. Pease then uses the information to create a price and a package for every possible type of fan, ranging from Champions Lounge members, to season ticket holders, to groups or families, to single-game fans. She also offers discounted tickets for students and children.

There are a lot of marketing activities taking place at the Galaxy. In fact, Casey Leppanen says, "My role here at the Galaxy is to integrate all the pieces of our marketing department." The integration is paying off, as attendance at LA Galaxy games is well above the league average. In addition, the team currently has 8,500 season ticket holders and plans to reach 12,500 in three years!

THE BUSINESS OF SOCCER

While ticket sales represent a substantial source of revenue for the Galaxy, there are several other important elements of the soccer "business"—broadcast rights, sponsorships, and merchandise—that the team must manage. Early in the league's history, MLS had to pay television and cable networks to broadcast its games. As the number of viewers increased, however, the league was able to attract coverage from ESPN, ABC, NBC, and Fox. The Galaxy recently began a ten-year, $55 million deal with the Time Warner Cable Sports network. Currently, all games have television and radio coverage in English and Spanish, and there is play-by-play coverage and webchat on LAGalaxy.com.

Sponsorships are also essential to the financial success of MLS and the Galaxy. Pepsi is the official soft drink and Aquafina is the official water of MLS. Similarly, Herbalife is the official nutrition company of the LA Galaxy. In addition, Herbalife recently announced a 10-year agreement to be the official jersey sponsor of the Galaxy. Herbalife pays $4 million annually to sponsor the team and place its logo on the front of the team jerseys. Other team sponsors include Chevrolet, Nestlé, Alaska Airlines, Shasta, and Buffalo Wild Wings. The sponsors participate in many of the team's contests, promotions, and events to support the team and to gain exposure to customers with similar values and interests.

The marketing team at the LA Galaxy is always busy. "There is a business to run," says Pease. "It is about driving revenue at the end of the day," she continues, "but the best part about it is you get to walk out on a game day and see a sold-out stadium." Seeing the sold-out stadium is a thrill not only because it's a business, however, but also because the marketing team loves soccer. Galaxy president Chris Klein, who studied business and marketing in college, is a good example of the attitude at Galaxy. "I went to college on a soccer scholarship," says Klein, "then I played professionally in our league, and I'm now president of a major club." He is thrilled by "the challenge of marketing a sport that I love, a sport that I've played, and a sport that has so much potential."

Questions

1 What is the LA Galaxy "product"?

2 Which of the seven elements of the service marketing mix are most important in the LA Galaxy marketing program?

3 How is promotion (advertising, personal selling, public relations, sales promotion, direct marketing) used by the LA Galaxy? Do these activities depend on the specific target markets?

4 How are social media integrated into the LA Galaxy's marketing strategy?

5 How does the LA Galaxy assess the impact of its marketing activities? Has its program been successful?

13 Building the Price Foundation

Learning Objectives

After reading this chapter you should be able to:

LO 13-1 Identify the elements that make up a price.

LO 13-2 Recognize the objectives a firm has in setting prices and the constraints that restrict the range of prices a firm can charge.

LO 13-3 Explain what a demand curve is and the role of revenues in pricing decisions.

LO 13-4 Describe what price elasticity of demand means to a manager facing a pricing decision.

LO 13-5 Explain the role of costs in pricing decisions.

LO 13-6 Describe how various combinations of price, fixed cost, and unit variable cost affect a firm's break-even point.

Mother "Was Not Thrilled": The Launch of StubHub.com!

"It was definitely something that my mother was *not* thrilled about," recalls Jeff Fluhr. The "it" Fluhr refers to was his dropping out of the Stanford University MBA program his first year there. She probably feels differently today, though, since her son's firm is a leader in the $5 billion online ticket industry![1]

Plan for the Start-up

Fluhr and his classmate, Eric Baker, had entered a class competition for the best business plan. Their idea: "Need A Ticket.com," a centralized website where people owning tickets to sporting events or concerts could auction them off. The idea seemed so appealing that Fluhr dropped out of graduate school to start the new business. But, as with most marketing or business plans for start-ups, actually turning the plan into reality wasn't as easy as the two entrepreneurs expected.

Launching their ticket-selling business in late 2000 right after the dot-com crash, Fluhr and Baker had trouble raising money from investors. Their original business plan focused on selling tickets on other websites and then splitting the revenues with them. Since 2003, the StubHub website has allowed sellers to sell their tickets online directly to buyers either at a fixed price, which declines as the date of the event approaches, or by auction. StubHub's "Where Do You Want to Sit?" slogan is apropos because customers no longer have to stand outside a venue haggling with ticket scalpers for an event they want to attend.

How StubHub's Pricing Works Now

The StubHub pricing formula is very straightforward. Suppose you want to sell a ticket to a Beyoncé concert for $100. The buyer pays $110 for the ticket, the extra $10 being the 10 percent commission StubHub receives. StubHub, in turn, pays you $85 for the ticket it sells on your behalf, earning a $15 or 15 percent commission from you, the seller. As a result of the transaction, StubHub makes $25 on the sale.

With over half of tickets to major events sold online, StubHub's website can help generate *extra ticket sales* for the original sponsors of the

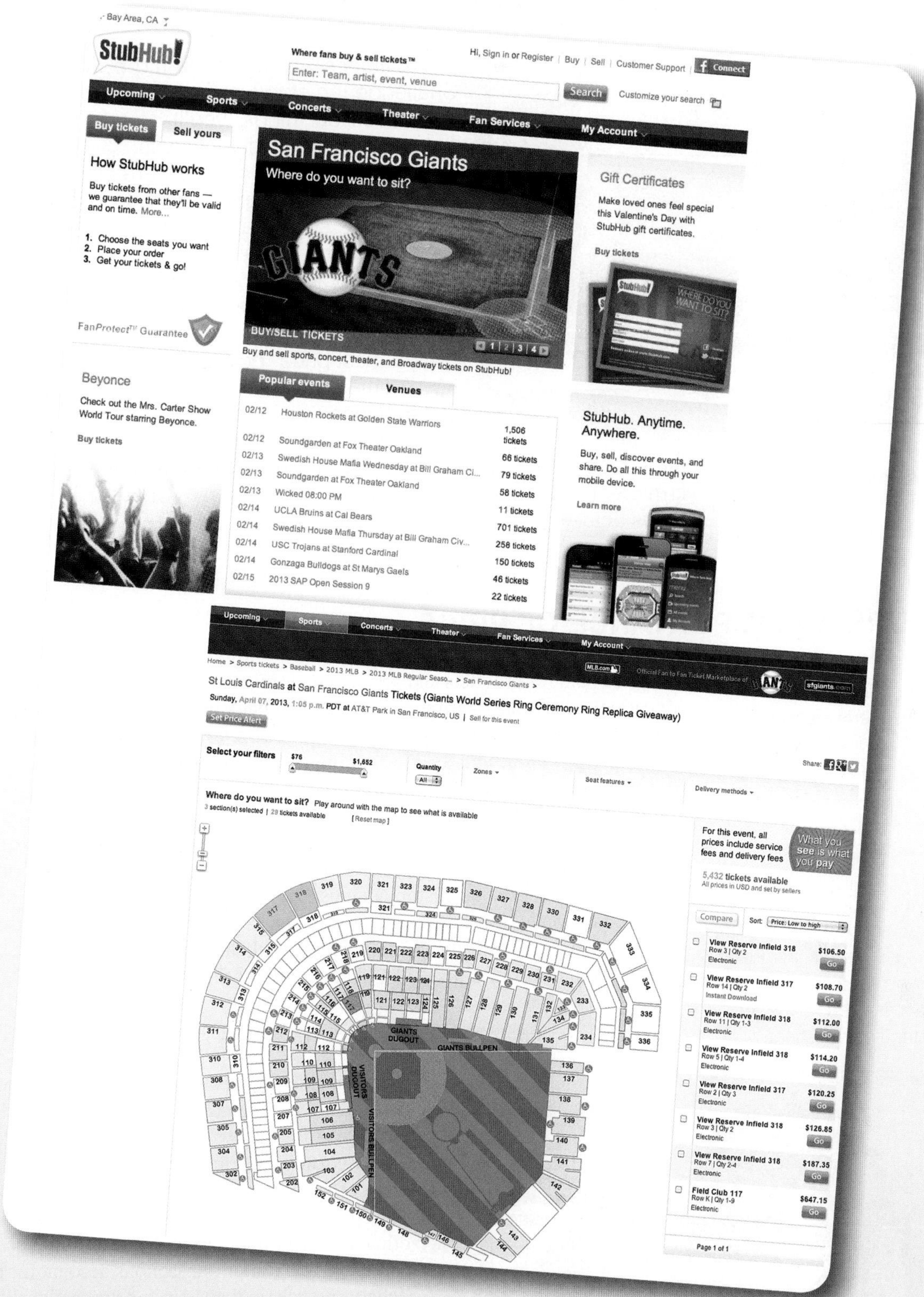

QR 13-1
StubHub
Pricing Ad

events. This is why StubHub now has formal relationships with not only professional sports leagues like Major League Baseball but also sports programs at major universities such as Alabama, Southern California, Stanford, Kansas State, and Purdue. As part of StubHub's partnership with the San Francisco Giants, fans buying resold tickets on StubHub (now part of eBay) are shown a simulated view of the field from the seats they are thinking about buying.[2]

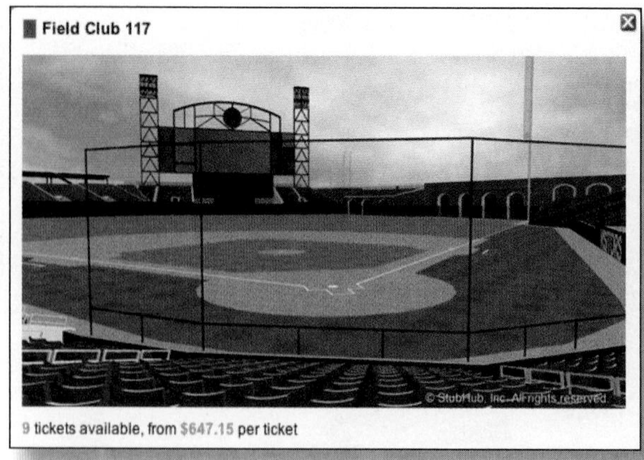

San Francisco Giants fans can get a simulated view of the field from the seat they are thinking about purchasing through StubHub.

Jeff Fluhr's advice for would-be entrepreneurs is: "Challenge the status quo. If you're disrupting the way businesses do things, you'll be told that's not how it works. But listen to your instincts!"[3]

Pricing decisions involve carefully assessing consumer demand, revenues, fixed costs, and variable costs before setting a final price. If the answers were easy, hundreds of failed dot-com firms with brilliant ideas, technologies, and marketing plans (such as Pets.com) would still be going strong today. In fact, many grocery product manufacturers run test markets to try to find the "best price" before introducing new products.

Welcome to the fascinating—and intense—world of pricing, where many forces come together in the price buyers are asked to pay. This chapter covers important factors used in setting prices, starting with the critical first step of having a firm identify its pricing objectives and constraints. Chapter 14 describes the steps actually used in setting a final price.

NATURE AND IMPORTANCE OF PRICE

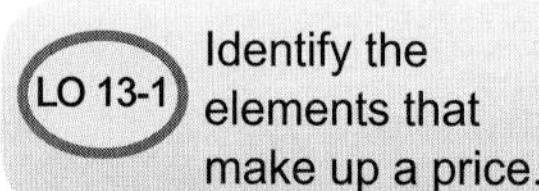
LO 13-1 Identify the elements that make up a price.

The price paid for products and services goes by many names. You pay *tuition* for your education, *rent* for an apartment, *interest* on a bank credit card, and a *premium* for car insurance. Your dentist or physician charges you a *fee*, a professional or social organization charges *dues*, and airlines charge a *fare*. In business, an executive is given a *salary*, a salesperson receives a *commission*, and a worker is paid a *wage*. And what you pay for clothes or a haircut is termed a *price*.

Among all marketing and operations factors in a business firm, price has a unique role. It is the place where all other business decisions come together. The price must be "right"—in the sense that customers must be willing to pay it; it must generate enough sales dollars to pay for the cost of developing, producing, and marketing the product; *and* it must earn a profit for the company. Small changes in price can have big effects on both the number of units sold and company profit.

How would you calculate the price of a new Bugatti Veyron, the world's fastest car? Read the text to see how the price equation is used to answer this intriguing question.

What Is a Price?

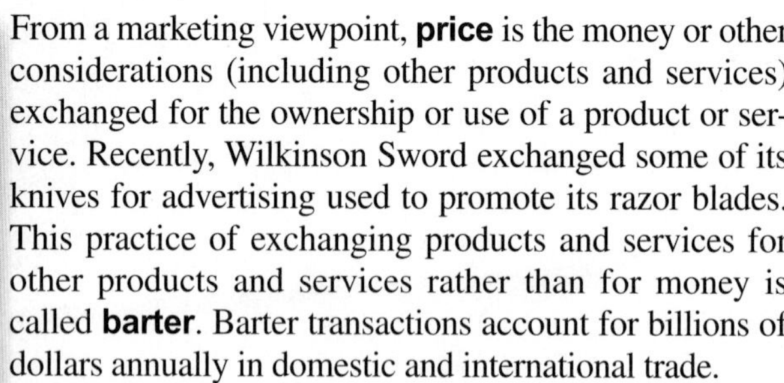
From a marketing viewpoint, **price** is the money or other considerations (including other products and services) exchanged for the ownership or use of a product or service. Recently, Wilkinson Sword exchanged some of its knives for advertising used to promote its razor blades. This practice of exchanging products and services for other products and services rather than for money is called **barter**. Barter transactions account for billions of dollars annually in domestic and international trade.

The Price Equation For most products, money is exchanged. However, the amount paid is not always the same as the list, or quoted, price because of discounts, allowances, and extra fees. One new 21st century pricing tactic involves using "special fees" and "surcharges." This practice is driven by consumers' zeal for low prices combined with the ease of making price comparisons on the

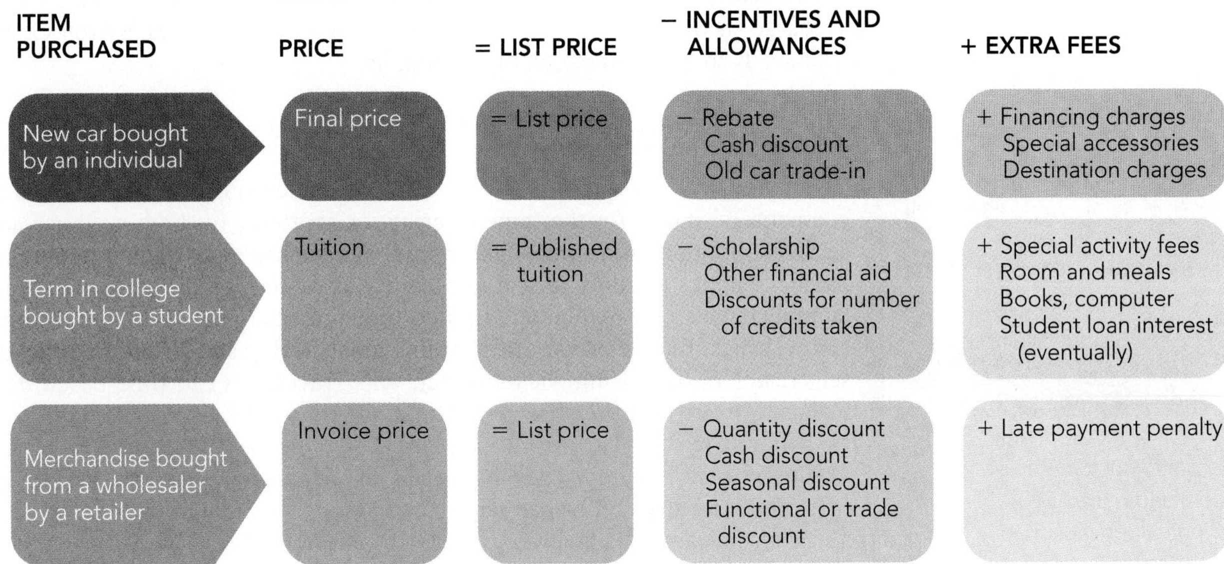

PRICE EQUATION
ITEM PURCHASED
PRICE
= LIST PRICE
– INCENTIVES AND ALLOWANCES
+ EXTRA FEES
New car bought by an individual
Final price
= List price
– Rebate
Cash discount
Old car trade-in
+ Financing charges
Special accessories
Destination charges
Term in college bought by a student
Tuition
= Published tuition
– Scholarship
Other financial aid
Discounts for number of credits taken
+ Special activity fees
Room and meals
Books, computer
Student loan interest (eventually)
Merchandise bought from a wholesaler by a retailer
Invoice price
= List price
– Quantity discount
Cash discount
Seasonal discount
Functional or trade discount
+ Late payment penalty

FIGURE 13–1
The "price" a buyer pays can take different names depending on what is purchased, and it can change depending on the price equation.

Internet. Buyers are more willing to pay extra fees than a higher list price, so sellers use add-on charges as a way of having the consumer pay more without raising the list price.

All the factors that increase or decrease the final price of an offering help construct a "price equation," which is shown for a few products in Figure 13–1. These are key considerations if you want to buy a 2013 Bugatti Veyron Grand Sport Vitesse (French for "speed"), the world's fastest and most expensive "open top" production car. The all-wheel car accelerates from 0 to 60 mph in just 2.5 seconds. With its 1,200 horsepower engine, top speed is 255 mph (roof on)! The aerodynamic body is made out of carbon fiber to safely handle the speed. But consider that: (1) fuel economy is a paltry 12.2 mpg, costing you about $10,000 per year, depending on premium gasoline prices; (2) every 10,000 miles, the four 20-inch Michelin tires, which cost a total of $40,000, must be replaced; and (3) maintenance will set you back about $20,000 every time the car needs servicing.[4]

QR 13-2
Bugatti Veyron Video

Calculating a Final Price The Bugatti Veyron Grand Sport Vitesse U.S. list price is a cool $2.5 million. But to get the special paint option seen in the photo, it will cost you an extra $430,000. An extended warranty will cost an additional $70,000. However, if you put $500,000 down and finance the balance, you will receive a $50,000 rebate off the list price. Also, the dealer has agreed to give you a trade-in allowance of $7,000 based on the *Kelley Blue Book* (www.kbb.com) trade-in value for your 2008 Honda Civic DX four-door sedan that has 75,000 miles and is in good condition. Other charges include: (1) an import duty of $50,000; (2) a gas-guzzler tax of $7,000; (3) a 7.5 percent sales tax of $229,125; (4) an auto registration fee of $5,000 to the state; and (5) a $50,000 destination charge to ship the car to you from France. Finally, your total finance charge is $377,168 based on a five-year loan with an annual interest rate of 5 percent, compounded monthly.[5]

Applying the price equation shown in Figure 13–1 to your Bugatti Veyron Grand Sport Vitesse purchase, your final price is:

$$\begin{aligned}
\text{Final price} &= [\text{List price}] - [(\text{Incentives}) + (\text{Allowances})] + [\text{Extra fees}] \\
&= [\$2{,}500{,}000] - [(\$50{,}000 + \$7{,}000)] + [\$430{,}000 + \$70{,}000 \\
&\quad + \$50{,}000 + \$7{,}000 + \$229{,}125 + \$5{,}000 + \$50{,}000 + \$377{,}168] \\
&= \$2{,}500{,}000 - \$57{,}000 + \$1{,}218{,}293 \\
&= \$3{,}661{,}293
\end{aligned}$$

Note that your final price is $1,161,293 more than the list price! Your monthly payment for the five-year loan of $3,161,293 ($2,784,125 principal plus $377,168 total finance charge) is $52,688.21. Are you still interested in the Bugatti Veyron Grand Sport Vitesse? If so, put yourself on the waiting list.[6]

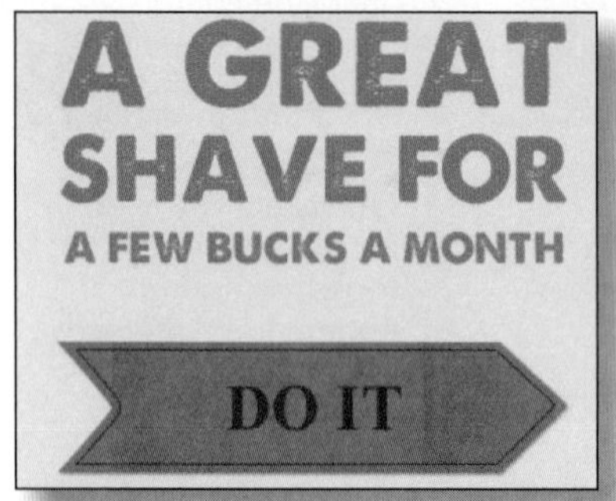

Benefits to customers, low prices, and a creative YouTube video launched Dollar Shave Club.

QR 13-3 Dollar Shave Club Video

Price Transparency Today

Revolutionary *price transparency*, a consumer's near-instantaneous access to competitors' prices for the same offering, exists today for both products and services through online websites, "apps," and smartphones. This price transparency applies not only to seat availability at venues, on airlines, and at restaurants but also for regular and limited-time price bargains at retailers' stores and websites. Examples vary from online giants (eBay and Amazon) to ticket/seat resellers (StubHub, Ticketmaster, and Travelocity) to time-based deal makers (Groupon) to retail and catalog marketers (Macy's, Lands' End, and Coldwater Creek).[7]

This price transparency revolution affects actions across marketing. It has reduced barriers to entry and helped launch countless online start-ups, like StubHub.com. Because they avoid the many expenses inherent in brick-and-mortar businesses, these firms are able to promote lower prices and other benefits to consumers. Dollar Shave Club, described in the Marketing Matters box, uses low prices, convenience, and its smash-hit YouTube video to market stainless steel razor blade cartridges.[8] Examples of price transparency and its marketing impact appear throughout this chapter.

Price and the Global Marketplace

To generate profits in today's global marketplace, international firms span the globe to find both (1) suppliers whose efficiencies and lower hourly wages can reduce the prices the buying firms must pay and (2) new markets to increase revenues. The global "playing field is being leveled," says the CEO of India's Infosys Technologies, Ltd., referring to Internet and computer technologies that enable research and development to be done around the world.[9]

IKEA, the huge Swedish retailer, understands this. It is both contracting with furniture manufacturers around the world *and* opening new stores. To compete in China, IKEA has slashed prices to appeal to consumers in the country's growing and affluent middle class. The strategy seems to be working: IKEA's first store in Beijing has floor space the size of eight football fields and can handle six million customers annually.

For how IKEA and other global marketers are profiting from today's more level global playing field, see the text.

At Toys "Я" Us, the firm's global strategy is focused on expanding both its brick-and-mortar and online marketing efforts to reach China's middle class. This includes doubling the 30 stores it already has there. Its mix of toys includes 35 percent that have an educational focus—many of which have been adapted for local appeal by using the multidomestic marketing strategy discussed in Chapter 7. And while Mattel closed its Shanghai-based flagship Barbie store in 2011, Toys "Я" Us offers the Barbie Beautiful Fairy doll on its Chinese website for $36.68—far above the $11.99 list price on its U.S. website.[10]

Price as an Indicator of Value

From a consumer's standpoint, price is often used to indicate value when it is compared with perceived benefits such as the quality or durability of a product or service. Specifically, **value** is the ratio of perceived benefits to price, or[11]

$$\text{Value} = \frac{\text{Perceived benefits}}{\text{Price}}$$

Marketing Matters

entrepreneurship

Dollar Shave Club: Razor Blade Cartridges Every Month . . . By Mail

Today, it seems that almost any type of consumer offering can be improved or priced lower by using the Internet.

The Idea

We've seen it with movie rentals, books, music, and now . . . shaving! The co-founders of Dollar Shave Club, Michael Dubin and Mark Levine, met at a party in 2010. They griped about the cost of razor blade cartridges—men can spend $40 a month or more on them. So, building on Dubin's marketing and Levine's manufacturing experiences, they came up with this idea: Use direct-to-consumer marketing via the Internet to sell razor blades in monthly subscription packages dirt cheap compared to those from Gillette or Schick. Men can now shave their beards (or heads!) cheaply without venturing to the local store and "scaling the walls of the razor fortress!"

The Launch

The company launched its business in early 2012 using a 94-second YouTube video that cost $4,500 to make. It immediately went "viral," generating more than 5 million hits. The key to the video's success? The great offer and an entertaining pitch. The video, starring Dubin, resonated with males around the country and sales skyrocketed: 12,000 people signed up in the first 48 hours after it aired. Scan the QR code to watch the video and judge for yourself!

The Pricing Strategy

Dollar Shave Club sends its members new razor blade cartridges each month—even throwing in the handle for free! Customers can choose from three different monthly fee plans, each of which includes shipping and handling. The $1 "Humble Twin" plan delivers a basic twin-blade shaver for "guys who dig simplicity and precision" with five cartridges a month. Want a better shave? Then check out "The 4X" plan and get four cartridges for $6 per month. This shaver has four stainless-steel blades and a 90-degree pivoting head. Still want more? Then go for "The Executive" plan for $9 per month and get a shaver that has six stainless-steel blades and a lubricating strip and three cartridges a month.

On the horizon: Razor blade cartridges for women as well as grooming products like shaving cream and after-shave lotion!

This relationship shows that for a given price, as perceived benefits increase, value increases. For example, if you're used to paying $7.99 for a medium frozen cheese pizza, wouldn't a large one at the same price be more valuable? Conversely, for a given price, value decreases when perceived benefits decrease.

Using Value Pricing Creative marketers engage in **value pricing**, the practice of simultaneously increasing product and service benefits while maintaining or decreasing price. For some products, price influences consumers' perception of overall quality and ultimately its value to them.[12] In a survey of home furnishing buyers, 84 percent agreed with the statement: "The higher the price, the higher the quality."[13] For example, Kohler introduced a walk-in bathtub that is safer for children and the elderly. Although priced higher than conventional step-in bathtubs, the product is successful because buyers are willing to pay a bit more for what they perceive as the value of extra safety.

In this context, "value" involves the judgment by a consumer of the worth of a product relative to substitutes that satisfy the same need. Through the process of comparing the costs and benefits of substitute items, a "reference value" emerges. For example, the recent price of a Big Mac, small soft drink, and small fries bought separately at McDonald's was $6.37. The three items bought together as a Big Mac "Extra Value Meal" bundle had a price of $5.59, a savings of 76 cents. In this example of value

A snapshot of today's deals and discounts: Gap offers a "buy one, get one" (or BOGO) deal of 60% off a second item (top), while Macy's offers 30% off plus an extra 20% off (bottom). For the actual prices buyers pay with such deals, work the text problems and see the Marketing Matters box.

pricing, a typical McDonald's customer uses the $5.59 bundle price of the three items bought together as his/her reference value, concludes the Extra Value Meal has great value, and buys it. Bundle pricing is explained further in Chapter 14.

Decoding Today's Consumer Prices In the holiday shopping season, retailers increasingly offer deals, discounts, and BOGOs—"buy one, get one" in retail slang—to entice shoppers to buy. The main problem is that shoppers have to have Albert Einstein's math skills to calculate in their heads the real percentage discount they receive and the actual price they pay.

Many brick-and-mortar retailers have taken lessons from fashion websites and now offer "flash sales"—those that involve cutting prices for only a few hours. Most shoppers can't take time to go home and work out the math. As a result, they are often fooled about the size of the "deal" they are getting or whether they are even getting one, and they make bad, snap-decision purchases.

For example, suppose you see a "77 & 7" deal "for today only" at your favorite local clothing store. This, as you discover, means you pay 77 percent of the ticket price, plus you get an additional 7 percent off that price. So you pay 70 percent of the ticket price, right? Not quite. You pay $0.77 \times (1.00 - 0.07) = 0.77 \times 0.93 = 71.6$ percent of the ticket price! Experiments involving consumers show they often err by *not* using the correct base when calculating the final price they must pay. This is the situation illustrated here, where the error is in using the base for the 7 percent discount as the original 100 percent—rather than the newly calculated base of 70 percent.[14]

Now that we've had some math practice, calculate your answers for the following three pricing questions posed recently by *The Wall Street Journal*:[15]

1. Which represents the biggest savings, in total dollars?
   a. A markdown from $85.27 to $70.66
   b. A markdown from $83.99 to $69.99
   c. A markdown from $80 to $70
2. Which represents the biggest percentage off a $2,000 item?
   a. 50% off
   b. 25% off, then another 25% off the reduced price
   c. 20% off, then another 20% off the reduced price, then 20% off the twice-reduced price
3. On a $40 pair of pants, which offer will yield the best discount?
   a. Buy one, get 50% off the second (a BOGO offer)
   b. $20 off all purchases of $50 or more
   c. A markdown of $10 on the pants

After your calculations, compare your answers with those in the Marketing Matters box. Also, read about some simple "hidden dangers" consumers face when in a hurry. Perhaps spending time on your smartphone calculator will pay off on your next visit to a retailer.

Price in the Marketing Mix

Pricing is a critical decision made by a marketing executive because price has a direct effect on a firm's profits. This is apparent from a firm's **profit equation**, where:

$$\begin{aligned}\text{Profit} &= \text{Total revenue} - \text{Total cost}\\ &= (\text{Unit price} \times \text{Quantity sold}) - (\text{Fixed cost} + \text{Variable cost})\end{aligned}$$

What makes this relationship even more complicated is that price affects the quantity sold, as illustrated with demand curves later in this chapter. Furthermore, since the quantity sold usually affects a firm's costs because of efficiency of production, price also indirectly affects costs. Thus, pricing decisions influence both total revenue (sales) and total cost, which makes pricing one of the most important decisions marketing executives face.

Marketing Matters

customer value

American Eagle "Buy One, Get One Free" Hoodies: A Good Deal?

American Eagle Outfitters (photo) sold its hoodies for $24.95 on a BOGO discount. A good deal?

Before you decide, compare your answers to the pricing questions in the text on the previous page to those below, study the "hidden dangers" that buyers face, and see if there are lessons for hoodie shoppers:

1. *Answer is (a):* Answering this requires three simple subtractions. Answer (a) ($14.61) may seem small, but it offers greater savings than (b) and (c) ($14 and $10, respectively). *Hidden Danger:* Pricing researchers say shoppers skip the math by taking cognitive shortcuts, such as associating precise prices with low prices. Also, those 9s at the end of the prices in choice (b) may help make the decline in the left-most digit (from 8 to 6) seem larger than the decline in choice (a) (from 8 to 7).
2. *Answer is (a):* Option (a) yields a sale price of $1,000, compared with a sale price of $1,125 in option (b). In option (c), the first reduction brings the price down to $1,600, the second to $1,280, and the third to $1,024. Those three discounts might appear to add up to 60%, but they save less than the one 50% discount in answer (a). *Hidden Danger:* Discounts layered on top of discounts sound more impressive than they really are, because each successive discount is taken off a lower price base.
3. *Answer is (c):* The discounts only look identical. When you buy two pairs of pants, you spend $60 to get the $20 discount. If you want just one pair, options (a) and (b) don't give any dollar savings. Option (c) saves only $10. *Hidden Danger:* A "good discount" on something you don't need isn't a smart deal. So with option (c), you don't end up with pants you may not need. Offers encouraging extra purchases—like BOGOs—play into a buyer's goal to get the best bargain possible.

Are the American Eagle hoodies a good deal? Probably . . . but only if you need two!

The importance of price in the marketing mix necessitates an understanding of six major steps in the process organizations go through in setting prices (see Figure 13–2):

1. Identify pricing objectives and constraints.
2. Estimate demand and revenue.
3. Determine cost, volume, and profit relationships.

FIGURE 13–2
The six steps in setting price. The first three steps are covered in this chapter, and the last three steps are covered in Chapter 14.

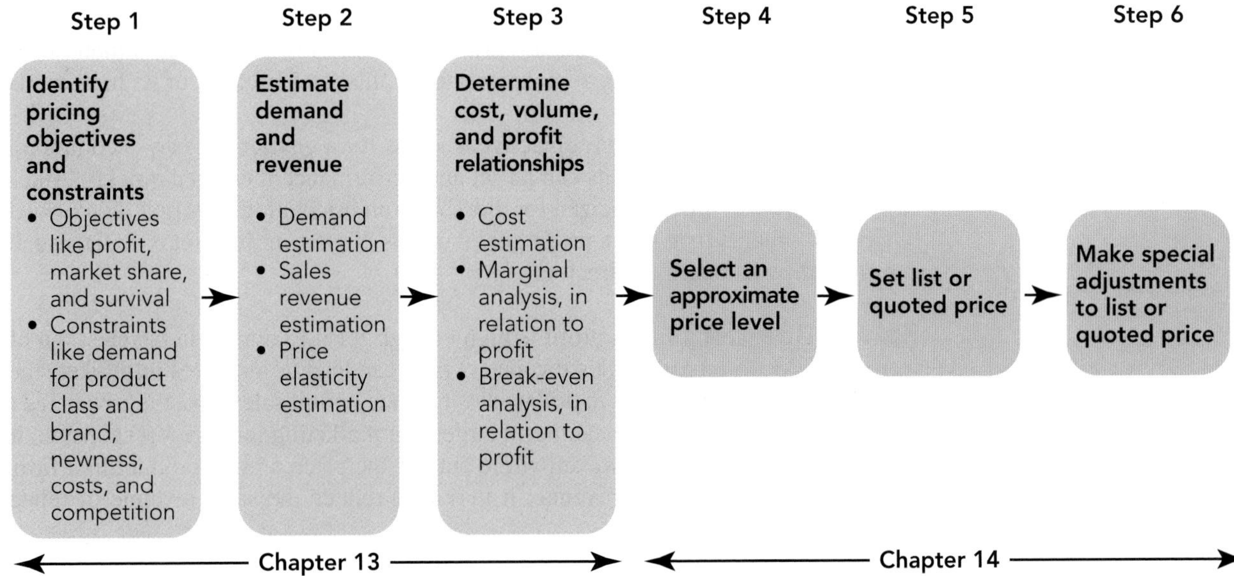

4. Select an approximate price level.
5. Set list or quoted price.
6. Make special adjustments to list or quoted price.

The first three steps are covered in this chapter, and the last three are discussed in Chapter 14.

learning review

13-1. What is price?

13-2. What factors impact the list price to determine the final price?

13-3. What is the profit equation?

STEP 1: IDENTIFY PRICING OBJECTIVES AND CONSTRAINTS

With such a variety of alternative pricing strategies available, a marketing manager must consider the pricing objectives and constraints that will narrow the range of choices. While pricing objectives frequently reflect corporate goals, pricing constraints often relate to conditions existing in the marketplace.

Identifying Pricing Objectives

Recognize the objectives a firm has in setting prices and the constraints that restrict the range of prices a firm can charge.

Pricing objectives involve specifying the role of price in an organization's marketing and strategic plans. To the extent possible, these pricing objectives are carried to lower levels in the organization, such as in setting objectives for marketing managers responsible for an individual brand. These objectives may change depending on the financial position of the company as a whole, the success of its products, or the segments in which it is doing business. H. J. Heinz, for example, has specific pricing objectives for its Heinz Ketchup brand that vary by country. Chapter 2 discussed broad objectives that an organization may pursue, which tie directly to the organization's pricing objectives covered next.

Profit Three different objectives relate to a firm's profit, which is often measured in terms of return on investment (ROI) or return on assets (ROA). These objectives have different implications for pricing strategy. One objective is *managing for long-run profits*, in which companies—such as many Japanese car or HDTV manufacturers—give up immediate profit by developing quality products to penetrate competitive markets over the long term. Products are priced relatively low compared to their cost to develop, but the firm expects to make greater profits later because of its high market share.

A *maximizing current profit* objective, such as for a quarter or year, is common in many firms because the targets can be set and performance measured quickly. American firms are sometimes criticized for this short-run orientation. A *target return* objective occurs when a firm sets a profit goal (such as 20 percent for pretax ROI), usually determined by its board of directors.

Sales Given that a firm's profit is high enough for it to remain in business, an objective may be to increase sales revenue, which can lead to increases in market share and profit. Objectives related to dollar sales revenue or unit sales have the advantage of being translated easily into meaningful targets for marketing managers responsible for a product line or brand. However, while cutting the price on one product in a firm's line may increase its sales revenue, it may also reduce the sales revenue of related products.

Market Share *Market share* is the ratio of the firm's sales revenues or unit sales to those of the industry (competitors plus the firm itself). Companies often pursue a market share objective when industry sales are relatively flat or declining. In the late 1990s, Boeing cut prices drastically to try to maintain its 60 percent share of the commercial airline market to compete with Airbus. As a result, it encountered huge losses. Although increased market share is a primary goal of some firms, others see it as a means to other ends: increasing sales and profits.

Unit Volume Many firms use *unit volume*, the quantity produced or sold, as a pricing objective. These firms often sell multiple products at very different prices and need to match the unit volume demanded by customers with price and production capacity. Using unit volume as an objective can be counterproductive if a volume objective is achieved, say, by drastic price cutting that drives down profit.

Survival In some instances, profits, sales, and market share are less important objectives of the firm than mere survival. Specialty-toy retailers increasingly are facing survival problems because they can't match the price cuts offered by big discount retailers like Walmart and Target. This was the dilemma faced by FAO Schwartz, which filed for bankruptcy and was recently bought by Toys "Я" Us.

Social Responsibility A firm may forgo higher profit on sales and follow a pricing objective that recognizes its obligations to customers and society in general. For example, Gerber supplies a specially formulated product free of charge to children who cannot tolerate foods containing cow's milk.

Identifying Pricing Constraints

Factors that limit the range of prices a firm may set are referred to as **pricing constraints**. Consumer demand for the product clearly affects the price that can be charged. Other constraints on price vary from factors within the organization to competitive factors outside the organization. Legal and regulatory constraints on pricing are discussed in Chapter 14.[16]

Demand for the Product Class, Product, and Brand The number of potential buyers for the product class (cars), product group (family sedans) and specific brand (Toyota Camry V6) clearly affects the price a seller can charge. Likewise, whether the item is a luxury—like the Bugatti Veyron—or a necessity—like bread and a roof over your head—also affects the price that can be charged. Generally, the greater the demand for a product, the higher the price that can be set. For example, the New York Mets set different ticket prices for their games based on the appeal of their opponent—prices are higher when they play the New York Yankees and lower when they play the Pittsburgh Pirates.[17]

The price for a specific brand—like the Toyota Camry V6 here—is also affected by general demand for its product class (cars) and product group (family sedans), as discussed in the text.

Newness of the Product: Stage in the Product Life Cycle The newer a product and the earlier it is in its life cycle, the higher the price that can usually be charged. Are you willing to spend $9,999 for an LG 55-inch 3D OLED HD Smart TV? The high initial price is possible because of patents and limited competition early in its product life cycle. By the time you read this, the price probably will be lower.

Element of Final Price	$ of Final Price	% of Final Price	
Fabric and Trim	$20	10%	Manufacturing = $32 or 16%
Labor	$6	3%	
Mfg. Contractor	$6	3%	
Brand Name Company	$68	34%	Marketing = $168 or 84%
Specialty Retailer	$100	50%	
Totals	$200	100%	

FIGURE 13–3
The text explains who gets the $200 you pay for your designer denim jeans.

Sometimes—when nostalgia or fad factors come into play—prices may rise later in the product's life cycle. For example, collectibles can experience skyrocketing prices. Recently, consumers on eBay paid $250 for a Zip the Cat Beanie Baby (with black paws), $200 for a 2001 Ichiro Suzuki rookie bobble-head doll, and $29,500 for a 1963 copy of the first "Amazing Spiderman" issue. But these prices can nosedive, too, when the fad wears off or a recession appears. To play it safe—and perhaps finance your retirement—save your perfect-condition, in-the-box Barbies, Hot Wheels, and Star Wars lightsabers.[18]

Cost of Producing and Marketing the Product Another profit consideration for marketers is to ensure that firms in their channels of distribution make an adequate profit. Without profits for channel members, a marketer is cut off from its customers. Figure 13–3 shows where the $200 a customer spends for a pair of designer denim jeans goes: 50 percent of each dollar spent by a customer goes to a specialty retailer to cover its costs and profit. The other 50 percent goes to the marketer (34 percent) and manufacturers and suppliers (16 percent).[19] So, the next time you buy a $200 pair of designer denim jeans, remember that $100 goes to the specialty retailer that stocked, displayed, and sold the jeans to you.

Cost of Changing Prices and Time Period They Apply If Scandinavian Airlines asks General Electric (GE) to provide spare jet engines to power the new Boeing 737 it just bought, GE can easily set a new price for the engines to reflect its latest information since only one buyer has to be informed. But if Coldwater Creek decides that sweater prices in its catalog are too low after thousands of catalogs have been mailed to customers, it has a big problem. It must consider the cost of changing prices and which prices apply to which time periods, as well as the cost of revising its price list and reprinting and mailing another edition of its catalog. However, for many of today's consumer products, prices can change from minute to minute due to the transparency of prices afforded by the Internet.

Setting hundreds of prices valid for the life of a catalog is risky.

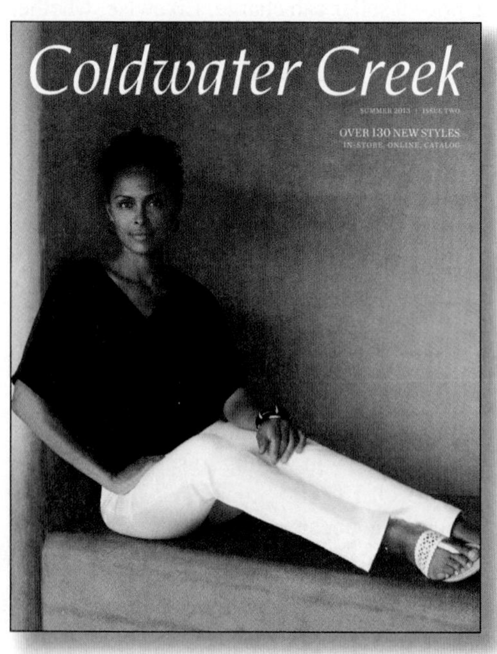

Single Product versus a Product Line When Apple introduced its iPhone in 2007, it was not only unique and in the introductory stage of its product life cycle, but it was also the first commercially successful smartphone sold. As a result, Apple had great latitude in setting and maintaining a premium price. However, by mid-2013, there was an onslaught of lower-cost rival smartphones, many of which were powered by Google's Android operating system. At that time, Apple had a market share of only about 15 percent of smartphone sales with its lone iPhone 5 model. Yet 48 percent of Apple's sales revenues were tied to sales of its iPhones and related services.

How should Apple respond to this competitive pressure? Apple's CEO Tim Cook has started to move away from the late Steve Jobs's strategy of having only a single model of a product that is targeted at high-end users. An example is Apple's iPad mini, which was introduced in October 2012 and broadened the iPad product line.

In late 2013, Apple launched the new iPhone 5S and the lower-priced iPhone 5C to broaden Apple's smartphone product line. The upside of this strategy is that it will increase Apple's sales revenues if the new product reaches new smartphone buyers not willing to pay the higher price of its iPhone 5S, which has more features. The downside:

What are the potential benefits and dangers of Apple's plan to offer a lower-priced iPhone mini? Read the text to find out.

If that doesn't happen, the new iPhone 5C could cannibalize sales from the higher-priced iPhone 5S and reduce overall sales revenues.[20]

Type of Competitive Market The seller's price is constrained by the type of market in which it competes. Economists generally delineate four types of competitive markets, as introduced in Chapter 3. From most competitive to least competitive, these are pure competition, monopolistic competition, oligopoly, and pure monopoly. Figure 13–4 shows that the type of competition dramatically influences the range of price competition and, in turn, the nature of product differentiation and the extent of advertising. A firm must recognize the general type of competitive market it is in to understand the range of both its price and nonprice strategies. Examples of how prices can be affected by the four competitive situations follow:

- *Pure competition.* Hundreds of local grain elevators sell corn whose price per bushel is set by the marketplace. Within strains, the corn is identical, so advertising only informs buyers that the seller's corn is available.
- *Monopolistic competition.* Dozens of regional, private brands of peanut butter compete with national brands like Skippy and Jif. Both price competition (regional, private brands being lower than national brands) and nonprice competition (product features and advertising) exist.
- *Oligopoly.* The few sellers of aluminum (Reynolds, Alcoa) or large jetliners (Boeing, Airbus) try to avoid price competition because it can lead to disastrous price wars in which they all lose money. Yet firms in such industries stay aware of a competitor's price cuts or increases and may follow suit. The products can be undifferentiated (aluminum) or differentiated (large jetliners), and informative advertising that avoids head-to-head price competition is used. In the early stages of the video game market, the Microsoft Xbox 360's oligopolistic competition with Sony and Nintendo was so severe that Microsoft lost $126 on every unit sold at its $399 introductory price.[21]
- *Pure monopoly.* In 1994, Johnson & Johnson (J&J) revolutionized the treatment of coronary heart disease by introducing the stent—a tiny mesh tube "spring" that props open clogged arteries. Initially a monopoly, J&J stuck with its early

FIGURE 13–4
Pricing, product, and advertising strategies available to firms in four types of competitive markets.

	TYPE OF COMPETITIVE MARKET			
STRATEGIES AVAILABLE	**PURE COMPETITION (Many sellers who follow the market price for identical, commodity products)**	**MONOPOLISTIC COMPETITION (Many sellers who compete on nonprice factors)**	**OLIGOPOLY (Few sellers who are sensitive to each other's prices)**	**PURE MONOPOLY (One seller who sets the price for a unique product)**
Extent of price competition	Almost none: market sets price	Some: compete over range of prices	Some: price leader or follower of competitors	None: sole seller sets price
Extent of product differentiation	None: products are identical	Some: differentiate products from competitors	Various: depends on industry	None: no other producers
Extent of advertising	Little: purpose is to inform prospects that seller's products are available	Much: purpose is to differentiate firm's products from competitors	Some: purpose is to inform but avoid price competition	Little: purpose is to increase demand for product class

Marketing Matters

customer value

Want to End "Showrooming"? Then Employ a Price-Matching Strategy!

As an oligopolist, Walmart has a few competitors in the broad range of products it sells: Target, Best Buy, and Amazon.com. Yet in terms of monopolistic competition, there are dozens of large chains like Kmart, Costco, or Walgreen's that are major competitors on one or several product lines and thousands of supermarkets, clothing stores, and appliance stores that compete locally or nationally.

EDLP and Ad Matching

Walmart's unique pricing strategy of "everyday low price," or EDLP, affects all of its competitors. Walmart's low prices result from the low prices it receives from its suppliers for its high-volume purchases. Walmart's EDLP is now supported by its "Ad Match Guarantee," in which its stores will "match the price of any local competitor's printed ad for an identical product." These include BOGOs (buy one, get one free) but *not* Internet prices! Insistent customers can now get a Walmart manager to approve the lower price for a product by mentioning a competitor's price from a print ad in the local newspaper *without* having to bring that ad to the store.

Showrooming

Walmart's low prices have caused its major competitors to employ price-matching strategies to end the practice of "showrooming." Showrooming occurs when shoppers go to a store, such as Best Buy, obtain the store price of a product, scan its SKU or barcode with a smartphone camera, and go online to compare prices with those of selected competitors (usually Amazon.com). If the store will not match or beat the best online price for the product, the shopper will leave the store and then buy it online from the store's competitor!

Competitive Price Matching

To combat showrooming, Target and Best Buy announced in early 2013 that they will match both in-store and online prices for selected retailers (Walmart, Amazon, Toys "Я" Us) all year round, not just during the holiday season, to win back customers and regain some of the market share that they had lost.

QR 13-4
Apple iPhone 5C Ad

$1,595 price and achieved $1 billion in sales and 91 percent market share by the end of 1996. But its reluctance to give price reductions to hospitals for large-volume purchases turned out to be a poor strategy. When competitors like Medtronic introduced an improved stent at lower prices, J&J's market share plummeted to 8 percent two years later.[22]

Because of Walmart's size and international operations, its actions and pricing strategies affect thousands of retailers, large and small. Over the 72-hour Black Friday weekend in November 2012, it launched the biggest mobile-advertising campaign in history on Facebook. Using 50 million prepurchased ads, Walmart's discounted prices on toys and televisions appeared in the Facebook mobile news feeds of tens of millions of people.[23] The Marketing Matters box describes the type of competitive market Walmart is in, its revolutionary pricing strategy, and how giant competitors like Target and Best Buy are responding.[24]

Competitors' Prices and Consumers' Awareness of Them A firm must know what specific prices its present and potential competitors are charging now as well as what they are likely to charge in the near future. The firm then develops a marketing mix strategy—including setting prices—to respond to its competitors' prices. But in recent years, the Internet has increased the number of "present and potential competitors" exponentially for many products.

Competitors' prices are important only if a prospective buyer both (1) knows about those prices and (2) can act to purchase them easily. A century ago, if you lived in San Francisco, it was interesting to know that your cousin in New York could buy the same item from a dealer there for $100 less than you could. But you couldn't benefit from that knowledge and act on it. There may even have been a dealer 25 miles away with the lower price, but you didn't know about it. Price changes and price transparency through the Internet and efficient distribution have changed the competitive rules. Two dimensions of this revolution in pricing are (1) consumer-driven pricing actions and (2) seller/retailer-driven pricing actions.

- *Consumer-Driven Pricing Actions.* With consumers able to compare prices on the Internet, they can make more efficient buying decisions. This occurs, say, when a consumer visits the HDTV section of a store to actually examine a TV— and then goes home and orders it online at a lower price. RedLaser, an eBay-owned smartphone app, enables consumers to scan a product's barcode on a store's shelf and then compare that price to those both online and in nearby stores.[25]
- *Seller/Retailer-Driven Pricing Actions.* Aggressive price changes through the Internet started in the 1990s when airlines constantly changed ticket prices to fill the seats on their planes using their yield management systems. Today, many sellers are changing online prices even faster. This is made possible by Internet-based *dynamic pricing*, in which the seller changes prices in response to its existing inventory and the prices of competitors. This can occur every 10 or 15 minutes.

Is dynamic pricing fair? Read how Amazon used it for the hot-selling Dance Central 3 video game, available for the Xbox.

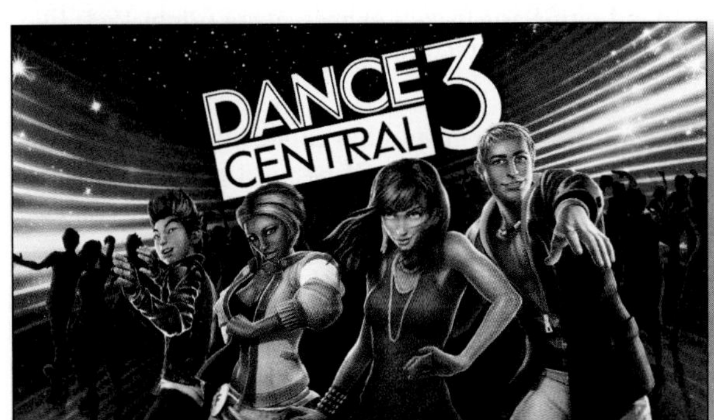

For example, the day before Thanksgiving 2012, online retailer Amazon.com sold the hugely popular Dance Central 3 (DC3) Xbox video game for $49.96—the same price as Walmart and 3 cents lower than Target. Then the pricing "dance moves" began. On Thanksgiving Day, Amazon lowered the game's price to $24.99, matching Best Buy. That same day, it dropped DC3's price to $15.00 to match Walmart. Then, over the next several days, Amazon raised and lowered the price *seven* times. If you were lucky, you paid a price that was two-thirds lower than those who were unlucky and bought DC3 at its highest price during that week!

Why did Amazon perform this dynamic price "dance?" To maximize short-term profits while beating its competition. However, in the long-run, Amazon and others who employ a vigorous dynamic pricing strategy can damage their relationships with customers, particularly those who unfortunately paid top dollar for items that could have been purchased for less. Some online systems can also vary prices depending on a customer's shopping history or on how far she lives from the store.[26]

Legal and Ethical Considerations Setting a final price is clearly a complex process. The task is further complicated by legal and ethical issues. Five pricing practices that have received special scrutiny are price fixing, price discrimination, deceptive pricing, geographical pricing, and predatory pricing, each of which is described more fully in Chapter 14.

learning review

13-4. What is the difference between pricing objectives and pricing constraints?

13-5. How does the type of competitive market a firm is in affect its range in setting prices?

13-6. What are examples of (*a*) consumer-driven and (*b*) seller/retailer-driven actions made possible through price transparency on the Internet?

STEP 2: ESTIMATE DEMAND AND REVENUE

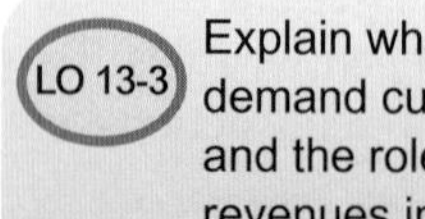

Explain what a demand curve is and the role of revenues in pricing decisions.

Basic to setting a product's price is the extent of customer demand for it. Marketing executives must also translate this estimate of customer demand into estimates of revenues the firm expects to receive.

Estimating Demand

What key factors affect the demand for Red Baron frozen cheese pizzas? Read the text to find out.

How much will you pay for a frozen cheese pizza you can pop in the oven for a quick dinner while you are studying for a marketing exam? $6? $8? $10? And what are some of the factors affecting this decision? Your preference for pizza compared to other quick-service food? The ease with which you can call Domino's or your local Chinese restaurant for an already-prepared meal delivered to your residence? How much money you have available in your credit card account while you're thinking about the tuition payment that's due next month? All these factors affect demand.

To illustrate the fundamentals of estimating demand, let's assume you are a consultant to the marketing manager at Red Baron® pizza and your job is to start analyzing the demand for its Red Baron frozen cheese pizzas. In the process, you'll have to consider what the demand curve for frozen cheese pizza might look like, how it affects Red Baron's sales revenues, and the price elasticity of demand.

The Demand Curve A **demand curve** is a graph that relates the quantity sold and price, showing the maximum number of units that will be sold at a given price. Based on secondary research you conducted regarding the annual demand for Red Baron frozen cheese pizza under circumstances that existed in 2013, you are able to construct the demand curve D_1 in Figure 13–5A, which you now need to update because market conditions have changed by 2014. Note the following relationship: As price falls, more people decide to buy Red Baron frozen cheese pizza, which increases its unit sales. But price is not the complete story when estimating demand. Economists emphasize three other key factors that influence demand for a product:

1. *Consumer tastes.* As we saw in Chapter 3, these depend on many forces such as demographics, culture, and technology. Because consumer tastes can change quickly, up-to-date marketing research is essential to estimate demand. For example, if research by nutritionists concludes that some pizzas are healthier (because they are now gluten-free or vegetarian), demand for them will probably increase.

FIGURE 13–5
Demand curves for Red Baron frozen cheese pizza showing the effect on annual sales (quantity demanded per year) by change in price caused by (A) a movement along the demand curve and (B) a shift of the demand curve.

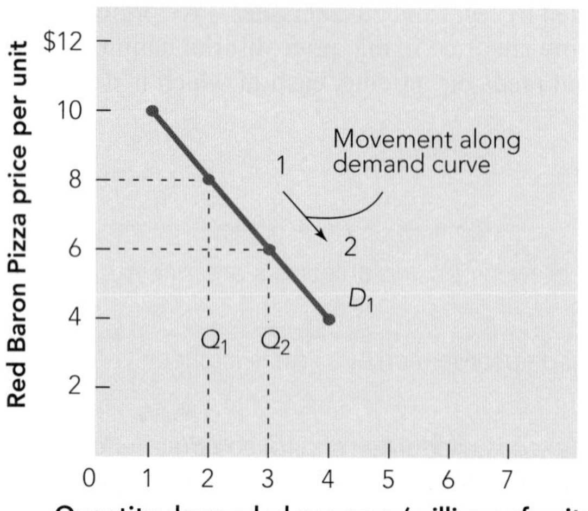

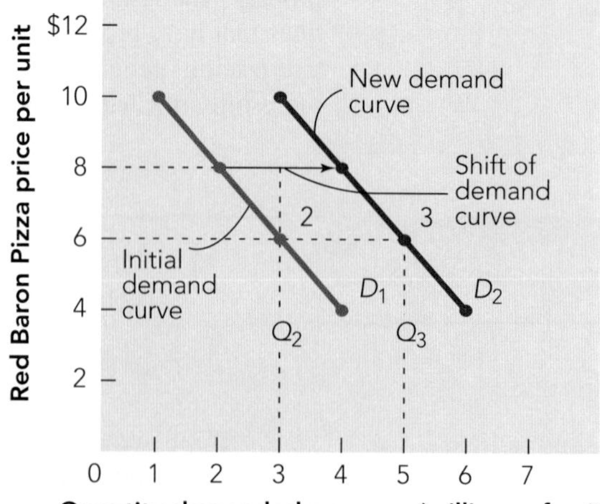

A wide range of brands of frozen pizza—for sale at various prices—can be found in huge display cabinets in the frozen foods section of your favorite supermarket, mass merchandiser, or warehouse club.

2. *Price and availability of similar products*. If the price of a competitor's pizza that is a substitute for yours—like Tombstone® pizza—falls, more people will buy it; its demand will rise and the demand for yours will fall. Other low-priced dinners are also substitutes for pizza. For example, if you want something fast so you can study, you could call Domino's or a local Chinese restaurant and order a meal for home delivery. So, as the price of a substitute falls or its availability increases, the demand for your Red Baron frozen cheese pizza will fall.
3. *Consumer income*. In general, as real consumers' incomes increase (allowing for inflation), demand for a product will also increase. So, if you get a scholarship and have extra cash for discretionary spending, you might eat more Red Baron frozen cheese pizzas and fewer peanut butter and jelly sandwiches to satisfy your appetite.

The first two factors influence what consumers *want* to buy, and the third factor affects what they *can* buy. Along with price, these are often called **demand factors**, or factors that determine consumers' willingness and ability to pay for products and services. As discussed in Chapters 8 and 10, it can be challenging to estimate demand for new products, especially because consumer likes and dislikes are often so difficult to read clearly. For example, Campbell's (yes, the soup company) spent seven years and $55 million on a super secret project to produce a line of Intelligent Quisine (IQ) food products "scientifically proven to lower high levels of cholesterol, blood sugar, and blood pressure." After 15 months in an Ohio test market, Campbell's yanked the entire IQ line because customers found the line too pricey and lacking in variety.[27]

Movement Along versus Shift of a Demand Curve The 2013 demand curve D_1 for Red Baron frozen cheese pizzas in Figure 13–5A shows that as its price is lowered from $8 (point 1) to $6 (point 2), the quantity sold (demanded) increases from 2 million (Q_1) to 3 million (Q_2) units per year. This is an example of a *movement along a demand curve* and it assumes that other factors (consumer tastes, price and availability of substitutes, and consumers' incomes) remain unchanged.

What if some of these factors do change? For example, if advertising causes more people to want Red Baron frozen cheese pizzas, demand will increase. Now the initial demand curve, D_1 (the blue line in Figure 13–5B), no longer represents the demand. Instead, the new demand curve, D_2 (the red line in Figure 13–5B) represents the new demand for Red Baron frozen cheese pizzas. Economists call this a *shift in the demand curve*—in this case, a shift to the right from D_1 to D_2. This increased demand means that more Red Baron frozen cheese pizzas are wanted for a given price. At a price of $6 (point 3), the demand is 5 million units per year (Q_3) on D_2 rather than 3 million units per year (Q_2) on D_1.

Estimating Revenue

While economists may talk about "demand curves," marketing executives are more likely to speak in terms of "sales revenues generated," which are the monies received by the firm for selling its products. Demand curves lead directly to three related revenue concepts critical to pricing decisions: **total revenue (TR)**, **average revenue (AR)**, and **marginal revenue (MR)** (see Figure 13–6 on the next page).

Let's next assume that in your consulting role at Red Baron, you are asked to do a more rigorous job in 2014 of measuring what the demand curve for your frozen cheese pizza might be. You decide to use four standard test markets, as discussed in Chapter 10. So you carefully select four U.S. metropolitan areas that are similar in demographic characteristics of consumers, media usage, and retail distribution.

FIGURE 13–6
Fundamental concepts about "revenues," which are the monies received from selling the product: total revenue, average revenue, and marginal revenue.

Total revenue (TR) is the total money received from the sale of a product.

If

TR = Total revenue
P = Unit price of the product
Q = Quantity of the product sold

Then:

$$TR = P \times Q$$

Average revenue (AR) is the average amount of money received for selling one unit of a product, or simply the price of that unit. Average revenue is the total revenue divided by the quantity sold:

$$AR = \frac{TR}{Q} = P$$

Marginal revenue (MR) is the change in total revenue that results from producing and marketing one additional unit of a product:

$$MR = \frac{\text{Change in TR}}{\text{1 unit increase in Q}} = \frac{\Delta TR}{\Delta Q} = \text{slope of TR curve}$$

You run the test markets for three months and use a different price point in each metropolitan area: $10, $8, $6, and $4, respectively. You pick these price points because you hope to raise prices from the $5 average frozen pizza price at supermarkets to perhaps $6 or $7. In fact, your test market price points are actually a penny less than whole dollar amounts—say, $6.99, rather than $7.00, but for simplicity we'll use the rounded number. This is an example of odd-even pricing, discussed later in Chapter 14. You then use historical data to project the three months of sales in your test markets to annual sales (see Chapter 8 on sales forcasting).

Demand and Total Revenue Curves

Figure 13–7A shows the demand curve you develop from the results in your four test markets—the solid red line running from points A to G. It is extended with the dotted lines to intersect both the price (Y) and quantity (X) axes. The specific results of the four test markets are the circled letters A, C, E, and G on the demand curve.

As expected, the demand curve shows that as price is changed, the quantity of your Red Baron frozen cheese pizzas sold annually also changes. Figure 13–7A shows that as the price per pizza is reduced from $10 to $8, the demand increases from 1 million to 2 million pizzas sold. Or conversely, if the price per pizza is increased from $4 to $6, the number sold falls from 4 million to 3 million pizzas.

Figure 13–7B shows the total revenue curve for Red Baron frozen cheese pizzas calculated from the demand curve shown in Figure 13–7A. As shown in the table in Figure 13–7, the total revenue curve is developed by simply multiplying the unit price times the quantity sold per pizza for each of the points on the demand curve. Total revenue is $0 at both ends of the demand curve and reaches a maximum of $18 million at point E in Figure 13–7B.

Figures 13–7A and 13–7B and the Figure 13–7 table show that as price is reduced from $10 to $8 per pizza, total revenue increases from $10 million to $16 million and total sales increase by 1 million pizzas. Reducing the price from $8 to $6 per pizza again increases sales by 1 million pizzas and increases total revenue to $18 million. And if we reduce the price from $6 to $4, we again increase sales by 1 million pizzas. However, in this case, the total revenue actually falls from $18 million to $16 million

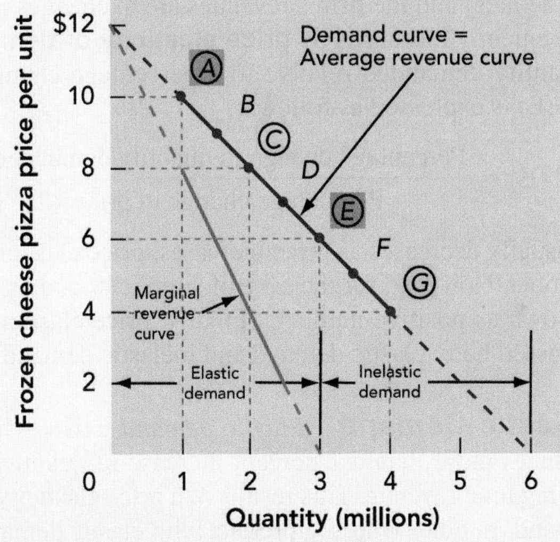

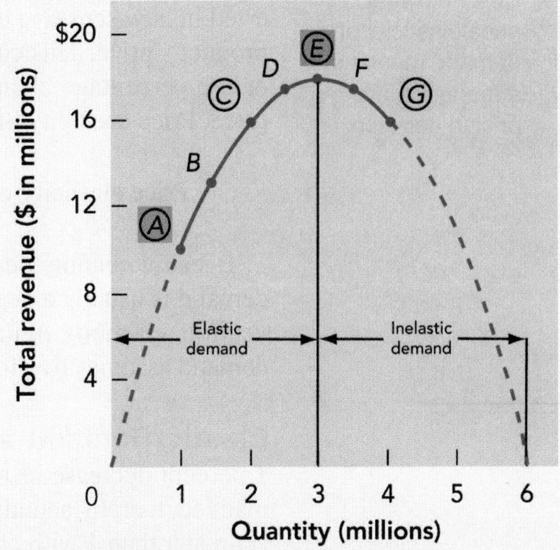

Point on Demand Curve	Price (P)	Quantity Sold (Q)	Total Revenue (P × Q)	Average Revenue (TR/Q = P)	Marginal Revenue (δTR/δQ)
Ⓐ	$10.00	1,000,000	$10,000,000	$10.00	$8.00
B	9.00	1,500,000	13,500,000	9.00	6.00
Ⓒ	8.00	2,000,000	16,000,000	8.00	4.00
D	7.00	2,500,000	17,500,000	7.00	2.00
Ⓔ	6.00	3,000,000	18,000,000	6.00	0
F	5.00	3,500,000	17,500,000	5.00	– 2.00*
Ⓖ	4.00	4,000,000	16,000,000	4.00	– 4.00*

*Not shown in Figure 13–7A. [Note that the marginal revenue (MR) curve in Figure 13–7A is the slope (dTR/dQ) of the total revenue (TR) curve in Figure 13–7B.][28]

FIGURE 13–7
How the downward-sloping demand curve for Red Baron frozen cheese pizza affects its total, average, and marginal revenues. Points A, C, E, and G show the results for the four test markets at $10, $8, $6, and $4 per pizza, respectively. The colored rows in the table are keyed to the colored points in the two graphs.

because the decrease in price more than offsets the increase in pizzas sold. This is related to price elasticity of demand, which is discussed next.

Marginal revenue, which is the slope of the total revenue curve, is positive but decreasing when the price lies in the range from $10 to $6 per pizza. Below $6 per pizza, though, marginal revenue is actually negative, showing that the extra quantity of pizzas sold is more than offset by the decrease in the price per pizza.

For any downward-sloping, straight-line demand curve, the marginal revenue curve always falls at a rate twice as fast as the demand curve. As shown in Figure 13–7A, the marginal revenue becomes $0 per unit at a quantity sold of 3 million units—the very point at which total revenue is maximized (see Figure 13–7B). A rational marketing manager would never operate in the region of the demand curve in which marginal revenue is negative—the region to the right of point E—because, as shown in Figure 13–7B, total revenue is actually decreasing.

After running your four test markets and empirically developing the demand curve for Red Baron frozen cheese pizzas, what will you recommend to management? It's pretty clear that raising prices to $7 or $8 per pizza actually lowers expected sales revenues. This is also true for price points of $4 or $5 per pizza. So, based on the information you collected in your test markets, you recommend that management price Red Baron frozen cheese pizzas at $6.00—or really $5.99 or $5.95—in supermarkets and other outlets.

Price Elasticity of Demand

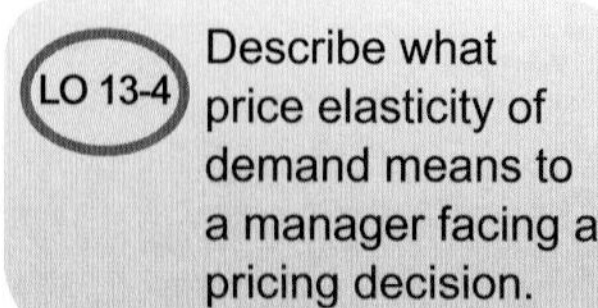

LO 13-4
Describe what price elasticity of demand means to a manager facing a pricing decision.

With a downward-sloping demand curve, marketing managers are especially interested in how sensitive consumer demand and the firm's revenues are to changes in the product's price. This can be conveniently measured by **price elasticity of demand**, or the percentage change in quantity demanded relative to a percentage change in price. Price elasticity of demand (E) is expressed as follows:

$$\text{Price elasticity of demand (E)} = \frac{\text{Percentage change in quantity demanded}}{\text{Percentage change in price}}$$

Because quantity demanded usually decreases as price increases, price elasticity of demand is usually a negative number. However, for the sake of simplicity and by convention, elasticity figures are shown as positive numbers. Finally, price elasticity of demand assumes two forms discussed here: elastic demand and inelastic demand.

Elastic Demand and Inelastic Demand *Elastic demand* exists when a 1 percent decrease in price produces more than a 1 percent increase in quantity demanded, thereby actually increasing total revenue. This results in a price elasticity that is greater than 1 with elastic demand. In other words, a product with elastic demand is one in which a slight decrease in price results in a relatively large increase in demand or units sold. The reverse is also true; with elastic demand, a slight increase in price results in a relatively large decrease in demand. So marketers may cut price to increase consumer demand, the units sold, and total revenue for a product with elastic demand, depending on what competitors' prices are.

Inelastic demand exists when a 1 percent decrease in price produces less than a 1 percent increase in quantity demanded, thereby actually decreasing total revenue. This results in a price elasticity that is less than 1 with inelastic demand. So a product with inelastic demand means that slight increases or decreases in price will not significantly affect the demand, or units sold, for the product. The concern for marketers is that while lowering price will increase the quantity sold, total revenue will actually fall.

Price elasticity is important to marketing managers because of its relationship to total revenue. So it is important that marketing managers recognize that price elasticity of demand is not the same over all possible prices of a product. Figure 13–7B illustrates this point using the Red Baron frozen cheese pizza demand curve shown in Figure 13–7A. As the price decreases from $10 (point A) to $6 (point E) per pizza, total revenue increases, indicating the elastic demand depicted in Figure 13–7B. However, when the price decreases from $6 (point E) to $4 (point G) per pizza, total revenue declines, indicating an inelastic demand, as shown in Figure 13–7B.

How Price Elasticity Affects Marketing and Public Policy Decisions Price elasticity of demand is determined by a number of factors. The more substitutes a product or service has, the more likely it is to be price elastic. For example, a new sweater, shirt, or blouse has many possible substitutes and is price elastic, but gasoline has almost no substitutes and is price inelastic. In fact, given America's love affair with cars and driving, we are surprisingly insensitive to price increases in gasoline: One study showed a 10 percent increase in price results in only a 0.6 percent decrease in gasoline consumption.[29] This could change in the future as gas-electric and electric cars become more cost competitive.

Products and services considered to be necessities are price inelastic, so open-heart surgery is price inelastic, whereas airline tickets for a vacation are price elastic. Toothpaste is an example of a consumer product with inelastic demand. So even during recessions, Procter & Gamble's and Colgate's toothpastes often show price *increases* on the shelves of retailers.[30] Items that require a large cash outlay compared with a person's disposable income are price elastic. Accordingly, cars and yachts are price elastic; soft drinks tend to be price inelastic.

A consumer product that is a necessity, like toothpaste, has an inelastic demand, which can result in an *increased* price during a recession.

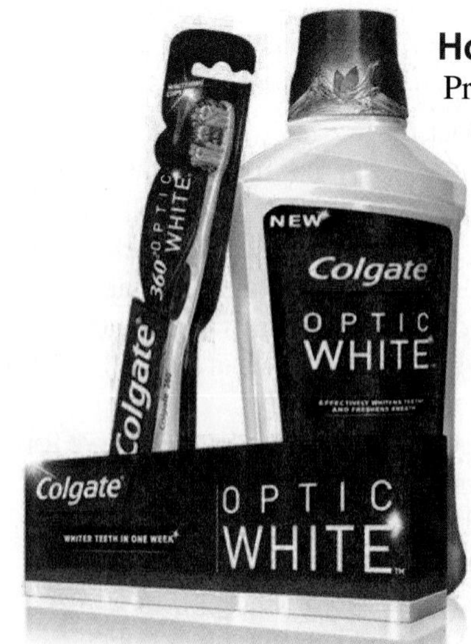

Because 12- to 17-year-olds often have limited spending money, this group is very price elastic in its demand for cigarettes. As a result, many legislators recommend far higher excise taxes on packs of cigarettes; by significantly increasing cigarette prices, they hope to reduce teenage smoking. In New York City recently, the combined taxes from federal, state, and local governments on a pack of Marlboro Light Kings cigarettes totaled $6.86. So the typical retail price in that city is more than $12 a pack. As a result of these inflated prices, high school student smoking in New York City has hit a new low of 13.8 percent, far below the national average.[31] Price elasticity is not only a relevant concept for marketing managers but also important for pricing practices involving public policy.

learning review

13-7. What is the difference between a movement along and a shift of a demand curve?

13-8. What is total revenue and how is it calculated?

13-9. What is the difference between elastic demand and inelastic demand?

STEP 3: DETERMINE COST, VOLUME, AND PROFIT RELATIONSHIPS

While revenues are the monies received by the firm from selling its products or services to customers, costs or expenses are the monies the firm pays out to its employees and suppliers. Marketing managers often use marginal analysis and break-even analysis to relate revenues and costs, topics covered in this section.

The Importance of Controlling Costs

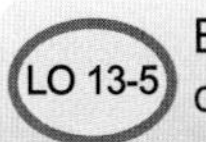

Explain the role of costs in pricing decisions.

Understanding the role and behavior of costs is critical for all marketing decisions, particularly pricing decisions. Five cost concepts are important in pricing decisions: **total cost (TC)**, **fixed cost (FC)**, **variable cost (VC)**, **unit variable cost (UVC)**, and **marginal cost (MC)** (see Figure 13–8).

FIGURE 13–8
Fundamental concepts about "costs," which are the monies the firm pays out to its employees and suppliers: total cost, fixed cost, variable cost, unit variable cost, and marginal cost.

Total cost (TC) is the total expense incurred by a firm in producing and marketing a product. Total cost is the sum of fixed cost and variable cost.

Fixed cost (FC) is the sum of the expenses of the firm that are stable and do not change with the quantity of a product that is produced and sold. Examples of fixed costs are rent on the building, executive salaries, and insurance.

Variable cost (VC) is the sum of the expenses of the firm that vary directly with the quantity of a product that is produced and sold. So, as the quantity sold doubles, the variable cost doubles. Examples are the direct labor and direct materials used in producing the product and the sales commissions that are tied directly to the quantity sold. As mentioned above:

$$TC = FC + VC$$

Unit variable cost (UVC) is variable cost expressed on a per unit basis for a product:

$$UVC = \frac{VC}{Q}$$

Marginal cost (MC) is the change in total cost that results from producing and marketing one additional unit of a product:

$$MC = \frac{\text{Change in TC}}{\text{1 unit increase in Q}} = \frac{\Delta TC}{\Delta Q} = \text{Slope of TC curve}$$

Many firms go bankrupt because their costs get out of control, causing their total costs to exceed their total revenues over an extended period. This is why sophisticated marketing managers make pricing decisions that balance both their revenues and costs.

The price of steel and other raw materials increased 20 percent in 2011. These are variable costs for manufacturers like Whirlpool, which uses steel in its products. In April 2011, Whirlpool raised the prices of its washing machines by an eye-popping 8 to 10 percent, considering this was during a recession. It did this because it wanted to remain profitable and hoped consumers would still buy its products at higher prices. The question Whirlpool asked itself: "In the oligopoly market of washing machines, what happens if South Korean rivals Samsung and LG do not raise prices and steal market share from us?"[32]

Marginal Analysis and Profit Maximization

A basic idea in business, economics, and indeed everyday life is **marginal analysis**, which is a continuing, concise trade-off of incremental costs against incremental revenues. In personal terms, marginal analysis means that people will continue to do something as long as the incremental return exceeds the incremental cost. So, if you know a sales call will generate $30 in revenue but will cost $25, you *make the sales call*. Conversely, if it only generates $20, you *don't make the sales call*. Marginal analysis also means that as long as revenue received from the sale of an additional unit of a product (marginal revenue) is greater than the additional cost of producing and selling it (marginal cost), a firm will expand its output of that product.

The message of marginal analysis, then, is to operate up to the quantity and price levels where marginal revenue equals marginal cost. Up to the output quantity at which they are equal, each increase in total revenue resulting from selling one additional unit exceeds the increase in the total cost of producing and marketing that unit. However, beyond the point at which marginal revenue equals marginal cost, the increase in total revenue from selling one more unit is less than the cost of producing and marketing that unit, so the output should be reduced to increase profit.

LO 13-6 Describe how various combinations of price, fixed cost, and unit variable cost affect a firm's bread-even point.

Break-Even Analysis

Break-even analysis is a technique that analyzes the relationship between total revenue and total cost to determine profitability at various levels of output. Figure 13–9 provides the data needed to conduct a break-even analysis. The **break-even point (BEP)** is the quantity at which total revenue and total cost are equal. Profit then comes from all units sold beyond the BEP. In terms of the definitions in Figure 13–8:

$$BEP_{Quantity} = \frac{\text{Fixed cost}}{\text{Unit price} - \text{Unit variable cost}} = \frac{FC}{P - UVC}$$

FIGURE 13–9 Calculating a break-even point for the picture frame shop in the text example shows that its profit starts at 400 pictures sold per year.

Quantity of Pictures Sold (Q)	Price per Picture (P)	Total Revenue (TR = P × Q)	Unit Variable Cost (UVC)	Total Variable Cost (VC = UVC × Q)	Fixed Cost (FC)	Total Cost (TC = FC + VC)	Profit (TR – TC)
0	$120	$0	$40	$0	$32,000	$32,000	($32,000)
400	$120	$48,000	$40	$16,000	$32,000	$48,000	$0
800	$120	$96,000	$40	$32,000	$32,000	$64,000	$32,000
1,200	$120	$144,000	$40	$48,000	$32,000	$80,000	$64,000
1,600	$120	$192,000	$40	$64,000	$32,000	$96,000	$96,000
2,000	$120	$240,000	$40	$80,000	$32,000	$112,000	$128,000

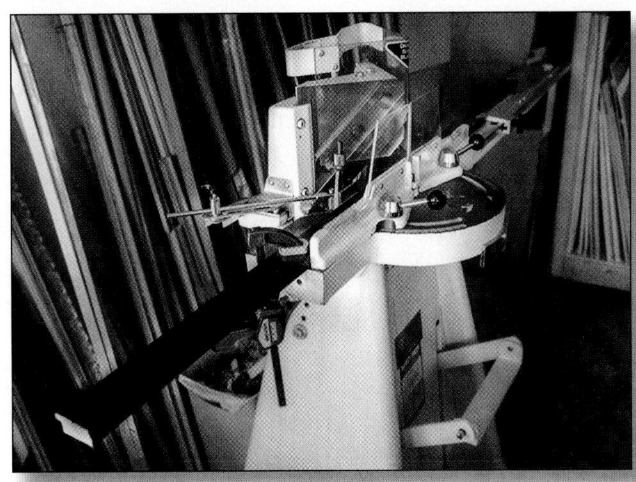

Calculating a Break-Even Point Suppose you are the owner of a picture frame shop and you wish to identify how many pictures you must sell to cover your fixed cost at a given price. Let's assume demand for your pictures is strong, so the average price customers are willing to pay for each picture is $120. Also, suppose your fixed cost (FC) is $32,000 (real estate taxes, interest on a bank loan, etc.) and unit variable cost (UVC) for a picture is now $40 (labor, glass, frame, and matting). Your break-even quantity (BEP) is 400 pictures, as follows:

$$\text{BEP}_{\text{Quantity}} = \frac{\$32{,}000}{\$120 - \$40}$$

$$\text{BEP}_{\text{Quantity}} = 400 \text{ pictures}$$

The text and Figure 13–10 explain the impact on the break-even point and the firm's profit of using a new cutting machine in a picture frame shop.

Developing a Break-Even Chart The row shaded in orange in Figure 13–9 shows that your break-even quantity at a price of $120 per picture is 400 pictures. At less than 400 pictures, your picture frame shop incurs a loss, and at more than 400 pictures, it makes a profit. Figure 13–10 depicts a graphic presentation of the break-even analysis, called a **break-even chart**. It shows that total revenue (line DE) and total cost (line AC) intersect and are equal at a quantity of 400 pictures sold, which is the break-even point (F) at which profit is exactly $0. You want to do better? If your picture frame shop could increase the quantity sold annually to 2,000 pictures, the graph in Figure 13–10A shows you can earn an annual profit of $128,000 ($240,000 − $112,000 or line EC), shown by the row shaded in green in Figure 13–9.

Break-Even Analysis, Technology, Automation, and 21st Century Jobs

Because of its simplicity, break-even analysis is used extensively in marketing, most frequently to study the impact of changes in price, quantity, fixed cost, and variable cost on profit. Marketers use computer programs such as Microsoft Excel

FIGURE 13–10
This break-even chart for a picture frame shop shows the break-even point at 400 pictures *without* a new cutting machine. With a new cutting machine, the break-even point rises to 500 pictures.

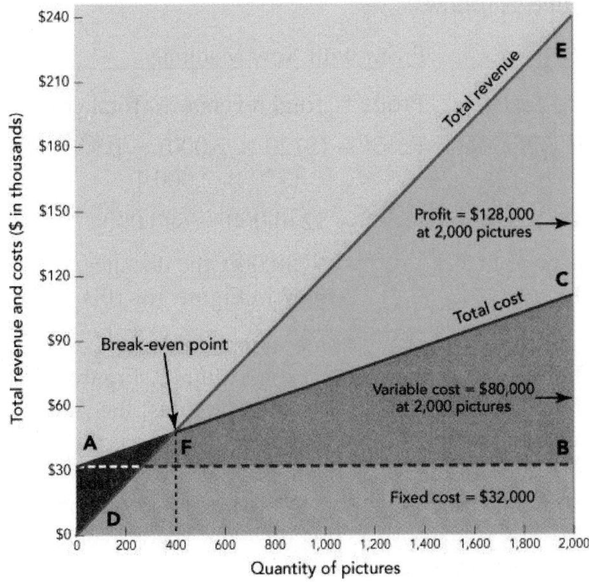

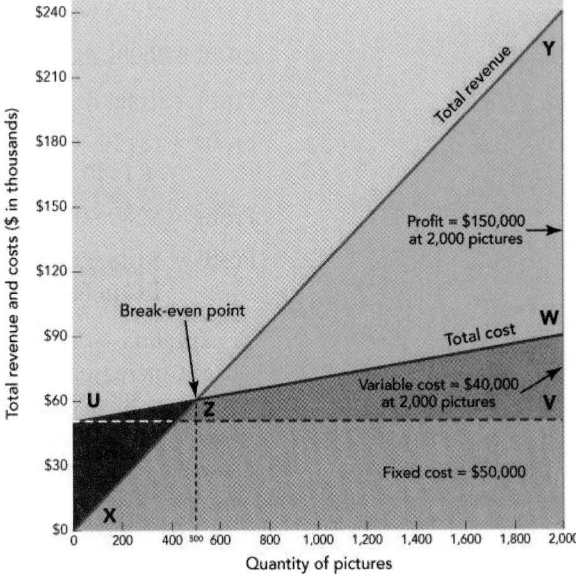

to develop models for break-even analysis to answer hypothetical "what if" questions about the effect of changes in demand and cost variables on profit. Let's (1) extend the picture frame shop example to analyze the impact of adding new technology to its operations and (2) analyze how it affects industries that you might consider for your career after graduation.

Impact of New Technology in the Picture Frame Shop As the owner of the picture frame shop, suppose you decide to rent a machine for $18,000 annually that will speed up the production of framed pictures. Using this machine, you simply key in the dimensions needed to automatically cut the frame, glass, and matting for any picture frame size. Automating the production process dramatically increases the output of framed pictures and reduces losses in miscut glass and mats.

As shown in Figure 13–10, this new technology increases annual fixed costs from $32,000 (dashed blue line AB in Figure 13–10A) to $50,000 (dashed red line UV in Figure 13–10B). However, it has the benefit of lowering variable cost from $40 to $20 per unit. The variable cost *with* the new machine is depicted by the flatter orange wedge WZV in Figure 13–10B. Compare this to the variable cost *without* the new machine, the larger orange wedge CFB in Figure 13–10A.

Assuming these same prices, fixed costs, and variable costs for your shop, you would calculate the break-even point (1) without the new machine and (2) with the new machine as follows:

BEP without New Machine	BEP with New Machine
$P = \$120$ per unit	$P = \$120$ per unit
$FC = \$32{,}000$	$FC = \$50{,}000$
$UVC = \$40$ per unit	$UVC = \$20$ per unit
$BEP_{Quantity} = \dfrac{FC}{P - UVC}$	$BEP_{Quantity} = \dfrac{FC}{P - UVC}$
$BEP_{Quantity} = \dfrac{\$32{,}000}{\$120 - \$40}$	$BEP_{Quantity} = \dfrac{\$50{,}000}{\$120 - \$20}$
$BEP_{Quantity} = 400$ pictures	$BEP_{Quantity} = 500$ pictures

And you would calculate the profit at 2,000 pictures sold (1) without the new machine and (2) with the new machine as follows:

Profit without New Machine	Profit with New Machine
Profit = Total revenue − Total cost	Profit = Total revenue − Total cost
Profit = ($120 × 2,000) − [($32,000) + ($40 × 2,000)]	Profit = ($120 × 2,000) − [($50,000) + ($20 × 2,000)]
Profit = $240,000 − $112,000	Profit = $240,000 − $90,000
Profit = $128,000, the distance EC in Figure 13–10A	Profit = $150,000, the distance YW in Figure 13–10B

Organizations—from car manufacturers to picture frame shops—add new technology because it increases their profitability at higher production volumes. Figure 13–10 demonstrates this. When producing and selling 2,000 framed pictures, the profit for your picture frame shop without the new technology (Figure 13–10A) is $128,000, represented by the green wedge EFC, with the break-even point at 400 picture frames (point F). However, using the new machine (Figure 13–10B) causes your profit to increase by $22,000 to $150,000, represented by the green wedge YZW, even though the break-even point rises to 500 picture frames (point Z).

Technology and Automation: Planning the Effect on Your Career

The key reason for adding new technology and automation is that with large production and sales volumes, say, in auto manufacturing plants, extra fixed costs and reduced variable costs can add tremendously to their existing profits beyond the break-even point. Also, firms in other industries that incur high fixed costs, such as airlines, railroads, and the hospitality (hotels/motels) industry, can reap large profits by using new technology when they go even slightly beyond their existing break-even points.

What does this mean to you personally? The addition of new technology and automation in manufacturing industries in recent decades has eliminated tens of millions of jobs around the world, while significantly increasing profits for these firms. This job elimination has affected countless other industries—from supermarkets, which have fewer check-out clerks because of barcode scanners, to travel agencies, which have fewer agents because of online airline reservation systems. So, in planning your career, consider industries where new technology or automation is *less likely* to eliminate your job!

learning review

13-10. What is the difference between fixed costs and variable costs?

13-11. What is a break-even point?

13-12. Why do firms add new technology and automation when it increases their fixed cost?

LEARNING OBJECTIVES REVIEW

LO 13-1 *Identify the elements that make up a price.*
Price is the money or other considerations (such as barter) exchanged for the ownership or use of a product or service. Although price typically involves money, the amount exchanged is often different from the list or quoted price because of incentives (rebates, discounts, etc.), allowances (trade), and extra fees (finance charges, surcharges, etc.). The price of an offering is often used to indicate value, which is the ratio of perceived benefits to price. Pricing has a direct effect on a firm's profits, which is determined by the profit equation: Profit = Total revenue − Total cost.

LO 13-2 *Recognize the objectives a firm has in setting prices and the constraints that restrict the range of prices a firm can charge.*
Pricing objectives specify the role of price in a firm's marketing strategy and may include profit, sales revenue, market share, unit volume, survival, or some socially responsible price level. Pricing constraints that restrict a firm's pricing flexibility include demand, product newness, other products sold by the firm, production and marketing costs, cost of price changes, type of competitive market, and the prices of competitive substitutes.

LO 13-3 *Explain what a demand curve is and the role of revenues in pricing decisions.*
A demand curve is a graph relating the quantity sold and price, which shows the maximum number of units that will be sold at a given price. Three demand factors affect price: (*a*) consumer tastes, (*b*) price and availability of substitute products, and (*c*) consumer income. These demand factors determine consumers' willingness and ability to pay for products and services. Assuming these demand factors remain unchanged, if the price of a product is lowered or raised, then the quantity demanded for it will increase or decrease, respectively.

Three important forms of revenues impact a firm's pricing decisions: (*a*) total revenue, which is the total money received from the sale of a product; (*b*) average revenue, which is the average amount of money received for selling one unit of a product (which is simply the price of the unit); and (*c*) marginal revenue, which is the change in total revenue that results from producing and marketing one additional unit.

LO 13-4 *Describe what price elasticity of demand means to a manager facing a pricing decision.*
Price elasticity of demand measures the responsiveness of units of a product sold to a change in price, which is expressed as the percentage change in the quantity of a product demanded divided by the percentage change in price. Price elasticity is important to marketing managers because a change in price usually has an important effect on the number of units of the product sold and on total revenue.

LO 13-5 *Explain the role of costs in pricing decisions.*
Five important costs impact a firm's pricing decisions: (*a*) total cost, or total expenses, is the sum of fixed cost and variable cost incurred by a firm in producing and marketing a product;

(*b*) fixed cost, is the sum of expenses of the firm that are stable and do not change with the quantity of a product that is produced and sold; (*c*) variable cost, is the sum of expenses of the firm that vary directly with the quantity of a product that is produced and sold; (*d*) unit variable cost, is variable cost expressed on a per unit basis; and (*e*) marginal cost, is the change in total cost that results from producing and marketing one additional unit of the product.

LO 13-6 *Describe how various combinations of price, fixed cost, and unit variable cost affect a firm's break-even point.*

Break-even analysis is a technique that analyzes the relationship between total revenue and total cost to determine profitability at various levels of output. The break-even point is the quantity at which total revenue and total cost are equal. Assuming no change in price, if the costs of a firm's product increase due to higher fixed costs (manufacturing or advertising) or variable costs (direct labor or materials), then its break-even point will be higher. And if total cost is unchanged, an increase in price will reduce the break-even point.

FOCUSING ON KEY TERMS

average revenue (AR) p. 337
barter p. 324
break-even analysis p. 342
break-even chart p. 343
break-even point (BEP) p. 342
demand curve p. 336
demand factors p. 337
fixed cost (FC) p. 341
marginal analysis p. 342
marginal cost (MC) p. 341
marginal revenue (MR) p. 337
price p. 324
price elasticity of demand p. 340
pricing constraints p. 331
pricing objectives p. 330
profit equation p. 328
total cost (TC) p. 341
total revenue (TR) p. 337
unit variable cost (UVC) p. 341
value p. 326
value-pricing p. 327
variable cost (VC) p. 341

APPLYING MARKETING KNOWLEDGE

1 How would the price equation apply to the purchase price of (*a*) gasoline, (*b*) an airline ticket, and (*c*) a checking account?

2 What would be your response to the statement, "Profit maximization is the only legitimate pricing objective for the firm"?

3 How is a downward-sloping demand curve related to total revenue and marginal revenue?

4 A marketing executive once said, "If the price elasticity of demand for your product is inelastic, then your price is probably too low." What is this executive saying in terms of the economic principles discussed in this chapter?

5 A marketing manager reduced the price on a brand of cereal by 10 percent and observed a 25 percent increase in quantity sold. The manager then thought that if the price were reduced by another 20 percent, a 50 percent increase in quantity sold would occur. What would be your response to the marketing manager's reasoning?

6 A student theater group at a university has developed a demand schedule that shows the relationship between ticket prices and demand based on a student survey (see the table that follows). (*a*) Graph the demand curve and the total revenue curve based on these data. What ticket price might be set based on this analysis? (*b*) What other factors should be considered before the final price is set?

Ticket Price	Number of Students Who Would Buy
$1	300
2	250
3	200
4	150
5	100

7 Touché Toiletries, Inc., has developed an addition to its Lizardman Cologne line tentatively branded Ode d'Toade Cologne. Unit variable costs are 45 cents for a three-ounce bottle, and heavy advertising expenditures in the first year would result in total fixed costs of $900,000. Ode d'Toade Cologne is priced at $7.50 for a three-ounce bottle. How many bottles of Ode d'Toade must be sold to break even?

8 Suppose that marketing executives for Touché Toiletries (see problem 7) reduced the price to $6.50 for a three-ounce bottle of Ode d'Toade and the fixed costs were $1,100,000. Suppose further that the unit variable cost remained at 45 cents for a three-ounce bottle. (*a*) How many bottles must be sold to break even?

(*b*) What dollar profit level would Ode d'Toade achieve if 200,000 bottles were sold?

9 Executives of Random Recordings, Inc., produced a digital album titled *Sunshine/Moonshine* by the Starshine Sisters Band. (*a*) Using the price and cost information in the table, prepare a chart like that in Figure 13–10 showing total cost, fixed cost, and total revenue for album quantity sold levels starting at 10,000 through 100,000 digital albums at 10,000 intervals, that is, 10,000; 20,000; 30,000; and so on. (*b*) What is the break-even point for the digital album?

Selling price	$10.00 per album
Album cover	$1.00 per album
Songwriter's royalties	$0.30 per album
Recording artists' royalties	$0.70 per album
Direct material and labor costs to produce the album	$1.00 per album
Fixed cost of producing an album (advertising, studio fee, etc.)	$100,000

BUILDING YOUR MARKETING PLAN

In starting to set a final price:

1 List two pricing objectives and three pricing constraints.

2 Think about your customers and competitors and set three possible prices.

3 Assume a fixed cost and unit variable cost and (*a*) calculate the break-even points and (*b*) plot a break-even chart for the three prices specified in step 2.

VIDEO CASE 13 Washburn Guitars: Using Break-Even Points to Make Pricing Decisions

QR 13-5 Washburn Guitars Video Case

"We offer a guitar at every price point for every skill level," explains Kevin Lello, vice president of marketing at Washburn Guitars. Washburn is one of the most prestigious guitar manufacturers in the world, offering instruments that range from one-of-a-kind, custom-made acoustic and electric guitars and basses to less-expensive, mass-produced guitars. Lello has responsibility for marketing Washburn's products and ensuring that the price of each product matches the company's objectives related to sales, profit, and market share. "We do pay attention to break-even points," adds Lello. "We need to know exactly how much a guitar costs us, and how much the overhead is for each guitar."

THE COMPANY

The modern Washburn Guitars company started in 1977 when a small Chicago firm bought the century-old Washburn brand name and a small inventory of guitars, parts, and promotional supplies. At that time, annual company sales of about 2,500 guitars generated revenues of $300,000. Washburn's first catalog, appearing in 1978, told a frightening truth:

> Our designs are translated by Japan's most experienced craftsmen, assuring the consistent quality and craftsmanship for which they are known.

At that time, the American guitar-making craft was at an all-time low. Guitars made by Japanese firms, such as Ibanez and Yamaha, were in use by an increasing number of professionals.

Times have changed for Washburn. Today, the company sells about 50,000 guitars each year and annual revenues exceed $40 million. All this resulted from Washburn's aggressive marketing strategies to develop product lines with different price points targeted at musicians in distinctly different market segments.

THE PRODUCTS AND MARKET SEGMENTS

One of Washburn's early successes was the trendsetting Festival Series of cutaway, thin-bodied flattops, with built-in bridge pickups and controls. This guitar became the standard for live performances as its popularity with rock and country stars increased. Over the years, several generations of musicians have used Washburn guitars. Early artists included Bob Dylan, Dolly Parton, Greg Allman, and the late George Harrison of the Beatles. In recent years, Mike Kennerty of The All-American Rejects, Rick Savage of Def Leppard, and Hugh McDonald of Bon Jovi have been among the many musicians who use Washburn products.

Until 1991, all Washburn guitars were manufactured in Asia. That year Washburn started building its high-end guitars in the United States. Today, Washburn marketing executives divide its product line into four categories to appeal to different market segments. From high-end guitars to low-end ones, these product groupings are:

- One-of-a-kind, custom instruments.
- Batch-custom instruments.
- Mass-customized instruments.
- Mass-produced instruments.

The one-of-a-kind custom products appeal to the many stars who use Washburn instruments as well as collectors. The batch-custom products appeal to professional musicians. The mass-customized products appeal to musicians with intermediate skill levels who may not yet be professionals. Finally, the mass-produced units are targeted at first-time buyers and are still manufactured in Asian factories.

PRICING ISSUES

Setting prices for its various lines presents a continuing challenge for Washburn. Not only do the prices have to reflect the changing tastes of its various segments of musicians, but the prices must also be competitive with the prices of other guitars manufactured and marketed globally. The price elasticity of demand, or price sensitivity, for Washburn's products varies between its segments. To reduce the price sensitivity for some of its products, Washburn uses endorsements by internationally known musicians who play its instruments and lend their names to lines of Washburn signature guitars. Stars playing Washburn guitars, such as Nuno Bettencourt of Extreme, Paul Stanley of KISS, Scott Ian of Anthrax, and Dan Donegan of Disturbed, have their own lines of signature guitars—the "batch-custom" units mentioned earlier. These guitars receive excellent reviews. *Total Guitar* magazine, for example, recently said, "If you want a truly original axe that has been built with great attention to detail . . . then the Washburn Maya Pro DD75 could be the one."

Bill Abel, Washburn's vice president of sales, is responsible for reviewing and approving prices for the company's lines of guitars. Setting a sales target of 2,000 units for a new line of guitars, he is considering a suggested retail price of $349 per unit for customers at one of the hundreds of retail outlets carrying the Washburn line. For planning purposes, Abel estimates half of the final retail price will be the price Washburn nets when it sells its guitar to the wholesalers and dealers in its channel of distribution.

Looking at Washburn's financial data for its present plant, Abel estimates that this line of guitars must bear these fixed costs:

Rent and taxes	= $14,000
Depreciation of equipment	= $ 4,000
Management and quality control program	= $20,000

In addition, he estimates the variable costs for each unit to be:

Direct materials	= $25/unit
Direct labor	= 15 hours/unit @ $8/hour

Carefully kept production records at Washburn's plant make Abel believe that these are reasonable estimates. He explains, "Before we begin a production run, we have a good feel for what our costs will be. The U.S.–built N-4, for example, simply costs more than one of our foreign-produced electrics."

Caught in the global competition for guitar sales, Washburn continually searches for ways to reduce and control costs. For example, Washburn recently purchased Parker Guitar, another guitar manufacturer that designed products for professionals and collectors, and will combine the two production facilities in a new location. Washburn expects the acquisition to lower its fixed and variable costs. Specifically, Washburn projects that its new factory location will reduce its rent and taxes expense by 40 percent, and the new skilled employees will reduce the hours of work needed for each unit by 15 percent.

By managing the prices of its products, Washburn also helps its dealers and retailers. In fact, Abel believes it is another reason for Washburn's success: "We have excellent relationships with the independent retailers. They're our lifeblood, and our outlet to sell our product. We sell through chains and online dealers, but it's the independent dealer that sells the guitars. So we take a smaller margin from them because they have to do more work. They appreciate it, and they go the extra mile for us."

Questions

1 What factors are most likely to affect the demand for the lines of Washburn guitars (*a*) bought by a first-time guitar buyer and (*b*) bought by a sophisticated musician who wants a signature model?

2 For Washburn, what are examples of (*a*) shifting the demand curve to the right to get a higher price for a guitar line (movement of the demand curve) and (*b*) pricing decisions involving moving along a demand curve?

3 In Washburn's factory, what is the break-even point for the new line of guitars if the retail price is (*a*) $349, (*b*) $389, and (*c*) $309? Also, (*d*) if Washburn achieves the sales target of 2,000 units at the $349 retail price, what will its profit be?

4 Assume that the merger with Parker leads to the cost reductions projected in the case. What will be the (*a*) new break-even point at a $349 retail price for this line of guitars and (*b*) new profit if it sells 2,000 units?

5 If, for competitive reasons, Washburn eventually has to move all its production back to Asia, (*a*) which specific fixed and variable costs might be lowered and (*b*) what additional fixed and variable costs might it expect to incur?

14 Arriving at the Final Price

Learning Objectives

After reading this chapter you should be able to:

LO 14-1 Describe how to establish the "approximate price level" using demand-oriented, cost-oriented, profit-oriented, and competition-oriented approaches.

LO 14-2 Recognize the major factors considered in deriving a final list or quoted price from the approximate price level.

LO 14-3 Identify the adjustments made to the approximate price level on the basis of discounts, allowances, and geography.

LO 14-4 Name the principal laws and regulations affecting specific pricing practices.

QR 14-1
VIZIO Ad

VIZIO, Inc.—Where Vision Meets Value™ in HDTV

Can you name North America's largest flat-panel HDTV company? Stumped? It's VIZIO, Inc., an entrepreneurial, Irvine, California–based company with a bold agenda. "Our goal is to be the next Sony in 20 to 30 years," says William Wang, VIZIO's co-founder and chief executive officer, who was born in Taiwan and immigrated to the United States at age 13.

In 2002, Mr. Wang was struck by an ad for a $10,000 flat-panel HDTV set and immediately saw an opportunity. Instead of marketing these sets as luxury items, Mr. Wang thought he could make and market an HDTV that would be affordable for the average customer.

Like many entrepreneurs, he borrowed money from friends and family and mortgaged his home. Within a year, he formed a company that is now known as VIZIO, Inc., and delivered the company's first VIZIO HDTV to Costco for distribution through that company's stores. VIZIO HDTVs are now sold through Costco, Walmart, BJ's Wholesale, Sears, Sam's Club, and Target stores nationwide, along with authorized online partners such as Amazon. The company has sold more than 30 million HDTV units since 2002.

VIZIO's ability to deliver affordable HDTVs to the average customer is based on a novel strategy. VIZIO didn't invest in expensive manufacturing facilities but instead relied on contract manufacturers in Taiwan to build its products. Product development and marketing specialists in the United States handle product design and marketing. That's where the company's motto, "Where Vision Meets Value," comes into play. "The whole goal is to ensure that we have the right product at the right time and the right price and really drive a seamless end-to-end value chain," says John Morriss, VIZIO's vice president of partner management.

"VIZIO HDTVs are more popular and in greater demand than ever," adds Laynie Newsome, VIZIO's co-founder and chief sales officer. "Consumers want to save money without sacrificing quality or technology, which is why we continue to be the fastest growing HDTV company in the United States." Matthew McRae, VIZIO's chief technology officer, adds that VIZIO's strategy is to make affordable products with innovative features, saying, "We're far from the cheapest brand on the market at present. Everybody deserves the latest technology too."

VIZIO's powerful and profitable price-value position clearly resonates with consumers—today the company produces annual sales of about $3 billion. VIZIO is now the largest seller of HDTVs in North America. For good measure, VIZIO was ranked "Highest in Customer Satisfaction" with HDTVs by J.D. Power and Associates in 2012. Also in 2012, VIZIO entered the personal computer market, offering desktop personal computers, home audio systems, tablet computers, and laptop computers. Not bad for a company with about 350 employees and just 12 years old![1]

STEP 4: SELECT AN APPROXIMATE PRICE LEVEL

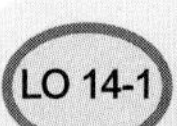

Describe how to establish the "approximate price level" using demand-oriented, cost-oriented, profit-oriented, and competition-oriented approaches.

This chapter describes how companies like VIZIO set an approximate price level for their offerings, highlights important considerations in setting a list or quoted price, and identifies various price adjustments that can be made to prices set by a company—the last three steps involved in setting prices (Figure 14–1). Legal and regulatory aspects of pricing are also described.

A key for a marketing manager setting a final price for a product is to find an approximate price level to use as a reasonable starting point. Four common approaches to helping find this approximate price level are (1) demand-oriented, (2) cost-oriented, (3) profit-oriented, and (4) competition-oriented approaches (see Figure 14–2). Although these approaches are discussed separately below, some of them overlap, and a seasoned marketing manager will consider several in selecting an approximate price level.

Demand-Oriented Pricing Approaches

Demand-oriented approaches weigh factors underlying expected customer tastes and preferences more heavily than such factors as cost, profit, and competition when selecting a price level.

Skimming Pricing A firm introducing a new or innovative product can use **skimming pricing**, setting the highest initial price that customers who really desire the product are willing to pay. These customers are not very price sensitive because they weigh the new product's price, quality, and ability to satisfy their needs against the same characteristics of substitutes. As the demand of these customers is satisfied, the firm lowers the price to attract another, more price-sensitive segment. Thus, skimming pricing gets its name from skimming successive layers of "cream," or customer segments, as prices are lowered in a series of steps.

Skimming pricing is an effective strategy when (1) enough prospective customers are willing to buy the product immediately at the high initial price to make these sales profitable, (2) the high initial price will not attract competitors, (3) lowering price has only a minor effect on increasing the sales volume and reducing the unit costs, and (4) customers interpret the high price as signifying high quality. These four conditions are most likely to exist when the new product is protected by patents or copyrights or its uniqueness is understood and valued by consumers. Gillette, for example, adopted

FIGURE 14–1
The six steps in setting price. The first three steps were covered in Chapter 13, and the last three steps are covered in this chapter.

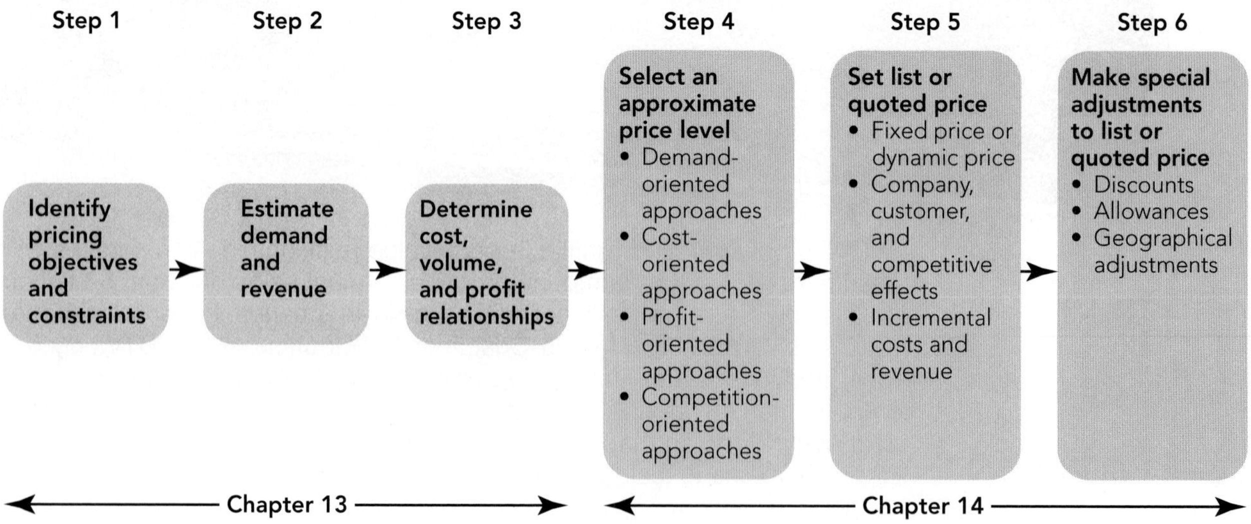

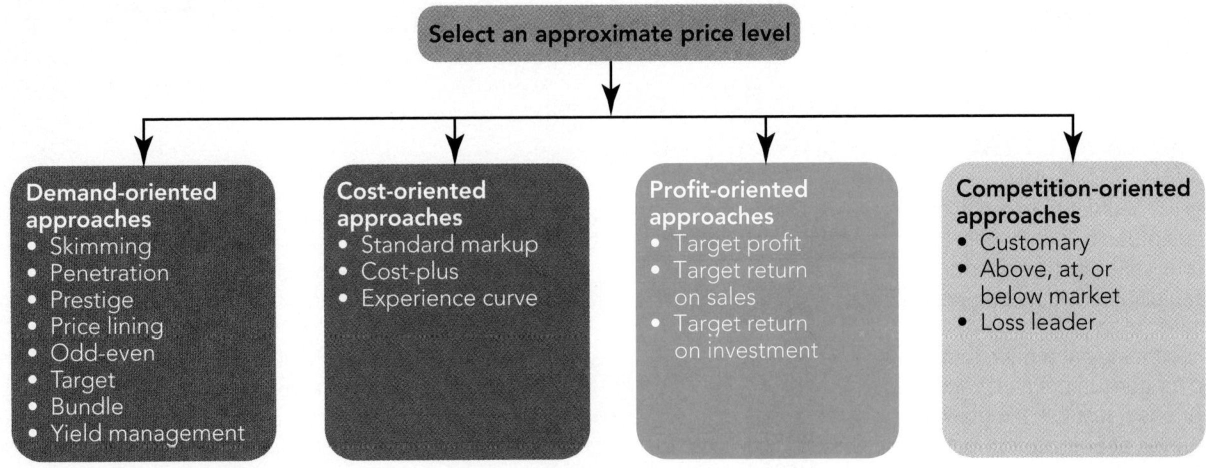

FIGURE 14–2
Four approaches for selecting an approximate price level.

a skimming strategy for its five-blade Fusion brand shaving system since many of these conditions applied. The Gillette Fusion shaving system has 70 patents that protect its product technology.

Penetration Pricing Setting a low initial price on a new product to appeal immediately to the mass market is **penetration pricing**, the exact opposite of skimming pricing. Amazon consciously chose a penetration strategy when it introduced its Amazon Kindle Fire tablet computer at $199 when competitive models were priced at $499.[2]

The conditions favoring penetration pricing are the reverse of those supporting skimming pricing: (1) many segments of the market are price sensitive, (2) a low initial price discourages competitors from entering the market, and (3) unit production and marketing costs fall dramatically as production volumes increase. A firm using penetration pricing may (1) maintain the initial price for a time to gain profit lost from its low introductory level or (2) lower the price further, counting on the new volume to generate the necessary profit.

In some situations, penetration pricing may follow skimming pricing. A company might initially price a product high to attract price-insensitive consumers and recoup initial research and development costs and introductory promotional expenditures. Once this is done, penetration pricing is used to appeal to a broader segment of the population and increase market share.[3]

FIGURE 14–3
For prestige pricing, the demand curve for high-quality products bought by status-conscious consumers is backward sloping.

Prestige pricing demand curve

A
Price P_0 B
C
Quantity

Prestige Pricing As noted in Chapter 13, consumers may use price as a measure of the quality or prestige of an item so that as price is lowered beyond some point, demand for the item actually falls. **Prestige pricing** involves setting a high price so that quality- or status-conscious consumers will be attracted to the product and buy it (see Figure 14–3). The demand curve slopes downward and to the right between points *A* and *B* but turns back to the left between points *B* and *C* because demand is actually reduced between points *B* and *C*. From *A* to *B*, buyers see the lowering of price as a bargain and buy more; from *B* to *C*, they become dubious about the quality and prestige and buy less. A marketing manager's pricing strategy here is to stay above price P_0 (the initial price).

Rolls-Royce cars, Chanel perfume, Cartier jewelry, Lalique crystal, and Swiss watches, such as Rolex, have an element of prestige pricing in them and may sell worse at lower prices than at higher ones.[4] The recent success of Swiss watchmaker TAG Heuer is an example. The company raised the average price of its watches from $250 to $1,000, and its sales volume jumped sevenfold.[5] Recently, Energizer learned that buyers of high-performance alkaline batteries tend to link a lower price with lower quality. The Marketing Matters box on the next page describes the pricing lesson learned by Energizer.[6]

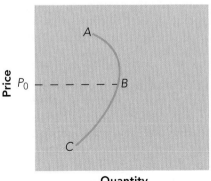

QR 14-2
Rolex Ad

Marketing Matters

customer value

Energizer's Lesson in Price Perception—Value Lies in the Eye of the Beholder

Battery manufacturers are as tireless as a certain drum-thumping bunny in their efforts to create products that perform better, last longer, and, not incidentally, outsell the competition. The commercialization of new alkaline battery technology at a price that creates value for consumers is not always obvious or easy. Just ask the marketing executives at Energizer about their experience with pricing Energizer Advanced Formula and Energizer e² AA alkaline batteries.

When Duracell launched its high-performance Ultra brand AA alkaline battery with a 25 percent price premium over standard Duracell batteries, Energizer quickly countered with its own high-performance battery—Energizer Advanced Formula. Believing that consumers would not pay the premium price, Energizer priced its Advanced Formula brand at the same price as its standard AA alkaline battery, expecting to gain market share from Duracell. It did not happen. Why? According to industry analysts, consumers associated Energizer's low price with inferior quality in the high-performance segment. Instead of gaining market share, Energizer lost market share to Duracell and Rayovac, the number three battery manufacturer.

Having learned its lesson, Energizer subsequently released its e² high-performance battery, this time priced 4 percent higher than Duracell Ultra and about 50 percent higher than Advanced Formula. The result? Energizer recovered lost sales and market share. The lesson learned? Value lies in the eye of the beholder.

Price Lining Often a firm that is selling not just a single product but a line of products may price them at a number of different specific pricing points, which is called **price lining**. For example, a department store manager may price a line of women's casual slacks at $59, $79, and $99. As shown in Figure 14–4, this assumes that demand is elastic at each of these price points but inelastic between these price points. In some instances, all the items might be purchased for the same cost and then marked up at different percentages to achieve these price points based on color, style, and expected demand. In other instances, manufacturers design products for different price points, and retailers apply approximately the same markup percentages to achieve the three or four different price points offered to consumers. Sellers often feel that a limited number of price points (such as 3 or 4) are preferable to 8 or 10, which may only confuse prospective buyers.[7]

FIGURE 14–4
For price lining, the demand curve is elastic at each price point but inelastic between price points.

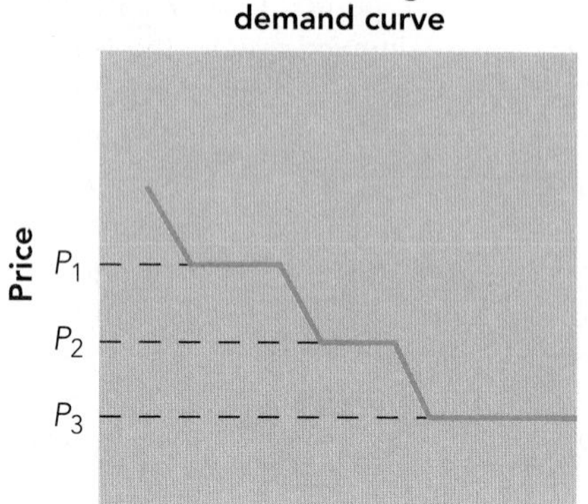

Odd-Even Pricing Sears offers a Craftsman radial saw for $499.99, the suggested retail price for the Gillette Fusion shaving system is $11.99, and Amazon sold a recent U2 CD for $3.99. Why not simply price these items at $500, $12, and $4, respectively? These firms are using **odd-even pricing**, which involves setting prices a few dollars or cents under an even number. The presumption is that consumers see the Craftsman radial saw as priced at "something over $400" rather than "about $500." In theory, demand increases if the price drops from $500 to $499.99. There is some evidence to suggest this does happen. However, research suggests that overuse of odd-ending prices tends to mute its effect on demand.[8]

Target Pricing Manufacturers will sometimes estimate the price that the ultimate consumer would be willing to pay for a product. They then work backward through markups taken by retailers and wholesalers to determine

Which pricing strategy is used by DIRECTV? Read the text to find out which one and why.

what price they can charge wholesalers for the product. This practice, called **target pricing**, results in the manufacturer deliberately adjusting the composition and features of a product to achieve the target price to consumers. Canon uses this practice for pricing its cameras.[9]

Bundle Pricing A frequently used demand-oriented pricing practice is **bundle pricing**—the marketing of two or more products in a single package price. For example, Delta Air Lines offers vacation packages that include airfare, car rental, and lodging. Bundle pricing is based on the idea that consumers value the package more than the individual items. This is due to benefits received from not having to make separate purchases and enhanced satisfaction from one item given the presence of another. This is the idea behind McDonald's Extra Value Meal and DIRECTV's TV, phone, and Internet bundles. Moreover, bundle pricing often provides a lower total cost to buyers and lower marketing costs to sellers.[10]

Yield Management Pricing Have you noticed seats on airline flights are priced differently within coach class? This is **yield management pricing**—the charging of different prices to maximize revenue for a set amount of capacity at any given time. As described in Chapter 12, service businesses engage in capacity management, and an effective way to do this is by varying prices by time, day, week, or season. Yield management pricing is a complex approach that continually matches demand and supply to customize the price for a service. Airlines, hotels, cruise ships, and car rental companies frequently use it. American Airlines estimates that yield management pricing produces an annual revenue that exceeds $500 million.[11]

learning review

14-1. In pricing a new product, what circumstances might support skimming or penetration pricing?

14-2. What is odd-even pricing?

Cost-Oriented Pricing Approaches

With cost-oriented approaches, a price setter stresses the cost side of the pricing problem, not the demand side. Price is set by looking at the production and marketing costs and then adding enough to cover direct expenses, overhead, and profit.

Standard Markup Pricing Managers of supermarkets and other retail stores have such a large number of products that estimating the demand for each product as a means of setting price is impossible. Therefore, they use **standard markup pricing**, which entails adding a fixed percentage to the cost of all items in a specific product class. This percentage markup varies depending on the type of retail store (such as furniture, clothing, or grocery) and the product involved. High-volume products usually have smaller markups than low-volume products. Supermarkets such as Kroger and Safeway have different markups for staple items and discretionary items. The markup on staple items such as sugar, flour, and dairy products varies from 10 percent to 23 percent. Markups on discretionary items like snack foods and candy range from 27 percent to 47 percent. These markups must cover all of the expenses of the store, pay for overhead costs, and contribute something to profits. Although these markups may appear very large, they result in only a 1 percent profit on sales revenue, assuming the supermarket is operating efficiently.

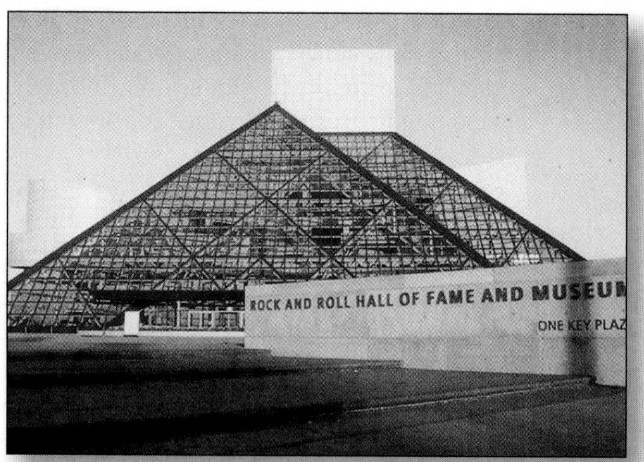

How was the price of the Rock and Roll Hall of Fame and Museum determined? Read the text to find out.

Rock and Roll Hall of Fame and Museum
www.rockhall.com

By comparison, consider the markups on snacks and beverages purchased at your local movie theater. The markup is 87 percent on soft drinks, 65 percent on candy bars, and 90 percent on popcorn. These markups might sound high, but consider the consequences. "If we didn't charge as much for concessions as we did, a movie ticket would cost $20," says the CEO of Regal Entertainment, the largest U.S. theater chain.[12] An explanation of how to compute a markup and markdown, along with operating statement data and other ratios, is given in Appendix B and Chapter 16.

Cost-Plus Pricing Many manufacturing, professional services, and construction firms use a variation of standard markup pricing. **Cost-plus pricing** involves summing the total unit cost of providing a product or service and adding a specific amount to the cost to arrive at a price. Cost-plus pricing generally assumes two forms. With *cost-plus percentage-of-cost pricing*, a fixed percentage is added to the total unit cost. This is often used to price one- or few-of-a-kind items, as when an architectural firm charges a percentage of the construction costs of, say, the $92 million Rock and Roll Hall of Fame and Museum in Cleveland, Ohio.

In buying highly technical, few-of-a-kind products such as hydroelectric power plants or space satellites, governments have found that general contractors are reluctant to specify a formal, fixed price for the procurement. Therefore, they use *cost-plus fixed-fee pricing*, which means that a supplier is reimbursed for all costs, regardless of what they turn out to be, but is allowed only a fixed fee as profit that is independent of the final cost of the project. For example, suppose the National Aeronautics and Space Administration agreed to pay Lockheed Martin $4 billion as the cost for its Orion lunar spacecraft and agreed to a $6.5 billion fee for providing the lunar spacecraft in 2016. Even if Lockheed Martin's cost increased to $5 billion for the lunar spacecraft, its fee would remain at $6.5 billion.

Cost-plus pricing is the most commonly used method to set prices for business products.[13] Increasingly, however, this method is finding favor among business-to-business marketers in the service sector. For example, the rising cost of legal fees has prompted some law firms to adopt a cost-plus pricing approach. Rather than billing business clients on an hourly basis, lawyers and their clients agree on a fixed fee based on expected costs plus a profit for the law firm. Many advertising agencies now use this approach. Here, the client agrees to pay the agency a fee based on the cost of its work plus some agreed-on profit, which is often a percentage of total cost.

Experience Curve Pricing The method of **experience curve pricing** is based on the learning effect, which holds that the unit cost of many products and services declines by 10 percent to 30 percent each time a firm's experience at producing and selling them doubles. This reduction is regular or predictable enough that the average cost per unit can be mathematically estimated. For example, if the firm estimates that costs will fall by 15 percent each time volume doubles, then the cost of the 100th unit produced and sold will be about 85 percent of the cost of the 50th unit, and the 200th unit will be 85 percent of the 100th unit. Therefore, if the cost of the 50th unit is $100, the 100th unit would cost $85, the 200th unit would be $72.25, and so on. Because prices often follow costs with experience curve pricing, a rapid decline in price is possible.

Japanese, Korean, and U.S. firms in the electronics industry often adopt this pricing approach. This cost-based pricing approach complements the demand-based pricing

VIZIO is a pioneer in the successful commercialization of affordable HDTVs. Like its competitors, VIZIO relies on experience curve pricing to drive down prices.

VIZIO
www.vizio.com

strategy of skimming followed by penetration pricing. For example, DVD player prices have decreased from $900 to about $50, fax machine prices have declined from $1,000 to under $100, and mobile telephones that once sold for $4,000 are now priced below $50. Sony, Samsung, LG, VIZIO, and other television manufacturers use experience curve pricing for HDTV sets. Consumers benefit because prices decline as cumulative sales volume grows. In fact, HDTV prices have fallen by 40 percent since 2007.[14]

Profit-Oriented Pricing Approaches

A price setter may choose to balance both revenues and costs to set price using profit-oriented approaches. These might either involve setting a target of a specific dollar volume of profit or expressing this target profit as a percentage of sales or investment.

Target Profit Pricing A firm that sets an annual target of a specific dollar volume of profit is using a **target profit pricing** approach. As the owner of a picture framing store, suppose you decide to use target profit pricing to establish a price for a typical framed picture. First, you need to make some assumptions, such as:

- Variable cost is a constant $22 per unit.
- Fixed cost is a constant $26,000.
- Demand is insensitive to price up to $60 per unit.
- A target profit of $7,000, at an annual volume of 1,000 units (framed pictures).

You can then calculate price as follows:

$$\begin{aligned}
\text{Profit} &= \text{Total revenue} - \text{Total cost}\\
\text{Profit} &= (\text{P} \times \text{Q}) - [\text{FC} + (\text{UVC} \times \text{Q})]\\
\$7{,}000 &= (\text{P} \times 1{,}000) - [\$26{,}000 + (\$22 \times 1{,}000)]\\
\$7{,}000 &= 1{,}000\text{P} - (\$26{,}000 + \$22{,}000)\\
1{,}000\text{P} &= \$7{,}000 + \$48{,}000\\
\text{P} &= \$55
\end{aligned}$$

Note that a critical assumption is that this higher average price for a framed picture will not cause the demand to fall.

Target Return-on-Sales Pricing A shortcoming with target profit pricing is that although it is simple and the target involves only a specific dollar volume, there is no benchmark of sales or investment used to show how much of the firm's effort is needed to achieve the target. Firms such as supermarket chains often use **target return-on-sales pricing** to set typical prices that will give them a profit that is a specified percentage, say, 1 percent, of the sales volume. Suppose you decide to use target return-on-sales pricing in your shop. To establish a price for a typical framed picture, you begin by making the same first three assumptions shown previously. However, for the fourth assumption, your target is now a 20 percent return on sales at an annual volume of 1,250 units. This results in the following price:

$$\begin{aligned}
\text{Target return on sales} &= \frac{\text{Target profit}}{\text{Total revenue}}\\
20\% &= \frac{\text{TR} - \text{TC}}{\text{TR}}\\
0.20 &= \frac{\text{P} \times \text{Q} - [\text{FC} + (\text{UVC} \times \text{Q})]}{\text{TR}}\\
0.20 &= \frac{\text{P} \times 1{,}250 - [\$26{,}000 + (\$22 \times 1{,}250)]}{\text{P} \times 1{,}250}\\
\text{P} &= \$53.50
\end{aligned}$$

So at a price of \$53.50 per unit and an annual quantity of 1,250 frames,

$$\begin{aligned}
\text{TR} &= \text{P} \times \text{Q} = \$53.50 \times 1{,}250 = \$66{,}875\\
\text{TC} &= \text{FC} + (\text{UVC} \times \text{Q}) = \$26{,}000 + (\$22 \times 1{,}250) = \$53{,}500\\
\text{Profit} &= \text{TR} - \text{TC} = \$66{,}875 - \$53{,}500 = \$13{,}375
\end{aligned}$$

As a check,

$$\text{Target return on sales} = \frac{\text{Target profit}}{\text{Total revenue}} = \frac{\$13{,}375}{\$66{,}875} = 20\%$$

Target Return-on-Investment Pricing Large, publicly owned corporations and many public utilities set annual return-on-investment (ROI) targets such as an ROI of 20 percent. **Target return-on-investment pricing** is a method of setting prices to achieve this target.

As the owner of the picture frame shop, suppose you decide to set a target ROI of 10 percent, which is twice that achieved the previous year. You consider raising the average price of a framed picture to \$54 or \$58—up from last year's average of \$50. To do this, you might improve product quality by offering better frames and higher-quality matting. This is likely to increase the cost, but higher prices will probably offset the decreased revenue from the lower number of units you are likely to sell next year.

Assumptions or Results	Financial Element	Last Year	SPREADSHEET SIMULATION A	B	C	D
ASSUMPTIONS	Price per unit (P)	$50	$54	$54	$58	$58
	Units sold (Q)	1,000	1,200	1,100	1,100	1,000
	Change in unit variable cost (UVC)	0%	+10%	+10%	+20%	+20%
	Unit variable cost	$22.00	$24.20	$24.20	$26.20	$26.40
	Total expenses	$8,000	Same	Same	Same	Same
	Owner's salary	$18,000	Same	Same	Same	Same
	Investment	$20,000	Same	Same	Same	Same
	State and federal taxes	50%	Same	Same	Same	Same
SPREADSHEET RESULTS	Net sales (P × Q)	$50,000	$64,800	$59,400	$63,800	$58,000
	Less: COGS (Q × UVC)	22,000	29,040	26,620	29,040	26,400
	Gross margin	$28,000	$35,760	$32,780	$34,760	$31,600
	Less: Total expenses	8,000	8,000	8,000	8,000	8,000
	Less: Owner's salary	18,000	18,000	18,000	18,000	18,000
	Net profit before taxes	$2,000	$9,760	$6,780	$8,760	$5,600
	Less: Taxes	1,000	4,880	3,390	4,380	2,800
	Net profit after taxes	$1,000	$4,880	$3,390	$4,380	$2,800
	Investment	$20,000	$20,000	$20,000	$20,000	$20,000
	Return on investment	5.0%	24.4%	17.0%	21.9%	14.0%

FIGURE 14–5
Results of a spreadsheet simulation used to select a price that will achieve a target return on investment.

To handle this wide variety of assumptions, managers use spreadsheets to project operating statements based on a set of assumptions. Figure 14–5 shows the results of a spreadsheet simulation, with assumptions shown at the top and the projected results at the bottom. A previous year's operating statement results are shown in the column headed "Last Year." The assumptions and spreadsheet results for four different sets of assumptions are shown in columns A, B, C, and D.

In choosing a price or another action using spreadsheet results, the manager must (1) study the results of the simulation projections and (2) assess the realism of the assumptions underlying each set of projections. For example, as the owner of the picture frame shop, you would look at the bottom row of Figure 14–5 and see that all four spreadsheet simulations exceed the after-tax target ROI of 10 percent. But after more thought, you might decide that it would be more realistic to set an average price of $58 per unit, allow the unit variable cost to increase by 20 percent to account for more expensive framing and matting, and settle for the same unit sales as the 1,000 units sold last year. Therefore, you would select simulation D in this spreadsheet approach to target ROI pricing, settling on a goal of 14 percent after-tax ROI.

Competition-Oriented Pricing Approaches

Rather than emphasize demand, cost, or profit factors, a price setter can stress what competitors or "the market" are doing.

Customary Pricing For some products where tradition, a standardized channel of distribution, or other competitive factors dictate the price, **customary pricing** is used. For example, tradition prevails in the pricing of Swatch watches. The $40 customary

Has Red Bull's price premium among energy-drink brands sold in convenience stores increased or decreased? The Using Marketing Dashboards box answers this question.

price for the basic model has changed little in 10 years. Candy bars offered through standard vending machines have a customary price of 75 cents. A significant departure from this price may result in a loss of sales for the manufacturer. Hershey changes the amount of chocolate in its candy bars depending on the price of raw chocolate rather than varying its customary retail price so that it can continue selling through vending machines.

Above-, At-, or Below-Market Pricing For most products, it is difficult to identify a specific market price for a product or product class. Still, marketing managers often have a subjective feel for the competitors' price or market price. Using this benchmark, they then may deliberately choose a strategy of **above-, at-, or below-market pricing**.

Among watch manufacturers, Rolex takes pride in emphasizing that it makes one of the most expensive watches you can buy, a clear example of above-market pricing. Manufacturers of national brands of clothing such as Hart Schaffner & Marx and Christian Dior and retailers such as Neiman Marcus deliberately set premium prices for their products.

Revlon cosmetics and Arrow brand shirts are generally priced "at market." As such, they also provide a reference price for competitors that use above- and below-market pricing.

A number of firms use below-market pricing. Manufacturers and retailers that offer private brands of products ranging from peanut butter to shampoo deliberately set prices for these products about 8 to 10 percent below the prices of nationally branded competitive products such as Skippy peanut butter and Vidal Sassoon shampoo. Below-market pricing also exists in business-to-business marketing. Hewlett-Packard, for instance, initially priced its office personal computers below those of competitors to promote a value image among corporate buyers.[15]

Companies use a "price premium" to assess whether their products and brands are above, at, or below the market. An illustration of how the price premium measure is calculated, displayed, and interpreted appears in the Using Marketing Dashboards box.[16]

Loss-Leader Pricing For a special promotion, retail stores deliberately sell a product below its customary price to attract attention to it. The purpose of this **loss-leader pricing** is not to increase sales but to attract customers in hopes they will buy other products as well, particularly the discretionary items with large markups. For example, Best Buy, Target, and Walmart sell CDs at about half of music companies' suggested retail prices to attract customers to their stores.[17]

learning review

14-3. What is standard markup pricing?

14-4. What profit-based pricing approach should a manager use if she wants to reflect the percentage of the firm's resources used in obtaining the profit?

14-5. What is the purpose of loss-leader pricing when used by a retail firm?

STEP 5: SET THE LIST OR QUOTED PRICE

Recognize the major factors considered in deriving a final list or quoted price from the approximate price level.

So far, we have covered four of the six steps involved in setting a price—steps 1–3, covered in Chapter 13, and step 4, covered in the preceding section. The result of these four steps is an approximate price level for the product that appears reasonable. But it still remains for the manager to set a specific list or quoted price in light of all relevant factors. In deciding upon the specific price for a product, the manager must choose a price policy; consider company, customer, and competitive effects on pricing; and balance incremental costs and revenues.

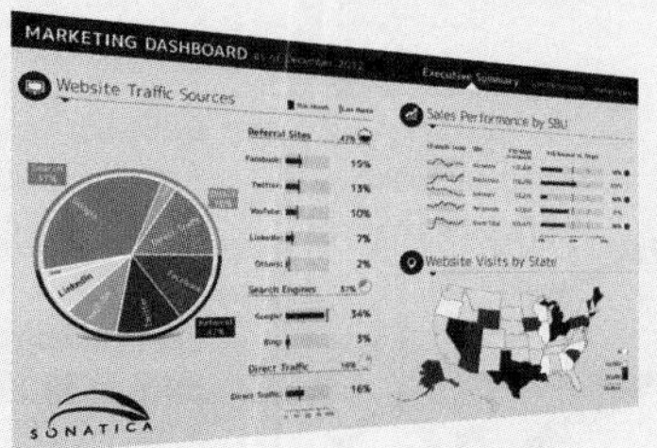

Using Marketing Dashboards

Are Red Bull Prices Above, At, or Below the Market?

How would you determine whether a firm's retail prices are above, at, or below the market? You might visit retail stores and record what prices retailers are charging for products or brands. However, this laborious activity can be simplified by combining dollar market share and unit volume market share measures to create a "price premium" display on your marketing dashboard.

Your Challenge Red Bull is the leading energy-drink brand in the United States in terms of dollar market share and unit market share (see the table below). Company marketing executives have research showing that Red Bull has a strong brand equity. What they want to know is whether the brand's price premium resulting from its brand equity has eroded due to heavy price discounting in the convenience store channel. This channel accounts for 60 percent of energy-drink sales.

A price premium is the percentage by which the actual price charged for a specific brand exceeds (or falls short of) a benchmark established for a similar product or basket of products. As such, a price premium shows whether a brand is priced above, at, or below the market. This premium is calculated as follows:

$$\text{Price premium (\%)} = \frac{\text{Dollar sales market share for a brand}}{\text{Unit volume market share for a brand}} - 1$$

Your Findings Using 2010 energy-drink brand market share data for U.S. convenience stores, the Red Bull price premium is 1.152, or 15.2 percent, calculated as follows: (38 percent ÷ 33 percent) −1 = .152. Red Bull's average price is 15.2 percent higher than the average price for energy-drink brands sold in convenience stores. Red Bull's price premium based on 2009 brand market share data was 1.121, or 12.1 percent, calculated as follows: (37 percent ÷ 33 percent) −1 = 12.1. Red Bull's price premium has increased relative to its competitors, notably Monster Energy and Rockstar. The price premiums for Red Bull and these two competitive brands for 2009 and 2010 are displayed in the marketing dashboard shown below.

Your Action Red Bull has increased its price premium while retaining its unit volume share, which is not only favorable news for the brand but also evidence of price discounting by other brands. Clearly, the company's brand-building effort, reflected in sponsorships and a singular focus on brand attributes valued by consumers, should be continued.

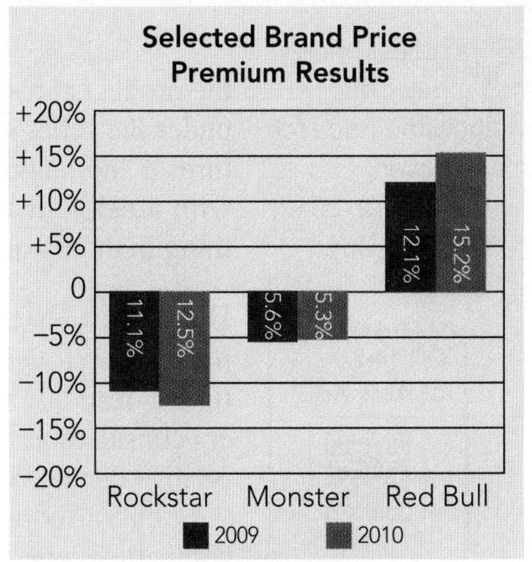

	Dollar Sales Market Share		Unit Volume Market Share	
Brand	**2010**	**2009**	**2010**	**2009**
Red Bull	38%	37%	33%	33%
Monster	18	17	19	18
Rockstar	7	8	8	9
Other brands	37	38	40	40
	100%	100%	100%	100%

Choose a Price Policy

Choosing a price policy is important in setting a list or quoted price. Two options are common—a fixed-price policy or a dynamic pricing policy.

Fixed-Price Policy A **fixed-price policy**, also called a *one-price policy*, is setting one price for all buyers of a product or service. For example, when you buy a Wilson Cirrus One BLX tennis racquet from a sporting goods store, you are offered

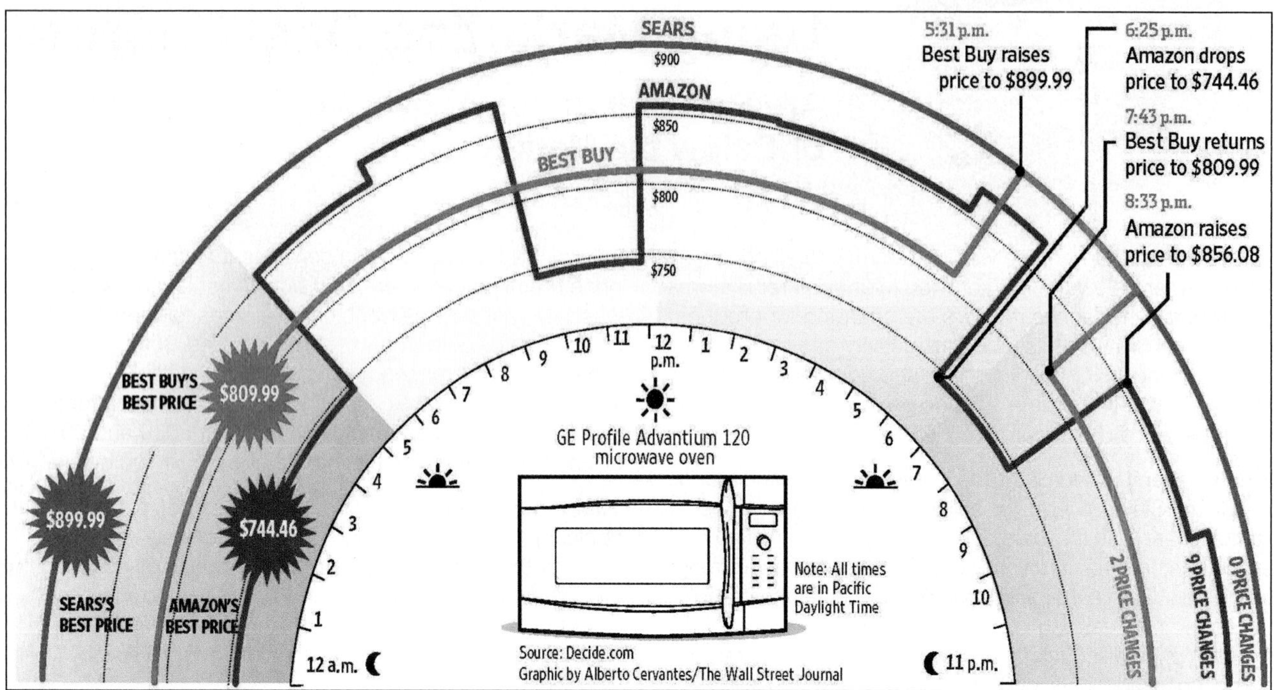

Online retailers adjust prices several times a day. This chart shows how the price for a GE microwave oven changed on August 12, 2012, on the Amazon, Best Buy, and Sears websites.

QR 14-3
CarMax Ad

the product at a single price. You can buy it or not, but there is no variation in the price under the seller's fixed-price policy. CarMax uses this approach in its stores and features a "no haggle, one price" price for cars. Some retailers have married this policy with a below-market approach. Dollar Value Stores and 99¢ Only Stores sell everything in their stores for $1 or less. Family Dollar Stores sell everything for $2.

Dynamic Pricing Policy In contrast, a **dynamic pricing policy**, also called a *flexible-price policy*, involves setting different prices for products and services in real time in response to supply and demand conditions. A dynamic pricing policy gives sellers considerable discretion in setting the final price in light of demand, cost, and competitive factors. Yield management pricing is a form of dynamic pricing because prices vary by an individual buyer's purchase situation, company cost considerations, and competitive conditions. Dell Inc. uses dynamic pricing. It continually adjusts prices in response to changes in its own costs, competitive pressures, and demand from customers, from one segment of the personal computer market to another. "Our flexibility allows us to be [priced] different even within a day," says a Dell spokesperson.[18]

Most companies use a fixed-price policy. However, dynamic pricing has grown in popularity because of increasingly sophisticated information technology. Today, many marketers have the ability to customize a price for an individual on the basis of his or her purchasing patterns, product preferences, and price sensitivity, all of which are stored in company data warehouses.[19] For example, online marketers like Amazon, described in Chapter 13, routinely adjust prices in response to purchase situations and past purchase behaviors of online buyers. Some online marketers monitor an online shopper's *clickstream*—the way that person navigates through the website. If the visitor behaves like a price-sensitive shopper—perhaps by comparing many different products and prices—that person may be offered a lower price.

Dynamic pricing means that some customers pay more and others pay less for the same product or service. Dynamic pricing is not without its critics because of this discriminatory potential. For example, car dealers have traditionally used dynamic pricing on the basis of buyer–seller negotiations to agree on a final sales price. However, dynamic pricing may result in discriminatory practices in car buying as detailed in the Making Responsible Decisions box.[20] Legal issues are also associated with dynamic

Making Responsible Decisions

ethics

Dynamic Pricing—Is There Discrimination in Bargaining for a New Car?

What do 60 percent of prospective buyers dread when looking for a new car? That's right! They dread negotiating the price. Price bargaining demonstrates the shortcomings of dynamic pricing when purchasing a new car: the potential for price discrimination.

A National Bureau of Economic Research study of 750,000 car purchases indicated that African Americans, Hispanics, and women, on average, paid roughly $423, $483, and $105 more, respectively, for a new car in the $21,000 range than the typical purchaser. Smaller price premiums remained after adjusting for income, education, and other factors that may affect price negotiations.

Research shows that searching automotive and car dealer websites before buying a new car reduces price premiums paid by African Americans, Hispanics, and women.

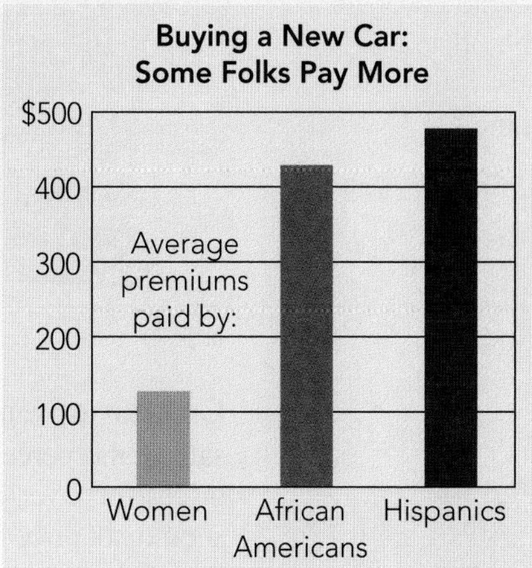

pricing. As noted later in this chapter, constraints under the *Robinson-Patman Act* prevent carrying a dynamic-pricing policy to the extreme of price discrimination.

Consider Company, Customer, and Competitive Effects on Pricing

In determining a final list or quoted price, the manager must next assess company, customer, and competitive effects on pricing.

Company Effects For a firm with more than one product, a decision on the price of a single product must consider the price of other items in its product line or related product lines in its product mix. Within a product line or mix there are usually some products that are substitutes for one another and some that complement each other.[21] Frito-Lay recognizes that its Baked Tostitos, Tostitos, and Doritos brands are partial substitutes for one another and its bean and cheese dips and salsas complement the products in its tortilla chip line.

A manager's challenge when marketing multiple products is **product-line pricing**, the setting of prices for all items in a product line. When setting prices, the manager seeks to cover the total cost and produce a profit for the complete line, not necessarily for each item. For example, a penetration price for Nintendo's Wii U video game console is probably at or below its cost, but the price of its video games (complementary products) is likely to be set high enough to cover the loss and deliver a handsome profit for the Nintendo product line.

Product-line pricing involves determining (1) the lowest-priced product and price, (2) the highest-priced product and price, and (3) price differentials for all other products in the line.[22] The lowest- and highest-priced items in the product line play important roles. The highest-priced item is typically positioned as the premium item in quality and features. The lowest-priced item is the traffic builder designed to capture the attention of the hesitant or first-time buyer. Price differentials between items in the line should make sense to customers and reflect differences in the perceived value of the products offered. Behavioral research also suggests that the price differentials should get larger as one moves up the product line.

Frito-Lay recognizes that its tortilla chip products are partial substitutes for one another. Its bean and cheese dips and salsas complement tortilla chips. This knowledge is used by Frito-Lay in its product-line pricing.

Frito-Lay, Inc.
www.frito-lay.com

Customer Effects In setting a price, marketers pay close attention to factors that satisfy the perceptions or expectations of ultimate consumers, such as the customary prices for a variety of consumer products. For example, retailers have found that they should not price their store brands 20 to 25 percent below manufacturers' brands.[23] When they do, consumers often view the lower price as a signal of lower quality and don't buy.

Manufacturers and wholesalers must choose prices that result in profit for resellers in the channel to gain their cooperation and support. Toro learned this lesson the hard way when it decided to augment its traditional hardware outlet distribution by also selling its lawn mower and snow thrower product lines through mass merchandisers. To do so, it set mass merchandiser prices far below those for its traditional hardware outlets. Unhappy hardware stores abandoned Toro products in favor of mowers and snow throwers from competitors.

Competitive Effects A manager's pricing decision is immediately apparent to most competitors, who may retaliate with price changes of their own. Therefore, a manager who sets a final list or quoted price must anticipate potential price responses from competitors. Regardless of whether a firm is a price leader or follower, it wants to avoid cutthroat price wars in which no firm in the industry makes a profit.

A **price war** involves successive price cutting by competitors to increase or maintain their unit sales or market share. Price wars erupt in a variety of industries, from consumer electronics to disposable diapers, from soft drinks to airlines, and from grocery retailing to smartphone services. Managers who engage in price wars do so expecting that a lower price will result in a larger market share, higher unit sales, and greater profit for their company. These results may occur. But, if competitors match the lower price, other things being equal, the expected market share, sales, and profit gain are lost. According to an analysis of large U.S. companies, a 1 percent price cut—assuming no change in unit volume or costs—lowers a company's net profit by an average of 8 percent.[24]

Marketers are advised to consider price cutting only when one or more conditions exist: (1) the company has a cost or technological advantage over its competitors, (2) primary demand for a product class will grow if prices are lowered, and (3) the price cut is confined to specific products or customers (as with airline tickets) and is not across the board.[25]

Balance Incremental Costs and Revenues

When a price is changed or new advertising or personal selling programs are planned, their effect on the quantity sold must be considered. This assessment, called *marginal analysis* (see Chapter 13), involves a continuing, concise trade-off of incremental costs against incremental revenues.

Do marketing and business managers really use marginal analysis? Yes, they do, but they often don't use phrases such as *marginal revenue*, *marginal cost*, and *elasticity of demand.*

FIGURE 14–6
Expected incremental revenue from pricing and other marketing actions must more than offset incremental costs to achieve an incremental profit.

Suppose the owner of a picture framing store is considering buying a series of magazine ads to reach her upscale target market. The cost of the ads is $1,000, the average price of a framed picture is $50, and the unit variable cost (materials plus labor) is $30.

This is a direct application of marginal analysis that an astute manager uses to estimate the incremental revenue or incremental number of units that must be obtained to at least cover the incremental cost. In this example, the number of extra picture frames that must be sold is obtained as follows:

$$\text{Incremental number of frames} = \frac{\text{Extra fixed cost}}{\text{Price} - \text{Unit variable cost}} = \frac{\$1{,}000 \text{ of advertising}}{\$50 - \$30} = 50 \text{ frames}$$

So unless there are other benefits of the ads, such as long-term goodwill, she should buy the ads only if she expects they will increase picture frame sales by at least 50 units.

Think about these managerial questions:

- How many extra units do we have to sell to pay for that $1,000 advertisement?
- Should we hire three more salespeople or not?

These questions are a form of marginal or incremental analysis discussed in Chapter 13, even though these exact words are not used.

Figure 14–6 uses an example of a picture frame store owner to illustrate the advantages and disadvantages of using marginal analysis to make marketing decisions. Note that the owner in this example must either conclude that a simple advertising campaign will more than pay for itself in additional sales or not undertake the campaign. The decision could also have been made to increase the average price of a framed picture to cover the cost of the campaign, but the principle still applies: Expected incremental revenues from pricing and other marketing actions must more than offset incremental costs.

The example in Figure 14–6 shows both the main advantage and the difficulty of marginal analysis. The advantage is its commonsense usefulness, and the difficulty is obtaining the necessary data to make decisions. The owner can measure the cost quite easily, but the incremental revenue generated by the ads is difficult to measure. To get a general idea, she might offer $2 off the purchase price with use of a coupon printed in the ad to see which sales resulted from the ad.

STEP 6: MAKE SPECIAL ADJUSTMENTS TO THE LIST OR QUOTED PRICE

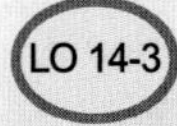

Identify the adjustments made to the approximate price level on the basis of discounts, allowances, and geography.

When you pay $1.00 for a bag of M&M's in a vending machine or receive a quoted price of $10,000 from a contractor to renovate a kitchen, the pricing sequence ends with the last step just described: setting the list or quoted price. But when you are a manufacturer of M&M candies or Wolf gas ranges and you sell your product to dozens or hundreds of wholesalers and retailers in your marketing channel, you may need to make special adjustments to the list or quoted price. Wholesalers adjust the list or quoted prices they set for retailers. Retailers, in turn, do the same for consumers. Three special adjustments to the list or quoted price are (1) discounts, (2) allowances, and (3) geographical adjustments (see Figure 14–7 on the next page).

FIGURE 14–7
Three special adjustments to the list or quoted price include discounts, allowances, and geographical adjustments. Each can substantially change the final price.

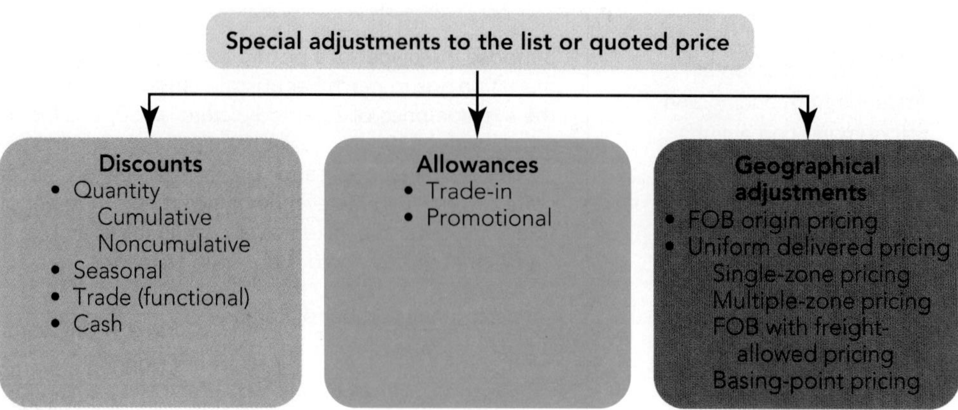

Discounts

Discounts are reductions from the list price that a seller gives a buyer as a reward for some activity of the buyer that is favorable to the seller. Four kinds of discounts are especially important in marketing strategy: (1) quantity, (2) seasonal, (3) trade (functional), and (4) cash.[26]

Quantity Discounts To encourage customers to buy larger quantities of a product, firms at all levels in the marketing channel offer **quantity discounts**, which are reductions in unit costs for a larger order. For example, a photocopying service such as AlphaGraphics might set a price of 10 cents a copy for 1 to 25 copies, 9 cents a copy for 26 to 100, and 8 cents a copy for 101 or more. Because the photocopying service gets more of the buyer's business and has longer production runs that reduce its order-handling costs, it is willing to pass on some of the cost savings in the form of quantity discounts to the buyer.

Quantity discounts are of two general kinds: noncumulative and cumulative. *Noncumulative quantity discounts* are based on the size of an individual purchase order. They encourage large individual purchase orders, not a series of orders. This discount is used by FedEx to encourage companies to ship a large number of packages at one time. *Cumulative quantity discounts* apply to the accumulation of purchases of a product over a given time period, typically a year. Cumulative quantity discounts encourage repeat buying by a single customer to a far greater degree than do noncumulative quantity discounts.

Seasonal Discounts To encourage buyers to stock inventory earlier than their normal demand would require, manufacturers often use *seasonal discounts*. A firm such as Toro that manufactures lawn mowers and snow throwers offers seasonal discounts to encourage wholesalers and retailers to stock up on lawn mowers in January and February and on snow throwers in July and August—five or six months before the seasonal demand by ultimate consumers. This enables Toro to smooth out seasonal manufacturing peaks and troughs, thereby contributing to more efficient production. It also rewards wholesalers and retailers for the risk they accept in assuming increased inventory carrying costs and having supplies in stock at the time they are wanted by customers.

Trade (Functional) Discounts To reward wholesalers and retailers for marketing functions they will perform in the future, a manufacturer often gives *trade*, or *functional, discounts*. These reductions off the list or base price are offered to resellers in the marketing channel on the basis of (1) where they are in the channel and (2) the marketing activities they are expected to perform in the future.

Discounts are a common adjustment to list prices. They are used to give a buyer a reward for some activity of the buyer that is favorable to the seller as described in the text.

Suppose a manufacturer quotes price in the following form: list price—$100 less 30/10/5. The first number in the percentage sequence always refers to the retail end of the channel. The last number always refers to the wholesaler or jobber closest to the manufacturer in the channel. The trade discounts are simply subtracted one at a time. This price quote shows $100 is the manufacturer's suggested retail price; 30 percent of the suggested retail price is available to the retailer to cover costs and provide a profit of $30 ($100 × 0.3 = $30); wholesalers closest to the retailer in the channel get 10 percent of their selling price ($70 × 0.1 = $7); and the final group of wholesalers in the channel (probably jobbers) that are closest to the manufacturer get 5 percent of their selling price ($63 × 0.05 = $3.15). Thus, starting with the manufacturer's suggested retail price and subtracting the three trade discounts shows that the manufacturer's selling price to the wholesaler or jobber closest to it is $59.85 (see Figure 14–8).

Traditional trade discounts have been established in various product lines such as hardware, food, and pharmaceutical items. Although the manufacturer may suggest the trade discounts shown in the example just cited, the sellers are free to alter the discount schedule depending on their competitive situation.

Cash Discounts To encourage retailers to pay their bills quickly, manufacturers offer them *cash discounts*. Suppose a retailer receives a bill quoted at $1,000, 2/10 net 30. This means that the bill for the product is $1,000, but the retailer can take a 2 percent discount ($1,000 × 0.02 = $20) if payment is made within 10 days and send a check for $980. If the payment cannot be made within 10 days, the total amount of $1,000 is due within 30 days. It is usually understood by the buyer that an interest charge will be added after the first 30 days of free credit.

Retailers provide cash discounts to consumers as well to eliminate the cost of credit granted to consumers. These discounts take the form of discount-for-cash policies.

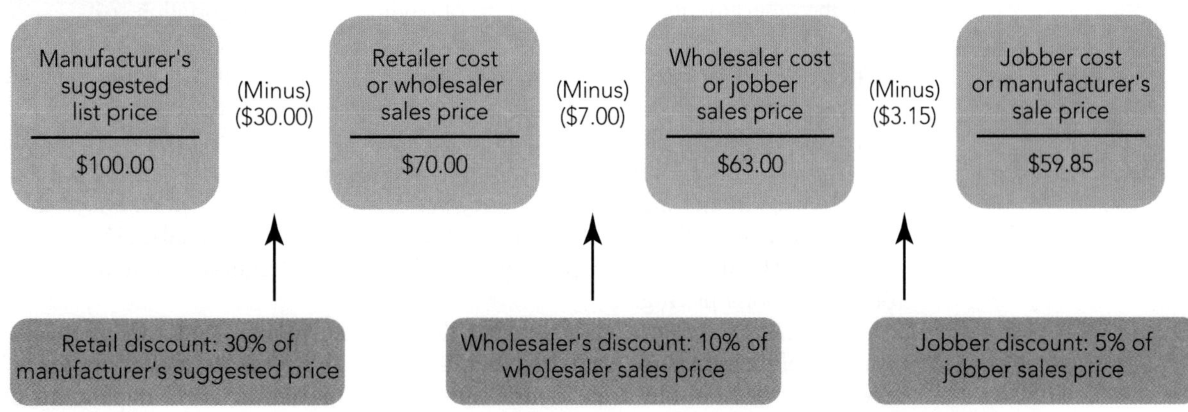

FIGURE 14–8
The structure of trade discounts affects the manufacturer's selling price and the margins made by resellers in a marketing channel.

Promotional allowances are used by retailers, such as Payless, to offer items at sale prices.

Allowances

Allowances, like discounts, are reductions from list or quoted prices to buyers for performing some activity. They include trade-in and promotional allowances.

Trade-in Allowances A new-car dealer can offer a substantial reduction in the list price of that new Toyota Camry by offering you a trade-in allowance of $1,000 for your Honda Civic. A *trade-in allowance* is a price reduction given when a used product is accepted as part of the payment on a new product. Trade-ins are an effective way to lower the price a buyer has to pay without formally reducing the list price.

Promotional Allowances Sellers in the marketing channel can qualify for **promotional allowances** by undertaking certain advertising or selling activities to promote a product. Various types of allowances include an actual cash payment or an extra amount of "free goods" (as with a free case of Red Baron frozen cheese pizzas to a retailer for every dozen cases purchased). Frequently, a portion of these savings is passed on to the consumer by retailers.

Some companies, such as Procter & Gamble, have chosen to reduce promotional allowances for retailers by using everyday low pricing. **Everyday low pricing (EDLP)** is the practice of replacing promotional allowances with lower manufacturer list prices. EDLP promises to reduce the average price to consumers while minimizing promotional allowances that cost manufacturers billions of dollars every year. However, EDLP does not necessarily benefit supermarkets, as described in the Marketing Matters box.[27]

Geographical Adjustments

Geographical adjustments to list or quoted prices are made by manufacturers or even wholesalers to reflect the cost of transportation of the products from seller to buyer. The two general methods for quoting prices related to transportation costs are (1) FOB origin pricing and (2) uniform delivered pricing.

FOB Origin Pricing FOB means "free on board" some vehicle at some location, which means the seller pays the cost of loading the product onto the vehicle that is used (such as a barge, railroad car, or truck). **FOB origin pricing** usually involves the seller's naming the location of this loading as the seller's factory or warehouse (such as "FOB Detroit" or "FOB factory"). The title to the goods passes to the buyer at the point of loading, so the buyer becomes responsible for picking the specific mode of transportation, for all the transportation costs, and for subsequent handling of the product. Buyers farthest from the seller face the big disadvantage of paying higher transportation costs.

Uniform Delivered Pricing When a **uniform delivered pricing** method is used, the price the seller quotes includes all transportation costs. It is quoted in a contract as "FOB buyer's location," and the seller selects the mode of transportation, pays the freight charges, and is responsible for any damage that may occur because the seller retains title to the goods until they are delivered to the buyer. Although they go by various names, there are four kinds of delivered pricing methods: (1) single-zone pricing, (2) multiple-zone pricing, (3) FOB with freight-allowed pricing, and (4) basing-point pricing.

In *single-zone pricing*, all buyers pay the same delivered price for the products, regardless of their distance from the seller. So, although a retail store offering free delivery in a metropolitan area incurs varying transportation costs depending on a customer's location in relation to the store, all customers pay the same delivered price.

Marketing Matters

customer value

Everyday Low Prices at the Supermarket = Everyday Low Profits—Creating Customer Value at a Cost

Who wouldn't welcome low retail prices every day? The answer is supermarket chains—76 percent of U.S. grocery stores have not adopted this practice. Supermarkets prefer Hi-Lo pricing based on frequent specials where prices are temporarily lowered and then raised again. Hi-Lo pricing reflects allowances that manufacturers give supermarkets to push their products. Consider a New York City supermarket whose advertisement is shown here. It regularly pays $1.15 for a can of Bumble Bee white tuna ($55.43 ÷ 48 = $1.15), but the allowances reduce the cost to 96 cents. A price special of 99 cents still provides a 3 cent retail markup ($0.99 retail price in ad − $0.96 cost). When the price on tuna returns to its regular level, the store's gross margin on tuna increases substantially on those cans that were bought with the allowance but not sold during the special price promotion.

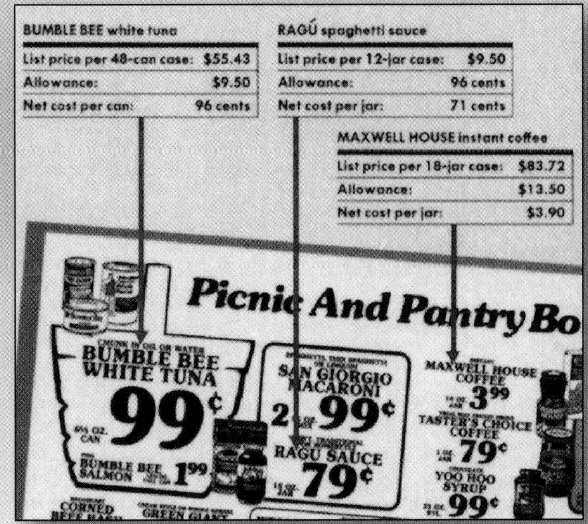

Everyday low pricing (EDLP) eliminates manufacturer allowances and can reduce average retail prices by up to 10 percent. While EDLP provides lower average prices than Hi-Lo pricing, EDLP does not allow for deeply discounted price specials. EDLP can create everyday customer value and modestly increase supermarket sales—but at a cost. Already slim supermarket chain profits can slip by 18 percent with EDLP without the benefit of allowances as described earlier. Also, some argue that EDLP without price specials is boring for many grocery shoppers who welcome price specials.

EDLP has been hailed as "value pricing" by manufacturers, but supermarkets view it differently. For them, EDLP means "Everyday Low Profits!"

In *multiple-zone pricing*, a firm divides its selling territory into geographic areas or zones. The delivered price to all buyers within any one zone is the same, but prices across zones vary depending on the transportation cost to each particular zone and the level of competition and demand within each zone.

With *FOB with freight-allowed pricing*, also called *freight absorption pricing*, the price is quoted by the seller as "FOB plant—freight allowed." The buyer is allowed to deduct freight expenses from the list price of the goods, so the seller agrees to pay, or "absorb," the transportation costs.

Basing-point pricing involves selecting one or more geographical locations (basing point) from which the list price for products plus freight expenses are charged to the buyer. For example, a company might designate St. Louis as the basing point and charge all buyers a list price of $100 plus freight from St. Louis to their location. Basing-point pricing methods have been used in the steel, cement, and lumber industries where freight expenses are a significant part of the total cost to the buyer and products are largely undifferentiated.

Legal and Regulatory Aspects of Pricing

LO 14-4 Name the principal laws and regulations affecting specific pricing practices.

Arriving at a final price is clearly a complex process. The task is further complicated by legal and regulatory restrictions. Five pricing practices have received the most scrutiny: (1) price fixing, (2) price discrimination, (3) deceptive pricing, (4) geographical pricing, and (5) predatory pricing (see Figure 14–9 on the next page).

Price Fixing A conspiracy among firms to set prices for a product is termed **price fixing**. Price fixing is illegal per se under the Sherman Act (*per se* means in and of

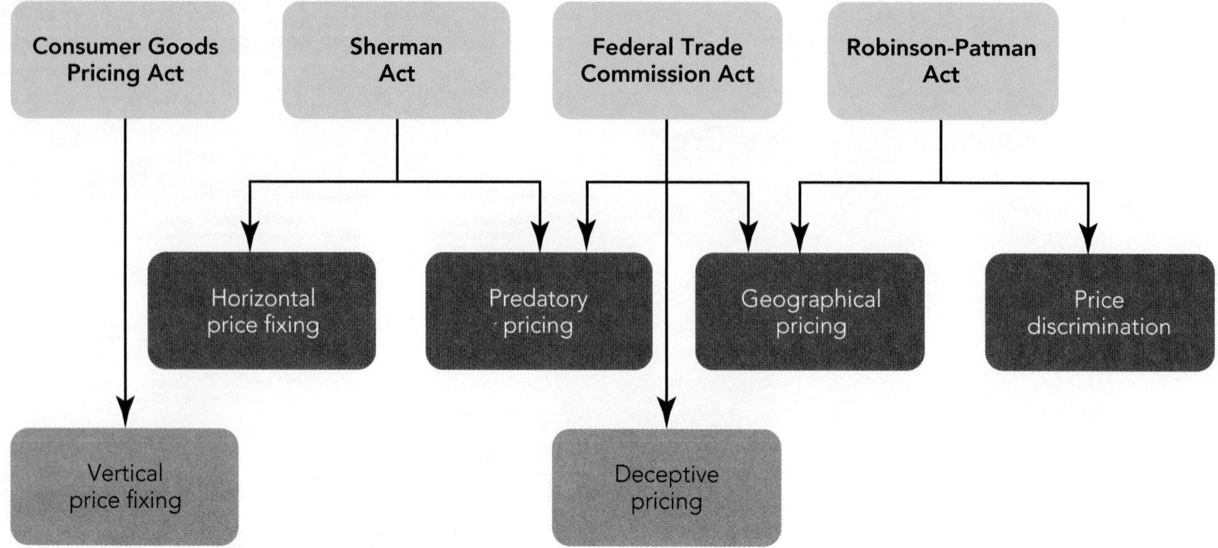

FIGURE 14–9
Several pricing practices are affected by legal and regulatory restrictions. These restrictions seek to benefit both consumers and companies.

itself). When two or more competitors explicitly or implicitly set prices, this practice is called *horizontal price fixing*. For example, in 2000, six foreign vitamin companies pled guilty to price fixing in the human and animal vitamin industry and paid the largest fine in U.S. history, a hefty $335 million.[28]

Vertical price fixing involves controlling agreements between independent buyers and sellers (a manufacturer and a retailer) whereby sellers are required to not sell products below a minimum retail price. This practice, called *resale price maintenance*, was declared illegal per se in 1975 under provisions of the *Consumer Goods Pricing Act*. Nevertheless, this practice is not uncommon. For example, shoe supplier Nine West was charged with restricting competition by coercing retailers to adhere to its resale prices. As part of its settlement, Nine West agreed to pay $34 million.[29] Although this type of coercive price fixing is illegal per se, manufacturers and wholesalers can fix the maximum retail price for their products provided the price agreement does not create an "unreasonable restraint of trade" or is anticompetitive.

It is important to recognize that a "manufacturer's suggested retail price," or MSRP, is not illegal per se. The issue of legality only arises when manufacturers enforce such a practice by coercion. Furthermore, there appears to be a movement toward a "*rule of reason*" in horizontal and vertical price fixing cases.[30] This rule holds that circumstances surrounding a practice must be considered before making a judgment about its legality. The rule of reason perspective is the direct opposite of the per se rule.

Price Discrimination The Clayton Act as amended by the Robinson-Patman Act prohibits **price discrimination**—the practice of charging different prices to different buyers for goods of like grade and quality. However, not all price differences are illegal; only those that substantially lessen competition or create a monopoly are deemed unlawful. Moreover, "goods" is narrowly defined and does not include discrimination in services.

A unique feature of the Robinson-Patman Act is that it allows for price differentials to different customers under the following conditions:

1. When price differences charged to different customers do not exceed the differences in the cost of manufacture, sale, or delivery resulting from differing methods or quantities in which such goods are sold or delivered to buyers. This condition is called the *cost justification defense*.
2. When price differences result from changing market conditions, avoiding obsolescence of seasonal merchandise, including perishables, or closing out sales.

3. When price differences are quoted to selected buyers in good faith to meet competitors' prices and are not intended to injure competition. This condition is called the *meet-the-competition defense*.

The Robinson-Patman Act also covers promotional allowances. To legally offer promotional allowances to buyers, the seller must do so on a proportionally equal basis to all buyers distributing the seller's products. In general, the rule of reason applies frequently in price discrimination disputes and is often applied to cases involving firms that use dynamic pricing policies.

Deceptive Pricing Price deals that mislead consumers fall into the category of *deceptive pricing*. Deceptive pricing is outlawed by the Federal Trade Commission Act. The FTC monitors such practices and has published a regulation titled "Guides against Deceptive Pricing" to help businesspeople avoid a charge of deception. The five most common deceptive pricing practices are described in Figure 14–10. As you read about these practices it should be clear that laws cannot be passed and enforced to protect consumers and competitors against all of these practices. So it is essential to rely on the ethical standards of those making and publicizing pricing decisions. An often used pricing practice is to promote products and services for free—a great price! It would seem that the meaning of "free" is obvious. Think again. Visit the FTC website described in the Marketing inSite box on the next page to learn what *free* means.

Geographical Pricing FOB origin pricing is legal, as are FOB freight-allowed pricing practices, providing no conspiracy to set prices exists. Basing-point pricing can be viewed as illegal under the Robinson-Patman Act and the Federal Trade Commission Act if there is clear-cut evidence of a conspiracy to set prices. In general, geographical pricing practices have been immune from legal and regulatory restrictions, except in those instances in which a conspiracy to lessen competition exists under the Sherman Act or price discrimination exists under the Robinson-Patman Act.

FIGURE 14–10
Five most common deceptive pricing practices used by businesses. Have you ever witnessed or experienced one or more of these practices?

DECEPTIVE PRICING PRACTICE	DESCRIPTION
Bait and switch	This deceptive practice exists when a firm offers a very low price on a product (the bait) to attract customers to a store. Once in the store, the customer is persuaded to purchase a higher priced item (the switch) using a variety of tricks, including (1) downgrading the promoted item, (2) not having the item in stock, or (3) refusing to take orders for the item.
Bargains conditional on other purchases	This practice may exist when a buyer is offered "1-Cent Sales," "Buy 1, Get 1 Free," and "Get 2 for the Price of 1." Such pricing is legal only if the first items are sold at the regular price, not a price inflated for the offer. Substituting lower quality items on either the first or second purchase is also considered deceptive.
Comparable value comparisons	Advertising such as "Retail Value \$100.00, Our Price \$85.00" is deceptive if a verified and substantial number of stores in the market area do not price the item at \$100.
Comparisons with suggested prices	A claim that a price is below a manufacturer's suggested or list price may be deceptive if few or no sales occur at that price in a retailer's market area.
Former price comparisons	When a seller represents a price as reduced, the item must have been offered in good faith at a higher price for a substantial previous period. Setting a high price for the purpose of establishing a reference for a price reduction is considered deceptive.

Marketing inSite

So You Think You Know What "Free" Means? Think Again

The offer of "free" merchandise or services is a promotional device often used to attract customers. The Federal Trade Commission (FTC) acknowledges that such offers are a useful and valuable marketing practice. However, the FTC also recognizes that such offers must be made with extreme care so as to avoid any possibility that consumers will be misled or deceived.

The FTC has issued its "Guide Concerning Use of the Word 'Free' and Similar Representations" at www.ftc.gov/bcp/guides/free.htm. This guide illustrates that the term *free* has multiple dimensions. Suppose a marketer substitutes similar words for *free*, such as *gift*, *given without charge*, or *bonus*. What is the FTC's position on this practice?

BUY THREE, GET ONE FREE

Predatory Pricing **Predatory pricing** is the practice of charging a very low price for a product with the intent of driving competitors out of business. Once competitors have been driven out, the firm raises its prices. This practice is illegal under the Sherman Act and the Federal Trade Commission Act. Proving the practice of predatory pricing is difficult and expensive, because it must be shown that the predator explicitly attempted to destroy a competitor and the predatory price was below the defendant's average cost.

learning review

14-6. Why would a seller choose a dynamic pricing policy over a fixed-price policy?

14-7. If a firm wished to encourage repeat purchases by a buyer throughout a year, would a cumulative or a noncumulative quantity discount be a better strategy?

14-8. Which pricing practices are covered by the Sherman Act?

LEARNING OBJECTIVES REVIEW

LO 14-1 *Describe how to establish the "approximate price level" using demand-oriented, cost-oriented, profit-oriented, and competition-oriented approaches.*
Demand, cost, profit, and competition influence the initial consideration of the approximate price level for a product or service. Demand-oriented pricing approaches stress consumer demand and revenue implications of pricing and include eight types: skimming, penetration, prestige, price lining, odd-even, target, bundle, and yield management. Cost-oriented pricing approaches emphasize the cost aspects of pricing and include three types: standard markup, cost-plus, and experience curve pricing. Profit-oriented pricing approaches focus on a balance between revenues and costs to set a price and include three types: target profit, target return-on-sales, and target return-on-investment pricing. And finally, competition-oriented pricing approaches stress what competitors or the marketplace are doing and include three types: customary; above-, at-, or below-market; and loss-leader pricing. Although these approaches are described separately, some of them overlap, and an effective marketing manager will consider several in searching for an approximate price level.

LO 14-2 *Recognize the major factors considered in deriving a final list or quoted price from the approximate price level.*
Given an approximate price level for a product or service, a manager sets a list or quoted price by considering three additional factors. First, a manager must decide whether to follow a fixed-price versus a dynamic pricing policy. Second, the manager should consider the effects of the proposed price on the company, customer, and competitors. Finally, consideration should be given to balancing incremental costs and revenues, particularly when price and cost changes are planned.

LO 14-3 *Identify the adjustments made to the approximate price level on the basis of discounts, allowances, and geography.*
Numerous adjustments can be made to the approximate price level. Discounts are reductions from the list or quoted price that a seller gives a buyer as a reward for some activity of the buyer that is favorable to the seller. These include quantity, seasonal, trade (functional), and cash discounts. Allowances offered to buyers also reduce list or quoted prices. Trade-in allowances and promotional allowances are most common. Finally, geographical adjustments are made to list or quoted prices to reflect

transportation costs from sellers to buyers. The two general methods for quoting prices related to transportation costs are FOB origin pricing and uniform delivered pricing.

LO 14-4 *Name the principal laws and regulations affecting specific pricing practices.*
There are four principal laws that affect six major pricing practices. The Sherman Act specifically prohibits horizontal price fixing and predatory pricing. The Consumer Goods Pricing Act makes it illegal for companies to engage in vertical price fixing (also called resale price maintenance agreements). The Federal Trade Commission Act outlaws deceptive pricing. Provisions in this act also address aspects of predatory pricing and geographical pricing. Finally, the Robinson-Patman Act prohibits price discrimination for goods of like grade and quality, covers the use of promotional allowances, and addresses certain aspects of geographical pricing.

FOCUSING ON KEY TERMS

above-, at-, or below-market pricing p. 360
basing-point pricing p. 369
bundle pricing p. 355
cost-plus pricing p. 356
customary pricing p. 359
dynamic pricing policy p. 362
everyday low pricing (EDLP) p. 368
experience curve pricing p. 356
fixed-price policy p. 361
FOB origin pricing p. 368
loss-leader pricing p. 360
odd-even pricing p. 354
penetration pricing p. 353
predatory pricing p. 372
prestige pricing p. 353
price discrimination p. 370
price fixing p. 369
price lining p. 354
price war p. 364
product-line pricing p. 363
promotional allowances p. 368
quantity discounts p. 366
skimming pricing p. 352
standard markup pricing p. 355
target pricing p. 355
target profit pricing p. 357
target return-on-investment pricing p. 358
target return-on-sales pricing p. 358
uniform delivered pricing p. 368
yield management pricing p. 355

APPLYING MARKETING KNOWLEDGE

1 Under what conditions would a digital camera manufacturer adopt a skimming price approach for a new product? A penetration approach?
2 What are some similarities and differences between skimming pricing, prestige pricing, and above-market pricing?
3 A producer of microwave ovens has adopted an experience curve pricing approach for its new model. The firm believes it can reduce the cost of producing the model by 20 percent each time volume doubles. The cost to produce the first unit was $1,000. What would be the approximate cost of the 4,096th unit?
4 The Hesper Corporation is a leading manufacturer of high-quality upholstered sofas. Current plans call for an increase of $600,000 in the advertising budget. If the firm sells its sofas for an average price of $850 and the unit variable costs are $550, then what dollar sales increase will be necessary to cover the additional advertising?
5 Suppose executives estimate that the unit variable cost for their DVD recorder is $100, the fixed cost related to the product is $10 million annually, and the target volume for next year is 100,000 recorders. What sales price will be necessary to achieve a target profit of $1 million?
6 A manufacturer of motor oil has a trade discount policy whereby the manufacturer's suggested retail price is $30 per case with the terms of 40/20/10. The manufacturer sells its products through jobbers, who sell to wholesalers, who sell to gasoline stations. What will the manufacturer's sale price be?
7 Suppose a manufacturer of exercise equipment sets a suggested price to the consumer of $395 for a particular piece of equipment to be competitive with similar equipment. The manufacturer sells its equipment to a sporting goods wholesaler who receives 25 percent of the selling price and a retailer who receives 50 percent of the selling price. What demand-oriented pricing approach is being used, and at what price will the manufacturer sell the equipment to the wholesaler?
8 Is there any truth in the statement, "Geographical pricing schemes will always be unfair to some buyers"? Why or why not?

BUILDING YOUR MARKETING PLAN

To arrive at the final price(s) for your offering(s):
1 In Chapter 13, you considered your customers and competitors and set three possible prices. Now, modify those three prices in light of (*a*) pricing considerations for demand-, cost-, profit-, and competition-oriented approaches described in this chapter and (*b*) possibilities for discounts, allowances, and geographic adjustments.
2 Do a break-even analysis for each of these three new prices.
3 Choose the final price(s).

VIDEO CASE 14 Carmex (B): Setting the Price of the Number One Lip Balm

"Carmex is dedicated to providing consumers with superior lip balm formulas—that heal, sooth and protect—while ensuring lips remain healthy and hydrated" exclaims Paul Woelbing, president of Carma Laboratories, Inc.

It's an ambitious mission, but the company has been extraordinarily successful with its 75-year-old-product. Woelbing and his management team at Carma Laboratories can attribute their success to a strong brand, a loyal customer base, a growing product line, financial strength, and an exceptional talent for setting prices that achieve company objectives and still provide value to customers. Even during the recession and periods of slow growth the company has been successful. "In a rough economy, shopping habits change," Woelbing says. "People buy smaller quantities more frequently, but they still need personal care products."

THE COMPANY

Carmex was created by Paul's grandfather, Alfred Woelbing, in his kitchen in Wauwatosa, Wisconsin, in 1937. Alfred had an entrepreneurial spirit and experimented with ingredients such as camphor, menthol, phenol, lanolin, salicylic acid, and cocoa seed butter to make the new product. The name didn't have any meaning other than Alfred liked the sound of "Carma" and "ex" was a popular suffix for many brands at the time. He packaged the balm in small glass jars and sold the product for 25 cents from the trunk of his car by making personal sales calls to pharmacies in Wisconsin, Illinois, and Indiana. From the beginning, price and value were important to the product's success. If pharmacies weren't initially interested in Carmex, Alfred would leave a dozen jars for free. The samples would sell quickly and soon the pharmacies would place orders for more!

As the company grew, Alfred's son, Don, joined the business and helped add new products to the company's offerings. For example, in the 1980's Carmex made its first significant packaging change by also offering the balm in squeezable tubes. In the 1990's Carmex became available in stick form, which had been used by two of Carma's major competitors – ChapStick and Blistex. In the 2000s Carmex became available in mint, cherry, and strawberry flavors (see Chapter 8 for a description of the research techniques used to identify new flavors). The company also expanded into larger manufacturing facilities, added a new distribution center, and hired its first marketing experts.

Today, the company is led by Alfred's grandsons, Paul and Eric Woelbing, who continue to manage the company to new levels of success. They appeared on *The Oprah Winfrey Show* to announce the sale of their billionth jar of Carmex. The governor of Wisconsin declared a Carmex commemoration day to celebrate its 75th anniversary. NBA all-star LeBron James became a promotional partner. In addition, *Pharmacy Times* magazine recently named Carmex the number one pharmacist-recommended brand of lip balm for the 15th consecutive year. "We are honored to receive this unprecedented acknowledgement," said Woelbing.

Industry observers estimate that Carma Labs holds approximately 10 percent of the lip balm market. The company distributes its products through major drug, food, and mass merchant retailers, convenience stores, and online in more than 25 countries around the world. The company's most recent products—Carmex Healing Cream and Carmex Hydrating Lotion—represent a significant step from lip care to skin care. The expanded product line, multichannel distribution, growing volume, international trade, and direct competition make pricing decisions even more important today than when Alfred started the business many years ago.

SETTING PRICES OF CARMEX PRODUCTS

"There are many factors that go into what results in the retail price in the store," explains Kirk Hodgdon of Bolin Marketing. As one of the marketing experts who helps Carma Labs with advertising, marketing research, and pricing decisions, Hodgdon uses information about consumer demand, production and material costs, profit goals, and competition to help Woelbing and Carmex retailers arrive at specific prices. The many factors often overlap and lead to different prices for different products, channels, and target markets. "It's a challenge!" says Hodgdon.

Consumers' tastes and preferences, for example, influence the price of Carmex products. Bolin director of marketing, Alisa Allen, explains: "Consumers will tell you that they love Carmex because it's a great value. That doesn't necessarily mean that it's the absolute lowest price. It means that it does so much; they pay a dollar and they get all kinds of benefits from the product above and beyond what they would expect." A single jar of original formula

Carmex may sell for $0.99 at mass retailers such as Walmart and Target, and between $1.59 and $1.79 in drug and food retailers such as Walgreens and Kroger. These prices are a good indication of how important it is to understand consumers when setting prices. "There are magic price points for consumers," says Allen, "Any time you can drop a penny off, the consumer responds to that price."

Carmex has also introduced a premium lip balm product, Carmex Moisture Plus, at a retail price between $2.49 and $2.99. Moisture Plus is a lip balm that is packaged in a sleek silver tube, offers a slant tip like lipstick, and is targeted toward women. The formula offers women a satin gloss shine and includes vitamin E and aloe for richer moisturization. The upscale package and additional product benefits help Carmex Moisture Plus command a higher price than the traditional Carmex jar and tube.

The cost of the ingredients that make up the Carmex lip balm formulas, the packaging, the manufacturing equipment, and the staffing are also factored into the price of the products. Volumes are a key driver of the cost of packaging and ingredients. For example, Carmex purchases up to 12 million yellow tubes each year for the traditional product, and 2 million sticks each year for the newer Moisture Plus product. The difference in quantities leads to a lower price for the traditional yellow tubes. Similarly, ingredient suppliers, label suppliers, and box suppliers all provide discounts for larger quantities. It is also more efficient for Carmex's manufacturing facility to make a large batch of traditional formula than it is to make a small batch of Moisture Plus. Carmex has also reduced its costs with efforts such as its new environmentally-friendly Carmex jar which holds the same amount of lip balm but uses 20 percent less plastic, eliminating 35 tons of raw material costs and the related shipping costs!

Carmex also considers retailer margins when it sets it prices. According to Allen, "We typically sell our product to two types of retailers." There are Everyday Low Price (EDLP) retailers such as Walmart, and High-Low retailers such as Walgreens. EDLP retailers offer consumers the lowest price every day without discounting through promotions. High-Low retailers charge consumers a higher price, but they occasionally discount the product through special promotions which Carmex often supports with "marketing discretionary funds." Carmex typically offers its products at different prices to EDLP and High-Low retailers to allow each retailer to achieve its profit margin goals and to account for Carmex's promotion expenditures. When the additional expenditures are considered, however, the cost to both types of retailer is similar.

Finally, Carmex considers competitors' prices when setting its prices. Burt's Bees, Chapstick, Blistex and many other brands offer lip balm products and consumers often compare their prices to the price of Carmex. "We have found through research that it is extremely important that the price gap is not too great," explains Allen. "If that gap becomes too wide consumers will leave the Carmex brand and purchase a competitor's product." When Carmex was preparing to launch its premium Moisture Plus product it conducted a thorough analysis of similar products to ensure that Moisture Plus was in an acceptable price range.

CARMEX IN THE FUTURE

The original, and now legendary, Carmex formula and packaging will continue into the future with occasional changes to its pricing practices. New products, however, are on the horizon and likely to challenge the perceptions of the traditional products and prices in the Carmex line. Carmex Moisture Plus products, for example, will be offered in limited edition designs that ask consumers "Which personality are you?" Paul Woelbing explains the new approach:

> "Lip care is an important component of a daily beauty regimen and consumers need a product they can rely on that protects and serves as an important foundation. The goal of the new Carmex Moisture Plus line is to offer our consumers a hard-working lip balm line that represent and reflects their unique style."

Some of the new styles include: *Chic* in houndstooth, *Fab* in a groovy retro look, *Adventurous* in a leopard print, *Whimsical* in an art deco design.

"We are so excited about the future of Carmex," says Hodgdon. "We are planning new products, we have new plans for retailers, and the future is nothing but bright!"

Questions

1. Which of the four approaches to setting a price does Carmex use for its products? Should one approach be used exclusively?
2. Why do many Carmex product prices end in 9? What type of pricing is this called? What should happen to demand when this approach is used?
3. Should cost be a factor in Carmex's prices? What do you think is a reasonable markup for Carmex and for its retailers?
4. What is the difference between an EDLP retailer and a High-Low retailer? Why does Carmex charge them different prices?
5. Conduct an online search of lip balm products and compare the price of a Carmex product with three similar products from competitors. How do you think the competitors are setting their prices?

APPENDIX

B FINANCIAL ASPECTS OF MARKETING

Basic concepts from accounting and finance provide valuable tools for marketing executives. This appendix describes an actual company's use of accounting and financial concepts and illustrates how they assist the owner in making marketing decisions.

THE CAPLOW COMPANY

An accomplished artist and calligrapher, Jane Westerlund decided to apply some of her experience to the picture framing business in Minneapolis. She bought an existing retail frame store, The Caplow Company, from a friend who owned the business and wanted to retire. She avoided the do-it-yourself end of the framing business and chose three kinds of business activities: (1) cutting the frame, mats, and glass for customers who brought in their own pictures or prints to be framed; (2) selling prints and posters that she had purchased from wholesalers; and (3) restoring high-quality frames and paintings.

To understand how accounting, finance, and marketing relate to each other, let's analyze (1) the operating statement for her frame shop, (2) some general ratios of interest that are derived from the operating statement, and (3) some ratios that pertain specifically to her pricing decisions.

The Operating Statement

The *operating statement* (also called an *income statement* or *profit-and-loss statement*) summarizes the profitability of a business firm for a specific time period, usually a month, quarter, or year. The title of the operating statement for The Caplow Company shows it is for a one-year period (Figure B–1). The purpose of an operating statement is to show the profit of the firm and the revenues and expenses that led to that profit. This information tells the owner or manager what has happened in the past and suggests actions to improve future profitability.

The left side of Figure B–1 shows that there are three key elements to all operating statements: (1) sales of the firm's products and services, (2) costs incurred in making and selling these products and services, and (3) profit or loss, which is the difference between sales and costs.

Sales Elements The sales elements of Figure B–1 have four terms that need explanation:

- *Gross sales* represent the total amount billed to customers. Dissatisfied customers or errors may reduce the gross sales through returns or allowances.
- *Returns* occur when a customer gives the item purchased back to the seller, who either refunds the purchase price or allows the customer a credit on subsequent purchases. In any event, the seller now owns the item again.
- *Allowances* are given when a customer is dissatisfied with the item purchased and the seller reduces the original purchase price. Unlike returns, in the case of allowances the buyer owns the item.
- *Net sales* are simply gross sales minus returns and allowances.

The operating statement for The Caplow Company shows that:

Gross sales	$80,500
Less: Returns and allowances	500
Net sales	$80,000

The low level of returns and allowances shows the shop generally has done a good job in satisfying customers, which is essential in building the repeat business necessary for success.

Cost Elements The *cost of goods sold* (COGS) is the total cost of the products sold during the period. This item varies according to the kind of business. A retail

FIGURE B–1
The Caplow Company operating statement.

THE CAPLOW COMPANY Operating Statement For the Year Ending December 31, 2013				
Sales	Gross sales			$80,500
	Less: Returns and allowances			500
	Net sales			$80,000
Costs	Cost of goods sold:			
	Beginning inventory at cost		$ 6,000	
	Purchases at billed cost	$21,000		
	Less: Purchase discounts	300		
	Purchases at net cost	20,700		
	Plus: freight-in	100		
	Net cost of delivered purchases		20,800	
	Direct labor (framing)		14,200	
	Cost of goods available for sale		41,000	
	Less: Ending inventory at cost		5,000	
	Cost of goods sold			36,000
	Gross margin (gross profit)			$44,000
	Expenses:			
	Selling expenses:			
	Sales salaries	2,000		
	Advertising expense	3,000		
	Total selling expense		5,000	
	Administrative expenses:			
	Owner's salary	18,000		
	Bookkeeper's salary	1,200		
	Office supplies	300		
	Total administrative expense		19,500	
	General expenses:			
	Depreciation expense	1,000		
	Interest expense	500		
	Rent expense	2,100		
	Utility expenses (heat, electricity)	3,000		
	Repairs and maintenance	2,300		
	Insurance	2,000		
	Social security taxes	2,200		
	Total general expense		13,100	
	Total expenses			37,600
Profit or loss	Profit before taxes			$ 6,400

store purchases finished products and resells them to customers without reworking them in any way. In contrast, a manufacturing firm combines raw and semifinished materials and parts, uses labor and overhead to rework these into finished products, and then sells them to customers. All these activities are reflected in the cost of goods sold item on a manufacturer's operating statement. Note that The Caplow Company has features of both a pure retailer (prints and posters it buys that are resold without alteration) and a pure manufacturer (assembling the raw materials of molding, matting, and glass to form a completed frame).

Some terms that relate to cost of goods sold need clarification:

- *Inventory* is the physical material that is purchased from suppliers, may or may not be reworked, and is available for sale to customers. In the frame shop, inventory includes molding, matting, glass, prints, and posters.

- *Purchase discounts* are reductions in the original billed price for reasons such as prompt payment of the bill or the quantity bought.
- *Direct labor* is the cost of the labor used in producing the finished product. For Caplow, this is the cost of producing the completed frames from the molding, matting, and glass.
- *Gross margin (gross profit)* is the money remaining to manage the business, sell the products or services, and provide some profit. Gross margin is net sales minus cost of goods sold.

The two right-hand columns in Figure B–1 between "Net sales" and "Gross margin" calculate the cost of goods sold:

Net sales		$80,000
Cost of goods sold		
Beginning inventory at cost	$ 6,000	
Net cost of delivered purchases	20,800	
Direct labor (framing)	14,200	
Cost of goods available for sale	41,000	
Less: Ending inventory at cost	5,000	
Cost of goods sold		36,000
Gross margin (gross profit)		$44,000

This section considers the beginning and ending inventories, the net cost of purchases delivered during the year, and the cost of the direct labor going into making the frames. Subtracting the $36,000 cost of goods sold from the $80,000 net sales gives the $44,000 gross margin.

Jane Westerlund (left) and an assistant assess the restoration of a gold frame for regilding.

Three major categories of expenses are shown in Figure B–1 below the gross margin:

- *Selling expenses* are the costs of selling the product or service produced by the firm. For The Caplow Company there are two such selling expenses: sales salaries of part-time employees waiting on customers and the advertising expense of simple newspaper ads and direct-mail ads sent to customers.
- *Administrative expenses* are the costs of managing the business, which for The Caplow Company include three expenses: the owner's salary, a part-time bookkeeper's salary, and office supplies expense.
- *General expenses* are miscellaneous costs not covered elsewhere; for the frame shop these include seven items: depreciation expense (on equipment), interest expense, rent expense, utility expenses, repairs and maintenance expense, insurance expense, and social security taxes.

As shown in Figure B–1, selling, administrative, and general expenses total $37,600 for The Caplow Company.

Profit Element What the company has earned, the *profit before taxes*, is found by subtracting cost of goods sold and expenses from net sales. For The Caplow Company, Figure B–1 shows that profit before taxes is $6,400.

General Operating Ratios to Analyze Operations

Looking only at the elements of Caplow's operating statement that extend to the right-hand column highlights the firm's performance on some important dimensions. Using operating ratios such as *expense-to-sales ratios* for expressing basic expense or profit elements as a percentage of net sales gives further insights:

Element in Operating Statement	Dollar Value	Percentage of Net Sales
Gross sales	$80,500	
Less: Returns and allowances	500	
Net sales	80,000	100%
Less: Cost of goods sold	36,000	45
Gross margin	44,000	55
Less: Total expenses	37,600	47
Profit (or loss) before taxes	$ 6,400	8%

Westerlund can use this information to compare her firm's performance from one time period to the next. To do so, it is especially important that she keep the same definitions for each element of her operating statement, also a significant factor in using the electronic spreadsheets discussed in Chapter 14. Performance comparisons between periods will be more difficult if she changes definitions for the accounting elements in the operating statement.

Westerlund can use either the dollar values or the operating ratios (the value of the element of the operating statement divided by net sales) to analyze the firm's performance. However, the operating ratios are more valuable than the dollar values for two reasons: (1) the simplicity of working with percentages rather than dollars and (2) the availability of operating ratios of typical firms in the same industry, which are published by Dun & Bradstreet and trade associations. Thus, Westerlund can compare her firm's performance not only with that of *other* frame shops but also with that of *small* frame shops that have annual net sales, for example, under $100,000. In this way, she can identify where her operations are better or worse than other similar firms. For example, if trade association data showed a typical frame shop of her size had a ratio of cost of goods sold to net sales of 37 percent, compared with her 45 percent, she might consider steps to reduce this cost through purchase discounts, reducing inbound freight charges, finding lower-cost suppliers, and so on.

Ratios to Use in Setting and Evaluating Price

Using The Caplow Company as an example, we can study four ratios that relate closely to setting a price: (1) markup, (2) markdown, (3) stockturns, and (4) return on investment. These terms are defined in Figure B–2 and explained below.

Markup Both *markup* and gross margin refer to the amount added to the cost of goods sold to arrive at the selling price, and they may be expressed in either dollar or percentage terms. However, the term *markup* is more commonly used in setting retail prices. Suppose the average price Westerlund charges for a framed picture is \$80. Then in terms of the first two definitions in Figure B–2 and the earlier information from the operating statement,

Element of Price	Dollar Value
Selling price	\$80
Cost of goods sold	\$36
Markup (or gross margin)	\$44

The third definition in Figure B–2 gives the percentage markup on selling price:

$$\text{Markup on selling price (\%)} = \frac{\text{Markup}}{\text{Selling price}} \times 100$$

$$= \frac{44}{80} \times 100 = 55\%$$

FIGURE B–2
How to calculate selling price, markups, markdown, stockturn rate, and return on investment.

Name of Financial Element or Ratio	What It Measures	Equation
Selling price (\$)	Price customer sees	Cost of goods sold (COGS) + Markup
Markup (\$)	Dollars added to COGS to arrive at selling price	Selling price − COGS
Markup on selling price (%)	Relates markup to selling price	$\frac{\text{Markup}}{\text{Selling price}} \times 100 = \frac{\text{Selling price} - \text{COGS}}{\text{Selling price}} \times 100$
Markup on cost (%)	Relates markup to cost	$\frac{\text{Markup}}{\text{COGS}} \times 100 = \frac{\text{Selling price} - \text{COGS}}{\text{COGS}} \times 100$
Markdown (%)	Ability of firm to sell its products at initial selling price	$\frac{\text{Markdowns}}{\text{Net sales}} \times 100$
Stockturn rate	Ability of firm to move its inventory quickly	$\frac{\text{COGS}}{\text{Average inventory at cost}}$ or $\frac{\text{Net sales}}{\text{Average inventory at selling price}}$
Return on investment (%)	Profit performance of firm compared with money invested in it	$\frac{\text{Net income}}{\text{Investment}} \times 100$

And the percentage markup on cost is obtained as follows:

$$\text{Markup on cost (\%)} = \frac{\text{Markup}}{\text{Cost of goods sold}} \times 100$$

$$= \frac{44}{36} \times 100 = 122.2\%$$

Inexperienced retail clerks sometimes fail to distinguish between the two definitions of markup, which (as the preceding calculations show) can represent a tremendous difference, so it is essential to know whether the base is cost or selling price. Marketers generally use selling price as the base for talking about markups unless they specifically state that they are using cost as a base.

Retailers and wholesalers that rely heavily on markup pricing (discussed in Chapter 14) often use standardized tables that convert markup on selling price to markup on cost, and vice versa. The two equations below show how to convert one to the other:

$$\text{Markup on selling price (\%)} = \frac{\text{Markup on cost (\%)}}{100\% + \text{Markup on cost (\%)}} \times 100$$

$$\text{Markup on cost (\%)} = \frac{\text{Markup on selling price (\%)}}{100\% - \text{Markup on selling price (\%)}}$$

Using the data from The Caplow Company gives:

$$\text{Markup on selling price (\%)} = \frac{\text{Markup on cost (\%)}}{100\% + \text{Markup on cost (\%)}} \times 100$$

$$= \frac{122.2}{100 + 122.2} \times 100 = 55\%$$

$$\text{Markup on cost (\%)} = \frac{\text{Markup on selling price (\%)}}{100\% - \text{Markup on selling price (\%)}} \times 100$$

$$= \frac{55}{100 - 55} \times 100 = 122.2\%$$

Consider the use of an incorrect markup base in Westerlund's business. A markup of 122.2 percent on her cost of goods sold for a typical frame she sells gives 122.2% × \$36 = \$44 of markup. Added to the \$36 cost of goods sold, this gives her a selling price of \$80 for the framed picture. However, a new clerk working for her who erroneously prices the framed picture at 55 percent of cost of goods sold sets the final price at \$55.80 (\$36 of cost of goods sold plus 55% × \$36 = \$19.80). The error, if repeated, could be disastrous: frames would be accidentally sold at \$55.80, or \$24.20 below the intended selling price of \$80.

Markdown A *markdown* is a reduction in a retail price that is necessary if the item will not sell at the full selling price to which it has been marked up. The item might not sell for a variety of reasons; perhaps the selling price was set too high or the item is out of style or has become soiled or damaged. The seller "takes a markdown" by lowering the price to sell it, thereby converting it to cash to buy future inventory that will sell faster.

The markdown percentage cannot be calculated directly from the operating statement. As shown in the fifth item of Figure B–2, the numerator of the markdown percentage is the total dollar markdowns. Markdowns are reductions in the prices of products that are purchased by customers. The denominator is net sales.

Suppose The Caplow Company had a total of \$700 in markdowns on the prints and posters that are stocked and available for sale. Since the frames are custom made for individual customers, there is little reason for a markdown there. Caplow's markdown percent is then:

Jane Westerlund discusses framing and matting choices with a customer.

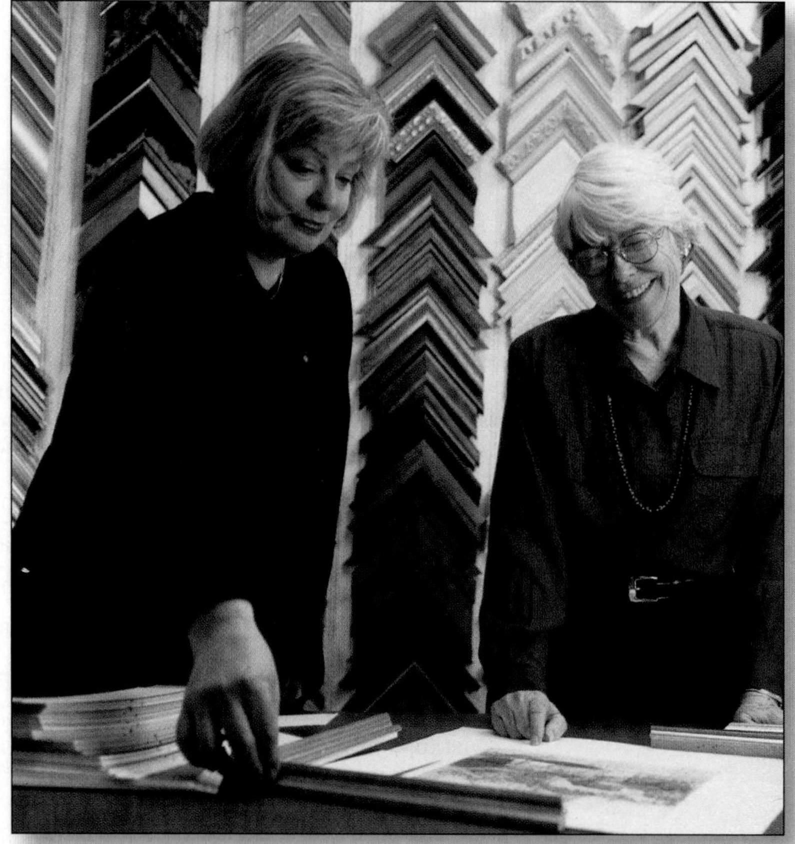

$$\text{Markdown (\%)} = \frac{\text{Markdowns}}{\text{Net sales}} \times 100$$

$$= \frac{\$700}{\$80{,}000} \times 100$$

$$= 0.875\%$$

Other kinds of retailers often have markdown ratios several times this amount. For example, women's dress stores have markdowns of about 25 percent, and menswear stores have markdowns of about 2 percent.

Stockturn Rate A business firm is eager to have its inventory move quickly, or "turn over." *Stockturn rate,* or simply *stockturns,* measures this inventory movement. For a retailer, a slow stockturn rate may show it is buying merchandise customers don't want, so this is a critical measure of performance. When a firm sells only a single product, one convenient way to measure stockturn rate is simply to divide its cost of goods sold by average inventory at cost. The sixth item in Figure B–2 shows how to calculate stockturn rate using information in the operating statement:

$$\text{Stockturn rate} = \frac{\text{Cost of goods sold}}{\text{Average inventory at cost}}$$

The dollar amount of average inventory at cost is calculated by adding the beginning and ending inventories for the year and dividing by 2 to get the average. From Caplow's operating statement, we have:

$$\text{Stockturn rate} = \frac{\text{Cost of goods sold}}{\text{Average inventory at cost}}$$

$$= \frac{\text{Cost of goods sold}}{\frac{\text{Beginning inventory} + \text{Ending inventory}}{2}}$$

$$= \frac{\$36{,}000}{\frac{\$6{,}000 + \$5{,}000}{2}}$$

$$= \frac{\$36{,}000}{\$5{,}500}$$

$$= 6.5 \text{ stockturns per year}$$

What is considered a "good stockturn" varies by industry. For example, supermarkets have limited shelf space for thousands of new products from manufacturers each year, so they watch stockturn carefully by product line. The stockturn rate in supermarkets for breakfast foods is about 17 times per year, for pet food about 22 times per year, and for paper products about 25 times per year.

Return on Investment A better measure of the performance of a firm than the amount of profit it makes in a year is its *return on investment* (ROI), which is the ratio of net income to the investment used to earn that net income. To calculate ROI, it is necessary to subtract income taxes from profit before taxes to obtain net income, then divide this figure by the investment that can be found on a firm's balance sheet (which is another accounting statement that shows the firm's assets, liabilities, and net worth). While financial and accounting experts have many definitions for *investment,* an often-used definition is "total assets."

For our purposes, let's assume that Westerlund has total assets (investment) of \$20,000 in The Caplow Company, which covers inventory, store fixtures, and framing equipment. If she pays \$1,000 in income taxes, her store's net income is \$5,400. Therefore, using the return on investment ratio illustrated in the last item in Figure B–2, The Caplow Company's ROI is:

$$\begin{aligned} \text{Return on investment} &= \text{Net income/Investment} \times 100 \\ &= \$5{,}400/\$20{,}000 \times 100 \\ &= 27\% \end{aligned}$$

If Westerlund wants to improve her store's ROI next year, the strategies she might take are found in this alternative equation for ROI:

$$\begin{aligned} \text{ROI} &= \text{Net sales/Investment} \times \text{Net income/Net sales} \\ &= \text{Investment turnover} \times \text{Profit margin} \end{aligned}$$

This equation suggests that The Caplow Company's ROI can be improved by raising investment turnover or increasing profit margin. Increasing stockturns will accomplish the former, whereas lowering cost of goods sold to net sales will cause the latter.

15 Managing Marketing Channels and Supply Chains

LEARNING OBJECTIVES

After reading this chapter you should be able to:

LO 15-1 Explain what is meant by a marketing channel of distribution and why intermediaries are needed.

LO 15-2 Distinguish among traditional marketing channels, electronic marketing channels, and different types of vertical marketing systems.

LO 15-3 Describe factors that marketing executives consider when selecting and managing a marketing channel.

LO 15-4 Explain what supply chain and logistics management are and how they relate to marketing strategy.

CALLAWAY GOLF: DESIGNING AND DELIVERING THE GOODS FOR GREAT GOLF

What do Morgan Pressel and Phil Mickelson, two world-class golf professionals, and Justin Timberlake, a pop icon and avid amateur golfer, have in common? All three use Callaway Golf equipment, accessories, and apparel when playing their favorite sport.

With annual sales exceeding $800 million, Callaway Golf is one of the most recognized and highly regarded companies in the golf industry. With its commitment to continuous product innovation and broad distribution in the United States and more than 100 countries worldwide, Callaway Golf has built a strong reputation for designing and delivering the goods for great golf for golfers of all skill levels, both amateur and professional.

Callaway Golf primarily markets its products through more than 15,000 on- and off-course authorized golf retailers and sporting goods retailers, such as Golf Galaxy, Inc., Dick's Sporting Goods, Inc., and PGA Tour Superstores, which sell quality golf products and provide a level of customer service appropriate for the sale of such products.

The company also has its own online store (Shop.Callawaygolf .com), which makes it a full-fledged multichannel marketer, and a successful one as well. Soon after the online store was launched, the chief executive of PGA of America called the store "innovative in that it combines that old legacy relationship with the retail channel with the new innovation of the Web." A Callaway spokesperson says Callaway's online store is useful for consumers who are looking for accessories or apparel and for those who know their preferred golf club specifications: "There are always going to be certain people that will not feel comfortable buying online. But for those that do feel comfortable, we really represent the most seamless process." Today, Callaway's online store is listed among the top Internet retailers in the United States with sales exceeding $30 million annually.

Callaway Golf considers its marketing channel partners a valued marketing asset. For example, when the company opened its online store, careful attention was given to how Callaway Golf "could satisfy the consumer but do so in a way that didn't violate our relationships with our loyal trade partners," according to a

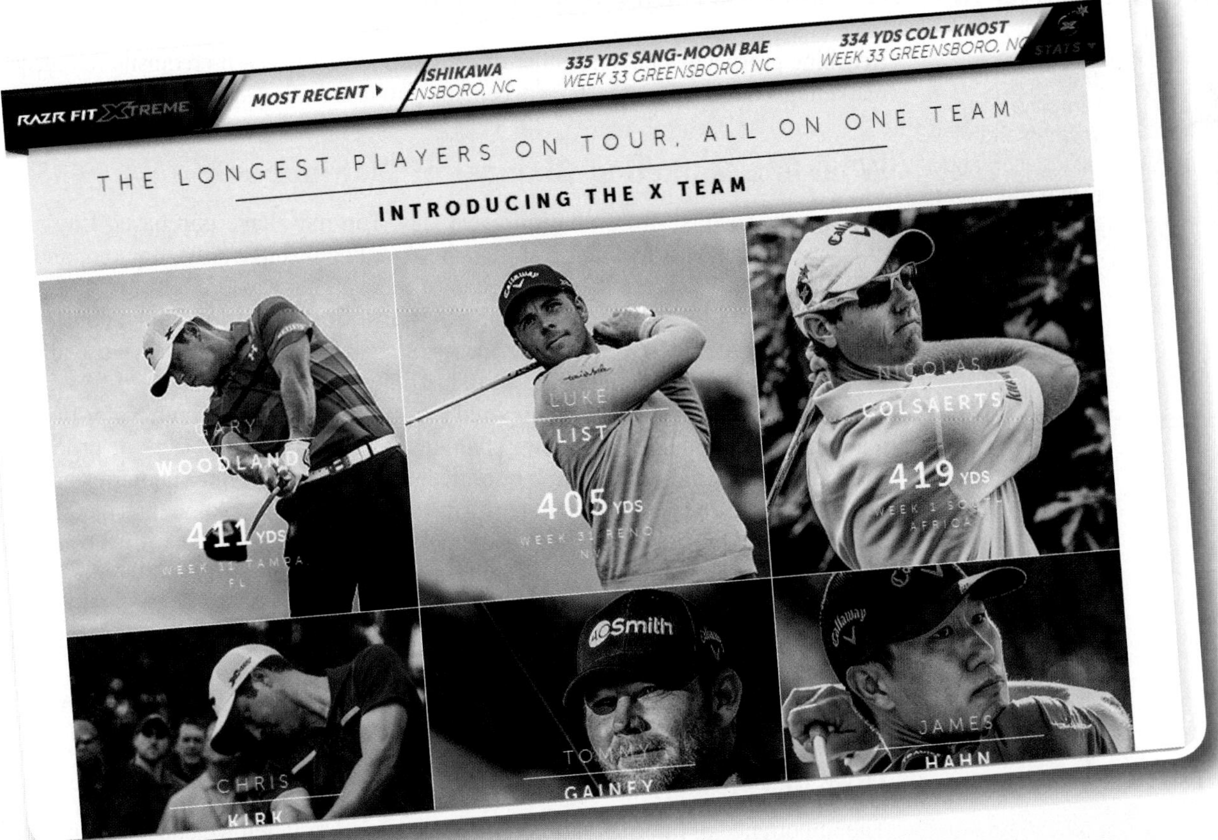

company spokesperson. The solution? Callaway Golf has one of its retailers get credit for the sale. This retailer then fulfills a buyer's order within 24 hours. Consumers, retailers, and Callaway Golf all benefit from this arrangement.[1]

Callaway Golf print advertisement featuring Phil Mickelson.

Providing Callaway's authorized golf retailers and sporting goods retailers with the right products, at the right place, at the right time, and in the right quantity and condition is the responsibility of the company's supply chain. Callaway sources raw materials for its golf equipment, accessories, and all apparel from around the world. At the same time, Callaway delivers its finished products to company retailers through external shipping companies, such as United Parcel Service (UPS).

This chapter first focuses on marketing channels of distribution and why they are an important component in the marketing mix. It then shows how such channels benefit consumers and the sequence of firms that make up a marketing channel. Finally, it describes factors that influence the choice and management of marketing channels, including channel conflict, cooperation, and legal restrictions. The discussion then turns to the significance of supply chains and logistics management. In particular, attention is placed on the necessary alignment between supply chain management and marketing strategy and the trade-offs managers make between total distribution costs and customer service.

NATURE AND IMPORTANCE OF MARKETING CHANNELS

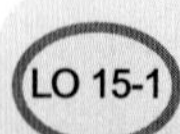

Explain what is meant by a marketing channel of distribution and why intermediaries are needed.

Reaching prospective buyers, either directly or indirectly, is a prerequisite for successful marketing. At the same time, buyers benefit from distribution systems used by companies.

What Is a Marketing Channel of Distribution?

You see the results of distribution every day. You may have purchased Lay's potato chips at a 7-Eleven convenience store, a book online through Amazon.com, and Levi's jeans at a Kohl's department store. Each of these items was brought to you by a marketing channel of distribution, or simply a **marketing channel**, which consists of individuals and firms involved in the process of making a product or service available for use or consumption by consumers or industrial users.

Marketing channels can be compared to a pipeline through which water flows from a source to a terminus. Marketing channels make possible the flow of products and services from a producer, through intermediaries, to a buyer. Intermediaries go by various names (see Figure 15–1) and perform various functions. Some intermediaries purchase items from the seller, store them, and resell them to buyers. For example, Celestial Seasonings produces specialty teas and sells them to food wholesalers. The wholesalers then sell these teas to supermarkets and grocery stores, which, in turn, sell them to consumers. Other intermediaries such as brokers and agents represent sellers but do not actually take title to products—their role is to bring a seller and buyer together. Century 21 real estate agents are examples of this type of intermediary.

How Is Value Created by Intermediaries?

The importance of intermediaries is made even clearer when we consider the functions they perform and the value they create for buyers.

Important Functions Performed by Intermediaries Intermediaries make possible the flow of products from producers to ultimate consumers by performing three basic functions (see Figure 15–2). Intermediaries perform a *transactional*

FIGURE 15–1
Terms used for marketing intermediaries vary in specificity and use in consumer and business markets.

TERM	DESCRIPTION
Middleman	Any intermediary between the manufacturer and end-user markets
Agent or broker	Any intermediary with legal authority to act on behalf of the manufacturer
Wholesaler	An intermediary who sells to other intermediaries, usually to retailers; term usually applies to consumer markets
Retailer	An intermediary who sells to consumers
Distributor	An imprecise term, usually used to describe intermediaries who perform a variety of distribution functions, including selling, maintaining inventories, extending credit, and so on; a more common term in business markets but may also be used to refer to wholesalers
Dealer	A more imprecise term than *distributor* that can mean the same as distributor, retailer, wholesaler, and so forth

TYPE OF FUNCTION	ACTIVITIES RELATED TO FUNCTION
Transactional function	• *Buying*: Purchasing products for resale or as an agent for supply of a product • *Selling*: Contacting potential customers, promoting products, and seeking orders • *Risk taking*: Assuming business risks in the ownership of inventory that can become obsolete or deteriorate
Logistical function	• *Assorting*: Creating product assortments from several sources to serve customers • *Storing*: Assembling and protecting products at a convenient location to offer better customer service • *Sorting*: Purchasing in large quantities and breaking into smaller amounts desired by customers • *Transporting*: Physically moving a product to customers
Facilitating function	• *Financing*: Extending credit to customers • *Grading*: Inspecting, testing, or judging products and assigning them quality grades • *Marketing information and research*: Providing information to customers and suppliers, including competitive conditions and trends

FIGURE 15–2
Marketing channel intermediaries perform these fundamental functions, each of which consists of different activities.

function when they buy and sell products or services. But an intermediary such as a wholesaler also performs the function of sharing risk with the producer when it stocks merchandise in anticipation of sales. If the stock is unsold for any reason, the intermediary—not the producer—suffers the loss.

The logistics of a transaction (described at length later in this chapter) involve the details of preparing and getting a product to buyers. Gathering, sorting, and dispersing products are some of the *logistical functions* of the intermediary—imagine the several books required for a literature course sitting together on one shelf at your college bookstore! Finally, intermediaries perform *facilitating functions* that, by definition, make a transaction easier for buyers. For example, Macy's issues credit cards to consumers so they can buy now and pay later.

All three functions must be performed in a marketing channel, even though each channel member may not participate in all three. Channel members often negotiate which specific functions they will perform and for what price.

Consumer Benefits Consumers also benefit from intermediaries. Having the products and services you want, when you want them, where you want them, and in the form you want them is the ideal result of marketing channels.

In more specific terms, marketing channels help create value for consumers through the four utilities described in Chapter 1: time, place, form, and possession. *Time utility* refers to having a product or service when you want it. For example, FedEx provides next-morning delivery. *Place utility* means having a product or service available where consumers want it, such as having a Chevron gas station located on a long stretch of lonely highway. *Form utility* involves enhancing a product or service to make it more appealing to buyers. Consider the importance of bottlers in the soft-drink industry. Coca-Cola and Pepsi-Cola manufacture the flavor concentrate (cola, lemon-lime) and sell it to bottlers—intermediaries—which then add sweetener and the concentrate to carbonated water and package the beverage in bottles and cans, which are then sold to retailers. *Possession utility* entails efforts by intermediaries to help buyers take possession of a product or service, such as having airline tickets delivered by a travel agency.

learning review

15-1. What is meant by a marketing channel?

15-2. What are the three basic functions performed by intermediaries?

MARKETING CHANNEL STRUCTURE AND ORGANIZATION

LO 15-2 Distinguish among traditional marketing channels, electronic marketing channels, and different types of vertical marketing systems.

A product can take many routes on its journey from a producer to buyers. Marketers continually search for the most efficient route from the many alternatives available. As you'll see, there are some important differences between the marketing channels used for consumer products and business products.

Marketing Channels for Consumer Products and Services

Figure 15–3 shows the four most common marketing channels for consumer products and services. It also shows the number of levels in each marketing channel, as evidenced by the number of intermediaries between a producer and ultimate buyers. As the number of intermediaries between a producer and buyer increases, the channel is viewed as increasing in length. Thus, the producer → wholesaler → retailer → consumer channel is longer than the producer → consumer channel.

Direct Channel Channel A represents a *direct channel* because the producer and the ultimate consumers deal directly with each other. Many products and services are distributed this way. Many insurance companies sell their services using a direct channel and branch sales offices. The Schwan's Food Company of Marshall, Minnesota, the largest direct-to-home provider of frozen foods in the United States, uses route sales representatives who sell from refrigerated trucks. Because there are no intermediaries with a direct channel, the producer performs all channel functions.

Indirect Channel The remaining three channel forms in Figure 15–3 are *indirect channels* because intermediaries are inserted between the producer and consumers and perform numerous channel functions. Channel B, with a retailer added, is most common when a retailer is large and can buy in large quantities from a producer or when the cost of inventory makes it too expensive to use a wholesaler. Automobile manufacturers such as Toyota use this channel, and a local car dealer acts as a retailer. Why is there no wholesaler?

FIGURE 15–3
Common marketing channels for consumer products and services differ by the kind and number of intermediaries involved.

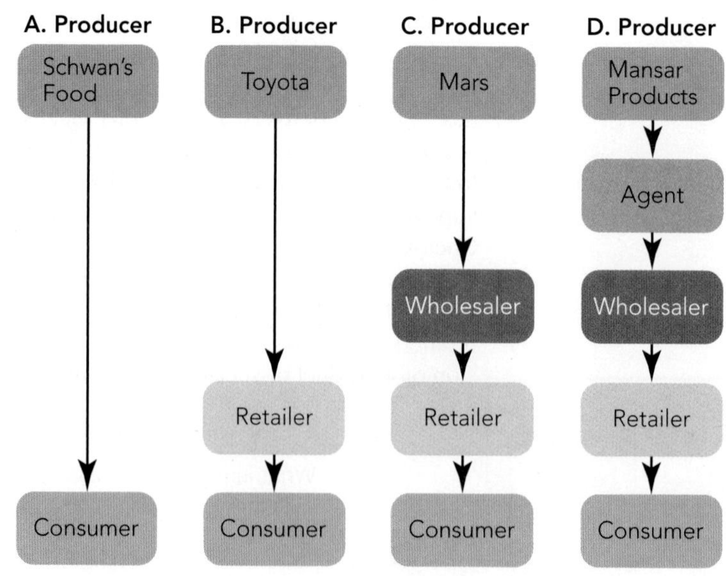

What kind of marketing channel does IBM use for its Watson computer—an artificially intelligent computer system capable of answering questions in natural language? Read the text to find out.

So many variations exist in the product that it would be impossible for a wholesaler to stock all the models required to satisfy buyers; in addition, the cost of maintaining an inventory would be too high. However, large retailers such as Target, 7-Eleven, Staples, Safeway, and Home Depot buy in sufficient quantities to make it cost effective for a producer to deal with only a retail intermediary.

Adding a wholesaler in Channel C is most common for low-cost, low-unit value items that are frequently purchased by consumers, such as candy, confectionary items, and magazines. For example, Mars sells case quantities of its line of candies to wholesalers, who then break down (sort) the cases so that individual retailers can order in boxes or much smaller quantities.

Channel D, the most indirect channel, is employed when there are many small manufacturers and many small retailers; in this type of channel, an agent is used to help coordinate a large supply of the product. Mansar Products, Ltd., is a Belgian producer of specialty jewelry that uses agents to sell to wholesalers in the United States, who then sell to many small independent jewelry retailers.

Marketing Channels for Business Products and Services

The four most common channels for business products and services are shown in Figure 15–4. In contrast with channels used for consumer products, business channels typically are shorter and rely on one intermediary or none at all because business users are fewer in number, tend to be more concentrated geographically, and buy in larger quantities.

Direct Channel Channel A in Figure 15–4, represented by IBM's large, mainframe computer business, is a direct channel. Firms using this channel maintain their own salesforce and perform all channel functions. This channel is employed when buyers are large and well defined, the sales effort requires extensive negotiations, and the products are of high unit value and require hands-on expertise in terms of installation or use. Not surprisingly, IBM's Watson supercomputer, priced at $3 million, is sold directly to buyers.

FIGURE 15–4
Common marketing channels for business products and services differ by the kind and number of intermediaries involved.

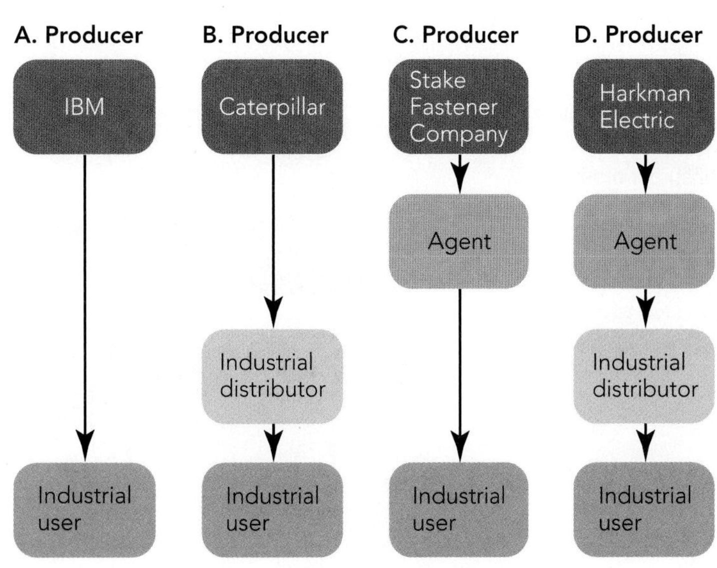

Indirect Channel Channels B, C, and D in Figure 15–4 are indirect channels with one or more intermediaries between the producer and the industrial user. In Channel B, an industrial distributor performs a variety of marketing channel functions, including selling, stocking, delivering a full product assortment, and financing. In many ways, industrial distributors are like wholesalers in consumer channels. Caterpillar uses industrial distributors to sell its construction and mining equipment in over 180 countries. In addition to selling, Caterpillar distributors stock 40,000 to 50,000 parts and service equipment using highly trained technicians.

Channel C introduces a second intermediary, an agent, who serves primarily as the independent selling arm of producers and represents a producer to industrial users. For example, Stake Fastener Company, a producer of industrial fasteners, has an agent call on industrial users rather than employing its own salesforce.

Channel D is the longest channel and includes both agents and industrial distributors. For instance, Harkman Electric, a producer of electric products, uses agents to call on electrical distributors who sell to industrial users.

Internet Marketing Channels

These common marketing channels for consumer and business products and services are not the only routes to the marketplace. Internet commerce offers new avenues for reaching buyers and creating customer value.

Interactive electronic technology has made possible *Internet marketing channels*, which employ the Internet to make products and services available for consumption or use by consumers or organizational buyers. A unique feature of these channels is that they combine electronic and traditional intermediaries to create time, place, form, and possession utility for buyers.

Figure 15–5 shows the Internet marketing channels for books (Amazon.com), automobiles (Autobytel.com), reservation services (Orbitz.com), and personal computers (Dell.com). Are you surprised that they look a lot like common consumer product marketing channels? An important reason for the similarity resides in the channel functions detailed in Figure 15–2. Electronic intermediaries can and do perform transactional and facilitating functions effectively and at a relatively lower cost than traditional intermediaries because of efficiencies made possible by Internet technology. But electronic intermediaries are incapable of performing elements of the logistical function, particularly for products such as books and automobiles. This function remains with traditional intermediaries or with the producer, as is evident with Dell Inc. and its direct channel.

FIGURE 15–5
Consumer Internet marketing channels look much like those for consumer products and services. Read the text to learn why.

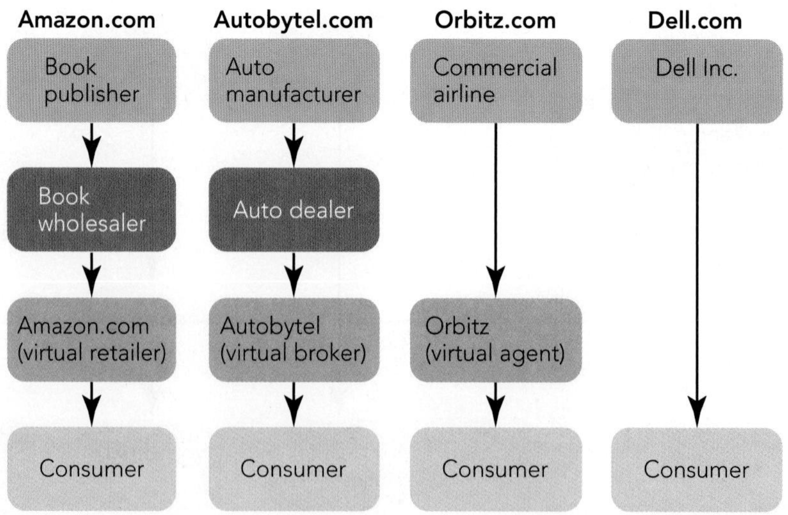

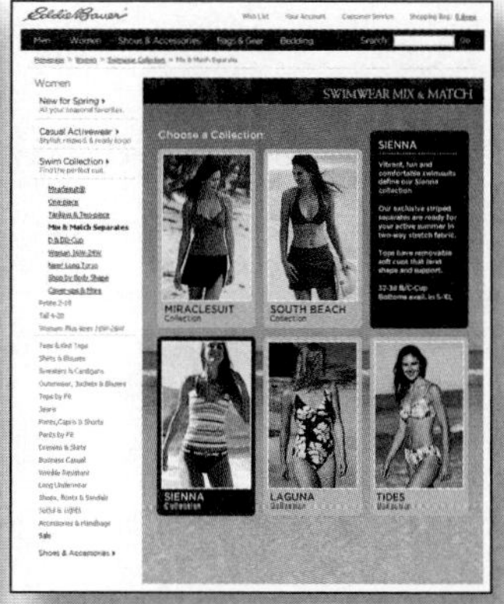

Eddie Bauer successfully engages in multichannel marketing through its 370 retail and outlet stores, its website, and its catalog.

Eddie Bauer
www.eddiebauer.com

Many services can be distributed through electronic marketing channels, such as car rental reservations marketed by Alamo.com, financial securities by Schwab.com, and insurance by MetLife.com. However, many other services, such as health care and auto repair, still involve traditional intermediaries.

Direct and Multichannel Marketing

Many firms also use direct and multichannel marketing to reach buyers. *Direct marketing channels* allow consumers to buy products by interacting with various advertising media without a face-to-face meeting with a salesperson. Direct marketing channels include mail-order selling, direct-mail sales, catalog sales, telemarketing, interactive media, and televised home shopping (the Home Shopping Network). Some firms sell products almost entirely through direct marketing. These firms include L.L. Bean (apparel) and Newegg.com (consumer electronics). Marketers such as Nestlé, in addition to using traditional channels composed of wholesalers and retailers, also employ direct marketing through catalogs and telemarketing to reach more buyers.

Multichannel marketing is the *blending* of different communication and delivery channels that are *mutually reinforcing* in attracting, retaining, and building relationships with consumers who shop and buy in traditional intermediaries and online. Multichannel marketing seeks to integrate a firm's electronic marketing and delivery channels. At Eddie Bauer, for example, every effort is made to make the apparel shopping and purchase experience for its customers the same across its retail store, catalog, and website channels. According to an Eddie Bauer marketing manager, "We don't distinguish between channels because it's all Eddie Bauer to our customers."[2]

Multichannel marketing also can leverage the value-adding capabilities of different channels. For example, retail stores leverage their physical presence by allowing customers to pick up their online orders at a nearby store or return or exchange nonstore purchases if they wish. Catalogs can serve as shopping tools for online purchasing, as they do for store purchasing. Websites can help consumers do their homework before visiting a store. Staples has leveraged its store, catalog, and website channels with impressive results. The company does about $10 billion in online retail sales annually and is the second largest Internet retailer in the United States.[3]

Dual Distribution and Strategic Channel Alliances

In some situations, producers use **dual distribution**, an arrangement whereby a firm reaches different buyers by employing two or more different types of channels for the same basic product. For example, GE sells its large appliances directly to home and apartment builders but uses retail stores, including Lowe's home centers, to sell to consumers. In some instances, firms pair multiple channels with a multibrand strategy (see Chapter 11). This is done to minimize cannibalization of the firm's family brand

Marketing Matters

customer value

Nestlé and General Mills—Cereal Partners Worldwide

Can you say Nestlé Cheerios *miel amandes*? Millions in France start their day with this European equivalent of General Mills's Honey Nut Cheerios, made possible by Cereal Partners Worldwide (CPW). CPW is a strategic alliance designed from the start to be a global business. It combines the cereal manufacturing and marketing capability of U.S.–based General Mills with the worldwide distribution clout of Swiss-based Nestlé.

From its headquarters in Switzerland, CPW first launched General Mills cereals under the Nestlé label in France, the United Kingdom, Spain, and Portugal in 1991. Today, CPW competes in more than 140 international markets.

The General Mills–Nestlé strategic channel alliance also increased the ready-to-eat cereal worldwide market share of these companies, which are already rated as the two best-managed firms in the world. CPW currently accounts for more than 8 percent of global breakfast cereal sales, with more than $3 billion in annual revenue.

and differentiate the channels. For example, Hallmark sells its Hallmark greeting cards through Hallmark stores and select department stores and its Ambassador brand of cards through discount and drugstore chains.

QR 15-1
Honey Nut Cheerios Ad

An innovation in marketing channels is the use of *strategic channel alliances*, whereby one firm's marketing channel is used to sell another firm's products. Strategic alliances are popular in global marketing, where the creation of marketing channel relationships is expensive and time-consuming. For example, General Mills and Nestlé have an extensive alliance that spans about 140 international markets from Mexico to China. Read the Marketing Matters box so you won't be surprised when you are served Nestlé (not General Mills) Cheerios when traveling outside North America.[4]

Vertical Marketing Systems

The traditional marketing channels described so far represent a loosely knit network of independent producers and intermediaries brought together to distribute products and services. However, other channel arrangements exist for the purpose of improving efficiency in performing channel functions and achieving greater marketing effectiveness. These arrangements are called vertical marketing systems. **Vertical marketing systems** are professionally managed and centrally coordinated marketing channels designed to achieve channel economies and maximum marketing impact.[5] Figure 15–6 depicts the three major types of vertical marketing systems: corporate, contractual, and administered.

Corporate Systems The combination of successive stages of production and distribution under a single ownership is a *corporate vertical marketing system*. For example, a producer might own the intermediary at the next level down in the channel. This practice, called *forward integration*, is exemplified by Ralph Lauren, which manufactures clothing and also owns apparel shops. Other examples of forward integration

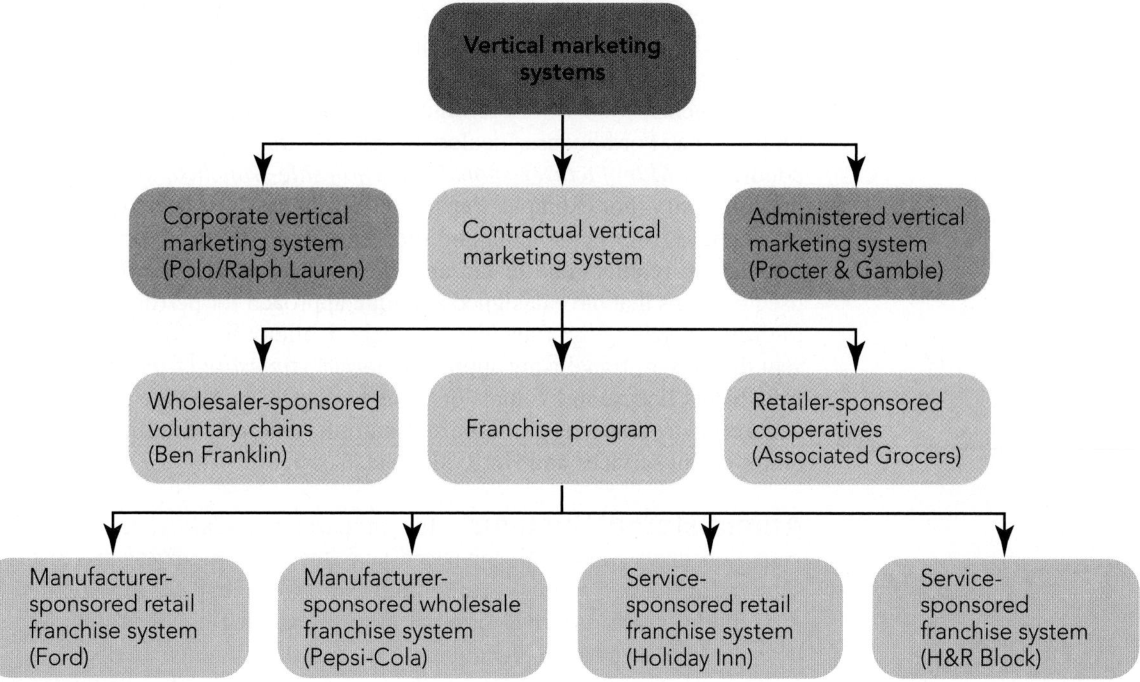

FIGURE 15–6
There are three major types of vertical marketing systems—corporate, contractual, and administered. Contractual systems are the most popular for reasons described in the text.

include Goodyear, Apple, and Sherwin-Williams. Alternatively, a retailer might own a manufacturing operation, a practice called *backward integration*. For example, Kroger supermarkets operate manufacturing facilities that produce everything from aspirin to cottage cheese for sale under the Kroger label. Tiffany & Co., the exclusive jewelry retailer, manufactures about half of the fine jewelry items for sale through its over 250 specialty stores and boutiques worldwide.

Companies seeking to reduce distribution costs and gain greater control over supply sources or resale of their products pursue forward and backward integration. However, both types of integration increase a company's capital investment and fixed costs. For this reason, many companies favor contractual vertical marketing systems to achieve channel efficiencies and marketing effectiveness.

Contractual Systems Under a *contractual vertical marketing system*, independent production and distribution firms integrate their efforts on a contractual basis to obtain greater functional economies and marketing impact than they could achieve alone. Contractual systems are the most popular among the three types of vertical marketing systems.

Three variations of contractual systems exist. *Wholesaler-sponsored voluntary chains* involve a wholesaler that develops a contractual relationship with small, independent retailers to standardize and coordinate buying practices, merchandising programs, and inventory management efforts. With the organization of a large number of independent retailers, economies of scale and volume discounts can be achieved to compete with chain stores. IGA and Ben Franklin variety and craft stores represent wholesaler-sponsored voluntary chains. *Retailer-sponsored cooperatives* exist when small, independent retailers form an organization that operates a wholesale facility cooperatively. Member retailers then concentrate their buying power through the wholesaler and plan collaborative promotional and pricing activities. Examples of retailer-sponsored cooperatives include Associated Grocers and Ace Hardware.

The most visible variation of contractual systems is franchising. *Franchising* is a contractual arrangement between a parent company (a franchisor) and an individual or firm (a franchisee) that allows the franchisee to operate a certain type of business under an established name and according to specific rules.

Four types of franchise arrangements are most popular. *Manufacturer-sponsored retail franchise systems* are prominent in the automobile industry, where a manufacturer such as Ford licenses dealers to sell its cars subject to various sales and service conditions. *Manufacturer-sponsored wholesale franchise systems* exist in the soft-drink industry. For example, Pepsi-Cola licenses wholesalers (bottlers) that purchase concentrate from Pepsi-Cola and then carbonate, bottle, promote, and distribute its products to retailers and restaurants. *Service-sponsored retail franchise systems* are used by firms that have designed a unique approach for performing a service and wish to profit by selling the franchise to others. Holiday Inn, Avis, and McDonald's represent this type of franchising approach. *Service-sponsored franchise systems* exist when franchisors license individuals or firms to dispense a service under a trade name and according to specific guidelines. Examples include Snelling and Snelling, Inc., employment services and H&R Block tax services.

Administered Systems In comparison, *administered vertical marketing systems* achieve coordination at successive stages of production and distribution by the size and influence of one channel member rather than through ownership. Procter & Gamble, given its broad product assortment ranging from disposable diapers to detergents, is able to obtain cooperation from supermarkets in displaying, promoting, and pricing its products. Walmart obtains cooperation from manufacturers in terms of product specifications, price levels, and promotional support due to its position as the world's largest retailer.

learning review

15-3. What is the difference between a direct and an indirect channel?

15-4. Why are channels for business products typically shorter than channels for consumer products?

15-5. What is the principal distinction between a corporate vertical marketing system and an administered vertical marketing system?

MARKETING CHANNEL CHOICE AND MANAGEMENT

Describe factors that marketing executives consider when selecting and managing a marketing channel.

Marketing channels not only link a producer to its buyers but also provide the means through which a firm implements various elements of its marketing strategy. Therefore, choosing a marketing channel is a critical decision.

Factors Affecting Channel Choice and Management

Marketing executives consider three questions when choosing a marketing channel and intermediaries:

1. Which channel and intermediaries will provide the best coverage of the target market?
2. Which channel and intermediaries will best satisfy the buying requirements of the target market?
3. Which channel and intermediaries will be the most profitable?

Target Market Coverage Achieving the best coverage of the target market requires attention to the *density*—that is, the number of stores in a geographical area—and type of intermediaries to be used at the retail level of distribution. Three degrees of distribution density exist: intensive, exclusive, and selective.

Marketing inSite

Visit an Apple Store to See What All the Excitement Is About

Interested in visiting an Apple store to see what all the excitement is about? Is one of Apple's over 400 stores in the world situated near you? If you answered "yes" to the first question and "no" to the second, then log on to www.ifoapplestore.com. Here you will find exterior and interior photographs and video tours of various Apple stores. To learn whether an Apple store is planned for your area, visit this website to find announcements of grand openings around the world.

Intensive distribution means that a firm tries to place its products and services in as many outlets as possible. Intensive distribution is usually chosen for convenience products or services such as candy, fast food, newspapers, and soft drinks. For example, Coca-Cola's retail distribution objective is to place its products "within an arm's reach of desire." Cash, yes cash, is distributed intensively by Visa. It operates over 1.8 million automatic teller machines in more than 200 countries.

Exclusive distribution is the extreme opposite of intensive distribution because only one retailer in a specified geographical area carries the firm's products. Exclusive distribution is typically chosen for specialty products or services, such as some women's fragrances and men's and women's apparel and accessories. Gucci, one of the world's leading luxury products companies, uses exclusive distribution in the marketing of its Yves Saint Laurent, Sergio Rossi, Boucheron, Opium, and Gucci brands.

Retailers and industrial distributors prefer exclusive distribution for two reasons. First, it limits head-to-head competition for an identical product. Second, it provides a point of difference for a retailer or distributor. For instance, luxury retailer Saks Inc. seeks exclusive product lines for its stores. According to the company CEO, "It's incumbent on us not to be just a place where you can buy the big brands. Those brands are still critical—the Chanels, the Pradas, the Guccis—but even with those brands, we need to find things unique to us."[6]

Selective distribution lies between these two extremes and means that a firm selects a few retailers in a specific geographical area to carry its products. Selective distribution weds some of the market coverage benefits of intensive distribution to the control over resale evident with exclusive distribution. For example, Dell Inc. chose selective distribution when it decided to sell its products through U.S. retailers along with its direct channel.[7] According to Michael Dell, the company CEO, "There were plenty of retailers who said, 'sell through us,' but we didn't want to show up everywhere." The company now sells a limited range of its products through Walmart, Sam's Club, Best Buy, and Staples, an office-products retailer. Dell's decision was consistent with current trends. Today, selective distribution is the most common form of distribution intensity.

Buyer Requirements A second consideration in channel choice is gaining access to channels and intermediaries that satisfy at least some of the interests buyers might want fulfilled when they purchase a firm's products or services. These interests fall into four broad categories: (1) information, (2) convenience, (3) variety, and (4) pre- or postsale services. Each relates to customer experience.

Information is an important requirement when buyers have limited knowledge or desire specific data about a product or service. Properly chosen intermediaries communicate with buyers through in-store displays, demonstrations, and personal selling. Consumer electronics manufacturers such as Apple have opened their own retail outlets staffed with highly trained personnel to communicate how their products can better satisfy each customer's needs. See the Marketing inSite box to learn more about Apple stores.

Which buying requirements are satisfied by Jiffy Lube and PetSmart? Read the text to find out.

Convenience has multiple meanings for buyers, such as proximity or driving time to a retail outlet. For example, 7-Eleven stores, with more than 50,000 outlets worldwide, many of which are open 24 hours a day, satisfy this interest for buyers. Candy and snack-food firms benefit by gaining display space in these stores. For other consumers, convenience means a minimum of time and hassle. Jiffy Lube, which promises to change engine oil and filters quickly, appeals to this aspect of convenience. For those who shop on the Internet, convenience means that websites must be easy to locate and navigate, and image downloads must be fast. A commonly held view among website developers is the "eight second rule": Consumers will abandon their efforts to enter or navigate a website if download time exceeds eight seconds.[8]

Variety reflects buyers' interest in having numerous competing and complementary items from which to choose. Variety is evident in the breadth and depth of products and brands carried by intermediaries, which enhances their attraction to buyers. Thus, manufacturers of pet food and supplies seek distribution through pet superstores such as Petco and PetSmart, which offer a wide array of pet products and services.

Pre- or postsale services provided by intermediaries are an important buying requirement for products such as large household appliances that require delivery, installation, and credit. Therefore, Whirlpool seeks dealers that provide such services.

Profitability The third consideration in choosing a channel is profitability, which is determined by the margins earned (revenue minus cost) for each channel member and for the channel as a whole. Channel cost is the critical dimension of profitability. These costs include distribution, advertising, and selling expenses associated with different types of marketing channels. The extent to which channel members share these costs determines the margins received by each member and by the channel as a whole.

Companies routinely monitor the performance of their marketing channels. Read the Using Marketing Dashboards box to see how Charlesburg Furniture views the sales and profit performance of its marketing channels.

Managing Channel Relationships: Conflict and Cooperation

Unfortunately, because channels consist of independent individuals and firms, there is always the potential for disagreements concerning who performs which channel functions, how profits are allocated, which products and services will be provided by whom, and who makes critical channel-related decisions. These channel conflicts necessitate measures for dealing with them.

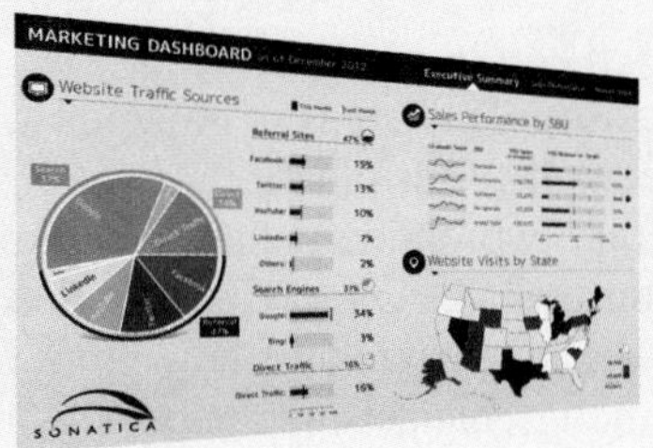

Using Marketing Dashboards

Channel Sales and Profit at Charlesburg Furniture

Charlesburg Furniture is one of 1,000 wood furniture manufacturers in the United States. The company sells its furniture through furniture store chains, independent furniture stores, and department store chains, mostly in the southern United States. The company has traditionally allocated its marketing funds for cooperative advertising, in-store displays, and retail sales support on the basis of dollar sales by channel.

Your Challenge As the vice president of sales & marketing at Charlesburg Furniture, you have been asked to review the company's sales and profit in its three channels and recommend a course of action. The question: Should Charlesburg Furniture continue to allocate its marketing funds on the basis of channel dollar sales or profit?

Your Findings Charlesburg Furniture tracks the sales and profit from each channel (and individual customer) and the three-year trend of sales by channel on its marketing dashboard. This information is displayed in the marketing dashboards below.

Several findings stand out. Furniture store chains and independent furniture stores account for 85.2 percent of Charlesburg Furniture sales and 93 percent of company profit. These two channels also evidence growth as measured by annual percentage change in sales. By comparison, the annual percentage sales growth of department store chains has declined, recording negative growth in 2013. This channel accounts for 14.8 percent of company sales and 7 percent of company profit.

Your Action Charlesburg Furniture should consider abandoning the practice of allocating marketing funds solely on the basis of channel sales volume. The importance of independent furniture stores to Charlesburg's profitability warrants further spending, particularly given this channel's favorable sales trend. Doubling the percentage allocation for marketing funds for this channel may be too extreme, however. Charlesburg Furniture might also consider the longer term role of department store chains as a marketing channel.

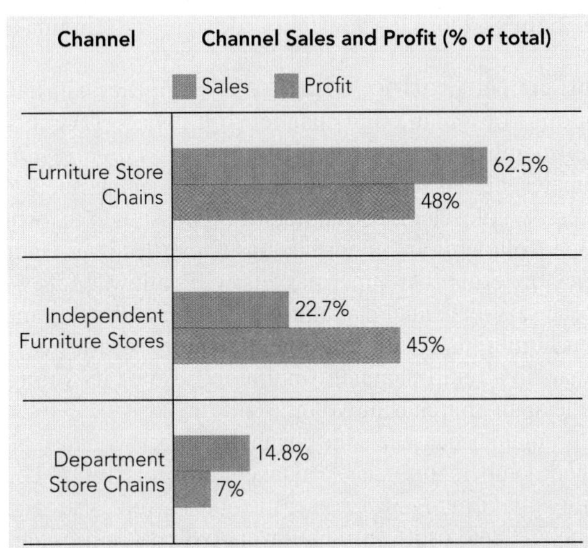

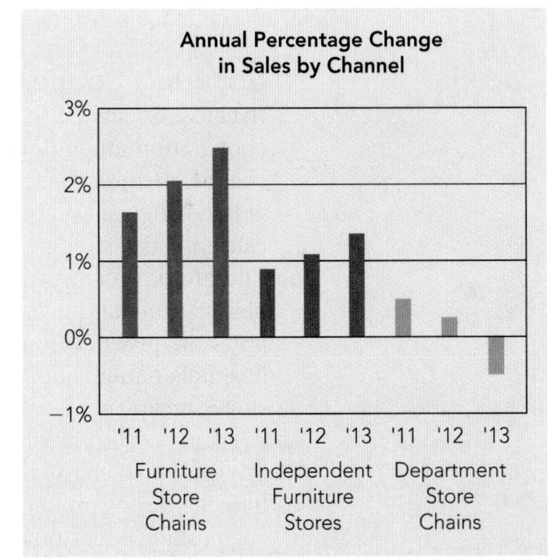

Sources of Conflict in Marketing Channels **Channel conflict** arises when one channel member believes another channel member is engaged in behavior that prevents it from achieving its goals. Two types of conflict occur in marketing channels: vertical conflict and horizontal conflict.

Vertical conflict occurs between different levels in a marketing channel—for example, between a manufacturer and a wholesaler or retailer or between a wholesaler and a retailer. Three sources of vertical conflict are most common.[9] First, conflict arises when a channel member bypasses another member and sells or buys products direct, a practice

Channel conflict is sometimes visible to consumers. Read the text to learn what type of channel conflict has antagonized this independent Goodyear tire dealer.

called **disintermediation**. This conflict emerged when American Airlines decided to terminate its relationship with Orbitz and Expedia, two online ticketing and travel sites, and sell directly through AA Direct Connect. Second, conflict occurs due to disagreements over how profit margins are distributed among channel members. This happened when the world's biggest music company, Universal Music Group, adopted a pricing policy for CDs that squeezed the profit margins for specialty music retailers. A third conflict situation arises when manufacturers believe wholesalers or retailers are not giving their products adequate attention. For example, Nike stopped shipping popular sneakers such as Nike Shox NZ to Foot Locker in retaliation for the retailer's decision to give more shelf space to shoes costing under $120.

Horizontal conflict occurs between intermediaries at the same level in a marketing channel, such as between two or more retailers (Target and Kmart) or two or more wholesalers that handle the same manufacturer's brands. Two sources of horizontal conflict are common.[10] First, horizontal conflict arises when a manufacturer increases its distribution coverage in a geographical area. For example, a franchised Buick dealer in Chicago might complain to General Motors that another franchised Buick dealer has located too close to its dealership. Second, dual distribution causes conflict when different types of retailers carry the same brands. For instance, independent Goodyear tire dealers became irate when Goodyear Tire Company decided to sell its brands through Sears, Walmart, and Sam's Club. Many switched to competing tire makers.

Securing Cooperation in Marketing Channels Conflict can have destructive effects on the workings of a marketing channel so it is necessary to secure cooperation among channel members. One means is through a *channel captain*, a channel member that coordinates, directs, and supports other channel members. Channel captains can be producers, wholesalers, or retailers. P&G assumes this role because it has a strong consumer following in brands such as Crest, Tide, and Pampers. Therefore, it can set policies or terms that supermarkets will follow. McKesson, a pharmaceutical drug wholesaler, is a channel captain because it coordinates and supports the product flow from numerous small drug manufacturers to drugstores and hospitals nationwide. Walmart is a retail channel captain because of its strong consumer image, number of outlets, and purchasing volume.

A firm becomes a channel captain because it is the channel member with the ability to influence the behavior of other members. Influence can take four forms. First, economic influence arises from the ability of a firm to *reward* other members given its strong financial position or customer franchise. Microsoft Corporation and Walmart have such influence. *Expertise* is a second source of influence. For example, American Hospital Supply helps its customers (hospitals) manage inventory and streamline order processing for hundreds of medical supplies. Third, *identification* with a particular channel member can create influence for that channel member. For instance, retailers may compete to carry the Ralph Lauren line, or clothing manufacturers may compete to be carried by Neiman Marcus, Nordstrom, or Bloomingdale's. In both instances, the desire to be identified with a channel member gives that firm influence over others. Finally, influence can arise from the *legitimate right* of one channel member to direct the behavior of other members. This situation is likely to occur in contractual vertical marketing systems where a franchisor can legitimately direct how a franchisee behaves.

Legal Considerations Conflict in marketing channels is typically resolved through negotiation or the exercise of influence by channel members. Sometimes

FIGURE 15–7
Channel strategies and practices are affected by legal restrictions. The Clayton Act and the Sherman Act restrict specific channel strategies and practices.

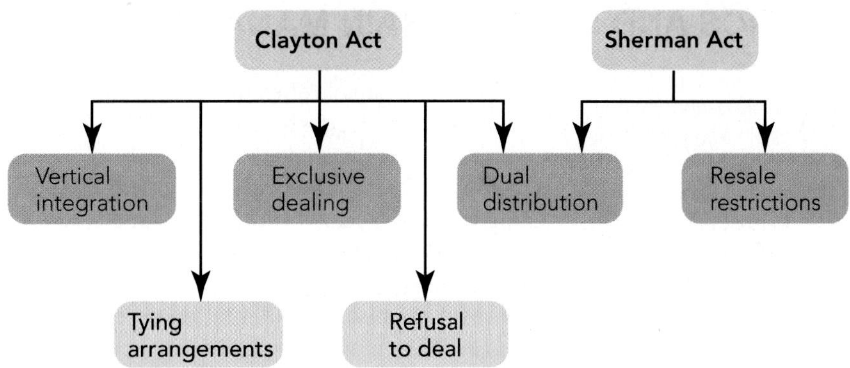

conflict produces legal action. Therefore, knowledge of legal restrictions affecting channel strategies and practices is important. Some restrictions were described in Chapter 14, namely vertical price fixing and price discrimination. However, other legal considerations are unique to marketing channels.[11]

In general, suppliers can select whomever they want as channel intermediaries and may refuse to deal with whomever they choose. However, the Federal Trade Commission and the Justice Department monitor channel practices that restrain competition, create monopolies, or otherwise represent unfair methods of competition under the Sherman Act (1890) and the Clayton Act (1914). Six channel practices have received the most attention (see Figure 15–7).

Dual distribution, although not illegal, can be viewed as anticompetitive in some situations. The most common situation arises when a manufacturer distributes through its own vertically integrated channel in competition with independent wholesalers and retailers that also sell its products. If the manufacturer's behavior is viewed as an attempt to lessen competition by eliminating wholesalers or retailers, then such action would violate both the Sherman and Clayton Acts.

Vertical integration is viewed in a similar light. Although not illegal, this practice is sometimes subject to legal action under the Clayton Act if it has the potential to lessen competition or foster monopoly.

The Clayton Act specifically prohibits exclusive dealing and tying arrangements when they lessen competition or create monopolies. *Exclusive dealing* exists when a supplier requires channel members to sell only its products or restricts distributors from selling directly competitive products. *Tying arrangements* occur when a supplier requires a distributor purchasing some products to buy others from the supplier. These arrangements often arise in franchising. They are illegal if the tied products could be purchased at fair market values from other suppliers at desired quality standards of the franchiser. *Full-line forcing* is a special kind of tying arrangement. This practice involves a supplier requiring that a channel member carry its full line of products in order to sell a specific item in the supplier's line.

Even though a supplier has a legal right to choose intermediaries to carry and represent its products, a *refusal to deal* with existing channel members may be illegal under the Clayton Act. *Resale restrictions* refer to a supplier's attempt to stipulate to whom distributors may resell the supplier's products and in what specific geographical areas or territories they may be sold. These practices have been prosecuted under the Sherman Act. Today, however, the courts apply the "rule of reason" in such cases and consider whether such restrictions have a "demonstrable economic effect."

learning review

15-6. What are the three questions marketing executives consider when choosing a marketing channel and intermediaries?

15-7. What are the three degrees of distribution density?

15-8. What is meant by exclusive dealing?

LOGISTICS AND SUPPLY CHAIN MANAGEMENT

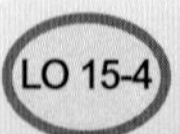

Explain what supply chain and logistics management are and how they relate to marketing strategy.

A marketing channel relies on logistics to make products available to consumers and industrial users. **Logistics** involves those activities that focus on getting the right amount of the right products to the right place at the right time at the lowest possible cost. The performance of these activities is *logistics management*, the practice of organizing the cost-effective flow of raw materials, in-process inventory, finished goods, and related information from point of origin to point of consumption to satisfy *customer requirements.*

Three elements of this definition deserve emphasis. First, logistics deals with decisions needed to move a product from the source of raw materials to consumption—that is, the *flow* of the product. Second, those decisions have to be *cost effective.* Third, while it is important to drive down logistics costs, there is a limit: A firm needs to drive down logistics costs as long as it can deliver expected *customer service,* which means satisfying customer requirements. The role of management is to see that customer needs are satisfied in the most cost-effective manner. When properly done, the results can be spectacular. Consider Procter & Gamble. The company set out to meet consumer needs more effectively by collaborating and partnering with its suppliers and retailers to ensure that the right products reached store shelves at the right time and at a lower cost. The effort was judged a success when, during an 18-month period, P&G's retail customers posted a $65 million savings in logistics costs and customer service increased.[12]

The Procter & Gamble experience is not an isolated incident. Companies now recognize that getting the right items needed for consumption or production to the right place at the right time in the right condition at the right cost is often beyond their individual capabilities and control. Instead, collaboration, coordination, and information sharing among manufacturers, suppliers, and distributors are necessary to create a seamless flow of products and services to customers. This perspective is represented in the concept of a supply chain and the practice of supply chain management.

Supply Chains versus Marketing Channels

A **supply chain** refers to the various firms involved in performing the activities required to create and deliver a product or service to consumers or industrial users. It differs from a marketing channel in terms of the firms involved. A supply chain includes suppliers that provide raw material inputs to a manufacturer as well as the wholesalers and retailers that deliver finished products to consumers. The management process is also different.

Supply chain management is the integration and organization of information and logistics activities *across firms* in a supply chain for the purpose of creating and delivering products and services that provide value to consumers. The relation among marketing channels, logistics management, and supply chain management is shown in Figure 15–8. An important feature of supply chain management is its application of sophisticated information technology that allows companies to share and operate systems for order processing, transportation scheduling, and inventory and facility management.

Sourcing, Assembling, and Delivering a New Car: The Automotive Supply Chain

All companies are members of one or more supply chains. A supply chain is essentially a series of linked suppliers and customers in which every customer is, in turn, a supplier to another customer until a finished product reaches the ultimate consumer. Even the simplified supply chain diagram for carmakers shown in Figure 15–9

FIGURE 15–8
Relating logistics management and supply chain management to supplier networks and marketing channels.

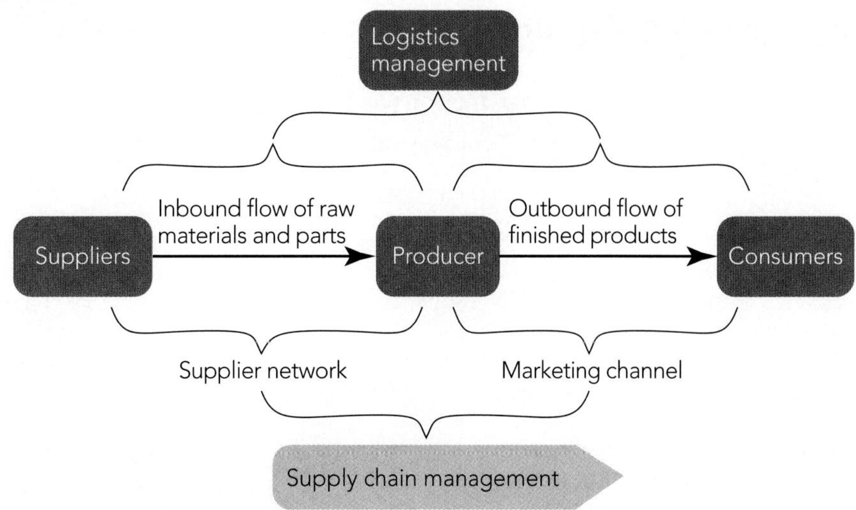

illustrates how complex a supply chain can be.[13] A carmaker's supplier network includes thousands of firms that provide the 2,000 functional components, 30,000 parts, and 10 million lines of software code in a typical automobile. They provide items ranging from raw materials, such as steel and rubber, to components, including transmissions, tires, brakes, and seats, to complex subassemblies such as chassis and suspension systems that make for a smooth, stable ride. The process of coordinating and scheduling the flow of materials and components for their assembly into actual automobiles by carmakers is heavily dependent on logistical activities, including transportation, order processing, inventory control, materials handling, and information technology. A central link is the carmaker's supply chain manager, who is responsible for translating customer requirements into actual orders and arranging for delivery dates and financial arrangements for automobile dealers.

Logistical aspects of the automobile marketing channel are also an important part of the supply chain. Major responsibilities include transportation (which involves the selection and oversight of external carriers—trucking, airline, railroad, and shipping companies—for cars and parts to dealers), the operation of distribution centers, the management of finished goods inventories, and order processing for sales. Supply chain managers also play an important role in the marketing channel. They work with car dealer networks to ensure that the right mix of automobiles is delivered to each location. In addition, they make sure that spare and service parts are available so that dealers can meet the car maintenance and repair needs of consumers. All of this is done with the help of information technology that links the entire automotive supply chain. What does all of this cost? It is estimated that logistics costs represent 25 to 30 percent of the retail price that you pay for a new car.

FIGURE 15–9
The automotive supply chain includes thousands of firms that provide the functional components, software codes, and parts in a typical car.

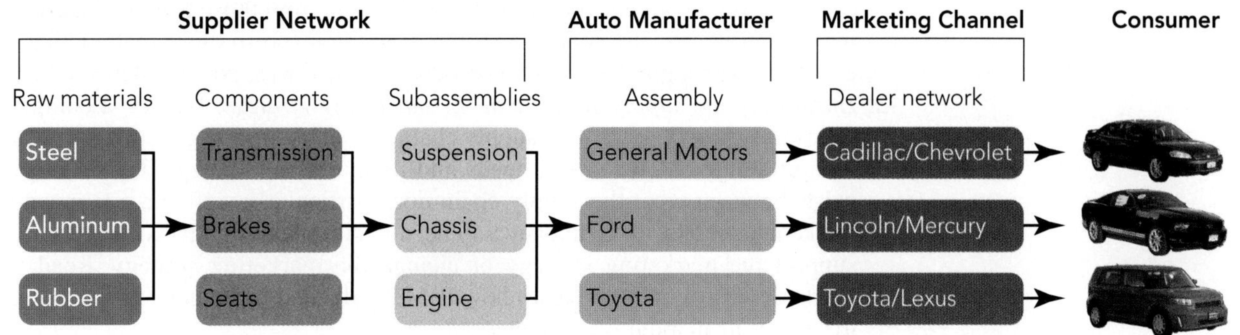

Marketing Matters

customer value

IBM's Integrated Supply Chain—Delivering a Total Solution for Its Customers

IBM is one of the world's great business success stories because of its ability to reinvent itself to satisfy shifting customer needs in a dynamic global marketplace. The company's transformation of its supply chain is a case in point.

IBM has built a single integrated supply chain that can handle raw material procurement, manufacturing, logistics, customer support, order entry, and customer fulfillment across all of IBM—something that has never been done before. Why would IBM undertake this task? According to IBM's former CEO, Samuel J. Palmisano, "You cannot hope to thrive in the IT industry if you are a high-cost, slow-moving company. Supply chain is one of the new competitive battlegrounds. We are committed to being the most efficient and productive player in our industry."

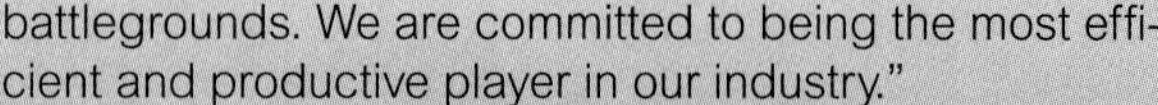

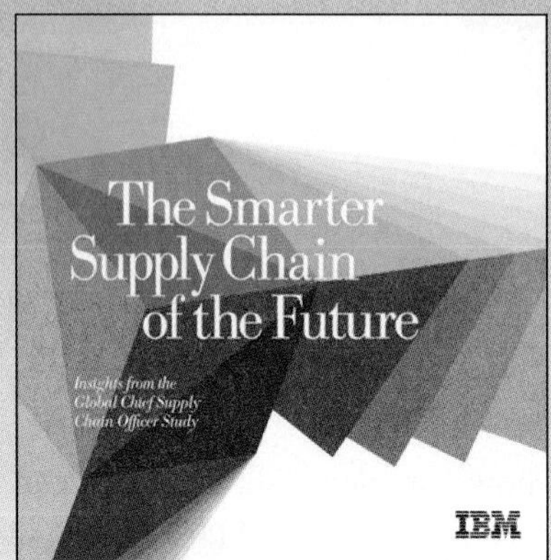

The task is not easy. IBM's supply chain management organization works out of 360 locations in 64 countries, tracking more than 1.5 million assets for both IBM and its clients. The organization also deals with about 23,000 suppliers in nearly 100 countries. Yet with surprising efficiency, IBM's supply chain is linked from raw material sourcing to postsales support.

Today, IBM is uniquely poised to configure and deliver a tailored mix of hardware, software, and service to provide a total solution for its customers. Not surprisingly, IBM's integrated supply chain is heralded as one of the best in the world!

QR 15-2
IBM Video

Supply Chain Management and Marketing Strategy

The automotive supply chain illustration shows how information and logistics activities are integrated and organized across firms to create and deliver a car to you, the consumer. What's missing from this illustration is the linkage between a specific company's supply chain and its marketing strategy. Just as companies have different marketing strategies, they also design and manage supply chains differently. The goals to be achieved by a firm's marketing strategy determine whether its supply chain needs to be more responsive or efficient in meeting customer requirements.

Aligning a Supply Chain with Marketing Strategy There are a variety of supply chain configurations, each of which is designed to perform different tasks well. Marketers today recognize that the choice of a supply chain follows from a clearly defined marketing strategy and involves three steps:[14]

1. *Understand the customer.* To understand the customer, a company must identify the needs of the customer segment being served. These needs, such as a desire for a low price or convenience of purchase, help a company define the relative importance of efficiency and responsiveness in meeting customer requirements.
2. *Understand the supply chain.* Second, a company must understand what a supply chain is designed to do well. Supply chains range from those that emphasize being responsive to customer requirements and demand to those that emphasize efficiency with a goal of supplying products at the lowest possible delivered cost.
3. *Harmonize the supply chain with the marketing strategy.* Finally, a company needs to ensure that what the supply chain is capable of doing well is consistent with the targeted customer's needs and its marketing strategy. If a mismatch exists between what the supply chain does particularly well and a company's marketing strategy, the company will need to either redesign the supply chain to support the marketing strategy or change the marketing strategy. Read the Marketing Matters box to learn how IBM overhauled its complete supply chain to support its marketing strategy.[15]

How are these steps applied and how are efficiency and responsiveness considerations built into a supply chain? Let's look at how two well-known companies—Dell and Walmart—have harmonized their supply chain and marketing strategy.[16]

Dell: A Responsive Supply Chain The Dell marketing strategy primarily targets customers who desire having the most up-to-date computer systems customized to their needs. These customers are also willing to (1) wait to have their customized computer system delivered in a few days, rather than picking out a model at a retail store, and (2) pay a reasonable, though not the lowest, price in the marketplace. Given Dell's customer segment, the company has the option of adopting an efficient or responsive supply chain.

An efficient supply chain may use inexpensive, but slower, modes of transportation, emphasize economies of scale in its production process by reducing the variety of system configurations offered, and limit its assembly and inventory storage facilities to a single location. If Dell opted only for efficiency in its supply chain, it would be difficult to satisfy its target customers' desire for rapid delivery and a wide variety of customizable products with its assembly and storage facilities confined to its headquarters in Austin, Texas.

Dell instead has opted for a responsive supply chain. It relies on more expensive express transportation for receipt of components from suppliers and delivery of finished products to customers. The company achieves product variety and manufacturing efficiency by designing common platforms across several products and using common components. Also, Dell has invested heavily in information technology to link itself with suppliers and customers.

Walmart: An Efficient Supply Chain Now let's consider Walmart. Walmart's marketing strategy is to be a reliable, lower-price retailer for a wide variety of mass consumption consumer goods. This strategy favors an efficient supply chain designed to deliver products to 200 million consumers each week at the lowest possible cost. Efficiency is achieved in a variety of ways. For instance, Walmart keeps relatively low inventory levels, and most of it is stocked in stores available for sale, not in warehouses gathering dust. The low inventory arises from Walmart's use of *cross-docking*—a practice that involves unloading products from suppliers, sorting products for individual stores, and quickly reloading products onto its trucks for a particular store. No warehousing or storing of products occurs, except for a few hours or, at most, a day. Cross-docking allows Walmart to operate only a small number of distribution centers to service its vast network of Walmart stores, Supercenters, Neighborhood Markets, Marketside stores, and Sam's Clubs, which contributes to efficiency. On the other hand, the company runs its own fleet of trucks to service its stores. This does increase cost and investment, but the benefits in terms of responsiveness justify the cost in Walmart's case.

Walmart has invested much more than its competitors in information technology to operate its supply chain. The company feeds information about customer requirements and demand from its stores back to its suppliers, which manufacture only what is being demanded. This large investment has improved the efficiency of Walmart's supply chain and made it responsive to customer needs.

Three lessons can be learned from these two examples. First, there is no one best supply chain for every company. Second, the best supply chain is the one that is consistent with the needs of the customer segment being served and complements a company's marketing strategy. And finally, supply chain managers are often called upon to make trade-offs between efficiency and responsiveness on various elements of a company's supply chain.

TWO CONCEPTS OF LOGISTICS MANAGEMENT IN A SUPPLY CHAIN

The objective of logistics management in a supply chain is to minimize total logistics costs while delivering the appropriate level of customer service.

Total Logistics Cost Concept

For our purposes, **total logistics cost** includes expenses associated with transportation, materials handling and warehousing, inventory, stockouts (being out of inventory), order processing, and return products handling. Note that many of these costs are interrelated so that changes in one will impact the others. For example, if a firm attempts to reduce its transportation costs by shipping in larger quantities, it will increase its inventory levels. While larger inventory levels will increase inventory costs, they should also reduce stockouts. It is important, therefore, to study the impact on all of the logistics decision areas when considering a change.

Customer Service Concept

Because a supply chain is a *flow*, the end of it—or *output*—is the service delivered to customers. Within the context of a supply chain, **customer service** is the ability of logistics management to satisfy users in terms of time, dependability, communication, and convenience. As suggested by Figure 15–10, a supply chain manager's key task is to balance these four customer service factors against total logistics cost factors.

Time In a supply chain setting, time refers to *order cycle* or *replenishment* time for an item, which means the time between the ordering of an item and when it is received and ready for use or sale. The various elements that make up the typical order cycle include recognition of the need to order, order transmittal, order processing, documentation, and transportation. A current emphasis in supply chain management is to reduce order cycle time so that the inventory levels of customers may be minimized. Another emphasis is to make the process of reordering and receiving products as simple as possible, often through inventory systems called *quick response* and *efficient consumer response* delivery systems. For example, at Saks Fifth Avenue, point-of-sale scanner technology records each day's sales. When stock falls below a minimum level, a replenishment order is automatically produced. Vendors such as Donna Karan (DKNY) receive the order, which is processed and delivered within 48 hours.[17]

FIGURE 15–10
Supply chain managers balance total logistics cost factors against customer service factors.

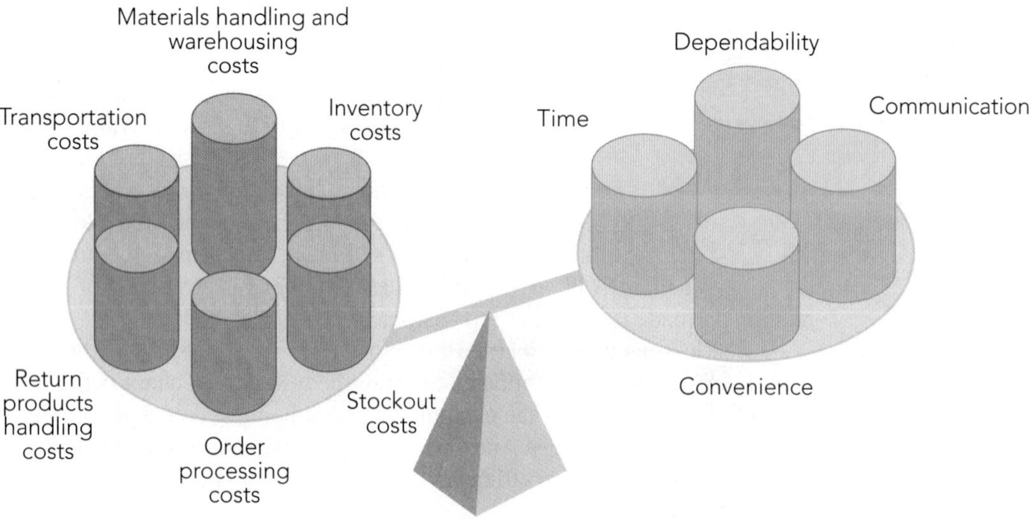

Making Responsible Decisions

sustainability

Reverse Logistics and Green Marketing Go Together at Hewlett-Packard: Recycling e-Waste

About 53 million tons of electronics and electronic equipment find their way to landfills around the world annually. Americans alone discarded over 400 million analog TV sets and computer monitors and Japanese consumers trashed more than 610 million cell phones in 2011. The result? Landfills are seeping lead, chromium, mercury, and other toxins prevalent in digital debris into the environment.

Fortunately, Hewlett-Packard has taken it upon itself to act responsibly and address this issue through its highly regarded reverse logistics program. Hewlett-Packard has recycled computer and printer hardware since 1987 and is an industry leader in this practice. The company's recycling service is available today in more than 67 countries, regions, and territories. By 2013, Hewlett-Packard will have recycled over 2 billion pounds of used electronic products and supplies to be refurbished for resale or donation or for recovery of materials.

The recycling effort at Hewlett-Packard is also part of the company's Design for Supply Chain program. Among other initiatives in this program, emphasis is placed on product and packaging changes to reduce reverse supply chain and environmental costs. For example, design changes have increased the recycling of its popular ink-jet supplies by 25 percent.

Dependability Dependability is the consistency of replenishment. This is important to all firms in a supply chain—and to consumers. How often do you return to a store if it fails to have in stock the item you want to purchase? Dependability can be broken into three elements: consistent lead time, safe delivery, and complete delivery. Consistent service allows planning (such as appropriate inventory levels), whereas inconsistencies create surprises. Intermediaries may be willing to accept longer lead times if they know about them in advance and can thus make plans.

Communication Communication is a two-way link between the buyer and seller that helps in monitoring service and anticipating future needs. Status reports on orders are a typical example of communication between the buyer and seller.

Convenience The concept of convenience for a supply chain manager means that there should be a minimum of effort on the part of the buyer in doing business with the seller. Is it easy for the customer to order? Are the products available from many outlets? Will the seller arrange all necessary details, such as transportation? This customer service factor has promoted the use of **vendor-managed inventory (VMI)**, whereby the *supplier* determines the product amount and assortment a customer (such as a retailer) needs and automatically delivers the appropriate items.

Campbell Soup's system illustrates how VMI works.[18] Every morning, retailers electronically inform the company of their demand for all Campbell products and the inventory levels in their distribution centers. Campbell uses that information to forecast future demand and determine which products need replenishment based on upper and lower inventory limits established with each retailer. Trucks leave the Campbell shipping plant that afternoon and arrive at the retailer's distribution centers with the required replenishments the same day.

CLOSING THE LOOP: REVERSE LOGISTICS

The flow of products in a supply chain does not end with the ultimate consumer or industrial user. Companies today recognize that a supply chain can work in reverse. **Reverse logistics** is a process of reclaiming recyclable and reusable materials, returns, and reworks from the point of consumption or use for repair, remanufacturing, redistribution, or disposal. The effect of reverse logistics can be seen in the reduced waste in landfills and lowered operating costs for companies. The Making Responsible Decisions box on the previous page describes the successful reverse logistics initiative at Hewlett-Packard.[19]

QR 15-3
UPS Video

Companies such as Motorola and Nokia (return and reuse of mobile phones), and Caterpillar, Xerox, and IBM (remanufacturing and recycling) have implemented acclaimed reverse logistics programs.[20] Other firms have enlisted third-party logistics providers such as UPS, FedEx, and Penske Logistics to handle this process along with other supply chain functions. GNB Technologies, Inc., a manufacturer of lead-acid batteries for automobiles and boats, has outsourced much of its supply chain activity to UPS Supply Chain Services.[21] The company contracts with UPS to manage its shipments between plants, distribution centers, recycling centers, and retailers. This includes movement of both new batteries and used products destined for recycling and covers both truck and railroad shipments. This partnership, along with the initiatives of other battery makers, has paid economic and ecological dividends. By recycling 90 percent of the lead from used batteries, manufacturers have kept the demand for new lead in check, thereby holding down costs to consumers. Also, solid waste management costs and the environmental impact of lead in landfills are reduced.

learning review

15-9. What is the principal difference between a marketing channel and a supply chain?

15-10. The choice of a supply chain involves what three steps?

15-11. A manager's key task is to balance which four customer service factors against which six logistics cost factors?

LEARNING OBJECTIVES REVIEW

LO 15-1 *Explain what is meant by a marketing channel of distribution and why intermediaries are needed.*

A marketing channel of distribution, or simply a marketing channel, consists of individuals and firms involved in the process of making a product or service available for use or consumption by consumers or industrial users. Intermediaries make possible the flow of products from producers to buyers by performing three basic functions. The transactional function involves buying, selling, and risk taking because intermediaries stock merchandise in anticipation of sales. The logistical function involves the gathering, storing, and dispensing of products. The facilitating function assists producers in making products and services more attractive to buyers. The performance of these functions by intermediaries creates time, place, form, and possession utility for consumers.

LO 15-2 *Distinguish among traditional marketing channels, electronic marketing channels, and different types of vertical marketing systems.*

Traditional marketing channels describe the route taken by products and services from producers to buyers. This route can range from a direct channel with no intermediaries, because a producer and the ultimate consumer deal directly with each other, to indirect channels where intermediaries (agents, wholesalers, distributors, or retailers) are inserted between a producer and consumer and perform numerous channel functions. Electronic marketing channels employ the Internet to make products and services available for consumption or use by consumer or business buyers. Vertical marketing systems are professionally managed and centrally coordinated marketing channels designed to achieve channel economies and maximum marketing impact. There are three major types of vertical marketing systems (VMSs). A corporate VMS combines successive stages of production and distribution under a single ownership. A contractual VMS exists when independent production and distribution firms integrate their efforts on a contractual basis to obtain greater functional economies and marketing impact than they could achieve alone. An administered VMS achieves coordination at successive stages of production and distribution by the size and influence of one channel member rather than through ownership.

LO 15-3 *Describe factors that marketing executives consider when selecting and managing a marketing channel.*
Marketing executives consider three questions when selecting and managing a marketing channel and intermediaries. (1) Which channel and intermediaries will provide the best coverage of the target market? Marketers typically choose one of three levels of market coverage: intensive, selective, or exclusive distribution. (2) Which channel and intermediaries will best satisfy the buying requirements of the target market? These buying requirements fall into four categories: information, convenience, variety, and pre- or postsale services. (3) Which channel and intermediaries will be the most profitable? Here marketers look at the margins earned (revenues minus cost) for each channel member and for the channel as a whole.

LO 15-4 *Explain what supply chain and logistics management are and how they relate to marketing strategy.*
A supply chain refers to the various firms involved in performing the various activities required to create and deliver a product or service to consumers or industrial users. Supply chain management is the integration and organization of information and logistics across firms for the purpose of creating value for consumers. Logistics involves those activities that focus on getting the right amount of the right products to the right place at the right time at the lowest possible cost. Logistics management includes the coordination of the flows of both inbound and outbound products, an emphasis on making these flows cost effective, and customer service. A company's supply chain follows from a clearly defined marketing strategy. The alignment of a company's supply chain with its marketing strategy involves three steps. First, a supply chain must reflect the needs of the customer segment being served. Second, a company must understand what a supply chain is designed to do well. Supply chains range from those that emphasize being responsive to customer requirements and demands to those that emphasize efficiency with the goal of supplying products at the lowest possible delivered cost. Finally, a supply chain must be consistent with the targeted customer's needs and the company's marketing strategy. The Dell and Walmart examples in the chapter illustrate how this alignment is achieved by two market leaders.

FOCUSING ON KEY TERMS

channel conflict p. 397
customer service p. 404
disintermediation p. 398
dual distribution p. 391
exclusive distribution p. 395
intensive distribution p. 395
logistics p. 400
marketing channel p. 386
multichannel marketing p. 391
reverse logistics p. 406
selective distribution p. 395
supply chain p. 400
total logistics cost p. 404
vendor-managed inventory (VMI) p. 405
vertical marketing systems p. 392

APPLYING MARKETING KNOWLEDGE

1 A distributor for Celanese Chemical Company stores large quantities of chemicals, blends these chemicals to satisfy the requests of customers, and delivers the blends to a customer's warehouse within 24 hours of receiving an order. What utilities does this distributor provide?

2 Suppose the president of a carpet manufacturing firm has asked you to look into the possibility of bypassing the firm's wholesalers (who sell to carpet, department, and furniture stores) and selling direct to these stores. What caution would you voice on this matter, and what type of information would you gather before making this decision?

3 What type of channel conflict is likely to be caused by dual distribution, and what type of conflict can be reduced by direct distribution? Why?

4 How does the channel captain idea differ among corporate, administered, and contractual vertical marketing systems with particular reference to the use of the different forms of influence available to firms?

5 List the customer service factors that would be vital to buyers in the following types of companies: (*a*) manufacturing, (*b*) retailing, (*c*) hospitals, and (*d*) construction.

BUILDING YOUR MARKETING PLAN

Does your marketing plan involve selecting channels and intermediaries? If the answer is "no," read no further and do not include this element in your plan. If the answer is "yes:"

1 Identify which channel and intermediaries will provide the best coverage of the target market for your product or service.

2 Specify which channel and intermediaries will best satisfy the important buying requirements of the target market.

3 Determine which channel and intermediaries will be the most profitable.

4 Select your channel(s) and intermediary(ies).

5 If inventory is involved, (*a*) identify the three or four major kinds of inventory needed for your organization (retail stock, finished products, raw materials, supplies, and so on), and (*b*) suggest ways to reduce their costs.

6 (*a*) Rank the four customer service factors (time, dependability, communication, and convenience) from most important to least important from your customers' point of view, and (*b*) identify actions for the one or two factors that are the most important in regard to your product or service.

VIDEO CASE 15 Amazon: Delivering the Goods . . . Millions of Times a Day

QR 15-4
Amazon
Video Case

"The new economy means that the balance of power has shifted toward the consumer," explains Jeff Bezos, CEO of Amazon.com, Inc. The global online retailer is a pioneer of fast, convenient, low-cost virtual shopping that has attracted millions of consumers. Of course, while Amazon has changed the way many people shop, the company still faces the traditional and daunting task of creating a seamless flow of deliveries to its customers—often millions of times each day.

THE COMPANY

Bezos started Amazon.com with a simple idea: to use the Internet to transform book buying into the fastest, easiest, and most enjoyable shopping experience possible. The company was incorporated in 1994 and opened its virtual doors in July 1995. At the forefront of a huge growth of dot-com businesses, Amazon pursued a get-big-fast business strategy. Sales grew rapidly and Amazon began adding products and services other than books. In fact, Amazon soon set its goal on being the world's most customer-centric company, where customers can find and discover anything they might want to buy online.

Today Amazon claims to have "Earth's Biggest Selection™" of products and services in the following categories: Books; Movies, Music & Games; Digital Downloads; Kindle; Computers & Office; Electronics; Home & Garden; Grocery, Health & Beauty; Toys, Kids & Baby; Clothing, Shoes & Jewelry; Sports & Outdoors;

and Tools, Auto & Industrial. Other services allow customers to:

- Search for a product or brand using all or part of its name.
- Place orders with one click using the "Buy Now with 1-Click" button.
- Receive personalized recommendations based on past purchases through opt-in e-mails.

These products and services have attracted millions of people around the globe. This has made Amazon.com, along with its international sites in Austria, Canada, the United Kingdom, Germany, Japan, France, and China, the leading online retailer.

SUPPLY CHAIN AND LOGISTICS MANAGEMENT AT AMAZON.COM

What happens after an order is submitted on Amazon's website but before it arrives at the customer's door? A lot. Amazon.com maintains huge distribution, or "fulfillment," centers where it keeps inventory of millions of products. This is one of the key differences between Amazon.com and some of its competitors—it actually stocks products. So Amazon must manage the flow of products from its 15 million suppliers to its distribution and customer service centers with the flow of customer orders from the distribution centers to individuals' homes or offices.

The process begins with the suppliers. "Amazon's goal is to collaborate with our suppliers to increase efficiencies and improve inventory turnover," explains Amazon's vice president of supply chain. "We want to bring to suppliers the kind of interactive relationship that has inspired customers to shop with us." For example, Amazon is using software to more accurately forecast purchasing patterns by region, which allows it to give its suppliers better information about delivery dates and volumes. Before the development of this software, 12 percent of incoming inventory was sent to the wrong location, leading to lost time and delayed orders. Now only 4 percent of the incoming inventory is mishandled.

At the same time, Amazon has been improving the part of the process that sorts the products into the individual orders. Amazon's senior vice president of operations says, "We spent the whole year really focused on increasing productivity." Again, technology has been essential. According to the senior vice president of operations, "The speed at which telecommunications networks allow us to pass information back and forth has enabled us to do the real-time work that we keep talking about. In the past, it would have taken too long to get this many items through a system." Once the order is in the system, computers ensure that all items are included in the box before it is taped and labeled. A network of trucks and regional postal hubs then concludes the process with delivery of the order.

The success of Amazon's logistics and supply chain management activities may be most evident during the year-end holiday shopping season. Amazon received orders for 37.9 million items between November 9 and December 21 one year, including orders for 450,000 Harry Potter books and products, and orders for 36,000 items placed just before the holiday delivery deadline. Well over 99 percent of the orders were shipped and delivered on time.

AMAZON'S CHALLENGES

Several sales growth options are possible for Amazon. First, it can continue to pursue growth through sales of hundreds of thousands of electronic books, magazines, and newspapers through its new Kindle devices and store. Second, Amazon can continue its expansion into new product and service categories. Recently, it launched its Outdoor Recreation store—the latest in over a dozen such categories. This approach would prevent Amazon from becoming a niche merchant and position it as a true online retail department store. Third, Amazon can increase the availability of products from other retailers through its Amazon WebStore. These retailers can create a customized, branded website that uses Amazon eCommerce technology. Finally, Amazon can pursue a strategy of providing access to its existing operations for other retailers through its Fulfillment by Amazon (FBA) service. Online retailers store their products at Amazon's distribution centers, and when they sell a product—Amazon ships it!

Amazon.com has come a long way toward proving that online retailing can work. Its logistics and supply chain management activities have provided Amazon with a cost-effective and efficient distribution system that combines automation and communication technology with superior customer service. To continue its drive to increase future sales, profits, and customer service, Amazon acquired Zappos.com in mid-2009. According to Bezos, "We see great opportunities for both companies to learn from each other and create even better experiences for our customers."

Questions

1 How do Amazon.com's logistics and supply chain management activities help the company create value for its customers?

2 What systems did Amazon develop to improve the flow of products from suppliers to Amazon distribution centers? What systems improved the flow of orders from the distribution centers to customers?

3 Why will logistics and supply chain management play an important role in the future success of Amazon.com?

16 Retailing and Wholesaling

LEARNING OBJECTIVES

After reading this chapter you should be able to:

LO 16-1 Identify retailers in terms of the utilities they provide.

LO 16-2 Explain the alternative ways to classify retail outlets.

LO 16-3 Describe the many methods of nonstore retailing.

LO 16-4 Classify retailers in terms of the retail positioning matrix, and specify retailing mix actions.

LO 16-5 Explain changes in retailing with the wheel of retailing and the retail life cycle concepts.

LO 16-6 Describe the types of firms that perform wholesaling activities and their functions.

IF YOU LIKE TO SHOP, YOU WILL LOVE GOOGLE GLASS(ES)!

You've shopped in a store. You've also shopped online. Now you can enjoy the benefits of both thanks to new technologies such as Google Glass!

Google Glass products resemble a pair of eyeglasses with a small display screen visible to the wearer. Image and voice recognition capabilities identify relevant information to display on the screen. The sound, video, and graphics accessed through the glasses create an *augmented reality* that overlays the physical, real-world environment being viewed at the same time. When used by shoppers, this technology adds rich content to the shopping experience, improving the purchase decision process. It's a perfect way to combine the fast, personalized, and customized information consumers enjoy when they shop online with the traditional brick-and-mortar in-store shopping experience!

In addition to the head-worn displays being developed by Google, other companies are developing augmented reality software and apps for smartphones, tablet devices, and 3D projectors. IBM, for example, is developing a mobile app that uses the camera in a smartphone to identify a product and then display information about the product (e.g., price, nutritional value, etc.) based on preferences specified by the consumer. Similarly, a company called Aurasma is developing image and pattern recognition technology to identify real-world objects and then activate interactive animations for consumers to view. Augmented reality technology platforms such as these are being used by Kellogg's, to provide additional information on 80 million cereal boxes; by Taylor Swift, to support her Wonderstruck fragrance; and by the Rolling Stones, to augment an advertising campaign in 50 cities around the world.

Retailers are excited about the opportunity to enhance the customer experience. IKEA's new catalog allows consumers to access information, videos, and 3D models through a tablet image recognition app. A Japanese furniture manufacturer is developing an app that allows customers to take a picture of a room in their house and then overlay digital images of furniture items in the photo to simulate the appearance of furniture arrangements before making a purchase. Toshiba offers a similar app that allows customers to see what a television will look like in their home. In addition, clothing retailers are developing augmented reality technology that allows consumers to take pictures of themselves and then superimpose images of clothing in the photo. The convenience of the technology encourages customers to try styles, combinations, and colors they might not take time to actually put on in a brick-and-mortar store.

QR 16-1
Google Glass Video

Augmented reality has the potential to significantly change the way consumers shop by making the experience faster, more effective, and more enjoyable. According to industry expert Stuart Nugent, "The future of augmented reality lies in offering potential customers much more valuable information about the products they're viewing."[1]

These are just a few examples of the many exciting changes occurring in retailing today. This chapter examines the critical role of retailing in the marketplace and the challenging decisions retailers face as they strive to create value for customers.

What types of products will consumers buy through catalogs, television, the Internet, or by telephone? In what type of store will consumers look for products they don't buy directly? How important is the location of the store? Will customers expect services such as alterations, delivery, installation, or repair? What price should be charged for each product? These are difficult and important questions that are an integral part of retailing. In the channel of distribution, retailing is where the customer meets the product. It is through retailing that exchange (a central aspect of marketing) occurs. **Retailing** includes all activities involved in selling, renting, and providing products and services to ultimate consumers for personal, family, or household use.

THE VALUE OF RETAILING

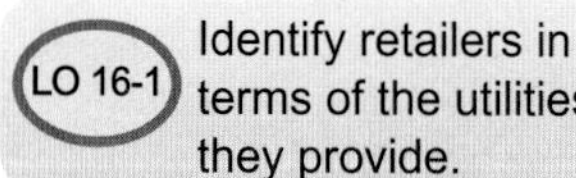
LO 16-1 Identify retailers in terms of the utilities they provide.

Retailing is an important marketing activity. Not only do producers and consumers meet through retailing actions, but retailing also creates customer value and has a significant impact on the economy. To consumers, the value of retailing is in the form of utilities provided (see Figure 16–1). Retailing's economic value is represented by the people employed in retailing as well as by the total amount of money exchanged in retail sales (see Figure 16–2).

Consumer Utilities Offered by Retailing

FIGURE 16–1
Which retailer best provides which utilities?

The utilities provided by retailers create value for consumers. Time, place, form, and possession utilities are offered by most retailers in varying degrees, but one utility is often emphasized more than others. Look at Figure 16–1 to see how

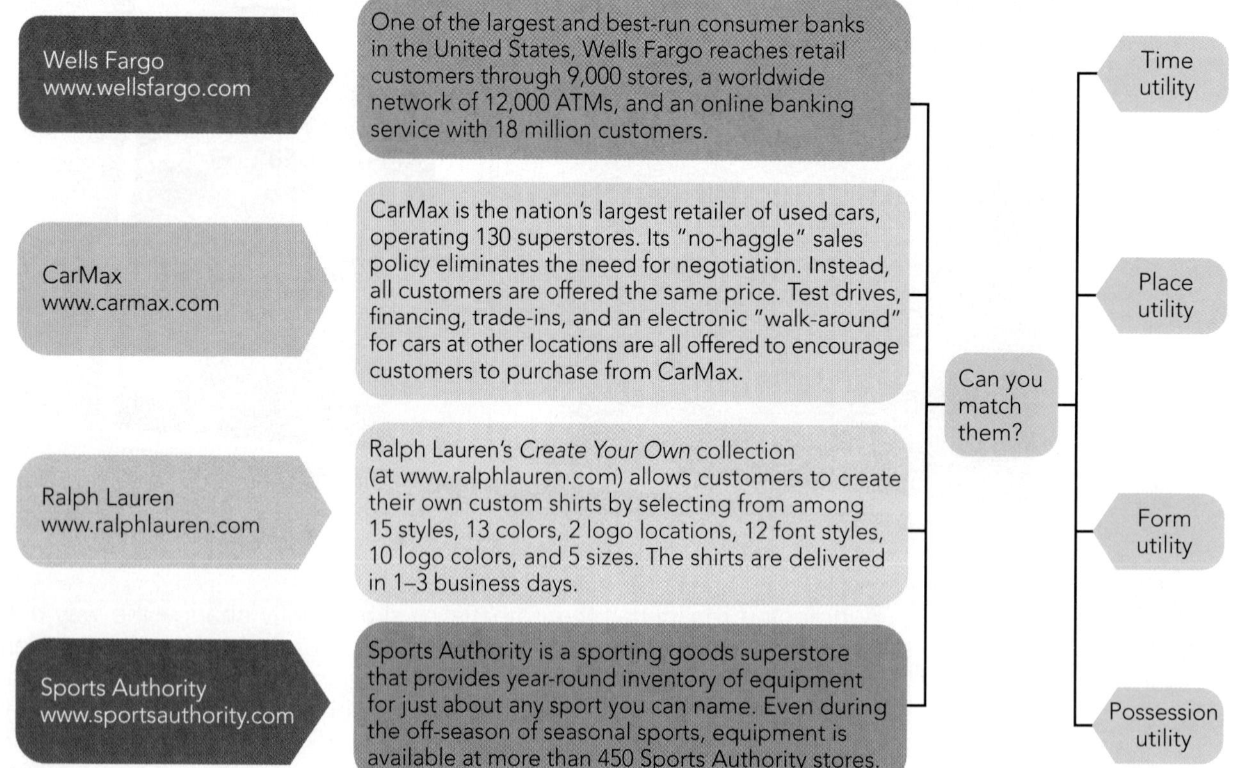

Wells Fargo
www.wellsfargo.com
One of the largest and best-run consumer banks in the United States, Wells Fargo reaches retail customers through 9,000 stores, a worldwide network of 12,000 ATMs, and an online banking service with 18 million customers.
CarMax
www.carmax.com
CarMax is the nation's largest retailer of used cars, operating 130 superstores. Its "no-haggle" sales policy eliminates the need for negotiation. Instead, all customers are offered the same price. Test drives, financing, trade-ins, and an electronic "walk-around" for cars at other locations are all offered to encourage customers to purchase from CarMax.
Ralph Lauren
www.ralphlauren.com
Ralph Lauren's Create Your Own collection (at www.ralphlauren.com) allows customers to create their own custom shirts by selecting from among 15 styles, 13 colors, 2 logo locations, 12 font styles, 10 logo colors, and 5 sizes. The shirts are delivered in 1–3 business days.
Sports Authority
www.sportsauthority.com
Sports Authority is a sporting goods superstore that provides year-round inventory of equipment for just about any sport you can name. Even during the off-season of seasonal sports, equipment is available at more than 450 Sports Authority stores.
Can you match them?
Time utility
Place utility
Form utility
Possession utility

Type of retailer	Sales ($ in billions)
Sporting goods, book, and music stores	90.1
Furniture and home furnishing stores	95.6
Electronics stores	99.2
Pharmacies and drugstores	227.9
Clothing and accessory stores	239.4
Building material and hardware stores	294.2
Nonstore retailers	440.0
Food services and drinking places	529.7
Gasoline stations	547.0
General merchandise stores	632.0
Food and beverage stores	634.2
Automotive dealers	759.8

0 200 400 600 800 1000

Sales ($ in billions)

FIGURE 16–2
Are you surprised by the relative sales of different types of retailers?

QR 16-2
CarMax Video

well you can match the retailer with the utility being emphasized in the description.

Providing mini banks in supermarkets, as Wells Fargo does, puts the bank's products and services close to the consumer, providing place utility. By providing financing or leasing and taking used cars as trade-ins, CarMax makes the purchase easier and provides possession utility. Form utility—production or alteration of a product—is offered by Ralph Lauren through its online *Create Your Own* program, which offers shirts that meet each customer's specifications. Finding the right sporting equipment during the off-season is the time utility provided by Sports Authority. Many retailers offer a combination of the four basic utilities. Some supermarkets, for example, offer convenient locations (place utility); are open 24 hours a day (time utility); customize purchases in the bakery, deli, and florist (form utility); and allow several payment and credit options (possession utility).

Carrefour is one of the largest retailers outside the United States.

The Global Economic Impact of Retailing

Retailing is important to the U.S. and global economies. Four of the 40 largest businesses in the United States are retailers (Walmart, Costco, Home Depot, and Target). Walmart's $469 billion in annual sales in 2012 surpassed the gross domestic product of all but 29 countries for that same year. Walmart, Costco, Home Depot, and Target together have more than 3 million employees—more than the combined populations of Jacksonville, Florida; El Paso, Texas; and Stockton, California.[2] Figure 16–2 shows that many types of retailers, including food stores, automobile dealers, and general merchandise outlets, are also significant contributors to the U.S. economy.[3]

Outside the United States large retailers include Aeon in Japan, Carrefour in France, Metro Group in Germany, and Tesco in Britain.[4] In emerging economies such as China and Mexico, a combination of local and global retailers is evolving. Walmart, for example, has more than 6,200 stores outside the United States, including stores in Argentina, Brazil, China, India, Japan, Mexico, and the United Kingdom. Despite the presence of these large retailers, however, most international markets are dominated by local retailers.[5]

learning review

16-1. When Ralph Lauren makes shirts to a customer's exact preferences, what utility is provided?

16-2. Two measures of the impact of retailing in the global economy are _____________ and ______________.

CLASSIFYING RETAIL OUTLETS

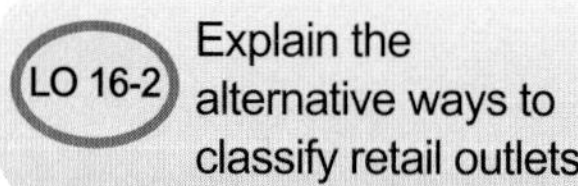

LO 16-2
Explain the alternative ways to classify retail outlets.

For manufacturers, consumers, and the economy, retailing is an important component of marketing that has several variations. Because of the large number of alternative forms of retailing, it is easier to understand the differences among retail institutions by recognizing that outlets can be classified in several ways. First, **form of ownership** distinguishes retail outlets based on whether independent retailers, corporate chains, or contractual systems own the outlet. Second, **level of service** is used to describe the degree of service provided to the customer. Three levels of service are provided by self-, limited-, and full-service retailers. Finally, the type of **merchandise line** describes how many different types of products a store carries and in what assortment. The alternative types of outlets are discussed in greater detail in the following pages. For many consumers today, retail outlets are also evaluated in terms of their environmentally friendly, or green, activities, in addition to their level of service and merchandise line. The Making Responsible Decisions box gives examples of the green activities of several retailers.[6]

Form of Ownership

There are three general forms of retail ownership—independent retailer, corporate chain, and contractual systems.

Independent Retailer One of the most common forms of retail ownership is the independent business owned by an individual. Independent retailers account for most of the 1.1 million retail establishments in the United States and include hardware stores, convenience stores, clothing stores, and computer and software stores. In addition, there are 26,700 jewelry stores, 18,500 florists, and 22,100 sporting goods and hobby stores. For the independent retailer, the advantage of this form of ownership is simple: The owner is the boss. For customers, the independent store can offer convenience, personal service, and lifestyle compatibility.[7]

Corporate Chain A second form of ownership, the corporate chain, involves multiple outlets under common ownership. Macy's, Inc., for example, operates 810 Macy's department stores in 45 states. Macy's also owns 37 Bloomingdale's, which compete with other chain stores such as Saks Fifth Avenue and Neiman Marcus.

In a chain operation, centralization in decision making and purchasing is common. Chain stores have advantages in dealing with manufacturers, particularly as the size of the chain grows. A large chain can bargain with a manufacturer to obtain good service or volume discounts on orders. Target's large volume makes it a strong negotiator with manufacturers of most products. For consumers, the buying power of chains translates into lower prices compared with other types of stores. Consumers also benefit in

Making Responsible Decisions

sustainability

What Color Is Your Retailer? Is It Green?

You might remember when "going green" was an expression used by consumers to describe their purchase and use of environmentally friendly products. Initially, retailers responded by offering products that matched consumers' new environmental interests. Over time, however, retailers have come to realize that consumers also want to purchase those products from like-minded retailers. Today, many retailers are developing comprehensive and sophisticated business practices that reflect a new focus on social and environmental responsibility.

U.S. GREEN RETAIL ASSOCIATION® GREEN CERTIFIED RETAIL OPERATIONS GUIDE

The U.S. Green Retail Association offers guidance for retailers implementing new practices, and it also provides a third-party certification that recognizes a commitment to "green" values. Some practices are intuitive and simple, such as encouraging the use of reusable shopping bags, installing LED lighting, and using nontoxic cleaning products. Many retailers are even using recyclable materials for credit and gift cards, rather than plastic. Other practices, such as using more economical delivery vehicles to reduce CO_2 emissions, using rainwater for landscape maintenance, or finding alternative uses for landfill waste, require a more concerted effort. Very often, however, these environmental initiatives also have financial benefits. When Home Depot switched light displays to CFL and LED light bulbs, painted the roofs of stores white, and installed solar panels, it reduced its energy use by 20 percent.

Many retailers are also requiring that their suppliers make similar efforts and meet the same standards. When Walmart noticed that some packaging led to waste, it required its toy suppliers to trim one square inch of packaging from their lines and reduce packaging by 3,500 tons. In addition, Walmart is taking these green initiatives overseas. For example, the company is working with the Chinese government to ensure that suppliers from that country comply with Chinese environmental laws and regulations.

Do sustainability practices such as these influence your purchase decisions? The issue is becoming so important that *Newsweek* now publishes rankings of retailers with the best green practices. Office Depot, Staples, Best Buy, Home Depot, and Walmart were at the top of the most recent list. Are your favorite retailers "green"?

dealing with chains because there are multiple outlets with similar merchandise and consistent management policies.

Retailing has become a high-tech business for many large chains. Walmart, for example, has developed a sophisticated inventory management and cost control system that allows rapid price changes for each product in every store. In addition, stores such as Walmart and Target are implementing pioneering new technologies such as radio frequency identification (RFID) tags to improve the quality of information available about products.

Contractual Systems Contractual systems involve independently owned stores that band together to act like a chain. Recall that in Chapter 15, we discussed three kinds of contractual vertical marketing systems: retailer-sponsored cooperatives, wholesaler-sponsored voluntary chains, and franchises (see Figure 15–6). One retailer-sponsored cooperative is Associated Grocers, which consists of neighborhood grocers that all agree with several other independent grocers to buy their goods directly from food manufacturers. In this way, members can take advantage of volume discounts commonly available to chains and also give the impression of being a large chain, which may be viewed more favorably by some consumers. Wholesaler-sponsored voluntary chains such as Independent Grocers Alliance (IGA) try to achieve similar benefits.

In a franchise system, an individual or firm (the franchisee) contracts with a parent company (the franchisor) to set up a business or retail outlet. The franchisor usually assists in selecting the location, setting up the store or facility, advertising, and training personnel. The franchisee usually pays a one-time franchise fee and an annual royalty, usually tied to the franchise's sales. There are two general types of franchises: *business-format franchises*, such as McDonald's, RadioShack, and Subway, and *product-distribution franchises*, such as a Ford dealership or a Coca-Cola distributor.

Franchise	Type of Business	Total Start-up Cost	Number of Franchises
Hampton Hotels	Hotels	$3,700,000–$13,520,000	1,917
Subway	Sandwiches	$85,200–$260,350	39,447
Jiffy Lube Int'l	Fast oil changes	$196,500–$304,000	2,086
7-Eleven	Convenience stores	$30,800–$1,500,000	47,298
Supercuts	Hair salons	$103,550–$196,500	2,316

FIGURE 16–3
The top five franchises in the United States vary from hotels to hair salons.

In business-format franchising, the franchisor provides step-by-step procedures for most aspects of the business and guidelines for the most likely decisions a franchisee will face. In product-distribution franchising, the franchisor provides a few general guidelines and the franchisee is much more independent.

Subway is a popular business-format franchisor.

Franchising is attractive because it offers an opportunity for people to enter a well-known, established business for which managerial advice is provided. Also, the franchise fee may be less than the cost of setting up an independent business. The International Franchise Association recently reported that there are 757,000 franchised businesses in the United States, which generate $802 billion in annual sales and employ more than 8 million people. Franchising is popular in international markets also: More than half of all U.S. franchisors have operations in other countries. What is one of the fastest-growing franchises? Subway now has 39,447 locations, including 13,549 stores outside the United States.[8]

Franchise fees paid to the franchisor can range from $15,000 for a Subway franchise to $45,000 for a McDonald's restaurant franchise. When the fees are combined with other costs such as real estate and equipment, however, the total investment can be much higher. Franchisees also pay an ongoing royalty fee that ranges from 5 percent for a Papa John's pizza franchise to 30 percent for an H&R Block tax preparation franchise. Figure 16–3 shows the top five franchises, as rated by *Entrepreneur* magazine, based on factors such as size, financial strength, stability, years in business, and costs. By selling franchises, an organization reduces the cost of expansion but loses some control. A good franchisor, however, will maintain strong control of the outlets in terms of delivery and presentation of merchandise and try to enhance recognition of the franchise name.[9]

Redbox provides a service without clerks.

Level of Service

Although most customers have little reason to notice form of ownership differences among retailers, they are typically aware of differences in terms of level of service. In some department stores, such as Loehmann's, very few services are provided. Some grocery stores, such as the Cub Foods chain, encourage customers to bag their groceries themselves. In contrast, outlets such as Neiman Marcus provide a wide range of customer services, from gift wrapping to wardrobe consultation.

Self-Service Self-service requires that customers perform many functions during the purchase process. Warehouse clubs such as Costco, for example, are usually self-service, with all nonessential customer services eliminated. Many gas stations, supermarkets, and airlines today also have self-service lanes and terminals. Video retailer Redbox has 35,500 kiosks throughout the United States—and operates without a single clerk. New forms of self-service are being developed at convenience stores, fast-food restaurants, and even coffee shops! Shop24 is building self-service, automated convenience stores in 15 countries, including the United States. At Pizza Hut, you can place an order through an iPhone app or on the website. Similarly, there will be more than 2,000 Marley Coffee Automated Cafes in the next two years. In general, the trend is toward retailing experiences that make customers co-creators of the value they receive. Experts estimate that automated sales will reach $1.1 trillion by 2015.[10]

Limited Service Limited-service outlets provide some services, such as credit and merchandise return, but not others, such as clothing alterations. General merchandise stores such as Walmart, Kmart, and Target are usually considered limited service outlets. Customers are responsible for most shopping activities, although salespeople are available in departments such as consumer electronics, jewelry, and lawn and garden.

Full Service Full-service retailers, which include most specialty stores and department stores, provide many services to their customers. Neiman Marcus, Nordstrom, and Saks Fifth Avenue, for example, all rely on better service to sell more distinctive, higher-margin goods and to retain their customers. Nordstrom offers a wide variety of services, including on-site alterations and tailoring; free exchanges and easy returns; gift cards; credit cards through Nordstrom Bank; a 7-days-a-week customer service line; a live chat line with beauty, design, and wedding specialists; online shopping with in-store pickup; catalogs; and a four-level loyalty program called Nordstrom Fashion Rewards. Some Nordstrom stores also offer a "Personal Stylist" department, which provides shopping assistants for consumers who need help with style, color, and size selection, as well as a concierge service for assistance with anything else. Nordstrom stores typically have 50 percent more salespeople on the floor than similarly sized stores, and the salespeople are renowned for their professional and personalized attention to customers. Nordstrom also offers e-mail, an RSS (rich site summary) feed, Twitter messages, a blog, a website, and mobile apps to notify customers about fashion trends, new merchandise, and sales. In the next few years, to continue to change its customer service to match its customers' interests, the company plans to replace cash registers with mobile checkout technology.[11]

Type of Merchandise Line

Retail outlets also vary by their merchandise lines, the key distinction being the breadth and depth of the items offered to customers (see Figure 16–4). **Depth of product line** means the store carries a large assortment of each item, such as a shoe store that offers running shoes, dress shoes, and children's shoes. **Breadth of product line** refers to the variety of different items a store carries, such as appliances and books.

Depth of Line Stores that carry a considerable assortment (depth) of a related line of items are limited-line stores. Sports Authority sporting goods stores carry considerable depth in sports equipment ranging from weight-lifting accessories to running shoes. Stores that carry tremendous depth in one primary line of merchandise are single-line

FIGURE 16–4
Stores vary in terms of the breadth and depth of their merchandise lines.

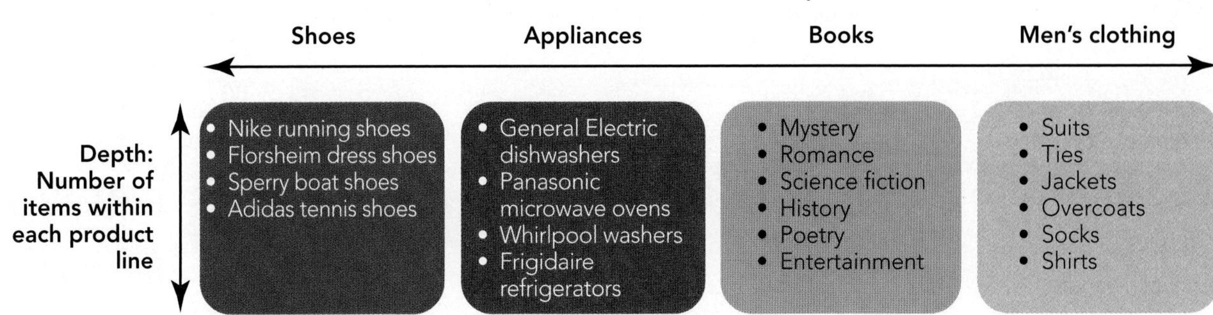

Staples is the category killer in office supplies because it dominates the market in that category.

stores. Victoria's Secret, a nationwide chain, carries great depth in women's lingerie. Both limited- and single-line stores are often referred to as *specialty outlets*.

Specialty discount outlets focus on one type of product, such as electronics (Best Buy), office supplies (Staples), or books (Barnes & Noble), at very competitive prices. These outlets are referred to in the trade as *category killers* because they often dominate the market. Best Buy, for example, is the largest consumer electronics retailer with more than 1,400 stores, Staples operates more than 2,000 office supply stores, and Barnes & Noble is the largest book retailer. Interesting trends in this form of retailing include a shift to smaller stores, such as Best Buy Mobile stores, and the use of price matching to compete with online retailers.[12]

Breadth of Line Stores that carry a broad product line, with limited depth, are referred to as *general merchandise stores*. For example, large department stores such as Dillard's, Macy's, and Neiman Marcus carry a wide range of different types of products but not unusual sizes. The breadth and depth of merchandise lines are important decisions for a retailer. Traditionally, outlets carried related lines of goods. Today, however, **scrambled merchandising**, offering several unrelated product lines in a single store, is common. For example, the modern drugstore carries food, camera equipment, magazines, paper products, toys, small hardware items, and pharmaceuticals. Supermarkets sell flowers and videos and print photos, in addition to selling groceries.

A form of scrambled merchandising, the **hypermarket**, has been successful in Europe. Hypermarkets are large stores (often more than 200,000 square feet) based on a simple concept: Offer "everything under one roof," thus eliminating the need to stop at more than one location. These stores provide variety, quality, and low prices for groceries and general merchandise items. Carrefour, one of the largest retailers in this category, has 1,366 hypermarkets, including 220 in France, 173 in Spain, and 218 in China. The growth of hypermarkets may be slowing in Europe, however, as consumers' interest in smaller stores and convenient locations has increased. In response, retailers have been cutting prices on food to attract customers and lure them away from competitors. Despite its declining popularity in some parts of the world, the original hypermarket concept is still growing in popularity in many countries; in China, for example, Carrefour, Tesco, and Walmart are expanding the number of stores they operate.[13]

QR 16-3
Walmart Video

In the United States, retailers have discovered that shoppers are uncomfortable with the huge size of hypermarkets. In response, they have developed a variation of the hypermarket called the *supercenter*, which combines a typical merchandise store with a full-size grocery store. Walmart, Kmart, and Target now use this concept at 3,211 Walmart Supercenters, 25 Kmart Supercenters, and more than 250 SuperTarget stores. Due to the increasing popularity of online retailers, however, the large size of these supercenters is no longer a certain advantage; Amazon.com, for example, is able to offer an even larger selection than these huge stores. Also, due to modern supply chain management techniques, smaller retailers are now able to keep shelves stocked without a lot of inventory. As customer interest shifts, retailers are modifying the supercenter concept to accommodate consumers' interest in smaller, more convenient stores. Walmart, for example, is introducing Walmart Express stores, which will stock only best-selling items, and expanding the number of its grocery stores, Walmart Neighborhood Markets. Figure 16–5 shows the differences between the supercenter and hypermarket concepts.[14]

FIGURE 16–5
Hypermarkets are popular in Europe, and supercenters are popular in the United States.

	Hypermarket	Supercenter
Region of Popularity	Europe	United States
Average size	90,000–300,000 sq. ft.	100,000–215,000 sq. ft.
Number of products	20,000–80,000	35,000
Annual revenue	$100,000,000 per store	$60,000,000 per store

Scrambled merchandising is convenient for consumers because it eliminates the number of stops required in a shopping trip. However, for the retailer this merchandising policy means there is competition between very dissimilar types of retail outlets, or **intertype competition**. A local bakery may compete with a department store, discount outlet, or even a local gas station. Scrambled merchandising and intertype competition make it more difficult to be a retailer.

learning review

16-3. Centralized decision making and purchasing are an advantage of ______________ ownership.

16-4. What are some examples of new forms of self-service retailers?

16-5. A shop for big men's clothes carries pants in sizes 40 to 60. Would this be considered a broad or a deep product line?

NONSTORE RETAILING

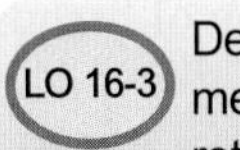

Describe the many methods of nonstore retailing.

Most of the retailing examples discussed thus far in the chapter, such as corporate chains, department stores, and limited- and single-line specialty stores, involve store retailing. Many retailing activities today, however, are not limited to sales in a store. Nonstore retailing occurs outside a retail outlet through activities that involve varying levels of customer and retailer involvement. Figure 16–6 shows six forms of nonstore retailing: automatic vending, direct mail and catalogs, television home shopping, online retailing, telemarketing, and direct selling.

Automatic Vending

Nonstore retailing includes vending machines, or *v-commerce*, which make it possible to serve customers when and where stores cannot. Machine maintenance, operating costs, and location leases can add to the cost of the products, so prices in vending machines are often higher than those in stores. About 31 percent of the products sold from vending machines are cold beverages, another 21 percent are candy and snacks, and

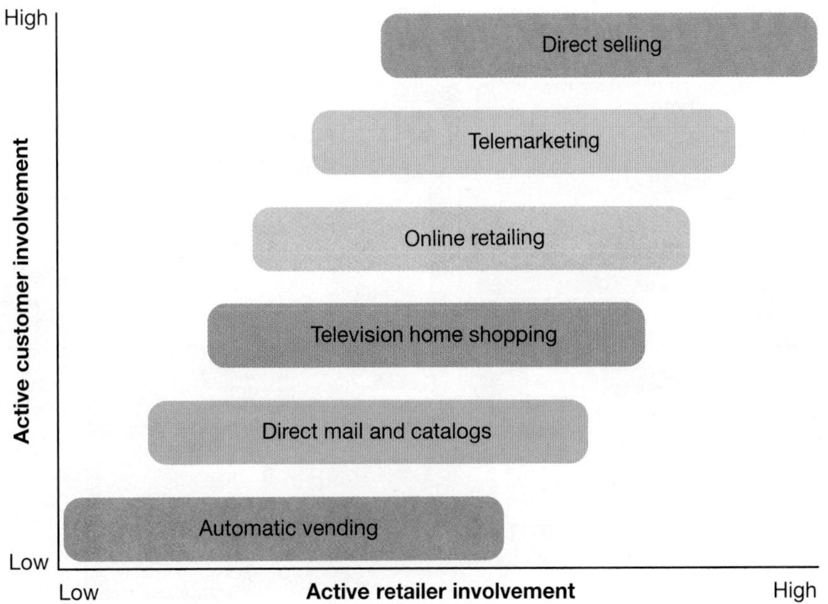

FIGURE 16–6 Many retailing activities do not involve a store. How many forms of nonstore retailing have you used?

Vending machines offer a variety of products. Which types of products are most common in a vending machine? For the answer, see the text.

5 percent are food. Many new types of products are quickly becoming available in vending machines. Best Buy now uses vending machines to sell mobile phone and computer accessories, digital cameras, flash drives, and other consumer electronics products in airports, hospitals, and businesses. Similarly, HealthyYou Vending manufactures machines designed to distribute healthy drinks, snacks, and entrées in offices, health clubs, hospitals, schools, and colleges. The 5.4 million vending machines currently in use in the United States generate more than $19 billion in annual sales.[15]

Improved technology is making vending easier to use. Many vending machines now have touchscreens and credit card readers. In addition, some vending machine companies are testing wireless technology to allow consumers to make vending machine purchases using their mobile phones. Wireless technology is also being used by companies to monitor sales; this information is used to schedule trips to restock machines when items are sold out. Another improvement in vending machines is the trend toward "green" machines, which consume less energy by using more efficient compressors, more efficient lighting, and better insulation. Vending machines are popular with consumers; recent consumer satisfaction research indicates that 82 percent of consumers believe purchasing from a vending machine is equal to or superior to a store purchase. For today's consumers, vending machines represent an extension of brands that are already available in stores, through catalogs, and online.[16]

Direct Mail and Catalogs

QR 16-4
IKEA Video

Direct-mail and catalog retailing has been called "the store that comes to the door." It is attractive for several reasons. First, it can eliminate the cost of a store and clerks. Dell, for example, is one of the largest computer and information technology retailers, and it does not have any stores. Second, direct mail and catalogs improve marketing efficiency through segmentation and targeting, and they create customer value by providing a fast and convenient means of making a purchase. Finally, many catalogs now serve as a tool to encourage consumers to visit a website, a social media page, or even a store. Online retailers such as Zappos, Amazon, and eBay, for example, now offer catalogs. The average U.S. household today receives 24 direct-mail items or catalogs each week. The Direct Marketing Association estimates that direct-mail and catalog retailing creates $642 billion in sales. Direct-mail and catalog retailing is popular outside the United States, also. Furniture retailer IKEA delivered 212 million copies of its catalog in 17 languages to 28 countries last year.[17]

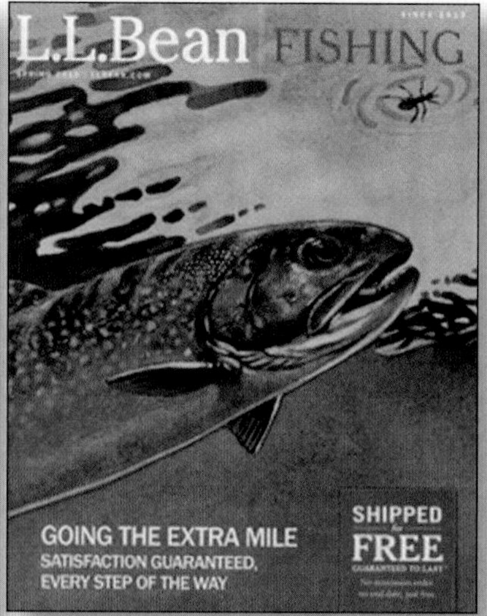

Specialty catalogs appeal to market niches. They create value by providing a fast and convenient way to shop.

Several factors have had an impact on direct-mail and catalog retailing in recent years. The influence of large retailers such as IKEA, Crate and Barrel, L.L. Bean, and others has been positive as their marketing activities have increased the number and variety of products consumers purchase through direct mail and catalogs. Higher paper costs and increases in postage rates, the growing interest in do-not-mail legislation, the concern for "green" mailings and catalogs, and the possibility of the U.S. Postal Service reducing delivery to five days, however, have caused direct-mail and catalog retailers to search for ways to provide additional customer value. One approach has been to focus on proven customers rather than prospective customers. Some merchants, such as Williams-Sonoma, reduce mailings to zip codes that have not been profitable. Another successful approach used by many catalog retailers is to send specialty catalogs to market niches identified in their databases. L.L. Bean, for example, has developed an individual catalog for fly-fishing enthusiasts.[18]

New, creative forms of direct-mail and catalog retailing are also being developed. Sears is investing in social media technologies to make its Wish Book available through smartphones and tablets. In addition, Sears and other retailers are creating digital versions of catalogs, which can be accessed through catalog-aggregating apps such as Google Catalogs. In the future, you will also see merchants using direct mail and catalogs to direct customers to personalized URLs (PURLs), such as www.JohnSmith.offer.com, which are web pages preloaded with information and offerings specific to an individual. To recognize companies that successfully integrate their direct-mail and catalog activities with other marketing activities, *Multichannel Merchant* magazine evaluates hundreds of entries to select the winners of the Multichannel Merchant Awards in 18 categories. Recent winners might be retailers you already know. They include L.L. Bean, EA Sports (Madden NFL), and Fairytale Brownies.[19]

Television Home Shopping

Television home shopping is possible when consumers watch a shopping channel on which products are displayed; orders are then placed over the telephone or the Internet. Currently, the three largest programs are QVC, HSN, and ShopNBC. QVC ("quality, value, convenience") broadcasts live 24 hours each day, 364 days a year, and reaches more than 200 million cable and satellite homes in the United States, United Kingdom, Germany, Japan, and Italy. The company generates sales of $8.3 billion from its 60 million customers by offering more than 1,150 products each week. The television home shopping channels offer apparel, jewelry, cooking, home improvement products, electronics, toys, and even food. Of all these products, the best-selling item ever was a Dell personal computer.[20]

In the past, television home shopping programs attracted mostly 40- to 60-year-old women. To attract a younger audience, QVC has invited celebrities onto the show. For example, Heidi Klum has been on the show promoting her jewelry collection, and Kim, Khloe, and Kourtney Kardashian have been hosts selling their apparel line. Rapper 50 Cent recently appeared on the show to sell his signature headphones. Broadcasting events such as the Red Carpet Style show at the Four Seasons Hotel in Beverly Hills also helps attract new customers. In addition, QVC supports its television program with retail stores, a website, mobile apps, text alerts, and online chats during programming. Similarly, Home Shopping Network now offers a multiplatform shopping experience. Some experts suggest that television shopping programs are becoming a modern version of door-to-door retailing by combining elements of reality TV programs, talk shows, and infomercials.[21]

Television home shopping programs serve millions of customers each year. See the text to learn how they are attracting new customers.

Marketing inSite

To Score Good Deals, Try Showrooming and Flash Sales!

If you love shopping, particularly for bargains, there are several new shopping techniques available to you. The first is called "showrooming," which involves going into a retail store to either (1) try on or test products before purchasing them online, or (2) use a mobile device to find the best available price online. Apps such as BuyVia and Price-Check scan barcodes or take pictures and look up comparison prices. Showrooming is estimated to lead to 50 percent of all online sales today!

Another new way to shop is to watch for "flash sales." Gilt, ideeli, HauteLook, Fab, and NoMoreRack are all examples of shopping sites that send text messages announcing limited-time offers at very steep discounts. Interested consumers then log on to the website to make a purchase. The sales last for several hours but sometimes sell out in a few minutes!

For some consumers, these new techniques are fun and engaging and make shopping a game. Quick, check your smartphone for price information or the next flash sale now!

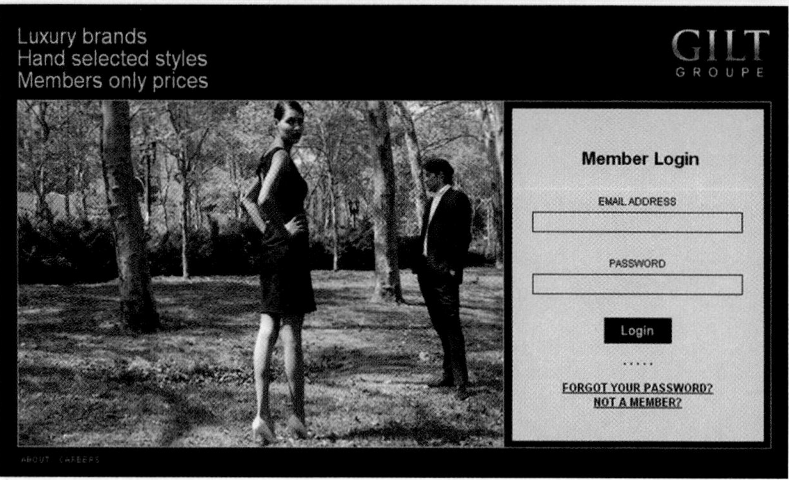

Online Retailing

Online retailing allows consumers to search for, evaluate, and order products through the Internet. For many consumers, the advantages of this form of retailing are the 24-hour access, the ability to comparison shop, in-home privacy, and variety. Early studies of online shoppers indicated that men were initially more likely than women to buy something online. As the number of online households has increased, however, the profile of online shoppers has changed to include all shoppers.

Today, traditional and online retailers—"bricks and clicks"—are melding, using experiences from both approaches to create better value and experiences for customers. For example, Walmart (www.walmart.com) offers its Site-to-Store service that allows customers to place an order online and pick it up at a Walmart store or a FedEx location. In addition, Walmart now offers its HomeFree option, which provides free shipping to customers' homes when they order $45 or more of selected items. The Walmart Mobile app allows shoppers to order products using their smartphones and tablets. Two of the biggest days for online retailing are the Friday after Thanksgiving—Black Friday—and the Monday after Thanksgiving—Cyber Monday—which generated $11.2 billion in total sales and $1.4 billion in online sales, respectively. Online sales account for approximately 5 percent of all retail sales and are expected to reach $327 billion in 2016.[22]

Shopping "bots" like mysimon.com find the best prices for products specified by consumers. Read the text on the next page to learn more!

Consumers can easily access the Internet in many locations today. How often do you use public Internet access?

Online retail purchases can be the result of several very different approaches. First, consumers can pay dues to become a member of an online discount service such as www.netmarket.com. The service offers thousands of products and hundreds of brand names at very low prices to its subscribers. Another approach to online retailing is to use a shopping "bot" such as www.mysimon.com. This site searches the Internet for a product specified by the consumer and provides a report listing retailers with the best prices. Consumers can also use the Internet to go directly to online malls (www.fashionmall.com), apparel retailers (www.gap.com), bookstores (www.amazon.com), computer manufacturers (www.dell.com), grocery stores (www.peapod.com), music and video stores (www.tower.com), and travel agencies (www.travelocity.com). A final approach to online retailing is the online auction, such as www.ebay.com, where 112 million users "trade practically anything."[23] See the Marketing inSite box for a description of new forms of online and mobile shopping.[24]

One of the biggest problems online retailers face is that nearly two-thirds of online shoppers make it to "checkout" and then leave the website to compare shipping costs and prices on other sites. Of the shoppers who leave, 70 percent do not return. One way online retailers are addressing this issue is to offer consumers a comparison of competitors' offerings. At Allbookstores.com, for example, consumers can use a "comparison engine" to compare prices with Amazon.com, Barnesandnoble.com, and as many as 25 other bookstores. Experts suggest that online retailers should think of their websites as dynamic billboards if they are to attract and retain customers, and they should be easy to use, customizable, and facilitate interaction to enhance the online customer experience.[25] For example, BMW, Mercedes, and Jaguar encourage website visitors to "build" a vehicle by selecting interior and exterior colors, packages, and options; view the customized virtual car; and then use Facebook, Twitter, or e-mail to share the configuration.

Online retailing is also evolving to include social shopping options, including: *intermediaries*, such as Groupon and LivingSocial, that match consumers with merchants; *marketplaces*, such as Google Offer and Storenvy, that provide a self-service advertising site; and *aggregators*, such as Yipit, that crawl the Web to find deals to list on their own site. Owning a computer isn't even a necessity for online shoppers; many hotels, bars, libraries, airports, and other public locations offer Internet kiosks. In China, there are 144,000 Internet cafes with over 14 million computers linked to the Internet.[26]

Telemarketing

Another form of nonstore retailing, called **telemarketing**, involves using the telephone to interact with and sell directly to consumers. Compared with direct mail, telemarketing is often viewed as a more efficient means of targeting consumers. Insurance companies, brokerage firms, and newspapers have often used this form of retailing as a way to cut costs but still maintain access to their customers. According to the Direct Marketing Association, annual telemarketing sales exceed \$332 billion.[27]

The telemarketing industry has recently gone through dramatic changes as a result of new legislation related to telephone solicitations. Issues such as consumer privacy, industry standards, and ethical guidelines have encouraged discussion among consumers, Congress, the Federal Trade Commission, and businesses. As a result, legislation created the National Do Not Call Registry (www.donotcall.gov) for consumers who do not want to receive telephone calls related to company sales efforts. Currently, there are more than 221 million phone numbers on the registry. Companies that use telemarketing have already adapted by adding compliance software to ensure that numbers on the list are not called.[28]

Direct Selling

MARY KAY

Direct selling, sometimes called door-to-door retailing, involves direct sales of products and services to consumers through personal interactions and demonstrations in their home or office. A variety of companies, including familiar names such as Avon, Fuller Brush, Mary Kay Cosmetics, and World Book, have created an industry with more than $29 billion in U.S. sales by providing consumers with personalized service and convenience. In the United States, there are more than 15 million direct salespeople working full-time and part-time in a variety of product categories, including wellness, home durables, and personal care.[29]

Growth in the direct-selling industry is the result of two trends. First, many direct selling retailers are expanding into markets outside of the United States. Avon, for example, has 6 million sales representatives in 100 countries. More than one-third of Amway's $11 billion in sales now comes from China. Similarly, other retailers such as Herbalife and Electrolux are rapidly expanding into new markets.[30] Direct selling is likely to continue to grow in markets where the lack of effective distribution channels increases the importance of door-to-door convenience and where the lack of consumer knowledge about products and brands increases the need for a person-to-person approach.

The second trend is the growing number of companies that are using direct selling to reach consumers who prefer one-on-one customer service and a social shopping experience rather than online shopping or big discount stores. The Direct Selling Association reports that the number of companies using direct selling is increasing. Pampered Chef, for example, has 60,000 independent sales reps who sell the company's products at in-home kitchen parties. Interest among potential sales representatives has grown during the recent economic downturn as people seek independence and control of their work activities.[31]

learning review

16-6. Successful catalog retailers often send ______________ catalogs to ______________ markets identified in their databases.

16-7. How are retailers increasing consumer interest and involvement in online retailing?

16-8. Where are direct selling retail sales growing? Why?

RETAILING STRATEGY

This section describes how a retailer develops and implements a retailing strategy. Research suggests that factors related to market and competitor characteristics may influence strategic choices and that the combination of choices is an important consideration for retailers.[32] Figure 16–7 identifies the relationship between strategy, positioning, and the retailing mix.

LO 16-4 Classify retailers in terms of the retail positioning matrix, and specify retailing mix actions.

Positioning a Retail Store

The classification alternatives presented in the previous sections help determine one store's position relative to its competitors. The **retail positioning matrix** is a matrix developed by the MAC Group, Inc., a management consulting firm.[33] This matrix positions retail outlets on two dimensions: breadth of product line and value added. As

FIGURE 16–7
Retailing strategy is related to store positioning and the retailing mix. Note the similarity between the retailing mix and the marketing mix.

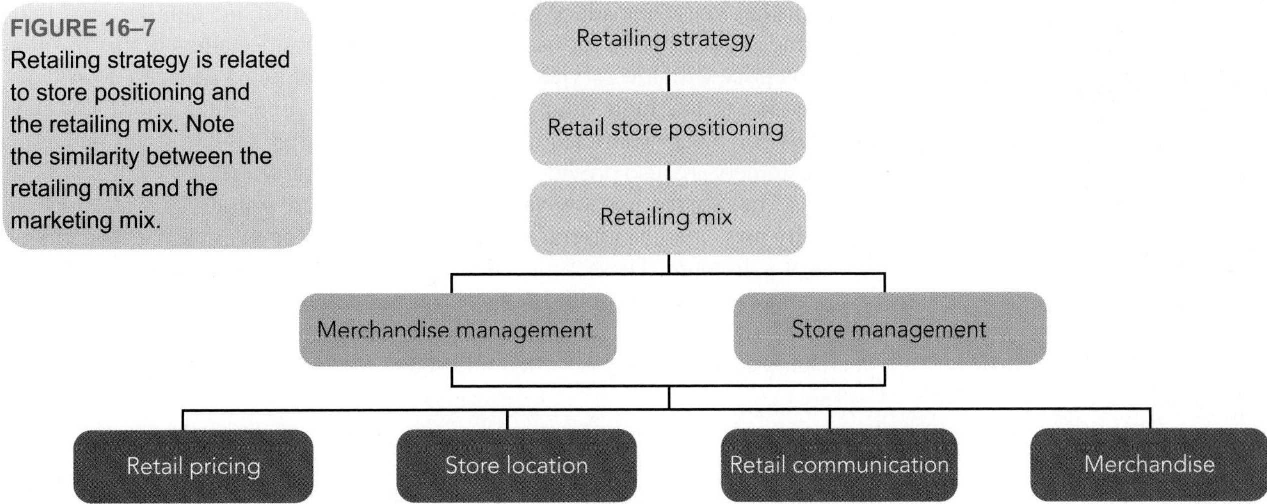

defined previously, *breadth of product line* is the range of products sold through each outlet. The second dimension, *value added*, includes elements such as location (as with 7-Eleven stores), product reliability (as with Holiday Inn or McDonald's), or prestige (as with Saks Fifth Avenue or Brooks Brothers).

The retail positioning matrix in Figure 16–8 shows four possible positions. An organization can be successful in any position, but unique strategies are required within each quadrant. Consider the four retailers shown in the matrix:

1. Bloomingdale's has high value added and a broad product line. Retailers in this quadrant pay great attention to store design and product lines. Merchandise often has a high margin of profit and is of high quality. The stores in this position typically provide high levels of service.

FIGURE 16–8
Positioning strategies for retailers are based on breadth of product line and value added.

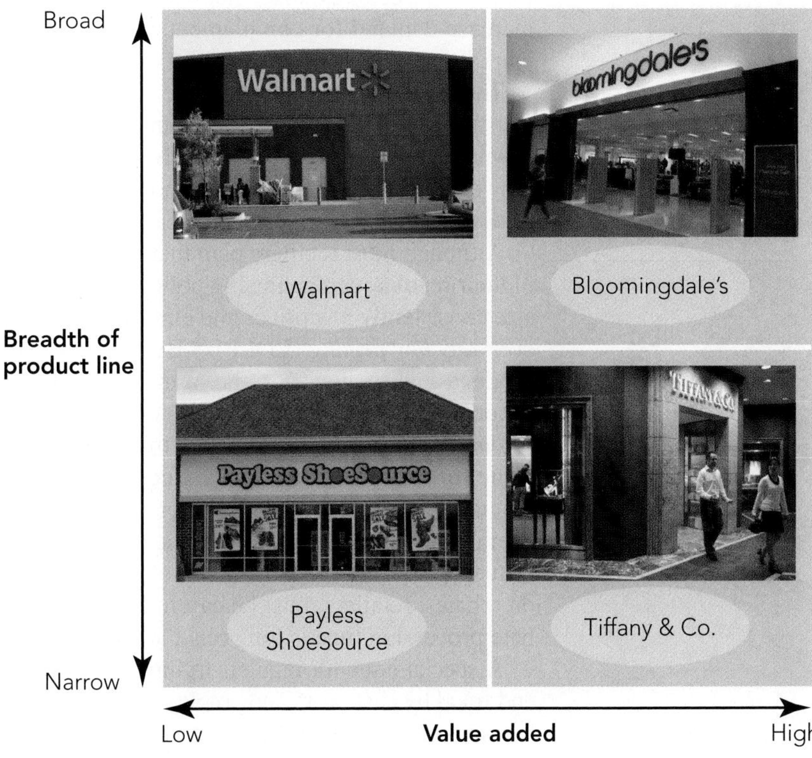

2. Walmart has low value added and a broad line. Walmart and similar firms typically trade a lower price for increased volume in sales. Retailers in this position focus on price with low service levels and an image of being a place for bargains.
3. Tiffany & Co. has high value added and a narrow line. Retailers of this type typically sell a very restricted range of products that are high in status and quality. Customers are also provided with high levels of service.
4. Payless ShoeSource has low value added and a narrow line. Such retailers are specialty mass merchandisers. Payless ShoeSource, for example, carries athletic shoes at a discount. These outlets appeal to value-conscious consumers. Economies of scale are achieved through centralized advertising, merchandising, buying, and distribution. Stores are usually the same in design, layout, and merchandise; hence they are often referred to as "cookie-cutter" stores.

Retailing Mix

In developing a retailing strategy, managers work with the **retailing mix**, which includes activities related to managing the store and the merchandise in the store. The retailing mix is similar to the marketing mix and includes retail pricing, store location, retail communication, and merchandise (see Figure 16–7).

Retail Pricing In setting prices for merchandise, retailers must decide on the markup, markdown, and timing for markdowns. As mentioned in Appendix B (following Chapter 14), the *markup* refers to how much should be added to the cost the retailer paid for a product to reach the final selling price. Retailers decide on the *original markup*, but by the time the product is sold, they end up with a *maintained markup*. The original markup is the difference between retailer cost and initial selling price. When products do not sell as quickly as anticipated, their price is reduced. The difference between the final selling price and retailer cost is the maintained markup, which is also called the *gross margin*.

Discounting a product, or taking a *markdown*, occurs when the product does not sell at the original price and an adjustment is necessary. Often new models or styles force the price of existing models to be marked down. Discounts may also be used to increase demand for complementary products.[34] For example, retailers might take a markdown on the price of cake mix to generate frosting purchases.

The *timing* of a markdown can be important. Many retailers take a markdown as soon as sales fall off to free up valuable selling space and cash. However, other stores delay markdowns to discourage bargain hunters and maintain an image of quality. There is no clear answer, but retailers must consider how the timing might affect future sales. Research indicates that frequent promotions increase consumers' ability to remember regular prices.[35]

Although most retailers plan markdowns, many retailers use price discounts as part of their regular merchandising policy. Walmart and Home Depot, for example, emphasize consistently low prices and eliminate most markdowns with a strategy often called *everyday low pricing* (EDLP).[36] Because consumers often use price as an indicator of product quality, however, the brand name of the product and the image of the store become important decision factors in these situations.[37] Another strategy, *everyday fair pricing*, is advocated by retailers that may not offer the lowest price but try to create value for customers through service and the total buying experience.[38] Consumers often use the prices of *benchmark* or *signpost* items, such as a can of Coke, to form an overall impression of a store's prices.[39] In addition, price is the most likely factor to influence consumers' assessment of merchandise value.[40] When store prices are based on rebates, retailers must be careful to avoid negative consumer perceptions if the rebate processing time is long (e.g., six weeks).[41]

A special issue for retailers trying to keep prices low is *shrinkage*, or breakage, theft, and fraud by customers and employees. The National Retail Federation estimates that the average retailer loses 1.4 percent of sales to shrinkage each year, totaling approximately

At off-price retail stores like T.J. Maxx, prices are low but selection may be unpredictable.

$34 billion. Fraudulent returns alone account for close to $9 billion. About 44 percent of retail shrinkage is due to employee theft. Some retailers have noticed an increase in theft and fraud as economic conditions have declined. In general, the issue has increased retailers' interest in new technical and surveillance techniques designed to detect and reduce shrinkage.[42]

Off-price retailing is a retail pricing practice that is used by retailers such as T.J. Maxx, Burlington Coat Factory, and Ross Stores. **Off-price retailing** involves selling brand-name merchandise at lower than regular prices. The difference between the off-price retailer and a discount store is that off-price merchandise is bought by the retailer from manufacturers with excess inventory at prices below wholesale prices. The discounter, however, buys at full wholesale prices but takes less of a markup than traditional department stores. Because of this difference in the way merchandise is purchased by the retailer, selection at an off-price retailer is unpredictable, and searching for bargains has become a popular activity for many consumers. "It's more like a sport than it is like ordinary shopping," says Christopher Boring of Columbus, Ohio's Retail Planning Associates.[43] Savings to the consumer at off-price retailers are reportedly as high as 70 percent off the prices of a traditional department store.

There are several variations of off-price retailing. One is the *warehouse club*. These large stores (100,000 to 140,000 square feet) are rather stark outlets that typically lack elaborate displays, customer service, or home delivery. Warehouse clubs require an annual membership fee (ranging from $30 to $100) for the privilege of shopping there. While a typical Walmart stocks 30,000 to 60,000 items, warehouse clubs carry 4,000 to 8,000 items and usually stock just one brand of appliance or food product. Service is minimal, and customers usually pay by cash or check. Customers are attracted by the ultra-low prices and surprise deals on selected merchandise, although several of the clubs have recently started to add ancillary services such as optical shops and pharmacies to differentiate themselves from competitors. The major warehouse clubs in the United States include Walmart's Sam's Club, BJ's Wholesale Club, and Costco's Warehouse Club. Sales of these off-price retailers have grown to approximately $390 billion annually.[44]

A second variation is the *outlet store*. Factory outlets, such as Van Heusen Factory Store, Bass Shoe Outlet, and Gap Factory Store, offer products for 25 to 75 percent off the suggested retail price. Manufacturers use the stores to clear excess merchandise and to reach consumers who focus on value shopping. Retail outlets such as Nordstrom Rack and Off 5th (an outlet for Saks Fifth Avenue) allow retailers to sell excess merchandise and still maintain an image of offering merchandise at full price in their primary store. Increasingly, retailers are offering merchandise made expressly for the outlet division. The recessionary economic climate has increased demand for this type of off-price retailing, and many retailers have responded by opening more outlet stores. For example, Bloomingdale's recently opened its first outlets. According to Michael Gould, Bloomingdale's CEO, "Outlets deliver a compelling combination of fashion, quality, and value."[45]

A third variation of off-price retailing is offered by *single-price*, or *extreme value*, *retailers* such as Family Dollar, Dollar General, and Dollar Tree. These stores average about 6,000 square feet in size and attract customers who want value and a "corner store" environment rather than a large supercenter experience. Some experts predict extraordinary growth of these types of retailers. Dollar General, for example, already has 10,000 stores in 40 states and plans to open more.[46]

Off 5th provides an outlet for excess merchandise from Saks Fifth Avenue.

Store Location A second aspect of the retailing mix involves choosing a location and deciding how many stores to operate. Department stores, which started downtown in most cities, have followed customers to the suburbs, and in recent years more stores have been opened in large regional malls. Most stores today are near several others in one of five settings: the central business district, the regional center, the community shopping center, the strip mall, or the power center.

The **central business district** is the oldest retail setting, the community's downtown area. Until the regional outflow to suburbs, it was the major shopping area, but the suburban population has grown at the expense of the downtown shopping area. Consumers often view central business district shopping as less convenient because of lack of parking, higher crime rates, and exposure to the weather. Many cities such as Louisville, Denver, and San Antonio have implemented plans to revitalize shopping in central business districts by attracting new offices, entertainment, and residents to downtown locations.

Regional shopping centers consist of 50 to 150 stores that typically attract customers who live or work within a 5- to 10-mile range. These large shopping areas often contain two or three *anchor stores*, which are well-known national or regional stores such as Sears, Saks Fifth Avenue, and Bloomingdale's. The largest variation of a regional center in North America is the West Edmonton Mall in Alberta, Canada. This shopping center is a conglomerate of more than 800 stores, the world's largest indoor amusement park, more than 100 restaurants, a movie complex, and two hotels, all of which attract 30 million visitors each year.[47]

A more limited approach to retail location is the **community shopping center**, which typically has one primary store (usually a department store branch) and often about 20 to 40 smaller outlets. Generally, these centers serve a population of consumers who are within a 10- to 20-minute drive.

Not every suburban store is located in a shopping mall. Many neighborhoods have clusters of stores, referred to as a **strip mall**, to serve people who are within a 5- to 10-minute drive. Gas station, hardware, laundry, grocery, and pharmacy outlets are commonly found in a strip mall. Unlike the larger shopping centers, the composition of these stores is usually unplanned. A variation of the strip mall is called the **power center**, which is a huge shopping strip with multiple anchor (or national) stores such as Home Depot, Best Buy, or jcpenney. Power centers combine the convenience of location provided by strip malls with the power of national stores. These large strip malls often have two to five anchor stores and contain a supermarket, which brings the shopper to the power center on a weekly basis.[48]

Retail Communication A retailer's communication activities can play an important role in positioning a store and creating its image. While the typical elements of communication and promotion are discussed in Chapter 18 on advertising, sales promotion, and public relations, Chapter 19 on social media, and Chapter 20 on personal selling, the message communicated by the many other elements of the retailing mix is also important.

Deciding on the image of a retail outlet is an important retailing mix factor that has been widely recognized and studied since the late 1950s. Pierre Martineau described image as "the way in which the store is defined in the shopper's mind," partly by its functional qualities and partly by an aura of psychological attributes.[49] In this definition, *functional* refers to mix elements such as price ranges, store layouts, and breadth and depth of merchandise lines. The psychological attributes are the intangibles such as a sense of belonging, excitement, style, or warmth. Image has been found to include impressions of the corporation that operates the store, the category or type of store, the product categories in the store, the brands in each category, merchandise and service quality, and the marketing activities of the store.[50]

Closely related to the concept of image is the store's atmosphere, or ambience. Many retailers believe that sales are affected by layout, color, lighting, music, scent,[51] and other elements of the retail environment. This concept leads many retailers to use **shopper marketing**—the use of displays, coupons, product samples, and other brand communications to influence shopping behavior in a store. Shopper marketing can also influence behavior in an online shopping environment and when shoppers use smartphone apps to identify shopping needs or make purchase decisions.[52] In creating the right image and atmosphere, a retail store tries to attract a target audience and

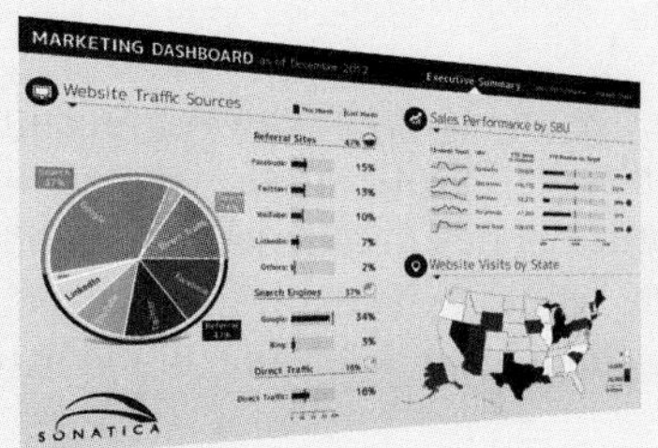

Using Marketing Dashboards

Why Apple Stores May Be the Best in the United States!

How effective is my retail format compared to other stores? How are my stores performing this year compared to last year? Information related to these questions is often displayed in a marketing dashboard using two measures: (1) sales per square foot and (2) same-store sales growth.

Your Challenge You have been assigned to evaluate the Apple Store retail format. The store's simple, inviting, and open atmosphere has been the topic of discussion among many retailers. Apple, however, is relatively new to the retailing business, and many experts have been skeptical of the format. To allow an assessment of Apple Stores, use *sales per square foot* as an indicator of how effectively retail space is used to generate revenue and *same-store sales growth* to compare the increase in sales of stores that have been open for the same period of time. The calculations for these two indicators are:

$$\text{Sales per square foot} = \frac{\text{Total sales}}{\text{Selling area in square feet}}$$

Same-stone sales growth

$$= \frac{\text{Store sales in year 2} - \text{Store sales in year 1}}{\text{Store sales in year 1}}$$

Your Findings You decide to collect sales information for Target, Neiman Marcus, Best Buy, Tiffany, and Apple Stores to allow comparisons with other successful retailers. The information you collect allows the calculation of *sales per square foot* and *same-store growth* for each store. The results are then easy to compare in the graphs below.

Your Action The results of your investigation indicate that Apple Stores' sales per square foot are higher than any of the comparison stores at $5,647. In addition, Apple's same-store growth rate of 41.9 percent is higher than all of the other retailers. You conclude that the elements of Apple's format are very effective and even indicate that Apple may currently be the best retailer in the United States.

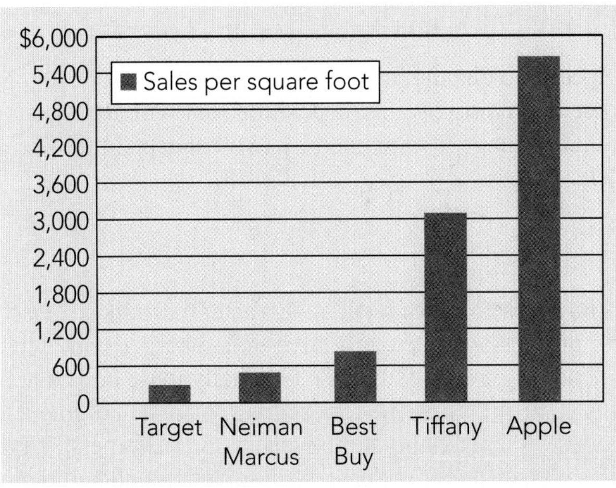

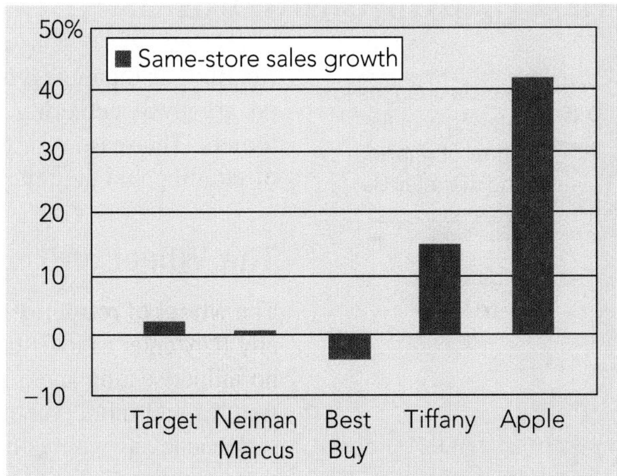

fortify beliefs about the store, its products, and the shopping experience in the store. While store image perceptions can exist independently of shopping experiences, consumers' shopping experiences influence their perceptions of a store.[53] In addition, the physical surroundings of the retail environment influence a store's employees.[54]

Merchandise The final element of the retailing mix is the merchandise offering. Managing the breadth and depth of the product line requires retail buyers who are familiar with both the needs of the target market and the alternative products available from the many manufacturers that might be interested in having a product available in the store. A popular approach to managing the assortment of merchandise today is called **category management**. This approach assigns a manager the responsibility for selecting all products that consumers in a market segment might view as substitutes for each other, with the objective of maximizing sales and profits in the category. For example, a category manager might be responsible for shoes in a department store or paper products in a grocery store. As such, he or she would consider trade deals, order costs, and the between-brand effects of price range changes to determine brand assortment, order quantities, and prices.[55]

Retailers have a variety of marketing metrics that can be used to assess the effectiveness of a store or retail format. First, there are measures related to customers such as the number of transactions per customer, the average transaction size per customer, the number of customers per day or per hour, and the average length of a store visit. Second, there are measures related to the stores and the products such as level of inventory, number of returns, inventory turnover, inventory carrying cost, and average number of items per transaction. Finally, there are financial measures, such as gross margin, sales per employee, return on sales, and markdown percentage.[56] The two most popular measures for retailers are *sales per square foot* and *same-store sales growth*. The Using Marketing Dashboards box on the previous page describes the calculation of these measures for Apple Stores.[57]

learning review

16-9. What are the two dimensions of the retail positioning matrix?

16-10. How does original markup differ from maintained markup?

16-11. A huge shopping strip mall with multiple anchor stores is a _____________ center.

THE CHANGING NATURE OF RETAILING

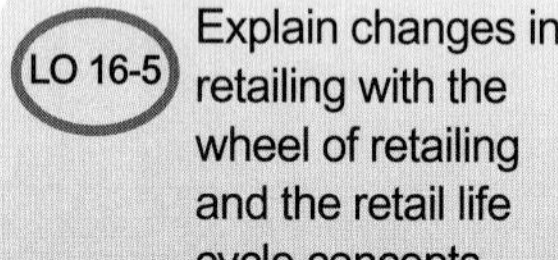

Explain changes in retailing with the wheel of retailing and the retail life cycle concepts.

Retailing is the most dynamic aspect of a channel of distribution. New types of retailers are always entering the market, searching for a new position that will attract customers. The reason for this continual change is explained by two concepts: the wheel of retailing and the retail life cycle.

The Wheel of Retailing

The **wheel of retailing** describes how new forms of retail outlets enter the market.[58] Usually they enter as low-status, low-margin stores such as a drive-in hamburger stand with no indoor seating and a limited menu (Figure 16–9, box 1). Gradually these outlets add fixtures and more embellishments to their stores (in-store seating, plants, and chicken sandwiches as well as hamburgers) to increase the attractiveness for customers. With these additions, prices and status rise (box 2). As time passes, these outlets add still more services and their prices and status increase even further (box 3). These retail outlets now face some new form of retail outlet that again appears as a low-status, low-margin operator (box 4), and the wheel of retailing turns as the cycle starts to repeat itself.

When Ray Kroc bought McDonald's in 1955, it opened shortly before lunch and closed just after dinner, and it offered a limited menu for the two meals without any inside seating for customers. Over time, the wheel of retailing has led to new products and services. In 1975, McDonald's introduced the Egg McMuffin and turned breakfast into a fast-food meal. Today, McDonald's offers an extensive menu, including oatmeal and premium coffee, and it provides seating and services such as wireless Internet connections and kid-friendly PlayPlaces. For the future, McDonald's is testing new food products, including a double-sausage McMuffin, a barbecued pork sandwich, and Spicy Chicken McBites, and new formats, such as in-car touchscreen ordering and table service![59]

QR 16-5
Checkers
Video

These changes are leaving room for new forms of outlets such as Checkers Drive-In Restaurants. The Checkers chain opened fast-food stores that offered only basics—

FIGURE 16–9
The wheel of retailing describes how retail outlets change over time. Read the text to find out the position of McDonald's and Checkers on the wheel of retailing.

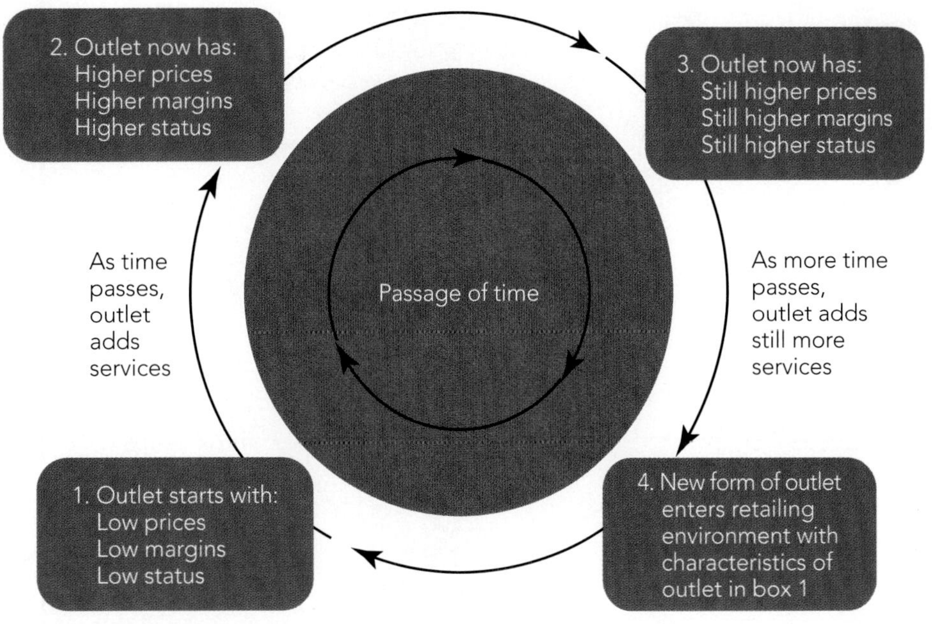

Outlets such as Checkers enter the wheel of retailing as low-status, low-margin stores.

burgers, fries, and cola, a drive-thru window, and no inside seating—and now has more than 800stores. The wheel is turning for other outlets, too—Boston Market has added pickup, delivery, and full-service catering to its original restaurant format, and it also provides Boston Market meal solutions through supermarket delis and Boston Market frozen meals in the frozen food sections of groceries. For still others, the wheel has come full circle. Taco Bell is now opening small, limited-offering outlets in gas stations, discount stores, or "wherever a burrito and a mouth might possibly intersect."[60]

The wheel of retailing is also evident in retail outlets outside the restaurant industry. Discount stores were a major new retailing form in the 1960s and priced their products below those of department stores. As prices in discount stores rose in the 1980s, they found themselves overpriced compared with a new form of retail outlet—the warehouse club. Today, off-price retailers and factory outlets are offering prices even lower than warehouse clubs.

The Retail Life Cycle

The process of growth and decline that retail outlets, like products, experience is described by the **retail life cycle**.[61] Figure 16–10 on the next page shows the stages of the retail life cycle and where various forms of retail outlets are currently positioned along its spectrum. *Early growth* is the stage of emergence of a retail outlet, with a sharp departure from existing competition. Market share rises gradually, although profits may be low because of start-up costs. In the next stage, *accelerated development*, both market share and profit achieve their greatest growth rates. Usually multiple outlets are established as companies focus on the distribution element of the retailing mix. In this stage, some later competitors may enter. Wendy's, for example, appeared on the hamburger chain scene almost 20 years after McDonald's had begun operation. The key goal for the retailer in this stage is to establish a dominant position in the fight for market share.

The battle for market share is usually fought before the *maturity stage*, and some competitors drop out of the market. In the war among hamburger chains, Jack in the Box, Gino's Hamburgers, and Burger Chef used to be more dominant outlets. In the

FIGURE 16–10
The retail life cycle describes stages of growth and decline for retail outlets.

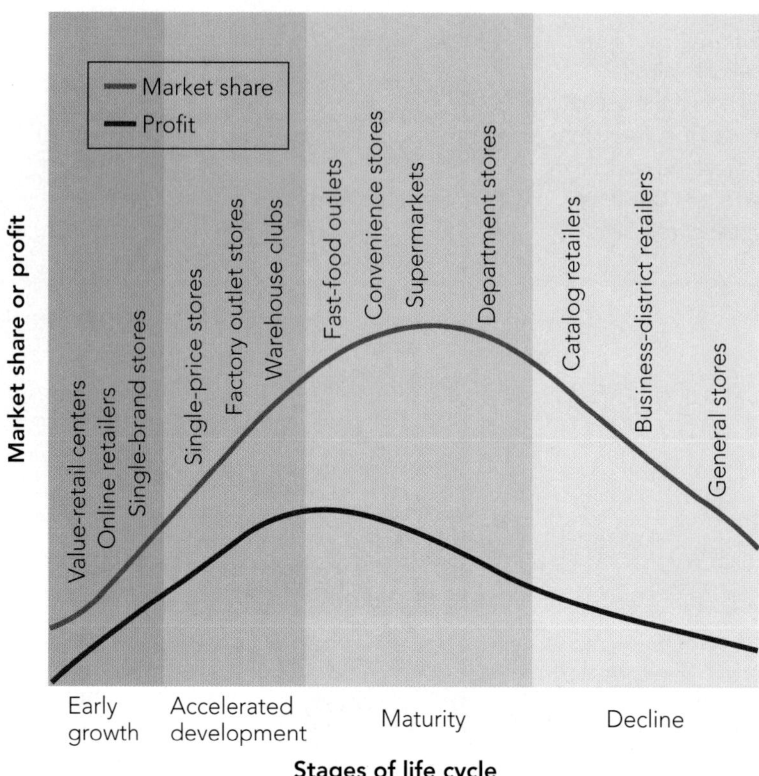

maturity stage, new retail forms enter the market (such as Fatburger and In-N-Out Burger in the hamburger chain industry), stores try to maintain their market share, and price discounting occurs.

The challenge facing retailers is to delay entering the *decline stage*, in which market share and profit fall rapidly. Specialty apparel retailers, such as the Gap, Limited, Benetton, and Ann Taylor, have noticed a decline in market share after years of growth. To prevent further decline, these retailers will need to find ways of discouraging their customers from moving to low-margin, mass-volume outlets or high-price, high-service boutiques.[62]

FUTURE CHANGES IN RETAILING

Two exciting trends in retailing—the growth of multichannel retailing and the increasing focus on customer experience management—are likely to lead to many changes for retailers and consumers in the future.

Multichannel Retailing

The retailing formats described previously in this chapter represent an exciting menu of choices for creating customer value in the marketplace. Each format allows retailers to offer unique benefits and meet the particular needs of various customer groups. While each format has many successful applications, retailers in the future are likely to combine many of the formats to offer a broader spectrum of benefits and experiences and to appeal to different segments of consumers.[63] These **multichannel retailers** will utilize and integrate a combination of traditional store formats and nonstore formats such as catalogs, television, home shopping, and online retailing.[64] Barnes & Noble, for example, created Barnesandnoble.com to compete with Amazon.com. Similarly, Office Depot has integrated its store, catalog, and Internet operations.

Marketing Matters

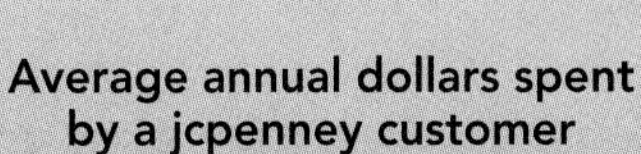

The Multichannel Marketing Multiplier

Multichannel marketing is the blending of different communication and delivery channels that are mutually reinforcing in attracting, retaining, and building relationships with consumers who shop and buy in the traditional marketplace and marketspace. Industry analysts refer to the complementary role of different communication and delivery channels as an *influence effect.*

Retailers that integrate and leverage their stores, catalogs, and websites have seen a sizable lift in yearly sales recorded from individual customers. Eddie Bauer is a good example. Customers who shop only one of its channels spend $100 to $200 per year. Those who shop in two channels spend $300 to $500 annually. Customers who shop all three channels—store, catalog, and website—spend $800 to $1,000 per year. Moreover, multichannel customers have been found to be *three times* as profitable as single-channel customers.

jcpenney has seen similar results. The company is a leading multichannel retailer and reports that a jcpenney customer who shops in all three channels—store, catalog, and website—spends *four to eight times* as much as a customer who shops in only one channel, as shown in the chart.

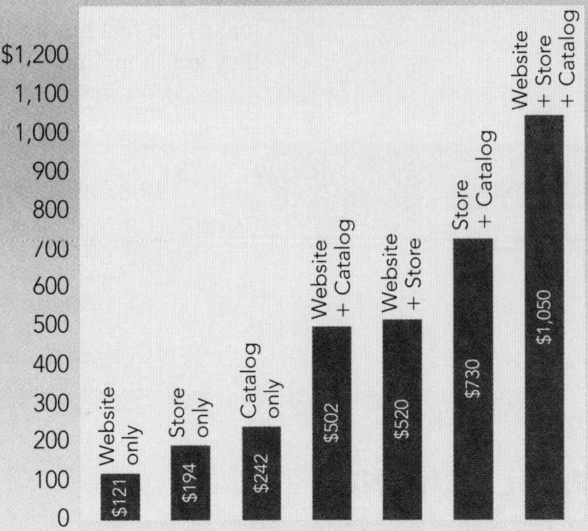

Multiple retail channels have often been viewed as alternatives that might cannibalize each other. When the channels are integrated, however, they can offer many opportunities to interact with and create value for a consumer. The various channels become a series of touch points. For example, a consumer might use a mobile app to scan a QR (quick response) code from a catalog, place an order online, pick up the product from the nearest store, call customer service for installation, and provide feedback on the retailer's social media page. In this way, the channels become complementary. Experts suggest this integration of various retail channels may lead to a new term—*omnichannel retailing*.

Multichannel retailers also benefit from the synergy of sharing information among the different channel operations. Online retailers have recognized that the Internet often serves as a source of information and a transactional tool rather than a relationship-building medium, and they are working to find ways to complement traditional customer interactions.[65] The benefits of multichannel marketing are also apparent in the spending behavior of consumers, as described in the Marketing Matters box.[66]

Managing the Customer Experience

Department stores are changing to create social retailing experiences. While many of those changes appeal to women and address the way women like to shop, retailers are also paying more attention to men and their shopping behavior. Men have typically been viewed as infrequent "mission shoppers" who go to a store only as a means of obtaining a product as efficiently as possible. Today's male shoppers, however, are changing their shopping behaviors. According to recent research, 84 percent of men now purchase their own clothes, compared with 65 percent just a few years ago; and 31 percent of grocery shopping is done by men.

To appeal to men, many department stores are creating stand-alone men's sections that combine clothes, accessories, and gadgets in one place. These new sections use "masculine" interior designs with simple colors, stainless-steel fixtures, and dark wood floors, and they often offer a dedicated lounge area with leather couches and possibly amenities such as a bar or a shoeshine station. Meanwhile, grocery stores are trying gender-neutral packaging and displays, while some chains such as Target and Walmart are considering launching "man aisles."

All of these changes are intended to create a better experience for male shoppers. As Jack Hruska, executive vice president at Bloomingdale's, explains, "We hope to make men feel more comfortable and at home by giving them a place to unwind while they are shopping."[67]

learning review

16-12. Using the wheel of retailing, describe the characteristics of a new retail form that has just entered the market.

16-13. Market share is usually fought out before the ____________ stage of the retail life cycle.

16-14. What is an influence effect?

WHOLESALING

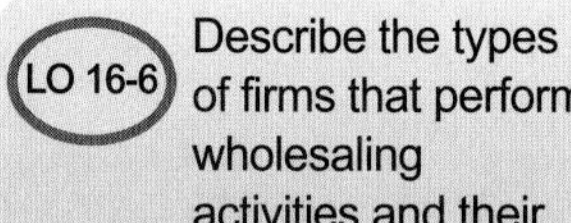

LO 16-6 Describe the types of firms that perform wholesaling activities and their functions.

Many retailers depend on intermediaries that engage in wholesaling activities—selling products and services for the purposes of resale or business use. There are several types of intermediaries, including wholesalers and agents (described briefly in Chapter 15), as well as manufacturers' sales offices, which are important to understand as part of the retailing process.

Merchant Wholesalers

Merchant wholesalers are independently owned firms that take title to the merchandise they handle. They go by various names, including *industrial distributor.* Most firms engaged in wholesaling activities are merchant wholesalers.

Merchant wholesalers are classified as either full-service or limited-service wholesalers, depending on the number of functions performed. Two major types of full-service wholesalers exist. *General merchandise* (or *full-line*) *wholesalers* carry a broad assortment of merchandise and perform all channel functions. This type of wholesaler is most prevalent in the hardware, drug, and clothing industries. However, these wholesalers do not maintain much depth of assortment within specific product lines. *Specialty merchandise* (or *limited-line*) *wholesalers* offer a relatively narrow range of products but have an extensive assortment within the product lines carried. They perform all channel functions and are found in the health foods, automotive parts, and seafood industries.

Four major types of limited-service wholesalers exist. *Rack jobbers* furnish the racks or shelves that display merchandise in retail stores, perform all channel functions, and sell on consignment to retailers, which means they retain the title to the products displayed and bill retailers only for the merchandise sold. Familiar products such as hosiery, toys, housewares, and health and beauty items are sold by rack jobbers. *Cash and carry wholesalers* take title to merchandise but sell only to buyers who call on them, pay cash for merchandise, and furnish their own transportation for merchandise. They carry a limited product assortment and do not make deliveries, extend credit, or supply market information. This type of wholesaler is common in electric supplies, office supplies, hardware products, and groceries.

Drop shippers, or *desk jobbers*, are wholesalers that own the merchandise they sell but do not physically handle, stock, or deliver it. They simply solicit orders from retailers and other wholesalers and have the merchandise shipped directly from a producer to a buyer. Drop shippers are used for bulky products such as coal, lumber, and chemicals, which are sold in extremely large quantities. *Truck jobbers* are small wholesalers that have a small warehouse from which they stock their trucks for distribution to retailers. They usually handle limited assortments of fast-moving or perishable items that are sold for cash directly from trucks in their original packages. Truck jobbers handle products such as bakery items, dairy products, and meat.

Agents and Brokers

Unlike merchant wholesalers, agents and brokers do not take title to merchandise and typically perform fewer channel functions. They make their profit from commissions or fees paid for their services, whereas merchant wholesalers make their profit from the sale of the merchandise they own.

Manufacturer's agents and selling agents are the two major types of agents used by producers. **Manufacturer's agents**, or *manufacturer's representatives*, work for several producers and carry noncompetitive, complementary merchandise in an exclusive territory. Manufacturer's agents act as a producer's sales arm in a territory and are principally responsible for the transactional channel functions, primarily selling. They are used extensively in the automotive supply, footwear, and fabricated steel industries. The Manufacturers' Agents National Association (MANA) facilitates the process of matching manufacturer's representatives with logical products and companies.

By comparison, *selling agents* represent a single producer and are responsible for the entire marketing function of that producer. They design promotional plans, set prices, determine distribution policies, and make recommendations on product strategy. Selling agents are used by small producers in the textile, apparel, food, and home furnishing industries.

Brokers are independent firms or individuals whose principal function is to bring buyers and sellers together to make sales. Brokers, unlike agents, usually have no continuous relationship with the buyer or seller but negotiate a contract between two parties and then move on to another task. Brokers are used extensively by producers of seasonal products (such as fruits and vegetables) and in the real estate industry.

A unique broker that acts in many ways like a manufacturer's agent is a food broker, representing buyers and sellers in the grocery industry. Food brokers differ from conventional brokers because they act on behalf of producers on a permanent basis and receive a commission for their services. For example, Nabisco uses food brokers to sell its candies, margarine, and Planters peanuts, but it sells its line of cookies and crackers directly to retail stores.

Manufacturer's Branches and Offices

Unlike merchant wholesalers, agents, and brokers, manufacturer's branches and sales offices are wholly owned extensions of the producer that perform wholesaling activities. Producers assume wholesaling functions when there are no intermediaries to perform these activities, customers are few in number and geographically concentrated, or orders are large or require significant attention. A *manufacturer's branch office* carries a producer's inventory and performs the functions of a full-service wholesaler. A *manufacturer's sales office* does not carry inventory, typically performs only a sales function, and serves as an alternative to agents and brokers.

learning review

16-15. What is the difference between merchant wholesalers and agents?

16-16. Under what circumstances do producers assume wholesaling functions?

LEARNING OBJECTIVES REVIEW

LO 16-1 *Identify retailers in terms of the utilities they provide.*
Retailers provide time, place, form, and possession utilities. Time utility is provided by stores with convenient time-of-day (e.g., open 24 hours) or time-of-year (e.g., seasonal sports equipment available all year) availability. Place utility is provided by the number and location of the stores. Possession utility is provided by making a purchase possible (e.g., financing) or easier (e.g., delivery). Form utility is provided by producing or altering a product to meet the customer's specifications (e.g., custom-made shirts).

LO 16-2 *Explain the alternative ways to classify retail outlets.*
Retail outlets can be classified by their form of ownership, level of service, and type of merchandise line. The forms of ownership include independent retailers, corporate chains, and contractual systems that include retailer-sponsored cooperatives, wholesaler-sponsored voluntary chains, and franchises. The levels of service include self-service, limited-service, and full-service outlets. Stores classified by their merchandise line include stores with depth, such as sporting goods specialty stores, and stores with breadth, such as large department stores.

LO 16-3 *Describe the many methods of nonstore retailing.*
Nonstore retailing includes automatic vending, direct mail and catalogs, television home shopping, online retailing, telemarketing, and direct selling. The methods of nonstore retailing vary by the level of involvement of the retailer and the level of involvement of the customer. Vending, for example, has low involvement, whereas both the consumer and the retailer have high involvement in direct selling.

LO 16-4 *Classify retailers in terms of the retail positioning matrix, and specify retailing mix actions.*
The retail positioning matrix positions retail outlets on two dimensions: breadth of product line and value added. There are four possible positions in the matrix—broad product line/low value added (Walmart), narrow product line/low value added (Payless ShoeSource), broad product line/high value added (Bloomingdale's), and narrow product line/high value added (Tiffany & Co.). Retailing mix actions are used to manage a retail store and the merchandise in a store. The mix variables include pricing, store location, communication activities, and merchandise. Two common forms of assessment for retailers are sales per square foot and same-store growth.

LO 16-5 *Explain changes in retailing with the wheel of retailing and the retail life cycle concepts.*
The wheel of retailing concept explains how retail outlets typically enter the market as low-status, low-margin stores. Over time, stores gradually add new products and services, increasing their prices, status, and margins, and leaving an opening for new low-status, low-margin stores. The retail life cycle describes the process of growth and decline for retail outlets through four stages: early growth, accelerated development, maturity, and decline.

LO 16-6 *Describe the types of firms that perform wholesaling activities and their functions.*
There are three types of firms that perform wholesaling functions. First, merchant wholesalers are independently owned and take title to merchandise. They include general merchandise wholesalers, specialty merchandise wholesalers, rack jobbers, cash and carry wholesalers, drop shippers, and truck jobbers. Merchant wholesalers can perform a variety of channel functions. Second, agents and brokers do not take title to merchandise and primarily perform marketing functions. Finally, manufacturer's branches, which may carry inventory, and sales offices, which perform sales functions, are wholly owned by the producer.

FOCUSING ON KEY TERMS

breadth of product line p. 417
brokers p. 435
category management p. 429
central business district p. 428
community shopping center p. 428
depth of product line p. 417
form of ownership p. 414
hypermarket p. 418
intertype competition p. 419
level of service p. 414
manufacturer's agents p. 435
merchandise line p. 414
merchant wholesalers p. 434
multichannel retailers p. 432
off-price retailing p. 427
power center p. 428
regional shopping centers p. 428
retail life cycle p. 431
retail positioning matrix p. 424
retailing p. 412
retailing mix p. 426
scrambled merchandising p. 418
shopper marketing p. 428
strip mall p. 428
telemarketing p. 423
wheel of retailing p. 430

APPLYING MARKETING KNOWLEDGE

1 Discuss the impact of the growing number of dual-income households on (*a*) nonstore retailing and (*b*) the retail mix.

2 How does value added affect a store's competitive position?

3 In retail pricing, retailers often have a maintained markup. Explain how this maintained markup differs from original markup and why it is so important.

4 What are the similarities and differences between the product and retail life cycles?

5 How would you classify Walmart in terms of its position on the wheel of retailing versus that of an off-price retailer?

6 Develop a chart to highlight the role of each of the four main elements of the retailing mix across the four stages of the retail life cycle.

7 Refer to Figure 16–8 and review the position of Payless ShoeSource on the retail positioning matrix. What strategies should Payless ShoeSource follow to move itself into the same position as Tiffany & Co.?

8 Breadth and depth are two important components in distinguishing among types of retailers. Discuss the breadth and depth implications of the following retailers discussed in this chapter: (*a*) Nordstrom, (*b*) Walmart, (*c*) L.L. Bean, and (*d*) Best Buy.

9 According to the wheel of retailing and the retail life cycle, what will happen to factory outlet stores?

10 The text discusses the development of online retailing in the United States. How does the development of this retailing form agree with the implications of the retail life cycle?

11 Comment on this statement: "The only distinction among merchant wholesalers and agents and brokers is that merchant wholesalers take title to the products they sell."

BUILDING YOUR MARKETING PLAN

Does your marketing plan involve using retailers? If the answer is "no," read no further and do not include a retailing element in your plan. If the answer is "yes":

1 Use Figure 16–8 to develop your retailing strategy by (*a*) selecting a position in the retail positioning matrix and (*b*) specifying the details of the retailing mix.

2 Develop a positioning statement describing the breadth of the product line (broad versus narrow) and value added (low versus high).

3 Describe an appropriate combination of retail pricing, store location, retail communication, and merchandise assortment.

4 Confirm that the wholesalers needed to support your retailing strategy are consistent with the channels and intermediaries you selected in Chapter 15.

VIDEO CASE 16 Mall of America®: Shopping and a Whole Lot More

QR 16-6
Mall of America Video Case

"If you build it, they will come" not only worked in the movie *Field of Dreams* but also applies—big time—to Mall of America®.

Located in a suburb of Minneapolis, Mall of America (www.mallofamerica.com) is the largest completely enclosed retail and family-entertainment complex in the United States. "We're more than a mall, we're a destination," explains Maureen Cahill, executive vice president at Mall of America. More than 100,000 people each day—40 million visitors each year—visit the one-stop complex offering retail shopping, guest services, convenience, a huge variety of entertainment, and fun for all. "Guest services" include everything from high school classrooms to a wedding chapel.

THE CONCEPT AND CHALLENGE

The idea for Mall of America came from the West Edmonton Mall in Alberta, Canada. The Ghermezian Brothers, who developed that mall, sought to create a unique mall that would attract not only local families but also tourists from the Upper Midwest, the nation, and even from abroad.

The two challenges for Mall of America: How can it (1) attract and keep the large number of retail establishments needed to (2) continue to attract even more millions of visitors than today? A big part of the answer is in Mall of America's positioning—"A place for fun!"

THE STAGGERING SIZE AND OFFERINGS

Opened August 1992 amid tremendous worldwide publicity, Mall of America faced skeptics who had their doubts because of its size, its unique retail-entertainment mix, and the nationwide recession. Despite these concerns, the mall opened with more than 80 percent of its space leased and attracted more than 1 million visitors its first week.

Mall of America is 4.2 million square feet, the equivalent of 88 football fields. This makes it three to four times the size of most other regional malls. It includes four anchor department stores: Nordstrom, Macy's, Bloomingdale's, and Sears. It also includes more than 520 specialty stores, from Armani Exchange to DSW (Designer Shoe Warehouse). Approximately 36 percent of Mall of America's space is devoted to anchors and 64 percent to specialty stores. This makes the space allocation the reverse of most regional malls.

The retail-entertainment mix of Mall of America is incredibly diverse. For example, there are more than 165 apparel and accessory stores, 14 jewelry stores, and 26 shoe stores. Two food courts with 27 restaurants, plus more than 20 other restaurants scattered throughout the building, meet most food preferences of visitors. Another surprise: Mall of America is home to many "concept stores," where retailers introduce a new type of store or design. In addition, it has an entrepreneurial program for people with an innovative retail idea and limited resources. They can open a kiosk, wall unit, or small store for a specified time period or as a temporary seasonal tenant.

Unique features of Mall of America include:

- Nickelodeon Universe®, a seven-acre theme park with more than 30 attractions and rides, including a roller coaster, Ferris wheel, and games in a glass-enclosed, skylighted area with more than 400 trees.
- Sea Life® Minnesota aquarium, where visitors are surrounded by sharks, stingrays, and sea turtles; can adventure among fish native to the north woods; and can discover what lurks at the bottom of the Mississippi River.
- Entertainment choices that include a 14-screen theater, A.C.E.S. Flight Simulation, the Amazing Mirror Maze, and Moose Mountain Adventure Golf.
- The House of Comedy, featuring comedians from *Last Comic Standing*, *Saturday Night Live*, and *Just for Laughs*.

As a host to corporate events and private parties, Mall of America has a rotunda that opens to all four floors, facilitating presentations, demonstrations, and exhibits. Organizations such as PepsiCo, Visa USA, and Ford have used the facilities to gain shopper awareness. Mall of America is a rectangle with the anchor department stores at the corners and an amusement park in the skylighted central area, making it easy for shoppers to understand and navigate. It has 12,550 free parking ramp spaces on-site and another 7,000 spaces nearby during peak times.

THE MARKET

The Minneapolis–St. Paul metropolitan area is a market with more than 3 million people. A total of 30 million people live within a day's drive of Mall of America. A survey of its shoppers showed that 32 percent of the shoppers travel 150 miles or more and account for more than 50 percent of the sales revenues. Located three miles from the Minneapolis/St. Paul International Airport, Mall of America has a light-rail service from the airport and downtown Minneapolis available.

Tourism accounts for 4 out of 10 visits to Mall of America. About 6 percent of visitors come from outside the United States. Some come just to see and experience Mall of America, while others take advantage of the cost savings available on goods (Japan) or taxes (Canada and states with sales taxes on clothing).

THE FUTURE: FACING THE CHALLENGES

Where is Mall of America headed in the future? "Mall of America is one of the most recognized brands in the world," Cahill says. "They might not know where we are sometimes, but they've heard of Mall of America and they know they want to come.

"What we've learned since 1992 is to keep Mall of America fresh and exciting," she explains. "We're constantly looking at what attracts people and adding to that. We're adding new stores, new attractions, and new events." For example, the mall holds more than 400 events each year, including book signings, an inventors fair, fashion shows, and live Cirque du Soleil performances.

Mall of America announced a plan for a 5.6 million-square-foot expansion, the area of another 117 football fields, connected by pedestrian skyway to the present building. "The second phase will not be a duplicate of what we have," Cahill says. "We have plans for boutique, family, and business hotels, 20,000 square feet of event space, an ice rink, a spa and wellness center, museum-quality exhibit space, and new restaurants and retail offerings."

The expansion is expected to attract an additional 20 million visitors annually. In addition, the development is designed to exceed environmental certification standards. All of these new additions and the many offerings of the current mall reinforce that Mall of America is a shopping destination and a whole lot more!

Questions

1 Why has Mall of America been such a marketing success so far?

2 What (*a*) retail and (*b*) consumer trends have occurred since Mall of America was opened in 1992 that it should consider when making future plans?

3 What criteria should Mall of America use in adding new facilities to its complex? Evaluate (*a*) retail stores, (*b*) entertainment offerings, and (*c*) hotels on these criteria.

4 What specific marketing actions would you propose that Mall of America managers take to ensure its continuing success in attracting visitors (*a*) from the local metropolitan area and (*b*) from outside of it?

17 Integrated Marketing Communications and Direct Marketing

Learning Objectives

After reading this chapter you should be able to:

Discuss integrated marketing communication and the communication process.

Describe the promotional mix and the uniqueness of each component.

Select the promotional approach appropriate to a product's target audience, life-cycle stage, and characteristics, as well as stages of the buying decision and channel strategies.

Describe the elements of the promotion decision process.

Explain the value of direct marketing for consumers and sellers.

What Are They Saying on the Twittersphere? Yo Quiero Taco Bell!

What company recently implemented its largest integrated marketing campaign ever? What company has mastered consumer engagement and interaction? What's the hottest brand on Twitter today? If you've ever had a late-night snack, you may have guessed—it's Taco Bell!

Taco Bell has been wildly successful with its Cool Ranch Doritos Locos Tacos campaign. It began three weeks before the new taco was launched with password-only social media events. Taco Bell listened to real-time conversations on Twitter (@TacoBell) and rewarded fans with "epic deliveries." A woman who asked Taco Bell to be her Valentine, a student who promised to gather enough friends to eat 1,000 tacos, and a fan who posted a message about tacos on YouTube all received early tastes of the new product.

The campaign then used television, radio, outdoor, and cinema ads, as well as public relations support. The television ads included two 15-second spots titled "Wow" and "Duh" that were supported by a contest (printed on taco wrappers) inviting customers to post photos to Instagram or Twitter using the #wow and #duh hashtags for a chance to have their entry appear on a billboard in Times Square. The most unique element of the campaign was a 3D ad showing a Dorito chip exploding and then morphing into a Cool Ranch Doritos Locos Taco chip. The ad appeared in more than 8,000 movie theaters nationwide, and the new product quickly became the company's most liked, shared, retweeted, and talked-about product on Facebook, Twitter, and Vine.

One reason for Taco Bell's success is that all of the elements of its Doritos Locos Tacos campaign are integrated to have the same message and tone, and they focus on engaging consumers. Some marketers have observed that our marketplace is in the midst of a shift from traditional branding to an "age of engagement" and that social media promotions are the best way to accommodate this shift. In addition, they suggest several aspects of social media promotions are essential to engage today's customers. They are:

1. Post relevant content about the benefits and uses of the product.
2. Supplement text with photos and videos.

3. Create sweepstakes, contests, and deals that reward current and new customers.
4. Encourage and respond to comments and feedback, both positive and negative.
5. Be current and timely with all interactions.

In addition to a presence on the Twittersphere, many brands are using other new forms of engagement, such as Facebook Pages, RSS (rich site summary) feeds, mobile apps, blogs, websites, and QR (quick response) codes. Even traditional media are engaging customers—for example, TV reality shows like *Dancing with the Stars* and *American Idol* encourage online and telephone voting. In the future, successful integrated marketing communications campaigns will certainly be engaging you![1]

Taco Bell's successful Doritos Locos Tacos campaign demonstrates the opportunity for engaging potential customers and the importance of integrating the various elements of a marketing communication program. Promotion represents the fourth element in the marketing mix. The promotional element consists of five communication tools, including advertising, personal selling, sales promotion, public relations, and direct marketing. The combination of one or more of these communication tools is called the **promotional mix**. All of these tools can be used to (1) inform prospective buyers about the benefits of the product, (2) persuade them to try it, and (3) remind them later about the benefits they enjoyed by using the product. In the past, marketers often viewed these communication tools as separate and independent. The advertising department, for example, often designed and managed its activities without consulting departments or agencies that had responsibility for sales promotion or public relations. The result was often an overall communication effort that was uncoordinated and, in some cases, inconsistent. Today, the concept of designing marketing communications programs that coordinate all promotional activities—advertising, personal selling, sales promotion, public relations, and direct marketing—to provide a consistent message across all audiences is referred to as **integrated marketing communications (IMC)**. By taking consumer expectations into consideration, IMC is a key element in a company's customer experience management strategy.[2]

This chapter provides an overview of the communication process, a description of the promotional mix elements, several tools for integrating the promotional mix, and a process for developing a comprehensive promotion program. One of the promotional mix elements, direct marketing, is also discussed in this chapter. Chapter 18 covers advertising, sales promotion, and public relations, Chapter 19 covers social media, and Chapter 20 discusses personal selling.

THE COMMUNICATION PROCESS

LO 17-1 Discuss integrated marketing communication and the communication process.

Communication is the process of conveying a message to others, and it requires six elements: a source, a message, a channel of communication, a receiver, and the processes of encoding and decoding[3] (see Figure 17–1). The **source** may be a company or person who has information to convey. The information sent by a source, such as a description of a new smartphone, forms the **message**. The message is conveyed by means of a **channel of communication** such as a salesperson, advertising media, or public relations tools. Consumers who read, hear, or see the message are the **receivers**.

FIGURE 17–1
The communication process consists of six key elements. See the text to learn about factors that influence the effectiveness of the process.

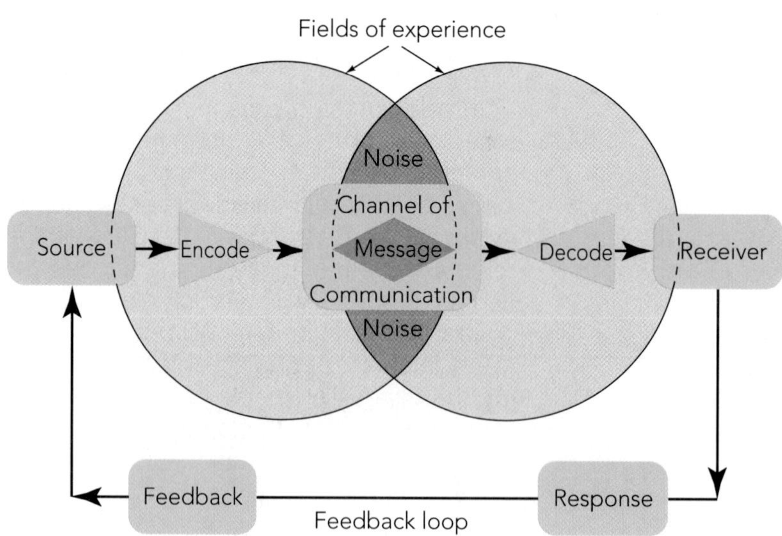

UNSTILL LIFE.
32
INTRODUCING MINI PACEMAN.
MINI

How would you decode this ad? What message is MINI trying to send?

MINI
www.miniusa.com

QR 17-1
MINI Ad

Encoding and Decoding

Encoding and decoding are essential to communication. **Encoding** is the process of having the sender transform an idea into a set of symbols. **Decoding** is the reverse, or the process of having the receiver take a set of symbols, the message, and transform the symbols into an idea. Look at the accompanying MINI USA advertisement: Who is the source, and what is the message?

Decoding is performed by the receivers according to their own frame of reference: their attitudes, values, and beliefs.[4] MINI USA is the source and the advertisement is the message, which appeared in *Wired* magazine (the channel). How would you interpret (decode) this advertisement? The picture and text in the advertisement show that the source's intention is to generate interest in its product with the headline "Unstill Life"—a statement the source believes will appeal to the readers of the magazine.

The process of communication is not always a successful one. Errors in communication can happen in several ways. The source may not adequately transform the abstract idea into an effective set of symbols, a properly encoded message may be sent through the wrong channel and never make it to the intended receiver, the receiver may not properly transform the set of symbols into the correct abstract idea, or finally, feedback may be so delayed or distorted that it is of no use to the sender. Although communication appears easy to perform, truly effective communication can be very difficult.

For the message to be communicated effectively, the sender and receiver must have a mutually shared **field of experience**—a similar understanding and knowledge they apply to the message. Figure 17–1 shows two circles representing the fields of experience of the sender and receiver, which overlap in the message. Some of the better-known message problems have occurred when U.S. companies have taken their messages to cultures with different fields of experience. Many misinterpretations are merely the result of bad translations. For example, KFC made a mistake when its "finger-lickin' good" slogan was translated into Mandarin Chinese as "eat your fingers off"![5]

Feedback

Figure 17–1 shows a line labeled *feedback loop*, which consists of a response and feedback. A **response** is the impact the message had on the receiver's knowledge, attitudes, or behaviors. **Feedback** is the sender's interpretation of the response and indicates whether the message was decoded and understood as intended. Chapter 18 reviews approaches called *pretesting*, which ensure that messages are decoded properly.

Noise

Noise includes extraneous factors that can work against effective communication by distorting a message or the feedback received (Figure 17–1). Noise can be a simple error, such as a printing mistake that affects the meaning of a newspaper advertisement or the use of words or pictures that fail to communicate the message clearly. Noise can also occur when a salesperson's message is misunderstood by a prospective buyer, such as when a salesperson's accent, use of slang terms, or communication style make hearing and understanding the message difficult.

learning review

17-1. What six elements are required for communication to occur?

17-2. A difficulty for U.S. companies advertising in international markets is that the audience does not share the same ______________.

17-3. A misprint in a newspaper ad is an example of ______________.

THE PROMOTIONAL ELEMENTS

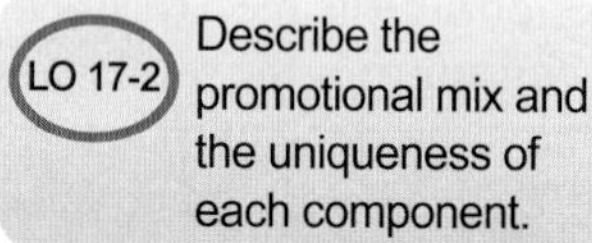

LO 17-2
Describe the promotional mix and the uniqueness of each component.

To communicate with consumers, a company can use one or more of five promotional alternatives: advertising, personal selling, public relations, sales promotion, and direct marketing. Figure 17–2 summarizes the distinctions among these five elements. Three of these elements—advertising, sales promotion, and public relations—are often said to use *mass selling* because they are used with groups of prospective buyers. In contrast, personal selling uses *customized interaction* between a seller and a prospective buyer. Personal selling activities include face-to-face, telephone, and interactive electronic communication. Direct marketing also uses messages customized for specific customers.

Magazines are a mass media outlet for advertising.

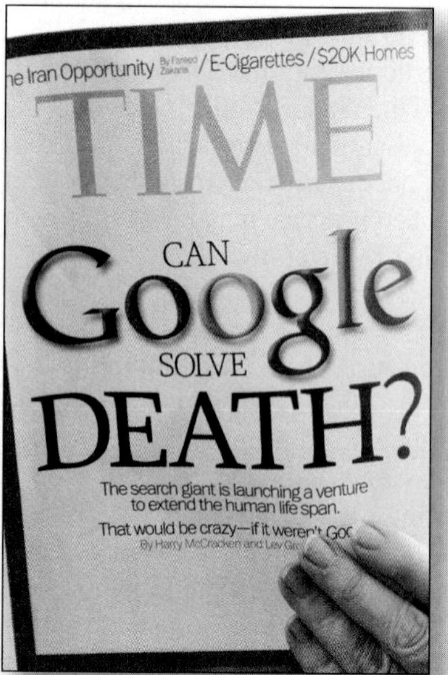

Advertising

Advertising is any paid form of nonpersonal communication about an organization, product, service, or idea by an identified sponsor. The *paid* aspect of this definition is important because the space for the advertising message normally must be bought. An occasional exception is the public service announcement, where the advertising time or space is donated. A full-page, four-color ad in *Time* magazine, for example, costs $339,400. The *nonpersonal* component of advertising is also important. Advertising involves mass media (such as TV, radio, and magazines), which are nonpersonal and do not have an immediate feedback loop as does personal selling. So before the message is sent, marketing research plays a valuable role; for example, it determines that the target market will actually see the medium chosen and that the message will be understood.

There are several advantages to a firm using advertising in its promotional mix. It can be attention-getting—as with the Columbia ad shown on page 446—and also communicate specific product benefits to prospective buyers. By paying

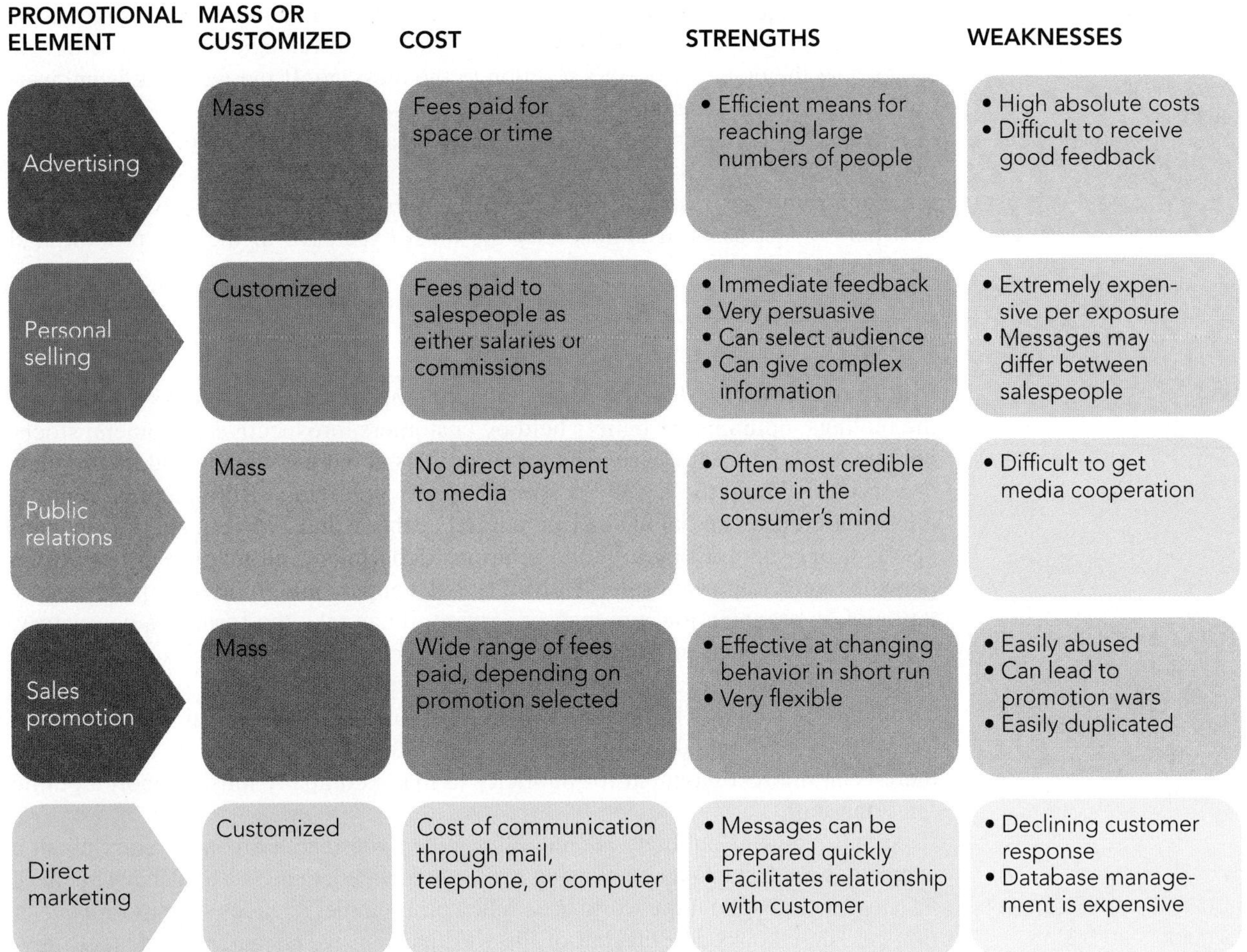

PROMOTIONAL ELEMENT	MASS OR CUSTOMIZED	COST	STRENGTHS	WEAKNESSES
Advertising	Mass	Fees paid for space or time	• Efficient means for reaching large numbers of people	• High absolute costs • Difficult to receive good feedback
Personal selling	Customized	Fees paid to salespeople as either salaries or commissions	• Immediate feedback • Very persuasive • Can select audience • Can give complex information	• Extremely expensive per exposure • Messages may differ between salespeople
Public relations	Mass	No direct payment to media	• Often most credible source in the consumer's mind	• Difficult to get media cooperation
Sales promotion	Mass	Wide range of fees paid, depending on promotion selected	• Effective at changing behavior in short run • Very flexible	• Easily abused • Can lead to promotion wars • Easily duplicated
Direct marketing	Customized	Cost of communication through mail, telephone, or computer	• Messages can be prepared quickly • Facilitates relationship with customer	• Declining customer response • Database management is expensive

FIGURE 17–2
Each of the five elements of the promotional mix has strengths and weaknesses.

for the advertising space, a company can control *what* it wants to say and, to some extent, to *whom* the message is sent. Advertising also allows the company to decide *when* to send its message (which includes how often). The nonpersonal aspect of advertising also has its advantages. Once the message is created, the same message is sent to all receivers in a market segment. If the pictorial, text, and brand elements of an advertisement are properly pretested, an advertiser can ensure the ad's ability to capture consumers' attention and trust that the same message will be decoded by all receivers in the market segment.[6]

Advertising has some disadvantages. As shown in Figure 17–2 and discussed in depth in Chapter 18, the costs to produce and place a message are significant, and the lack of direct feedback makes it difficult to know how well the message was received.

Personal Selling

The second major promotional alternative is **personal selling**, which is the two-way flow of communication between a buyer and seller designed to influence a person's or group's purchase decision. Unlike advertising, personal selling is usually face-to-face communication between the sender and receiver. Why do companies use personal selling?

There are important advantages to personal selling, as summarized in Figure 17–2. A salesperson can control to *whom* the presentation is made, reducing the amount of *wasted coverage*, or communication with consumers who are not in the target audience. The personal component of selling has another advantage in that the seller can see or hear the potential buyer's reaction to the message. If the feedback is unfavorable, the salesperson can modify the message.

The flexibility of personal selling can also be a disadvantage. Different salespeople can change the message so that no consistent communication is given to all customers. The high cost of personal selling is probably its major disadvantage. On a cost-per-contact basis, it is generally the most expensive of the five promotional elements.

Public Relations

Public relations is a form of communication management that seeks to influence the feelings, opinions, or beliefs held by customers, prospective customers, stockholders, suppliers, employees, and other publics about a company and its products or services.[7] Many tools such as special events, lobbying efforts, annual reports, press conferences, social media (including Facebook and Twitter), and image management may be used by a public relations department, although publicity often plays the most important role.[8] **Publicity** is a nonpersonal, indirectly paid presentation of an organization, product, or service. It can take the form of a news story, editorial, or product announcement. A difference between publicity and both advertising and personal selling is the "indirectly paid" dimension. With publicity a company does not pay for space in a mass medium (such as television or radio) but attempts to get the medium to run a favorable story on the company. In this sense, there is an indirect payment for publicity in that a company must support a public relations staff.

An advantage of publicity is credibility. When you read a favorable story about a company's product (such as a glowing restaurant review), there is a tendency to believe it. Travelers throughout the world have relied on Frommer's guides such as *Frommer's France.* These books describe out-of-the-way, inexpensive restaurants and hotels, giving invaluable publicity to these establishments. Such businesses do not (nor can they) buy a mention in the guide. Publicity is particularly effective when consumers lack prior knowledge of the product or service.[9]

The Columbia ad, Frommer's travel guide, and M&M's sweepstakes are examples of three elements of the promotional mix—advertising, public relations, and sales promotion.

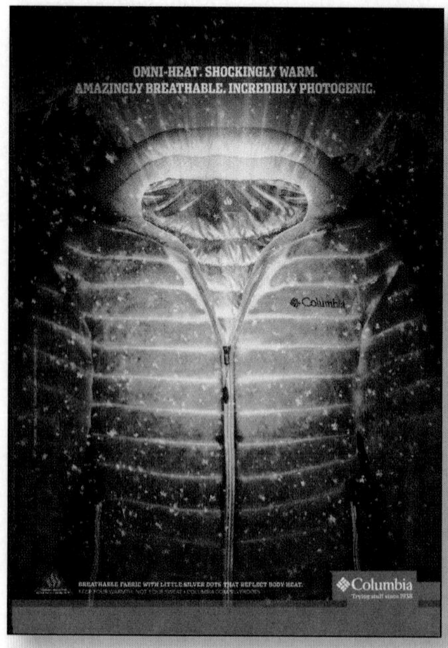

McDonald's facilitates online discussions with its blog.

The disadvantage of publicity relates to the lack of the user's control over it. A company can invite media to cover an interesting event such as a store opening or a new-product release, but there is no guarantee that a story will result, that it will be positive, or that the target audience will receive the message. Social media, such as blogs, have grown dramatically and allow uncontrollable public discussions of almost any company activity. Many public relations departments now focus on facilitating and responding to online discussions. McDonald's, for example, responds to comments about McDonald's products and promotions on its corporate social responsibility blog, *Let's Talk*. Generally, publicity is an important element of most promotional campaigns, although the lack of control means that it is rarely the primary element. Research related to the sequence of IMC elements, however, indicates that publicity followed by advertising with the same message increases the positive response to the message.[10]

QR 17-2 McDonald's Video

Sales Promotion

A fourth promotional element is **sales promotion**, a short-term inducement of value offered to arouse interest in buying a product or service. Used in conjunction with advertising or personal selling, sales promotions are offered to intermediaries as well as to ultimate consumers. Coupons, rebates, samples, contests, and sweepstakes such as the M&M's promotion are just a few examples of sales promotions discussed later in this chapter.

The advantage of sales promotion is that the short-term nature of these programs (such as a coupon or sweepstakes with an expiration date) often stimulates sales for their duration. Offering value to the consumer in terms of a cents-off coupon or rebate may increase store traffic from consumers who are not store-loyal.[11]

Sales promotions cannot be the sole basis for a campaign because gains are often temporary and sales drop off when the deal ends. Advertising support is needed to convert the customer who tried the product because of a sales promotion into a long-term buyer. If sales promotions are conducted continuously, they lose their effectiveness. Customers begin to delay purchase until a coupon is offered, or they question the product's value. Some aspects of sales promotions also are regulated by the federal government.[12] These issues are reviewed in detail in Chapter 18.

Direct Marketing

Another promotional alternative, **direct marketing**, uses direct communication with consumers to generate a response in the form of an order, a request for further information, or a visit to a retail outlet. The communication can take many forms, including face-to-face selling, direct mail, catalogs, telephone solicitations, direct response advertising (on television and radio and in print), and online marketing.[13] Like personal selling, direct marketing often consists of interactive communication. It also has the advantage of being customized to match the needs of specific target markets. Messages can be developed and adapted quickly to facilitate one-to-one relationships with customers.

While direct marketing has been one of the fastest-growing forms of promotion, it has several disadvantages. First, most forms of direct marketing require a comprehensive and up-to-date database with information about the target market. Developing and maintaining the database can be expensive and time-consuming. In addition, growing concern about privacy has led to a decline in response rates among some customer groups. Companies with successful direct marketing programs are sensitive to these issues and often use a combination of direct marketing alternatives together, or direct marketing combined with other promotional tools, to increase value for customers.

learning review

17-4. Explain the difference between advertising and publicity when both appear on television.

17-5. Cost per contact is high with the ______________ element of the promotional mix.

17-6. Which promotional element should be offered only on a short-term basis?

INTEGRATED MARKETING COMMUNICATIONS—DEVELOPING THE PROMOTIONAL MIX

LO 17-3 Select the promotional approach appropriate to a product's target audience, life-cycle stage, and characteristics, as well as stages of the buying decision and channel strategies.

A firm's promotional mix is the combination of one or more of the promotional tools it chooses to use. In putting together the promotional mix, a marketer must consider two issues. First, the balance of the elements must be determined. Should advertising be emphasized more than personal selling? Should a promotional rebate be offered? Would public relations activities be effective? Several factors affect such decisions: the target audience for the promotion, the stage of the product's life cycle, the characteristics of the product, the decision stage of the buyer, and even the channel of distribution. Second, because the various promotional elements are often the responsibility of different departments, coordinating a consistent promotional effort is necessary. A promotional planning process designed to ensure integrated marketing communications (IMC) can facilitate this goal.

The Target Audience

Promotional programs are directed to the ultimate consumer, to an intermediary (retailer, wholesaler, or industrial distributor), or to both. Promotional programs directed to buyers of consumer products often use mass media because the number of potential buyers is large. Personal selling is used at the place of purchase, generally the retail store. Direct marketing may be used to encourage first-time or repeat purchases. Combinations of many media alternatives are a necessity for some target audiences today. The Marketing Matters box describes how today's college students can be reached through mobile marketing programs.[14]

Advertising directed to business buyers is used selectively in trade publications such as *Restaurant Business* magazine for buyers of restaurant equipment and supplies. Because business buyers often have specialized needs or technical questions, personal selling is particularly important. The salesperson can provide information and the necessary support after the sale.

Intermediaries are often the focus of promotional efforts. As with business buyers, personal selling is the major promotional ingredient. The salespeople assist intermediaries in making a profit by coordinating promotional campaigns sponsored by the manufacturer and by providing marketing advice and expertise. Intermediaries' questions often pertain to the allowed markup, merchandising support, and return policies.

Publications such as *Restaurant Business* reach business buyers.

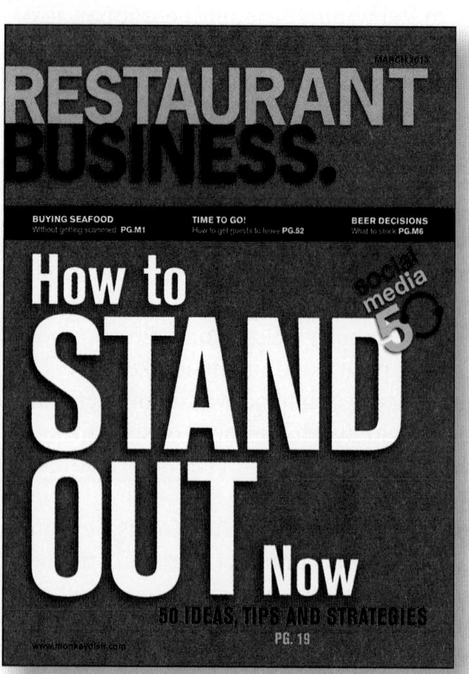

Marketing Matters

technology

How Can You Reach Today's College Students? With Mobile Marketing!

Today's college students include the tail end of Generation Y and the new generation of young consumers often called Millennials. Nationwide Bank estimates that college students spend more than $400 billion each year, making them an attractive market for many businesses. In an effort to reach students with their offerings, marketers are tailoring their activities to match the segment's unique characteristics.

College students consist of "digital natives" who have grown up with technology. They have and use laptop computers, high-definition televisions, video game consoles, tablet devices, and smartphones. In fact, a recent study of university and college students found that 82 percent of new college students own a smartphone. They access Facebook, Twitter, YouTube, and Instagram; they download apps, coupons, and information 24/7; and they communicate with e-mail, text messages, and blogs. For many businesses, these facts suggest that marketing through smartphones, or mobile marketing, will be an essential element in integrated marketing communications campaigns in the future.

Several guidelines can help ensure the success of mobile marketing. First, it is important to create a mobile-ready app that is flashy, fun, and has the potential to "go viral." In addition, because the recession has created financial hardships for Millennials, successful mobile apps should help shoppers make price comparisons and match product characteristics to their needs, preferences, and lifestyles. Communication must be short (140 characters on Twitter!), honest, authentic, and transparent about the purpose and value of the brand. Finally, mobile marketing campaigns should facilitate multitasking. According to one expert, marketers "should picture students looking at text and images while traveling on a bus, rushing to a lecture, or out socializing."

Examples of successful mobile marketing campaigns include MTV's use of a Twitter jockey to provide messages to its viewers and the Starbucks Mobile Card application to make payments easier. Coming soon are Volkswagen's SmileDrive app that measures fun on the road and Coca-Cola's use of classic ads in mobile advertising.

Watch for other brands that use mobile marketing as part of their campaigns to reach college students in the future.

The Product Life Cycle

All products have a product life cycle (see Chapter 11), and the composition of the promotional mix changes over the four life-cycle stages, as shown in Figure 17–3 on the next page.

Advertising in *Dog Fancy* can build awareness of a new dog food.

Introduction Stage Informing consumers in an effort to increase their level of awareness is the primary promotional objective in the introduction stage of the product life cycle. In general, all the promotional mix elements are used at this time, although the use of specific mix elements during any stage depends on the product and situation. News releases about a new dog food, for example, are sent to veterinary magazines, trial samples are sent to registered dog owners, advertisements are placed in *Dog Fancy* magazine, and the salesforce begins to approach supermarkets and pet stores to get orders. Advertising is particularly important as a means of reaching as many people as possible to build awareness and interest. Publicity may even begin slightly before the product is commercially available.

Growth Stage The primary promotional objective of the growth stage is to persuade the consumer to buy the product rather than substitutes, so the marketing manager seeks to gain brand preference and solidify distribution. Sales promotion assumes less importance in this stage, and publicity is not a factor because it depends on novelty of the product. The primary promotional element is advertising, which stresses brand differences. Personal selling is used to solidify the channel of distribution. For consumer products such as dog food, the salesforce calls on the wholesalers and retailers in hopes of increasing inventory levels and gaining shelf space. For business

FIGURE 17–3
The product life cycle illustrates how promotional objectives and activities change over the four stages.

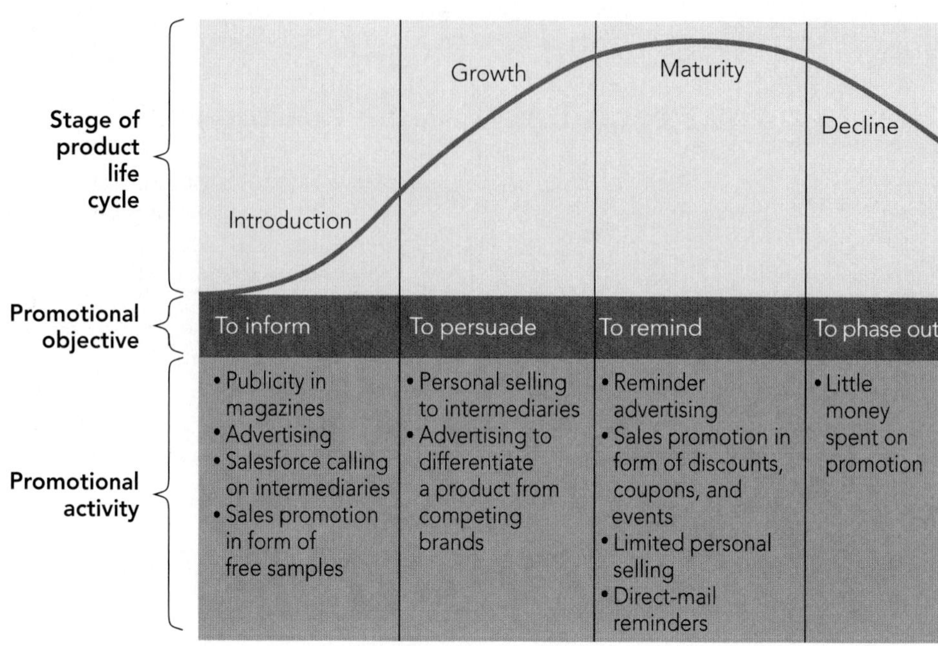

products, the salesforce often tries to get contractual arrangements to be the sole source of supply for the buyer.

Stage of product life cycle
Introduction
Growth
Maturity
Decline
Promotional objective
To inform
To persuade
To remind
To phase out
Promotional activity
• Publicity in magazines
• Advertising
• Salesforce calling on intermediaries
• Sales promotion in form of free samples
• Personal selling to intermediaries
• Advertising to differentiate a product from competing brands
• Reminder advertising
• Sales promotion in form of discounts, coupons, and events
• Limited personal selling
• Direct-mail reminders
• Little money spent on promotion

Maturity Stage In the maturity stage, the need is to maintain existing buyers, and advertising's role is to remind buyers of the product's existence. Sales promotion, in the form of discounts and coupons offered to both ultimate consumers and intermediaries, is important in maintaining loyal buyers. In a test of one mature consumer product, it was found that 80 percent of the product's sales at this stage resulted from sales promotions.[15] Sponsoring events can also help maintain loyalty. For the past 15 years, Purina has sponsored the Purina Pro Plan Incredible Dog Challenge, which is covered by a live stream on the Bark Network. In addition, Purina has developed an iPhone app called P5 to teach viewers how to train their dogs in the events they see performed during the Challenge.[16] Direct marketing actions such as direct mail are used to maintain involvement with existing customers and to encourage repeat purchases. Price cuts and discounts can also significantly increase a mature brand's sales. The salesforce at this stage seeks to satisfy intermediaries. An unsatisfied customer who switches brands is hard to replace.

Decline Stage The decline stage of the product life cycle is usually a period of phase-out for the product, and little money is spent in the promotional mix. The rate of decline can be rapid, as is the case when a product is replaced by an improved or lower-cost product, for example, or slow, as often happens when there is a loyal group of customers.

Product Characteristics

The proper blend of elements in the promotional mix also depends on the type of product. Three specific characteristics should be considered: complexity, risk, and ancillary services. *Complexity* refers to the technical sophistication of the product and hence the amount of understanding required to use it. It's hard to provide much information in a one-page magazine ad or a 30-second television ad, so the more complex the product, the greater the emphasis on personal selling. Gulfstream asks potential customers to call a representative identified in its ads. On the other hand, very little information is provided for simple products such as Tropicana orange juice.

How do Gulfstream aircraft and Tropicana orange juice differ on complexity, risk, and ancillary services?

Gulfstream
www.gulfstream.com

Tropicana
www.tropicana.com

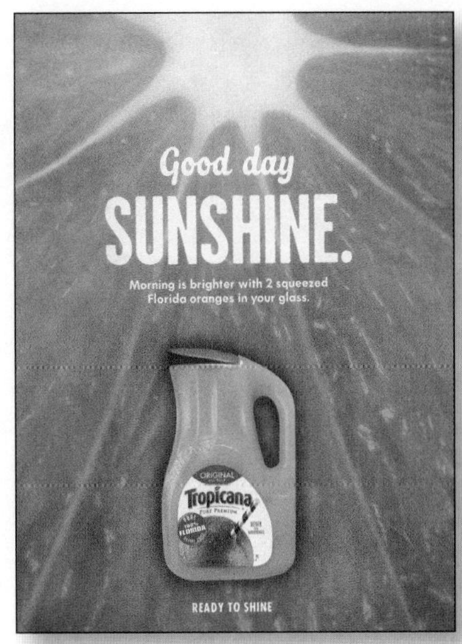

A second element is the degree of risk represented by the product's purchase. *Risk* for the buyer can be assessed in terms of financial risk, social risk, and physical risk. A private jet, for example, might represent all three risks—it is expensive, employees and customers may see and evaluate the purchase, and safety and reliability are important. Although advertising helps, the greater the risk, the greater the need for personal selling. Consumers are unlikely to associate any of these risks with a candy bar.

The level of ancillary services required by a product also affects the promotional strategy. *Ancillary services* pertain to the degree of service or support required after the sale. This characteristic is common to many industrial products and consumer purchases. Who will provide maintenance for the plane? Advertising's role is to establish the seller's reputation. Direct marketing can be used to describe how a product or service can be customized to meet individual needs. However, personal selling is essential to build buyer confidence and provide evidence of customer service.

Stages of the Buying Decision

Knowing the customer's stage of decision making can also affect the promotional mix. Figure 17–4 on the next page shows how the importance of the promotional elements varies with the three stages in the consumer purchase decision process.

Prepurchase Stage In the prepurchase stage, advertising is more helpful than personal selling because advertising informs the potential customer of the existence of the product and the seller. Sales promotion in the form of free samples also can play an important role to gain low-risk trial. When the salesperson calls on the customer after heavy advertising, there is some recognition of what the salesperson represents. This is particularly important in industrial settings in which sampling of the product is usually not possible.

Purchase Stage At the purchase stage, the importance of personal selling is highest, whereas the impact of advertising is lowest. Sales promotion in the form of coupons, deals, point-of-purchase displays, and rebates can be very helpful in encouraging demand. In this stage, social media can play an important role in the final decision by delivering promotions and giving consumers control of the process. Research

FIGURE 17–4
The importance of promotional elements varies during the stages of the consumer purchase decision process.

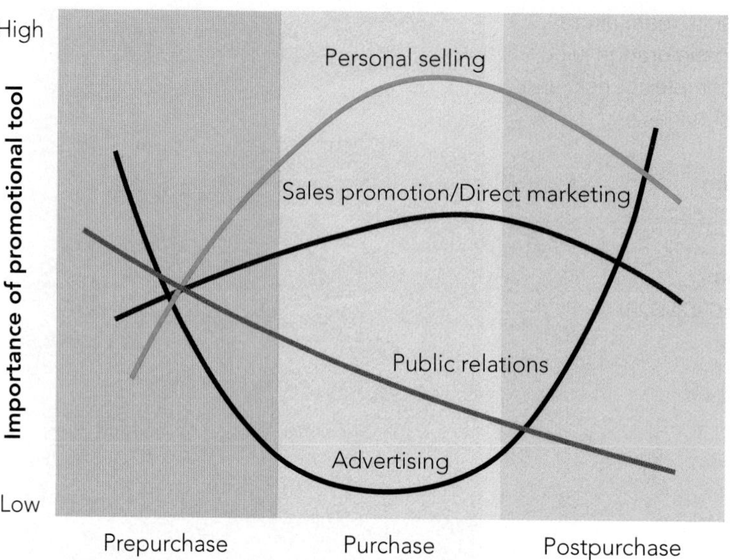

indicates that direct marketing activities shorten the time consumers take to adopt a product or service.[17]

Postpurchase Stage In the postpurchase stage, the salesperson is still important. In fact, the more personal contact after the sale, the more the buyer is satisfied. Advertising is also important to assure the buyer that the right purchase was made. Advertising and personal selling help reduce the buyer's postpurchase anxiety. Sales promotion in the form of coupons and direct marketing reminders can help encourage repeat purchases from satisfied first-time triers. Public relations plays a small role in the postpurchase stage.[18]

Channel Strategies

Chapter 15 discussed the channel flow from a producer to intermediaries to consumers. Achieving control of the channel is often difficult for the manufacturer, and promotional strategies can assist in moving a product through the channel of distribution. This is where a manufacturer has to make an important decision about whether to use a push strategy, pull strategy, or both in its channel of distribution.[19]

Why does this ad for a drug that helps lower cholesterol suggest readers should "Ask your doctor if Zetia is right for you"? For the answer, see the text.

Push Strategy Figure 17–5A shows how a manufacturer uses a **push strategy**, directing the promotional mix to channel members to gain their cooperation in ordering and stocking the product. In this approach, personal selling and sales promotions play major roles. Salespeople call on wholesalers to encourage orders and provide sales assistance. Sales promotions, such as case discount allowances (20 percent off the regular case price), are offered to stimulate demand. By pushing the product through the channel, the goal is to get channel members to push it to their customers.

Ford Motor Company, for example, provides support and incentives for its 3,290 Ford dealers. Through a multilevel program, Ford provides incentives to reward dealers for meeting sales goals. Dealers receive an incentive when they are near a goal, another when they reach a goal, and an even larger one if they exceed sales projections. Ford also offers some dealers special incentives for maintaining superior facilities or improving customer service. All of these actions are intended to encourage Ford dealers to "push" the Ford products through the channel to consumers.[20]

FIGURE 17–5
Push and pull strategies direct the promotional mix to different points in the channel of distribution.

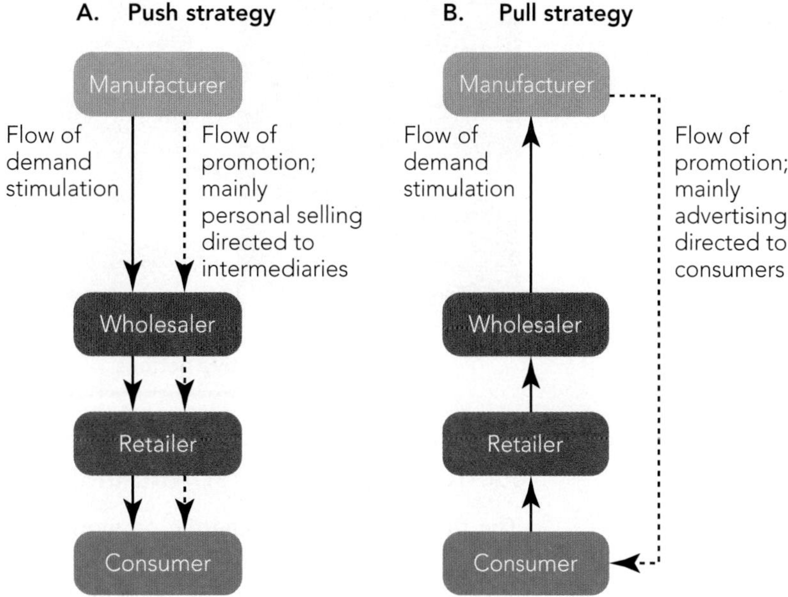

Pull Strategy In some instances, manufacturers face resistance from channel members who do not want to order a new product or increase inventory levels of an existing brand. As shown in Figure 17–5B, a manufacturer may then elect to implement a **pull strategy** by directing its promotional mix at ultimate consumers to encourage them to ask the retailer for a product. Seeing demand from ultimate consumers, retailers order the product from wholesalers and thus the item is pulled through the intermediaries. Pharmaceutical companies, for example, now spend more than $3.4 billion annually on *direct-to-consumer* prescription drug advertising, to complement traditional personal selling and free samples directed only at doctors.[21] The strategy is designed to encourage consumers to ask their doctor for a specific drug by name—pulling it through the channel. Successful campaigns such as the print ad which says, "Ask your doctor if Zetia is right for you," can have dramatic effects on the sales of a product.

learning review

17-7. Describe the promotional objective for each stage of the product life cycle.

17-8. At what stage of the consumer purchase decision process is the importance of personal selling highest? Why?

17-9. Explain the differences between a push strategy and a pull strategy.

DEVELOPING AN IMC PROGRAM

LO 17-4 Describe the elements of the promotion decision process.

Because media costs are high, promotion decisions must be made carefully, using a systematic approach. Paralleling the planning, implementation, and evaluation steps described in the strategic marketing process (Chapter 2), the promotion decision process is divided into (1) developing, (2) executing, and (3) assessing the promotion program (see Figure 17–6 on the next page). Development of the promotion program focuses on the four *W*s:

- *Who* is the target audience?
- *What* are (1) the promotion objectives, (2) the amounts of money that can be budgeted for the promotion program, and (3) the kinds of promotion to be used?
- *Where* should the promotion be run?
- *When* should the promotion be run?

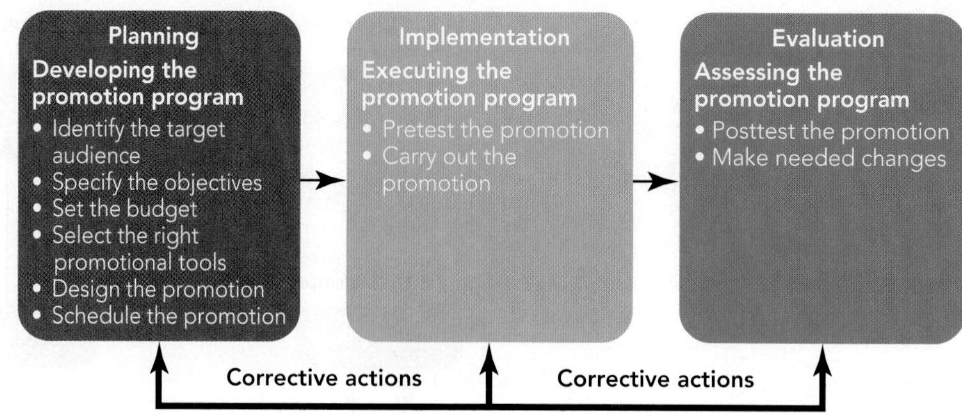

FIGURE 17–6
The promotion decision process includes planning, implementation, and evaluation.

Identifying the Target Audience

The first step in developing the promotion program involves identifying the *target audience*, the group of prospective buyers toward which a promotion program will be directed. To the extent that time and money permit, the target audience for the promotion program is the target market for the firm's product, which is identified from primary and secondary sources of marketing information. The more a firm knows about its target audience—including demographics, interests, preferences, media use, and purchase behaviors—the easier it is to develop a promotional program. A firm might use a profile based on gender, age, and income, for example, to place ads during specific TV programs or in particular magazines. Similarly, a firm might use *behavioral targeting*—collecting information about your web-browsing behavior to determine the banner and display ads that you will see as you surf the Web. Behavioral targeting is discussed in more detail in Chapter 21.[22]

Specifying Promotion Objectives

After the target audience has been identified, a decision must be reached on what the promotion should accomplish. Consumers can be said to respond in terms of a **hierarchy of effects**, which is the sequence of stages a prospective buyer goes through from initial awareness of a product to eventual action (either trial or adoption of the product).[23] The five stages are:

- *Awareness*—the consumer's ability to recognize and remember the product or brand name.
- *Interest*—an increase in the consumer's desire to learn about some of the features of the product or brand.
- *Evaluation*—the consumer's appraisal of the product or brand on important attributes.
- *Trial*—the consumer's actual first purchase and use of the product or brand.
- *Adoption*—through a favorable experience on the first trial, the consumer's repeated purchase and use of the product or brand.

For a totally new product, the sequence applies to the entire product category, but for a new brand competing in an established product category, it applies to the brand itself. These steps can serve as guidelines for developing promotion objectives.

Although sometimes an objective for a promotion program involves several steps in the hierarchy of effects, it often focuses on a single stage. Regardless of what the specific objective might be, from building awareness to increasing repeat purchases, promotion objectives should possess three important qualities. They should (1) be designed for a well-defined target audience, (2) be measurable, and (3) cover a specified time period.

Rank	Company	Advertising ($ in millions)	+	All Other Promotion ($ in millions)	=	Total ($ in millions)
1	Procter & Gamble	$3,143		$1,687		$4,830
2	General Motors	$1,655		$1,412		$3,067
3	Comcast	$1,772		$1,217		$2,989
4	AT&T	$1,592		$1,318		$2,910
5	Verizon	$1,439		$942		$2,381
6	Ford	$1,065		$1,212		$2,277
7	L'Oréal	$1,508		$732		$2,240
8	JPMorgan Chase	$447		$1,640		$2,087
9	American Express	$349		$1,722		$2,071
10	Toyota	$1,245		$763		$2,008

FIGURE 17–7
U.S. promotion expenditures of the top 10 companies. Note that Ford, JPMorgan Chase, and American Express spend more on promotion than on advertising.

Setting the Promotion Budget

From Figure 17–7, it is clear that the promotion expenditures needed to reach U.S. households are enormous. Note that each of the companies spends a total of more than $2 billion annually on promotion.[24]

After setting the promotion objectives, a company must decide how much to spend. Determining the ideal amount for the budget is difficult because there is no precise way to measure the exact results of spending promotion dollars. However, several methods can be used to set the promotion budget.[25]

Percentage of Sales In the **percentage of sales budgeting** approach, funds are allocated to promotion as a percentage of past or anticipated sales, in terms of either dollars or units sold. A common budgeting method, this approach is often stated in terms such as, "Our promotion budget for this year is 3 percent of last year's gross sales."[26] The advantage of this approach is obvious: It is simple and provides a financial safeguard by tying the promotion budget to sales. However, there is a major fallacy in this approach, which implies that sales cause promotion. Using this method, a company may reduce its promotion budget because of a downturn in past sales or an anticipated downturn in future sales—situations in which it may need promotion the most. See the Using Marketing Dashboards box on the next page for an application of the promotion-to-sales ratio to the soft-drink industry.[27]

Competitive Parity A second common approach, **competitive parity budgeting**, is matching the competitor's absolute level of spending or the proportion per point of market share. This approach has also been referred to as *matching competitors* or *share of market*. It is important to consider the competition in budgeting. Consumer responses to promotion are affected by competing promotional activities, so if a competitor runs 30 radio ads each week, it may be difficult for a firm to get its message across with only 5 ads. The competitor's budget level, however, should not be the only determinant in setting a company's budget. The competition might have very different promotional objectives, which require a different level of promotion expenditures.[28]

All You Can Afford Common to many small businesses is **all-you-can-afford budgeting**, in which money is allocated to promotion only after all other budget items are covered. As one company executive said in reference to this budgeting process, "Why, it's simple. First, I go upstairs to the controller and ask how much they can afford to give us this year. She says a million and a half. Later, the boss comes to me and

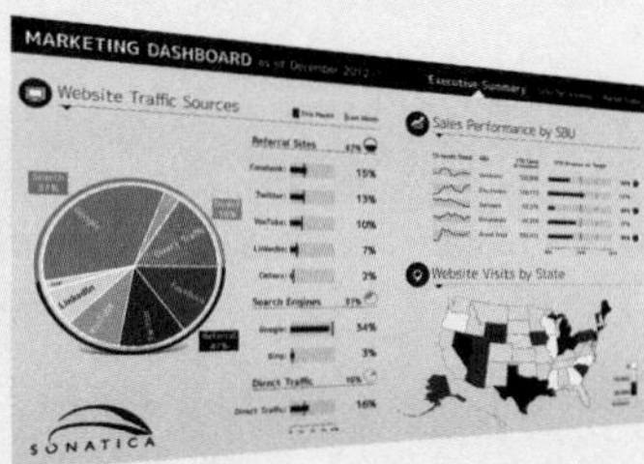

Using Marketing Dashboards

How Much Should You Spend on IMC?

Integrated marketing communications (IMC) programs coordinate a variety of promotion alternatives to provide a consistent message across audiences. The amount spent on the various promotional elements, or on the total campaign, may vary depending on the target audience, the type of product, where the product is in the product life cycle, and the channel strategy selected. Managers often use the promotion-to-sales ratio on their marketing dashboard to assess how effective the IMC program expenditures are at generating sales.

Your Challenge As a manager at PepsiCo, you've been asked to assess the effectiveness of all promotion expenditures during the past year. The promotion-to-sales ratio can be used to make year-to-year comparisons of a company's promotional programs, to compare the effectiveness of a company's program with competitors' programs, or to make comparisons with industry averages. You decide to calculate the promotion-to-sales ratio for PepsiCo. In addition, to allow a comparison, you decide to make the same calculation for one of your competitors, Coca-Cola, and for the entire nonalcoholic beverage industry. The ratio is calculated as follows:

Promotion-to-sales ratio =
Total promotion expenditures ÷ Total sales

Your Findings The information needed for these calculations is readily available from trade publications and annual reports. The following graph shows the promotion-to-sales ratio for PepsiCo, Coca-Cola, and the entire nonalcoholic beverage industry. PepsiCo spent $196 million on its promotion program to generate $2.3 billion in sales for a ratio of 8.5 (percent). In comparison, Coca-Cola's ratio was 5.3, and the industry average was 5.5.

Your Action PepsiCo's promotion-to-sales ratio is higher than Coca-Cola's and higher than the industry average. This suggests that the current mix of promotional activities and the level of expenditures may not be creating an effective IMC program. In the future, you will want to monitor the factors that may influence the ratio.

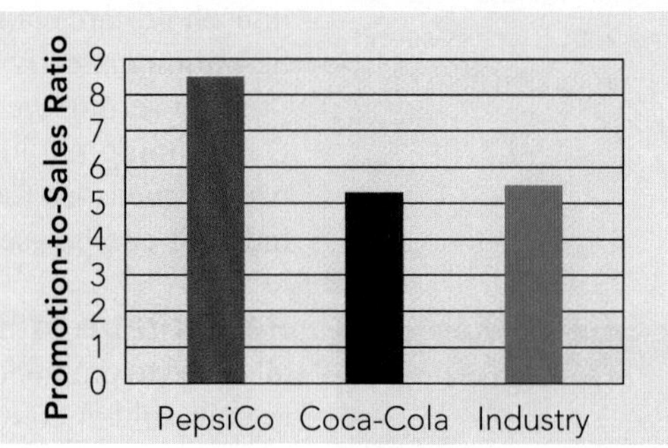

asks how much we should spend, and I say, 'Oh, about a million and a half.' Then we have our promotion appropriation."[29]

Fiscally conservative, this approach has little else to offer. Using this budgeting philosophy, a company acts as though it doesn't know anything about a promotion-sales relationship or what its promotion objectives are.

Objective and Task The best approach to budgeting is **objective and task budgeting**, whereby the company (1) determines its promotion objectives, (2) outlines the tasks it will undertake to accomplish those objectives, and (3) determines the promotion cost of performing those tasks.[30] This method takes into account what the company wants to accomplish and requires that the objectives be specified.[31] Strengths of the other budgeting methods are integrated into this approach because each previous method's strength is tied to the objectives. For example, if the costs are beyond what the company can afford, objectives are reworked and the tasks revised. The difficulty with this method is the judgment required to determine the tasks needed to accomplish objectives.

Selecting the Right Promotional Tools

Once a budget has been determined, the combination of the five basic IMC tools—advertising, personal selling, sales promotion, public relations, and direct marketing—can be specified. While many factors provide direction for selection of the appropriate

This logo for the 2016 Summer Olympics in Rio de Janeiro, Brazil, is part of a comprehensive IMC program.

QR 17-3
Olympics Video

mix, the large number of possible combinations of the promotional tools means that many combinations can achieve the same objective. Therefore, an analytical approach and experience are particularly important in this step of the promotion decision process. The specific mix can vary from a simple program using a single tool to a comprehensive program using all forms of promotion.

The Olympics have become a very visible example of a comprehensive integrated communications program. Because the Games are repeated every two years, the promotion is continuous during "on" and "off" years. Included in the program are advertising campaigns, personal selling efforts by the Olympic committee and organizers, sales promotion activities such as product tie-ins and sponsorships, public relations programs managed by the host cities, online and social media communication, and direct marketing efforts targeted at a variety of audiences, including governments, organizations, firms, athletes, and individuals.[32] At this stage, it is also important to assess the relative importance of the various tools. While it may be desirable to utilize and integrate several forms of promotion, one may deserve emphasis. The Olympics, for example, place primary importance on public relations and publicity.

Designing the Promotion

The central element of a promotion program is the promotion itself. Advertising consists of advertising copy and the artwork that the target audience is intended to see or hear. Personal selling efforts depend on the characteristics and skills of the salesperson. Sales promotion activities consist of the specific details of inducements such as coupons, samples, and sweepstakes. Public relations efforts are readily seen in tangible elements such as news releases, and direct marketing actions depend on written, verbal, and electronic forms of delivery. The design of the promotion will play a primary role in determining the message that is communicated to the audience. This design activity is frequently viewed as the step requiring the most creativity. In addition, successful designs are often the result of insight regarding consumers' interests and purchasing behavior. All of the promotion tools have many design alternatives. Advertising, for example, can utilize fear, humor, attractiveness, or other themes in its appeal. Similarly, direct marketing can be designed for varying levels of personal or customized appeals. One of the challenges of IMC is to design each promotional activity to communicate the same message.[33]

What promotional tools did Disney use to support the release of *Oz: The Great and Powerful*?

Scheduling the Promotion

Once the design of each of the promotional program elements is complete, it is important to determine the most effective timing of their use. The promotion schedule describes the order in which each promotional tool is introduced and the frequency of its use during the campaign.

Walt Disney Pictures movie studio, for example, uses a schedule of several promotional tools for its movies. To generate interest in a movie such as *Oz: The Great and Powerful*, the studio first invited the television program *Entertainment Tonight* to visit the set to film a behind-the-scenes story about the movie. The trailer for the movie was then released in regular format and in 3D format. In addition, a television commercial for the movie debuted during the Super Bowl, and the studio created a website with movie information, links to Twitter and Facebook, and games such as "Journey to Oz." An app called "Temple Run: Oz" was also created for the iPhone, iPad, and Android phones. As the premiere of the movie approached, Disney began a hot air balloon tour of the United States, added an Oz garden at Epcot Center, and sent the lead actor from the movie, James Franco, to serve as the grand marshal of the Daytona 500. Disney also launched a sweepstakes with partner World Market and collaborated with Home Shopping Network to create an exclusive collection of fashions, jewelry, and accessories based on the movie. After the movie was released, Disney used online promotions to encourage fans to purchase the DVD.[34]

Overall, the scheduling of the various promotions was designed to generate interest, bring consumers into theaters, and then encourage additional purchases after seeing the movie. Several factors such as seasonality and competitive promotion activity can also influence the promotion schedule. Businesses such as ski resorts, airlines, and professional sports teams are likely to reduce their promotional activity during the off-season. Similarly, restaurants, retail stores, and health clubs are likely to increase their promotional activity when new competitors enter the market.

EXECUTING AND ASSESSING THE PROMOTION PROGRAM

Carrying out the promotion program can be expensive and time-consuming. One researcher estimates that "an organization with sales less than $10 million can successfully implement an IMC program in one year, one with sales between $200 million and $500 million will need about three years, and one with sales between $2 billion and $5 billion will need five years." In addition, firms with a market orientation are more likely to implement an IMC program, and firms with support from top management have more effective IMC programs.[35] To facilitate the transition, approximately 200 integrated marketing communications agencies are in operation. In addition, some of the largest agencies are adopting approaches that embrace "total communications solutions."

QR 17-4
Carat Video

Media agency Carat, which recently won *Advertising Age* magazine's Media Agency of the Year award, for example, is part of a global network of 5,000 people in 70 countries who "help clients get the most from the new era of media." In fact, the agency website proclaims that it is "Redefining Media." The agency's services include sponsorship; product placement; direct marketing; strategy and planning; and digital, social, mobile, search, and out-of-home media buying. One of its integrated campaigns for Nokia included television and print advertising, banner ads, and online video ads. The campaign resulted in 5.1 million video views and a 61 percent increase in purchase intent. Other Carat clients include Home Depot, Disney, General Motors, Macy's, and GoPro. CEO Doug Ray explains that "clients are trying to globalize their brands," so Carat helps them "go to market faster, in a consistent way, across markets." While many agencies may still be specialists, the trend today is clearly toward an integrated perspective that includes all forms of promotion. Agencies can accomplish this by including account managers, channel experts, media specialists, and planning personnel in their campaign design efforts.[36]

An important factor in developing successful IMC programs is to create a process that facilitates their design and use. A tool used to evaluate a company's current process is the IMC audit. The audit analyzes the internal communication network of the company; identifies key audiences; evaluates customer databases; assesses messages in recent advertising, public relations releases, packaging, websites, e-mail and social media communication, signage, sales promotions, and direct mail; and determines the IMC expertise of company and agency personnel.[37] This process is becoming increasingly important as consumer-generated media such as blogs, RSS, podcasts, and social networks become more popular and as the use of search engines increases. Now, in addition to ensuring that traditional forms of communication are integrated, companies must be able to monitor consumer content, respond to inconsistent messages, and even answer questions from individual customers. According to Professor Judy Franks, marketers should also be cognizant of consumers she calls "accelerators." These individuals easily move content from medium to medium—from TV to YouTube to a mobile phone text message, for example—without any influence or control from the message source.[38]

As shown earlier in Figure 17–6, the ideal execution of a promotion program involves pretesting each design before it is actually used to allow for changes and modifications that improve its effectiveness. Similarly, posttests are recommended to evaluate the impact of each promotion and the contribution of the promotion toward achieving the program objectives. The most sophisticated pretest and posttest procedures have been developed for advertising and are discussed in Chapter 18. Testing procedures for sales promotion and direct marketing efforts currently focus on comparisons of different designs or responses of different segments. To fully benefit from IMC programs, companies must create and maintain a test-result database that allows comparisons of the relative impact of the promotional tools and their execution options in varying situations. Information from the databasc will allow informed design and execution decisions and provide support for IMC activities during internal reviews by financial or administrative personnel. The San Diego Padres baseball team, for example, developed a database of information relating attendance to its integrated campaign, which included a new logo, special events, merchandise sales, and a loyalty program.

As many as three-fourths of businesses may individually test new communication elements such as digital advertising, while one-fourth of all businesses may assess "most of their communication tactics" using new and traditional measures of effectiveness.[39] For most organizations, the assessment focuses on trying to determine which element of promotion works better. In an integrated program, however, media advertising might be used to build awareness, sales promotion to generate an inquiry, direct mail to provide additional information to individual prospects, and a personal sales call to complete the transaction. The tools are used for different reasons, and their combined use creates a synergy that should be the focus of the assessment. In addition, the effectiveness of IMC programs is strongly related to overall company performance.[40] Another level of assessment is necessary when firms have international promotion programs.

learning review

17-10. What are the characteristics of good promotion objectives?

17-11. What is the weakness of the percentage of sales budgeting approach?

17-12. How have advertising agencies changed to facilitate the use of IMC programs?

DIRECT MARKETING

Explain the value of direct marketing for consumers and sellers.

Direct marketing takes many forms and utilizes a variety of media. Several forms of direct marketing—direct mail and catalogs, television home shopping, telemarketing, and direct selling—were discussed as methods of nonstore retailing in Chapter 16. In addition, although advertising is discussed in Chapter 18, a form of advertising—direct response advertising—is an important form of direct marketing. Finally, interactive marketing is discussed in detail in Chapter 21. In this section, the growth of direct marketing, its value for consumers and sellers, and key global, technological, and ethical issues are discussed.

The Growth of Direct Marketing

The increasing interest in customer relationship management is reflected in the dramatic growth of direct marketing. The ability to customize communication efforts and

FIGURE 17–8
Business expenditures and response rates of four popular forms of direct marketing. Read the text to learn why the use of direct marketing is increasing.

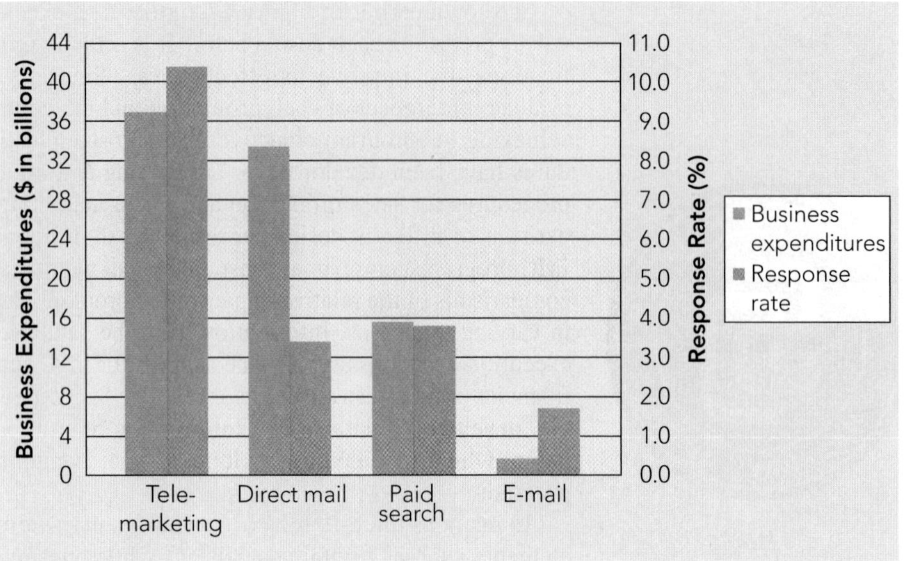

create one-to-one interactions is appealing to most marketers, particularly those with IMC programs, because it leads to more favorable attitudes from the recipients. While many direct marketing methods are not new, the ability to design and use them has increased with the availability of customer information databases and new printing technologies. In recent years, direct marketing growth has outpaced total economic growth. Direct marketing expenditures exceed $168 billion and are growing at a rate of 3.4 percent. Similarly, revenues are expected to grow to $2.4 trillion by 2016. Direct marketing currently accounts for 8.7 percent of the total U.S. gross domestic product. Figure 17–8 shows the annual expenditures on four popular forms of direct marketing and their typical response rates. For example, marketers spend over $33 billion on direct mail each year, and direct mail generates a 3.4 percent response rate.[41]

While telemarketing receives the highest level of expenditures, most campaigns use several methods. jcpenney is one company that has integrated its direct marketing activities. The company begins a campaign by sending coupons to customers through e-mail and text messages. Consumers also receive direct-mail postcards and "Look Books" that invite them to visit the company's e-commerce website www.jcpenney.com or mobile commerce site www.m.jcpenney.com. A special social commerce app is also available for purchases on jcpenney's Facebook "Fan" Page. Many companies also integrate their direct marketing with other forms of promotion. Porsche, for example, recently launched television ads to change consumer perceptions of its cars and supported the campaign with direct-mail brochures, a mobile application, and an online video contest. As part of its campaign, Porsche parked its cars in the driveways of selected homes, took photos, and then created customized cards for delivery to each of the homes! Mobile direct marketing sales and social network direct marketing sales are growing at 33 percent and 20 percent, respectively—the fastest of all direct marketing tools.[42]

The Value of Direct Marketing

One of the most visible indicators of the value of direct marketing for consumers is its increasing level of use in its various forms. For example, in the past year, 52 percent of the U.S. population ordered merchandise or services by mail; more than 110 million people made purchases online; and consumers spent more than $147 billion on products available through television offers. In addition, 57 percent of social media users say that they are more likely to purchase a product after seeing a positive post.

For consumers, direct marketing offers a variety of benefits, including: They don't have to go to a store; they can usually shop 24 hours a day; buying direct saves time; they avoid hassles with salespeople; they can save money; it's fun and entertaining; and it offers more privacy than in-store shopping. Many consumers also believe that direct marketing provides excellent customer service. Toll-free telephone numbers, customer service representatives with access to information regarding purchasing preferences, overnight delivery services, and unconditional guarantees all help create value for direct marketing customers. At Landsend.com, when customers need assistance they can click the "Live Help" icon to receive help from a sales representative on the phone or through online chat or online video until the correct product is found. "It's like we were walking down the aisle in a store!" says one Lands' End customer.[43]

QR 17-5
Priceline Ad

The value of direct marketing for sellers can be described in terms of the responses it generates. **Direct orders** are the result of offers that contain all the information necessary for a prospective buyer to make a decision to purchase and complete the transaction. Priceline.com, for example, will send *PriceBreaker* RSS alerts to people in its database. The messages offer discounted fares and rates to customers who can travel on very short notice. **Lead generation** is the result of an offer designed to generate interest in a product or service and a request for additional information. Four Seasons Hotels now sell private residences in several of their properties and send direct mail to prospective residents asking them to request additional information on the telephone or through a website. Finally, **traffic generation** is the outcome of an offer designed to motivate people to visit a business. Home Depot, for example, uses an opt-in e-mail alert to announce special sales that attract consumers to the store. Similarly, Target uses direct mail to generate traffic in new and remodeled stores.[44]

Target uses direct mail to motivate people to visit its stores.

Technological, Global, and Ethical Issues in Direct Marketing

The information technology and databases described in Chapter 8 are key elements in any direct marketing program. Databases are the result of organizations' efforts to create profiles of customers so that direct marketing tools, such as e-mail and catalogs, can be directed at specific customers. While most companies try to keep records of their customers' past purchases, many other types of data are needed to use direct marketing to develop one-to-one relationships with customers. Some data, such as lifestyles, media use, and demographics, are best collected from the consumer. Other types of data, such as price, quantity, and brand, are best collected from the businesses where purchases are made. New integrated marketing databases match consumers' postal addresses, telephone numbers, and e-mail addresses. In addition, many businesses are beginning to match their customer records with Facebook profiles, Twitter following behavior, and Google search activity.[45]

Increases in postage rates and the decline in the economy have also increased the importance of information related to the cost of direct marketing activities. For example, the Direct Marketing Association estimates that e-mail advertising expenditures outperform social media advertising by a ratio of 3-to-1. Similarly, catalog businesses have found they can reduce the cost of printing by using innovations such as soy-based ink and recycled paper, and they can reduce postage fees through database list analysis. Related to postage fees, many direct marketers are assessing the potential impact of the USPS plan for a five-day mail delivery cycle.[46]

Direct marketing faces several challenges and opportunities in global markets today. Many countries, including the United Kingdom, Australia, the European Union, and Japan, have requirements for a mandatory "opt-in"—that is, potential customers must give permission to be included on a list for direct marketing solicitations. In addition, the mail, telephone, and Internet systems in many countries are not as well developed as they are in the United States. The need for improved reliability and security in these countries has slowed the growth of direct mail, while the dramatic growth of mobile phone penetration has created an opportunity for direct mobile marketing campaigns.

Making Responsible Decisions

ethics

What Is the Future of Your Privacy?

In 2003, the Federal Trade Commission opened the National Do Not Call Registry to give Americans a tool for maintaining their privacy on home and cellular telephone lines. More than 70 percent of all Americans registered. Since then, several state legislatures have also passed laws to create do-not-call lists for automated (robo) telephone calls. In addition, new discussions about privacy related to mail and computer use are now taking place.

Generally, the question being debated is, "What information is private?" Are telephone numbers, addresses of residences, and online activities private or public information? Proponents of a do-not-mail registry argue that, like telephone calls, citizens should be able to stop unsolicited mail. Proponents of do-not-track regulations suggest that website owners who use cookies to collect information about consumers' shopping habits should only do so with a consumer's consent. Marketers counter that consumers who share this information are more likely to receive messages and advertising that better match their interests.

The Direct Marketing Association currently advocates several solutions. First, it has created DMAchoice, an online tool to help consumers manage the types of mail and e-mail they receive. Second, the organization endorses a self-regulatory program for online behavioral advertising (OBA) that encourages advertisers to include an "Ad Choices" icon in the corner of online ads to allow consumers to opt out of having data collected about their online activities. Moving beyond self-regulation, the European Union recently passed the *E-Privacy Directive* to provide explicit laws for website owners. And in the United States, the Senate is evaluating the "Do Not Track Online Act." These guidelines and regulations, of course, have huge implications for advertisers, portals such as Facebook and Google, and consumers.

What is your opinion? What types of information should be private? Can we find a balance between self-regulation and legislation?

QR 17-6
Ad Choices
Video

Another issue for global direct marketers is payment. The availability of credit and credit cards varies throughout the world, creating the need for alternatives such as C.O.D. (cash on delivery), bank deposits, and online payment accounts.[47]

Global and domestic direct marketers both face challenging ethical issues today. Concerns about privacy, for example, have led to various attempts to provide guidelines that balance consumer and business interests. The European Union passed a consumer privacy law, called the *Data Protection Directive*, after several years of discussion with the Federation of European Direct Marketing and the U.K.'s Direct Marketing Association. A new version of the law, called the *General Data Protection Regulation*, will address new developments such as social networks and cloud computing and is scheduled to take effect in 2016.

In the United States, the Federal Trade Commission and many state legislatures have also been concerned about privacy. Several bills that call for a do-not-mail registry similar to the Do Not Call Registry are being discussed. Similarly, there are growing concerns about the web "tracking" tools used by direct marketers to segment consumers and match them with advertising. The Making Responsible Decisions box describes some of the issues under consideration.[48]

learning review

17-13. The ability to design and use direct marketing programs has increased with the availability of ___________ and ___________.

17-14. What are the three types of responses generated by direct marketing activities?

LEARNING OBJECTIVES REVIEW

LO 17-1 *Discuss integrated marketing communication and the communication process.*
Integrated marketing communication is the concept of designing marketing communications programs that coordinate all promotional activities—advertising, personal selling, sales promotion, public relations, and direct marketing—to provide a consistent message across all audiences. The communication process conveys messages with six elements: a source, a message, a channel of communication, a receiver, and encoding and decoding. The communication process also includes a feedback loop and can be distorted by noise.

LO 17-2 *Describe the promotional mix and the uniqueness of each component.*
There are five promotional alternatives. Advertising, sales promotion, and public relations are mass selling approaches, whereas personal selling and direct marketing use customized messages. Advertising can have high absolute costs but reaches large numbers of people. Personal selling has a high cost per contact but provides immediate feedback. Public relations is often difficult to obtain but is very credible. Sales promotion influences short-term consumer behavior. Direct marketing can help develop customer relationships, although maintaining a database can be very expensive.

LO 17-3 *Select the promotional approach appropriate to a product's target audience, life-cycle stage, and characteristics, as well as stages of the buying decision and channel strategies.*
The promotional mix depends on the target audience. Programs for consumers, business buyers, and intermediaries might emphasize advertising, personal selling, and sales promotion, respectively. The promotional mix also changes over the product life-cycle stages. During the introduction stage, all promotional mix elements are used. During the growth stage advertising is emphasized, while the maturity stage utilizes sales promotion and direct marketing. Little promotion is used during the decline stage. Product characteristics also help determine the promotion mix. The level of complexity, risk, and ancillary services required will determine which element is needed. Knowing the customer's stage in the buying process can help marketers select appropriate promotions. Advertising and public relations can create awareness in the prepurchase stage, personal selling and sales promotion can facilitate the purchase, and advertising can help reduce anxiety in the postpurchase stage. Finally, the promotional mix can depend on the channel strategy. Push strategies require personal selling and sales promotions directed at channel members, while pull strategies depend on advertising and sales promotion directed at consumers.

LO 17-4 *Describe the elements of the promotion decision process.*
The promotional decision process consists of three steps: planning, implementation, and evaluation. The planning step consists of six elements: identify the target audience, specify the objectives, set the budget, select the right promotional elements, design the promotion, and schedule the promotion. The implementation step includes pretesting. The evaluation step includes posttesting.

LO 17-5 *Explain the value of direct marketing for consumers and sellers.*
The value of direct marketing for consumers is indicated by its increasing level of use. For example, during the past year, 52 percent of the U.S. population made a purchase by mail and more than 110 million people shopped online. The value of direct marketing for sellers can be measured in terms of three types of responses: direct orders, lead generation, and traffic generation.

FOCUSING ON KEY TERMS

advertising p. 444
all-you-can-afford budgeting p. 455
channel of communication p. 442
communication p. 442
competitive parity budgeting p. 455
decoding p. 443
direct marketing p. 447
direct orders p. 461
encoding p. 443
feedback p. 444
field of experience p. 443
hierarchy of effects p. 454
integrated marketing communications (IMC) p. 442
lead generation p. 461
message p. 442
noise p. 444
objective and task budgeting p. 456
percentage of sales budgeting p. 455
personal selling p. 445
promotional mix p. 441
public relations p. 446
publicity p. 446
pull strategy p. 453
push strategy p. 452
receivers p. 442
response p. 444
sales promotion p. 447
source p. 442
traffic generation p. 461

APPLYING MARKETING KNOWLEDGE

1 After listening to a recent sales presentation, Mary Smith signed up for membership at the local health club. On arriving at the facility, she learned there was an additional fee for racquetball court rentals. "I don't remember that in the sales talk; I thought they said all facilities were included with the membership fee," complained Mary. Describe the problem in terms of the communication process.

2 Develop a matrix to compare the five elements of the promotional mix on three criteria—to *whom* you deliver the message, *what* you say, and *when* you say it.

3 Explain how the promotional tools used by an airline would differ if the target audience were (*a*) consumers who travel for pleasure and (*b*) corporate travel departments that select the airlines to be used by company employees.

4 Suppose you introduced a new consumer food product and invested heavily both in national advertising (pull strategy) and in training and motivating your field salesforce to sell the product to food stores (push strategy). What kinds of feedback would you receive from both the advertising and your salesforce? How could you increase both the quality and quantity of each?

5 Fisher-Price Company, long known as a manufacturer of children's toys, has introduced a line of clothing for children. Outline a promotional plan to get this product introduced in the marketplace.

6 Many insurance companies sell health insurance plans to companies. In these companies the employees pick the plan, but the set of offered plans is determined by the company. Recently, Blue Cross–Blue Shield, a health insurance company, ran a television ad stating, "If your employer doesn't offer you Blue Cross–Blue Shield coverage, ask why." Explain the promotional strategy behind the advertisement.

7 Identify the sales promotion tools that might be useful for (*a*) Tastee Yogurt, a new brand introduction, (*b*) 3M self-sticking Post-it® Notes, and (*c*) Wrigley's Spearmint gum.

8 Design an integrated marketing communications program—using each of the five promotional elements—for Rhapsody, the online music service.

9 BMW recently introduced its first sport activity vehicle, the X6, to compete with other popular crossover vehicles such as the Mercedes-Benz R-Class. Design a direct marketing program to generate (*a*) leads, (*b*) traffic in dealerships, and (*c*) direct orders.

10 Develop a privacy policy for database managers that provides a balance of consumer and seller perspectives. How would you encourage voluntary compliance with your policy? What methods of enforcement would you recommend?

BUILDING YOUR MARKETING PLAN

To develop the promotion strategy for your marketing plan, follow the steps suggested in the planning phase of the promotion decision process described in Figure 17–6.

1 You should (*a*) identify the target audience, (*b*) specify the promotion objectives, (*c*) set the promotion budget, (*d*) select the right promotion tools, (*e*) design the promotion, and (*f*) schedule the promotion.

2 Also specify the pretesting and posttesting procedures needed in the implementation and evaluation phases.

3 Finally, describe how each of your promotion tools is integrated to provide a consistent message.

VIDEO CASE 17 Mountain Dew: Using IMC and Social Media to Create and Promote a New Flavor

QR 17-7
Mountain Dew Video Case

"When you look at a brand like Mountain Dew, and actually many of our brands, we absolutely used to have a focus on creating iconic TV advertising. That was how the marketing model worked. Right now when you look at what the brand needs going forward, that's just not going to do it. That's not going to be able to break through. So we are completely changing our approach," observes Lauren Hobart, chief marketing officer for Sparkling Beverages at PepsiCo, Inc. Pepsi's new model is to apply an integrated marketing communications (IMC) approach that utilizes traditional promotion tools and new social media to engage consumers. Mountain Dew has based its extraordinarily successful "DEWmocracy" campaigns on this new model. "No longer is it OK to just stand and talk to your consumers one way," observes Hobart.

THE BRAND

Mountain Dew is a citrus-flavored carbonated soft drink invented by Barney and Ally Hartman in Tennessee during the 1940s. The name was derived from a slang term for moonshine whiskey and matched the unique energizing effect created by carbonated water, extra sugar, caffeine, concentrated orange juice, and citric acid. The beverage became very popular in local markets and attracted the attention of PepsiCo, Inc., in the early 1960s, when it acquired Mountain Dew as its first flavored soft drink.

During the past 50 years, terms used to describe the brand image have changed from "hillbilly," to "country cool," to "young and irreverent," but all have conveyed a common underlying theme. As Frank Cooper, senior vice president and chief consumer engagement officer, explains, "There is a thread that went throughout the Mountain Dew experience throughout the years." The thread had three dimensions:

- A "do-it-yourself" ethic
- An "operating outside of the mainstream" perspective
- A "remain true to yourself" attitude

These elements were part of all of Mountain Dew's advertising campaigns as it moved from popularity in rural areas to distribution in suburbs and metropolitan areas. The expansion really took off when the "Do the Dew" campaign began. This campaign positioned Mountain Dew as a product for "edgy" young consumers involved in activities such as skateboarding, snowboarding, skydiving, windsurfing, extreme sports, and video gaming.

Today Mountain Dew is a megabrand in the soft-drink category, with about 6 percent of all carbonated soft-drink sales in the United States and about 80 percent of the citrus soft-drink market. Mountain Dew has more than 30 flavors and variations including caffeine-free, diet, Code Red, LiveWire, Pitch Black, Baja Blast, Voltage, Throwback, Cherry Fusion, and White Out. Its main competition includes Mello Yello and Sun Drop. It is one of 19 brands at PepsiCo with sales greater than $1 billion, and it is the company's second largest beverage, behind only Pepsi-Cola. PepsiCo, Inc., has annual revenues of approximately $60 billion from several businesses, which also include the Frito-Lay, Quaker, Tropicana, and Gatorade brands.

THE DEWMOCRACY CAMPAIGNS

The general concept of the DEWmocracy campaigns is to harness the passion of Mountain Dew's loyal customers. The need for the concept resulted from several changes in the marketplace. First, the carbonated beverage market became very competitive. Hobart describes the situation: "There has been a proliferation of new products. With the rise of energy drinks, with the rise of enhanced water, there has been growth coming from all places, and the model of how we compete has dramatically had to change over the last few years." Second, consumers became more

Stage	Name	Description
1	Truck Stop: Taste the Flavors	In the first stage, trucks traveled to 17 markets in 12 states, giving consumers a chance to sample seven possible new flavors.
2	Make Your Voice Heard: Flavor Nations	The top three flavors from Stage One were sent to 4,000 loyal Dew consumers. Each participant selected their favorite flavor and joined the corresponding Flavor Nation.
3	Shoot Your Shade: Color Selection	The members of each Flavor Nation selected three colors from an 18-color palette, and then all consumers voted on Facebook to select the best of the nine final colors.
4	Name Game: Name the Product	Flavor Nation members submitted name suggestions and then selected the top three. Dew fans could become followers of their favorite name on Twitter. The winners of the Twitter race were Typhoon, Distortion, and White Out.
5	Dew Art: Design Your Can	Mountain Dew asked designers, art schools, and Dew fans to submit labels for each flavor. Fan votes were used to select the top 10 labels, and each Flavor Nation selected the best of the top 10. Dew brand teams then adjusted them to look good on the shelf.
6	Creative Juices: Advertising	Advertising agencies, film students, and individuals were asked to submit 12-second commercials on 12seconds.tv, where fans voted to select the top ads. The winners then prepared 15-second versions to air on television.
7	Vote in the Flavor Battle	The three products were introduced in stores and consumers voted for their favorite. The winner was added to the Dew product line!

FIGURE 1
The seven stages of the DEWmocracy 2 campaign.

interested in authentic, high-involvement brand experiences. These types of experiences were difficult to offer through a single media outlet. "We had noticed that traditional ways of connecting with consumers weren't working as well," observes Mark Hanson, brand manager for Mountain Dew.

The first DEWmocracy campaign began in late 2007 by asking consumers to choose the next Dew's flavor, color, name, and graphics. More than 1 million people participated in the process, which utilized a website, DEWmocracy.com, and featured gaming elements and a discussion board. The results led to three final concepts—Supernova, Revolution, and Voltage—being introduced to the market. Three months later, Voltage, which featured a citrus-charged flavor and a deep blue color, was announced as the winner. Voltage has gone on to exceed its sales volume projections, selling more than 17 million cases after its introduction as the winner.

The success of the first DEWmocracy campaign led to another DEWmocracy campaign and the integration of more communication tools. In addition to the website, the second campaign utilized many forms of social media, such as Facebook, Twitter, 12seconds.tv, and YouTube. DEWmocracy 2 involved a seven-stage process (described in Figure 1). Stage One was a truck stop tour that allowed consumers to try seven new flavors of Mountain Dew. During this stage Mountain Dew also gave away home testing kits to winners of a video testimonial contest. The second stage organized loyal fans into "Flavor Nations" based on their preference for one of the top three flavors from Stage One. In the third stage, fans chose product colors. Stage Four used a Twitter race to determine the names of each flavor. Stage Five determined the design of the cans and Stage Six selected television advertising for each flavor. The seventh and final stage introduced each of the three flavors to the market for voting.

Each Flavor Nation used Facebook and Twitter to generate votes for their flavor. After two months of competition and voting, Mountain Dew White Out was declared the winner with 44 percent of the votes. Consumers had played an active role in the design and selection of a new Mountain Dew flavor. In addition, for the first time, consumers also had played a role in the selection of paid media, which ran on television.

THE RESULTS

The effectiveness of the DEWmocracy 2 campaign can be measured in many ways. Each stage of the process can be evaluated in terms of a variety of statistics. For example:

- The truck stop tour generated a total attendance of 1.5 million people.
- The color selection stage generated 538 total viewer hours.
- The Twitter race attracted more than 1,900 followers.
- The advertising challenge videos received 202,000 views.
- The final stage, the flavor battle, generated almost 3 million votes.

In addition, there was dramatic growth in the general interest in Mountain Dew. Prior to the campaign Mountain Dew had about 125,000 Facebook members. By the end of the campaign, Mountain Dew had 1 million Facebook members. This is critically important because, as Frank Cooper explains, "You have to move cases, so volume is important," however, "the second piece of it is . . . deepening the connection with the people who love the brand."

DEWmocracy 2 represents an excellent example of an integrated marketing communications campaign utilizing many media alternatives to reinforce a central message. The process included sales promotion activities such as the truck events, video contests, and retail displays; advertising such as the online messages during the seven-stage process and traditional (television) advertising following the selection of the winner; and public relations activities such as the press releases and news coverage generated by the interest in the DEWmocracy campaign. Mountain Dew also used new forms of communication such as prompting Xbox users to vote for one of the new flavors.

Mark Hanson offers a good summary of the DEWmocracy approach: "I think what DEWmocracy 1 and ultimately DEWmocracy 2 have done, is solidify Mountain Dew's position as a brand that acknowledges and embraces the desires of its fans. There is tangible proof that we are listening to the voice of the consumer throughout. It uniquely situates Mountain Dew in the consumer landscape as a brand for the people, by the people." Since the first two DEWmocracy campaigns have been so successful, watch for the announcement of a third one soon!

Questions

1 What changes in the environment provided the opportunity for the DEWmocracy approach?

2 Which of the promotional elements described in Figure 17–2 were used by Mountain Dew in its DEWmocracy 2 campaign?

3 What are some of the different ways Mountain Dew can assess the success of its campaign?

18 Advertising, Sales Promotion, and Public Relations

Learning Objectives

After reading this chapter you should be able to:

LO 18-1 Explain the differences between product advertising and institutional advertising and the variations within each type.

LO 18-2 Describe the steps used to develop, execute, and evaluate an advertising program.

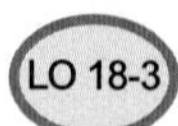
LO 18-3 Explain the advantages and disadvantages of alternative advertising media.

LO 18-4 Discuss the strengths and weaknesses of consumer-oriented and trade-oriented sales promotions.

LO 18-5 Recognize public relations as an important form of communication.

What Is the Killer App of Advertising? Television!

By every measure, television represents the single largest medium for advertisers. The combination of broadcast TV and cable/satellite TV has a powerful grip on consumers. Watch closely, though, and in the next few years you will see the newest version of television—online TV—become a key third element to television advertising!

Television has been a dominant part of the advertising landscape for decades. Over the years there have been many changes to the technology, including the invention of remote controls, VCRs, DVRs, pay-per-view, videotape and DVD rental, and high-definition transmission. The changing technology has also led to changes in television advertising. For example, the potential for skipping ads encouraged a shift from traditional 60-second ads to 30-, 15-, 5-, and even 1-second ads. As viewers increased their use of rentals, advertisers increased their focus on live events and reality programming that was more likely to be viewed in real time. As technology improved, advertisers experimented with 3D formats. All of these changes were attempts to adjust to the behaviors and preferences of consumers. None of them, however, are likely to compare to the changes coming during the next few years.

What's the next big thing in TV? In addition to traditional broadcast, cable, and satellite television, programming will be available through the Internet. OTV, or online TV, is the growing capability to view streaming video that is available online. This new capability makes it possible to view programming on desktop computers, laptops, tablets, and smartphones—anywhere and anytime. In fact, the availability of programming on these devices has prompted some households to stop using cable and satellite services and to view all of their programming through the Internet. Television rating company Nielsen has labeled this group "Zero TV" households. They watch television programming, just not on televisions!

You may already be familiar with some versions of OTV. Hulu, for example, is an ad-supported subscription service offering streaming video of TV shows, movies, and other content from NBC, Fox, ABC, and other networks. Similarly, Machinima is a YouTube channel that offers how-to clips, user-generated video, and original series such as *Mortal Kombat: Legacy* and *Bite Me*. The channel currently has more than 8 million subscribers. Netflix, Apple, and Amazon also offer video-on-demand services.

Many companies are preparing to participate in this transformation. Microsoft is talking to TV networks about providing a package of channels to its 76 million Xbox users and 46 million Xbox Live subscribers. In addition, the company recently opened the Xbox Entertainment Studio to create original programming. Verizon is setting up a new business unit, Verizon Digital Media Services, to deliver live TV on the Web to any network-connected device. In addition, YouTube is developing premium-content offerings in categories ranging from sports, to cooking, to video games. "It's going to be the Wild West for a while until it settles down and matures and the economics settle out," explains David Rips, president of Verizon's TV service.

Advertisers are excited because OTV will offer targeted audiences who are engaged in the programming. According to Allen DeBevoise, CEO of Machinima, "People are not only watching these videos, they're also embedding, ranking, and replying to them." Early evidence suggests that OTV will provide many challenges and opportunities for advertisers. There is no question that television is becoming advertising's killer app![1]

The growth of OTV is just one of the many exciting changes occurring in the field of advertising today. They illustrate the importance of advertising as one of the five promotional mix elements in marketing communications programs. This chapter describes three of the promotional mix elements—advertising, sales promotion, and public relations. Direct marketing was covered in Chapter 17, and personal selling is covered in Chapter 20.

TYPES OF ADVERTISEMENTS

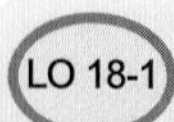

LO 18-1 Explain the differences between product advertising and institutional advertising and the variations within each type.

Chapter 17 described **advertising** as any paid form of nonpersonal communication about an organization, a product, a service, or an idea by an identified sponsor. As you look through any magazine, watch television, listen to the radio, or browse the Internet, the variety of advertisements you see or hear may give you the impression that they have few similarities. Advertisements are prepared for different purposes, but they basically consist of two types: product advertisements and institutional advertisements.

Product Advertisements

Focused on selling a good or service, **product advertisements** take three forms: (1) pioneering (or informational), (2) competitive (or persuasive), and (3) reminder. Look at the ads for DIGIORNO®, Fidelity Investments, and Dove Chocolate to determine the type and objective of each ad.

Used in the introductory stage of the product life cycle, *pioneering* advertisements tell people what a product is, what it can do, and where it can be found. The key objective of a pioneering advertisement (such as the ad for DIGIORNO® PIZZERIA!™ pizza) is to inform the target market. Informational ads, particularly those with specific message content, have been found to be interesting, convincing, and effective.[2]

Advertising that promotes a specific brand's features and benefits is *competitive*. The objective of these messages is to persuade the target market to select the firm's brand rather than that of a competitor. An increasingly common form of competitive advertising is *comparative* advertising, which shows one brand's strengths relative to those of competitors.[3] The Fidelity ad, for example, highlights the competitive advantages of Fidelity's online trading service compared to Schwab, E*TRADE, and TD Ameritrade. Studies indicate that comparative ads attract more attention and increase the perceived quality of the advertiser's brand although their impact may vary by product type, message content, and audience gender.[4] Firms that use comparative advertising need market research to provide legal support for their claims.[5]

Reminder advertising is used to reinforce previous knowledge of a product. The Dove Promises® ad reminds consumers about a special event, in this case, Valentine's

Product advertisements take three forms—pioneering, competitive, or reminder—depending on their objective. See if you can correctly identify the ads shown here.

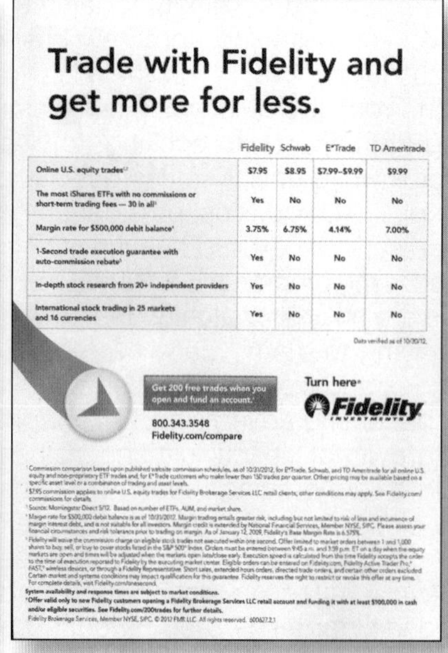

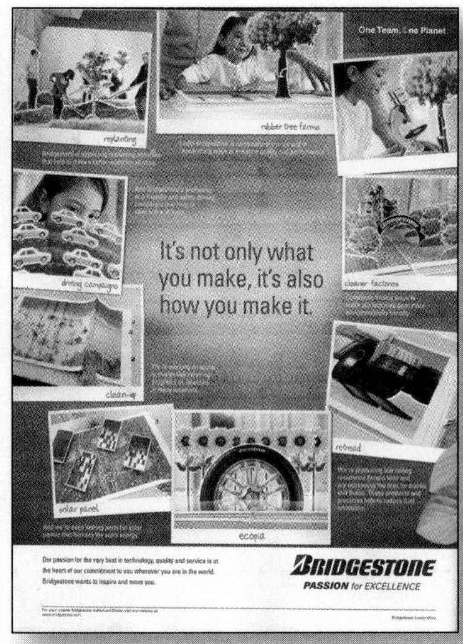

Chevron uses an advocacy ad to communicate its position on "protecting the planet." Bridgestone uses a pioneering ad to inform readers about how it makes its products.

Day. Reminder advertising is good for products that have achieved a well-recognized position and are in the mature phase of their product life cycle. Another type of reminder ad, *reinforcement*, is used to assure current users they made the right choice. For example, consider the tag line used in Dial soap advertisements: "Aren't you glad you use Dial? Don't you wish everybody did?"

Institutional Advertisements

The objective of **institutional advertisements** is to build goodwill or an image for an organization rather than promote a specific good or service. Institutional advertising has been used by companies such as Texaco, Pfizer, and IBM to build confidence in the company name.[6] Often this form of advertising is used to support the public relations plan or counter adverse publicity. Four alternative forms of institutional advertisements are often used:

QR 18-1 Chevron Video

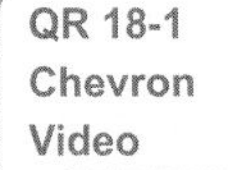

1. *Advocacy* advertisements state the position of a company on an issue. Chevron's "We Agree" campaign places ads stating its position on issues such as renewable energy, protecting the planet, and community development. Another form of advocacy advertisement is used when organizations make a request related to a particular action or behavior, such as a request by the American Red Cross for blood donations.
2. *Pioneering institutional* advertisements, like the pioneering ads for products discussed earlier, are used for announcements about what a company is, what it can do, or where it is located. Recent Bayer ads stating, "We cure more headaches than you think," are intended to inform consumers that the company produces many products in addition to aspirin. Bridgestone uses pioneering institutional ads in its "One Team. One Planet" campaign to inform people about its rubber tree farms, tire recycling, and environmentally friendly factories.
3. *Competitive institutional* advertisements promote the advantages of one product class over another and are used in markets where different product classes compete for the same buyers. America's milk processors and dairy farmers use their "Got Milk?" campaign, shown on the next page, to increase demand for milk as it competes against other beverages.
4. *Reminder institutional* advertisements, like reminder ads for products, simply bring the company's name to the attention of the target market again. The Army branch of the U.S. military sponsors a campaign to remind potential recruits of the opportunities available in the Army.

A competitive institutional ad by dairy farmers tries to increase demand for milk, and a reminder institutional ad by the U.S. Army tries to keep the attention of the target market.

Finishing touch.
got milk?

YOU'RE GOOD AT
STANDING OUT,
BUT CAN YOU
BLEND IN?
U.S. ARMY
ARMY STRONG.

learning review

18-1. What is the difference between pioneering and competitive ads?

18-2. What is the purpose of an institutional advertisement?

DEVELOPING THE ADVERTISING PROGRAM

LO 18-2 Describe the steps used to develop, execute, and evaluate an advertising program.

The promotion decision process described in Chapter 17 can be applied to each of the promotional elements. Advertising, for example, can be managed by following the three steps (developing, executing, and evaluating) of the process.

Identifying the Target Audience

To develop an effective advertising program, advertisers must identify the target audience. All aspects of an advertising program are likely to be influenced by the characteristics of the prospective consumer. Understanding the lifestyles, attitudes, and demographics of the target market is essential. Diet Mountain Dew, for example, is targeted at Generation X males, while Kraft's Crystal Light Liquid is targeted at calorie-conscious women. Both campaigns emphasize advertising techniques that match their target audiences. To appeal to Generation X males, Diet Mountain Dew became the sponsor of Dale Earnhardt Jr.'s NASCAR team. Meanwhile, to attract calorie-conscious women, Crystal Light began providing nutritional information on a dedicated Facebook Page and on Twitter.

Under Armour places its ads to reach competitive women.

NO
MATTER
WHAT
SWEAT
EVERY
DAY
I WILL.

Similarly, the placement of the advertising depends on the audience. When Under Armour introduced its recent "What's Beautiful" campaign featuring women's apparel, it ran ads with the tag line, "No matter what, sweat every day. I will." on ESPNW, DailyCandy, and Gilt Groupe to reach competitive women. Even scheduling can depend on the audience. Nike schedules advertising, sponsorships, deals, and endorsements to correspond with the Olympics to appeal to amateur, college, and professional athletes.[7]

To eliminate possible bias that might result from subjective judgments about some population segments, the Federal Communications Commission suggests that advertising program decisions be based on market research about the target audience.[8]

Specifying Advertising Objectives

The guidelines for setting promotion objectives described in Chapter 17 also apply to setting advertising objectives. This step helps advertisers with other choices in the promotion decision process, such as selecting media and evaluating a campaign. Advertising with an objective of creating awareness, for example, would be better matched with a magazine than a directory such as the Yellow Pages. The Association of Magazine Media believes objectives are so important that it is developing an awards program to recognize magazine advertising campaigns that demonstrate both creative excellence and effectiveness in meeting campaign objectives. Similarly, the Advertising Research Foundation sponsors research forums to advance the practice of measuring and evaluating the effectiveness of advertising and marketing communication.[9]

Experts believe that factors such as product category, brand, and consumer involvement in the purchase decision may change the importance—and, possibly, the sequence—of the stages of the hierarchy of effects (see Chapter 17). Snickers, for example, knew that its consumers were unlikely to engage in elaborate information processing when it designed a recent campaign. The result was ads with simple humorous messages rather than extensive factual information. New managerial perspectives also consider that advertising can have a long-term impact on the financial value of the organization.[10]

Setting the Advertising Budget

In 1990, advertisers paid $700,000 to place a 30-second ad during the Super Bowl. By 2013, the cost of placing a 30-second ad during Super Bowl XLVII was $3.8 million (see Figure 18–1). The escalating cost is related to the growing number of

FIGURE 18–1
The Super Bowl delivers a huge audience, if you can afford the cost of placing an ad.

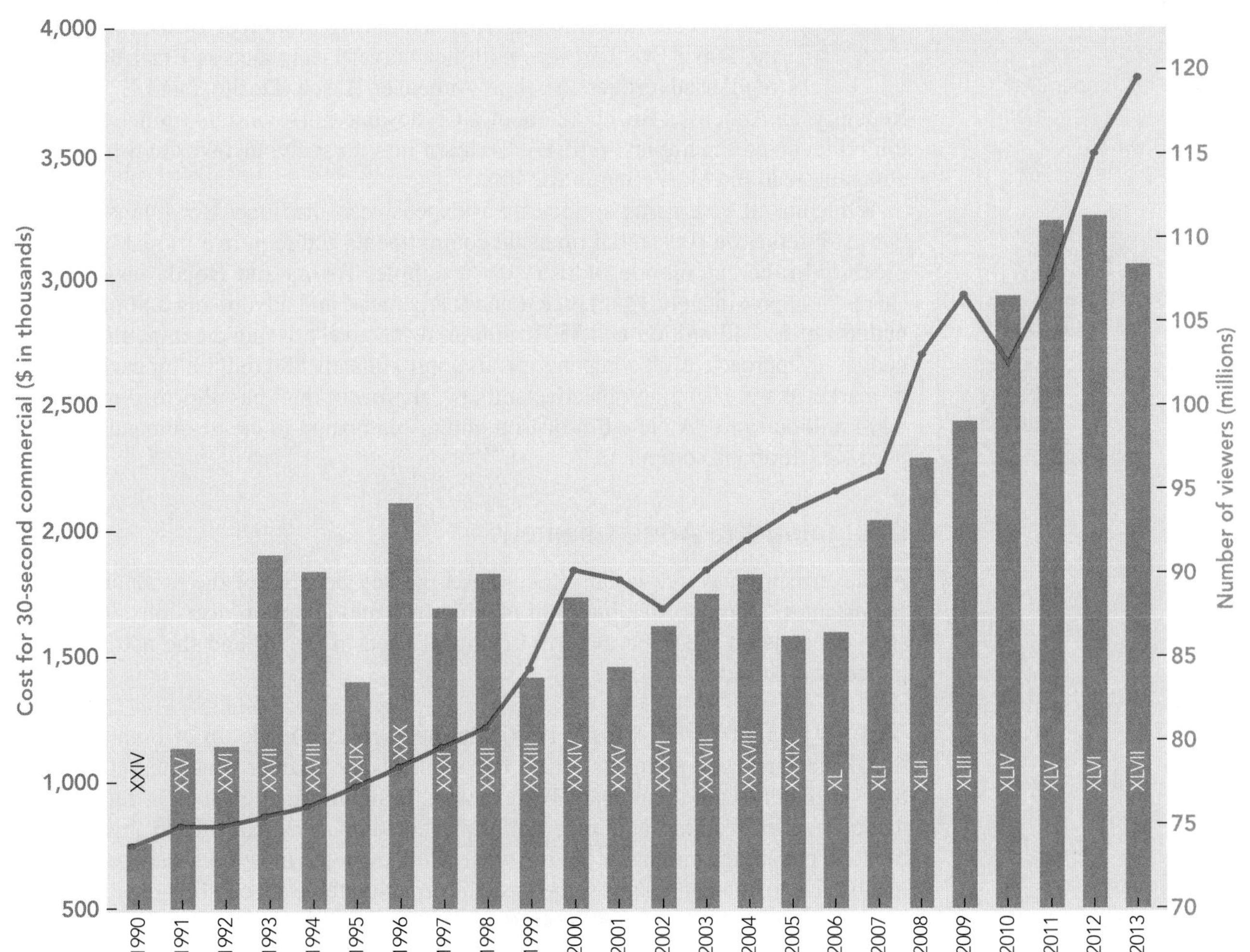

Marketing inSite

See Your Favorite Super Bowl Ads Again, and Again!

If you missed some of the ads during the last Super Bowl, or if you liked some of them so much you want to see them again, you can view the ads again at www.superbowl-ads.com. All ads for the past 15 Super Bowls, as well as some classics, are available on this website. According to *Advertising Age*, the best Super Bowl ads of all time are the Apple "1984" ad (1984), the Monster.com "When I Grow Up" ad (1999), the EDS "Cat Herders" ad (2000), the Coke "Mean Joe Greene" ad (1980), and the Budweiser "Wassup?" ad (2000).

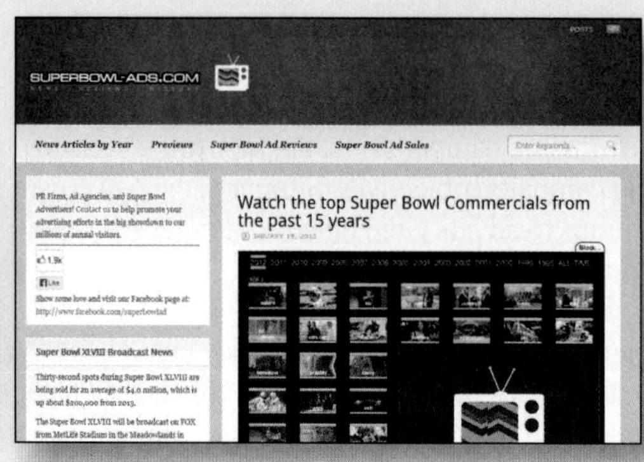

Which ads are your favorites? Compare the best ads or ads from the same advertiser in different years. For example, take a look at the Coke "Open Happiness" ads from the past three Super Bowls. Do you notice any changes?

Do you remember this GoDaddy ad from the Super Bowl?

viewers: 108 million people watch the game. In addition, the audience is attractive to advertisers because research indicates it is equally split between men and women and many viewers look forward to watching the ads. The ads are effective too: GoDaddy reported that the day following its Super Bowl ad was the "biggest sales day in company history;" Coca-Cola generated 11 million visits to its website; and Mercedes-Benz reported that its number of inquiries increased by 122 percent after running four ads during the Super Bowl. As a result, the Super Bowl attracts both new advertisers, such as BlackBerry, and regular advertisers, such as Anheuser-Busch, Doritos, and E*TRADE. Recently, an Anheuser-Busch ad about a Clydesdale horse and its trainer being reunited received the highest rating.[11] To learn how to see your favorite Super Bowl ad again, read the Marketing inSite box.[12]

QR 18-2
E*TRADE
Video

While not all advertising options are as expensive as the Super Bowl, most alternatives still represent substantial financial commitments and require a formal budgeting process. In the automobile industry, for example, Toyota and Honda have market shares of approximately 14.4 percent and 9.8 percent, and advertising and promotion budgets of $1,245 million and $851 million, respectively. Using a competitive parity budgeting approach, each company spends approximately $86 million for each percent of market share. Using an objective and task approach, Intel has allocated more than $200 million to its "A New Era of Computing" campaign to create demand for thin, portable Ultrabook computers.[13]

Designing the Advertisement

An advertising message usually focuses on the key benefits of the product that are important to a prospective buyer in making trial and adoption decisions. The message depends on the general form or appeal used in the ad and the actual words included in the ad.

Message Content Most advertising messages are made up of both informational and persuasive elements. These two elements are so intertwined that it is sometimes difficult to tell them apart. For example, basic information such as the product name, benefits, features, and price can be presented in a way that tries to attract attention and encourage purchase. On the other hand, even the most persuasive advertisements have to contain at least some basic information to be successful.

Information and persuasive content can be combined in the form of an appeal to provide a basic reason for the consumer to act. Although the marketer can use many different types of appeals, common advertising appeals include fear, sex, and humor.

Fear appeals suggest to the consumer that he or she can avoid some negative experience through the purchase and use of a product or service, a change in behavior, or a reduction in the use of a product. Examples with which you may be familiar include automobile safety ads that depict an accident or injury; political candidate endorsements that warn against the rise of other, unpopular ideologies; or social cause ads warning of the serious consequences of drug and alcohol use. Insurance companies often try to show the negative effects on the relatives of those who die prematurely without carrying enough life or mortgage insurance. Food producers encourage the purchase of low-carb, low-fat, and high-fiber products as a means of reducing weight, lowering cholesterol levels, and preventing a heart attack. The World Wide Fund for Nature (WWF) recently ran an ad with a fear appeal in which the headline read: "Stop Climate Change Before It Changes You." The image shows a person who has changed to resemble a fish.

When using fear appeals, the advertiser must be sure that the appeal is strong enough to get the audience's attention and concern but not so strong that it will lead them to tune out the message. In fact, research on antismoking ads indicates that stressing the severity of long-term health risks may actually enhance smoking's allure among youth.[14]

In contrast, *sex appeals* suggest to the audience that the product will increase the attractiveness of the user. Sex appeals can be found in almost any product category, from automobiles to toothpaste. The contemporary women's clothing store Bebe, for example, designs its advertising to "attract customers who are intrigued by the playfully sensual and evocative imagery of the Bebe lifestyle." Studies indicate that sex appeals increase attention by helping advertising stand out in today's cluttered media environment. Unfortunately, sexual content does not always lead to changes in recall, recognition, or purchase intent. Experts suggest that sexual content is most effective when there is a strong fit between the use of a sex appeal in the ad and the image and positioning of the brand, as seen in the Candie's ad below.[15]

Humorous appeals imply either directly or subtly that the product is more fun or exciting than competitors' offerings. As with fear and sex appeals, the use of humor is widespread in advertising and can be found in many product categories. You may have

Read the text to learn why the World Wide Fund for Nature (WWF), Candie's, and Geico use fear, sex, and humor appeals.

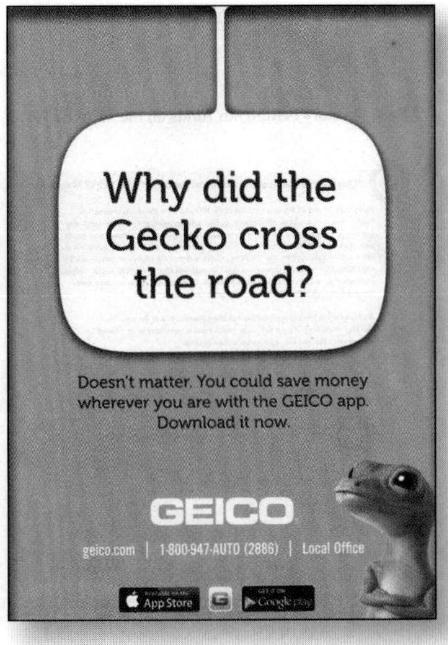

smiled at the popular Geico ads that use a talking pig, cavemen, a gecko, a stack of money with eyes named Kash, and a Rod Serling look-alike actor. These ads use humor to differentiate the company from its competitors. Geico has also created viral videos and posted them on video-sharing websites such as YouTube, where millions of viewers watch them within days.[16] You may have a favorite humorous ad character, such as the Energizer battery bunny, the AFLAC duck, or Travelocity's gnome. Advertisers believe that humor improves the effectiveness of their ads, although some studies suggest that humor wears out quickly, losing the interest of consumers. Another problem with humorous appeals is that their effectiveness may vary across cultures if used in a global campaign.[17]

QR 18-3
72andSunny
Video

Creating the Actual Message Advertising agency 72andSunny was recently designated *Advertising Age* magazine's U.S. Agency of the Year for using an optimistic and collaborative style to help shape its clients' voices for consumers. Examples of the agency's approach include its "The Next Big Thing Is Already Here" campaign for Samsung Galaxy smartphones, its "The Eat Like You Mean It," campaign for Carl's Jr. burgers, and its "Unleash Your Music" campaign for Sonos wireless HiFi systems. 72andSunny was also recognized at the Cannes Lions International Festival for its use of online media. Its K-Swiss athletic shoe campaign, for example, generated millions of views of online videos, a 1,256 percent increase in Facebook fans, designation on the "biggest buzz" list in trade publication *Footwear News*, and a 250 percent increase in online sales![18]

72andSunny and other agencies use many forms of advertising to create their messages. A very popular form of advertising today is the use of a celebrity spokesperson. 72andSunny's use of well-known personalities such as LeBron James, Seth Rogen, and Paul Rudd in Samsung ads, Sam Worthington and Jonah Hill in Call of Duty ads, and Danny McBride in K-Swiss ads are examples. Many companies use athletes, film and television stars, musicians, and other celebrities to talk to consumers through their ads.

QR 18-4
K-Swiss
Video

Advertisers who use a celebrity spokesperson believe that the ads are more likely to influence brand equity and sales. The popular "Got Milk?" campaign has successfully reversed a steady decline in milk consumption. These ads feature a wide variety of celebrities, among them actor Hugh Jackman, singer Taylor Swift, NASCAR driver Danica Patrick, fictional characters such as Batman and Ronald McDonald, and many others. Other ads feature Beyoncé (Pepsi), Alec Baldwin (the Capital One Venture Card), and William Shatner (Priceline.com).

Some of the top spokespersons today are Danica Patrick, Ashton Kutcher, LeBron James, and Catherine Zeta Jones. L'Oréal Paris recently signed actress Lea Michele from *Glee* as a spokeswoman for the company and its brands. Karen Fondu, president, explains that Lea was selected because she is "a beautiful woman inside and out," and "truly exemplifies our brand philosophy 'Because You're Worth It'."[19]

The K-Swiss campaign created by *Advertising Age*'s Agency of the Year, 72andSunny, attracted millions of online viewers.

One potential shortcoming of this form of advertising is that the spokesperson's image may change over time, becoming inconsistent with the image of the company or brand. For example, Tour de France cyclist Lance Armstrong lost endorsement contracts with Nike and golf pro Tiger Woods lost contracts with AT&T and Accenture after the athletes received negative public attention. Many companies now probe the backgrounds of potential endorsers and consider retired athletes and legacy (deceased) athletes who are low risk and still have lasting appeal in the marketplace. Some companies are also using licensing agreements where the spokesperson's compensation is directly related to the success of the product they endorse.[20]

Another issue involved in creating the message is the complex process of translating the copywriter's ideas into an actual advertisement. Designing quality artwork, layout, and production for advertisements is costly and time-consuming. The American Association of Advertising Agencies reports that a high-quality, 30-second TV commercial typically costs about $354,000 to produce. One reason for the high cost is that as companies have developed global campaigns, the need to shoot commercials in several locations has increased. Actors are also expensive: Compensation for a typical TV ad is $19,000.[21]

learning review

18-3. What other decisions can advertising objectives influence?

18-4. What is a potential shortcoming of using a celebrity spokesperson?

Selecting the Right Media

Every advertiser must decide where to place its advertisements. The alternatives are the *advertising media*, the means by which the message is communicated to the target audience. Newspapers, magazines, radio, and TV are examples of advertising media. Media selection is related to the target audience, type of product, nature of the message, campaign objectives, available budget, and the costs of the alternative media. Figure 18–2 shows the distribution of the $214 billion spent on advertising by medium.[22]

Choosing a Medium and a Vehicle within That Medium In deciding where to place advertisements, a company has several media to choose from and a number of alternatives, or vehicles, within each medium. Often advertisers use a mix of media forms and vehicles to maximize the exposure of the message to the target audience while at the same time minimizing costs. These two conflicting goals are of central importance to media planning.

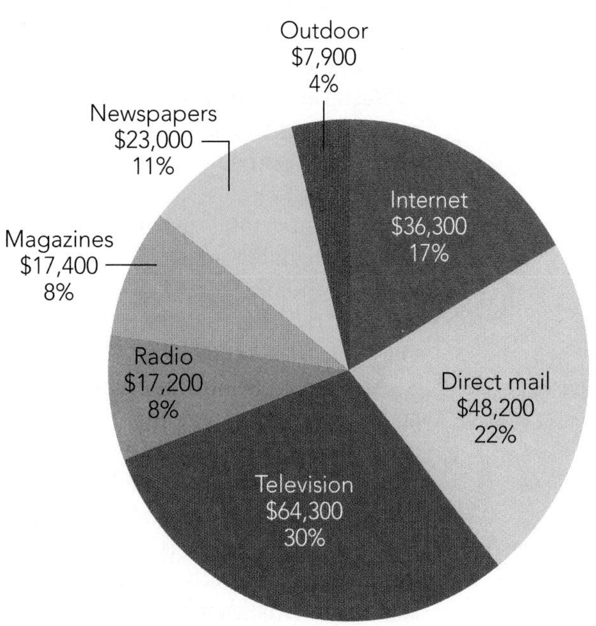

FIGURE 18–2
Television, direct mail, and newspapers account for more than 60 percent of all advertising expenditures ($ in millions).

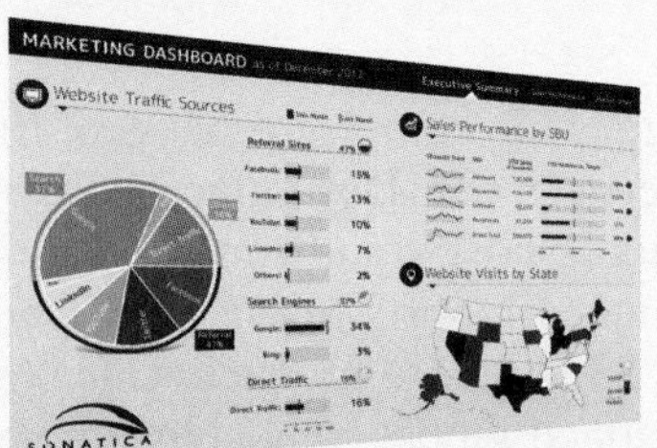

Using Marketing Dashboards

What Is the Best Way to Reach 1,000 Customers?

Marketing managers must choose from many advertising options as they design a campaign to reach potential customers. Because there are so many media alternatives (television, radio, magazines, etc.) and multiple options within each medium, it is important to monitor the efficiency of advertising expenditures on your marketing dashboard.

Your Challenge As the marketing manager for a company about to introduce a new soft drink into the U.S. market, you are preparing a presentation in which you must make recommendations for the advertising campaign. You have observed that competitors use magazine ads, newspaper ads, and even Super Bowl ads! To compare the cost of some of the alternatives you decide to use one of the most common measures in advertising: cost per thousand impressions (CPM). The CPM is calculated as follows:

$$\text{CPM} = \left(\frac{\text{Cost of ad}}{\text{Audience size}}\right) \times 1000$$

Your challenge is to determine the most efficient use of your advertising budget.

Your Findings Your research department helps you collect cost and audience size information for three options: full-page color ads in *Bloomberg Businessweek* magazine and *USA Today* newspaper, and a 30-second television ad during the Super Bowl. With this information you are able to calculate the cost per thousand impressions for each alternative.

Media Alternative	Cost of Ad	Audience Size	Cost per Thousand Impressions
Bloomberg Businessweek (magazine)	$161,600	980,000	$165
USA Today (newspaper)	$199,000	1,662,766	$120
Super Bowl (television)	$3,800,000	108,400,000	$35

Your Action Based on the calculations for these options, you see that there is a large variation in the cost of reaching 1,000 potential customers (CPM) and also in the absolute cost of the advertising. Although advertising during the Super Bowl has the lowest CPM, $35 for each 1,000 impressions, it also has the largest absolute cost! Your next step will be to consider other factors such as your total available budget, the profiles of the audiences each alternative reaches, and whether the type of message you want to deliver is better communicated in print or on television.

Basic Terms Media buyers speak a language of their own, so all advertisers involved in selecting the right media for their campaigns must be familiar with some common terms used in the advertising industry.

Because advertisers try to maximize the number of individuals in the target market exposed to the message, they must be concerned with reach. **Reach** is the number of different people or households exposed to an advertisement. The exact definition of reach sometimes varies among alternative media. Newspapers often use reach to describe their total circulation or the number of different households that buy the paper. Television and radio stations, in contrast, describe their reach using the term **rating**—the percentage of households in a market that are tuned to a particular TV show or radio station. In general, advertisers try to maximize reach in their target market at the lowest cost.

Although reach is important, advertisers are also interested in exposing their target audience to a message more than once. This is because consumers often do not pay close attention to advertising messages, some of which contain large amounts of relatively complex information. When advertisers want to reach the same audience more than once, they are concerned with **frequency**, the average number of times a person in the target audience is exposed to a message or advertisement. Like reach, greater frequency is generally viewed as desirable. Studies indicate that with repeated exposure to advertisements consumers respond more favorably to brand extensions.[23]

When reach (expressed as a percentage of the total market) is multiplied by frequency, an advertiser will obtain a commonly used reference number called **gross rating points (GRPs)**. To obtain the appropriate number of GRPs to achieve an advertising campaign's objectives, the media planner must balance reach and frequency. The balance will also be influenced by cost. **Cost per thousand (CPM)** refers to the cost of reaching 1,000 individuals or households with the advertising message in a given medium (*M* is the Roman numeral for 1,000). See the Using Marketing Dashboards box for an example of the use of CPM in media selection.

Different Media Alternatives

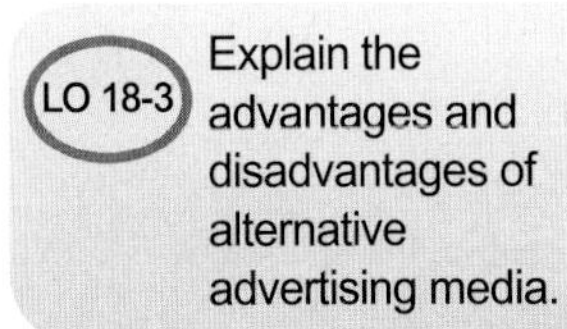

Figure 18–3 on the next page summarizes the advantages and disadvantages of the major advertising media, which are described in more detail below. For detailed coverage of direct mail, refer to Chapter 17.

Television Television is a valuable medium because it communicates with sight, sound, and motion. Print advertisements alone could never give you the sense of a sports car accelerating from a stop or cornering at high speed. In addition, television reaches more than 96 percent of all households—115.6 million, including 5 million "Zero TV" households that watch only through a broadband connection. There are also many opportunities for out-of-home TV viewing, as televisions are present in many bars, hotels, offices, airports, and college campuses.[24]

Several aspects of traditional television viewing are changing. First, research at the Nielsen Company indicates that the amount of time allocated to television viewing is increasing. American viewers now spend 41 hours each week watching television programming on multiple screens, including traditional TVs, computers, tablets, and smartphones. In addition, viewers are increasingly timeshifting their viewing with DVRs, DVDs, subscription services such as Netflix, and Internet options such as Hulu and Apple TV. Technologies are changing, too. In recent years, many consumers have purchased high-definition and 3D televisions. The future, however, will include 4K televisions, which are four times as sharp as high-definition televisions, can convert ordinary television into 3D, offer voice-activated and motion controls, and allow two programs to be watched simultaneously on their huge screens.[25]

Television's major disadvantage is cost: The price of a prime-time, 30-second ad can range from $545,142 to run on *Sunday Night Football*, to $296,062 to run on *American Idol*, to $69,690 to run on *America's Funniest Home Videos*. Because of these high charges, many advertisers choose less expensive "spot" ads, which run between programs, or 15-second ads, rather than investing in ads that run the more traditional length of 30 or 60 seconds. In fact, approximately 34 percent of all TV ads are now 15 seconds long. Recent studies suggest that the placement of an ad within a program and relative to other ads in a sequence of ads may influence the ad's effectiveness. In addition, there is some indication that advertisers are shifting their interest to live events rather than programs that might be watched on a DVR days later.[26]

Another problem with television advertising is the likelihood of *wasted coverage*—having people outside the market for the product see the advertisement. The cost and wasted coverage problems of TV advertising can be reduced through the specialized cable and satellite channels. Advertising time is often less expensive on cable and satellite channels than on the broadcast networks. According to the National Cable and Telecommunication Association, there are 900 cable channels such as Disney, ESPN, History, MTV, Oxygen, and Lifetime. Cable channels are also "tagging" their programs to allow advertisers to place ads in scenes with particular themes. Advertisements for golf equipment, for example, might be placed after a program scene that shows characters playing golf.[27]

Oxygen is one of many specialized channels available to advertisers on cable networks.

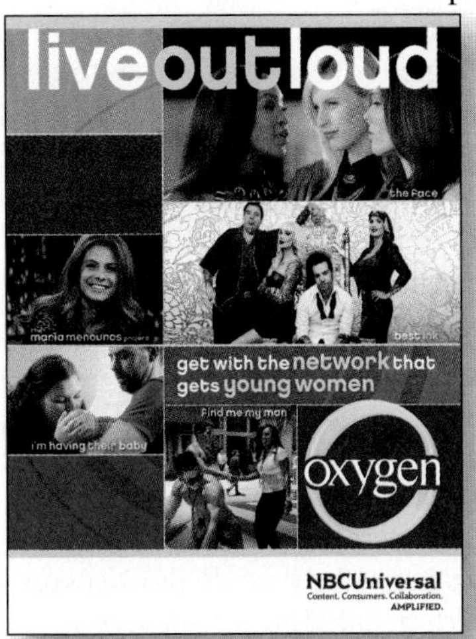

MEDIUM	ADVANTAGES	DISADVANTAGES
Television	Reaches extremely large audience; uses picture, print, sound, and motion for effect; can target specific audiences	High cost to prepare and run ads; short exposure time and perishable message; difficult to convey complex information
Radio	Low cost; can target specific local audiences; ads can be placed quickly; can use sound, humor, and intimacy effectively	No visual element; short exposure time and perishable message; difficult to convey complex information
Magazines	Can target specific audiences; high-quality color; long life of ad; ads can be clipped and saved; can convey complex information	Long time needed to place ad; relatively high cost; competes for attention with other magazine features
Newspapers	Excellent coverage of local markets; ads can be placed and changed quickly; ads can be saved; quick consumer response; low cost	Ads compete for attention with other newspaper features; short life span; poor color
Yellow Pages	Excellent coverage of geographic segments; long use period; available 24 hours/365 days	Proliferation of competitive directories in many markets; difficult to keep up to date
Internet	Video and audio capabilities; animation can capture attention; ads can be interactive and link to advertiser	Animation and interactivity require large files and more time to load; effectiveness is still uncertain
Outdoor	Low cost; local market focus; high visibility; opportunity for repeat exposures	Message must be short and simple; low selectivity of audience; criticized as a traffic hazard
Direct mail	High selectivity of audience; can contain complex information and personalized messages; high-quality graphics	High cost per contact; poor image (junk mail)

FIGURE 18–3
Advertisers must consider the advantages and disadvantages of the many media alternatives.

Another popular form of television advertising is the infomercial. **Infomercials** are program-length (30-minute) advertisements that take an educational approach to communication with potential customers. You may remember seeing infomercials for the Magic Bullet, ThighMaster, and OxiClean products, using Ron Popeil, Suzanne, Somers, and Anthony Sullivan, respectively, as the spokesperson.

Infomercials are increasingly popular because they can be both informative and entertaining, and because the average cost of a 30-minute block of television time is only $425. Each year, *Response Magazine* and Infomercial Monitoring Service Inc. publish a list of the top 50 infomercials during the past 12 months. Recent popular infomercials included the Insanity body fitness DVDs, Total Gym exercise equipment, Keurig coffee makers, and Nutrisystem weight loss products. The industry generates more than $150 billion in annual sales and has facilitated the long-term success of many products. The Total Gym infomercials featuring Chuck Norris and Christie Brinkley, for example, have led to more than $1 billion in sales![28]

Radio The United States has more than 27,800 radio stations. These stations consist of approximately 4,700 AM, 10,600 FM, and 12,800 HD and Internet stations. The major advantage of radio is that it is a segmented medium. For example, the Farm Radio Network, the Family Life Network, Business Talk Radio, and the Performance Racing Network are all

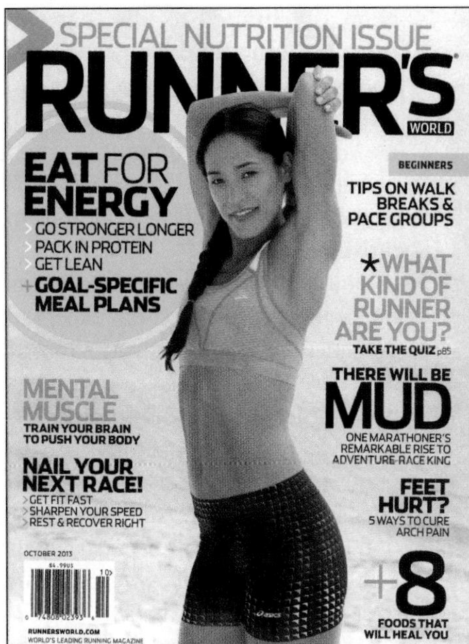

Magazines such as *Runner's World* appeal to narrowly defined segments such as athletes who are interested in running.

listened to by different market segments. Satellite radio service SiriusXM offers more than 165 commercial-free, digital, coast-to-coast channels to consumers for a monthly fee, and Internet radio service Pandora offers up to 100 personalized channels to each listener. The large number of media options today has reduced the amount of time spent listening to radio, although radio still reaches 77 percent of all adults daily. The average 18- to 34-year-old listens to radio an average of 13.7 hours each week, making radio an important medium for businesses with college students and recent graduates as a target market.[29]

A disadvantage of radio is that it has limited use for products that must be seen. Another problem is the ease with which consumers can tune out a commercial by switching stations. Radio is also a medium that competes for people's attention as they do other activities, such as driving, working, or relaxing. Radio listening time reaches its peak during the morning drive time (7 to 8 A.M.), remains high during the day, and then begins to decline in the afternoon (after 4 P.M.) as people return home and start evening activities.[30]

Magazines Magazines have become a very specialized medium. In fact, there are currently more than 7,179 consumer magazines. Some 213 new magazines were introduced last year, including *As If*, a large-format quarterly magazine focusing on creative visionaries; *Ink and Hustle*, a magazine about tattoos and tattoo artists; *Modern Farmer*, a magazine for people who want to be part of the "new food culture"; and *Click*, a bimonthly magazine designed and written for female photographers. Many publishers are also adding digital versions of existing magazines. *Skateboarder*, for example, can now also be read on the magazine's website, an iPad, or a smartphone. Some magazines, such as *Auto Trader* and *Computer Weekly*, are dropping their print format to offer only an online version.[31]

The marketing advantage of this medium is the great number of special-interest publications that appeal to narrowly defined segments. Runners read *Runner's World*, sailors buy *Yachting*, gardeners subscribe to *Garden Design*, and children peruse *Sports Illustrated for Kids*. More than 675 publications focus on travel, 146 are dedicated to interior design and decoration, and 98 are related to golf. Each magazine's readers often represent a unique profile. Take the *Rolling Stone* reader, who tends to listen to music more than most people. SiriusXM Satellite Radio knows an ad in *Rolling Stone* is reaching the desired target audience. In addition, recent studies comparing advertising in different media suggest that magazine advertising is perceived to be more "inspirational" than other media.[32]

The cost of advertising in national magazines is a disadvantage, but many national publications publish regional and even metro editions, which reduces the absolute cost and wasted coverage. *Time* publishes well over 400 editions, including Latin American, Canadian, Asian, South Pacific, European, and U.S. editions. The U.S. editions include geographic and demographic options. In addition to cost, another limitation to magazines is their infrequency. At best, magazines are printed on a weekly basis, with many specialized publications appearing only monthly or less often. Although specialization can be an advantage of this medium, consumer interests can be difficult to translate into a magazine theme—a fact made clear by the hundreds of magazine failures during the past decade. *U.S. News and World Report*, *GamePro*, *CosmoGirl*, *Teen People*, *Business 2.0*, *PC Magazine*, *Men's Vogue*, *Gourmet*, and *Esquire Sportsman*, for example, all failed to attract and keep a substantial number of readers or advertisers. Which magazine has the highest circulation? It's *AARP The Magazine*, with a circulation of 22 million![33]

Newspapers Newspapers are an important local medium with excellent reach potential. Daily publication allows advertisements to focus on specific current events, such as a 24-hour sale. Local retailers often use newspapers as their sole advertising medium. Newspapers are rarely saved by the purchaser, however, so companies are generally limited to ads that call for an immediate customer response (although customers can clip and save ads they select). Companies also cannot expect newspapers to offer the same quality color reproduction available in most magazines.

The Huffington Post is one example of the trend toward new types of news organizations.

National advertising campaigns rarely include this medium except in conjunction with local distributors of their products. In these instances, both parties often share the advertising costs using a cooperative advertising program, which is described later in this chapter. Another exception is the use of newspapers such as *The Wall Street Journal* and *USA Today*, which have national distribution of more than 2.4 and 1.7 million readers, respectively. One newspaper, *Metro*, offers a global audience of 18 million daily readers in Boston, New York, Philadelphia, and 100 cities in Europe, North and South America, and Asia.[34]

Several important trends are influencing newspapers today. First is the decline in circulation and advertising revenue. A recent report by the Alliance for Audited Media showed that circulation declined at 9 of the 25 largest newspapers during the past year. The shift is attributed to readers' growing preference for free websites and mobile services, as half of all Americans now get some form of local news on a mobile device. In addition, classified advertising revenue has declined as Craigslist and similar sites have become more popular with consumers.

The second trend is the growth in online newspapers. Today, hundreds of newspapers, including *The New York Times*, *The Wall Street Journal*, *Chicago Sun-Times*, and the *San Francisco Chronicle*, offer online versions of their printed newspapers. In fact, online subscriptions now account for 19 percent of all newspaper subscriptions. *The New York Times* now has more digital subscribers than print subscribers. Many newspapers also have online readers who are not subscribers. *USA Today*, for example, reports that it has 32 million readers on the free portion of its website. A final trend is the growth in new types of news organizations such as *The Huffington Post*, which covers entertainment, media, living, business, and politics and has more than 3 million Twitter followers, and *Examiner.com*, which utilizes a large group of freelance reporters.[35]

Print yellow pages are used more than 11 billion times each year. See the text for advantages and disadvantages of this media alternative.

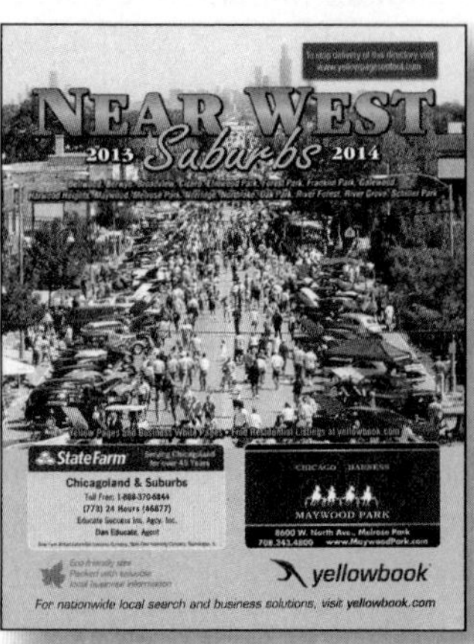

Yellow Pages Yellow pages represent an advertising media alternative comparable to outdoor advertising in terms of expenditures—about $8 billion in the United States. According to the Local Search Association, consumers turn to print yellow pages approximately 11 billion times annually and online yellow pages (desktop, tablet, and mobile) an additional 5.6 billion times per year. One reason for this high level of use is that the 6,500 yellow pages directories reach almost all households. Yellow pages are a "directional" medium because they direct consumers to where purchases can be made after other media have created awareness and demand.

The yellow pages face several disadvantages today. First is the proliferation of directories. AT&T (*Real Yellow Pages*), Dex Media (*Dex One* and *Superpages*), and Hibu (*Yellowbook*) now produce competing directories for many cities, neighborhoods, and ethnic groups. Second, relative to other advertising options, the yellow pages have limited accountability and ROI metrics. Many advertisers believe that yellow pages need to improve their audience measurement research and circulation auditing practices. Finally, yellow pages publishers are facing increasing public concern about the environmental impact of the directories. The cities of San Francisco

FIGURE 18–4
Google, Microsoft, and Yahoo! have the largest shares of Internet searches and offer opportunities for online advertising.

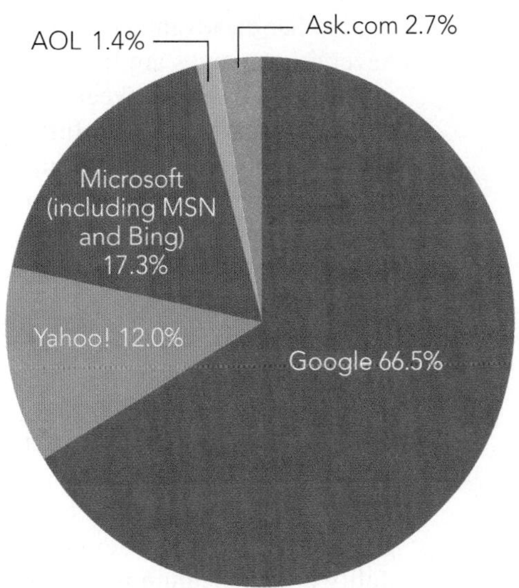

and Seattle, for example, have proposed legislation banning the distribution of yellow pages to residences, and residents in Winnipeg, Canada, now have an opt-out option if they prefer not to receive print directories.[36]

Internet The Internet represents a relatively new medium for many advertisers, although it has already attracted a wide variety of industries. Online advertising is similar to print advertising in that it offers a visual message. It has additional advantages, however, because it can also use the audio and video capabilities of the Internet. Sound and movement may simply attract more attention from viewers, or they may provide an element of entertainment to the message. Online advertising also has the unique feature of being interactive. Called *rich media,* these interactive ads have drop-down menus, built-in games, or search engines to engage viewers. Although online advertising is relatively small compared to other traditional media, it offers an opportunity to reach younger consumers who have developed a preference for online communication.

There are a variety of online advertising options. The most popular options are paid search, display (banner) ads, classified ads, and video. Paid search is one of the fastest-growing forms of Internet advertising, as approximately 80 percent of all Internet traffic begins at a search engine such as Google or Yahoo! (see Figure 18–4). Experts estimate that consumers conduct 20 billion searches each month. Now search engine agencies help firms add tags, wikis, and RSS (rich site summary) to the content of a site to increase search rankings. Firms such as 24/7 Real Media provide assessment of the effectiveness of a website. While the use of banner ads is growing also, there is some concern that consumers are developing "banner blindness" because the click-through rate has been declining to its current level of 0.1 percent.

Classified ads, such as those on Craigslist, and video ads also contribute to the growth of online advertising by providing many of the advantages and characteristics of other media such as yellow pages, magazines, newspaper, and television. Video ads also have the benefit of "going viral" when people share the ads with friends.[37]

One disadvantage of online advertising is that because the medium is relatively new, technical and administrative standards for the various formats are still evolving. This situation makes it difficult for advertisers to run national online campaigns across multiple sites. The Interactive Advertising Bureau provides "Guidelines, Standards & Best Practices" and creative guidelines to facilitate the use and growth of online advertising.

24/7 Real Media's service can provide an assessment of the effectiveness of a website by monitoring "click-through" rates.

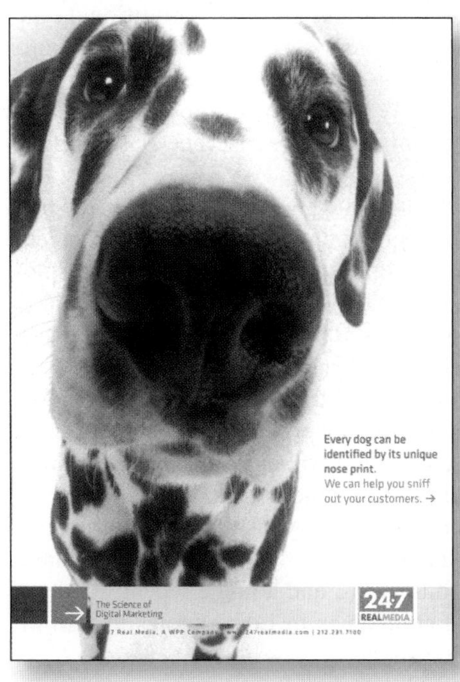

Every dog can be identified by its unique nose print.
We can help you sniff out your customers. →
The Science of Digital Marketing
24·7 REALMEDIA

Another disadvantage to online advertising is the difficulty of measuring impact. Several companies are testing methods of tracking where viewers go on their computer in the days and weeks after seeing an ad. Nielsen's online rating service, for example, measures actual Internet use through meters installed on the computers of 500,000 individuals in 20 countries. Measuring the relationship between online and offline behavior is also important. Research by comScore, which studied 139 online ad campaigns, revealed that online ads didn't always result in a "click," but they increased the likelihood of a purchase by 17 percent and they increased visits to the advertiser's website by 40 percent.[38] The Making Responsible Decisions box describes how click fraud is increasing the necessity of assessing online advertising effectiveness.[39]

Outdoor A very effective medium for reminding consumers about your product is outdoor advertising, such as the scoreboard at San Diego's Qualcomm Stadium. The most common form of outdoor advertising, called *billboards*, often results in good reach and frequency and has been shown to increase purchase rates.[40] The visibility of this medium is good supplemental reinforcement for well-known products, and it is a relatively low-cost, flexible alternative. Also, a company can buy space in a specific, targeted geographical market. A disadvantage to billboards, however, is that no opportunity exists for lengthy advertising copy. Also, a good billboard site depends on traffic patterns and sight lines.

If you have ever lived in a metropolitan area, chances are you might have seen another form of outdoor advertising, *transit advertising*. This medium includes messages on the interior and exterior of buses, subway and light-rail cars, and taxis. As the use of mass transit grows, transit advertising may become increasingly important. Selectivity is available to advertisers, who can buy space by neighborhood or bus route. One disadvantage to this medium is that the heavy travel times, when the audiences are the largest, are not conducive to reading advertising copy. People are standing shoulder to shoulder on the subway, hoping not to miss their stop, and little attention is paid to the advertising.

The outdoor advertising industry has experienced a growth surge recently. According to the Outdoor Advertising Association of America, outdoor advertising expenditures have grown to $6.7 billion annually. Much of the growth is the result of creative forms of outdoor advertising and the conversion to digital billboards, which allow advertisers to quickly present *conditional content*. Conditional content ads are based on current events, weather, business conditions, and even sports scores. Radio stations, for example, can display the title of the song currently playing on their station, newspapers can display current headlines, and retailers can advertise umbrellas or sunscreen based on the weather forecast.

Outdoor advertising can be an effective medium for reminding consumers about a product.

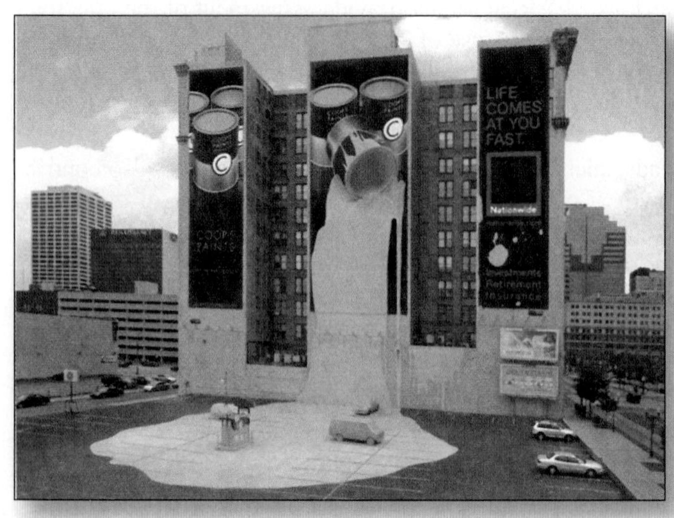

Digital billboard companies have also donated billboard time to display public service announcements. For example, in Minnesota digital billboards display National Weather Service tornado warnings, and in Houston messages from the police department are displayed to help apprehend fugitives. A recent study found that 80 percent of U.S. residents can be reached daily through outdoor advertising and that many commuters think that digital billboards make the commute more interesting. While these are positive trends, the outdoor advertising industry also faces important environmental concerns. For example, several states have banned billboards, and a judge recently ordered two billboard companies in Los Angeles to turn off about 80 digital signs.[41]

Making Responsible Decisions

ethics

Who Is Responsible for Click Fraud?

Spending on Internet advertising is expected to exceed $20 billion in 2014 as many advertisers shift their budgets from print and TV to the Internet. For most advertisers one advantage of online advertising is that they pay only when someone clicks on their ad. Unfortunately, the growth of the medium has led to "click fraud," which is the deceptive clicking of ads solely to increase the amount advertisers must pay. There are several forms of click fraud. One method is the result of Paid-to-Read (PTR) websites that recruit and pay members to simply click on ads. Another method is the result of "clickbots," which are software programs that produce automatic clicks on ads, sometimes through mobile devices. The activity is difficult to detect and stop. Experts estimate that up to 20 percent of clicks may be the result of fraud and may be costing advertisers as much as $800 million each year!

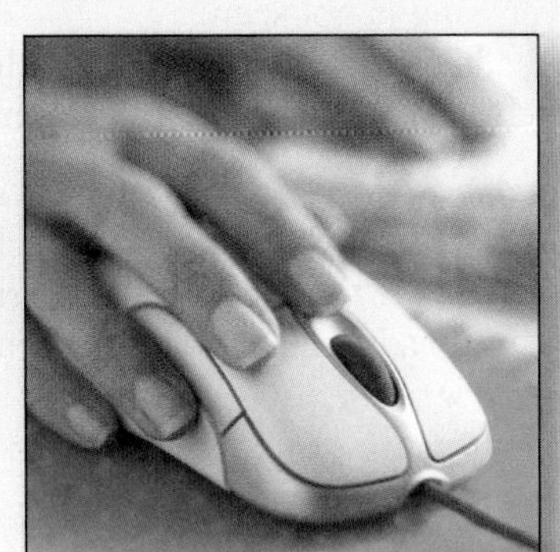

Two of the largest portals for Internet advertising are Google and Yahoo! Both firms try to filter out illegitimate clicks, although some advertisers claim that they are still being charged for PTR and clickbot traffic. Although the laws that govern click fraud are not very clear, Google and Yahoo! have each settled class action lawsuits and agreed to provide rebates or credits to advertisers who were charged for fraudulent clicks.

Investigations of the online advertising industry have discovered a related form of click fraud that occurs when legitimate website visitors click on ads without any intention of looking at the site. As one consumer explains, "I always try and remember to click on the ad banners once in a while to try and keep the sites free." Stephen Dubner calls this "webtipping"!

As the Internet advertising industry grows it will become increasingly important to resolve the issue of click fraud. Consumers, advertisers, websites that carry paid advertising, and the large web portals are all involved in a complicated technical, legal, and social situation. Who do you think is responsible for click fraud? Who should lead the way in the effort to find a solution?

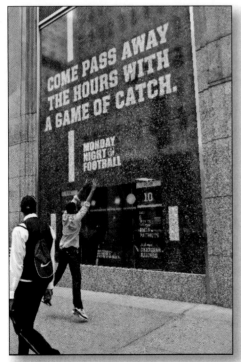

Out-of-home advertising such as this storefront display is becoming interactive to engage consumers.

Other Media As traditional media have become more expensive and cluttered, advertisers have been attracted to a variety of nontraditional advertising options called out-of-home advertising, or *place-based media*. Messages are placed in locations that attract a specific target audience such as airports, doctors' offices, health clubs, theaters (where ads are played on the screen before the movies are shown), grocery stores, storefronts, and even the bathrooms of bars, restaurants, and nightclubs. Soon there will be advertising on video screens on gas pumps, ATMs, and in elevators, and increasingly it will be interactive.

The $2.5 billion industry has attracted advertisers such as AT&T and jcpenney, which use in-store campaigns, and Geico, Sprint, and FedEx, which use out-of-home advertising to reach mobile professionals in health clubs, airports, and hotels. Research suggests that creative use of out-of-home advertising, such as preshow theater ads, enhances consumer recall of the ads.[42]

Selection Criteria Choosing between these alternative media is difficult and depends on several factors. First, knowing the media habits of the target audience is essential to deciding among the alternatives. Second, occasionally product attributes necessitate that certain media be used. For example, if color is a major aspect of product appeal, radio is excluded. Newspapers allow advertising for quick actions to confront competitors, and magazines are more appropriate for complicated messages because the reader can spend more time reading the message. The final factor in selecting a medium is cost. When possible, alternative media are compared using a common denominator that reflects both reach and cost—a measure such as CPM.

Scheduling the Advertising

There is no correct schedule to advertise a product, but three factors must be considered. First is the issue of *buyer turnover*, which is how often new buyers enter the market to buy the product. The higher the buyer turnover, the greater the amount of advertising required. A second issue in scheduling is the *purchase frequency*; the more frequently the product is purchased, the less repetition is required. Finally, companies must consider the *forgetting rate*, the speed with which buyers forget the brand if advertising is not seen.

Setting schedules requires an understanding of how the market behaves. Most companies tend to follow one of three basic approaches:

1. *Continuous (steady) schedule.* When seasonal factors are unimportant, advertising is run at a continuous or steady schedule throughout the year.
2. *Flighting (intermittent) schedule.* Periods of advertising are scheduled between periods of no advertising to reflect seasonal demand.
3. *Pulse (burst) schedule.* A flighting schedule is combined with a continuous schedule because of increases in demand, heavy periods of promotion, or introduction of a new product.

For example, products such as breakfast cereals have a stable demand throughout the year and would typically use a continuous schedule of advertising. In contrast, products such as snow skis and suntan lotions have seasonal demands and receive flighting-schedule advertising during the seasonal demand period. Some products such as toys or automobiles require pulse-schedule advertising to facilitate sales throughout the year and during special periods of increased demand (such as holidays or new car introductions). Some evidence suggests that pulsing schedules are superior to other advertising strategies.[43] In addition, research indicates the effectiveness of a particular ad wears out quickly and, therefore, many alternative forms of a commercial may be more effective.[44]

learning review

18-5. You see the same ad in *Time* and *Fortune* magazines and on billboards and TV. Is this an example of reach or frequency?

18-6. Why has the Internet become a popular advertising medium?

18-7. What factors must be considered when choosing among alternative media?

EXECUTING THE ADVERTISING PROGRAM

Executing the advertising program involves pretesting the advertising copy and actually carrying out the advertising program. John Wanamaker, the founder of Wanamaker's Department Store in Philadelphia, remarked, "I know half my advertising is wasted, but I don't know what half." By evaluating advertising efforts, marketers can try to ensure that their advertising expenditures are not wasted.[45] Evaluation is done usually at two separate times: before and after the advertisements are run in the actual campaign. Several methods used in the evaluation process at the stages of idea formulation and copy development are discussed below.

Pretesting the Advertising

To determine whether the advertisement communicates the intended message or to select among alternative versions of the advertisement, **pretests** are conducted before the advertisements are placed in any medium.

Portfolio Tests Portfolio tests are used to test copy alternatives. The test ad is placed in a portfolio with several other ads and stories, and consumers are asked to read through the portfolio. Afterward, subjects are asked for their impressions of the ads on several evaluative scales, such as from "very informative" to "not very informative."

Jury Tests Jury tests involve showing the ad copy to a panel of consumers and having them rate how they liked it, how much it drew their attention, and how attractive they thought it was. This approach is similar to the portfolio test in that consumer reactions are obtained. However, unlike the portfolio test, a test advertisement is not hidden within other ads.

Theater Tests Theater testing is the most sophisticated form of pretesting. Consumers are invited to view new television shows or movies in which test commercials are also shown. Viewers register their feelings about the advertisements either on handheld electronic recording devices used during the viewing or on questionnaires afterward.

Carrying Out the Advertising Program

The responsibility for actually carrying out the advertising program can be handled in one of three ways, as shown in Figure 18–5. The **full-service agency** provides the most complete range of services, including market research, media selection, copy development, artwork, and production. In the past, agencies that assisted a client by both developing and placing advertisements often charged a commission of 15 percent of the media costs. As corporations introduced integrated marketing communication approaches, however, many advertisers switched from paying commissions to incentive plans based on performance. These plans typically pay for agency costs and a 5 to 10 percent profit, plus bonuses if specific performance goals related to brand preference, lead generation, sales, and market share are met. The Association of National Advertisers estimates that 46 percent of all agency clients currently use this approach.

Anheuser-Busch recently introduced a new version of the full-service agency approach when it announced it would begin to compensate agencies for their costs based on rigid scope-of-work agreements. Vice President of Marketing Keith Levy explains, "We want partner agencies really tied to the strategy of the brand." In the future, clients may move to a value-based approach where compensation is dependent on sales of the advertised product or brand. This approach will add additional emphasis on agency contributions beyond advertising. In some instances, such as specialized direct-response agencies, compensation is already a percentage of revenue generated.[46]

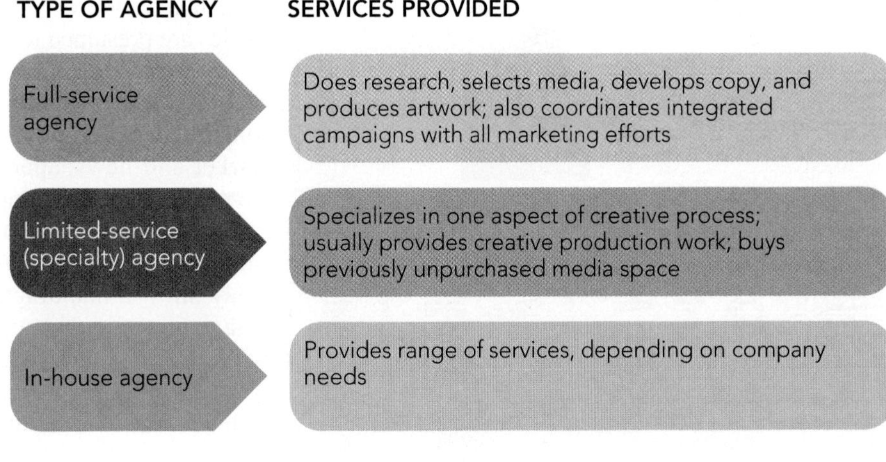

TYPE OF AGENCY
SERVICES PROVIDED
Full-service agency
Does research, selects media, develops copy, and produces artwork; also coordinates integrated campaigns with all marketing efforts
Limited-service (specialty) agency
Specializes in one aspect of creative process; usually provides creative production work; buys previously unpurchased media space
In-house agency
Provides range of services, depending on company needs

FIGURE 18–5 Alternative structures of advertising agencies used to carry out the advertising program.

Limited-service agencies specialize in one aspect of the advertising process, such as providing creative services to develop the advertising copy, buying previously unpurchased media (media agencies), or providing Internet services (Internet agencies). Limited-service agencies that deal in creative work are compensated by a contractual agreement for the services performed. Finally, **in-house agencies** made up of the company's own advertising staff may provide full services or a limited range of services.

ASSESSING THE ADVERTISING PROGRAM

The advertising decision process does not stop with executing the advertising program. The advertisements must be evaluated to determine whether they are achieving their intended objectives, and results may indicate that changes must be made in the advertising program.

Posttesting the Advertising

An advertisement may go through **posttests** after it has been shown to the target audience to determine whether it accomplished its intended purpose. Five approaches common in posttesting are discussed here.[47]

Aided Recall After being shown an ad, respondents are asked whether their previous exposure to it was through reading, viewing, or listening. The Starch test shown in the accompanying photo uses aided recall to determine the percentage of those who (1) remember seeing a specific ad (*noted*), (2) saw or read any part of the ad identifying the product or brand (*seen-associated*), (3) read any part of the ad's copy (read some), and (4) read at least half of the ad (*read most*). Elements of the ad are then tagged with the results, as shown in the photo.[48]

Unaided Recall The unaided recall approach involves asking respondents a question such as, "What ads do you remember seeing yesterday?" without any prompting to determine whether they saw or heard advertising messages.

Attitude Tests Attitude tests involve asking respondents questions to measure changes in their attitudes after an advertising campaign. For example, they might be asked whether they now have a more favorable attitude toward the product advertised. Recent research suggests that attitudes can be influenced by many factors, including the increasingly popular use of co-creation to develop consumer-generated ads.[49]

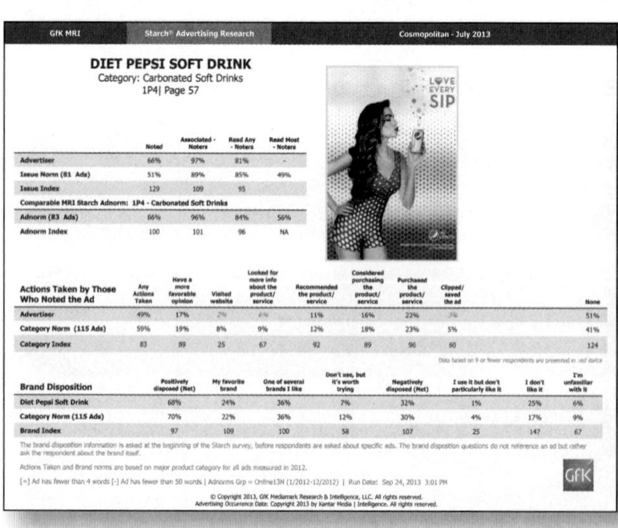

GfK MRI | Starch® Advertising Research | Cosmopolitan - July 2013

DIET PEPSI SOFT DRINK
Category: Carbonated Soft Drinks
1P4| Page 57

	Noted	Associated - Noters	Read Any - Noters	Read Most - Noters
Advertiser	66%	97%	81%	-
Issue Norm (81 Ads)	51%	89%	85%	49%
Issue Index	129	109	95	
Comparable MRI Starch Adnorm: 1P4 - Carbonated Soft Drinks				
Adnorm (83 Ads)	66%	96%	84%	56%
Adnorm Index	100	101	96	NA

Actions Taken by Those Who Noted the Ad	Any Actions Taken	Have a more favorable opinion	Visited website	Looked for more info about the product/ service	Recommended the product/ service	Considered purchasing the product/ service	Purchased the product/ service	Clipped/ saved the ad	None
Advertiser	49%	17%	2%	6%	11%	16%	22%	3%	51%
Category Norm (115 Ads)	59%	19%	8%	9%	12%	18%	23%	5%	41%
Category Index	83	89	25	67	92	89	96	60	124

Data based on 9 or fewer respondents are presented in *red italics*

Brand Disposition	Positively disposed (Net)	My favorite brand	One of several brands I like	Don't use, but it's worth trying	Negatively disposed (Net)	I use it but don't particularly like it	I don't like it	I'm unfamiliar with it
Diet Pepsi Soft Drink	68%	24%	36%	7%	32%	1%	25%	6%
Category Norm (115 Ads)	70%	22%	36%	12%	30%	4%	17%	9%
Brand Index	97	109	100	58	107	25	147	67

The brand disposition information is asked at the beginning of the Starch survey, before respondents are asked about specific ads. The brand disposition questions do not reference an ad but rather ask the respondent about the brand itself.

Actions Taken and Brand norms are based on major product category for all ads measured in 2012.

[≈] Ad has fewer than 4 words [-] Ad has fewer than 50 words | Adnorms Grp = Online13N (1/2012-12/2012) | Run Date: Sep 24, 2013 3:01 PM

© Copyright 2013, GfK Mediamark Research & Intelligence, LLC. All rights reserved.
Advertising Occurrence Data: Copyright 2013 by Kantar Media | Intelligence. All rights reserved.

The Starch test uses aided recall to evaluate an ad on four dimensions. See the text to learn more.

Inquiry Tests Inquiry tests involve offering additional product information, product samples, or premiums to an ad's readers or viewers. Ads generating the most inquiries are presumed to be the most effective.

Sales Tests Sales tests involve studies such as controlled experiments (e.g., using radio ads in one market and newspaper ads in another and comparing the results) and consumer purchase tests (measuring retail sales that result from a given advertising campaign). The most sophisticated experimental methods today allow a manufacturer, a distributor, or an advertising agency to manipulate an advertising variable (such as schedule or copy) through cable systems and observe subsequent sales effects by monitoring data collected from checkout scanners in supermarkets.[50]

Making Needed Changes

Results of posttesting the advertising copy are used to reach decisions about changes in the advertising program. If the posttest results show that an advertisement is doing poorly in terms of awareness, cost efficiency, or sales, it may be dropped and other ads run in its place in the future. On the other hand, sometimes an advertisement may be so successful it is run repeatedly or used as the basis of a larger advertising program.

learning review

18-8. Explain the difference between pretesting and posttesting advertising copy.

18-9. What is the difference between aided and unaided recall posttests?

SALES PROMOTION

LO 18-4 Discuss the strengths and weaknesses of consumer-oriented and trade-oriented sales promotions.

Sales promotion is a key element of the promotional mix today; it now accounts for more than $70 billion in annual expenditures. In a recent forecast by ZenithOptimedia, sales promotion expenditures accounted for 19 percent of all promotional spending.[51] The large allocation of marketing expenditures to sales promotion reflects the trend toward integrated marketing communications programs, which often include a variety of sales promotion elements. Selection and integration of the many promotion techniques require a good understanding of the advantages and disadvantages of each kind of sales promotion.[52] The two major kinds of sales promotions, consumer-oriented and trade-oriented, are discussed below.

Consumer-Oriented Sales Promotions

Directed to ultimate consumers, **consumer-oriented sales promotions**, or simply *consumer promotions*, are sales tools used to support a company's advertising and personal selling. A variety of consumer-oriented sales promotion tools may be used, including coupons, deals, premiums, contests, sweepstakes, samples, loyalty programs, point-of-purchase displays, rebates, and product placements (see Figure 18–6 on the next page).

Coupons encourage trial by offering a discounted price. See the text to learn if coupons increase sales.

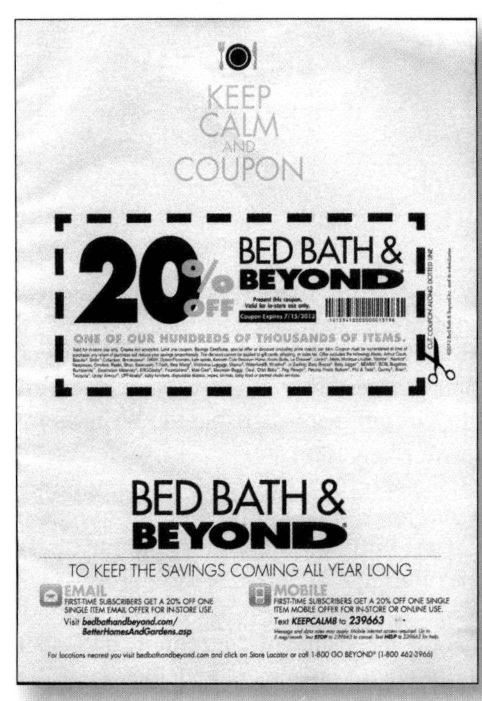

Coupons Coupons are sales promotions that usually offer a discounted price to the consumer, which encourages trial. Approximately 305 billion coupons worth $467 billion are distributed in the United States each year. More than 90 percent of all coupons are distributed as freestanding inserts in newspapers. Research indicates that consumer use of coupons rose during the recession and has remained at 79 percent in subsequent years. Consumers redeemed 2.8 billion of the coupons last year, for a savings of approximately $3.7 billion.

Companies that have increased their use of coupons include Procter & Gamble, Nestlé, and Kraft, while the top retailers for coupon redemption were Walmart, Kroger, and Target. The number of coupons generated at Internet sites (e.g., www.valpak.com and www.coupon.com) and on mobile phones has been increasing as well, although they account for less than 2 percent of all coupons. The redemption rate for online coupons—approximately 14 percent—however, is substantially higher than other forms of coupons. The TV show

KIND OF SALES PROMOTION	OBJECTIVES	ADVANTAGES	DISADVANTAGES
Coupons	Stimulate demand	Encourage retailer support	Consumers delay purchases
Deals	Increase trial; retaliate against competitor's actions	Reduce consumer risk	Consumers delay purchases; reduce perceived product value
Premiums	Build goodwill	Consumers like free or reduced-price merchandise	Consumers buy for premium, not product
Contests	Increase consumer purchases; build business inventory	Encourage consumer involvement with product	Require creative or analytical thinking
Sweepstakes	Encourage present customers to buy more; minimize brand switching	Get customer to use product and store more often	Sales drop after sweepstakes
Samples	Encourage new-product trial	Low risk for consumer	High cost for company
Loyalty programs	Encourage repeat purchases	Help create loyalty	High cost for company
Point-of-purchase displays	Increase product trial; provide in-store support for other promotions	Provide good product visibility	Hard to get retailer to allocate high-traffic space
Rebates	Encourage customers to purchase; stop sales decline	Effective at stimulating demand	Easily copied; steal sales from future; reduce perceived product value
Product placements	Introduce new products; demonstrate product use	Positive message in a noncommercial setting	Little control over presentation of product

FIGURE 18–6
Consumer-oriented sales promotion makes use of many different tools to achieve a variety of objectives.

Extreme Couponing: All Stars and "daily deal" sites like Groupon and Living-Social have helped fuel the growth in couponing. Today, coupons are available in almost every product category and they are used by men and women of all ages.[53]

Do coupons help increase sales? Studies suggest that market share does increase during the period immediately after coupons are distributed.[54] There are also indications, however, that couponing can reduce gross revenues by lowering the price paid by already-loyal consumers.[55] Therefore, the 9,000 manufacturers that currently use coupons are particularly interested in coupon programs directed at potential first-time buyers. One means of focusing on these potential buyers is through electronic in-store coupon machines that match coupons to your most recent purchases.

Coupons are often far more expensive than the face value of the coupon; a 25-cent coupon can cost three times that after paying for the advertisement to deliver it, dealer handling, clearinghouse costs, and redemption. In addition, misredemption, or attempting to redeem a counterfeit coupon or a valid coupon when the product was not purchased, should be added to the cost of the coupon. The Coupon Information Corporation estimates that companies pay out refunds worth hundreds of millions of dollars each year as a result of coupon fraud. Recent growth in coupon fraud has marketers considering adding holograms and visual aids to help cashiers identify valid coupons.[56]

Deals Deals are short-term price reductions, commonly used to increase trial among potential customers or to retaliate against a competitor's actions. For example, if a rival manufacturer introduces a new cake mix, the company responds with a "two packages for the price of one" deal. This short-term price reduction builds up the stock on the kitchen shelves of cake mix buyers and makes the competitor's introduction more difficult.

Premiums A promotional tool often used with consumers is the premium, which consists of merchandise offered free or at a significant savings over its retail price. This latter type of premium is called self-liquidating because the cost charged to the consumer covers the cost of the item. McDonald's, for example, used a free premium in a promotional partnership with 20th Century Fox during the release of the movie *Epic*. Collectible toys that portrayed movie characters were given away free with the purchase of a Happy Meal. What are the most popular premiums? According to the Promotional Products Association International, the top premiums are apparel, writing instruments, shopping bags, cups and mugs, and desk accessories. By offering a premium, companies encourage customers to return frequently or to use more of the product. Research suggests that deal-prone consumers and value seekers are attracted to premiums.[57]

Contests As shown in Figure 18–6, contests are another sales promotion tool used with consumers. Contests encourage consumers to apply their skill or analytical or creative thinking to try to win a prize. This form of promotion has been growing as requests for videos, photos, and essays are a good match with the trend toward consumer-generated content. For example, Doritos sponsors the "Crash the Super Bowl" ad contest, asking people to create their own 30-second ad about Doritos. A panel of judges then selects five finalists, posts the submissions on the Doritos Facebook Page, and opens up voting by the public. The two winners are aired during the Super Bowl, and if one of the ads is ranked No. 1 on *USA Today's* Super Bowl Ad Meter, the winner is awarded a $1 million prize! If you like contests, you can enter online now at websites such as www.contests.about.com.[58]

McDonald's Monopoly sweepstakes offers a grand prize of $1 million.

Sweepstakes Sweepstakes are sales promotions that require participants to submit some kind of entry but are purely games of chance requiring no analytical or creative effort by the consumer. Popular sweepstakes include the HGTV "Dream Home Giveaway," which receives more than 76 million entries each year, and McDonald's Monopoly, which offers a grand prize of $1 million.[59]

Two variations of sweepstakes are popular now. First are sweepstakes that offer products that consumers value as prizes. Mars Chocolate, for example, created a sweepstakes where consumers enter a UPC code from M&M's products for a chance to win one of five Toyota automobiles. Coca-Cola has a similar sweepstakes called "My Coke Rewards" that allows consumers to use codes from bottle caps to enter to win prizes or to collect points to be redeemed for rewards.

The second type of sweepstakes offers an "experience" as the prize. For example, one of television's most popular series, *American Idol*, and AT&T sponsor a sweepstakes for a chance to win a trip for two to the season finale of *American Idol* in Los Angeles. Similarly, StumbleUpon and the Academy of Motion Picture Arts and Sciences created a sweepstakes where consumers entered for a chance to win a trip to the Oscars in Hollywood.

The Dial sweepstakes attracts prospective customers, while the Hilton loyalty program rewards frequent customers.

Dial
www.dial.com

Hilton
www. hilton.com

Federal laws, the Federal Trade Commission, and state legislatures have issued rules covering sweepstakes, contests, and games to regulate fairness, ensure that the chance for winning is represented honestly, and guarantee that the prizes are actually awarded. Several well-known sweepstakes created by Publishers Clearing House and *Reader's Digest* have paid fines and agreed to new sweepstakes guidelines in response to regulatory scrutiny.[60]

Samples Another common consumer sales promotion is sampling, which is offering the product free or at a greatly reduced price. Often used for new products, sampling puts the product in the consumer's hands. A trial size is generally offered that is smaller than the regular package size. If consumers like the sample, it is hoped they will remember and buy the product. Taco Bell has offered free tacos nationwide six times in the past to encourage customers to try new products. Most recently, Taco Bell gave a free Doritos Locos Taco to each guest on the day of the promotion. The taco has become the company's most successful new product. Similarly, Ben & Jerry's offers a complimentary scoop of ice cream on "Free Cone Day." Some consumers watch for free samples online at sites such as www.startsampling.com. According to Stacy Fisher, who started trying free samples in college and now blogs about them, free samples are "a great way to try new things and save money."[61]

Loyalty Programs Loyalty programs are a sales promotion tool used to encourage and reward repeat purchases by acknowledging each purchase made by a consumer and offering a premium as purchases accumulate. The most popular loyalty programs today are credit card reward programs. More than 75 percent of all cards offer incentives for use of their card. Citibank, for example, offers "Thank You" points for using Citi credit or debit cards. The points can be redeemed for books, music, gift cards, cash, travel, and special limited time rewards. Airlines, retailers, hotels, and grocery stores also offer popular loyalty programs. Specialty retailers such as Toys 'Я' Us and Best Buy have enhanced their reward programs to add value to their offerings as they compete with low-cost merchandise. There are now more than 2 billion loyalty program memberships, for an average of 18 for each household in the United States, with point balances close to $50 billion.[62]

Point-of-purchase displays help increase consumers' attention in a store.

One trend in loyalty programs today is to customize the rewards and benefits for different segments of program members. This approach leads to promotions targeted at new members, members with unique purchase histories, or members who have self-selected into "elite" status groups. American Airlines, for example, has offered bonus points for new members, an additional 50 percent of award points for members who fly first class, and special benefits for members who join the American Airlines Admirals Club. Another trend is the shift from programs where points and rewards can be earned from only one operator to an "open economy" for loyalty where points and rewards can be earned from many interchangeable programs. An example of a program moving in this direction is the Chase Ultimate Rewards program, which was recently rated highest in terms of overall customer satisfaction.[63]

Point-of-Purchase Displays In a store aisle, you often encounter a sales promotion called a point-of-purchase display. These product displays take the form of advertising signs, which sometimes actually hold or display the product, and are often located in high-traffic areas near the cash register or the end of an aisle. The point-of-purchase display for the *Twilight Saga* movies is designed to maximize the consumer's attention to a DVD release and provide storage for the products. Annual expenditures on point-of-purchase promotions now exceed $20.3 billion and are expected to grow as point-of-purchase becomes integrated with all forms of promotion.

Some studies estimate that one-third of a consumer's buying decisions are made in the store. Grocery product manufacturers want to get their message to you at the instant you are next to their brand in your supermarket aisle, perhaps through a point-of-purchase display. At a growing number of supermarkets, this may be done with digital signage. Walmart, for example, is replacing its satellite-based in-store TV network with an Internet protocol system called Walmart Smart Network, which includes welcome screens, category screens, and "endcap" screens that display information about product categories, brands, and new products, respectively. The advantage of these methods of promotion is that they do not rely on the consumers' ability to remember the message for long periods. Other in-store promotions such as interactive kiosks are also becoming popular.[64]

Rebates Another consumer sales promotion tool in Figure 18–6, the cash rebate, offers the return of money based on proof of purchase. For example, Virgin Mobile recently offered a $100 rebate to T-Mobile subscribers who switched their service during a seven-week period. When a rebate is offered on lower-priced items, the time and trouble of mailing in a proof of purchase to get the rebate check often means that many buyers never take advantage of it. However, this "slippage" is less likely to occur with frequent users of rebate promotions. In addition, online consumers are more likely to take advantage of rebates.[65]

Product Placements A final consumer promotion tool, **product placement**, involves the use of a brand-name product in a movie, television show, video game, or commercial for another product. It was Steven Spielberg's placement of Hershey's Reese's Pieces in *E.T. the Extra Terrestrial* that first brought a lot of interest to the candy. Similarly, when Tom Cruise wore Bausch and Lomb's Ray-Ban sunglasses in *Risky Business* and its Aviator glasses in *Top Gun*, sales skyrocketed from 100,000 pairs to 7,000,000 pairs in five years. After *Toy Story*, Etch-A-Sketch sales increased 4,500 percent and Mr. Potato Head sales increased 800 percent.

More recently, you might remember seeing products from Apple, JanSport, Mercedes, and Steinway & Sons in *The Twilight Saga*: *Breaking Dawn Part 2*; Aston Martin, Coca-Cola Zero, and Omega in *Skyfall*; and Brooks Brothers, Prada, and Tiffany in *The Great Gatsby*. Product placement has also grown in television programs. *American Idol* ranks No. 1 with Coca-Cola, Ford, and AT&T product appearances, followed by *The*

Product placement can take many forms today. Are you familiar with these examples?

Biggest Loser and *Celebrity Apprentice.* Companies are usually eager to gain exposure for their products, and studios believe that product placements can add authenticity to the film or program. The producers sometimes receive fees in exchange for the exposure, although they often do not. BlackBerry phones, for example, were donated in exchange for their use in *Zero Dark Thirty*.

The annual value of all product placements is estimated to be $8.3 billion. Complaints that product placement has become excessive have led the Federal Communications Commission to begin developing guidelines for TV product placements. Meanwhile, the British government recently passed a law allowing product placement only if a bold "P" logo is shown before and after the program.[66]

New forms of product placement may appear to be integrated into the program. An episode of *Modern Family*, for example, includes a scene in an Apple store. Some programs have recently begun digital product placement in programs after they have been filmed. Similarly, some companies such as Amway are creating partnerships with game developers in order to be included in video games. A variation of product placement, called *reverse product placement*, brings fictional products to the marketplace. Bertie Bott's Every Flavour Beans, for example, began as an imaginary brand in Harry Potter books. Similarly, the movie *Forrest Gump* led to the Bubba Gump Shrimp Company restaurant chain. And fans of *The Office* can purchase Dunder Mifflin office supplies from www.quill.com![67]

Trade-Oriented Sales Promotions

Trade-oriented sales promotions, or simply *trade promotions*, are sales tools used to support a company's advertising and personal selling directed to wholesalers, retailers, or distributors. Some of the sales promotions just reviewed are used for this purpose, but three other common approaches are targeted uniquely to these intermediaries: (1) allowances and discounts, (2) cooperative advertising, and (3) training of distributors' salesforces.

Allowances and Discounts Trade promotions often focus on maintaining or increasing inventory levels in the channel of distribution. An effective method for encouraging such increased purchases by intermediaries is the use of allowances and discounts. However, overuse of these price reductions can lead to retailers changing their ordering patterns in the expectation of such offerings. Although there are many variations that manufacturers can use with discounts and allowances, three common approaches are the merchandise allowance, the case allowance, and the finance allowance.[68]

Reimbursing a retailer for extra in-store support or special featuring of the brand is a *merchandise allowance*. Performance contracts between the manufacturer and trade member usually specify the activity to be performed, such as a picture of the product in a newspaper with a coupon good at only one store. The merchandise allowance then consists of a percentage deduction from the list case price ordered during the promotional period. Allowances are not paid by the manufacturer until it sees proof of performance (such as a copy of the ad placed by the retailer in the local newspaper).

A second common trade promotion, a *case allowance*, is a discount on each case ordered during a specific time period. These allowances are usually deducted from the invoice. A variation of the case allowance is the "free goods" approach, whereby retailers receive some amount of the product free based on the amount ordered, such as 1 case free for every 10 cases ordered.[69]

A final trade promotion, the *finance allowance*, involves paying retailers for financing costs or financial losses associated with consumer sales promotions. This trade promotion is regularly used and has several variations. One type is the floor stock protection program—manufacturers give retailers a case allowance price for products in their warehouse, which prevents shelf stock from running down during the promotional period. Also common are freight allowances, which compensate retailers that transport orders from the manufacturer's warehouse.

Cooperative Advertising Resellers often perform the important function of promoting the manufacturer's products at the local level. One common sales promotional activity is to encourage both better quality and greater quantity in the local advertising efforts of resellers through **cooperative advertising**. These are programs by which a manufacturer pays a percentage of the retailer's local advertising expense for advertising the manufacturer's products.

Usually, the manufacturer pays a percentage, often 50 percent, of the cost of advertising up to a certain dollar limit, which is based on the amount of the manufacturer's products purchased by the retailer. In addition to paying for the advertising, the manufacturer often furnishes the retailer with a selection of different ad executions, sometimes suited for several different media. A manufacturer may provide, for example, several different print layouts as well as a few broadcast ads for the retailer to adapt and use.[70]

Training of Distributors' Salesforces One of the many functions the intermediaries perform is customer contact and selling for the producers they represent. Both retailers and wholesalers employ and manage their own sales personnel. A manufacturer's success often rests on the ability of the reseller's salesforce to represent its products. Thus, it is in the best interest of the manufacturer to help train the reseller's salesforce.

Because the reseller's salesforce is often less sophisticated and knowledgeable about the products than the manufacturer might like, training can increase their sales performance. Training activities include producing manuals and brochures to educate the reseller's salesforce. The salesforce then uses these aids in selling situations. Other activities include national sales meetings sponsored by the manufacturer and field visits to the reseller's location to inform and motivate the salesperson to sell the products. Manufacturers also develop incentive and recognition programs to motivate a reseller's salespeople to sell their products.

learning review

18-10. What is the difference between a coupon and a deal?

18-11. Which sales promotional tool is most common for new products?

18-12. Which trade promotion approach is used on an ongoing basis?

PUBLIC RELATIONS

LO 18-5
Recognize public relations as an important form of communication.

As noted in Chapter 17, public relations is a form of communications management that seeks to influence the image of an organization and its products and services. Public relations efforts may utilize a variety of tools and may be directed at many distinct audiences. While public relations personnel usually focus on communicating positive aspects of the business, they may also be called on to minimize the negative impact of a problem or crisis. Carnival Cruises, BP, and Goldman Sachs, for example, faced substantial negative publicity for passengers stranded on disabled ships, the worst oil spill in U.S. history, and securities fraud charges, respectively.[71] The most frequently used public relations tool is publicity.

Publicity Tools

In developing a public relations campaign, several methods of obtaining nonpersonal presentation of an organization, product, or service without direct cost—**publicity tools**—are available to the public relations director. Many companies frequently use the *news release*, consisting of an announcement regarding changes in the company or the product line. The objective of a news release is to inform a newspaper, radio station, or other medium of an idea for a story.

A second common publicity tool is the *news conference*. Representatives of the media are all invited to an informational meeting, and advance materials regarding the content are sent. This tool is often used when new products are introduced or significant changes in corporate structure and leadership are being made.

Lucy Liu receives publicity for her movies by visiting programs such as *Late Night with Jimmy Fallon.*

Nonprofit organizations rely heavily on *public service announcements* (PSAs), which are free space or time donated by the media. For example, the charter of the American Red Cross prohibits any local chapter from advertising, so to solicit blood donations local chapters often depend on PSAs on radio or television to announce their needs.

Finally, today many high-visibility individuals are used as publicity tools to create visibility for their companies, their products, and themselves. Richard Branson uses visibility to promote the Virgin Group, Lucy Liu uses it to promote her movies, and U.S. senators use it to promote themselves as political candidates. These publicity efforts are coordinated with news releases, conferences, advertising, donations to charities, volunteer activities, endorsements, and any other activities that may have an impact on public perceptions.[72]

INCREASING THE VALUE OF PROMOTION

Today's customers seek value from companies that provide leading-edge products, hassle-free transactions at competitive prices, and customer intimacy.[73] Promotion practices have changed dramatically to improve transactions and increase customer intimacy by (1) emphasizing long-term relationships and (2) increasing self-regulation.

Building Long-Term Relationships

Many changes in promotional techniques have been driven by marketers' interest in developing long-term relationships with their customers. Promotion can contribute to brand and store loyalty by improving a company's ability to target individual preferences and by engaging customers in valuable and entertaining communication. New social and mobile media have provided immediate opportunities for personalized promotion activities. In addition, technological developments have helped traditional media such as TV and radio focus on individual preferences through services such as TiVo and SiriusXM Satellite Radio. Although the future holds extraordinary promise for the personalization of promotion, the industry will need to manage and balance consumers' concerns about privacy as it proceeds.

Changes that help engage consumers have also been numerous. Marketers have attempted to utilize interactive technologies and to integrate new media and technologies into the overall creative process. Ad agencies are increasingly integrating public relations, direct marketing, advertising, and sales promotion into comprehensive IMC campaigns. In fact, some experts predict that advertising agencies will soon become "communications consulting firms." Further, increasingly diverse and global audiences necessitate multimedia approaches and sensitivity communication techniques that engage the varied groups.[74] Overall, companies hope that these changes will build customer relationships for the long term—emphasizing a lifetime of purchases rather than a single transaction.

Self-Regulation

Unfortunately, over the years, many consumers have been misled, or even deceived, by some promotions. Examples include sweepstakes in which the gifts were not awarded, rebate offers that were a terrible hassle, and advertisements whose promises were great, until the buyer read the small print. In one of the worst scandals in promotion history, McDonald's assisted an FBI investigation of the firm responsible for the fast-food chain's sweepstakes because the promotion agency security director was suspected of stealing winning game pieces.[75]

Promotions targeted at special groups such as children and the elderly also raise ethical concerns. For example, providing free samples to children in elementary schools or linking product lines to TV programs and movies has led to questions about the need for restrictions on promotions.[76] Although the Federal Trade Commission does provide some guidelines to protect consumers and special groups from misleading promotions, some observers believe more government regulation is needed.

Formal regulation of all promotional activities by federal, state, and local governments would be very expensive. As a result, advertising agencies, trade associations, and marketing organizations are increasing their efforts toward *self-regulation*.[77] By imposing standards that reflect the values of society on their promotional activities, marketers can (1) facilitate the development of new promotional methods, (2) minimize regulatory constraints and restrictions, and (3) help consumers gain confidence in the communication efforts used to influence their purchases. As organizations strive for effective self-regulation, marketing executives will need to make sound ethical judgments about the use of existing and new promotional practices.

learning review

18-13. What is a news release?

18-14. What is the difference between government regulation and self-regulation?

LEARNING OBJECTIVES REVIEW

LO 18-1 *Explain the differences between product advertising and institutional advertising and the variations within each type.*
Product advertisements focus on selling a good or service and take three forms: Pioneering advertisements tell people what a product is, what it can do, and where it can be found; competitive advertisements persuade the target market to select the firm's brand rather than a competitor's; and reminder advertisements reinforce previous knowledge of a product. Institutional advertisements are used to build goodwill or an image for an organization. They include advocacy advertisements, which state the position of a company on an issue, and pioneering, competitive, and reminder advertisements, which are similar to the product ads but focused on the institution.

LO 18-2 *Describe the steps used to develop, execute, and evaluate an advertising program.*
The promotion decision process can be applied to each of the promotional elements. The steps to develop an advertising program include the following: identify the target audience, specify the advertising objectives, set the advertising budget, design the advertisement, create the message, select the media, and schedule the advertising. Executing the program requires pretesting, and evaluating the program requires posttesting.

LO 18-3 *Explain the advantages and disadvantages of alternative advertising media.*
Television advertising reaches large audiences and uses picture, print, sound, and motion; its disadvantages, however, are that it is expensive and perishable. Radio advertising is inexpensive and can be placed quickly, but it has no visual element and is perishable. Magazine advertising can target specific audiences and can convey complex information, but it takes a long time to place the ad and is relatively expensive. Newspapers provide excellent coverage of local markets and can be changed quickly, but they have a short life span and poor color. Yellow pages advertising has a long use period and is available 24 hours per day; its disadvantages, however, are that there is a proliferation of directories and they cannot be updated frequently. Internet advertising can be interactive, but its effectiveness is difficult to measure. Outdoor advertising provides repeat exposures, but its message must be very short and simple. Direct mail can be targeted at very selective audiences, but its cost per contact is high.

LO 18-4 *Discuss the strengths and weaknesses of consumer-oriented and trade-oriented sales promotions.*
Coupons encourage retailer support but may delay consumer purchases. Deals reduce consumer risk but also reduce perceived value. Premiums offer consumers additional merchandise they want, but they may be purchasing only for the premium. Contests create involvement but require creative thinking. Sweepstakes encourage repeat purchases, but sales drop after the sweepstakes. Samples encourage product trial but are expensive. Loyalty programs help create loyalty but are expensive to run. Displays provide visibility but are difficult to place in retail space. Rebates stimulate demand but are easily copied. Product placements provide a positive message in a noncommercial setting that is difficult to control. Trade-oriented sales promotions include (*a*) allowances and discounts, which increase purchases but may change retailer ordering patterns, (*b*) cooperative advertising, which encourages local advertising, and (*c*) salesforce training, which helps increase sales by providing the salespeople with product information and selling skills.

LO 18-5 *Recognize public relations as an important form of communication.*
Public relations activities usually focus on communicating positive aspects of the business. A frequently used public relations tool is publicity. Publicity tools include news releases and news conferences. Nonprofit organizations often use public service announcements.

FOCUSING ON KEY TERMS

advertising p. 470
consumer-oriented sales promotions p. 489
cooperative advertising p. 495
cost per thousand (CPM) p. 479
frequency p. 478
full-service agency p. 487
gross rating points (GRPs) p. 479
infomercials p. 480
in-house agencies p. 488
institutional advertisements p. 471
limited-service agencies p. 488
posttests p. 488
pretests p. 486
product advertisements p. 470
product placement p. 493
publicity tools p. 496
rating p. 478
reach p. 478
trade-oriented sales promotions p. 494

APPLYING MARKETING KNOWLEDGE

1 How does competitive product advertising differ from competitive institutional advertising?

2 Suppose you are the advertising manager for a new line of children's fragrances. Which form of media would you use for this new product?

3 You have recently been promoted to be director of advertising for the Timkin Tool Company. In your first meeting with Mr. Timkin, he says, "Advertising is a waste! We've been advertising for six months now and sales haven't increased. Tell me why we should continue." Give your answer to Mr. Timkin.

4 A large life insurance company has decided to switch from using a strong fear appeal to a humorous approach. What are the strengths and weaknesses of such a change in message strategy?

5 Some national advertisers have found that they can have more impact with their advertising by running a large number of ads for a period and then running no ads at all for a period. Why might such a flighting schedule be more effective than a continuous schedule?

6 Which medium has the lowest cost per thousand (CPM)?

Medium	Cost of Ad	Audience Size
TV show	$5,000	25,000
Magazine	2,200	6,000
Newspaper	4,800	7,200
FM radio	420	1,600

7 Each year, managers at Bausch and Lomb evaluate the many advertising media alternatives available to them as they develop their advertising program for contact lenses. What advantages and disadvantages of each alternative should they consider? Which media would you recommend to them?

8 What are two advantages and two disadvantages of the advertising posttests described in the chapter?

9 Federated Banks is interested in consumer-oriented sales promotions that would encourage senior citizens to direct deposit their Social Security checks with the bank. Evaluate the sales promotion options, and recommend two of them to the bank.

10 How can public relations be used by Firestone and Ford following investigations into complaints about tire failures?

11 Describe a self-regulation guideline you believe would improve the value of (*a*) an existing form of promotion and (*b*) a new promotional practice.

BUILDING YOUR MARKETING PLAN

To augment your promotion strategy from Chapter 17:

1 Use Figure 18–3 to select the advertising media you will include in your plan by analyzing how combinations of media (e.g., television and Internet advertising, radio and yellow pages advertising) can complement each other.

2 Use Figure 18–6 to select your consumer-oriented sales promotion activities.

3 Specify which trade-oriented sales promotions and public relations tools you will use.

VIDEO CASE 18 Google, Inc.: The Right Ads at the Right Time

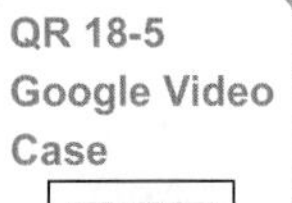

QR 18-5 Google Video Case

"So what we did, in essence, is we said advertising should be useful to a consumer just as much as the organic search results, and we don't want people just to buy advertising and be able to show an ad if it's irrelevant to the consumer's need," says Richard Holden, director of product management at Google. To accomplish this, Google developed a "Quality Score" model to predict how effective an ad will be. The model uses many factors such as click-through rates, advertiser history, and keyword performance to develop a score for each advertisement. "Essentially, what we're trying to do is predict ahead, before we actually show an ad, how a consumer will react to that ad, and our interest is in showing fewer ads, not more ads; just the right ads at the right time," Holden continues. The Google advertising model has revolutionized the advertising industry, and it continues to improve every day!

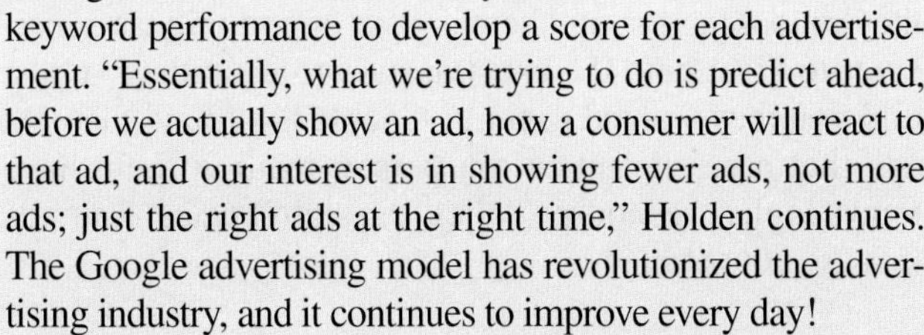

THE COMPANY

Google began in 1996 as a research project for Stanford computer science students Larry Page and Sergey Brin. They started with a simple idea—that a search engine based on the relationships between websites would provide a better ranking than a search engine based only on the number of times a key term appeared on a website. The success of their model led to rapid growth, and the founders moved the company from their dorm room, to a friend's garage, to offices in Palo Alto, California, and eventually to its current location, known as the Googleplex, in Mountain View, California. In 2000, Google began selling advertising as a means of generating revenue. Its advertising model allowed advertisers to bid on search words and pay for each "click" by a search-engine user. The ads were required to be simple and text-based so that the search result pages remained uncluttered and the search time was as fast as possible.

Page and Brin's first search engine was called "BackRub" because their technique was based on relationships, or backlinks, between websites. The name quickly changed, however. The name "Google" is a misspelling of the word "googol," which is a mathematical term for a 1 followed by 100 zeros. Page and Brin used the name in the original domain, www.google.stanford.edu, to reflect their interest in organizing the immense amount of information available on the Web. The domain name, of course, became www.google.com and eventually Webster's dictionary added the verb "google" with the definition "to use the Google search engine to obtain information on the Internet." The name has become so familiar that *Advertising Age* recently reported that Google is "the world's most powerful brand"!

Today, Google receives several hundred million inquiries each day as it pursues its mission: to organize the world's information and make it universally accessible and useful. The company generates more than $21 billion in annual revenue and has more than 20,000 employees. As Google has grown, it has developed 10 guidelines that represent the corporate philosophy. They are:

1. Focus on the user and all else will follow.
2. It's best to do one thing really, really well.
3. Fast is better than slow.
4. Democracy on the Web works.
5. You don't need to be at your desk to need an answer.
6. You can make money without doing evil.
7. There's always more information out there.
8. The need for information crosses all borders.
9. You can be serious without a suit.
10. Great just isn't good enough.

Using these guidelines, Google strives to continually improve its search engine. "The perfect search engine," explains Google co-founder Larry Page, "would understand exactly what you mean and give back exactly what you want."

ONLINE ADVERTISING

Google generates revenue by offering online advertising opportunities—next to search results or on specific web pages. The company always distinguishes ads from the search results or the content of a web page and it never sells placement in the search results. This approach ensures that Google website visitors always know when someone has paid to put a message in front of them. The advantage of online advertising is that it is measurable and allows immediate assessment of its effectiveness. As Gopi Kallayil, product marketing manager, explains: "There is a very high degree of measurability and trackability that you get through online advertising." In addition, he says, "With online advertising you can actually track the value of every single dollar that you spend, understand which particular customers the ad reached, and what they did after they received the advertising message."

The online advertising market has grown from its initial focus on simple text ads to a much larger set of options. There are five key categories of online advertising. They are:

- Search: 47%
- Display: 35%
- Classified: 10%
- Referral: 7%
- E-mail: 1%

Google is the dominant provider of online search requests and receives more than 60 percent of the search advertising revenue. The fastest-growing advertising category, however, is display advertising, where Yahoo! and Microsoft are established providers. Google believes that there is an opportunity to grow its display advertising sales by making the ads useful information instead of visual clutter. According to Google co-founder Sergey Brin, "It's like search—matching people with information they want. It just happens to be promotional."

Several improvements in technology and business practice tools contributed to Google's success. First, Google developed its patented PageRank™ algorithm, which evaluates the entire link structure of the Web and uses the link structure to determine which pages are most important. Then the process uses hypertext-matching analysis to determine which pages are relevant to a specific search. A combination of the importance and the relevance of web pages provides the search results—in just a fraction of a second. Second, Google developed two business practice tools—AdWords and AdSense—to help (1) advertisers create ads, and (2) content providers generate advertising revenue. Both tools have become essential elements of Google's advertising model.

AdWords

To help advertisers place ads on their search-engine results, Google developed an online tool called AdWords. Advertisers can use AdWords to create ad text, select target keywords, and manage their account. The process allows advertisers to reach targeted audiences. Frederick Vallaeys, AdWords evangelist, explains: "One of my favorite things about AdWords is the fact that it really helps you find the right customer at the right time and show them the right message. With AdWords you can very specifically target your market because you're targeting them at a time when they do a search on Google. At that time they've told you a keyword, you know exactly what they're looking for, and here is your opportunity as a marketer to give them the exact answer to what they've just told you they wanted to find." Google has found that text ads that are relevant to the person reading them have much higher response ("click-through") rates than ads that are not targeted.

AdWords is also easy for any advertiser to use. Large or small businesses can simply open an account with a credit card and have ads appear within minutes. "When AdWords rolled out their self-service product, it really was one of the first times when it was very easy for a small business to put their ad up on the Internet on a search engine and compete on a level playing field alongside *Fortune* 1000 companies," says Vallaeys. Google has an experienced sales and service team available to help any advertiser select appropriate keywords, generate ad copy, and monitor campaign performance. The team is dedicated to helping its advertisers improve click-through rates because high click-through rates are an indication that ads are relevant to a user's interests. Methods of improving advertising performance include changing the keywords and rewriting copy. Because there is no limit to the number of keywords that an advertiser can select and each keyword can be matched with different ad copy, the potential for many very customer-specific options is high.

Another advantage of Google's AdWords program is that it allows advertisers to easily control costs. The ads appear as a "Sponsored Link" next to search results each time the Google search engine matches the search request with the ad's keywords and Quality Score, although the advertiser is not charged unless someone "clicks" on the link. In a traditional advertising model, advertisers were charged using a CPM (cost-per-thousand) approach, which charged for the impressions made by an ad. According to Holden, the Google model "transformed that to what we call a CPC, or a cost-per-click model, and this is a model that an advertiser, instead of paying for an impression, only pays when somebody actually clicks on that ad and is delivered to their website. So, in effect, they may be getting the benefit from impressions being shown, but we're not actually charging them anything unless there's a definite lead being delivered to their website." Google also offers advertisers real-time analytical services to allow assessment of and changes to any component of an advertising campaign.

AdSense

The AdSense program was designed for website owners as a tool for placing ads next to their web page content rather than next to search results. Currently, thousands of website managers use AdSense to place ads on their sites and generate revenue. Google applies the same general philosophy to matching ads with websites as it does to matching ads to search requests. By delivering ads that precisely target the content on the site's pages, Google believes the advertising enhances the experience for visitors to the website. In this way advertisers, website publishers, and information seekers all benefit.

AdSense is one of the tools Google is using to pursue its goal of increasing its display advertising business. Yahoo! and Microsoft's Bing are leaders in display advertising because they can put ads on their own websites such as Yahoo! Finance and MSN Money. To provide additional outlets for display ads, Google recently purchased YouTube. In addition, Google purchased DoubleClick, an advertising exchange where websites put space up for auction and ad agencies bid to place ads for their clients. Google is also trying to make it easy for anyone to create a display ad by introducing a new tool called Display Ad Builder. Some experts observe that because Google is so dominant at search advertising, its future growth will depend on success in display advertising.

GOOGLE'S FUTURE STRATEGY

How will Google continue its success? One possibility is that it will begin to try to win advertising away from the U.S. TV industry. While this is a new type of advertising requiring creative capabilities and relationships with large advertising agencies, Google has dedicated many of its resources to becoming competitive for television advertising expenditures. For example, Google recently helped Volvo develop a campaign that included a YouTube ad and Twitter updates. Google is also likely to develop new websites, establish blogs, and build relationships with existing sites.

Another opportunity for Google will be mobile telephone advertising. There are currently more than 5.4 billion mobile phones in use, and 1 billion of those are Internet-capable. Just as Google's search engine provides a means to match relevant information with consumers, phones offer a chance to provide real-time and location-specific information. Some of the challenges in mobile advertising will be that the networks are not fast and that the ad formats are not standardized. Google believes its new phone and its Android operating system will also help.

Finally, as Google pursues its mission it will continue to expand throughout the world. Search results are already available in 35 languages, and volunteers are helping with many others. It is obvious that Google is determined to "organize the world's information" and make it "accessible and useful."

Questions

1 Describe several unique characteristics about Google and its business practices.

2 What is Google's philosophy about advertising? How can less advertising be preferred to more advertising?

3 Describe the types of online advertising available today. Which type of advertising does Google currently dominate? Why?

4 How can Google be successful in the display advertising business? What other areas of growth are likely to be pursued by Google in the future?

19 Using Social Media to Connect with Consumers

Learning Objectives

After reading this chapter you should be able to:

LO 19-1 Define social media and describe how they differ from traditional advertising media.

LO 19-2 Identify the four major social networks and how brand managers integrate them into marketing actions.

LO 19-3 Describe the differing roles of those receiving messages through traditional versus social media and how brand managers select a social network.

LO 19-4 Explain how social media can produce sales revenues for a brand and compare the performance measures linked to costs versus revenues.

LO 19-5 Describe how the convergence of the real and digital worlds affects the future of social media.

How to Connect with Today's College Student? Use Facebook and Twitter!

Like Kimmy Summers at the University of North Carolina (wearing cap in the photo), thousands of "brand ambassadors" at U.S. colleges and universities face a special challenge right before freshman week.[1]

Finding Volunteers for Freshman Move-In Day

The challenge: How can she recruit student volunteers to help incoming freshmen during campus move-in day? Use the campus newspaper?

The answer is a no-brainer for most upperclassmen working as brand ambassadors for firms like American Eagle Outfitters (AE), Target, and Apple: Use Facebook and Twitter! Here's a somewhat generic marketing plan they use for freshman week, with AE as an example:

- Use the college Facebook Page and Twitter messages to recruit about 40 volunteers to assist freshmen on move-in day.
- Tell incoming freshmen about the volunteers on the college Facebook Page with teasers like: "Need help moving in? No worries. AE will be there."
- Have these volunteers help freshmen move into their college dorms.
- Give each freshman who was helped a coupon for a free pair of AE flip-flops.

The volunteers often get a free American Eagle T-shirt (photo).

College Students and Social Media

"College students are wary of old-school marketing," says Paul Himmelfarb, managing director of Youth Marketing Connection, which links marketers with college students. "You have to take a brand and incorporate it into the college lifestyle by peer-to-peer marketing."[2]

In the past decade, college students have more than doubled their use of the Internet and social media to collect information and buy products. College marketers increasingly use social media to reach students because they work better than traditional print and TV ads.[3] More than 10,000 student brand ambassadors on the 4,000 U.S. college campuses use social media to connect with other students.

This chapter defines social media, describes four widely used social networks, explains how organizations use them in developing marketing strategies, and considers where social media are headed in the future.

facebook
DOT
StuffDot
354 likes · 13 talking about this
Liked
Message
Website
A smarter way to share. Get rewarded for your recommendations! Check us out at www.stuffdot.com
354
About
Photos
Likes
StuffDot
February 23
Trending on StuffDOT: Travel. Dotters are dreaming of warm places! bit.ly/Xo7qfS
StuffDot
March 30
Have a look at our top three favorite beauty-themed posts of the week! http://bit.ly/10VzUPs
YouTube
ok go this too shall pass
OK Go - This Too Shall Pass - Rube Goldberg Machine version - ...
40,623,460
2013 DODGE DART GT
Linkedin
Welcome, Michael! See Who You Already Know on LinkedIn
Get started by adding your email address.
Your email:
Email password:
Continue
PEOPLE YOU MAY KNOW
Maggie
Connect
Lee
Connect
THE $249 LAPTOP FROM GOOGLE
chromebook
Learn more
Share with: Public
Share
All Updates
LinkedIn Today recommends this news for you
HELP! I'm Too Smart for My Job
WHO'S VIEWED YOUR PROFILE
1 Your profile has been viewed by 1 person in the past 90 days.
YOUR LINKEDIN NETWORK
10 Connections link you to 256,389+ professionals
4.580 New people in your Network since August 13
CARMEX
Carmex
@Carmex
Tweets
Following
Followers
Favorites
Lists
Tweet to Carmex
Photos and videos
Who to follow
Trends
healing
hydra

UNDERSTANDING SOCIAL MEDIA

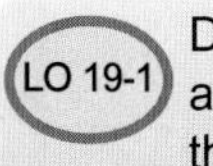

LO 19-1 Define social media and describe how they differ from traditional advertising media.

Defining *social media* is challenging, but it's necessary to help a brand or marketing manager select the right one. This section defines social media, positions a number of social networks, and compares social and traditional media. As you read this, consider how you might choose a social network if *you*—like college students around the globe—were using one to launch a start-up business or expand a small business.

The text describes how Web 2.0 and user-generated content are the foundations of today's social media.

What Are Social Media?

This section describes how social media came about (remember that the word "media" is plural—"medium" being singular), defines social media, and provides a means of classifying the countless social media networks available to assist marketing managers in choosing among them.

Defining Social Media Social media represent a unique blending of technology and social interaction to create personal value for users. **Social media** are online media where users submit comments, photos, and videos—often accompanied by a feedback process to identify "popular" topics.[4] Most social media involve a genuine online conversation among people about a subject of mutual interest, one built on their personal thoughts and experiences. However, other social media sites involve games and virtual worlds, in which the online interaction includes playing a game, completing a quest, controlling an avatar, and so on. Business firms also refer to social media as "consumer-generated media." A single social media site with millions of users interacting with each other, like Facebook, Twitter, LinkedIn, and YouTube, is referred to as a *social network*.

How Social Media Came About Researchers Andreas M. Kaplan and Michael Haenlein note that the term "social media" is sometimes used interchangeably with the terms "Web 2.0" and "user-generated content"—two concepts that are the foundations of today's social media.[5]

The term "Web 2.0" first appeared in 2004 to describe a new way to utilize the World Wide Web. Web 2.0 does not refer to any technical update of the World Wide Web, but identifies functionalities that make possible today's high degree of interactivity among users. So with Web 2.0, content is no longer seen as being created and published in final form exclusively by one author. Instead, the content can be modified continuously by all users in a participatory fashion, such as with blogs and wikis.

A **blog**—a contraction of "web log"—is a web page that serves as a publicly accessible personal journal and online forum for an individual or organization. Companies like Hewlett-Packard and Frito-Lay routinely monitor blogs to gain insights into customer complaints and suggestions. A *wiki* is a website whose content is created and edited by the ongoing collaboration of end users—such as generating and improving new-product ideas. They differ in that a blog is a diary that shows a sequential journey while a wiki shows the end result as a single entry.[6]

User-generated content (UGC) refers to the various forms of online media content that are publicly available and created by end users. The term "user-generated content" (also referred to as *consumer-generated content*) was in common use by 2005 and covers all the ways people can use social media. UGC satisfies three basic criteria:[7]

1. It is published either on a publicly accessible website or on a social networking site, so it is not simply an e-mail.
2. It shows a significant degree of creative effort, so it is more than simply posting a newspaper article on a personal blog without editing or comments.
3. It is consumer-generated by an individual outside of a professional organization, without a commercial market in mind.

FIGURE 19–1
A sample of social media, classified by media richness and self-disclosure. Note that in moving from words to photos, videos, and animation, media richness increases. Also, in moving from very impersonal messages to highly personal ones, self-disclosure increases.

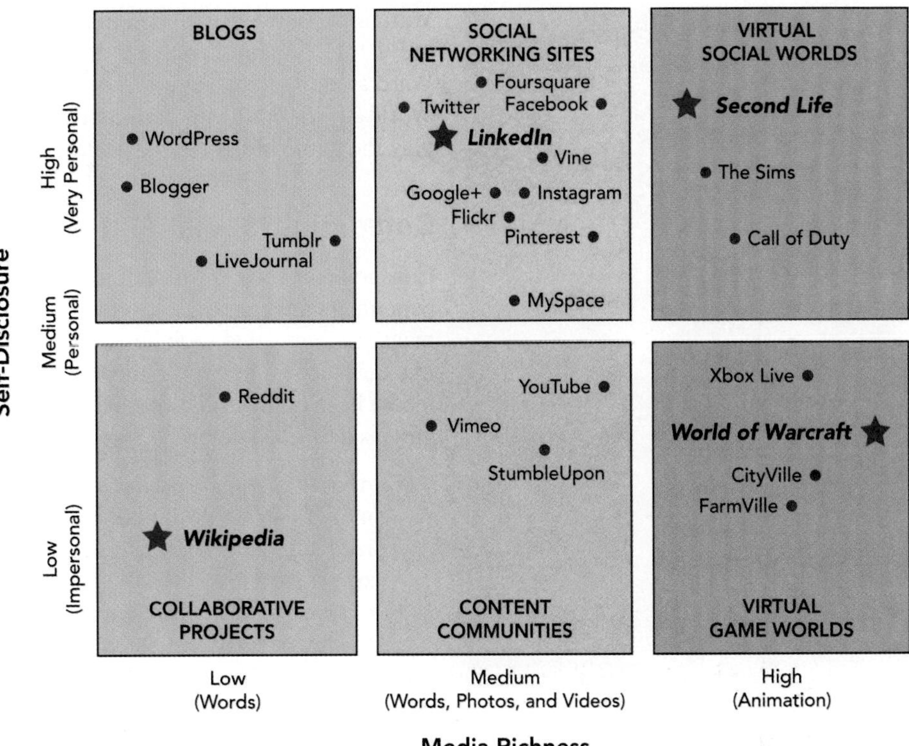

With the countless social networks available on smartphones and computer screens, how do marketing managers choose the best ones to reach their target markets? As a first step, the text describes how social media can be classified and how they differ from traditional media.

Classifying Social Media Most of us would probably say that Facebook, Twitter, LinkedIn, and YouTube are well-known social networks. But marketing managers trying to reach potential customers need a system to classify the more than 400 specialized and diverse social networks to select the best among them. Kaplan and Haenlein have proposed a classification system for marketers based on two factors:[8]

1. *Media richness.* This involves the degree of acoustic, visual, and personal contact between two communication partners—face-to-face communications, say, being higher in media richness than telephone or e-mail communications. The higher the media richness and quality of presentation, the greater the social influence that communication partners have on each other's behavior.
2. *Self-disclosure.* In any type of social interaction, individuals want to make a positive impression to achieve a favorable image with others. This favorable image is affected by the degree of self-disclosure about a person's thoughts, feelings, likes, and dislikes—where greater self-disclosure is likely to increase one's influence on those reached.

Figure 19–1 uses these two factors of media richness and self-disclosure to position a number of social media sites in two-dimensional space. For example, Wikipedia is a collaborative project that is low on both self-disclosure and media richness.[9] At the other extreme, Second Life, high in both self-disclosure and media richness, is a 3D virtual social world where users create a personal avatar to explore and interact with others in that world to "live a life without boundaries." LinkedIn, on the other hand, contains detailed career and résumé information for business networking and is high in self-disclosure but only moderate in media richness.

Marketing managers look carefully at the positioning of the social networks shown in Figure 19–1 when selecting those to use in their plans. For example, World of

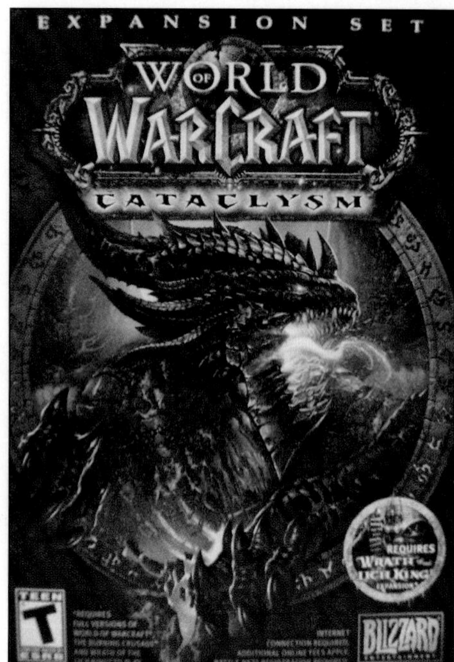

World of Warcraft is a multiplayer, online role-playing game where players control a character avatar within a fantasy world. For how WoW was used by Toyota to reach consumers in this social network, see the text.

Warcraft (WoW), positioned in the Virtual Game Worlds segment in Figure 19–1, is a multiplayer, online role-playing game in the fantasy Warcraft universe. Toyota recently used mechanics and pictures from World of Warcraft in a commercial to reach the millions of people who play the game in the United States.

Comparing Social and Traditional Media

Consumers receive information, news, and education from print (newspapers, magazines) and electronic media (radio, television). But marketing managers know that social media are very different from traditional media like newspapers or even radio or television. Social media and traditional media have both similarities and differences that impact marketing strategies, as described below:[10]

- *Ability to reach both large and niche audiences.* Both kinds of media can be designed to reach either a mass market or specialized segments; however, good execution is critical, and audience size is not guaranteed.
- *Expense and access.* Messages and ads in traditional media like newspapers or television generally are expensive to produce and have restricted access by individuals. Also, traditional media are typically owned privately or by the government. In contrast, messages on social media networks are generally accessible everywhere to those with smartphones, computers, and tablet devices and can be produced cheaply.
- *Training and number of people involved.* Producing traditional media typically requires specialized skills and training and often involves teams of people. In contrast, sending messages on social media requires only limited skills, so practically anyone can post a message that includes words and images.
- *Time to delivery.* Traditional media can involve days or even months of continuing effort to deliver the communication, and time lags can be extensive. In contrast, individuals using social media can post virtually instantaneous content.
- *Permanence.* Traditional media, once created, cannot be altered. For example, once a magazine article is printed and distributed, it cannot be changed. But social media message content can be altered almost instantaneously by comments or editing.
- *Credibility and social authority.* Individuals and organizations can establish themselves as "experts" in their given field, thereby becoming "influencers" in that field. For example, *The New York Times* has immense credibility among newspaper media. But with social media, a sender often simply begins to participate in the "conversation," hoping that the quality of the message will establish credibility with the receivers, thereby enhancing the sender's influence.

In terms of privacy, with minor exceptions, recipients of traditional media like TV or radio ads are completely anonymous. Subscribers to newspapers or magazines are somewhat less so because publishers can sell subscription lists to advertisers. Social media users have much less privacy and anonymity. When social media sites breach expectations for privacy, unethical outsiders can access users' names.

learning review

19-1. What are social media?

19-2. In classifying social media, what do we mean by (*a*) media richness and (*b*) self-disclosure?

19-3. Compare traditional media and social media in terms of time to delivery of the communication.

A LOOK AT FOUR IMPORTANT SOCIAL NETWORKS

LO 19-2 Identify the four major social networks and how brand managers integrate them into marketing actions.

Facebook, Twitter, LinkedIn, and YouTube are four widely used networks in the world of social media. So marketing managers need a special understanding of these four platforms as they integrate social media into their marketing strategies to supplement the traditional media they already use. This section briefly compares, defines, and explains each of these four major social media and shows how brand managers can use them. Because of its importance, Facebook merits more detailed coverage.

Comparing Four Social Networks

Figure 19–2 compares four major social networks (Facebook, Twitter, LinkedIn, and YouTube) from the point of view of a brand manager.[11] The green boxes in the figure show the special strengths of each social network. These suggest that using Facebook can increase brand exposure by encouraging brand-loyal customers to share their opinions with their Facebook friends and involving them in brand conversations. Twitter is effective in sending crisp messages about a brand and learning what people say about it. While powerful in helping users find jobs, LinkedIn has found a niche in helping small businesses network to reach potential customers. YouTube's videos make it especially useful in explaining a complex product.

Facebook

Facebook is the first choice among people seeking to create and maintain online connections with others by using photos, videos, and short text entries.[12] Facebook enhanced its photo-sharing capability with its acquisition of Instagram in early 2012. With over 1 billion active users—1 in every 7 people on the planet—Facebook is truly the 900-pound gorilla among all social media.[13]

Facebook: An Overview **Facebook** is a website where users create a personal profile, add other users as friends, and exchange comments, photos, videos, and "likes" with them. Facebook users today can keep friends and family updated on what they are

FIGURE 19–2
How brand managers can use four social networks in developing their marketing strategies.

BASIS OF COMPARISON	SOCIAL NETWORKS			
	facebook	twitter	LinkedIn	YouTube
User Characteristics	49% male, 51% female; 30% income under $30,000; 39% under 35 years old	54% male, 46% female; 26% income under $30,000; 34% under 35 years old	56% male, 44% female; 17% income under $30,000; 25% under 35 years old	53% male, 47% female; 29% income under $30,000; 36% under 35 years old
Brand Exposure	Great for brand exposure; jump-start it through the Facebook ad platform; connect with other brand pages.	Offers unique opportunities for website integration and engagement with customers.	Effective to demonstrate an organization's professionalism; have employees maintain complete profiles to do this.	Can be a powerful tool to build your channel, to explain a complex product, and to brand your videos.
Customer Communication	Great for engaging people who like your brand, want to share their opinions and have customer service questions.	Use Twitter monitoring programs such as CoTweet or HootSuite to track what people are saying about your brand.	Not the primary focus, but small businesses find it valuable as a networking service to reach potential customers.	Whether you seek to entertain, inform, or both, video is a powerful tool for quickly engaging your customers.
Traffic to Website	Traffic is decent and on the rise; use sponsored ads, links, and customized tabs to direct visitors back to your website.	Potential can be large; focus on sending out info relevant to your brand and audience interested in your tweets.	Traffic may be small, but can be valuable from a B2B and business development perspective.	Traffic goes to the YouTube channel or website; to get traffic back to your site, add a hyperlink in the video description.

GOOD! OK! BAD!

thinking, doing, and feeling. In addition, users may chat with friends and create and join common-interest groups organized by workplace, high school, college, and Pages—some of the latter maintained by organizations as a means of advertising. Facebook is open to anyone age 13 and older.

Time magazine's selection of Mark Zuckerberg as its "Person of the Year" reflects the staggering impact of Facebook today.[14] Consider that Facebook:

- Surpassed 1 million active advertisers.[15]
- Has more than 800 million people who tap into Facebook on mobile phones.[16]
- Introduced 15-second video uploads to its Instagram site, where 5 million were uploaded in the first 24 hours.[17]

The average American Facebook user has 303 friends on the site, but those users who are 18 to 24 years old have 510![18]

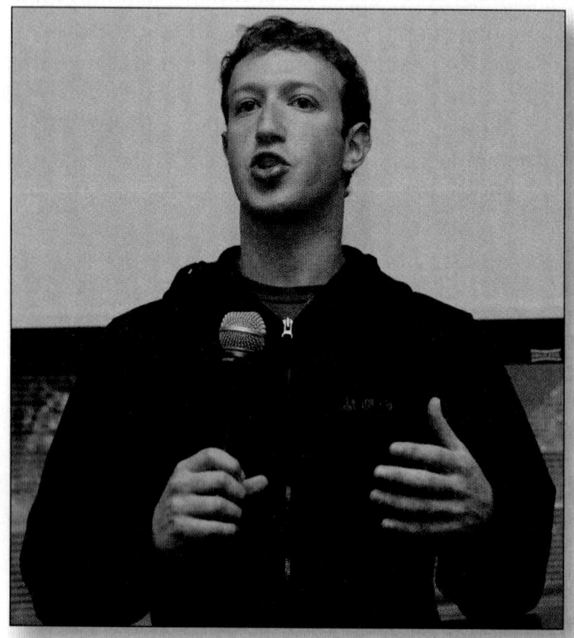

Mark Zuckerberg, a *Time* magazine "Person of the Year," now connects over a billion Facebook users.

Facebook in a Brand Manager's Strategy Facebook Pages were created as a method for brand managers to generate awareness for their product, service, or brand within Facebook. They allow brand managers to promote their business on Facebook, separate from their private and personal profiles. Done well, these are magnets for feedback. Additionally, Facebook Page information is generally public and cataloged by search engines so brand managers can identify influencers within their customer base.

To generate new customers and increase traffic to their Facebook Pages, brand managers can use paid ads and sponsored stories within the Facebook advertising platform.[19] Most ads within Facebook appear on the right-hand side of the website. An advantage of these Facebook ads is that the content can migrate into Facebook conversations among friends—to the delight of advertisers.

The marketing challenge for an organization's Facebook Page is to post content that will generate the best response. Brand managers using Facebook seek to maintain a conversation with their fans. Recent research suggests the following guidelines to engage fans on Facebook:[20]

- *Make it familiar, but with a twist.* Focus content strategy on imagery and messaging that is familiar to fans—punctuated with something unique. For example, Aflac uses its Aflac Duck—the well-known "spokes-duck"—to treat fans to Aflac Duck commercials and virtual Duck gifts. These, in turn, link to a point-of-purchase site for supplemental insurance.
- *Keep it fresh.* Redbox uses frequent posts to keep fans informed about its latest film releases.
- *Learn users' passions and let them guide content.* Taco Bell polls users to see which menu item they'd like featured in the following week's menu profile photo.

Gaining meaningful user loyalty enables a company to target promotional offers to its best customers. A recent study found that "Likes" or "Friends" on a brand's Facebook Page are worth an astounding $174 in terms of product spending, brand loyalty, and "propensity to recommend" the site to others.[21]

Launching a New Social Network Using Facebook Want to launch your own social network? For example, StuffDOT—"where sharing meets rewards"—is a place for people to post the things they like and earn rewards for

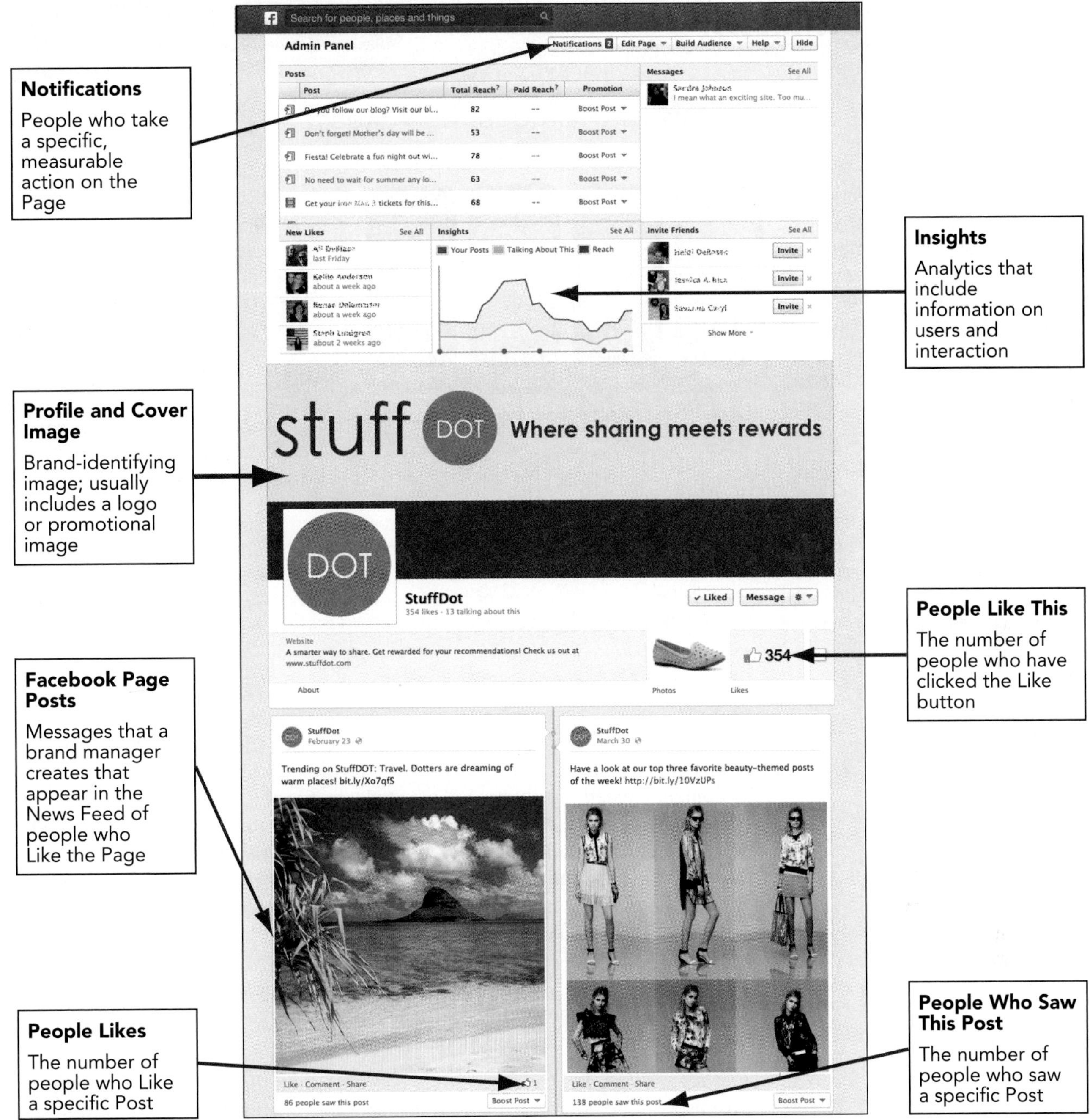

FIGURE 19–3 This Facebook Page for StuffDOT, a social network start-up "where sharing meets rewards," shows elements that are of interest to its brand manager.

their recommendations and online purchases. It differs from other social-sharing websites because users "dot" their favorite things to StuffDOT and *receive cash rewards* when someone purchases that item. Reward money can be cashed in via PayPal or redeemed for gift cards with many major retailers, including Amazon and Target.

Figure 19–3 shows the Facebook Page for StuffDOT. This new start-up targets college-aged women. The notes in the margin in Figure 19–3 show how elements on the StuffDOT Facebook Page seek to connect with fans and generate conversations. Several also help measure the success of the Facebook Page. With dozens of new social networks launched annually, StuffDOT's challenge is to break through the clutter and attract loyal users. So the brand manager for StuffDOT works continuously with

Marketing Matters

entrepreneurship

When Giants Stumble: How Facebook's Mark Zuckerberg Overcame One of His "Biggest Mistakes"!

In 2010, Mark Zuckerberg goofed. He put his engineers to work designing a version of Facebook that could operate on any smartphone. On the surface it sounded brilliant!

Zuckerberg was betting that stand-alone apps would disappear and Facebook users would simply surf websites on their smartphones—like they do on PCs. But he turned out to be very, very wrong. "It's probably one of the biggest mistakes we've made," says Zuckerberg.

The reason: Facebook's app worked very poorly on Apple's iOS and Google's Android mobile operating systems, the market leaders. Its app often crashed. Another nightmare: Around the world, people were abandoning PCs for smartphones—the very devices where Facebook was the weakest.

Zuckerberg put his mobile developers to work for a year on finding a way to provide Facebook users with a rich, exciting experience on their mobile phones. In April 2013, the result appeared: Facebook Home. It offers Facebook users a more "immersive experience" than Facebook's current app for either the Apple iPhone or Android phones.

Facebook Home gives easier access to its features on a smartphone—like friends' photos, messages, and status updates. In the process, Facebook hopes to keep smartphone users engaged longer, while convincing advertisers to place more ads on the smartphones' small screens.

Are you a Facebook Home user yet? If so, what do you think of the more "immersive experience" compared to the old Facebook app?

its website designer to present an attention-getting, user-friendly Facebook Page to achieve that goal.[22]

With content created mostly by college students, StuffDOT is also a place to find the latest news and trends. As a start-up, StuffDOT set out to find new users and website testers by recruiting college campus ambassadors. StuffDOT campus ambassadors are a major force behind the platform's growth and actively promote the site nationally through workshops, social media marketing, word-of-mouth, and promotional partnerships with events and businesses on college campuses.

Updating Facebook Keeping a billion user "customers" happy is a tall order—even for Facebook. To achieve this goal, Facebook continually refreshes elements of its social network site. Some recent updates include:

- *Privacy settings*. In December 2012, Facebook simplified its privacy settings to give users more control over what personal information they share. Still, users need to be aware that they cannot entirely opt out of Facebook data searches.[23]
- *Ads on mobile devices*. These didn't exist until early 2012. But as more Facebook users access their friends with mobile devices, Facebook is seeking ways to generate revenues by placing ads on the small screens.[24]
- *Customizing Facebook's News Feed*. In March 2013, Facebook announced that a version of its News Feed was being tailored for images to appear on mobile devices. This is important because about half of the average Facebook user's News Feed consists of photos and videos.[25]
- *Hashtag roll-out*. In June 2013, Facebook introduced hashtags in its network "to help people more easily discover what others are saying about a specific topic and participate in public conversations."[26]

QR 19-1
Facebook Home Ad

The Marketing Matters box describes how Mark Zuckerberg overcame one of his "biggest mistakes" with the 2013 launch of Facebook Home.[27]

Carmex (@Carmex) used Twitter to partner with members of TeamLeBron to give away a jar of Carmex lip balm with a 14 karat gold cap.

Twitter

Now that "tweets" have become part of our everyday language, it's apparent that Twitter has entered the mainstream of American life. Twitter now has over 500 million registered users worldwide, with more than 200 million active users who post an average of 400 million tweets per day.[28]

Twitter: An Overview **Twitter** is a website that enables users to send and receive *tweets*, messages up to 140 characters long. Twitter is based on the principle of "followers." So when you choose to follow another Twitter user, that user's tweets appear in reverse chronological order on your Twitter page.

Because of its short message length, the ease of posting and receiving tweets, and its convenience on a smartphone, Twitter can be a good source of information about a brand or product. Carma Laboratories, the maker of Carmex lip balm and skin care products, uses Twitter as an important tool in its social media program to communicate brand messages to its followers. As part of Carmex's social media outreach, the brand is active on Twitter with daily messages, retweets, and replies.

The immediacy of Twitter messaging allows brands like Carmex to operate promotions in real time. For example, Carmex partnered with LeBronJames.com to conduct a scavenger hunt on Twitter where members of TeamLeBron tweeted clues to their location. The first person to arrive at the destination won a jar of Carmex with a 14 karat gold cap.

Beyond sending out messages, Carmex relies on Twitter as a listening device. Carmex's social media team monitors mentions of Carmex on Twitter to see what people are saying. If there are product concerns, Carmex can reach out to consumers to make sure their concerns are quickly addressed. For more on Carmex and how it uses social media to conduct marketing research, see Chapter 8.

Twitter in a Brand Manager's Strategy With the 140-character limit on tweets, brand managers cannot expect extensive comments on their brands. But they can use social media management tools like CoTweet to see what Twitter users are saying—good and bad—about both their own brands and competitive ones. They can then respond to the negative comments and retweet the positive ones.

Brand managers have various other strategies for listening to and interacting with current and potential consumers using Twitter. For example, they can:[29]

- Generate brand buzz by developing an official Twitter profile, recruiting followers, and showing photos of their products.
- Follow the Twitter profiles that mention their product and monitor what is being said, responding to user criticisms to develop happier customers.
- Tweet on topics that provide information of value to their consumers.

As with Facebook, Twitter can actively engage customers if done creatively. Starbucks successfully used Twitter to supplement its "Free Pastry Day" on Facebook—a promotion awarding a free pastry to those buying a Starbucks beverage.

Professor Steven Hartley, a coauthor of this textbook, uses LinkedIn to connect with a network of educators and businesspeople.

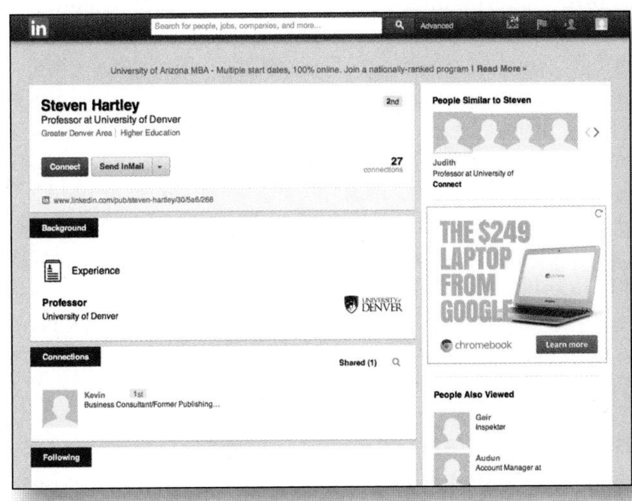

LinkedIn

Unlike Facebook and Twitter, the LinkedIn site's main purpose is professional networking and job searching.

LinkedIn: An Overview **LinkedIn** is a business-oriented website that lets users post their professional profiles to connect to a network of businesspeople, who are also called *connections*. This social network has almost 240 million registered members who have conducted about 6 billion professionally oriented searches. Because of its popularity, over 3 million companies have LinkedIn Company Pages to post news and job openings.[30] Of growing importance, LinkedIn has over 30 million students and recent college graduates as members.

Experts offer the following tips to job seekers using LinkedIn:

- Focus your profile to make sure it is both complete and current and includes who you are professionally, who you can help, and how you can help them.
- Brand yourself as an expert with "answers" by searching through relevant questions to let your answers showcase your abilities.

Also, make a point of growing your network to connect with new people.[31]

LinkedIn in a Brand Manager's Strategy Marketing managers can use LinkedIn to promote their brand in subtle ways. This is done mainly for business-to-business (B2B) image building and networking with industry-related groups. Using LinkedIn, brand managers can demonstrate the organization's expertise and create and moderate discussion groups. According to a 2013 survey of small business owners, 41 percent see LinkedIn as potentially beneficial to their company—more than twice that for Facebook, Twitter, or YouTube. In using LinkedIn to recruit qualified employees, owners can use the website's algorithms, which actually "recommend potential job candidates." Owners also use LinkedIn for business development to identify sales leads and locate vendors. In 2013, LinkedIn acquired Pulse, a news-reading app, with the goal of expanding its market by publishing timely articles for business professionals.[32]

YouTube

The ability of YouTube to reach its audience stretches the imagination. Think about this: In mid-2013, YouTube's 1-billion-plus users: (1) watched over 6 billion hours of video each month; (2) uploaded 100 hours of video each minute; and (3) had over 1 *trillion* page views![33]

YouTube: An Overview **YouTube** is a video-sharing website in which users can upload, view, and comment on videos. YouTube uses streaming video technology to display user-generated video content that includes movie and TV clips, music videos, and original videos developed by amateurs. While most of the content is uploaded by amateurs, many companies offer material on the site through a YouTube channel.

Rebecca Black uses a YouTube channel to promote her music, which allows her fans to "like," "share," and "comment" on her videos.

In December 2011, YouTube redesigned its home page—to the dismay of many of its loyal users. Its goal was to provide a more organized structure to steer users to "channels," rather than simply encourage them to browse like in the past.[34] An interesting issue is whether the greater structure might hurt single YouTube videos like Rebecca Black's "Friday" (over 50 million views), which went viral."[35] More recently, YouTube has redesigned the format for its YouTube channels. These channels serve as home pages for organizations and individuals and allow them to upload their own videos, as well as post and share videos created by others. For example, Rebecca Black now has a YouTube channel that aggregates all her music and other videos she has uploaded for fans and other users to view.

YouTube in a Brand Manager's Strategy YouTube offers great opportunity for a brand manager to produce and show a video

Marketing Matters

technology

What Are Some of Your Other Favorite Social Networks?

Other social networks that are popular among college students with diverse interests include the following:

Vimeo—A community of creative people who are passionate about sharing the videos they make.

Google+—A social-sharing network from Google that allows you to organize friends in "circles" for easy sharing, host "hangouts," and more.

Foursquare—A location-based mobile platform that helps you explore cities through "check-ins" and rewards.

StumbleUpon—A discovery engine for finding and sharing the best content on the Web.

Flickr—An online photo management and sharing network that allows you to show off and organize your favorite photos and videos.

Pinterest—A content sharing network where members "pin" images, videos, and more to "boards" they create, which are categorized into different themes.

Tumblr—A feature-rich, micro-blogging platform that allows users to share text, photos, music, links, videos, and more.

Instagram—A fast and fun way to share photos; users simply snap a photo, choose a specialized filter to alter the look and feel of the image, and share the image with family and friends.

QR 19-2
OK Go Music Video

that explains the benefits of a complex product (Figure 19–2). Since YouTube is owned by Google, it incorporates a search engine so users interested in a specific topic can find it easily. In terms of cost advantages, while a brand manager must pay the cost of creating a video, launching a new channel on YouTube is free.

In 2012, YouTube announced a new program to help small businesses create video ads on its social network. Small businesses can now buy and manage key words for their video ads on YouTube. So, a baker who runs a YouTube video ad for her bakery can buy words like "baking," "cookies," and "cake," and her video will appear when someone searches for those terms on YouTube.[36] For the hundreds of social networks in the secondary tier, the ones discussed in the Marketing Matters box are among the most widely used by college students today.

OK Go, a music group, watched downloaded songs from the Internet cause a meltdown in its CD sales and experienced difficulty in getting its own record label. So it used YouTube to win fans, licensees, and sponsors for its *very* offbeat music creations. OK Go's YouTube music videos—what it calls "treadmill videos"—are the foundation for its

For how OK Go has used "Here It Goes Again" (18 million views) and "This Too Shall Pass" (40 million views) on YouTube to gain fans, licensees, live shows, and sponsors, see the text.

success. Examples include: an animation with 2,300 pieces of toast, a dance with a dozen trained dogs, and the first-ever Rube Goldberg machine that operates in time to music.[38]

YouTube is revolutionizing the pop music scene. It pays for the views that copyrighted content achieves, usually 60 cents per 1,000 views. South Korea's Psy, whose "Gangnam Style" is YouTube's biggest video, made his fortune with its over 1.7 billion views. The "Harlem Shake" song by the Brooklyn producer Baauer appeared in early 2012 as a free download. "Harlem Shake" used iTune downloads and 500 million YouTube views—featuring talent ranging from Miami Heat basketball players to Austin Mahone—to do the same. The result is that unknown musicians are using YouTube to achieve music success, a route far different than trying to attract attention from a music label company.[37]

Guidelines for marketing and promoting a brand using YouTube videos include:[39]

- Exploit visual aspects of your message, perhaps sacrificing product messages to tell a more entertaining story.
- Create a branded channel rich in key words to improve the odds of the video showing up in user searches.
- Target viewers by using YouTube's insights and analytics research to reveal the number of views, the number of visits to your website, and what key words are driving user visits.

As with all social networks, YouTube is continuously innovating and changing.

learning review

19-4. How is user-generated content presented by someone using Facebook?

19-5. What are some ways brand managers use Facebook to converse with a brand's fans?

19-6. What are the major differences between Facebook and YouTube that are of interest to brand managers?

INTEGRATING SOCIAL MEDIA INTO TODAY'S MARKETING STRATEGIES

Describe the differing roles of those receiving messages through traditional versus social media and how brand managers select a social network.

Thousands of marketing managers around the globe understand how to use traditional media to generate sales for their brand. Some are successful, and others are not. But many of these same managers will admit that social networks are so complex they are not sure how best to use them.

This section looks at (1) how social media tie to the strategic marketing process, (2) how to select a social network, (3) how social media can be used to generate sales, and (4) how to measure the results of social media programs. The section closes by describing Carmex's "Shot Seen 'Round the World" promotion. The ultimate dream for a brand manager, this Carmex–LeBronJames.com promotion went viral on YouTube!

Social Media and the Strategic Marketing Process

The strategic marketing process described in Chapter 2 and the communication process from sender to receiver in Chapter 17 apply to both traditional and social media. But note these important differences in the communication process:

- Traditional media like magazine or TV ads generally use one-way communication from sender to receiver, those whom the marketer hopes will buy the product advertised. A little word-of-mouth chatting may occur among the "passive receivers," but communications generally end with the receiver.

- Social media deliberately seek to ensure that the message *does not end* with an individual receiver. Instead, the goal is to reach "active receivers," those who will become "influentials" and be "delighted" with the brand advertised. These customers will then become "evangelists," who will send messages to their online friends and then back to the advertiser about the joys of using the brand.

Success in social media marketing relies heavily on the ability of a marketing program to convert passive "receivers" of the message to active "evangelists" who will spread favorable messages about the brand.

Selecting the Social Network

In using social media, a brand manager tries to select and use one or more social networks from the hundreds that exist. This often entails assessing (1) the characteristics of these visitors and (2) the number of users or unique visitors to the website.

Audience Data Available for Social Networks Each social network and other website analysis firms provide user profile data for the social networks to help brand managers choose among them. As presented earlier, the top row of Figure 19–2 shows a recent profile of audience demographics for four major social networks. As shown in the figure, Facebook users are 51 percent female and 49 percent male; 30 percent earn income under $30,000 per year; and 39 percent are under 35 years of age.[40]

Recent Growth of the Four Social Networks Figure 19–4 shows the recent growth of Facebook, Twitter, LinkedIn, and YouTube. In terms of millions of unique U.S. visitors to the website per month, it shows the dramatic growth of Facebook, which reached 139 million visitors in August 2013. At that time, Figure 19–4 shows that YouTube had 175 million unique visitors, while Twitter had 92 million and LinkedIn had 78 million.[41]

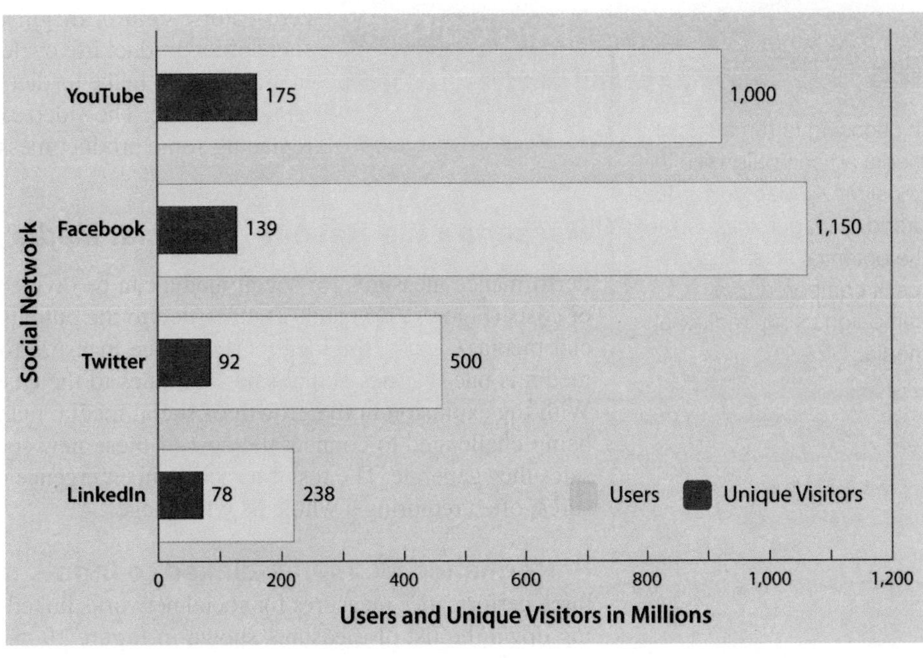

FIGURE 19–4
The number of users and unique visitors for four social network sites: YouTube, Facebook, Twitter, and LinkedIn as of August 2013.

How Social Media Produce Sales

LO 19-4 Explain how social media can produce sales revenues for a brand and compare the performance measures linked to costs versus revenues.

An example shows how a PepsiCo brand manager can use social media to produce sales and profits for her product or brand. Consider the roles of both the PepsiCo brand manager and social media in the following example.[42]

Role of the PepsiCo Brand Manager The PepsiCo brand manager composes title, copy, and images or photos for the social network ad. She often specifies the web address to which its ad should link based on the brand's social media marketing goals. To increase awareness and build up a fan base, she might link the ad to the PepsiCo website or its Facebook, Twitter, or Pinterest sites. Ideally, to encourage and produce new sales that can be tracked, she must link the ad to a coupon code, a specific product on the PepsiCo website, or other promotional offer.

The brand manager then defines the characteristics of the one or more market segments she wants to reach on the social media she has selected. This starts with demographic characteristics like geographic region, sex, age range, and education. She then adds factors like relationship status and user interests.

QR 19-3
Pepsi MAX
Video

Role of Social Media Ads and videos on social media like YouTube and Facebook are less likely than traditional print ads to have a marketing objective of immediate sales. This is because social network images are often on the screen for only seconds. A more likely goal is to have viewers go to the advertiser's website and post it on their Facebook Pages or forward it to friends. The key for a brand manager using social media is to gain viewers' attention for a few extra seconds.

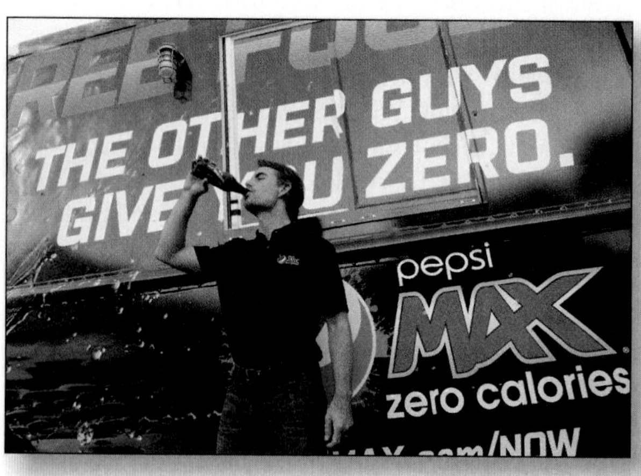

In choosing to run a social media ad campaign like this Pepsi MAX video on YouTube, brand managers must assess the potential sales likely to result compared to a campaign using traditional media.

PepsiCo's 2013 "Test Drive" YouTube video is an example of this strategy. Building on its highly successful "Uncle Drew" videos and TV ads, PepsiCo used its entertaining "Test Drive" video to promote its Pepsi MAX beverages—a zero-calorie cola. In the video, NASCAR driver Jeff Gordon is disguised as "Mike," an average guy taking a test drive at a local dealership. The unsuspecting car salesman riding along will never forget it!

"Test Drive" was a huge hit for Pepsi MAX, with over 35 million views in its first two months. Even better, the video reinforces the product's tag line of "a great-tasting, zero-calorie cola in disguise." As a product in the mature stage of its product life cycle, Pepsi MAX uses an entertaining message to make its diet beverages relevant to a younger target audience. The video captures the viewer's attention by replacing some product messaging with entertainment.[43]

Measuring the Results of Social Media Programs

Performance measures for social media can be divided into (1) those linked to inputs or costs (Figure 19–5) and (2) those tied to the outputs or revenues resulting from social media. Clearly, the ideal performance measure for both conventional and social media is one that ties actual sales revenues to the cost of the ad or other promotion. With the explosion in the growth of social media, marketing and brand managers are being challenged to connect the cost of these new social network promotions to the sales they generate. The result has been an emergence of many new performance measures, often requiring a whole new language.

Performance Measures Linked to Inputs or Costs Figure 19–5 shows three performance measures for social networks linked mainly to inputs or costs. Moving down the list of measures shown in Figure 19–5, one starts with a measure tied

Performance Measure	Costs to Advertisers	Who Provides It	Who Uses It	An Assessment	
				Advantages	Disadvantages
Cost per thousand (CPM)	"I will pay $0.50 for every 1,000 times this ad loads, up to $100 per month."	Small websites that sell ads directly (may be using a third-party service)	Advertisers who simply want to build "awareness"	Simple to use	Impressions don't always lead to sales
Cost per click (CPC)	"I will pay $1.00 for every visitor who clicks on this ad and goes from your website to mine."	Most websites use this method—executed by a third party like Google/AdWords	Advertisers who want to pay for success, but may not be able to track sales from advertisement to purchase	I only pay for a visitor who has expressed an interest in my ad.	Ads may not display if they are a poor fit for the viewing audience
Cost per action (CPA)	"I will pay $5 for every purchase that originates from an ad on your site."	Usually executed through third parties; Google AdSense offers this feature	Sophisticated advertisers who want to pay for success	I only pay for what works.	Similar to CPC but harder to track and more expensive per action

FIGURE 19–5
Performance measures for social networks linked mainly to inputs or costs, as seen by a brand manager.

only to costs (the cost per thousand measure) and then moves to a measure linked more closely to the sales revenues generated from the social media ad or action (cost per action, or CPA).

The cost per thousand (CPM) measure ties to the number of times the ad loads and a user might see it—but not whether the user has actually reacted to it. This measure is roughly equivalent to the CPM for traditional media discussed in Chapter 18. The cost per click (CPC) measure gives the rate the advertiser pays, say to Facebook, every time a visitor clicks on the ad and jumps from that page to the advertiser's website. Finally, the cost per action (CPA) measure ties loosely to actual sales—for example, paying $5 for every purchase that originates from an ad, say, on the Facebook site. By summing up the revenues from all these purchases, a difficult task, this CPA measure most closely ties the cost of the social media ad to the sales revenues the ad generates.

Performance Measures Linked to Outputs or Revenues Many of the measures for evaluating how a brand manager's social network promotion is doing reflect the two-way communications present in social media. These measures often tie to output results in terms of "fans," "friends," "followers," or "visitors" to a social network site, which can be a first step to estimating the sales revenue generated. From a brand manager's viewpoint, here are some of the frequently used Facebook measures, moving from the more general to the more specific:

- *Users/members.* Individuals who have registered on a social networking site by completing the process involved, such as providing their name, user ID (usually an e-mail address), and password, as well as answering a few questions (date of birth, gender, etc.).
- *Fans.* The number of people who have opted in to a brand's messages through a social media platform at a given time.
- *Share of voice.* The brand's share or percentage of all the online social media chatter related to, say, its product category or a topic.
- *Page views.* The number of times a Facebook Page is loaded in a given time period.
- *Visitors.* The total number of visitors to a Facebook Page in a given time period; if someone visits three times in one day, she is counted three times.

Pinterest allows users to "pin" or share images of favorite interests on its site, which is useful for brand managers promoting their company's products.

- *Unique visitors.* The total number of unique visitors to a Facebook Page in a given time period; if someone visits three times in one day, he is counted only once.
- *Average Page views per visitor.* Page views divided by visitors in a given time period.
- *Interaction rate.* The number of people who interact with a Post ("like," make a comment, and so on) divided by the total number of people seeing the Post.
- *Click-through rate (CTR).* Percentage of recipients who have clicked on a link on the Page to visit a specific site.
- *Fan source.* Where a social network following comes from—with fans coming from a friend being more valuable than those coming from an ad.

Note that while sales revenues resulting from social media do not appear in these measures, as we move down the list, the measures are often more specific than comparable ones used in traditional media. This is because it is far simpler to electronically track the social network users who click on a website or ad than it is to track consumers who watch, listen to, or read traditional media.

Specialized Focus for Other Social Networks One of the advantages of social media is that communities can form around ideas and commonalities, regardless of the physical location of their members. While major social networks such as Facebook or YouTube may garner the majority of the traffic, smaller networks like Pinterest may be more successful for some products and services.

Pinterest, a virtual pinboard and content-sharing social network, allows people to "pin" or share images of their favorite things such as clothing, craft ideas, home décor, and recipes. Pinterest members create customized, themed "pinboards" to categorize their images such as "Odds & Ends," "Food," and "Knitting" shown on the Pinterest screen. These images are shared with other members of the Pinterest community. Members can also share their pinned images on Facebook and Twitter.[44]

Pinterest has over 70 million users, 80 percent of whom are women. So it has become a major sales driver for retailers and manufacturers that target women. In using Pinterest, brand managers can post images of their company's products on their Pinterest board and link them back to their websites. This can be done effectively by ensuring that all website links are associated with unique images and adding share features like the "Pin It" button to the brand's online content.

For the way Nestlé's Kit Kat Facebook Page was "brand-jacked" with Greenpeace activists dressed as orangutans, see the text.

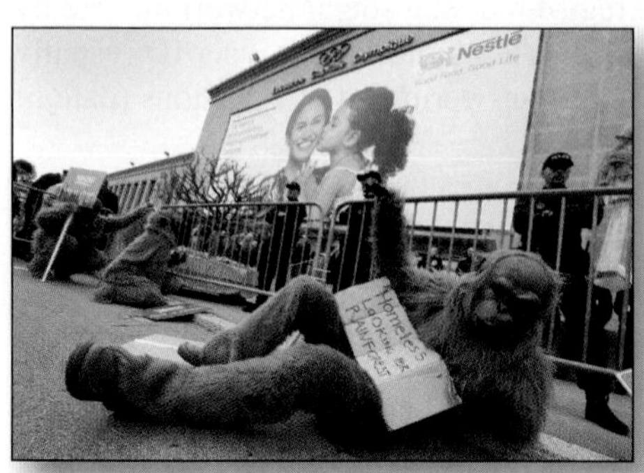

Greenpeace vs. Nestlé's Kit Kat: A Nightmarish Meltdown

While an intense level of social media communications on Facebook or Twitter can be a brand manager's dream, it can also be his worst nightmare. The Greenpeace campaign against Nestlé and its Kit Kat candy bar brand is an example.[45]

The Background Currently, palm oil is an ingredient in several of Nestlé's products, including the Kit Kat chocolate bar. In March 2010, Nestlé reported that 18 percent of its palm oil was "nonsustainable," meaning its suppliers were cutting down rainforests in places like Indonesia without enough concern for the environmental harm or equivalent remediation. These Indonesian rainforests are home to orangutans. Nestlé announced that its goal was to be using "100 percent sustainable palm oil" by 2015. Nestlé's plan seemed to demonstrate a sense of social responsibility and to support the goal of global sustainability.

Greenpeace's Actions and Results Greenpeace, a social and environmental advocacy organization, decided that Nestlé's effort to find sustainable palm oil suppliers was moving too slowly. So it launched an all-out "shock campaign" against Nestlé with the proclamation: "Caught Red-Handed: How Nestlé's Use of Palm Oil Is Having a Devastating Impact on Rainforests, the Climate, and Orangutans." Then Greenpeace posted a very graphic and provocative video on YouTube, including activists dressed as orangutans. The Greenpeace campaign triggered customer complaints on the Kit Kat Facebook Page, some with a "Killer Kat" logo (at left), a play on Nestlé's "Kit Kat" logo. Also, Nestlé management received 200,000 e-mails, and its 1-800 customer service numbers were jammed by protest calls.

QR 19-4
Greenpeace
Kit Kat Video

Nestlé's Overreaction and Its Effects Nestlé's response unwittingly led to increased online attention and animosity. At Nestlé's request, YouTube removed the video that Nestlé believed infringed on its Kit Kat brand. The result: Views of the video on other sites like Flickr and Vimeo skyrocketed in the next 24 hours.

Nestlé's Kit Kat Facebook users who were violently opposed to its deforestation actions swelled. One commentator noted that Greenpeace had "brand-jacked" the Nestlé Kit Kat Facebook Page. Within 60 days, Nestlé's management capitulated. It took steps to drop palm oil suppliers linked to deforestation—in effect recognizing the power of social media.

Social Media Lessons for Brand Managers Rather than being aggressive, brand managers should respond to a crisis situation with transparency. They should communicate directly with "key influencers," emphasizing the company's concern about the issue and using relevant social media. Above all, brand managers should have an emergency social media plan for the brand in place—*before* an actual crisis erupts.

Carmex Goes Viral with Luck and a LeBron James Bear Hug

In contrast to the social media nightmare faced by Kit Kat's brand managers, consider the wild success enjoyed by Carmex lip balm. Brand managers dream about their stars aligning—having their promotions go viral and reaping millions of dollars worth of free brand exposure. Carmex lip balm had this experience!

The Background As noted earlier in the chapter, Carmex has a partnership with LeBronJames.com. It started in 2011 when the firm found out that LeBron James of the NBA's Miami Heat professional basketball team uses Carmex as part of his pregame routine.

QR 19-5
Carmex Video

The Half-Court Hero Contest As part of their partnership, Carmex created the "Carmex and LeBronJames.com Half-Court Hero" promotion in April 2012. The promotion featured an online entry form and weekly prizes leading up to a grand prize

Getting Set

The Shot

Nothing but Net!

The Celebration

The Lift

LeBron's Bear Hug

Achieving a brand manager's wildest dream! The text describes how the Carmex "shot seen 'round the world" achieved this dream—including 30 million YouTube viewers.

drawing for one lucky winner to travel to Miami and have the chance to take a half-court shot worth $75,000. The "Hero" part meant that if the winner hit the shot (i.e., made the basket), Carmex would also donate $75,000 to the LeBron James Family Foundation and the Boys and Girls Clubs of America.

On January 25, 2013, Michael Drysch walked to center court at American Airlines Arena between the third and fourth quarters of the Miami Heat–Detroit Pistons game in front of a sold-out crowd of 20,000 fans. Michael carefully aligned himself just left of center court, took two steps, and launched a one-handed hook shot.

Nothing but net!! And $75,000 richer!

The crowd erupted as Michael turned and pumped his fist. But before he could celebrate any further, LeBron himself came running out of his Miami Heat huddle to bear-hug Michael to the ground in a moment of pure jubilation.

The "Shot Seen 'Round the World" Goes Viral Instantly, the footage of Half-Court Hero winner Michael Drysch's incredible hook shot and the celebratory bear hug from LeBron James went viral online. Michael was interviewed immediately after the shot by Fox Sports South, and NBATV interviewed him side-by-side with James after the game. It was the #1 Play of the Day on ESPN's SportsCenter. The Carmex brand team immediately arranged a public relations tour for Michael Drysch that included four Miami area news stations and a trip to New York City for appearances on *Fox and Friends*, *Good Morning America*, *Inside Edition*, *CNN Early Start*, and *HuffPost Live*, as well as ESPN.com and dozens of local radio shows.

Meanwhile, the Carmex marketing team kept Carmex's social media accounts and website updated throughout the weekend with Twitter and Facebook Posts from the public relations tour. The team actively monitored social media tracking software for up-to-the-minute brand mentions resulting from the shot. Within three months, Carmex's Half-Court Hero shot had been seen by over 30 million YouTube viewers and became the most-watched video of all time on the National Basketball Association's YouTube page. In all, the promotion earned Carmex over 500 million media impressions across TV, print, online, and social media.[46]

Michael Drysch receives his reward for sinking his unlikely hook shot in the "Carmex and LeBronJames.com 'Half-Court Hero'" promotion. Also benefiting are the LeBron James Family Foundation and the Boys and Girls Clubs of America!

Social Media Lessons for Brand Managers The lesson for brand managers is: Watch for opportunities to "manage luck." Small, smart investments can pay off in big ways when your brand gets lucky. Find ways to use *both* social and traditional media—as the Carmex team did—to help the campaign go viral and to maximize the opportunity to achieve even greater success. Be ready.

learning review

19-7. What is the difference between (and marketing significance of) a "passive receiver" for conventional media and an "active receiver" for social media?

19-8. Stated simply, how can an advertiser on Facebook expect to generate sales?

19-9. What did the Carmex team do to exploit its incredible good fortune after seeing Michael Drysch make his "Half-Court Hero" shot?

THE FUTURE: SOCIAL MEDIA + SMARTPHONES + EXOTIC APPS

LO 19-5 Describe how the convergence of the real and digital worlds affects the future of social media.

Trends in marketing's use of social media reflect what scientists call "mirror worlds" or "smart systems" that are really the convergence of the real and digital worlds. A *smart system* is a computer-based network that triggers actions by sensing changes in the real or digital world. This section discusses: (1) the convergence of real and digital worlds; (2) how this convergence links social media to marketing actions; and (3) where all this *may* be headed in *your* future.

The Convergence of Real and Digital Worlds

Saying that our physical and virtual worlds are converging sounds like science fiction. This convergence of real and digital worlds is the result of a proliferation of interlinked smartphones, tablet devices, sensors, special identification tags, databases, algorithms, apps, and other elements. A look at several of these elements in Figure 19–6 on the next page helps explain this real world–digital world convergence and what it means for marketing.

Smartphones Seeing today's smartphones, users often forget how far they've come in 15 years and how they've changed marketing. In 1998, the RIM 950 revolutionized mobile e-mail. The device had a screen and a keyboard—but *no phone*. The revolution was completed in 2007 with Apple's legendary iPhone. It had all three basics—screen, multitouch keyboard, and phone. Combined with other elements in Figure 19–6, today's GPS-enabled smartphones give mobile consumers access to online ads, local restaurant promotions, and time-sensitive discounts at retailers.[47]

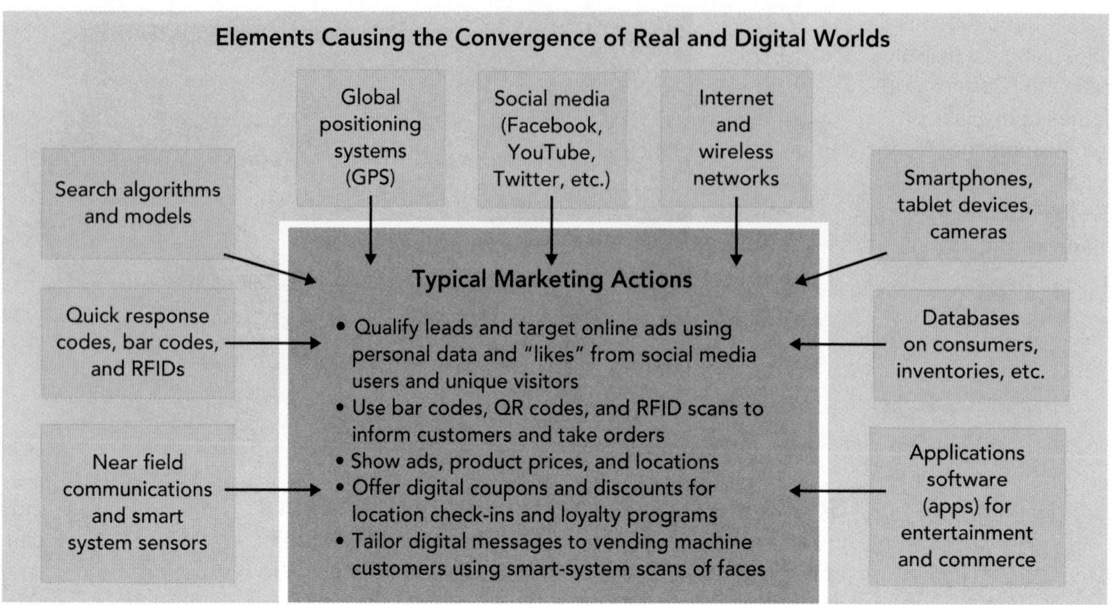

FIGURE 19–6
An array of diverse elements leads to a convergence of the real and digital worlds. This, in turn, triggers marketing actions whose results are often more easily measurable.

Databases and Algorithms As discussed in Chapters 8 and 9, finding prospective customers often involves market segmentation that requires databases searched with exotic algorithms—models used to query, organize, manipulate, and present data. The owners of these databases, among them Google and Facebook, must make them as useful as possible to potential advertisers in order to succeed.

Among databases, Google is the hands-down winner—indexing 30 trillion unique web pages across 230 million sites. Its search engine now gives results in answers to research queries in photos, facts, and "direct answers," and not just the "blue links" of website addresses. Google now offers its own social networking service, Google+, to obtain data about individuals by name, personal interests, and identities of friends.[48]

In January 2013, Facebook entered Google's territory by announcing Graph Search, its own search engine algorithm. Facebook users can conduct their own queries about people, places, photos, and interests. An example is "restaurants recommended by friends." This lets Facebook give advertisers real value in the "likes" found on its site. For example, a small chocolate retail shop in New York City can target (1) young parents (2) who buy lots of organic food products.[49] So it's not difficult to see how a casual "like" for a brand by a user in a database's "digital world" can converge into an actual "real world" purchase by the user through a very targeted promotion planned by a brand manager.

Success in video game apps doesn't last forever. The text and Marketing Matters box reassess the "business" of Angry Birds and look at new competitors.

Apps The apps for smartphones are accelerating the convergence of the real and digital worlds. **Apps** (or *mobile apps* or *applications*) are small, downloadable software programs that run on smartphones and tablet devices. When Apple launched its iPhone, it didn't expect smartphone apps to be very important. Wrong! By 2013, Apple's App Store offered over 900,000 apps either free or for sale. Google Play has over 800,000 apps for users of Android devices. With the wide array of apps to choose from, today's consumers typically spend two hours a day using about eight apps.[50]

Many apps are video games. Rovio's Angry Birds has achieved astounding success. Angry Birds has been downloaded over 2 billion times for use on smartphones, tablet devices, video game consoles, PCs, and soon—Internet-connected "Smart" TVs and cable boxes. Due to intense competition, however, the product life cycle (PLC) of even successful video game apps is often a mere two or three years—or less. By 2013, even

Marketing Matters

technology

The Coolest, Wildest, Weirdest, and . . . Best . . . Apps???

Here are six apps that were popular among college students in mid-2013.

Draw Something—The fastest-growing social drawing game where two players cooperate and take turns drawing a picture for the other to guess.

Spotify—A music-streaming app that makes it easy to find the right music for every moment. With a catalog of over 20 million songs, users can browse by artist, album, record label, genre, and playlist.

Fruit Ninja—A game where the player slices fruit with a blade controlled by a touchscreen. Extra points are awarded for slicing multiple fruit in one slice. If a player accidentally slices a bomb, the game ends.

Pandora—An app offering free, personalized radio that helps listeners discover new music based on the artists and songs the listener likes.

Temple Run—An action video game where wandering explorers attempting to steal an idol from a temple navigate through a maze of booby traps and try to outrun demonic monkeys.

4Pics1Word—A game where the player is shown four pictures that have a common word between them. The word is hidden in the scrambled letters that appear below the pictures.

How popular are these apps as you read this? Your answer relates to the product life cycle for today's apps, which is discussed in the text.

Angry Birds appeared to be in the decline stage of its PLC. So, as described in Chapter 2, Rovio redefined its business model to see itself in the "entertainment business" with an animated cartoon series for TV (*Angry Birds Toons*), board games, merchandise, and entertainment parks.[51]

The Marketing Matters box describes six popular apps among college students for use on digital devices. While apps like Words With Friends and Tiny Wings were favored in 2012, a year later these have been replaced by apps like Spotify and Fruit Ninja. And, for every popular app, there are hundreds of thousands that die a quiet death each year.[52]

Mobile Marketing: Tightening Links to Marketing Actions

This convergence of the real and digital worlds has resulted in increasing use of *mobile marketing*, or any marketing activity conducted through several Internet networks to which consumers are continuously connected using a personal mobile device.[53] This continuous connection present in mobile marketing has led to important smartphone apps, such as:[54]

- *Price-comparison searches.* Scan product bar codes or QR codes and research 500,000 stores, synchronizing searches between your computer and your smartphone.
- *Location-based promotions.* Use your GPS-enabled smartphone for location check-ins to receive discounts at stores such as jcpenney.
- *Loyalty programs.* Win loyalty points for walking into stores like Target or Macy's and receive discounts from them.

The number of smartphone shopping searches and purchases has exploded in recent years, causing huge challenges (such as showrooming) for conventional brick-and-mortar retailers.

Where to Now?

The clear point of difference in mobile marketing is its unique ability to empower users by connecting with them individually and continuously—learning about their likes and personal characteristics and sharing this information with online friends and (often) marketers selling products.[55] This shifting mind-set to a socially networked world will lead to connected users having more influence in the marketplace.[56] In the future, it is likely we will see:

- New, creative ways to personalize social media connections.
- An enhanced focus on socially networked "communities"—loyal users of a brand, alumni associations, and other groups with common interests.
- An increased emphasis on measuring the marketing return on investment for social media initiatives.

Soon, purchases will be made with smartphones and other devices using *near field communications* technology, which uses wireless (radio) connections and apps between devices through touching or close proximity. Using this technology, when a consumer purchases a product, information is transmitted between the buyer's smartphone and the seller's "smart register," which may be a tablet device. For example, this technology allows immediate transmission of product purchase data, such as a product's SKU, price, coupon, rebate, and so on; personal data, such as name, credit card number, and address; and details regarding product warranty, credit approval, and so on.

The convergence of social media, smartphones, tablet devices, and new apps will lead to companies having a more dynamic interaction with their customers.[57] But is this an unqualified success for buyers? Consider the following perspectives.

A Consumer Purchase Where the Buyer Controls All Tesco Home Plus, a South Korean supermarket chain, provides a quick spur-of-the-moment opportunity for grocery shopping. Shoppers use their smartphones to scan images on the wall of a subway station to buy Tesco's grocery products while waiting for their train. They use the smartphone app to pay for the groceries, which are delivered to their door right after they get home.[58] In this example, buyers achieve great convenience—probably an unqualified success.

Too busy to visit your grocery store this week? If you are in South Korea, you can shop on the wall of your subway station with your smartphone—and have your purchases delivered to your door!

A Consumer Purchase Where Sensors Have Some Control A vending machine scans your face to identify your age and sex and changes its display and—in the future—may give you a quantity discount for buying two of your favorite candy bars (it knows about your Facebook "likes") while showing an electronic dinner coupon for a nearby restaurant if you appear between 7:00 and 9:00 P.M. this evening. The results of the candy and dinner offer are directly measurable for marketers. Note how many of the "convergence elements" in Figure 19–6 are present in this scenario. While it offers unusual convenience, does this buying situation start to interfere with your personal privacy?

On Privacy: How Much "Convergence" Is Too Much? Smart systems are fine up to a point. For example, most of us are comfortable letting convergence find us a timely deal at a local restaurant using a location-based app on our smartphone. It may even be all right if Google's latest database breakthrough automatically proposes an "ideal vacation plan" for us based on our normal preferences, weather conditions, and available hotel and airline prices.

But we may start to disagree among ourselves about having facial recognition sensors automatically propose a local restaurant or movie that meets our database criteria. Why be squeamish? If those sensors know we are 10 miles from home, might someone be able to hack the system so burglars know it's a good time to break in and rob us?

Here's where most of us would probably say, "Enough is enough." A recent analysis of 58,000 Facebook users revealed that the "likes" they post can reveal their political and religious views, drug use, and marital status. In the study, researchers could distinguish between Republicans and Democrats 85 percent of the time. Comments Helen Nissenbaum, director of the Information Law Institute at New York University, "When people today agree to volunteer information, they have no idea what can be inferred from that information."[59]

learning review

19-10. What is an example of how the real (physical) and digital (virtual) worlds are converging?

19-11. What are apps and why are they important?

19-12. Can personal privacy become a problem as the real and digital worlds converge with smart systems?

LEARNING OBJECTIVES REVIEW

LO 19-1 *Define social media and describe how they differ from traditional advertising media.*
Social media are online media where users submit comments, photos, and videos, often accompanied by a feedback process to identify "popular" topics. Social media can be classified based on two factors: (1) media richness, which involves the degree of acoustic, visual, and personal contact between the social network and the user, and (2) self-disclosure, which is the degree to which individuals can control the impressions they want to make on others. Social media differ from traditional advertising media (newspapers, magazines, radio, and television) in that user-generated content (1) is relatively inexpensive to create, publish, and access, (2) requires little training to develop, (3) can deliver virtually instantaneous responses, (4) can quickly alter and repost, and (5) may not be as private or anonymous as users expect.

LO 19-2 *Identify the four major social networks and how brand managers integrate them into marketing actions.*
The four major social networks are Facebook, Twitter, LinkedIn, and YouTube. Facebook is a social network where users create a personal profile, add other users as "friends," and exchange comments, photos, videos, and "likes" with them. To increase traffic to a Facebook Page, brand managers can use paid ads and sponsored stories. Twitter enables users to send and receive "tweets," messages up to 140 characters long. For Twitter, brand managers can use monitoring programs to track what people are saying about their organization's brand. LinkedIn lets users post their personal profiles to a network of businesspeople. LinkedIn can be used to create a company profile to share brand information and career opportunities with LinkedIn users and to demonstrate the company's expertise and professionalism. YouTube is a video-sharing website where users can upload, view, and comment on videos. YouTube also allows marketers to create a brand channel to promote a product, show ads for it, and have viewers comment on it. A company can use YouTube to inform consumers about itself and direct traffic by featuring a link back to its website.

LO 19-3 *Describe the differing roles of those receiving messages through traditional versus social media and how brand managers select a social network.*
With promotional messages received through traditional media, recipients are generally "passive receivers" and the communication ends with them. In contrast, recipients of social media messages are "active receivers," and the company sending them messages hopes they will become "evangelists" and send positive messages back to the company and to online friends. The factors a marketer uses to select a specific social network involve assessing (1) the number of registered users and unique visitors to the company's website, (2) the characteristics (or profile) of those visitors, and (3) the focus of the social network. Of the four major social networks, Facebook has the largest number of daily visitors, followed by YouTube, Twitter, and LinkedIn. Each of these has a unique user profile that allows marketers to develop marketing programs to reach specific target segments. Also, because each social network has a unique focus (videos, short text messaging, and so on), marketers can modify their marketing programs to take advantage of these differences.

LO 19-4 *Explain how social media can produce sales revenues for a brand and compare the performance measures linked to costs versus revenues.*
Measuring the sales generated from social media is more difficult than with traditional media because in many cases there is no direct link between a social network user and a sale. Brand

managers can use social media platforms to send messages or paid advertisements to the brand's audience that include links to the special promotions, coupon codes, or specific products in an online store. By tracking the performance of these links, the brand manager can identify the ones that produce sales revenues. Performance measures linked to inputs and costs include (1) cost per thousand (similar to the CPM for a print ad), which is the number of times an ad is displayed to a user; (2) cost per click (CPC), which gives the rate the advertiser pays each time a visitor clicks on the ad and then jumps to the advertiser's web page; and (3) cost per action (CPA), which is the amount paid for every purchase that originates from an ad on a social media network site. Examples of performance measures linked to outputs or revenues include (1) users/members that have registered on social media websites; (2) the number of unique monthly users viewing the website at a given time; (3) page views, or the number of times a specific web page is loaded; and (4) visitors, or the total number of users viewing a particular web page during a specified time period.

LO 19-5 *Describe how the convergence of the real and digital worlds affects the future of social media.*
The convergence of the real and digital worlds in social networking is the result of the proliferation of interlinked smartphones, tablet devices, sensors, RFIDs, databases, algorithms, apps, and other elements. Apps are small, downloadable software programs that run on smartphones and tablet devices to add functionality to these devices. In the future, there will be: (1) new ways to personalize social media connections; (2) an increased focus on socially networked "communities;" (3) an increased emphasis on measuring the marketing return on investment for social media initiatives; and (4) the use of devices equipped with near field communications technology that allows consumers and marketers to exchange personal and product-related information with each other. The convergence of social media, smartphones, tablet devices, and new apps will lead to companies having a more dynamic interaction with their customers. For consumers, however, this could lead to a loss of privacy and possible exploitation by unscrupulous marketers.

FOCUSING ON KEY TERMS

apps p. 522
blog p. 504
Facebook p. 507
LinkedIn p. 512
social media p. 504
Twitter p. 511
user-generated content (UGC) p. 504
YouTube p. 512

APPLYING MARKETING KNOWLEDGE

1 In the chapter opener, why was Kimmy Summers more successful using Facebook and Twitter to get volunteers and promote freshman move-in day at her university than she might have been using more conventional print media?

2 You and three college friends have decided to launch an online business selling clothes college students wear—T-shirts, shorts, sweats, and so on. You plan to use Facebook ads. What "likes" or interests do (*a*) college men and (*b*) college women have that might help you in planning your Facebook strategy?

3 You are about to graduate from college and want a job in marketing research or sales. Go to the LinkedIn site, register, and determine what information you would put on your LinkedIn profile to help you find a new job.

4 What is the significance of user-generated content when contrasted with social media and traditional media?

5 You are a brand manager for a sneaker manufacturer like Nike or New Balance and are trying to use Facebook to reach (*a*) college-age women and (*b*) men over 55 years of age. What three or four "likes" or interests would you expect each segment to have when you try to reach it with Facebook?

6 In measuring the results of a social network, what are the (*a*) advantages and (*b*) disadvantages of performance measures linked directly to revenues versus costs?

7 Looking back with perfect hindsight, what should the brand manager for Nestlé's Kit Kat have done when the Greenpeace e-mails first appeared?

BUILDING YOUR MARKETING PLAN

Remembering the target market segments you identified in Chapter 9 for your marketing plan:

1 (*a*) Identify which one of the four social networks described in the chapter would be most useful and (*b*) give your reasons. Would you consider other social networks like Pinterest? Why or why not?

2 Briefy describe (*a*) how you would use this social network to try to increase sales of your products and (*b*) why you expect target market customers to respond to it.

VIDEO CASE 19 StuffDOT™, Inc.: Rewarding Social Media Users for Shopping and Sharing

"Coming from a rewards and loyalty background, I often wondered how to combine the best of rewards with the expanding universe of social media," says Jennifer Katz, founder and chief executive officer of StuffDOT, Inc.

"Further, it seemed really unfair that only a few people were benefiting from all the content millions of people were providing for free online. I believe the individuals creating all this online content deserve to benefit from their efforts," says Katz.

"Thinking about this, one day our marketing director came into a meeting and explained how a really cute ankle bracelet that she posted on a social sharing site went viral. But now she faced a six-week backlog to purchase it. So we all said, if she made a commission on every ankle bracelet that was sold because of that one post, she could have bought five. Right then and there, StuffDOT was born," explains Katz.

StuffDOT's VISION, BRAND NAME, AND LOGO

StuffDOT's vision is to reward users for shopping and sharing online. Most other sites tend to keep all the affiliate fees and commissions for themselves. StuffDOT, however, enables users to benefit from all this online shopping and sharing. This is the first time, to StuffDOT's knowledge, that a firm has developed a platform where the people posting to social media are the same people who are rewarded for it. In addition, the StuffDOT team plans to add coupons and loyalty elements that will broaden its reach, as well as its value to merchants.

"We chose the brand name StuffDOT because it was catchy and [we] felt we could really build on it," says Katz. "With the name StuffDOT, we could use Stuff, DOT, and StuffDOT, which also gives flexibility. The name also is great for campaigns like 'Dare to Dot,' 'Spot it, Dot it, Got it,' or 'Stuff I Like,' just to name a few. The team tried other names, but they just didn't have that fun stickiness that the name StuffDOT does," says Jennifer Katz.

The StuffDOT team tried and tested several different logos before coming up with its memorable, attention-getting logo shown here. People see the orange dot as friendly, familiar, and eye-catching. It has proven to be an easy logo to build on.

HOW StuffDOT WORKS

"To really see how StuffDOT works and its key benefits, you have to understand 'Dotting' and how users earn and use the resulting rewards," says Amanda Axvig, StuffDOT's director of marketing. Kelsey Fisher, a StuffDOT marketing associate, explains to a group of student interns what a "Dot" is and the steps in "Dotting."

What Is a "Dot"?

"Dots are posts ranging all the way from products, Do-It-Yourself projects, recipes, and news stories to funny videos to random photos," Fisher explains. "A Dot is something posted to view, to share, or to track for a future purchase. A Dot is simply a post of anything you want to display on the StuffDOT site," she says.

How to "Dot"

Kelsey Fisher walks the interns through the three steps to Dot:

1. "Use the simple drag-and-drop process to add the 'Dot It' button to your toolbar in your web browser.
2. "Dot or post items you 'like' online by clicking on that button on your toolbar. For example, if you are browsing Macy's online store and see something you like, you can click on the 'Dot It' button in your toolbar and it will show up on your StuffDOT page.
3. "Watch your rewards grow as people share, buy, or click on the stuff you've 'Dotted.' You can also earn rewards on your own purchases!" she concludes.

Earning and Redeeming StuffDOT Rewards

So how does an online user actually earn rewards? "When you find things you like online, you Dot or post the item to StuffDOT," says Amanda Axvig. "If the item appears with a magenta border around it, this means it is from one of our 18,000+ retail sites and qualifies for rewards."

"If your StuffDOT followers view, click, share, repost, or buy the item, you see your rewards balance increase," Axvig says. "You can also earn rewards by posting and purchasing your own items. Once your balance reaches $15, you can start redeeming gift cards from a variety of popular retailers."

TARGET MARKET SEGMENTS AND COMPETITION

StuffDOT targets three initial market segments:

- Students—18- to 24-year-old college students who are already sharing online things like fashion, music, books, high-tech gadgets, and so on. This target segment also regularly posts to Facebook, Twitter, Pinterest, and Instagram.
- Loyal online shoppers—People who are making purchases online and are regularly seeking online coupons, discounts, or rewards.
- Moms—Mothers, often the family "purchasing agents," who are sharing advice about products, parenting, recipes, and craft ideas with their peers.

As StuffDOT gains traction within these communities, the team plans to reach out to new market segments, as research and measurable actions dictate.

At the present time, StuffDOT sees no "direct" competitors. However, StuffDOT views all social-sharing, affiliate marketing, shopping, and couponing sites as indirect competitors and possible threats. Pinterest also remains on StuffDOT's radar as a potential competitor solely because of its social-sharing aspects.

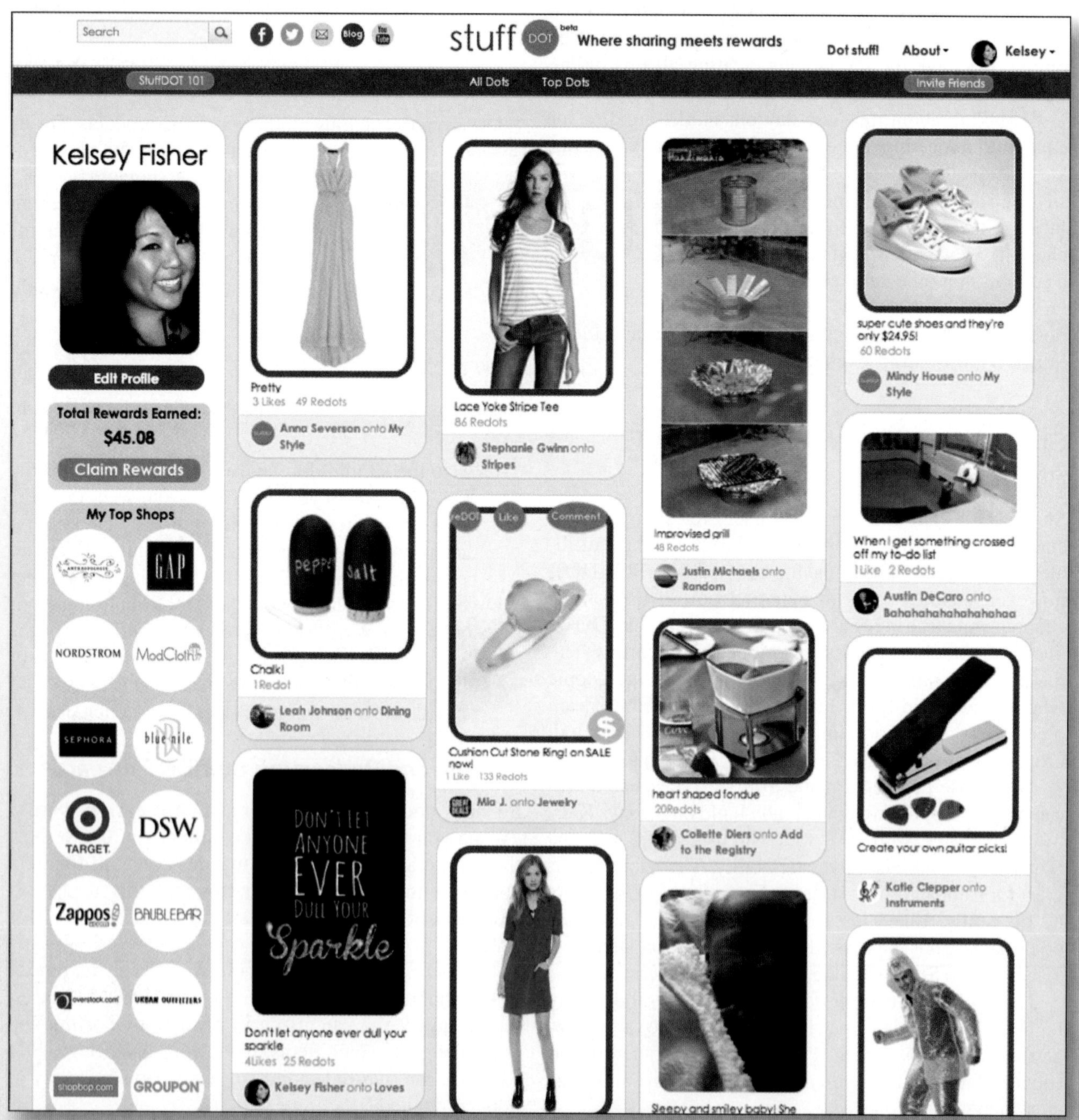

MAKING StuffDOT USER-FRIENDLY

A challenge for the StuffDOT team is keeping it simple, yet having features that make StuffDOT fun and rewarding.

"I work closely with the StuffDOT team to turn the concepts they create into user-friendly features on StuffDOT," says Sudipta Tripathy, StuffDOT's chief technology officer. "For example, we want to ensure that all new features have the same look and feel across all parts of the StuffDOT platform—website, Android app, or iOS app," he says.

Starting with the first version, a special challenge was developing a unique look for the social-sharing site while keeping it familiar and user-friendly. The team focused on the round "Dot" theme throughout the development phase. Details like ensuring that all corners on the site are rounded and that buttons have a consistent look impacts the site's "stickiness" among users. StuffDOT has also added social-sharing features to make the site accessible to a larger audience and provide users with more ways to showcase the things they post.

One of the biggest challenges was making sure all the features were available and easy to use on the mobile apps as well. When creating Android (Google) versus iOS (Apple) apps, there were many levels and versions to consider. What may look great on an Android device may not render well on an iPad or iPhone, and so on. All of these things need attention when launching new platforms.

MARKETING StuffDOT

StuffDOT has focused its initial marketing efforts on three areas: (1) partnerships, (2) the StuffDOT Internship and Campus Ambassador Program, and (3) social sharing.

StuffDOT's partnership works with online affiliate aggregators that give users access to 18,000+ online retailers that share affiliate fees and rewards. In addition, StuffDOT has been working with select retailers at a deeper level to create unique promotional programs that benefit users and make the partner brand more prominent. For example, a recent promotion featured a free pair of running shoes for signing up, referring friends, and Dotting. This not only built awareness for the brand of running shoes, but it also created a new user base for StuffDOT.

The StuffDOT Internship and Campus Ambassador Program (photo) not only gives students a rich experience working in new social media, but it has greatly enhanced the benefits of the StuffDOT platform. Many of the features on the StuffDOT platform emerged from suggestions from student interns and address weaknesses in other social media platforms. Student interns work both at the home office and on campus to create StuffDOT promotions. Depending on their interests, students may focus on organizing new-user workshops and street-team promotions or finding new partners and users through social networks. StuffDOT regularly posts its new campus ambassador opportunities in the "Careers" section of StuffDOT.com.

Major social-sharing features throughout the StuffDOT site make it very convenient for users to share items with friends. For example, a student who wants a new laptop for her birthday can share that item with friends on Facebook, and she can also e-mail that item with an embedded link to her parents as a reminder. That student can also earn a StuffDOT reward on the purchase—a "double" birthday present.

Questions

1 (*a*) Who are StuffDOT's target markets and (*b*) what items are most likely to be Dotted by each of these user groups?

2 (*a*) Who are StuffDOT's major competitors and (*b*) what point(s) of difference should StuffDOT use to distinguish itself from them?

3 How should StuffDOT be marketed so that it becomes an integral part of everyday life?

4 How can the team create "buzz" for StuffDOT and grow its user base most effectively (*a*) using social media platforms (like Facebook and Twitter) and (*b*) using its own website?

20 Personal Selling and Sales Management

Learning Objectives

After reading this chapter you should be able to:

Discuss the nature and scope of personal selling and sales management in marketing.

Identify the different types of personal selling.

Explain the stages in the personal selling process.

Describe the major functions of sales management.

Meet Today's Sales Professional

Have you been considering sales as a career opportunity? If so, then consider Lindsey Smith as a role model (see opposite page).

Ms. Smith began her career representing Molecular Imaging Products within the Medical Diagnostics Division of GE Healthcare Americas. She joined the company eleven years ago right out of college with a BBA degree. The epitome of today's sales professional, she lists integrity, motivation, trust and relationship building, and a team orientation as just a few of the ingredients necessary for a successful sales career today.

As a sales professional, she recognizes the importance of constantly updating and refining her product knowledge, analytical and communication skills, and strategic thinking about opportunities to more fully satisfy each customer's clinical, economic, and technical requirements. And for good reason. Her customer contacts include physicians (radiologists, neurologists, and cardiologists), medical technologists, nurses, and health care provider CEOs, CFOs, and other administrators.

Lindsey Smith's selling orientation and customer relationship philosophy rest on four pillars:

1. *A commitment to creating value for clients*. Lindsey believes "every sales call and client interaction should create value for both the customer and the company."
2. *Seek to serve clients as a trusted consultant*. Lindsey emphasizes "being a resource for my customers by providing novel solutions for them."
3. *Reinforce the company's competitive advantage*. Lindsey continually reinforces GE Healthcare Americas' competitive advantage: "I emphasize my company's value proposition and showcase the company's product innovation, solutions, and service."
4. *Regard challenges as opportunities*. Lindsey says, "I consider challenges as opportunities to provide innovative solutions and resources to customers and to build client trust and long-term relationships."

Lindsey Smith's approach to selling and customer relationships has served her customers and her well. She is among the company's top revenue producers and has a long list of loyal customers. Not surprisingly, Ms. Smith has been a recipient of the company's Commercial Excellence Award in six of the last eight years.

In 2011, Lindsey Smith was promoted to Client Director at GE Healthcare Americas. In this capacity, she represents and manages the entire GE Healthcare Americas company portfolio, including medical technology, health care consulting, information technology, and finance solutions for one of GE's largest strategic health care systems.[1]

This chapter describes the scope and significance of personal selling and sales management in marketing and creating value for customers. It first highlights the many forms of personal selling. Next, the major steps in the selling process are outlined with an emphasis on building buyer–seller relationships.

The chapter then focuses on salesforce management and its critical role in achieving a company's broader marketing objectives. Three major salesforce management functions are then detailed. They are sales plan formulation, sales plan implementation, and salesforce evaluation. Finally, technology's persuasive influence on how selling is done and how salespeople are managed is described.

SCOPE AND SIGNIFICANCE OF PERSONAL SELLING AND SALES MANAGEMENT

Chapter 17 described personal selling and management of the sales effort as being part of the firm's promotional mix. Although it is important to recognize that personal selling is a useful vehicle for communicating with present and potential buyers, it is much more. Take a moment to answer the questions in the personal selling and sales management quiz in Figure 20–1. As you read on, compare your answers with those in the text.

Nature of Personal Selling and Sales Management

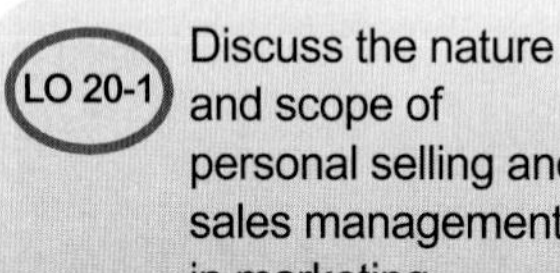

Discuss the nature and scope of personal selling and sales management in marketing.

Personal selling involves the two-way flow of communication between a buyer and seller, often in a face-to-face encounter, designed to influence a person's or group's purchase decision. However, with advances in telecommunications, personal selling also takes place over the telephone and through video teleconferencing and Internet-enabled links between buyers and sellers.

Personal selling remains a highly human-intensive activity despite the use of technology. Accordingly, the people involved must be managed. **Sales management** involves planning the selling program and implementing and evaluating the personal selling effort of the firm. The tasks involved in managing personal selling include setting objectives; organizing the salesforce; recruiting, selecting, training, and compensating salespeople; and evaluating the performance of individual salespeople.

Selling Happens Almost Everywhere

"Everyone lives by selling something," wrote author Robert Louis Stevenson a century ago. His observation still holds true today. The U.S. Bureau of Labor Statistics reports that about 14 million people are employed in sales positions in the United States. Included in this number are manufacturing sales personnel, real estate brokers, stockbrokers, and salesclerks who work in retail stores. In reality, however, virtually every occupation that involves customer contact has an element of personal selling. For example, attorneys, accountants, bankers, and company

FIGURE 20–1
Personal selling and sales management quiz. Check your answers as you read the chapter.

1. What percentage of chief executive officers in the largest U.S. companies have significant sales experience in their work history? (check one)

   10% ______ 30% ______ 50% ______

   20% ______ 40% ______ 60% ______

2. About what percentage of an average field sales representative's time each work-week is spent actually selling to customers by phone or face-to-face? (check one)

   40% ______ 50% ______ 60% ______

3. "A salesperson's job is finished when a sale is made." True or false? (circle one)

   True False

4. About what percentage of U.S. companies include customer satisfaction as a measure of salesperson performance? (check one)

   10% ______ 30% ______ 50% ______

   20% ______ 40% ______ 60% ______

Could this be a salesperson in the operating room? Read the text to find out why Medtronic salespeople visit hospital operating rooms.

Medtronic
www.medtronic.com

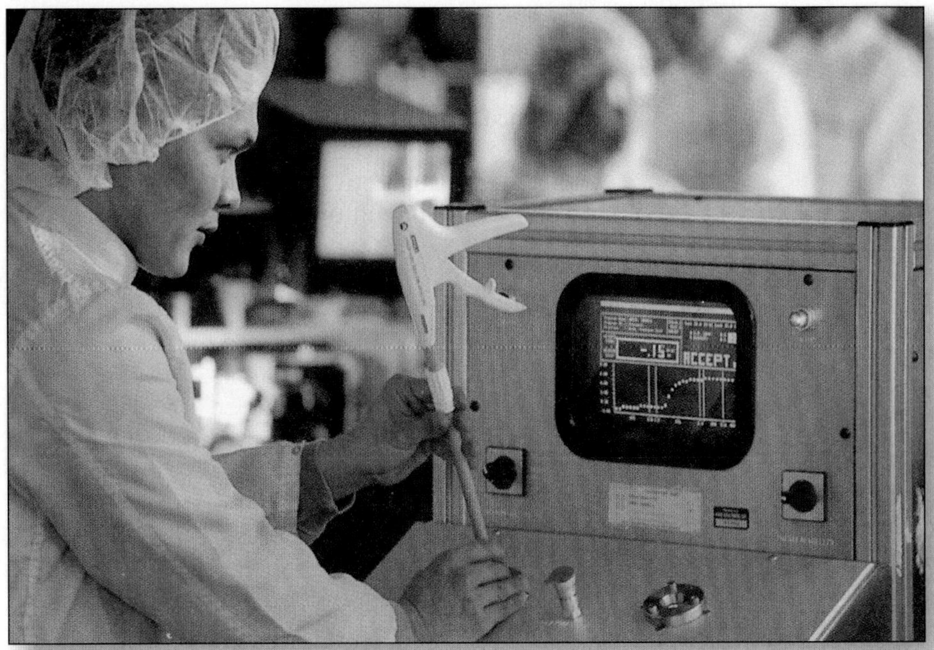

personnel recruiters perform sales-related activities, whether or not they acknowledge it.

About 20 percent of chief executive officers in the largest U.S. corporations have significant sales experience in their work history.[2] (*What percentage did you check for question 1 in Figure 20–1?*) Thus, selling often serves as a stepping-stone to top management, as well as being a career path itself.

Personal Selling in Marketing

QR 20-1
Cambridge
Sales Video

Personal selling serves three major roles in a firm's overall marketing effort. First, salespeople are the critical link between the firm and its customers. This role requires that salespeople match company interests with customer needs to satisfy both parties in the exchange process. Second, salespeople *are* the company in a consumer's eyes. They represent what a company is or attempts to be and are often the only personal contact a customer has with the company. For example, as acknowledged by IBM's former chief executive officer, the company's 40,000-strong salesforce is "our face to the client."[3] Third, personal selling may play a dominant role in a firm's marketing program. This situation typically arises when a firm uses a push marketing strategy, described in Chapter 17. Avon, for example, pays almost 40 percent of its total sales dollars for selling expenses. Pharmaceutical firms and office and educational equipment manufacturers also rely heavily on personal selling in the marketing of their products.

Creating Customer Solutions and Value through Salespeople: Relationship and Partnership Selling

As the critical link between the firm and its customers, salespeople can create customer value in many ways. For instance, by being close to the customer, salespeople can identify creative solutions to customer problems. Salespeople at Medtronic, Inc., the world leader in the heart pacemaker market, are in the operating room for more than 90 percent of the procedures performed with their product and are on call 24 hours a day. "It reflects the willingness to be there in every situation, just in case a problem arises—even though nine times out of ten the procedure goes just fine," notes a satisfied customer.[4]

Salespeople can create value by easing the customer buying process. This happened at TE Connectivity, a producer of electrical products. Salespeople and customers had a difficult time getting product specifications and performance data on the company's 70,000 products quickly and accurately. The company now has all of its information on its website, which can be downloaded instantly by salespeople and customers.

Customer value is also created by salespeople who follow through after the sale. At Jefferson Smurfit Corporation, a multibillion-dollar supplier of packaging products, one of its salespeople juggled production from three of the company's plants to satisfy an unexpected demand for boxes from General Electric. This person's action led to the company being given GE's Distinguished Supplier Award.

Relationship Selling Customer value creation is made possible by **relationship selling**, the practice of building ties to customers based on a salesperson's attention and commitment to customer needs over time. Relationship selling involves mutual respect and trust among buyers and sellers. It focuses on creating long-term customers, not a one-time sale. A survey of 300 senior sales executives revealed that 96 percent consider "building long-term relationships with customers" to be the most important activity affecting sales performance. Companies such as Xerox, American Express, and Owens Corning have made relationship building a core focus of their sales effort.[5]

Partnership Selling Some companies have taken relationship selling a step further and forged partnerships between buyer and seller organizations. With **partnership selling**, sometimes called *enterprise selling*, buyers and sellers combine their expertise and resources to create customized solutions; commit to joint planning; and share customer, competitive, and company information for their mutual benefit and, ultimately, the benefit of the customer.

As an approach to sales, partnership selling relies on cross-functional business specialists who apply their knowledge and expertise to achieve better customer solutions, lower cost, and greater customer value. Partnership selling complements the supply partnerships described in Chapter 6. This practice is embraced by General Electric, Honeywell, DuPont, and IBM. For example, on any given day, IBM has 30 information technology hardware and software specialists, business consultants, and engineers working at Charles Schwab, a large brokerage firm, all under the direction of a senior IBM sales executive. Their job? To create and manage a complex state-of-the-art financial planning system that assists Schwab clients with their retirement planning.[6]

Relationship and partnership selling represent another dimension of customer relationship management. Both emphasize the importance of first learning about customer needs and wants and then tailoring solutions to customer problems as a means to customer value creation. Recent research suggests that a salesperson may have a genetic predisposition to create customer value. See the Marketing Matters box for details.[7]

learning review

20-1. What is personal selling?

20-2. What is involved in sales management?

Marketing Matters

customer value

Science and Selling: Is Customer Value Creation in Your Genes?

Is a predisposition to create customer value in your genes? Are you a born salesperson? Recent research by University of Michigan Marketing Professor Richard P. Bagozzi and his colleagues offers a novel insight into this question that may or may not surprise you.

Their research identifies a genetic marker, the 7R variant of the DRD_4 gene, that is correlated with a salesperson's predisposition or willingness to interact with customers and learn about their problems in order to meet their needs. The researchers also found that the presence of the A1 variant of the DRD_2 gene is correlated with predisposition or tendency to try to persuade customers to buy a given product rather than listen to their needs.

These two different genetic markers help explain the difference between a salesperson's customer orientation versus sales orientation. A customer orientation is guided by such ideas as, "I try to align customers who have problems with products that will help them solve their problems," where the aim is to satisfy mutual needs and the hope is to build a long-term relationship.

In contrast, a sales orientation is driven by notions such as, "I try to sell customers all I can convince them to buy, even if I think it is more than a wise customer should buy." In this case, the motivation is to satisfy one's own short-term interests and not necessarily the needs of the customer.

Faced with a selling situation, do you have a sales orientation or a customer orientation? Customer value creation may be in your genes!

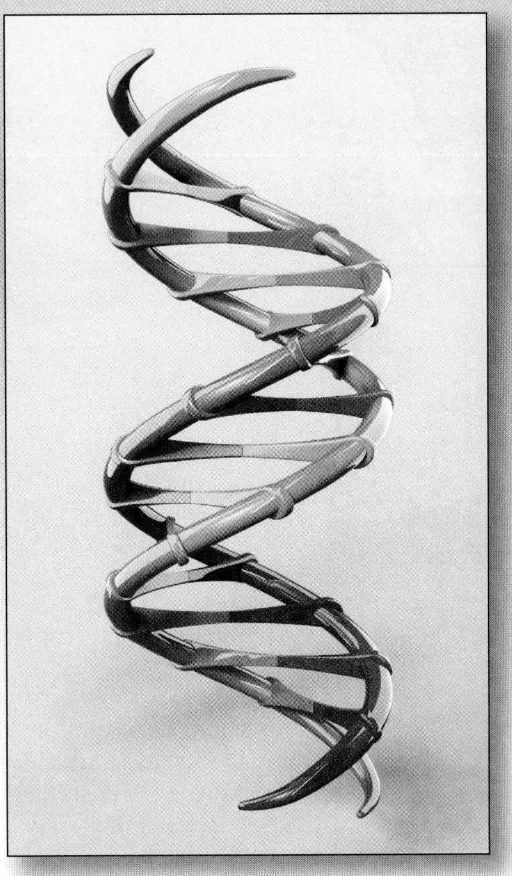

THE MANY FORMS OF PERSONAL SELLING

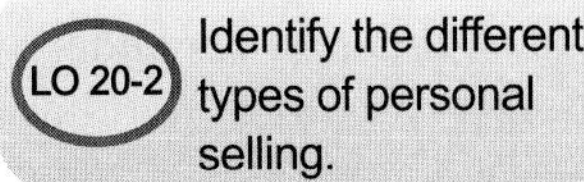

LO 20-2 Identify the different types of personal selling.

Personal selling assumes many forms based on the amount of selling done and the amount of creativity required to perform the sales task. Broadly speaking, three types of personal selling exist: order taking, order getting, and customer sales support activities. While some firms use only one of these types of personal selling, others use a combination of all three.

Order-Taking Salespeople

Typically, an **order taker** processes routine orders or reorders for products that were already sold by the company. The primary responsibility of order takers is to preserve an ongoing relationship with existing customers and maintain sales.

Two types of order takers exist. *Outside order takers* visit customers and replenish inventory stocks of resellers, such as retailers or wholesalers. For example, Frito-Lay

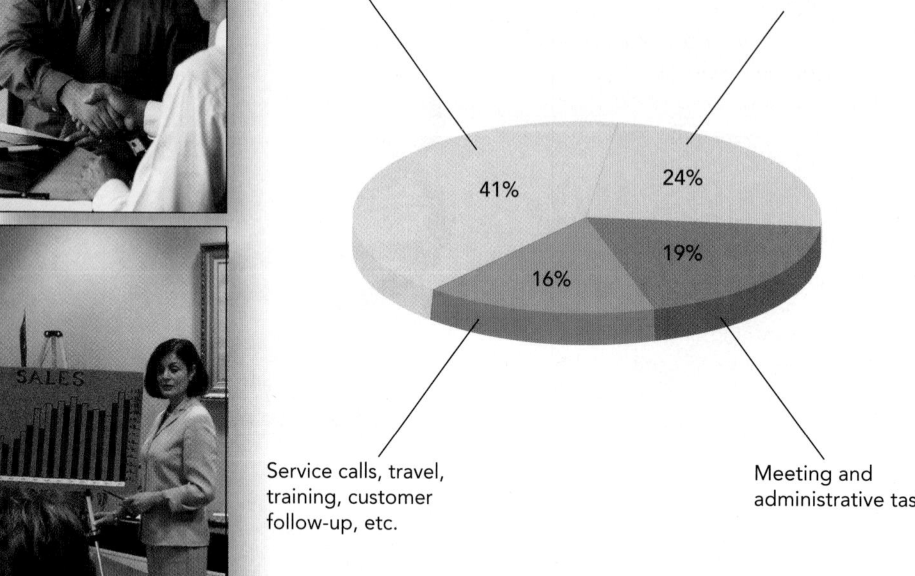

FIGURE 20–2
How do outside order-getting salespeople spend their time each week? You might be surprised after reading the text.

salespeople call on supermarkets, convenience stores, and other establishments to ensure that the company's line of snack products (such as Lay's potato chips and Doritos and Tostitos tortilla chips) is in adequate supply. In addition, outside order takers often provide assistance in arranging displays.

Inside order takers, also called *order clerks* or *salesclerks*, typically answer simple questions, take orders, and complete transactions with customers. Many retail clerks are inside order takers. Inside order takers are often employed by companies that use *inbound telemarketing*, the use of toll-free telephone numbers that customers can call to obtain information about products or services and make purchases. In business-to-business settings, order taking arises in straight rebuy situations as described in Chapter 6.

Order takers generally do little selling in a conventional sense. They engage in modest problem solving with customers. They often represent products that have few options, such as magazine subscriptions and highly standardized industrial products. Inbound telemarketing is also an essential selling activity for more "customer service" driven firms, such as Dell. At these companies, order takers undergo extensive training so that they can better assist callers with their purchase decisions.

Order-Getting Salespeople

An **order getter** sells in a conventional sense and identifies prospective customers, provides customers with information, persuades customers to buy, closes sales, and follows up on customers' use of a product or service. Like order takers, order getters can be inside (an automobile salesperson) or outside (a Xerox salesperson).

Order getting involves a high degree of creativity and customer empathy and is typically required for selling complex or technical products with many options, so considerable product knowledge and sales training are necessary. In modified rebuy or new-buy purchase situations in business-to-business selling, an order getter acts as a problem solver who identifies how a particular product may satisfy a customer's need. Similarly, in the purchase of a service, such as insurance, an insurance agent can provide a mix of plans to satisfy a buyer's needs depending on income, stage of the family's life cycle, and investment objectives.

Order getting is not a 40-hour-per-week job. Industry research shows that outside order getters, or field service representatives, often work over 50 hours per week. As shown in Figure 20–2, 41 percent of an average field sales representative's time is actually spent selling by phone or face-to-face. (*What percentage did you check for question 2 in Figure 20–1?*) Another 24 percent is devoted to generating leads and researching customer accounts. The remainder of a sales representative's workweek is occupied by administrative tasks, meetings, service calls, travel, training, and customer follow-up.[8]

Order getting by outside salespeople is also expensive. It is estimated that the average cost of a single field sales call on a business customer is about $350, factoring in the salesperson's compensation, benefits, and travel-and-entertainment expenses. This cost illustrates why outbound telemarketing is popular. *Outbound telemarketing* is the practice of using the telephone rather than personal visits to contact current and prospective customers. A much lower cost per sales call (from $20 to $25) and little or no field expense accounts for its widespread appeal.[9]

Customer Sales Support Personnel

Customer sales support personnel augment the selling effort of order getters by performing a variety of services. For example, *missionary salespeople* do not directly solicit orders but rather concentrate on performing promotional activities and introducing new products. They are used extensively in the pharmaceutical industry, where they persuade physicians to prescribe a firm's product. Actual sales are made through wholesalers or directly to pharmacists who fill prescriptions. *Sales engineers* specialize in identifying, analyzing, and solving customer problems. These salespeople bring know-how and technical expertise to the selling situation but often do not actually sell products and services. Sales engineers are popular in selling business products such as chemicals and heavy equipment.

Many firms engage in cross-functional **team selling**, the practice of using an entire team of professionals in selling to and servicing major customers.[10] Team selling is used when specialized knowledge is needed to satisfy the different interests of individuals in a customer's buying center. A selling team might consist of a salesperson, a sales engineer, a service representative, and a financial executive, each of whom would deal with a counterpart in the customer's firm.

Selling teams take different forms. In *conference selling*, a salesperson and other company resource people meet with buyers to discuss problems and opportunities. In *seminar selling*, a company team conducts an educational program for a customer's technical staff, describing state-of-the-art developments. IBM and Xerox pioneered cross-functional team selling in working with prospective buyers. Since then, other firms have embraced this practice to create and sustain value for their customers as well, as described in the Marketing Matters box on the next page.[11]

learning review

20-3. What is the principal difference between an order taker and an order getter?

20-4. What is team selling?

Marketing Matters

customer value

Creating and Sustaining Customer Value through Cross-Functional Team Selling

The day of the lone salesperson calling on a customer is rapidly becoming history. Today, 75 percent of companies employ cross-functional teams of professionals to work with customers to improve relationships, find better ways of doing things, and, of course, create and sustain value for their customers.

Xerox and IBM pioneered cross-functional team selling, but other firms have been quick to follow as they spotted the potential to create and sustain value for their customers. Recognizing that corn growers needed a herbicide they could apply less often, a DuPont team of chemists, sales and marketing executives, and regulatory specialists created just the right product that recorded sales of $57 million in its first year. Procter & Gamble uses teams of marketing, sales, advertising, computer systems, and supply chain personnel to work with its major retailers, such as Walmart, to identify ways to develop, promote, and deliver products. Pitney Bowes, Inc., which produces sophisticated computer systems that weigh, rate, and track packages for firms such as UPS and FedEx, also uses sales teams to meet customer needs. These teams consist of sales personnel, "carrier management specialists," and engineering and administrative executives who continually find ways to improve the technology of shipping goods across town and around the world.

Efforts to create and sustain customer value through cross-functional team selling have become a necessity as customers seek greater value for their money. According to the vice president for procurement of a *Fortune* 500 company, "Today, it's not just getting the best price but getting the best value—and there are a lot of pieces to value."

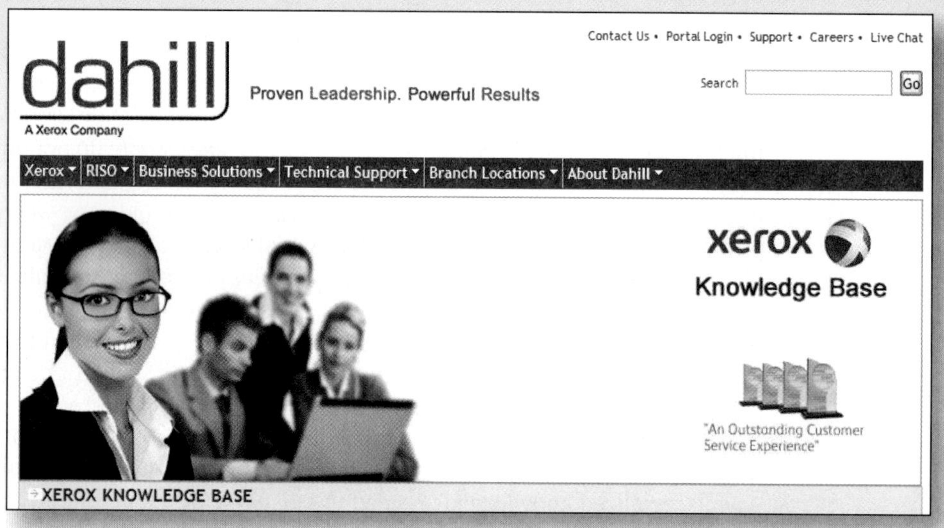

THE PERSONAL SELLING PROCESS: BUILDING RELATIONSHIPS

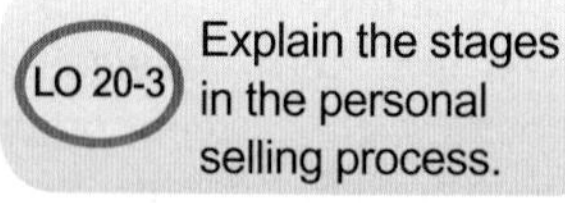

LO 20-3
Explain the stages in the personal selling process.

Selling, and particularly order getting, is a complicated activity that involves building buyer–seller relationships. Although the salesperson–customer interaction is essential to personal selling, much of a salesperson's work occurs before this meeting and continues after the sale itself. The **personal selling process** consists of six stages: (1) prospecting, (2) preapproach, (3) approach, (4) presentation, (5) close, and (6) follow-up (see Figure 20–3).

Prospecting: Identifying and Qualifying Prospective Customers

Personal selling begins with the *prospecting* stage—the search for and qualification of potential customers. There are three types of prospects. A *lead* is the name of a person who may be a possible customer. A *prospect* is a customer who wants or needs the product. If an individual wants the product, can afford to buy it, and is the decision maker, this individual is a *qualified prospect*.

FIGURE 20–3
Stages and objectives of the personal selling process. Each stage is critical for successful selling and building a customer relationship.

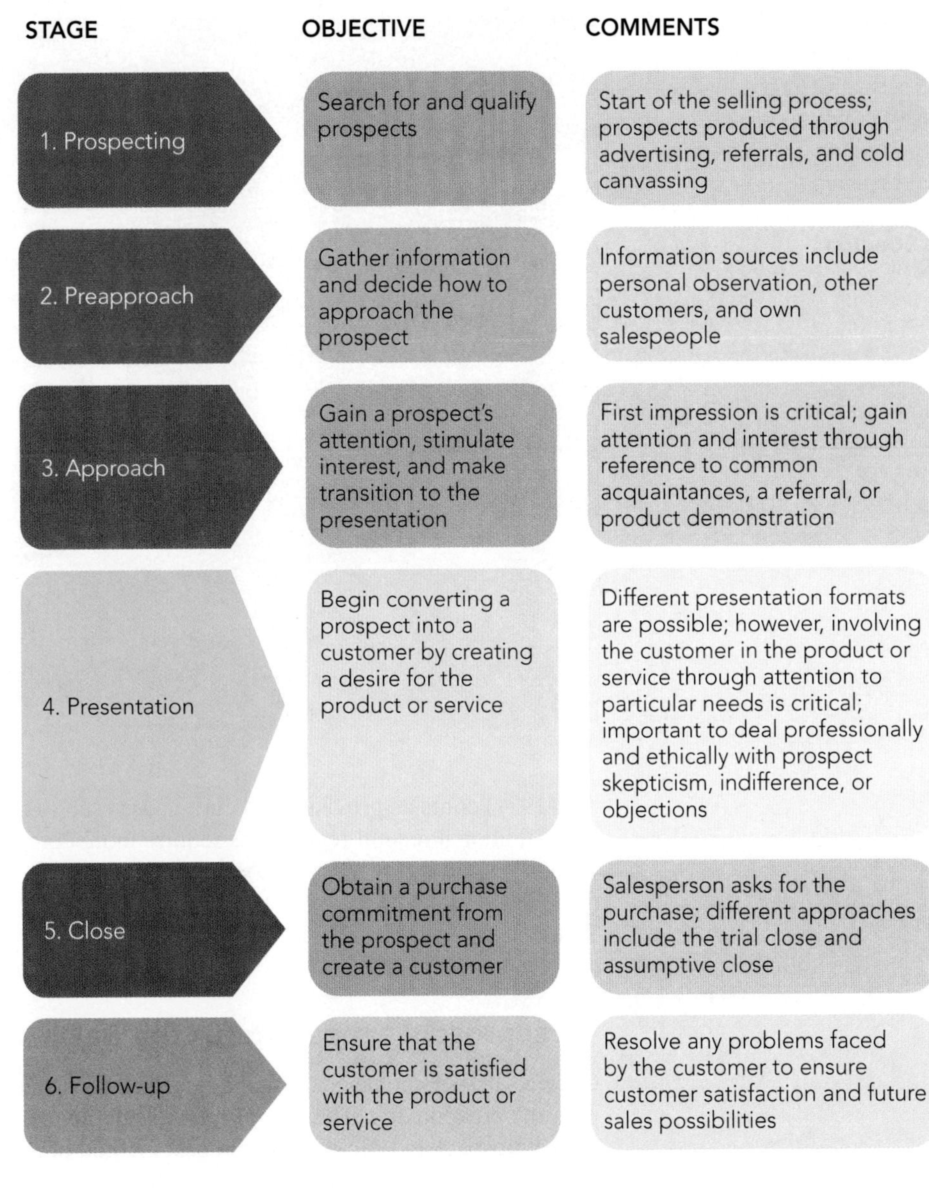

STAGE
OBJECTIVE
COMMENTS
1. Prospecting
Search for and qualify prospects
Start of the selling process; prospects produced through advertising, referrals, and cold canvassing
2. Preapproach
Gather information and decide how to approach the prospect
Information sources include personal observation, other customers, and own salespeople
3. Approach
Gain a prospect's attention, stimulate interest, and make transition to the presentation
First impression is critical; gain attention and interest through reference to common acquaintances, a referral, or product demonstration
4. Presentation
Begin converting a prospect into a customer by creating a desire for the product or service
Different presentation formats are possible; however, involving the customer in the product or service through attention to particular needs is critical; important to deal professionally and ethically with prospect skepticism, indifference, or objections
5. Close
Obtain a purchase commitment from the prospect and create a customer
Salesperson asks for the purchase; different approaches include the trial close and assumptive close
6. Follow-up
Ensure that the customer is satisfied with the product or service
Resolve any problems faced by the customer to ensure customer satisfaction and future sales possibilities

Leads and prospects are generated using several sources. For example, advertising may contain a coupon or a toll-free number to generate leads. Some companies use exhibits at trade shows, professional meetings, and conferences to generate leads or prospects. Staffed by salespeople, these exhibits are used to attract the attention of prospective buyers and share information. Others utilize the Internet for generating leads and prospects. Today, salespeople are using websites, e-mail, and social networks, such as LinkedIn, to connect to individuals and companies that may be interested in their products or services.

Another approach for generating leads is through *cold canvassing* or *cold calling*, either in person or by telephone. This approach simply means that a salesperson may open a directory, pick a name, and contact that individual or business. Despite its high refusal rate, cold canvassing can be successful.[12] However, cold canvassing is frowned upon in some cultures. For example, in most Asian and Latin American societies, personal visits, based on referrals, are expected.

Cold canvassing is often criticized by U.S. consumers and is now regulated. Research shows that 75 percent of U.S. consumers consider this practice an intrusion on their privacy, and 72 percent find it distasteful.[13] The *Telephone Consumer Protection*

Trade shows are a popular source for leads and prospects. Companies like TSCentral provide comprehensive trade show information.

TSCentral
www.tscentral.com

Act (1991) contains provisions to curb abuses such as early morning or late night calling. Additional federal regulations require more complete disclosure regarding solicitations, include provisions that allow consumers to avoid being called at any time through the Do Not Call Registry, and impose fines for violations. For example, satellite television provider DirecTV was fined \$5.3 million for making thousands of calls to consumers who had put their telephone numbers on the Do Not Call Registry.[14]

Preapproach: Preparing for the Sales Call

Once a salesperson has identified a qualified prospect, preparation for the sale begins with the preapproach. The *preapproach* stage involves obtaining further information on the prospect and deciding on the best method of approach. Knowing how the prospect prefers to be approached and what the prospect is looking for in a product or service is essential, regardless of industry or cultural setting.

For instance, a Merrill Lynch stockbroker will need information on a prospect's discretionary income, investment objectives, and preference for discussing brokerage services over the telephone or in person. For business product companies such as Texas Instruments, the preapproach involves identifying the buying role of a prospect (for example, influencer or decision maker), important buying criteria, and the prospect's receptivity to a formal or informal presentation. Identifying the best time to contact a prospect is also important. Northwestern Mutual Life Insurance Company suggests that the following are the best times to call on people in different occupations: dentists before 9:30 A.M., lawyers between 11:00 A.M. and 2:00 P.M., and college professors between 7:00 and 8:00 P.M.

The preapproach stage is especially important in international selling, where customs dictate appropriate protocol. In many South American countries, for example, buyers expect salespeople to be punctual for appointments. However, prospective buyers are routinely 30 minutes late. South Americans take negotiating seriously and prefer straightforward presentations, but a hard-sell approach will not work.[15]

Successful salespeople recognize that the preapproach stage should never be shortchanged. Their experience coupled with research on customer complaints indicates that failure to learn as much as possible about the prospect is unprofessional and the ruin of a sales call.

Approach: Making the First Impression

The *approach* stage involves the initial meeting between the salesperson and the prospect, where the objectives are to gain the prospect's attention, stimulate interest, and build the foundation for the sales presentation itself and the basis for a working relationship. The first impression is critical at this stage, and it is common for salespeople to begin the conversation with a reference to common acquaintances, a referral, or even the product or service itself. Which tactic is taken will depend on the information obtained in the prospecting and preapproach stages.

How business cards are exchanged with Asian customers is very important. Read the text to learn the appropriate protocol in the approach stage of the personal selling process.

The approach stage is very important in international settings.[16] In many societies outside the United States, considerable time is devoted to nonbusiness talk designed to establish a rapport between buyers and sellers. For instance, it is common for two or three meetings to occur before business matters are discussed in the Middle East and Asia. Gestures are also very important. The initial meeting between a salesperson and a prospect in the United States customarily begins with a firm handshake. Handshakes also apply in France, but they are gentle, not firm. Forget the handshake in Japan. An appropriate bow is expected. What about business cards? Business cards should be printed in English on one side and the language of the prospective customer on the other. Knowledgeable U.S. salespeople know that their business cards should be handed to Asian customers using both hands, with the name facing the receiver. In Asia, anything involving a person's name demands respect.

Presentation: Tailoring a Solution for a Customer's Needs

The *presentation* stage is at the core of the order-getting selling process, and its objective is to convert a prospect into a customer by creating a desire for the product or service. Three major presentation formats exist: (1) stimulus-response format, (2) formula selling format, and (3) need-satisfaction format.

Stimulus-Response Format The **stimulus-response presentation** format assumes that given the appropriate stimulus by a salesperson, the prospect will buy. With this format the salesperson tries one appeal after another, hoping to hit the right button. A counter clerk at McDonald's is using this approach when he or she asks whether you'd like an order of french fries or a dessert with your meal. The counter clerk is engaging in what is called *suggestive selling*. Although useful in this setting, the stimulus-response format is not always appropriate, and for many products a more formalized format is necessary.

Formula Selling Format The **formula selling presentation** format is based on the view that a presentation consists of information that must be provided in an accurate, thorough, and step-by-step manner to inform the prospect. A popular version of this format is the *canned sales presentation*, which is a memorized, standardized message conveyed to every prospect. Used frequently by firms in telephone and door-to-door selling of consumer products (for example, Kirby vacuum cleaners), this approach treats every prospect the same, regardless of differences in needs or preferences for certain kinds of information.

Canned sales presentations can be advantageous when the differences between prospects are unknown or with novice salespeople who are less knowledgeable about the product and selling process than experienced salespeople. Although it guarantees a thorough presentation, it often lacks flexibility and spontaneity. More important, it does not provide for feedback from the prospective buyer—a critical component in the communication process and the start of a relationship.

Need-Satisfaction Format The stimulus-response and formula selling formats share a common characteristic: The salesperson dominates the conversation. By comparison, the **need-satisfaction presentation** format emphasizes probing and listening by the salesperson to identify the needs and interests of prospective buyers. Once these are identified, the salesperson tailors the presentation to the prospect and highlights product benefits that may be valued by the prospect. The need-satisfaction format, which emphasizes problem solving and customer solutions, is the most consistent with the marketing concept and relationship building.

Two selling styles are common with this format.[17] **Adaptive selling** involves adjusting the presentation to fit the selling situation, such as knowing when to offer solutions and when to ask for more information. Sales research and practice show that knowledge of the customer and sales situation are key ingredients for adaptive selling. Many consumer service firms such as brokerage and insurance firms and consumer product firms like Rockport, AT&T, and Gillette effectively apply this selling style.

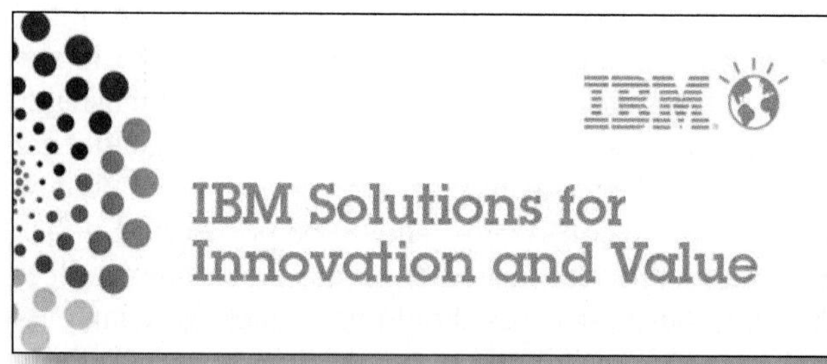

IBM is a leader in consultative selling with its focus on developing novel solutions that create customer value.

Consultative selling focuses on problem identification, where the salesperson serves as an expert on problem recognition and resolution. With consultative selling, problem solution options are not simply a matter of choosing from an array of existing products or services. Rather, novel solutions often arise, thereby creating unique value for the customer.

Consultative selling is prominent in business-to-business marketing. Johnson Controls's Automotive Systems Group, IBM's Global Services, DHL Worldwide Express, GE Healthcare Americas, and Xerox offer customer solutions through their consultative selling style. According to a senior Xerox sales executive, "Our business is no longer about selling boxes. It's about selling digital, networked-based information management solutions, and this requires a highly customized and consultative selling process. So we look for consultative and business-savvy salespeople." But what does a customer solution really mean? The Marketing Matters box offers a unique answer.[18]

Handling Objections A critical concern in the presentation stage is handling objections. *Objections* are excuses for not making a purchase commitment or decision. Some objections are valid and are based on the characteristics of the product or service or price. However, many objections reflect prospect skepticism or indifference. Whether valid or not, experienced salespeople know that objections do not put an end to the presentation. Rather, techniques can be used to deal with objections in a courteous, ethical, and professional manner. The following six techniques are the most common:[19]

1. *Acknowledge and convert the objection.* This technique involves using the objection as a reason for buying. For example, a prospect might say, "The price is too high." The reply: "Yes, the price is high because we use the finest materials. Let me show you. . . . "
2. *Postpone.* The postpone technique is used when the objection will be dealt with later in the presentation: "I'm going to address that point shortly. I think my answer would make better sense then."
3. *Agree and neutralize.* Here a salesperson agrees with the objection, then shows that it is unimportant. A salesperson would say, "That's true. Others have said the same. But, they thought that issue was outweighed by other benefits."

Marketing Matters

customer value

Imagine This . . . Putting the Customer into Customer Solutions!

Solutions for problems are what companies are looking for from suppliers. At the same time, suppliers focus on customer solutions to differentiate themselves from competitors. So what is a customer solution and what does it have to do with selling?

Sellers view a solution as a customized and integrated combination of products and services for meeting a customer's business needs. But what do buyers think? From a buyer's perspective, a solution is one that (1) meets their requirements, (2) is designed to uniquely solve their problem, (3) can be implemented, and (4) ensures follow-up.

This insight arose from a field study conducted by three researchers at Emory University. Their in-depth study also yielded insight into what an effective customer solution offers. According to one buyer interviewed in their study:

> They (the supplier) make sure that their sales and marketing guys know what's going on. The sales and technical folks know what's going on, and the technical and support guys know what's going on with me. All these guys are in the loop, and it's not a puzzle for them.

So what does putting the customer into customer solutions have to do with selling? Three things stand out. First, considerable time and effort is necessary to fully understand a specific customer's requirements. Second, effective customer solutions are based on relationships among sellers and buyers. And finally, consultative selling is central to providing novel solutions for customers, thereby creating value for them.

4. *Accept the objection.* Sometimes the objection is valid. Let the prospect express such views, probe for the reason behind it, and attempt to stimulate further discussion on the objection.
5. *Denial.* When a prospect's objection is based on misinformation and clearly untrue, it is wise to meet the objection head on with a firm denial.
6. *Ignore the objection.* This technique is used when it appears that the objection is a stalling mechanism or is clearly not important to the prospect.

Each of these techniques requires a calm, professional interaction with the prospect and is most effective when objections are anticipated in the preapproach stage. Handling objections is a skill requiring a sense of timing, appreciation for the prospect's state of mind, and adeptness in communication. Objections also should be handled ethically. Lying or misrepresenting product or service features are grossly unethical practices.

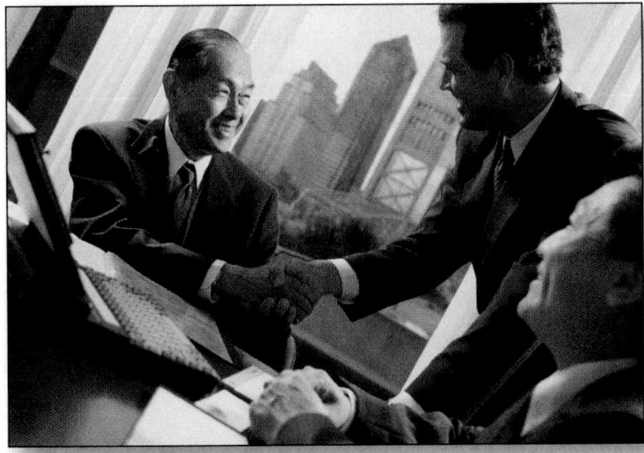

The closing stage involves obtaining a purchase commitment from the prospect. Read the text to learn how the close itself can take several forms.

Close: Asking for the Customer's Order or Business

The *closing* stage in the selling process involves obtaining a purchase commitment from the prospect. This stage is the most important and the most difficult because the salesperson must determine when the prospect is ready to buy. Telltale signals indicating a readiness to buy include body language (prospect reexamines the product or contract closely), statements ("This equipment should reduce our maintenance costs"), and questions ("When could we expect delivery?").

The close itself can take several forms. Three closing techniques are used when a salesperson believes a buyer is about ready to make a purchase: (1) trial close, (2) assumptive close, and (3) urgency close. A *trial close* involves asking the prospect to make a decision on some aspect of the purchase: "Would you prefer the blue or gray model?" An *assumptive close* entails asking the prospect to consider choices concerning delivery, warranty, or financing terms under the assumption that a sale has been finalized. An *urgency close* is used to commit the prospect quickly by making reference to the timeliness of the purchase: "The low interest financing ends next week," or "That is the last model we have in stock." Of course, these statements should be used only if they accurately reflect the situation; otherwise, such claims would be unethical. When a prospect is clearly ready to buy, the final close is used, and a salesperson asks for the order.

Follow-up: Solidifying the Relationship

The selling process does not end with the closing of a sale; rather, professional selling requires customer follow-up. One marketing authority equated the follow-up with courtship and marriage by observing, "The sale merely consummates the courtship. Then the marriage begins. How good the marriage is depends on how well the relationship is managed."[20] The *follow-up* stage includes making certain the customer's purchase has been properly delivered and installed and addressing any difficulties experienced with the use of the item. Attention to this stage of the selling process solidifies the buyer–seller relationship. Research shows that the cost and effort to obtain repeat sales from a satisfied customer is roughly half of that necessary to gain a sale from a new customer.[21] In short, today's satisfied customers become tomorrow's qualified prospects or referrals. (*What was your answer to question 3 in the Figure 20–1 quiz?*)

learning review

20-5. What are the six stages in the personal selling process?

20-6. What is the distinction between a lead and a qualified prospect?

20-7. Which presentation format is most consistent with the marketing concept? Why?

THE SALES MANAGEMENT PROCESS

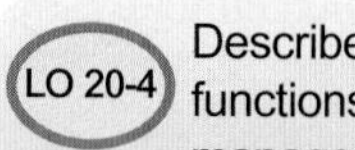

LO 20-4 Describe the major functions of sales management.

Selling must be managed if it is going to contribute to a firm's marketing objectives. Although firms differ in the specifics of how salespeople and the selling effort are managed, the sales management process is similar across firms. Sales management consists of three interrelated functions: (1) sales plan formulation, (2) sales plan implementation, and (3) salesforce evaluation (see Figure 20–4).

FIGURE 20–4 The sales management process involves sales plan formulation, sales plan implementation, and salesforce evaluation.

Sales plan formulation
- Setting objectives
- Organizing the salesforce
- Developing account management policies

→

Sales plan implementation
- Salesforce recruitment and selection
- Salesforce training
- Salesforce motivation and compensation

→

Salesforce evaluation
- Quantitative assessment
- Behavioral evaluation

Making Responsible Decisions

ethics

The Ethics of Asking Customers about Competitors

Salespeople are a valuable source of information about what is happening in the marketplace. By working closely with customers and asking good questions, salespeople often have firsthand knowledge of customer problems and wants. They also are able to spot the activities of competitors. However, should salespeople explicitly ask customers about competitor strategies such as pricing practices, product development efforts, and trade and promotion programs?

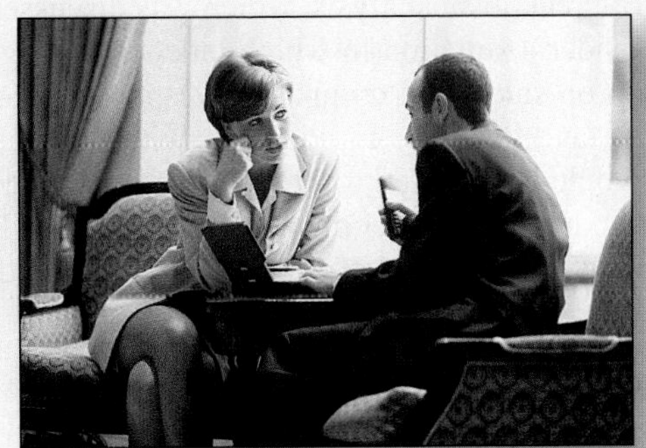

Gaining knowledge about competitors by asking customers for information is a ticklish ethical issue. Research indicates that 25 percent of U.S. salespeople engaged in business-to-business selling consider this practice unethical, and their companies have explicit guidelines for this practice.

It is also noteworthy that Japanese salespeople consider this practice to be more unethical than do U.S. salespeople.

Do you believe that asking customers about competitor strategies and practices is unethical? Why or why not?

Sales Plan Formulation: Setting Direction

Formulating the sales plan is the most basic of the three sales management functions. According to the vice president of the Harris Corporation, a global communications company, "If a company hopes to implement its marketing strategy, it really needs a detailed sales planning process."[22] The **sales plan** is a statement describing what is to be achieved and where and how the selling effort of salespeople is to be deployed. Sales plan formulation involves three tasks: (1) setting objectives, (2) organizing the salesforce, and (3) developing account management policies.

Setting Objectives Setting objectives is central to sales management because this task specifies what is to be achieved. In practice, objectives are set for the total salesforce and for each salesperson.

Selling objectives can be output related and focus on dollar or unit sales volume, number of new customers added, or profit. Alternatively, they can be input related and emphasize the number of sales calls and selling expenses. Output- and input-related objectives are used for the salesforce as a whole and for each salesperson. A third type of objective that is behaviorally related is typically specific for each salesperson and includes his or her product knowledge, customer service satisfaction ratings, and selling and communication skills.

Increasingly, firms are also emphasizing knowledge of competition as an objective since salespeople are calling on customers and should see what competitors are doing. In fact, 89 percent of companies encourage their salespeople to gather competitive intelligence.[23] But should salespeople explicitly ask their customers for information about competitors? Read the Making Responsible Decisions box to see how salespeople view this practice.[24]

Whatever objectives are set, they should be precise and measurable and specify the time period over which they are to be achieved. Once established, these objectives serve as performance standards for the evaluation of the salesforce, the third function of sales management.

Organizing the Salesforce Organizing a selling organization is the second task in formulating the sales plan. Three questions are related to organization. First, should the company use its own salesforce, or should it use independent agents such as manufacturer's representatives? Second, if the decision is made to employ company salespeople, then should they be organized according to geography, customer type, or product or service? Third, how many company salespeople should be employed?

The decision to use company salespeople or independent agents is made infrequently. The decision itself is based on an analysis of economic and behavioral factors. An economic analysis examines the costs of using both types of salespeople and is a form of break-even analysis, which was discussed in Chapter 13.

Consider a situation in which independent agents would receive a 5 percent commission on sales, and company salespeople would receive a 3 percent commission, salaries, and benefits. In addition, with company salespeople, sales administration costs would be incurred for a total fixed cost of $500,000 per year. At what sales level would independent or company salespeople be less costly? This question can be answered by setting the costs of the two options equal to each other and solving for the sales level amount, as shown in the equation:

$$\text{Total cost of company salespeople} = \text{Total cost of independent agents}$$
$$[0.03(X) + \$500{,}000] = 0.05(X)$$

where X = sales volume. Solving for X, sales volume equals $25 million, indicating that below $25 million in sales independent agents would be cheaper, but above $25 million a company salesforce would be cheaper. This relationship is shown in Figure 20–5.

Economics alone does not answer this question. A behavioral analysis is also necessary and should focus on issues related to the control, flexibility, effort, and availability of independent and company salespeople.[25] A firm must weigh the pros and cons of the economic and behavioral factors before making this decision.

If a company elects to employ its own salespeople, then it must choose an organizational structure based on (1) geography, (2) customer, or (3) product (see Figure 20–6). A *geographical sales organization* is the simplest structure, where the United States, or indeed the globe, is first divided into regions and each region is divided into districts or territories. Salespeople are assigned to each district with defined geographical boundaries and call on all customers and represent all products sold by the company. An advantage of this structure is that it can minimize travel time, expenses, and duplication of selling effort. However, if a firm's products or customers require specialized knowledge, then a geographical structure is unsuitable.

When different types of buyers have different needs, a *customer sales organization* is used. In practice this means that a different salesforce calls on each separate type of

FIGURE 20–5
A break-even chart for comparing independent agents and a company salesforce includes an analysis of selling costs and sales. The break-even point occurs when company salesforce selling cost equals independent agent selling cost.

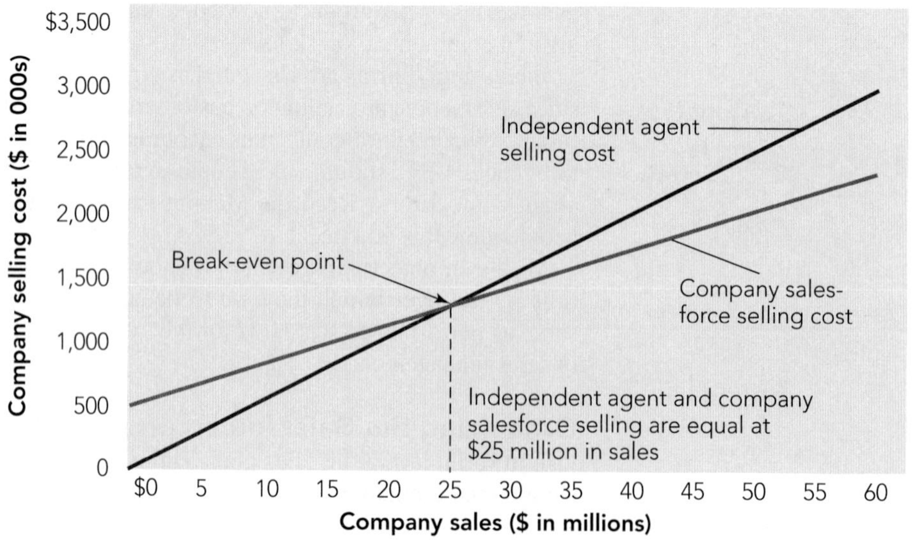

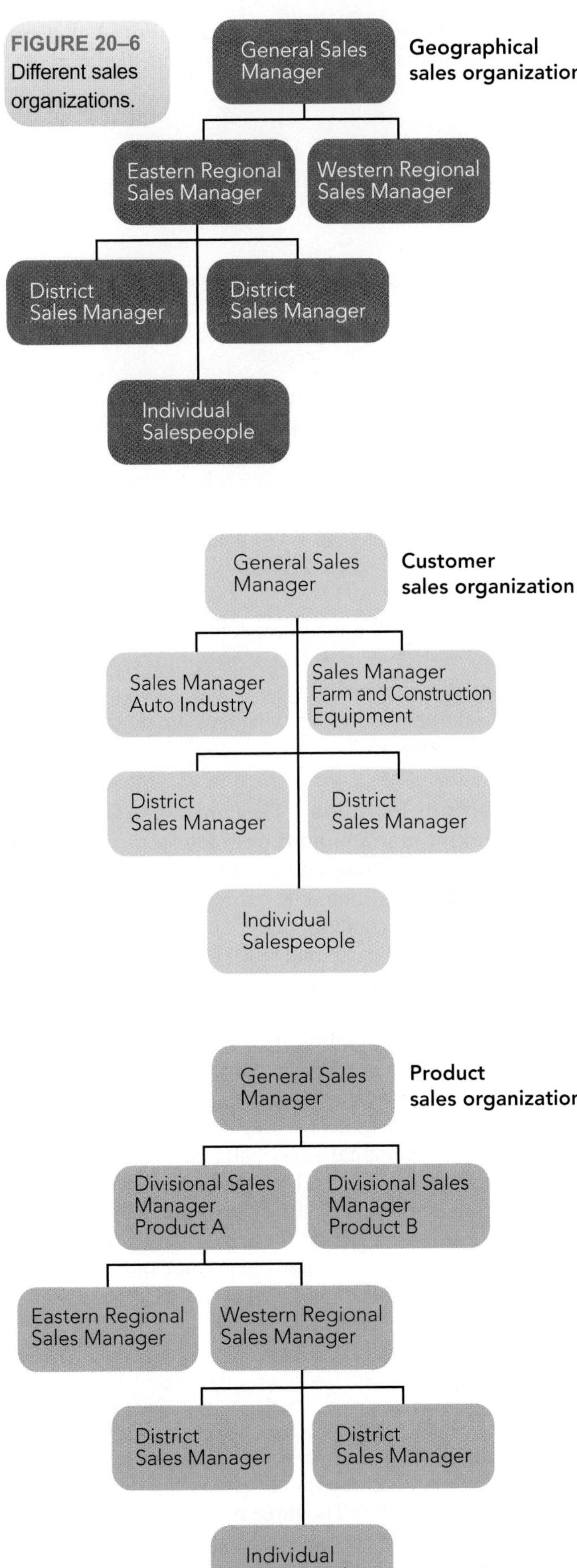

FIGURE 20–6 Different sales organizations.

buyer or marketing channel. For example, Konica switched from a geographical to a marketing channel structure with different sales teams serving specific retail channels: mass merchandisers, photo specialty outlets, and food and drug stores. The rationale for this approach is that more effective, specialized customer support and knowledge are provided to buyers. However, this structure often leads to higher administrative costs and some duplication of selling effort, because several salesforces are used to represent the same products.

An important variation of the customer organizational structure is **key account management**—the practice of using team selling to focus on important customers so as to build mutually beneficial, long-term, cooperative relationships.[26] Key account management involves teams of sales, service, and often technical personnel who work with purchasing, manufacturing, engineering, logistics, and financial executives in customer organizations. This approach, which often assigns company personnel to a customer account, results in "customer specialists" who can provide exceptional service. Procter & Gamble uses this approach with Walmart, as does Black & Decker with Home Depot.

When specific knowledge is required to sell certain types of products, then a *product sales organization* is used. For example, Maxim Steel has a salesforce that sells drilling pipe to oil companies and another that sells specialty steel products to manufacturers. The advantage of this structure is that salespeople can develop expertise with technical characteristics, applications, and selling methods associated with a particular product or family of products. However, this structure produces high administrative costs and duplication of selling effort, because two company salespeople may call on the same customer.

In short, there is no one best sales organization for all companies in all situations.[27] Rather, the organization of the salesforce should reflect the marketing strategy of the firm. Each year about 10 percent of U.S. firms change their sales organizations to implement new marketing strategies.

The third question related to salesforce organization involves determining the size of the salesforce. For example, why do you think Frito-Lay has about 18,000 salespeople who call on supermarkets, convenience stores, and other establishments to sell snack foods? The answer lies in the number of accounts (customers) served, the frequency of calls on accounts, the length of an average call, and the amount of time a salesperson can devote to selling.

A common approach for determining the size of a salesforce is the **workload method**. This formula-based method integrates the number of customers served, call frequency, call length, and available selling time to arrive at a figure for the salesforce size. For example, Frito-Lay needs about 18,000 route salespeople according to the following workload method formula:

$$NS = \frac{NC \times CF \times CL}{AST}$$

Where,

NS = Number of salespeople

NC = Number of customers

CF = Call frequency necessary to service a customer each year

CL = Length of an average call

AST = Average amount of selling time available per year

How many route salespeople does Frito-Lay need to sell and service its retail accounts?

Frito-Lay route salespeople sell and display products in 350,000 supermarkets, convenience stores, and other establishments. Salespeople should call on these accounts at least once a week, or 52 times a year. The average sales call lasts an average of 83 minutes (1.38 hour). An average salesperson works 2,000 hours a year (50 weeks × 40 hours a week), but 12 hours a week are devoted to nonselling activities such as travel and administration, leaving 1,400 hours a year. Using these guidelines, Frito-Lay needs

$$NS = \frac{350{,}000 \times 52 \times 1.38}{1{,}400} = 17{,}940 \text{ route salespeople}$$

The value of this formula is apparent in its flexibility; a change in any one of the variables will affect the number of salespeople needed. Changes are determined, in part, by the firm's account management policies.

Developing Account Management Policies The third task in formulating a sales plan involves developing **account management policies** specifying whom salespeople should contact, what kinds of selling and customer service activities should be engaged in, and how these activities should be carried out. These policies might state which individuals in a buying organization should be contacted, the amount of sales and service effort that different customers should receive, and the kinds of information salespeople should collect before or during a sales call.

An example of an account management policy in Figure 20–7 shows how different accounts or customers can be grouped according to level of opportunity and the firm's competitive sales position.[28] When specific account names are placed in each cell, salespeople clearly see which accounts should be contacted, with what level of selling and service activity, and how to deal with them. Accounts in cells 1 and 2 might have high frequencies of personal sales calls and increased time spent on a call. Cell 3 accounts will have lower call frequencies, and cell 4 accounts might be contacted through telemarketing or direct mail rather than in person. For example, Union Pacific Railroad put its 20,000 smallest accounts on a telemarketing program. A subsequent survey of these accounts indicated that 84 percent rated Union Pacific's sales effort "very effective" compared with 67 percent before the switch.

Sales Plan Implementation: Putting the Plan into Action

The sales plan is put into practice through the tasks associated with sales plan implementation. Whereas sales plan formulation focuses on "doing the right things," implementation emphasizes "doing things right." The three major tasks involved in implementing a sales plan are (1) salesforce recruitment and selection, (2) salesforce training, and (3) salesforce motivation and compensation.

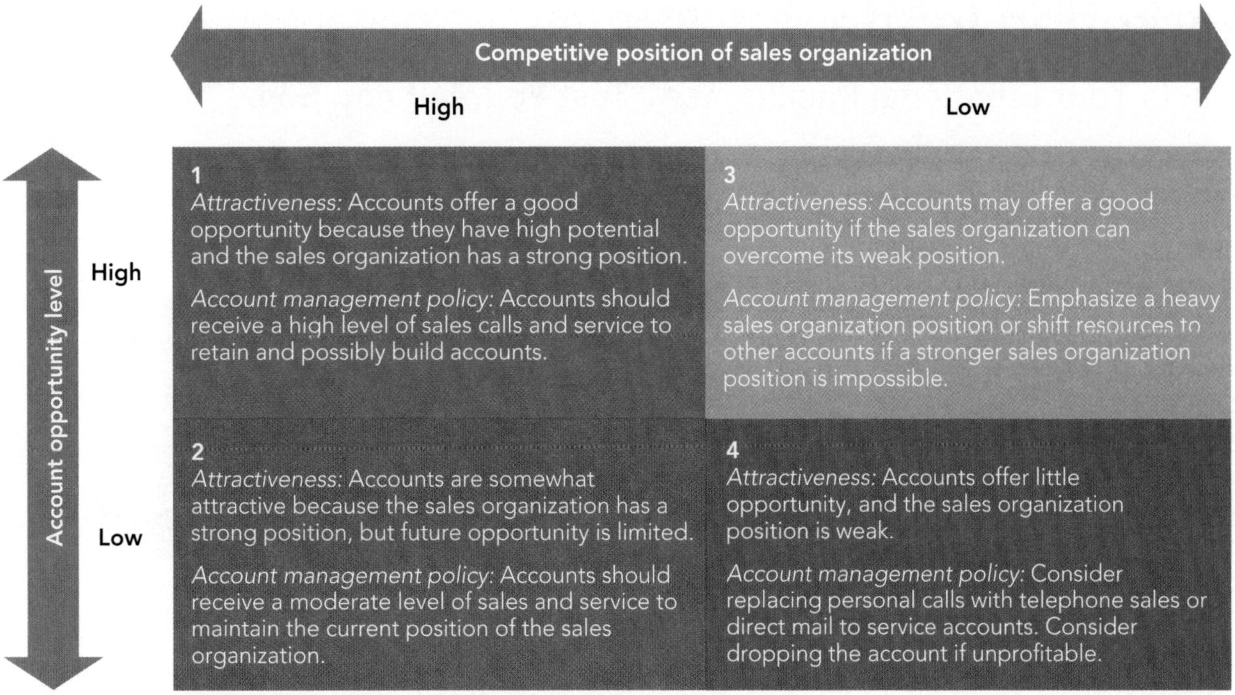

Competitive position of sales organization

	High	Low
Account opportunity level: High	1 *Attractiveness:* Accounts offer a good opportunity because they have high potential and the sales organization has a strong position. *Account management policy:* Accounts should receive a high level of sales calls and service to retain and possibly build accounts.	3 *Attractiveness:* Accounts may offer a good opportunity if the sales organization can overcome its weak position. *Account management policy:* Emphasize a heavy sales organization position or shift resources to other accounts if a stronger sales organization position is impossible.
Account opportunity level: Low	2 *Attractiveness:* Accounts are somewhat attractive because the sales organization has a strong position, but future opportunity is limited. *Account management policy:* Accounts should receive a moderate level of sales and service to maintain the current position of the sales organization.	4 *Attractiveness:* Accounts offer little opportunity, and the sales organization position is weak. *Account management policy:* Consider replacing personal calls with telephone sales or direct mail to service accounts. Consider dropping the account if unprofitable.

FIGURE 20–7
An account management policy grid grouping customers according to level of opportunity and the firm's competitive sales position.

Salesforce Recruitment and Selection Effective recruitment and selection of salespeople is one of the most crucial tasks of sales management. It entails finding people who match the type of sales position required by a firm. Recruitment and selection practices will differ greatly between order-taking and order-getting sales positions, given the differences in the demands of these two jobs. Therefore, recruitment and selection begin with a carefully crafted job analysis and job description followed by a statement of job qualifications.

A *job analysis* is a study of a particular sales position, including how the job is to be performed and the tasks that make up the job. Information from a job analysis is used to write a *job description*, a written document that describes job relationships and requirements that characterize each sales position. It explains (1) to whom a salesperson reports, (2) how a salesperson interacts with other company personnel, (3) the customers to be called on, (4) the specific activities to be carried out, (5) the physical and mental demands of the job, and (6) the types of products and services to be sold.

The job description is then translated into a statement of job qualifications, including the aptitudes, knowledge, skills, and a variety of behavioral characteristics considered necessary to perform the job successfully. Qualifications for order-getting sales positions often mirror the expectations of buyers: (1) imagination and problem-solving ability, (2) strong work ethic, (3) honesty, (4) intimate product knowledge, (5) effective communication and listening skills, and (6) attentiveness reflected in responsiveness to buyer needs and customer loyalty and follow-up. Firms use a variety of methods for evaluating prospective salespeople. Personal interviews, reference checks, and background information provided on application forms are the most frequently used methods.[29]

Successful selling also requires a high degree of emotional intelligence. **Emotional intelligence** is the ability to understand one's own emotions and the emotions of people with whom one interacts on a daily basis. These qualities are important for adaptive selling and may spell the difference between effective and ineffective order-getting salespeople.[30] Are you interested in what your emotional intelligence might be? Read the Marketing inSite box on the next page and test yourself.

Marketing inSite

What Is Your Emotional Intelligence? Test Yourself and See.

A person's success at work depends on many talents, including intelligence and technical skills. Recent research indicates that an individual's emotional intelligence or EI is also important, if not more important!

Evidence suggests that emotional intelligence is two times more important in contributing to performance than intellect and expertise alone. Emotional intelligence has five dimensions: (1) self-motivation skills; (2) self-awareness, or knowing one's own emotions; (3) the ability to manage one's emotions and impulses; (4) empathy, or the ability to sense how others are feeling; and (5) social skills, or the ability to handle the emotions of other people.

What is your emotional intelligence? Visit the website at www.ihhp.com/quiz.php and answer the 24 questions to learn what your emotional intelligence is and obtain additional insights.

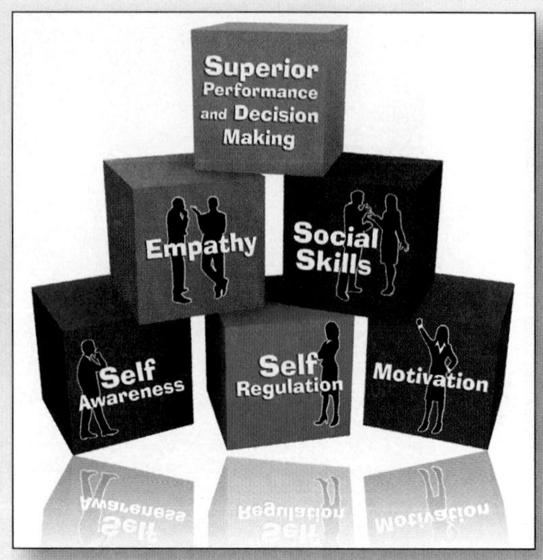

Salesforce Training Whereas the recruitment and selection of salespeople is a one-time event, salesforce training is an ongoing process that affects both new and seasoned salespeople.[31] Sales training covers much more than selling practices. For example, IBM Global Services salespeople, who sell consulting and various information technology services, take at least two weeks of in-class and Internet-based training on both consultative selling and the technical aspects of business.

Training new salespeople is an expensive process. Salespeople in the United States receive employer-sponsored training annually at a cost of over $7 billion per year. On-the-job training is the most popular type of training, followed by individual instruction taught by experienced salespeople. Formal classes, seminars taught by professional sales trainers, and computer-based training are also popular.

Salesforce Motivation and Compensation A sales plan cannot be successfully implemented without motivated salespeople. Research on salesperson motivation suggests that (1) a clear job description, (2) effective sales management practices, (3) a personal need for achievement, and (4) proper compensation, incentives, or rewards will produce a motivated salesperson.[32]

The importance of compensation as a motivating factor means that close attention must be given to how salespeople are financially rewarded for their efforts. Salespeople are paid using one of three plans: (1) straight salary, (2) straight commission, or (3) a combination of salary and commission. Under a *straight salary compensation plan*, a salesperson is paid a fixed fee per week, month, or year. With a *straight commission compensation plan*, a salesperson's earnings are directly tied to the sales or profit generated. For example, an insurance agent might receive a 2 percent commission of $2,000 for selling a $100,000 life insurance policy. A *combination compensation plan* contains a specified salary plus a commission on sales or profit generated.

Each compensation plan has its advantages and disadvantages.[33] A straight salary plan is easy to administer and gives management a large measure of control over how salespeople allocate their efforts. However, it provides little incentive to expand sales volume. This plan is used when salespeople engage in many nonselling activities, such as account or customer servicing. A straight commission plan provides the maximum

Why is Jamie Cruse Vrinios, a successful Mary Kay Cosmetics Independent National Sales Director, posing with a Cadillac Escalade Hybrid? Read the text to learn how Mary Kay rewards its top sales performers.

Mary Kay Cosmetics, Inc.
www.marykay.com

amount of selling incentive but can discourage salespeople from providing customer service. This plan is common when nonselling activities are minimal. Combination plans are most preferred by salespeople and attempt to build on the advantages of salary and commission plans while reducing the potential shortcomings of each. A majority of companies use combination plans today.

Nonmonetary rewards are also given to salespeople for meeting or exceeding objectives. These rewards include trips, honor societies, distinguished salesperson awards, and letters of commendation. Some unconventional rewards include the new pink Cadillacs and Buicks and jewelry given by Mary Kay Cosmetics to outstanding salespeople. Mary Kay, with 12,000 cars, has the largest fleet of General Motors cars in the world.[34]

Effective recruitment, selection, training, motivation, and compensation programs combine to create a productive salesforce. Ineffective practices often lead to costly salesforce turnover. The expense of replacing and training a new salesperson, including the cost of lost sales, can be high. Also, new recruits are often less productive than seasoned salespeople.[35]

Salesforce Evaluation: Measuring Results

The final function in the sales management process involves evaluating the salesforce. It is at this point that salespeople are assessed as to whether sales objectives were met and account management policies were followed. Both quantitative and behavioral measures are used to tap different selling dimensions.

Quantitative Assessments Quantitative assessments are based on input- and output-related objectives set forth in the sales plan. Input-related measures focus on the actual activities performed by salespeople such as those involving sales calls, selling expenses, and account management policies. The number of sales calls made, selling expense related to sales made, and the number of reports submitted to superiors are frequently used input measures.

Output measures often appear in a sales quota. A **sales quota** contains specific goals assigned to a salesperson, sales team, branch sales office, or sales district for a stated time period. Dollar or unit sales volume, last year/current year sales ratio, sales of specific products, new accounts generated, and profit achieved are typical goals. The time period can range from one month to one year.

Behavioral Evaluation Behavioral measures are also used to evaluate salespeople. These include assessments of a salesperson's attitude, attention to customers, product knowledge, selling and communication skills, appearance, and professional demeanor. Even though these assessments are sometimes subjective, they are frequently considered and, in fact, inevitable, in salesperson evaluation. Why? These factors are often important determinants of quantitative outcomes.

About 60 percent of U.S. companies now include customer satisfaction as a behavioral measure of salesperson performance. (*What percentage did you check for question 4 in Figure 20–1?*) The relentless focus on customer satisfaction by Eastman Chemical Company salespeople contributed to the company being named a recipient of the prestigious Malcolm Baldrige National Quality Award.[36] Eastman surveys its customers with multiple versions of its customer satisfaction questionnaire delivered in nine languages. Some 25 performance items are studied, including on-time and correct delivery, product quality, pricing practice, and sharing of market information. Salespeople review the results with customers. Eastman salespeople know that "the second most important thing they have to do is get their customer satisfaction

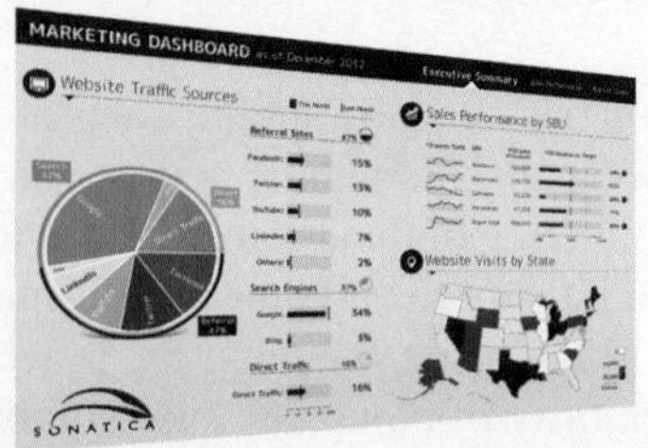

Using Marketing Dashboards

Tracking Salesperson Performance at Moore Chemical & Sanitation Supply, Inc.

Moore Chemical & Sanitation Supply, Inc. (MooreChem) is a large midwestern supplier of cleaning chemicals and sanitary products. MooreChem sells to janitorial companies that clean corporate and professional office buildings.

MooreChem recently installed a sales and account management planning software package that included a dashboard for each of its sales representatives. Salespeople had access to their dashboards as well. These dashboards included seven metrics—sales revenue, gross margin, selling expense, profit, average order size, new customers, and customer satisfaction. Each metric was gauged to show actual salesperson performance relative to target goals.

Your Challenge As a newly promoted district sales manager at MooreChem, your responsibilities include tracking each salesperson's performance in your district. You are also responsible for directing the sales activities and practices of district salespeople.

In anticipation of a performance review with one of your salespeople, Brady Boyle, you review his dashboard for the previous quarter. This information can be used to provide a constructive review of his performance.

Your Findings Brady Boyle's quarterly performance is displayed below. Boyle has exceeded targeted goals for sales revenue, selling expenses, and customer satisfaction. All of these metrics show an upward trend. He has met his target for gaining new customers and average order size. But, Boyle's gross margin and profit are below targeted goals. These metrics evidence a downward trend as well. Brady Boyle's mixed performance requires a constructive and positive correction.

Your Action Brady Boyle should already know how his performance compares with targeted goals. Remember, Boyle has access to his dashboard. Recall that he has exceeded his sales target, but is considerably under his profit target. Boyle's sales trend is up, but his profit trend is down.

You will need to focus attention on Boyle's gross margin and selling expense results and trend. Boyle, it seems, is spending time and money selling lower-margin products that produce a targeted average order size. It may very well be that Boyle is actually expending effort selling more products to his customers. Unfortunately, the product mix yields lower gross margins, resulting in a lower profit.

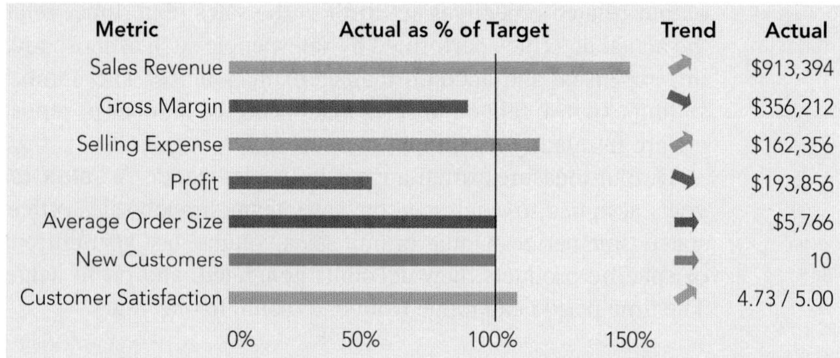

surveys out to and back from customers," says Eastman's sales training director. "Number one, of course, is getting orders."

Increasingly, companies are using marketing dashboards to track salesperson performance for evaluation purposes. An illustration appears in the Using Marketing Dashboards box.

Salesforce Automation and Customer Relationship Management

Personal selling and sales management have undergone a technological revolution with the integration of salesforce automation into customer relationship management processes. In fact, the convergence of computer, information, communication, and

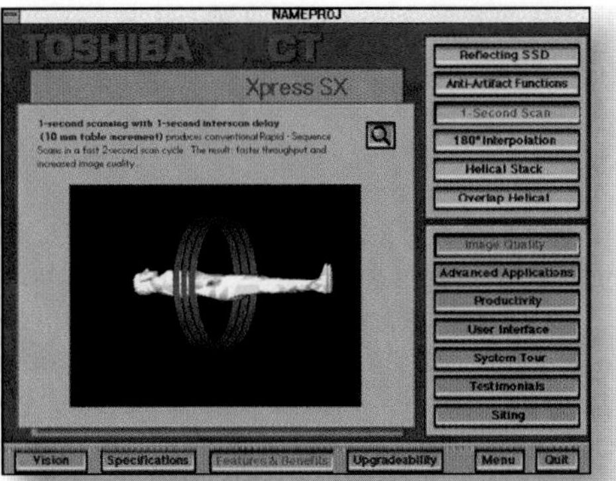

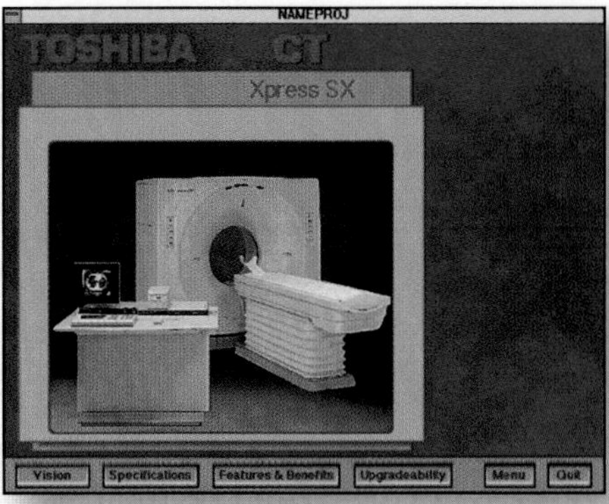

Toshiba America Medical Systems salespeople have found computer technology to be an effective sales presentation tool and training device.

Toshiba America Medical Systems
www.toshiba.com

Internet technologies has transformed the sales function in many companies and made the promise of customer relationship management a reality. **Salesforce automation (SFA)** is the use of these technologies to make the sales function more effective and efficient. SFA applies to a wide range of activities, including each stage in the personal selling process and management of the salesforce itself.[37]

Salesforce automation exists in many forms. Examples of SFA applications include computer hardware and software for account analysis, time management, order processing and follow-up, sales presentations, proposal generation, and product and sales training. Each application is designed to ease administrative tasks and free time for salespeople to be with customers building relationships, designing solutions, and providing service.

Salesforce Technology Technology has become an integral part of field selling. Today, most companies supply their field salespeople with laptop computers. For example, salespeople for Godiva Chocolates use their laptop computers to process orders, plan time allocations, forecast sales, and communicate with Godiva personnel and customers. While in a department store candy buyer's office, such as Neiman Marcus, a salesperson can calculate the order cost (and discount), transmit the order, and obtain a delivery date within minutes from Godiva's order processing department.

Toshiba America Medical Systems salespeople use laptop computers with built-in DVD capabilities to provide interactive presentations for their computerized tomography (CT) and magnetic resonance imaging (MRI) scanners. The computer technology allows the customer to see elaborate three-dimensional animations, high-resolution scans, and video clips of the company's products in operation as well as narrated testimonials from satisfied customers. Toshiba has found this application to be effective both for sales presentations and for training its salespeople.

Salesforce Communication Technology has changed the way salespeople communicate with customers, other salespeople and sales support personnel, and management. Facsimile, electronic mail, and voice mail are common communication technologies used by salespeople today. Mobile phone and tablet device technologies now allow salespeople to exchange data, text, and voice transmissions. Whether traveling or in a customer's office, these technologies provide information at the salesperson's fingertips to answer customer questions and solve problems.

Advances in communication and computer technologies have made possible the mobile and home sales office. Some salespeople now equip minivans with a fully functional desk, swivel chair, light, multifunctional printer, fax machine, mobile phone, and a satellite dish. Jeff Brown, an agent manager with U.S. Cellular, uses such a mobile office. He says, "If I arrive at a prospect's office and they can't see me right away, then I can go outside to work in my office until they're ready to see me."[38]

Home offices are now common. Hewlett-Packard is a case in point. The company shifted its U.S. salesforce into home offices, closed several regional sales offices, and saved millions of dollars in staff salaries and office rent. A fully equipped home office for each salesperson includes a notebook computer, fax/copier, cellular phone, two phone lines, and office furniture.

Perhaps the greatest impact on salesforce communication is the application of Internet technology. Today, salespeople are using their company's intranet for a variety of purposes. At HP Enterprise Services, a professional services firm, salespeople access its intranet to download client material, marketing content, account information, technical papers, and competitive profiles. In addition, HP Enterprise Services offers 7,000 training classes that salespeople can take anytime and anywhere.

Salesforce automation is clearly changing how selling is done and how salespeople are managed. Its numerous applications promise to boost selling productivity, improve customer relationships, and decrease selling cost.

learning review

20-8. What are the three types of selling objectives?

20-9. What three factors are used to structure sales organizations?

20-10. How does emotional intelligence tie to adaptive selling?

LEARNING OBJECTIVES REVIEW

LO 20-1 *Discuss the nature and scope of personal selling and sales management in marketing.*
Personal selling involves the two-way flow of communication between a buyer and seller, often in a face-to-face encounter, designed to influence a person's or group's purchase decision. Sales management involves planning the selling program and implementing and controlling the personal selling effort of the firm. The scope of selling and sales management is apparent in three ways. First, virtually every occupation that involves customer contact has an element of personal selling. Second, selling plays a significant role in a company's overall marketing effort. Salespeople occupy a boundary position between buyers and sellers; they *are* the company to many buyers and account for a major cost of marketing in a variety of industries; and they can create value for customers. Finally, through relationship and partnership selling, salespeople play a central role in tailoring solutions to customer problems as a means to customer value creation.

LO 20-2 *Identify the different types of personal selling.*
Three types of personal selling exist: (*a*) order taking, (*b*) order getting, and (*c*) customer sales support activities. Each type differs from the others in terms of actual selling done and the amount of creativity required to perform the sales task. Order takers process routine orders or reorders for products that were already sold by the company. They generally do little selling in a conventional sense and engage in only modest problem solving with customers. Order getters sell in a conventional sense and identify prospective customers, provide customers with information, persuade customers to buy, close sales, and follow up on customers' use of a product or service. Order getting involves a high degree of creativity and customer empathy and is typically required for selling complex or technical products with many options. Customer sales support personnel augment the sales effort of order getters by performing a variety of services. Sales support personnel are prominent in cross-functional team selling, the practice of using an entire team of professionals in selling to and servicing major customers.

LO 20-3 *Explain the stages in the personal selling process.*
The personal selling process consists of six stages: (*a*) prospecting, (*b*) preapproach, (*c*) approach, (*d*) presentation, (*e*) close, and (*f*) follow-up. Prospecting involves the search for and qualification of potential customers. The preapproach stage involves obtaining further information on the prospect and deciding on the best method of approach. The approach stage involves the initial meeting between the salesperson and prospect. The presentation stage involves converting a prospect into a customer by creating a desire for the product or service. The close involves obtaining a purchase commitment from the prospect. The follow-up stage involves making certain that the customer's purchase has been properly delivered and installed and addressing any difficulties experienced with the use of the item.

LO 20-4 *Describe the major functions of sales management.*
Sales management consists of three interrelated functions: (*a*) sales plan formulation, (*b*) sales plan implementation, and (*c*) salesforce evaluation. Sales plan formulation involves setting objectives, organizing the salesforce, and developing account management policies. Sales plan implementation involves salesforce recruitment, selection, training, motivation, and compensation. Finally, salesforce evaluation focuses on quantitative assessments of sales performance and behavioral measures such as customer satisfaction that are linked to selling objectives and account management policies.

FOCUSING ON KEY TERMS

account management policies p. 548
adaptive selling p. 542
consultative selling p. 542
emotional intelligence p. 549
formula selling presentation p. 541
key account management p. 547
need-satisfaction presentation p. 542
order getter p. 536
order taker p. 535
partnership selling p. 534
personal selling p. 532
personal selling process p. 538
relationship selling p. 534
sales management p. 532
sales plan p. 545
sales quota p. 551
salesforce automation (SFA) p. 553
stimulus-response presentation p. 541
team selling p. 537
workload method p. 547

APPLYING MARKETING KNOWLEDGE

1 Jane Dawson is a new sales representative for the Charles Schwab brokerage firm. In searching for clients, Jane purchased a mailing list of subscribers to *The Wall Street Journal* and called them all regarding their interest in discount brokerage services. She asked if they have any stocks and if they have a regular broker. Those people without a regular broker were asked their investment needs. Two days later, Jane called back with investment advice and asked if they would like to open an account. Identify each of Jane Dawson's actions in terms of the personal selling process.

2 For the first 50 years of business, the Johnson Carpet Company produced carpets for residential use. The salesforce was structured geographically. In the past five years, a large percentage of carpet sales have been to industrial users, hospitals, schools, and architects. The company also has broadened its product line to include area rugs, Oriental carpets, and wall-to-wall carpeting. Is the present salesforce structure appropriate, or would you recommend an alternative?

3 Where would you place each of the following sales jobs on the order-taker/order-getter continuum shown below? (*a*) Burger King counter clerk, (*b*) automobile insurance salesperson, (*c*) Hewlett-Packard computer salesperson, (*d*) life insurance salesperson, and (*e*) shoe salesperson.

Order taker —————————————— Order getter

4 Listed here are two different firms. Which compensation plan would you recommend for each firm, and what reasons would you give for your recommendations? (*a*) A newly formed company that sells lawn care equipment on a door-to-door basis directly to consumers; and (*b*) the Nabisco Company, which sells heavily advertised products in supermarkets by having the salesforce call on these stores and arrange shelves, set up displays, and make presentations to store buying committees.

5 Tyler Automotive, Inc., supplies 1,000 independent auto parts stores throughout the United States. Each store is called on 12 times a year, and the average sales call lasts 30 minutes. Assuming a salesperson works 40 hours a week, 50 weeks a year, and devotes 75 percent of the time to actual selling, how many salespeople does Tyler Automotive need?

6 A furniture manufacturer is currently using manufacturer's representatives to sell its line of living room furniture. These representatives receive an 8 percent commission. The company is considering hiring its own salespeople and has estimated that the fixed cost of managing and paying their salaries would be $1 million annually. The salespeople would also receive a 4 percent commission on sales. The company has sales of $25 million, and sales are expected to grow by 15 percent next year. Would you recommend that the company switch to its own salesforce? Why or why not?

7 Suppose someone said to you, "The only real measure of a salesperson is the amount of sales produced." How might you respond?

BUILDING YOUR MARKETING PLAN

Does your marketing plan involve a personal selling activity? If the answer is "no," read no further and do not include a personal selling element in your plan. If the answer is "yes":

1 Identify the likely prospects for your product or service.

2 Determine what information you should obtain about the prospect.

3 Describe how you would approach the prospect.

4 Outline the presentation you would make to the prospect for your product or service.

5 Develop a sales plan, focusing on the organizational structure you would use for your salesforce (geographic, product, or customer).

VIDEO CASE 20 Xerox: Building Customer Relationships through Personal Selling

QR 20-2
Xerox Video
Case

"I'm like the quarterback of the team. I manage 250 accounts, and anything from billing issues, to service issues, to selling the products. I'm really the face to the customer," says Alison Capossela, a Washington, DC–based Xerox sales representative.

As the primary company contact for Xerox customers, Alison is responsible for developing and maintaining customer relationships. To accomplish this she uses a sophisticated selling process that requires many activities from making presentations, to attending training sessions, to managing a team of Xerox personnel, to monitoring competitors' activities. The face-to-face interactions with customers, however, are the most rewarding for Capossela. "It's an amazing feeling; the more they challenge me the more I fight back. It's fun!" she explains.

THE COMPANY

Xerox Corporation's mission is to "help people find better ways to do great work by constantly leading in document technologies, products, and services that improve customers' work processes and business results." To accomplish this mission Xerox employs 130,000 people in 160 countries. Xerox is the world's leading document management enterprise and a *Fortune* 500 company.

Xerox offers a wide range of products and services. These include printers, copiers and fax machines, multifunction and network devices, high-speed color presses, digital imaging and archiving products and services, and supplies such as toner, paper, and ink. The entire company is guided by customer-focused and employee-centered core values (e.g., "We succeed through satisfied customers") and a passion for innovation, speed, and adaptability.

THE SELLING PROCESS AT XEROX

In 2001, Xerox began a shift to a consultative selling model that focused on helping customers solve their business problems rather than just placing more equipment in their office. The shift meant that sales reps needed to be less product-oriented and more relationship- and value-oriented. Xerox wanted to be a provider of total solutions.

Today, Xerox has more than 8,000 sales professionals throughout the world who spend a large amount of their day developing customer relationships. Capossela explains: "Fifty percent of my day is spent with my customers, 25 percent is following up with phone calls or e-mails, and another 25 percent involves preparing proposals." The approach has helped Xerox attract new customers and keep existing customers.

The sales process at Xerox typically follows the six stages of the personal selling process identified in Figure 20–3: (1) Xerox identifies potential clients through responses to advertising, referrals, and telephone calls; (2) the salesforce prepares for a presentation by familiarizing themselves with the potential client and its document needs; (3) a Xerox sales representative approaches the prospect and suggests a meeting and presentation; (4) as the presentation begins, the salesperson summarizes relevant information about potential solutions Xerox can offer, states what he or she hopes to get out of the meeting, explains how the products and services work, and reinforces the benefits of working with Xerox; (5) the salesperson engages in an action close (gets a signed document or a firm confirmation of the sale); and then (6) continues to meet and communicate with the client to provide assistance and monitor the effectiveness of the installed solution.

Xerox sales representatives also use the selling process to maintain relationships with existing customers. In today's competitive environment it is not unusual to have customers who have been approached by competitors or who are required to obtain more than one bid before renewing a contract. Xerox has teams of people who collect and analyze information about competitors and their products. The information is sent out to sales reps or offered to them through workshops and seminars. The most difficult competitors are the ones that have also invested in customer relationships. The selling process allows Xerox to continually react and respond to new information and take advantage of opportunities in the marketplace.

THE SALES MANAGEMENT PROCESS AT XEROX

The Xerox salesforce is divided into four geographic organizations: North America, which includes the United States and Canada; Europe, which includes 17 countries; Global Accounts, which manages large accounts that operate in multiple locations; and Developing Markets, which includes all other geographic territories that may require Xerox products and services. Within each geographic area, the majority of Xerox products and services are typically sold through its direct salesforce.

Xerox also utilizes a variety of other channels, including value-added resellers, independent agents, dealers, systems integrators, telephone, and Internet sales channels.

Motivation and compensation are important aspects of any salesforce. At Xerox there is a passion for winning that provides a key incentive for sales reps. Compensation also plays an important role. In addition, Xerox has a recognition program called the President's Club where the top performers are awarded a five-day trip to one of the top resorts in the world. The program has been a huge success and has now been offered for more than 30 years.

Perhaps the most well-known component of Xerox's sales management process is its sales representative recruitment and training program. "For recruitment, Xerox looks for seasoned businesspeople who can talk to customers," says Kevin Warren, president of United States customer operations at Xerox. "Our value proposition is that we take care of document management to help run your business," Warren explains. "So we look for consultative and business-savvy salespeople."

On the training front, Xerox developed the "Create and Win" program to help sales reps learn the consultative selling approach. The components of the program consist of interactive training sessions and distance-learning webinars. Every new sales representative at Xerox receives eight weeks of training development in the field and at the Xerox Corporate University in Virginia. "The training program is phenomenal!" according to Capossela. The training and its focus on the customer is part of the Xerox culture outside of the sales organization also. Every senior executive at Xerox is responsible for working with at least one customer. They also spend a full day every month responding to incoming customer calls and inquiries.

WHAT IS IN THE FUTURE FOR THE XEROX SALESFORCE?

The recent growth and success at Xerox is creating many opportunities for the company and its sales representatives. For example, Xerox is accelerating the development of its top salespeople. Mentors are used to provide advice for day-to-day issues and long-term career planning. In addition, globalization has become such an important initiative at Xerox that experienced and successful sales representatives are quickly given opportunities to manage large global accounts.

Xerox is also moving toward an approach that empowers sales representatives to make decisions about how to handle accounts. The large number of Xerox customers means there are a variety of different corporate styles, and the sales reps are increasingly the best qualified to manage the relationship. This approach is just one more example of Xerox's commitment to customers and creating customer value.

Questions

1 How does Xerox create customer value through its personal selling process?

2 How does Alison Capossela provide solutions for Xerox customers?

3 Why is the Xerox training program so important to the company's success?

21 Implementing Interactive and Multichannel Marketing

Learning Objectives

After reading this chapter you should be able to:

 LO 21-1 Describe what interactive marketing is and how it creates customer value, customer relationships, and customer experiences.

 LO 21-2 Identify the demographic and lifestyle profile of online consumers.

 LO 21-3 Explain why certain types of products and services are particularly suited for interactive marketing.

 LO 21-4 Describe why consumers shop and buy online and how marketers influence online purchasing behavior.

 LO 21-5 Define cross-channel shoppers and the role of transactional and promotional websites in reaching these shoppers.

Seven Cycles Delivers Just One Bike. Yours.

"One Bike. Yours." is the company tagline for Seven Cycles, Inc., located in Watertown, Massachusetts. And for good reason.

Seven Cycles is the world's largest custom bicycle frame builder. The company produces a broad range of road, mountain, cyclocross, tandem, touring, single-speed, and commuter bikes annually, and no two bikes are exactly alike.

At Seven Cycles, attention is focused on each customer's unique cycling experience through the optimum fit, function, performance, and comfort of his or her very own bike. According to one satisfied customer, "Getting a Seven is more of a creation than a purchase."

While Seven Cycles does offer stock frames in more than 200 sizes, each is still built-to-order and a full 95 percent of the bicycle frames that Seven ships are completely custom made. Customized elements include frame size, frame geometry, tubing diameters, and wall thickness, as well as countless options such as cable routing, water bottle mounts, paint color, and decal color. Every custom option is available at no additional charge and the number of combinations is virtually infinite.

The marketing success of Seven Cycles is due to its state-of-the-art bicycle frames. But as Rob Vandermark, company founder and president, says, "Part of our success is that we are tied to a business model that includes the Internet."

Seven uses its multilanguage (English, German, Chinese, Japanese, Korean, and Flemish) website (www.sevencycles.com) to let customers get deeply involved in the frame-building process and the selection of components to outfit their complete bike. It enables customers to collaborate on the design of their own bike using the company's Custom Kit fitting system, which considers the rider's size, aspirations, and riding habits. Then customers can monitor their bike's progress through the development and production process by clicking "Where's My Frame?" on the Seven Cycles website.

This customization process and continuous feedback make for a collaborative relationship between Seven Cycles, its nearly 200 authorized retailers in the United States, some 30 international distributors, and customers in 40 countries. "Our whole process is designed to keep the focus on the rider the bike is being built for, so it ends up being a very different and more interactive experience than most people

seven cycles

are used to. That experience is a large part of the value we sell, above and beyond the bike," explains Jennifer Miller, operations manager at Seven Cycles.

In addition to the order process, website visitors can peruse weekly news stories and learn about new product introductions to get a unique perspective on the business. They can read employee biographies online to learn more about the people who build the bikes. The website also offers a retailer-specific section as a 24/7 repository of updated information for the company's channel partners.

Beyond the website, current Seven owners can interact with the company on the Seven Cycles blog to learn about its activities and products. Seven Cycles also uses its company Facebook Page and Twitter account to post brief and timely updates and build a stronger sense of community around the brand.[1]

This chapter describes how companies design and implement interactive marketing programs. It begins by explaining how Internet technology can create customer value, build customer relationships, and produce customer experiences in novel ways. Next, it describes how Internet technology affects and is affected by consumer behavior and marketing practice. Finally, the chapter shows how marketers integrate and leverage their communication and delivery channels using Internet technology to implement multichannel marketing programs to better serve cross-channel shoppers.

CREATING CUSTOMER VALUE, RELATIONSHIPS, AND EXPERIENCES IN MARKETSPACE

LO 21-1 Describe what interactive marketing is and how it creates customer value, customer relationships, and customer experiences.

Consumers and companies populate two market environments today. One is the traditional *marketplace*. Here buyers and sellers engage in face-to-face exchange relationships in a material environment characterized by physical facilities (stores and offices) and mostly tangible objects. The other is the *marketspace*, an Internet-enabled digital environment characterized by face-to-screen exchange relationships and electronic images and offerings.

The existence of two market environments has been a boon for consumers. Today, consumers can shop for and purchase a wide variety of products and services in either market environment. Actually, many consumers now browse and buy in both market environments. More are expected to do so in the future as mobile devices, notably smartphones, expand their capabilities.

Figure 21–1 shows the growth in online shoppers and estimated retail sales in the United States since 2011. About 90 percent of Internet users ages 15 and older shop online in the United States. They are expected to buy $327 billion worth of products and services in 2016 (excluding travel, automobile, and prescription drugs).[2]

Marketing in two market environments poses significant challenges for companies. Companies with origins in the traditional marketplace, such as Procter & Gamble, Walmart, and General Motors, are continually challenged to define the nature and scope of their marketspace presence. These companies consistently refine the role of Internet technology in attracting, retaining, and building consumer relationships to improve their competitive positions in the traditional marketplace while also bolstering their marketspace presence.

On the other hand, companies with marketspace origins, including Amazon.com, Google, eBay, E*TRADE, and others, are challenged to continually refine, broaden, and deepen their marketspace presence. At the same time, these companies must consider what role, if any, the traditional marketplace will play in their future. Regardless of origin, a company's success in achieving a meaningful marketspace presence hinges largely on its ability to design and execute a marketing program that capitalizes on the unique value-creation and relationship-building capabilities of Internet technology in delivering a favorable customer experience.[3]

Customer Value Creation in Marketspace

Why has the marketspace captured the eye and imagination of marketers worldwide? Recall from Chapter 1 that marketing creates time, place, form, and possession

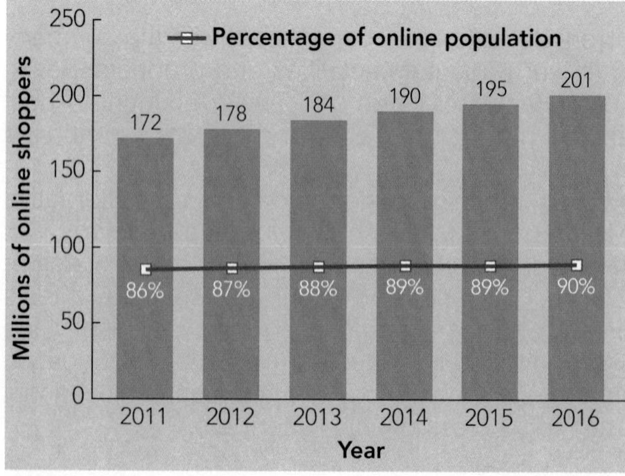

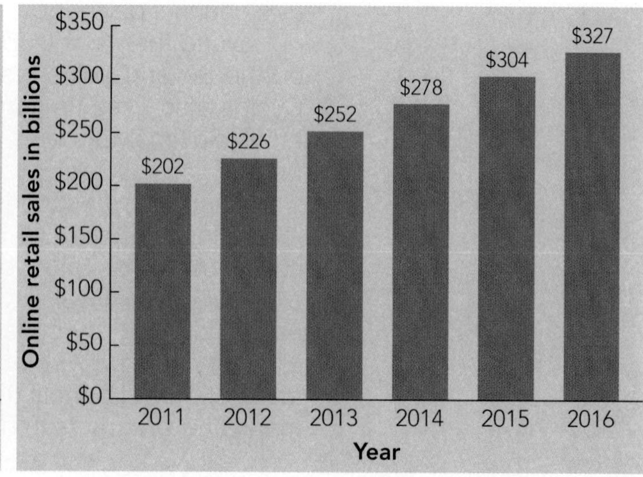

FIGURE 21–1 Trends in online shoppers and online retail sales revenue in the United States.

utilities, thereby providing value. Marketers believe that the possibilities for customer value creation are greater in the digital marketspace than in the physical marketplace.

Consider place and time utility. In marketspace, the provision of direct, on-demand information is possible from marketers *anywhere* to customers *anywhere, at any time*. Why? Operating hours and geographical constraints do not exist in marketspace. For example, Recreational Equipment, Inc. (www.rei.com), an outdoor gear marketer, reports that 35 percent of its orders are placed between 10:00 P.M. and 7:00 A.M., long after and before retail stores are open for business. Similarly, a U.S. consumer from Chicago can access Marks & Spencer (www.marks-and-spencer.co.uk), the well-known British department store, to shop for clothing as easily as a person living near London's Piccadilly Square.

Possession utility—getting a product or service to consumers so they can own or use it—is accelerated. Airline, car rental, and lodging electronic reservation systems such as Orbitz (www.orbitz.com) allow comparison shopping for the lowest fares, rents, and rates and almost immediate access to and confirmation of travel arrangements and accommodations.

The greatest marketspace opportunity for marketers, however, lies in its potential for creating form utility. Interactive two-way Internet-enabled communication capabilities in marketspace invite consumers to tell marketers specifically what their requirements are, making customization of a product or service to fit their exact needs possible. Today, 35 percent of online consumers are interested in customizing product features or in purchasing build-to-order products that use their specifications.[4] At Seven Cycles, customers can arrange for a custom-made mountain bike to fit their specifications, as described in the chapter-opening example.

Seven Cycles offers form utility by creating customized bikes for customers in 40 countries.

Seven Cycles, Inc.
www.sevencycles.com

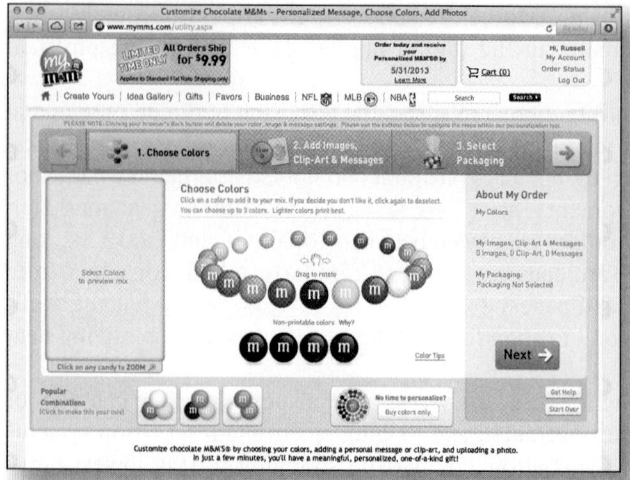

Mars, Inc., uses choiceboard technology to decorate M&M's® candies with personal photos and messages.

Mars, Inc.
www.mymms.com

Interactivity, Individuality, and Customer Relationships in Marketspace

Marketers also benefit from two unique capabilities of Internet technology that promote and sustain customer relationships. One is *interactivity*; the other is *individuality*.[5] Both capabilities are important building blocks for buyer–seller relationships. For these relationships to occur, companies need to interact with their customers by listening and responding to their needs. Marketers must also treat customers as individuals and empower them to (1) influence the timing and extent of the buyer–seller interaction and (2) have a say in the kind of products and services they buy, the information they receive, and in some cases, the prices they pay.

Internet technology allows for interaction, individualization, and customer relationship building to be carried out on a scale never before available and makes interactive marketing possible. **Interactive marketing** involves two-way buyer–seller electronic communication in a computer-mediated environment in which the buyer controls the kind and amount of information received from the seller. Interactive marketing is characterized by sophisticated choiceboard and personalization systems that transform information supplied by customers into customized responses to their individual needs.

Choiceboards A **choiceboard** is an interactive, Internet-enabled system that allows individual customers to design their own products and services by answering a few questions and choosing from a menu of product or service attributes (or components), prices, and delivery options. Customers today can design their own computers with Dell's online configurator, style their own athletic shoe at www.reebok.com, assemble their own investment portfolios with Schwab's mutual fund evaluator, build their own bicycle at www.sevencycles.com, create a diet and fitness program to fit their lifestyle at www.ediet.com, and decorate M&M's® with photos of themselves and unique messages at www.mymms.com. Because choiceboards collect precise information about the preferences and behavior of individual buyers, a company becomes more knowledgeable about a customer and better able to anticipate and fulfill that customer's needs.

QR 21-1
My M&M's®
Video

Most choiceboards are essentially transaction devices. However, companies have expanded the functionality of choiceboards using collaborative filtering technology. **Collaborative filtering** is a process that automatically groups people with similar buying intentions, preferences, and behaviors and predicts future purchases.[6] For example, say two people who have never met buy a few of the same DVDs over time. Collaborative filtering software is programmed to reason that these two buyers might have similar musical tastes: If one buyer likes a particular DVD, then the other will like it as well. The outcome? Collaborative filtering gives marketers the ability to make a dead-on sales recommendation to a buyer in *real time*. You see collaborative filtering applied each time you view a selection at Amazon.com and see "Customers who bought this (item) also bought. . . ."

Personalization Choiceboards and collaborative filtering are marketer-initiated efforts to provide customized responses to the needs of individual buyers. Personalization systems are typically buyer-initiated efforts. **Personalization** is the consumer-initiated practice of generating content on a marketer's website that is custom tailored to an individual's specific needs and preferences.

Today, one-half of the largest online retailers in the United States use personalization techniques.[7] For example, Yahoo! (www.yahoo.com) allows users to create personalized

Reebok uses choiceboard technology to create customized athletic shoes for its customers.

Reebok
www.reebok.com

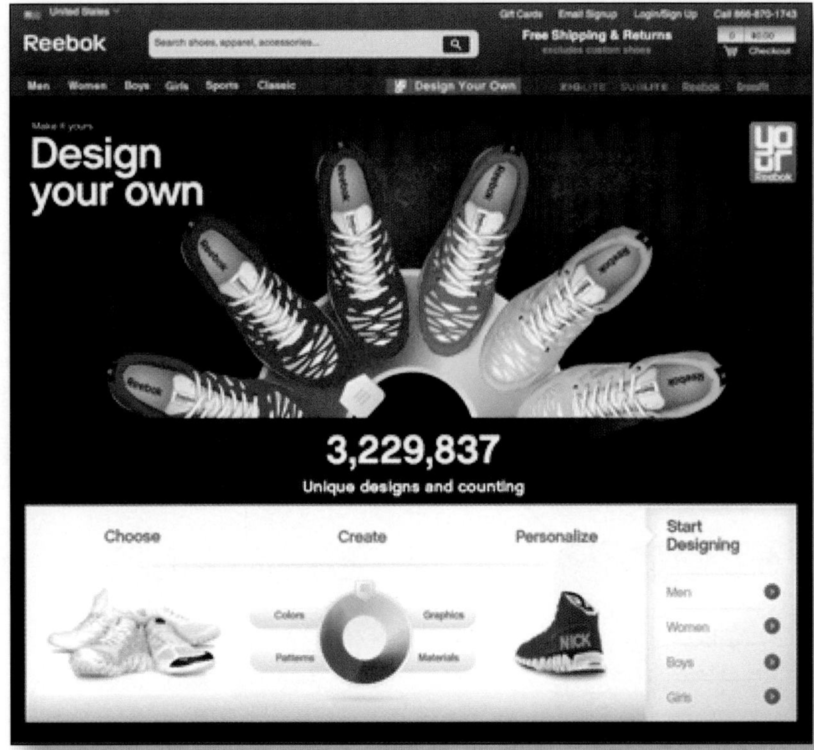

MyYahoo! pages. Users can add or delete a variety of types of information from their personal pages, including specific stock quotes, weather conditions in any city in the world, and local television schedules. In turn, Yahoo! uses the buyer profile data entered when users register at the site to tailor e-mail messages, advertising, and content to the individual—and post a happy birthday greeting on the user's special day.

An important aspect of personalization is a buyer's willingness to have tailored communications brought to his or her attention. Obtaining this approval is called **permission marketing**—the solicitation of a consumer's consent (called *opt-in*) to receive e-mail and advertising based on personal data supplied by the consumer. Permission marketing is a proven vehicle for building and maintaining customer relationships, provided it is properly used.

Companies that successfully employ permission marketing adhere to three rules.[8] First, they make sure opt-in customers receive only information that is relevant and meaningful to them. Second, their customers are given the option to *opt-out*, or change the kind, amount, or timing of information sent to them. Finally, their customers are assured that their name or buyer profile data will not be sold or shared with others. This assurance is important because 76 percent of adult Internet users are concerned about the privacy of their personal information.[9]

Creating an Online Customer Experience

A continuing challenge for companies is the design and execution of marketing programs that capitalize on the unique customer value-creation capabilities of Internet technology. Companies realize that applying Internet technology to create time, place, form, and possession utility is just a starting point for creating a meaningful marketspace presence. Today, the quality of the customer experience produced by a company is the standard by which a meaningful marketspace presence is measured.

From an interactive marketing perspective, *customer experience* is defined as the sum total of the interactions that a customer has with a company's website, from the

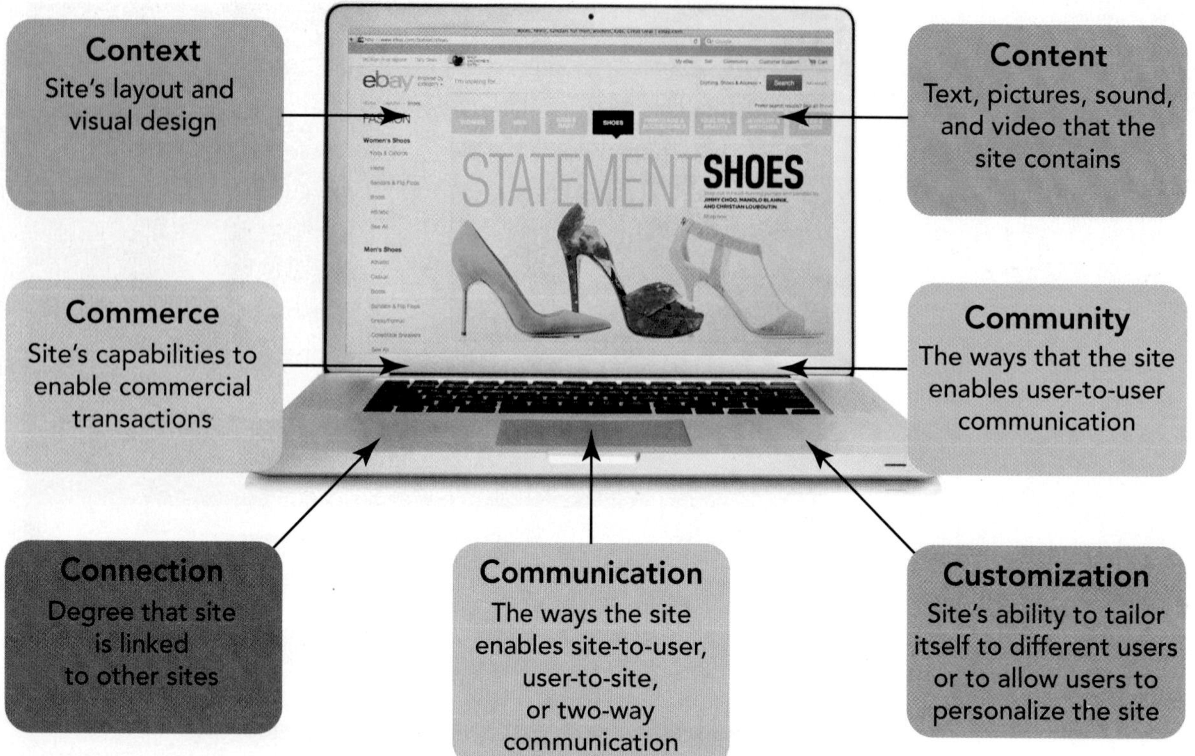

FIGURE 21–2
Seven website design elements that drive customer experience.

initial look at a home page through the entire purchase decision process.[10] Companies produce a customer experience through seven website design elements. These elements are context, content, community, customization, communication, connection, and commerce. Each is summarized in Figure 21–2. A closer look at these elements illustrates how each contributes to customer experience.

Context *Context* refers to a website's aesthetic appeal and the functional look and feel of the site's layout and visual design. A functionally oriented website focuses largely on the company's offering, be it products, services, or information. Deal-oriented travel websites, such as Priceline.com, tend to be functionally oriented with an emphasis on destinations, scheduling, and prices. In contrast, beauty websites, such as Revlon.com, are more aesthetically oriented. As these examples suggest, context attempts to convey the core consumer benefit provided by the company's offerings.

Content *Content* applies to all digital information on a website, including the presentation form—text, video, audio, and graphics. Content quality and presentation along with context dimensions combine to engage a website visitor and provide a platform for the five remaining design elements.

Customization Website *customization* is the ability of a site to modify itself to, or be modified by and for, each individual user. This design element is prominent in websites that offer personalized content, such as My eBay and MyYahoo!

Connection The *connection* element is the network of linkages between a company's site and other sites. These links are embedded in the website; appear as highlighted words, a picture, or graphic; and allow a user to effortlessly visit other sites with a mouse click. Connection is a major design element for informational websites such as *The New York Times*. Users of NYTimes.com can access the book

Travelocity pays close attention to creating a favorable customer experience by employing all seven website design elements.

Travelocity
www.travelocity.com

review section and link to Barnes & Noble to order a book or browse related titles without ever visiting a store.

Communication *Communication* refers to the dialogue that unfolds between the website and its users. Consumers—particularly those who have registered at a site—now expect that communication to be interactive and individualized in real time much like a personal conversation. In fact, some websites now enable a user to talk directly with a customer representative while shopping the site. For example, two-thirds of the sales through Dell.com involve human sales representatives.

Community In addition, many company websites encourage user-to-user communications hosted by the company to create virtual communities, or simply, *community*. This design element is popular because it has been shown to enhance customer experience and build favorable buyer–seller relationships. Examples of communities range from the Pampers Village hosted by Procter & Gamble (www.pampers.com) to the Harley Owners Group (HOG) sponsored by Harley-Davidson (www.harley-davidson.com).

Commerce The seventh design element is *commerce*—the website's ability to conduct sales transactions for products and services. Online transactions are quick and simple in well-designed websites. Amazon.com has mastered this design element with "one-click shopping," a patented feature that allows users to order products with a single mouse click.

Most websites do not include every design element. Although every website has context and content, they differ in the use of the remaining five elements. Why? Websites have different purposes. For example, only websites that emphasize the actual sale of products and services include the commerce element. Websites that are used primarily for advertising and promotion purposes emphasize the communication element. The difference between these two types of websites is discussed later in the chapter in the description of multichannel marketing.

Companies use a broad array of measures to assess website performance. For example, the amount of time per month visitors spend on their website, or "stickiness," is used to gauge customer experience.[11] Read the Using Marketing Dashboards box on the next page to learn how stickiness is measured and interpreted at one of the largest automobile dealerships in the United States.

learning review

21-1. The consumer-initiated practice of generating content on a marketer's website that is custom tailored to an individual's specific needs and preferences is called ____________.

21-2. What are the seven website design elements that companies use to produce a customer experience?

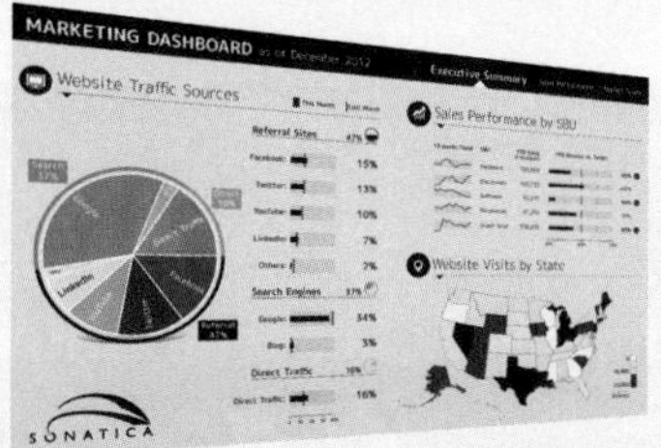

Using Marketing Dashboards

Sizing Up Site Stickiness at Sewell Automotive Companies

Automobile dealerships have invested significant time, effort, and money in their websites. Why? Car browsing and shopping on the Internet is now commonplace.

Dealerships commonly measure website performance by tracking visits, visitor traffic, and "stickiness"—the amount of time per month visitors spend on their website. Website design, easy navigation, involving content, and visual appeal combine to enhance the interactive customer experience and website stickiness.

To gauge stickiness, companies monitor the average time spent per unique monthly visitor (in minutes) on their websites. This is done by tracking and displaying the average visits per unique monthly visitor and the average time spent per visit, in minutes, in their marketing dashboards. The relationship is as follows:

Average Time Spent per Unique Monthly Visitor (minutes) =

$$\left(\text{Average Visits per Unique Monthly Visitor}\right) \times \left(\text{Average Time Spent per Visit (minutes)}\right)$$

Your Challenge As the manager responsible for Sewell.com, the Sewell Automotive Companies's website, you have been asked to report on the effect that recent improvements in the company's website have had on the amount of time per month visitors spend on the website. Sewell ranks among the largest U.S. automotive dealerships and is a recognized customer service leader in the automotive industry. Its website reflects the company's commitment to an unparalleled customer experience at its family of dealerships.

Your Findings Examples of monthly marketing dashboard traffic and time measures are displayed below for June 2008, three months before the website improvements (green arrow), and June 2009, three months after the improvements were made (red arrow).

The average time spent per unique monthly visitor increased from 8.5 minutes in June 2008 to 11.9 minutes in June 2009—a sizable jump. The increase is due primarily to the upturn in the average time spent per visit from 7.1 minutes to 8.5 minutes. The average number of visits also increased, but the percentage change was much less.

Your Action Improvements in the website have noticeably "moved the needle" on average time spent per unique monthly visitor. Still, additional action may be required to increase average visits per unique monthly visitor. These actions might include an analysis of Sewell's web advertising program, search engine initiatives with Google, links to automobile manufacturer corporate websites, and broader print and electronic media advertising.

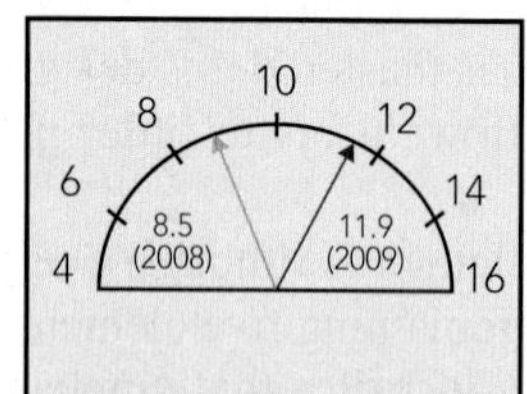

Average Time Spent per Unique Monthly Visitor (minutes)

=

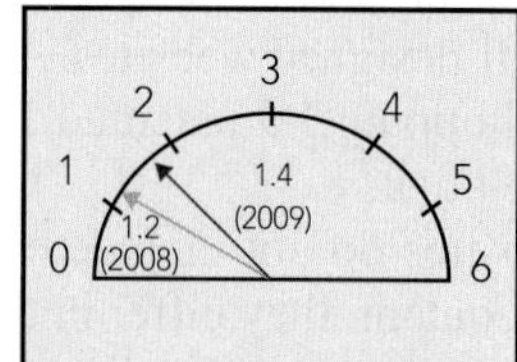

Average Visits per Unique Monthly Visitor

×

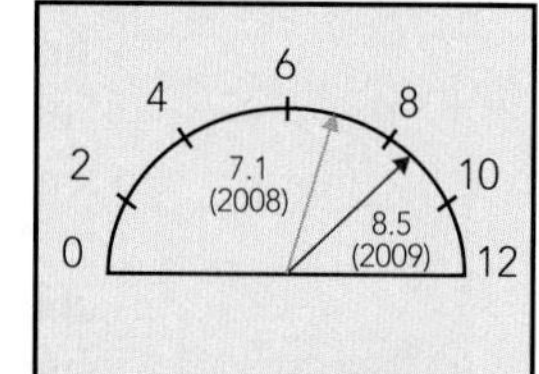

Average Time Spent per Visit (minutes)

ONLINE CONSUMER BEHAVIOR AND MARKETING PRACTICE IN MARKETSPACE

Who are online consumers, and what do they buy? Why do they choose to shop and purchase products and services in the digital marketspace rather than (or in addition to) the traditional marketplace? Answers to these questions have a direct bearing on marketspace marketing practices.

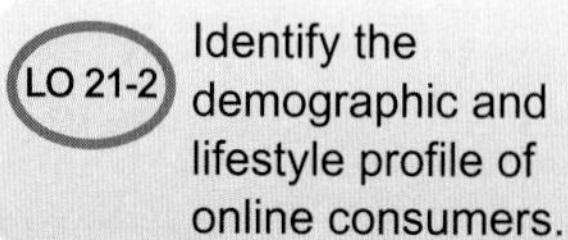

LO 21-2
Identify the demographic and lifestyle profile of online consumers.

Who Is the Online Consumer?

Many labels are given to online consumers—cybershoppers, Netizens, and e-shoppers—suggesting they are a homogeneous segment of the population. They are not, but as a group, they do differ demographically from the general population.

Marketing inSite

Are You a Roving Node, a Mobile Newbie, or a Drifting Surfer?

Consumers differ in their use of information and communication technology. With that in mind, the researchers at the Pew Internet & American Life Project conducted a survey of adults ages 18 and older to classify people into different groups of information and communication technology users. Nine unique groups were identified and labeled with names such as Roving Node, Mobile Newbie, and Drifting Surfer.

Which group best describes you? To find out, simply go to www.pewinternet.org, click "Participate," and then click "What Kind of Tech User Are You?" Answer the 14 questions and then press the "What Kind of User Am I?" button. You will be told the group into which you fit, along with a description of the general characteristics of that group. Do you agree with the quiz results?

Profiling the Online Consumer Online consumers differ from the general population in one important respect. They own or have access to a personal computer or an Internet-enabled mobile device, such as a smartphone.

Online consumers are the subsegment of all Internet users who employ this technology to research products and services and make purchases. As a group, online consumers are equally likely to be women and men, and they tend to be better educated, younger, and more affluent than the general U.S. population.[12] This makes them an attractive market. Even though online shopping and buying is popular, a small percentage of online consumers still account for a disproportionate share of online retail sales in the United States. It is estimated that 20 percent of online consumers account for 69 percent of total consumer online sales. Also, women tend to purchase more products and services online than men.[13]

In general, online consumers also tend to use a range of information and communication technology as a platform to express themselves online and engage with the digital marketspace. Research sponsored by the Pew Internet & American Life Project has categorized information and communication technology users into nine groups based on their use of devices to connect to the Internet, the activities they engage in, and their attitudes toward the marketspace. To learn which group you fall into, take the quiz described in the Marketing inSite box.

Online Consumer Lifestyle Segmentation Not all Internet users use the technology the same way, nor are they likely to be exclusive online consumers. Numerous marketing research firms have studied the lifestyles and shopping and spending habits of online consumers. A recurrent insight is that online consumers are diverse and represent different kinds of people seeking different kinds of online experiences. As an illustration, Harris Interactive, a large U.S. research firm, has identified six distinct online consumer lifestyle segments.[14]

The largest online consumer lifestyle segment, called *click-and-mortar*, consists of women who tend to browse retailer websites but actually buy products in traditional retail outlets. They make up 23 percent of online consumers and represent an important segment for multichannel retailers that also feature catalog and store operations, such as J. Crew.

Twenty percent of online consumers are *hunter-gatherers*—married couples with children at home who use the Internet like a consumer magazine to gather information and compare products and prices. They can be found visiting comparison shopping websites such as DealCatcher.com and mySimon.com on a regular basis. The Marketing Matters box on the next page provides an in-depth look at today's "Internet mom."[15]

Nineteen percent of online consumers are *brand loyalists* who regularly visit their favorite bookmarked websites and spend the most money online. They are better-educated

Marketing Matters

technology

Meet Today's Internet Mom on a Mission

Do you have fond childhood memories of surfing the Internet with your mother?

Research indicates that 95 percent of mothers with children under 18 years old will be online regularly by 2015. Internet moms are typically 38 years old. They tend to be married, college educated, and work outside the home.

Results from a recent Disney Online M.O.M.—Mom on a Mission—study show how today's mother uses the Internet. Consider that:

1. Internet moms spend the most time online between the hours of 5 A.M. and noon.
2. Seventy-five percent of moms go online with a specific task or goal in mind. They are not surfers.
3. Moms spend an average of 6.9 hours per week online connecting with family and friends: 84 percent stay connected through e-mail and 69 percent through social networks.
4. For subjects other than their child's health, moms turn to the Internet as their primary source of information about: (a) shopping deals or discounts; (b) cooking/baking recipes and nutrition/dieting; (c) family activities, entertainment, and travel; (d) holiday planning and activities; (e) beauty/style suggestions; and (f) financial planning.

According to a Disney Online spokesperson, "Moms juggle so many roles, from being the caregiver and household CEO, to coordinating the family's activities. Our study results showed that the Internet is helping to make moms' lives more manageable, so they can spend more quality time with their families."

and more affluent Internet users who effortlessly navigate familiar and trusted websites and enjoy the online browsing and buying experience.

Next there are *time-sensitive materialists* who regard the Internet as a convenience tool for buying music, books, computer software, and electronics. They account for 17 percent of online consumers and can be found visiting Amazon.com and Dell.com.

The *hooked, online, and single* segment consists of young, affluent, and single online consumers who bank, play games, and spend more time online than any other segment. They make up 16 percent of online consumers, enjoy auction websites such as eBay, and visit game websites like Slingo.com and Jigzone.com.

Five percent of online consumers are the *e-bivalent newbies*—relative newcomers to the Internet who rarely spend money online but seek product information. Do any of these segments describe your online lifestyle and spending habits?

What Online Consumers Buy

LO 21-3 Explain why certain types of products and services are particularly suited for interactive marketing.

Much still needs to be learned about online consumer purchase behavior. Although research has documented the most frequently purchased products and services bought online, marketers also need to know *why* these items are popular in the digital marketspace.

Five general product and service categories account for about two-thirds of online consumer buying today and for the foreseeable future, as shown in Figure 21–3.[16] One category consists of items for which product information is an important part of the purchase decision, but prepurchase trial is not necessarily critical. Items such as computers, computer accessories, and consumer electronics fall into this category. So

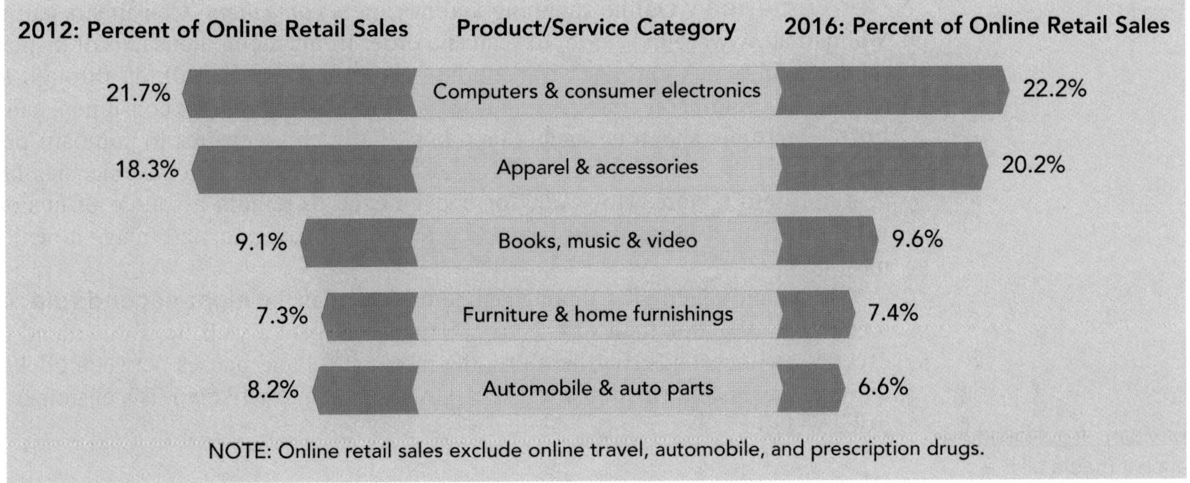

FIGURE 21–3
Five product categories account for about two-thirds of online retail sales today—a trend that is projected to continue in the future.

do books. Booksellers like Barnes & Noble publish short reviews of new books that visitors to their websites can read before making a purchase decision.

A second category includes items for which audio or video demonstration is important. The third category contains items that can be delivered digitally, including computer software, music, and video.

Unique items, such as specialty products, foods, beverages, and gifts, represent a fourth category. A fifth category includes items that are regularly purchased and where convenience is very important. Many consumer packaged goods, such as grocery products, personal care items, and office products, fall into this category. A final category of items consists of highly standardized products and services for which information about price is important. Certain kinds of home and automotive products, casual apparel, and toys make up this category.

LO 21-4 Describe why consumers shop and buy online and how marketers influence online purchasing behavior.

Why Consumers Shop and Buy Online

Why do consumers shop and buy online? Marketers emphasize the customer value-creation possibilities, the importance of interactivity, individuality, and relationship building, and their ability to produce a positive customer experience in the new marketspace. However, consumers typically refer to six reasons they shop and buy online: convenience, choice, customization, communication, cost, and control (Figure 21–4).

FIGURE 21–4
Why do consumers shop and buy online? Read the text to learn how convenience, choice, customization, communication, cost, and control result in a favorable customer experience.

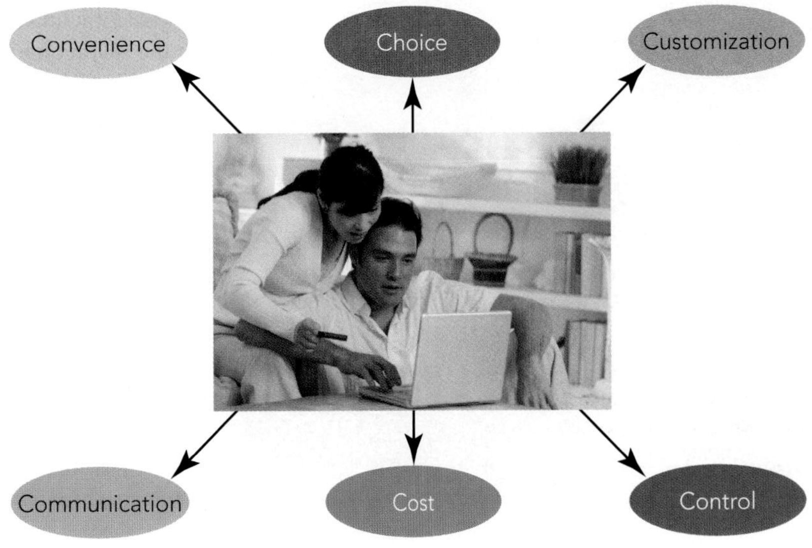

Convenience Online shopping and buying is *convenient*. Consumers can visit Walmart at www.walmart.com to scan and order from among thousands of displayed products without fighting traffic, finding a parking space, walking through long aisles, and standing in store checkout lines. Alternatively, online consumers can use **bots**, electronic shopping agents or robots that comb websites to compare prices and product or service features. In either instance, an online consumer has never ventured into a store. However, for convenience to remain a source of customer value creation, websites must be easy to locate and navigate, and image downloads must be fast.

A commonly held view among online marketers is the **eight-second rule**: Customers will abandon their efforts to enter and navigate a website if download time exceeds eight seconds. Furthermore, the more clicks and pauses between clicks required to access information or make a purchase, the more likely it is a customer will exit a website.

Zappos.com is successful because it meets all the requirements necessary for consumers to shop and buy online. In less than 10 years, the company has posted significant annual sales of shoes, apparel, bags, accessories, housewares, and jewelry.

Zappos.com
www.zappos.com

Choice *Choice*, the second reason consumers shop and buy online, has two dimensions. First, choice exists in the product or service selection offered to consumers. Buyers desiring selection can avail themselves of numerous websites for almost anything they want. For instance, online buyers of consumer electronics can shop individual manufacturers such as Bose (www.bose.com) and QVC.com, a general merchant that offers more than 100,000 products.

Choice assistance is the second dimension. Here, the interactive capabilities of Internet-enabled technologies invite customers to engage in an electronic dialogue with marketers for the purpose of making informed choices. Choice assistance is one of the reasons for the continued success of Zappos.com. The company offers an online chat room that enables prospective buyers to ask questions and receive answers in real time. In addition, carefully designed search capabilities permit consumers to review products by brand and particular items.

Customization Even with a broad selection and choice assistance, some customers prefer one-of-a-kind items that fit their specific needs. *Customization* arises from Internet-enabled capabilities that make possible a highly interactive and individualized information and exchange environment for shoppers and buyers. Remember the earlier Reebok, Schwab, Dell, and Seven Cycles examples? To varying degrees, online consumers also benefit from **customerization**—the growing practice of not only customizing a product or service but also personalizing the marketing and overall shopping and buying interaction for each customer.[17]

Customerization seeks to do more than offer consumers the right product, at the right time, and at the right price. It combines choiceboard and personalization systems to expand the exchange environment beyond a transaction and makes shopping and buying an enjoyable, personal experience.

Communication Online consumers particularly welcome the *communication* capabilities of Internet-enabled technologies. This communication can take three forms: (1) marketer-to-consumer e-mail notification, (2) consumer-to-marketer buying and service requests, and (3) consumer-to-consumer chat rooms and

Staffers in Gatorade's "Mission Control" room in Chicago, Illinois, monitor Internet and social media outlets, such as Facebook and Twitter, 24 hours a day. Whenever someone uses Twitter to say they are drinking a Gatorade or mentions the brand on Facebook or in a blog, it pops up on-screen at Mission Control. In this way, conversations featuring Gatorade provide useful consumer insights into how the brand is viewed and used.

Gatorade
www.gatorade.com

instant messaging, in addition to social networking websites such as Twitter and Facebook.

Communication has proven to be a double-edged sword for online consumers. On the one hand, the interactive communication capabilities of Internet-enabled technologies increase consumer convenience, reduce information search costs, and make choice assistance and customization possible. Communication also promotes the development of company-hosted and independent **web communities**—websites that allow people to congregate online and exchange views on topics of common interest. For instance, Coca-Cola hosts MyCoke.com, and iVillage.com is an independent web community for women and includes topics such as career management, personal finances, parenting, relationships, beauty, and health.

Web logs, or blogs, are another form of communication. A *blog* is a web page that serves as a publicly accessible personal journal for an individual or organization. Blogs are popular because they provide online forums on a wide variety of subjects ranging from politics to car repair. Companies such as Hewlett-Packard, PepsiCo, and Harley-Davidson routinely monitor blogs and social media posts to gather customer insights.[18]

On the other hand, communications can take the form of electronic junk mail or unsolicited e-mail, called **spam**. In fact, 67 percent of e-mail messages in the world are spam.[19] The prevalence of spam has prompted many online services to institute policies and procedures to prevent spammers from spamming their subscribers, and several states have antispamming laws. The 2004 *CAN-SPAM (Controlling the Assault of Non-Solicited Pornography and Marketing) Act* restricts information collection and unsolicited e-mail promotions on the Internet.

Careerbuilder.com, an online career placement company, has produced a great viral marketing success with its Monk-e-mail featuring talking monkeys. People can stylize their monkeys by choosing headgear, clothes, glasses, backgrounds, and other features. They can also record a message using one of four monkey voices, or their own voice. Monk-e-mail can be sent to friends or posted on Twitter.

CareerBuilder
www.careerbuilder.com

Internet-enabled communication capabilities also make possible *buzz*, a popular term for word-of-mouth behavior in marketspace. Chapter 5 described the importance of word of mouth in consumer behavior. Internet technology has magnified its significance. According to Jeff Bezos, president of Amazon.com, "If you have an unhappy customer on the Internet, he doesn't tell his six friends, he tells his 6,000 friends!"[20] Buzz is particularly influential for toys, cars, sporting goods, motion pictures, apparel, consumer electronics, pharmaceuticals, health and beauty products, and health care services. Some marketers have capitalized on this phenomenon by creating buzz through viral marketing.

Viral marketing is an Internet-enabled promotional strategy that encourages individuals to forward marketer-initiated messages to others via e-mail, social networking websites, and blogs. There are three approaches to viral marketing. First, marketers can embed a message in the product or service so that customers hardly realize they are passing it along. The classic example is Hotmail, which was one of the first companies to provide free, Internet-based e-mail. Each outgoing e-mail message had the tagline: "Get Your Private, Free Email from MSN Hotmail." This effort produced more than 350 million users.

QR 21-2
Frito-Lay Video

Second, marketers can make the website content so compelling that viewers want to share it with others. Careerbuilder.com has done this with its Monk-e-mail site, which allows users to send personalized, private-themed e-cards for all occasions. More than 100 million Monk-e-mails have been sent since 2006. Finally, marketers can offer incentives (discounts, sweepstakes, or free merchandise). For example, Burger King asked, "What do you love more, your friend or the Whopper?" in its Whopper Sacrifice campaign. Facebook users were asked to "unfriend" 10 people from their Facebook friends list in exchange for a free burger.[21]

Cost Consumer *cost* is a fifth reason for online shopping and buying. Many popular items bought online can be purchased at the same price or cheaper than in retail stores. The likelihood of lower online prices has given rise to a consumer practice called **showrooming**. Recall that showrooming is when a shopper visits a retail store to inspect merchandise but then purchases the merchandise online (see the Marketing inSite box in Chapter 16). While obtaining a lower price is the primary motivator for showrooming, shoppers also engage in this practice to gather additional merchandise information, look for online promotions or deals, and check merchandise reviews and ratings. About half of U.S. online shoppers engage in showrooming. Consumer electronics, apparel, books, and home appliances are the most popular showrooming product categories.

Lower prices also result from Internet-enabled software that permits **dynamic pricing**, the practice of changing prices for products and services in real time in response to supply and demand conditions. As described in Chapter 14, dynamic pricing is a form of flexible pricing and can often result in lower prices. It is typically used for pricing time-sensitive items such as airline seats, scarce items found at art or collectible auctions, and out-of-date items such as last year's models of computer equipment and accessories. Ticketmaster has recently experimented with dynamic pricing to adjust the price of sports and concert tickets in response to demand.[22]

A consumer's cost of external information search, including time spent and often the hassle of shopping, is also reduced. Greater shopping convenience and lower external search costs are two major reasons for the popularity of online shopping and buying among women—particularly those who work outside the home.

Control The sixth reason consumers prefer to buy online is the *control* it gives them over their shopping and purchase decision process. Online shoppers and buyers are empowered consumers. They deftly use Internet technology to seek information, evaluate alternatives, and make purchase decisions on their own time, terms, and conditions. For example, studies show that shoppers spend an average of five hours researching cars online before setting foot in a showroom.[23] The result of these activities is a more informed and discerning shopper.

Even though consumers have many reasons for shopping and buying online, a segment of Internet users refrains from making purchases for privacy and security reasons. These consumers are concerned about a rarely mentioned seventh C—cookies.

Cookies are computer files that a marketer can download onto the computer and mobile phone of an online shopper who visits the marketer's website. Cookies allow the marketer's website to record a user's visit, track visits to other websites, and store and retrieve this information in the future. Cookies also contain visitor information such as expressed product preferences, personal data, passwords, and credit card numbers.

Cookies make possible customized and personal content for online shoppers. They also make possible the practice of behavioral targeting for marketers. **Behavioral targeting** uses information provided by cookies for directing online advertising from marketers to those online shoppers whose behavioral profiles suggest they would be interested in such advertising. A controversy surrounding cookies is summed up by an authority on the technology: "At best cookies make for a user-friendly web world: like a salesclerk who knows who you are. At worst, cookies represent a potential loss of privacy."[24] Read the Making Responsible Decisions box on the next page to learn more about privacy and security issues in the digital marketspace.[25]

When and Where Online Consumers Shop and Buy

Shopping and buying also happen at different times in marketspace than in the traditional marketplace.[26] About 80 percent of online retail sales occur Monday through Friday. The busiest shopping day is Wednesday. By comparison, 35 percent of retail store sales are registered on the weekend. Saturday is the most popular shopping day. Monday through Friday online shopping and buying often occur during normal work hours—some 30 percent of online consumers say they visit websites from their place of work, which partially accounts for the sales level during the workweek.

Favorite websites for workday shopping and buying include those featuring event tickets, auctions, online periodical subscriptions, flowers and gifts, consumer electronics, and travel. Websites offering health and beauty items, apparel and accessories, and music and video tend to be browsed and bought from a consumer's home.

learning review

21-3. Which online consumer lifestyle segment spends the most money online and which spends the most time online?

21-4. What are the six reasons consumers prefer to shop and buy online?

21-5. What is the eight-second rule?

Making Responsible Decisions

ethics

Who Is Responsible for Internet Privacy and Security?

Privacy and security are two key reasons consumers are leery of online shopping and buying. A recent Pew Internet & American Life Project poll reported that 76 percent of online consumers have privacy and security concerns about the Internet. And, 73 percent of online consumers considered it an invasion of privacy if a search engine tracked their activity to personalize future search results. Even more telling, many have stopped shopping a website or forgone an online purchase because of these concerns. Industry analysts estimate that over $30 million in e-commerce sales are lost annually because of privacy and security concerns among online shoppers.

Consumer concerns are not without merit. According to the Federal Trade Commission, 46 percent of fraud complaints are Internet related, costing consumers $560 million. In addition, consumers lose millions of dollars each year due to identity theft resulting from breaches in company security systems.

A percolating issue is whether the U.S. government should pass more stringent Internet privacy and security laws. About 70 percent of online consumers favor such action. Companies, however, favor self-regulation. For example, TRUSTe (www.truste.com) awards its trademark to company websites that comply with standards of privacy protection and disclosure. Still, consumers are ultimately responsible for using care and caution when engaging in online behavior, including e-commerce. Consumers have a choice of whether or not to divulge personal information and are responsible for monitoring how their information is being used.

What role should the U.S. government, company self-regulation, and consumer vigilance play in dealing with privacy and security issues in the digital marketspace?

CROSS-CHANNEL SHOPPERS AND MULTICHANNEL MARKETING

LO 21-5 Define cross-channel shoppers and the role of transactional and promotional websites in reaching these shoppers.

Consumers are more likely to browse than buy online. Consumer marketspace browsing and buying in the traditional marketplace has given rise to the cross-channel shopper and the importance of multichannel marketing.

Who Is the Cross-Channel Shopper?

The opposite of showrooming, a **cross-channel shopper** is an online consumer who researches products online and then purchases them at a retail store.[27] Recent research shows that 51 percent of U.S. online consumers are cross-channel shoppers. These shoppers represent both genders equally and are only slightly younger than online consumers. They tend to have a higher education, earn significantly more money, and are more likely to embrace technology in their lives than online consumers who don't cross-channel shop.

Cross-channel shoppers want the right product at the best price, and they don't want to wait several days for delivery. The top reasons these shoppers research items online before buying in stores include (1) the desire to compare products among different retailers; (2) the need for more information than is available in stores; and (3) the ease of comparing their options without having to trek to multiple retail locations.

Research shows that sales arising from cross-channel shoppers dwarf exclusive online retail sales. Retail sales revenue from cross-channel shoppers is estimated to be about five times greater than online retail sales.

Implementing Multichannel Marketing

The prominence of cross-channel shoppers has focused increased attention on multichannel marketing. Recall from Chapter 15 that *multichannel marketing* is the blending of different communication and delivery channels that are mutually reinforcing in attracting, retaining, and building relationships with consumers who shop and buy in the traditional marketplace and online—the cross-channel shopper.

The most common cross-channel shopping and buying path is to browse one or more websites and then purchase an item at a retail store. This shopping path might suggest that company websites for cross-channel shoppers should be similar. But they are not. Websites play a multifaceted role in multichannel marketing because they can serve as either a communication or delivery channel. Two general applications of websites exist based on their intended purpose: (1) transactional websites and (2) promotional websites.

Cross-channel shoppers routinely browse online and shop retail stores, often during the same shopping trip.

Multichannel Marketing with Transactional Websites *Transactional websites* are essentially electronic storefronts. They focus principally on converting an online browser into an online, catalog, or in-store buyer using the website design elements described earlier. Transactional websites are most common among store and catalog retailers and direct selling companies, such as Tupperware. Retailers and direct selling firms have found that their websites, while cannibalizing sales volume from stores, catalogs, and sales representatives, attract new customers and influence sales. Consider Victoria's Secret, the well-known specialty retailer of intimate apparel for women ages 18 to 45. It reports that almost 60 percent of its website customers are men, most of whom generate new sales volume for the company.[28]

Transactional websites are used less frequently by manufacturers of consumer products. A recurring issue for manufacturers is the threat of *channel conflict*, described in Chapter 15, and the potential harm to trade relationships with their retailing intermediaries. Still, manufacturers do use transactional websites, often cooperating with retailers. For example, Callaway Golf Company markets its golf merchandise at www.callawaygolf.com but relies on a retailer close to the buyer to fill the order. The retailer ships the order to the buyer within 24 hours and is credited with the sale. The majority of retailers that sell Callaway merchandise participate in this relationship, including retail chains Golf Galaxy and Dick's Sporting Goods. According to Callaway's chief executive officer, "This arrangement allows us to satisfy the consumer but to do so in a way that didn't violate our relationship with our loyal trade partners—those 15,000 outlets that sell Callaway products."[29] For more on the unique arrangement between Callaway Golf and its marketing channel partners, see the opening example in Chapter 15.

Promotional websites seek to engage the visitor in an interactive experience involving games, contests, and quizzes with electronic coupons and other gifts as prizes.

In addition, Callaway, like other manufacturers, lists stores on its website where its merchandise can be shopped and bought. More often than not, however, manufacturers using multichannel marketing channels employ websites for advertising and promotion purposes.

Multichannel Marketing with Promotional Websites *Promotional websites* have a very different purpose than transactional sites. They advertise and promote a company's products and services and provide information on how items can be used and where they can be purchased. They often engage the visitor in an interactive experience involving games, contests, and

FIGURE 21–5
Implementing multichannel marketing with promotional websites is common today. Two successes are found at Hyundai Motor America and the Clinique Division of Estée Lauder, Inc.

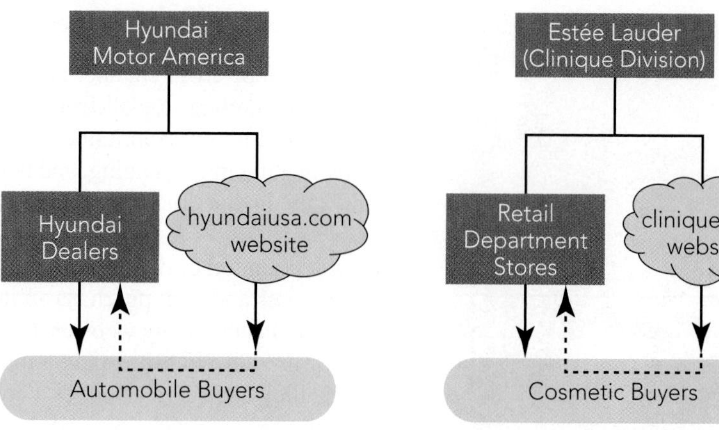

- 70% of Hyundai leads come from its website.
- 80% of people visiting a Hyundai dealer first visited its website.

- 80% of current Clinique buyers who visit its website later purchase a Clinique product at a store.
- 37% of non-Clinique buyers make a Clinique purchase after visiting its website.

QR 21-3
Pampers
Video

quizzes with electronic coupons and other gifts as prizes. Procter & Gamble maintains separate websites for many of its leading brands, including Scope mouthwash (www.getclose.com) and Pampers diapers (www.pampers.com). Promotional sites are effective in generating interest in and trial of a company's products (see Figure 21–5).[30] Hyundai Motor America reports that 80 percent of the people visiting a Hyundai store first visited the brand's website (www.hyundaiusa.com) and 70 percent of Hyundai leads come from its website.

Promotional websites also can be used to support a company's traditional marketing channel and build customer relationships. This is the objective of the Clinique Division of Estée Lauder, Inc., which markets cosmetics through department stores. Clinique reports that 80 percent of current customers who visit its website (www.clinique.com) later purchase a Clinique product at a department store, while 37 percent of non-Clinique buyers make a Clinique purchase after visiting the company's website.

The popularity of multichannel marketing is apparent in its growing impact on online retail sales.[31] Fully 70 percent of U.S. online retail sales are made by companies that practice multichannel marketing. Multichannel marketers are expected to register about 90 percent of U.S. online retail sales in 2014.

learning review

21-6. A cross-channel shopper is ________________.

21-7. Channel conflict between manufacturers and retailers is likely to arise when manufacturers use ______________ websites.

LEARNING OBJECTIVES REVIEW

LO 21-1 *Describe what interactive marketing is and how it creates customer value, customer relationships, and customer experiences.*

Interactive marketing involves two-way buyer–seller electronic communication in a computer-mediated environment in which the buyer controls the kind and amount of information received from the seller. It creates customer value by providing time, place, form, and possession utility for consumers. Customer relationships are created and sustained through two unique capabilities of Internet technology: interactivity and individuality. From an interactive marketing perspective, customer experience represents the sum total of the interactions that a customer has with a company's website, from the initial look at a home page through the entire purchase decision process. Companies produce a customer experience through seven website design elements. These elements are context, content, community, customization, communication, connection, and commerce.

LO 21-2 *Identify the demographic and lifestyle profile of online consumers.*
As a group, online consumers are more likely to be women than men and tend to be better educated, younger, and more affluent than the general U.S. population. Women tend to purchase more products and services online than men. The lifestyle profile of online consumers reflects the different kinds of online experiences they seek. Six lifestyle segments have been identified. The click-and-mortar segment consists of women who browse retailer websites but actually buy products at retail outlets. Hunter-gatherers use the Internet like a consumer magazine to gather information and compare products and services. Brand loyalists regularly visit their favorite bookmarked websites and spend the most money online. Time-sensitive materialists regard the Internet as a convenient tool for buying. The hooked, online, and single segment spends more time online than any segment. E-bivalent newbies are relative newcomers to the Internet who rarely spend money online, but seek product information.

LO 21-3 *Explain why certain types of products and services are particularly suited for interactive marketing.*
Certain types of products and services seem to be particularly suited for interactive marketing. One category consists of items for which product information is an important part of the purchase decision, but prepurchase trial is not necessarily critical. A second category involves items for which audio or video demonstration is important. A third category contains items that can be digitally delivered. Unique items represent a fourth category. A fifth category includes items that are regularly purchased and where convenience is very important. A final category consists of highly standardized items for which information about price is important.

LO 21-4 *Describe why consumers shop and buy online and how marketers influence online purchasing behavior.*
There are six reasons consumers shop and buy online. They are convenience, choice, customization, communication, cost, and control. Marketers have capitalized on these reasons through a variety of means. For example, they provide choice assistance using choiceboard and collaborative filtering technology, which also provides opportunities for customization. Company-hosted web communities and viral marketing practices capitalize on the communications dimensions of Internet-enabled technologies. Dynamic pricing provides real-time responses to supply and demand conditions, often resulting in lower prices for consumers. Permission marketing is popular given consumer interest in control.

LO 21-5 *Define cross-channel shoppers and the role of transactional and promotional websites in reaching these shoppers.*
A cross-channel shopper is an online consumer who researches products online and then purchases them at a retail store. These shoppers are reached through multichannel marketing. Websites play a multifaceted role in multichannel marketing because they can serve as either a delivery or communication channel. In this regard, transactional websites are essentially electronic storefronts. They focus principally on converting an online browser into an online, catalog, or in-store buyer using the website design elements described earlier. On the other hand, promotional websites serve to advertise and promote a company's products and services and provide information on how items can be used and where they can be purchased.

FOCUSING ON KEY TERMS

behavorial targeting p. 573
bots p. 570
choiceboard p. 562
collaborative filtering p. 562
cookies p. 573
cross-channel shopper p. 574
customerization p. 570
dynamic pricing p. 572
eight-second rule p. 570
interactive marketing p. 562
online consumers p. 567
permission marketing p. 563
personalization p. 562
showrooming p. 572
spam p. 571
viral marketing p. 572
web communities p. 571

APPLYING MARKETING KNOWLEDGE

1 Have you made an online purchase? If so, why do you think so many people who have access to the Internet are not also online buyers? If not, why are you reluctant to do so? Do you think that electronic commerce benefits consumers even if they don't make a purchase?

2 Like the traditional marketplace, the digital marketspace offers marketers opportunities to create time, place, form, and possession utility. How do you think Internet-enabled technology rates in terms of creating these values? Take a shopping trip at a virtual retailer of your choice (don't buy anything unless you really want to). Then compare the time, place, form, and possession utility provided by the virtual retailer to that provided by a traditional retailer in the same product category.

3 Visit Amazon.com (www.amazon.com) or Barnes & Noble (www.barnesandnoble.com). As you tour the website, think about how shopping for books online compares with a trip to your university bookstore to buy books. Specifically, compare and contrast your shopping experiences with respect to convenience, choice, customization, communication, cost, and control.

4 You are planning to buy a new car so you visit www.edmunds.com. Based on your experience visiting that site, do you think you will enjoy more or less control in negotiating with the dealer when you actually purchase your vehicle?

5 Visit the website for your university or college. Based on your visit, would you conclude that the site is a transactional site or a promotional site? Why? How would you rate the site in terms of the six website design elements that affect customer experience?

BUILDING YOUR MARKETING PLAN

Does your marketing plan involve a marketspace presence for your product or service? If the answer is "no," read no further and do not include this element in your plan. If the answer is "yes," then attention must be given to developing a website in your marketing plan. A useful starting point is to:

1 Describe how each website element—context, content, community, customization, communication, connection, and commerce—will be used to create a customer experience.
2 Identify a company's website that best reflects your website conceptualization.

VIDEO CASE 21 Pizza Hut and imc²: Becoming a Multichannel Marketer

QR 21-4
Pizza Hut
Video Case

It's no surprise that Pizza Hut is the world's largest pizza chain with more than 10,000 restaurants in 100 countries. But did you know that Pizza Hut became one of the top 35 U.S. Internet retailers in 2009?

According to Brian Niccol, Pizza Hut's chief marketing officer (CMO), "We've done what many would say is impossible. We successfully built an online business in three years that produces hundreds of millions of dollars in annual revenue. Today, Pizza Hut is a category leader in the interactive and emerging marketplace." So how did they do it? Pizza Hut simply revolutionized the quick serve restaurant (QSR) world through a multichannel marketing approach that created a customer experience and a customer engagement platform that was second to none.

THE RETAIL PIZZA BUSINESS

With three national competitors dominating the marketplace, the pizza business is very competitive. Even customers who could be considered heavy users of a particular brand regularly purchase from competitors on the basis of timing, pricing, and convenience.

In general, Pizza Hut's most frequent customers (and likely those of the other two major competitors) divide into two categories: (1) families, primarily time-starved mothers, looking for a quick and simple mealtime solution; and (2) young adult males who fuel their active lifestyle with one of the world's most versatile and convenient foods (no cooking, no utensils, no cleanup, and leftovers are perfect for breakfast). While these two groups could not be more dissimilar on the surface, value and convenience are important for both groups. Cost-conscious mothers look for a good quality product and a hassle-free eating experience. Deal-seeking young adult males seek more of the food they love with less time and cash invested in the process.

The importance of the take-home and delivery segment of the U.S. pizza market is illustrated by the fact that Pizza Hut's principal national competitors focus exclusively on this aspect of the business. Most take-home and delivery sales are ordered before a customer enters the restaurant. By 2006, a growing number of retail pizza customers had become comfortable ordering pizza online. Pizza ordering, as it turned out, was an ideal product for the digital world. People understood the basic menu, generally knew that they could customize their order in a variety of ways, and were accustomed to not being in the store when ordering. Brand retail presence and established customer delivery networks also made the shift to online ordering easier for national pizza chains than other national quick serve restaurants.

But, as Pizza Hut understood, there is still an incredible level of complexity in making something truly sophisticated simple and easy for the customer.

CREATING A PLAN OF ACTION

For the most part, the intent of online ordering for the pizza business was to make transactions with the customer easier and cheaper for the brand. Pizza Hut recognized the opportunity to engage people with its brand and with other people directly and do something special; namely, build sustainable relationships with its customers and enable Pizza Hut to engage people in a more meaningful and profitable way. In short, Pizza Hut set about to reinvent the retail pizza business by breaking away from a transactional platform to an efficient and powerful customer engagement platform by reaching out to customers' kitchens and couches to offer a better mealtime ordering, delivery, and dining experience.

Pizza Hut selected imc² (www.imc2.com) as one of its lead agencies to plan a comprehensive interactive strategy that focused first on the redesign of the Pizza Hut corporate website (including redefining the customer experience online and across all of the brand's touchpoints) and then on a series of progressively sophisticated and industry-leading customer engagement strategies. imc² brought 15 years of experience in interactive marketing and brand engagement to the assignment. Its clients have included Coca-Cola, Johnson & Johnson, Pfizer, Omni Hotels, Hasbro, Procter & Gamble, and Samsung, among a host of other companies, large and small.

PIZZAHUT.COM, CUSTOMER EXPERIENCE, AND BRAND ENGAGEMENT

Pizza Hut and imc² executives agreed that the strategy for reinventing the retail pizza business would involve developing opportunities for customers to engage with the brand by using the right technologies to enable and encourage interaction. A new website was necessary to better address all major design elements. How Pizza Hut and imc² executed these design elements not only created value for its customers, but also served as a basis for differentiation in the retail pizza business. Let's look at these design elements and PizzaHut.com's performance.

The Pizza Hut website was completely redesigned to support nationwide online ordering in 2007 (including all franchise locations for the first time) and is updated frequently to keep up with the company's fast-paced marketing strategy and ambitious product innovation rollout schedule. Since promotions are an important expectation in pizza purchasing and speak to the brand's consumers in a language that clearly connects with their desire for value, the website *context* and *content* balance the ability to shop for a deal with quick and easy ordering access for people who arrive at PizzaHut.com ready to purchase. The site presents a number of Pizza Hut's current offers in the central viewing window as well as

through the rolling navigation directly underneath the main content. Primary navigation for information, such as the menu, locations, and nutrition facts, are displayed horizontally across the top of the rotating content.

Website *customization* is achieved in several ways, but the primary utility is to simplify ordering. For customers who have already registered, there are several personalization options, including rapid ordering called *Express Checkout*—a feature that's based on saved preferences similar to a "playlist." For example, if you have a group of friends that likes to watch movies together, you might create an order named *Movie Night* that has your group's favorite pizzas. Using the *Express Checkout* option accessible directly on the home page, you can select *Movie Night*, quickly review the order, click the "submit" button, and the pizzas are on their way, relying on saved delivery and payment options through a stored *cookie* (a piece of digital code that is used to identify previous visitors) to speed the transaction. With this type of functionality, you can think of convenience as an investment that creates loyalty and somewhat insulates the brand against switching down the line when customers would have to register with and learn a competitor's system, and where access to their favorite features might not be available.

Website *content* and *communications* are integrated with the company's overall communications programs—including traditional media—with product innovations, promotions, and special events shared across platforms. True to the brand, communications are fun and energetic, matching bold images and vibrant color with a smart, clever, and lighthearted voice. One noteworthy example includes the 2008 April Fools' Day rebranding of the company as "Pasta Hut" to coincide with the launch of the brand's innovative line of Tuscani Pastas. This campaign included online support in the form of display media (banner ads) and the temporary rebranding of PizzaHut.com as PastaHut.com with special imagery and copy supporting the name change. Not only did the brand get plenty of coverage in the press, but it deepened the connection with customers by showing their willingness to be spontaneous and fun, inviting people to play along with the joke.

Pizza Hut's integrated marketing communications approach enables the company to easily test and incorporate other items and brands under the larger corporate umbrella, such as the WingStreet operation and the pasta extension. This demonstrates the brand's ability to stretch the QSR concept way beyond its pizza roots and suggests the kind of direction the company may pursue in the future.

PizzaHut.com and the brand's other online assets are all about getting the world's favorite pizza and signature products into the hands and stomachs of customers. Since *commerce* is a huge consideration on the site, there are multiple pathways for ordering, including several onsite methods, a Facebook app (the first national pizza chain to produce an ordering application for the world's leading social networking site), a branded desktop widget, mobile ordering (also known as Total Mobile Access, added in 2008, that includes both a WAP [wireless application protocol] site and text ordering), and a sophisticated and simple iPhone app released in 2009 that lets customers build and submit their order visually. Additional revenue streams can also be quickly built online, as demonstrated by the eGift Card program conceived and implemented by imc^2 over a weekend during the 2008 holiday season.

Realizing that it did not make sense for the company or its customers to create a *community* on the site, Pizza Hut tapped into Facebook to achieve results in a very cost-effective manner. With approximately 1 million fans and the first of its kind Facebook ordering application, the brand can efficiently engage a huge group of people in a very natural way without disrupting their daily routine. Again, the brand understands that if you make something convenient, you can increase trust while securing greater transactional loyalty. Pizza Hut's 2009 program to identify a summer intern, or *Twintern*, responsible for monitoring and encouraging dialogue on Twitter and other social media networks is another example of how the brand is building on existing platforms and making effective use of the massive social marketing infrastructure.

PizzaHut.com connects mobile, desktop, social networks, and other digital gateways to complement traditional media and its retail presence. So when Pizza Hut thinks about the *connection* design element, it includes more than just linking to other websites online. Rather, it provides a comprehensive approach to creating a seamless customer experience wherever and whenever people want to engage with the brand.

PERFORMANCE MEASUREMENT AND OUTCOMES

Pizza Hut diligently measures the performance of Pizza Hut.com. The company created a customized marketing dashboard that allows the Pizza Hut management team to monitor various aspects of the brand's marketing program and provides an almost constant stream of fresh information that it can use to optimize engagement with people or tweak various aspects of performance.

The results have been remarkable, but understand that due to the highly competitive nature of the industry, they are fluid and only represent a moment in time. Consider, for example:

1. PizzaHut.com dominates the pizza category with number one rankings in website traffic and search volume. According to comScore, a global leader in digital analytics and measurement, the Pizza Hut site achieves the most traffic per online dollars spent in the pizza category.
2. PizzaHut.com became one of the top 35 Internet retailers in the United States in 2009, up from 45th in 2008.
3. Pizza Hut's iPhone app had more than 100,000 downloads in the first two weeks after release.

WHAT'S NEXT

So what's next for PizzaHut.com? While the brand has made huge gains in a very short time period, staying on top in the rapidly evolving digital marketplace requires constant attention. Pizza Hut envisions that its online business will surpass the $1 billion mark within the next five years, and that digital transactions will lead all revenue within a decade.

While understandably protective of the company's future strategy, Pizza Hut CMO Niccol has ambitious goals and he's not joking when he deadpans, "I want Pizza Hut to become the Amazon of food service and be pioneers for the digital space. I do not want us to be a brick-and-mortar company that just dabbles in the space." The transition to something along the lines of the Amazon model suggests that the brand might further evolve its identity as a pizza business and stretch or completely redefine the QSR model.

Most brands that want to grow in the evolving economy will have to think and plan long-term and be able to act swiftly as marketplace conditions change. imc^2 Chief Marketing Officer Ian Wolfman, when assessing the future of marketing, sums up the opportunity neatly. "Our agency believes that marketing's current transformation will result in a complete reorientation of how brands and companies engage with their consumers and other stakeholders. Brands that thrive will be those, like Pizza Hut, that can efficiently build sustainable relationships with people—relationships that have both high trust and high transactions" (see Figure 1). He goes on to explain that "brands taking a longer view have an unexpected advantage over traditional models that often focus too tightly on hitting near-term quarterly targets." Referring

FIGURE 1

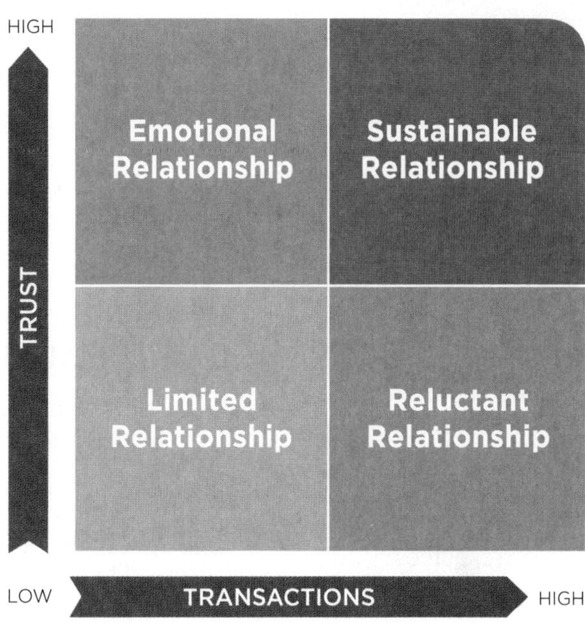

to research his agency has done on the subject, Wolfman points out that the most successful brands in the future will likely be those that resonate with people on a deeply emotional level and operate with a clearly defined sense of purpose.

Pizza Hut, with its focus on digitally enabled customer convenience and category innovation, is ideally positioned to connect with people on a level that builds trust and increases transactions. Referring to the initial time investment, however modest, that customers have to make in registering with the system and enabling various devices, Niccol sees the landscape as very promising for brands that put their customers' interests and preferences first. "If we do our job right—creating authentic engagement and making it convenient and valuable for people to interact with the brand—the numbers follow."

Questions

1 What kind of website is PizzaHut.com?

2 How does PizzaHut.com incorporate the seven website design elements?

3 How are choiceboard and personalization systems used in the PizzaHut.com website?

22 Pulling It All Together: The Strategic Marketing Process

LEARNING OBJECTIVES

After reading this chapter you should be able to:

LO 22-1 Explain how marketing managers allocate resources.

LO 22-2 Describe Porter's generic business strategies and synergy analysis planning frameworks.

LO 22-3 Explain what makes an effective marketing plan.

LO 22-4 Use a time-based agenda and an action item list to conduct a meeting.

LO 22-5 Describe an organization's marketing department and the role of a product manager.

LO 22-6 Explain the use of marketing ROI, metrics, and dashboards in evaluating marketing programs.

WARM DELIGHTS FOR TODAY'S ON-THE-GO CONSUMERS

"Sometimes you have to break the rules at every level," says Vivian Milroy Callaway about her challenges at General Mills.[1]

Breaking the Rules at "Big G"

Callaway "broke the rules" in developing a new dessert concept at General Mills. The company gets its nickname—"Big G"—from the logo on its breakfast cereals, which is the biggest business at General Mills.[2] Callaway did not look at the new dessert concept *alone* by itself—but in relation to *all* the other sweet treats people were eating. "One of my challenges," she says, "is that consumers often say one thing in marketing research studies and then do something else when facing a supermarket shelf."

To overcome this problem, Callaway and her team ran marketing experiments that involved putting a prototype dessert in a store, measuring the results, improving the prototype, and repeating the process. The result: The launch of its highly successful Warm Delights microwavable desserts, followed quickly by the product line extension Warm Delights Minis. The special packaging is based on the team's research, which revealed that extending the black microwavable bowl outside the edges of the Warm Delights package communicated its cooking convenience to prospective buyers.

As vice president of the Center for Learning and Experimentation at Big G, Callaway is responsible for helping uncover new-product ideas for the company, which gets 25 percent of its sales internationally.[3] A day with Callaway reveals just how competitive today's cereal business is, as well as a few of General Mills's creative initiatives.

Cereal Industry Facts of Life

A quick environmental scan of the cereal industry shows the fierce competition General Mills faces and why it is searching for non-cereal products:

- *Expense.* The launch of a new cereal typically costs up to $30 million and usually involves replacing one of more than 300 competing breakfast cereals already sitting on retailers' shelves.
- *Success rate.* Only one out of four brands "succeeds," which is defined as maintaining distribution for three to four years in the $9.5 billion-a-year U.S. ready-to-eat (RTE) cereal market. Adding

to the somber outlook: The RTE market has had flat or slightly declining sales in recent years.[4]

QR 22-1
Fiber One Ad

- *Market decline.* The decline in the RTE cereal market is being caused by a number of factors: Americans are following low-carbohydrate diets, munching breakfast bars, and eating breakfast at fast-food restaurants; consumers are buying lower priced "bagged" or generic private-label brands; and shoppers are avoiding the higher shelf prices of RTE cereal, which are the result of rising grain prices.[5]

What may be on the breakfast horizon from General Mills? It's BFast, a dairy-based drink that may compete with a similar offering from Kellogg's, known as Breakfast To Go.

Creative Initiatives at Big G

General Mills introduces more than 300 new food products each year around the world that respond to what consumers are asking for: the ability to eat the product on the go, the option of healthier products, and the convenience of single portions and microwave cooking. Sometimes it's possible to get all these features in the same new product; other times it is not. So, in light of these consumer trends and the intense competition it faces in the consumer packaged foods industry, Big G is offering a variety of new products, among them:

- Single-portion entrees (Betty Crocker Hamburger Helper Microwave Singles).
- New high-fiber, low-calorie cereals (Fiber One 80 Calories Chocolate).
- New healthier snacks (Green Giant Veggie Snack Chips).
- A new line of high-protein yogurt targeted at "tweens" to capitalize on the Greek-style yogurt trend (Yoplait Pro-Force).
- A breakfast drink (BFast) rolled out nationally in 2013 that contains protein, fiber, and vitamins and is targeted at "on-the-go" Millennials.[6]

The success or failure of these and other products is related to the planning, implementation, and evaluation phases of the strategic marketing process General Mills uses. This chapter elaborates on some of the issues and techniques presented in Chapter 2 and introduces additional tools and strategies to help marketing, product, and brand managers succeed in the ever-changing, competitive marketplace. Marketing strategies now emerging at General Mills and other firms provide examples.

MARKETING BASICS: DOING WHAT WORKS AND ALLOCATING RESOURCES

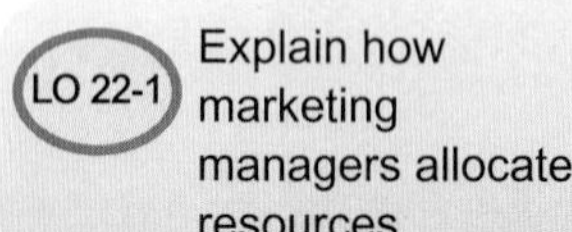
LO 22-1 Explain how marketing managers allocate resources.

As noted in Chapter 2, corporate and marketing executives search continuously to find a competitive advantage—a unique strength relative to what competitors are doing now and likely to do in the future.[7] Having identified this competitive advantage, they then must figure out how to exploit it.[8] This involves (1) finding and using what works for their organization and industry and (2) allocating resources effectively.

Finding and Using What Really Works

In a five-year study, researchers conducted an in-depth analysis of 160 companies and more than 200 management tools and techniques, such as supply chain management or use of an intranet. Their findings? Individual management tools and techniques had no direct relationship to superior business performance in the companies.[9]

What *does* matter? The researchers concluded that four basic business and management practices are what matter—"what really works," to use their phrase. These are (1) strategy, (2) execution, (3) culture, and (4) structure. Firms with excellence in all four of these areas are likely to achieve superior business performance. The researchers concluded that which of these basic practices a firm chooses to use is less important than flawless execution of the ones it does use.

Industry leaders such as Home Depot do all four of the basic practices extremely well, not just two or three, and are vigilant about continuing to do them well when conditions change. In contrast, Dell and, more recently, Groupon are struggling today to get these basics right and regain their past success. Let's look at companies that stand out today in each of the four key business practices:

Costco and Smucker's achieve excellence in what really matters—a clear, focused strategy (Costco) and a performance-oriented culture (Smucker's).

QR 22-2 Smucker's TV Ad

- *Strategy: Devise and maintain a clearly stated, focused strategy.* While Walmart may be the unstoppable force in mass-merchandise retailing, its Sam's Club comes up short in warehouse club retailing. The winner: Costco Wholesale, the largest membership warehouse club chain in the United States. A key reason is its focused strategy based on the knowledge that of all U.S. retail channels, warehouse clubs attract the largest proportion of affluent shoppers. Costco's strategy: Sell a limited selection of branded high-end merchandise at low prices.[10]
- *Execution: Develop and maintain flawless operational execution.* Toyota is generally acknowledged as the best in the world in revolutionizing auto manufacturing. It created the doctrine of *kaizen*, or continuous improvement, which is now used across the auto industry. While Toyota stumbled with massive recalls in 2009, new CEO Akio Toyoda has used this "wake-up call" to focus on execution: "Always better cars."[11]
- *Culture: Develop and maintain a performance-oriented culture.* Always near the top of *Fortune*'s list of the 100 Best Companies to Work For is Smucker's—yes, the "With a name like Smucker's" company. Its straightforward culture is based on four key elements in its code of conduct: "Listen with your full attention, look for the good in others, have a sense of humor, and say thank you for a job well done." The performance result? Low employee turnover and a large increase in the value of its stock.
- *Structure: Build and maintain a fast, flexible, flat organization.* Successful small organizations often grow into bureaucratic large ones with layers of managers and red tape that slow decision making. The unquestioned all-time leader in delivering world-class aircraft with only a small team of engineers, designers, and machinists: Lockheed Martin's Skunk Works. Discussed later in the chapter, its first director set key organizational guidelines, like "use a small number of good people who can talk to anyone in the organization to solve a problem."[12] France and Russia have attempted to apply Skunk Works guidelines to their aircraft production.

Of course, in practice a firm cannot allocate unlimited resources to achieving each of these business basics. It must make choices based on where its resources can produce the greatest return, the topic of the next section.

Allocating Marketing Resources Using Sales Response Functions

A **sales response function** relates the expense of the marketing effort to the marketing results obtained.[13] To simplify the examples that follow, only the effects of annual marketing effort on annual sales revenue will be analyzed, but keep in mind that the concept applies to other measures of marketing success—such as profit or units sold.

Maximizing Incremental Revenue Minus Incremental Cost Economists give managers a specific guideline for optimal resource allocation: Allocate the firm's marketing, production, and financial resources to the markets and products where the excess of incremental revenues over incremental costs is greatest. This parallels the marginal revenue–marginal cost analysis discussed in Chapter 13.

Figure 22–1 on the next page illustrates the resource allocation principle that is inherent in the sales response function. The firm's annual marketing effort, such as advertising, personal sales, sales promotion, direct marketing, and public relations expenses, is plotted on the horizontal axis. As the annual marketing effort increases, so does the resulting annual sales revenue, which is plotted on the vertical axis. The relationship is assumed to be S-shaped, showing that an additional $1 million of marketing effort, from $3 million to $4 million at Point A, results in far greater increases of sales revenue in the midrange ($20 million) of the curve than at either end. This is because

FIGURE 22–1
A sales response function shows the impact of various levels of marketing effort on annual sales revenue for two different years.

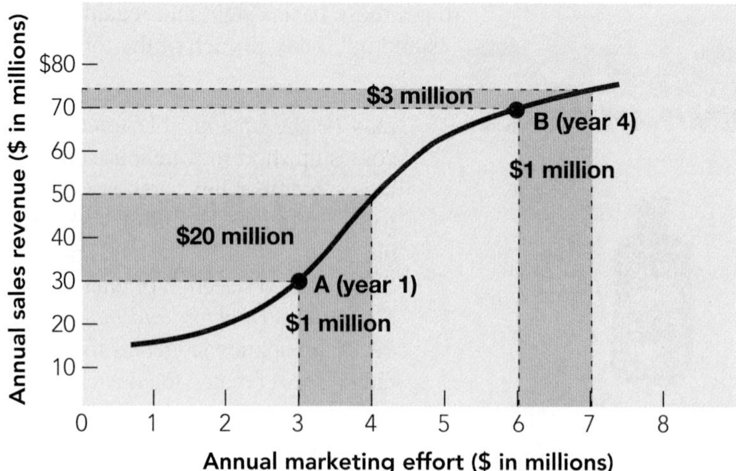

at the left end of the S-curve, the cost of the marketing effort to gain new customers is high for they must be made aware of the product. In contrast, at the right end of the S-curve, the easy-to-get customers are already buying the product and gaining new customers is again very costly—as illustrated by Point B at the right end.

An Example of Resource Allocation Suppose Figure 22–1 shows the situation for a new General Mills product such as Honey Nut Cheerios Medley Crunch, with one-third of the daily recommended amount of whole grains. It is targeted at health-conscious consumers who want a great-tasting cereal. Honey Nut Cheerios Medley Crunch is an extension of Honey Nut Cheerios and, in turn, the Cheerios name, the best-selling ready-to-eat cereal brand in the United States.[14]

Also assume that the sales response function in Figure 22–1 doesn't change through time as a result of changing consumer tastes and incomes. Point A shows the position of the firm in year 1, whereas Point B shows it three years later in year 4. Now suppose General Mills decides to launch new advertising and sales promotions that increase its marketing effort for the brand from $3 million to $6 million a year. If the relationship in Figure 22–1 holds true and is a good picture of consumer purchasing behavior, the sales revenues of Honey Nut Cheerios Medley Crunch should increase from $30 million to $70 million a year.

Let's look at the major resource allocation question: What are the probable increases in sales revenue for Honey Nut Cheerios Medley Crunch in year 1 and year 4 if General Mills spends an additional $1 million in marketing effort? As Figure 22–1 reveals,

A careful study of the words on the packages of these recently introduced General Mills products reveals the company's increased emphasis on healthy eating.

Year 1

Increase in marketing effort from $3 million to $4 million = $1 million.

Increase in sales revenue from $30 million to $50 million = $20 million.

Ratio of incremental sales revenue to effort = $20 million:$1 million = 20:1.

Year 4

Increase in marketing effort from $6 million to $7 million = $1 million.

Increase in sales revenue from $70 million to $73 million = $3 million.

Ratio of incremental sales revenue to effort = $3 million:$1 million = 3:1.

Thus, in year 1 a dollar of extra marketing effort returned $20 in sales revenue, whereas in year 4 it returned only $3. If no other expenses are incurred, it might make sense to spend $1 million in year 4 to gain $3 million in incremental sales revenue. However, it may be far wiser for General Mills to invest the money in one of its other brands, such as its new line of Green Giant Veggie Snack Chips.

The essence of resource allocation is simple: Put incremental resources where the incremental returns are greatest over the foreseeable future. For General Mills, this means that it must allocate its available resources (talent and dollars) more efficiently when developing its broad portfolio of products and brands and creating the marketing actions required to reach their respective target market segments. For example, General Mills is increasingly using social media like blogs and Facebook.

Allocating Marketing Resources in Practice General Mills, like many firms in the consumer packaged foods industry, does extensive analysis using **share points**, or percentage points of market share, as the common basis of comparison to allocate marketing resources effectively for different product lines within the same firm. This practice allows the company to explore questions like, "How much is it worth to us to try to increase our market share by another 1 (or 2, or 5, or 10) percentage point(s)?"

This analysis enables higher-level managers to make resource allocation trade-offs among different kinds of strategic business units owned by the company. To make these resource allocation decisions, marketing managers must estimate: (1) the market share for the product; (2) the revenues associated with each point of market share (a share point in breakfast cereals may be five times what it is in cake mixes); (3) the contribution to overhead and profit (or gross margin) of each share point; and (4) possible cannibalization effects on other products in the line (for example, sales of new Honey Nut Cheerios Medley Crunch might reduce sales of regular Cheerios).

Resource Allocation and the Strategic Marketing Process Company resources are allocated effectively in the strategic marketing process by converting marketing information into marketing actions. Figure 22–2 summarizes the strategic marketing process introduced in Chapter 2, along with the pertinent marketing actions and information. Figure 22–2 is really a simplification of the actual strategic marketing process. In practice, marketing actions and the information needed to develop them overlap throughout the three phases of the strategic marketing process.

FIGURE 22–2
The actions in the strategic marketing process are supported and directed by detailed reports, studies, and memos.

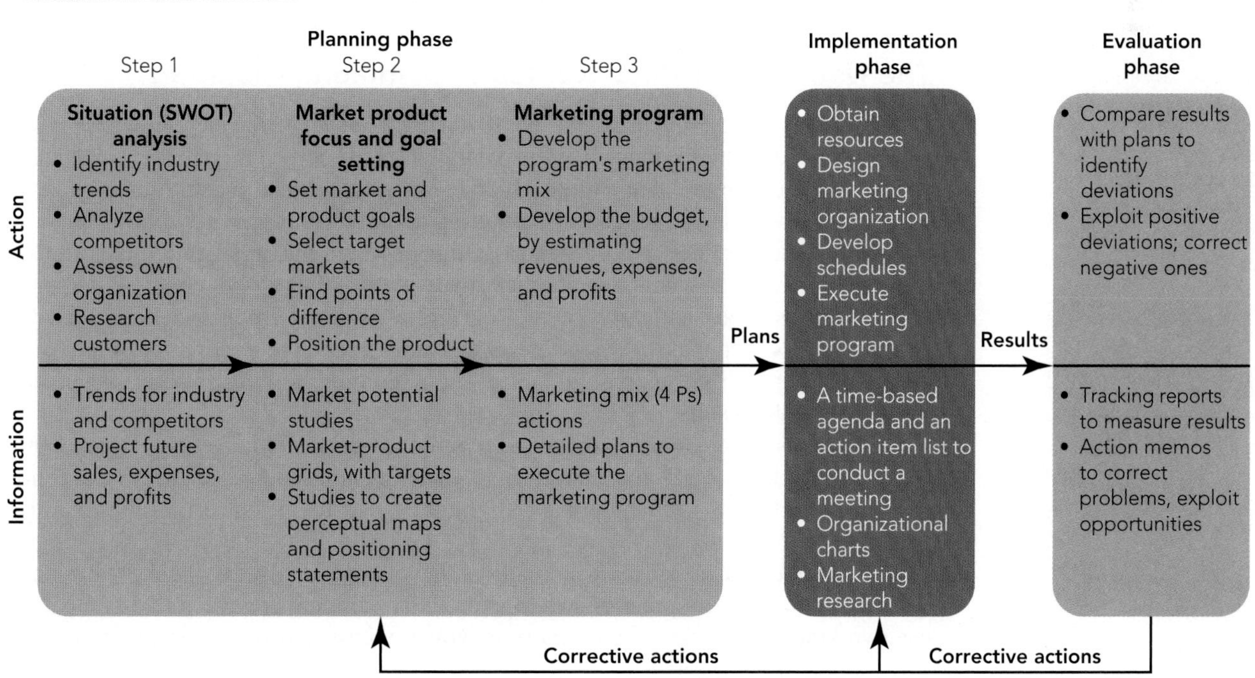

The upper half of each box in Figure 22–2 highlights the actions involved in that part of the strategic marketing process, and the lower half summarizes the information and reports used. Note that each phase has an output report, as shown below:

Phase	Output Report
Planning	Marketing plans (or programs) that define goals (with pertinent marketing metrics) and the marketing mix strategies to achieve them
Implementation	Action memos that tell (1) *who* is (2) to do *what* (3) by *when*
Evaluation	Corrective action memos, triggered by comparing results with goals, often using the firm's marketing metrics and displayed in marketing dashboards

The corrective action memos become feedback loops in Figure 22–2 that help improve decisions and actions in earlier phases of the strategic marketing process.

learning review

22-1. What are the four basic practices "that really work" that characterize industry-leading firms?

22-2. What is the significance of the S-shape of the sales response function in Figure 22–1?

THE PLANNING PHASE OF THE STRATEGIC MARKETING PROCESS

Four aspects of the strategic marketing process deserve special mention: (1) the vital importance of marketing metrics in marketing planning; (2) the variety of marketing plans; (3) marketing planning frameworks that have proven useful; and (4) some key marketing planning and strategy lessons.

The Use of Marketing Metrics in Marketing Planning

Planners have a tongue-in-cheek truism: "If you don't know where you're going, any road will get you there." In making marketing plans, the "road" chosen is really the quantitative goal *plus* the quantitative metric used to measure whether the goal is being achieved.

Today, measuring the results of marketing actions has become a central focus in many organizations. This boils down to defining "where the organization is going"—the quantitative goals—and "whether it is really getting there"—the quantitative marketing metrics used to measure actual performance. This emphasizes the need for data-driven decision making (mentioned in Chapter 2) and the importance of choosing and displaying the right marketing metrics in marketing dashboards so managers can quickly view the results.[15]

Most firms stress innovation to help achieve growth. Marketing departments work closely with R&D and operations departments to complete successful innovation projects.[16] So what metrics might they use to measure their innovation performance?

A recent study asked firms what metrics they used in analyzing their performance on innovation and new-product development.[17] The findings revealed that companies use two kinds of metrics: *output metrics*, which measure results, and *input metrics*, which measure efforts going into developing new products. Areas of performance most often measured using these metrics are:

- Revenue growth due to new products or services and customer satisfaction with new products or services (*output metrics*).
- Number of ideas or concepts in the new-product pipeline and R&D spending as a percentage of sales (*input metrics*).

A careful look at these innovation metrics reveals that it is generally far easier to measure marketing inputs rather than marketing outputs. For example, measuring "the number of ideas or concepts in the new-product pipeline" (an input) is far easier than measuring "customer satisfaction with new products or services" (an output). But the evaluation phase of the strategic marketing process seeks to compare actual results—an output metric—with the goals set. So where possible, marketing managers prefer to use effective output metrics if they are available.

Consumer packaged goods firms like Campbell Soup Company create detailed annual marketing plans to focus their strategies.

The Variety of Marketing Plans

The planning phase of the strategic marketing process usually results in a marketing plan that sets the direction for the marketing activities of an organization. As noted earlier in Appendix A, a marketing plan is the heart of a business plan. Like business plans, marketing plans aren't all from the same mold; they vary with the length of the planning period, their purpose, and their audience. Let's look briefly at two kinds: long-range and annual marketing plans.

Long-Range Marketing Plans Typically, long-range marketing plans cover marketing activities from two to five years into the future. Except for firms in industries such as automobiles, steel, or forest products, marketing plans rarely go beyond five years into the future because the tremendous number of uncertainties makes the benefits of planning less than the effort expended. Such plans are often directed at senior-level executives and the board of directors.

Annual Marketing Plans Annual marketing plans are usually developed by a marketing or product manager (discussed later in the chapter) in a consumer products firm such as Campbell Soup Company. These plans detail marketing goals and strategies for a product, product line, or entire firm for a single year. Suppose Campbell's annual planning cycle starts with a detailed marketing research study of current users and ends after 42 weeks with the approval of the plan by the division general manager, 10 weeks before the fiscal year starts. Between these points there are continuing efforts to uncover new ideas through key-issues sessions with specialists both inside and outside the firm. The plan is fine-tuned through a series of often excruciating reviews by several levels of management, which leaves few surprises and little to chance.

Marketing Planning Frameworks: The Search for Growth

LO 22-2 Describe Porter's generic business strategies and synergy analysis planning frameworks.

Marketing planning for a firm with many products competing in many markets is a complex process. Yet in a business firm, all these planning efforts are directed at finding the means for increased growth in sales and profits. Two marketing planning frameworks that help executives make important resource allocation decisions are (1) Porter's generic business strategies and (2) synergy analysis. Both frameworks relate to elements introduced in earlier chapters.

Porter's Generic Business Strategies As shown in Figure 22–3 on the next page, Michael E. Porter has developed a framework in which he identifies four basic, or "generic," business strategies.[18] A **generic business strategy** is one that can be adopted by any firm, regardless of the product or industry involved, to achieve a competitive advantage.

FIGURE 22–3
Porter's four generic business strategies involve combinations of (1) competitive scope, or the breadth of the target markets, and (2) a stress on lower cost versus product differentiation.

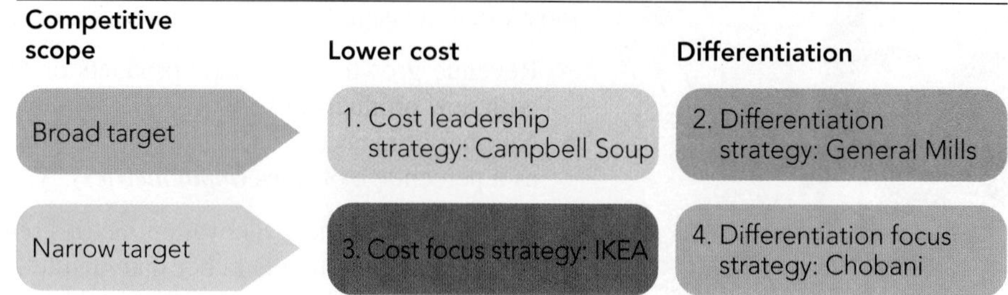

SOURCE OF COMPETITIVE ADVANTAGE
Competitive scope
Lower cost
Differentiation
Broad target
1. Cost leadership strategy: Campbell Soup
2. Differentiation strategy: General Mills
Narrow target
3. Cost focus strategy: IKEA
4. Differentiation focus strategy: Chobani

Although all the techniques discussed here involve generic strategies, the phrase is most often associated with Porter's framework. In this framework, the columns identify the two fundamental alternatives a firm can use in seeking a competitive advantage: (1) It can become the low-cost producer within the markets in which it competes or (2) it can differentiate itself from competitors by developing points of difference in its product offerings or marketing programs. In contrast, the rows identify the competitive scope: Choosing a broad target means the firm will be competing in many market segments, whereas choosing a narrow target means the firm will be competing in only a few segments or even a single segment. The columns and rows result in four generic business strategies, which can provide a competitive advantage among similar strategic business units in the same industry. These four strategies are as follows:

1. A **cost leadership strategy** (cell 1) focuses on reducing expenses and, in turn, lowers product prices while targeting a broad array of market segments. This may be done by securing less expensive raw materials from lower-cost suppliers or investing in new production equipment to reduce unit costs and improve quality. Campbell Soup's sophisticated product development and supply chain systems have led to huge cost savings. So its cost leadership strategy has resulted in lower prices for customers—causing its market share to increase in the current recession.
2. A **differentiation strategy** (cell 2) requires products to have significant points of difference in product offerings, brand image, higher quality, advanced technology, or superior service to charge a higher price while targeting a broad array of market segments. This strategy allows the firm to charge a price premium. General Mills uses this strategy in stressing its nutritious, high-quality brands in reaching a diverse array of customer segments.
3. A **cost focus strategy** (cell 3) involves controlling expenses and, in turn, lowering product prices targeted at a narrow range of market segments. Retail chains targeting only a few market segments in a restricted group of products often use a cost focus strategy successfully. IKEA has become the world's largest furniture retailer by selling flat-pack, self-assembly furniture, accessories, and bathroom and kitchen items to cost-conscious consumers.
4. Finally, a **differentiation focus strategy** (cell 4) requires products to have significant points of difference in order to target one or only a few market segments. Chobani Greek Yogurt, discussed in Chapter 1, uses a differentiation focus strategy. Its 2007 launch of a healthy, high-quality, great-tasting yogurt using natural ingredients successfully reached the small but now exploding segment of consumers who favor Greek-style yogurt.

These four generic business strategies are the basis for Michael Porter's theory about what makes a nation's industries successful, as discussed in Chapter 7.

Which of Porter's generic strategies is IKEA using? For the answer and a discussion of these strategies, see the text and Figure 22–3.

There is no wrong side of this bed.

Marketing Matters

customer value

A Test of Your Skills: Where Are the Synergies?

To try your hand at this multibillion-dollar synergy game, assume you are the vice president of marketing for Great States Corp., which markets a line of nonpowered, powered walking, and powered riding lawn mowers throughout North America. A market-product grid for your business is shown to the right. You distribute your nonpowered mowers in all three market segments, but you offer your walking powered mowers only in suburban markets. Your powered riding mowers are not offered in any of the three market segments.

Here are your strategy dilemmas:

1. Where are the marketing synergies (efficiencies)?
2. Where are the R&D–manufacturing synergies (efficiencies)?
3. What would a market-product grid look like for an ideal company that Great States could merge with to achieve both marketing and R&D–manufacturing synergies (efficiencies)?

To consider these questions, read the text and study Figure 22–4 and the figure below.

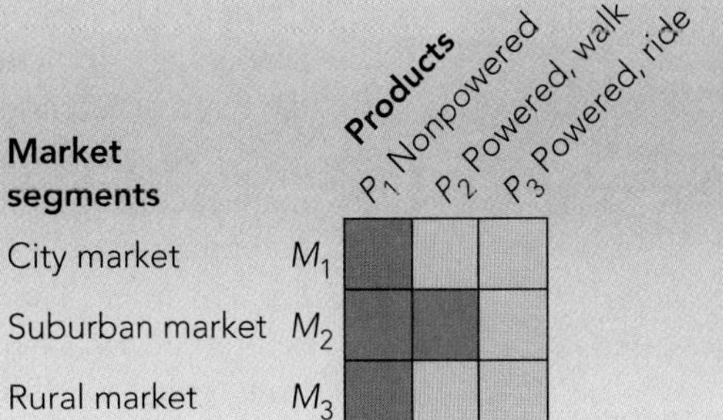

Synergy Analysis **Synergy analysis** seeks market-product opportunities by finding the optimum balance between marketing efficiencies versus R&D–manufacturing efficiencies. Using diversification analysis from Chapter 2 and the market-product grid framework from Chapter 9, we can see two kinds of synergy that are critical in developing corporate and marketing strategies: (1) marketing synergy and (2) R&D–manufacturing synergy.

While the search for synergies starts within the organization itself, marketing and manufacturing synergies can also come about through mergers and acquisitions that perform organizational functions more efficiently. For example, as noted in the Marketing Matters box, assume you are the vice president of marketing for Great States Corp.'s line of nonpowered lawn mowers and powered walking mowers sold to the consumer market. You are looking for new product and new market opportunities to increase your revenues and profits.

You conduct a market segmentation study and develop a market-product grid to analyze future opportunities. You identify three major segments in the consumer market based on geography: (1) city, (2) suburban, and (3) rural households. These market segments relate to the size of lawn a consumer must mow. The product groupings are (1) nonpowered, (2) powered walking, and (3) powered riding mowers.

Five alternative marketing strategies are shown in the market-product grids in Figure 22–4.[19] As mentioned in Chapter 9, the important marketing synergies, or

FIGURE 22–4
Market-product grids show alternative strategies for a lawn mower manufacturer. Try to find synergies in each strategy—if any exist.

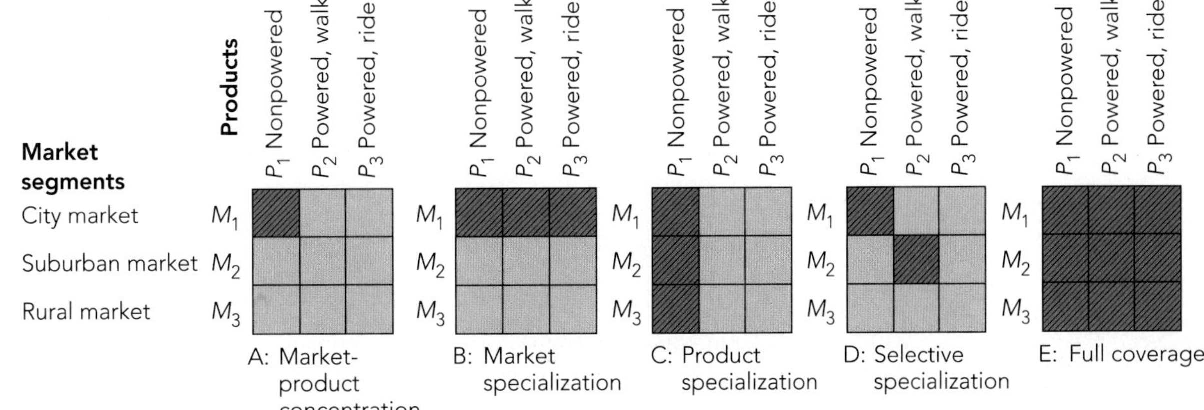

How might you segment the lawn mower market? What marketing synergies might result? For the answers, see the text.

efficiencies, run horizontally across the rows in Figure 22–4. Conversely, the important R&D–manufacturing synergies, or efficiencies, run vertically down the columns. Let's look at the synergy effects for the five combinations in Figure 22–4.

A. *Market-product concentration.* The firm benefits from its focus on a single product line and market segment, but it loses opportunities for significant synergies in both marketing and R&D–manufacturing.

B. *Market specialization.* The firm gains marketing synergy through providing a complete product line for the city market segment, but R&D–manufacturing has the difficulty of developing and producing three different products.

C. *Product specialization.* The firm gains R&D–manufacturing synergy through producing only a nonpowered lawn mower, but gaining market distribution in the three different geographic areas will be costly.

D. *Selective specialization.* The firm doesn't gain either marketing or R&D–manufacturing synergies because of the uniqueness of the market-product combinations.

E. *Full coverage.* The firm receives the maximum potential synergies in both marketing and R&D–manufacturing. The critical question to be answered: Is the firm spread too thin because of the resource requirements needed to reach all market-product combinations?

The Marketing Matters box poses the question of what the ideal partner for Great States would be if it merged with another firm, given the market-product combinations shown. If you want to follow a full-coverage strategy, then the ideal merger partner is shown in Figure 22–5. This partnership would give the maximum potential synergies—if you are not spreading the resources of your merged companies too thin. Marketing gains by having a complete product line in all regions, and R&D–manufacturing gains by achieving production efficiencies through the firm's access to new markets and its ability to produce larger volumes of its existing products.

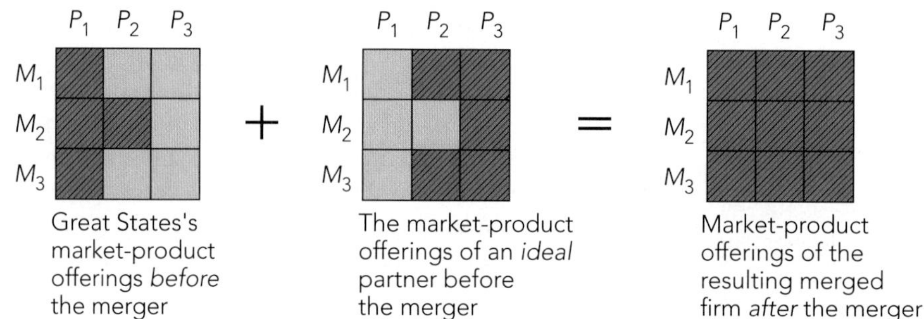

FIGURE 22–5
This is the ideal merger for Great States to obtain full market-product coverage. The ideal partner offers lawn mower products to the exact segments of customers not being served by Great States.

learning review

22-3. What is the difference between an input metric and an output metric?

22-4. Describe Porter's four generic business strategies.

22-5. Where do (*a*) marketing synergies and (*b*) R&D–manufacturing synergies appear when using the synergy analysis framework?

Some Marketing Planning and Strategy Lessons

Explain what makes an effective marketing plan.

Applying marketing planning frameworks is not automatic; in fact, it requires a great deal of managerial judgment. Commonsense requirements of an effective marketing plan are discussed next, followed by problems that can arise.

Guidelines for an Effective Marketing Plan President Dwight D. Eisenhower, when he commanded Allied armies in World War II, made his classic observation, "Plans are nothing; planning is everything." It is the process of careful planning that focuses an organization's efforts and leads to success. The plans themselves, which change with events, are often secondary. Effective planning and plans are inevitably characterized by identifiable objectives, specific strategies or courses of action, and the means to execute them. Here are some guidelines for developing effective marketing plans:[20]

- *Set measurable, achievable goals.* Ideally, goals should be quantified and measurable in terms of what is to be accomplished and by when. So, "Increase market share from 18 percent to 22 percent by December 31, 2014," is preferable to "Maximize market share given our available resources." Also, to motivate people, the goals must be achievable.
- *Use a base of facts and valid assumptions.* The more a marketing plan is based on facts and valid assumptions, rather than guesses, the less uncertainty and risk are associated with executing it. Good marketing research helps.
- *Use simple, but clear and specific, plans.* Effective execution of plans requires that people at all levels in the firm understand what, when, and how they are to accomplish their tasks. Involve people with the right skills and experience in the planning effort.
- *Have complete and feasible plans.* Marketing plans must incorporate all the key marketing mix factors and be supported by adequate resources.
- *Make plans controllable and flexible.* Marketing plans must enable results to be compared with planned targets, often using precise marketing metrics. This allows replanning—the flexibility to alter the original plans based on recent results.
- *Find the right person to implement the plans.* But make sure that person is heavily involved in making the plans.
- *Work toward consensus-building.* "Ownership" of the plan by team members and stakeholders increases the chances for its success.

Problems in Marketing Planning and Strategy An all-too-frequent problem in marketing planning and strategy is that bad news is filtered out as information goes up each organizational level (see Chapter 2), giving top management a very rosy picture. J.D. Power III did marketing research at Ford four decades ago. "There was no interest in finding out what customers really thought," he says. "Instead, we were constantly asked to 'torture the data until it confessed,' giving us the answers the execs wanted."[21]

So he founded J.D. Power & Associates to do customer satisfaction studies. One of his first marketing research clients was Toyota, which listened and has used hundreds of J.D. Power studies over the years. Today, J.D. Power & Associates is one of the world's best-known marketing information companies and now serves not only the auto industry but also the health care, telecommunications, insurance, financial services, and other industries. Other key problems that emerge from a firm engaging in the strategic marketing process include the following:

1. *Plans may be based on very poor assumptions about environmental forces,* especially changing economic conditions and competitors' actions. A Western Union plan failed because it didn't reflect the impact of deregulation and competitors' actions on business.
2. *Planners and their plans may have lost sight of their customers' needs.* But not at the Papa John's pizza chain. The "better ingredients, better pizza" slogan makes the hair stand up on the back of the necks of competing Pizza Hut executives. The reason is that this Papa John's slogan reflects the firm's obsessive attention to detail, which is stealing market share from the much-bigger Pizza Hut. Sample detail: If the cheese on the pizza shows a single air bubble or the crust is not golden brown, the offending pizza is not served to the customer.

QR 22-3
Papa John's
Video

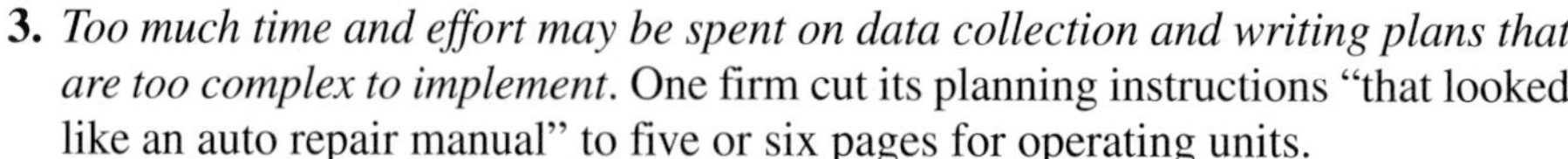

3. *Too much time and effort may be spent on data collection and writing plans that are too complex to implement.* One firm cut its planning instructions "that looked like an auto repair manual" to five or six pages for operating units.
4. *Line operating managers often feel no sense of ownership in implementing the plans.* Andy Grove, when he was CEO of Intel, observed, "We had the very ridiculous system . . . of delegating strategic planning to strategic planners. The strategies these [planners] prepared had no bearing on anything we actually did."[22] The solution is to assign more planning activities to line operating managers—the people who actually carry them out.

General Mills's successful introduction of French-developed Yoplait yogurt to U.S. consumers . . .

Big G: Global Strategies to Find Synergies, Segments, and Partners Competing in today's global marketplace, General Mills is concerned with *both* selling its products and brands in countries around the world *and* obtaining ideas for new products from anyone, anywhere, who has a great product or technology. The company's joint venture with Swiss-based Nestlé in Cereal Partners Worldwide provides General Mills access to European, Latin American, and Asian consumers—offering everything from cereals to ice cream bars.

Big G now conducts a global search for new ideas, products, and technologies. The success of Yoplait yogurt ("The Yogurt of France") has led the firm to broaden its yogurt offerings—including the recently introduced Yoplait Greek 100, a 100-calorie Greek-style yogurt. Big G also has brought other products developed outside the United States to our shores. Wanchai Ferry brand dinners are an adaptation of frozen dumplings developed by Madame Kin Wo Chong, a Hong Kong entrepreneur who started by selling her dumplings in 1977 from a cart on the city's Wanchai Ferry pier. General Mills first introduced Wanchai Ferry as a dry dinner kit to which one added meat. And surprise! The brand is now one of General Mills's new stars in China and is sold in about 100 Chinese cities.[23]

Have a great idea for a new technology or product General Mills might use? Under the General Mills Worldwide Innovation Network (G-WIN), the company wants your idea to help accelerate its innovation efforts. You can contact General Mills online at www.generalmills.com/Company/Innovation/G-Win.aspx to submit your idea. But the new product or technology must uniquely meet a large unmet consumer need, be technically feasible, fit within Big G's product categories or brands, and be a "game-changer"![24]

. . . led the way to its global search for new products today, such as Wanchai Ferry dinner kits from Hong Kong.

Balancing Value and Values in Strategic Marketing Plans Two important trends are likely to influence the strategic marketing process in the future. The first, *value-based planning*, combines marketing planning ideas and financial planning techniques to assess how much a division or strategic business unit (SBU) contributes to the price of a company's stock (or shareholder wealth). Value is created when the financial return of a strategic activity exceeds the cost of the resources allocated to the activity.

The second trend is the increasing interest in *value-driven strategies*, which incorporate concerns for ethics, integrity, employee health and safety, and environmental safeguards with more common corporate values such as growth, profitability, customer service, and quality. Some experts have observed that although many corporations cite broad corporate values in advertisements, press releases, and company newsletters, they have not yet changed their strategic plans to reflect these stated values. U.S. firms, like those around the world, are increasingly called on to be good global citizens and to support sustainable development.

Marketing Matters

entrepreneurship

Ask Disruptive Questions to Achieve Disruptive Innovations

The glamour of successfully launching a Google, Apple, or Facebook hides one blatant fact: Launching a revolutionary new product or service is incredibly difficult! Research on disruptive innovations suggests that precise, focused questions can be used in developing new products or reaching key market segments. This involves invoking powerful questions "to help see beneath the surface of everyday action and discover what's never been."

"Disruptive innovators" often start by exploring *what currently is* and then moving to a powerful search for *what might be*. Rather than simply ask for "any questions" or "any suggestions" in a meeting, disruptive innovators often:

1. Ask "what is" questions. This helps reveal *what is happening* here and now.
2. Ask "what caused" questions. This helps explain *why things are the way they are.*
3. Ask "why" and "why not" questions. This helps reveal changes to reach *what might be.*
4. Ask "what if" questions. This helps suggest and *get reactions to new actions*—perhaps a new-product concept.

Using these questions effectively can reveal solutions to a variety of problems, not just new-product innovations. Try asking these questions in your next group-project meeting.

Disruptive Innovations and Long-Range Marketing Plans *Disruptive innovations* create a new market by initially reaching new customers through displacing an existing market's low-end product. The innovation eventually displaces the original product or technology, creating havoc for organizations that operate in the old, displaced market and disrupting their long-range marketing plans.

However, these disruptive innovations don't replace an existing product or technology overnight. Instead, established firms in the industry initially conclude the disruptive innovation isn't worth pursuing because the new market is too small and takes scarce resources away from improving their existing products. Eventually, the disruptive innovation becomes pervasive enough to invade the large, traditional markets, often driving the original firms out of business. Examples include Wikipedia, which caused *Encyclopedia Britannica* to stop print production in 2012 after 244 years, and liquid-crystal displays (LCDs), which replaced cathode ray tubes (CRTs) in TVs in the 2000s.[25]

How can marketing managers recognize and incorporate disruptive innovations in their long-range plans? While no perfect answer exists, the Marketing Matters box shows the first giant step toward an answer: Ask tough, focused, disruptive questions. Research shows that (1) disruptive innovators ask more questions than they get answers to and (2) good questions provide greater value than good answers![26]

THE IMPLEMENTATION PHASE OF THE STRATEGIC MARKETING PROCESS

The post-game summary provided by a losing football coach often runs something like, "We had an excellent game plan; we just didn't execute it." The planning-versus-execution issue applies to the strategic marketing process as well: When a marketing plan fails, it's difficult to determine whether the failure is due to a poor plan or poor implementation.

Is Planning or Implementation the Problem?

Effective managers tracking progress on a struggling plan first try to identify whether the problems involve (1) the plan and strategy, (2) its implementation, or (3) both, and then they try to correct the problems. But as discussed earlier in the chapter, research on what really works shows that successful firms have excellence on both the planning and strategy side and the implementation and execution side.

At the other extreme, most of the hundreds of dot-com firms like Pets.com that failed in the late 1990s had both planning *and* implementation problems. Their bad planning often resulted from their focus on getting start-up money from investors rather than providing real value to customers. Bad implementation by some of these dot-coms led to their spending huge sums on wasteful Super Bowl television ads to try to promote their failing websites. Also, many of these Internet firms didn't understand key implementation issues that involved inventories, warehouses, and physical distribution.

Increasing Emphasis on Marketing Implementation

Today, the implementation phase of the strategic marketing process often involves moving many planning activities from planners to the line managers responsible for implementing the plans. General Electric's legendary CEO Jack Welch is credited with making GE more efficient and far better at implementation. When Welch became CEO, GE was bogged down with 25,000 managers and close to a dozen layers between him and the factory floor.

In his "delayering strategy," Welch sought to cut GE's levels in half and to speed up decision making and implementation by building an atmosphere of trust and autonomy among his managers and employees. Where possible, he made the people planning the project responsible for carrying it out. Today, businesses around the world use GE's focus on implementation as a benchmark.[27]

Improving Implementation of Marketing Programs

No magic formula exists to guarantee the effective implementation of marketing plans. In fact, the answer seems to be a balance between good management skills and good practices, from which have come some guidelines for improving program implementation.

Open communications at Lockheed Martin's Skunk Works have led to state-of-the-art aircraft like this F-35 Lightning II Joint Strike Fighter.

Take Action and Avoid Paralysis by Analysis Management experts warn against "paralysis by analysis," the tendency to excessively analyze a problem instead of taking action. To overcome this pitfall, they call for a "bias for action" and recommend a "do it, fix it, try it" approach.[28] Their conclusion: Perfectionists finish last, so getting it 90 percent perfect and letting the marketplace help in the fine-tuning makes good sense in implementation.

Lockheed Martin's Skunk Works got its name from the comic strip *L'il Abner*. Led by Kelly Johnson, Skunk Works developed its legendary reputation for achieving superhuman technical feats by stressing teamwork and working within the constraints of small budgets and tight deadlines. Under Johnson, the Skunk Works turned out a series of world-class aircraft, such as the F-35 Lightning II Joint Strike Fighter. Two of Kelly Johnson's basic tenets: (1) Make decisions promptly, and (2) Avoid paralysis by analysis. One U.S. Air Force audit showed that Johnson's Skunk Works could carry out a program on schedule with

126 people, whereas a competitor in a comparable program was behind schedule with 3,750 people.[29]

QR 22-4
F-35 Video

Surface Problems with Open Communications Two more Kelly Johnson axioms from Lockheed Martin's Skunk Works apply here: (1) When trouble develops, surface the problem immediately, and (2) Get help—don't keep the problem to yourself. Success often lies in fostering a work setting that is open enough so employees are willing to speak out when they see problems, without fear of punishment. The focus is placed on trying to solve the problem as a group rather than finding someone to blame. In this "open communications" environment, solutions are solicited from anyone who has a creative idea to suggest—from the janitor to the president.

Communicate Goals and the Means of Achieving Them Those called on to implement plans need to understand both the goals sought and how they are to be accomplished. Historically, Toyota's growth has been built on a foundation of QDR—quality, dependability, and reliability. Besides emphasizing "always better cars" under new CEO Akio Toyoda, the Toyota design team encourages a more "emotional" link between buyers and Toyota vehicles. And it continues to stress *genchi genbutsu*—"go and see"—a message about *both* a goal and a means of achieving it.[30]

Its RAV4 EV, an all-electric SUV, reflects Toyota's *genchi genbutsu*—"go and see"—message that shows *both* a goal and a means of achieving it.

Have a Responsible Program Champion Willing to Act Successful programs almost always have a **program champion**, a person who is willing and able to "cut the red tape" to move the program forward. Such a person often has the uncanny ability to move back and forth between the "big picture" and the specific details as the situation warrants. Program champions can be notoriously brash in overcoming organizational hurdles. The U.S. Navy's Admiral Grace Murray Hopper gave the world not only an early computer language but also her famous advice for cutting through an organization's red tape: "Better to ask forgiveness than permission."

Reward Success but Don't Punish Failure Sara Blakely, founder and 100 percent owner of Spanx, has a simple mantra: "Failure just leads you to the next great thing"—so learn takeaway lessons from your failures. Her vision for her start-up was to eliminate "visible panty lines" when women dressed in stylish outfits. So she cut the feet off her control-top pantyhose, wrote her own patent application, and made all her initial sales calls. Blakely sent a basket of her prototypes to Oprah Winfrey, who selected Spanx as her Product of the Year. Today, Spanx has 200 products, including a men's line of undershirts, underwear, and socks.[31]

When an individual or a team is rewarded for achieving an organization's goal, they have maximum incentive to see a program implemented successfully because

Founder Sara Blakely launched Spanx with a simple mantra: "Failure just leads you to the next great thing."

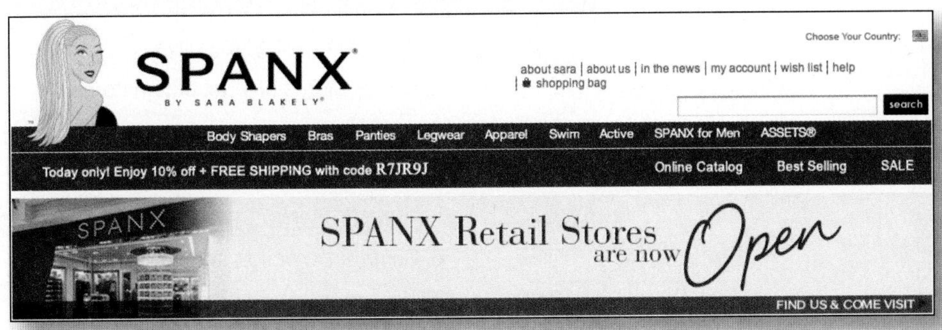

Marketing Matters

entrepreneurship

From Dragons and Cows to Clash of Clans and Hay Day

Tiny Finnish mobile game start-up Supercell is a virtual poster child for succeeding by failing. Asked to explain Supercell's success, 34-year-old CEO and founder Ilkka Paananen says simply, "The truth is we're very good at failing." For specifics, he goes on, "What really made us successful were the four games we killed before release." Not punishing failures—but learning difficult lessons from them—is a characteristic of many successful firms.

Supercell's success ties to dragons and cows. This two-year-old company released its two free games in mid-2012. Downloads surged and by early 2013, its revenues from in-game purchases made Clash of Clans No. 1 and Hay Day No. 3 on Apple's App Store ranking of the highest grossing apps in the United States. Set in medieval times, Clash of Clans lets players build villages, train troops, and join other clans. With Hay Day, players grow virtual crops and livestock like Zynga's FarmVille.

Killing poor mobile games before their release is only part of the planning and implementation strategy at Supercell. It minimizes bureaucracy and assembles small project teams of 10 employees or less—rare for game developers—that have great freedom from bosses and the need for continual approval. And its teams can apparently read the minds of the players of its first two games, who log in an average of 12 times a day!

they have personal ownership and a stake in that success. At the same time, many firms owe their success to learning important lessons from their failures—as was the case with mobile game start-up Supercell. See the Marketing Matters box for how this tiny Finnish firm succeeded by failing.[32]

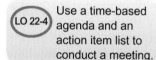

Use a time-based agenda and an action item list to conduct a meeting.

Schedule Precise Tasks, Responsibilities, and Deadlines Successful implementation requires that members of the program team understand its goals, the tasks they are responsible for to help reach those goals, and the deadlines for completing them. To implement the thousands of tasks for a new aircraft design, Lockheed Martin typically holds weekly program meetings.

In most organizations, the meeting chairperson calls the meeting to order and hands out an agenda with the topics listed sequentially. The difficulty with this is that if the critical topic is an agenda item near the end of the list, meeting members don't know this, and they waste a lot of the meeting time on earlier agenda items. A better approach is a **time-based agenda**, a meeting agenda that shows the running time allocated to each agenda item. In a time-based agenda, time is shown as *running time* (2:00, 2:03, etc.) and not *target time* (3 minutes, 10 minutes, etc.), which lets participants know better how the meeting is progressing. A sample time-based agenda for a marketing department meeting is shown below:

Running Time	Topic	Who Leads	– Objective – Info	Action
2:00	1. Review meeting objectives	Gina	×	
2:03	2. Check status of past action items	Gina	×	
2:13	3. Analyze client's marketing needs	Gina		×
2:25	4. Assess client's promotion options	Roger		×
2:30	5. Agree on client's promotion goals, media	Steve		×
2:57	6. Summarize action items	Gina	×	
3:00	7. Adjourn meeting	Gina		×

In the time-based agenda above, everyone knows topic #5—Steve's leading the discussion to agree on the client's promotion goals and media to use—is especially critical and is allocated the most time. They also know if a topic is for "info" (information), they are to listen and not spend valuable time discussing it. Sharing ideas is only for items with an "×" in the "Action" column.

The outcome of each of these program meetings is an **action item list**, an aid to implementing a plan that consists of four columns: (1) the task; (2) the person responsible for completing that task; (3) the date to finish the task; and (4) what is to be delivered. Note that topic #6 in the time-based agenda is "Summarize action items," so that everyone in the meeting knows the actions for which they are responsible. A sample action item list is shown below:

Action/Task	Who Does	By When	Deliverable
1. Write Client A proposal	Lisa	March 3	Draft proposal
2. Identify new clients	Kris	March 6	Draft client call list
3. Develop Client B print ad	Mike	March 10	Submit final ad

It is clear from this example that Kris knows she is responsible for providing a list of new clients by March 6. Within hours of completing a program meeting, the action item list is circulated to those attending. This then serves as a starting point for the next meeting, shown as topic #2 in the time-based agenda on the previous page. Meeting minutes are viewed as secondary and backward-looking. Action item lists are forward-looking, clarify the targets, and put strong pressure on people to achieve their designated tasks by the specified deadlines.

Related to the action item lists are formal *program schedules*, which show the relationships through time of the various program tasks. Scheduling an action program involves: (1) identifying the main tasks; (2) determining the time required to complete each task; (3) arranging the activities to meet the deadline; and (4) assigning responsibility for completing each task. The most widely used program schedule is the Gantt chart, described in Chapter 2 (see Figure 2–10, which illustrates the use of a Gantt chart to schedule tasks and complete a team project on time).

learning review

22-6. What is the meaning and importance of a program champion?

22-7. Describe one or two lessons from Lockheed Martin's Skunk Works that can be applied to implementing marketing programs.

22-8. How are (*a*) a time-based agenda and (*b*) an action item list used in a marketing program meeting?

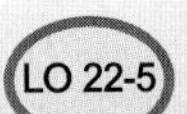

Describe an organization's marketing department and the role of a product manager.

Organizing for Marketing

A marketing organization is needed to implement the firm's marketing plans. Today's marketing organizations understand: (1) the evolving role of the chief marketing officer; (2) how line versus staff positions and divisional groupings interrelate to form a cohesive marketing organization; and (3) the role of the product manager.

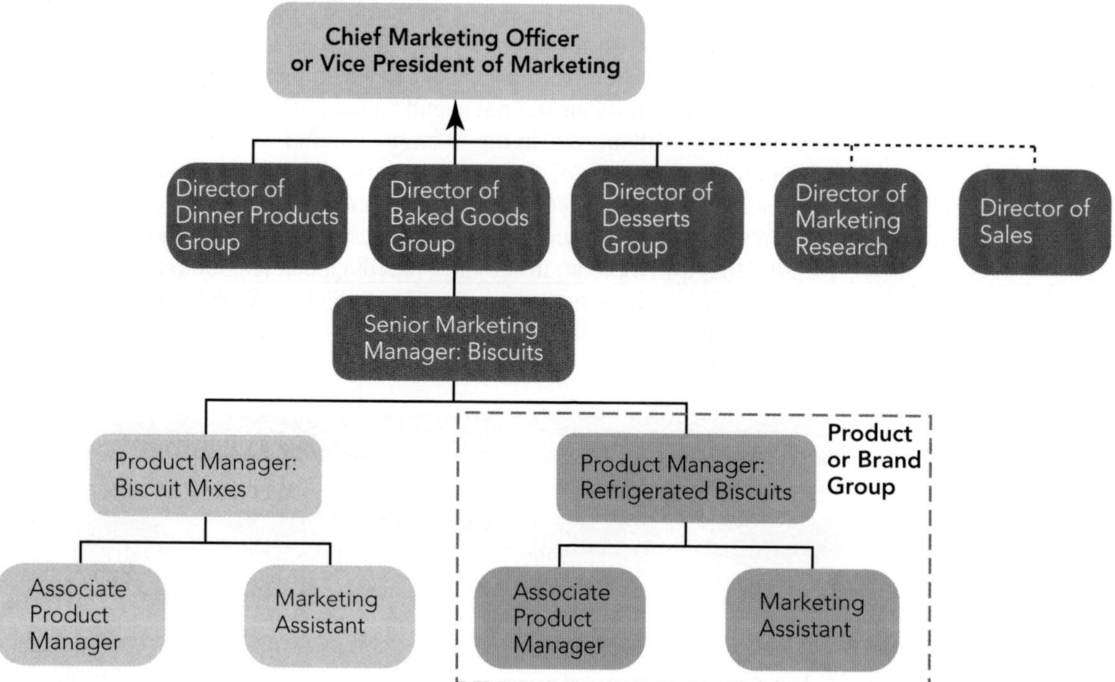

FIGURE 22–6
This organization of a strategic business unit in a typical consumer packaged goods firm shows two product or brand groups—biscuit mixes and refrigerated biscuits.

The Evolving Role of the Chief Marketing Officer The senior executive responsible for a firm's marketing activities shown in Figure 22–6 is increasingly given the title of chief marketing officer (CMO) rather than vice president of marketing. This reflects the broadening of the CMO's role as the inside-the-company "voice of the consumer." So today, it is critical that CMOs understand (1) the changing characteristics of the global consumer segments served and (2) how to market to consumers who increasingly combine Internet online research with offline purchasing at a local store and vice versa.[33] Along with these broadened responsibilities is higher turnover among CMOs. A recent sample of 100 large firms revealed the average CMO held the job for less than two years.[34]

Line versus Staff and Divisional Groupings Although simplified, Figure 22–6 shows the organization of a typical strategic business unit in a consumer packaged goods firm like Procter & Gamble, Kraft, or General Mills. It consists of the Dinner Products, Baked Goods, and Desserts groups and highlights the distinction between line and staff positions. Managers in **line positions**, such as the senior marketing manager for Biscuits, have the authority and responsibility to issue orders to people who report to them, such as the two product managers shown in Figure 22–6. In this organizational chart, line positions are connected with solid lines. People in **staff positions** (connected by dotted lines) have the authority and responsibility to advise people in line positions but cannot issue direct orders to them.

Most marketing organizations use divisional groupings—such as product line, functional, geographical, and market-based—to implement plans and achieve objectives. Only the first of these appears in the organizational chart in Figure 22–6. The top of the chart shows organization by **product line groupings** in which a unit is responsible for specific product offerings, such as Dinner Products or Desserts.

At higher levels than what is shown in Figure 22–6, grocery products firms are organized by **functional groupings**—such as manufacturing, marketing, and finance—that represent the different departments or business activities within a firm.

Most grocery products firms use **geographical groupings**, in which sales territories are subdivided according to geographical location. Each director of sales has several regional sales managers reporting to him or her, such as western, southern, and so on. These, in turn, have district managers reporting to them, with the field sales representatives operating at the lowest level.

A fourth method of organizing a company is to use **market-based groupings**, which utilize specific customer segments, such as the banking, health care, or manufacturing segments. When this method of organizing is combined with product groupings, the result is a *matrix organization*.

A relatively new position in consumer products firms is the *category manager* (the senior marketing manager in Figure 22–6), who is responsible for an entire product line—all biscuit brands, for example. These marketers attempt to reduce the possibility of one brand's actions hurting another brand in the same category. Procter & Gamble uses category managers to organize by "global business units," such as baby care and beauty care. Cutting across country boundaries, these global business units implement standardized worldwide pricing, promotion, and distribution.

Role of the Product Manager The key person in the product or brand group is the manager who heads it. As mentioned in Chapter 11, this person is often called the *product manager* or *brand manager*. This person and his or her assistants comprise the *product group* or *brand group*, enclosed by the dashed red line in Figure 22–6. These product or brand groups are the basic building blocks in the marketing department of most consumer and business product firms. The function of a product manager is to plan, implement, and evaluate the annual and long-range plans for the products for which he or she is responsible.

There are both benefits and dangers to the product manager system. On the positive side, product managers become strong advocates for the assigned products, cut red tape to work with people in various functions both inside and outside the organization, and assume profit-and-loss responsibility for the product line. On the negative side, even though product managers have major responsibilities, they have relatively little direct authority, so they must use persuasion rather than issue direct orders to implement their marketing plans.

THE EVALUATION PHASE OF THE STRATEGIC MARKETING PROCESS

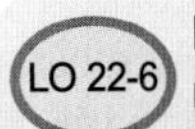

Explain the use of marketing ROI, metrics, and dashboards in evaluating marketing programs.

Evaluation, the final phase of the strategic marketing process, involves (1) the marketing evaluation process itself and (2) the use of marketing ROI, metrics, and dashboards. We conclude this section with a look at how General Mills uses marketing metrics and dashboards.

The Marketing Evaluation Process

The essence of marketing evaluation involves (1) comparing results with planned goals to identify deviations and then (2) taking corrective actions.

Identifying Deviations from Goals Figure 22–7 on the next page shows that marketing plans made in the planning phase have both quantified goals and a specific marketing metric used to measure whether the goal is actually achieved. Marketing actions are taken in the implementation phase to attempt to achieve the goals set in the planning phase. In the evaluation phase, as Figure 22–7 shows, the quantitative results are measured using the marketing metrics and compared with the actual results of the marketing actions. For speed and efficiency, the results are compared with goals and often shown to marketing managers on marketing dashboards to enable them to take timely actions.

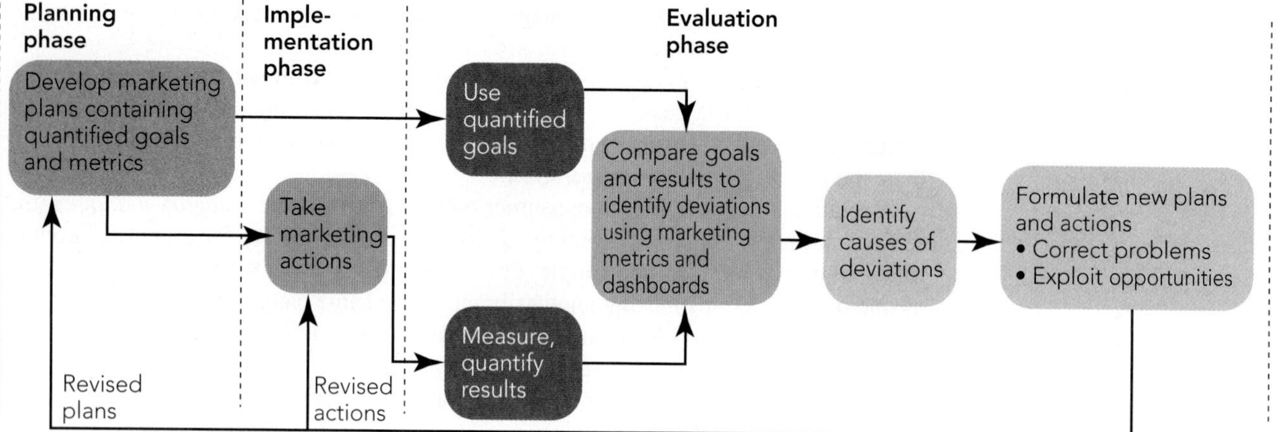

FIGURE 22–7
The evaluation phase of the strategic marketing process ties results and actions to goals, often using marketing metrics and dashboards.

Acting on Deviations from Goals A marketing manager interprets the marketing dashboard information using *management by exception*, which involves identifying results that deviate from plans to diagnose their causes and take new actions. The marketing manager looks for two kinds of deviations, each triggering a different kind of action:

- *Actual results exceed goals.* In this case, marketing must act quickly to exploit unforeseen opportunities. In 2012, Starbucks added a "blonde roast" and more food items for U.S. customers. It also opened hundreds of new stores for Asian customers. The result: Starbucks' first quarter 2013 profits grew by 13 percent. Having exceeded its goals, Starbucks recently announced aggressive plans to add thousands of additional stores worldwide, make 60 percent of new U.S. stores drive-thrus, and develop new coffee varieties on its just-purchased 600-acre Costa Rican research farm.[35]
- *Actual results fall short of goals.* This requires a corrective action. Beaten badly for years in the U.S. toothpaste market by P&G's Crest, Colgate used new technology to introduce its Total toothpaste, the first "oral pharmaceutical" approved by the U.S. Food and Drug Administration. Total not only cleans teeth, but its germ-fighting technology helps heal gingivitis, a bleeding-gum disease. Colgate marketed this feature aggressively, enabling Total to become No. 1 in the U.S. toothpaste market.[36]

What recession? With over 33 million Facebook fans and over 17,000 stores worldwide—like this one in London, England—Starbucks is planning thousands more, including 900 new ones with drive-thrus by 2017.

"Hiring a Milkshake" and Digging Beneath the Numbers The "goals" used in marketing metrics are almost always *quantitative* goals. But sometimes the numbers can hide what is really happening and digging beneath the surface is needed to reveal the insights that lead to better marketing actions. A product and service example illustrate this issue.

A fast-food chain asked a team of consultants to beef up sales of its milkshakes. The chain had huge files about the likes of loyal milkshake customers. Changing the milkshakes based on those likes had no impact on sales. So consultants tried a different approach and asked: "What job is a customer trying to do when he hires a milkshake?" After looking at the results, the consultants found that: (1) half the milkshakes were bought by men in the early morning; (2) it was the only thing they bought; and (3) they then drove off in their car with it.

For how the Detroit Institute of Arts uses direct observation and interviews to measure the results of its marketing actions, see the text.

◀ The Meeting of David and Abigail' by Peter Paul Rubens. It is one of the gallery's big draws.
Matt Sikora, the museum's director of evaluation, with his hand-held computer. ▼
After noticing that visitors overlooked the gallery summary panel, the museum moved it next to this Rubens. ▲
Museum visitor from Youngstown, OH. ▶

Research on why these customers "hired the milkshake" revealed they (1) all had a similar job (2) with a long, boring drive to work and (3) needed something to do while driving.

> One hand had to be on the wheel, but, jeez, somebody gave me another hand and there isn't anything in it. And I'm not hungry yet but I know I'll be hungry by ten o'clock. So what do I hire? If you promise not to tell my wife, I hire doughnuts a lot, but they crumb all over my clothes and they're gone too fast. . . . But, let me tell you, this milkshake is so viscous that it takes twenty-five minutes to suck it up that little straw. And you can turn it sideways and it doesn't fall out![37]

By understanding what job the customers were trying to get done, how to improve the milkshake product became clear: You make the milkshake more viscous and put chunks of fruit into it to make sucking through a straw on the commute more unpredictable, interesting, and rewarding!

With services, measuring results that lead to actions becomes even more intangible. As shown in the photo, the Detroit Institute of Arts observes and interviews visitors to make its galleries more appealing. It discovered that visitors were often confused by the museum's panels—the written descriptions next to the art. So it made the panels more user-friendly by:

- Moving them closer to the art.
- Reducing the maximum word count from 250 to 150.
- Increasing readability by breaking up blocks of text with bullet points, subheadings, color, and graphics.

The result: These changes have significantly increased the "readership" of these descriptive panels, some of which in the past were read by only 2 percent of gallery visitors.[38]

Marketing ROI, Metrics, and Dashboards

In the past decade, measuring the performance of marketing activities has become a central focus in many organizations. This boils down to some form of the question, "What measure can I use to determine if my company's marketing is effective?"

No single measure exists to determine if a company's marketing is effective. In finance, the return on investment (ROI) metric relates the total investment made to the total return generated from the investment. The concept has been extended to measuring the effectiveness of marketing expenditures with **marketing ROI**, the application of modern measurement technologies to understand, quantify, and optimize marketing spending.[39]

The strategic marketing process tries to improve marketing ROI through the effective use of marketing metrics and dashboards:

- *Marketing metrics.* Depending on the specific goal or objective sought, one or a few key marketing metrics are chosen, such as market share, cost per sales lead, cost per click, sales per square foot, and so on.[40] This is step 2 (set market and product goals) of the planning phase shown in Figure 22–2.
- *Marketing dashboards.* Ideally, the marketing metrics are displayed—often daily or weekly—on the marketing dashboard on the manager's computer. With today's syndicated scanner data, website hits, and TV viewership tracking, the typical manager faces information overload. So an effective marketing dashboard highlights actual results that vary significantly from plans. This alerts the manager to potential problems.[41]

These highlighted exceptions or deviations from the marketing plan (shown in the evaluation phase in Figure 22–2) are the immediate focus of the marketing manager, who then tries to improve the firm's marketing ROI.

You've eaten healthy all day and now you want something quick and tasty to satisfy your sweet tooth. Try Warm Delight Minis—the 150 calorie, microwavable dessert! Just add water in the container and cook for 1 minute. Then, enjoy!

Evaluation Using Marketing Metrics and Marketing Dashboards at General Mills

Let's assume it is mid-January and you are part of Vivian Callaway's Warm Delights team at General Mills. Your team is using the marketing data and metrics shown in the marketing dashboard in Figure 22–8. We can summarize the evaluation step of the strategic marketing process using this dashboard and the three-step Challenge-Findings-Actions format used in the Using Marketing Dashboard boxes in the book.

The Distribution Challenge for Warm Delights Minis You've been asked to analyze the channel of distribution strategy of the Warm Delights Minis product. This hypothetical example is based on the type of scanner data that might appear in a computer display used by General Mills. However, details have been modified to simplify the data and analysis.

The marketing dashboard in Figure 22–8 focuses on the distribution of the six existing Warm Delights Minis flavors and the impact of adding two new flavors introduced in the fall—Lemon Swirl cake and Cinnamon Swirl cake.[42] As with all new grocery products, the challenge is to gain distribution on retailers' shelves. So the marketing metrics in Figure 22–8 show the distribution of Warm Delights Minis in the five main channels of distribution used by General Mills. These five channels and their shortened names in Figure 22–8 are:

- Grocery stores/supermarkets—Grocery
- Mass merchandisers—Mass
- Warehouse/club stores—Warehouse
- Convenience stores—Convenience
- Drugstores/pharmacies—Drug

The Findings for Warm Delights Minis The Figure 22–8 marketing dashboard describing the 2013 performance of Warm Delights Minis is divided into four charts, each with different marketing metrics:

- *Chart A: Monthly Sales by Channel ($ millions).* This shows the sales revenues for warehouse and convenience stores are flat or trending downward while those for mass merchandisers and grocery are up slightly. The grocery channel is clearly the most important. But the really encouraging news is the jump in sales in the drugstore channel from September to December.

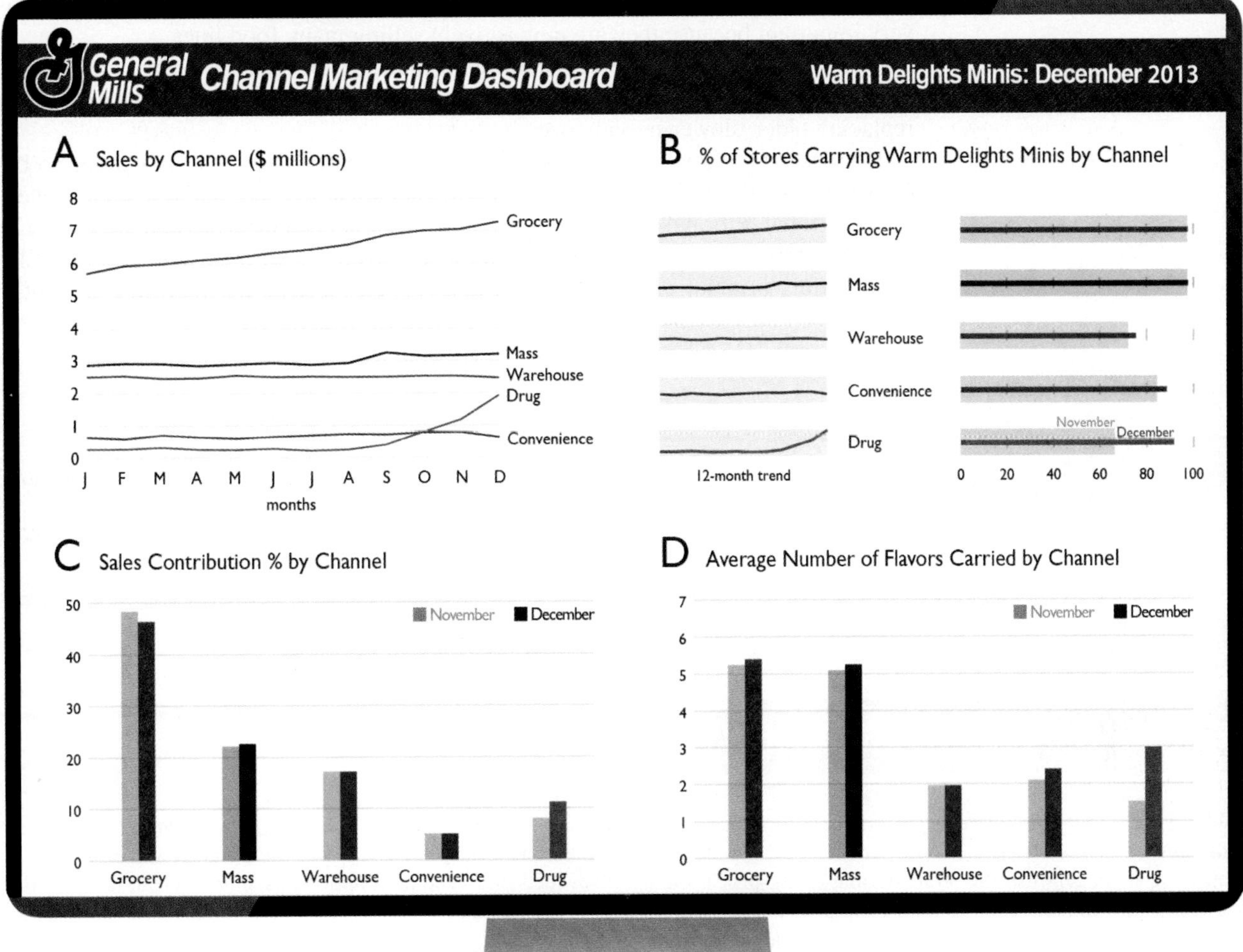

FIGURE 22–8
As a member of the Warm Delights team at General Mills, here is the marketing dashboard you see on your computer screen. You can use this dashboard to update the distribution channels strategy for the recently introduced line of Warm Delights Minis.

Source: Nelson Ng, Data Visualization Advisor, Dundas Data Visualization, Inc.

- *Chart B: % of Stores Carrying Warm Delights Minis by Channel.* The horizonal bar chart—a narrow December bar within the wider November bar—explains much of the major increase in September to December drugstore dollar sales seen in Chart A. Chart B shows that from November to December the percentage of drugstores carrying the Warm Delights Minis jumped from about 64 percent to 91 percent.
- *Chart C: Sales Contribution % by Channel.* The monthly bars total 100 percent. While the chart shows the importance of the grocery channel, it also shows the increased monthly sales revenue in the drug channel.
- *Chart D: Average Number of Flavors Carried by Channel.* This paints the picture more clearly. An important reason for the increased dollar sales from the drug channel is due to increasing the average number of flavors carried in a drugstore from 1.4 to 3.0 from November to December.

The Actions for Warm Delights Minis Further analysis of the marketing dashboard showing the sales by channel of individual flavors of Warm Delights Minis reveals the jump in sales in the drugstore channel is because (1) a major chain (like

Walgreens) added the line and (2) drugstores are embracing the new flavors, which is very important because they are now actively selling many food lines.

Your investigation also reveals a different situation for the four channels other than drugstores. The minor changes in sales there are due to the two new flavors simply replacing older, slower-moving ones.

Hot desserts normally experience an increased seasonal demand in winter. So because sales and distribution are growing, you decide to invest in the brand and schedule additional national TV advertising in late January and throughout February to exploit both the seasonal demand and recent sales trends. Seeing the jump in sales from adding a major drugstore chain, you research ways to attract other potential chains in all the five main channels Warm Delights Minis uses.

learning review

22-9. What are four groupings used within a typical marketing organization?

22-10. How do marketing metrics tie the goal-setting element of the planning phase of the strategic marketing process to the evaluation phase?

LEARNING OBJECTIVES REVIEW

LO 22-1 *Explain how marketing managers allocate resources.*
Marketing managers use the strategic marketing process and marketing information, such as marketing plans, sales reports, and action memos, to effectively allocate their scarce resources to exploit the competitive advantages of their products. Marketers may use techniques like sales response functions or market share (share point) analysis to help them assess what the market's response will be to additional marketing efforts.

LO 22-2 *Describe Porter's generic business strategies and synergy analysis planning frameworks.*
Porter identifies four generic business strategies that firms can adopt: (1) a cost leadership strategy, which focuses on reducing expenses to lower product prices while targeting many market segments; (2) a differentiation strategy, which requires products to have significant points of difference to charge a premium price while targeting many market segments; (3) a cost focus strategy, which involves controlling costs to lower prices of products targeting only a few market segments; and (4) a differentiation focus strategy, which requires products to have significant points of difference to reach one or only a few market segments.

The synergy analysis framework focuses on two kinds of synergies: marketing synergies (efficiencies), which run horizontally across the row of the various products offered by the firm to a single market segment; and R&D–manufacturing synergies (efficiencies), which run vertically down a column of the various market segments targeted for a given product or product class. This results in five alternative combinations: market-product concentration, market specialization, product specialization, selective specialization, and full coverage.

LO 22-3 *Explain what makes an effective marketing plan.*
An effective marketing plan has measurable, achievable goals; uses facts and valid assumptions; is simple, clear, and specific; is complete and feasible; and is controllable and flexible.

LO 22-4 *Use a time-based agenda and an action item list to conduct a meeting.*
Successful implementation of a marketing program requires that meetings be run efficiently and that team members know what they are to do. A time-based agenda for a meeting shows the running time allocated to each agenda item, thereby reducing irrelevant discussion. An action item list helps program implementation and consists of four columns: (1) the task; (2) the person responsible for completing the task; (3) the date to finish the task; and (4) what is to be delivered—such as a draft proposal or a client call list.

LO 22-5 *Describe an organization's marketing department and the role of a product manager.*
First, marketing departments must distinguish between line positions, those individuals who have the authority and responsibility to issue orders to people who report to them, and staff positions, those individuals who have the authority and responsibility to advise but cannot directly order people in line positions to do something.

Second, marketing organizations use one of four divisional groupings to implement marketing plans: product line groupings, which are responsible for specific product offerings; functional groupings, which represent the different departments and business activities within a firm; geographical groupings, in which sales territories are subdivided on a geographical basis; and market-based groupings, which utilize specific customer segments.

Product managers interact with many people and groups both inside and outside the firm to coordinate the planning, implementation, and evaluation of the marketing plan and its budget on an annual and long-term basis for the products for which they are responsible.

LO 22-6 *Explain the use of marketing ROI, metrics, and dashboards in evaluating marketing programs.*
The evaluation phase of the strategic marketing process involves measuring the results of the marketing actions from the implementation phase and comparing them with goals set in the planning phase. Marketing metrics, used to help quantify the goals in the planning stage, are of two kinds: input metrics and output metrics. The marketing manager then takes action to exploit positive deviations from the plan and to correct negative ones. Today, managers want an answer to the question, "Are my marketing activities effective?" One answer is in using marketing ROI, which is the application of modern measurement technologies to understand, quantify, and optimize marketing spending. Quantifying a marketing goal with a carefully defined output metric and tracking this metric on a marketing dashboard can improve marketing ROI.

FOCUSING ON KEY TERMS

APPLYING MARKETING KNOWLEDGE

1 Assume a firm faces an S-shaped sales response function. What happens to the ratio of incremental sales revenue to incremental marketing effort at the (*a*) bottom, (*b*) middle, and (*c*) top of this curve?
2 What happens to the ratio of incremental sales revenue to incremental marketing effort when the sales response function is an upward-sloping straight line?
3 Assume General Mills has to decide how to invest millions of dollars to try to expand its dessert and yogurt businesses. To allocate this money between these two businesses, what information would General Mills like to have?
4 Suppose your Great States lawn mower company has the market-product concentration situation shown in Figure 22–4A. What are both the synergies and potential pitfalls of following expansion strategies of (*a*) market specialization and (*b*) product specialization?
5 The first Domino's Pizza restaurant was near a college campus. What implementation problems are (*a*) similar and (*b*) different for restaurants near a college campus versus a military base?
6 A common theme among managers who succeed repeatedly in program implementation is fostering open communication. Why is this so important?
7 In regard to implementing a marketing program, what are the advantages of (*a*) a time-based agenda over a traditional agenda and (*b*) an action item list over traditional meeting minutes?
8 In the organizational chart for the consumer packaged goods firm in Figure 22–6, where do product line, functional, and geographical groupings occur?
9 Why are quantified goals in the planning phase of the strategic marketing process important for the evaluation phase?

BUILDING YOUR MARKETING PLAN

Do the following activities to complete your marketing plan:
1 Draw a simple organization chart for your organization.
2 Develop a Gantt chart (see Chapter 2) to schedule the key activities required to implement your marketing plan.
3 In terms of the evaluation, list (*a*) the four or five critical factors (such as revenues, number of customers, variable costs) and (*b*) how frequently (monthly, quarterly) you will monitor them to determine if special actions are needed to exploit opportunities or correct deviations.
4 Finalize your marketing plan based on the outline presented in Appendix A.

VIDEO CASE 22 General Mills Warm Delights: Indulgent, Delicious, and Gooey!

QR 22-5
Warm Delights
Video Case

Vivian Milroy Callaway, vice president for the Center for Learning and Experimentation at General Mills, retells the story for the "indulgent, delicious, and gooey" Warm Delights product. She summarizes, "When you want something that is truly innovative, you have to look at the rules you have been assuming in your category and break them all!"

When a new business achieves a breakthrough, it looks easy to outsiders. The creators of Betty Crocker Warm Delights stress that if the marketing decisions had been based on the traditions and history of the cake category, a smaller, struggling business would have resulted. The team chose to challenge the assumptions and expectations of accumulated cake category business experience. The team took personal and business risks, and Warm Delights became a roaring success.

PLANNING PHASE: INNOVATION, BUT A SHRINKING MARKET

"In the typical grocery store, the baking mix aisle is a quiet place," says Callaway. Shelves sigh with flavors, types, and brands. Prices are low, but there is little consumer traffic. Cake continues to be a tradition for birthdays and social occasions. But, consumer demand has declined. The percentage of U.S. households that bought at least one baking mix in 2000 was 80 percent. Four years later, the percentage was 77 percent, a very significant decline.

Today, a promoted price of 89 cents to make a 9×12 inch cake is common. Many choices, but little differentiation, gradually falling sales, and low uniform prices are the hallmarks of a mature category. But it's not that consumers don't buy cake-like treats. In fact, indulgent treats are growing. The premium prices for ice cream ($3.00 a pint) and chocolate ($3.00 a bar) are not slowing consumer purchases.

The Betty Crocker marketing team challenged the food scientists at General Mills to create a great-tasting, easy-to-prepare, single-serve cake treat. The goal: Make it indulgent, delicious, and gooey. The team focused the scientists on a product that would have:

- Consistent great taste.
- Quick preparation.
- A single portion.
- No cleanup.

The food scientists delivered the prototype! Now, the marketing team began hammering out the four Ps. They started with a descriptive name "Betty Crocker Dessert Bowls" (see photo) and a plan to shelve it in the "quiet" cake aisle. This practical approach would meet the consumer need for a "small, fast, microwave cake" for dessert. Several marketing challenges emerged:

- *The comparison problem.* The easy shelf price comparison to 9 × 12 inch cakes selling for 89 cents would make it harder to price Dessert Bowls at $2.00.
- *The communication problem.* The product message "a small, faster-to-make cake" wasn't compelling. For example, after-school snacks should be fast and small, but "dessert" sounds too indulgent.
- *The quiet aisle problem.* The cake-aisle shopper is probably not browsing for a cake innovation.
- *The dessert problem.* Consumers' on-the-go, calorie-conscious meal plans don't generally include a planned dessert.
- *The microwave problem.* Consumers might not believe it tastes good.

In sum, the small, fast-cake product didn't resonate with a compelling consumer need. But it would be a safe bet because the Dessert Bowl positioning fit nicely with the family-friendly Betty Crocker brand.

IMPLEMENTATION PHASE: LEAVING THE SECURITY OF FAMILY BEHIND

The consumer insights team really enjoyed the hot, gooey cake product. But they feared it would languish in the cake aisle under the "Dessert Bowl" name since this didn't capture the essence of what the food delivered. They explored who the indulgent treat customers really are. The data revealed that the heaviest buyers of premium treats are women without children. This focused the team on a target consumer: "What does she want?" They enlisted an ad agency and consultants to come up with a name that would appeal to "her." Several independently suggested the "Warm Delights" name, which became the brand name.

An interesting postscript to the team's brand name research: A competitor apparently liked not only the idea of a quick, gooey, microwavable dessert but also the "Dessert Bowls" name! You may now see its competitive product on your supermarket's shelves.

Targeting on-the-go women who want a small, personal treat had marketing advantages:

- The $2.00 Warm Delights price compared favorably to the price of many single-serve indulgent treats.
- The product food message "warm, convenient, delightful" is compelling.
- On-the-go women's meal plans do include the occasional delicious treat.

One significant problem remained: The cake-aisle shopper is probably not browsing for an indulgent, single-serve treat.

The marketing team solved this shelving issue by using advertising and product point-of-purchase displays outside the cake aisle. This would raise women's awareness of Warm Delights. Television advertising and in-store display programs are costly, so Warm Delights sales would have to be strong to pay back the investment.

Vivian Callaway and the team turned to market research to fine-tune the plan. The research put Warm Delights (and Dessert Bowls) on the shelf in real grocery stores. A few key findings emerged. First, the name "Warm Delights" beat "Dessert Bowls." Second, the Warm Delights with nuts simply wasn't easy to prepare, so nuts were removed. Third, the packaging with a disposable bowl beat the typical cake-mix packaging involving using your own bowl. Finally, by putting the actual product on supermarket shelves and in displays in these stores, sales volumes could be analyzed.

EVALUATION PHASE: TURNING THE PLAN INTO ACTION!

The marketing plan isn't action. Sales for Warm Delights required the marketing team to (1) get the retailers to stock the product, preferably somewhere other than the cake aisle, and (2) appeal to consumers enough to have them purchase, like, and repurchase the product.

The initial acceptance of a product by retailers is important. But each store manager must experience good sales of Warm Delights to be motivated to keep its shelves stocked with the product. Also, the Warm Delights team must monitor the display activity in the store. Are the displays placed in the locations as expected? Do the sales increase when a display is present? Watching distribution and display execution on a new product is very important so that sales shortfalls can be addressed proactively.

Did the customer buy one or two Warm Delights? Did the customer return for a second purchase a few days later? The syndicated services that sell household panel purchase data can provide these answers. The Warm Delights team evaluates these reports to see if the number of people who tried the product matches with expectations and how the repeat purchases occur. Often, the "80/20 rule" applies. So, in the early months, is there a group of consumers who buy repeatedly and will fill this role?

For ongoing feedback, calls by Warm Delights consumers to the toll-free consumer information line are monitored. This is a great source of real-time feedback. If a pattern emerges and these calls are mostly about the same problem, that is bad. However, when consumers call to say "thank you" or "it's great," that is good. This is an informal quick way to identify if the product is on track or further investigation is warranted.

GOOD MARKETING MAKES A DIFFERENCE

The team took personal and business risks by choosing the Warm Delights plan over the more conservative Dessert Bowls plan. Today, General Mills has loyal Warm Delights consumers who are open to trying new flavors, new sizes, and new forms. If you were a consultant to the Warm Delights team, what would you do to grow this brand in terms of product line and brand extensions?

Questions

1 What is the competitive set of desserts in which Warm Delights is located?

2 (*a*) Who is the target market? (*b*) What is the point of difference on the positioning for Warm Delights? (*c*) What are the potential opportunities and hindrances of the target market and positioning?

3 (*a*) What marketing research did Vivian Callaway execute? (*b*) What were the critical questions that led her to conduct research and seek expert advice? (*c*) How did this affect the product's marketing mix price, promotion, packaging, and distribution decisions?

4 (*a*) What initial promotional plan directed to consumers in the target market did Callaway use? (*b*) Why did this make sense to Callaway and her team when Warm Delights was launched?

5 If you were a consultant to Vivian Callaway, what product changes would you recommend to increase sales of Warm Delights?

APPENDIX C

PLANNING A CAREER IN MARKETING

GETTING A JOB: THE PROCESS OF MARKETING YOURSELF

Getting a job is usually a lengthy process, and it is exactly that—a *process* that involves careful planning, implementation, and evaluation. You may have everything going for you: a respectable grade point average (GPA), relevant work experience, several extracurricular activities, superior communication skills, and demonstrated leadership qualities. Despite these, you still need to market yourself systematically and aggressively; after all, even the best products lie dormant on retailers' shelves unless marketed effectively.

The process of getting a job involves the same activities marketing managers use to develop and introduce products and brands into the marketplace.[1] The only difference is that you are marketing yourself, not a product. You need to conduct marketing research by analyzing your personal qualities (performing a self-audit) and by identifying job opportunities.

Based on your research results, select a target market—those job opportunities that are compatible with your interests, goals, skills, and abilities—and design a marketing mix around that target market. *You* are the "product"; you must decide how to "position" and "brand" yourself in the job market.[2]

The price component of the marketing mix is the salary range and job benefits (such as health and life insurance, vacation time, and retirement benefits) that you hope to receive. Promotion involves communicating with prospective employers through written and electronic correspondence (advertising) and job interviews (personal selling). The place element focuses on how to reach prospective employers—at the career services office, job fairs, or online, for example.

This appendix will assist you in career planning by (1) providing information about careers in marketing and (2) outlining a job search process.

CAREERS IN MARKETING

The diversity of marketing opportunities is reflected in the many types of marketing jobs, including product management, marketing research, and public relations. While many of these jobs are found at traditional employers such as manufacturers, retailers, and advertising agencies, there are also many opportunities in a variety of other types of organizations.

Professional services such as law, accounting, and consulting firms, for example, have a growing need for marketing expertise. Similarly, nonprofit organizations such as universities, the performing arts, museums, and government agencies are developing marketing functions. Event organizations such as athletic teams, golf and tennis tournaments, and the Olympics are also new and visible sources of marketing jobs.

The diversity of marketing jobs is also changing because of changes in the marketing discipline. The growth of interactive marketing and social media has created a variety of new jobs such as data miners and social media managers. The growth of multichannel marketing has led to the need for communication channel managers and integration specialists. The increasing involvement and control by consumers has required public relations personnel to become social networking experts and consumer-generated content managers. Specialties in demand now include digital marketing, multicultural marketing, and viral marketing.[3]

Examples of companies that have opportunities for graduates with degrees in marketing include Altria, AT&T,

Enterprise Rent-A-Car, GEICO, General Electric, International Paper, Johnson & Johnson, Macy's, McGraw-Hill Companies, Merck, PepsiCo, State Farm, Toys "Я" Us, and Vector Marketing. Many of these companies have also appeared on *Fortune's* list of the "100 Best Companies to Work For."[4] Most of these career opportunities offer a chance to work with interesting people on stimulating and rewarding problems. Comments one product manager, "I love marketing as a career because there are different challenges every day."[5]

Recent studies of career paths and salaries suggest that marketing careers can also provide excellent opportunities for advancement and substantial pay. For example, one of every eight chief executive officers (CEOs) of the nation's 500 most valuable publicly held companies held positions in marketing before becoming CEO.[6] Similarly, reports of average starting salaries of college graduates indicate that salaries in marketing compare favorably with those in many other fields. The average starting salary of new marketing undergraduates in 2013 was $51,000, compared with $40,400 for journalism majors and $46,600 for advertising majors.[7] The future is likely to be even better. The U.S. Department of Labor reports that employment of advertising, marketing, promotion, public relations, and sales managers is expected to grow at a rate of 14 percent through 2020. This growth is being spurred by the introduction of new products to the marketplace and the growing need to "manage digital media campaigns which often target customers through the use of websites, social media, and live chats."[8]

QR C-1
Careers Video

Figure C–1 on the next page describes marketing occupations in seven major categories: product management and physical distribution, advertising and promotion, retailing, sales, marketing research, global marketing, and nonprofit marketing. One of these may be right for you. Additional sources of marketing career information are provided at the end of this appendix.

Product Management and Physical Distribution

Many organizations assign one manager the responsibility for a particular product. For example, Procter & Gamble (P&G) has separate managers for Tide, Cheer, Gain, and Bold. Product or brand managers are involved in all aspects of a product's marketing program, such as marketing research, sales, sales promotion, advertising, and pricing, as well as manufacturing. Managers of similar products typically report to a category manager, or marketing director, and may be part of a *product management team* to encourage interbrand cooperation.[9]

Product or brand managers are involved in all aspects of a product's marketing program.

College graduates with bachelor's and master's degrees—often in marketing and business—enter P&G as assistant brand managers, the only starting position in its product or brand groups. As assistant brand managers, their responsibilities include developing a detailed marketing plan for a specific brand and learning consumer, shopper, and customer insights. With good performance and demonstrated leadership, after three to six years the assistant brand manager is promoted to brand manager, then after four to eight years to associate marketing director, and after three to eight years to marketing director. These promotions often involve several brand groups. For example, a new employee might start as assistant brand manager for Folger's coffee, be promoted to brand manager for Crest toothpaste, become an associate marketing director for P&G's soap products, and finally a marketing director for a different brand group. Other positions important at P&G include launch leader, account manager, and market manager.[10]

Several other jobs related to product management (see Figure C–1) deal with physical distribution issues such as storing the manufactured product (inventory), moving the product from the firm to the customers (transportation), and engaging in many other aspects of the manufacture and sale of goods. Prospects for these jobs are likely to increase as a wider range of products and technologies lead to increased demand. In addition, as manufacturers cut costs, they are increasingly shifting more responsibilities to wholesalers.[11]

Advertising and Promotion

Although we may see hundreds of advertisements in a day, what we can't see easily is the fascinating and complex advertising profession. The entry-level advertising

PRODUCT MANAGEMENT AND PHYSICAL DISTRIBUTION

Product development manager creates a road map for new products by working with customers to determine their needs and with designers to create the product.

Product or brand manager is responsible for integrating all aspects of a product's marketing program including research, sales, sales promotion, advertising, and pricing.

Supply chain manager oversees the part of a company that transports products to consumers and handles customer service.

Operations manager supervises warehousing and other physical distribution functions and often is directly involved in moving products on the warehouse floor.

Inventory control manager forecasts demand for products, coordinates production with plant managers, and tracks shipments to keep customers supplied.

Physical distribution specialist is an expert in the transportation and distribution of products and also evaluates the costs and benefits of different types of transportation.

SALES

Direct or retail salesperson sells directly to consumers in the salesperson's office, the consumer's home, or a retailer's store.

Trade salesperson calls on retailers or wholesalers to sell products for manufacturers.

Industrial or semitechnical salesperson sells supplies and services to businesses.

Complex or professional salesperson sells complicated or custom-designed products to businesses. This requires understanding of the product technology.

Customer service manager maintains good relations with customers by coordinating the sales staff, marketing management, and physical distribution management.

NONPROFIT MARKETING

Marketing manager develops and directs marketing campaigns, fund-raising, and public relations.

GLOBAL MARKETING

Global marketing manager is an expert in world-trade agreements, international competition, cross-cultural analysis, and global market-entry strategies.

ADVERTISING AND PROMOTION

Account executive maintains contact with clients while coordinating the creative work among artists and copywriters. Account executives work as partners with the client to develop marketing strategy.

Media buyer deals with media sales representatives in selecting advertising media and analyzes the value of media being purchased.

Copywriter works with art director in conceptualizing advertisements and writes the text of print or radio ads or the storyboards of television ads.

Art director handles the visual component of advertisements.

Sales promotion manager designs promotions for consumer products and works at an ad agency or a sales promotion agency.

Public relations manager develops written or video messages for the public and handles contacts with the press.

Online marketing manager develops and executes the e-business marketing plan and manages all aspects of the advertising, promotion, and content for the online business.

Social media marketing manager plans and manages the delivery of marketing messages through all social media and monitors and responds to the feedback received.

RETAILING

Buyer selects products a store sells, surveys consumer trends, and evaluates the past performance of products and suppliers.

Store manager oversees the staff and services at a store.

MARKETING RESEARCH

Project manager for the supplier coordinates and oversees the market studies for a client.

Account executive for the supplier serves as a liaison between client and market research firm, like an advertising agency account executive.

In-house project director acts as project manager (see above) for the market studies conducted by the firm for which he or she works.

Competitive intelligence researcher uses new information technologies to monitor the competitive environment.

Marketing database manager compiles and analyzes consumer data to identify behavior patterns, preferences, and user profiles for personalized marketing programs.

Source: Adapted from Lila B. Stair and Leslie Stair, *Careers in Marketing* (New York: McGraw-Hill, 2008); and David W. Rosenthal and Michael A. Powell, *Careers in Marketing*, ©1984, pp. 352–54.

FIGURE C–1
Seven major categories of marketing occupations.

positions filled every year include jobs with a variety of firms. Advertising professionals often remark that they find their jobs appealing because the days are not routine and they involve creative activities with many interesting people.

Advertising positions are available in three kinds of organizations: advertisers, media companies, and agencies. Advertisers include manufacturers, retail stores, service firms, and many other types of companies. Often they have an advertising department responsible for preparing and placing their own ads. Advertising careers are also possible with the media: television, radio stations, magazines, and newspapers. Finally, advertising agencies offer job opportunities through their use of account management, research, media, and creative services.

Starting positions with advertisers and advertising agencies are often as assistants to employees with several years of experience. An assistant copywriter facilitates the development of the message, or copy, in an advertisement. An assistant art director participates in the design of visual components of advertisements. Entry-level media positions involve buying the media that will carry the ad or selling airtime on radio or television or page space in print media. Some agencies are encouraging employees to develop skills in multiple roles. Advancement to supervisory positions requires planning skills, a broad vision, and an affinity for spotting an effective advertising idea. Students interested in advertising should develop good communication skills and try to gain advertising experience through summer employment opportunities or internships.[12]

Growing interest in integrated marketing programs has increased opportunities for sales promotion managers, public relations managers, and Internet marketing managers. These positions require an understanding of the potential synergy of all promotional tools. Responsibilities include the design and implementation of sweepstakes, sampling programs, events and partnerships, newsletters, press releases and conferences, e-mail promotions, web-content management, and permission marketing campaigns. In addition, as advertisers increase search marketing budgets, the number of search marketing positions is increasing. Finally, many companies have decided that they need social media managers to ensure that messages can be sent to and received from the millions of people now on Facebook, Twitter, and other social media websites.[13]

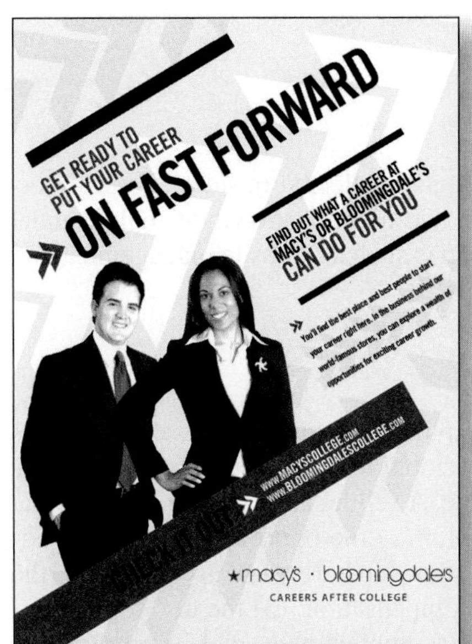

Retailers such as Macy's and Bloomingdale's offer careers in merchandise management and store management.

Retailing

There are two separate career paths in retailing: merchandise management and store management (see Figure C–2). The key position in merchandising is that of a buyer, who is responsible for selecting merchandise, guiding the promotion of the merchandise, setting prices, bargaining with wholesalers, training the salesforce, and monitoring the competitive environment. The buyer must also be able to organize and coordinate many critical activities under severe time constraints. In contrast, store management involves the supervision of personnel in all departments and the general management of all facilities, equipment, and merchandise displays. In addition, store managers are responsible for the financial performance of each department and for the store as a whole. Typical positions beyond the store manager level include district manager, regional manager, and divisional vice president.[14]

Most starting jobs in retailing are trainee positions. A trainee is usually placed in a management training program and then given a position as an assistant buyer or assistant department manager. Advancement and responsibility can be achieved quickly because there is a shortage of qualified personnel in retailing and because superior

FIGURE C–2
Two common retailing career paths include merchandise management and store management.

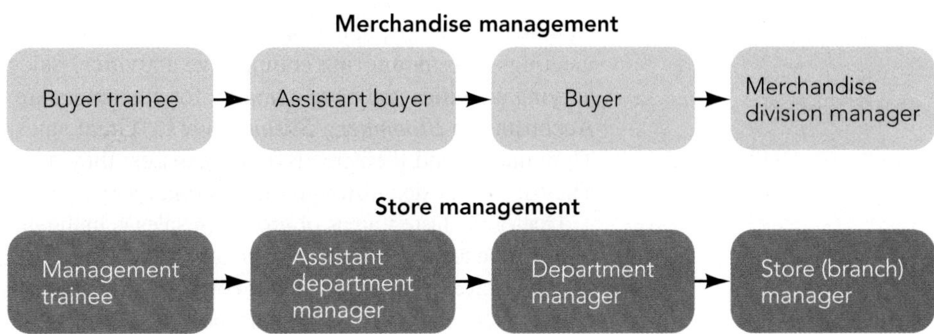

FIGURE C–3
Employment opportunities in selected sales occupations (2010 to 2020).

Occupation	2010 Employment	2020 Employment	Percentage Change 2010–2020	Growth
Insurance sales agents	411,500	501,700	22%	90,200
Real estate brokers and sales agents	466,100	518,600	11%	52,500
Retail salespersons	4,261,600	4,968,400	17%	706,800
Manufacturers' and wholesalers' sales representatives	1,830,000	2,118,900	16%	288,900
Securities and financial services sales agents	312,200	359,700	15%	47,500

Source: "Job Prospects," *Occupational Outlook Handbook, 2012–13 Edition* (Washington, DC: U.S. Department of Labor, Bureau of Labor Statistics).

Xerox is well known for its sales career opportunities.

performance of an individual is quickly reflected in sales and profits—two visible measures of success. In addition, the growth of multichannel retailing has created new opportunities such as website management and online merchandise procurement.[15]

Sales

College graduates from many disciplines are attracted to sales positions because of the increasingly professional nature of selling jobs and the many opportunities they can provide. A selling career offers benefits that are hard to match in any other field: (1) the opportunity for rapid advancement (into management or to new territories and accounts); (2) the potential for extremely attractive compensation; (3) the development of personal satisfaction, feelings of accomplishment, and increased self-confidence; and (4) independence—salespeople often have almost complete control over their time and activities.

Employment opportunities in sales occupations are found in a wide variety of organizations, including insurance agencies, retailers, and financial service firms (see Figure C–3). In addition, many salespeople work as manufacturers' representatives for organizations that have selling responsibilities for several manufacturers.[16] Activities in sales jobs include *selling duties*, such as prospecting for customers, demonstrating the product, or quoting prices; *sales-support duties*, such as handling complaints and helping solve technical problems; and *nonselling duties*, such as preparing reports, attending sales meetings, and monitoring competitive activities. Salespeople who can deal with these varying activities and have empathy for customers are critical to a company's success. According to *Bloomberg Businessweek*, "Great salespeople feel for their customers. They understand their needs and pressures; they get the challenges of their business. They see every deal through the customer's eyes."[17]

One of the fastest areas of growth in sales is in the direct marketing industry. Interest in information technology, customer relationship management (CRM), and integrated marketing has increased the demand for contact with customers. For many firms this means increasing the amount of time salespeople spend with clients; for other firms it means increased use of web conferencing technology; for still others it means sophisticated e-mail

Garmin is an example of a company that encourages students to think about a career and the culture of the company.

marketing. *Sales & Marketing Management* magazine's People's Choice Awards recently recognized companies such as GoToMeeting, Salesforce.com, and WebEx for providing innovative solutions that provide better relationships between salespeople and customers. Consultant Susan Aldrich observes that customers always say, "I want you to know about me and offer me things that are relevant to me."[18]

Marketing Research

Marketing researchers play important roles in many organizations today. They are responsible for obtaining, analyzing, and interpreting data to facilitate making marketing decisions. This means marketing researchers are basically problem solvers. Success in the area requires not only an understanding of statistical analysis, research methods, and programming, but also a broad base of marketing knowledge, writing and verbal presentation skills, and an ability to communicate with colleagues and clients. According to Stan Sthanunathan, vice president of marketing strategy and insights at Coca-Cola, a researcher's job "is to bring out opportunities."[19] Individuals who are inquisitive, methodical, analytical, and solution-oriented find the field particularly rewarding.

The responsibilities of the men and women currently working in the market research industry include defining the marketing problem, designing the questions, selecting the sample, collecting and analyzing the data, and, finally, reporting the results of the research. These jobs are available in three kinds of organizations. *Marketing research consulting firms* contract with large companies to provide research about their products or services.[20] *Advertising agencies* may provide research services to help clients with questions related to advertising and promotional problems. Finally, some companies have an *in-house research staff* to design and execute their research projects. Online marketing research, which is likely to become the most common form of marketing research in the near future, requires an understanding of new tools such as dynamic scripting, response validation, intercept sampling, instant messaging surveys, and online consumer panels.[21]

Although marketing researchers may start as assistants performing routine tasks, they quickly advance to broader responsibilities. Survey design, interviewing, report writing, and all aspects of the research process create a challenging career. In addition, research projects typically deal with such diverse problems as consumer motivation, pricing, forecasting, and competition. Successful candidates "like what they're doing and get excited over their work, whether it be listening to a focus group or running a complex data mining model," according to Carolyn Marconi, director of marketing research for the Vanguard Group, Inc.[22]

Merck seeks diverse and collaborative employees and offers them challenging career opportunities throughout the world.

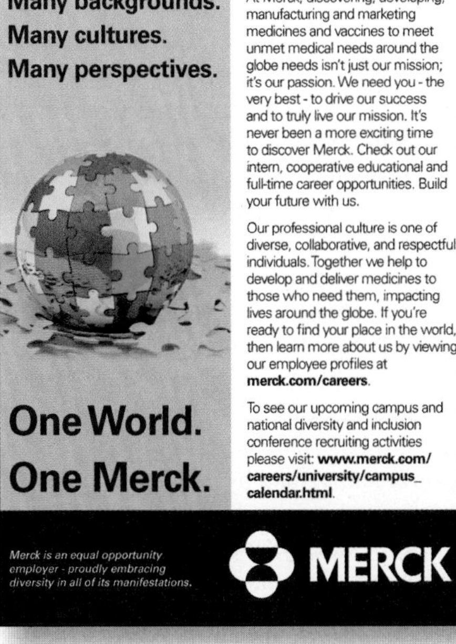

International Careers

Many of the careers just described can be found in international settings—in large multinational U.S. corporations, small- to medium-size firms with export business, and franchises. The international consulting firm Accenture, for example, has thousands of consultants around the world. Similarly, many franchises such as 7-Eleven, which has 42,316 foreign locations, are rapidly expanding outside of the United States.[23] The changes in the European Union, Brazil, Russia, India, China, and other growing markets are likely to provide many opportunities for international careers.

Several methods of gaining international experience are possible. For example, some companies may alternate periods of work at domestic locations with assignments outside of the United States. In addition, working for a firm with headquarters outside of the United States at one of its local offices may be appealing. In many organizations, international experience has become a necessity for promotion and career advancement. "If you are going to succeed, an expatriate assignment is essential," says Eric Kraus of Gillette Co. in Boston.[24]

Applicants for international positions need language skills and an ability to adapt to different business models, management styles, and local practices. In addition, as multinational firms use worldwide communication technologies to build global teams of people who have never met, collaboration skills become increasingly important. Accenture uses instant messaging, voice, video and online meetings, and telepresence technology to help its 259,000 employees serve clients in more than 120 countries. Similarly, IBM helps thousands of its employees be a part of "innovation jams" with a team home page on the company intranet.[25]

THE JOB SEARCH PROCESS

Activities you should consider during your job search process include assessing yourself, identifying job opportunities, preparing your résumé and related correspondence, and going on job interviews.

Assessing Yourself

You must know your product—you—so that you can market yourself effectively to prospective employers. Consequently, a critical first step in your job search is conducting a self-inquiry or self-assessment. This activity involves understanding your interests, abilities, personality, preferences, and individual style. You must be confident that you know what work environment is best for you, what makes you happy, the balance you seek between personal and professional activities, and how you can be most effective at reaching your goals. This process helps ensure that you are matching your profile to the right job, or as business consultant and author Jim Collins explains, "Finding the right seat on the bus."[26]

Asking Key Questions A self-analysis, in part, entails asking yourself some very important and difficult questions (see Figure C–4). It is critical that you respond to the questions honestly, because your answers ultimately will be used as a guide in your job selection.[27] A less-than-candid appraisal of yourself might result in a job mismatch.

Identifying Strengths and Weaknesses After you have addressed the questions posed in Figure C–4, you are ready to identify your strengths and weaknesses. To do so, draw a vertical line down the middle of a sheet of paper and label one side of the paper "strengths" and the other side "weaknesses." Based on your answers to the questions, record your strong and weak points in their respective columns. Ideally, this cataloging should be done over a few days to give you adequate time to reflect on your attributes. In addition, you might seek input from others who know you well (such as parents, close relatives, friends, professors, or employers) and can offer more objective viewpoints. They might even evaluate you on the questions in Figure C–4, and you can compare the results with your own evaluation. A hypothetical list of strengths and weaknesses is shown in Figure C–5 on page 618.

What skills are most important? The answer, of course, varies by occupation and employer. Recent studies, however, suggest that problem-solving skills, communication skills, interpersonal skills, analytical and computer skills, and leadership skills are all valued by employers. Personal characteristics employers seek in a job candidate include honesty, integrity, motivation, initiative, self-confidence, flexibility, and enthusiasm. Finally, most employers also look for work experience, internship experience, or co-op experience. Internships "give you hands-on experience and make you

INTERESTS

How do I like to spend my time?
Do I enjoy working with people?
Do I like working with tangible things?
Do I enjoy working with data?
Am I a member of many organizations?
Do I enjoy physical activities?
Do I like to read?

ABILITIES

Am I adept at analysis?
What are my hardware, software, and operating system skills?
Do I have good verbal and written communication skills?
What special talents do I have?
At which abilities do I wish I were more adept?

EDUCATION

How have my courses and extracurricular activities prepared me for a specific job?
Which were my best subjects? My worst?
Is my GPA a good indication of my academic ability? Why?
Do I aspire to a graduate degree? Is this something I want to pursue before beginning my job? Or after?
Why did I choose my major?

PERSONAL GOALS

What are my short-term and long-term goals? Why?
Am I career oriented, or do I have broader interests?
What are my career goals?
What jobs are likely to help me achieve my goals?
What do I hope to be doing in 5 years? In 10 years?
What do I want out of life?
What work–life balance do I prefer?

PERSONALITY

What are my good and bad traits?
Am I competitive?
Do I work well with others?
Am I outspoken?
Am I a leader or a follower?
Do I work well under pressure?
Do I work quickly, or am I methodical?
Do I get along well with others?
Am I ambitious?
Do I work well independently of others?

DESIRED JOB ENVIRONMENT

Am I willing to relocate? Why?
Do I have a geographical preference? Why?
Would I mind traveling in my job?
Do I have to work for a large or nationally known firm to be satisfied?
Must my job offer rapid promotion opportunities?
If I could design my own job, what characteristics would it have?
How important is high initial salary to me?

EXPERIENCE

What previous jobs have I held? What were my responsibilities in each job?
What internships or co-op positions have I held? What were my responsibilities?
What volunteer positions have I held? What were my responsibilities?
Were any of my jobs or positions applicable to positions I may be seeking? How?
What did I like the most about my previous jobs? What did I like the least?
If I had it to do over again, would I work in these jobs? Why?

FIGURE C–4
Questions to ask in your self-analysis.

a stronger job candidate," explains Arlene Hill, director of career development at American University's Kogod School of Business.[28]

Taking Job-Related Tests Personality and vocational interest tests, provided by many colleges and universities, can give you other ideas about yourself. After tests have been administered and scored, test takers meet with testing service counselors to discuss the results. Test results generally suggest jobs for which students have an inclination. The most common tests at the college level are the Strong Interest Inventory and the Campbell Interest and Skill Survey. Some counseling centers and career coaches also use the Myers-Briggs® Type Indicator personality inventory and the Peoplemap™ assessments to help identify professions you may enjoy.[29] If you have not already done so, you may wish to see whether your school offers such testing services.

Identifying Your Job Opportunities

To identify and analyze the job market, you must conduct some marketing research to determine what industries *and* companies offer promising job opportunities that relate to the results of your self-analysis. Several sources that can help in your search are discussed next.

FIGURE C–5
Hypothetical list of a job candidate's strengths and weaknesses.

Strengths	Weaknesses
I enjoy being with people.	I am very demanding of team members.
I am an avid reader.	I have minimal work experience.
I have good communication skills.	I have a mediocre GPA.
I am involved in many extracurricular activities.	I am sometimes impatient.
I work well with others.	I resent close supervision.
I work well independently.	I work methodically (slowly).
I am honest and dependable.	I will not relocate.
I am willing to travel in the job.	I procrastinate unless there is a deadline.
I am a good problem solver.	I lack a customer orientation.
I have a good sense of humor.	I have poor technical skills.

Career Services Office Your campus career services office is an excellent source of job information. Personnel in that office can (1) inform you about which companies will be recruiting on campus; (2) alert you to unexpected job openings; (3) advise you about short-term and long-term career prospects; (4) offer advice on résumé construction; (5) assess your interviewing strengths and weaknesses; and (6) help you evaluate a job offer. Career services offices are also expanding to help students connect with companies that might not recruit on campus.[30]

In addition, the office usually contains a variety of written materials focusing on different industries and companies and tips on job hunting. One major publication available in most career services offices is the National Association of Colleges and Employers publication *Job Choices*, which contains a list of employers, kinds of job openings for college graduates, and who to contact about jobs in those firms. Another publication for students is *jobpostings*, which is published two times during the academic year and distributed to more than 550 colleges and universities across the United States.

Campus career centers and online databases such as Monster.com are excellent sources for job information.

Online Career and Employment Services Many companies no longer make frequent on-campus visits. Instead, they may use the many online services available to advertise an employment opportunity or to search for candidate information. The National Association of Colleges and Employers, for example, maintains a site on the Internet called JobWeb (www.jobweb.org). Similarly, Monster.com and Careerbuilder.com are online databases of employment ads, candidate résumés, and other career-related information. Some of the information resources include career guidance, a cover letter library, occupational profiles, résumé templates, and networking services.[31] Employers may contact students directly when the candidate's qualifications meet their specific job requirements. The advantage of this system for students is that regardless of the size or location of the campus they are attending, many companies have access to their résumé. Some job boards even allow applicants to post audio and video clips of themselves. One advantage for recruiters is that some of the job boards utilize software for performing background verification.[32] Your school's career center may also have a home page that offers online job search information and links to other Internet sites.

Library The public or college library can provide you with reference material that, among other things, describes successful firms and their operations, defines the content of various jobs, and forecasts job opportunities. For example, *Fortune* publishes a list of the 1,000 largest U.S. and global companies and their respective sales and profits, and Dun & Bradstreet publishes directories of more than 26 million companies in the United States. The *Occupational Outlook Handbook* is an annual publication of the U.S. Department of Labor that provides projections for specific job prospects, as well as information pertaining to those jobs. A librarian can indicate reference materials that will be most pertinent to *your* job search.

Advertisements Help-wanted advertisements provide an overview of what is happening in the job market. Local (particularly Sunday editions) and college newspapers, trade press (such as *Marketing News* or *Advertising Age*), and business magazines (such as *Sales & Marketing Management*) contain classified advertisement sections that generally have job opening announcements, often for entry-level positions. Reviewing the want ads can help you identify what kinds of positions are available and their requirements and job titles, which firms offer certain kinds of jobs, and levels of compensation.

Employment Agencies An employment agency can make you aware of several job opportunities very quickly because of its large number of job listings available through computer databases. Many agencies specialize in a particular field (such as sales and marketing). The advantages of using an agency include that it (1) reduces the cost of a job search by bringing applicants and employers together, (2) often has exclusive job listings available only by working through the agency, (3) performs much of the job search for you, and (4) tries to find a job that is compatible with your qualifications and interests.[33] In the past, some employment agencies have engaged in questionable business practices, so check with the Better Business Bureau (www.bbb.org) or your business contacts to determine the quality of the various agencies.

Personal Contacts and Networking An important source of job information that students often overlook is their personal contacts. People you know often may know of job opportunities, so you should advise them that you're looking for a job. Relatives and friends might aid your job search. Instructors you know well and business contacts can provide a wealth of information about potential jobs and even help arrange an interview with a prospective employer. They may also help arrange *informational interviews* with employers that do not have immediate openings. These interviews allow you to collect information about an industry or an employer and give you an advantage if a position does become available. It is a good idea to leave your résumé with all your personal contacts so they can pass it along to those who might be in need of your services.

Student organizations (such as the student chapter of the American Marketing Association and Pi Sigma Epsilon, the professional sales fraternity) may be sources of job opportunities, particularly if they are involved with the business community. Local chapters of professional business organizations (such as the American Marketing Association and Sales and Marketing Executives International) also can provide job information; contacting their chapter president is a first step in seeking assistance from these organizations. Creating and maintaining a network of professional contacts is one of the most important career-building activities you can undertake.[34]

There are many popular social networking sites available to job seekers. LinkedIn, for example, has 225 million users, including recruiters. Other sites include Plaxo, Twitter, Jobster, Facebook, Craigslist, MyWorkster, VisualCV, and JobFox. Some of the sites allow users to create and post a traditional résumé while others facilitate personalized web pages with video, audio, images, and even work samples. BranchOut .com can link to Facebook and pull education and work history from pages to help identify a network of friends who have worked for a specific company. Even Pinterest has job-related and personal-brand pinboards. Using all or many of these sites provides greater exposure. Remember, however, to be consistent in the image and information presented online.[35]

State Employment Office State employment offices have listings of job opportunities in their state and counselors to help arrange a job interview for you. Although state employment offices perform functions similar to employment agencies, they differ in listing only job opportunities in their state and providing their services free of charge.

Direct Contact Another means of obtaining job information is direct contact—personally communicating to prospective employers (either by mail, e-mail, or in person) that you would be interested in pursuing job opportunities with them. Often you may not even know whether jobs are available in these firms. If you correspond with the companies in writing, a letter of introduction and an attached résumé should serve as your initial form of communication. One way to make direct contact with companies is to attend a career or job fair. These events allow many employers, recruiters, and prospective job seekers to meet in one location.[36] Your goals in direct contact are to create a positive impression and, ultimately, to arrange a job interview.

Writing Your Résumé

A résumé is a document that communicates to prospective employers who you are. An employer reading a résumé is looking for a snapshot of your qualifications to decide if you should be invited to a job interview. It is imperative that you design a résumé that presents you in a favorable light and allows you to get to that next important step.[37] Personnel in your career services office can provide assistance in designing résumés.

The Résumé Itself A well-constructed résumé generally contains up to nine major sections: (1) identification (name, address, telephone number, and e-mail address); (2) job or career objective; (3) educational background; (4) honors and awards; (5) work experience or history; (6) skills or capabilities (that pertain to a particular kind of job for which you may be interviewing); (7) extracurricular activities; (8) personal interests; and (9) personal references.[38]

There is no universally accepted format for a résumé, but three are more frequently used: chronological, functional, and targeted. A *chronological* format presents your work experience and education according to the time sequence in which they occurred (i.e., in chronological order). If you have had several jobs or attended several schools, this approach is useful to highlight what you have done. With a *functional* format, you group your experience into skill categories that emphasize your strengths. This option is particularly appropriate if you have no experience or only minimal experience related to your chosen field. A *targeted* format focuses on the capabilities you have for a specific job. This alternative is desirable if you know what job you want and are qualified for it.

In any of the formats, if possible, you should include quantitative information about your accomplishments and experience, such as "increased sales revenue by 20 percent" for the year you managed a retail clothing store. A résumé that illustrates the chronological format is shown in Figure C–6.[39]

Technology has created a need for a new type of résumé—the digital résumé. Although traditional versions of résumés may be visually appealing, today most career experts suggest that résumés accommodate delivery through mail, e-mail, and fax machines. In addition, résumés must accommodate employers who use scanning technology to enter résumés into their own databases or who search commercial online databases.

To fully utilize online opportunities, an electronic résumé with a popular font (e.g., Times New Roman) and relatively large font size (e.g., 10–14 pt.)—and without italic text, graphics, shading, underlining, or vertical lines—must be available. In addition, because online recruiting starts with a keyword search, it is important to include keywords, focus on nouns rather than verbs, and avoid abbreviations. Related to this use of technology—don't forget that many employers may visit social networking sites such as Facebook, or may simply "Google" your name, to see what comes up. Review your online profiles before you start your job search to provide a positive and accurate image![40]

FIGURE C–6
A chronological résumé presents your education and work experience in the sequence in which they occurred.

Sally Winter

Campus address (until 6/1/2014):	Home address:
Elm Street Apartments #2B	123 Front Street
College Town, Ohio 44042	Teaneck, NJ 07666
Mobile phone: (555) 424-1648	Phone: (555) 836-4995
Email: swinter@osu.stu.edu	
LinkedIn: www.linkedin.com/in/sallywinter	

Education

B.S. in Business Administration, Ohio State University, 2014, cum laude
3.3 overall GPA—3.6 GPA in major

Work Experience

Paid for 70 percent of my college expenses through the following part-time and summer jobs:

Summer 2013 Legal Secretary, Smith, Lee & Jones, Attorneys at Law, New York, NY

- Took dictation and transcribed tapes of legal proceedings
- Typed contracts and other legal documents
- Reorganized client files for easier access
- Answered the phone and screened calls for the partners

2011–2013 Academic Years Salesclerk, College Varsity Shop, College Town, Ohio

- Helped customers with buying decisions
- Arranged stock and helped with window displays
- Assisted in year-end inventories
- Took over responsibilities of store manager when she was on vacation or ill

2008–2011 Assistant Manager, Treasure Place Gift Shop, Teaneck, NJ

- Supervised two salesclerks
- Helped select merchandise at trade shows
- Handled daily accounting
- Worked comfortably under pressure during busy seasons

Campus Activities

- Elected captain of the women's varsity tennis team for two years
- Worked as a reporter and night editor on campus newspaper for two years
- Elected historian for Mortar Board chapter, a senior women's honorary society

Computer Skills

- Word, Excel, PowerPoint, Outlook

Personal Interests

- Collecting antique clocks, listening to jazz, swimming

References Available on Request

Letter Accompanying a Résumé The letter accompanying a résumé, or cover letter, serves as the job candidate's introduction. As a result, it must gain the attention and interest of the reader or it will fail to give the incentive to examine the résumé carefully. In designing a letter to accompany your résumé, address the following issues:[41]

- Address the letter to a specific person.
- Identify the position for which you are applying and how you heard of it.
- Indicate why you are applying for the position.
- Summarize your most significant credentials and qualifications.
- Refer the reader to the enclosed résumé.
- Request a personal interview, and advise the reader when and where you can be reached.

A sample letter comprising these six factors is presented in Figure C–7 on the next page.

FIGURE C–7
A sample letter accompanying a résumé provides the job candidate's introduction.

Sally Winter
Elm Street Apartments, #2B
College Town, Ohio 44042
January 31, 2014

Mr. J. B. Jones
Sales Manager
Hilltop Manufacturing Company
Minneapolis, MN 55406

Dear Mr. Jones:

Dr. William Johnson, Professor of Business Administration at the Ohio State University, recently suggested that I write to you concerning your opening and my interest in a sales position. With a B.S. degree in business administration and courses in personal selling and sales management, I am confident that I could make a positive contribution to your firm.

During the past four years, I have been a salesclerk in a clothing store and an assistant manager in a gift shop. These two positions required my performing a variety of duties including selling, purchasing, stocking, and supervising. As a result, I have developed an appreciation for the viewpoints of the customer, salesperson, and management. Given my background and high energy level, I feel that I am particularly well qualified to assume a sales position in your company.

My enclosed résumé better highlights my education and experience. My extracurricular activities should strengthen and support my abilities to serve as a sales representative.

I am eager to talk with you because I feel I can demonstrate to you why I am a strong candidate for the position. I have friends in Minneapolis with whom I could stay on weekends, so Fridays or Mondays would be ideal for an appointment. I will call you in a week to see if we can arrange a mutually convenient time for a meeting. I am hopeful that your schedule will allow this.

Thank you for your kind consideration. If you would like some additional information, please feel free to contact me at (555) 424-1648. I look forward to talking with you.

Sincerely,

Sally Winter

enclosure

Interviewing for Your Job

The job interview is a conversation between a prospective employer and a job candidate that focuses on determining whether the employer's needs can be satisfied by the candidate's qualifications. The interview is a "make or break" situation: If the interview goes well, you have increased your chances of receiving a job offer; if it goes poorly, you probably will be eliminated from further consideration.

Preparing for a Job Interview To be successful in a job interview, you must prepare for it so you can exhibit professionalism and indicate to a prospective employer that you are serious about the job. When preparing for the interview, several critical activities need to be performed.

Before the interview, gather facts about the industry, the prospective employer, and the job. Relevant information might include the general description for the occupation; the firm's products or services; the firm's size, number of employees, and financial and competitive position; the requirements of the position; and the name and personality of the interviewer. Obtaining this information will provide you with additional insight into the firm and help you formulate questions to ask the interviewer. This information might be gleaned, for example, from corporate annual reports, *The Wall Street Journal*, Moody's manuals, Standard & Poor's *Register of Corporations, Directors, and Executives,*

The Directory of Corporate Affiliations, selected issues of *Bloomberg Businessweek*, or trade publications. You should also study the LinkedIn profiles, Twitter feeds, and blogs of the people you'll be meeting. If information is not readily available, you could call the company and indicate that you wish to obtain some information about the firm before your interview.[42]

Preparation for the job interview should also involve role playing, or pretending that you are in the "hot seat" being interviewed. Before role playing, anticipate questions interviewers may pose and how you might address them (see Figure C–8). Do not memorize your answers, though, because you want to appear spontaneous, yet logical and intelligent. Nonetheless, it is helpful to practice how you might respond to the questions. In addition, develop questions you might ask the interviewer that are important and of concern to you (see Figure C–9 on the next page). "It's an opportunity to show the recruiter how smart you are," comments one recruiter.[43]

When role playing, you and someone with whom you feel comfortable should engage in a mock interview. Afterward, ask the stand-in interviewer to candidly appraise your interview content and style. You may wish to make a video of the mock interview; ask the personnel in your career services office where video equipment can be obtained for this purpose.

Before the job interview you should attend to several details. Know the exact time and place of the interview; write them down—do not rely on your memory. Get the full company name straight. Find out what the interviewer's name is and how to pronounce it. Bring a notepad and pen along to the interview in case you need to record anything. Make certain that your appearance is clean, neat, professional, and conservative. And be punctual; arriving tardy to a job interview gives you an appearance of being unreliable.

FIGURE C–8
Anticipate questions frequently asked by interviewers and practice how you might respond.

Interviewer Questions
1. How would you describe yourself?
2. What do you consider to be your greatest strengths and weaknesses?
3. Describe your most rewarding college experiences.
4. What do you see yourself doing in 5 years? In 10 years?
5. What are three important leadership qualities that you have demonstrated?
6. What do you really want out of life?
7. What are your long-range and short-range career goals?
8. Why did you choose your college major?
9. In which extracurricular activities did you participate? Why?
10. What jobs have you enjoyed the most? The least? Why?
11. How has your previous work experience prepared you for a marketing career?
12. Why do you want to work for our company?
13. What qualifications do you think a person needs to be successful in a company like ours?
14. Describe a creative idea you produced that led to the success of a project.
15. What criteria are you using to evaluate the company for which you hope to work?
16. Describe a project where you worked as part of a team.
17. What can I tell you about our company?
18. Are you willing to relocate?
19. Are you willing to spend at least six months as a trainee?
20. Why should we hire you?

FIGURE C–9
Interviewees should develop questions about topics that are important to them.

Interviewee Questions
1. Why would a job candidate want to work for your firm?
2. What makes your firm different from its competitors?
3. What is the company's promotion policy?
4. Describe the typical first-year assignment for this job.
5. How is an employee evaluated?
6. What are the opportunities for personal growth?
7. Do you have a training program?
8. What are the company's plans for future growth?
9. What is the retention rate of people in the position for which I am interviewing?
10. How can you use my skills?
11. Why is this position vacant?
12. How would you describe the ideal candidate?
13. Why do you enjoy working for your firm?
14. How much responsibility would I have in this job?
15. What is the corporate culture in your firm?

Succeeding in Your Job Interview You have done your homework, and at last the moment arrives and it is time for the interview. Although you may experience some apprehension, view the interview as a conversation between the prospective employer and you. Both of you are in the interview to look over the other party, to see whether there might be a good match. When you meet the interviewer, greet him or her by name, be cheerful, smile, and maintain good eye contact. Take your lead from the interviewer at the outset. Sit down after the interviewer has offered you a seat. Sit up straight in your chair, and look alert and interested at all times. Appear relaxed, not tense. Be enthusiastic.

During the interview, be yourself. If you try to behave in a manner that is different from the real you, your attempt may be transparent to the interviewer or you may ultimately get the job but discover that you aren't suited for it. However, remember that the interview is not the time to tweet, text, or take a telephone call.[44] In addition to assessing how well your skills match those of the job, the interviewer will probably try to assess your long-term interest in the firm.

As the interview comes to a close, leave it on a positive note. Thank the interviewer for his or her time and the opportunity to discuss employment opportunities. If you are

View the interview as a conversation between the prospective employer and you.

still interested in the job, express this to the interviewer. The interviewer will normally tell you what the employer's next step is—probably a visit to the company.[45] Rarely will a job offer be made at the end of the initial interview. If it is and you want the job, accept the offer; if there is any doubt in your mind about the job, however, ask for time to consider the offer.

Following Up on Your Job Interview After your interview, send a thank-you note to the interviewer and indicate whether you are still interested in the job. If you want to continue pursuing the job, polite persistence may help you get it. The thank-you note is a gesture of appreciation and a way of maintaining visibility with the interviewer. (Remember the adage, "Out of sight, out of mind.") Even if the interview did not go well, the thank-you note may impress the interviewer so much that his or her opinion of you changes.

After you have sent your thank-you note, you may wish to call the prospective employer to determine the status of the hiring decision. If the interviewer told you when you would hear from the employer, make your telephone call *after* this date (assuming, of course, that you have not yet heard from the employer); if the interviewer did not tell you when you would be contacted, make your telephone call a week or so after you have sent your thank-you note. While e-mail is a common form of communication today, it is often viewed as less personal than a letter or telephone call, so be confident that e-mail is preferred before using it to correspond with the interviewer.[46]

As you conduct your follow-up, be persistent but polite. If you are too eager, one of two things could happen to prevent you from getting the job: The employer might feel that you are a nuisance and would exhibit such behavior on the job, or the employer may perceive that you are desperate for the job and thus are not a viable candidate.

Handling Rejection You have put your best efforts into your job search. You developed a well-designed résumé and prepared carefully for the job interview. Even the interview appears to have gone well. Nevertheless, a prospective employer may send you a rejection letter. ("We are sorry that our needs and your superb qualifications don't match.") Although you will probably be disappointed, not all interviews lead to a job offer because there normally are more candidates than there are positions available.

If you receive a rejection letter, you should think back through the interview. What appeared to go right? What went wrong? Perhaps personnel from your career services office can shed light on the problem, particularly if they are accustomed to having interviewers rate each interviewee. Try to learn lessons to apply in future interviews. Keep interviewing and gaining interview experience; your persistence will eventually pay off.

SELECTED SOURCES OF MARKETING CAREER INFORMATION

The following is a selected list of marketing information sources that you should find useful during your academic studies and professional career.

Business and Marketing Publications

Business Periodicals Index (BPI) (New York: H.W. Wilson Company). This is a monthly (except August) index of 604 periodicals from all fields of business and marketing.

Scott Dacko, *The Advanced Dictionary of Marketing: Putting Theory to Use* (Oxford University Press, 2008). This dictionary focuses on leading-edge terminology for individuals who are serious about the theory and practice of marketing. Each term includes six elements: description, key insights, key words, implications, applications, and a bibliography.

Paul Hague, Nick Hague, and Carol-Ann Morgan, *Market Research in Practice: How to Get Greater Insight from Your Market* (Sterling, VA: Kogan Page, 2013). This practical book offers a clear, step-by-step guide to the market research process and explains how to use research tools and methods effectively to obtain reliable results.

Eric J. Forte, Cassandra J. Hartnett, and Andrea L. Sevetson, *Fundamentals of Government Information: Mining, Finding, Evaluating, and Using Government Resources* (New York: Neal-Schuman Publishers, 2011). This manual provides the background knowledge and tools needed to access online and print government information resources. Key topics include consumer information, census data, and summaries from the *Statistical Abstract of the United States*.

Hoover's Handbook of World Business (Austin, TX: Hoover's Business Press, 2012). A detailed source of information about companies outside of the United States, including firms from Canada, Europe, Japan, China, India, and Taiwan.

Jagdish Sheth and Naresh Malhotra, eds., *Wiley International Encyclopedia of Marketing* (West Sussex: John Wiley & Sons Ltd., 2011). This six-volume reference contains 360 entries from over 500 global experts. Entries are arranged alphabetically within each subject volume, and each volume carries an index.

Ray Poynter, *The Handbook of Online and Social Media Research: Tools and Techniques for Market Researchers* (West Sussex: John Wiley & Sons Ltd., 2010). This reference book covers new innovations in the fields of online and social media research, including community panels, blog mining, social networks, mobile research, and e-ethnography.

Kirk Tyson, *The Complete Guide to Competitive Intelligence* (Lees Summit, MO: Leading Edge Publications, 2010). This book provides detailed instructions on how to establish networks, conduct interviews, and gather and analyze intelligence to create a comprehensive competitive intelligence process.

Linda D. Hall, *Encyclopedia of Business Information Sources*, 27th ed. (Detroit: Gale Group, 2010). A bibliographic guide to over 35,000 citations covering more than 1,100 primary subjects of interest to business personnel.

Career Planning Publications

Richard N. Bolles, *What Color Is Your Parachute? 2014: A Practical Manual for Job-Hunters and Career-Changers* (Berkeley, CA: Ten Speed Press, 2013). A companion workbook is also available. See www.jobhuntersbible.com.

Dennis V. Damp, *The Book of U.S. Government Jobs: Where They Are, What's Available & How to Complete a Federal Résumé*, 11th ed. (McKees Rocks, PA: Bookhaven Press, 2011).

Alison Doyle, *Internet Your Way to a New Job*, 3rd ed. (Cupertino, CA: Happy About, 2011).

Jay Conrad Levinson and David E. Perry, *Guerrilla Marketing for Job Hunters 3.0: How to Stand Out from the Crowd and Tap Into the Hidden Job Market Using Social Media and 999 Other Tactics Today* (Hoboken, NJ: John Wiley & Sons, Inc., 2011).

Miriam Salpeter, *Social Networking for Career Success: Using Online Tools to Create a Personal Brand* (New York: Learning Express, 2011).

Lila B. Stair and Leslie Stair, *Careers in Marketing,* 4th ed. (New York: McGraw-Hill, 2009).

Martin Yate, *Knock'em Dead 2013: The Ultimate Job Search Guide* (Holbrook, MA: Adams Media Corporation, 2012). See www.adamsmedia.com.

Also see the following websites for additional information related to job searches, résumé writing, interviewing, and U.S. and international job postings:

www.accessalesjobs.com
www.careerbuilder.com
www.careers.org
www.careers-in-marketing.com
www.careerXroads.com
www.jobbankinfo.org
www.jobbankusa.com
www.monster.com
www.simplyhired.com
www.studentcentral.com
www.truecareers.com
www.usajobs.gov
www.vault.com
www.wetfeet.com

Selected Periodicals

Ad Week, Neilsen Business Media, Inc. (weekly). See www.adweek.com. (Subscription rate: $149 per year)

Advertising Age, Crain Communications, Inc. (weekly). See www.adage.com. (Subscription rate: $99 per year)

Barron's, Dow Jones & Co., Inc. (weekly). See www.barrons.com (Subscription rates: $99 print; $79 online; $149 online and print)

Bloomberg Businessweek, McGraw-Hill Companies (weekly). See www.businessweek.com. (Subscription rate: $39.97)

Business Horizons, Indiana University c/o Elsevier Science Publishing (bimonthly). See www.elsevier.com. (Subscription rate: $120)

Chain Store Age, Lebhar-Friedman, Inc. (monthly). See www.chainstoreage.com. (Subscription rate: $150)

eCommerce Times, ECT News Network, Inc. (daily). See www.ecommercetimes.com.

Forbes, Forbes, Inc. (17 issues) See www.forbes.com. (Subscription rates: $14.99)

Fortune, Time, Inc. (28 issues). See www.money.cnn.com. (Subscription rate: $19.99)

Harvard Business Review, Harvard University (monthly). See www.hbr.org. (Subscription rate: $99 online; $79 print; $129 premium subscription)

Industrial Marketing Management, Elsevier Science Publishing (8 issues). See www.elsevier.com. (Subscription rate: $167)

International Journal of Electronic Commerce, M. E. Sharpe Publishing (quarterly). See www.mesharpe.com. (Subscription rate: $92)

Journal of Advertising Research, Springer Science+Business Media (quarterly). See www.springer.com. (Subscription rate: $340)

Journal of Consumer Marketing, Emerald Group Publishing, Ltd. (7 issues). See www.emeraldinsight.com. (Subscription rate: $3,549)

Journal of Consumer Research, University of Chicago Press (quarterly). See www.journals.uchicago.edu. (Subscription rates: $145 non-members; $70 members; $25 students)

Journal of Interactive Marketing, Direct Marketing Educational Foundation (quarterly). See www.elsevier.com. (Subscription rate: $313)

Journal of International Marketing, American Marketing Association (quarterly). See www.marketingpower.com. (Subscription rates: $120 print; $145 print + online)

Journal of Marketing, American Marketing Association (quarterly). See www.marketingpower.com. (Subscription rates: $135 print; $162 print + online)

Journal of Marketing Communications, Routledge Publishing (5 times per year). See www.tandfonline.com. (Subscription rate: $184)

Journal of Marketing Education, Sage Publications (3 times per year). See www.sagepub.com. (Subscription rate: $109)

Journal of Marketing Research, American Marketing Association (bimonthly). See www.marketingpower.com. (Subscription rates: $135 print; $162 print + online)

Journal of Personal Selling and Sales Management, American Marketing Association (quarterly). See www.jpssm.org. (Subscription rate: $79)

Journal of Public Policy and Marketing, American Marketing Association (semiannually). See www.marketingpower.com. (Subscription rates: $90 print; $115 print + online)

Journal of Retailing, Elsevier Science Publishing (quarterly). See www.elsevier.com. (Subscription rate: $173)

Journal of the Academy of Marketing Science, Springer Science and Business Media LLC (6 issues). See www.springer.com. (Subscription rate: $193)

Marketing Education Review, CTC Press (3 times per year). See www.marketingeducationreview.com. (Subscription rate: $55)

Marketing Health Services, American Marketing Association (quarterly). See www.marketingpower.com. (Subscription rate: $100)

Marketing Insights, American Marketing Association (quarterly). See www.marketingpower.com. (Subscription rate: $100)

Marketing News, American Marketing Association (biweekly). See www.marketingpower.com. (Subscription rates: $85 nonmembers; $53 members; $65 students)

Media Week, Quantum Business Media (weekly). See www.mediaweek.co.uk. (Subscription rate: $825)

Sales and Marketing Management, Lakewood Media Group, LLC. See www.salesandmarketing.com. (Subscription rate: free)

Stores, National Retail Federation (weekly). See www.nrf.com or www.stores.org. (Subscription rates: $120 for nonmembers; free for members)

The Wall Street Journal Interactive, Dow Jones & Company, Inc. (weekly). See www.wsj.com. (Subscription rates: $103 online; $119 print; $140 online and print)

Professional and Trade Associations

American Advertising Federation
1101 Vermont Ave. N.W., Suite 500
Washington, DC 20005-6306
(202)898-0089
www.aaf.org

American Association of Advertising Agencies
405 Lexington Ave.
New York, NY 10174-1801
(212)682-2500
www.aaaa.org

American e-Commerce Association
2346 Camp St.
New Orleans, LA 70130
(504)495-1748
www.aeaus.com

American Marketing Association
311 S. Wacker Dr., Suite 5800
Chicago, IL 60606
(800)AMA-1150
www.marketingpower.com

American Society of Transportation and Logistics
P.O. Box 3363
Warrenton, VA 20188
(202)580-7270
www.astl.org

Business Marketing Association
1833 Centre Point Circle, Suite 123
Naperville, IL 60563
(630)544-5054
www.marketing.org

Direct Marketing Association
1120 Avenue of the Americas
New York, NY 10036-6700
(212)768-7277
www.the-dma.org

Direct Selling Association
1667 K Street, N.W., Suite 1100
Washington, DC 20006
(202)452-8866
www.dsa.org

Institute for Supply Management
2055 E. Centennial Circle
Tempe, AZ 85284
(480)752-6276
www.ism.ws

International Advertising Association
World Service Center
257 Madison Ave., Suite 2102
New York, NY 10016
(212)557-1133
www.iaaglobal.org

International Franchise Association
1501 K Street, N.W., Suite 350
Washington, DC 20005
(202)628-8000
www.franchise.org

Internet Marketing Association
10 Mar Del Rey
San Clemente, CA 92673
(949)443-9300
www.imanetwork.org

Marketing Research Association
110 National Drive
Glastonbury, CT 06033-1212
(860)682-1000
www.mra-net.org

Marketing Science Institute
1000 Massachusetts Ave.
Cambridge, MA 02138-5396
(617)491-2060
www.msi.org

National Association of Wholesale Distributors
1325 G Street, N.W., Suite 1000
Washington, DC 20005
(202)872-0885
www.naw.org

National Mail Order Association
2807 Polk St. NE
Minneapolis, MN 55418-2954
(612)788-1673
www.nmoa.org

National Retail Federation
325 7th St. N.W., Suite 1100
Washington, DC 20004
(800)NRF-HOW2
www.nrf.com

Product Development and Management Association
15000 Commerce Parkway, Suite C
Mount Laurel, NJ 08054
(800)232-5241
www.pdma.org

Public Relations Society of America
33 Maiden Lane
New York, NY 10038-5150
(212)460-1400
www.prsa.org

Sales and Marketing Executive International
P.O. Box 1390
Suma, WA 98295-1390
(312)893-0751
www.smei.org

Society for Marketing Professional Services
44 Canal Center Plaza, Suite 444
Alexandria, VA 22314
(800)292-7667
www.smps.org

APPENDIX

D ALTERNATE CASES

Available online at www.12e.kerin.tv/AppD

GLOSSARY

80/20 rule A concept that suggests 80 percent of a firm's sales are obtained from 20 percent of its customers. p. 231
above-, at-, or below-market pricing Setting a market price for a product or product class based on a subjective feel for the competitors' price or market price as the benchmark. p. 360
account management policies Policies that specify who salespeople should contact, what kinds of selling and customer service activities should be engaged in, and how these activities should be carried out. p. 548
action item list An aid to implementing a plan that consists of four columns: (1) the task; (2) the person responsible for completing that task; (3) the date to finish the task; and (4) what is to be delivered. p. 599
adaptive selling A need-satisfaction presentation format that involves adjusting the presentation to fit the selling situation, such as knowing when to offer solutions and when to ask for more information. p. 542
advertising Any paid form of nonpersonal communication about an organization, product, service, or idea by an identified sponsor. pp. 444, 470
all-you-can-afford budgeting Allocating funds to promotion only after all other budget items are covered. p. 455
apps Small, downloadable software programs that can run on smartphones and tablet devices. p. 522
attitude A learned predisposition to respond to an object or class of objects in a consistently favorable or unfavorable way. p. 123
average revenue (AR) The average amount of money received for selling one unit of a product, or simply the price of that unit. p. 337

baby boomers Includes the generation of 76 million children born between 1946 and 1964. p. 69
back translation The practice where a translated word or phrase is retranslated into the original language by a different interpreter to catch errors. p. 175
balance of trade The difference between the monetary value of a nation's exports and imports. p. 163
barriers to entry Business practices or conditions that make it difficult for new firms to enter the market. p. 81
barter The practice of exchanging products and services for other products and services rather than for money. p. 324
basing-point pricing Selecting one or more geographical locations (basing point) from which the list price for products plus freight expenses are charged to the buyer. p. 369
behavioral targeting Uses information provided by cookies for directing online advertising from marketers to those online shoppers whose behavioral profiles suggest they would be interested in such advertising. p. 573
beliefs A consumer's subjective perception of how a product or brand performs on different attributes based on personal experience, advertising, and discussions with other people. p. 123
bidder's list A list of firms believed to be qualified to supply a given item. p. 151
blended family A family formed by merging two previously separated units into a single household. p. 70
blog A contraction of "web log," a web page that serves as a publicly accessible personal journal and online forum for an individual or organization. p. 504
bots Electronic shopping agents or robots that comb websites to compare prices and product or service features. p. 570
bottom of the pyramid The largest but poorest socioeconomic group of people in the world. p. 177
brand community A specialized group of consumers with a structured set of relationships involving a particular brand, fellow customers of that brand, and the product in use. p. 128
brand equity The added value a brand name gives to a product beyond the functional benefits provided. p. 284
brand licensing A contractual agreement whereby one company (licensor) allows its brand name(s) or trademark(s) to be used with products or services offered by another company (licensee) for a royalty or fee. p. 285
brand loyalty A favorable attitude toward and consistent purchase of a single brand over time. p. 122
brand name Any word, device (design, sound, shape, or color), or combination of these used to distinguish a seller's products or services. p. 283
brand personality A set of human characteristics associated with a brand name. p. 284
branding A marketing decision in which an organization uses a name, phrase, design, symbols, or combination of these to identify its products and distinguish them from those of competitors. p. 283
breadth of product line The variety of different product items a store carries. p. 417
break-even analysis A technique that analyzes the relationship between total revenue and total cost to determine profitability at various levels of output. p. 342
break-even chart A graphic presentation of the break-even analysis that shows when total revenue and total cost intersect to identify profit or loss for a given quantity sold. p. 343
break-even point (BEP) The quantity at which total revenue and total cost are equal. p. 342
brokers Independent firms or individuals whose principal function is to bring buyers and sellers together to make sales. p. 435
bundle pricing The marketing of two or more products in a single package price. p. 355
business The clear, broad, underlying industry or market sector of an organization's offering. p. 30
business analysis The stage of the new-product process that specifies the features of the product and the marketing strategy needed to bring it to market and make financial projections. p. 261
business marketing The marketing of products and services to companies, governments, or not-for-profit organizations for use in the creation of products and services that they can produce and market to others. p. 140
business plan A road map for the entire organization for a specified future period of time, such as one year or five years. p. 50
business portfolio analysis A technique that managers use to quantify performance measures and growth targets to analyze their firms' strategic business units (SBUs) as though they were a collection of separate investments. p. 35

business products Products organizations buy that assist in providing other products for resale. Also called *B2B products* or *industrial products*. p. 248
buy classes Consist of three types of organizational buying situations: straight rebuy, new buy, and modified rebuy. p. 148
buying center The group of people in an organization who participate in the buying process and share common goals, risks, and knowledge important to a purchase decision. p. 147

capacity management Integrating the service component of the marketing mix with efforts to influence consumer demand. p. 315
category management An approach to managing the assortment of merchandise in which a manager is assigned the responsibility for selecting all products that consumers in a market segment might view as substitutes for each other, with the objective of maximizing sales and profits in the category. p. 429
cause marketing Occurs when the charitable contributions of a firm are tied directly to the customer revenues produced through the promotion of one of its products. p. 102
caveat emptor The legal concept of "let the buyer beware" that was pervasive in the American business culture prior to the 1960s. p. 95
central business district The oldest retail setting, usually located in the community's downtown area. p. 428
channel conflict Arises when one channel member believes another channel member is engaged in behavior that prevents it from achieving its goals. p. 397
channel of communication The means (e.g., a salesperson, advertising media, or public relations tools) of conveying a message to a receiver during the communication process. p. 442
choiceboard An interactive, Internet-enabled system that allows individual customers to design their own products and services by answering a few questions and choosing from a menu of product or service attributes (or components), prices, and delivery options. p. 562
code of ethics A formal statement of ethical principles and rules of conduct. p. 98
cognitive dissonance The feeling of postpurchase psychological tension or anxiety consumers may experience when faced with two or more highly attractive alternatives. p. 115
collaborative filtering A process that automatically groups people with similar buying intentions, preferences, and behaviors and predicts future purchases. p. 562
commercialization The stage of the new-product process that positions and launches a new product in full-scale production and sales. p. 263
communication The process of conveying a message to others that requires six elements: a source, a message, a channel of communication, a receiver, and the processes of encoding and decoding. p. 442
community shopping center A retail location that typically has one primary store (usually a department store branch) and often 20 to 40 smaller outlets, serving a population of consumers who are within a 10- to 20-minute drive. p. 428
competition The alternative firms that could provide a product to satisfy a specific market's needs. p. 80
competitive parity budgeting Allocating funds to promotion by matching the competitor's absolute level of spending or the proportion per point of market share. Also called *matching competitors* or *share of market*. p. 455
consideration set The group of brands that a consumer would consider acceptable from among all the brands in the product class of which he or she is aware. p. 113
constraints In a decision, the restrictions placed on potential solutions to a problem. p. 196
consultative selling A need-satisfaction presentation format that focuses on problem identification, where the salesperson serves as an expert on problem recognition and resolution. p. 542
consumer behavior The actions a person takes in purchasing and using products and services, including the mental and social processes that come before and after these actions. p. 112
***Consumer Bill of Rights* (1962)** A law that codified the ethics of exchange between buyers and sellers, including the rights to safety, to be informed, to choose, and to be heard. p. 95
consumer ethnocentrism The tendency to believe that it is inappropriate, indeed immoral, to purchase foreign-made products. p. 176
consumer products Products purchased by the ultimate consumer. p. 248
consumer socialization The process by which people acquire the skills, knowledge, and attitudes necessary to function as consumers. p. 128
consumerism A grassroots movement started in the 1960s to increase the influence, power, and rights of consumers in dealing with institutions. p. 83
consumer-oriented sales promotion Sales tools used to support a company's advertising and personal selling directed to ultimate consumers. Also called *consumer promotions*. p. 489
convenience products Items that the consumer purchases frequently, conveniently, and with a minimum of shopping effort. p. 249
cookies Computer files that a marketer can download onto the computer and mobile phone of an online shopper who visits the marketer's website. p. 573
cooperative advertising Advertising programs whereby a manufacturer pays a percentage of the retailer's local advertising expense for advertising the manufacturer's products. p. 495
core values The fundamental, passionate, and enduring principles of an organization that guide its conduct over time. p. 29
cost focus strategy One of Porter's generic business strategies that involves controlling expenses and, in turn, lowering product prices targeted at a narrow range of market segments. p. 590
cost leadership strategy One of Porter's generic business strategies that focuses on reducing expenses and, in turn, lowers product prices while targeting a broad array of market segments. p. 590
cost per thousand (CPM) The cost of reaching 1,000 individuals or households with the advertising message in a given medium (M is the Roman numeral for 1,000). p. 479
cost-plus pricing Summing the total unit cost of providing a product or service and adding a specific amount to the cost to arrive at a price. p. 356
countertrade The practice of using barter rather than money for making global sales. p. 162
cross tabulation A method of presenting and analyzing data involving two or more variables to discover relationships in the data. Also known as *cross tab*. p. 211

cross-channel shopper An online consumer who researches products online and then purchases them at a retail store. p. 574
cross-cultural analysis The study of similarities and differences among consumers in two or more nations or societies. p. 173
cultural symbols Things that represent ideas and concepts. p. 174
culture The set of values, ideas, and attitudes that are learned and shared among the members of a group. p. 73
currency exchange rate The price of one country's currency expressed in terms of another country's currency. p. 179
customary pricing Setting a price that is dictated by tradition, a standardized channel of distribution, or other competitive factors. p. 359
customer contact audit A flowchart of the points of interaction or "service encounters" between consumers and a service provider. p. 309
customer experience The internal response that customers have to all aspects of an organization and its offering. p. 16
customer experience management (CEM) The process of managing the entire customer experience within the company. pp. 260, 314
customer relationship management (CRM) The process of identifying prospective buyers, understanding them intimately, and developing favorable long-term perceptions of the organization and its offerings so that buyers will choose them in the marketplace. p. 15
customer service The ability of logistics management to satisfy users in terms of time, dependability, communication, and convenience. p. 404
customer value The unique combination of benefits received by targeted buyers that includes quality, convenience, on-time delivery, and both before-sale and after-sale service at a specific price. p. 11
customer value proposition The cluster of benefits that an organization promises customers to satisfy their needs. p. 10
customerization The growing practice of not only customizing a product or service but also personalizing the marketing and overall shopping and buying interaction for each customer. p. 570
customs What is considered normal and expected about the way people do things in a specific country. p. 174

data The facts and figures related to the project that are divided into two main parts: secondary data and primary data. p. 198
decoding The process of having the receiver take a set of symbols, the message, and transform them back to an idea during the communication process. p. 443
demand curve A graph that relates the quantity sold and price, showing the maximum number of units that will be sold at a given price. p. 336
demand factors Factors that determine consumers' willingness and ability to pay for products and services. p. 337
demographics Describing a population according to selected characteristics such as age, gender, ethnicity, income, and occupation. p. 68
depth of product line The store carries a large assortment of each product item. p. 417
derived demand The demand for industrial products and services that is driven by, or derived from, the demand for consumer products and services. p. 143
development The stage of the new-product process that turns the idea on paper into a prototype. p. 261
differentiation focus strategy One of Porter's generic business strategies that requires products to have significant points of difference to target one or only a few market segments. p. 590
differentiation strategy One of Porter's generic business strategies that requires products to have significant points of difference to charge a higher price while targeting a broad array of market segments. p. 590
direct investment A global market-entry strategy that entails a domestic firm actually investing in and owning a foreign subsidiary or division. p. 184
direct marketing A promotion alternative that uses direct communication with consumers to generate a response in the form of an order, a request for further information, or a visit to a retail outlet. p. 447
direct orders The result of direct marketing offers that contain all the information necessary for a prospective buyer to make a decision to purchase and complete the transaction. p. 461
discretionary income The money that remains after paying for taxes and necessities. p. 77
disintermediation Channel conflict that arises when a channel member bypasses another member and sells or buys products direct. p. 398
disposable income The money a consumer has left after paying taxes to use for necessities such as food, housing, clothing, and transportation. p. 76
diversification analysis A technique that helps a firm search for growth opportunities from among current and new markets as well as current and new products. p. 38
dual distribution An arrangement whereby a firm reaches different buyers by employing two or more different types of channels for the same basic product. p. 391
dumping Occurs when a firm sells a product in a foreign country below its domestic price or below its actual cost. p. 187
dynamic pricing The practice of changing prices for products and services in real time in response to supply and demand conditions. p. 572
dynamic pricing policy Setting different prices for products and services in real time in response to supply and demand conditions. Also called a *flexible-price policy*. p. 362

economic espionage The clandestine collection of trade secrets or proprietary information about a company's competitors. p. 96
***Economic Espionage Act* (1996)** A law that makes the theft of trade secrets by foreign entities a federal crime in the United States. p. 165
economy Pertains to the income, expenditures, and resources that affect the cost of running a business and household. p. 75
eight-second rule A view that customers will abandon their efforts to enter and navigate a website if download time exceeds eight seconds. p. 570
electronic commerce Any activity that uses some form of electronic communication in the inventory, exchange, advertisement, distribution, and payment of products and services. p. 80
e-marketplaces Online trading communities that bring together buyers and supplier organizations to make possible the real time exchange of information, money, products, and services. Also called *B2B exchanges* or *e-hubs*. p. 153

emotional intelligence The ability to understand one's own emotions and the emotions of people with whom one interacts on a daily basis. p. 549

encoding The process of having the sender transform an idea into a set of symbols during the communication process. p. 443

environmental forces The uncontrollable forces that affect a marketing decision and consist of social, economic, technological, competitive, and regulatory forces. p. 11

environmental scanning The process of continually acquiring information on events occurring outside the organization to identify and interpret potential trends. p. 66

ethics The moral principles and values that govern the actions and decisions of an individual or group. p. 92

evaluative criteria Factors that represent both the objective attributes of a brand and the subjective ones a consumer uses to compare different products and brands. p. 113

everyday low pricing (EDLP) The practice of replacing promotional allowances with lower manufacturer list prices. p. 368

exchange The trade of things of value between buyer and seller so that each is better off after the trade. p. 5

exclusive distribution A level of distribution density whereby only one retailer in a specific geographical area carries the firm's products. p. 395

experience curve pricing A method of pricing based on the learning effect, which holds that the unit cost of many products and services declines by 10 percent to 30 percent each time a firm's experience at producing and selling them doubles. p. 356

exporting A global market-entry strategy in which a company produces products in one country and sells them in another country. p. 181

Facebook A website where users may create a personal profile, add other users as friends, and exchange comments, photos, videos, and "likes" with them. p. 507

family life cycle The distinct phases that a family progresses through from formation to retirement, each phase bringing with it identifiable purchasing behaviors. p. 129

feedback In the feedback loop, the sender's interpretation of the response, which indicates whether a message was decoded and understood as intended during the communication process. p. 444

field of experience A mutually shared understanding and knowledge that the sender and receiver apply to the message so that it can be communicated effectively during the communication process. p. 443

fixed cost (FC) The sum of the expenses of the firm that are stable and do not change with the quantity of a product that is produced and sold. p. 341

fixed-price policy Setting one price for all buyers of a product or service. Also called a *one-price policy*. p. 361

FOB origin pricing The "free on board" (FOB) price the seller quotes that includes only the cost of loading the product onto the vehicle and specifies the name of the location where the loading is to occur (seller's factory or warehouse). p. 368

***Foreign Corrupt Practices Act* (1977)** A law, amended by the *International Anti-Dumping and Fair Competition Act* (1998), that makes it a crime for U.S. corporations to bribe an official of a foreign government or political party to obtain or retain business in a foreign country. p. 174

form of ownership Distinguishes retail outlets based on whether independent retailers, corporate chains, or contractual systems own the outlet. p. 414

formula selling presentation A sales presentation format that consists of information that must be provided in an accurate, thorough, and step-by-step manner to inform the prospect. p. 541

four I's of services The four unique elements to services: intangibility, inconsistency, inseparability, and inventory. p. 301

frequency The average number of times a person in the target audience is exposed to a message or an advertisement. p. 478

full-service agency An advertising agency that provides the most complete range of services, including market research, media selection, copy development, artwork, and production. p. 487

functional groupings Organizational groupings that represent the different departments or business activities within a firm. p. 600

gap analysis A type of analysis that compares the differences between the consumer's expectations about and experiences with a service based on dimensions of service quality. p. 308

Generation X Includes the 50 million people born between 1965 and 1976. Also called the *baby bust*. p. 69

Generation Y Includes the 72 million Americans born between 1977 and 1994. Also called the *echo-boom* or the *baby boomlet*. p. 70

generic business strategy A strategy that can be adopted by any firm, regardless of the product or industry involved, to achieve a competitive advantage. p. 589

geographical groupings Organizational groupings in which sales territories are subdivided according to geographical location. p. 600

global brand A brand marketed under the same name in multiple countries with similar and centrally coordinated marketing programs. p. 171

global competition Exists when firms originate, produce, and market their products and services worldwide. p. 169

global consumers Consumer groups living in many countries or regions of the world who have similar needs or seek similar features and benefits from products or services. p. 171

global marketing strategy A strategy used by transnational firms that employ the practice of standardizing marketing activities when there are cultural similarities and adapting them when cultures differ. p. 170

goals Statements of an accomplishment of a task to be achieved, often by a specific time. Also called *objectives*. p. 31

gray market A situation where products are sold through unauthorized channels of distribution. Also called *parallel importing*. p. 187

green marketing Marketing efforts to produce, promote, and reclaim environmentally sensitive products. p. 102

gross domestic product (GDP) The monetary value of all products and services produced in a country during one year. p. 162

gross income The total amount of money made in one year by a person, household, or family unit. Also known as *money income* at the Census Bureau. p. 76

gross rating points (GRPs) A reference number used by advertisers that is obtained by multiplying reach (expressed as a percentage of the total market) by frequency. p. 479

hierarchy of effects The sequence of stages a prospective buyer goes through from initial awareness of a product to eventual action that includes awareness, interest, evaluation, trial, and adoption of the product. p. 454

hypermarket A form of scrambled merchandising, which consists of a large store (more than 200,000 square feet) that offers everything in a single outlet, eliminating the need for consumers to shop at more than one location. p. 418

idea generation The stage of the new-product process that develops a pool of concepts to serve as candidates for new products, building upon the previous stage's results. p. 257

idle production capacity Occurs when the service provider is available but there is no demand for the service. p. 303

infomercials Program-length (30-minute) advertisements that take an educational approach to communication with potential customers. p. 480

information technology Involves operating computer networks that can store and process data. p. 208

in-house agencies Consist of the company's own advertising staff, who may provide full services or a limited range of services. p. 488

institutional advertisements Advertisements designed to build goodwill or an image for an organization rather than promote a specific product or service. p. 471

integrated marketing communications (IMC) The concept of designing marketing communications programs that coordinate all promotional activities—advertising, personal selling, sales promotion, public relations, and direct marketing—to provide a consistent message across all audiences. p. 442

intensive distribution A level of distribution density whereby a firm tries to place its products and services in as many outlets as possible. p. 395

interactive marketing Two-way buyer–seller electronic communication in a computer-mediated environment in which the buyer controls the kind and amount of information received from the seller. p. 562

internal marketing The notion that a service organization must focus on its employees, or internal market, before successful programs can be directed at customers. p. 313

intertype competition Competition between very dissimilar types of retail outlets that results from a scrambled merchandising policy. p. 419

involvement The personal, social, and economic significance of the purchase to the consumer. p. 115

ISO 9000 Standards for the registration and certification of a manufacturer's quality management and assurance system based on an on-site audit of practices and procedures developed by the International Standards Organization (ISO). p. 145

joint venture A global market-entry strategy in which a foreign company and a local firm invest together to create a local business in order to share ownership, control, and profits of the new company. p. 183

key account management The practice of using team selling to focus on important customers so as to build mutually beneficial, long-term, cooperative relationships. p. 547

label An integral part of the package that typically identifies the product or brand, who made it, where and when it was made, how it is to be used, and package contents and ingredients. p. 290

laws Society's values and standards that are enforceable in the courts. p. 92

lead generation The result of a direct marketing offer designed to generate interest in a product or service and a request for additional information. p. 461

learning Those behaviors that result from (1) repeated experience and (2) reasoning. p. 122

level of service Describes the degree of service provided to the customer from three types of retailers: self-, limited-, and full-service. p. 414

lifestyle A mode of living that is identified by how people spend their time and resources, what they consider important in their environment, and what they think of themselves and the world around them. p. 124

limited-service agencies Advertising agencies that specialize in one aspect of the advertising process, such as providing creative services to develop the advertising copy, buying previously unpurchased media space, or providing Internet services. p. 488

line positions Managers who have the authority and responsibility to issue orders to the people who report to them. p. 600

LinkedIn A business-oriented website that lets users post their professional profiles to connect to a network of businesspeople. p. 512

logistics Those activities that focus on getting the right amount of the right products to the right place at the right time at the lowest possible cost. p. 400

loss-leader pricing Deliberately selling a product below its customary price, not to increase sales, but to attract customers' attention to it in hopes that they will buy other products with large markups as well. p. 360

make-buy decision An evaluation of whether components and assemblies will be purchased from outside suppliers or built by the company itself. p. 151

manufacturer's agents Agents who work for several producers and carry noncompetitive, complementary merchandise in an exclusive territory. Also called *manufacturer's representatives.* p. 435

marginal analysis A continuing, concise trade-off of incremental costs against incremental revenues. p. 342

marginal cost (MC) The change in total cost that results from producing and marketing one additional unit of a product. p. 341

marginal revenue (MR) The change in total revenue that results from producing and marketing one additional unit of a product. p. 337

market People with both the desire and the ability to buy a specific offering. p. 9

market modification Strategies by which a company tries to find new customers, increase a product's use among existing customers, or create new use situations. p. 281

market orientation An organization that focuses its efforts on (1) continuously collecting information about customers' needs, (2) sharing this information across departments, and (3) using it to create customer value. p. 15

market segmentation Involves aggregating prospective buyers into groups, or segments, that (1) have common needs and (2) will respond similarly to a marketing action. pp. 40, 224

market segments The relatively homogeneous groups of prospective buyers that (1) have common needs and (2) will respond similarly to a marketing action. p. 12

market share The ratio of sales revenue of the firm to the total sales revenue of all firms in the industry, including the firm itself. p. 31

market testing The stage of the new-product process that exposes actual products to prospective consumers under realistic purchase conditions to see if they will buy. p. 262

market-based groupings Organizational groupings that use specific customer segments. p. 601

marketing The activity for creating, communicating, delivering, and exchanging offerings that benefit customers, the organization, its stakeholders, and society at large. p. 5

marketing channel Consists of individuals and firms involved in the process of making a product or service available for use or consumption by consumers or industrial users. p. 386

marketing concept The idea that an organization should (1) strive to satisfy the needs of consumers while also (2) trying to achieve the organization's goals. p. 15

marketing dashboard The visual computer display of the essential information related to achieving a marketing objective. p. 32

marketing metric A measure of the quantitative value or trend of a marketing action or result. p. 32

marketing mix The marketing manager's controllable factors—product, price, promotion, and place—that can be used to solve a marketing problem. p. 10

marketing plan A road map for the marketing actions of an organization for a specified future time period, such as one year or five years. p. 32

marketing program A plan that integrates the marketing mix to provide a good, service, or idea to prospective buyers. p. 12

marketing research The process of defining a marketing problem and opportunity, systematically collecting and analyzing information, and recommending actions. p. 194

marketing ROI The application of modern measurement technologies to understand, quantify, and optimize marketing spending. p. 603

marketing strategy The means by which a marketing goal is to be achieved, usually characterized by a specified target market and a marketing program to reach it. p. 44

marketing tactics The detailed day-to-day operational marketing actions for each element of the marketing mix that contribute to the overall success of marketing strategies. p. 44

market-product grid A framework to relate the market segments of potential buyers to products offered or potential marketing actions. p. 225

marketspace An information- and communication-based electronic exchange environment mostly occupied by sophisticated computer and telecommunication technologies and digitized offerings. p. 80

measures of success Criteria or standards used in evaluating proposed solutions to the problem. p. 196

merchandise line Describes how many different types of products a store carries and in what assortment. p. 414

merchant wholesalers Independently owned firms that take title to the merchandise they handle. p. 434

message The information sent by a source to a receiver during the communication process. p. 442

microfinance The practice of offering small, collateral-free loans to individuals who otherwise would not have access to the capital necessary to begin small businesses or other income-generating activities. p. 179

mission A statement of the organization's function in society that often identifies its customers, markets, products, and technologies. Often used interchangeably with *vision*. p. 29

mixed branding A branding strategy where a firm markets products under its own name(s) and that of a reseller because the segment attracted to the reseller is different from its own market. p. 290

moral idealism A personal moral philosophy that considers certain individual rights or duties as universal, regardless of the outcome. p. 100

motivation The energizing force that stimulates behavior to satisfy a need. p. 118

multibranding A branding strategy that involves giving each product a distinct name when each brand is intended for a different market segment. p. 288

multichannel marketing The blending of different communication and delivery channels that are mutually reinforcing in attracting, retaining, and building relationships with consumers who shop and buy in traditional intermediaries and online. p. 391

multichannel retailers Retailers that utilize and integrate a combination of traditional store formats and nonstore formats such as catalogs, television home shopping, and online retailing. p. 432

multicultural marketing Combinations of the marketing mix that reflect the unique attitudes, ancestry, communication preferences, and lifestyles of different races. p. 72

multidomestic marketing strategy A strategy used by multinational firms that have as many different product variations, brand names, and advertising programs as countries in which they do business. p. 170

multiproduct branding A branding strategy in which a company uses one name for all its products in a product class. p. 288

need-satisfaction presentation A sales presentation format that emphasizes probing and listening by the salesperson to identify the needs and interests of prospective buyers. p. 542

new-product process The seven stages an organization goes through to identify opportunities and convert them into salable products or services. p. 256

new-product strategy development The stage of the new-product process that defines the role for a new product in terms of the firm's overall objectives. p. 257

noise Extraneous factors that can work against effective communication by distorting a message or the feedback received during the communication process. p. 444

North American Industry Classification System (NAICS) Provides common industry definitions for Canada, Mexico, and the United States, which makes it easier to measure economic activity in the three member countries of the *North American Free Trade Agreement* (NAFTA). p. 141

objective and task budgeting Allocating funds to promotion whereby the company: (1) determines its promotion objectives; (2) outlines the tasks to accomplish those objectives; and (3) determines the promotion cost of performing those tasks. p. 456

objectives Statements of an accomplishment of a task to be achieved, often by a specific time. Also called *goals*. p. 31

observational data Facts and figures obtained by watching, either mechanically or in person, how people actually behave. p. 200

odd-even pricing Setting prices a few dollars or cents under an even number. p. 354

off-peak pricing Charging different prices during different times of the day or during different days of the week to reflect variations in demand for the service. p. 312

off-price retailing Selling brand-name merchandise at lower than regular prices. p. 427

online consumers The subsegment of all Internet users who employ this technology to research products and services and make purchases. p. 567

opinion leaders Individuals who exert direct or indirect social influence over others. p. 126

order getter Sells in a conventional sense and identifies prospective customers, provides customers with information, persuades customers to buy, closes sales, and follows up on customers' use of a product or service. p. 536

order taker Processes routine orders or reorders for products that were already sold by the company. p. 535

organizational buyers Those manufacturers, wholesalers, retailers, and government agencies that buy products and services for their own use or for resale. pp. 18, 140

organizational buying behavior The decision-making process that organizations use to establish the need for products and services and identify, evaluate, and choose among alternative brands and suppliers. p. 149

organizational buying criteria The objective attributes of the supplier's products and services and the capabilities of the supplier itself. p. 144

organizational culture The set of values, ideas, attitudes, and norms of behavior that is learned and shared among the members of an organization. p. 30

packaging A component of a product that refers to any container in which it is offered for sale and on which label information is conveyed. p. 290

partnership selling The practice whereby buyers and sellers combine their expertise and resources to create customized solutions, commit to joint planning, and share customer, competitive, and company information for their mutual benefit and, ultimately, the benefit of the customer. Also called *enterprise selling*. p. 534

penetration pricing Setting a low initial price on a new product to appeal immediately to the mass market. p. 353

perceived risk The anxiety felt because the consumer cannot anticipate the outcomes of a purchase but believes there may be negative consequences. p. 121

percentage of sales budgeting Allocating funds to promotion as a percentage of past or anticipated sales, in terms of either dollars or units sold. p. 455

perception The process by which an individual selects, organizes, and interprets information to create a meaningful picture of the world. p. 120

perceptual map A means of displaying in two dimensions the location of products or brands in the minds of consumers to enable a manager to see how they perceive competing products or brands, as well as the firm's own product or brand. p. 241

permission marketing The solicitation of a consumer's consent (called "opt-in") to receive e-mail and advertising based on personal data supplied by the consumer. p. 563

personal selling The two-way flow of communication between a buyer and seller, often in a face-to-face encounter, designed to influence a person's or group's purchase decision. pp. 445, 532

personal selling process Sales activities occurring before, during, and after the sale itself, consisting of six stages: (1) prospecting, (2) preapproach, (3) approach, (4) presentation, (5) close, and (6) follow-up. p. 538

personality A person's consistent behaviors or responses to recurring situations. p. 119

personalization The consumer-initiated practice of generating content on a marketer's website that is custom tailored to an individual's specific needs and preferences. p. 562

points of difference Those characteristics of a product that make it superior to competitive substitutes. p. 41

posttests Tests conducted after an advertisement has been shown to the target audience to determine whether it accomplished its intended purpose. p. 488

power center A retail location consisting of a huge shopping strip with multiple anchor (or national) stores. p. 428

predatory pricing The practice of charging a very low price for a product with the intent of driving competitors out of business. p. 372

prestige pricing Setting a high price so that quality- or status-conscious consumers will be attracted to the product and buy it. p. 353

pretests Tests conducted before an advertisement is placed in any medium to determine whether it communicates the intended message or to select among alternative versions of the advertisement. p. 486

price (P) The money or other considerations (including other products and services) exchanged for the ownership or use of a product or service. p. 324

price discrimination The practice of charging different prices to different buyers for products of like grade and quality. p. 370

price elasticity of demand The percentage change in quantity demanded relative to a percentage change in price. p. 340

price fixing A conspiracy among firms to set prices for a product. p. 369

price lining Setting the price of a line of products at a number of different specific pricing points. p. 354

price war Successive price cutting by competitors to increase or maintain their unit sales or market share. p. 364

pricing constraints Factors that limit the range of prices a firm may set. p. 331

pricing objectives Specifying the role of price in an organization's marketing and strategic plans. p. 330

primary data Facts and figures that are newly collected for the project. p. 198

private branding A branding strategy used when a company manufactures products but sells them under the brand name of a wholesaler or retailer. Also called *private labeling* or *reseller branding*. p. 289

product A good, service, or idea consisting of a bundle of tangible and intangible attributes that satisfies consumers' needs and is received in exchange for money or something else of value. pp. 18, 248

product advertisements Advertisements that focus on selling a product or service and which take three forms: (1) pioneering (or informational), (2) competitive (or persuasive), and (3) reminder. p. 470

product class Refers to the entire product category or industry. p. 278

product differentiation A marketing strategy that involves a firm using different marketing mix actions to help consumers perceive the product as being different and better than competing products. p. 224

product form Pertains to variations of a product within the product class. p. 278

product item A specific product that has a unique brand, size, or price. p. 250

product life cycle Describes the stages a new product goes through in the marketplace: introduction, growth, maturity, and decline. p. 272

product line A group of product or service items that are closely related because they satisfy a class of needs, are used together, are sold to the same customer group, are distributed through the same outlets, or fall within a given price range. p. 250

product line groupings Organizational groupings in which a unit is responsible for specific product offerings. p. 600

product mix Consists of all of the product lines offered by an organization. p. 250

product modification Strategies that alter one or more of a product's characteristics, such as its quality, performance, or appearance, to increase the product's value to customers and increase sales. p. 281

product placement A consumer sales promotion tool that uses a brand-name product in a movie, television show, video game, or a commercial for another product. p. 493

product positioning The place a product occupies in consumers' minds based on important attributes relative to competitive products. p. 240

product repositioning Changing the place a product occupies in a consumer's mind relative to competitive products. p. 240

product-line pricing The setting of prices for all items in a product line to cover the total cost and produce a profit for the complete line, not necessarily for each item. p. 363

profit The money left after a for-profit organization subtracts its total expenses from its total revenues and is the reward for the risk it undertakes in marketing its offerings. p. 26

profit equation Profit = Total revenue – Total cost; or Profit = (Unit price × Quantity sold) – (Fixed cost + Variable cost). p. 328

program champion A person who is able and willing to "cut the red tape" to move the program forward. p. 597

promotional allowances Cash payments or an extra amount of "free goods" awarded sellers in the marketing channel for undertaking certain advertising or selling activities to promote a product. p. 368

promotional mix The combination of one or more communication tools used to: (1) inform prospective buyers about the benefits of the product, (2) persuade them to try it, and (3) remind them later about the benefits they enjoyed by using the product. p. 441

protectionism The practice of shielding one or more industries within a country's economy from foreign competition through the use of tariffs or quotas. p. 166

protocol A statement that, before product development begins, identifies: (1) a well-defined target market; (2) specific customers' needs, wants, and preferences; and (3) what the product will be and do to satisfy consumers. p. 253

public relations A form of communication management that seeks to influence the feelings, opinions, or beliefs held by customers, prospective customers, stockholders, suppliers, employees, and other publics about a company and its products or services. p. 446

publicity A nonpersonal, indirectly paid presentation of an organization, product, or service. p. 446

publicity tools Methods of obtaining nonpersonal presentation of an organization, product, or service without direct cost, such as news releases, news conferences, and public service announcements (PSAs). p. 496

pull strategy Directing the promotional mix at ultimate consumers to encourage them to ask the retailer for a product. p. 453

purchase decision process The five stages a buyer passes through in making choices about which products and services to buy: (1) problem recognition, (2) information search, (3) alternative evaluation, (4) purchase decision, and (5) postpurchase behavior. p. 112

push strategy Directing the promotional mix to channel members to gain their cooperation in ordering and stocking the product. p. 452

quantity discounts Reductions in unit costs for a larger order. p. 366

questionnaire data Facts and figures obtained by asking people about their attitudes, awareness, intentions, and behaviors. p. 202

quota A restriction placed on the amount of a product allowed to enter or leave a country. p. 167

rating The percentage of households in a market that are tuned to a particular TV show or radio station. p. 478

reach The number of different people or households exposed to an advertisement. p. 478

receivers Consumers who read, hear, or see the message sent by a source during the communication process. p. 442

reciprocity An industrial buying practice in which two organizations agree to purchase each other's products and services. p. 146

reference groups People to whom an individual looks as a basis for self-appraisal or as a source of personal standards. p. 128

regional shopping centers A retail location consisting of 50 to 150 stores that typically attract customers who live or work within a 5- to 10-mile range, often containing two or three anchor stores. p. 428

regulation Restrictions state and federal laws place on a business with regard to the conduct of its activities. p. 82

relationship marketing Links the organization to its individual customers, employees, suppliers, and other partners for their mutual long-term benefit. p. 12

relationship selling The practice of building ties to customers based on a salesperson's attention and commitment to customer needs over time. p. 534

response In the feedback loop, the impact the message had on the receiver's knowledge, attitudes, or behaviors during the communication process. p. 444

retail life cycle The process of growth and decline that retail outlets, like products, experience, consisting of the early growth, accelerated development, maturity, and decline stages. p. 431

retail positioning matrix A matrix that positions retail outlets on two dimensions: breadth of product line and value added, such as location, product reliability, or prestige. p. 424

retailing All activities involved in selling, renting, and providing products and services to ultimate consumers for personal, family, or household use. p. 412

retailing mix The activities related to managing the store and the merchandise in the store, which includes retail pricing, store location, retail communication, and merchandise. p. 426

reverse auction In an e-marketplace, an online auction in which a buyer communicates a need for a product or service and would-be suppliers are invited to bid in competition with each other. p. 154

reverse logistics A process of reclaiming recyclable and reusable materials, returns, and reworks from the point of consumption or use for repair, remanufacturing, redistribution, or disposal. p. 406

sales forecast The total sales of a product that a firm expects to sell during a specified time period under specified environmental conditions and its own marketing efforts. p. 215

sales management Planning the selling program and implementing and evaluating the personal selling effort of the firm. p. 532

sales plan A statement describing what is to be achieved and where and how the selling effort of salespeople is to be deployed. p. 545

sales promotion A short-term inducement of value offered to arouse interest in buying a product or service. p. 447

sales quota Specific goals assigned to a salesperson, sales team, branch sales office, or sales district for a stated time period. p. 551

sales response function Relates the expense of the marketing effort to the marketing results obtained. p. 585

salesforce automation (SFA) The use of computer, information, communication, and Internet technologies to make the sales function more effective and efficient. p. 553

scrambled merchandising Offering several unrelated product lines in a single store. p. 418

screening and evaluation The stage of the new-product process that internally and externally evaluates new-product ideas to eliminate those that warrant no further effort. p. 260

secondary data Facts and figures that have already been recorded prior to the project at hand. p. 198

selective distribution A level of distribution density whereby a firm selects a few retailers in a specific geographical area to carry its products. p. 395

self-concept The way people see themselves and the way they believe others see them. p. 119

self-regulation An alternative to government control whereby an industry attempts to police itself. p. 85

semiotics A field of study that examines the correspondence between symbols and their role in the assignment of meaning for people. p. 175

service continuum The range of offerings companies bring to the market, from the tangible to the intangible or the product-dominant to the service-dominant. p. 303

services Intangible activities or benefits that an organization provides to satisfy consumers' needs in exchange for money or something else of value. pp. 248, 300

seven Ps of services marketing An expanded marketing mix concept for services that includes the four Ps (product, price, promotion, and place or distribution) as well as people, physical environment, and process. p. 311

share points An analysis that uses percentage points of market share as the common basis of comparison to allocate marketing resources effectively for different product lines within the same firm. p. 587

shopper marketing The use of displays, coupons, product samples, and other brand communications to influence shopping behavior in a store. p. 428

shopping products Items for which the consumer compares several alternatives on criteria such as price, quality, or style. p. 249

showrooming Occurs when a shopper visits a retail store to inspect merchandise but then goes online to compare prices from other retail and online sellers to attempt to make the best purchase. p. 572

situation analysis Taking stock of where the firm or product has been recently, where it is now, and where it is headed in terms of the organization's marketing plans and the external forces and trends affecting it. p. 39

situational influences The five aspects of the purchase situation that impact the consumer's purchase decision process: (1) the purchase task, (2) social surroundings, (3) physical surroundings, (4) temporal effects, and (5) antecedent states. p. 117

skimming pricing Setting the highest initial price that customers really desiring the product are willing to pay when introducing a new or innovative product. p. 352

social audit A systematic assessment of a firm's objectives, strategies, and performance in terms of social responsibility. p. 103

social class The relatively permanent, homogeneous divisions in a society into which people sharing similar values, interests, and behaviors can be grouped. p. 130

social forces The demographic characteristics of the population and its culture. p. 68

social media Online media where users submit comments, photos, and videos—often accompanied by a feedback process to identify "popular" topics. p. 504

social responsibility The idea that organizations are part of a larger society and are accountable to that society for their actions. p. 100

societal marketing concept The view that organizations should satisfy the needs of consumers in a way that provides for society's well-being. p. 17

source A company or person who has information to convey during the communication process. p. 442

spam Communications that take the form of electronic junk mail or unsolicited e-mail. p. 571

specialty products Items that the consumer makes a special effort to search out and buy. p. 249

staff positions People who have the authority and responsibility to advise people in line positions but cannot issue direct orders to them. p. 600

standard markup pricing Adding a fixed percentage to the cost of all items in a specific product class. p. 355

stimulus-response presentation A sales presentation format that assumes that given the appropriate stimulus by a salesperson, the prospect will buy. p. 541

strategic alliances Agreements among two or more independent firms to cooperate for the purpose of achieving common goals such as a competitive advantage or customer value creation. p. 169

strategic marketing process The approach whereby an organization allocates its marketing mix resources to reach its target markets. p. 39

strategy An organization's long-term course of action designed to deliver a unique customer experience while achieving its goals. p. 26

strip mall A retail location consisting of a cluster of neighborhood stores to serve people who are within a 5- to 10-minute drive. p. 428

subcultures Subgroups within the larger, or national, culture with unique values, ideas, and attitudes. p. 131

subliminal perception Seeing or hearing messages without being aware of them. p. 121

supplier development The deliberate effort by organizational buyers to build relationships that shape suppliers' products, services, and capabilities to fit a buyer's needs and those of its customers. p. 145

supply chain The various firms involved in performing the activities required to create and deliver a product or service to ultimate consumers or industrial users. p. 400

supply partnership A relationship that exists when a buyer and its supplier adopt mutually beneficial objectives, policies, and procedures for the purpose of lowering the cost or increasing the value of products and services delivered to the ultimate consumer. p. 146

sustainable development Conducting business in a way that protects the natural environment while making economic progress. p. 103

SWOT analysis An acronym describing an organization's appraisal of its internal **S**trengths and **W**eaknesses and its external **O**pportunities and **T**hreats. p. 39

synergy analysis Seeks market-product growth opportunities by finding the optimum balance between marketing efficiencies versus R&D–manufacturing efficiencies. p. 591

target market One or more specific groups of potential consumers toward which an organization directs its marketing program. p. 10

target pricing Consists of (1) estimating the price that ultimate consumers would be willing to pay for a product, (2) working backward through markups taken by retailers and wholesalers to determine what price to charge wholesalers, and then (3) deliberately adjusting the composition and features of the product to achieve the target price to consumers. p. 355

target profit pricing Setting an annual target of a specific dollar volume of profit. p. 357

target return-on-investment pricing Setting a price to achieve an annual target return on investment (ROI). p. 358

target return-on-sales pricing Setting a price to achieve a profit that is a specified percentage of the sales volume. p. 358

tariffs Government taxes on products or services entering a country that primarily serve to raise prices on imports. p. 166

team selling The practice of using an entire team of professionals in selling to and servicing major customers. p. 537

technology Inventions or innovations from applied science or engineering research. p. 78

telemarketing Using the telephone to interact with and sell directly to consumers. p. 423

time-based agenda A meeting agenda that shows the running time allocated to each agenda item. p. 598

total cost (TC) The total expense incurred by a firm in producing and marketing a product. Total cost is the sum of fixed cost and variable cost. p. 341

total logistics cost The expenses associated with transportation, materials handling and warehousing, inventory, stockouts (being out of inventory), order processing, and return products handling. p. 404

total revenue (TR) The total money received from the sales of a product. p. 337

trade name A commercial, legal name under which a company does business. p. 283

trademark Identifies that a firm has legally registered its brand name or trade name so the firm has its exclusive use, thereby preventing others from using it. p. 284

trade-oriented sales promotions Sales tools used to support a company's advertising and personal selling directed to wholesalers, distributors, or retailers. Also called *trade promotions*. p. 494

trading down Reducing a product's number of features, quality, or price of the product. p. 283

trading up Adding value to the product (or line) through additional features or higher-quality materials. p. 282

traditional auction In an e-marketplace, an online auction in which a seller puts an item up for sale and would-be buyers are invited to bid in competition with each other. p. 154

traffic generation The outcome of a direct marketing offer designed to motivate people to visit a business. p. 461

triple-bottom line The recognition of the need for organizations to improve the state of people, the planet, and profit simultaneously if they are to achieve sustainable, long-term growth. p. 102

Twitter A website that enables users to send and receive "tweets," messages up to 140 characters long. p. 511

ultimate consumers The people who use the products and services purchased for a household. Also called *consumers*, *buyers*, or *customers*. p. 18

uniform delivered pricing The price the seller quotes that includes all transportation costs. p. 368

unit variable cost (UVC) Variable cost expressed on a per unit basis for a product. p. 341

unsought products Items that the consumer does not know about or knows about but does not initially want. p. 249

usage rate The quantity consumed or patronage (store visits) during a specific period. Also called *frequency marketing*. p. 230

user-generated content (UGC) The various forms of online media content that are publicly available and created by end users. Also called *consumer-generated media*. p. 504

utilitarianism A personal moral philosophy that focuses on "the greatest good for the greatest number" by assessing the costs and benefits of the consequences of ethical behavior. p. 100

utility The benefits or customer value received by users of the product. p. 19

value The ratio of perceived benefits to price; or Value = (Perceived benefits ÷ Price). p. 326

value analysis A systematic appraisal of the design, quality, and performance of a product to reduce purchasing costs. p. 151

value consciousness The concern for obtaining the best quality, features, and performance of a product or service for a given price that drives consumption behavior. p. 75

value pricing The practice of simultaneously increasing product and service benefits while maintaining or decreasing price. p. 327

values A society's personally or socially preferable modes of conduct or states of existence that tend to persist over time. p. 173

variable cost (VC) The sum of the expenses of the firm that vary directly with the quantity of a product that is produced and sold. p. 341

vendor-managed inventory (VMI) An inventory management system whereby the supplier determines the product amount and assortment a customer (such as a retailer) needs and automatically delivers the appropriate items. p. 405

vertical marketing systems Professionally managed and centrally coordinated marketing channels designed to achieve channel economies and maximum marketing impact. p. 392

viral marketing An Internet-enabled promotional strategy that encourages individuals to forward marketer-initiated messages to others via e-mail, social networking websites, and blogs. p. 572

warranty A statement indicating the liability of the manufacturer for product deficiencies. p. 293

web communities Websites that allow people to congregate online and exchange views on topics of common interest. p. 571

wheel of retailing A concept that describes how new forms of retail outlets enter the market. p. 430

whistle-blowers Employees who report unethical or illegal actions of their employers. p. 99

word of mouth The influencing of people during conversations. p. 127

workload method A formula-based method for determining the size of a salesforce that integrates the number of customers served, call frequency, call length, and available selling time to arrive at a figure for the salesforce size. p. 547

World Trade Organization (WTO) A permanent institution that sets rules governing trade between its members through panels of trade experts who decide on trade disputes between members and issue binding decisions. p. 167

yield management pricing The charging of different prices to maximize revenue for a set amount of capacity at any given time. p. 355

YouTube A video-sharing website in which users can upload, view, and comment on videos. p. 512

LEARNING REVIEW ANSWERS

CHAPTER 1

1-1. What is marketing?
Answer: Marketing is the activity for creating, communicating, delivering, and exchanging offerings that benefit customers, the organization, its stakeholders, and society at large.

1-2. Marketing focuses on ______ and ______ consumer needs.
Answer: discovering; satisfying

1-3. What four factors are needed for marketing to occur?
Answer: The four factors are: (1) two or more parties (individuals or organizations) with unsatisfied needs; (2) a desire and ability on their part to have their needs satisfied; (3) a way for the parties to communicate; and (4) something to exchange.

1-4. An organization can't satisfy the needs of all consumers, so it must focus on one or more subgroups, which are its ______.
Answer: target market

1-5. What are the four marketing mix elements that make up the organization's marketing program?
Answer: product, price, promotion, place

1-6. What are environmental forces?
Answer: Environmental forces are the uncontrollable forces that affect a marketing decision. They consist of social, economic, technological, competitive, and regulatory forces.

1-7. What are the two key characteristics of the marketing concept?
Answer: An organization should (1) strive to satisfy the needs of consumers while also (2) trying to achieve the organization's goals.

1-8. What is the difference between ultimate consumers and organizational buyers?
Answer: Ultimate consumers are the people who use the products and services purchased for a household. Organizational buyers are those manufacturers, wholesalers, retailers, and government agencies that buy products and services for their own use or for resale.

CHAPTER 2

2-1. What is the difference between a for-profit organization and a nonprofit organization?
Answer: A for-profit organization is a privately owned organization that serves its customers to earn a profit so that it can survive. A nonprofit organization is a nongovernmental organization that serves its customers but does not have profit as an organizational goal. Instead, its goals may be operational efficiency or client satisfaction.

2-2. What are examples of a functional level in an organization?
Answer: The functional level in an organization is where groups of specialists from the marketing, finance, manufacturing/operations, accounting, information systems, research & development, and/or human resources departments focus on a specific strategic direction to create value for the organization.

2-3. What is the meaning of an organization's mission?
Answer: A mission is a clear, concise, meaningful, inspirational, and long-term statement of the organization's function in society, often identifying its customers, markets, products, and technologies. It is often used interchangeably with *vision*.

2-4. What is the difference between an organization's business and its goals?
Answer: An organization's business describes the clear, broad, underlying industry or market sector of an organization's offering. An organization's goals (or objectives) are statements of an accomplishment of a task to be achieved, often by a specific time. Goals convert an organization's mission and business into long- and short-term performance targets to measure how well it is doing.

2-5. What is the difference between a marketing dashboard and a marketing metric?
Answer: A marketing dashboard is the visual computer display of the essential information related to achieving a marketing objective. Each variable displayed in a marketing dashboard is a marketing metric, which is a measure of the quantitative value or trend of a marketing action or result.

2-6. What is business portfolio analysis?
Answer: Business portfolio analysis is a technique that managers use to quantify performance measures and growth targets to analyze their firms' strategic business units (SBUs) as though they were a collection of separate investments. The purpose of this tool is to determine which SBU or offering generates cash and which one requires cash to fund the organization's growth opportunities.

2-7. Explain the four market-product strategies in diversification analysis.
Answer: The four market-product strategies in diversification analysis are: (1) Market penetration, which is a marketing strategy to increase sales of current products in current markets. There is no change in either the basic product line or the markets served. Rather, selling more of the product or selling the product at a higher price generates increased sales. (2) Market development, which is a marketing strategy to sell current products to new markets. (3) Product development, which is a marketing strategy of selling new products to current markets. (4) Diversification, which is a marketing strategy of developing new products and selling them in new markets. This is a potentially high-risk strategy because the firm has neither previous production nor marketing experience on which to draw in marketing a new product to a new market.

2-8. What are the three steps of the planning phase of the strategic marketing process?
Answer: The three steps of the planning phase of the strategic marketing process are: (1) Situation analysis, which involves taking stock of where the firm or product has been recently, where it is now, and where it is headed in terms of the organization's marketing plans and the external forces and trends affecting it. To do this, an organization uses a SWOT analysis, an acronym that describes an organization's appraisal of its internal **S**trengths and **W**eaknesses and its external **O**pportunities and **T**hreats. (2) Market-product focus and goal setting, which determines what products an organization will offer to which customers. This is often based on market segmentation—aggregating prospective buyers into groups or segments that have common needs and will respond similarly to a marketing action. (3) Marketing program, which is where an organization develops the marketing mix elements and budget for each offering.

2-9. What are points of difference and why are they important?
Answer: Points of difference are those characteristics of a product that make it superior to competitive substitutes—offerings the organization faces in the marketplace. They are important factors in the success or failure of a new product.

2-10. What is the implementation phase of the strategic marketing process?
Answer: The implementation phase carries out the marketing plan that emerges from the planning phase and consists of: (1) obtaining resources; (2) designing the marketing organization; (3) defining precise tasks, responsibilities, and deadlines; and (4) executing the marketing program designed in the planning phase.

2-11. How do the goals set for a marketing program in the planning phase relate to the evaluation phase of the strategic marketing process?
Answer: The planning phase goals or objectives are used as the benchmarks with which the actual performance results are compared in the evaluation phase to identify deviations from the written marketing plans and then exploit positive ones or correct negative ones.

CHAPTER 3

3-1. Describe three generational cohorts.

Answer: (1) Baby boomers are the generation of 76 million children among the U.S. population born between 1946 and 1964. These Americans are growing older and will all be 65 or older by 2030. Their workforce participation has made them the wealthiest generation in history, accounting for an estimated 50 percent of consumer spending. (2) Generation X are the 50 million people born between 1965 and 1976. Also known as the *baby bust* cohort because of declining birth rates, these well-educated Americans have a collective net worth that is less than the baby boomer generation. (3) Generation Y are the 72 million Americans among the U.S. population born between 1977 and 1994. The rising birth rate of this *echo-boom* or *baby boomlet* cohort is the result of baby boomers having children. A subset of this generational cohort are millennials, who are younger Americans born since 1994. Because each generational cohort has its distinct attitudes and behaviors, marketers have developed generational marketing programs for each of them.

3-2. Why are many companies developing multicultural marketing programs?

Answer: Multicultural marketing programs consist of combinations of the marketing mix that reflect the unique attitudes, ancestry, communication preferences, and lifestyles of different races and ethnic groups. The reasons for developing these programs are: (1) The racial and ethnic diversity of the United States is changing rapidly due to increases in the African American, Asian, and Hispanic populations, which increases their economic impact. (2) An accurate understanding of the culture of each group is essential if marketing efforts are to be successful. (3) Based on an analysis of population demographic data, racial and ethnic groups tend to be concentrated in specific geographic regions.

3-3. How are important values such as sustainability reflected in the marketplace today?

Answer: Many Americans desire and practice sustainability to preserve the environment. Specifically, these consumers are buying hybrid cars and energy-efficient light bulbs. Consumers also prefer brands that have a strong link to social action. Companies are responding to this consumer trend by using renewable energy and reducing the amount of packaging used by their products.

3-4. What is the difference between a consumer's disposable and discretionary income?

Answer: Disposable income is the money a consumer has left after paying taxes to use for necessities such as food, housing, clothing, and transportation. Discretionary income is the money that remains after paying for taxes and necessities and is usually spent on luxury items.

3-5. How does technology impact customer value?

Answer: (1) Because the cost of technology is plummeting, this allows consumers to assess the value of technology-based products on other dimensions, such as quality, service, and relationships. (2) Technology provides value through the development of new products. (3) Technology has changed the way existing products are produced through recycling and precycling.

3-6. In pure competition there are a ______ number of sellers.

Answer: large

3-7. The ______ Act was punitive toward monopolies, whereas the ______ Act was preventive.

Answer: *Sherman Antitrust*; *Clayton*

3-8. Describe some of the recent changes in trademark law.

Answer: From Chapter 11, a trademark identifies that a firm has legally registered its brand name or trade name so the firm has its exclusive use, thereby preventing others from using it. Trademarks are intended to protect both the firm selling a trademarked product and the consumer buying it. The *Lanham Act* (1946) provides for registration of a company's trademarks. Historically, the first user of a trademark in commerce had the exclusive right to use that particular word, name, or symbol in its business. The *Trademark Law Revision Act* (1988), which modified the *Lanham Act*, allows companies to secure rights to a name before its actual use by declaring an intent to use the name. In 2003, the United States agreed to participate in the *Madrid Protocol*, which is a treaty that facilitates the protection of U.S. trademark rights. Also, the U.S. Supreme Court recently ruled that a company may obtain trademarks for colors associated with their products. Finally, the *Federal Dilution Act* (1995, 2006) prevents someone from using a trademark on a noncompeting product (such as the "Cadillac" of brushes).

3-9. How does the Better Business Bureau encourage companies to follow its standards for commerce?

Answer: The Better Business Bureau (BBB) uses moral suasion to get members to comply with its standards. Companies, which join the BBB voluntarily, must agree to follow these standards before they are allowed to display the BBB Accredited Business logo.

CHAPTER 4

4-1. What are ethics?

Answer: Ethics are the moral principles and values that govern the actions and decisions of an individual or group. They serve as guidelines on how to act rightly and justly when faced with moral dilemmas.

4-2. What are four possible reasons for the present state of ethical conduct in the United States?

Answer: (1) Increased pressure on businesspeople to make decisions in a society with diverse value systems. (2) A growing tendency for business decisions to be judged publicly by groups with different values and interests. (3) The public's expectations of ethical business behavior have increased. (4) Ethical business conduct may have actually declined.

4-3. What rights are included in the Consumer Bill of Rights?

Answer: The Consumer Bill of Rights (1962) codified the ethics of exchange between buyers and sellers. These are the rights to safety, to be informed, to choose, and to be heard.

4-4. Economic espionage includes what kinds of activities?

Answer: Economic espionage is the illegal and unethical clandestine collection of trade secrets or proprietary information about a company's competitors. This practice includes trespassing, theft, fraud, misrepresentation, wiretapping, searching competitors' trash, and violations of written and implicit employment agreements with noncompete clauses.

4-5. What is meant by moral idealism?

Answer: Moral idealism is a personal moral philosophy that considers certain individual rights or duties as universal, regardless of the outcome; it is the philosophy embodied in the Consumer Bill of Rights and favored by consumer interest groups.

4-6. What is meant by social responsibility?

Answer: Social responsibility means that organizations are part of a larger society and are accountable to that society for their actions. It comprises three concepts: (1) profit responsibility—maximizing profits for the organization's owners or shareholders; (2) stakeholder responsibility—focusing on the obligations organizations have to those who can effect the achievement of its objectives; and (3) societal responsibility—focusing on the obligations organizations have to preserve the ecological environment and to the general public.

4-7. Marketing efforts to produce, promote, and reclaim environmentally sensitive products are called ______.

Answer: green marketing

4-8. What is a social audit?

Answer: A social audit is a systematic assessment of a firm's objectives, strategies, and performance in terms of social responsibility. It consists of five steps: (1) Recognition of a firm's social expectations and the rationale for engaging in social responsibility endeavors. (2) Identification of social responsibility causes or programs consistent with the company's mission. (3) Determination of organizational objectives and priorities for programs and activities it will undertake. (4) Specification of the type and amount of resources necessary to achieve social responsibility objectives. (5) Evaluation of social responsibility programs and activities undertaken and assessment of future involvement.

CHAPTER 5

5-1. What is the first stage in the consumer purchase decision process?
Answer: problem recognition—perceiving a need

5-2. The brands a consumer considers buying out of the set of brands in a product class of which the consumer is aware are collectively called the ______.
Answer: consideration set

5-3. What is the term for postpurchase anxiety?
Answer: cognitive dissonance

5-4. The problem with the Toro Snow Pup was an example of selective ______.
Answer: comprehension—Consumers perceived the name to mean that Snow Pup was a toy that was too light to do any serious snow removal.

5-5. What three attitude-change approaches are most common?
Answer: (1) Change beliefs about the extent to which a brand has certain attributes. (2) Change the perceived importance of these attributes. (3) Add new attributes to the product.

5-6. What does *lifestyle* mean?
Answer: Lifestyle is a mode of living that is identified by how people spend their time and resources, what they consider important in their environment, and what they think of themselves and the world around them.

5-7. What are the two primary forms of personal influence?
Answer: (1) Opinion leadership—persons considered to be knowledgeable about or users of particular products and services and (2) word of mouth—the influencing of people (friends, family, and colleagues) during conversations.

5-8. Marketers are concerned with which types of reference groups?
Answer: Three reference groups have clear marketing implications: (1) associative groups—ones to which a person actually belongs, such as a brand community that consists of a specialized group of consumers with a structured set of relationships involving a particular brand; (2) aspiration groups—ones that people wish to be a member of or identified with; and (3) dissociative groups—ones that people wish to maintain a distance from because of differences in values or behaviors.

5-9. What two challenges must marketers overcome when marketing to Hispanic consumers?
Answer: (1) The diversity of nationalities among this subculture that affect product preferences. (2) The language barrier that can lead to misinterpretation or mistranslation of commercial messages when translated into Spanish.

CHAPTER 6

6-1. What are the three main types of organizational buyers?
Answer: (1) industrial firms, which in some way reprocess a product or service they buy before selling again to the next buyer; (2) resellers, which are wholesalers and retailers that buy physical products and resell them again without any reprocessing; and (3) government units, which are the federal, state, and local agencies that buy products and services for the constituents they serve.

6-2. What is the North American Industry Classification System (NAICS)?
Answer: The NAICS provides common industry definitions for Canada, Mexico, and the United States, which makes it easier to measure economic activity in the three member countries of the North American Free Trade Agreement (NAFTA).

6-3. What one department is almost always represented by a person in the buying center?
Answer: purchasing department

6-4. What are the three types of buying situations or buy classes?
Answer: (1) new buy—the organization is a first-time buyer of the product or service; (2) straight rebuy—the organization reorders an existing product or service from a list of acceptable suppliers; and (3) modified rebuy—an organization's buying center changes the product's specifications, price, delivery schedule, or supplier.

6-5. What is a make-buy decision?
Answer: A make-buy decision is an evaluation of whether components and assemblies will be purchased from outside suppliers or built by the company itself.

6-6. What is a bidder's list?
Answer: A bidder's list is a list of forms generated from a company's purchasing database that is believed to be qualified to supply a given item.

6-7. What are e-marketplaces?
Answer: E-marketplaces are online trading communities that bring together buyers and supplier organizations to make possible the real-time exchange of information, money, products, and services.

6-8. In general, which type of online auction creates upward pressure on bid prices and which type creates downward pressure on bid prices?
Answer: traditional auction; reverse auction

CHAPTER 7

7-1. What is the trade feedback effect?
Answer: The phenomenon in which one country's imports affect the exports of other countries and vice versa, thus stimulating economic activity in all the nations involved.

7-2. What variables influence why some companies and industries in a country succeed globally while others lose ground or fail?
Answers: Porter identifies four key elements to explain a nation's competitive advantage and why some industries and firms within a specific nation are successful and others are not: (1) Factor conditions—a nation's ability to turn its natural resources, education, and infrastructure into a competitive advantage. (2) Demand conditions—includes both the number and sophistication of domestic customers for an industry's product. (3) Related and supporting industries—clusters of world-class suppliers that accelerate innovation. (4) Company strategy, structure, and rivalry—the conditions governing the way a nation's businesses are organized and managed, along with the intensity of domestic competition.

7-3. What is protectionism?
Answer: Protectionism is the practice of shielding one or more industries within a country's economy from foreign competition through the use of (1) tariffs, which are a government tax on products or services entering a country that primarily serve to raise prices on imports and (2) quotas, which are restrictions on the amount of product allowed to enter or leave a country.

7-4. The North American Free Trade Agreement was designed to promote free trade among which countries?
Answer: The United States, Canada, and Mexico

7-5. What is the difference between a multidomestic marketing strategy and a global marketing strategy?
Answer: Multinational firms view the world as consisting of unique markets. As a result, they use a multidomestic marketing strategy

because they have as many different product variations, brand names, and advertising programs as countries in which they do business. Transnational firms view the world as one market. As a result, they use a global marketing strategy to standardize marketing activities when there are cultural similarities and adapt it when cultures differ.

7-6. Semiotics involves the study of ______.
Answer: examining the correspondence between symbols and their role in the assignment of meaning for people

7-7. When foreign currencies can buy more U.S. dollars, are U.S. products more or less expensive for a foreign consumer?
Answer: less expensive

7-8. What mode of entry could a company follow if it has no previous experience in global marketing?
Answer: indirect exporting through intermediaries

7-9. How does licensing differ from a joint venture?
Answer: Under licensing, a company (licensor) offers the right to a trademark, patent, trade secret, or other similarly valued item of intellectual property in return for a fee or royalty. It is a low-risk, capital-free strategy to enter a foreign country. However, the licensor forgoes control of its offerings and potential profits are reduced while the licensee gains information that may give it a competitive advantage in the future. In a joint venture, a foreign company and a local firm invest together to create a local business to produce some product or service. The two companies share ownership, control, and profits of the new entity. Neither firm may have the resources necessary to enter the foreign market on its own. However, the two companies may disagree about policies or courses of action or when government bureaucracy bogs down the efforts.

7-10. Products may be sold globally in three ways. What are they?
Answer: Products can be sold: (1) in the same form as in their home market (product extension); (2) with some adaptations to make them more appealing to local consumers (product adaptation); and (3) as totally new products to satisfy consumers' needs across countries (product invention).

7-11. What is dumping?
Answer: Dumping is when a firm attempts to build a company's market share by selling a product in a foreign country below its domestic price or below its actual production cost or when a surplus exists because the company cannot sell the product domestically.

CHAPTER 8

8-1. What is marketing research?
Answer: Marketing research is the process of defining a marketing problem and opportunity, systematically collecting and analyzing information, and recommending actions to reduce the risk of and thereby improve marketing decisions.

8-2. What is the five-step marketing research approach?
Answer: The five-step marketing research approach provides a systematic checklist for making marketing decisions and actions. The five steps are: (1) define the problem; (2) develop the research plan; (3) collect relevant information (data); (4) develop findings; and (5) take marketing actions.

8-3. What are constraints, as they apply to developing a research plan?
Answer: Constraints in a decision are the restrictions placed on potential solutions to a problem, such as time and money. These set the parameters for the research plan—due dates, budget, etc.

8-4. What is the difference between secondary and primary data?
Answer: Secondary data are facts and figures that have already been recorded prior to the project at hand, whereas primary data are facts and figures that are newly collected for the project.

8-5. What are some advantages and disadvantages of secondary data?
Answer: Advantages of secondary data are the time savings, the low cost, and the greater level of detail that may be available. Disadvantages of secondary data are that the data may be out of date, unspecific, or have definitions, categories, or age groupings that are wrong for the project.

8-6. What is the difference between observational data and questionnaire data?
Answer: Observational data are facts and figures obtained by watching, either mechanically or in person, how people actually behave. Questionnaire data are facts and figures obtained by asking people about their attitudes, awareness, intentions, and behaviors.

8-7. Which type of survey provides the greatest flexibility for asking probing questions: mail, telephone, or personal interview?
Answer: personal interview (or individual/depth interview)

8-8. What is cross tabulation?
Answer: Cross tabulation, or "cross tab," is a method of presenting and analyzing data involving two or more variables to discover relationships in the data. As the most widely used technique for organizing and presenting marketing data, the simple format and flexibility of cross tabulations permit the direct interpretation of and an easy means to communicate the data.

8-9. In the marketing research for Tony's Pizza, what is an example of (*a*) a finding and (*b*) a marketing action?
Answer: (*a*) Figure 8-7A depicts annual sales from 2010 to 2013; the finding is that annual sales are relatively flat, rising only 5 million units over the 4-year period. (*b*) Figure 8-7D shows a finding (the decline in pizza consumption) that leads to a recommendation to develop an ad targeting children 6 to 12 years old (the marketing action).

8-10. In evaluating marketing actions, what are the two dimensions on which they should be evaluated?
Answer: There are two aspects marketers use to evaluate the results of marketing actions: (1) evaluate the decision itself, which involves monitoring the marketplace to determine if action is necessary in the future and (2) evaluate the decision process used to determine whether (*a*) the marketing research and analysis used to develop the recommendations was effective or flawed in some way and (*b*) the process could be improved for similar situations in the future.

8-11. What are the three kinds of sales forecasting techniques?
Answer: They are: (1) judgments of the decision maker who acts on the results of a sales forecast; (2) surveys of knowledgeable groups, those who are likely to know something about future sales; and (3) statistical methods such as trend extrapolation, which involves extending a pattern observed in past data into the future.

8-12. How do you make a lost-horse forecast?
Answer: To make a lost-horse forecast, begin with the last known value of the item being forecast, list the factors that could affect the forecast, assess whether they have a positive or negative impact, and then make the final forecast.

CHAPTER 9

9-1. Market segmentation involves aggregating prospective buyers into groups that have two key characteristics. What are they?
Answer: The groups (1) should have common needs and (2) will respond similarly to a marketing action.

9-2. In terms of market segments and products, what are the three market segmentation strategies?
Answer: The three market segmentation strategies are: (1) one product and multiple market segments; (2) multiple products and multiple market segments; and (3) "segments of one," or mass customization—the next step beyond build-to-order.

9-3. The process of segmenting and targeting markets is a bridge between which two marketing activities?
Answer: identifying market needs and executing the marketing program

9-4. What is the difference between the demographic and behavioral bases of market segmentation?
Answer: Demographic segmentation is based on some objective physical (gender, race), measurable (age, income), or other classification attribute (birth era, occupation) of prospective customers. Behavioral segmentation is based on some observable actions or attitudes by prospective customers—such as where they buy, what benefits they seek, how frequently they buy, and why they buy.

9-5. What factor is estimated or measured for each of the cells in a market-product grid?
Answer: Each cell in the grid can show the estimated market size of a given product sold to a specific market segment.

9-6. What are some criteria used to decide which segments to choose for targets?
Answer: Possible criteria include market size, expected growth, competitive position, cost of reaching the segment, and compatibility with the organization's objectives and resources.

9-7. How are marketing and product synergies different in a market-product grid?
Answer: Marketing synergies run horizontally across a market-product grid. Each row represents an opportunity for efficiency in the marketing efforts to a market segment. Product synergies run vertically down the market-product grid. Each column represents an opportunity for efficiency in research and development (R&D) and production. Marketing synergies often come at the expense of product synergies because a single customer segment will likely require a variety of products, each of which will have to be designed and manufactured. The company saves money on marketing but spends more on production. Conversely, if product synergies are emphasized, marketing will have to address the concerns of a wide variety of consumers, which costs more time and money.

9-8. What is the difference between product positioning and product repositioning?
Answer: Product positioning refers to the place a product occupies in consumers' minds based on important attributes relative to competitive products. Product repositioning involves changing the place a product occupies in a consumer's mind relative to competitive products.

9-9. Why do marketers use perceptual maps in product positioning decisions?
Answer: Perceptual maps are a means of displaying in two dimensions the location of products or brands in the minds of consumers. Marketers use perceptual maps to see how consumers perceive competing products or brands as well as their own product or brand. Then they can develop marketing actions to move their product or brand to the ideal position.

CHAPTER 10

10-1. What are the four main types of consumer products?
Answer: They are: (1) convenience products—items that the consumer purchases frequently, conveniently, and with a minimum of shopping effort; (2) shopping products—items for which the consumer compares several alternatives on criteria such as price, quality, or style; (3) specialty products—items that the consumer makes a special effort to search out and buy; and (4) unsought products—items that the consumer does not know about or knows about but does not initially want.

10-2. What is the difference between a product line and a product mix?
Answer: A product line is a group of product or service items that are closely related because they satisfy a class of needs, are used together, are sold to the same customer group, are distributed through the same outlets, or fall within a given price range. The product mix consists of all the product lines offered by an organization.

10-3. What kind of innovation would an improved electric toothbrush be?
Answer: continuous innovation—no new learning is required by consumers

10-4. Why can an "insignificant point of difference" lead to new-product failure?
Answer: The product must have superior characteristics that deliver unique benefits to the user compared to those of competitors that must be sufficient enough to motivate a change in consumption behavior. Without these points of difference, the product will probably fail.

10-5. What marketing metric might you use in a marketing dashboard to discover which states have weak sales?
Answer: The marketing metric—annual percentage change in unit volume by state—will help identify those states that are underperforming.

10-6. What is the new-product strategy development stage in the new-product process?
Answer: New-product strategy development is the first stage of the new-product process that defines the role for a new product in terms of the firm's overall objectives. During this stage, the firm uses both a SWOT analysis and environmental scanning to assess its strengths and weaknesses relative to the trends it identifies as opportunities or threats. The outcome not only defines the vital "protocol" for each new-product idea but also identifies the strategic role it might serve in the firm's business portfolio.

10-7. What are the main sources of new-product ideas?
Answer: Many firms obtain ideas externally using open innovation, in which an organization finds and executes creative new-product ideas by developing strategic relationships with outside individuals and organizations. Some of these sources include employee and coworker suggestions, customer and supplier suggestions (either directly, through the firm's salesforce or purchasing department or through crowd sourcing—soliciting ideas via the Internet from large numbers of people), R&D laboratories (both internal to the firm and professional innovation firms like IDEO), competitive products (analyzing their points of difference that lead to a competitive advantage for them), and smaller, nontraditional technology firms, university technology transfer centers that partner with business firms to commercialize faculty inventions, and lone inventors or entrepreneurs.

10-8. How do internal and external screening and evaluation approaches differ?
Answer: In internal screening, company employees evaluate the technical feasibility of new-product ideas to determine whether they meet the objectives defined in the new-product strategy development stage. For services, employees are assessed to determine whether they have the commitment and skills to meet customer expectations and sustain customer loyalty. In external screening, evaluation consists of preliminary concept testing of the new-product idea (not the actual product itself) using written descriptions, sketches, mockups, or promotional literature with consumers.

10-9. How does the development stage of the new-product process involve testing the product inside and outside the firm?
Answer: Development is the stage of the new-product process that turns the idea on paper into a prototype, which results in a demonstrable, producible product that can be efficiently manufactured. Internally, laboratory tests are done to see if the product achieves the physical, quality, and safety standards set for it. Externally, market testing is done to expose actual products to prospective consumers under realistic purchase conditions to see if they will buy.

10-10. What is a test market?
Answer: Test marketing involves offering a product for sale on a limited basis in a defined area for a specific time period. The three

main kinds of test markets are: (1) standard, (2) controlled, and (3) simulated. In a standard test market, a city (or cities) is selected that is viewed as being demographically representative of the markets targeted for the new product and has both cable TV systems that can deliver different ads to different homes and retailers with checkout counter scanners to measure sales results. In a controlled test market, the firm contracts the entire test program to an outside service, which pays retailers for shelf space to guarantee a specified percentage of the test product's potential distribution volume. In a simulated (or laboratory) test market (STM), the firm attempts to replicate a full-scale test market by creating a fictitious storefront in a shopping mall and exposing prospective customers to the product (or concept) and ads from both it and its competitors to see if they will buy.

10-11. What is the commercialization of a new product?
Answer: Commercialization, the most expensive stage for most new products, is the last stage of the new-product process that involves positioning and launching a new product in full-scale production and sales.

CHAPTER 11

11-1. Advertising plays a major role in the ______ stage of the product life cycle, and ______ plays a major role in maturity.
Answer: introduction; product differentiation or finding new buyers

11-2. How do high-learning and low-learning products differ?
Answer: A high-learning product requires significant customer education and there is an extended introductory period. A low-learning product requires little customer education because the benefits of purchase are readily understood, resulting in immediate sales.

11-3. What are the five categories of product adopters in the diffusion of innovations?
Answer: The five categories of product adopters based on the diffusion of innovation are: (1) innovators—2.5%; (2) early adopters—13.5%; (3) early majority—34%; (4) late majority—34%; and (5) laggards—16%.

11-4. How does a product manager help manage a product's life cycle?
Answer: A product manager shepherds a product through its life cycle by (1) modifying the product, which involves altering one or more of its characteristics to increase its value to customers and thus increase sales; (2) modifying the market, which involves finding new customers, increasing a product's use among existing customers, or creating new use situations; and (3) repositioning the product, which involves changing the place it occupies in consumers' minds relative to competitive products.

11-5. What does "creating a new use situation" mean in managing a product's life cycle?
Answer: Creating a new use situation means finding new uses or applications for an existing product.

11-6. Explain the difference between trading up and trading down in product repositioning.
Answer: Trading up involves adding value to the product (or line) through additional features or higher-quality materials. Trading down involves reducing the number of features, quality, price, or downsizing—reducing the content of packages without changing package size and maintaining or increasing the package price.

11-7. What are the six criteria mentioned most often when selecting a good brand name?
Answer: A good brand name should: (1) suggest the product benefits; (2) be memorable, distinctive, and positive; (3) fit the company or product image; (4) have no legal or regulatory restrictions; (5) be simple and emotional; and (6) have favorable phonetic and semantic associations in other languages.

11-8. What are the three major benefits of packaging and labeling?
Answer: Packaging and labeling provide important benefits for the manufacturer, retailer, and ultimate consumer that can create a competitive advantage for the firm. The three benefits are: (1) communication benefits through label information; (2) functional benefits through storage, convenience, protection, or product quality; and (3) perceptual benefits such as package and label shape, color, and graphics that can both position a firm's brand relative to others and build brand equity.

11-9. What is the difference between an express and an implied warranty?
Answer: Express warranties are written statements of liabilities. Implied warranties assign responsibility for product deficiencies to the manufacturer even if the retailer sells the product.

CHAPTER 12

12-1. What are the four I's of services?
Answer: The four I's of services are: (1) intangibility, which means that they can't be held, touched, or seen; (2) inconsistency, which means that their quality varies with each person's capabilities and day-to-day job performance; (3) inseparability, which means that the consumer cannot (and does not) separate the deliverer of the service from the service itself; and (4) inventory, which means that inventory carrying costs are more subjective and are related to idle production capacity—when the service provider is available but there is no demand for the service.

12-2. To eliminate service inconsistencies, companies rely on ______ and ______.
Answer: standardization; training

12-3. Would inventory carrying costs for an accounting firm with certified public accountants be (*a*) high, (*b*) low, or (*c*) nonexistent?
Answer: Inventory carrying costs are related to idle production capacity, which is when the service provider is available but there is no demand. A CPA typically earns a high fixed cost salary. Therefore, if he/she is available but there is no demand for his/her service, the inventory cost of this service is (*a*) "high," because the cost of the accountant's salary must be paid regardless of whether or not the service is performed.

12-4. What are the differences between search, experience, and credence properties?
Answer: Search properties, such as color, size, and style, can be determined before purchase. Experience properties, such as with restaurants, can only be assessed during or after consumption. Credence properties, which are characteristics of services provided by specialized professionals such as legal advice or medical diagnostics, may be impossible to evaluate even after purchase and consumption.

12-5. Hertz created its differential advantage at the points of ______ in its customer contact audit.
Answer: interaction between consumer and service provider

12-6. How does a movie theater use off-peak pricing?
Answer: Off-peak pricing consists of charging different prices during different times of the day or during different days of the week to reflect variations in demand for the service. Movie theaters reduce prices for matinees and often for Monday through Thursday shows due to the lower demand for this service during this time of day or days of the week.

12-7. Matching demand with capacity is the focus of ______ management.
Answer: capacity

12-8. What factors will influence future changes in services?
Answer: Technology advances, improved understanding of service delivery and consumption, and the social imperative for sustainability are factors that will influence future changes in services.

CHAPTER 13

13-1. What is price?
Answer: Price is the money or other considerations (including other products and services) exchanged for the ownership or use of a product or service.

13-2. What factors impact the list price to determine the final price?
Answer: Several factors increase or decrease the final price of an offering that the consumer pays. These factors help construct the price equation, which includes incentives, such as cash discounts, allowances, and rebates, that decrease the final price and extra fees or surcharges that increase the final price.

13-3. What is the profit equation?
Answer: Price has a direct effect on a firm's profits, which can be expressed in the following profit equation: Profit = Total revenue – Total cost or [(Unit price × Quantity sold) – (Fixed cost + Variable cost)].

13-4. What is the difference between pricing objectives and pricing constraints?
Answer: Pricing objectives involve specifying the role of price in an organization's marketing and strategic plans whereas pricing constraints are factors that limit the range of prices a firm may set.

13-5. How does the type of competitive market a firm is in affect its range in setting prices?
Answer: The seller's price is constrained by the type of market in which it competes. Economists generally delineate four types of competitive markets: (1) With pure competition, there are many sellers who follow the market price for identical, commodity products. (2) With monopolistic competition, there are many sellers who compete on nonprice factors such as product features and advertising. (3) With an oligopoly, there are *(a)* a few sellers who are sensitive to each other's prices and *(b)* a firm that is a price leader that sets the market price that other firms follow. The firms that are price followers set a price based on the prices set by their competitors to avoid a price war. (4) With a pure monopoly, there is one seller in the market who can set any price it wants for its unique product.

13-6. What are examples of (1) consumer-driven and (2) seller- or retailer-driven pricing actions made possible through price transparency on the Internet?
Answer: Price transparency occurs as a result of a consumer's near-instantaneous access to competitors' prices for the same offering through the Internet. Two dimensions of price transparency are: (1) Consumer-driven pricing actions, in which consumers make more efficient buying decisions by comparing the price of an item first in the store and then on the Internet using a smartphone. If the price is lower on the Internet, they'll ask the store to match the price or go home and buy the item online. This behavior is called showrooming. (2) Seller- or retailer-driven pricing actions, in which sellers can quickly change their online prices. This is made possible by Internet-based dynamic pricing, in which the seller changes prices in response to its existing inventory and the prices of its competitors.

13-7. What is the difference between a movement along and a shift of a demand curve?
Answer: A demand curve is a graph that relates the quantity sold and price, showing the maximum number of units that will be sold at a given price. A movement along a demand curve (up or down) for a product occurs when its price is lowered or increased and the quantity demanded for it correspondingly increases or decreases, assuming that other factors such as consumer tastes, promotion (advertising and/or sales promotion), price and availability of substitute products, and/or consumer incomes remain unchanged. However, if one or more of these factors do change, then the demand curve for a product will shift to the right or left based on whether the change(s) was favorable or not. This means that there will be either an increase or decrease in demand for the product based on the change in the factor(s).

13-8. What is total revenue and how is it calculated?
Answer: Total revenue (TR) is the total money received from the sale of a product. Total revenue (TR) equals the product's unit price (P) times the quantity sold (Q) or TR = P × Q.

13-9. What is the difference between elastic demand and inelastic demand?
Answer: Price elasticity of demand is the percentage change in the quantity demanded relative to a percentage change in price and is expressed as follows: Price elasticity of demand (E) = Percentage change in quantity demanded (%Δ in Q) ÷ Percentage change in price (%Δ in P). Elastic demand exists when a 1 percent decrease in price produces more than a 1 percent increase in quantity demanded, thereby actually increasing total revenue. This results in a price elasticity that is greater than 1. Inelastic demand exists when a 1 percent decrease in price produces less than a 1 percent increase in quantity demanded, thereby actually decreasing total revenue. This results in a price elasticity that is less than 1.

13-10. What is the difference between fixed costs and variable costs?
Answer: Fixed cost (FC) is the sum of the expenses of the firm that are stable and do not change with the quantity of a product that is produced and sold. Examples of fixed costs are rent on the building, executive salaries, and insurance. Variable cost (VC) is the sum of the expenses of the firm that vary directly with the quantity of a product that is produced and sold. Examples are the direct labor and direct materials used in producing the product and the sales commissions that are tied directly to the quantity sold.

13-11. What is a break-even point?
Answer: Break-even analysis is a technique that analyzes the relationship between total revenue and total cost to determine profitability at various levels of output. The break-even point (BEP) is the quantity at which total revenue and total cost are equal. Profit then comes from all units sold beyond the BEP. Break-even point (BEP) = [Fixed cost ÷ (Unit price – Unit variable cost)].

13-12. Why do firms add new technology and automation when they increases their fixed costs?
Answer: Adding new technology, such as automation equipment, can increase profitability beyond the break-even point due to higher production volumes that result from reductions in variable costs (materials waste, labor savings due to increased efficiency, etc.) even though fixed costs are increased.

CHAPTER 14

14-1. In pricing a new product, what circumstances might support skimming or penetration pricing?
Answer: Skimming pricing is an effective strategy when: (1) the firm may want to recoup the initial R&D and promotion costs in developing and promoting the product; (2) enough prospective customers are willing to buy the product immediately at the high initial price to make these sales profitable because they are not very price sensitive; (3) the high initial price will not attract competitors; (4) lowering the price has only a minor effect on increasing the sales volume and reducing the unit costs; and (5) customers interpret the high price as signifying high quality. These conditions are most likely to exist when the new product is protected by patents or copyrights or its uniqueness is understood and valued by consumers. Penetration pricing is an effective strategy when: (1) used after a skimming strategy to appeal to a broader segment of the population and increase market share; (2) many segments of the market are price sensitive; (3) a low initial price discourages competitors from entering the market; (4) unit production and marketing costs fall dramatically as production volumes increase; (5) a firm wants to maintain the initial price for a time to gain profit lost from its low introductory level; and (6) a firm wants to lower the price further, counting on the new volume to generate the necessary profit.

14-2. What is odd-even pricing?
Answer: Odd-even pricing involves setting prices a few dollars or cents under an even number. Psychologically, a $499.99 price feels lower than $500.00, even though the difference is just 1¢.

14-3. What is standard markup pricing?
Answer: Standard markup pricing entails adding a fixed percentage to the cost of all items in a specific product class. The price varies based on the type of product and the retail store within which it is sold.

14-4. What profit-based pricing approach should a manager use if or she wants to reflect the percentage of the firm's resources used in obtaining the profit?
Answer: target return-on-investment pricing

14-5. What is the purpose of loss-leader pricing when used by a retail firm?
Answer: Loss-leader pricing involves deliberately selling a product below its customary price not to increase sales but to attract customers in hopes they will buy other products as well, such as discretionary items with large markups.

14-6. Why would a seller choose a dynamic pricing policy over a fixed-price policy?
Answer: A dynamic pricing policy sets different prices for products and services in real time in response to supply and demand conditions. Sellers have considerable discretion in setting the final price in light of demand, cost, and competitive factors. Moreover, sellers can continually adjust prices due to the implementation of sophisticated information technology that gives them the ability to customize a price on the basis of customer purchasing patterns, product preferences, and price sensitivity. A fixed-price policy sets one price for all buyers of a product or service. Consumers can choose to buy or not buy, but there is no variation in the price from the seller.

14-7. If a firm wished to encourage repeat purchases by a buyer throughout a year, would a cumulative or a noncumulative quantity discount be a better strategy?
Answer: Cumulative quantity discounts apply to the accumulation of purchases of a product over a given time period (typically a year) and encourage repeat buying by a single customer to a far greater degree than do noncumulative quantity discounts.

14-8. Which pricing practices are covered by the Sherman Act?
Answer: The Sherman Act prohibits (1) horizontal price fixing, which is when two or more competitors explicitly or implicitly set prices and (2) predatory pricing, which is the practice of charging a very low price for a product with the intent of driving competitors out of business. Once competitors have been driven out, the firm raises its prices.

CHAPTER 15

15-1. What is meant by a marketing channel?
Answer: A marketing channel consists of individuals and firms involved in the process of making a product or service available for use or consumption by ultimate consumers or industrial users.

15-2. What are the three basic functions performed by intermediaries?
Answer: Intermediaries perform three basic functions: (1) Transactional, which occurs when customers buy and sell products and services. Intermediaries share the risk in the ownership of inventory in anticipation of sales. (2) Logistical, which involves gathering, storing, sorting, and transporting products for and to customers. (3) Facilitating, which makes transactions easier for buyers through financing, grading, and marketing information and research.

15-3. What is the difference between a direct and an indirect channel?
Answer: A direct channel is one in which a producer of consumer or business products and services and ultimate consumers or industrial users deal directly with each other. In an indirect channel, intermediaries are inserted between the producer and ultimate consumers or industrial users and perform numerous channel functions.

15-4. Why are channels for business products typically shorter than channels for consumer products?
Answer: Business channels are typically shorter than consumer channels because business users are fewer in number, tend to be more concentrated geographically, and buy in larger quantities.

15-5. What is the principal distinction between a corporate vertical marketing system and an administered vertical marketing system?
Answer: A corporate vertical marketing system combines successive stages of production and distribution under a single ownership. In forward integration, a producer owns an intermediary; in backward integration, an intermediary owns a producer. An administered vertical marketing system achieves coordination at successive stages of production and distribution by the size and influence of one channel member rather than through ownership.

15-6. What are the three questions marketing executives consider when choosing a marketing channel and intermediaries?
Answer: The three questions to consider when choosing a marketing channel and intermediaries are: (1) Which will provide the best coverage of the target market? (2) Which will best satisfy the buying requirements of the target market? (3) Which will be the most profitable?

15-7. What are the three degrees of distribution density?
Answer: Three degrees of distribution density exist: (1) Intensive distribution means that a firm tries to place its products and services in as many outlets as possible. (2) Exclusive distribution is the extreme opposite of intensive distribution because only one retailer in a specified geographical area carries the firm's products. (3) Selective distribution lies between these two extremes and means that a firm selects a few retailers in a specific geographical area to carry its products.

15-8. What is meant by exclusive dealing?
Answer: Exclusive dealing exists when a supplier requires channel members to sell only its products or restricts distributors from selling directly competitive products. It is specifically prohibited under the Clayton Act when it lessens competition or creates monopolies.

15-9. What is the principal difference between a marketing channel and a supply chain?
Answer: A marketing channel consists of individuals and firms involved in the process of making a product or service available for use or consumption by ultimate consumers or industrial users. A supply chain refers to the various firms involved in performing the activities required to create and deliver a product or service to ultimate consumers or industrial users. A supply chain differs from a marketing channel in terms of membership. It includes suppliers who provide raw materials to a manufacturer as well as the wholesalers and retailers—the marketing channel—that deliver the finished goods to ultimate consumers.

15-10. The choice of a supply chain involves what three steps?
Answer: (1) Understand the customer—identify its needs. (2) Understand the supply chain—determine what it is designed to do well. (3) Harmonize the supply chain with the marketing strategy—match supply chain capabilities with the targeted customers' needs and the firm's marketing strategy.

15-11. A manager's key task is to balance which four customer service factors against which six logistics cost factors?

Answer: The four supply chain customer service factors designed to satisfy users are: (1) Time, which means the time between the ordering of an item and when it is received and ready for use or sale. (2) Dependability, which is the consistency of replenishment. (3) Communication, the two-way link between the buyer and seller that helps in monitoring service and anticipating future needs. (4) Convenience, which means that there should be a minimum of effort on the part of the buyer in doing business with the seller. The six supply chain logistics cost factors are transportation costs, materials handling and warehousing costs, inventory costs, stockout costs (being out of inventory), order processing costs, and return products handling costs.

CHAPTER 16

16-1. When Ralph Lauren makes shirts to a customer's exact preferences, what utility is provided?

Answer: form utility—involves the production or alteration of a product

16-2. Two measures of the impact of retailing in the global economy are _______ and _______.

Answer: the total annual sales—four of the 40 largest businesses in the United States are retailers; the number of employees working at large retailers

16-3. Centralized decision making and purchasing are an advantage of _______ ownership.

Answer: corporate chain

16-4. What are some examples of new forms of self-service retailers?

Answer: New forms of self-service are being developed at warehouse clubs, gas stations, supermarkets, airlines, convenience stores, fast-food restaurants, and even coffee shops.

16-5. A shop for big men's clothes carries pants in sizes 40 to 60. Would this be considered a broad or deep product line?

Answer: deep product line; the range of sizes relates to the assortment of a product item (pants) rather than the variety of product lines (pants, shirts, shoes, etc.)

16-6. Successful catalog retailers often send _______ catalogs to _______ markets identified in their databases.

Answer: specialty; niche

16-7. How are retailers increasing consumer interest and involvement in online retailing?

Answer: Retailers have improved the online retailing experience by adding experiential or interactive activities to their websites, allowing customers to "build" virtual products by customizing their purchases. And to minimize "checkout," when consumers leave a website to compare prices and shipping costs on other sites, some firms now offer them the ability to compare competitors' offerings. Another way is to offer consumers "flash sales," in which retailers will send a text message to consumers' mobile phones informing them of a limited-time, discounted offer.

16-8. Where are direct selling retail sales growing? Why?

Answer: Direct selling, sometimes called door-to-door retailing, involves direct sales of products and services to consumers through personal interactions and demonstrations in their homes or offices. Direct-selling retailers are (1) expanding into other global markets outside the United States and (2) reaching consumers who prefer one-on-one customer service and a social shopping experience rather than shopping online or at big discount stores.

16-9. What are the two dimensions of the retail positioning matrix?

Answer: The two dimensions of the retail positioning matrix are: (1) breadth of product line, which is the range of products sold through each outlet and (2) value added, which includes elements such as location, product reliability, or prestige.

16-10. How does original markup differ from maintained markup?

Answer: The original markup is the difference between retailer cost and initial selling price, whereas maintained markup is the difference between the final selling price and retailer cost, which is also called the gross margin.

16-11. A huge shopping strip mall with multiple anchor stores is a _______ center.

Answer: power

16-12. Using the wheel of retailing, describe the characteristics of a new retail form that has just entered the market.

Answer: a low-status, low-margin, low-price outlet

16-13. Market share is usually fought out before the _______ stage of the retail life cycle.

Answer: maturity

16-14. What is an influence effect?

Answer: An influence effect is the complementary role that different communication and delivery channels have on sales.

16-15. What is the difference between merchant wholesalers and agents?

Answer: Merchant wholesalers are independently owned firms that take title to the merchandise they handle and make their profit from the sale of merchandise they own. Agents do not take title to merchandise, typically perform fewer channel functions, and make their profit from commissions or fees paid for their services.

16-16. Under what circumstances do producers assume wholesaling functions?

Answer: Producers assume wholesaling functions when there are no intermediaries to perform these activities, customers are few in number and geographically concentrated, or orders are large or require significant attention.

CHAPTER 17

17-1. What six elements are required for communication to occur?

Answer: The six elements required for communication to occur are: (1) a source, which is a company or person who has information to convey; (2) a message, which is the information sent; (3) a channel of communication, which is how the information is conveyed; (4) a receiver, which is the consumer who reads, hears, or sees the message; and the processes of (5) encoding, in which the sender transforms the idea into a set of symbols; and (6) decoding, in which the receiver takes the symbols, or the message, and transforms it back into an idea.

17-2. A difficulty for U.S. companies advertising in international markets is that the audience does not share the same _______.

Answer: field of experience, which is a similar understanding and knowledge that is applied to a message

17-3. A misprint in a newspaper ad is an example of _______.

Answer: noise, the extraneous factors that distort a message

17-4. Explain the difference between advertising and publicity when both appear on television.

Answer: Since advertising space on TV is paid for, a firm can control what it wants to say and to whom and how often the message is sent over a broadcast, cable, satellite, or local TV network. Since publicity is an indirectly paid presentation of a message about a firm or its products or services, the firm has little control over what is said to whom or when. Instead, it can only suggest to the TV medium that it run a favorable story about the firm or its offerings.

17-5. Cost per contact is high with the _______ element of the promotional mix.

Answer: personal selling

17-6. Which promotional element should be offered only on a short-term basis?

Answer: sales promotion

17-7. Describe the promotional objective for each stage of the product life cycle.

Answer: Introduction—to inform consumers of the product's existence; growth—to persuade consumers to buy the product; maturity—to remind consumers that the product still exists; and decline—to phase out the product.

17-8. At what stage of the consumer purchase decision process is the importance of personal selling highest? Why?

Answer: Personal selling is most important at the purchase stage of the consumer purchase decision process because salespeople can provide sales assistance to prospective customers and negotiate terms of the sale.

17-9. Explain the differences between a push strategy and a pull strategy.

Answer: In a push strategy, a firm directs the promotional mix to channel members to gain their cooperation in ordering and stocking the product. In a pull strategy, a firm directs the promotional mix at ultimate consumers to encourage them to ask retailers for the product, who then order it from wholesalers or the firm itself.

17-10. What are the characteristics of good promotion objectives?

Answer: Promotion objectives should possess three important qualities. They should (1) be designed for a well-defined target audience, (2) be measurable, and (3) cover a specified time period.

17-11. What is the weakness of the percentage of sales budgeting approach?

Answer: In the percentage of sales budgeting approach, funds are allocated to promotion based on a percentage of past or anticipated dollar or unit sales. The major fallacy of this method is that sales cause promotion. By using this method, a company may reduce its promotion budget because of actual or projected downturns in past or future sales—situations where promotion may be needed the most.

17-12. How have advertising agencies changed to facilitate the use of IMC programs?

Answer: Some agencies have adopted: (1) a total communications solutions approach; (2) a long-term perspective in which all forms of promotion are integrated; (3) an IMC audit to analyze the internal communication network of their clients, identify key audiences, evaluate customer databases, assess messages contained in recent advertising, press releases, packaging, websites, social media, direct marketing, etc., and determine the IMC expertise of company and agency personnel; and (4) strategies to monitor consumer content, respond to inconsistent messages, answer questions from individual customers, and recognize that consumers easily move content from medium to medium without any influence or control from the message source.

17-13. The ability to design and use direct marketing programs has increased with the availability of ______ and ______.

Answer: customer information databases; new printing technologies

17-14. What are the three types of responses generated by direct marketing activities?

Answer: They are: (1) direct orders, the result of offers that contain all the information necessary for a prospective buyer to make a decision to purchase and complete the transaction; (2) lead generation, the result of an offer designed to generate interest in a product or service and a request for additional information; and (3) traffic generation, the outcome of an offer designed to motivate people to visit a business.

CHAPTER 18

18-1. What is the difference between pioneering and competitive ads?

Answer: Pioneering (or informational) ads, used in the introductory stage of the product life cycle, tell people what a product is, what it can do, and where it can be found. The key objective of a pioneering ad is to inform the target market. Competitive (or persuasive) ads promote a specific brand's features and benefits to persuade the target market to select the firm's brand rather than that of a competitor. An increasing form of a competitive ad is the comparative ad that shows one brand's strengths relative to those of competitors. Both are forms of product advertisements.

18-2. What is the purpose of an institutional advertisement?

Answer: The purpose of an institutional advertisement is to build goodwill or an image for an organization rather than a specific offering. This form of advertising is often used to support the public relations plan or counter adverse publicity.

18-3. What other decisions can advertising objectives influence?

Answer: Advertising objectives can influence decisions such as selecting media, evaluating an advertising campaign, creating awareness, and establishing the importance and sequence of the stages of the hierarchy of effects.

18-4. What is a potential shortcoming of using a celebrity spokesperson?

Answer: The spokesperson's image may change to be inconsistent with the image of the company or brand.

18-5. You see the same ad in *Time* and *Fortune* magazines and on billboards and TV. Is this an example of reach or frequency?

Answer: Reach—using more of the same media type (magazines) as well as using more of different types of media (magazines, billboards, and TV)—is an attempt to maximize the number of individuals in a target market that are exposed to the advertisement. Frequency uses the same medium/media more than once to present the advertising message.

18-6. Why has the Internet become a popular advertising medium?

Answer: The Internet offers a visual message, can use both audio and video, is interactive through rich media, and tends to reach younger consumers.

18-7. What factors must be considered when choosing among alternative media?

Answer: Choosing among alternative media depends on: knowing the media habits of the target audience; understanding the product's attributes, such as color, a quick competitive response, or the message is complicated; and calculating the cost, as measured by CPM.

18-8. Explain the difference between pretesting and posttesting advertising copy.

Answer: Pretests are conducted before ads are placed in any medium to determine whether they communicate the intended message or to select among alternative versions of the ad. Posttests are conducted after the ads are shown to the target audience to determine whether they accomplished their intended purpose.

18-9. What is the difference between aided and unaided recall posttests?

Answer: Aided and unaided recall posttests are conducted after the ads are shown to the target audience. Aided recall involves showing an ad to respondents who then are asked if their previous exposure to it was through reading, viewing, or listening. Aided recall is used to determine the percentage of those (1) who remember seeing a specific magazine ad (*noted*), (2) who saw or read any part of the ad identifying the product or brand (*seen-associated*), (3) who read any part of the ad's copy (*read some*), and (4) who read at least half of the ad (*read most*). Unaided recall involves specifically asking respondents if they remember an ad without any prompting to determine if they saw or heard its message.

18-10. What is the difference between a coupon and a deal?
Answer: Coupons and deals are consumer-oriented sales promotion tools used to support a company's advertising and personal selling. A coupon provides a reduced price for an item based on redemption to encourage the trial of an offering. A deal is a short-term price reduction used to increase trial among potential customers or to retaliate against a competitor's actions.

18-11. Which sales promotional tool is most common for new products?
Answer: A product sample (or sampling) is a consumer-oriented sales promotion tool that is given to consumers through the use of a trial size package, which is generally smaller than the regular size.

18-12. Which trade promotion is used on an ongoing basis?
Answer: Trade-oriented sales promotions (or simply trade promotions) are sales tools used to support a company's advertising and personal selling directed to wholesalers, retailers, or distributors. One of these tools is the use of allowances and discounts, which encourage increased purchases by intermediaries to maintain or increase inventory levels in the channel of distribution.

18-13. What is a news release?
Answer: A news release is a publicity tool that consists of an announcement regarding changes in the company or the product line to inform the media of an idea for a story.

18-14. What is the difference between government regulation and self-regulation?
Answer: Government regulation involves laws or other controls that are set by an agency of local, state, or federal government and restrict some promotion activities. The Federal Trade Commission (FTC) issues guidelines to protect consumers from misleading promotions. Self-regulation involves imposing standards and ethical guidelines for business practices set by advertising agencies, trade associations, and marketing organizations that reflect the values of society.

CHAPTER 19

19-1. What are social media?
Answer: Social media are online media where users submit comments, photos, and videos—often accompanied by a feedback process to identify "popular" topics. Business firms also refer to social media as "consumer-generated media." A single social media site is a social network.

19-2. In classifying social media, what do we mean by (*a*) media richness and (*b*) self-disclosure?
Answer: Social media can be classified based on two factors: (*a*) Media richness involves the degree of acoustic, visual, and personal contact between two communication partners. For example, face-to-face communication is higher in media richness than telephone or e-mail communication. The higher the media richness and quality of presentation, the greater the social influence that these communication partners have on each other's behavior. (*b*) Self-disclosure involves the degree to which an individual shares his or her thoughts, feelings, likes, and dislikes when engaged in a social interaction. Typically, this person wants to make a positive impression to achieve a favorable image with others. The greater the self-disclosure, the greater the likelihood that the person will increase his or her influence on those reached.

19-3. Compare traditional media and social media in terms of time to delivery of the communication.
Answer: Traditional media can involve days or even months of continuing effort to deliver the communication, and time lags can be extensive. In contrast, individuals using social media can post virtually instantaneous content.

19-4. How is user-generated content presented by someone using Facebook?
Answer: User-generated content (UGC) refers to the various forms of online media content that are publicly available and created by end users. Facebook is a website where users create a personal profile, add other users as friends, and exchange comments, photos, videos, and "likes" with them. Facebook users today can keep friends and family updated on what a user is thinking, doing, and feeling. Additionally, users may chat with friends and create and join common-interest groups.

19-5. What are some ways brand managers use Facebook to converse with a brand's fans?
Answer: A brand manager can create awareness for a product, service, or brand by creating a Facebook Page for it. Done well, this is a magnet for feedback. Facebook allows brand managers to request a range of user data like addresses and phone numbers—with the users' permission (an "opt-in" approach). To generate new customers and increase traffic to their Facebook Pages, brand managers can use paid ads and sponsored stories within the Facebook advertising platform. The marketing challenge for a Facebook Page is to post and create the content that will generate the best response. Most ads for a brand on a Facebook site appear on the right-hand side of the page. An advantage of a Facebook ad for a brand is that it can migrate into Facebook conversations among friends—to the delight of advertisers.

19-6. What are the major differences between Facebook and YouTube that are of interest to brand managers?
Answer: According to Figure 19-2, Facebook has slightly more female users than YouTube. So, if a brand manager wants to reach males with an ad for a brand, he/she more likely would use YouTube. Both Facebook and YouTube enable a brand manager to promote the brand but in different ways: Facebook has a platform that connects with the firm's brand website. YouTube allows brand managers to create an actual brand channel to host its advertisements and other video clips that can explain or demonstrate complex products. YouTube can also link to a brand's website. Both Facebook and YouTube allow users to share their opinions with other users through their respective "Like" and "Comment" features. However, YouTube, because it is a more visual medium, allows a brand manager to entertain as well as inform users about the brand. YouTube traffic goes directly to the video; a hyperlink is needed to get users back to the brand's website. Facebook, on the other hand, uses customized tabs and buttons to direct users to the brand's website.

19-7. What is the difference between (and marketing significance of) a "passive receiver" for conventional media and an "active receiver" for social media?
Answer: Traditional media, like magazine or TV ads, generally use one-way communication from the sender to the receiver, whom the marketer hopes will buy the product advertised. A little word-of-mouth chatting may occur among the consumer "passive receivers," but communications generally end with the receiver. Social media deliberately seek to ensure that the message does not end with an individual receiver. Instead, the goal is to reach "active receivers," those who will become "influentials" and be "delighted" with the brand advertised. These will then become "evangelists," who will send messages—user-generated content—to their online friends and then back to the advertiser about the joys of using the brand. So success in social media marketing relies heavily on the ability of a marketing program to convert passive "receivers" of the message to active "evangelists" who will spread favorable messages about the brand.

19-8. Stated simply, how can an advertiser on Facebook expect to generate sales?

Answer: The brand manager composes title, copy, and images or photos for an ad to be placed on Facebook. A website address links the ad to the brand's website or its Facebook Page. To encourage and produce new sales that can be tracked, the brand manager might also link the ad to a coupon code or some other promotional offer.

19-9. What did the Carmex team do to exploit its incredible good fortune after seeing Michael Drysch make his "Half-Court Hero" shot?

Answer: In April 2012, Carmex created the "Carmex and LeBronJames.com Half-Court Hero" contest: the grand prize was a trip to Miami and a chance to win $75,000 if s/he made a basket from half court. Carmex would donate the same amount to two charities selected by LeBron James if the shot was made. On January 25, 2013, at a Miami Heat–Detroit Pistons game, Michael Drysch did the impossible and made the shot. LeBron James came running out of his Miami Heat huddle—congratulating Michael with a bear hug. Instantly, the footage of Half-Court Hero winner Michael Drysch's incredible hook shot and the celebratory bear hug from LeBron James went viral online. Drysch was immediately interviewed after the shot by Fox Sports South, and NBATV interviewed him side-by-side with James after the game. It was the #1 Play of the Day on ESPN's SportsCenter. The Carmex brand team immediately arranged a public relations tour for Drysch that included four Miami area news stations and a trip to New York City for appearances on several TV and radio shows. Meanwhile, the Carmex marketing team kept Carmex's social media accounts and website updated throughout the weekend with Twitter and Facebook posts from the public relations tour. The team actively monitored social media tracking software for up-to-the-minute brand mentions resulting from the shot. Within three months, Carmex's Half-Court Hero shot had been seen by over 20 million YouTube viewers and became the most-watched video of all time on the National Basketball Association's YouTube page. In all, the promotion earned Carmex over 500 million media impressions across TV, print, online, and social media.

19-10. What is an example of how the real (physical) and digital (virtual) worlds are converging?

Answer: The convergence of real and digital worlds is the result of a proliferation of interlinked smartphones, tablet devices, sensors, special identification tags, databases, algorithms, apps, and other elements (see Figure 19-6). For example, GPS-enabled smartphones give mobile consumers access to online ads, local restaurant promotions, and time-sensitive discounts at retailers. In addition, apps for smartphones are accelerating the convergence of the real and digital worlds as they make the devices more productive and provide users with entertainment. Finally, marketers can tailor specific messages to targeted users by using their personal data and preferences so that they can order products and services as a result of receiving these offers.

19-11. What are apps and why are they important?

Answer: Apps are small, downloadable software programs that run on smartphones and tablet devices. They are speeding up the convergence of the real (physical) and digital (virtual) worlds. Many apps are related to social media, such as programs for (1) price-comparison searches, (2) loyalty programs, (3) location-based promotions, and (4) entertainment, such as video games, music, and others.

19-12. Can personal privacy become a problem as the real and digital worlds converge with smart systems?

Answer: The convergence of social media, smartphones, tablet devices, and new apps will lead to companies having a more dynamic interaction with their customers. This convergence allows for the collection of users' personal data, preferences, and behaviors, which allows marketers to tailor offerings based on these data. A recent analysis of 58,000 Facebook users revealed that the "likes" they posted can reveal their political and religious views, drug use, and marital status. The issue is, do we want others to know all this information about us?

CHAPTER 20

20-1. What is personal selling?

Answer: Personal selling involves the two-way flow of communication between a buyer and seller, often in a face-to-face encounter, designed to influence a person's or group's purchase decision.

20-2. What is involved in sales management?

Answer: Sales management involves planning the selling program and implementing and evaluating the personal selling effort of the firm. The tasks involved in managing personal selling include setting objectives; organizing the salesforce; recruiting, selecting, training, and compensating salespeople; and evaluating the performance of individual salespeople.

20-3. What is the principal difference between an order taker and an order getter?

Answer: An order taker processes routine orders or reorders for products that were already sold by the company. The primary responsibility of order takers is to preserve an ongoing relationship with existing customers and maintain sales. An order getter sells in a conventional sense and identifies prospective customers, provides customers with information, persuades customers to buy, closes sales, and follows up on customers' use of a product or service. Order getting involves a high degree of creativity, customer empathy, considerable product knowledge, and sales training.

20-4. What is team selling?

Answer: Team selling is the practice of using an entire team of professionals in selling to and servicing major customers. Team selling is used when specialized knowledge is needed to satisfy the different interests of individuals in a customer's buying center.

20-5. What are the six stages in the personal selling process?

Answer: The six stages in the personal selling process are: (1) prospecting—searching for qualified potential customers; (2) preapproach—obtaining further information on prospects and deciding on the best method of approach; (3) approach—setting up the first meeting between the salesperson and the prospect to gain his/her attention, stimulate interest, and establish a foundation for the relationship and eventual sales presentation; (4) presentation—converting a prospect into a customer by creating a desire for the offering; (5) close—obtaining a purchase commitment from the prospect; and (6) follow-up—delivering, installing, and/or resolving any difficulties with the purchase.

20-6. What is the distinction between a lead and a qualified prospect?

Answer: A lead is the name of a person who may be a possible customer whereas a qualified prospect is an individual who wants the product, can afford to buy it, and is the decision maker.

20-7. Which presentation format is most consistent with the marketing concept? Why?

Answer: The need-satisfaction presentation format emphasizes probing and listening by the salesperson to identify the needs and interests of prospective buyers and then tailors the presentation to the prospect and highlights product benefits, which is consistent with the marketing concept and its focus on relationship building.

20-8. What are the three types of selling objectives?

Answer: The three types of selling objectives are: (1) output-related (dollars or unit sales, number of new customers, profit); (2) input-related (number of sales calls, selling expenses); and (3) behavior-related (product and competitive knowledge, customer service satisfaction ratings, selling and communication skills).

20-9. What three factors are used to structure sales organizations?

Answer: Three questions need to be answered when structuring a sales organization: (1) Should the company use its own salesforce or independent agents such as manufacturer's representatives? (2) If the decision is made to employ company salespeople, then should they be organized according to geography, customer type, or product or service? (3) How many company salespeople should be employed?

20-10. How does emotional intelligence tie to adaptive selling?
Answer: Emotional intelligence is the ability to understand one's own emotions and the emotions of people with whom one interacts on a daily basis. Evidence suggests that emotional intelligence is two times more important in contributing to performance than intellect and expertise alone. Emotional intelligence has five dimensions: (1) self-motivation skills; (2) self-awareness, or knowing one's own emotions; (3) the ability to manage one's emotions and impulses; (4) empathy, or the ability to sense how others are feeling; and (5) social skills, or the ability to handle the emotions of other people. These qualities are important for adaptive selling.

CHAPTER 21

21-1. The consumer-initiated practice of generating content on a marketer's website that is custom tailored to an individual's specific needs and preferences is called ______.
Answer: personalization

21-2. What are the seven website design elements that companies use to produce a customer experience?
Answer: From an interactive marketing perspective, customer experience is defined as the sum total of the interactions that a customer has with a company's website, from the initial look at a home page through the entire purchase decision process. Companies produce a customer experience through seven website design elements, which are: (1) context—a website's aesthetic appeal and functional look and feel reflected in site layout and visual design; (2) content—all digital information on a website, including the text, video, audio, and graphics; (3) community—the user-to-user communications hosted by the company to create virtual communities; (4) customization—the ability of a site to modify itself to, or be modified by, each individual user; (5) communication—the dialogue that unfolds between the website and its users; (6) connection—the network of linkages between a company's site and other sites; and (7) commerce—the website's ability to conduct sales transactions for products and services. Most websites do not include every design element. Although every website has context and content, they differ in the use of the remaining five elements. See Figure 21-2.

21-3. Which online consumer lifestyle segment spends the most money online and which spends the most time online?
Answer: The "brand loyalists" segment spends the most money online whereas the "hooked, online, and single" segment spends more time online.

21-4. What are the six reasons consumers prefer to shop and buy online?
Answer: The six reasons consumers prefer to shop and buy online are: convenience, choice, customization, communication, cost, and control. See Figure 21-4. A potential seventh reason is cookies.

21-5. What is the eight-second rule?
Answer: The eight-second rule is a view that customers will abandon their efforts to enter and navigate a website if download time exceeds eight seconds.

21-6. A cross-channel shopper is ______.
Answer: an online consumer who researches products online and then purchases them at a retail store

21-7. Channel conflict between manufacturers and retailers is likely to arise when manufacturers use ______ websites.
Answer: transactional

CHAPTER 22

22-1. What are the four basic practices "that really work" that characterize industry-leading firms?
Answer: The four basic business and management practices that matter are: (1) strategy—devise and maintain a clearly stated, focused strategy; (2) execution—develop and maintain flawless operational execution; (3) culture—develop and maintain a performance-oriented culture; and (4) structure—build and maintain a fast, flexible, flat organization.

22-2. What is the significance of the S-shape of the sales response function in Figure 22–1?
Answer: The sales response function relates the expense of marketing effort to the marketing results obtained. Different levels of marketing effort will cause different rates of sales revenue growth. In Figure 22-1, an additional $1 million of marketing effort results in far greater increases of sales revenue in the midrange of the curve than at either end. At the left end of the S-curve, the cost of the marketing effort to gain new customers is high for they must be made aware of the product. In contrast, at the right end of the S-curve, the easy-to-get customers are already buying the product and getting every new one is again very costly.

22-3. What is the difference between an input metric and an output metric?
Answer: Marketing metrics are used to measure actual organizational performance—whether its goals have been achieved. An output metric is a measure of actual results, such as sales revenues due to new offerings and customer satisfaction with new offerings during a specified time period. An input metric measures the efforts that go into developing new offerings, such as the number of ideas or concepts in the new-product pipeline and R&D spending as a percentage of sales.

22-4. Describe Porter's four generic business strategies.
Answer: A generic business strategy is one that can be adopted by any firm, regardless of the product or industry involved, to achieve a competitive advantage. Porter's four generic business strategies are: (1) Cost leadership strategy, which focuses on reducing expenses and, in turn, lowers product prices while targeting a broad array of market segments. (2) Differentiation strategy, which requires products to have significant points of difference to charge a higher price while targeting a broad array of market segments. (3) Cost focus strategy, which involves controlling expenses and, in turn, lowering product prices targeted at a narrow range of market segments. (4) Differentiation focus strategy, which requires products to have significant points of difference to target one or only a few market segments.

22-5. Where do (*a*) marketing synergies and (*b*) R&D–manufacturing synergies appear when using the synergy analysis framework?
Answer: Synergy analysis seeks market-product opportunities by finding the optimum balance between marketing efficiencies versus R&D–manufacturing efficiencies. This can be accomplished by using both diversification analysis and the market-product grid framework. (*a*) Marketing synergies run horizontally across the rows. As a result, a firm may experience the market specialization effect if it provides a complete product line for a given market segment. (*b*) R&D–manufacturing synergies run vertically down the columns. As a result, a firm may experience the product specialization effect if it provides a product item for all market segments. A firm can experience both marketing and R&D–manufacturing efficiencies if it offers full coverage: a complete product line targeted at all market segments.

22-6. What is the meaning and importance of a program champion?
Answer: A program champion is able and willing to cut red tape and move the program forward to get it implemented. Such a person often has the uncanny ability to move back and forth between the "big picture" and the specific details as the situation warrants. Program champions can be notoriously brash in overcoming organizational hurdles. An adage voiced by a program champion: "Better to ask forgiveness than permission."

22-7. Describe one or two lessons from Lockheed Martin's Skunk Works that can be applied to implementing marketing programs.
Answer: Examples of lessons from Lockheed's Skunk Works are: (1) make decisions promptly; (2) avoid "paralysis by analysis," which is the tendency to excessively analyze a problem instead of taking action; (3) when trouble develops, surface the problem immediately; (4) get help—don't keep the problem to yourself; (5) hold weekly meetings using a time-based agenda, which is one that shows the running time allocated to each agenda item; and (6) create an action item list, which is an aid to implementing a plan consisting of four columns: (*a*) the task, (*b*) the person responsible for completing that task, (*c*) the date to finish the task, and (*d*) what is to be delivered.

22-8. How are (*a*) a time-based agenda and (*b*) an action item list used in a marketing program meeting?
Answer: Successful implementation requires that members of the program team understand its goals, the tasks they are responsible for to help reach those goals, and the deadlines for completing them. Time-based agendas and action item lists are two tools to assist program champions and others on the project to manage meetings and deadlines. A time-based agenda shows the running time allocated to each agenda item. It sets the agenda for the next meeting and its minutes become secondary and backward-looking. An action item list is the outcome of these meetings. It is an aid that consists of four columns: (*a*) the task, (*b*) the person responsible for completing that task, (*c*) the date to finish the task, and (*d*) what is to be delivered. Action item lists are forward-looking, clarify the targets, and put strong pressure on people to achieve their designated tasks by the specified deadlines.

22-9. What are four groupings used within a typical marketing organization?
Answer: The four marketing organizational groupings are: (1) product line, in which a unit is responsible for specific product offerings; (2) functional, where different departments or business activities within a firm are represented, such as manufacturing, marketing, and finance; (3) geographical, in which sales territories are subdivided according to geographical location; and (4) market-based, which uses specific customer segments. When this method of organizing is combined with product groupings, the result is a matrix organization.

22-10. How do marketing metrics tie the goal-setting element of the planning phase of the strategic marketing process to the evaluation phase?
Answer: For each marketing plan goal developed in the planning phase for an organization's offering, a marketing metric is created to measure whether the goal actually has been achieved. Marketing actions are then taken in the implementation phase with these goals in mind. In the evaluation phase, actual results are measured using this marketing metric to compare the established goal with the results to identify any deviations that need to be either exploited or corrected when revising the marketing plans for the next period.

CHAPTER NOTES

Chapter 1

1. Dave Fusaro, "Chobani Selected as *Food Processing* 2012 Processor of the Year," *Food Processing,* December 5, 2012, see http://www.foodprocessing.com/articles/2012/processor-of-the-year.html.
2. Meghan Walsh, "Chobani Takes Gold in the Yogurt Aisle," *Bloomberg Businessweek*, July 31, 2012, see http://www.businessweek.com/articles/2012-07-31/chobani-takes-gold-in-the-yogurt-aisle.
3. Fusaro, "Chobani Selected as *Food Processing* 2012 Processor of the Year."
4. "Chobani Brings the Heart of Central New York to the London 2012 Olympic Games," Chobani press release, July 26, 2012, see http://chobani.com/who-we-are/news/page/5/; and Samuel Greengard, "How Chobani Yogurt Used Social Media to Boost Sales," *Entrepreneur,* September 16, 2012, see http://www.entrepreneur.com/article/223999.
5. Stuart Elliott, "Anything-but-Ordinary Mom Pitches for Chobani Yogurt," *The New York Times,* June 14, 2012, see http://www.nytimes.com/2012/06/15/business/media/jennie-finch-pitches-for-childs-version-of-chobani-yogurt.html; and "Maker of America's Leading Yogurt Brand to Open First-of-Its-Kind Mediterranean Yogurt Bar in New York City," Chobani press release, July 24, 2012, see http://chobani.com/who-we-are/news/page/5/.
6. E. J. Schultz, "Chobani's Head of Marketing Doron Stern Exits," *Advertising Age,* November 21, 2012, see http://adage.com/article/news/chobani-s-head-marketing-doron-stern-exits/238446; and Elliott, "Maker of America's #1 Yogurt Brand Announces Chobani Bite, Chobani Champions Tubes, Chobani Flip, and Two New Chobani Fan-Sourced Flavors," Chobani press release, December 19, 2012.
7. Bryan Gruley, "How a Turkish Immigrant Made a Billion Dollars in Eight Years Selling...Yogurt," *Bloomberg Businessweek*, January 31, 2013, pp. 60–64; Julie Cruz, "A Culture Clash in the Yogurt Aisle," *Bloomberg Businessweek*, September 9–September 15, 2013, pp. 20–21; "Translating Chobani's Success," *Convenience Store Products*, April 23, 2013, pp. 1, 2; and Sarah Nassauer, "The Greek Yogurt Culture War," *The Wall Street Journal*, September 4, 2013, pp. D1, D3.
8. Lev Grossman, "2010 Person of the Year: Mark Zuckerberg," *Time,* December 27, 2010–January 3, 2011, pp. 44–75; and Ben Mezrich, *The Accidental Billionaire* (New York: Anchor Books, 2009), pp. 92–150.
9. To compare the 2004 and 2007 American Marketing Association (AMA) definitions of "marketing," see Lisa M. Keefe, "Marketing Defined," *Marketing News,* January 15, 2008, pp. 28–29. The 2007 AMA approved definition is: "Marketing is the activity, set of institutions, and processes for creating, communicating, delivering, and exchanging offerings that have value for customers, clients, partners, and society at large."
10. Richard P. Bagozzi, "Marketing as Exchange," *Journal of Marketing,* October 1975, pp. 32–39; and Gregory T. Gundlach and Patrick E. Murphy, "Ethical and Legal Foundations of Relational Marketing Exchanges," *Journal of Marketing,* October 1993, pp. 35–46.
11. "The Rise of the Creative Consumer," *The Economist,* March 12, 2005, pp. 54–60.
12. Productscan® Online database of new products, from *Marketing Intelligence Service,* December 17, 2003. See www.productscan.com. [NOTE: Now known as Datamonitor's Product Launch Analytics.]
13. Robert M. McMath and Thom Forbes, *What* Were *They Thinking*? (New York: Times Business, 1998), pp. 3–22; see also http://www.gfkamerica.com/practice_areas/gfk_innovation/newproductworks/index.en.html.
14. Ibid.
15. W. J. Hennigan, "Wheels Up," *Star Tribune,* April 27, 2012, p. M1; see also the Terrafugia website, http://www.terrafugia.com.
16. Martinne Geller, "Pepsi Counts on 'Next' to Lure Back Lost Drinkers," *Reuters,* March 13, 2012. See http://www.reuters.com/article/2012/03/13/pepsico-idUSL2E8E9HSP20120313.
17. Kara McGuire, "New Credit Rules Are No Reason to Let Guard Down," *Star Tribune,* January 31, 2010, pp. D1, D2; and Sandra Block, "How the Credit Card Reforms Will Affect You," *USA Today,* February 22, 2010, p. 38.
18. Jerome McCarthy, *Basic Marketing: A Managerial Approach* (Homewood, IL: Richard D. Irwin, 1960); and Walter van Waterschool and Christophe Van den Bulte, "The 4P Classification of the Marketing Mix Revisited," *Journal of Marketing,* October 1992, pp. 83–93.
19. David J. Collis and Michael G. Rukstad, "Can You Say What Your Strategy Is?" *Harvard Business Review,* April 2008, pp. 82–90; and Roger A. Kerin and Robert A. Peterson, *Strategic Marketing Problems: Cases and Comments,* 12th ed. (Upper Saddle River, NJ: Prentice-Hall, 2010), p. 12.
20. Ashish Kothari and Joseph Lackner, "A Value Based Approach to Management," *Journal of Business and Industrial Marketing* 21, no. 4, pp. 243–49; and James C. Anderson, James A. Narius, and Wouter van Rossum, "Customer Value Propositions in Business Markets," *Harvard Business Review,* March 2006, pp. 91–99.
21. V. Kumar, *Managing Customers for Profit* (Upper Saddle River, NJ: Pearson Education, 2008); and "What's a Loyal Customer Worth?" *Fortune,* December 11, 1995, p. 182.
22. Michael Treacy and Fred D. Wiersema, *The Discipline of Market Leaders* (Reading, MA: Addison-Wesley, 1995); Michael Treacy and Fred Wiersema, "How Market Leaders Keep Their Edge," *Fortune* (February 6, 1995), pp. 88–89; and Michael Treacy, "You Need a Value Discipline—But Which One?" *Fortune* (April 17, 1995), p. 195.
23. Target and Starbucks corporate websites; and personal interview with Jennifer Neuman, U.S. Bank Corporation.
24. Robert W. Palmatier, Rajiv P. Dant, Dhruv Grewal, and Kenneth R. Evans, "Factors Influencing the Effectiveness of Relationship Marketing: A Meta-Analysis," *Journal of Relationship Marketing,* October 2006, pp. 136–53; and William Boulding, Richard Staelin, Michael Ehret, and Wesley J. Johnson, "A Customer Relationship Management Roadmap: What Is Known, Potential Pitfalls, and Where to Go," *Journal of Marketing,* October 2005, pp. 155–66.
25. Susan Foumier, Susan Dobscha, and David Glen Mick, "Preventing the Premature Death of Relationship Marketing," *Harvard Business Review,* January–February 1998, pp. 42–51.
26. The 3M Post-it® Flag Highlighter and 3M Post-it® Flag Pen examples are based on a series of interviews and meetings with 3M inventor and researcher David Windorski from 2004 to 2011.
27. See www.oprah.com for January 15, 2008; and "Post-it® Flags Co-Sponsors Oprah's Live Web Event," *3M Stemwinder,* March 4–17, 2008, p. 3.

28. Reservations about and elaborations of these simplified stages appear in D. G. Brian Jones and Eric H. Shaw, "A History of Marketing Thought," Chapter 2 in *Handbook of Marketing,* edited by Barton Weitz and Robin Wensley (London: Sage Publications, 2006), pp. 39–65; Frederick E. Webster, Jr., "The Role of Marketing and the Firm," Chapter 3 in *Handbook of Marketing,* ed. Barton Weitz and Robin Wensley (London: Sage Publications, 2006), pp. 66–82; and Frederick E. Webster, Jr., "Back to the Future: Integrating Marketing as Tactics, Strategy and Organizational Culture," *Journal of Marketing*, October 2005, pp. 4–8.
29. Robert F. Keith, "The Marketing Revolution," *Journal of Marketing,* January 1960, pp. 35–38.
30. *Annual Report* (New York: General Electric Company, 1952), p. 21.
31. John C. Narver, Stanley F. Slater, and Brian Tietje, "Creating a Market Orientation," *Journal of Market Focused Management,* no. 2 (1998), pp. 241–55; Stanley F. Slater and John C. Narver, "Market Orientation and the Learning Organization," *Journal of Marketing,* July 1995, pp. 63–74; and George S. Day, "The Capabilities of Market-Driven Organizations," *Journal of Marketing,* October 1994, pp. 37–52.
32. The definition of customer relationship management is adapted from Rajendra K. Srivastava, Tasadduq A. Shervani, and Liam Fahey, "Marketing, Business Processes, and Shareholder Value: An Embedded View of Marketing Activities and the Discipline of Marketing," *Journal of Marketing,* special issue (1999), pp. 168–79; Gary F. Gebhardt, Gregory S. Carpenter, and John F. Sherry Jr., "Creating a Market Orientation: A Longitudinal, Multifirm, Grounded Analysis of Cultural Transformation," *Journal of Marketing,* October 2006, pp. 37–55; and Christopher Meyer and Andre Schwager, "Understanding Customer Experience," *Harvard Business Review,* February 2007, pp. 117–26.
33. Gary F. Gebhardt, Gregory S. Carpenter, and John F. Sherry Jr., "Creating a Market Orientation: A Longitudinal, Multifirm, Grounded Analysis of Cultural Transformation," *Journal of Marketing,* October 2006, pp. 37–55.
34. Beth Kowitt, "Inside Trader Joe's," *Fortune,* September 6, 2010, p. 87.
35. Christopher Meyer and Andre Schwager, "Understanding Customer Experience," *Harvard Business Review,* February 2007, pp. 117–26.
36. Philip Kotler and Sidney J. Levy, "Broadening the Concept of Marketing," *Journal of Marketing,* January 1969, pp. 10–15; and Jim Rendon, "When Nations Need a Little Marketing," *The New York Times,* November 23, 2003, p. BU6.
37. Peter Gumbel, "Louvre, Inc." *Time,* August 11, 2008, pp. 51–52; and Stella Wai-Art Law, *A Branding Context: The Guggenheim and the Louvre* (Columbus, OH: The Ohio State University, M.A. Thesis, 2008).
38. William L. Wilkie and Elizabeth S. Moore, "Marketing's Relationship to Society," Chapter 1 in *Handbook of Marketing,* ed. Barton Weitz and Robin Wensley (London: Sage Publications, 2006), pp. 9–38.

Chobani, Inc.: This case was written by William Rudelius, based on personal interviews with Chobani executives Joshua Dean, Sujean Lee, and Kyle O'Brien. Other sources include "The Chobani Story," MEDIA@CHOBANI.COM, 2013; Megan Durisin, "Chobani CEO: Our Success Has Nothing to Do with Yogurt," *Business Retail Insider*, May 3, 2013, p. 1; and Sarah E. Needleman, "Old Factory, Snap Decision Spawn Greek Yogurt Craze," *The Wall Street Journal*, June 21, 2012, pp. B1, B2.

Chapter 2

1. Information obtained from selected web pages and press releases from the Ben & Jerry's website; see www.benjerry.com and "Ice Cream History Revealed! What Was Ben & Jerry's First Ice Cream Flavor?" *BusinessWire,* November 15, 2011; see http://www.businesswire.com/news/home/20111115007275/en/Ice-Cream-History-Revealed!-Ben-Jerry's-Ice.
2. Joe Van Brussel, "Ben & Jerry's Become B-Corp Certified, Adds Credibility to Impact Investing Movement," *Huffington Post: Business,* October 23, 2012; see http://www.huffingtonpost.com/2012/10/23/ben-and-jerrys-b-corp-impact-investing_n_2005315.html and "What Are B-Corps?" B-Corporation website; see http://www.bcorporation.net/what-are-b-corps.
3. "Ice Cream: Global Industry Guide," *Datamonitor,* April 27, 2010, press release posted at MarketResearch.com; see http://www.marketresearch.com/MarketLine-v3883/Ice-cream-Global-Guide-6509861.
4. Roger Kerin and Robert Peterson, *Strategic Marketing Problems: Cases and Comments,* 12th ed. (Upper Saddle River, NJ: Prentice Hall, 2010), p. 140.
5. See http://www.teachforamerica.org and Wendy Kaufman, "Ex-Starbucks Exec Helps Develop Global Eye Banks," *National Public Radio,* March 8, 2011.
6. For a discussion on how industries are defined and offerings are classified, see the following: the American Marketing Association website, which provides one definition of an industry (www.marketingpower.com/mg-dictionary-view1509.php) and the Census Bureau's Economic Classification Policy Committee Issues Paper #1 (www.census.gov/epcd/naics/issues1), which aggregates industries in the NAICS (www.census.gov/epcd/www/naicsdev.htm) from a "production-oriented" view.
7. W. Chan Kim and Reneé Mauborgne, "Blue Ocean Strategy: From Theory to Practice," *California Management Review* 47, no. 3 (Spring 2005), p. 105; and Michael E. Porter, "What Is Strategy?" *Harvard Business Review* OnPoint Article, November–December 1996, p. 2.
8. The definition of *strategy* reflects thoughts appearing in Porter, "What Is Strategy?" pp. 4, 8; a condensed definition of strategy is found on the American Marketing Association website www.marketingpower.com; Gerry Johnson, Kevan Scholes, and Richard Wittington, *Exploring Corporate Strategy* (Upper Saddle River, NJ: Prentice Hall, 2005), p. 10; and Costas Markides, "What Is Strategy and How Do You Know If You Have One?" *Business Strategy Review* 15, no. 2 (Summer 2004), p. 5.
9. Geoff Colvin, "Building a Super Brand—Superfast," *Fortune,* September 3, 2012, pp. 60–64; George S. Day and Robert Malcolm, "The CMO and the Future of Marketing," *Marketing Management,* Spring 2012, pp. 34–43; Gordon Wyner, "Getting Engaged," *Marketing Management,* Fall, 2012, pp. 4–9; Christine Moorman, "Ten Trends from The CMO Survey™," *Marketing Management,* Fall 2012, pp. 15–17; John Kador, "The View from Marketing: How to Get the Most from Your CMO," *Chief Executive,* July/August 2011, pp. 60–61; Jessica Shambora, "Wanted: Fearless Marketing Execs," *Fortune,* April 15, 2011, p. 27; Roger A. Kerin, "Strategic Marketing and the CMO," *Journal of Marketing,* October 2005, pp. 12–13; and The CMO Council: Biographies of Selected Advisory Board Members. See www.cmocouncil.org/advisory-board.php.
10. Taken in part from Jim Collins and Jerry I. Porras, *Built to Last: Successful Habits of Visionary Companies* (New York: HarperCollins Publishers, 2002), p. 54.
11. Ibid., p. 73; Patrick M. Lencioni, "Make Your Values Mean Something," *Harvard Business Review,* July 2002, p. 6; and Aubrey Malphurs, *Values-Driven Leadership: Discovering and Developing Your Core Values for Ministry,* 2nd ed. (Grand Rapids, MI: BakerBooks, 2004), p. 31.
12. Collins and Porras, *Built to Last,* p. 73; and Lencioni, "Make Your Values Mean Something," p. 6.

13. Catherine M. Dalton, "When Organizational Values Are Mere Rhetoric," *Business Horizons* 49 (September–October 2006), p. 345.

14. Collins and Porras, *Built to Last,* pp. 94–95; and Tom Krattenmaker, "Write a Mission Statement That Your Company Is Willing to Live," *Harvard Management Communication Letter,* March 2002, pp. 3–4.

15. Janet Moore, "Change of Pace," *Star Tribune,* May 23, 2010, pp. D1, D8.

16. Tom Holloran, "Remarks to Medtronic Employees at the Celebration of the 50th Anniversary of Earl Bakken's Invention of the Wearable Pacemaker," December 6, 2007; and Janet Moore, "An Enduring Mission," *Star Tribune,* December 27, 2010, pp. D1, D2.

17. For the Southwest Airlines mission statement, see http://www.southwest.com/html/about-southwest/index.html and click on the "Mission" link. For the American Red Cross mission statement, see http://www.redcross.org/about-us/mission.

18. Collins and Porras, *Built to Last*, pp. 219–233.

19. Kenneth E. Goodpaster and Thomas E. Holloran, "Anatomy of Spiritual and Social Awareness: The Case of Medtronic, Inc.," *Third International Symposium on Catholic Social Thought and Management Education,* Goa, India, 1999, pp. 9–11.

20. Theodore Levitt, "Marketing Myopia," *Harvard Business Review,* July–August 1960, pp. 45–56.

21. David Phelps, "Debt Threat," *Star Tribune,* January 26, 2009, pp. D1, D6.

22. Jeffrey A. Trachtenberg, "E-Books Rewrite Bookselling," *The Wall Street Journal,* May 20, 2010, pp. A1, A12.

23. John McDermott, "With 'Angry Birds Star Wars,' Rovio Has Another Gaming, Merchandise Hit on Its Hands," *Advertising Age,* November 13, 2012. See http://adage.com/article/digital/angry-birds-star-wars-rovio-gaming-merchandise-hit-hands/238280; Sven Grundberg, "Finland's Angry Birds Flock Takes Wing," *The Wall Street Journal,* November 27, 2012. See http://online.wsj.com/article/SB10001424127887323330604578141082379307840.html; Earnest Cavalli, "Angry Birds Hits Theaters in Summer 2016," *Digital Trends,* December 11, 2012. See http://www.digitaltrends.com/gaming/angry-birds-hits-theaters-in-summer-2016; Anthony John Agnello, "Angry Birds Is Still Big Business but Rovio Thinks It's Time for New IP," *Digital Trends*, December 19, 2012. See http://www.digitaltrends.com/mobile/angry-birds-is-still-big-business-but-rovio-thinks-its-time-for-new-ip; Neil Long, "Bigger Than Star Wars: What's Next for Angry Birds Developer Rovio," *Edge,* December 19, 2012. See http://www.edge-online.com/features/bigger-than-star-wars-whats-next-for-angry-birds-developer-rovio; Jim Muehlhausen, "Is the Angry Birds Business Model Unique?" Business Model Institute. See http://businessmodelinstitute.com/is-the-angry-birds-business-model-unique; "Angry Birds Space," Wikipedia. See http://en.wikipedia.org/wiki/Angry_Birds_Space; and "Angry Birds Star Wars," Wikipedia. See http://en.wikipedia.org/wiki/Angry_Birds_Star_Wars.

24. The definition is adapted from Stephen Few, *Information Dashboard Design: The Effective Visual Communication of Data* (Sebastopol, CA: O'Reilly Media, Inc., 2006), pp. 2–46.

25. Koen Pauwels, et al., *Dashboards & Marketing: Why, What, How and What Research Is Needed?* (Hanover, NH: Tuck School, Dartmouth, May 2008).

26. Few, *Information Dashboard Design;* Bruce H. Clark, Andrew V. Abela, and Tim Ambler, "Behind the Wheel," *Marketing Management,* May–June 2006, pp. 19–23; Spencer E. Ante, "Giving the Boss the Big Picture," *BusinessWeek,* February 13, 2006, pp. 48–49; and *Dashboard Tutorial* (Cupertino, CA: Apple Computer, Inc., 2006).

27. Few, *Information Dashboard Design,* p. 13.

28. Mark Jeffery, *Data-Driven Marketing: The 15 Metrics Everyone in Marketing Should Know* (Hoboken, NJ: John Wiley & Sons, Inc., 2010), Chapter 1; Michael Krauss, "Balance Attention to Metrics with Intuition," *Marketing News,* June 1, 2007, pp. 6–8; John Davis, *Measuring Marketing: 103 Key Metrics Every Marketer Needs* (Singapore: John Wiley & Sons [Asia] Pte Ltd., 2007); and Paul W. Farris, Neil T. Bendle, Phillip E. Pfeifer, and David J. Reibstein, *Marketing Metrics,* 2nd ed. (Upper Saddle River, NJ: Wharton School Publishing, 2010).

29. Art Weinstein and Shane Smith, "Game Plan," *Marketing Management,* Fall 2012, pp. 24–31; Alexander Chiang, "Special Interview with Stephen Few, Dashboard and Data Visualization Expert," *Dundas Dashboard,* July 14, 2011; Stephen Few, *Now You See It* (Oakland, CA: Analytics Press, 2009), Chapters 1–3; and Jacques Bughin, Amy Guggenheim Shenkan, and Mark Singer, "How Poor Metrics Undermine Digital Marketing," *The McKinsey Quarterly,* October 2008.

30. The now-classic reference on effective graphic presentation is Edward R. Tufte, *The Visual Display of Quantitative Information,* 2nd ed. (Cheshire, CT: Graphics Press, 2001); see also Few, *Information Dashboard Design,* Chapters 3–5.

31. George Stalk, Phillip Evans, and Lawrence E. Shulman, "Competing on Capabilities: The New Rules of Corporate Strategy," *Harvard Business Review,* March–April 1992, pp. 57–69; and Darrell K. Rigby, *Management Tools 2007: An Executive's Guide* (Boston: Bain & Company, 2007), p. 22.

32. Michael Arndt, "High-Tech and Handcrafted," *Businessweek,* July 5, 2004, pp. 86–87.

33. Kerin and Peterson, *Strategic Marketing Problems,* pp. 2–3; and Derek F. Abell, *Defining the Business* (Englewood Cliffs, NJ: Prentice Hall, 1980), p. 18.

34. Robert D. Hof, "How to Hit a Moving Target," *Businessweek,* August 21, 2006, p. 3; and Peter Kim, *Reinventing the Marketing Organization* (Cambridge, MA: Forrester, July 13, 2006), pp. 7, 9, and 17.

35. Adapted from *The Experience Curve Reviewed, IV: The Growth Share Matrix of the Product Portfolio* (Boston: The Boston Consulting Group, 1973). See also https://www.bcgperspectives.com/content/classics/strategy_the_product_portfolio (registration and login required for access).

36. Roger A. Kerin, Vijay Mahajan, and P. Rajan Varadarajan, *Contemporary Perspectives on Strategic Marketing Planning* (Boston: Allyn & Bacon, 1990), p. 52.

37. "The Top 100 Brands: Best Global Brands 2012," Interbrand. See http://www.interbrand.com/en/best-global-brands/2012/Best-Global-Brands-2012-Brand-View.aspx.

38. See the Apple press release library at http://www.apple.com/pr/library.

39. "May PC shipments Reflect Slow Second Quarter, According to IDC," IDC press release, June 28, 2013. See http://www.idc.com/getdoc.jsp?containerId=prUS24202913; Apple Worldwide Developer Conference Keynote Address, June 10, 2013; "Gartner Says Declining Worldwide PC Shipments in Fourth Quarter of 2012 Signal Structural Shift of PC Market," Gartner press release, January 14, 2013; see http://www.gartner.com/it/page.jsp?id=2301715; Lance Whitney, "Apple to Buck the Trend in Sour Computer Market, Says Analyst," *CNET,* January 4, 2013; see http://news.cnet.com/8301-13579_3-57562068-37/apple-to-buck-the-trend-in-sour-computer-market-says-analyst.

40. "iPod Still Has 70% of MP3 Player Market," *MacTech.* See http://www.mactech.com/2012/07/24/ipod-still-has-70-mp3-player-market; Liau Yun Qing, "Niche Markets to Secure MP3 Players' Future," *ZDNet,* October 29, 2012; see http://www.zdnet.com/niche-markets-to-secure-mp3-players-future-7000006505; James Hall, "MP3 Players Are Dead," *Business Insider,* December 26, 2012; see http://www.businessinsider.com/mp3-players-are-dead-2012-12; Zak Islam, "Smartphones Heavily Decrease Sales of iPod, MP3 Players," *Tom's Hardware,* December 31, 2012. See http://www.tomshardware.com/news/Smartphones-iPod-MP3-Players-Sales,20062.html.

41. "Gartner: Apple Falls Below 20% in Smartphone Market Share," *MacDailyNews,* May 14, 2013. See http://macdailynews.com/2013/05/14/gartner-apple-falls-below-20-in-smartphone-market-share; Ingrid Lunden, "IDC: Android OEMs Shipped 162M Smartphones in Q1, More Than 4X Apple's Rate; Windows Phone Now in (Distant) Third, *Tech Crunch,* May 16, 2013. See http://techcrunch.com/2013/05/16/idc-android-oems-shipped-162m-smartphones-in-q1-more-than-4x-apples-rate-windows-phone-now-a-distant-third/; Wayne Lam, "Samsung Displaces Nokia as Top Cellphone Brand in 2012 and Takes Decisive Lead Over Apple," iSuppli press release, December 18, 2012. See http://www.isuppli.com/Mobile-and-Wireless-Communications/News/Pages/Samsung-Displaces-Nokia-as-Top-CellphoneBrand-in-2012-and-Takes-Decisive-Smartphone-Lead-Over-Apple.aspx.

42. Larry Magid, "Apple's Tablets Selling Well but Market Share Slips While Samsung Grows, *Forbes,* May 1, 2013. See http://www.forbes.com/sites/larrymagid/2013/05/01/apples-tablet-market-share-slips-and-samsung-grows; "Worldwide Tablet Market Surges Ahead on Strong First Quarter Sales, Says IDC," IDC press release, May 1, 2013. See http://www.idc.com/getdoc.jsp?containerId=prUS24093213; JP Mangalindan, "America's 11th Largest Tech Company (It's Apple's iPad)," *CNNMoney,* January 8, 2013. See http://tech.fortune.cnn.com/2013/01/08/americas-11th-largest-tech-company-ipad; Lisa Rapaport, "Tablet Sales to More Than Double by 2016," *SFGate,* December 5, 2012. See http://www.sfgate.com/technology/article/Tablet-sales-to-more-than-double-by-2016-4094671.php.

43. Strengths and weaknesses of the BCG technique are based on Derek F. Abell and John S. Hammond, *Strategic Market Planning: Problem and Analytic Approaches* (Englewood Cliffs, NJ: Prentice Hall, 1979); Yoram Wind, Vijay Mahajan, and Donald Swire, "An Empirical Comparison of Standardized Portfolio Models," *Journal of Marketing,* Spring 1983, pp. 89–99; and J. Scott Armstrong and Roderick J. Brodie, "Effects of Portfolio Planning Methods on Decision Making: Experimental Results," *International Journal of Research in Marketing,* Winter 1994, pp. 73–84.

44. H. Igor Ansoff, "Strategies for Diversification," *Harvard Business Review,* September–October 1957, pp. 113–24.

45. Geoff Colvin, "How to Fix a Great American Business," *Fortune,* November 12, 2012, pp. 96–100; and Linda Swenson and Kenneth E. Goodpaster, *Medtronic in China (A)* (Minneapolis, MN: University of St. Thomas, 1999), pp. 4–5.

46. Wyner, pp. 4–9; and Moorman, pp. 16–17.

IBM: This case was written by Steven Hartley. Sources: Jessi Hempel, "IBM's Super Second Act," *Fortune,* March 21, 2011, pp. 114–24; Bruce Upbin, "IBM Plays Jeopardy!" *Forbes,* January 17, 2011, pp. 36–37; Kurt Badenhausen, "The World's Most Valuable Brands," *Forbes,* August 30, 2010, p. 34; Jeffrey M. O'Brien, "IBM's Grand Plan to Save the Planet," *Fortune,* May 4, 2009, pp. 84–91; *IBM 2009 Annual Report; IBM 2010 Annual Report;* Samuel J. Palmisano, "Our Values at Work on Being an IBMer," IBM website, see http://www.ibm.com/ibm/values/us; and "Welcome to the Decade of Smart," IBM website. See http://www.ibm.com/smarterplanet/us/en/events/sustainable_development/12jan2010/files/palmisano_decadeofsmart-12jan2010.pdf.

Appendix A

1. Personal interview with Arthur R. Kydd, St. Croix Management Group.

2. Examples of guides to writing marketing plans include William A. Cohen, *The Marketing Plan,* 5th ed. (New York: Wiley and Sons, 2006); and Roman G. Hiebing, Jr., and Scott W. Cooper, *The Successful Business Plan: A Disciplined and Comprehensive Approach* (New York: McGraw-Hill, 2008).

3. Examples of guides to writing business plans include Rhonda Abrams, *Business Plan in a Day,* 2nd ed. (Palo Alto, CA: The Planning Shop, a Division of Rhonda, Inc., 2009); Rhonda Abrams, *The Successful Business Plan,* 5th ed. (Palo Alto, CA: The Planning Shop, a Division of Rhonda, Inc., 2010); Joseph A. Covello and Brian J. Hazelgren, *The Complete Book of Business Plans,* 2nd ed. (Naperville, IL: Sourcebooks, 2006); Joseph A. Covello and Brian J. Hazelgren, *Your First Business Plan,* 5th ed. (Naperville, IL: Sourcebooks, 2005); and Mike McKeever, *How to Write a Business Plan,* 8th ed. (Berkeley, CA: Nolo, 2007).

4. Abrams, *The Successful Business Plan,* p. 41.

5. Some of these points are adapted from Abrams, *The Successful Business Plan,* pp. 41–49; others were adapted from William Rudelius, *Guidelines for Technical Report Writing* (Minneapolis: University of Minnesota, undated). See also William Strunk, Jr., and E.B. White, *The Elements of Style,* 4th ed. (Needham Heights, MA: Allyn & Bacon, 2000).

6. Personal interviews with Randall F. and Leah E. Peters, Paradise Kitchens, Inc.

7. Rebecca Zimoch, "The Dawn of the Frozen Age," *Grocery Headquarters,* December 2002; see www.groceryheadquarters.com.

8. ACNielsen Strategic Planner as reported to the National Frozen & Refrigerated Foods Association for the week ending February 24, 2007; see www.nfraweb.org.

9. Chuck Van Hyning, *NPD's National Eating Trends;* see www.npdfoodworld.com.

10. Jeffrey M. Humphreys, "The Multicultural Economy 2009," *Georgia Business and Economic Conditions* 69, no. 3 (Third Quarter, 2009), pp. 1–13.

Chapter 3

1. Ashlee Vance, "Facebook: The Making of 1 Billion Users," *Bloomberg Businessweek*, October 8–14, 2012, pp. 64–70; Miguel Helft and Jessi Hempel, "Inside Facebook," *Fortune,* March 19, 2012, pp. 112–22; Miguel Helft and Jessi Hempel, "Facebook vs. Google: The Battle for the Future of the Web," *Fortune,* November 21, 2011, pp. 114–24; David Kirkpatrick, *The Facebook Effect* (New York: Simon and Schuster, 2010); Barry Libert, *Social Nation* (Hoboken, NJ: John Wiley & Sons, Inc.); and Lev Grossman, "2010 Person of the Year: Mark Zuckerberg," *Time,* December 27, 2010/January 3, 2011, pp. 44–75.

2. "Past Day Penetration of Coffee by Type," *2012 National Coffee Drinking Trends Study* (New York: National Coffee Association of U.S.A., Inc., February 2013); Tim Sanford, "NCA Study Finds Daily Coffee Consumption Outpacing Soft Drinks," *Vending Times,* 52, no. 8 (August 2012); "Strong Future for Coffee Likely as Younger Generation's Consumption Rebounds," *VendingMarketWatch.com,* May 23, 2011; "Starbucks Card Mobile Goes National," http://www.starbucks.com/blog/archive/mobile%20payment, January 19, 2011; and "Consumers Still Want Quality Coffee: National Coffee Association Drinking Trends Survey Reveals That Coffee Drinkers Look for Quality More Than Price, Even in Recession," *Automatic Merchandiser,* June 1, 2010.

3. "McDonald's to Offer Bagged Coffee," *The Toronto Star,* October 26, 2012, p. B2; Leslie Patton, "The Next American Tea Party," *Bloomberg Businessweek,* January 31, 2011, p. 76; and Judith Crown, "A Wake-Up Call for Coffee," *BusinessWeek,* October 22, 2007, p. 23.

4. "The Future Issue," *Fortune*, January 14, 2013, p. 49; "10 Crucial Consumer Trends for 2013," www.trendwatching.com, January 14, 2013; Brian Steinberg, "Digital Natives Are Restless–Switching

Media 27 Times an Hour," *Advertising Age,* April 9, 2012, p. 1; Christine Birkner, "Marketing in 2012: The End of the Middle," *Marketing News,* January 31, 2012, p. 22; Matt Carmichael, "More Cash for Marketers to Chase as Savings Rate Drops," *Advertising Age,* December 5, 2011, p. 4; Bill Clinton, "The Case for Optimism," *Time,* October 1, 2012, p. 38; "The HBR Agenda," *Harvard Business Review,* January–February 2011, pp. 47–59; Christine Birkner and Piet Levy, "Marketing in 2011," *Marketing News,* January 30, 2011, pp. 16–21; "Predictions 2011," *Bloomberg Businessweek,* January 3, 2011, pp. 14–36; and Thomas Miner, "FTC Releases Revised Green Guides for Public Input," www.sustainablelifemedia.com, October 7, 2010.

5. *2012 World Population Data Sheet* (Washington, DC: Population Reference Bureau, 2010), pp. 2, 5.
6. "GNI per Capita, Atlas Method," *World Development Indicators Database* (Washington DC: World Bank, January 2013); and *World Population Prospects: The 2012 Revision,* Population Aging and Development 2012 (Geneva: United Nations, Department of Economic and Social Affairs, Population Division).
7. Population and Housing Unit Estimates, 2012 National Total Population Estimates, United States Census, www.census.gov, December 20, 2012; Ellen Byron, "How to Market to an Aging Boomer: Flattery, Subterfuge and Euphemism," *The Wall Street Journal,* February 5, 2011, p. A1; "U.S. Census Bureau Projections Show a Slower Growing, Older, More Diverse Nation a Half Century from Now," U.S. Census Bureau, December 12, 2012; and "Projections of the Population by Selected Age Groups and Sex for the United States: 2015 to 2060," U.S. Census Bureau, Table 2, December 2012.
8. Tom Sightings, "How Baby Boomers Will Change the Economy," *USNews.com,* January 15, 2013; "Lay's Unveils 2 New Kettle Cooked Potato Chip Varieties," *Entertainment Close-Up,* July 11, 2012; and Byron, "How to Market to an Aging Boomer, p. A1.
9. Leonard Klie, "Gen X: Stuck in the Middle," *destinationCRM.com,* February 1, 2012; Michele Hammond, "Gen X Pips Boomers to Lead Online Retail Spending," www.startupsmart.com.au, January 10, 2013; Chris Johns, "Hotels for Hipsters," *The Globe and Mail,* November 13, 2012, p. E1; and Piet Levy, "Segmentation by Generation," *Marketing News,* May 15, 2011, p. 20.
10. "Generations X, Y Adopt Smartphones as Media Hubs," *Business Wire,* July 31, 2012; "The Truth about Millennials—Are You Ready for These New Professionals?" *States News Service*, March 30, 2012; "The Millennials Speak, and They Want Their Packaging to Respond Boldly," *Packaging Strategies,* April 30, 2012; Elizabeth Olson, "For Millennials, It's More about Personal Style Than Luxury," *The New York Times,* November 3, 2010, p. 3; Laura Vanderkam, "Graduates, You Can Have It All," *USA Today,* May 27, 2010, p. 11A; Carla Seaquist, "Hope for Reversing America's Decline: the Millennial Generation," *The Christian Science Monitor,* September 24, 2010; Geoff Gloeckler, "Here Come the Millennials," *BusinessWeek,* November 24, 2008, p. 47; Sarah Littman, "Welcome to the New Millennials," *Response,* May 1, 2008, p. 74; "The Echo Boom Gets Louder," *Multi-Housing News,* December 4, 2008; Eileen P. Gunn, "Is Your Company Really Eco-Conscious?" *USNews.com,* October 9, 2008; "Welcome Generation Y," *Management Today,* July 10, 2008; and Eileen P. Gunn, "10 Hot Green Careers for You," *USNews.com,* February 15, 2009.
11. Daphne Lofquist, Terry Lugaila, Martin O'Connell, and Sarah Feliz, "Households and Families," U.S. Census Bureau, April 2012, p. 5; "U.S. Census Bureau Reports Men and Women Wait Longer to Marry," U.S. Census Bureau, released November 10, 2010, revised February 2, 2011; Historical Time Series, U.S. Census Bureau, Table HH-1: Households, by Type: 1940 to Present; Rose M. Kreider, "Increase in Opposite-Sex Cohabiting Couples from 2009 to 2010 in the Annual Social and Economic Supplement (ASEC) to the Current Population Survey (CPS), U.S. Bureau of the Census, September 15, 2010; and "Young Careers Will Carry Scars of Great Recession," *Chattanooga Times Free Press,* November 7, 2010, p. C1.
12. National Marriage and Divorce Rate Trends, National Center for Health Statistics, National Vital Statistics System, January 10, 2012; "Births, Marriages, Divorces, and Deaths: Provisional Data for 2009," National Vital Statistics Reports, August 27, 2010, Table A; Gail Sheehy, "The Gray Divorce," *Harper's Bazaar,* November 1, 2010, p. 189; and Alexandra Montgomery, "U.S. Families 2025: In Search of Future Families," *Futures,* May 2008, p. 377.
13. "Estimates of Resident Population Change for the United States, Regions, States, and Puerto Rico and Region and State Rankings: July 1, 2010, to July 1, 2011 (NST-EST2011-03), U.S. Census Bureau, Population Division, released December 2011.
14. "Pulling Back from the Exurbs," *The New York Times,* April 10, 2012, p. 22; David Peterson and Katie Humphrey, "Reverse Migration: Flight to the Exurbs Stops Cold," *StarTribune.com,* April 12, 2010; and Conor Dougherty, "In the Exurbs, the American Dream Is Up for Rent," *The Wall Street Journal,* March 1, 2009.
15. 2010 Standards for Delineating Metropolitan and Micropolitan Statistical Areas, Office of Management and Budget, *Federal Register* 75, no. 123, June 28, 2010; Update of Statistical Area Definitions and Guidance on Their Uses, OMB Bulletin, No. 10-02, December 1, 2009; and "About Metropolitan and Micropolitan Statistical Areas," U.S. Census Bureau, www.census.gov/population/www/estimates/aboutmetro.html.
16. "2010 Census Shows America's Diversity," U.S. Census Bureau, CB11–CN.125, March 24, 2011; "An Older and More Diverse Nation by Midcentury," Public Information Office, U.S. Census Bureau, Last Revised: February 2, 2011, Table 4: Projections of the Population by Sex, Race, and Hispanic Origin for the United States: 2010 to 2050 (NP2008-T4), Population Division, U.S. Census Bureau, August 14, 2008; and "Mapping Census 2000: The Geography of U.S. Diversity," Population Division, U.S. Census Bureau.
17. "Research: Latino Purchasing Power Now Pegged at $1 Trillion, *Hispanically Speaking News,* May 3, 2011; "Black Buying Power to Reach $1.1 Trillion, Report Finds," *Huffington Post,* November 10, 2011; *State of the Asian American Consumer,* The Nielsen Company, Quarter 3, 2012, p. 14; and "The New Now: Defining the Future Together," *PR Newswire,* February 18, 2011.
18. Laurel Wentz, "Multicultural Agency of the Year: Latinworks," *Advertising Age,* January 28, 2013, p.26; "Our Purpose," LatinWorks website, www.latinworks.com, accessed April 17, 2013; Laurel Wentz, "Retailers Break Out of Multicultural Silo," *Advertising Age,* March 19, 2012, p. 12; Laurel Wentz, "Multicultural Marketing Dollars Flowing to Mobile, Online Video," *Advertising Age,* November 8, 2010, p. 10; and Michael Bush, "Is Cross-Cultural an Industry Breakthrough or Threat to Ethnic Shops?" *Advertising Age,* January 31, 2011, p. 4.
19. Hannah Weinberger, "Where Are All the Millennial Feminists?" *CNN Wire,* November 9, 2012; "Salary Survey 2011: Taking a Lead on Gender Issues," *Marketing Week,* January 13, 2011, p. 17; and "From 18 to 80: Women on Politics and Society," 2008 Women's Monitor Study, *PR Newswire,* August 20, 2008.
20. Elizabeth Sweet, "Guys and Dolls No More?" *The New York Times,* December 23, 2012, p. 12; "Domestic Duties: A Clean Break with Tradition on Home Front," *Marketing Week,* February 24, 2011, p. 22; Patricia Odell, "UGG VP Marketing on Tom Brady's Impact on the Brand," *Chief Marketer,* November 29, 2012; Howard French, "Lego Construction Toys for Girls a Best-seller," *The Associated Press State and Local Wire,* January 5, 2013; and Debra D. Bass,

"Follow Your Nose: Scents Are Subjective, So Feel Free to Ignore the Gender-Specific Labels," *Canwest News Service,* July 12, 2011.

21. Robin M. Williams, Jr., *American Society: A Sociological Interpretation,* 3rd ed. (New York: Knopf, 1970); L. Robert Kohls, "Why Do Americans Act Like That?" International Programs, San Francisco State University; Eric Pooley, David Welch, and Alan Ohnsman, "Charged for Battle," *Bloomberg Businessweek,* January 3, 2011, pp. 48–56; Edwin R. Stafford and Cathy L. Hartman, "Promoting the Value of Sustainably Minded Purchase Behaviors," *Marketing News,* January 2013, p. 28; and Juan Rodriguez, "Selling the Righteous Life," *The Gazette,* September 18, 2010, p. B3.
22. "Consumers Cut Back on Toilet Paper, Pampers, Huggies," *Mish's Global Economic Trend Analysis,* January 14, 2013; Adam Davidson, "New Normal for Post-Recession Consumers," *The International Herald Tribune,* January 5, 2013, p. 8; Michelle Groenke, "Consumers Say 'Show Me the Bargains'," *UPI,* November 22, 2012; Devin Leonard, "The New Abnormal," *Bloomberg Businessweek,* August 2, 2010, p. 50; and Chris Burritt, "Came for the Bargains, Stayed for the Brands," *Bloomberg Businessweek,* August 2, 2010, p. 23–24.
23. "Tuition and Fees and Room and Board Charges over Time in Current Dollars and 2012 Dollars," College Board, http://trends.collegeboard.org/college-pricing/figures-tables/tuition-and-fee-and-room-and-board-charges-over-time-unweighted; and Carmen DeNavas-Walt, Bernadette D. Proctor, and Jessica C. Smith, "Income, Poverty, and Health Insurance Coverage in the United States: 2011," *Current Population Reports* (Washington, DC: U.S. Census Bureau, September 2012).
24. Azhar Iqbal and Mark Vitner, "The Deeper the Recession, the Stronger the Recovery: Is It Really That Simple?" *Business Economics* (2011), pp. 22–31.
25. "Monthly Chart 1: The Index of Consumer Sentiment," Surveys of Consumers (Ann Arbor, MI: Survey Research Center, University of Michigan, June 2012).
26. DeNavas-Walt, Proctor, and Smith, "Income, Poverty and Health Insurance Coverage in the United States: 2011," pp. 6, 31.
27. Betsy Bohlen, Steve Carlotti, and Liz Mihas, "How the Recession Has Changed U.S. Consumer Behavior," *McKinsey Quarterly,* Issue 1 (2010), pp. 17–20; and Mark Trumbull, "In Tough Times, U.S. Consumers Forging New Behaviors," *Christian Science Monitor,* February 3, 2009, p. 25.
28. Tiffany Hsu, "High Prices Lift Consumer Spending: But the Savings Rate Slips in August as Americans Spend More for Food and Gas," *Los Angeles Times,* September 29, 2012, p. 2; "Consumer Expenditure Survey: 2008–2011," U.S. Department of Labor, Bureau of Labor Statistics, April 2013, Table B; and Mark Trumbull, "Consumers Holding Back on Spending," *Christian Science Monitor,* August 4, 2010.
29. Kelli B. Grant, "4 Future Tech Trends," *MarketWatch,* January 15, 2013; Gillian Shaw, "Deloitte Predicts 10 Tech Trends for 2013," *The Vancouver Sun,* January 17, 2013, p. B8; "The Biggest Tech Trends Coming in 2013," *First Digital Media,* January 22, 2013; "5 Important Tech Trends of 2013," *Business2Community.com,* January 8, 2013; "7 Engineering and Tech Trends to Watch in 2013," *Green and Clean,* January 16, 2013; Ullekh NP, "How GE's Over $100 Billion Investment in 'Industrial Internet' Will Add $15 Trillion to World GDP," *The Economic Times,* December 17, 2012; Eric Savitz, "CES: Looking Spiffy in the FaceCake Digital Dressing Room," *Forbes.com,* January 13, 2013; and "CEA's Five Technology Trends to Watch," *Business Wire,* October 18, 2010.
30. Eric Griffith, "The Best Free Software of 2012," *PCMag.com,* April 2, 2012; "Should Carriers End Smartphone Subsidies?" *Trefis,* January 17, 2013; and Koen Pauwels and Allen Weiss, "Moving from Free to Fee: How Online Firms Market to Change Their Business Model Successfully," *Journal of Marketing,* May 2008, pp. 14–31.
31. "CES 2013 and Amazing New Products," *CIOL,* January 15, 2013; "2013 Best New Product Awards, *Better Homes and Gardens,* www.bhg.com, January 2013; and Steven Levy, "The A.I. Revolution," *Wired,* January 2011, p. 88.
32. "2011 Report on Postconsumer PET Container Recycling Activity," National Association for PET Container Resources, October 10, 2012; Paul Fattig, "Big Step, Smaller Footprints," *Mail Tribune,* January 26, 2012; and Becky Ebenkam, "'Precycling' Catches on with Consumers," *Brandweek.com,* August 12, 2008.
33. Marguerite Reardon, "Competitive Wireless Carriers Take on AT&T and Verizon," *CNET News,* September 10, 2012; "Market Share of Subscriptions Held by Wireless Carriers in the U.S. from 1st to 3rd Quarter 2011 and 2012," Chetan Sharma Consulting, *statista.com,* 2013; www.fiercewireless.com/special-reports/grading-top-10-us-carriers-first-quarter-2013; and "Economic Consequences of Armaments Production: Institutional Perspectives of J.K. Galbraith and T.B. Veblen," *Journal of Economic Issues,* March 1, 2008, p. 37.
34. James Kanter, "E.U. Accuses Microsoft of Violating Antitrust Deal," *The International Herald Tribune,* October 25, 2012, p. 17; "Google Wins an Antitrust Battle," *The New York Times,* January 6, 2013, p. 10; and "Microsoft Anti-Trust Ruling: April 3, 2000, No Monopoly," *Dataquest,* December 30, 2010.
35. Michael Porter, *Competitive Advantage* (New York: Free Press, 1985); and Michael Porter, *Competitive Strategy* (New York: Free Press, 1980).
36. Jessica Silver-Greenberg, "New Rules for Money Transfers, but Few Limits," *The New York Times,* www.nytimes.com, June 1, 2012.
37. "Frequently Asked Questions," Small Business Administration, Office of Advocacy, www.sba.gov/advocacy, September 2012; "Small Business Trends," Small Business Administration, www.sba.gov/content/small-business-trends; and Kathryn Kobe, "Small Business GDP: Update 2002–2010," Small Business Administration, Office of Advocacy, January 2012.
38. "One Year Later, SOPA Activists Reignite Copyright Conversation," *CBS News,* January 18, 2013; and "Legal Roundup," *Billboard,* January 31, 2009.
39. "Ben & Jerry's Supports GMO Right-to-Know Labeling Movement," *Business Wire,* January 24, 2013; and Julie Ann Grimm, "Bill Would Require Labeling of Genetically Modified Food," *Las Cruces Sun-News,* January 19, 2013.
40. Dorothy Cohen, "Trademark Strategy Revisited," *Journal of Marketing,* July 1991, pp. 46–59.
41. Matthew Himich, "United States: Madrid Protocol: Is It for You?" *Mondaq Business Briefing,* February 10, 2012; and Madrid System for the International Registration of Marks, World Intellectual Property Organization, http://www.wipo.int/madrid/en/, January 25, 2013.
42. Paul Barrett, "High Court Sees Color as Basis for Trademarks," *The Wall Street Journal,* March 29, 1995, p. A6; Paul Barrett, "Color in the Court," *The Wall Street Journal,* January 5, 1995, p. A1; and David Kelly, "Rainbow of Ideas to Trademark Color," *Advertising Age,* April 24, 1995, pp. 20, 22.
43. Vasilios Peros, "Famous Trademarks: Dilution versus Confusion," *Mondaq,* April 18, 2011; and Maxine L. Retsky, "Dilution of Trademarks Hard to Prove," *Marketing News,* May 12, 2003, p. 6.
44. Dick Mercer, "Tempest in a Soup Can," *Advertising Age,* October 17, 1994, pp. 25–29.
45. Cotton Delo, "You Are Big Brother (But That Isn't So Bad)," *Advertising Age,* April 23, 2012, p. 1; Ana Radelat, "Online Privacy, Postal Hikes Top List of DMA Concerns," *Advertising Age,* April 23, 2012, p. 3; Kate Kaye, "Capitol Hill Focuses on Mobile Privacy with Spate of Actions," *Advertising Age,* December 17, 2012, p. 9; "Twitter to Honor Do Not Track Requests," *Marketing News,* July 31, 2012, p. 7;

"The Internet Browsing Cops," *The Wall Street Journal,* January 21, 2011, p. A12; Edmund Lee, "Government Says Self-Regulation of Online Privacy Is Coming Up Short," *Advertising Age,* December 6, 2010, p. 1; and Julia Angwin and Jennifer Valentino-DeVries, "Web Privacy 'Inadequate,'" *The Wall Street Journal,* December 2, 2010, p. B1.

46. "The New Internet Tax Freedom Act," JD Supra, May 16, 2008.
47. BBB Online Program Standards, http://us.bb.org, accessed January 25, 2013.

Geek Squad: This case was written by Steven Hartley. Sources: Thomas Lee, "Best Buy Stakes Big Share of Its Future on Geek Squad," *San Jose Mercury News,* August 7, 2012; Natalie Zmuda, "Best Buy Gets Back in the Game with New Tagline," *Advertising Age,* June 25, 2012, p. 4; "Best Buy Continues to Diversify by Selling Geek Squad Services," *Trefis,* October 9, 2012; Mike Snider and Edward C. Baig, "Companies Foresee Record Electronics Sales This Year," *USA Today,* January 10, 2011, p. 8A; "3D TV Surpasses HD Sales Success," *Broadcast,* February 25, 2011; "Ford Working with Best Buy to Offer Focus Electric Charging Station Sales and Support," *ENP Newswire,* January 10, 2011; Mary Ellen Lloyd, "Camp Teaches Power of Geekdom," *The Wall Street Journal,* July 11, 2007; Dean Foust, Michael Mandel, Frederick F. Jespersen, and David Henry, "The Business Week 50—The Best Performers," *BusinessWeek,* March 26, 2007, p. 58; Jessica E. Vascellaro, "What's a Cellphone For? Businesses Are Finding All Sorts of New Uses for Mobile Devices," *The Wall Street Journal,* March 26, 2007, p. R5; Cade Metz, "Just How Stupid Are You? Geek Squad War Stories," *PC Magazine,* February 1, 2006; Brad Stone, "Lore of the Geek Squad," *Newsweek,* February 20, 2006, p. 44; Michelle Conlin, "Smashing the Clock," *BusinessWeek,* December 11, 2006, p. 60; "Best Buy: How to Break Out of Commodity Hell," *BusinessWeek,* March 27, 2006, p. 76; Pallavi Gogoi, "Meet Jane Geek," *BusinessWeek,* November 28, 2005, p. 94; Desiree J. Hanford, "Geek Squad Is Popular at Best Buy," *The Wall Street Journal,* December 14, 2005, p. 1; Michelle Higgins, "Getting Your Own IT Department," *The Wall Street Journal,* May 20, 2004, p. D1; and information contained on the Geek Squad website (www.geeksquad.com).

Chapter 4

1. www.anheuser-busch.com, downloaded June 20, 2013; "Anheuser-Busch 2012 Corporate Social Responsibility Report," www.anheuser-busch.com, downloaded February 15, 2013; and "America's Most Admired Companies," *Fortune,* March 17, 2012, p. 38.
2. For a discussion of the definition of ethics, see Patrick E. Murphy, Gene R. Laezniak, Norman E. Bowie, and Thomas A. Klein, *Ethical Marketing: Basic Ethics in Action* (Upper Saddle River, NJ: Prentice Hall, 2005).
3. Verne E. Henderson, "The Ethical Side of Enterprise," *Sloan Management Review,* Spring 1982, pp. 37–47. See also, Joseph L. Badaracco, Jr., *Defining Moments: When Managers Must Choose between Right and Right* (Boston: Harvard Business School Press, 1997).
4. "Honorable?" *Business 2.0,* February 2000, p. 92.
5. Roger O. Crockett, "Hauling in the Hollywood Hackers," *Businessweek,* May 15, 2006, pp. 80–82; "Exporting Death," *Time,* April 13, 1998, p. 63; Ray O. Werner, "Marketing and the Supreme Court in Transition, 1982–1984," *Journal of Marketing,* Summer 1985, pp. 97–105; and Jane Bryant Quinn, "Computer Program Deceives Consumers," *Dallas Morning News,* March 2, 1998, p. B3.
6. *The 2011 National Business Ethics Survey* (Washington, DC: Ethics Resource Center, 2012); and "Congress Retains Low Honesty Rating," www.gallup.com, December 3, 2012.
7. See, for example, Linda K. Trevino and Katherine A. Nelson, *Managing Business Ethics: Straight Talk about How to Get It Right,* 5th ed. (New York: John Wiley & Sons, 2011).
8. Thomas Donaldson, "Values in Tension: Ethics Away from Home," *Harvard Business Review,* September–October 1996, pp. 48–62.
9. Ethisphere Institute, "2012 World's Most Ethical Companies," www.ethisphere.com, accessed January 3, 2013.
10. These statistics were obtained from Recording Industry Association of America (www.riaa.com), Motion Picture Association of America (www.mpaa.com), and the Business Software Alliance (www.bsa.org).
11. June Jamich Parsons and Dan Oja, *Computer Concepts 2010* (Florence, KY: Cengage Publishing, 2009), p. 171.
12. Vern Terpstra and Kenneth David, *The Cultural Environment of International Business,* 3rd ed. (Cincinnati: South-Western Publishing, 1991), p. 12.
13. Hukari Kane, "Recall Shows Battery Limits," *The Wall Street Journal,* August 18, 2006, p. A13; and "Dell Announces Recall of Notebook Computer Batteries Due to Fire Hazard," U.S. Consumer Product Safety Commission press release, August 15, 2006.
14. "Child Web Privacy Law Gets Updated," *The Wall Street Journal,* December 20, 2012, pp. B1, B2; and Timothy Muris, "Protecting Consumers' Privacy," www.ftc.gov, downloaded January 3, 2005.
15. For an extensive examination of slotting fees, see Paul N. Bloom, Gregory T. Gundlach, and Joseph P. Cannon, "Slotting Allowances and Fees: Schools of Thought and Views of Practicing Managers," *Journal of Marketing,* April 2000, pp. 92–109. Also see, K. Sudhir and Vithala R. Rao, "Do Slotting Allowances Enhance Efficiency or Hinder Competition?" *Journal of Marketing Research* (May 2006), pp. 137–55.
16. Hedich Nasheri, *Economic Espionage and Industrial Spying* (Cambridge: Cambridge University Press, 2005).
17. "Coke Employee Faces Charges in Plot to Sell Secrets," *The Wall Street Journal,* July 6, 2006, p. B6; "Do the Right Thing? Not with a Rival's Inside Info," *Advertising Age,* July 17, 2006, p. 4; and "You Can't Beat the Real Thing," *Time,* July 17, 2006, pp. 10–11.
18. www.transparency.org, downloaded January 20, 2013.
19. "Interview with Michael A. Monts, UTC Vice President, Business Practices, on Ethics at UTC," United Technologies Corporation press release, July 26, 2011; and Trevino and Nelson, *Managing Business Ethics.*
20. "Coca-Cola Unit Head Resigns after Rigged Test," www.forbes.com, downloaded August 25, 2003.
21. *The 2011 National Business Ethics Survey.*
22. *The 2011 National Business Ethics Survey;* and "Critics Blow Whistle on Law," *The Wall Street Journal,* November 1, 2010, pp. B1, B11.
23. "Scotchgard Working Out Recent Stain on Its Business," www.mercurynews.com, downloaded June 22, 2003.
24. James Q. Wilson, "Adam Smith on Business Ethics," *California Management Review,* Fall 1989, pp. 57–72.
25. Alix M. Freedman, "Bad Reaction: Nestlé's Bid to Crash Baby-Formula Market in U.S. Stirs a Row," *The Wall Street Journal,* February 16, 1989, pp. A1, A6; and Alix Freedman, "Nestlé to Drop Claim on Label of Its Formula," *The Wall Street Journal,* March 13, 1989, p. B5.
26. Harvey S. James and Farhad Rassekh, "Smith, Friedman, and Self-Interest in Ethical Society," *Business Ethics Quarterly,* July 2000, pp. 659–74.
27. "When a Drug Costs $300,000," www.nytimes.com, March 23, 2008; and "Cost of Living," *The Economist,* March 1, 2003, p. 60.
28. "Perrier—Overresponding to a Crisis," in Robert F. Hartley, *Marketing Mistakes and Successes,* 10th ed. (New York: John Wiley & Sons, 2006), pp. 119–30.
29. Michael Connor, "Toyota Recall: Five Critical Lessons," www.business_ethics.com, January 31, 2010.
30. Andrew W. Savitz with Karl Weber, *The Triple Bottom Line: How Today's Best Run Companies Are Achieving Economic, Social and Environmental Success* (San Francisco, CA: Josey Bass, 2006).

31. 3M 2012 Sustainability Report, downloaded May 25, 2012; "Levi's Has a New Color for Blue Jeans: Green," *Businessweek,* October 22–October 28, 2012, pp. 26, 28; and "Walmart 2012 Global Sustainability Report," www.walmart.com downloaded January 30, 2013.

32. *The ISO Survey of Management System Standard Classifications—2011* (Geneva, Switzerland: International Organization for Standardization, 2012).

33. For a seminal discussion on this topic, see P. Rajan Varadarajan and Anil Menon, "Cause-Related Marketing: A Coalignment of Marketing Strategy and Corporate Philanthropy," *Journal of Marketing*, July 1988, pp. 58–74.

34. "Even as Cause Marketing Grows, 83 Percent of Consumers Still Want to See More," press release, Cone LLC, September 15, 2010; and Larry Chiagouris and Ipshita Ray, "Saving the World with Cause-Related Marketing," *Marketing Management,* July–August 2007, pp. 48–51.

35. These steps are adapted from J. J. Corson and G. A. Steiner, *Measuring Business's Social Performance: The Corporate Social Audit* (New York: Committee for Economic Development, 1974). See also Risako Morinoto, John Ash, and Chris Hope, "Corporate Social Responsibility Audit: From Theory to Practice," *Journal of Business Ethics* (December 2005), pp. 315–25; and William B. Werther, Jr., and David Chandler, *Strategic Corporate Social Responsibility* (Thousand Oaks, CA: Sage Publications, Inc., 2006).

36. Unmesh Kher, "Getting Smart at Being Good . . . Are Companies Better Off for It?" *Time,* January 2006, pp. A1–A37; and Pete Engardio, "Beyond the Green Corporation," *Businessweek,* January 29, 2007, pp. 50–64.

37. "Economics—Creating Environmental Capital," *The Wall Street Journal,* March 24, 2008, Section R; Remi Trudel and June Cotte, "Does Being Ethical Pay?" *The Wall Street Journal,* May 12, 2008, p. R4; and Pete Engardio, "Beyond the Green Corporation," *Businessweek,* January 29, 2007, pp. 50–64.

38. This discussion is based on Wayne D. Hoyer, Deborah J. MacInnis, and Rik Pieters, *Consumer Behavior,* 6th ed. (New York: Houghton Mifflin Company, 2013), pp. 535–37; "Retail Group: 'Return Fraud' Costs $9B a Year," USAToday.com, December 11, 2012; and www.shopliftingprevention.org, downloaded January 7, 2013.

39. "A Pirate and His Penance," *Time,* January 26, 2004, p. 60; and Crockett, "Hauling in the Hollywood Hackers."

40. Jack Neff, "As More Marketers Go Green, Fewer Consumers Willing to Pay for It," *Advertising Age,* September 24, 2012, p. 6; and Jack Neff, "Has Green Stopped Giving?" *Advertising Age,* November 8, 2010, pp. 1, 19.

41. "Misleading Claims on 'Green' Labeling," *The Wall Street Journal,* October 26, 2010, p. D4.

42. Jack Neff, "FTC Green Guidelines May Leave Marketers Red-Faced," *Advertising Age,* August 23, 2010, pp. 1, 21.

Toyota Inc.: This case was written by Steven Hartley. Sources: "Global 500: The World's Largest Corporations," *Fortune,* July 23, 2012, p. F-1; *2010 North America Environmental Report,* Toyota Motor North America, Inc., p. 1; "Toyota's Mobile Hybrid Tour and The Power of Partnership," Presentation by Mary Nickerson, National Marketing Manager, Toyota Motor sales, U.S.A., Inc.; Toyota web site, http://www.toyota.com/sitemap.html, accessed July 6, 2013; "Lexus Seeks To Regain Luxury Crown with New Advertisement," *AutoShopper.com,* June 28, 2013; Tim Higgins, "Luxury Cars Are Neck and Neck in the U.S.," Bloomberg *BusinessWeek,* October 18, 20 10, p. 26; Lucy Tobin, "Recall Tarnishes Toyota's Reputation, *The Evening Standard,* July 3,2013, p. 45; and Mark Rechtin, "Toyota Reputation Starts to Recover," *Advertising Age,* January 24, 2011, p. 34.

Chapter 5

1. "Car-Buying Tips Men Can Learn from Women," www.leasetrader.com, January 30, 2012; Jerry Hirsh, "Car Buying: How Men and Women Compare," www.latimes.com, April 7, 2011; "What Matters the Most When People Buy Cars," *BrandWeek,* October 11, 2010, p. 23; "Gender Wars and Car Shopping: Men Want Power, Women Want Cloth Seats," www.autos.aol.com, July 16, 2010; and Michael J. Silverstein and Kate Sayre, "The Female Economy," *Harvard Business Review,* September 2009, pp. 46–53.

2. Roger D. Blackwell, Paul W. Miniard, and James F. Engel, *Consumer Behavior,* 10th ed. (Mason, OH: South-Western Publishing, 2006).

3. For thorough descriptions of consumer expertise, see Joseph W. Alba and J. Wesley Hutchinson, "Knowledge Calibration: What Consumers Know and What They Think They Know," *Journal of Consumer Research,* September 2000, pp. 123–57.

4. For in-depth studies on external information search patterns, see Brian T. Ratchford, Debabrata Talukdar, and Myung-Soo Lee, "The Impact of the Internet on Consumers' Use of Information Sources for Automobiles: A Re-Inquiry," *Journal of Consumer Research,* June 2007, pp. 111–19; Joel E. Urbany, Peter R. Dickson, and William L. Wilkie, "Buyer Uncertainty and Information Search," *Journal of Consumer Research,* March 1992, pp. 452–63; and Sharon E. Beatty and Scott M. Smith, "External Search Effort: An Investigation across Several Product Categories," *Journal of Consumer Research,* June 1987, pp. 83–95.

5. "Ratings: Smart Phones," *Consumer Reports,* January 2013, p. 39.

6. For an extended discussion on evaluative criteria, see Delbert I. Hawkins, David L. Mothersbaugh, and Roger Best, *Consumer Behavior: Building Marketing Strategy,* 12th ed. (Burr Ridge, IL: McGraw-Hill/Irwin, 2013).

7. John A. Howard, *Buyer Behavior in Marketing Strategy,* 2nd ed. (Englewood Cliffs, NJ: Prentice Hall, 1994). For an extended discussion on consumer choice sets, see Allan D. Shocker, Moshe Ben-Akiva, Brun Boccara, and Prakesh Nedungadi, "Consideration Set Influences on Consumer Decision Making and Choice: Issues, Models, and Suggestions," *Marketing Letters,* August 1991, pp. 181–98.

8. Robert J. Donovan, John R. Rossiter, Gillian Marcoolyn, and Andrew Nesdale, "Store Atmosphere and Purchasing Behavior," *Journal of Retailing,* Fall 1994, pp. 283–94; and Eric A. Greenleaf and Donald R. Lehmann, "Reasons for Substantial Delay in Consumer Decision Making," *Journal of Consumer Research,* September 1995, pp. 186–99.

9. "Phone-Wielding Shoppers Strike Fear into Retailers," *The Wall Street Journal,* December 16, 2010, pp. A1, A9.

10. Sunil Gupta and Valarie Zeithaml, "Customer Metrics and Their Impact on Financial Performance," *Marketing Science,* November–December 2006, pp. 718–39.

11. These estimates are given in Jagdish N. Sheth and Banwari Mitral, *Consumer Behavior,* 2nd ed. (Mason, OH: South-Western Publishing, 2003), p. 32.

12. For an in-depth examination of this topic, see Sunil Gupta and Donald R. Lehmann, *Managing Customers as Investments* (Upper Saddle River, NJ: Pearson Education, Inc., 2005).

13. For an overview of research on involvement, see Wayne D. Hoyer, Deborah J. MacInnis, and Rik Pieters, *Consumer Behavior,* 6th ed. (Florence, KY: South-Western Education Publishing, 2013).

14. Russell Belk, "Situational Variables and Consumer Behavior," *Journal of Consumer Research,* December 1975, pp. 157–63. The examples in this section are taken from Martin Lindstrom, *buy.ology: Truth and Lies about Why We Buy* (New York: Doubleday Publishing, 2008).

15. A. H. Maslow, *Motivation and Personality* (New York: Harper & Row, 1970). Also see Richard Yalch and Frederic Brunel, "Need Hierarchies in Consumer Judgments of Product Design: Is It Time to Reconsider Maslow's Hierarchy?" in Kim Corfman and John Lynch, eds., *Advances in Consumer Research* (Provo, UT: Association for Consumer Research, 1996), pp. 405–10.
16. Bernardo J. Carducci, *The Psychology of Personality,* 2nd ed. (Oxford, UK: John Wiley & Sons, 2009), pp. 182–84.
17. Jane Spencer, "Lenovo Puts Style in New Laptop," *The Wall Street Journal,* January 3, 2008, p. B5.
18. This example is provided in Michael R. Solomon, *Consumer Behavior,* 4th ed. (Upper Saddle River, NJ: Prentice Hall, 1999), p. 59.
19. For further reading on subliminal perception, see Lindstrom, *buy.ology;* B. Bahrami, N. Lavie, and G. Rees, "Attentional Load Modulates Responses of Human Primary Visual Cortex to Invisible Stimuli," *Current Biology,* March 2007, pp. 39–47; and J. Karremans, W. Stroebe, and J. Claus, "Beyond Vicary's Fantasies: The Impact of Subliminal Priming and Brand Choice," *Journal of Experimental Social Psychology* 42 (2006), pp. 792–98.
20. August Bullock, *The Secret Sales Pitch* (San Jose, CA: Norwich Publishers, 2004); and Dave Lakhani, *Subliminal Persuasion* (Hoboken, NJ: John Wiley & Sons, 2008).
21. Steve Olenski, "Is Brand Loyalty Dying a Slow and Painful Death?" www.forbes.com, January 7, 2013; and Sholnn Freeman, "Brand Breakdown," *The Washington Post,* March 26, 2006, p. F1ff.
22. Martin Fishbein and I. Aizen, *Belief, Attitude, Intention and Behavior: An Introduction to Theory and Research* (Reading, MA: Addison-Wesley, 1975), p. 6.
23. Richard J. Lutz, "Changing Brand Attitudes through Modification of Cognitive Structure," *Journal of Consumer Research,* March 1975, pp. 49–59.
24. This discussion is based on "The VALS™ Types," www.strategicbusinessinsights.com, downloaded February 1, 2013.
25. This discussion is based on Ed Keller and Jon Berry, *The Influentials* (New York: Simon and Schuster, 2003).
26. Ed Keller and Brad Fay, "Word-of-Mouth Advocacy: A New Key to Advertising Effectiveness," *Journal of Advertising Research,* December 2012, pp. 459–64.
27. Emanuel Rosen, *The Anatomy of Buzz Revisited* (New York: Crown Business, 2009).
28. www.bzzAgent.com, downloaded January 10, 2013; and Laura Burkett, "Word-of-Mouth Marketing Evolution" www.forbes.com, May 21, 2009.
29. Emanuel Rosen, "Conversation Starter," *BrandWeek,* April 12, 2010, p. 16.
30. Hoyer, MacInnis, and Pieters, *Consumer Behavior.*
31. Elizabeth Holmes, "Abercrombie and Fitch Offers to Pay 'The Situation' to Stop Wearing Its Clothes," *The Wall Street Journal,* August 16, 2011, p. B2.
32. For an extensive review on consumer socialization of children, see Deborah Roedder John, "Consumer Socialization of Children: A Retrospective Look at Twenty-Five Years of Research," *Journal of Consumer Research,* December 1999, pp. 183–213. Also see, Gwen Bachmann Achenreinver and Deborah Roedder John, "The Meaning of Brand Names to Children: A Developmental Investigation," *Journal of Consumer Psychology* 13, no. 3 (2003), pp. 205–19; and Elizabeth S. Moore, William L. Wilkie, and Richard J. Lutz, "Passing the Torch: Intergenerational Influences as a Source of Brand Equity," *Journal of Marketing,* April 2002, pp. 17–37.
33. J. Paul Peter and Jerry C. Olson, *Consumer Behavior and Marketing Strategy,* 9th ed. (Burr Ridge, IL: McGraw-Hill/Irwin, 2010); "Grocers Catering More to Men" *Dallas Morning News,* January 13, 2013, p. 3D; "Who Makes the Call at the Mall, Men or Women?" *The Wall Street Journal,* April 23–24, 2011, p. A1; and Rich Morin and D'Vera Cohn, "Women Call the Shots at Home: Public Mixed on Gender Roles in Jobs," www.pewresearch.org, downloaded February 4, 2011. Also see, Rex Y. Du and Wagner A. Kamakura, "Household Life Cycles and Lifestyles in the United States," *Journal of Marketing Research,* February 2006, pp. 121–32.
34. This discussion is based on Hawkins, Mothersbaugh, and Best, *Consumer Behavior: Building Marketing Strategy*; Jack Neff, "Time to Rethink Your Message: Now the Cart Belongs to Daddy," *Advertising Age*, January 17, 2011, pp. 1, 20; *The Kids and Tweens Market in the U.S.*, 9th ed. (Rockville, MD: Packaged Facts, August 1, 2008); and "How Teens Use Media" (New York: Neilsen Company, June 2009).
35. Harold R. Kerbo, *Social Stratification and Inequality* (Burr Ridge, IL: McGraw-Hill, 2000). For an extensive discussion on social class, see Eric Arnould, Linda Price, and George Zinkhan, *Consumers,* 2nd ed. (Burr Ridge, IL: McGraw-Hill/Irwin, 2004).
36. Jeffrey M. Humphreys, "The Multicultural Economy in 2012," Selig Center for Economic Growth, Terry College of Business, The University of Georgia, p. 7.
37. The remainder of this discussion is based on Hoyer, MacInnis, and Pieters, *Consumer Behavior*; "The Lust for Latino Lucre," *The Economist*, May 11, 2013, p. 71; and *The State of Hispanic Consumer: Hispanic Market Imperative* (New York: The Nielsen Company, 2012); and *10th Annual Hispanic Fact Pack* (New York: Advertising Age, 2013).
38. The remainder of this discussion is based on Peter and Olson, *Consumer Behavior and Marketing Strategy;* and *The State of the African-American Consumer: Still Vital, Still Growing* (New York: The Nielsen Company, 2012).
39. The remainder of this discussion is based on *The State of the Asian American Consumer: Growing Market, Growing Impact* (New York: The Nielsen Company, 2012); Christine Birkner, "Asian-Americans in Focus," *Marketing News*, March 2013, p. 14; and Lee Siegel, "Rise of the Tiger Nation," *The Wall Street Journal,* October 27–28, 2012, pp. C1, C2.

Groupon: This case was written by Steven Hartley. Sources: Bari Weiss, "The Journal Interview with Andrew Mason: Groupon's $6 Billion Gambler," *Wall Street Journal,* December 20, 2010, p. 12; Brad Stone and Douglas MacMillan, "Are Four Words Worth $25 Billion?" *Bloomberg Businessweek,* March 21, 2011, pp. 70–75; Brendan Coffey, "What's The Deal?" *Forbes,* April 25, 2011, pp. 20–22; Brad Stone and Douglas MacMillan, "Groupon's $6 Billion Snub," *Bloomberg Businessweek,* December 13, 2010, pp. 6–7; Christopher Steiner, "Meet the Fastest Growing Company Ever," *Forbes,* August 30, 2010; Rupal Parekh, "Groupon," *Advertising Age,* November 15, 2010, p. 20; "10 Big Stories for the Week," *Advertising Age,* December 13, 2010, pp. 12–13; Jessi Hempel, "Social Media Meets Retailing," *Fortune,* March 22, 2010, p. 30; Kunur Patel, "Suddenly, Everyone Wants to be Groupon," *Advertising Age,* November 1, 2010, p. 1; Brad Stone, "Coupon Deathmatch, Party of Two?" *Bloomberg Businessweek,* October 4, 2010, pp. 37–38; "Q1 2013 Fact Sheet," and "2012 Letter to Shareholders," on Groupon website, http://investor.groupon.com/, accessed July 8, 2013.

Chapter 6

1. Interview with Kim Nagele, JCPenney, February 1, 2013.
2. International Business Machines Form 10-K, for the period ending December 31, 2011, February 17, 2012.
3. Figures reported in this discussion are found in *Statistical Abstract of the United States: 2013,* 132nd ed. (Washington, DC: U.S. Census Bureau, 2013).

4. "NASA Needs More Money for Lockheed Martin's Orion," *Denver Business Journal,* January 16, 2011.
5. Aleda V. Roth, Andy A. Tay, Madeleine E. Pullman, and John V. Gray, "Reaping What You Sow?" *International Commerce Review,* Autumn 2008, pp. 37–47.
6. "2012 North American Industry Classification System," www.census.gov/eos/www/naics.
7. This list of characteristics and portions of the discussion in this section are based on F. Robert Dwyer and John F. Tanner, Jr., *Business Marketing,* 4th ed. (Burr Ridge, IL: McGraw-Hill/Irwin, 2009); and Michael D. Hutt and Thomas W. Speh, *Business Marketing Management: B2B,* 11th ed. (Mason, OH: South-Western, 2012).
8. "Siemens Receives Contract for High-Efficiency Power Plant in the United States," Siemens USA press release, July 18, 2012.
9. www.at&t.com, downloaded February 25, 2013.
10. Hutt and Speh, *Business Marketing Management: B2B.*
11. For an overview on ISO 9000 certification, see Thomas H. Stevenson and Frank C. Barnes, "What Industrial Marketers Need to Know about ISO 9000 Certification: A Review, Update, and Integration with Marketing," *Industrial Marketing Management,* November 2002, pp. 695–703.
12. This example is found in Sandy D. Jap and Jakki J. Mohr, "Leveraging Internet Technologies in B2B Relationships," *California Management Review,* Summer 2002, pp. 24–38.
13. "IBM's 'Sequoia' Unseats Fujitsu; Tops the List as Fastest Supercomputer," www.washingtonpost.com, June 6, 2012.
14. "HP Finalizes $3 Billion Outsourcing Agreement to Manage Procter & Gamble's IT Infrastructure," Hewlett-Packard news release, May 6, 2003.
15. "About Us," www.milsco.com, downloaded January 25, 2013; and "Milsco Manufacturing: Easy Rider," *Industry Today,* February 2010, pp. 86–87.
16. Helen Walker and Wendy Phillips, "Sustainable Procurement: Emerging Issues," *International Journal of Procurement Management,* 2, no. 1 (2009), pp. 41–61.
17. Thomas V. Bonoma, "Major Sales: Who Really Does the Buying?" *Harvard Business Review,* May–June 1982, pp. 11–19. Also see, Philip L. Dawes, Don Y. Lee, and Grahame R. Dowling, "Information Control and Influence in Emerging Buying Centers," *Journal of Marketing,* July 1998, pp. 55–68; and Thomas Tellefsen, "Antecedents and Consequences of Buying Center Leadership: An Emergent Perspective," *Journal of Business-to-Business Marketing,* 13, no. 1 (2006), pp. 53–59.
18. These definitions are adapted from Frederick E. Webster, Jr., and Yoram Wind, *Organizational Buying Behavior* (Englewood Cliffs, NJ: Prentice Hall, 1972), p. 6.
19. "Can Corning Find Its Optic Nerve?" *Fortune,* March 19, 2001, pp. 148–50.
20. Jeffrey E. Lewin and Naveen Donthu, "The Influence of Purchase Situation on Buying Center Structure and Involvement: A Select Meta-Analysis of Organizational Buying Behavior Research," *Journal of Business Research,* October 2005, 1381–90. Representative studies on the buy-class framework that document its usefulness include Erin Anderson, Wujin Chu, and Barton Weitz, "Industrial Purchasing: An Empirical Exploration of the Buy-Class Framework," *Journal of Marketing,* July 1987, pp. 71–86; and Thomas W. Leigh and Arno J. Ethans, "A Script-Theoretic Analysis of Industrial Purchasing Behavior," *Journal of Marketing,* Fall 1984, pp. 22–32. Studies not supporting the buy-class framework include Donald W. Jackson, Janet E. Keith, and Richard K. Burdick, "Purchasing Agents' Perceptions of Industrial Buying Center Influences: A Situational Approach," *Journal of Marketing,* Fall 1984, pp. 75–83; R. Vekatesh, Ajay Kohli, and Gerald Zaltman, "Influence Strategies in Buying Centers," *Journal of Marketing,* October 1995, pp. 61–72; Gary L. Lilien and Anthony Wong, "An Exploratory Investigation of the Structure of the Buying Center in the Metal Working Industry," *Journal of Marketing Research,* February 1984, pp. 1–11; and Wesley J. Johnston and Thomas V. Bonoma, "The Buying Center: Structure and Interaction Patterns," *Journal of Marketing,* Summer 1981, pp. 143–56.
21. *Global Machine Vision and Vision Guided Robotics Market: 2011–2015* (Elmhurst, IL: Infiniti Research, Inc., 2011).
22. "Machine Vision Looks Well Beyond Inspection," *Packaging Digest,* August 2005, pp. 32–35.
23. This discussion is based on "W. W. Grainger Budgets $40 Million for Online Growth," www.InternetRetailer.com, March 12, 2012; "B2B, Take 2," *Business Week Online,* November 25, 2005; and Jennifer Reinhold, "What We Learned in the New Economy," *Fast Company,* March 4, 2004, pp. 56ff.
24. "Meet the eBay Millionaires," www.huffingtonpost.com, August 4, 2011; "Former eBay CEO Urges Action on Small Business," www.washingtonpost.com, June 11, 2008; "New Study Reveals 724,000 Americans Rely on eBay Sales for Income," eBay press release, July 21, 2005; Robyn Greenspan, "Net Drives Profits to Small Biz," www.clickz.com, downloaded March 25, 2006; and "eBay Realizes Success in Small-Biz Arena," *Marketing News,* May 1, 2004, p. 11.
25. This discussion is based on Robert J. Dolan and Youngme Moon, "Pricing and Market Making on the Internet," *Journal of Interactive Marketing,* Spring 2000, pp. 56–73; and Ajit Kambil and Eric van Heck, *Making Markets: How Firms Can Benefit from Online Auctions and Exchanges* (Boston: Harvard Business School Press, 2002).
26. Susan Avery, "Supply Management Is Core of Success at UTC," *Purchasing,* September 7, 2006, pp. 36–39.
27. Shawn P. Daley and Prithwiraz Nath, "Reverse Auctions for Relationship Marketers," *Industrial Marketing Management,* February 2005, pp. 157–66; and Sandy Jap, "The Impact of Online Reverse Auction Design on Buyer–Seller Relationships," *Journal of Marketing,* January 2007, pp. 146–59.

Trek: This case was written by Steven Hartley. Sources: "Trek Bicycle Corporation," Hoovers, 2011; "Alliance Data Signs Long-Term Extension Agreement with Trek Bicycle Corporation," *PR Newswire,* November 22, 2010; Lou Massante, "Trek Bicycle Buys Villiger, A Leader in the Swiss Market," *Bicycle Retailer & Industry News,* January 1, 2003, p. 10; "Trek Bicycle Corporation," Wikipedia, accessed September 4, 2011; and Trek website, http://www.trekbikes.com/us/en/company/believe, accessed September 4, 2011.

Chapter 7

1. Dell's Next Big Agenda," www.crn.in, February 21, 2012; Dell India Opens Its Exclusive Store in Hyderabad, www.greatandhra.com, September 12, 2012; "How Dell Conquered India," www.CNNMoney.com, February 10, 2011; and "Dell Plans to Up Focus on India Biz," www.AdAge.com, October 24, 2008.
2. "International Trade Statistics: 2012" (Geneva: World Trade Organization, 2013). Global trade statistics in this chapter come from this source, unless otherwise indicated.
3. "World Trade Follows New Rules: First of Four Parts," www.Annapolisinstitute.net, May 23, 2011.
4. "Export Shift Turns Rivals into Allies," *The Wall Street Journal,* February 12–13, 2011, p. A3.
5. Michael E. Porter, *The Competitive Advantage of Nations* (New York: Free Press, 1990), pp. 577–615. For another view that emphasizes cultural differences, see David S. Landes, *The Wealth and Poverty of Nations* (New York: Norton, 1998).
6. "Industrial Espionage: Data Out the Door," *Financial Times,* February 1, 2011, p. 8; and "FBI's New Campaign Targets Corporate Espionage," *The Wall Street Journal,* May 11, 2012, p. B4.

7. Dennis R. Appleyard and Alfred J. Field, *International Economics,* 8th ed. (Burr Ridge, IL: McGraw-Hill/Irwin, 2013), Chapter 15; Tansa Mesa, "Africa and Carribbean Fear EU Latam Banana Tariff Cuts," *International Herald Tribune,* August 26, 2008, p. 8; Yuri Kageyama, "Selling Rice to Japan? U.S. Plans to Try," www.msnbc.com, March 7, 2004; "A Shoe Tariff with a Big Footprint," *The Wall Street Journal,* November 23, 2012, p. A13; and *Economic Report of the President* (Washington, DC: U.S. Government Printing Office, 2012).

8. This discussion is based on information provided by the World Trade Organization, www.wto.org, downloaded February 10, 2013.

9. This discussion on the European Union is based on information provided at www.europa.eu, downloaded March 5, 2013.

10. This discussion is based on "Probable Effect of Certain Modifications to the North American Free Trade Agreement Rules of Origin" (Washington, DC: U.S. International Trade Commission, 2006); and "Target Is Going Abroad to Canada," *The Wall Street Journal,* January 14, 2011, pp. B1, B2.

11. For an overview of different types of global companies and marketing strategies, see, for example, Masaaki Kotabe and Kristiaan Helsen, *Global Marketing Management,* 5th ed. (New York: Wiley, 2011), p. 221; Warren J. Keegan and Mark C. Green, *Global Marketing,* 4th ed. (Upper Saddle River, NJ: Prentice Hall, 2005); and Michael Czinkota and Ilkka A. Ronkainen, *International Marketing,* 10th ed. (Mason, OH: South-Western, 2013).

12. Johnny K. Johansson and Ilkka A. Ronkainen, "The Brand Challenge," *Marketing Management,* March–April 2004, pp. 54–55.

13. Kevin Lane Keller, *Strategic Brand Management,* 4th ed. (Upper Saddle River, NJ: Prentice Hall, 2008); and Michael Fielding, "Global Brands Need Balance of Identity, Cultural Respect," *Marketing News,* September 1, 2006, pp. 8–10.

14. "Coca-Cola, Nike and Adidas Top Brands for Teens Globally, TRU Study Finds," www.teenresearch.com, March 2, 2009; "Global Habbo Youth Survey," marketinginsight@sulake.com, downloaded March 20, 2009; www.mtv.com/company, downloaded January 10, 2011; Bay Fong, "Spending Spree," *U.S. News & World Report,* May 1, 2006, pp. 42–50; and "Burgeoning Bourgeoisie," *The Economist,* February 14, 2009. Special report on the new middle classes.

15. "The Pocket World in Figures: 2013 Edition," *The Economist.*

16. For comprehensive references on cross-cultural aspects of marketing, see Paul A. Herbig, *Handbook of Cross-Cultural Marketing* (New York: Halworth Press, 1998); Jean Claude Usunier, *Marketing Across Cultures,* 4th ed. (London: Prentice Hall Europe, 2005); and Philip K. Cateora, Mary Gilly, and John L. Graham, *International Marketing,* 16th ed. (Burr Ridge, IL: McGraw-Hill/Irwin, 2013). Unless otherwise indicated, examples found in this section appear in these excellent sources.

17. "Bribery Law Dos and Don'ts," *The Wall Street Journal,* November 15, 2012, pp. B1, B2.

18. These examples appear in Del I. Hawkins and David L. Mothersbaugh, *Consumer Behavior,* 10th ed. (Burr Ridge, IL: McGraw-Hill/Irwin, 2010), Chapter 2.

19. "Greeks Protest Coke's Use of Parthenon," *Dallas Morning News,* August 17, 1992, p. D4.

20. "Attaching Importance to 'Made in America'," *BrandWeek,* October 4, 2010, p. 17; "Some Will Not Be Eager to Buy 'Made in USA'," *AdweekMedia,* January 19, 2009, p. 14; and Cateora, Gilly, and Graham, *International Marketing.*

21. "How Did Kit Kat Become King of Candy in Japan?" www.cnnmoney.com, February 2, 2012.

22. Terence A. Shimp and Subhash Sharma, "Consumer Ethnocentrism: Construction and Validation of the CETSCALE," *Journal of Marketing Research,* August 1987, pp. 280–89.

23. Representative research on consumer ethnocentrism includes: Srinivas Durvasula, J. Craig Andrews, and Richard G. Netemeyer, "A Cross-Cultural Comparison of Consumer Ethnocentrism in the United States and Russia," *Journal of International Consumer Marketing* 9, no. 4 (1997), pp. 73–93; Hyokjin Kwak, Anupam Jaju, and Trina Larsen, "Consumer Ethnocentrism Offline and Online: The Mediating Role of Marketing Efforts and Personality Traits in the United States, South Korea, and India," *Journal of the Academy of Marketing Science* 34 (2006), pp. 367–85; and Heiner Evanschitzky, et al., "Consumer Ethnocentrism in the German Market," *International Marketing Review* 25, no. 1 (2008), pp. 7–32.

24. Jennifer Reingold, "Can P&G Make Money in Places Where People Earn $2 a Day?" *Fortune,* January 17, 2011, pp. 86–91.

25. Vijay Mahajan and Kamini Banga, *The 86 Percent Solution: How to Succeed in the Biggest Market Opportunity of the Next 50 Years* (Upper Saddle River, NJ: Pearson Education, 2006); and C. K. Pralahad, *The Fortune at the Bottom of the Pyramid: Eradicating Poverty Through Profits* (Upper Saddle River, NJ: Pearson Education, 2005).

26. www.wto.org, downloaded January 25, 2013.

27. www.unilever.com, downloaded February 4, 2013.

28. "Burgeoning Bourgeoisie," *The Economist.*

29. "Mattel Plans to Double Sales Abroad," *The Wall Street Journal,* February 11, 1998, pp. A3, A11.

30. These examples are found in Cateora, Gilly, and Graham, *International Marketing.*

31. Eric Clark, *The Real Toy Story* (New York: The Free Press, 2007); and Cateora, Gilly, and Graham, *International Marketing.*

32. For an extensive and recent examination of these market-entry options, see for example, Johnny K. Johansson, *Global Marketing: Foreign Entry, Local Marketing, and Global Management,* 5th ed. (Burr Ridge, IL: McGraw Hill/Irwin, 2008); A. Coskun Samli, *Entering & Succeeding in Emerging Countries: Marketing to the Forgotten Majority* (Mason, OH: South-Western, 2004); and Keegan and Green, *Global Marketing.*

33. Based on an interview with Pamela Viglielmo, Director of International Marketing, Fran Wilson Creative Cosmetics; and "Foreign Firms Think Their Way into Japan," www.successstories.com/nikkei, downloaded March 24, 2003.

34. *Small and Medium Sized Exporting Companies: Statistical Overview, 2010* (Washington, DC: International Trade Administration, April 16, 2012).

35. "Made in Taiwan," *Forbes,* April 2, 2001, pp. 64–66.

36. "About Us," www.strauss-group.com, downloaded March 15, 2011.

37. "Dannon Pulls Out of Disputed China Venture," *The Wall Street Journal,* October 1, 2009, p. B1.

38. "FedEx Expands Reach in China with Buyout of Joint Venture," *The Wall Street Journal,* January 25, 2006; and www.harley-davidson.com, downloaded January 10, 2013.

39. "After Losses at Grocery Stores, Tesco to Retreat from U.S. Operations," www.nytimes.com, December 5, 2012.

40. This discussion is based on Keller, *Strategic Brand Management,* pp. 709–10; "Global Sales of Lay's Chips Top $10 Billion in '11," *Dallas Morning News,* March 12, 2012, pp. D1, 10D; "Machines for the Masses," *The Wall Street Journal,* December 9, 2003, pp. A19, A20; "The Color of Beauty," *Forbes,* November 22, 2000, pp. 170–76; "It's Goo, Goo, Goo, Goo Vibrations at the Gerber Lab," *The Wall Street Journal,* December 4, 1996, pp. A1, A6; Donald R. Graber, "How to Manage a Global Product Development Process," *Industrial Marketing Management,* November 1996, pp. 483–98; and Herbig, *Handbook of Cross-Cultural Marketing.*

41. Jagdish N. Sheth and Atul Parvatiyar, "The Antecedents and Consequences of Integrated Global Marketing," *International Marketing Review* 18, no. 1 (2001), pp. 16–29. Also see, D. Szymanski, S. Bharadwaj, and R. Varadarajan, "Standardization versus Adaptation of International Marketing Strategy: An Empirical Investigation," *Journal of Marketing,* October 1993, pp. 1–17.

42. "With Profits Elusive, Wal-Mart to Exit Germany," *The Wall Street Journal,* July 29, 2006, pp. A1, A6.
43. "Rotten Apples," *Dallas Morning News,* April 7, 1998, p. 14A.

Mary Kay India: This case was prepared by Roger A. Kerin based on company interviews.

Chapter 8

1. Rachel Dodes, "What's in a Name?" *The Wall Street Journal,* October 19, 2012, pp. D1–D2; "'Hunger Games' One for the Record Books," *Star Tribune,* March 26, 2012, p. E8; and Michelle Tauber, "Game On," *People,* March 26, 2012, pp. 66–74.
2. John Horn, "Studios Play Name Games," *Star Tribune,* August 10, 1997, p. F11; and "Flunking Chemistry," *Star Tribune,* April 11, 2003, p. E13.
3. Tad Friend, "The Cobra," *The New Yorker,* January 19, 2009, pp. 41–49.
4. Willow Bay, "Test Audiences Have Profound Effect on Movies," *CNN Newsstand & Entertainment Weekly,* September 28, 1998. See www.cnn.com/SHOWBIZ/Movies/9809/28/screen.test.
5. Helene Diamond, "Lights, Camera . . . Research!" *Marketing News,* September 11, 1989, pp. 10–11; and "Killer!" *Time,* November 16, 1987, pp. 72–79.
6. Carl Diorio, "Tracking Projections: Box Office Calculations an Inexact Science," *Variety,* May 24, 2001.
7. Ronald Grover, Tom Lowry, and Michael White, "King of the World (Again)," *Bloomberg Businessweek,* February 1 & 8, 2010, pp. 48–56; and Richard Corliss, "Avatar Ascendant," *Time,* February 8, 2010, pp. 50–51.
8. A lengthier, expanded definition from 2004 is found on the American Marketing Association's website. See http://www.marketingpower.com/AboutAMA/Pages/DefinitionofMarketing.aspx. For a researcher's comments on this and other definitions of marketing research, see Lawrence D. Gibson, "Quo Vadis, Marketing Research?" *Marketing Research,* Spring 2000, pp. 36–41.
9. Harry McCracken, "Build-A-Bot," *Time,* January 21, 2013, pp. 52–53; and Warren Buckleitner, "Lego Updates Its Mindstorms Robotics Kit," *The New York Times,* January 9, 2013; see http://gadgetwise.blogs.nytimes.com/2013/01/09/lego-updates-its-mindstorms-robotics-kit.
10. Lawrence D. Gibson, "Defining Marketing Problems," *Marketing Research,* Spring 1998, pp. 4–12.
11. David A. Aaker, V. Kumar, George S. Day, and Robert P. Leone, *Marketing Research,* 10th ed. (Hoboken, NJ: John Wiley & Sons, 2010), pp. 114–16.
12. Meg James, "Nielsen 'People Meter' Changed the TV Ratings Game 25 Years Ago," *Los Angeles Times,* August 31, 2012. See http://articles.latimes.com/2012/aug/31/entertainment/la-et-ct-nielsen-people-meter-anniversary-20120830.
13. "Cross-Platform Measurement," The Nielsen Company. See Brian Stelter, "New Nielsen Ratings Measure TV and Online Ads Together," *The New York Times Media Decoder,* March 18, 2012; and Andrew Hamp, "Nielsen Adds Ratings for Away-from-Home TV Networks," *Advertising Age—Creativity,* June 14, 2010, p. 13.
14. "Local Television Market Universe (DMA) Estimates: 2013 TV Homes," The Nielsen Company. See http://nielsen.com/content/dam/corporate/us/en/public%20factsheets/tv/2012-2013%20DMA%20Ranks.pdf, p.4.
15. "U.S. Spending Totals by Medium: ZenithOptimedia Forecast 2012," *Advertising Age,* June 25, 2012, p. 22.
16. Jessica E. Vascellaro, "On TV, New Ways to Gauge the Ads," *The Wall Street Journal,* February 4, 2011, p. B10.
17. David Kiley, "Counting the Eyeballs," *BusinessWeek,* January 16, 2006, pp. 84–85; and "The Ultimate Marketing Machine," *The Economist,* July 8, 2006, pp. 61–64.
18. Colleen Moore-Mezler, "Mystery Shoppers Are an Important Resource," *Alert! Magazine,* Marketing Research Association 46, no. 4 (April 2008), pp. 10, 12; and Robert Frank, "How to Live Large and Largely for Free, Jennifer Voitle's Way," *The Wall Street Journal,* June 9, 2003, pp. A1, A8.
19. Sarah Ellison, "P&G Chief's Turnaround Recipe: Find Out What Women Want," *The Wall Street Journal,* June 1, 2005, p. A1; Mark Maremont, "New Toothbrush Is Big-Ticket Item," *The Wall Street Journal,* October 27, 1998, pp. B1, B6; and Emily Nelson, "P&G Checks Out Real Life," *The Wall Street Journal,* May 17, 2001, pp. B1, B4.
20. Gavin Johnson and Melinda Rea-Holloway, "Ethnography: How to Know If It's Right for Your Study," *Alert! Magazine,* Marketing Research Association 47, no. 2 (February 2009), pp. 1–4. See www.mra-net.org/alert.
21. Kenneth Chang, "Enlisting Science's Lessons to Entice More Shoppers to Spend More," *The New York Times,* September 19, 2006, p. D3; and Janet Adamy, "Cooking Up Changes at Kraft Foods," *The Wall Street Journal,* February 20, 2007, p. B1.
22. Martin Lindstrom, *Buyology: Truth and Lies about Why We Buy* (New York: Doubleday, 2008), pp. 8–36; C. B. Whittemore, "Martin Lindstrom's *Buyology,*" *Flooring the Consumer blogspot,* March 1, 2009; Seth Brown, "*Buyology* Offers a Peek Inside Buyers' Heads," *USA Today,* October 29, 2008; and Andrea Sachs, "Business Books," *Time,* October 23, 2008.
23. Ilan Brat, "The Emotional Quotient of Soup Shopping," *The Wall Street Journal,* February 17, 2010, p. B6.
24. For a more complete discussion of questionnaire methods, see Joseph F. Hair, Jr., Robert P. Bush, and David J. Ortinau, *Marketing Research,* 4th ed. (New York: McGraw-Hill/Irwin, 2009), Chapters 6 and 13.
25. See www.trendhunter.com/about-trend-hunter.
26. "What Is Online Research?" Marketing Research Association at http://www.marketingresearch.org/?q=node/221. See also, www.surveymonkey.com.
27. For more discussion on wording questions effectively, see Gilbert A. Churchill, Jr., Tom J. Brown, and Tracy A. Suter, *Basic Marketing Research,* 7th ed. (Mason, OH: South-Western, Cengage Learning, 2010), pp. 289–307.
28. Stephanie Clifford, "Social Media Act as a Guide for Marketers," *The New York Times,* July 31, 2012, pp. A1, A3; and Noam Cohen, "The Breakfast Meeting: Social Media as Focus Group," *The New York Times,* July 31, 2012, p. A3.
29. Jeff Gerst of Bolin Marketing provided the Carmex example, with the permission of Carma Laboratories, Inc.
30. Mark Jeffery, *Data-Driven Marketing: The 15 Metrics Everyone in Marketing Should Know* (Hoboken, NJ: John Wiley & Sons, Inc., 2010), pp. 156–86.
31. Douglas D. Bates, "The Future of Qualitative Research Is Online," *Alert! Magazine,* Marketing Research Association 47, no. 2 (February 2009); Jack Neff, "The End of Consumer Surveys?" *Advertising Age,* September 15, 2008; Jack Neff, "Marketing Execs: Researchers Could Use a Softer Touch," *Advertising Age,* January 27, 2009; Bruce Mendelsohn, "Social Networking: Interactive Marketing Lets Researchers Reach Consumers Where They Are," *Alert! Magazine,* Marketing Research Association 46, no. 4 (April 2008); Toby, "Social Media Research: Interview with Joel Rubinson of ARF: Part 1," *Diva Marketing Blog,* February 16, 2009; and Toby, "Social Media Research: Interview with Joel Rubinson of ARF: Part 2," *Diva Marketing Blog,* February 23, 2009.
32. "Big Data: Before You Start Restricting It, Be Aware of All the Opportunities," *The Wall Street Journal,* November 19, 2012, p. R10;

"Mining the Big Data Gold Mine," *Fortune:* Special Advertising Section, March 30, 2012; Byron Acohido, "Online Tracking Takes a Scary Turn," *USA Today,* August 4, 2011, pp. B1, B2; and "Data, Data Everywhere—A Special Report on Managing Information: A Different Game," *The Economist,* February 27, 2010, pp. 6–8.

33. Joel Stein, "Your Data, Yourself," *Time,* March 21, 2011, pp. 39–46; Ryan Flinn, "The Big Business of Sifting through Social Media Data," *Bloomberg Businessweek,* October 25–October 31, 2010, pp. 20–22; Michael Lev-Ram, "The Hot New Gig in Tech," *Fortune,* September 5, 2011, p. 29; and Geoffrey A. Fowler and Emily Steel, "Facebook Says User Data Sold to Broker," *The Wall Street Journal,* November 1, 2010, p. B3.
34. The Step 4 discussion was written by David Ford and Don Rylander of Ford Consulting Group, Inc.; the Tony's Pizza example was provided by Teré Carral of Tony's Pizza.
35. See http://www.newbalance.com/NB-Minimus/minimus,default,pg.html and http://www.goodformrunning.com.

Carmex: This case was written by Jeff Gerst of Bolin Marketing.

Chapter 9

1. Kimberly Weisal, "A Shine in Their Shoes," *BusinessWeek,* December 5, 2005, p. 84; and information from the "Executive Biographies" section of the Zappos.com website.
2. Dinah Eng, "Zappos's Silent Founder," *Fortune,* September 3, 2012, pp. 19–22; Jeffrey M. O'Brien, "Zappos Knows How to Kick It," *Fortune,* February 2, 2009, pp. 55–60; and Max Chafkin, "Get Happy," *Inc.,* May 2009, pp. 66–71.
3. Weisal, "A Shine in Their Shoes," p. 84.
4. Duff McDonald, "Zappos.com: Success through Simplicity," *CIO-Insight,* November 10, 2006.
5. Jena McGregor, "Zappos' Secret: It's an Open Book," *Bloomberg Businessweek,* March 23 and 30, 2009, p. 62; and Jeffrey M. O'Brien, "The 10 Commandments of Zappos," *Fortune,* January 22, 2009, see http://money.cnn.com/2009/01/21/news/companies/obrien_zappos10.fortune and Zappos.com.
6. Motoko Rich, "Why Is This Man Smiling?" *The New York Times,* April 10, 2011, pp. ST1, ST10; Christopher Palmeri, "Now for Sale, the Zappos Culture," *Bloomberg Businessweek,* January 11, 2010, p. 57; and see https://twitter.com/zappos.
7. Natalie Zmuda, "Marketer of the Year: Zappos," *Advertising Age,* October 20, 2008, p. 36.
8. Eric N. Berkowitz, Roger A. Kerin, and William Rudelius, *Marketing* (St. Louis, MO: Times Mirror/Mosby College Publishing, 1986), pp. 189–91; Sleep Research Institute, the National Sleep Foundation, and the International Sleep Products Association (March 20, 2007); and Frederick G. Crane, Roger A. Kerin, Steven W. Hartley, and William Rudelius, *Marketing,* 8th Canadian ed. (Toronto, Canada: McGraw-Hill Ryerson Ltd., 2011), pp. 229–32.
9. Ellen Byron, "As Middle Class Shrinks, P&G Aims High and Low," *The Wall Street Journal,* September 12, 2011, pp. A1, A16; Ellen Byron, "P&G Puts Spotlight on Newer Products," *The Wall Street Journal,* October 21, 2010, pp. B1, B2; Anthony Bianco, "The Vanishing Mass Market," *BusinessWeek,* July 12, 2004, pp. 61–65; and Geoff Colvin, "Selling P&G," *Fortune,* September 17, 2007, pp. 163–69.
10. Jeffrey A. Trachtenberg and Ann Paul Sonne, "Rowling Casts E-Book Spell," *The Wall Street Journal,* June 24, 2011, pp. B1, B2; and Larry Neumeister, "Rowling to Testify Against Fan in Bid to Block Publication of 'Harry Potter' Encyclopedia," StarTribune.com from an Associated Press article, April 13, 2008; www.startribune.com/entertainment/17761909.html.
11. James Cook, "Where's the Niche?" *Forbes,* September 24, 1984, p. 54.
12. J. P. Donlon, "The Road Ahead," *Chief Executive,* July/August, 2011, pp. 31–37; "Epiphany in Dearborn," *The Economist,* December 11, 2010, pp. 72–74; and Bill Saporito, "How to Make Cars and Make Money Too," *Time,* August 9, 2010, pp. 36–39.
13. *2010 Ann Taylor Annual Report* and selected press releases.
14. Ann D'Innocenzio, "Wal-Mart to Accelerate Small Store Growth," *Associated Press,* October 10, 2012, see http://bigstory.ap.org/article/wal-mart-accelerate-small-store-growth; Alissa Skelton, "Wal-Mart to Test Small Store Format," *The Wall Street Journal,* June 2, 2011, see http://www.nytimes.com/2011/06/03/business/03walmart.html; and Miguel Bastillo, "Walmart Sees Small Stores in Big Cities," *The Wall Street Journal,* October 14, 2010, pp. B1, B6.
15. The relation of these criteria to implementation is discussed in Jacqueline Dawley, "Making Connections: Enhance the Implementation of Value of Attitude-Based Segmentation," *Marketing Research,* Summer 2006, pp. 16–22.
16. Ian Michiels, "Customer Analytics: Segmentation beyond Demographics," *The Aberdeen Group,* August 2008, p. 11.
17. The discussion of fast-food trends and market share is based on Experian Simmons Fall 2012 NCS/NHCS Full-Year Adult Survey 12 OneView[SM] Crosstabulation Report © Experian Simmons 2013. See http://www.experian.com/simmons-research/consumer-study.html.
18. Julie Jargon, "McDonald's Is Feeling Fried," *The Wall Street Journal,* November 9, 2012, pp. B1–B2.
19. Julie Jargon, "McDonald's to Start Posting Calorie Counts Across U.S.," *The Wall Street Journal,* September 13, 2012, pp. B1–B2; Mariko Sanchanta and Yoree Kuh, "McDonald's in Japan Gives New Meaning to Supersize," *The Wall Street Journal,* January 12, 2011, pp. B1, B2; and Julie Jargon, "On the McDonald's Menu: Variety, Caution," *The Wall Street Journal,* November 9, 2010, p. B5.
20. Burt Helm, "An Expensive Face-Lift on Burger King's Menu," *Bloomberg Businessweek,* October 11–17, 2010, pp. 21–22; and Julie Jargon and Gina Chon, "BK's Strategy: Play Catch Up," *The Wall Street Journal,* September 3, 2010, p. B1.
21. Julie Jargon, "Fast Food Aspires to Move Up the Food Chain," *The Wall Street Journal,* October 11, 2012, p. B11; Josh Sanburn, "Fast-Casual Nation," *Time,* April 23, 2012, pp. 60–61; Don Jacobson, "Fast-Casual Restaurants Are Just What Landlords Ordered," *Star Tribune,* January 20, 2012, p. D5; Tiffany Hsu, "Fast, Casual, Trendy," *Star Tribune,* January 5, 2012, pp. D1, D3; and Al Reis, "Viewpoint," *Advertising Age,* January 20, 2011, p. 16.
22. Keith O'Brien, "Supersize," *The New York Times Magazine,* May 6, 2012, pp. 44–48; and "A Look Ahead: 2011—Fast Food," *Advertising Age,* January 20, 2011, p. 4.
23. Julie Jargon, "Costlier Food Puts Restaurants in Bind," *The Wall Street Journal,* August 29, 2012, p. B8; and Julie Jargon, "Wendy's Stages a Palace Coup," *The Wall Street Journal,* December 21, 2011, pp. B1, B2.
24. Julie Jargon, "New Menu Helps Burger King," *The Wall Street Journal,* October 30, 2012, p. B8; and "The 2012 Zagat Fast-Food Survey," September 29, 2012. See http://blog.zagat.com/2012/09/2012-fast-food-survey-results-are-live.html.
25. The discussion of Apple's segmentation strategies through the years is based on information from its website, www.apple.com and www.apple-history.com/history.html.
26. Much of the discussion about positioning and perceptual maps is based on Roger A. Kerin and Robert A. Peterson, *Strategic Marketing Problems: Cases and Comments,* 12th ed. (Upper Saddle River, NJ: Prentice Hall, 2010), pp. 146–47; and John M. Mullins, Orville C. Walker, Jr., and Harper W. Boyd, Jr., *Marketing Management: A Strategic Decision-Marketing Approach,* 7th ed. (New York: McGraw-Hill/Irwin, 2010), p. 202.

27. Nicholas Zamiska, "How Milk Got a Major Boost by Food Panel," *The Wall Street Journal,* August 30, 2004, pp. B1, B5; and Rebecca Winter, "Chocolate Milk," *Time,* April 30, 2001, p. 20.

Prince Sports: This case was written by William Rudelius and is based on personal interviews with Linda Glassel, Tyler Herring, and Nick Skally.

Chapter 10

1. Edward C. Baig, "On New iPad, Looks Are Everything," *USA Today,* March 16, 2012, p. B3; Walter Isaacson, "American Icon," *Time,* October 17, 2011, pp. 32–35; Lev Grossman and Harry McCracken, "The Inventor of the Future," *Time,* October 17, 2011, pp. 36–44; Brad Stone, "1997–2011: The Return," *Bloomberg Businessweek,* October 10–16, 2011, pp. 36–42; Sean Wilsey, "The Products," *Bloomberg Businessweek,* October 10–16, 2011, pp. 48–61; Beth Snyder Bulik, "Marketer of the Decade," *Advertising Age,* October 18, 2010, p. 14; and Geoff Colvin, "The World's Most Admired Companies: 2012," *Fortune*. See http://money.cnn.com/magazines/fortune/most-admired/2012/snapshots/670.html; Adam Lashinsky, "The Decade of Steve," *Fortune,* November 23, 2009, pp. 92–100; and Michael Arndt and Bruce Einhorn, "The 50 Most Innovative Companies," *Bloomberg Businessweek,* April 25, 2010, pp. 34–40.
2. Andy Serwer, "Steve Jobs vs. Sam Walton," *Fortune,* December 3, 2012, pp. 123–30.
3. Ian Sherr, "Apple's Magic Wears Thin As Its Earnings Disappoint," *The Wall Street Journal,* January 24, 2013, pp. A1, A2; and Lev Grossman, "The Technologist: Tim Cook," *Time,* December 31, 2012–January 7, 2013, pp. 112–18.
4. Apple Special Event, June 6, 2011. See http://www.apple.com/apple-events/wwdc-2011.
5. Jessica E. Vascellaro, "Apple Tries to Keep Edge," *The Wall Street Journal,* March 8, 2012, pp. B1, B4; Jessica E. Vascellaro, Erica Orden, and Sam Schechner, "Hollywood Studios Warm to Apple's iCloud Effort," *The Wall Street Journal,* March 12, 2012, pp. B1, B6; Lev Grossman, "Cloud Control. Apple's iCloud Is a Great Service—and a Blow to the Power of the PC," *Time,* June 20, 2011, p. 51; and William J. Holstein, "Can Cloud Live Up to Its Promise?" *ChiefExecutive.Net,* July/August, 2011, pp. 46–50.
6. "Gross Domestic Product: Fourth Quarter and Annual 2012 (Advance Estimate)," news release from the Bureau of Economic Analysis: U.S. Department of Commerce, January 30, 2013, Table 3. Gross Domestic Product and Related Measures, p. 8—calculation from data for 2012, column 1. See http://www.bea.gov/newsreleases/national/gdp/2013/pdf/gdp4q12_adv.pdf.
7. Todd Nelson, "On a Run with Crapola Granola," *Star Tribune,* January 14, 2013, p. D2; and James Norton, "Brian and Andrea Strom of Crapola Granola," *Heavy Table,* January 16, 2013. See http://heavytable.com/brian-and-andrea-strom-of-crapola-granola; Jess Fleming, "Made in Minnesota: Crapola Granola Is Better Than It Sounds," *Pioneer Press,* December 19, 2012. See http://www.twincities.com/restaurants/ci_22223106/crapola-granola-is-better-than-it-sounds; and Abe Sauer, "Minnesota's Crapola Proud to Be Number Two Brand, *Brandchannel,* December 12, 2011. See http://www.brandchannel.com/home/post/2011/12/12/Minnesota-Brand-Crapola-121211.aspx.
8. Barbara Ortutay, "Sony Likely to Unveil Next PlayStation on Feb. 20," *Associated Press,* February 1, 2013. See http://bigstory.ap.org/article/sony-likely-unveil-next-playstation-feb-20; and Daisuke Wakabayashi and Ian Sherr, "Nintendo Sticks to Its Guns," *The Wall Street Journal,* November 17–18, 2012, pp. B1, B2.
9. Interview with Geek Squad founder Robert Stephens on *60 Minutes,* January 28, 2007, www.geeksquad.com; Debora Viana Thompson, Rebecca W. Hamilton, and Roland Rust, "Feature Fatigue: When Product Capabilities Become Too Much of a Good Thing," *Journal of Marketing Research,* November 2005, pp. 431–42; and Ronald T. Rust, Debora Viana Thompson, Rebecca W. Hamilton, "Defeating Feature Fatigue," *Harvard Business Review,* February 2006, pp. 98–107.
10. Youngme Moon, "Break Free from the Product Life Cycle," *Harvard Business Review,* May 2005, pp. 86–94.
11. See "The 25 Biggest Product Flops of All Time," www.walletpop.com/photos/top-25-biggest-product-flops-of-all-time; and Zac Frank and Tania Khadder, "The 20 Worst Product Failures," www.saleshq.monster.com/news/articles/2655-the-20-worst-product-failures.
12. Joan Schneider and Julie Hall, "Why Most Product Launches Fail," *Harvard Business Review,* April 2011, pp. 21–23.
13. Robert G. Cooper, "New Products: What Separates the Winners from the Losers?" in *The PDMA Handbook of New Product Development,* eds. M. D. Rosenau, A. Griffin, G. Castellion, and N. Anscheutz (New York: Wiley and Sons, 1996), pp. 3–18; Robert G. Cooper, "The Impact of Product Innovativeness on Performance," *Journal of Product Innovation Management,* April 1999, pp. 115–33; Thomas D. Kuczmarski, "Measuring Your Return on Innovation," *Marketing Management,* Spring 2000, pp. 25–32; and Merle Crawford and Anthony Di Benedetto, *New Products Management,* 9th ed. (New York: McGraw-Hill/Irwin, 2008), pp. 61–71.
14. Julie Fortser, "The Lucky Charm of Steve Sanger," *BusinessWeek,* March 26, 2001, pp. 75–76.
15. The Avert Virucidal tissues, Hey! There's A Monster In My Room spray, and Garlic Cake examples are adapted from Robert M. McMath and Thom Forbes, *What Were They Thinking?* (New York: Random House, 1998).
16. Schneider and Hall, "Why Most Product Launches Fail," p. 22.
17. Dan P. Lovallo and Olivier Sibony, "Distortions and Deceptions in Strategic Decisions," *The McKinsey Quarterly* 1 (2006), pp. 19–29; and Byron G. Augusto, Eric P. Harmon, and Vivek Pandit, "The Right Service Strategies for Product Companies," *The McKinsey Quarterly* 1 (2006), pp. 41–51.
18. "The 25 Biggest Product Flops of All Time"; Isabelle Royer, "Why Bad Projects Are So Hard to Kill," *Harvard Business Review,* February 2003, pp. 48–56; John T. Morn, Dan P. Lovallo, and S. Patrick Viguerie, "Beating the Odds in Market Entry," *The McKinsey Quarterly* 4 (2005), pp. 35–45; Leslie Perlow and Stephanie Williams, "Is Silence Killing Your Company?" *Harvard Business Review,* May 2003, pp. 52–58; Beverly K. Brockman and Robert M. Morgan, "The Moderating Effect of Organizational Cohesiveness in Knowledge Use and New Product Development," *Journal of Marketing Science* 3 (Summer 2006), pp. 295–306; Eyal Biyalogorsky, William Boulding, and Richard Staelin, "Stuck in the Past: Why Managers Persist with New Product Failures," *Journal of Marketing,* April 2006, pp. 108–21; and Irwin L. Janis, *Groupthink* (New York: Free Press, 1988).
19. Walter Isaacson, *Steve Jobs* (New York: Simon & Schuster, 2011), pp. 94–101.
20. Robert G. Cooper, "What Leading Companies Are Doing to Reinvent Their NPD Process," *PDMA Visions Magazine,* September 2008, pp. 6–10; Robert G. Cooper, "The Stage-Gate Idea-to-Launch Process—Update: What's New and NexGen Systems," *Journal of Product Innovation Management,* May 2008, pp. 213–32; Leland D. Shaeffer and Michael Zirkle, "Beyond 'Phase Gate'—Why Not a Tailored Solution?" *PDMA Visions Magazine,* June 2008, pp. 21–25; and Gloria Barczak, Abbie Griffin, and Kenneth B. Kahn, "Perspective: Trends and Drivers of Success in NPD Practices: Results of the 2003 PDMA Best Practices Study," *Journal of Product Innovation Management,* January 2009, pp. 3–23.

21. Walter Isaacson, *Steve Jobs,* pp. 98–101; and Malcolm Gladwell, "Creation Myth: Xerox PARC, Apple, and the Truth about Innovation," *The New Yorker,* May 16, 2011. See www.newyorker.com/reporting/2011/05/16/110516ta_fact_gladwell.

22. Hal B. Greyersen, Jeff Dyer, and Clayton M. Christensen, "Why Ask Why?" *ChiefExecutive.Net,* January/February, 2012, pp. 40–43.

23. Peter Erickson, "One Food Company's Foray into Open Innovation," *PDMA Visions Magazine,* June 2008, pp. 12–14; Benn Lawson, Kenneth J. Petersen, Paul D. Cousins, and Robert B. Handfield, "Knowledge Sharing in Interorganizational Product Development Teams: The Effect of Formal and Informal Socialization Mechanisms," *Journal of Product Innovation Management,* March 2009, pp. 156–72; and James I. Cash, Jr., Michael J. Earl, and Robert Morison, "Teaming Up to Crack Innovation and Enterprise Integration," *Harvard Business Review,* November 2008, pp. 90–100.

24. "Epiphany in Dearborn," *The Economist,* December 11, 2010, pp. 72–74; and Bill Saporito, "How to Make Cars and Make Money Too," *Time,* August 9, 2010, pp. 36–39.

25. Bryce G. Hoffman, "Inside Ford's Fight to Avoid Disaster," *The Wall Street Journal,* March 9, 2012, B1, B7; and J. P. Donlon, "CEO of the Year: The Road Ahead," *ChiefExecutive.Net,* July/August 2011, pp. 31–37.

26. Kimberly Judson, Denise D. Schoenbachler, Geoffrey L. Gordon, Rick E. Ridnour, and Dan C. Weilbaker, "The New Product Development Process: Let the Voice of the Salesperson Be Heard," *Journal of Product & Brand Management* 15, no. 3 (2006), pp. 194–202.

27. Morgan L. Swink and Vincent A. Mabert, "Product Development Partnerships: Balancing Needs of OEMs and Suppliers," *Business Horizons,* May–June 2000, pp. 59–68.

28. C. K. Prahalad and Venkat Ramswamy, *The Future of Competition* (Boston: Harvard Business School Press, 2004); Steve Hamm, "Adding Customers to the Design Team," *BusinessWeek,* March 1, 2004, pp. 22–23; and Anthony W. Ulwick, "Turn Customer Input into Innovation," *Harvard Business Review,* January 2002, pp. 91–97.

29. Sarah Ellison, "P&G Chief's Turnaround Recipe: Find Out What Women Want," *The Wall Street Journal,* June 1, 2005, pp. A1, A16.

30. Jack Neff, "Tide Pods Winning $7 Billion Detergent Wars by Defining Value," *Advertising Age,* December 18, 2012. See http://adage.com/article/news/tide-pods-winning-7-billion-detergent-wars-redefining/23877; and Dale Buss, "P&G Awash in Success of Tide Pods Despite Wrinkles Along the Way, *Brandchannel,* December 18, 2012. See http://www.brandchannel.com/home/post/2012/12/18/PG-Tide-Pods-121812.aspx; Emily Glazer, "Tide Rides Convenience Wave," *The Wall Street Journal,* February 23, 2012, p. 138; Jack Neff, "P&G Reinvents Laundry with $150 Million Tide Pods Launch," *Advertising Age,* April 26, 2011, downloaded April 28, 2011; and Emily Glazer, "P&G to Alter Tide Pods Packaging," *The Wall Street Journal,* May 26–27, 2012, p. B3.

31. Elisabeth A. Sullivan, "A Group Effort," *Marketing News,* February 28, 2010, pp. 22–29.

32. Adam Lashinsky, "Inside Apple," *Fortune,* May 23, 2011, p. 128; Daniel Turner, "The Secret of Apple Design," *MIT Technology Review,* May/June 2007; Leander Kahney, "Silicon Valley Loves Transparency and Cooperation. Not Steve Jobs. How Apple Got Everything Right by Doing Everything Wrong," *Wired Business Trends,* April 2008, pp. 137–43; and Karl T. Ulrich and Stephen D. Eppinger, *Product Design and Development*, 4th ed. (New York: McGraw-Hill/Irwin, 2008), Chapter 10.

33. Joseph Weber, Stanley Holmes, and Christopher Palmeri, "'Mosh Pits' of Creativity," *BusinessWeek,* November 7, 2005, pp. 98–100.

34. Charlie Rose, "How to Design Breakthrough Inventions," *CBS 60 Minutes,* air date January 6, 2013. See http://www.cbsnews.com/8301-18560_162-57562201/how-to-design-breakthrough-inventions; Bruce Nussbaum, "The Best Global Design of 2008," *BusinessWeek,* July 28, 2008, pp. 44–46; Tim Brown, "He Prizes Questions More Than Answers," *The New York Times,* October 25, 2009, p. BU2; Bruce Nussbaum, "The Power of Design," *BusinessWeek,* May 17, 2004, pp. 86–94; the article gives many techniques for idea and concept generation, as do Appendixes A and B in Merle Crawford and Anthony Di Benedetto, *New Products Management,* 10th ed. (New York: McGraw-Hill/Irwin, 2011).

35. Erickson, "One Food Company's Foray into Open Innovation," p. 12.

36. Ibid., p. 13.

37. Simona Covel, "My Brain, Your Brawn," *The Wall Street Journal,* October 13, 2008, p. R12.

38. Kristin Tillotson, "Crowdfunding Gears Up for a Fresh Kick Start," *Star Tribune,* November 6, 2012, pp. A1, A10.

39. Steve Hoeffler, "Measuring Preferences for Really New Products," *Journal of Marketing Research,* November 2003, pp. 406–20.

40. Christopher Lovelock and Jochen Wirtz, *Services Marketing* (Englewood Cliffs, NJ: Prentice Hall, 2007), pp. 260–84.

41. Chunka Mui, "Google's Trillion Dollar Driverless Car: Sooner Than You Think," *Forbes,* January 30, 2013. See http://www.forbes.com/sites/chunkamui/2013/01/30/googles-trillion-dollar-driverless-car-part-3-sooner-than-you-think; Chunka Mui, "Google's Trillion Dollar Driverless Car: The Ripple Effects," *Forbes,* January 24, 2013. See http://www.forbes.com/sites/chunkamui/2013/01/24/googles-trillion-dollar-driverless-car-part-2-the-ripple-effects; Chunka Mui, "Fasten Your Seat Belts: Google's Driverless Car Is Worth Trillions," *Forbes,* January 22, 2013. See http://www.forbes.com/sites/chunkamui/2013/01/22/fasten-your-seatbelts-googles-driverless-car-is-worth-trillions; Abby Haglage, "Google, Audi, Toyota, and the Brave New World of Driverless Cars," *The Daily Beast,* January 16, 2013. See http://www.thedailybeast.com/articles/2013/01/16/google-audi-toyota-and-the-brave-new-world-of-driverless-cars.html; Henry Fountain, "Yes, Driverless Cars Know the Way to San Jose," *The New York Times,* October 26, 2012. See http://www.nytimes.com/2012/10/28/automobiles/yes-driverless-cars-know-the-way-to-san-jose.html; and Shane McGlaun, "Google Self-Driving Cars Log 300,000 Accident-Free Miles," *DailyTech,* August 13, 2012. See http://www.dailytech.com/Google+SelfDriving+Cars+Log+300000+AccidentFree+Miles/article25382.htm;

42. Ben Fritz and Keach Hagey, "Netflix Hires DreamWorks," *The Wall Street Journal*, June 18, 2013, p. 83; Cecilia Kang, "Netflix Takes on Hollywood with Original Programming," *The Washington Post,* February 4, 2013, p. 5B; Brian Stelter, "New Way to Deliver a Drama: All 13 Episodes in One Sitting," *The New York Times,* February 1, 2013, pp. 1, 3; Greg Bensinger, "Amazon, Netflix Battle Over Content," *The Wall Street Journal,* February 2, 2013, p. B3; Tom Gliatto, "*House of Cards,*" *People*, February 1, 2013, p. 43; Roger Yu, "New Customers Boost Netflix," *USA Today,* January 24, 2013, p. B1; Greg Bensinger, "Netflix Shares Surge 35% on Profit," *The Wall Street Journal,* January 24, 2013, p. B1; John Jannarone, "Netflix Signs Streaming Deal with Time Warner," *The Wall Street Journal,* January 8, 2013, p. B9.

43. Gilbert A. Churchill, Jr., Tom J. Brown, and Tracy A. Suter, *Basic Marketing Research,* 7th ed. (Mason, OH: South-Western, Cengage Learning, 2010), pp. 122–30.

44. Daniel Michaels, "Innovation Is Messy Business," *The Wall Street Journal,* January 24, 2013, pp. B1, B2; Christopher Drew, "Dreamliner Troubles Put Boeing on Edge," *The New York Times,* January 20, 2013. See http://www.nytimes.com/2013/01/21/business/battery-fire-resolution-may-weigh-on-boeing.html; Andy Pasztor and Jon Ostrower, "Probe of Boeing 787 Battery

Fire Expands," *The Wall Street Journal,* January 24, 2013. See http://online.wsj.com/article/SB10001424127887324624404578253010041254492.html; and Brad Stone and Susanna Roy, "Don't Dream It's Over, "*Bloomberg Businessweek,* January 28–February 3, 2013, pp. 4–16.

45. "The French Fry Wars: Burger King Cooks Up a New Recipe," *The Miami Herald,* December 12, 2011. See http://www.miamiherald.com/2011/12/07/2535291/the-french-fry-wars-burger-king.html; "New Fries at Burger King Restaurants," Burger King press release, November 30, 2011. See http://www.bk.com/en/us/company-info/news-press/detail/new-fries-at-burger-king-restaurants-559.html; "Burger King Introduces Hotter, Crispier, Better-Tasting French Fries," *PRNewswire,* December 10, 2011. See http://www2.prnewswire.com/cgi-bin/stories.pl?ACCT=104&STORY=www/story/12-10-97/375783&EDATE; and Jennifer Ordonez, "How Burger King Got Burned in Quest to Make the Perfect Fry," *The Wall Street Journal,* January 16, 2001, pp. A1, A8.

46. Kerry A. Dolan, "Speed: The New X Factor," *Forbes,* December 26, 2005, pp. 74–77.

X-1: This case was written by Steven Hartley. Sources: "X-1 Breaks the Barriers of Sound with Innovative Rebranding and Website," *PR.com,* February 23, 2013; "US Patent Issued to H2O Audio on July 17 for 'Waterproof Enclosure for Audio Device,' *US Fed News,* July 23, 2012; "NetSuite Announces Outdoor Retail Customer Wins," *ENP Newswire,* August 6, 2012; X-1 website, www.x-1.com, accessed July 18, 2013; and personal interviews with X-1 personnel.

Chapter 11

1. "Gatorade's New Selling Point: We're Necessary Performance Gear," www.adage.com, January 2, 2012; "The Best Goes On," *BrandWeek,* May 10, 2010, p. 22; "Gatorade: Before and After," *The Wall Street Journal,* April 23, 2010, p. B8; "Pepsi Turns to Innovation to Boost Gatorade," *The Wall Street Journal,* October 21, 2009, p. B7; "Gatorade Refreshes Look," *BrandWeek,* January 15, 2009, p. 4; Darren Rovell, *First in Thirst: How Gatorade Turned the Science of Sweat into a Cultural Phenomenon* (New York: AMACOM, 2005); and www.Gatorade.com.

2. For an extended discussion of the generalized product life cycle, see Donald R. Lehmann and Russell S. Winer, *Product Management,* 5th ed. (Burr Ridge, IL: McGraw-Hill, 2008).

3. *Gillette Fusion Case Study* (New York: Datamonitor, June 6, 2008). All subsequent references to Gillette Fusion are based on this case study.

4. Orville C. Walker, Jr., and John W. Mullins, *Marketing Management: A Strategic Decision-Making Approach,* 8th ed. (Burr Ridge, IL: McGraw-Hill/Irwin, 2014), p. 209.

5. Portions of this discussion on the fax machine product life cycle are based on Mike Elgan, "Tired Technologies That Should Die Off in 2010," www.pcworld.com, December 30, 2009; Karen Prema, "Faxes Are Evolving," *Purchasing Magazine Online,* March 16, 2006; and "Atlas Electronics Corporation," in Roger A. Kerin and Robert A. Peterson, *Strategic Marketing Problems: Cases and Comments,* 8th ed. (Upper Saddle River, NJ: Prentice Hall, 1998), pp. 494–506.

6. "Email Statistics Report, 2012–2016," (Palo Alto, CA: The Radicati Group, 2012); and "Why Are Faxes Still Around?" *Wired,* January 2009, p. 47.

7. Kate MacArthur, "Coke Energizes Tab, Neville Isdell's Fave," *Advertising Age,* August 29, 2005, pp. 3, 21.

8. "Hosiery Sales Hit Major Snag," *Dallas Morning News,* December 18, 2006, p. 50.

9. "Year-End Marketing Reports on U.S. Recorded Music Shipments," (New York: Recording Industry Association of America, 2013); and "U.S. Music Forecast: 2011–2015," Forrester Research Reports, www.forrester.com, downloaded January 17, 2013.

10. Everett M. Rogers, *Diffusion of Innovations,* 5th ed. (New York: Free Press, 2003).

11. Jagdish N. Sheth and Banwasi Mitral, *Consumer Behavior: A Managerial Perspective,* 2nd ed. (Mason, OH: South-Western College Publishing, 2003).

12. "Why Honda's Unloading Electric Cars for a Song," *Bloomberg Businessweek,* June 24–30, 2013, pp. 33–34.

13. "When Free Samples Become Saviors," *The Wall Street Journal,* August 14, 2001, pp. B1, B4.

14. "Dockers Adds Diversity to Message," *BrandWeek,* September 11, 2006, p. 18.

15. "New Balance Steps Up Marketing Drive," *The Wall Street Journal,* March 21, 2008, p. B3.

16. Sheth and Mitral, *Consumer Behavior*; and Marsha Cohen, *Marketing to the 50+ Population* (New York: EPM Communications, Inc., 2007).

17. "Pop(sicle) Quiz," *Consumer Reports,* August 2012, p. 63; "Downsized: More and More Products Lose Weight," *Consumer Reports,* February 2011, p. 32ff; "P&G Lightens the Load on Diapers," *The Wall Street Journal,* September 9, 2013, p. B2; and Bruce Horovitz, "Shoppers Beware: Products Shrink but Prices Stay the Same," www.usatoday, June 11, 2008.

18. "The 5 Most Counterfeited Products," www.money.msn.com, March 2, 2013.

19. This discussion is based on Kevin Lane Keller, *Strategic Brand Management,* 4th ed. (Upper Saddle River, NJ: Prentice Hall, 2013). Also see, Susan Fornier, "Building Brand Community on the Harley-Davidson Posse Ride," Harvard Business School Note #5-501–502 (Boston: Harvard Business School, 2001); and Tulin Erdem, Joffre Swait, and Ana Valenzuela, "Brands as Signals: A Cross-Country Validation Study," *Journal of Marketing,* January 2006, pp. 34–49.

20. Keller, *Strategic Brand Management.*

21. This discussion is based on John Deighton, "How Snapple Got Its Juice Back," *Harvard Business Review,* January 2002, pp. 47–53; and "Breakfast King Agrees to Sell Bagel Business," *The Wall Street Journal,* September 28, 1999, pp. B1, B6. Also see, Vithala R. Rao, Manoj K. Agarwal, and Denise Dahlhoff, "How Is Manifest Branding Strategy Related to the Value of a Corporation?" *Journal of Marketing,* October 2004, 125–41.

22. Keach Hagey, "Rebuilding Playboy: Less Smut, More Money," *The Wall Street Journal,* February 20, 2013, pp. B1, B2; "Judge Pooh-poohs Lawsuit over Disney Licensing Fees," USATODAY.com, March 30, 2004; and Keller, *Strategic Brand Management.*

23. John Brodie, "The Many Faces of Ralph Lauren," www.Fortune.com, August 29, 2007; and "Polo Ralph Lauren Enters into Licensing Agreement with Luxottica Group, S.p.A., www.thebusinessedition.com, February 28, 2006.

24. Marc Fetscherin, et al., "In China? Pick Your Brand Name Carefully," *Harvard Business Review,* September 2012, p. 26; Beth Snyder Bulik, "What's in a (Good) Product Name? Sales," *Advertising Age,* February 2, 2009, p. 10; and Keller, *Strategic Brand Management.* Also see Chiranjeev Kohli and Douglas W. LaBahn, "Creating Effective Brand Names: A Study of the Naming Process," *Journal of Advertising Research,* January–February 1997, pp. 67–75.

25. Jack Neff, "The End of the Line for Line Extensions?" *Advertising Age,* July 7, 2008, pp. 3, 28; and "When Brand Extension Becomes Brand Abuse," *BrandWeek,* October 26, 1998, pp. 20, 22.

26. For an in-depth discussion on co-branding, see Akshay R. Rao and Robert W. Ruekert, "Brand Alliances as Signals of Product Quality," *Sloan Management Review,* Fall 1994, pp. 87–97.

27. David Aaker, *Brand Portfolio Strategy* (New York: Free Press, 2004).
28. Mark Ritson, "Should You Launch a Fighter Brand?" *Harvard Business Review,* October 2009, pp. 87–94.
29. "Ribbons Roll Out on Rides," *Dallas Morning News* (September 30, 2005), p. 8D.
30. "Why Delete Brands from Your Portfolio?" www.cnnmoney.com, May 14, 2010.
31. "Store Brand Share on the Rise," www.storebranddecisions.com, October 16, 2012; "Wal-Mart Spices Up Private Label," *The Wall Street Journal,* February 6–7, 2010, p. B16; "Consumers Flock to Private Labels," *Advertising Age,* February 2, 2009, p. 27; and Lien Lamey, Barbara Deleersnyder, Marnik G. Dekimpe, and Jan-Benedict E. M. Steenkamp, "How Business Cycles Contribute to Private-Label Success: Evidence from the United States and Europe," *Journal of Marketing,* January 2007, pp. 1–15.
32. www.pez.com, downloaded February 1, 2013; "So Sweet: William and Kate PEZ Dispensers," www.today.msnbc.com, March 30, 2012; David Welch, *Collecting Pez* (Murphysboro, IL: Bubba Scrubba Publications, 1995); and "Elements Design Adds Dimension to Perennial Favorite Pez Brand," *Package Design Magazine,* May 2006, pp. 37–38.
33. "Market Statistics," www.Packaging-Gateway.com, downloaded March 25, 2008.
34. "Green Bean Casserole Turns 50," *Dallas Morning News,* November 19, 2005, p. 10D.
35. "L'eggs Hatches a New Hosiery Package," *BrandWeek,* January 1, 2001, p. 6.
36. Representative scholarly research on packaging and labeling perceptions include: Priya Raghubir and Eric A. Greenleaf, "Ratios in Proportion: What Should the Shape of the Package Be?" *Journal of Marketing,* April 2006, pp. 95–107; Peter H. Bloch, Frederic F. Brunel, and Todd Arnold, "Individual Differences in the Centrality of Visual Product Aesthetics: Concept and Measurement," *Journal of Consumer Research,* March 2003, pp. 551–65; and Pamela Anderson, Joan Giese, and Joseph A. Cote, "Impression Management Using Typeface Design," *Journal of Marketing,* October 2004, pp. 60–72.
37. "Pepsi-Cola Global Brand Restyle," www.junkfoodnews.com, June 27, 2012.
38. "Asian Brands Are Sprouting English Logos in Pursuit of Status, International Image," *The Wall Street Journal,* August 7, 2001, p. B7C.
39. Stephanie Strom, "Companies Pick Up Used Packaging and Recycling's Cost," www.nytimes.com, March 23, 2012; and Betsy McKay, "Pepsi to Cut Plastic Used in Bottles," *The Wall Street Journal,* May 6, 2008, p. B2.
40. "Wal-Mart: Use Less Packaging," *Dallas Morning News,* September 23, 2006, p. 2D. For an overview of Procter & Gamble's environmental efforts, see *Sustainability Report 2011* (Cincinnati, OH: Procter & Gamble Company, 2012).
41. "Packaging," www.hp.com, downloaded January 17, 2007.
42. Christian Twigg-Flesner, *Consumer Product Guarantees* (Aldershot, England: Ashgate Publishing, 2003).

P&G's Secret Deodorant: This case was prepared by Jana Boone. Used with permission.

Chapter 12

1. Tomio Geron, "The Share Economy," *Forbes,* February 11, 2013, pp. 58–66; "How Couchsurfing Epitomizes the 'Sharing Economy,'" *The Huffington Post,* January 25, 2013; "adverCar Invites Drivers to Rent Car 'Real Estate' to Showcase Favorite Brands," *GlobeNewswire,* January 14, 2013; "Will You Leave Your Job to Join the Sharing Economy?" *VentureBeat,* January 22, 2013; Dana Hull, "Sharing Economy Raises Tensions," *Dayton Daily News,* December 31, 2012, p. A10; "Airbnb's Brian Chesky: It's Only Day Two in the Sharing Economy," *PandoDaily,* January 11, 2013; and "A Step Forward for Ride-Sharing: California Suspends Fines against Lyft," *VentureBeat,* January 30, 2013.
2. "Gross Domestic Product: Fourth Quarter and Annual 2012," News Release, Bureau of Economic Analysis, U.S. Department of Commerce, January 30, 2013; "International Trade Statistics 2011," World Trade Organization, p. 12; "Table 2.1 Employment by Major Industry Sector, 2000, 2010, and Projected 2020," Bureau of Labor Statistics, U.S. Department of Labor, February 1, 2012; "Table 1.1.5. Gross Domestic Product," Bureau of Economic Analysis, National Income and Product Accounts Table, February 25, 2011.
3. "One Concierge Makes Hard-to-Get Gift Ideas Easier with GiftVault .com," *PR.com,* October 6, 2012; One Concierge Announces Partnership with Paramount Business Jets," *American Consumer News,* March 4, 2011; "Ubitus to Launch Cloud Gaming Services on Google TV," *PR Newswire,* January 7, 2013; and The Breakers Palm Beach website, www.thebreakers.com, accessed January 30, 2013.
4. Janet R. McColl-Kennedy and Tina White, "Service Provider Training Programs at Odds with Customer Requirements in Five Star Hotels," *Journal of Services Marketing* 11, no. 4 (1997), pp. 249–64; Ellyn A. McColgan, "How Fidelity Invests in Service Professionals," *Harvard Business Review,* January–February 1997, pp. 137–43; and Frederick F. Reichheld and W. Earl Sasser, Jr., "Zero Defections: Quality Comes to Services," *Harvard Business Review,* September–October 1990, pp. 105–11.
5. Christian Gronroos, "Value Co-creation in Service Logic: A Critical Analysis," *Marketing Theory,* September 2011, pp. 279–301; and Stephen L. Vargo and Robert F. Lusch, "Evolving to a New Dominant Logic for Marketing," *Journal of Marketing,* January 2004, p. 1.
6. Alana Semuels, "Self-Service Machines Replacing Retail Workers," *The Star-Ledger,* March 13, 2011, p. 1; Zhen Zhu, Cheryl Nakata, and K. Sivakumar, "Self-Service Technology Effectiveness: The Role of Design Features and Individual Traits," *Journal of the Academy of Marketing Science,* Winter 2007, pp. 492–506; and Lawrence F. Cunningham, Clifford E. Young, and James Gerlach, "A Comparison of Consumer Views of Traditional Services and Self-Service Technologies," *Journal of Services Marketing* 1 (2009), pp. 11–23.
7. Ashlee Vance and Aaron Ricadela, "Hewlett-Packard's Free Fall," *Bloomberg Businessweek,* January 14–20, 2013, pp. 44–50; and "HP to Invest $1 Billion to Launch New Era of Enterprise Services," *Business Wire,* June 1, 2010.
8. Christopher Lovelock and Jochen Wirtz, *Services Marketing: People, Technology, Strategy,* 7th ed., (Upper Saddle River, NJ: Pearson Prentice-Hall, 2011); Lance A. Bettencourt, Stephen W. Brown, and Nancy J. Sirianni, "The Secret to True Service Innovation," *Business Horizons,* February 2013, pp. 13–22; and Thomas J. Delong and Vineeta Vijayaraghavan, "Should You Listen to the Customer?" *Harvard Business Review,* September 2012, pp. 129–33.
9. Suzanne C. Makarem, Susan M. Mudambi, Jeffrey S. Podoshen, "Satisfaction in Technology-Enabled Service Encounters," *The Journal of Services Marketing* 3 (2009), p. 134; Peter C. Honebein and Roy F. Cammarano, "Customers at Work: Self-Service Customers Can Reduce Costs and Become Cocreators of Value," *Marketing Management,* January/February 2006, pp. 26–31; and Matthew L. Meuter, Amy L. Ostrom, Robert I. Roundtree, and Mary Jo Bitner, "Self-Service Technologies: Understanding Customer Satisfaction with Technology-Based Service Encounters," *Journal of Marketing,* July 2000, pp. 50–64.
10. Katie L. Roeger, Amy S. Blackwood, and Sarah L. Pettijohn, *The Nonprofit Almanac,* 2012; and "Quick Facts about Nonprofits," National Center for Charitable Statistics, http://nccsdataweb.urban.org, 2012.

11. Don Knapp, "Ten Nonprofit Myths—and How to Debunk Them," *Nonprofit World,* September/October 2010, pp. 12–14; and Jessi Hempl, "Selling a Cause? Better Make It Pop," *BusinessWeek,* February 13, 2006, p. 75.
12. Elyse Dupre, "The American Red Cross Braves the Campaign Storm," *DMNews,* January 2013; "American Red Cross Launches New Ad Campaign," *India Pharma News,* January 11, 2013; "Storytellers Campaign Shows Powerful Red Cross Moments," *States News Service,* December 13, 2012; Jane L. Levere, "To Tell Its Story, Red Cross Goes to Those It Helped," *The New York Times,* December 13, 2012, p. 3; "Corporate Partners Support Red Cross Holiday Campaign," *PR Newswire,* December 12, 2012; Christine Birkner, "The American Red Cross Took a Centralized Approach to Protect Its Brand Message," *Marketing News,* July 30, 2011, p. 10; "National Celebrity Cabinet Members," American Red Cross website, http://www.redcross.org/supporters/celebrities/2012-cabinet-members, accessed February 3, 2013; and "AMA and AMAF Honor the 2012 Nonprofit Marketer of the Year," American Marketing Association, press release, July 10, 1012.
13. Doug Donovan, "Fiscal Cliff Deal Could Hurt Charitable Giving," *The Chronicle of Philanthropy,* January 1, 2013; Michele Nichols, "U.S. Charitable Giving Approaches $300 Billion in 2011," *Reuters,* June 19, 2012; "The American Red Cross and Dell Launch First-of-Its-Kind Social Media Digital Operations Center," *Business Wire,* March 7, 2012; Alex Goldmark, "Everyone Chip In, Please; Crowdfunding Sandy," National Public Radio (transcript), December 10, 2012; "People Can Support Response by Giving to Red Cross Disaster Relief," American Red Cross, press release, October 29, 2012; Christine Birkner, "Give—And Give Again," *Marketing News,* May 31, 2012, p. 8; Pete Born, "Komen Foundation to Launch Fragrance," *Women's Wear Daily,* January 3, 2011, p. 4; "Telescope Inc. and Susan G. Komen for the Cure Los Angeles Join Forces to 'Text for the Cure,'" *PR Newswire,* December 15, 2010; Ann Marie Kerwin, "How to Get the Social-Media Generation Behind Your Cause," *Advertising Age,* June 28, 2010, p. 8; "American Red Cross Responds to Japan Earthquake and Pacific Tsunami," *PR Newswire,* March 11, 2011; Michael Bush, "Red Cross Delivers Real Mobile Results for a Real Emergency," *Advertising Age,* February 22, 2010, p. 38; and Maureen West, "How Nonprofits Can Use Social Media to Spark Change," *The Chronicle of Philanthropy,* February 20, 2011.
14. "U.S. Postal Service Details Free Package Pickup in New TV Ad," *Wireless News,* December 30, 2012; Ryan Joe, "The U.S. Postal Service Steps Up Its Mobile Game," *DMNews,* December 2012; "Hallmark and the U.S. Postal Service Launch Postage-Paid Greeting Cards," *PR Newswire,* February 17, 2011; "Postal Service Begins 2011 with Loss in First Quarter, Recession Eases, but First-Class Mail Volume Continues to Decline," *States News Service,* February 9, 2011; and Diane C. Lade, "Postal Service Learns to Love the Internet," *South Florida Sun-Sentinel,* March 15, 2007.
15. Keith B. Murray, "A Test of Services Marketing Theory: Consumer Information Acquisition Activities," *Journal of Marketing,* January 1991, pp. 10–25.
16. Dawn Iacobucci, "An Empirical Examination of Some Basic Tenets in Services: Goods-Services Continua," in *Advances in Services Marketing and Management,* vol. 1, eds. Teresa Swartz, David E. Bowen, and Stephen W. Brown (Greenwich, CT: JAI Press), pp. 23–52; and Valerie A. Zeithaml, "How Consumer Evaluation Processes Differ between Goods and Services," in *Marketing of Services,* eds. James H. Donnelly and William R. George (Chicago: American Marketing Association, 1981).
17. Ebrahim Mazaheri, Richard Marie-Odile, and Michel Laroche, "The Role of Emotions in Online Consumer Behavior: A Comparison of Search, Experience, and Credence Services," *Journal of Services Marketing* 7 (2012), pp. 535–50; Michael J. Dorsch, Stephen J. Grove, and William Darden, "Consumer Intentions to Use a Services Category," *Journal of Services Marketing* 2 (2000), pp. 92–117; and Murray, "A Test of Services Marketing Theory: Consumer Information Acquisition Activities," *Journal of Marketing,* January 1991, pp. 10–25.
18. Leonard L. Berry and Neeli Bendapudi, "Clueing in Customers," *Harvard Business Review,* February 2003, pp. 100–6.
19. John Ozment and Edward Morash, "The Augmented Service Offering for Perceived and Actual Service Quality," *Journal of the Academy of Marketing Science,* Fall 1994, pp. 352–63.
20. A. Parasuraman, Valerie A. Zeithaml, and Leonard L. Berry, "Reassessment of Expectations as a Comparison Standard in Measuring Service Quality: Implications for Further Research," *Journal of Marketing,* January 1994, pp. 111–24; and Leonard L. Berry, *On Great Service* (New York: Free Press, 1995).
21. Valerie A. Zeithaml, A. Parasuraman, and Leonard L. Berry, *Delivering Quality Service* (New York: Free Press, 1990); and Stephen W. Brown and Teresa Swartz, "A Gap Analysis of Professional Service Quality," *Journal of Marketing,* April 1989, pp. 92–98.
22. Amy Ostrom and Dawn Iacobucci, "Consumer Trade-Offs and the Evaluation of Services," *Journal of Marketing,* January 1995, pp. 17–28; and J. Joseph Cronin, Jr., and Steven A. Taylor, "Measuring Service Quality: A Reexamination and Extension," *Journal of Marketing,* July 1992, pp. 55–68.
23. L. Jean Harrison-Walker, "The Role of Cause and Affect in Service Failure," *Journal of Services Marketing* 2 (2012), pp. 115–23; Kriengsin Prasongsukarn and Paul G. Patterson, "An Extended Service Recovery Model: The Moderating Impact of Temporal Sequence of Events," *Journal of Services Marketing* 7 (2012), pp. 510–20; Anna S. Mattila, "Do Women Like Options More Than Men? An Examination in the Context of Service Recovery," *Journal of Services Marketing* 7 (2012), pp. 499–508; Leslie M. Fine, "Service Marketing," *Business Horizons,* May–June 2008, pp. 163–68; and James G. Maxham III and Richard G. Netermeyer, "A Longitudinal Study of Complaining Customers' Evaluations of Multiple Service Failures and Recovery Efforts," *Journal of Marketing,* October 2002, pp. 57–71.
24. "How To Earn Extreme Trust: The True Story of Domino's Pizza," *Fearless Competitor,* June 27, 2012; "Becoming Crystal Clear: The Hits and Misses of Brand Transparency," *Business 2 Community.com,* November 14, 2012; "Culture of Openness Gets the Thumbs Up," *Marketing Week,* August 4, 2011, p. 20; and Charles Enman, "Social Media Monitoring Firm Is Looking to Hire," *The Daily Gleaner,* March 8, 2011, p. D1.
25. Vicki Clift, "Everyone Needs Service Flow Charting," *Marketing News,* October 23, 1995, pp. 41, 43; Mary Jo Bitner, Bernard H. Booms, and Mary Stanfield Tetreault, "The Service Encounter: Diagnosing Favorable and Unfavorable Incidents," *Journal of Marketing,* January 1990, pp. 71–84; Eberhard Scheuing, "Conducting Customer Service Audits," *Journal of Consumer Marketing,* Summer 1989, pp. 35–41; and W. Earl Susser, R. Paul Olsen, and D. Daryl Wyckoff, *Management of Service Operations* (Boston: Allyn & Bacon, 1978).
26. Chi Kin (Bennett) Yim, Kimmy Wa Chan, and Simon S. K. Lam, "Do Customers and Employees Enjoy Service Participation? Synergistic Effect of Self- and Other-Efficacy," *Journal of Marketing,* November 2012, pp. 121–40; Joseph Pine and James H. Gilmore, *The Experience Economy,* Revised Edition, (Boston: Harvard Business School Publishing, 2011); Mary Jo Bitner, Amy L. Ostrom, and Felicia N. Morgan, "Service Blueprinting: A Practical Technique for Service Innovation," *California Management Review,* Spring 2008, pp. 66–94; Thorsten Hennig-Thurau, Markus Groth, Michael Paul, and Dwayne D. Gremler, "Are All Smiles Created Equal? How Emotional Contagion and Emotional Labor Affect Service Relationships," *Journal of Marketing,* July 2006, pp. 58–73.

27. Leonard L. Berry, "Relationship Marketing of Services—Growing Interest, Emerging Perspectives," *Journal of the Academy of Marketing Science,* Fall 1995, pp. 236–45; Mary Jo Bitner, "Building Service Relationships: It's All about Promises," *Journal of the Academy of Marketing Science,* Fall 1995, pp. 246–51; Kevin P. Gwinner, Dwayne D. Gremler, and Mary Jo Bitner, "Relational Benefits in Services Industries: The Customer's Perspective," *Journal of the Academy of Marketing Science,* Spring 1998, pp. 101–14; Susan Fournier, Susan Dobscha, and David Glen Mick, "Preventing the Premature Death of Relationship Marketing," *Harvard Business Review,* January–February 1998, pp. 42–51; and John V. Petrof, "Relationship Marketing: The Wheel Reinvented?" *Business Horizons,* November–December 1997, pp. 26–31.

28. Katherine N. Lemon, Tiffany Barnett White, and Russell S. Winer, "Dynamic Customer Relationship Management: Incorporating Future Considerations into the Service Retention Decision," *Journal of Marketing,* January 2002, pp. 1–14.

29. Michael Paul, Thorsten Hennig-Thurau, Dwayne D. Gremler, Kevin P. Gwinner, and Caroline Wiertz, "Toward a Theory of Repeat Purchase Drivers for Consumer Services," *Journal of the Academy of Marketing Science,* Summer 2009, pp. 215–37.

30. Thomas S. Gruca, "Defending Service Markets," *Marketing Management* 1 (1994), pp. 31–38; and Leonard L. Berry, Jeffrey S. Conant, and A. Parasuraman. "A Framework for Conducting a Services Marketing Audit," *Journal of the Academy of Marketing Science,* Summer 1991, pp. 255–68.

31. Christopher Lovelock and Jochen Wirtz, *Service Marketing: People, Technology, Strategy,* 7th ed. (Upper Saddle River, NJ: Prentice Hall, 2011); Valerie A. Zeithaml, Mary Jo Bitner, and Dwayne D. Gremler, *Services Marketing,* 6th ed. (New York: McGraw-Hill, 2013), p. 26; and Brian Solis, "Exploring the Fifth and Sixth Ps of Marketing," *Marketing News,* January 2013, p. 7.

32. Dan R. E. Thomas, "Strategy Is Different in Service Businesses," *Harvard Business Review,* July–August 1978, pp. 158–65.

33. Sundar G. Bharedwaj, P. Rajan Varadarajan, and John Fahy, "Sustainable Competitive Advantage in Service Industries: A Conceptual Model and Research Propositions," *Journal of Marketing,* October 1993, pp. 83–99.

34. "Fairmont Hotels and Resorts to Offer Local Shuttle Service with BMW Vehicles," *Entertainment Close-Up,* January 30, 2013; "Westin Hotels Celebrates Anniversary of the Heavenly Bed with Limited-Time Sale," *Manufacturing Close-Up,* September 10, 2012; Abby Ellin, "No Place Like Home—Or a Hotel with the Gym You Use When You're There," *The International Herald Tribune,* November 2, 2011, p. 20; Elisabeth A. Sullivan, "Brand Power2: Fairmont Hotels Partners with Lifestyle Brands to Leverage Their Combined Reach and Add to Its Customer Experience," *Marketing News,* February 28, 2010, p. 11; and Daniel B. Honigman, "Hotels at Home: In-Room Catalog and E-Commerce Service Leverages Guest Experience While Increasing Brand Awareness," *Marketing News,* March 15, 2008, p. 12.

35. Kent B. Monroe, "Buyers' Subjective Perceptions of Price," *Journal of Marketing Research,* February 1973, pp. 70–80; and Jerry Olson, "Price as an Informational Cue: Effects on Product Evaluation," in *Consumer and Industrial Buying Behavior,* eds. A. G. Woodside, J. N. Sheth, and P. D. Bennett (New York: Elsevier North-Holland, 1977), pp. 267–86.

36. Hean Tat Keh and Jun Pang, "Customer Reactions to Service Separation," *Journal of Marketing,* March 2010, pp. 55–70; Leonard L. Berry, Kathleen Seiders, and Dhruv Grewal, "Understanding Service Convenience," *Journal of Marketing* 66 (July 2002), pp. 1–17; and Charles L. Colby and A. Parasuraman, "Technology Still Matters: E-Services Are Alive and Well and Positioned for Growth," *Marketing Management* 12 (July–August 2003), pp. 28–33.

37. Robert E. Hite, Cynthia Fraser, and Joseph A. Bellizzi, "Professional Service Advertising: The Effects of Price Inclusion, Justification, and Level of Risk," *Journal of Advertising Research* 30 (August–September 1990), pp. 23–31; William R. George and Leonard L. Berry, "Guidelines for the Advertising of Services," *Business Horizons,* July–August 1981, pp. 52–56; and Eugene M. Johnson, Eberhard E. Scheuing, and Kathleen A. Gaida, *Profitable Service Marketing* (Homewood, IL: Dow Jones-Irwin, 1986).

38. Kathleen Mortimer, "Identifying the Components of Effective Service Advertisements," *Journal of Services Marketing* 22 (2008), pp. 104–13.

39. Joe Adams, "Why Public Service Advertising Doesn't Work," *Adweek,* November 17, 1980, p. 72.

40. Patriya Tansuhaj, Donna Randall, and Jim McCullough, "A Services Marketing Management Model: Integrating Internal and External Marketing Functions," *Journal of Sciences Marketing,* Winter 1998, pp. 31–38.

41. Christian Gronroos, "Internal Marketing Theory and Practice," in *Services Marketing in a Changing Environment,* eds. Thomas Bloch, G. D. Upah, and V. A. Zeithaml (Chicago: American Marketing Association, 1984).

42. Ibid.

43. Rita Di Mascio, "The Service Models of Frontline Employees," *Journal of Marketing,* July 2010, pp. 63–80; Yong-Ki Lee, Jung-Heon Nam, Dae-Hwan Park, and Kyung Ah Lee, "What Factors Influence Customer-Oriented Prosocial Behavior of Customer-Contact Employees?" *Journal of Services Marketing* 20, no. 4 (2006), pp. 251–64; Stephen W. Brown, "The Employee Experience," *Marketing Management* 12 (March–April 2003), pp. 12–13; Lawrence A. Crosby and Sheree L. Johnson, "Watch What I Do," *Marketing Management* 12 (November–December 2003), pp. 10–11; and March C. Gilly and Mary Wolfinbarger, "Advertising's Internal Audience," *Journal of Marketing,* January 1998, pp. 69–88.

44. Adrian Palmer, "Customer Experience Management: A Critical Review of an Emerging Idea," *Journal of Service Marketing* 3 (2010), pp. 196–208; Gabriel M. Gelb and John M. McKeever, "In Their Shoes," *Marketing Management,* July/August 2006, pp. 40–45; Lynette Ryals, "Making Customer Relationship Management Work: The Measurement and Profitable Management of Customer Relationships," *Journal of Marketing,* October 2005, pp. 252–61; Bernd H. Schmitt, *Customer Experience Management* (Hoboken, NJ: Wiley and Sons, 2003); and Shaun Smith and Joe Wheeler, *Managing the Customer Experience* (Englewood Cliffs, NJ: Prentice Hall, 2002).

45. Lance A. Bettencourt, "Fundamental Tenets of Service Excellence," *Marketing Management,* Fall 2012, pp. 19–23; "Zappos Family Core Values," Zappos website, http://about.zappos.com/our-unique-culture/zappos-core-values, accessed February 5, 2013; and Paula Andruss, "Delivering WOW Through Service," *Marketing News,* October 15, 2008, p. 10.

46. F. G. Crane, *Professional Services Marketing: Strategy and Tactics* (London: Haworth Press, 1993); and Leonard L. Berry and Neeli Bendapudi, "Clueing in Customers," *Harvard Business Review,* February 2003, pp. 100–6.

47. Frederick H. deB. Harris and Peter Peacock, "Hold My Place, Please," *Marketing Management,* Fall 1995, pp. 34–46.

48. Christopher Lovelock and Jochen Wirtz, *Services Marketing* (Englewood Cliffs, NJ: Prentice Hall, 2007), pp. 260–84.

49. Angel Moscaritolo, "AT&T Rebrands U-verse as Mobile TV," *PC Magazine,* February 4, 2013; and "This New Google TV Watches You and Chooses Shows Based on Your Behavior," *The Business Insider,* January 10, 2013.

50. Anyuan Shen and A. Dwayne Ball, "Is Personalization of Services Always a Good Thing? Exploring the Role of Technology-Mediated Personalization (TMP) in Service Relationships," *Journal of Services Marketing* 23 (2009), pp. 80–92.

51. Kamalini Ramdas, Elizabeth Teisberg, and Amy L. Tucker, "4 Ways to Reinvent Service Delivery," *Harvard Business Review,* December 2012, pp. 99–106; Michael K. Brady, Clay M. Voorhees, and Michael J. Brusco, "Service Sweethearting: Its Antecedents and Customer Consequences," *Journal of Marketing,* March 2012, pp. 81–98.

52. "Washington: Green Teams Help U.S. Postal Service Save Millions," *Plus Media Solutions,* February 3, 2013; Hilton Worldwide website, Corporate Responsibility, http://www.hiltonworldwide.com/corporate-responsibility/sustainability/, February 10, 2013; Lawrence Crosby, "Sustainable Relationships," *Marketing Management,* Spring 2010, pp. 12–13; David A. Lubin and Daniel C. Esty, "The Sustainability Imperative," *Harvard Business Review,* May 2010, pp. 42–50; "Consumer Interest in 'Green' Service Doubled from 2008–2010," *PR Newswire,* March 8, 2011; "Choice Energy Services Enables Trump SoHo Hotel to Access 100 Percent Green Power through Innovative Energy Procurement and Management Program," *Business Wire,* March 16, 2011; E. Robinot and J. L. Giannelloni, "Do Hotels' "Green" Attributes Contribute to Customer Satisfaction?" *Journal of Services Marketing* 2 (2010), pp. 157–169; and "Green Team Helps Postal Service Save Millions," *PR Newswire,* January 25, 2011.

53. Mary Jo Bitner and Stephen W. Brown, "The Service Imperative," *Business Horizons,* January–February 2008, pp. 39–46; and Valerie Zeithaml, Mary Jo Bitner, and Dwayne Gremler, "Services Marketing Strategy," *Marketing Strategy Encyclopedia* (Hoboken, NJ: Wiley and Sons, 2009).

LA Galaxy: This case was written by Steven Hartley. Sources: "Galaxy's Home Has New Name," *The Daily News of Los Angeles,* March 5, 2013, p. A1; Kevin Baxter, "Beckham Will Hang Up His Boots: A Star In Europe, His Late Career Move to the Galaxy Brought U.S. Fans to Soccer and Put MLS on Map," *Los Angeles Times,* May 17, 2013, p. C2; "Galaxy, Tim Warner Strike 10-Year, $55 Million Deal," *The Daily News of Los Angeles,* November 16, 2011, p. C6; denz@rslsoapbox, "For Major League Soccer It Is All About the Numbers, TV, Attendance, and Season Tickets," rslsoapbox.com, May 18, 2012; Karl Greenberg, "Chevrolet Cleats Up for L.A. Galaxy Sponsorship," *Marketing Daily,* May 28, 2013; LA Galaxy website, www.lagalaxy.com, accessed July 26, 2013; and personal interviews with LA Galaxy personnel.

Chapter 13

1. Steve Stecklow, "StubHub's Ticket to Ride," *The Wall Street Journal,* January 17, 2006, pp. B1–B2; Neal Karlinsky, "StubHub: Revolutionizing the Modern-Day Ticket Scalper," *ABC News: Nightline,* February 6, 2013; and *ABC NewsRadio: Perspective,* February 8, 2013. See http://abcnews.go.com/Business/stubhub-revolutionizing-modern-day-ticket-scalper/story?id=18421695 and http://abcnewsradioonline.com/perspective, respectively.

2. Eric Young, "Giants Strike Online Ticket Deal," *Silicon Valley/San Jose Business Journal,* February 9, 2009.

3. Dinah Eng, "StubHub: "The Anatomy of a Game-Changing Idea," *Fortune,* July 23, 2012, pp. 57–60.

4. "Premiere of the Bugatti Grand Sport Vitesse at the Qatar Motor Show 2013," Bugatti press release, January 28, 2013. See http://www.bugatti.com/press/detail.php?mode=press&dbid=120 (login required—press:bugatti) and http://www.bugatti.com/en/vitesse.html; Jason H. Harper, "Bugatti's $2.5 Million Vitesse Zooms to 233 MPH," *Bloomberg,* September 12, 2012. See http://www.bloomberg.com/news/2012-09-12/bugatti-s-2-5-million-vitesse-zooms-to-233-mph.html; and Jim Holder, "First Drive Review: Bugatti Veyron Vitesse," *Autocar,* June 7, 2012. See http://www.autocar.co.uk/car-review/bugatti/veyron/first-drives/first-drive-review-bugatti-veyron-vitesse and for the video review, see http://www.youtube.com/watch?v=st_hE-2Cy0Y.

5. Edmunds allows prospective car buyers the opportunity to calculate a total cost of ownership (TCO), which includes insurance, repairs, depreciation, etc., over a specified period of time, such as five years, for a variety of vehicles. See http://www.edmunds.com/tco.html to perform such a calculation for a vehicle of choice. The calculation here used several assumptions to illustrate the price equation.

6. Kirby Garlitos, "2014 Bugatti SuperVeyron," *TopSpeed,* November 19, 2012. See http://www.topspeed.com/cars/bugatti/2014-bugatti-superveyron-ar138038.html.

7. Brad Stone and Douglass MacMillan, "Are Four Words Worth $25 Billion?" *Bloomberg Businessweek,* March 21–27, 2011, pp. 72–74; and Ben Sisario, "Ticketmaster Plans to Use a Variable Pricing Policy," *The New York Times,* April 19, 2011, p. B5.

8. The Marketing Matters box on Dollar Shave Club was written by Professor Nancy Harrower, Concordia University, St. Paul, MN.

9. Thomas L. Friedman, *The World Is Flat* (New York: Farrar, Straus, and Giroux, Expanded Edition, 2006), pp. 5–9; "The Secret of IKEA's Success," *The Economist,* February 26, 2011, pp. 67–68; Jason Dean and Peter Wonacott, "Tech Firms Woo 'Next Billion' Users," *The Wall Street Journal,* November 3, 2006 p. A2; and Dexter Roberts, "China Mobile's Hot Signal," *BusinessWeek,* February 5, 2007, pp. 42–44.

10. Laurie Burkitt and Ann Zimmerman, "Toys "Я" Us Grows in China with 'Tiger Moms' in Mind," *The Wall Street Journal,* November 20, 2012, pp. B1, B7.

11. Adapted from Kent B. Monroe, *Pricing: Making Profitable Decisions,* 3rd ed. (New York: McGraw-Hill, 2003); and David J. Curry, "Measuring Price and Quality Competition," *Journal of Marketing,* Spring 1985, pp. 106–17.

12. Numerous studies have examined the price-quality-value relationship. See, for example, Jacob Jacoby and Jerry C. Olsen, eds., *Perceived Quality* (Lexington, MA: Lexington Books, 1985); William D. Dodds, Kent B. Monroe, and Dhruv Grewal, "Effects of Price, Brand, and Store Information on Buyers' Product Evaluations," *Journal of Marketing Research,* August 1991, pp. 307–19; and Roger A. Kerin, Ambuj Jain, and Daniel Howard, "Store Shopping Experience and Consumer Price-Quality-Value Perceptions," *Journal of Retailing,* Winter 1992, pp. 235–45. For a thorough review of the price-quality-value relationship, see Valerie A. Zeithaml, "Consumer Perceptions of Price, Quality, and Value," *Journal of Marketing,* July 1998, pp. 2–22.

13. Roger A. Kerin and Robert A. Peterson, "Crestfield Furniture Industries, Inc. (A)," *Strategic Marketing Problems: Cases and Comments,* 11th ed. (Upper Saddle River, NJ: Prentice Hall, 2007), pp. 275–86.

14. Haipeng (Allan) Chen, Howard Marmorstein, Michael Tsiros, and Akshay R. Rao, "When More Is Less: The Impact of Base Value Neglect on Consumer Preferences for Bonus Packs over Price Discounts," *Journal of Marketing* 76 (July 2012), pp. 64–77.

15. Carl Bialik, Elizabeth Holmes, and Ray A. Smith, "Many Discounts, Few Deals," *The Wall Street Journal,* December 15, 2010, pp. D1–D2; and Jayne O'Donnell and Kate Coughlin, "Retailers Try to Entice Customers into Buying Blitz," *USA Today,* April 1, 2011, pp. 1A, 2A.

16. Ajaero Tony Martins, "7 Factors That Will Influence Your Product Pricing Strategy," www.StrategicBusinessTeam.com. See http://www.strategicbusinessteam.com/small-business-marketing-strategy/7-critical-factors-that-will-influence-the-pricing-of-your-product.
17. Ken Belson, "Mets Going for the Gold on Tickets for More Games," *The New York Times,* April 8, 2009, p. B13.
18. Ann Zimmerman, "How Toy Crazes Are Born," *The Wall Street Journal,* December 15, 2010, pp. D1–D2; Mike Dodd, "Cards Hold 50 Years of Memories," *USA Today,* March 27, 2001, pp. 1A, 2A; and J. C. Conklin, "Don't Throw Out Those Old Sneakers, They're a Gold Mine," *The Wall Street Journal,* September 21, 1998, pp. A1, A20. Prices quoted on eBay.com on February 17, 2013.
19. Christina Binkley, "How Can Jeans Cost $300?" *The Wall Street Journal,* July 7, 2011, pp. D1–D2.
20. Jessica E. Lessin, "A Low-Priced iPhone Awaits," *The Wall Street Journal,* January 9, 2013, p. B1; Ian Sheer, "Tablet War Is an Apple Rout," *The Wall Street Journal,* August 12, 2011, pp. B1–B2; and Apple's website. See http://www.apple.com/ipad.
21. Arik Hesseldahl, "For Every Xbox, a Big Fat Loss," *BusinessWeek,* December 5, 2005, p. 13; and Akshay R. Rao, Mark E. Bergen, and Scott Davis, "How to Fight a Price War," *Harvard Business Review,* March–April 2000, pp. 107–16.
22. Ron Winslow, "How a Breakthrough Quickly Broke Down for Johnson & Johnson," *The Wall Street Journal,* September 18, 1988, pp. A1, A5.
23. Evelyn M. Rusli and Shelly Banjo, "Facebook's Wal-Mart Gambit," *The Wall Street Journal,* December 17, 2012, pp. B1–B2.
24. John Ewoldt, "Best Buy Makes Its Online Price-Match Policy Permanent," *Star Tribune,* February 22, 2013. See http://www.startribune.com/business/192413341.html; Chris Burritt, "Best Buy Makes Price Match Permanent to Win Back Clients," *Bloomberg Businessweek,* February 15, 2013. See http://www.bloomberg.com/news/2013-02-15/best-buy-makes-price-match-permanent-to-win-back-clients.html; John Vomhof, Jr., "Target Now Will Match Online Prices Year-Round, *Minneapolis/St. Paul Business Journal,* January 23, 2013. See http://www.bizjournals.com/twincities/news/2013/01/08/target-online-price-match-year-round.html; John Ewoldt, "Big-Box Retailers Take on the Internet, *The Wall Street Journal,* November 18, 2012, pp. A1, A13; and Matt Townsend, Sapna Maheshwari, and Cotten Timberlake, "Holiday Shopping: Retailers Aim to Thwart Online Rivals, *Bloomberg Businessweek,* November 5–November 11, 2012, pp. 19–21. See also Walmart's Ad Match Guarantee at http://corporate.walmart.com/ad-match-guarantee; Target's Low Price Promise at https://corporate.target.com/about/shopping-experience/our-low-price-promise; and Best Buy's Price Match Guarantee at http://www.bestbuy.com/site/Payment-Pricing/Best-Buy-Price-Match-Guarantee/pcmcat204400050011.c?id=pcmcat204400050011.
25. Rob Veres, "Find the Lowest Price for Anything in a Store," *Time,* October 15, 2012, p. 40.
26. Jennifer Valentino-DeVries, Jeremy Singer-Vine, and Ashkan Soltani, "Websites Vary Prices, Deals Based on Users' Information." *The Wall Street Journal,* December 24, 2012. See http://online.wsj.com/article_email/SB10001424127887323777204578189391-8138815341MyQjAxMTAyMDIwMzEyNDMyWj.html; Rafi Mohammed, "Why Online Retailers' New Pricing Strategy Will Backfire," *Harvard Business Review,* December 19, 2012. See http://blogs.hbr.org/es/2012/12/why_online_retailers_new_prici.html; and Stephanie Clifford, "Retail Frenzy: Prices on the Web Change Hourly," *The New York Times,* November 30, 2012. See http://www.nytimes.com/2012/12/01/business/online-retailers-rush-to-adjust-prices-in-real-time.html.
27. Vanessa O'Connell, "How Campbell Saw a Breakthrough Menu Turn into Leftovers," *The Wall Street Journal,* October 6, 1998, pp. A1, A12.
28. A detailed explanation of the calculation of marginal revenue appears in the Instructor's Manual; and Sydney Weintraub, *Price Theory* (New York: Pitman Publishing Corporation, 1956), pp. 36–45.
29. Peter Coy, "Can't Stop Guzzling," *BusinessWeek,* July 31, 2006, pp. 26–29.
30. Ellen Byron and Anjali Cordeiro, "P&G, Others Are Confident Higher Prices Will Stick," *The Wall Street Journal,* February 20, 2009, pp. B1, B2; and Jeff D. Opdyke, "In Colgate's Profit, a Breath of Fresh Air," *The Wall Street Journal,* January 29, 2009, p. C1.
31. "Message Is Clear: Higher Prices Deter Smoking," *USA Today,* April 9, 2009, p. 10A.
32. "Everyday Higher Prices," *The Economist,* February 26, 2011, pp. 68–69.

Washburn Guitar: This case was edited by Steven Hartley. Sources: Burkhard Bilger, "String Theory, Building a Better Guitar," *The New Yorker,* May 14, 2007, p. 79; and the Washburn Guitar website (www.washburn.com).

Chapter 14

1. "How Vizio Conquered TV," *CNNMoney*, July 25, 2012; "America's Largest Private Companies," www.forbes.com, November 28, 2012; "Vizio Extends Battle Plan," *The Wall Street Journal,* January 3, 2011, p. B3; "How Vizio Beat Sony in High-Def TV," www.bloombergbusinessweek.com, April 22, 2010; "U.S. Upstart Takes On TV Giants in Price War," *The Wall Street Journal,* April 15, 2008, pp. B1, B6; and "The VIZIO Story," www.vizio.com, downloaded March 10, 2013.
2. "Amazon Fights the iPad with 'Fire,'" *The Wall Street Journal,* September 29, 2011, pp. B1, 10.
3. The conditions favoring skimming versus penetration pricing are described in Kent B. Monroe, *Pricing: Making Profitable Decisions,* 3rd ed. (Burr Ridge, IL: McGraw-Hill/Irwin, 2003).
4. Jean-Noel Kapferer, *The New Strategic Brand Management: Creating and Sustaining Brand Equity,* 4th ed. (London: Kogan Page Ltd, 2008).
5. Stacy Meichtry, "What Your Time Is Really Worth," *The Wall Street Journal,* April 7–8, 2007, pp. P1, P4.
6. "Premium AA Alkaline Batteries," *Consumer Reports,* March 21, 2002, p. 54; Kemp Powers, "Assault and Batteries," *Forbes,* September 4, 2000, pp. 54, 56; and "Razor Burn at Gillette," *BusinessWeek,* June 18, 2001, p. 37.
7. Michael Levy and Barton A. Weitz, *Retailing Management,* 7th ed. (Burr Ridge, IL: McGraw-Hill/Irwin, 2010), pp. 501–2.
8. "Bet Your Bottom Dollar on 99 Cents," www.nytimes.com, February 8, 2009. For further reading on odd-even pricing, see Mark Stiving and Russell S. Winer, "An Empirical Analysis of Price Endings with Scanner Data," *Journal of Consumer Research,* June 1997, pp. 57–67; and Robert M. Schindler, "Patterns of Rightmost Digits Used in Advertised Prices: Implications for Nine-Ending Effects," *Journal of Consumer Research,* September 1997, pp. 192–201.
9. For an overview on target pricing, see Stephan A. Butscher and Michael Laker, "Market Driven Product Development," *Marketing Management,* Summer 2000, pp. 48–53.
10. Thomas T. Nagle and Reed K. Holden, *The Strategy and Tactics of Pricing,* 4th ed. (Englewood Cliffs, NJ: Prentice Hall, 2009), pp. 243–49.
11. Robert J. Dolan and Hermann Simon, *Power Pricing: How Managing Price Transforms the Bottom Line* (New York: Free Press, 1996),

p. 249; and Scott McCartney, "You Paid What for That Flight?" *The Wall Street Journal,* August 26, 2010, pp. D1, D2.

12. "What Popcorn Prices Mean for Movies," *Advertising Age,* May 19, 2008, p. 4.
13. Peter M. Noble and Thomas S. Gruca, "Industrial Pricing: Theory and Managerial Practice," *Marketing Science* 18, no. 3 (1999), pp. 435–54.
14. Ann Zimmerman, "Can Electronics Stores Survive?" *The Wall Street Journal,* August 31, 2012, pp. B1, B2.
15. "In Lean Times, Big Companies Make a Grab for Market Share," *The Wall Street Journal,* September 5, 2003, pp. A1, A6.
16. "A New Beverage Attitude," *Convenience Store/Petroleum News,* May 2010, pp. 110–12.
17. "Is the Music Store Over?" *Business 2.0,* March 2004, pp. 115–19.
18. "Dell Fine-Tunes Its PC Pricing to Gain an Edge in Slow Market," *The Wall Street Journal,* June 8, 2001, pp. A1, A8.
19. Bill Saporito, "This Offer Won't Last," *Time,* January 21, 2013, p. 56; "Don't Like This Price? Wait a Minute," *The Wall Street Journal,* September 5, 2012, pp. A1, A2; and "Online Retailers Vary Prices Based on a User's Location," *The Wall Street Journal,* December 24, 2012, pp. A1, A10.
20. Brad Tuttle, "When Consumers Pay More Due to Race and Gender," www.business.time.com, May 18, 2012; "Are Minority Shoppers Treated Unfairly? An Expensive Reason to Care," www.diversity.com, downloaded May 18, 2003; Florian Zettelmeyer, Fiona Scott Morton, and Jorge Silva-Risso, "How the Internet Lowers Prices: Evidence from Matched Survey and Automobile Transaction Data," *Journal of Marketing Research,* May 2006, pp. 168–81; and Fiona Scott Morton, Florian Zettelmeyer, and Jorge Silva-Risso, "Consumer Information and Discrimination: Does the Internet Affect the Pricing of New Cars to Women and Minorities?" *Quantitative Marketing and Economics* 1 (2003), pp. 65–92.
21. For an extended discussion on product complements and substitutes, see Allan D. Shocker, Barry L. Bayus, and Namwoon Kim, "Product Complements and Substitutes in the Real World: The Relevance of 'Other Products,'" *Journal of Marketing,* January 2004, pp. 28–40.
22. Monroe, *Pricing,* pp. 396–97; and "Deciding When the Price Is Right," *Dallas Morning News,* May 23, 2007, pp. 1D, 3D.
23. Jagmohan S. Raju, Raj Sethuraman, and Sanjay K. Dhar, "National Brand-Store Brand Price Differential and Store Brand Market Share," *Pricing Strategy & Practice* 3, no. 2 (1995), pp. 17–24; and Akshay R. Rao, "The Quality of Price as a Quality Cue," *Journal of Marketing Research,* November 2005, pp. 401–5.
24. Tim J. Smith, *Pricing Strategy* (Mason, OH: South-West Cengage Learning, 2012). Also see, Kevin P. Coyne and John Horn, "Predicting Your Competitor's Reaction," *Harvard Business Review,* April 2009, pp. 90–97.
25. For an extended discussion about price wars, see Akshay R. Rao, Mark E. Bergen, and Scott Davis, "How to Fight a Price War," *Harvard Business Review,* March–April 2000, pp. 107–16.
26. Monroe, *Pricing*, Chapters 16 and 17.
27. Kenneth C. Manning, William O. Bearden, and Randall L. Rose, "Development of a Theory of Retailer Response to Manufacturers' Everyday Low Cost Programs," *Journal of Retailing,* Spring 1998, pp. 107–37; "Everyday Low Profits," *Harvard Business Review,* March–April 1994, p. 13; Stephen J. Hoch, Xavier Dreze, and Mary E. Purk, "EDLP, Hi-Lo, and Margin Arithmetic," *Journal of Marketing,* October 1994, pp. 16–27; and Tibbett Speer, "Do Low Prices Bore Shoppers?" *American Demographics,* January 1994, pp. 11–13. Also see Barbara E. Kahn and Leigh McAlister, *The Grocery Revolution: The New Focus on the Consumer* (Reading, MA: Addison-Wesley Educational Publishers, 1996).
28. "Six Vitamin Firms Agree to Settle Price-Fixing Suit," *The Wall Street Journal,* October 11, 2000, p. B10.
29. "Price Fixing," *USA Today,* March 7, 2000, p. C1.
30. Ronald A. Cass, "When Price 'Fixing' Makes Sense," *The Wall Street Journal,* March 24–25, 2007, p. A10; and Joseph Pereira, "Discounters, Monitors Face Battle on Minimum Pricing," *The Wall Street Journal,* December 4, 2008, pp. A1, A8.

Carmex (B): This case was written by Steven Hartley and Alisa Allen. Sources: Kristen Scheuing, "The Man Behind Carmex," *Wisconsin Trails,* March/April 2011; "Carmex and Carma Laboratories: *Pharmacy Times* Names Carmex Number One Recommended Lip Balm," *India Pharma News,* June 21, 2013; "New Lip Balm Offers Sun Protection While Drenching Lips in Moisture," *Postmedia Breaking News,* May 21, 2013; Carma Laboratories website, www.mycarmex.com, accessed September 2, 2013; and interviews with Bolin Media personnel.

Chapter 15

1. www.callawaygolf.com, downloaded April 15, 2013; "Integrated Demand Planning at Callaway Golf," www.supplychainbrain.com, June 11, 2012; Stephanie Kang, "Callaway Will Use Retailers to Sell Goods Directly to Consumers Online," *The Wall Street Journal,* November 6, 2006, p. B5; "Justin Timberlake Putting the 'Sexy' Back in Callaway Golf," www.sportingoodsnewswire.com, November 19, 2008; and Internet Retailer Top 500 Guide, 2013 Edition.
2. www.eddiebauer.com, March 20, 2013; and "Eddie Bauer's Banner Time of Year," *Advertising Age,* October 1, 2001, p. 55.
3. Internet Retailer Top 500 Guide, 2013 Edition.
4. "Second-Largest Cereal Producer Turns 20, with Style," General Mills Press Release, September 13, 2010.
5. For an overview of vertical marketing systems, see Lou Pelton, Martha Cooper, David Strutton, and James R. Lumpkin, *Marketing Channels,* 3rd ed. (Burr Ridge, IL: McGraw-Hill/Irwin, 2005).
6. "Saks to Add Exclusive Lines," *The Wall Street Journal,* February 25, 2010, p. B2.
7. "Dell Treads Carefully into Selling PCs in Stores," *The Wall Street Journal,* January 3, 2008, p. B1.
8. "8-second rule," www.pcmag.com, retrieved March 15, 2013.
9. Ben Mutzabaugh, "American Airlines Yanks Its Flights Off Travel Site Orbitz," www.USAtoday.com, December 23, 2010; Ethan Smith, "Why a Grand Plan to Cut CD Prices Went Off the Track," *The Wall Street Journal,* June 4, 2004, pp. A1, A6; and "Feud with Seller Hurts Nike Sales, Shares," *Dallas Morning News,* June 28, 2003, p. 30.
10. For an extensive discussion on channel influence and power, see Anne T. Coughlan, Erin Anderson, Louis W. Stern, and Adel I. El-Ansary, *Marketing Channels,* 7th ed. (Upper Saddle River, NJ: Prentice-Hall, 2006), Chapters 6 and 7.
11. For a contemporary and comprehensive treatment of legal issues pertaining to marketing channels, see *Antitrust Law and Economics of Product Distribution* (Chicago: American Bar Association, 2006).
12. David Simchi-Levi, Philip Kaminsky, and Edith Simchi-Levi, *Designing and Managing the Supply Chain,* 4th ed. (Burr Ridge, IL: McGraw-Hill/Irwin, 2011).
13. *The Smarter Supply Chain of the Future: Industry Edition* (Somers, NY: IBM Corporation, 2009); and John Paul MacDuffie and Takahiro Fujimoto, "Why Dinosours Will Keep Ruling the Automobile Industry," *Harvard Business Review,* June 2010, pp. 23–25.
14. Major portions of this discussion are based on Sunil Chopra and Peter Meindl, *Supply Chain Management: Strategy, Planning, and Operations,* 5th ed. (Upper Saddle River, NJ: Prentice Hall, 2013), Chapters 1–3; and Hau L. Lee, "The Triple-A Supply Chain," *Harvard Business Review* (October 2004), pp. 102–12.

15. James A. Cooke, "From Many, One: IBM's Unified Supply Chain," *Supply Chain Quarterly,* Quarter 4, 2012, pp. 2–4; Jessi Hempel, "IBM's Super Second Act," *Fortune,* March 21, 2011, pp. 115 ff; and Thomas A. Foster, "World's Best-Run Supply Chains Stay on Top Regardless of the Competition," *Global Logistics & Supply Chain Strategies,* February 2006, pp. 27–41.
16. This discussion is based on Brett Booen, "Wal-Mart's Supply Chain Acts As If Every Day Is Black Friday," *Supply Chain Digital,* November 19, 2010; Kathryn Jones, "The Dell Way," *Business 2.0,* February 2003, pp. 61–66; Charles Fishman, "The Wal-Mart You Don't Know," *Fast Company,* December 2003, pp. 68–80; "Michael Dell: Still Betting on the Future of Online Commerce and Supply Chain Efficiencies," Knowledge@Wharton, September 7, 2006; and Chopra and Meindl, *Supply Chain Management.*
17. Christina Passariello, "Logistics Are in Vogue with Designers," *The Wall Street Journal,* June 27, 2008, p. B1.
18. Jean Murphy, "Better Forecasting, S&OP Support Transformation at Campbell's Soup Co.," *Global Logistics & Supply Chain Strategies,* June 2004, pp. 28–30.
19. "A Cadmium Lining," *The Economist,* January 26, 2013, p. 56; "Rewriting the Rules for E-Cycling," *Fortune,* March 22, 2010, Special Section; Steve Miller, "Recycling Becomes Electric for GE Brands," *BrandWeek,* May 13, 2008, p. 4; "Don't Toss Out That Old Gadget," *Newsweek,* November 3, 2008, p. E8; and Lorraine Woellert, "HP Wants Your Old PCs Back," *BusinessWeek,* April 10, 2006, pp. 82–83.
20. Brian Hindo, "Everything Old Is New Again," *BusinessWeek,* September 25, 2006, pp. 64–70.
21. Doug Bartholomew, "IT Delivers for UPS," *Industry Week,* August 2002, pp. 35–36.

Amazon.com: This case is based on material available on the company website and the following sources: Robert D. Hof and Heather Green, "How Amazon Cleared That Hurdle," *BusinessWeek,* February 4, 2002, p. 60; Heather Green, "How Hard Should Amazon Swing?" *BusinessWeek,* January 14, 2002, p. 38; Robert D. Hof, "We've Never Said We Had to Do It All," *BusinessWeek,* October 15, 2001, p. 53; and Bob Walter, "Amazon Leases Distribution Center from Sacramento, Calif., Development Firm," *Sacramento Bee,* July 19, 2001.

Chapter 16

1. "Augmented Reality's Real Implications for Hardware, Software and Advertising: A Roadmap for Success," *PR Newswire,* February 5, 2013; Yomiuri, "Will Augmented Reality Technology Replace Fitting Rooms with Apps, Tablets?" *The Daily Yomiuri,* February 19, 2013, p. 6; Chris Ciaccia, "Google Glass Edges Closer to Reality," *The Street,* February 20, 2013; "Virtual Shopping: What Augmented Reality Means for Retailers," *Marketing Thought Leaders,* February 2013; "How Augmented Reality Is Changing the Consumer Experience," *Business 2 Community.com,* December 11, 2012; "Augmented Reality: A Growing Force in Retail," *Retailcustomerexperience.com,* October 5, 2012; and "Augmented Reality Makes Shopping More Personal," www.research.ibm.com, accessed February 20, 2013.
2. "The Fortune 500," *Fortune,* May 20, 2013, p. F-1; *The World Factbook* (Washington, DC: Central Intelligence Agency), www.cia.gov, accessed April 7, 2011; *Statistical Abstract of the United States: 2009,* 128th ed. (Washington, DC: U.S. Department of Commerce, Bureau of the Census, 2008), Table 19, Large Metropolitan Statistical Areas.
3. "Monthly and Annual Retail Trade," United States Census Bureau, http://www.census.gov/retail/, February 13, 2013.
4. "The Global 2000," *Forbes,* May 7, 2012, p. 99; and http://www.forbes.com/global2000.
5. "Where in the World Is Walmart?" Walmart website, http://corporate.walmart.com/our-story/locations, accessed February 22, 2013; and Marcel Corstjens and Rajiv Lal, "Retail Doesn't Cross Borders," *Harvard Business Review,* April 2012, pp. 104–11.
6. "Some Actions Last a Lifetime," *Home Depot 2012 Sustainability Report;* Edwin R. Stafford and Cathy L. Hartman, "Promoting the Value of Sustainably Minded Purchase Behaviors," *Marketing News,* January 2013, p. 28; "Neenah Paper Gives Retailers a 'Green' Option with Environmental Retail Card," *Product News Network,* December 10, 2012; "Green Rankings 2012: U.S. Companies," *Newsweek,* October 22, 2012; "Can Green Marketing Work?" *Advertising Age,* November 8, 2010, p. 19; Nathalie Atkinson, "Green Army, Sure Companies Are Jumping on the Eco-Bandwagon but It's This Sort of Retailing We Should Encourage," *National Post,* April 17, 2010, p. TO4; and "The Company of the Future: Fact Sheet," Wal-Mart, Inc., www.walmartfacts.com, accessed April 8, 2011.
7. "Retail Trade—Establishments, Employees, and Payroll," *County Business Patterns,* U.S. Census Bureau, July 2010, Table 1048.
8. "Franchise Business Economic Outlook for 2013," International Franchise Association, IHS Global Insight, December 17, 2012.
9. "2013 Franchise 500," *Entrepreneur,* http://www.entrepreneur.com/franchise500/index.html#.
10. "The Next Generation of Retailing Driven by Automated, Self-Service Solutions," *Market News Publishing,*" February 4, 2013; "Apartment Complex Readies for Automated C-Store," *States News Service,* September 10, 2012; "Marley Coffee and AVT Bet Big on the Future of Automated Cafes," *Market News Publishing,* February 6, 2013; "Automated Retailing Industry Expected to Grow to More Than $1.1 Trillion in 2015," *PR Newswire,* January 24, 2013; Alana Semuels, "Self-Service Machines Replacing Retail Workers," *The Star-Ledger,* March 13, 2011, p. 1; and Bridget Carey, "You Can Get Most Anything at a Kiosk," *The Miami Herald,* August 20, 2010.
11. "Wealthy Customers Sing Praises of Shopping Experiences at Bergdorf, Nordstrom and Barneys," *Marketwire,* February 5, 2013; Anne D'Innocenzio and Mae Anderson, "Nordstrom 4th-Quarter Net Income Rises," *StarTribune,* February 21, 2013; Megan Conniff, "Customer Service Is Changing, and So Is Nordstrom," www.Shop.org, September 12, 2012; Peter King, "Personal Shoppers Find Clothes to Make the Man," *The Wall Street Journal,* August 12, 2010, p. D3; Will Ashworth, "Retail Customer Service Excellence Pays," *Investopedia Advisor,* December 9, 2010; and Michael A. Wiles, "The Effect of Customer Service on Retailers' Shareholder Wealth: The Role of Availability and Reputation Cues," *Journal of Retailing,* 2007, pp. 19–31.
12. "Best Buy Adopts Price-Matching in U.S., Big Box Retailer Takes on Amazon, Apple," *The Toronto Star,* February 20, 2013, p. B2; John Ewoldt, "Big-Box Retailers Take on Internet," *StarTribune,* November 18, 2012, p. 1A; and Michael Shedlock, "Big-Box Retailers Reconsider Size," *Mish's Global Economic Trend Analysis,* March 5, 2011.
13. Nadya Masidlover, "Corporate News: Carrefour Stems a Slide in Its Domestic Market," *The Wall Street Journal,* January 18, 2013, p. B7; "Mass Grocery Retail-Q3 2012," *BMI Food & Drink Report,* July 2012; Tom Orlik and Bob David, "Relief on China Growth Comes with Caveats," *The Wall Street Journal,* January 19, 2013, p. A10; "Research and Markets: Carrefour: Hypermarket Reinvention—European Hypermarkets Account for 70% of Carrefour's Total Sales," *Business Wire,* January 13, 2011; "Supermarket and Hypermarket Retailing in China 2010: A Market Analysis," *M2 Presswire,* February 11, 2011; and Carrefour website, http://www.carrefour.com/content/hypermarkets.
14. Dana Mattioli, "Déjà vu for Sears CEO: Fix Kmart," *The Wall Street Journal,* January 24, 2013, p. B1; Andria Cheng, "Corporate News: Wal-Mart Lays Out Strategy," *The Wall Street Journal,* October 11, 2012, p. B8; Miguel Bustillo, "As Big Boxes Shrink, They Also

Rethink," *The Wall Street Journal,* March 3, 2011, B1; and Miguel Bustillo, "Boss Talk: With Sales Flabby, Wal-Mart Turns to Its Core," *The Wall Street Journal,* March 21, 2011, p. B1; Walmart website, http://corporate.walmart.com/our-story/locations#/united-states, accessed February 25, 2013; and Kmart website, http://searsmedia.com/kmart/kmart.htm, accessed February 25, 2013.

15. "No Time to Shop for Your Valentine? From Flowers to Caviar, a Vending Machine Can Save the Day," *Targeted News Service,* February 11, 2013; Jill Becker, "Vending Machines for All Your Needs," www.CNN.com, August 15, 2012; Jackie Crosby, "Vending Machine Variety Goes beyond Snack Food Offerings," *Los Angeles Times,* January 18, 2011, p. B2; Carlie Kollath, "Veggies in Vending Machines?" *Biz Buzz,* April 6, 2011; "2012 State of the Vending Industry Report," *Automatic Merchandiser,* June/July 2012, pp. 8–19; and http://www.vendingmarketwatch.com/document/10756834/2012-state-of-the-vending-industry-report-pdf.

16. Yukihiro Omoto, "Coca-Cola Setting Up More Green Vending Machines," *The Nikkei Weekly,* February 18, 2013; Ilan Brat, "Business Technology: Restocking the Snack Machine—Sales Pinched, Vending-Machine Operators Add Touch Screen, Card Readers," *The Wall Street Journal,* August 3, 2010, p. B5.

17. *Statistical Fact Book* (New York: Direct Marketing Association, 2010), pp. 4, 33; David Kaplan, "Catalogs Thinner but Still Carry Weight, Retailers Use Them to Draw Consumers to Stores, Web or Social Media Sites," *The Houston Chronicle,* November 28, 2010, p. 1; Mercedes Cardona, "Catalog Role Is Communications, Not Sales," *DM News,* November 1, 2010; and IKEA website, http://www.ikea.com/ms/en_CA/customer_service/faq/faq.html#/0100, accessed February 25, 2013.

18. "How Much Will Postal Cuts Hurt?" *Advertising Age,* February 11, 2013, p. 3; Ira Teinowitz and Nat Ives, "No Day Is a Good Day for No Mail," *Advertising Age,* February 9, 2009, p. 8; "A Zip-Code Screen for Catalog Customers," *The Wall Street Journal,* June 24, 2008, p. B1; and Richard H. Levey, "It's All about Me," *Direct,* November 1, 2008.

19. Katherine Boehret, "The Digital Solution: Is Browsing a Catalog More Fun on a Tablet?" *The Wall Street Journal,* March 28, 2012, p. D2; Dianna Dilworth, "Print Stages a Comeback," *DM News,* March 1, 2011; and Chris Daniels, "Retailers Testing Out e-Catalog Versions, *DM News,* January 1, 2011. See award information at http://multichannelmerchant.com/2012-mcm-awards-winners/, accessed February 25, 2013.

20. "Fact Sheet" from the QVC website, http://www.qvc.com/AboutQVCFacts.content.html, accessed February 26, 2013.

21. Bianca Carneiro, "Mum Camila McConaughey Outshines Supermodels Miranda Kerr and Heidi Klum at QVC's Red Carpet Style Event," *Mail Online,* February 23, 2013; Jordan Zakarin, "Inside QVC: The Semi-Scripted Reality of the $8 Billion Business Next Door," *The Hollywood Reporter,* December 17, 2012; and Elizabeth Holmes, "The Golden Age of TV Shopping," *The Wall Street Journal,* November 11, 2010, p. D1.

22. Ian Thomas, William Davie, and Deanna Weidenhamer, "Quarterly Retail e-Commerce Sales," *U.S. Census Bureau News,* February 15, 2013; Brad Tuttle, "Cyber Monday Was a Monster—But We Still Love Shopping in Stores," www.Time.com, November 28, 2012; "Black Friday 2012 Retail Foot Traffic Rises 3.5%," *International Business Times News,* November 25, 2012; "Cyber Monday Spending Soars to $1.46 Billion," *comScore,* November 28, 2012; Thad Rueter, "e-Retail Spending to Increase 62% by 2016," www.internetretailer.com, February 27, 2012; and "Enjoy Free Shipping on All These Essentials," Wal-Mart website, http://www.walmart.com/cp/HomeFree/1089999#422750, accessed February 26, 2013.

23. "eBay Marketplaces Fast Facts At-a-Glance," eBay website, http://www.ebayinc.com/assets/pdf/fact_sheet/eBay_Marketplaces_Fact_Sheet_Q42012.pdf, accessed February 26, 2013.

24. "Going Showrooming," *Brand-e.biz,* February 26, 2013; Johanna Cox, "Brands Adapting to Showrooming," *L2 Think Tank,* February 21, 2013; and Jacqueline Curtis, "How to Use the Best Flash Sale Sites to Score Deals," *Money Crashers,* February 20, 2013.

25. Susan Rose, Moira Clark, Phillip Samouel, and Neil Hair, "Online Customer Experience in e-Retailing: An Empirical Model of Antecedents and Outcomes," *Journal of Retailing* 2 (2012), pp. 308–22; and Feng Zhu and Xiaoquan (Michael) Zhang, "Impact of Online Consumer Reviews on Sales: The Moderating Role of Product and Consumer Characteristics," *Journal of Marketing* 74 (March 2010), pp. 133–48.

26. In Lee and Kyoochun Lee, "Social Shopping Promotions from a Social Merchant's Perspective," *Business Horizons,* October 2012, pp. 441–51; and "A Look Inside the Smoky World of Chinese Internet Cafes," *Kotaku,* August 13, 2012.

27. "DM-Driven Sales by Medium and Market," *Statistical Fact Book* (New York: Direct Marketing Association, 2010), p. 5.

28. "FTC Issues FY 2012 National Do Not Call Registry Data Book," *Federal Trade Commission Documents and Publications,* October 16, 2012; and Nate Anderson, "Do Not Call List Tops 200 Million, Some Scammers Still Ignore It," www.Wired.com, July 31, 2010.

29. "Direct Selling USA—Pinpoint Growth Sectors and Identify Factors Driving Change," *M2 Presswire,* April 12, 2011; and *Fact Sheet,* Direct Selling Association, http://www.dsa.org/research/industry-statistics/11gofactsheet.pdf, accessed February 27, 2013.

30. "Amway Says China Sales Increase to 27.1b Yuan," *China Daily,* February 21, 2013; "Avon Announces Management Realignments," *PR Newswire,* February 24, 2011; and "Herbalife Ltd. Receives Approval of Additional Direct-Selling Licenses in China," *Business Wire,* July 19, 2010.

31. Virginia Bridges, "In a Slow Economy, Some Try the Direct Approach," *The Virginian-Pilot,* February 17, 2013, p. K1; Maria Croce, "Recession Sparks a Massive Boom in Direct Selling Parties but Gone Are the Days of Selling Tupperware," *Daily Record,* June 2, 2012, pp. 34–35; Olivera Perkins, "Direct Sales Proves Attractive to Long-Term Jobless Workers; Companies Selling Retail Goods at Home Parties See Profits Climbing," *Plain Dealer,* February 6, 2011, p. D1; Carol Lewis, "Calling All Avon Ladies—Direct Selling Is Back," *The Times,* December 28, 2010, p. 40; and "Company Facts," The Pampered Chef website, http://www.pamperedchef.com/company-facts.jsp, accessed February 27, 2013.

32. Dinesh Kumar Gauri, Minakshi Trivedi, and Dhruv Grewal, "Understanding the Determinants of Retail Strategy: An Empirical Analysis," *Journal of Retailing,* September 2008, p. 256.

33. The following discussion is adapted from William T. Gregor and Eileen M. Friars, *Money Merchandizing: Retail Revolution in Consumer Financial Services* (Cambridge, MA: Management Analysis Center, Inc., 1982).

34. Francis J. Mulhern and Robert P. Leon, "Implicit Price Bundling of Retail Products: A Multiproduct Approach to Maximizing Store Profitability," *Journal of Marketing,* October 1991, pp. 63–76.

35. Marc Vanhuele and Xavier Dreze, "Measuring the Price Knowledge Shoppers Bring to the Store," *Journal of Marketing,* October 2002, p. 72–85.

36. "Are Sales a Thing of the Past?" *Newstex,* www.jennstrathman.com, January 10, 2013; and Gwen Ortmeyer, John A. Quelch, and Walter Salmon, "Restoring Credibility to Retail Pricing," *Sloan Management Review,* Fall 1991, pp. 55–66.

37. "On Sale! But Does Inexpensive Mean Cheap?" www.Futurity.org, November 27, 2012; Rajneesh Suri, Jane Zhen Cai, Kent B. Monroe, and Mrugank V. Thakor, "Retailers' Merchandise Organization and Price Perceptions," *Journal of Retailing* 1 (2012), pp. 168–79; and William Dodds, "In Search of Value: How Price and Store Name Information Influence Buyers' Product Perceptions," *Journal of Consumer Marketing,* Spring 1991, pp. 15–24.
38. Stephanie Clifford, "Stores Bend to Cost-Savvy Shoppers: Experiments in Pricing Move Away from Usual Markups and Discounts," *The International Herald Tribune,* March 29, 2012, p. 18; and Leonard L. Berry, "Old Pillars of New Retailing," *Harvard Business Review,* April 2001, pp. 131–37.
39. Eric Anderson and Duncan Simester, "Mind Your Pricing Cues," *Harvard Business Review,* September 2003, pp. 96–103.
40. Julie Baker, A. Parasuraman, Dhruv Grewal, and Glenn B. Voss, "The Influence of Multiple Store Environment Cues on Perceived Merchandise Value and Patronage Intentions," *Journal of Marketing,* April 2002, pp. 120–41.
41. Hyeong Min Kim, "Consumers' Responses to Price Presentation Formats in Rebate Advertisements," *Journal of Retailing,* 4 (2006), pp. 309–17.
42. Kathy Grannis, "Retail Theft Decreased in 2011, According to Preliminary National Retail Security Survey Findings," press release, National Retail Federation, June 22, 2012; Shari Brown and Kathy Grannis, "Return Fraud to Cost Retailers $2.9 Billion This Holiday Season, According to NRF Survey," press release, National Retail Federation, December 4, 2012; Lloyd C. Harris, "Fraudulent Return Proclivity: An Empirical Analysis," *Journal of Retailing,* December 2008, p. 461; Sharna Johnson, "Businesses See Shoplifting Spike," *Clovis News Journal,* February 1, 2009; and "Nedap Retail Introduces New 'Invisible' Anti-Theft Tags in Partnership with Kovio," *PR Newswire,* November 13, 2012.
43. Rita Koselka, "The Schottenstein Factor," *Forbes,* September 28, 1992, pp. 104, 106.
44. "Research and Markets: 2012 Report on the $390 Billion U.S. Warehouse Clubs & Superstores Industry Featuring Wal-Mart, Costco, BJs and Meijer," *M2 Presswire,* September 28, 2012; and "Industry Overview: Warehouse Clubs and Superstores," *Hoover's,* www.hoovers.com, accessed February 27, 2013.
45. "The Deal on Outlet Store Deals," *WalletPop,* March 22, 2011; and "Macy's to Launch 3 New Bloomingdale's Outlet Stores," *Entertainment Close-Up,* April 28, 2011.
46. "About Dollar General," Dollar General website, http://www2.dollargeneral.com/About-Us/Pages/index.aspx, accessed February 27, 2013.
47. "About WEM," West Edmonton Mall website, http://www.wem.ca/#/about-wem/overview, accessed February 27, 2013.
48. Ernesto Portillo, "Home Depot Part of Center Plan," *McClatchy-Tribune Business News,* November 20, 2008; and Lisa A. Bernard, "Anchor ID'd for 'Big Box' Power Center," *Dayton Daily News,* July 19, 2007.
49. Pierre Martineau, "The Personality of the Retail Store," *Harvard Business Review,* January–February 1958, p. 47.
50. Julie Baker, Dhruv Grewal, and A. Parasuraman, "The Influence of Store Environment on Quality Inferences and Store Image," *Journal of the Academy of Marketing Science,* Fall 1994, pp. 328–39; Howard Barich and Philip Kotler, "A Framework for Marketing Image Management," *Sloan Management Review,* Winter 1991, pp. 94–104; Susan M. Keaveney and Kenneth A. Hunt, "Conceptualization and Operationalization of Retail Store Image: A Case of Rival Middle-Level Theories," *Journal of the Academy of Marketing Science,* Spring 1992, pp. 165–75; James C. Ward, Mary Jo Bitner, and John Barnes, "Measuring the Prototypicality and Meaning of Retail Environments," *Journal of Retailing,* Summer 1992, p. 194; and Dhruv Grewal, R. Krishnan, Julie Baker, and Norm Burin, "The Effect of Store Name, Brand Name and Price Discounts on Consumers' Evaluations and Purchase Intentions," *Journal of Retailing,* Fall 1998, pp. 331–52. For a review of the store image literature, see Mary R. Zimmer and Linda L. Golden, "Impressions of Retail Stores: A Content Analysis of Consumer Images," *Journal of Retailing,* Fall 1988, pp. 265–93.
51. Andreas Herrmann, Manja Zidansek, David E. Sprott, and Eric R. Spangenberg, "The Power of Simplicity: Processing Fluency and the Effects of Olfactory Cues on Retail Sales," *Journal of Retailing* 1 (2013), pp. 30–43.
52. Jack Neff, "Shopper Marketing's New Frontier: e-Commerce," *Advertising Age,* March 14, 2011, p. 14; Andrew Adam Newman, "Taking Pickles Out of the Afterthought Aisle," *The New York Times,* April 26, 2011, p. 3: Piet Levy, "Snack Attack," *Marketing News,* February 28, 2011, p. 12; Yong Jian Wang, Michael S. Minor, and Jie Wei, "Aesthetics and the Online Shopping Environment: Understanding Consumer Responses," *Journal of Retailing* 87, no. 1 (2011), pp. 46–58; and Els Breugelmans and Katia Campo, "Effectiveness of In-Store Displays in a Virtual Store Environment," *Journal of Retailing* 87, no. 1 (2011), pp. 75–89.
53. Jans-Benedict Steenkamp and Michel Wedel, "Segmenting Retail Markets on Store Image Using a Consumer-Based Methodology," *Journal of Retailing,* Fall 1991, p. 300; Philip Kotler, "Atmospherics as a Marketing Tool," *Journal of Retailing* 49 (Winter 1973–74), p. 61; and Roger A. Kerin, Ambuj Jain, and Daniel L. Howard, "Store Shopping Experience and Consumer Price-Quality-Value Perceptions," *Journal of Retailing,* Winter 1992, pp. 376–97.
54. Mary Jo Bitner, "Servicescapes: The Impact of Physical Surroundings on Customers and Employees," *Journal of Marketing,* April 1992, pp. 57–71.
55. Joseph M. Hall, Praveen K. Kopale, and Aradhna Krishna, "Retailer Dynamic Pricing and Ordering Decisions: Category Management versus Brand-by-Brand Approaches," *Journal of Retailing* 86, no. 2 (2010), pp. 172–83; and "Category Management Professionals Can Benefit from Integration of Leading Category and Space Management Suite with Comprehensive and Accurate Product Information," *Business Wire,* April 28, 2011.
56. Kevin Peters, "How I Did It: Office Depot's President on How 'Mystery Shopping' Helped Spark a Turnaround," *Harvard Business Review,* November 2011, pp. 47–50; and John Davis, *Measuring Marketing* (Singapore: Wiley and Sons, 2007), p. 46.
57. Tom Webb, "Retail Ramifications: Best Buy and Apple Seem a Perfect Pair—Except for Apple's Store Ambitions," *St. Paul Pioneer Press,* February 19, 2011; Paul W. Farris, Neil T. Bendle, Phillip E. Pfeifer, and David J. Reibstein, *Marketing Metrics* (Philadelphia: Wharton School Publishing, 2006), p. 106; Jerry Useem, "Simply Irresistible," *Fortune,* March 19, 2007, pp. 107–12; "Apple 2.0," blogs.business2.com/apple/the_evil_empire/index.html; Steve Lohr, "Apple, a Success at Stores, Bets Big on Fifth Avenue," *The New York Times,* May 19, 2006; Jim Dalrymple, "Inside the Apple Stores," *MacWorld,* June 2007, pp. 16–17; John Davis, *Measuring Marketing,* pp. 280–81; and Retailsails 2011 Chain Store Productivity Report, September 23, 2011, http://retailsails.files.wordpress.com/2011/09/rs_spsf.pdf, accessed October 7, 2011.
58. The wheel of retailing theory was originally proposed by Malcolm P. McNair, "Significant Trends and Developments in the Postwar Period," in *Competitive Distribution in a Free, High-Level Economy and Its Implications for the University,* ed. A. B. Smith, (Pittsburgh: University of Pittsburgh Press, 1958), pp. 1–25; also see Stephen Brown, "The Wheel of Retailing—Past and Future," *Journal of Retailing,* Summer 1990, pp. 143–49; and Malcolm P. McNair and Eleanor May, "The Next Revolution of the Retailing Wheel," *Harvard Business Review,* September–October 1978, pp. 81–91.

59. Lorene Yue, "Putting More on the Menu: McDonald's Promises New Products to Drive Revenue Growth," *Crain's Chicago Business,* February 18, 2013, p. 1; "The Special Tonight: Big Mac Served with Style," *The New York Times,* February 13, 2013; and Ashley Lutz, "Starbucks Could Be Laying the Groundwork for the Next Generation of Ordering," *Business Insider,* January 29, 2013.
60. "Our Story," Checkers website, http://checkerscompany.com/our_story, accessed February 28, 2013; and "Company Milestones," Boston Market website, http://www.bostonmarket.com/newsroom/index.jsp?page=milestones, accessed February 29, 2013.
61. William R. Davidson, Albert D. Bates, and Stephen J. Bass, "Retail Life Cycle," *Harvard Business Review,* November–December 1976, pp. 89–96.
62. Anne Marie Doherty, "Who Will Weather Economic Storms on the High Street?" *The Western Mail,* January 1, 2009, p. 29.
63. "A Business Survival Guide to Multi-Channel Retail," www.Business2Community.com, December 3, 2012; Umut Konus, Peter C. Verhoef, and Scott A. Neslin," Multichannel Shopper Segments and Their Covariates," *Journal of Retailing,* December 2008, p. 398; and Robert A. Peterson and Sridhar Balasubramanian, "Retailing in the 21st Century: Reflections and Prologue to Research," *Journal of Retailing,* Spring 2002, pp. 9–16.
64. "PWC's Annual Survey of Online Shoppers Debunks 10 Myths of Multichannel Retailing," *PR Newswire,* February 6, 2013; Lawrence A. Crosby, "Multi-Channel Relationships," *Marketing Management,* Summer 2011, pp. 12–13; and Jim Carter and Norman Sheehan, "From Competition to Cooperation: E-Tailing's Integration with Retailing," *Business Horizons,* March–April 2004, pp. 71–78.
65. Darrel Rigby "The Future of Shopping," *Harvard Business Review,* December 2011, pp. 65–76; "Multi-Channel Retailing: The Way Forward," *Images Retail,* November 12, 2012; Ranjay Gulati and Jason Garino, "Getting the Right Mix of Bricks and Clicks," *Harvard Business Review,* May–June 2000, pp. 107–14; Marshal L. Fisher, Ananth Raman, and Anna Sheen McClelland, "Rocket Science Retailing Is Almost Here: Are You Ready?" *Harvard Business Review,* July–August 2000, pp. 115–24; Charla Mathwick, Naresh Malhotra, and Edward Rigdon, "Experiential Value: Conceptualization, Measurement and Application in the Catalog and Internet Shopping Environment," *Journal of Retailing,* Spring 2001, pp. 39–56; Lawrence M. Bellman, "Bricks and Mortar: 21st Century Survival," *Business Horizons,* May–June 2001, pp. 21–28; Zhan G. Li and Nurit Gery, "E-Tailing—for All Products?" *Business Horizons,* November–December 2000, pp. 49–54; and Bill Hanifin, "Go Forth and Multichannel: Loyalty Programs Need Knowledge Base," *Marketing News,* August 27, 2001, p. 23.
66. Robert Berner, "J.C. Penney Gets the Net," *BusinessWeek,* May 7, 2007, p. 70; Multi-Channel Integration: *The New Retail Battleground* (Columbus, OH: PricewaterhouseCoopers, March 2001); and Richard Last, "JC Penney Internet Commerce," presentation at Southern Methodist University, February 12, 2001.
67. Georgina Gustin, "Grocery Stores Work to Appeal to Male Shoppers," *The Augusta Chronicle,* January 13, 2013, p. D1; Courtney Shea, "A Field Guide to the Difficult Male Shopper," *Canadian Business,* Winter 2012/2013, p. 58; Nanette Byrnes, "Secrets of the Male Shopper," *BusinessWeek,* September 4, 2006, p. 44; Simon Brooke, "It's Different for Guys. Retailers Are Rethinking the Shop Floor with Men in Mind," *Financial Times,* April 28, 2007, p. 7; and Velitchka D. Kaltcheva and Barton A. Weitz, "When Should a Retailer Create an Exciting Store Environment?" *Journal of Marketing,* January 2006, p. 107–18.

Mall of America: This case was written by David P. Brennan and is based on an interview with Maureen Cahill and materials provided by Mall of America.

Chapter 17

1. Jenni Romaniuk, "Are You Ready for the Next Big Thing?" *Journal of Advertising Research,* December 2012, pp. 397–99; "Taco Bell Implements Its Largest Marketing Campaign Ever," *QSRweb,* March 7, 2013; "Highly Anticipated, Most Socially Requested Taco Bell Product Launch to Be Largest Marketing Campaign in Brand's History," *Business Wire,* March 7, 2013; "Yo Quiero Engagement? Taco Bell Charms the Twittersphere," www.Business2Community.com, February 4, 2013; Lynne D. Johnson, "Customer Engagement Is the New Marketing," *Journal of Advertising Research,* June 2010, pp. 118–19; Natalie Zmuda, "QR Codes Gaining Prominence Thanks to a Few Big Players," *Advertising Age,* March 21, 2011, p. 8; Alyssa S. Groom, "Integrated Marketing Communication Anticipating the 'Age of Engage'," *Communication Research Trends,* December 1, 2008, p. 3; "How to Get More Followers on Twitter: Engage with Social Promotions," www.Business2Community.com, March 16, 2013; and "How to Engage Your Audience on Social Media," www.Business2Community.com, March 28, 2013.
2. Sita Mishra and Sushma Muralie, "Managing Dynamism of IMC—Anarchy to Order," *Journal of Marketing and Communication,* September 2010, pp. 29–37; Philip J. Kitchen, Ilchul Kim, and Don E. Schultz, "Integrated Marketing Communications: Practice Leads Theory," *Journal of Advertising Research,* December 2008, pp. 531–46; Bob Liodice, "Essentials for Integrated Marketing," *Advertising Age,* June 9, 2008, p. 26; and Shu-pei Tsai, *Journal of Advertising* 34 (Winter 2005), pp. 11–23.
3. Wilbur Schramm, "How Communication Works," in *The Process and Effects of Mass Communication,* Wilbur Schramm, ed., (Urbana, IL: University of Illinois Press, 1955), pp. 3–26.
4. E. Cooper and M. Jahoda, "The Evasion of Propaganda," *Journal of Psychology* 22 (1947), pp. 15–25; H. Hyman and P. Sheatsley, "Some Reasons Why Information Campaigns Fail," *Public Opinion Quarterly* 11 (1947), pp. 412–23; and J. T. Klapper, *The Effects of Mass Communication* (New York: Free Press, 1960), Chapter VII.
5. "Mistakes in Advertising," on the Learn English website, http://www.learnenglish.de/mistakes/HorrorMistakes.htm, accessed March 18, 2013; and Bianca Bartz, "International Ads Lost in Translation," TrendHunter Marketing website, http://www.trendhunter.com/trends/advertising-bloopers-international-ads-lost-in-translation, accessed March 18, 2013.
6. Rik Pieters and Michel Wedel, "Attention Capture and Transfer in Advertising: Brand, Pictorial, and Text-Size Effects," *Journal of Marketing,* April 2004, pp. 36–50.
7. Adapted from American Marketing Association, Resource Library Dictionary, http://www.marketingpower.com/_layouts/Dictionary.aspx?dLetter=P, accessed March 18, 2013.
8. Dave Folkens, "3 Ways Social Media Is Changing Public Relations," *Online Marketing Blog,* February 17, 2011; Michael Bush, "How Social Media Is Helping the Public-Relations Sector Not Just Survive, but Thrive," *Advertising Age,* August 23, 2010, p. 1; David Robinson, "Public Relations Comes of Age," *Business Horizons* 49 (2006), pp. 247–56; and Dick Martin, "Gilded and Gelded: Hard-Won Lessons from the PR Wars," *Harvard Business Review,* October 2003, pp. 44–54.
9. Martin Eisend and Franziska Kuster, "The Effectiveness of Publicity versus Advertising: A Meta-Analytic Investigation of Its Moderators," *Journal of the Academy of Marketing Science,* December 2011, pp. 906–21; and Joan Stewart, "Pros and Cons of Free Publicity in Newspapers, Magazines," www.Business2Community.com, January 30, 2013.
10. "The Public Relations Metamorphosis: Social Media Is Here to Stay," www.Business2Community.com, December 21, 2012;

Piet Levy, "CSR Take Responsibility," *Marketing News,* May 30, 2010, p. 20; *Let's Talk,* McDonald's corporate blog, http://community.aboutmcdonalds.com/t5/Let-s-Talk/bg-p/blog1, accessed March 18, 2013; Jooyoung Kim, Hye Jin Yoon, and Sun Young Lee, "Integrating Advertising and Publicity: A Theoretical Examination of the Effects of Exposure Sequence, Publicity Valence, and Product Attribute Consistency," *Journal of Advertising,* Spring 2010, p. 97; and Marsha D. Loda and Barbara Carrick Coleman, "Sequence Matters: A More Effective Way to Use Advertising and Publicity," *Journal of Advertising Research* 45 (December 2005), pp. 362–71.

11. Kusum L. Ailawadi, Scott A. Neslin, and Karen Gedenk, "Pursuing the Value-Conscious Consumer: Store Brands versus National Brand Promotions," *Journal of Marketing,* January 2001, pp. 71–89.

12. Nikki Hopewell, "The Rules of Engagement: A Bevy of Rules and Best Practices Govern Promotions and Contests," *Marketing News,* June 1, 2008, p. 6; and Gerard Prendergast, Yi-Zheng Shi, and Ka-Man Cheung, "Behavioural Response to Sales Promotion Tools," *International Journal of Advertising* 24 (2005), pp. 467–86.

13. Adapted from American Marketing Association, Resource Library Dictionary, http://www.marketingpower.com/_layouts/Dictionary.aspx?dLetter=D, accessed March 18, 2013.

14. "Top 5 Brands Using Mobile Marketing Successfully," www.Business2Community.com, March 11, 2013; "Eight Out of Ten Freshers Have Smartphones, According to New UCAS Media Survey," *M2 Presswire,* March 13, 2013; "Mysteries and Myths of Millennials in Social Media," www.Business2Community.com, July 21, 2012; Stuart Elliott, "In an Upgrade, Google Adds to Its Model for Mobile Marketing," *The New York Times,* March 7, 2013, p. 3; "Tailoring Your Mobile Strategy to the New Millennials," *VentureBeat,* July 18, 2012; Nationwide Bank website, http://www.nationwide.com/cps/college-student-spending-habits-infographic.htm, accessed March 19, 2013; Antje Cockrill, Mark M. Goode, and Amy White, "The Bluetooth Enigma: Practicalities Impair Potential," *Journal of Advertising Research,* March 2011, pp. 298–312; Thomas Pardee, "Media-Savvy Gen Y Finds Smart and Funny Is 'New Rock-N-Roll'," *Advertising Age,* October 11, 2010, p. 17; and "5 Tips for Marketing to Millennials," *Advertising Age,* October 11, 2010, p. 17.

15. Dunn Sunnoo and Lynn Y. S. Lin, "Sales Effects of Promotion and Advertising," *Journal of Advertising Research* 18 (October 1978), pp. 37–42.

16. Don Kaplan, "Every Dog Has Its Day at Purina Challenge," *Daily News,* January 12, 2013, p. 1; and Art Eddy, "15th Annual Purina Pro Plan Incredible Dog Challenge National Finals Airs January 12th," *Yahoo! Voices,* http://voices.yahoo.com/15th-annual-purina-pro-plan-incredible-dog-challenge-11964522.html?cat=53, accessed April 1, 2013.

17. Todd Powers, Dorothy Advincula, Manila S. Austin, Stacy Graiko, and Jasper Snyder, "Digital and Social Media in the Purchase Decision Process," *Journal of Advertising Research,* December 2012, pp. 479–89; and Remco Prins and Peter C. Verhoef, "Marketing Communication Drivers of Adoption Timing of a New E-Service among Existing Customers," *Journal of Marketing* 71 (April 2007), pp. 169–83.

18. Anders Parment, "Distribution Strategies for Volume and Premium Brands in Highly Competitive Consumer Markets," *Journal of Retailing and Consumer Services,* July 2008, p. 250; and R. Srinivasan and Archana K. Murthy, "Integrated Brand Building Process: A Special Case," *International Journal of Business Research,* June 1, 2008, p. 174.

19. "Push vs. Pull Strategies," *Daily News,* May 3, 2011; "Question: Should B2B Be Focusing All Its Efforts on 'Pull' Marketing Therefore Turning Its Back on 'Push' Marketing Techniques?" *B2B Marketing Magazine,* September 2009; and Michael Levy, John Webster, and Roger Kerin, "Formulating Push Marketing Strategies: A Method and Application," *Journal of Marketing,* Winter 1983, pp. 25–34.

20. Bradford Wernle, "Quality, Market Share, Leasing Top Ford Dealers' Agenda," *Automotive News,* February 10, 2013; Jamie LaReau, "Ford Dealers Revamp Pay Plans; Some Efforts Resemble Stair-Step Programs," *Automotive News,* February 14, 2011, p. 10; and *Ford Motor Company Annual Report, 2012,* p. 14.

21. Tracy Staton, "Pharma DTC Ad Spending Sinks 11.5%," *FiercePharma,* April 2, 2013, www.fiercepharma.com; John Mack, "DTC Not as Dead as We Thought," *Pharma Marketing Blog,* April 2, 2013, www.pharmamkting.blogspot.com; Beth Snyder Bulik, "Ad Spending: 15 Years of DTC," *Advertising Age Insights White Paper,* October 17, 2011; Sheng Yuan, "Public Response to Direct-to-Consumer Advertising of Prescription Drugs," *Journal of Advertising Research,* March 2008, pp. 30–41; and Fusun F. Gonul, Franklin Carter, Elina Petrova, and Kannan Srinivasan, "Promotion of Prescription Drugs and Its Impact on Physicians' Choice Behavior," *Journal of Marketing,* July 2001, pp. 79–90.

22. Don E. Shultz, Martin P. Block, and Kaylan Raman, "Understanding Consumer-Created Media Synergy," *Journal of Marketing Communications,*" July 2012, pp. 173-87; "Why Behavioral Targeting Is Effective," www.Business2Community.com, January 15, 2013; Lauren Drell, "4 Ways Behavioral Targeting Is Changing the Web," *Mashable,* April 26, 2011; and adapted from American Marketing Association, Resource Library Dictionary, http://www.marketingpower.com/_layouts/Dictionary.aspx?dLetter=B, accessed April 2, 2013.

23. Robert J. Lavidge and Gary A. Steiner, "A Model for Predictive Measurement of Advertising Effectiveness," *Journal of Marketing,* October 1961, p. 61.

24. "100 Leading National Advertisers," *Advertising Age,* June 24, 2013, p. 16.

25. George S. Low and Jakki J. Mohr, "Setting Advertising and Promotion Budgets in Multi-Brand Companies," *Journal of Advertising Research,* January/February 1999, pp. 67–78; Don E. Schultz and Anders Gronstedt, "Making Marcom an Investment," *Marketing Management,* Fall 1997, pp. 41–49; and J. Enrique Bigne, "Advertising Budget Practices: A Review," *Journal of Current Issues and Research in Advertising,* Fall 1995, pp. 17–31.

26. John Philip Jones, "Ad Spending: Maintaining Market Share," *Harvard Business Review,* January–February 1990, pp. 38–42; and Charles H. Patti and Vincent Blasko, "Budgeting Practices of Big Advertisers," *Journal of Advertising Research* 21 (December 1981), pp. 23–30.

27. "U.S. Market Leaders," *Advertising Age,* June 25, 2012, pp. 24–25.

28. Brenda Marlin, "Adding It Up: You Can Save Time by Trying One of Three Short-Cut Approaches to an Annual Budget," *ABA Banking,* October 1, 2007, p. 36; James A. Shroer, "Ad Spending: Growing Market Share," *Harvard Business Review,* January–February 1990, pp. 44–48; and Jeffrey A. Lowenhar and John L. Stanton, "Forecasting Competitive Advertising Expenditures," *Journal of Advertising Research* 16, no. 2 (April 1976), pp. 37–44.

29. Daniel Seligman, "How Much for Advertising?" *Fortune,* December 1956, p. 123.

30. James E. Lynch and Graham J. Hooley, "Increasing Sophistication in Advertising Budget Setting," *Journal of Advertising Research* 30 (February–March 1990), pp. 67–75.

31. Jimmy D. Barnes, Brenda J. Muscove, and Javad Rassouli, "An Objective and Task Media Selection Decision Model and Advertising Cost Formula to Determine International Advertising Budgets," *Journal of Advertising* 11, no. 4 (1982), pp. 68–75.

32. "The Olympic Brand Maintains Its Global Strength and Recognition," *States News Service,* February 12, 2013; Graham Ruddock, "London Olympics Sponsors Are Already into Their Stride," *The Daily Telegraph,* May 6, 2011, p. 8; "The Olympics Come But Once Every Two Years," *Marketing News,* November 1, 2008, p. 12; "Olympics Will Bring Online Opportunities for Many Brands," *Revolution,* July 14,

2008, p. 13; and Don E. Schultz, "Olympics Get the Gold Medal in Integrating Marketing Event," *Marketing News,* April 27, 1998, pp. 5, 10.

33. "It's Time to Take an Integrated Marketing Approach," www.Business2Community.com, January 22, 2013; "Integrated Marketing: One Message, Many Media," *Marketing Week,* September 18, 2008, p. 31; and Cornelia Pechman, Guangzhi Zhao, Marvin E. Goldberg, and Ellen Thomas Reibling, "What to Convey in Antismoking Advertisements for Adolescents: The Use of Protection Motivation Theory to Identify Effective Message Themes," *Journal of Marketing,* April 2003, pp. 1–18.

34. Brooks Barnes, "Great and Powerful Opening for New 'Oz' Movie," *The New York Times,* March 11, 2013, p. 3; "Small Bits of First Look Footage Unveiled from Sam Raimi's 'Oz: The Great and Powerful,'" *indieWire,* July 11, 2012; "Cost Plus World Market Collaborates with Disney for the Release of "'Oz the Great and Powerful,'" *Business Wire,* February 19, 2013; "HSN and Disney Collaborate for Oz the Great and Powerful Retail Experience," www.chipandco.com, January 23, 2013.

35. Sabine A. Einwiller and Michael Boenigk, "Examining the Link between Integrated Communication Management and Communication Effectiveness in Medium-Sized Enterprises," *Journal of Marketing Communications,* December 2012, pp. 335–61; and Mike Reid, "Performance Auditing of Integrated Marketing Communication (IMC) Actions and Outcomes," *Journal of Advertising* 34 (Winter 2005), p. 41.

36. Alexandra Bruell, "Agency A-List: Media Agency of the Year Carat," *Advertising Age,* January 28, 2013, p. 26; "Nokia Connects with South East Asia," *Microsoft Advertising,* http://advertising.microsoft.com/asia/WWDocs/User/Asia/ResearchLibrary/CaseStudy/MSA_Nokia%20Case%20Study.pdf; and the Carat website, http://www.carat.com, accessed April 5, 2013.

37. "Integrated Marketing: The Benefits of Integrated Marketing," *Marketing Week,* September 18, 2008, p. 33; and Tom Duncan, "Is Your Marketing Communications Integrated?" *Advertising Age,* January 24, 1994, p. 26.

38. Don E. Schultz, "The Media Circuits Evolution," *Marketing News,* March 30, 2011, p. 11; "Integrated Marketing: Digital Fuels Integration Boom," *Marketing Week,* December 11, 2008, p. 27; Don E. Schultz, "IMC Is Do or Die in New Pull Marketplace," *Marketing News,* August 15, 2006, p. 7; and Don E. Schultz, "Integration's New Role Focuses on Customers," *Marketing News,* September 15, 2006, p. 8.

39. Yunjae Cheong, John D. Leckenby, and Tim Eakin, "Evaluating the Multivariate Beta Binomial Distribution for Estimating Magazine and Internet Exposure Frequency Distributions," *Journal of Advertising,* Spring 2011, p. 7; Jack Neff, "Copy Testing Coming to Digital Marketing," *Advertising Age,* February 28, 2011, p.18; and "Measure for Measure," *Marketing Management,* January–February 2004, p. 7.

40. T. Reinold and J. Tropp, "Integrated Marketing Communications: How Can We Measure Its Effectiveness?" *Journal of Marketing Communications,* April 2012, pp. 113–32; Maria Angeles Navarro-Bailon, "Strategic Consistent Messages in Cross-Tool Campaigns: Effects on Brand Image and Brand Attitude," *Journal of Marketing Communications,* July 2012, pp. 189–202; and Don E. Shultz, "Measure IMC's Whole—Not Just Each Part," *Marketing News,* February 15, 2006, p. 8.

41. Tae Hyun Baek and Mariko Morimoto, "Stay Away from Me," *Journal of Advertising,* Spring 2012, pp. 59–76; and *Statistical Fact Book 2012* (New York: Direct Marketing Association, 2012), pp. 5, 16.

42. "Direct Mail Strategy: JCPenney's New Postcard Campaign," www.Business2Community.com, April 18, 2012; Cindy Waxer, "Automotive Brands Are Test-Driving New Marketing Strategies," *DMNews,* October 2012; "JCPenney America's Shopping Destination This Christmas," *Business Wire,* November 10, 2010; "JCPenney Kicks Off Christmas Gift Program," *Wireless News,* November 16, 2010; Alex Palmer, "JCPenney Launches Facebook e-Commerce Store," *DMNews,* December 15, 2010; Tim Peterson, "Porsche Launches Integrated Campaign to Shift Consumer Perception," *DMNews,* March 25, 2011; and *Statistical Fact Book 2012* (New York: Direct Marketing Association, 2012), p. 5.

43. *Statistical Fact Book 2012* (New York: Direct Marketing Association, 2012), pp. 24, 67; and "Six Ways Lands' End Makes Online Shopping a Joy," *PR Newswire,* November 21, 2007.

44. Theresa Howard, "E-mail Grows as Direct-Marketing Tool: They're Quicker to Make, Cheap to Send," *USA Today,* November 28, 2008, p. 5B.

45. Cotton Delo, "Facebook Testing Effort to Match Offline Purchases to Online Profiles," *Advertising Age,* February 25, 2013, p. 6; Michael Learmonth, "Facebook Goes the Route of Direct Marketing, While Twitter Plays It Safe with Focus on User Interests," *Advertising Age,* September 10, 2012, p. 20; and "Infogroup Targeting Solution Launches Sapphire™, a New Integrated Marketing Database," *GlobeNewswire,* August 7, 2012.

46. Sapna Maheshwari and Matt Townsend, "BC-E-MAIL-MARKETING-RETA," *Postmedia Breaking News,* March 14, 2013; "A-Catalog-Printer.com Uses Revolutionary Soy Ink Technology to Help the Environment and Reduce Costs of Printing," *SBWire,* March 22, 2013; Charley Howard, "Help USPS Help You: 3 Ways to Cut Mail Costs through Workshare Discounts," http://www.targetmarketingmag.com/article/3-ways-cut-mail-costs-through-workshare-discounts-417119/1#, February 2011 and "How Much Will Postal Cuts Hurt?" *Advertising Age,* February 11, 2013, p. 3.

47. "Companies Opposing Anti-Spam Laws," *The Toronto Star,* February 9, 2013, p. B5; Beth Negus Viveiros, "New Bill Takes Permission Beyond Opt-In in EU," *Chief Marketer,* April 19, 2011; "China: New Media Blossoming as Business Models Revamp," BBC Monitoring World Media, December 9, 2008; "The Data Dilemma," *Marketing Direct,* February 6, 2007, p. 37; and Marc Nohr, "South Africa—A Worthy Contender," *Marketing Direct,* March 5, 2007, p. 20.

48. "Protecting Your Identity and Your Privacy," *Targeted News Service,* March 1, 2013; "The Do Not Track Online Act Was Reintroduced in Congress," *The Business Insider,* March 1, 2013; "Online Behavioral Advertising," in the DMA OBA Guidelines, Direct Marketing Association website, http://thedma.org/issues/dma-oba-guidelines, accessed April 6, 2013; Don E. Shultz, "The Bugaboo of Behaviors," *Marketing Management,* Summer 2011, pp. 10–11; "Cell Phones Now Protected by the Do Not Call List," *States News Service,* May 16, 2011; Jonathan Brunt, "'Do Not Mail' Can't Gain Traction," *Spokesman Review,* May 5, 2010, p. 7; "DMA: 'Do Not Track Online Act' Is Unnecessary," *States News Service,* May 9, 2011; "DMA Updates Its 'Guidelines for Ethical Business Practice,'" *States News Service,* May 25, 2011; Martin Courtney and Tony Lock, "Keep It Safe, Keep It Legal," *Computing,* May 26, 2011; Siobhain Butterworth, "Cookie Law Shambles Really Takes the Biscuit," *Guardian Unlimited,* May 27, 2011; and Lara O'Reilly, "New Cookie Law: What You Need to Know," *Marketing Week,* May 26, 2011.

Mountain Dew: This case was written by Steven Hartley. Sources: "DEWmocracy Campaign Overview," www.dewmocracymediahub.com; "The Mountain Dew DEWmocracy 2 Campaign Empowers Brand Loyalists Nationwide to Create and Launch the Next New Dew," press release, http://www.dewmocracymediahub.com/images/press_release_041910.pdf; "Fresh Dew," *Prepared Foods,* June 2010, vol. 179, p. 39; "Mountain Dew Embraces the Spirit of 'DEWmocracy,' 'Most Memorable New Product Launch website, http://mmnpl.wordpress.com/?s=mountain; "Marketing Campaign: Winner: DEWmocracy 2," *Beverage World* 129, p. 35; "Program Overview and DEWmocracy 2—

Campaign Statistics, www.dewmocracymediahub.com; Jessica E. Vascellaro and Suzanne Vranica, "Shaping Ads for Web-Connected TV—Software Offers New Real Estate to Tout Products, Ability to Target Messages," *The Wall Street Journal,* September 20, 2010, p. B9; and Natalie Zmuda, "Why Mtn Dew Let Skater Dudes Take Control of Its Marketing," *Advertising Age,* March 22, 2010, p. 30.

Chapter 18

1. Geoffrey Precourt, "What We Know about TV Today (and Tomorrow)," *Journal of Advertising Research,* March 2013, pp. 3–4; "Television Advertising: Destined for Eternity?" *Branding Strategy Insider,* May 3, 2013; Verne Gay, "Small Screen, Big Troubles: Television Networks Finding It Harder to Draw Conventional Audiences," *Spokesman Review,* March 8, 2013; Ryan Nakashima, "'Zero TV' Viewers Are Pulling the Plug on Traditional Television," *The Washington Post,* April 8, 2013, p. A14; "More U.S. Consumers Shun Traditional Television," *Multichannel News,* March 18, 2013; Dan Farber, "Microsoft's Xbox Entertainment Studio Working on Interactive TV," *CNET News,* February 11, 2013; Brian Steinberg, "12 Minutes, 10 Ideas That Tried to Change TV Ad Time Forever," *Advertising Age,* April 18, 2011, p. 12; Michael Learmonth, "Web TV? Xbox, Verizon and Others Appear to Be Up for the Challenge," *Advertising Age,* April 18, 2011, p. 6; Andrew Hampp, "The Next Big Thing in TV? Well, It's Not on TV," *Advertising Age,* May 16, 2011, p. 4; Michael Learmonth, "Beyond TV, Marketers Look to 'Earn' Love for Video Ads," *Advertising Age,* May 16, 2011, p. 14; Kelty Logan, "Hulu.com or NBC? Streaming Video versus Traditional TV," *Journal of Advertising Research,* March 2011, pp. 276–85; and Mark Yi-Cheon Yim, Vincent J. Cicchirillo, and Minette E. Drumwright, "The Impact of Stereoscopic Three-Dimensional (3D) Advertising," *Journal of Advertising,* Summer 2012, pp. 113–28.
2. Karen V. Fernandez and Dennis L. Rosen, "The Effectiveness of Information and Color in Yellow Pages Advertising," *Journal of Advertising,* Summer 2000, p. 61; David A. Aaker and Donald Norris, "Characteristics of TV Commercials Perceived as Informative," *Journal of Advertising Research* 22, no. 2 (April–May 1982), pp. 61–70.
3. Larry D. Compeau and Dhruv Grewal, "Comparative Price Advertising: An Integrative Review," *Journal of Public Policy & Marketing,* Fall 1998, pp. 257–73; and William Wilkie and Paul W. Farris, "Comparison Advertising: Problems and Potentials," *Journal of Marketing,* October 1975, pp. 7–15.
4. Chingching Chang, "The Relative Effectiveness of Comparative and Noncomparative Advertising: Evidence for Gender Differences in Information-Processing Strategies," *Journal of Advertising,* Spring 2007, p. 21; Jerry Gotlieb and Dan Sarel, "The Influence of Type of Advertisement, Price, and Source Credibility on Perceived Quality," *Journal of the Academy of Marketing Science,* Summer 1992, pp. 253–60; and Cornelia Pechmann and David Stewart, "The Effects of Comparative Advertising on Attention, Memory, and Purchase Intentions," *Journal of Consumer Research,* September 1990, pp. 180–92.
5. Kathy L. O'Malley, Jeffrey J. Bailey, Chong Leng Tan, and Carl S. Bozman, "Effects of Varying Web-Based Advertising-Substantiation Information on Attribute Beliefs and Perceived Product Quality," *Academy of Marketing Studies Journal,* 2007, p. 19; Bruce Buchanan and Doron Goldman, "Us vs. Them: The Minefield of Comparative Ads," *Harvard Business Review,* May–June 1989, pp. 38–50; Dorothy Cohen, "The FTC's Advertising Substantiation Program," *Journal of Marketing,* Winter 1980, pp. 26–35; and Michael Etgar and Stephen A. Goodwin, "Planning for Comparative Advertising Requires Special Attention," *Journal of Advertising* 8, no. 1 (Winter 1979), pp. 26–32.
6. David W. Schumann, Jan M. Hathcote, and Susan West, "Corporate Advertising in America: A Review of Published Studies on Use, Measurement, and Effectiveness," *Journal of Advertising,* September 1991, p. 35; Lewis C. Winters, "Does It Pay to Advertise in Hostile Audiences with Corporate Advertising?" *Journal of Advertising Research,* June–July 1988, pp. 11–18; and Robert Selwitz, "The Selling of an Image," *Madison Avenue,* February 1985, pp. 61–69.
7. "New Crystal Light Liquid Drink Mix Frees You from the Choice between Taste or Calories," *PR Newswire,* February 11, 2013; Natalie Zmuda, "Diet Mtn Dew Steps Out from Shadow of Flagship Brand," *Advertising Age,* March 5, 2012, p. 4; E. J. Schultz and Natalie Zmuda, "No Solo Mio: Kraft's Smash Product Attracts Rival in Coke's Dasani," *Advertising Age,* November 5, 2012, p. 10; Natalie Zmuda, "No More 'Shrinking It and Pinking It' at Under Armour," *Advertising Age,* September 24, 2012, p. 46; Molly Soat, "Moving Beyond Shrink IT & Pink IT," *Marketing News,* February 2013, p. 32; Katie Smith, "US: Nike in Uniform Deal with International Olympic Committee," *Just-Style Global News,* October 17, 2012; and Shareen Pthak, "How Nike Ambushed the Olympics with This Neon Shoe," *Advertising Age,* August 20, 2012, p. 1.
8. Ira Teinowitz, "Self-Regulation Urged to Prevent Bias in Ad Buying," *Advertising Age,* January 18, 1999, p. 4.
9. See the Advertising Research Foundation website, http://thearf.org/advancing-marketing-forum.php, accessed May 4, 2013.
10. Demetrios Vakratsas and Tim Ambler, "How Advertising Works: What Do We Really Know?" *Journal of Marketing,* January 1999, pp. 26–43; and Amit Joshi and Dominique M. Hanssens, "The Direct and Indirect Effects of Advertising Spending on Firm Value," *Journal of Marketing,* January 2010, pp. 20–33.
11. Chris Sorensen, "Tackling the Super Bowl," *MacLean's,* February 11, 2013, p. 47; Andrea Morabito, "Super Bowl Viewership Down for First Time Since 2005," *Broadcasting and Cable,* February 4, 2013; "Super Bowl XLVII Live Stream Establishes Viewership Records," *Entertainment Close-Up,* February 16, 2013; Stuart Elliott, "Replaying Super Bowl Ads' Effectiveness," *The New York Times Blogs,* February 6, 2013; "Mercedes-Benz 'Soul' Shines Through," *PR Newswire,* February 7, 2013; "The Complete 2013 USA Today Ad Meter Results," February 3, 2013, http://admeter.usatoday.com/articles/view/the-results; Sara Bibel, "CBS's Super Bowl Sunday Delivers 108.5 Million Viewers," www.tvbythenumbers.com, February 5, 2013; and Rama Ylkur, Chuck Tomkovick, and Patty Traczyk, "Super Bowl Effectiveness: Hollywood Finds the Games Golden," *Journal of Advertising Research,* March 2004, pp. 143–59.
12. "Creativity Picks the Best Super Bowl Ads of All Time," *Advertising Age,* February 7, 2011, p. 23.
13. "100 Leading National Advertisers," *Advertising Age,* June 24, 2013, p. 16; "Market Leaders," *Advertising Age,* July 8, 2013, pp. 14–19; Beth Snyder Bulik, "Thin Is In as Lenovo Launches Massive Ultrabook Campaign," *Advertising Age,* June 4, 2012, p. 2; "Despite Setbacks, Intel Moves Ahead with New Ultrabook Campaign," *Impact,* November 18, 2012.
14. Ioni Lewis, Barry Watson, Richard Tay, and Katherine M. White, "The Role of Fear Appeals in Improving Driver Safety," *The International Journal of Behavioral Consultation and Therapy,* June 22, 2007, p. 203; Lenore Skenazy, "Take the Fat Out of Your Food," *Advertising Age,* January 14, 2008, p. 12; Cornelia Pechmann, Guangzhi Zhao, Marvin E. Goldberg, and Ellen Thomas Reibling, "What to Convey in Antismoking Advertisements for Adolescents: The Use of Protection Motivation Theory to Identify Effective Message Themes," *Journal of Marketing,* April 2003, pp. 1–18; Jeffrey D. Zbar, "Fear!" *Advertising Age,* November 14, 1994,

pp. 18–19; and John F. Tanner, Jr., James B. Hunt, and David R. Eppright, "The Protection Motivation Model: A Normative Model of Fear Appeals," *Journal of Marketing,* July 1991, pp. 36–45.

15. "About Bebe," Bebe website, www.bebe.com, accessed June 16, 2011; and Sanjay Putrevu, "Consumer Responses toward Sexual and Nonsexual Appeals: The Influence of Involvement, Need for Cognition (NFC), and Gender," *Journal of Advertising,* Summer 2008, p. 57.

16. Rupal Parekh, "With Strong Work for Walmart and Geico, Martin Agency Is Creating a New Specialty: Making Marketers Recession-Proof," *Advertising Age,* January 19, 2009, p. 30; and Louis Llovio, "Geico Gecko's Viral Videos," *Richmond Times Dispatch,* March 28, 2009, p. B-9.

17. Thomas W. Cline and James J. Kellaris, "The Influence of Humor Strength and Humor-Message Relatedness on Ad Memorability: A Dual Process Model," *Journal of Advertising,* Spring 2007, p. 55; Yong Zhang and George M. Zinkham, "Responses to Humorous Ads," *Journal of Advertising,* Winter 2006, p. 113; and Yih Hwai Lee and Elison Ai Ching Lim, "What's Funny and What's Not: The Moderating Role of Cultural Orientation in Ad Humor," *Journal of Advertising,* Summer 2008, p. 71.

18. Rupal Parekh, "Agency of the Year," *Advertising Age*, January 28, 2013, p. 15; and Teressa Iezzi, "Kenny Powers Returns for Second K-Swiss Campaign," posted on 72andSunny website, www.72andsunny/work/k-swiss/mfceo.com, no date.

19. Judith Anne Garretson Folse, Richard G. Netemeyer, and Scot Burton, "Spokescharacters," *Journal of Advertising,* Spring 2012, pp. 17–32; "Pepsi/Beyoncé and Chanel/Brad Pitt Battle for Most Celebrity Spokesperson Chatter: NetBase Evaluates Endorsement Buzz Winners," *Marketwire,* April 10, 2013; "L'Oreal Paris Announces Lea Michele as Newest Brand Ambassador," *PR Newswire,* September 18, 2012.

20. "Celebrities and the Art of High-Risk Marketing," *Postmedia Breaking News,* April 25, 2013; Chris Isidore, "Lance Armstrong: How He'll Make Money Now," *CNN Wire,* January 16, 2013; Francois A. Carrillat, Alain D'Astous, and Josianne Lazure, "For Better, for Worse? What to Do When Celebrity Endorsements Go Bad," *Journal of Advertising Research,* March 2013, pp. 15–30; and Chris Isidore, "Tiger Woods No Longer Top-Paid Athlete," *CNNMoney.com,* July 17, 2012.

21. "Results of 4A's 2011 Television Production Cost Survey," *4A's Bulletin,* January 22, 2013 (New York: American Association of Advertising Agencies); and "Washington: Results of 4A's 2011 Television Production Cost Survey," *Plus Media Solutions,* January 23, 2013.

22. "U.S. Ad Spending Totals by Medium," *Advertising Age,* December 31, 2012, p. 13.

23. Vicki R. Lane, "The Impact of Ad Repetition and Ad Content on Consumer Perceptions of Incongruent Extensions," *Journal of Marketing,* April 2000, pp. 80–91.

24. "Nielsen Includes Internet Viewers for the First Time, Estimates That There Are Now 115.6 Million TV Homes in the U.S.," *Engadget HD,* May 8, 2013; "Rise of the 'Zero TV' Home: Ratings Altered to Take into Account the People Who Only Watch Online," *Mail Online,* April 8, 2013; and "Nielsen Estimates 115.6 Million TV Homes in the U.S., Up 1.2%," Nielsen website, www.nielsen.com/us/en/newswire, May 7, 2013.

25. "Free to Move between Screens: The Cross-Platform Report," The Nielsen Company (New York), March 2013; and Ryan Kisiel, "Forget HD or 3D, 4K Television Is the Next Big Thing," *Daily Mail,* January 28, 2013.

26. Brian Steinberg, "TV Ad Prices: 'Idol' No Match for Football," *Advertising Age,* October 22, 2012, pp. 18–19; Emily Fredrix, "TV Commercials Shrink to Match Attention Spans," *USA Today,* October 30, 2010; Kate Newstead and Jenni Romaniuk, "Cost per Second: The Relative Effectiveness of 15- and 30-Second Television Advertisements," *Journal of Advertising Research,* 2009, pp. 68–76; and Srinivasan Swaminathan and Robert Kent, "Second-by-Second Analysis of Advertising Exposure in TV Pods," *Journal of Advertising Research,* March 2013, pp. 91–100.

27. "Michael Powell Testimony to House Energy & Commerce Subcommittee on Communications & Technology," press release, National Cable & Telecommunications Association, www.ncta.com, June 25, 2012; and Brian Steinberg, "Turner Experiments with Building a Smarter Ad for Its Cable Networks," *Advertising Age,* April 11, 2011, p. 3.

28. Mike Pewterbaugh, "IMS Top 50 Infomercials and Spots of 2012," *Response Magazine,* December 2012, pp. 36–40; "10 Best-Selling Infomercial Products," *Gizmodo,* May 1, 2013; "All the Info on Infomercials," www.Backstage.com, November 18, 2010; and Herb Weisbaum, "ConsumerMan: Busting Infomercial Myths," www.MSNBC.com, December 16, 2010.

29. "National Radio Format Shares and Station Counts," *Radio Today 2013: How America Listens to Radio,* Arbitron, 2013; "Radio Today by the Numbers," Arbitron, Spring 2013; "Radio's Weekly Reach: Hours per Week Spent Listening," "Daily Media Reach," and "Radio Listeners Listen," *Why Radio Fact Sheet,* Radio Advertising Bureau, April 2012; and Anthony Ha, "Pandora Resurrects Its 40-Hour Limit on Free Music," www.techcrunch.com, February 27, 2013.

30. "Hour-by-Hour Listening," in *Radio Today,* 2010 Edition, Arbitron, p. 89.

31. "A Magazine for Everyone," *Magazine Media Factbook 2012/13* (New York: The Association of Magazine Media), p. 85; "April Arrives; Brings 74 New Titles to the Nation's Newsstands," mr.magazine website, www.mrmagazine.com, May 2, 2013; "Skateboarder Magazine Changes the Game with Innovative Digital-First Platform," *States News Service,* April 16, 2013; and Rebecca Clancy, "*Auto Trader* Print Edition to Stop as Focus Shifts to Digital," *The Telegraph,* May 7, 2013.

32. "Number of Magazines by Category," The Association of Magazine Media, http://www.magazine.org/insights-resources/research-publications/trends-data/magazine-industry-facts-data/1998-2010-number, accessed May 13, 2013; and "Magazines Mean Engagement," *Magazine Media Factbook 2012/13* (New York: The Association of Magazine Media), p. 14.

33. "Defunct or Suspended Magazines," The Association of Magazine Media, http://www.magazine.org/insights-resources/research-publications/trends-data/magazine-industry-facts-data/publishing-trends, accessed May 13, 2013; "Circulation Averages for All ABC Magazines," The Association of Magazine Media, http://www.magazine.org/insights-resources/research-publications/trends-data/magazine-industry-facts-data/circulation-trends, accessed May 13, 2013; and AARP website, http://advertise.aarp.org/media_properties/publications/, accessed May 13, 2013.

34. "Top 25 U.S. Newspapers for March 2013," Research and Data, Alliance for Audited Media, http://www.auditedmedia.com/news/research-and-data/top-25-us-newspapers-for-march-2013.aspx; "About Us," *Metro* website, http://www.metro.us/newyork/about-us/; and "Metro Newspaper Is the #1 Free Daily Newspaper in Boston," *Business Wire,* June 13, 2011.

35. Tom Baxter, "Big News: Newspapers, Long Mourned, Aren't Really Dead," *SaportaReport,* May 13, 2013; "Top 25 U.S. Newspapers for September 2012," Research and Data, Alliance for Audited Media, http://www.auditedmedia.com/news/research-and-data/top-25-us-newspapers-for-september-2012.aspx; Christine Haughney, "Newspapers Post Gains in Digital Circulation," *The New York Times,* May 1, 2013, p. 5; "Digital Fees Pay Off for 2 Top-Selling

Newspapers," *The Associated Press,* April 30, 2013; and "Huffington Post Twitter: 3 Million Follower Giveaway," *The Huffington Post,* May 10, 2013.

36. "U.S. Ad Spending Forecast from ZenithOptimedia," *Advertising Age,* December 31, 2012, p. 13; "Can Yellow Pages Make a Come Back?" *Zacks Investment Research,* March 21, 2013; Chris Silver Smith, "Are Yellow Pages Toast?" www.searchengineland.com, March 26, 2012; "Mobile Searches for Local Business Info Replacing Desktop and Yellow Pages," *SBWire,* April 10, 2013; "Yellow Page Group Reminds Winnipeg Residents of Directory Opt-Out Program," *Marketwire,* March 18, 2013; Heather Knight, "Yellow Pages Ruling Endangers SF Ban," *SFGate,* October 15, 2012; and "As Media Habits Evolve, Yellow Pages and Search Engines Firmly Established as Go-To Sources for Consumer Shopping Locally," *PR Newswire,* June 13, 2011.

37. "comScore Releases April 2013 U.S. Search Engine Rankings," Press Release, comScore website, http://www.comscore.com/Insights/Press_Releases/2013/5/comScore_Releases_April_2013_US_Search_Engine_Rankings, May 15, 2013; "10 Ways to Improve the Banner Ad Design and Enhance the Click Through Rate," *Tech and Techie,* May 6, 2013; "'Banner Blindness' Now a Major Marketing Concern," *Bulldog Reporter's Daily Dog,* March 29, 2013; and Thales Teixeira, "The New Science of Viral Ads," *Harvard Business Review,* March 2012, pp. 25–27.

38. See "Guidelines, Standards & Best Practices," at the Interactive Advertising Bureau website, http://www.iab.net/guidelines; "IAB Releases New Standard Ad Unit Portfolio," press release, International Advertising Bureau, February 26, 2012; "Online Measurement," Nielsen website, http://www.nielsen.com/us/en/nielsen-solutions/nielsen-measurement/nielsen-online-measurement.html, accessed May 16, 2013; and Abbey Klaassen, "Why the Click Is the Wrong Metric for Online Ads," *Advertising Age,* February 23, 2009, p. 4.

39. "Why We Need to Pivot in the Fight against Ad Fraud," *VentureBeat,* April 18, 2013; "Three Ways Advertisers Can Avoid Click Fraud, *ReadWriteWeb,* September 6, 2012; "Click Fraud Rate Drops to 19.1 Percent in Q4 2010," *Business Wire,* January 26, 2011; Sara Yin, "Click Fraud Skyrockets," *PC Magazine,* October 21, 2010; Alex Mindlin, "Click Fraud Climbs with Mobile Gear," *The New York Times,* November 1, 2010, p. 2; and Gareth Jones, "Briefing—Paid Search—Advertisers Stung by Rising Click Fraud," *Revolution,* May 1, 2009, p. 18.

40. Arch G. Woodside, "Outdoor Advertising as Experiments," *Journal of the Academy of Marketing Science* 18 (Summer 1990), pp. 229–37.

41. "OOH Revenue Grew to $6.7 Billion in 2012," Outdoor Advertising Association of America website, http://www.oaaa.org/ResourceCenter/MarketingSales/Factsamp;Figures/Revenue/HistoricalRevenue.aspx, accessed May 17, 2013; "New Report Evaluates Consumer Lifestyles to Determine Value of Out of Home Advertising," press release, Outdoor Advertising Association of America, May 2, 2012; "Clear Channel Outdoor Digital Billboards Help Houston Crime Stoppers Take a Bite Out of Crime," www.DigitalSignageToday.com, April 25, 2013; "Clear Channel Digital Billboards Will Carry Twin Cities Weather Warnings," www.DigitalSignageToday.com, April 26, 2013; "Judge Hits 'Off' Switch on Digital Billboards," *Plus Media Solutions,* April 26, 2013; "Beer, Donuts and Digital Billboard Advertising," www.DigitalSignageToday.com, March 19, 2013; and "Council Limits Supergraphics in Hollywood, Signs: Action Comes as Judge Upholds City's Billboard Ban," *The Daily News of Los Angeles,* September 29, 2010, p. A3.

42. "Clear Channel Outdoor Holdings Releases 'Out-of-Home Advertising and the Retail Industry' Report," *Professional Services Close-Up,* January 25, 2011; Andrew Hampp, "What's New with Outdoor Ads, and What's This Digital Out-of-Home I Keep Hearing About?" *Advertising Age,* September 27, 2010, p. 48; "The Year Ahead for … Outdoor," *Campaign,* January 9, 2009, p. 28; Andrew Hampp, "Digital Out of Home. That's Those Pixilated Billboards, Right?" *Advertising Age,* March 30, 2009; Andrew Hampp, "Out of Home That Stood Out," *Advertising Age,* December 15, 2008, p. 22; and Daniel W. Baack, Rick T. Wilson, and Brian D. Till, "Creativity and Memory Effects," *Journal of Advertising,* Winter 2008, p. 85.

43. Sehoon Park and Minhi Hahn, "Pulsing in a Discrete Model of Advertising Competition," *Journal of Marketing Research,* November 1991, pp. 397–405.

44. Peggy Masterson, "The Wearout Phenomenon," *Marketing Research,* Fall 1999, pp. 27–31; and Lawrence D. Gibson, "What Can One TV Exposure Do?" *Journal of Advertising Research,* March–April 1996, pp. 9–18.

45. Rik Pieters, Michel Wedel, and Rajeev Batra, "The Stopping Power of Advertising: Measure and Effects of Visual Complexity," *Journal of Marketing,* September 2010, pp. 48–60; Rob Norton, "How Uninformative Advertising Tells Consumers Quite a Bit," *Fortune,* December 26, 1994, p. 37; and "Professor Claims Corporations Waste Billions on Advertising," *Marketing News,* July 6, 1992, p. 5.

46. "ANA Survey Finds Fees Persist as Dominant Method of Agency Compensation, Even with the Emergence of Other Models," *Target News Service,* July 27, 2010; Rance Crain, "Why Agencies—and the Media—Are Reluctant to Bet It All on Value-Compensation Systems," *Advertising Age,* June 7, 2010, p. 31; Stephen Fajen, "The Agency Model Is Bent but Not Broken," *Advertising Age,* July 7, 2008, p. 17; Jeremy Mullman, "Anheuser-Busch Whacks Retainers for Its Agencies," *Advertising Age,* February 16, 2009, p. 1; and Jack Neff, "No One-Size-Fits-All Snuggie Model Exists for DRTV Shops," *Advertising Age,* March 23, 2009.

47. The discussion of posttesting is based on William F. Arens, Michael F. Weigold, and Christian Arens, *Contemporary Advertising,* 12th ed. (New York: McGraw-Hill Irwin, 2009), pp. 228–30.

48. "ROI Metric Available in MRI Starch Syndicated," Mediamark Research & Intelligence, www.mediamark.com, accessed April 23, 2009.

49. Debora V. Thompson and Prashant Malaviya, "Consumer-Generated Ads: Does Awareness of Advertising Co-Creation Help or Hurt Persuasion?" *Journal of Marketing,* May 2013, pp. 33–47; David A. Aaker and Douglas M. Stayman, "Measuring Audience Perceptions of Commercials and Relating Them to Ad Impact," *Journal of Advertising Research* 30 (August–September 1990), pp. 7–17; and Ernest Dichter, "A Psychological View of Advertising Effectiveness," *Marketing Management* 1, no. 3 (1992), pp. 60–62.

50. David Krugel, "Television Advertising Effectiveness and Research Innovation," *Journal of Consumer Marketing,* Summer 1988, pp. 43–51; and Laurence N. Gold, "The Evolution of Television Advertising Sales Measurement: Past, Present, and Future," *Journal of Advertising Research,* June–July 1988, pp. 19–24.

51. "U.S. Ad Spending Forecast From ZenithOptimedia," *Advertising Age,* June 24, 2013, p. 22.

52. Tom Hansen, "Media Mash," *Promo,* February 1, 2007, p. 66; Magid M. Abraham and Leonard M. Lodish, "Getting the Most Out of Advertising and Promotion," *Harvard Business Review,* May–June 1990, pp. 50–60; Steven W. Hartley and James Cross, "How Sales Promotion Can Work For and Against You," *Journal of Consumer Marketing,* Summer 1988, pp. 35–42; Robert D. Buzzell, John A. Quelch, and Walter J. Salmon, "The Costly Bargain of Trade Promotion," *Harvard Business Review,* March–April 1990, pp. 141–49; and Mary L. Nicastro, "Break-Even Analysis Determines Success of Sales Promotions," *Marketing News,* March 5, 1990, p. 11.

53. "Annual Coupon Facts," NCH Marketing Services, 2013; "NCH Annual Topline U.S. CPG Coupon Facts Report for Year-End 2012," NCH Marketing Services, January 2013; "2012 NCH Consumer Survey: Demographic Profile of Coupon Users," NCH Marketing Services, 2012; Claudia Buck, "Coupon Industry: No Scissors Required," *The State Journal-Register,* February 24, 2013, p. 40; "Coupons.com Report Shows Upward Trend among Digital Coupon Users," *Wireless News,* May 19, 2013; and "How Mobile Coupons Are Driving an Explosion in Mobile Commerce," *The Business Insider,* May 22, 2013.

54. Kapil Bawa and Robert W. Shoemaker, "Analyzing Incremental Sales from a Direct-Mail Coupon Promotion," *Journal of Marketing,* July 1998, pp. 66–78.

55. Robert A. Strang, "Sales Promotion—Fast Growth, Faulty Management," *Harvard Business Review* 54 (July–August 1976), pp. 115–24; and Ronald W. Ward and James E. Davis, "Coupon Redemption," *Journal of Advertising Research* 18 (August 1978), pp. 51–58. Similar results on favorable mail-distributed coupons were reported by Alvin Schwartz, "The Influence of Media Characteristics on Coupon Redemption," *Journal of Marketing* 30 (January 1966), pp. 41–46.

56. "What Is Coupon Fraud?" The Coupon Information Corporation, http://www.couponinformationcenter.com, accessed May 26, 2013; Josh Elledge, "Coupon Fraud Hurts Us All," *Grand Rapids Press,* April 19, 2011, p. B1; and Amy Johannes, "Flying the Coup," *Promo,* July 1, 2008, p. 28.

57. *Epic* website, http://www.epicthemovie.com, accessed May 27, 2013; "The Influence of Promotional Products on Consumer Behavior," Promotional Product Association International, November 2012; Amy Johannes, "Premium Connections," *Promo,* October 2008, p. 34; and Gerard P. Prendergast, Alex S. L. Tsang, Derek T. Y. Poon, "Predicting Premium Proneness," *Journal of Advertising Research,* June 2008, p. 287.

58. "Two Consumer-Created Doritos Ads Crash the Super Bowl Advertising Stage, Now Compete for $1 Million Bonus Prize," *PR Newswire,* February 3, 2013; "Official Rules," Doritos Crash the Super Bowl Ad Contest, Frito-Lay Inc., https://ctsb.grindnetworks.com/voting_finalists_winners_phase/officialrules.php; and "User Content Offers a New Perspective," *PR Week,* February 23, 2009, p. 21.

59. Sarah Firshein, "HGTV Dream Home Winner Revealed!: Here's a Warm 'n' Fuzzy Story … " *Curbed NY,* March 11, 2011; and Charlotte McEleny, "Social Media and Mobile Boost Participation for McDonald's Monopoly," *New Media Age Online,* April 18, 2011.

60. "Mars Chocolate North America Launches 5 Characters, 5 Cars Promotion," *Travel & Leisure Close-Up,* June 20, 2011; "Buy a Large Coke at Carl's Jr. and Win—Guaranteed; Guests Can Win Big with My Coke Rewards Point and Food Prizes," *Business Wire,* May 27, 2011; and "StumbleUpon Partners with the Academy of Motion Picture Arts and Sciences for Sweepstakes," *Marketwire,* January 17, 2013.

61. Tiffany Hsu, "Taco Bell Gives Away Free Doritos Locos Tacos after World Series," *Money and Company,* October 30, 2012; "Free Doritos Locos Tacos Available at Taco Bell if Bases Stolen in World Series," *Huff Post,* October 19, 2012; Elana Ashanti Jefferson, "Sample Hunters Offer Advice for Trying—Before You Buy," *Denver Post,* July 16, 2012, p. 3C; and Schuyler Velasco, "Ben & Jerry's Free Cone Day," *The Christian Science Monitor,* April 9, 2013.

62. "Who Says Loyalty Is Dead? Americans Have More Than 2B Loyalty Memberships," *PandoDaily on Facebook,* February 22, 2013; Kelly Hlavinka and Jim Sullivan, *The Billion Member March: The 2011 Colloquy Loyalty Census*, LoyaltyOne Colloquy, http://www.colloquy.com/files/2011-COLLOQUY-Census-Talk-White-Paper.pdf, 2011; Kara McGuire, "Retailers Work to Make Shopping Its Own Reward," *Star Tribune,* December 19, 2010, p. 1A; and "Loyalty Rewards Membership on the Rise," *Brandweek.com,* April 17, 2009.

63. Richard Postrel and Kelly Hlavinka, "An Open Economy: The Evolution of Loyalty in the United States," Colloquy, September 2012, http://colloquy.com/white-view.asp?uid=38; "Maritz Loyalty Marketing Survey Updates on Consumers' Top-Rated Loyalty Programs," *Entertainment Close-Up,* May 19, 2013; and David Rosen, "Exclusively Yours," *Promo,* February 1, 2009, p. 12.

64. Walmart Smart Network website, http://www.walmartsmartnetwork.com/default.aspx, accessed May 27, 2013; and Amy Johannes, "Watching the Carts," *Promo,* October 2008, p. 36.

65. "Virgin Mobile Offers $100 Rebate to T-Mobile Turncoats," *Engadget HD*, April 9, 2013; Nathalia Dens, Patrick De Pelsmacker, Marijke Wouters, and Nathalia Purnawirawan, "Do You Like What You Recognize?" *Journal of Advertising,* Fall 2012, pp. 35–53; "The Case for Rebates," *Chief Marketer,* July 1, 2011; and Marvin A. Jolson, Joshua L. Wiener, and Richard B. Rosecky, "Correlates of Rebate Proneness," *Journal of Advertising Research,* February–March 1987, pp. 33–43.

66. "Primetime Shows with the Most Product Placement," www.CNBC.com, http://www.cnbc.com/id/45884892/page/1, accessed May 27, 2013; Misty Harris, "Subtlety Is No Longer in Style: Great Gatsby Epitomizes Product Placement Trend," *Edmonton Journal,* May 2, 2013, p. D1; "Celebrity Product Brands … Now Showing!" www.Business2Community.com, May 8, 2013; Alex Biles, "Keep Your Eyes Peeled for These Product Placements in *The Great Gatsby,*" *Benzinga,* May 10, 2013; "FCC Examines Product Placement Rules," *Marketing News,* July 15, 2008, p. 8; Josh Halliday, "Product Placement: P Logo Stands for Puzzled Public," *Guardian Unlimited,* June 20, 2011; Kate Ward, "'American Idol' Product Placement: Does It Distract from the Show?" www.popwatch.com, April 19, 2011; Brandchannel.com website, http://www.brandchannel.com/brandcameo_films.asp?movie_year=2011#movie_list, accessed May 27, 2013; and Ekaterina V. Karniouchina, Can Uslay, and Grigori Erenburg, "Do Marketing Media Have Life Cycles? The Case of Product Placement in Movies," *Journal of Marketing,* May 2011, pp. 27–49.

67. "Direct Selling Leader Amway Leverages Product Placement in the Video Gaming World," *India Retail News,* April 5, 2013; Stuart Elliott, "Expanding Line of Dunder Mifflin Products Shows Success in Reverse Product Placement," *The New York Times Blogs,* November 23, 2012; Karen Idelson, "Product Placements Don't Derail Nom Hopes," *Daily Variety,* June 1, 2011, p. A8; Andrew Hampp, "Why Viewers and Marketers Are Loving 'Modern Family,'" *Advertising Age,* April 18, 2011, p. 4; "Sky and Discovery Launch Digital Product Placement," *Broadcast*, May 17, 2011; and Amy Johannes, "Simpson Mania," *Promo,* November 1, 2008, p. 8.

68. This discussion is drawn particularly from John A. Quelch, *Trade Promotions by Grocery Manufacturers: A Management Perspective* (Cambridge, MA: Marketing Science Institute, August 1982).

69. Michael Chevalier and Ronald C. Curhan, "Retail Promotions as a Function of Trade Promotions: A Descriptive Analysis," *Sloan Management Review* 18 (Fall 1976), pp. 19–32.

70. G. A. Marken, "Firms Can Maintain Control over Creative Co-op Programs," *Marketing News,* September 28, 1992, pp. 7, 9.

71. Kathleen Cleeren, Harald J. van Heerde, and Marnik G. Dekimpe, "Rising from the Ashes: How Brands and Categories Can Overcome Product-Harm Crises," *Journal of Marketing,* March 2013, pp. 58–77; "Carnival Cruises Tries to Dig Themselves Out of Another PR Crisis," *Bulldog Reporter's Daily Dog,* February 22, 2013; and Peter S. Goodman, "From Corporate Crises, a Handbook on Lost Love and Publicity: Missteps by Toyota, BP, and Goldman Show Trust Is Tough to Win Back," *The International Herald Tribune,* August 23, 2010, p. 1.

72. Irving Rein, Philip Kotler, and Martin Stoller, *High Visibility* (New York: Dodd, Mead, 1987); and Steven Colford, "Ross Perot: A Winner after All," *Advertising Age,* December 21, 1992, pp. 4, 18.

73. Michael Treacy and Fred Wiersema, "Customer Intimacy and Other Value Disciplines," *Harvard Business Review,* January–February 1993, pp. 84–93.
74. Gerry Khermouch and Tom Lowry, "The Future of Advertising," *BusinessWeek,* March 26, 2001, p. 139; and "Outlook 2001: Advertising," *Marketing News,* January 1, 2001, p. 10.
75. Betsy Spethmann, "McFallout," *Promo,* October 2001, pp. 31–38.
76. "Kid Stuff," *Promo,* January 1991, pp. 25, 42; Steven W. Colford, "Fine-Tuning Kids' TV," *Advertising Age,* February 11, 1991, p. 35; and Kate Fitzgerald, "Toys Star-Struck for Movie Tie-Ins," *Advertising Age,* February 18, 1991, pp. 3, 45.
77. Herbert J. Rotfeld, Avery M. Abernathy, and Patrick R. Parsons, "Self-Regulation and Television Advertising," *Journal of Advertising* 19, no. 4 (1990), pp. 18–26.

Google, Inc.: This case was written by Steven Hartley. Sources: "Mobile Cellular Subscriptions: 2000–2010," International Telecommunication Union, accessed October 15, 2011, http://www.itu.int/ITU-D/ict/material/FactsFigures2010.pdf; Jessica E. Vascellaro, "Google Decides to Find Its Creative Side," *The Wall Street Journal,* October 7, 2009; Robert D. Hof, "Google's New Ad Weapon," *BusinessWeek,* June 22, 2009, p. 52; Maria Bartiromo, "Eric Schmidt on Where Google Is Headed," *BusinessWeek,* August 17, 2009, p. 11; "Why Microsoft-Yahoo Deal Could Be Good for Google," *Advertising Age,* August 10, 2009, p. 10; Peter Burrow, "Apple and Google: Another Step Apart," *BusinessWeek,* August 17, 2009, p. 24; Jeff Jarvis, "How The Google Model Could Help," *BusinessWeek,* February 9, 2009, p. 32; Abbey Klaassen, "Google Says Print Ads Isn't the Answer for Newspapers," *Advertising Age,* January 26, 2009, p. 17; Matthew Creamer, "Recession Doesn't Dent Total Value of Top 100 Brands," *Advertising Age,* April 27, 2009; "The 500 Largest U.S. Corporations," *Fortune,* May 4, 2009, F-1; "ComScore Releases August 2009 U.S. Search Engine Rankings," www.comscore.com, October 10, 2009; interviews with Google personnel; and information contained on the Google website (www.google.com).

Chapter 19

1. Natasha Singer, "On Campus, It's One Big Commercial," *The New York Times,* September 11, 2011, pp. BU1, BU4; Natalie Zmuda, "Marketers Hitting Campus Harder Than Ever," *Advertising Age,* October 17, 2011, pp. 26, 28; and Bruce Horovitz, "Marketers Pull an Inside Job on College Campuses," *USA Today,* October 4, 2010, pp. 2A, 2B.
2. Ibid.
3. Ibid.
4. Dave Evans, *Social Media Marketing: An Hour a Day* (Indianapolis, IN: Wiley Publishing, Inc., 2009), pp. 57–59.
5. Andreas M. Kaplan and Michael Haenlein, "Users of the World, Unite! The Challenges and Opportunities of Social Media," *Business Horizons* 53, no. 1 (2010), pp. 59–68.
6. Dave Evans, *Social Media Marketing: An Hour a Day,* pp. 57–59; Jason Miletsky, *Principles of Internet Marketing* (Boston, MA: Course Technology, Cengage Learning, 2010), pp. 75–76; Kristin Tillotson, "Blogging's Getting Old These Days," *Star Tribune,* December 22, 2010, p. E1; and Soumitra Dutta and Matthew Fraser, "Web 2.0: The ROI Case," *CEO Magazine,* May/June 2009, pp. 42–44.
7. "Participative Web and User-Created Content: Web 2.0, Wikis, and Social Networking" (Paris: Organization for Economic Co-operation and Development, 2007); and Jason Daley, "Tearing Down the Walls," *Entrepreneur,* December 2010, pp. 57–60.
8. Kaplan and Haenlein, "Users of the World, Unite!" pp. 62–64.
9. Drake Bennett, "Ten Years of Inaccuracy and Remarkable Detail," *Bloomberg Businessweek,* January 10–January 16, 2011, pp. 57–61.
10. Starr Hall and Chadd Rosenberg, *Get Connected: The Social Networking Toolkit for Business* (Madison, WI: Entrepreneur Press, 2009), pp. 17–20.
11. Figure 19–2 is adapted from "The CMO's Guide to the Social Landscape," prepared by 97th Floor, CMO.com, March 20, 2012, Website demographic data as of late August 2013 for Facebook, Twitter, LinkedIn, and YouTube were provided by Quantcast. See http://www.quantcast.com.
12. This discussion of Facebook and Twitter uses material on the Ford Consulting Group website provided by David Ford and Clara Shih, *The Facebook Era* (Boston, MA: Pearson Education, Inc., 2009), pp. 25–51.
13. "Facebook Reports First Quarter 2013 Results," Facebook news release. See http://investor.fb.com/releasedetail.cfm?ReleaseID=761090.
14. Lev Grossman, "2010 Person of the Year: Mark Zuckerberg," *Time,* December 27, 2010–January 3, 2011, pp. 44–75; and Randall Stross, "Social Networks, Small and Smaller," *The New York Times,* April 15, 2012, p. BU3.
15. Facebook Reports Second Quarter 2013 Results," Facebook news release. See http://investor.fb.com/releasedetail.cfm?ReleaseID=780093.
16. Ibid.
17. Ibid.
18. The Infinite Dial 2013: Navigating Digital Platforms— "Average Number of Facebook Friends by Age Group," p. 48. See http://www.edisonresearch.com/wpcontent/uploads/2013/04/Edison_Research_Arbitron_Infinite_Dial_2013.pdf.
19. Ben Pickering, "How to Use Facebook Ads: An Introduction," www.socialmediaexaminer.com, May 3, 2012; and Martin Peers, "Facebook Pokes Its Rivals," *The Wall Street Journal,* November 16, 2010, p. C12.
20. "Top 10 Ways to Engage Fans on Facebook," Buddy Media, Inc., 2010.
21. Ned Smith, "How Much Is a Facebook Friend Worth? $174.17," *BusinessNewsDaily,* April 26, 2013. See http://www.businessnewsdaily.com/4402-value-facebook-friend-marketing.html.
22. The discussion of StuffDOT was provided by Jennifer Katz and Amanda Axvig of StuffDOT, Inc.
23. Evelyn M. Rusli, "Facebook Simplifies Privacy Settings," *The Wall Street Journal,* December 13, 2013, p. B4.
24. Sarah E. Needleman and Evelyn M. Rusli, "Putting a Value on Facebook Followers," *The Wall Street Journal,* October 11, 2012, p. B9.
25. Rachael Metz, "Facebook Gets More Visual to Keep Its Users Engaged," *MIT Technology Review,* March 7, 2013.
26. Evelyn M. Rusli, "Facebook Unveils Hashtags," *The Wall Street Journal,* June 13, 2013, p. B7.
27. Jessi Hempel, "The Second Coming of Facebook," *Fortune,* April 29, 2013, pp. 72–78; Brian Womack, "Facebook Goes After Phony Ads," *Star Tribune,* April 5, 2013, p. D3; Walter S. Mossberg, "Facebook Gets a Hold on Phones," *The Wall Street Journal,* April 10, 2013, pp. D1–D2; and Evelyn M. Rusli, "Facebook Shows Off Its New 'Home,'" *The Wall Street Journal,* April 5, 2013, p. B1.
28. Richard Holt, "Twitter in Numbers," *The Telegraph,* March 21, 2013. See http://www.telegraph.co.uk./technology/twitter/9945505/Twitter-in-numbers.html; and Karen Wickre, "Celebrating #Twitter7," Twitter press release, March 21, 2013. See http://blog.twitter.com/2013.celebrating-twitter7.
29. Thomas Lee, "Social-Media Bees Create Target Buzz," *Star Tribune,* April 13, 2013, pp. A1, A6; and Jeff Herring and Maritza Parra, "Make the Most of Tweeting," *Star Tribune,* January 6, 2011, p. E4.
30. Katherine Jacobsen, "LinkedIn Targets College-Bound High Schoolers," *The Christian Science Monitor,* August 20, 2013. See http://www.csmonitor.com/Innovation/Tech-Culture/2013/0820/LinkedIn-targets-college-bound-high-schoolers; and "About US: LinkedIN Facts." See http://press.linkedin.com/about.

31. Kristin Burnham, "5 LinkedIn Tips for Career Success in 2012," January 5, 2012. See www.c10.com.
32. "LinkedIn Is Trying to Quicken Its Pulse," *Bloomberg Businessweek,* April 22–April 28, 2013, pp. 32–33; Emily Moltby and Shira Ovide, "Which Social Media Work?" *The Wall Street Journal,* January 31, 2013, p. B8; and Brandon Bailey, "Who Needs Friends? LinkedIn Has Success with Members," *Star Tribune,* April 25, 2013, pp. D1, D3.
33. YouTube Statistics. See http://www.youtube.com/yt/press/statistics.html; and Amanda Axvig, Vice President of Marketing, AOI Marketing, Inc.
34. Mike Hale, "Is YouTube's New Design a Sign of Things to Come?" *Star Tribune,* December 19, 2011, p. E2.
35. Alex Perry, "The Warlord vs. the Hipsters," *Time,* March 26, 2012, pp. 36–41; and Solomon Moore, "U.S. Plays a Bigger Part in Hunt for Kony," *The Wall Street Journal,* April 30, 2012, p. A16.
36. Brad Stone and Andy Fixmar, "MustSee YouTube," *Bloomberg Businessweek,* May 7–May 13, 2012, pp. 42–44; and Tanzina Vega, "Your Ad, as Seen on YouTube," *Media Decoder: The New York Times,* April 23, 2012.
37. Jonah Weiner, "Video Makes the Radio Star," *Bloomberg Businessweek,* April 1–April 7, 2013, pp. 75–77; and Amanda Axvig, Vice President of Marketing, AOI Marketing, Inc.
38. Damian Kulash, Jr., "The New Rock Star Paradigm," *The Wall Street Journal,* December 17, 2010, p. D1; and "YouTube Press Room: Statistics." See http://www.youtube.com/t/press_statistics.
39. Christa Toole, "Ten Tips for Those Who Still Aren't Using YouTube," *Advertising Age* (www.adage.com), October 19, 2010; and Felix Gillette, "On YouTube, Seven-Figure Views, Six-Figure Paychecks," *Bloomberg Businessweek,* September 27–October 3, 2010, pp. 35–36.
40. Website demographic data as of late August 2013 for Facebook, Twitter, LinkedIn, and YouTube were provided by Quantcast. See https://www.quantcast.com.
41. Ibid.
42. This example and the section on measuring results were provided by Brian Stuckey and Amanda Axvig of StuffDOT, Inc.
43. The Jeff Gordon–Pepsi Max example was provided by Nancy Harrower, Concordia University–St. Paul; and Sheila Shayon, "Pepsi Continues to Bask in Branded Content Glory with Top YouTube Views," *Brand Channel,* April 8, 2013. See http://www.brandchannel.com/home/post/2013/04/08/Pepsi-Tops-YouTube-Leaderboard-040813.aspx.
44. See http://www.huffingtonpost.com/2012/04/06/pinteresttraffic-growth_n_1408088.html.
45. The Greenpeace-Nestlé example uses material on the Ford Consulting Group website provided by David Ford.
46. The Carmex "Half-Court Hero" example was written by Patrick Hodgdon, Manager of Digital Marketing, Bolin Marketing.
47. Sam Grobart, "Think Colossal," *Bloomberg Businessweek,* April 1, 2013, pp. 58–64.
48. Evelyn M. Rusli and Amir Efrati, "Facebook on Collision Course with Google on Web Searches," *The Wall Street Journal,* January 16, 2013, pp. A1, A10.
49. Evelyn M. Rusli, "Buy Signal: Facebook Widens Data Targeting," *The Wall Street Journal,* April 10, 2013, p. B4; and Hayley Tsukayama, "Facebook's Big Reveal: Social Search," *Star Tribune,* January 16, 2013, p. D6.
50. Jessi Hempel, "Smartphones: The War to Be No. 3," *Fortune,* February 4, 2013, pp. 35–36.
51. Juhana Rossi, "Angry Birds' Maker Perches for Global Growth Takeoff," *The Wall Street Journal,* April 4, 2013, p. B4; Spencer E. Ante, "Rovio Mines Video with 'Angry Birds Toons,'" *The Wall Street Journal,* March 12, 2013, p. B6; and John Gaudiosi, "Rovio Execs Explain What Angry Birds Toons Channel Opens Up to Its 1.7 Billion Gamers," *Forbes,* March 13, 2013. See http://www.forbes.com/sites/johngaudiosi/2013/03/11/rovio-execs-explain-what-angry-birds-toons-channel-opens-up-to-its-1-7-billion-gamers.
52. Jessica E. Lessen and Spencer E. Ante, "Apps Bloom into Industry Set to Hit $25 Billion," *The Wall Street Journal,* March 4, 2013, pp. B1, B4; and Rolf Winkler, "The Apps Fall Far from Apple's Tree," *The Wall Street Journal,* April 4, 2013, p. C1.
53. Andreas M. Kaplan, "If You Love Something, Let It Go Mobile: Mobile Marketing and Mobile Social Media 4x4," *Business Horizons* 55, no. 2(2012), pp. 129–39.
54. Geoffrey A. Fowler, "A High-Tech Edge on Black Friday," *The Wall Street Journal,* November 24, 2010, pp. D1, D3.
55. Geoffrey A. Fowler and Vauhini Vara, "Using 'Likes' for Gift Ideas," *The Wall Street Journal,* December 22, 2010, p. B1.
56. Dave Evans, *Social Media Marketing: An Hour a Day,* pp. 127–49.
57. Mike Swift, "Smart Phones Ring Up a Bigger Slice of Holiday Sales," *Star Tribune,* December 30, 2010, pp. A1, A10; Evan Ramsted, "TV Makers Turn Their Hopes to Apps," *The Wall Street Journal,* January 4, 2011, pp. A1, A2; Randall Stross, "Someday, Store Coupons May Tap You on the Shoulder," *The New York Times,* December 26, 2010, p. BU3; and Jackie Crosby, "Just Call It V-Commerce," *Star Tribune,* January 2, 2011, p. D1.
58. Kara McGuire, "Shoppers Hunt Bargains via Their Smart Phones," *Star Tribune,* November 28, 2010, pp. D1, D10; Michelle Higgins, "Smart Phone Apps Can Help You Avoid Holiday Travel Headaches," *Star Tribune,* December 19, 2010, p. 63; Sue Stock, "Code Alert for Smart Phones," *Star Tribune,* November 17, 2010, p. D8; Miguel Bustillo and Ann Zimmerman, "Phone-Wielding Shoppers Strike Fear into Retailers," *The Wall Street Journal,* December 16, 2010, pp. A1, A19; and Roger Cheng, "The Phone Delivers Gift Cards," *The Wall Street Journal,* November 24, 2010, p. D3.
59. Evan Ramstad, "Big Brother, Now at the Mall," *The Wall Street Journal,* October 9, 2012, p. B6; Robert Lee Hotz, "When 'Likes' Can Shed Light," *The Wall Street Journal,* March 12, 2013, p. A2; and Miguel Helft, "Larry Page Looks Ahead," *Fortune,* January 14, 2013, pp. 50–57.

StuffDOT, Inc.: This case was written by Jennifer Katz, Amanda Axvig, and William Rudelius.

Chapter 20

1. Interview with Lindsey Smith, GE Healthcare Americas, April 17, 2013.
2. "Emerging Leaders Study," prepared by Beresford Research for The Week Marketing Solutions, November 2011, www.theweek.com.
3. Jessi Hempel, "IBM's All-Star Salesman," www.cnnmoney.com, September 26, 2008.
4. "Surgical Visits," *Business 2.0,* April 2006, p. 94.
5. Mark W. Johnston and Greg W. Marshall, *Relationship Selling,* 3rd ed. (Burr Ridge, IL: McGraw-Hill/Irwin, 2010).
6. David Kirkpatrick, "Inside Sam's $100 Billion Growth Machine," *Fortune,* June 14, 2004, pp. 80ff.
7. Richard P. Bagozzi, et al., "Genetic and Neurological Foundations of Customer Orientation: Field and Experimental Evidence," *Journal of the Academy of Marketing Science,* September 2012, pp. 639–58; and "Does Your Salesperson Have the Right Genes?" *Harvard Business Review,* April 2013, p. 24.
8. Gerhard Gschwandtner, "How Much Time Do Your Salespeople Spend Selling?" *Selling Power,* March/April 2011, p. 8.
9. "The New Willy Loman Survives by Staying Home," *Bloomberg Businessweek,* January 14–January 20, 2013, pp. 16–17.

10. For an overview of team selling, see Eli Jones, Andrea Dickson, Lawrence B. Chonko, and Joseph P. Cannon, "Key Accounts and Team Selling: A Review, Framework, and Research Agenda," *Journal of Personal Selling & Sales Management,* Spring 2005, pp. 181–98.
11. "Team Selling Works!" www.sellingpower.com, March 24, 2013; "Group Dynamics," *Sales & Marketing Management,* January/February 2007, p. 8; and Steve Atlas and Elise Atlas, "Team Approach," *Selling Power,* May 2000, pp. 126–28.
12. Scott Sterns, "Cold Calls Have Yet to Breathe Their Last Gasp," *The Wall Street Journal,* December 14, 2006, p. D2.
13. Jim Edwards, "Dinner, Interrupted," *BrandWeek,* May 26, 2003, pp. 28–32.
14. Christopher Conkey, "Record Fine Levied for Telemarketing," *The Wall Street Journal,* December 14, 2005, pp. D1, D4.
15. Paul A. Herbing, *Handbook of Cross-Cultural Marketing* (New York: Haworth Press, 1998).
16. Philip R. Cateora, Mary C. Gilly, and John L. Graham, *International Marketing,* 16th ed. (Burr Ridge, IL: McGraw-Hill/Irwin, 2013).
17. This discussion is based on Johnston and Marshall, *Relationship Selling;* and "In Transition—Xerox," www.sellingpower.com, June 15, 2011.
18. Kapil R. Tuli, Ajay K. Kohli, and Sundar G. Bharadwaj, "Rethinking Customer Solutions: From Product Bundles to Relational Processes," *Journal of Marketing,* July 2007, pp. 1–17.
19. For an extensive discussion of objections, see Charles M. Futrell, *Fundamentals of Selling,* 13th ed. (Burr Ridge, IL: McGraw-Hill/Irwin, 2014), chapter 12.
20. Theodore Levitt, *The Marketing Imagination* (New York: Free Press, 1983), p. 111.
21. Barton A. Weitz, Stephen B. Castleberry, and John F. Tanner, Jr., *Selling: Building Partnerships,* 8th ed. (Burr Ridge, IL: McGraw-Hill/Irwin, 2012).
22. *Management Briefing: Sales and Marketing* (New York: Conference Board, October 1996), pp. 3–4.
23. Ellen Neuborne, "Know Thy Enemy," *Sales & Marketing Management,* January 2003, pp. 29–33.
24. Stephen Schultz, "Capturing CI through Your Sales Force," *Competitive Intelligence Magazine*, January–February 2002, pp. 15–17; Alan J. Dubinsky, Marvin A. Jolson, Ronald E. Michaels, Masaaki Katobe, and Chea Un Lim, "Ethical Perceptions of Field Sales Personnel: An Empirical Assessment," *Journal of Personal Selling & Sales Management,* Fall 1992, pp. 9–21; and Alan J. Dubinsky, Marvin A. Jolson, Masaaki Katobe, and Chae Un Lim, "A Cross-National Investigation of Industrial Sales People's Ethical Perceptions," *Journal of International Business Studies* (Fourth Quarter, 1991), pp. 651–70.
25. See Mark W. Johnston and Greg W. Marshall, *Sales Force Management,* 9th ed. (Burr Ridge, IL: McGraw-Hill/Irwin, 2010), pp. 100–4; and William T. Ross, Jr., Frederic Dalsace, and Erin Anderson, "Should You Set Up Your Own Sales Force or Should You Outsource It? Pitfalls in the Standard Analysis," *Business Horizons,* January–February 2005, pp. 23–36.
26. Eli Jones, et al., "Key Accounts and Team Selling." Also see, Arun Sharma, "Success Factors in Key Accounts," *Journal of Business & Industrial Marketing* 21, no. 3 (2006), pp. 141–50.
27. William L. Cron and David W. Cravens, "Sales Force Strategy," in Robert A. Peterson and Roger A. Kerin, eds., *Wiley International Encyclopedia of Marketing: Volume 1—Marketing Strategy* (West Sussex, UK: John Wiley & Sons, Ltd., 2011), pp. 197–207.
28. This discussion is based on William L. Cron and Thomas E. DeCarlo, *Dalrymple's Sales Management,* 10th ed. (Hoboken, NJ: John Wiley & Sons, Inc., 2009).
29. René Y. Darmon, *Leading the Sales Force* (New York: Cambridge University Press, 2007).
30. Blair Kidwell, David M. Hardesty, Brian R. Murtha, and Shibin Sheng, "Emotional Intelligence in Marketing Exchanges," *Journal of Marketing,* January 2011, pp. 78–93; and Elizabeth J. Rozell, Charles E. Pettijohn, and R. Stephen Parker, "Customer-Oriented Selling: Exploring the Roles of Emotional Intelligence and Organizational Commitment," *Psychology & Marketing,* June 2004, pp. 405–24.
31. Rosann L. Spiro, Gregory A. Rich, and William J. Stanton, *Management of a Sales Force,* 12th ed. (Burr Ridge, IL: McGraw-Hill/Irwin, 2008), chapter 7; and Thomas L. Powers, Thomas E. DeCarlo, and Gouri Gupte, "An Update on the Status of Sales Management Training," *Journal of Personal Selling & Sales Management,* Fall 2010, pp. 319–26.
32. Spiro, et al., *Management of a Sales Force,* chapter 8. Also see, Julia Chang, "Wholly Motivated," *Sales & Marketing Management,* March 2007, pp. 24ff.
33. This discussion is based on Johnston and Marshall, *Sales Force Management,* chapter 11; and Andris Zoltners, Prabhakant Sinha, and Sally E. Lorimer, *The Complete Guide to Sales Force Incentive Compensation* (New York: AMACOM, 2006).
34. www.MaryKay.com, downloaded April 10, 2013.
35. Jeffrey E. Lewin and Jeffrey K. Sager, "The Influence of Personal Characteristics and Coping Strategies on Salespersons' Turnover Intentions," *Journal of Personal Selling & Sales Management,* Fall 2010, pp. 355–70; and René Y. Darmon, "The Concept of Salesperson Replacement Value: A Sales Force Turnover Management Tool," *Journal of Personal Selling & Sales Management,* Summer 2008, pp. 211–32.
36. Gary Hallen and Robert Latino, "Eastman Chemical's Success Story," *Quality Progress,* June 2003, pp. 50–54.
37. Mark Cotteleer, Edward Inderrieden, and Felissa Lee, "Selling the Sales Force on Automation," *Harvard Business Review,* July–August 2006, pp. 18–22.
38. Darmon, *Leading the Sales Force.*

Xerox: This case was written by Steven Hartley and Roger Kerin. Sources: "In Transition—Xerox," www.sellingpower.com, June 15, 2011; Joseph Kornik, "Table Talk: A Sales Leaders Roundtable," *Sales & Marketing Management,* February 2007; Philip Chadwick, "Xerox Global Service," *Printweek,* October 11, 2007, p. 32; Sarah Campbell, "What It's Like Working for Xerox," *The Times,* September 14, 2006, p. 9; Simon Avery, "CEO's HR Skills Turn Xerox Fortunes," *The Globe and Mail,* June 2, 2006, p. B3; Julia Chang, "Ultimate Motivation Guide: Happy Sales Force, Happy Returns," *Sales & Marketing Management,* March 2006; and resources available on the Xerox website, www.xerox.com.

Chapter 21

1. Interview with John Lewis, account executive at Seven Cycles, Inc., April 19, 2013; and www.sevencycles.com, April 20, 2013.
2. "U.S. Online Retail Forecast: 2011–2016," www.forrester.com, March 5, 2012.
3. "Mixing Bricks with Clicks," www.economist.com, March 23, 2013; and Stephanie Clifford, "Once Proudly Web Only, Shopping Sites Hang Out Real Shingles," www.nytimes.com, December 18, 2012.
4. Rupal Parekh, "Personalized Products Please But Can They Create Profit?" *Advertising Age,* May, 21, 2013, p. 4.
5. Rafi A. Mohammed, Robert J. Fisher, Bernard J. Jaworski, and Gordon J. Paddison, *Internet Marketing: Building Advantage in a Networked Economy,* 2nd ed. (Burr Ridge, IL: McGraw-Hill/Irwin, 2004).

6. Ward A. Hanson and Kirthi Kalyanam, *Internet Marketing & Electronic Commerce* (Mason, OH: Thompson Higher Education, 2007).
7. Natasha Singer, "E-Tailer Customization: Convenient or Creepy?" www.nytimes.com, June 23, 2012.
8. Judy Strauss, Adel El-Ansary, and Raymond Frost, *E-Marketing,* 5th ed. (Upper Saddle River, NJ: Prentice Hall, 2009).
9. Piet Levy, "The Data Dilemma," *Marketing News,* January 30, 2011, pp. 20–21.
10. This discussion is drawn from Jeffrey F. Rayport and Bernard J. Jaworski, *e-Commerce,* 2nd ed. (Burr Ridge, IL: McGraw-Hill/Irwin, 2004); and *The Essential Guide to Best Practices in eCommerce* (Portland, OR: Webtrends, Inc., 2006).
11. Mylene Mangalindan, "Web Sites Want You to Stick Around," *The Wall Street Journal,* April 15, 2008, p. B5.
12. "Demographics of Internet Users," www.pewinternet.org, downloaded March 1, 2013.
13. "State of the U.S. Online Retail Economy," www.comscore.com, April 6, 2013.
14. "Statistics: U.S. Online Shoppers," www.pewinternet.org, April 5, 2013.
15. "Infographic: The Digital Lives of American Moms," www.nielson.com, May 11, 2012; Beth Bulik, "Technology No Longer Just Kid Stuff," *Advertising Age,* February 2, 2009, p. 12; "Internet Moms," www.newmediatrend.com, April 28, 2011; "Today's New Mom Is Never Disconnected, Says a New Survey," www.internetretailer.com, June 30, 2009; and "New Study Reveals Internet Is the Medium Moms Rely on Most," Disney Online news release, March 25, 2008.
16. Category online retail sales estimates are based on *Statistical Abstract of the United States: 2012* (Washington, DC: Government Printing Office, 2012); and "U.S. Online Retail Forecast: 2011–2016."
17. Jerry Wind and Arvind Ranaswamy, "Customerization: The Next Wave in Mass Customization," *Journal of Interactive Marketing,* Winter 2001, pp. 13–32.
18. Valerie Bauerkin, "Gatorade's Mission: Sell More Drinks," *The Wall Street Journal,* September 14, 2010, p. B6; Tom Hayes and Michael S. Malone, "Marketing in the World of the Web," *The Wall Street Journal,* November 29–30, 2008, p. A13. Also see, Kate Fitzgerald, "Blogs Fascinate, Frighten Marketers Eager to Tap Loyalists," *Advertising Age,* March 5, 2007, p. S-4.
19. "Read This and Win Million$!!!" *The Economist,* January 26, 2013, p. 60.
20. Quoted in Strauss, et al., *E-Marketing,* p. 357.
21. Victoria Taylor, "The Best-Ever Social Media Campaigns," www.forbes.com, August 17, 2010.
22. "State of the U.S. Online Retail Economy"; and Rob Veres, "Find the Lowest Price for Anything in a Store," *Time,* October 15, 2012, p. 40.
23. Stephen Baker, "The Online Ad Surge," *BusinessWeek,* November 22, 2004, pp. 76–81.
24. "Cookies Cause Bitter Backlash," *The Wall Street Journal,* September 20, 2010, pp. B1, B2.
25. Joseph Turow, "Behavior Aside, Consumers Do Want Control of Their Privacy," *Advertising Age,* January 28, 2013, p. 32; "Are Digital Foxes Guarding the Web's Privacy Hen House?" *The Wall Street Journal,* December 14, 2012, p. B1; "Ad Industry Takes Another Look at 'Do Not Track' in Browsers," *The Wall Street Journal,* March 31, 2011, p. B5; Edmund Lee, "Online Self-Regulation May Not Satisfy Administration," *Advertising Age,* March 21, 2011, p. 3; *2012 Internet Crime Report,* www.ic3.gov; and Joel Stein, "Your Data, Yourself," *Time,* March 21, 2011, pp. 40–46.
26. Kathleen Kim, "More Employers Letting Employees Shop Online at Work," www.inc.com, November 14, 2012; and "Survey: Many Admit to Online Shopping at Work," www.moneycentral.msn.com, December 2, 2008.
27. This discussion is based on "Attention Shoppers: Online Product Research," www.pewresearch.org, September 29, 2010; "Online Research Drives Offline Sales," www.emarketer.com, February 26, 2008; "Study: More Consumers Do Research Online, Shop Offline," *Brandweek,* November 3, 2008, p. 8; and Tamera Mendelsohn, "The State of Multichannel Consumers in the U.S. and Europe," www.forresterresearch.com, June 25, 2007.
28. "Retailers' Panty Raid on Victoria's Secret," *The Wall Street Journal,* June 20, 2007, pp. B1, B12.
29. www.Callaway.com, May 5, 2011; and Stephanie Kang, "Callaway Will Use Retailers to Sell Goods Directly to Consumers Online," *The Wall Street Journal,* November 6, 2006, p. B5.
30. Erik Hauser and Max Lenderman, "Experiential Marketing," *Brandweek,* September 20, 2008.
31. "Attention Shoppers: Online Product Research."

Pizza Hut: This case was prepared by Pizza Hut and imc² executives for exclusive use in this text.

Chapter 22

1. Personal interviews with Vivian Milroy Callaway.
2. Mike Hughlett, "Ups & Downs at General Mills," *Star Tribune,* February 17, 2013, pp. D1, D6; and General Mills Overview: 2012 Fiscal Year. See http://www.generalmills.com/~/media/Files/company_overviews/overview_2012.ashx.
3. Mike Hughlett, "General Mills Expects a More Profitable Year in 2014," *Star Tribune,* February 20, 2013, pp. D1, D3; Mike Hughlett, "Global Growth Helps General Mills as Core U.S. Products Struggle," *Star Tribune,* December 20, 2012, pp. D1, D2; and General Mills Overview: 2012 Fiscal Year.
4. General Mills Overview: 2012 Fiscal Year.
5. Mike Hughlett, "Bagged Cereal Boom," *Star Tribune,* June 3, 2012, pp. D1, D8; Mike Hughlett, "Demonized Gluten Means Major Dough," *Star Tribune,* May 8, 2011, pp. A1, A10; and Mike Hughlett, "General Mills Reformulates Some Products to Boost Health," *Star Tribune,* November 20, 2010, pp. D1, D2.
6. Mike Hughlett, "Breakfast on the Go," *Star Tribune,* June 2, 2013, p. D4; and "Bigger, Differentiated New Products Drive Growth for General Mills," news release dated December 19, 2012. See http://www.generalmills.com/en/Media/NewsReleases/Library/2012/December/NewProductInnovationFY13.aspx.
7. Hugh Courtney, John T. Horn, and Jayanti Kar, "Getting Into Your Competitor's Head," *The McKinsey Quarterly,* February 2009.
8. Roger A. Kerin, P. Rajan Varadarajan, and Robert A. Peterson, "First-Mover Advantage: A Synthesis, Conceptual Framework, and Research Proposition," *Journal of Marketing,* October 1992, pp. 33–52; and Pankaj Ghemawat, "Sustainable Advantage," *Harvard Business Review,* September–October 1986, pp. 53–58.
9. Nitin Nohria, William Joyce, and Bruce Roberson, "What Really Works," *Harvard Business Review,* July 2003, pp. 42–52; and "Who Gets Eaten and Who Gets to Eat," *The Economist,* July 12, 2003, pp. 61–63.
10. Armin Harris, et al., "The Directors: Costco Wholesale," *Fortune,* May 4, 2009, pp. 100–1.
11. Geoff Colvin, "How It Works," *Fortune,* February 27, 2012, pp. 71–79; and Kathleen Kerwin and Paul Magnusson, "Can Anything Stop Toyota?" *BusinessWeek,* November 17, 2003, pp. 114–22.
12. Ben R. Rich and Leo Janos, *Skunk Works* (Boston: Little, Brown and Company, 1994).
13. Murali K. Mantrala, Probhakant Sirha, and Andris A. Zoltners, "Impact of Resource Allocation Rules on Marketing Investment-Level Decisions and Profitability," *Journal of Marketing Research,* May 1992, pp. 162–75.

14. "No. 1 Cereal Gets a New Buddy," General Mills news release, December 27, 2012. See http://www.generalmills.com/Home/Media/Inside_General_Mills_live_archive/Library/2012/cereal_2013.aspx.
15. Steve Lohr, "When There's No Such Thing as Too Much Information," *The New York Times,* April 24, 2011, p. BU3; and Mark Jeffery, *Data-Driven Marketing* (Hoboken, NJ: John Wiley & Sons, Inc., 2010), chapters 1 and 2.
16. Lisa C. Troy, Tanawat Hirunyawipada, and Audhesh K. Paswan, "Cross-Functional Integration and New Product Success: An Empirical Investigation of the Findings," *Journal of Marketing,* November 2008, pp. 132–46.
17. Vanessa Chan, Chris Musso, and Venkatesh Shankar, "Assuming Innovation Metrics," *The McKinsey Quarterly,* October 2008; and Jacques Bughin, Amy Guggenheim Shenkan, and Marc Singer, "How Poor Metrics Undermine Digital Marketing," *The McKinsey Quarterly,* October 2008.
18. Michael E. Porter, *Competitive Advantage: Creating and Sustaining Superior Performance* (New York: The Free Press, a Division of Simon & Schuster, Inc., 1985), adapted with permission.
19. Adapted from Philip Kotler and Kevin Lane Keller, *Marketing Management*, 12th ed. (Upper Saddle River, NJ: Prentice Hall, 2006), pp. 262–63.
20. Several of the items in the list are adapted from Massimo Garbuio, Dan Lovallo, and Patrick Viguerie, "How Companies Make Good Decisions," *The McKinsey Quarterly,* December 2008; Renee Dye and Olivier Sibony, "How to Improve Strategic Planning," *The McKinsey Quarterly,* August 2007; and Jungkiu Choi, Dan Lovallo, and Anna Tarasova, "Better Strategy for Business Units," *The McKinsey Quarterly,* June 2007.
21. University of Pennsylvania Wharton Alumni Emeritus Society, *Spring 2009 Newsletter,* p. 2.
22. Stratford Sherman, "How Intel Makes Spending Pay Off," *Fortune,* February 22, 1993, pp. 57–61.
23. Mike Hughlett, "From Pushcart to Grocery Cart," *Star Tribune,* February 7, 2011, pp. D1, D2; and Julie Jargon, "General Mills Tries to Convince Americans to Cook Chinese," *The Wall Street Journal,* May 29, 2007, pp. B1, B3.
24. "Submit Your Novel Ideas," General Mills website. See http://www.generalmills.com/en/Company/Innovation/G-Win/Submit_ideas.aspx; Matt McKinney, "General Public, Meet General Mills," *Star Tribune,* April 6, 2007, pp. D1, D; Julie Jargon, "General Mills Seeks Help from Iron Chef," *The Wall Street Journal,* April 4, 2007, p. B4; and "General Mills Supports Creation of New Food Science Division at YourEncore™," General Mills news release, July 10, 2007.
25. Clayton M. Christensen, *The Innovator's Dilemma: When New Technologies Cause Great Firms to Fail* (Boston, MA: Harvard Business School Press, 1997).
26. Hal B. Gregerson, Jeff Dyer, and Clayton M. Christensen, "Why Ask Why?" *Chief Executive.Net,* January/February, 2012, pp. 40–43.
27. Anne Fisher, "America's Most Admired Companies," *Fortune,* March 19, 2007, pp. 88–94.
28. Thomas J. Peters and Robert H. Waterman, Jr., *In Search of Excellence: Lessons from America's Best-Run Companies* (New York: Harper & Row, 1982).
29. Tom Peters, "Winners Do Hundreds of Percent over Norm," *StarTribune,* January 8, 1985, p. 5B; and Rich and Janos, *Skunk Works,* pp. 51–53.
30. Geoff Colvin, "How It Works," p. 75.
31. "The Best Advice I Ever Got: Sara Blakely," *Fortune,* November 12, 2012, p. 124; and the Spanx website. See www.spanx.com.
32. Sven Grundberg and Juhana Rossi, "Finland's Newest Hit Maker: Supercell," *The Wall Street Journal,* March 8, 2013, p. B4.
33. David Court, "The Downturn's New Rules for Marketers," *The McKinsey Quarterly,* December 2008; and David Court, "The Evolving Role of the CMO," *The McKinsey Quarterly,* August 2007.
34. Alexander Krasnikov and Satish Jayachandran, "The Relative Impact of Marketing, Research-and-Development, and Operations Capabilities on Firm Performance," *Journal of Marketing,* July 2008, pp. 1–11.
35. Julie Jargon, "Starbucks Buys Its First Coffee Farm," *The Wall Street Journal,* March 19, 2013, p. B3; Sheila Shayon, "Why Starbucks' Customer Loyalty Is More Lucrative Than Any Ad Campaign," *Brandchannel,* March 8, 2013; Walter Loeb, "Starbucks: Global Coffee Giant Has New Growth Plans," *Forbes,* January 31, 2013; and Bill Saporito, "Starbucks' Big Mug," *Time,* June 25, 2012, pp. 52–54.
36. Nelson D. Schwartz, "Colgate Cleans Up," *Fortune,* April 16, 2001, pp. 179–80.
37. Larissa MacFarquhar, "When Giants Fail," *The New Yorker,* May 14, 2012, pp. 81–95.
38. Isaac Arnsdorf, "The Museum Is Watching You," *The Wall Street Journal,* August 18, 2010, pp. D1, D2.
39. James D. Lenskold, *Marketing ROI* (New York: McGraw-Hill, 2003).
40. Michael Krauss, "Balance Attention to Metrics with Intuition," *Marketing News,* June 1, 2007, pp. 6–8; John Davis, *Measuring Marketing: 103 Key Metrics Every Marketer Needs* (Singapore: Wiley and Sons, 2007); and Paul W. Farris, Neil T. Bendle, Phillip E. Pfeifer, and David J. Reibstein, *Marketing Metrics* (Upper Saddle River, NJ: Wharton School Publishing, 2006).
41. Malcolm Craig, *Thinking Visually: Business Applications of 14 Core Diagrams* (New York and London: Continuum, 2000).
42. The illustrative example of using a marketing dashboard at General Mills was developed by David Ford and Vivian Milroy Callaway.

Warm Delights: This case was prepared by David Ford based on interviews with Vivian Milroy Callaway.

Appendix C

1. Catherine Kaputa, *You Are a Brand!: How Smart People Brand Themselves for Business Success* (Nicholas Brealey Publishing, Boston: MA, 2010); Diane Brady, "Creating Brand You," *Bloomberg Businessweek,* August 22, 2007, pp. 72–73; and Denny E. McCorkle, Joe F. Alexander, and Memo F. Diriker, "Developing Self-Marketing Skills for Student Career Success," *Journal of Marketing Education,* Spring, 1992, pp. 57–67.
2. Morag Cuddeford-Jones, "Managing a Marketing Career Is Academic," *Marketing Week,* January 16, 2013; Linda J. Popky, *Marketing Your Career: Positioning, Packaging and Promoting Yourself for Success,* Woodside Business Press, 2009; Marianne E. Green, "Marketing Yourself: From Student to Professional," *Job Choices for Business & Liberal Arts Students,* 50th ed., 2007, pp. 30–31; and Joanne Cleaver, "Find a Job through Self-Promotion," *Marketing News,* January 31, 2000, pp. 12, 16.
3. Kevin Cochrane, "The 21st Century Marketer," *Marketing News,* March 30, 2011, p. 22; and John N. Frank, "Stand Out from the Crowd, Landing a Marketing Job Today Means Touting Your Specialty and Staying Positive," *Marketing News,* January 30, 2009, p. 22.
4. "Opportunities by Occupation," *Job Choices for Business & Liberal Arts Students, 2013*, National Association of Colleges and Employers, p. 93; "Opportunities by Occupation," *Job Choices, Diversity Edition*, 2013, National Association of Colleges and Employers, p. 84; www.Monster.com, accessed June 3, 2013; and Milton Moskowitz

and Robert Levering, "100 Best Companies to Work For," *Fortune*, February 4, 2013, pp. 85–96.

5. Nicholas Basta, "The Wide World of Marketing," *BW's Guide to Careers,* February–March 1984, pp. 70–72.
6. Anjali Bansal, David S. Daniel, John T. Mitchell, and Patrick B. Walsh, "The CEO Today: Sharing Leadership at the Top," *Research & Insight*, SpencerStuart, March 2013, http://www.spencerstuart.com/research/articles/1642/; Jonathan Harper and Frank Birkel, "From CMO to CEO: The Route to the Top," *Research & Insight*, SpencerStuart, December 2009, http://www.spencerstuart.com/research/articles/1329/; and "Leading CEOs: A Statistical Snapshot of S&P 500 Leaders," *Research & Insight*, SpencerStuart, December 2008, http://www.spencerstuart.com/research/ceo/975/.
7. Salary Survey (Bethlehem, PA: National Association of Colleges and Employers, April 2013), p. 4.
8. "Advertising, Promotions, and Marketing Managers," *Occupational Outlook Handbook*, 2012–13 Edition (Washington, DC: US Department of Labor), http://www.bls.gov/ooh/management/advertising-promotions-and-marketing-managers.htm#tab-6, accessed June 4, 2013.
9. Matthew Creamer, "P&G Primes Its Pinpoint Marketing," *Advertising Age*, May 7, 2007.
10. "P&G Profiles," P&G website, http://www.experiencepg.com/our-people/profiles.aspx, accessed June 3, 2013.
11. "Wholesale and Manufacturing Sales Representatives," *Occupational Outlook Handbook,* 2012–13 Edition, (Washington, DC: US Department of Labor), http://www.bls.gov/ooh/sales/wholesale-and-manufacturing-sales-representatives.htm#tab-6, accessed June 4, 2013.
12. "Freedom to Explore Different Career Paths Makes for a More Well-Rounded, Dedicated Staff," *Advertising Age*, March 26, 2012, p. 14; S. William Pattis, *Careers in Advertising* (New York: McGraw-Hill, 2004).
13. "13 Professional Skills for a Rewarding Career in Digital Marketing," Business2Community.com, January 9, 2013; Sarah Lundy, "Job Opportunities Multiply in Social Media: With More People Connecting Online, Businesses Rush to Join the Party," *Buffalo News,* January 10, 2011, p. C1; Duane Forrester, "Search Can Offer Jobs, Decent Salaries," *Advertising Age,* May 26, 2008, p. 28; and Tanya Lewis, "Talent in Demand," *PR Week Career Guide,* 2006, pp. 4–6.
14. Roslyn Dolber, *Opportunities in Retailing Careers* (New York: McGraw-Hill, 2008).
15. Peter Coy, "Help Wanted," *Bloomberg Businessweek,* May 11, 2009, pp. 40–46; and "The Way We'll Work," *Time,* May 25, 2009, pp. 39–50.
16. **"**Wholesale and Manufacturing Sales Representatives," Occupational Outlook Handbook, 2012–13 Edition (Washington, DC: U.S. Department of Labor), http://www.bls.gov/ooh/sales/wholesale-and-manufacturing-sales-representatives.htm#tab-6, accessed June 4, 2013.
17. Jack and Suzy Welch, "Dear Graduate . . . To Stand Out among Your Peers, You Have to Overdeliver," *Bloomberg Businessweek,* June 19, 2006, p. 100.
18. "People's Choice Awards. And the Winners Are . . ." *Sales and Marketing Management,* November/December 2008, p. 20; and Elisabeth A. Sullivan, "One-to-One," *Marketing News,* June 15, 2009, pp. 10–13.
19. Piet Levy, "10 Minutes with Stan Sthanunathan, Vice President of Marketing Strategy and Insights, The Coca-Cola Co.," *Marketing News,* February 28, 2011, p. 34; and Edmund Hershberger and Madhav N. Segal, "Ads for MR Positions Reveal Desired Skills," *Marketing News,* February 1, 2007, p. 28.
20. "Market Research Analyst," in Les Krantz, ed., *Jobs Rated Almanac,* 6th ed. (New York: St. Martin's Press, 2002).
21. Deborah L. Vence, "In an Instant, More Researchers Use IM for Fast, Reliable Results," *Marketing News,* March 1, 2006, p. 53; and Joshua Grossnickle and Oliver Raskin, "What's Ahead on the Internet," *Marketing Research,* Summer 2001, pp. 9–13.
22. Carolyn D. Marconi, "Desperately Looking for New Talent Is a Recurring Theme," *Marketing Research,* Spring 2000, pp. 4–6.
23. "2013 Franchise 500," *Entrepreneur* website, at www.entrepreneur.com, accessed June 5, 2013.
24. Lisa Bertagnoli, "Marketing Overseas Excellent for Career," *Marketing News,* June 4, 2001, p. 4.
25. "Global Consulting Firm Accenture Opens Office in Calgary," *Postmedia Breaking News*, February 6, 2013; and "Managing Collaborators No Matter Where They Sit," *The Huffington Post*, April 17, 2013.
26. Barbara Flood, "Turbo Charge Your Job Search, Job Searching and Career Development Tips," *Information Outlook,* May 1, 2007, p. 40.
27. Robin T. Peterson and J. Stuart Devlin, "Perspectives on Entry-Level Positions by Graduating Marketing Seniors," *Marketing Education Review,* Summer 1994, pp. 2–5.
28. Louis Lavelle, "Business Schools Embrace the Liberal Arts," *Bloomberg Businessweek*, April 10, 2013; Regina Pefanis Schlee and Katrin R. Harich, "Knowledge and Skill Requirements for Marketing Jobs in the 21st Century," *Journal of Marketing Education,* December 2010, pp. 341–52; "10 Job Hunting Tips," *Marketing News,* November 15, 2010, p. 19; "Succeeding in the Job Market for the Class of 2007," *Job Choices for Business & Liberal Arts Students,* 50th ed., 2007, pp. 14–15; Callum J. Floyd and Mary Ellen Gordon, "What Skills Are Most Important? A Comparison of Employer, Student, and Staff Perceptions," *Journal of Marketing Education,* August 1998, pp. 103–09; and "About Us: LinkedIn Facts," accessed October 15, 2011, www.press.linkedin.com/about.
29. Barbara Flood, "Turbo Charge Your Job Search, Job Searching and Career Development Tips," *Information Outlook,* May 1, 2007, p. 40.
30. Geoff Gloecker, "The Best Business Schools 2012, *Bloomberg Businessweek*, November 19, 2012, p. 57–61; and "More MBA Grads Take the Road Less Traveled," *Bloomberg Businessweek,* April 18–24, 2011, p. 53.
31. Barbara Kiviat, "The New Rules of Web Hiring," *Time,* November 24, 2003, p. 57; Karen Epper Hoffman, "Recruitment Sites Changing Their Focus," *Internet World,* March 15, 1999; Pamela Mendels, "Now That's Casting a Wide Net," *Bloomberg Businessweek,* May 25, 1998: and James C. Gonyea, *The Online Job Search Companion* (New York: McGraw-Hill, 1995).
32. Peter Cappelli, "Making the Most of On-Line Recruiting," *Harvard Business Review,* March 2001, pp. 139–46.
33. Ronald B. Marks, *Personal Selling: A Relationship Approach,* 6th ed. (New York: Pearson, 1996).
34. Chris Farrell, "It's Not What Grads Know, It's Who They Know," *Bloomberg Businessweek,* June 18, 2012, pp. 9–10; Sima Dahl, "A New Job Is No Excuse to Ease Up on Networking," *Marketing News,* February 28, 2011, p. 4; Leonard Felson, "Undergrad Marketers Must Get Jump on Networking Skills," *Marketing News,* April 8, 2001, p. 14; Wayne E. Baker, *Networking Smart* (New York: McGraw-Hill, 1994); and Piet Levy, "AMA Chapters across the Country Are Increasingly Using Job Boards, Networking Events and Other Techniques to Help Members in This Economy," *Marketing News,* March 15, 2009, p. 14.
35. "Careers in Marketing: Utilizing Social Networking to Improve Your Job Prospects," *CareerAlley*, July 22, 2012; "Finding Job Candidates Who Aren't Looking," *Bloomberg Businessweek*, December 17, 2012, pp. 41–42; Sima Dahl, "Pinning Your Career Hopes on Pinterest," Marketing News, May 15, 2012, p. 5; Tim Post, "New Graduates Use Social Media to Look for Jobs," *St. Paul Pioneer Press,* June 3, 2011; Susan Berfield, "Dueling Your Facebook Friends for a New Job," *Bloomberg Businessweek,* March 7, 2011, p. 35; and Dan Schawbel, "Top 10 Social Sites for Finding a Job," *Mashable,* February 24, 2009.

36. "Stand Out at the Career Fair," *Job Choices for Business & Liberal Arts Students: 2009,* 52nd ed. (Bethlehem, PA: National Association of Colleges and Employers, 2008), pp. 22–23.
37. Amy Diepenbrock, "Will Your Resume Open the Door to an Interview?" *Job Choices for Business & Liberal Arts Students, 2011,* National Association of Colleges and Employers, p. 31; and Marianne E. Green, "Marketing Yourself: From Student to Professional," *Job Choices for Business & Liberal Arts Students: 2009* (Bethlehem, PA: National Association of Colleges and Employers, 2008), pp. 28–29.
38. Marianne E. Green, "Resume Writing: Sell Your Skills to Get the Interview!" *Job Choices for Business & Liberal Arts Students,* 50th ed., 2007, pp. 39–47.
39. C. Randall Powell, "Secrets of Selling a Résumé," in Peggy Schmidt, ed., *The Honda How to Get a Job Guide* (New York: McGraw-Hill, 1984), pp. 4–9.
40. Sima Dahl, "Social Media and Your Job Search: How the Age of the Referral May Impact Your Career," *Marketing News*, September 30, 2012, p. 6; "Post with Caution: Your Online Profile and Our Job Search," *Job Choices for Business & Liberal Arts Students: 2009* (Bethlehem, PA: National Association of Colleges and Employers, 2008), p. 30; "If I 'Google' You, What Will I Find?" *Job Choices for Business and Liberal Arts Students,* 50th ed., 2007, p. 16; Joyce Lain Kennedy, "Computer-Friendly Résumé Tips," Planning Job Choices: 1999, 42nd ed. (Bethlehem, PA: National Association of Colleges and Employers, 1998), p. 49; and Joyce Lain Kennedy and Thomas J. Morrow, *Electronic Résumé Revolution* (New York: Wiley and Sons, 1994).
41. William J. Banis, "The Art of Writing Job-Search Letters," *Job Choices for Business and Liberal Arts Students,* 50th ed., 2007, pp. 32–38; and Arthur G. Sharp, "The Art of the Cover Letter," *Career Futures* 4, no. 1 (1992), pp. 50–51.
42. Lindsey Pollak, "The 10 Commandments of Social Media Job Seeking," *Job Choices for Business & Liberal Arts Students, 2011,* National Association of Colleges and Employers, p. 20; Alison Damast, "Recruiters' Top 10 Complaints," *Bloomberg Businessweek,* April 26, 2007; and Marilyn Moats Kennedy, "'Don't List' Offers Important Tips for Job Interviews," *Marketing News,* March 15, 2007, p. 26.
43. Sima Dahl, "Where Do You See Yourself in Five Years?" *Marketing News,* November 15, 2010, p. 4; and Dana James, "A Day in the Life of a Corporate Recruiter," *Marketing News*, April 10, 2000, pp. 1, 11.
44. Paul Davidson, "Managers to Millennials: Job Interview No Time to Text," *USA Today*, April 29, 2013.
45. Robert M. Greenberg, "The Company Visit—Revisited," *NACE Journal,* Winter 2003, pp. 21–27.
46. Mary E. Scott, "High-Touch vs. High-Tech Recruitment," *NACE Journal,* Fall 2002, pp. 33–39.

Appendix D (Online)

1. The Nike MaxSight case was prepared by Professor Linda Rochford, University of Minnesota, Duluth, based on the following sources: Bausch and Lomb website, www.bausch.com/enUS/consumer/visioncare/product/softcontacts/nikemaxsight.aspx; Nike website, www.nike.com/nikevision/main.html; "A Brief History of Contact Lenses," Contact Lens Manufacturers Association, February 2007, www.contactlenses.org/timeline.htm; Richard Edlich, "A Tribute to Dr. Robert C. Allen, an Inspirational Teacher, Humanitarian and Friend," *Journal Long Term Effects of Medical Implants,* no. 163 (2006), pp. 261–64; MayoClinic.com, "Tools for Better Health: Melanoma," www.mayoclinic.com/health/melanoma/DS00439/DSECTION-1; MayoClinic.com, "Tools for Better Health: Eye Melanoma," www.mayoclinic.com/health/eye-melanoma/DS00707; and MayoClinic.com, "Tools for Better Health: Contact Lenses: What to Know Before You Buy," www.mayoclinic.com/health/contact-lenses/WL00010.
2. The Daktronics, Inc., case was prepared by William Rudelius based on conversations with Dr. Al Kurtenbach, internal sources, and these other sources: Bill Syken, "Bright Lights, Little City," *Sports Illustrated,* May 11, 2004; Dick Youngblood, "Signs of Success," *Star Tribune,* April 6, 2003, pp. D1, D2; Marilyn Alva, "Shifting Technology Helps It Score Big Wins," *Investor's Business Daily,* January 12, 2004; and Michael Hiestand, "S.D. Company Lights Up Sports World," *USA Today,* May 4, 2004, pp. C1, Cs.
3. The Jamba Juice case was prepared by Professor Linda Rochford, University of Minnesota, Duluth, and Steven Hartley from the following sources: Jamba Juice Corporation website and press releases: www.jambajuice.com; "Juicy Prospects," *Star Tribune,* August 27, 2001, pp. D1–D2; Scott Hume, "Segment Rankings," *Restaurants and Institutions,* July 1, 2004, p. 61; Celeste Ward, "Riney Creates Good Karma for Jamba Juice," *Adweek.com,* March 18, 2004; and John Agoglia, "Squeezing Profits," *Club Industry,* December 1, 2003, p. 12.
4. This case was prepared by Leslie L. Kendrick, The Center for Leadership Education, Johns Hopkins University, based on the following sources: Russel Gold, "Rig's Final Hours Probed," *The Wall Street Journal,* July 18, 2010, http://online.wsj.com; Clifford Krauss, "Static Kill of the Well Is Working, Officials Say," *The New York Times,* Aug. 4, 2010, www.nytimes.com; Sarah Lyall, "In BPs Record, a History of Boldness and Costly Blunders," *The New York Times,* July 12, 2010, http://dealbook.blogs.nytimes.com; Justin Gillis and Leslie Kaufman, "The Corrosive Legacy of Oil Spills," *The New York Times,* July 18, 2010, p. 1; Ben Casselman and Russell Gold, "BP Decisions Set Stage for Disaster," *The Wall Street Journal,* May 27, 2010, http://online.wsj.com; John Schwartz, "BP Wants Partners to Help Shoulder Spill Costs," July 4, 2010, www.nytimes.com; Ben Casselman and Russell Gold, "BP Managers Named in Disaster Probe," *The Wall Street Journal,* July 22, 2010, http://www.onlince.wsj.com; "Times Topic: The Minerals Management Service," *The New York Times,* May 14, 2010, http://topics.nytimes.com; "Big Oil Turns Its Back on BP," *Bloomberg Businessweek,* July 19–25, 2010, pp. 22–24; "Reported Number of Bird Deaths Grow on Gulf Coast," *The Associated Press,* July 23, 2010, www.google.com/hostednews; Jay Reeves, John Flesher, and Tamara Lush, "Sea Creatures Flee Oil Spill, Gather Near Shore," *The Associated Press,* June 17, 2010, www.nytimes.com; Matthew L. Wald, "Despite Directive, BP Used Dispersant Often, Panel Finds," *The New York Times,* Aug. 1, 2010, p. 20; Daniel Stone, "BP Continues Stealth Public Relations during Its Crisis," *Newsweek,* May 19, 2010, http://www.newsweek.com; Ariel Schwartz, "BP's Latest Tactic: Buying Gulf Oil Disaster-Related Links on Google," June 8, 2010, www.fastcompany.com; Dionne Searcey and Stephen Power, "Oil Spill Puts a Target on BP's Back," *The Wall Street Journal,* July 19, 2010, http://www.online.wsj.com; Clifford Krauss, "BP Moves Chief Executive to Lesser Role in Spill Response," *The New York Times,* June 18, 2010, www.nytimes.com; Jad Mouawad and Clifford Krauss, "BP's Blueprint for Emerging from Crisis," *The New York Times,* July 27, 2010, www.nytimes.com; and Scott Wilson and Joel Achenbach, "BP Agrees to $20 Billion Fund for Gulf Oil Spill Claims," *The Washington Post,* June 17, 2010, www.washingtonpost.com.
5. The Jamisons case was prepared by Professor Roy D. Adler, Pepperdine University, Malibu. Used with permission.

6. The Motetronix Technology case was prepared by Roger A. Kerin, based on company sources.
7. The Callaway case was prepared by Professor Linda Rochford, University of Minnesota, Duluth, from the following sources: James Achenback, "From Hickory Stick to Callaway, Ely Sought to Please Golfers," *Golfweek,* July 14, 2001, pp. 26–27; "China the Largest Growth Market for Equipment," *Golf Today,* March 2004, www.golftoday.co.uk/news/yeartodate/news04/china.html; "Opportunities in Global Golf Club Market: Market to Grow over 25% in India and China According to E-Composites, Inc.," PR Newswire, February 18, 2004, www.pmewswire.com; "2006 Participation by Sport," National Sporting Goods Association, www.nsga.org; "Callaway Golf Co.: Company Description, Financial Summary," Reuters, 2007; Bennet Galloway, "Adrift in a Sea of Golf Balls," *Golf In Japan,* June 10, 2006, www.golf-in-japan.com/bennetts; John Steinbreder, "Partnership Could Strengthen NGF's Research," *Golfweek Business,* June 4, 2007; Bradley Klein, "Klein: Remedies for the Malaise," *Golfweek Business,* March 5, 2007; Beth Ann Baldry, "Dispatch from South Korea," *Golfweek Business,* July 20, 2007; Paul Jones, "Japan Golf: The State of the Game," *Golf In Japan,* February 14, 2006, www.golf-in-japan.com/pauls; John Paul Newport, "Golf Journal: Spin Control; Golf's Police Are Tweaking Clubhead Rules, but a Bigger Issue Looms: The Balls," *The Wall Street Journal* (Eastern Edition), March 3, 2007, p. 7; and John Paul Newport, "Golf Journal: Crazy Driver: The Clubs About to Shake Up Golf: Bizarre New Designs Could Improve Players' Shots—And Many in the Game Worry That's a Bad Thing," *The Wall Street Journal* (Eastern Edition), January 6, 2007, p. 1.
8. The HOM Furniture case was prepared by Kathy Chadwick based on interviews with Wayne Johansen and internal HOM Furniture materials.
9. The Lawn Mowers case was prepared by Professor Linda Rochford, University of Minnesota, Duluth, based on the following sources: Don Babwin, "Reel Mowers Cut in Quietly," *Denver Post,* May 28, 2007, www.denverpost.com; Felicity Barringer, "A Greener Way to Cut the Grass Runs Afoul of a Powerful Lobby," *The New York Times,* April 24, 2006; "It All Adds Up; Lawnmowers," *The Economist,* June 9, 2007, p. 36; "Lawn and Garden Tractors and Home Lawn and Garden Equipment," *Encyclopedia of American Industries, Online Edition,* Thomson Gale, 2007; "Canadians Switch to Push-Reel Lawn Mowers for Health and Environment," Associated Press Financial Wire, July 2, 2007; Mindy Fetterman, "Compared with Today's Mowers, Yesterday's Just Don't Cut It," *USA Today,* May 4, 2007, p. 4B; Charles J. Murray, "Mowing on Autopilot: With the Introduction of the RoboMower in the U.S., Two Israeli Inventors May Open New Door to the Fledgling Home Robotics Market," *Design News,* June 26, 2006, p. 37; Jonathan Welsh, "Splendor in the Grass; Big, Fast, 'Zero-Turn' Mowers Are Latest Status Symbol; Cruise Control and Cupholders," *The Wall Street Journal,* June 13, 2007, p. D1; Virginia Smith, "A Luscious Lawn's Lure: For Some, It's an Obsession They Never Outgrow," *Philadelphia Inquirer;* May 5, 2006; "Lawn Mowers," *Consumer Reports Buying Guide 2006,* pp. 92–95; Ray Routhier, "Mowers—They're Not Just for Grass Anymore," *Portland Press Herald,* July 15, 2007, p. A1; and Rachel Sauer, "Get Your Mower Runnin'; Speeds Reached: 30 Mph, Goal: To Mow Down the Competition," *Palm Beach Post,* June 5, 2007, p. 1E.
10. The Medtronic in China case was prepared by Mark T. Spriggs and Kenneth E. Goodpaster based on Medtronic annual reports and three Medtronic cases: *Medtronic in China (A), (B),* and *(C)* prepared by research assistant Linda Swenson under the supervision of Kenneth E. Goodpaster (Minneapolis-St. Paul, MN: University of St. Thomas).
11. The Pampered Pooches case was prepared by Professor Linda Rochford, University of Minnesota, Duluth, based on the following sources: American Pet Products Manufacturers Association, Inc., "Industry Trends, 2007–2008," Pet Owners Survey Summary, www.appma.org/press-industrytrends.asp; Diane Brady and Christopher Palmeri, "The Pet Economy," *Business Week,* August 2007; John Woestendisk, "Statistics, Trends Reflect Growing Importance of Pets in the Home," *Baltimore Sun,* July 22, 2007; Sarah Casey Newman, "Traveling with Terriers and Tabbies," *St. Louis Post-Dispatch,* July 21, 2007; Leanne Ritchie, "Airline Bans Pets from Travel on Regular Flights," *Daily News,* July 20, 2007; "New Dolce Vita™ Traveler™ Pet Products Let Your Dog Travel in Warmth and Comfort; Take Your Pets Anywhere You Go," PR Newswire, February 22, 2007; and "Traveling with Pets for the Dogs, according to TripAdvisor Survey; TripAdvisor Names Top 10 Pet-Friendly Accommodations," PR Newswire, July 18, 2007.
12. The DigitalThink case was adapted by Monica Noordam and Steven Hartley from a case titled "LearningByte International" written by Giana Eckardt. Sources: Personal interviews with Umberto Milletti and Shelly Berkowitz; DigitalThink's website, www.digitalthink.com; Lisa Vaas, "The E-Training of America," *PC Magazine,* December 26, 2001; DigitalThink press release, "DigitalThink Ranked Number 22 Fastest Growing Technology Company in North America on 2003 Deloitte Technology Fast 500," October 14, 2003; and "Making E-Learning More than 'Pixie Dust,'" *Workforce Management,* March 1, 2003, p. 58.
13. The Health Cruises, Inc., case was prepared by Professors Maurice Mandell and Larry Rosenberg, Reprinted with permission.
14. The Glitzz case was prepared by Lau Geok Theng, based on company sources.
15. The Shiseido case was prepared by Lau Geok Theng based on the following sources: "The Shiseido Story," www.shiseido.co.jp/e/story/html/sto10100.htm, downloaded June 2008; Geoffrey Jones, Akiko Kanno, and Masako Egawa, "Making China Beautiful: Shiseido and the China Market," Harvard Business School, Case 9-805-003, December 19, 2005; Miyakawa Katsu, "Make Chinese Women and Girls Bonnier: Shiseido's Business Development in China," *Investment Shanghai,* October 27, 2005, www.investment.gov.cn/2005-10-27/1130425544124.html, downloaded June 2008; Azusa Iizumi, "Shiseido Establishes Nationwide Network of Outlets in China," *Nikkei Business Online,* April 24, 2006, business.nikkeibp.co.jp/article/eng/20061206/115034/, downloaded June 2008; Shiseido news release, "Shiseido to Operate Cosmetics Specialty Stores and Establish a Holding Company in China," www.shiseido.co.jp/releimg/467-e.pdf, downloaded June 2008; Azusa Iizumi, "Shiseido Established Nationwide Network of Outlets in China," *Nikkei Business Online,* April 24, 2006, business.nikkeibp.co.jp/article/eng/20061206/115034/, downloaded June 2008; Fraser Newham, "China Puts Its Best Face Forward," *Asia Times Online,* April 6, 2006, www.atimes.com/atimes/china_business/hd06cb05.html, downloaded June 2008; Leah Genuario, "Asian Market: A Mixed Bag," *Beauty Packaging,* January/February 2006, www.beautypackaging.com/articles/2006/01/asian-market-the-china-factor.php, downloaded June 2008; and Letian Pan, "More Companies Licensed for Direct Sales Market," *Shanghai Daily,* February 1, 2007.
16. The Trader Joe's case was prepared by Professor Linda Rochford, associate professor of marketing, University of Minnesota, Duluth, from the following sources: "Trader Joe's Company," www.hovers.com; SN's Top 75 Retailers for 2009, supermarketnews.com, accessed October 15, 2009; David Orgel, "Trader Joe's President Shares Secrets of Success," *Supermarket News,* February 6, 2006; Joy Buchanan, "More Than Just Goat Cheese," Knight-Ridder/Tribune Business News, December 9, 2005; Mark Hamstra

"Convenience Only One Small Part of Total Value Equation," *Supermarket News,* July 17, 2006; and "Behind the Scenes at Trader Joe's," *Private Label Buyer* 20, no. 4 (April 2006).

17. The Banyan Tree Holding case was prepared by Lau Geok Theng based on the following sources: Banyan Tree website, www.banyantree.com/; Angsana Hotels and Resorts website, www.angsana.com/; Factsheet: Banyan Tree Private Collection, October 2006, www.btprivatecollection.com/aboutus/press.html; www.angsana.com/en/deer_park/index.html, downloaded May 2008; www.angsana.com/en/gyalthang_dzong/index.html, downloaded May 2008; www.lagunaphuket.com/spa/banyantreespa.html, downloaded May 2008; www.angsanaspa.com/, downloaded May 2008; www.spatime.com/udaivilas.htm, downloaded May 2008; www.oberoibali.com/Hotel/Spa_Fitness.aspx, downloaded May 2008; "Best Marketing Campaign for Regional Brand Development," Media, June 30, 2006; www.kiwicollection.com/property/banyan-tree-lijiang, downloaded January 10, 2008; www.thecoolhunter.net/travel/BANYAN-TREE-PHUKET---REVIEW/, downloaded January 10, 2008; "What Makes a Banyan Tree Grow?" *Hotels' Investment Outlook* 10, no. 3 (September 2007), pp. 23–30; *Sustainability Report 2006,* Banyan Tree Holding Limited; and *Country Factfile,* Euromonitor International.

18. The Target case was prepared by Professor Linda Rochford, assistant professor of marketing, University of Minnesota, Duluth, from the following sources: Target Corporation website, www.target.com; "Target Makes Itself Ubiquitous," *MMR* 22, no. 16 (October 3, 2005), p. 16; "Target's Advertising Savvy," *MMR* 24, no. 1 (January 8, 2007), p. 32; Laura Heller, "Target Sweeps Awards Honoring Best Advertising; Office Max Also Wins Nod; Target Stores Inc.," *DSN Retailing Today,* February 25, 2005, p. 6; "Target Dominates RAC Awards," *Chain Store Age,* April 2004, p. 65; "Target Sees 'Red' with In-Store TV Network," *DSN Retailing Today,* March 27, 2006, p. 6; and "The New Yorker Is Scolded over Single-Sponsor Issue," *The New York Times,* September 19, 2005, p. C7.

19. The Morgantown Furniture case was prepared by Roger A. Kerin, based on company sources.

20. The Crate and Barrel case was prepared by Professor Linda Rochford, University of Minnesota, Duluth, based on the following sources: Crate and Barrel website, www.crateandbarrel.com; Crate and Barrel 2007 catalogs; "Crate and Barrel Selects Unica Corporation's Affinium to Increase Effectiveness of its Multi-Channel Marketing Campaigns," *Business Wire,* April 28, 2004; "Euromarket Design, Inc.," RDS Business and Company Resource Center, 2007; and "Otto Group Takes the Lead in Online Business," Otto Group Media Centre press release, March 28, 2007, www.ottogroup.com/press.

21. The Naked Juice case was prepared by Professor Linda Rochford, University of Minnesota, Duluth, based on the following sources: Anjali Cordeiro, "Beverage Deal Gets Fuel from Desire for Less Fizz," *The Wall Street Journal,* February 14, 2007; Paul Ziobro, "Health Drinks Reward Backers," *The Wall Street Journal,* January 4, 2007, p. B10A; "Naked Juice Company," Hoovers.com; Naked Juice website, www.nakedjuice.com, and promotional materials; Hansen's Natural website, www.hansens.com; Kate MacArthur, "Pepsi Primes Brand Overhauls: Exclusive: $50M Effort from BBDO Looks to Restore the Tone and Spirit of the 1970s Work," *AA* 77, no. 42, p. 1; Bureau of Labor Statistics, *Who's Buying Alcoholic and Nonalcoholic Beverages* (Ithaca, NY: New Strategist Publications, 2005); Odwalla Products website, www.odwalla.com; "A Healthy Glow: Consumers Soak Up the Health Benefits of Juice and Juice Drinks," *Beverage Industry,* January 12, 2007; "Naked Juice Expands DSD, Taps Team of R&D Experts," *Beverage Industry,* August 8, 2006; "2006 State of the Industry," *Beverage Industry,* July 22, 2006; "Soda Industry to Stop Selling Non-Diet Soft Drinks in Schools," *Food Chemical News* 48, no. 13 (May 8, 2006); and "Beverages," *Media Week,* May 1, 2006, p. SR16.

CREDITS

CHAPTER 1

P. 3, Courtesy Chobani, Inc. Used with permission. P. 4, Courtesy Chobani, Inc. Used with permission. P. 4, ©Lee Jae0Won/Reuters/Corbis. P. 5, ©Martin Schoeller. P. 7, Courtesy Domino's Pizza. P. 8, Courtesy New Product Works. P. 8, ©Terrafugia, Inc. P. 8, ©M. Hruby. P. 9, Courtesy Nestle USA. P. 11, ©M. Hruby. P. 11, ©M. Hruby. P. 11, Courtesy U.S. Bank. P. 12, Courtesy Apple, Inc. P. 13, Courtesy 3M. P. 14, Courtesy 3M. P. 16, ©Brian Henn. P. 17, ©M. Hruby. P. 17, Courtesy Zaha Hadid Architects. P. 18, ©DeA Picture Library/Art Resource, NY. P. 18, Courtesy of the Peace Corps. P. 22, Courtesy Chobani, Inc. Used with permission. P. 22, See above. P. 23, Courtesy Chobani, Inc. Used with permission.

CHAPTER 2

P. 25, *All images:* Courtesy Ben & Jerry's Homemade, Inc. Used with permission. P. 26, Used with permission. Courtesy Cree, Inc. P. 27, Courtesy Teach for America. P. 27, Courtesy SightLife. P. 28, Imaginechina via AP Images. P. 29, *Both images:* Courtesy of Medtronic, Inc. P. 30, Photography by Sean Lamb, 2004. P. 30, AP Photo/Lehtikuva, Jukka Töyli. P. 31, AP Photo/Lucasfilm, Gary He. P. 32, Juho Kuva/Bloomberg/Getty Images. P. 33, ©1999-2013 Dundas Data Visualization, Inc. ©1999-2013 Dundas Data Visualization, Inc. P. 35, ©Rick Armstrong. P. 36, *All:* Courtesy Apple, Inc. P. 37, *All images:* Courtesy Apple, Inc. P. 38, Courtesy Ben & Jerry's Homemade, Inc. Used with permission. P. 41, Courtesy Medtronic. P. 45, Courtesy Apple, Inc. P. 45, Photo by Mickey Pfleger/Time & Life Pictures/Getty Images. P. 45, Photographer: Jerome Favre/Bloomberg via Getty Images. P. 48, ©IBM. P. 49, ©IBM.

APPENDIX A

P. 54, 57, 59, 60, 61: ©1996 Paradise Kitchens, Inc. All photos & ads reprinted with permission.

CHAPTER 3

P. 65, Fotosearch Stock Photography. P. 67, ®McDonald's Corporation. P. 68, Courtesy United Nations Publications. P. 69, Provided Courtesy of Frito-Lay North America, Inc. P. 69, Courtesy of Prudential Financial. P. 69, Courtesy American Airlines. P. 69, ©2013 HTC Corporation. All rights reserved. P. 70, Courtesy Hallmark Cards, Inc. P. 71, Copyright© NetImpact. http://www.netimpact.org. P. 72, Source: United States Census Bureau. P. 73, Client: General Motors; Agency: latinworks/Austin, Texas; Talent: Suzy Kaye, Myrna Velasco, Jeannette Sousa and Esmeralda Leon. P. 73, PR NewsFoto/AP Images. P. 74, Courtesy Diesel. P. 74, Courtesy Ford Motor Company. P. 77, Source: United States Census Bureau; www.census.gov. P. 77, Courtesy Cunard Line. P. 78, Courtesy Logitech, Inc. P. 78, ©General Motors. P. 78, Courtesy Nike, Inc. P. 79, *Both photos:* Courtesy TOMRA of North America. P. 83, ©M. Hruby. P. 84, Source: United States Federal Trade Commission; www.ftc.gov. P. 86, Courtesy of Better Business Bureau, Inc. P. 88, Photo by Tim Boyle/Getty Images. P. 89, Photo by Tim Boyle/Getty Images.

CHAPTER 4

P. 91, Copyright Anheuser-Busch, LLC. All rights reserved. Reproduced by permission. P. 95, ©Lisa Young/Inmagine LLC. P. 96, ©5 Creative, L.P. Illustration C. Tew & J. Robinson. P. 97, webphotographeer/Getty Images. P. 100, ©M. Hruby. P. 102, Courtesy of Procter & Gamble Babycare Western Europe and unicef/United Nations Children's Fund. Used with permission. P. 103, PhotoDisc Blue. P. 104, ©Dylan Slagle/Carroll County Times. P. 105, AP Photo/Richard Vogel. P. 108, PRNewsFoto/Toyota.

CHAPTER 5

P. 111, ©Masterfile. P. 114, Press Association via AP Images. P. 115, Trademarks of Kimberly-Clark Worldwide, Inc. ©KCWW Used with permission.P. 117, Courtesy Campbell Soup Company. P. 120, The Secret Sales Pitch: An Overview of Subliminal Advertising. Copyright ©2004 by August Bullock. All Rights Reserved. Used with permission. SubliminalSex.com. P. 121, ©2013 The Clorox Pet Products Company. Reprinted with permission. P. 121, ©2001 Mary Kay, Inc. Photos by: Grace Huang for Sarah Laird. P. 122, With permission of McNeil Consumer Healthcare Division of McNeil-PPC, Inc. P. 123, Courtesy Colgate-Palmolive Company. P. 123, Reproduced with kind permission of Unilever N.V. and/or its group companies. P. 124, *Both:* Courtesy SRI Consulting Business Intelligence (SRIC-BI), Menlo Park, CA. VALS™ is a trademark of SRI Consulting Business Intelligence. Reprinted with permission. P. 126, *Both images:* Courtesy Citizen Watch Company of America, Inc. P. 127, Courtesy BzzAgent, LLC. P. 128, Joseph Eid/AFP/Getty Images. P. 130, Jochen Sand/Getty Images. P. 131, Courtesy ACH Food Companies, Inc. P. 132, Courtesy Maybelline/L'Oreal USA, Inc. P. 135, Daniel Acker/Bloomberg via Getty Images. P. 137, ©Iain Masterton/Alamy.

CHAPTER 6

P. 139, Courtesy J.C. Penney Company, Inc. P. 141, Courtesy Lockheed Martin Company. P. 144, Used with permission Pitney Bowers Inc. P. 145, Courtesy of AT&T Intellectual Property. Used with permission. P. 146, Lluis Gene/AFP/Getty Images. P. 147, Jewel Samad/AFP/Getty Images. P. 148, VEER Mark Adams/Photonica/Getty Images. P. 152, ©Keyence Corporation. P. 154, PR Newswire/AP Images. P. 155, Jim Esposito/blend Images/Getty Images. P. 155, Comstock Images/Getty Images. P. 155, Comstock Images/Getty Images. P. 155, Jim Esposito/blend Images/Getty Images. P. 158, Courtesy Trek Bicycle Corporation. P. 159, Courtesy Trek Bicycle Corporation.

CHAPTER 7

P. 161, *Both images:* Courtesy Enfatico Agency/New York. P. 165, Courtesy Sony Electronics, Inc. P. 165, Courtesy of Bruno Magli. P. 167, Frans Lemmens/The Image Bank/Getty Images. P. 170, Courtesy ALMAP/BBDO Sãu Paulo. P. 171, Courtesy Saatchi & Saatchi/Beijing. P. 172, Kainaz Amaria/Bloomberg via Getty Images. P. 172, Courtesy Nestlé S.A. P. 173, AP Photo/McDonald's Corp. P. 174, Sylvain Sonnet/Photographer's Choice RF/Getty Images. P. 174, Antonio M. Rosario/The Image Bank/Getty Images. P. 175, Courtesy of Nestlé S.A. P. 176, *Both images:* Courtesy MINI USA. P. 176, ©R. Kerin. P. 178, Courtesy The Coca-Cola Company. P. 179, Courtesy Levi Strauss Asia Pacific. P. 179, Courtesy Unilever U.S. P. 180, Courtesy The PRS Group Inc. P. 182, Courtesy McDonald's Corporation. P. 183, Courtesy Fran Wilson Creative Cosmetics, Inc. P. 183, Courtesy Elite Industries, Ltd. P. 184, Courtesy Nestlé S.A. P. 186, *All* Courtesy The Gillette Company/Procter & Gamble. P. 191, Courtesy Mary Kay, Inc.

CHAPTER 8

P. 193, ©Lionsgate/Photofest, Inc. P. 194, ©Andy Kropa 2010/Redux. P. 195, Courtesy LEGO Company. P. 196, Courtesy LEGO Company. P. 199, Pixtal/AGE Fotostock. P. 200, Photo by M. Caulfield/American Idol 2008/Getty Images. P. 201, Macduff Everton/The Image Bank/Getty Images. P. 202, ©iStock. P. 203, ©Spencer Grant/PhotoEdit. P. 203, AP Photo/Paul Vernon. P. 204-205, The Wendy's name, design and logo are trademarks of Oldemark LLC and are licensed to Wendy's International, Inc. P. 206, *Both images:* Provided Courtesy of Frito-Lay North America, Inc. P. 206, Courtesy Carma Laboratories; Bolin Marketing/Minneapolis. P. 208, ©Imaginechine/Corbis. P. 209, Todd Warnock/Lifesize/Getty Images. P. 209, ©Brent Jones. P. 210, The Wendy's name, design and logo are trademarks of Oldemark LLC and are licensed to Wendy's International, Inc. P. 212, Courtesy Schwan's Consumer Brands North America, Inc. P. 214, Courtesy Schwan's Consumer Brands North America, Inc. P. 215, Courtesy New Balance. P. 219 & P. 220, *Al imagesl:* Courtesy Carma Laboratories; Bolin Marketing/Minneapolis.

CHAPTER 9

P. 223, *Both images:* ©Zappos Development, Inc. P. 225, ©Zappos Development, Inc. P. 226, *All* Courtesy of Sporting News Yearbooks. P. 227, Courtesy Ann, Inc. P. 227, ©Marc F. Henning/ Alamy. P. 228, The Wendy's name, design and logo are trademarks of Oldemark LLC and are licensed to Wendy's International, Inc. P. 230, Microfridge® Courtesy Mac-Gray. P. 232, The Wendy's name, design and logo are trademarks of Oldemark LLC and are licensed to Wendy's International, Inc. P. 232, Chris Ratcliffe/ Bloomberg via Getty Images. P. 232, ®McDonald's Corporation. P. 232, ©2013 Xerox Corporation. All Rights Reserved. P. 234, *All* ©2011 Oldemark, LLC. Reprinted with permission. The Wendy's name, design and logo are trademarks of Oldemark LLC and are licensed to Wendy's International, Inc. P. 236, Courtesy Wendy's International, Inc. P. 238, Courtesy Five Guys Enterprises, LLC. P. 239, *All photos:* Courtesy Apple, Inc. P. 239, Courtesy Apple Computer. P. 240, Courtesy Apple, Inc. P. 241, ©M. Hruby. P. 241, ©M. Hruby. P. 244, Courtesy Prince Sports. P. 245, Courtesy Prince Sports.

CHAPTER 10

P. 247, *All images:* Courtesy Apple, Inc. P. 247, Julian Stratenschulte/dpa/Corbis. P. 248, Wrigley's Doublemint and all affiliated designs owned by and used courtesy of the Wm. Wrigley Jr. Company. P. 250, Photo courtesy Brain Storm Bakery. P. 251, AP Photo/Dino Vournas. P. 252, ©M. Hruby. P. 253, Courtesy Nestle Purina Pet Care Company. P. 253, ©M. Hruby. P. 254, Courtesy The New Product Works. P. 254, Courtesy of the Original Pet Drink. P. 255, Courtesy The New Product Works. P. 255, ©GfK Custom Research, LLC. P. 257, Courtesy Eastman Kodak Company; Agency Ketchum Communications. P. 258, ©Ford Motor Company. P. 259, ©M. Hruby. P. 259, Courtesy of IDEO. P. 259, Courtesy Gary Schwarzberg. P. 260,AP Photo/Mary Altaffer. P. 261,AP Photo/Eric Risberg.P. 261, ©1997–2013 Netflix Inc. P. 263, Courtesy General Mills; Photo: Bolin Marketing. P. 263, KiyoshiOta/ Bloomberg via Getty Images. P. 264, ©M. Hruby. P. 268, ©2013 X-1. Used with permission.

CHAPTER 11

P. 271, ©Lauren Greenfield/INSTITUTE.P. 271, Photo by J. Meric/Getty Images. P. 272, ©M. Hruby. P. 274, Getty Images. P. 275, Photo by Kevork Djansezian/Getty Images. P. 275, Courtesy Amazon.com Inc. P. 281, ©2009 Blue Moon. P. 282, Courtesy Lowe Worldwide; Photo: Brian Kuhlman; Talent: Cameo Amato. P. 283, *Both images:* "Selling It" ©2012 Consumers Union of U.S., Inc. Yonkers, NY 10703-1057, a nonprofit organization. Reprinted with permission from the August 2012 issue of Consumer Reports® for educational purposes only. www.ConsumerReports.org. P. 284, DR. PEPPER is a registered trademark of Dr. Pepper/Seven Up, Inc. Used with permission. P. 286, Photo by Rebecca Sapp/WireImage for Mediaplacement/Getty Images. P. 287, ©Fotosearch Stock/Publitek, Inc. Photography. P. 288, ©M. Hruby. P. 289, *Both images:* Courtesy The Black & Decker Corporation. P. 290, ©M. Hruby. P. 291, Courtesy QPG Sherpa. P. 292, ©M. Hruby. P. 293, Courtesy Hyundai Motor America. P. 295, ©2013 Procter & Gamble. Used with permission. P. 296, ©M. Hruby.

CHAPTER 12

P. 299, ©The Economist Newspaper Limited 2013. All rights reserved. P. 301, Agency:TM Advertising; Creative Team: Bernard Park and Shep Kellam; Art Buyer: Ranelle Fowler. P. 301, Courtesy American Express Company.P. 302, Courtesy Hill Holliday/Boston, MA.; Photography ©Pat Molnar and John Dolan. P. 303, ©2013 Hewlett-Packard Development Company, L.P. Reproduced with Permission. P. 304, Courtesy of Southwest Airlines. P. 305, Courtesy Outward Bound/Voca PR. P. 305, Courtesy Girl Scouts of the USA. P. 306, Used with permission of the American Red Cross. P. 307, Courtesy of the Peace Corps.P. 309, ©Hertz System, Inc. Hertz is a registered service mark and trademark of Hertz System, Inc. P. 310,©M. Hruby. P. 310, ©F1online digitale Bildagentur GmbH/Alamy. P. 311, Momahhad Kheirkhah/UPI/Newscom. P. 311, Courtesy Sprint Nextel Corporation. P. 311, Logo used with permission of the American Red Cross. P. 312, ©Redirections Sign Design. P. 313, Courtesy Accenture. P. 313, Courtesy Space Adventures, Ltd. P. 314, ©Zappos Development, Inc. P. 315, ©Caro/ Alamy. P. 319, *All:* Robert Mora/LA Galaxy.

CHAPTER 13

P. 323, *Both:* Courtesy StubHub. P. 324, Courtesy StubHub. P. 324, Courtesy Bugatti Automobiles S.A.S.P. 326, ©Dollar Shave Club, Inc. P.326, Doug Kanter/Bloomberg News/Getty. P.327, ©Dollar Shave Club, Inc.P. 328,©Bryan Derballa. P. 328, ©Bryan Derballa. P. 329, ©Bryan Derballa. P. 331,©M. Hruby. P. 332, Courtesy Coldwater Creek, Inc. Used with permission. P. 333, AP Photo/Marcio Jose Sanchez. P. 334, PR NewsFoto/ AP Images. P. 335, ©2012 Harmonix Music Systems, Inc. P. 336, ©M. Hruby. P. 337, ©M. Hruby. P. 340, Courtesy Colgate-Palmolive Company. P. 343, ©Ben Osborn. P.347, Photo by Paul Kane/ Getty Images. P. 348, ©2013 Washburn Guitars. Used with permission U.S. Music Corp.

CHAPTER 14

P. 351, Courtesy Vizio, Inc. P. 354, ©Terry McElroy. P. 355, Courtesy of DIRECTV. P. 356, Courtesy of Rock & Roll Hall of Fame. P. 357, PRNewsFoto/Vizio, Inc./AP Images. P. 360, ©M. Hruby. P. 362, ©Illustration: Alberto Cervantes/The Wall Street Journal. P. 364, ©M. Hruby. P. 367, ©2001-2011 Fengtao Software Inc. All rights reserved. P. 368, Courtesy Payless ShoeSource, Inc. P. 369, Photography by Monci Jo Williams, FORTUNE; ©1983 Time, Inc. All rights reserved. P. 374 and P. 375, *All:* Courtesy Carma Laboratories; Bolin Marketing/Minneapolis.

APPENDIX B

P. 378, *Both* Courtesy The Caplow Company.

CHAPTER 15

P. 385, *Both images:* ©2013 Callaway Golf Company. All rights reserved. P. 388, Courtesy M. Booth & Associates/New York. P. 389, Courtesy IBM Corporation. P. 391, ©Bonnie Kamin/ PhotoEdit. All Rights Reserved. P. 391, PR Newswire/AP Images. P. 391, PR Newswire/AP Images. P. 392, Courtesy Nestle SA. P. 395, Justin Sullivan/Getty Images. P. 396, Laura Embry/ ZUMA Press/Newscom. P. 396, ©PetSmart, Inc. Used with permission. P. 398, ©Joe & Kathy Heiner. P. 401, *All photos:* ©M. Hruby. P. 402, Courtesy IBM Corporation. P. 403, Courtesy of Dell, Inc. P. 403, PR NewsFoto/AP Images. P. 405, ©2013 Hewlett-Packard Development Company, L.P. Reproduced with Permission. P. 408, Courtesy Amazon.com Inc.

CHAPTER 16

P. 411, AP Photo/Google. P. 411, Google/ ZUMAPRESS.com. P. 411, *All images:* AP Photo/ Google. P. 413, ©TAO Images Limited/Alamy. P. 414, ©2013 macys.com is a registered trademark. All rights reserved. Used with permission. P. 415, Courtesy Green Retail Association. P. 416, Courtesy Doctor's Associates, Inc. P. 416, ©2013, Redbox Automated Retail, LLC. All rights reserved. P. 418, Courtesy Staples, Inc. P. 418, AP Photo/ Christoiphe Ena. P. 418, AP Photo/Sue Ogrocki. P. 420, Courtesy Healthy You Vending. P. 420, ©M. Hruby. P. 420, ©M. Hruby. P. 420, Courtesy L.L.Bean, Inc. P. 421, ©QVC, Inc. P. 422, ©K. Rousonelos. P. 422,Handout/MCT., P. 422, Courtesy CBS Interactive. Used with permission. P. 423, AP Photo/Jacques Brinon. P. 423, Frederic J. Brown/AFP/Getty Images. P. 424, Courtesy Mary Kay, Inc. P. 425, ©M. Hruby. P. 425, ©Najlah Feanny/Corbis. P. 425, ©M. Hruby. P. 425, AP Photo/Michael Dwyer. P. 426, Courtesy The Home Depot. P. 427, Courtesy TJX Companies, Inc. P. 427, AP Photo/Paul Sakuma. P. 428, Courtesy Sears, Roebuck and Co. P. 431, Supplied by: Checkers Drive-In Restaurants, Inc. P. 435, Courtesy www.manaonline.org. P. 438, *Both:* Courtesy Mall of America.

CHAPTER 17

P. 441, Courtesy Taco Bell. Used with permission. P. 443, Courtesy MINI USA. P. 444, ©M. Hruby. P. 446, Courtesy Columbia Sportswear Company. Used with permission. P.446,

©M. Hruby. P. 446, M&M's is a registered trademark of Mars, Incorporated. This trademark and advertisement are used with permission. Mars, Incorporated is not associated with McGraw-Hill Higher Education. P. 447, Used with permission from McDonald's Corporation. P. 447, ©Fotosearch, LLC. P. 448, Courtesy of Restaurant Business Magazines. P. 449, Press Association via AP Images. P. 449, ©M. Hruby. P. 451, Courtesy Gulfstream Aerospace Corporation. P. 451, ©2013 Tropicana Products, Inc. Used with permission. P. 452, Artwork supplied by Merck-Schering/Plough Pharmaceuticals. P. 455, ©General Motors Company. P. 455, ©2013 Verizon. P. 457, Carr/MCT/Newscom. P. 457, ©Walt Disney Studios Motion Pictures/Photofest, Inc. P. 459, The San Diego Padres word mark and primary logo are used with permission of Major League Baseball Properties, Inc. P. 460, Courtesy J.C. Penney Company, Inc. P. 461, Created for Target by CatalystStudios.com. P. 462, Courtesy 463 Communications. Used with permission. P. 465, ©M. Hruby.

CHAPTER 18

P. 469, Courtesy AIO TV, Inc. Used with permission. P. 470, NESTLÉ®, DIGIORNO® and PIZZERIA! ™ are trademarks of Société des Produits Nestlé S.A., Vevey, Switzerland. P.470, ©2013 FMR LLC. All rights reserved. Used by permission. P. 470, DOVE and DOVE PROMISES are registered trademarks of Mars, Incorporated. These trademarks are used with permission. Mars, Incorporated is not associated with McGraw-Hill Higher Education. P. 471, Trademarks held by Chevron Intellectual Property LLC and © owned by Chevron U.S.A. Inc. and used with permission. P. 471, Courtesy Bridgestone Corporation. P. 472, PRNewFoto/Milk Processor Education Program/AP Images. P. 472, Ad developed by McCann Worldgroup on behalf of the U.S. Army. P. 472, Courtesy Under Armour, Inc. Used with permission. P. 474, ©M. Hruby. P. 474, ©1999-2013 GoDaddy Operating Company LLC. All Rights Reserved. Used with permission. P. 475, Courtesy Worldwildlife Fund. P. 475, Courtesy Candies. P. 475, Courtesy GEICO. P. 476,Client: K-Swiss; Agency: 72 & Sunny. Used with permission. P. 479, Courtesy NBCUniversal, Inc. Used with permission. P. 481, ©M. Hruby. P. 481, Courtesy USA Today. P. 482, AP Photo/Mark Lennihan. P. 482, ©M. Hruby. P. 483, Courtesy 24/7 Real Media Inc. P. 484, Courtesy Nationwide Insurance. P. 485, Spike Mafford/Getty Images. P. 485, Courtesy Wieden + Kennedy/New York. P. 488, Courtesy GfK Mediamark Research & Intelligence, LLC. Used with permission. P. 489, ©M. Hruby. P. 491, ©M. Hruby. P. 492, Courtesy Henkel Corporation. Used with permission. P. 492, Courtesy Hilton Worldwide. Used with permission. P. 493, Courtesy Landaal Packaging Systems. Used with permission. P. 494, ©Geffen Pictures/Zuma Press. P. 494, AP Photo/FOX, Michael Becker. P. 494, Hand-out/STAPLES CANADA INC./Newscom. P. 496, Photo by Jamie McCarthy/Getty Images. P. 499, Courtesy Google Inc.

CHAPTER 19

P. 503, Center Photo by: ©Jeremy M. Lange. P. 503, Courtesy of StuffDOT, Inc. Used with permission. P. 503, AP Photo/Craig Ruttle. P. 503, ©OK GO Partnership. P. 503, Photo by Todd Williamson/Invision for YouTube/AP Images. P. 503, Courtesy Carma Laboratories; Bolin Marketing/Minneapolis. P. 503, Picture Alliance/Frank May/Newscom. P. 503, Courtesy Steven W. Hartley/author. P. 503, RNewsFoto/PwC/AP Images. P. 504, ©Ford Consulting Group. P. 505, ©Ford Consulting Group. P. 506, ©K. Rousonelos. P. 508, AP Photo/Marcio Jose Sanchez. P. 509, Courtesy of StuffDOT, Inc. Used with permission. AP Photo/Craig Ruttle. Picture Alliance/Frank May/Newscom. PRNewsFoto/PwC/AP Images. Photo by Todd Williamson/Invision for YouTube/AP Images. P. 510, ©2013 Facebook. P. 511, Courtesy Carma Laboratories; Bolin Marketing/Minneapolis. P. 511, Courtesy Steven W. Hartley/author. P. 512, Courtesy Karen Black; Agency: SpinLab Public Relations. Used with permission. P. 513, ©2013 Vimeo, LLC. All rights reserved. P. 513, ©2013 Google. P. 513, Foursquare ©2013. P. 513, ©2013 StumbleUpon. Used with permission. P. 513, ©2013 Yahoo! Inc. Used with permission. P. 513,©PhotoEdit/Alamy. P. 513, Aaron M. Sprecher/AP Images for Tumblr. P. 513, Lionel Bonaventure/AFP/Getty Images. P. 513, *Both photos:* ©OK GO Partnership. P. 516, Photo by Brian Blanco/Invision for Pepsi/AP Images. P. 518, P. 518, AP Photo/KEYSTONE/ Laurent Gillieron. P. 519, AP Photo/Irwin Fedriansyah. P. 520 and P. 521, *All images:* Courtesy Carma Laboratories; Bolin Marketing/Minneapolis. P. 522, ©2012 Rovio Entertainment Ltd. P. 523, Courtesy of Zynga. Used with permission. P. 523, ©2007-2013 Spotify Ltd.; Courtesy The OutCast Agency. P. 523, Courtesy Halfbrick Studios. P. 523, Courtesy Pandora Media, Inc. Used with permission. P. 523, ©2013 Imangi Studios, LLC. All rights reserved. P. 523, LOTUM ©2013. P. 524, Courtesy Tesco PLC; Agency: Cheil Worldwide/Korea. P. 527, P. 528 and P. 529, *All images:* Courtesy of StuffDOT, Inc. Used with permission.

CHAPTER 20

P. 531, ©Hillsman Stuart Jackson. P. 533, Courtesy Medtronic. P. 535, Dimitri Otis/Photographer's Choice/Getty Images. P. 536, Asia Images/Getty Images. P. 536, ©Susan Van Etten/PhotoEdit, Inc. P. 536, Tetra Images/Getty Images. P. 536, ©Royalty-Free/Corbis. P. 538, Courtesy Xerox Corporation. P. 540, ©Einzig Photography. P. 541, Phillip Jarrell/Taxi/Getty Images. P. 542, Courtesy IBM Corporation. P. 543, Frank Herholdt/Stone/Getty Images. P. 543, Purestock/GettyImages. P. 545, Image Bank/Color Day Productions/Getty Images. P. 548, David Goldman/AP Images for Frito Lay. P. 550, Courtesy DTS International Human Performance Technology. P. 551, Courtesy Mary Kay, Inc. P. 553, *Both* Courtesy of Toshiba Medical Systems & Interactive Media. P. 557, Courtesy Xerox Corporation.

CHAPTER 21

P. 559 and P. 561, *Both images:* Courtesy Seven Cycles, Inc. P. 562, M&M's is a registered trademark of Mars, Incorporated. This trademark and advertisement are used with permission. Mars, Incorporated is not associated with McGraw-Hill Higher Education. P. 563, Courtesy Reebok International Ltd. P. 564, ©NetPhotos/Alamy. P.565, Courtesy Travelocity. P. 567, PeskyMonkey/Vetta/Getty Images. P. 568, ©Paul Barton/Corbis. P. 569, ©Tom Grill/Corbis. P. 570, ©2008 Zappos.com., Inc. P. 571, ©Clayton Hauck Photography. P. 572, Courtesy Career Builder.com. P. 574, ©Fotosearch/ Publitek, Inc. P. 575, Cultura/Seb Oliver/StockImage/Getty Images. P. 575, ©Inmagine LLC. P. 578, P. 579 and P. 583, *All images:* Courtesy Pizza Hut, Inc.

CHAPTER 22

P. 583, Courtesy General Mills; Photo: Bolin Marketing. P. 584, ©M. Hruby. P. 585, ©1998-2013 Costco Wholesale Corporation. All rights reserved. P. 585, ©M. Hruby. P. 586, Courtesy General Mills; Photo: Bolin Marketing. P. 589, Courtesy Campbell Soup Company. P. 590, Courtesy Ikea. P. 592, Fotosearch. P. 594, Courtesy General Mills; Photo: Bolin Marketing. P. 594, ©M. Hruby. P. 595, Courtesy Google, Inc. P. 595, Ralph Orlowski/Bloomberg via Getty Images. P. 595, Thomas Coex/AFP/Getty Images. P. 596, Courtesy Lockheed Matin Corp. P. 597, Patrick T. Fallon/Bloomberg via Getty Images. P. 597, *Both images:* ©2013 SPANX, Inc. P. 598, *Both images:* ©2013 Supercell. All rights reserved. P. 602, Photo by Dan Kitwood/Getty Images. P. 603, ©Fabrizio-Costantini. P. 604, Courtesy General Mills: Photo: Bolin Marketing. P. 605, Courtesy Apple, Inc. P. 609, Courtesy General Mills.

APPENDIX C

P. 610, ©Kheng Guan Toh/Inmagine LLC. P. 611, ©Paul Elledge. P. 613, Used with the permission of Macy's, Inc. P. 614, Courtesy Xerox Corporation. P. 615, Courtesy Garmin International, Inc. P. 615, Courtesy Merck/Schering-Plough Pharmaceuticals; Agency: JWT INSIDE. P. 616, ©Stuart Miles/Inmagine LLC. P. 618, Reprinted from Job Choices 2002, with permission of the National Association of Colleges & Employers. P. 618, ©Monster Worldwide, Inc. Used with permission. P. 619, PRNewsFoto/PwC/AP Images. P. 619, ©2002-2013 Plaxo, Inc. All rights reserved. P. 624, ©Jeff Shesol. P. 625, White Packert/The Image Bank/Getty Images. P. 626, ©M. Hruby. P. 626, ©M. Hruby. P. 626, Reprinted with permission from Journal of Marketing, published by the American Marketing Association. P. 627, Reprinted with permission from Journal of Marketing published by the American Marketing Association.

NAME INDEX

D

E

F

G

H

I

J

N

P

Q

R

S

T

U

V

W

Z

COMPANY/PRODUCT INDEX

A

B

C

D

E

H

I

J

K

L

T

U

V

W

X

Y

Z

SUBJECT INDEX

Note: Glossary terms and the page numbers where they are defined are **boldface**.

A

C

D

E

G

N

O

P

Q

T

U

McGraw Hill Education **connect**®

Kerin/Hartley/Rudelius: *Marketing*, 12e, offers a seamless content and technology solution to improve student engagement and comprehension, automation of assignments and grading, and easy reporting to ensure that learning objectives are being met.

Connect® Marketing provides a wide array of tools and content to improve instructor productivity and student performance. In fact, the aggregated results of 34 Connect adoptions showed an 11% improvement in pass rates, a 16% improvement in retention, two times as many students receiving an A, and a 77% reduction in instructor grading time.

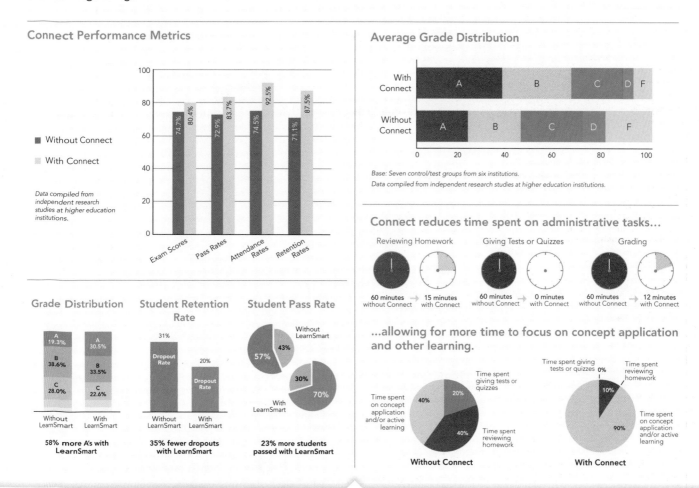

Connect Performance Metrics

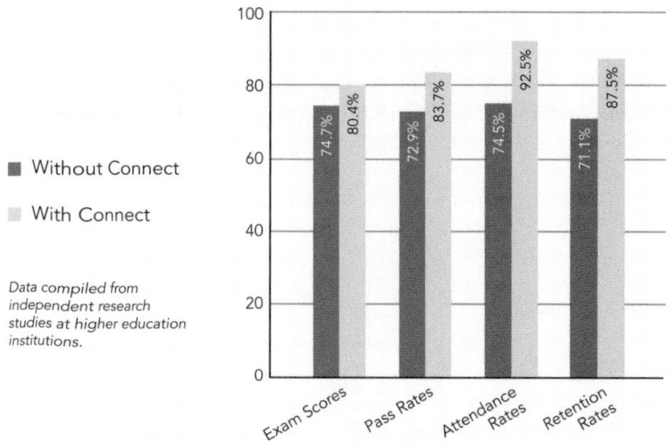

	Without Connect	With Connect
Exam Scores	74.7%	80.4%
Pass Rates	72.9%	83.7%
Attendance Rates	74.5%	92.5%
Retention Rates	71.1%	87.5%

Data compiled from independent research studies at higher education institutions.

Average Grade Distribution

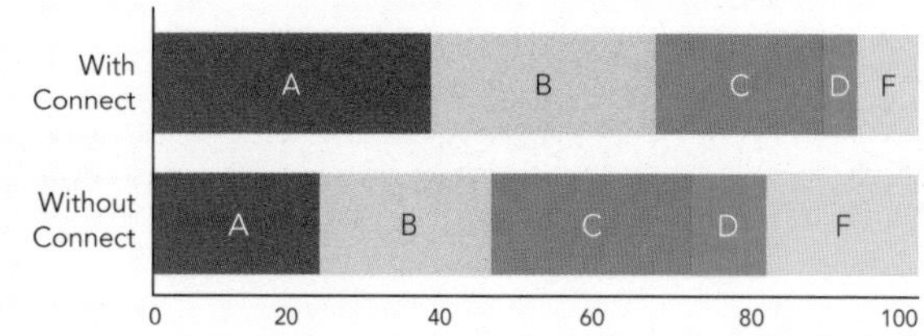

With Connect: A, B, C, D, F

Without Connect: A, B, C, D, F

Base: Seven control/test groups from six institutions.
Data compiled from independent research studies at higher education institutions.

Grade Distribution

	Without LearnSmart	With LearnSmart
A	19.3%	30.5%
B	38.6%	33.5%
C	28.0%	22.6%

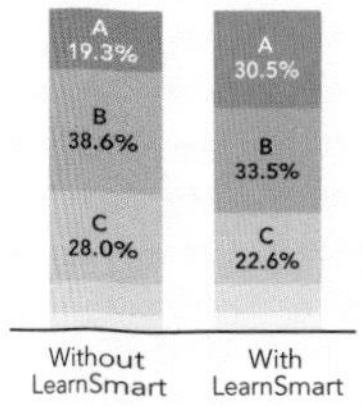

58% more A's with LearnSmart

Student Retention Rate

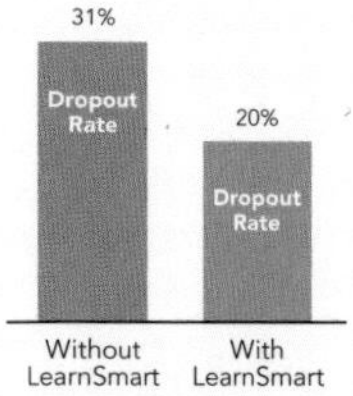

	Without LearnSmart	With LearnSmart
Dropout Rate	31%	20%

35% fewer dropouts with LearnSmart

Student Pass Rate

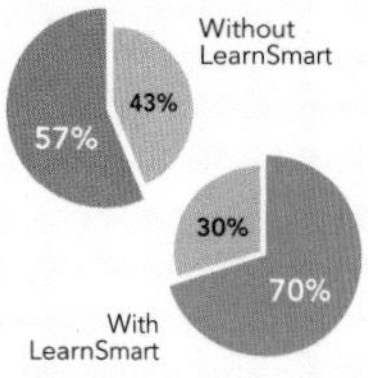

Without LearnSmart: 57% / 43%

With LearnSmart: 70% / 30%

23% more students passed with LearnSmart

Connect reduces time spent on administrative tasks...

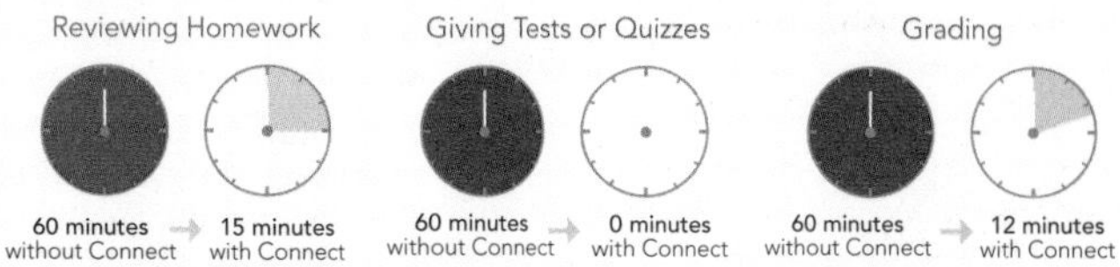

	Without Connect	With Connect
Reviewing Homework	60 minutes	15 minutes
Giving Tests or Quizzes	60 minutes	0 minutes
Grading	60 minutes	12 minutes

...allowing for more time to focus on concept application and other learning.

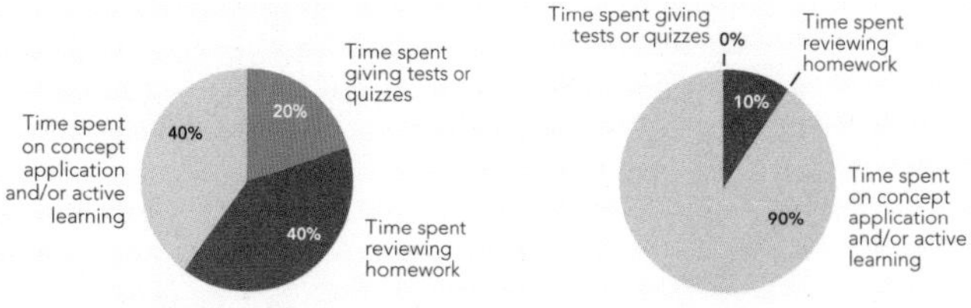

Without Connect: Time spent on concept application and/or active learning 40%; Time spent giving tests or quizzes 20%; Time spent reviewing homework 40%

With Connect: Time spent giving tests or quizzes 0%; Time spent reviewing homework 10%; Time spent on concept application and/or active learning 90%

LEARNSMART ADVANTAGE

LearnSmart®

LearnSmart, the most widely used adaptive learning resource, is proven to improve grades. By focusing each student on the most important information they need to learn, LearnSmart personalizes the learning experience so they can study as efficiently as possible.

Smartbook™

SmartBook—an extension of LearnSmart—is an adaptive eBook that helps students focus their study time more effectively. As students read, SmartBook assesses comprehension and dynamically highlights where they need to study more.

CONNECT FEATURES

Interactive Applications

Interactive Applications offer a variety of automatically graded exercises that require students to **apply** key concepts. Whether the assignment includes a *click and drag*, *video case*, or *decision generator*, these applications provide instant feedback and progress tracking for students and detailed results for the instructor.

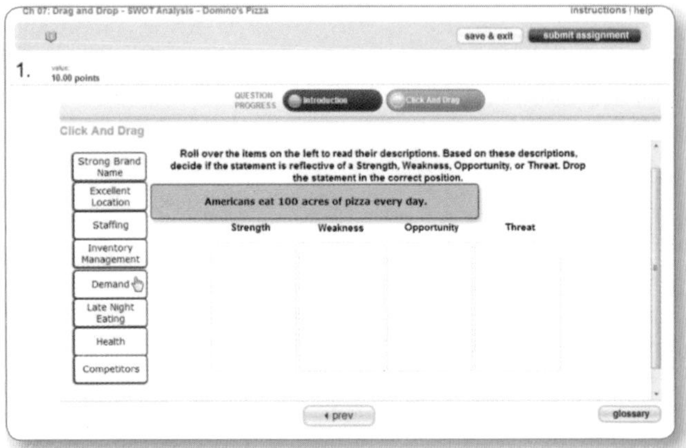

eBook

Connect Plus includes a media-rich eBook that allows you to share your notes with your students. Your students can insert and review their own notes, highlight the text, search for specific information, and interact with media resources. Using an eBook with Connect Plus gives your students a complete digital solution that allows them to access their materials from any computer.

Tegrity

Make your classes available anytime, anywhere. With simple, one-click recording, students can search for a word or phrase and be taken to the exact place in your lecture that they need to review.

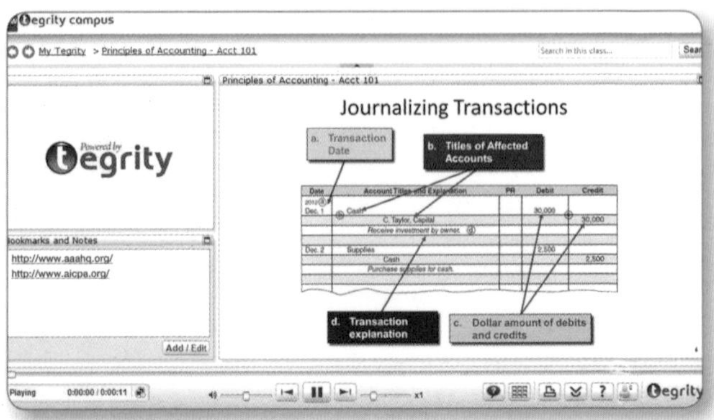